The Battle of Prokhorovka

The Battle of Prokhorovka

The Tank Battle at Kursk, the Largest Clash of Armor in History

Christopher A. Lawrence
The Dupuy Institute

STACKPOLE
BOOKS

ESSEX, CONNECTICUT
BLUE RIDGE SUMMIT, PENNSYLVANIA

STACKPOLE BOOKS
An imprint of Globe Pequot, the trade division of
The Rowman & Littlefield Publishing Group, Inc.
4501 Forbes Blvd., Ste. 200
Lanham, MD 20706
www.rowman.com

Distributed by NATIONAL BOOK NETWORK

First paperback edition 2024

British Library Cataloguing in Publication Information available

Library of Congress Cataloging-in-Publication Data

ISBN 978-0-8117-3807-1 (cloth : alk. paper)
ISBN 978-0-8117-7548-9 (pbk : alk. paper)
ISBN 978-0-8117-6812-2 (ebook)

∞™ The paper used in this publication meets the minimum requirements of American National Standard for Information Sciences—Permanence of Paper for Printed Library Materials, ANSI/NISO Z39.48-1992.

This book is dedicated to

Colonel Dr. Fyodor Davidovich Sverdlov

(Soviet Army), 1921 to 2002

In my very first meeting with Colonel Sverdlov on 11 October 1993,
he stated, "I was at Prokhorovka right after the war,
and I didn't see a hundred tigers."

Contents

Illustrations and Maps

The Battle of Prokhorovka

Acknowledgements

THIS BOOK HAS been created based upon my 1,662-page mega-book: *Kursk: The Battle of Prokhorovka*. That book covered the entire German Belgorod offensive in the south, from 4 July to 24 July 1943. It incorporated the actions of two German infantry corps and three German panzer corps against most of the Soviet Voronezh Front and reinforcing forces. It was a massive battle that was detailed down to division-level for each day of the operation.

This book is based upon the action of the SS Panzer Corps and the supporting III Panzer Corps from 9 to 18 July. It is a part of this larger battle, but it is the part that includes the legendary Battle of Prokhorovka. It still tracks, for better or worse, the operations of each division for each day of the battle. While this may drag the reader into the weeds by covering the details of secondary operations where nothing significant happened, it is felt that to give a full and comprehensive story; these operations needed to be addressed. This is not a Hollywood film, where there is a central antagonist and protagonist driving towards a climatic finish. Granted many books have been written that way, with the fight between the SS and Rotmistrov's Fifth Guards Tank Army resolved on the tank fields of Prokhorovka on 12 July. In fact, it was discussed whether to shorten my books by cutting back most of the material after 12 July. This is, of course, bastardizing the history for the sake of making a good story. I choose not to do this.

THE BATTLE OF Kursk was the subject of a large data base that we assembled at *The Dupuy Institute* from 1993 to 1996 for the U.S. Army Concepts Analysis Agency (CAA), now called the Center for Army Analysis. I was the program manager for this large research and database effort. We assembled unit records from the German side, and uniquely, obtained access to the Soviet Army files from the Russian Military Archives just outside of Moscow, at Podolsk. This effort included over a dozen people and resulted in a database being delivered to CAA for use in model validation. CAA never used it for such.

As we were sitting on a collection of unique material, I felt an obligation to prepare a book using this unique material. The original Kursk book was written from late 1999 to around the middle of 2003 and almost completed then. Because of the large amount of material we had assembled, the draft of the book came out much larger than I originally planned. Because of the work load at *The Dupuy Institute*, I was unable to complete it at that time. Therefore, I was only able to start back to work on it in late 2009 and the behemoth was published in 2015.

A detailed description of this effort is provided in my original book and in articles written since then.[1] Many people were important in this effort and there are all acknowledged in that book. The key personnel that are acknowledged are: Colonel Trevor N. Dupuy (USA); E. G. Vandiver, Director of the Center for Army Analysis; Dr. Fyodor Davidovich Sverdlov (Colonel, USSR); Dr. Anatolii Vainer (Colonel, USSR); Major General G. G.

1 See Christopher A. Lawrence, *Kursk: The Battle of Prokhorovka* (Aberdeen Books, Sheridan, Colorado, 2015), 19–24 (Preface: The Kursk Data Base) and 25–26 (Acknowledgements). Also see Christopher A. Lawrence, "Did I Just Write the Largest History Book Ever?" at http://www.aberdeenbookstore.com/the-largest-history-book-ever, and a shorter version of the same article at the *History News Network* at https://historynewsnetwork.org/article/161443, dated January 2016.

Nessonov (USSR); Colonel Valerii Akimov (Russia); Vyacheslav Viktorovich Stepashkin; Dr. Richard Harrison; Colonel John Sloan (USA, Ret.); Richard C. Anderson; Major General Dieter Brand (Bundeswehr, Ret.); L. Jay Karamales; Major General Nicholas Krawciw (USA, Ret.) and Dr. Arthur Volz. They all played a major role in assisting with the Kursk Data Base or in preparing the book. Also among other people who provided help and are acknowledged in the original book are: Walter Baumen, Dr. Ronald Bellamy (Col. USA, Ret.), Christer Bergstrom, Wulf-Dietrich Brand, Frederick L. Clemens, Jeff Chrisman, Dr. George Daoust (Col. USA), Alexander Dinsmoor, Gary Dickson, Anders Frankson, Dr. Karl-Heinz Frieser (Col. Bundeswehr), David M. Glantz (Col. USA, Ret.), Harvey Gough, Alex Hellmund, Jukka Juutinen, Grigori A. Kultonov (Col. USSR), Paul Krawciw, Thomas Peters, Tom Petteys (Aberdeen Books), Dr. Yan Mann, Edward Milligan (Lt. Col. USA), Dmitri Myslivschenko. Rainer Prill (Lt. Col. Bundeswehr, Ret.), Dr. Dmitri Ryabushkin, Jonna Schwarz, Susan Sims, Mikhail Serykh, Ariane C. Smith, Howard Whitley, Niklas Zetterling, Yun Zhang, and, of course, Tatiana Samsonova Lawrence. All of these people played a role in completing the Kursk Data Base or helping with the original Kursk book.

I put Kursk aside for a couple of years and focused on other books.[2] When I first realized back in 2002 how large my original draft had become, I changed my plans to actually write two Kursk books: a large definitive book, which was completed, and a smaller book for the general reader. I am finally getting around to addressing the second part of that plan, although this book is more specifically focused on just the Battle of Prokhorovka. There is still not a single good general reader book addressing the Belgorod Offensive. Perhaps I will attempt this later.

Central to this new effort has been David Reisch (Stackpole Books) and my original editor for the first Kursk book, Ariane C. Smith (Capital A). I would also like to thank Tom Petteys of Aberdeen Books for so graciously allowing us to use the electronic files from my original Kursk book. Also assisting me in research and reviewing of this book is Frederick L. Clemens, L. Jay Karamales, Thomas Peters, Dr. Shawn Woodford, and Niklas Zetterling. I would also like to thank Kevin Connor, the British film director, for providing me with encouragement for my various Kursk related projects.

---

2 See *America's Modern Wars: Understanding Iraq, Afghanistan and Vietnam* (Casemate Publishers, Philadelphia and Oxford, 2015) and *War by Numbers: Understanding Conventional Combat* (Potomac Books, Lincoln, NE, 2017).

Prologue

I feel as if I am pushing open the door to a dark room never seen before,
without knowing what lies behind the door.

ADOLF HITLER
21 JUNE 1941[1]

On 19 November 1942, moving through the snow of Russia's bitter winter, the Soviet Union unleashed a massive attack by three Fronts (army groups) on both flanks of the German positions around Stalingrad. The attack on the northern flank was by two Fronts, the Don Front, headed by Lieutenant General Konstantin K. Rokossovskii, and the newly created Southwestern Front, headed by Lieutenant General Nikolai F. Vatutin.

The Soviet offensive completed its encirclement of the German and Romanian defenders around Stalingrad on 23 November 1943. German attempts to resupply them by air fell short while a German relief effort in mid-December also failed. This relief effort was commanded by Field Marshal Erich von Manstein and was led by the Fourth Panzer Army under command of Colonel General Hermann Hoth. The German Army was then driven back away from Stalingrad by Soviet offensives, leaving the German Sixth Army behind to starve and die.

Many of these units and commanders would meet again at Kursk. Manstein would later command Army Group South and Hoth would continue to command the Fourth Panzer Army during the Kursk offensive. Vatutin would later command the Voronezh Front, which was defending the southern part of the Kursk bulge, during battles which are the focus of this book. Rokossovskii would later command the Central Front, which defended the northern part of the Kursk bulge during the Battle of Kursk.

The leading formation in Vatutin's attack was the powerful Fifth Tank Army. This attack also included the Twenty-first Army, commanded by Lieutenant General Ivan Chistyakov. This army, which would later fight at Kursk, was renamed the Sixth Guards Army. Of the six infantry divisions under its command, two of these (the 63rd and 76th Rifle Divisions) would still be under its command at Kursk, although renamed the 52nd and 51st Guards Rifle Divisions. Also under its command was the IV Tank Corps, which would appear at Kursk as the V Guards Tank Corps.

Supporting these attacks in the north were three armies belonging to the neighboring Don Front. These included Lieutenant General Alexei Zhadov's Sixty-sixth Army (later the Fifth Guards Army) which would be sent into the battle at Kursk as reinforcements. Three of its divisions (293rd, 226th and 343rd Rifle Divisions) would be with it for the Kursk battle, as the 66th, 95th, and 97th Guards Rifle Divisions.

These armies were supported by four air armies, including the Seventeenth Air Army and Second Air

1 V. E. Tarrant, *Stalingrad, Anatomy of an Agony* (Leo Cooper, London, 1992), page 18.

Army, both of the Southwestern Front and supporting the main attack. Both of these air armies would later appear at Kursk. The opposing German air unit was the VIII Air Corps, part of the Fourth Air Army, which would also appear at Kursk, but under a new commander.

Of the 21 rifle divisions fielded by the three guards armies near Belgorod in July 1943, 12 of them had operated together eight months earlier in surrounding the German Sixth Army at Stalingrad.

THE STALINGRAD DISASTER had cost Germany some 300,000 troops. A total of 22 divisions were destroyed completely and six others mauled. A total of 107,800 prisoners were taken; only around 7,000 would ever return from captivity.

Soviet losses were equally horrendous. Russian researcher G. F. Krivosheyev reports total losses from 19 November to 2 February as 154,885 killed and missing and 330,892 wounded. Their losses in the defense of Stalingrad (17 July–18 November) are reported as 323,856 killed and missing and 319,986 wounded.[2] Still, it was an overwhelmingly decisive victory on the part of the Soviet Union, and the resulting continuous offensives sent the German Army reeling back to where it had started in the summer of 1942.

DURING THE WINTER of 1942/43, the Soviet Armies continued to advance across the southern half of Russia, repeatedly attacking weak points in the German line, often the Germans' Romanian and Italian allies. In mid-February, they had taken Kharkov and were advancing to the southwest towards Field Marshal Manstein's Army Group South headquarters at Zaparorzhye. In the midst of this unprecedented military disaster, the dictator of Germany, Adolf Hitler, flew out to Manstein's headquarters in the middle of February. Manstein was confident he could throw back this offense and was already thinking about what German operations were going to be once the Soviet attack was halted.

Manstein tried to outline for Hitler what German operations should be after the spring thaw (called Rasputitsa in Russian). In less than 30 days, perhaps sooner, the thaw would arrive and effectively halt all serious military operations for about two months. After the thaw, Manstein would still be left with a situation where he would be holding a 750 kilometer front (470 miles) with some thirty-two divisions, or more than 20 kilometers per division. Hitler deferred a decision on post-Rasputitsa operations and left the afternoon of the 19th February to his forward headquarters at Vinnitsa, Ukraine, where he remained until the 13th of March.

On 20 February, Manstein launched his counteroffensive against the scattered, exhausted, but still advancing Soviet armies. The SS Panzer Corps, with two of its SS divisions (Das Reich and Totenkopf), initially pushed to the southeast into Vatutin's advancing forces, while the Fourth Panzer Army, spearheaded by the XLVIII (48th) Panzer Corps (consisting of the 6th and 17th Panzer Divisions), struck to the northwest. This attack was supported on its right by the XL (40th) Panzer Corps (7th and 11th Panzer Divisions and Viking SS Panzer Grenadier Division), which were part of the First Panzer Army and were dealing with the strong Lieutenant General Markian M. Popov's armored group on their front. Further to the east was the III Panzer Corps (3rd and 19th Panzer Divisions), which was still primarily in a defensive role. The III Panzer Corps had been one of the units transferred from Army Group A, and would later be one of the three panzer corps attacking the southern flank at Kursk. The engagements with the Popov group pitted the X and XVIII (18th) Tank Corps against the 7th and 11th Panzer Divisions and the Viking SS Panzer Grenadier Division. At the end of this action, these two Soviet tank corps were very depleted and started the Battle of Kursk in July in rearward reserve positions.

2 Krivosheyev, G. F., ed., *Grif Sekretnosti Snyat: Poteri Vooruzhennyikh sil SSSR v Voinakh, Boyevyikh Deistviyakh i Voyennyikh Konfliktakh. Statisticheskoye Issledovaniye* [The Mark of Secrecy has been Removed: Losses of the USSR Armed Forces in Wars, Combat Actions and Military Conflicts. A Statistical Study] (Voyennoye Izdatelstvo, Moscow, 1993).

On the 28th of February, Manstein issued orders to push the attack toward Kharkov and the Voronezh Front. The Fourth Panzer Army attack had by the 5th of March driven back the Soviet Third Tank Army, with few prisoners, and then continued to push due north with its two panzer corps, supported by drives from the west from Provisional Army Kempf's forces, including Corps Raus and the Gross Deutschland Division. As the ground was starting to thaw and the ice was breaking up on the Donets River, the options for maneuver became more limited and the Fourth Panzer Army was forced to race north. Meanwhile the Adolf Hitler SS Division was added to the attack, and to the east was now the newly inserted LVII (57th) Panzer Corps with the reassigned 17th Panzer Division (and the 6th and 11th Panzer Divisions now assigned to the XLVIII Panzer Corps). The Provisional Army Kempf and Fourth Panzer Army attacks went forward led by seven panzer and panzer grenadier divisions.[3]

Meanwhile the Soviet Army began shifting its forces in response to this drive, which would take the pressure off of Provisional Army Kempf. The Soviets sent in the II Guards Tank Corps as reinforcements and began moving three new armies, the Twenty-first, the Sixty-fourth, and the First Tank, to the area to bolster the defense.

MANSTEIN'S COUNTERATTACK WAS now not only steamrolling its way across the German southern front, but was beginning to take pressure off the entire German line. On the 10th of March, Hitler had paid a brief return visit to Manstein's headquarters, where Manstein once again discussed plans for after the spring thaw.

On the 9th of March, the German attack had advanced to the west of Kharkov. General Hoth, commander of the Fourth Panzer Army, ordered the SS Panzer Corps to surround Kharkov and then see if they could take it. The Fourth Panzer Army's main objective had not been to retake Kharkov, but to destroy the Soviet forces around Kharkov. SS General Hausser, in violation of Hoth's direct orders, on the 11th sent Das Reich and the Adolf Hitler SS Divisions into Kharkov while Totenkopf shielded the attack from the north. The city was taken with three days of fighting although not with particularly heavy losses. Meanwhile, elements of Totenkopf and Das Reich moved behind Kharkov, which almost completed the encirclement. The SS Panzer Corps, violating orders for a second time in a month, had retaken the city for their Fuehrer. Hoth declined to bring charges against Hausser. Meanwhile, the Gross Deutschland Division, against strong Soviet armored forces, was pushing on Belgorod.

Placed in the way above Belgorod was the 52nd Guards Rifle Division under commander of Major General N. D. Kozin. An advance detachment of the 155th Guards Rifle Regiment under Lieutenant Colonel G. G. Pentyukhov was sent toward Belgorod with the objective of engaging the enemy and taking prisoners. This detachment, near Shopino, succeeded in capturing prisoners from the Totenkopf SS Division.[4] The 52nd Guards Rifle Division was able to emplace itself solidly north of Belgorod, halting the German progress out of Belgorod. By the 20th/21st of March, the main forces of the Twenty-first Army had organized a strong defense north of Belgorod, and parts of the First Tank Army were about to mass in reserve south of Oboyan.

Manstein would have liked to clear out, with the help of Army Group Center, the large Soviet occupied bulge in order to shorten the German front. This idea had to be abandoned as Army Group Center declared itself unable to co-operate. Its commander, General Guenther von Kluge claimed that his Second Army and Second Panzer Army were in no shape to attack after their hard fight to stabilize their front. As a result the Kursk bulge remained, with its southern boundary established by these operations. As we will see, the weaknesses of Army Group Center continued to plague the Kursk operations.

By the 23rd and 24th of March, the northern limits of Manstein's counteroffensive were reached with the Gross Deutschland, 167th and 320th Infantry Divisions

3 Gross Deutschland was officially called an infantry division, even with its armored components.

4 Totenkopf SS Division reported 72 men missing-in-action from 25 January 1943 to 31 March 1943.

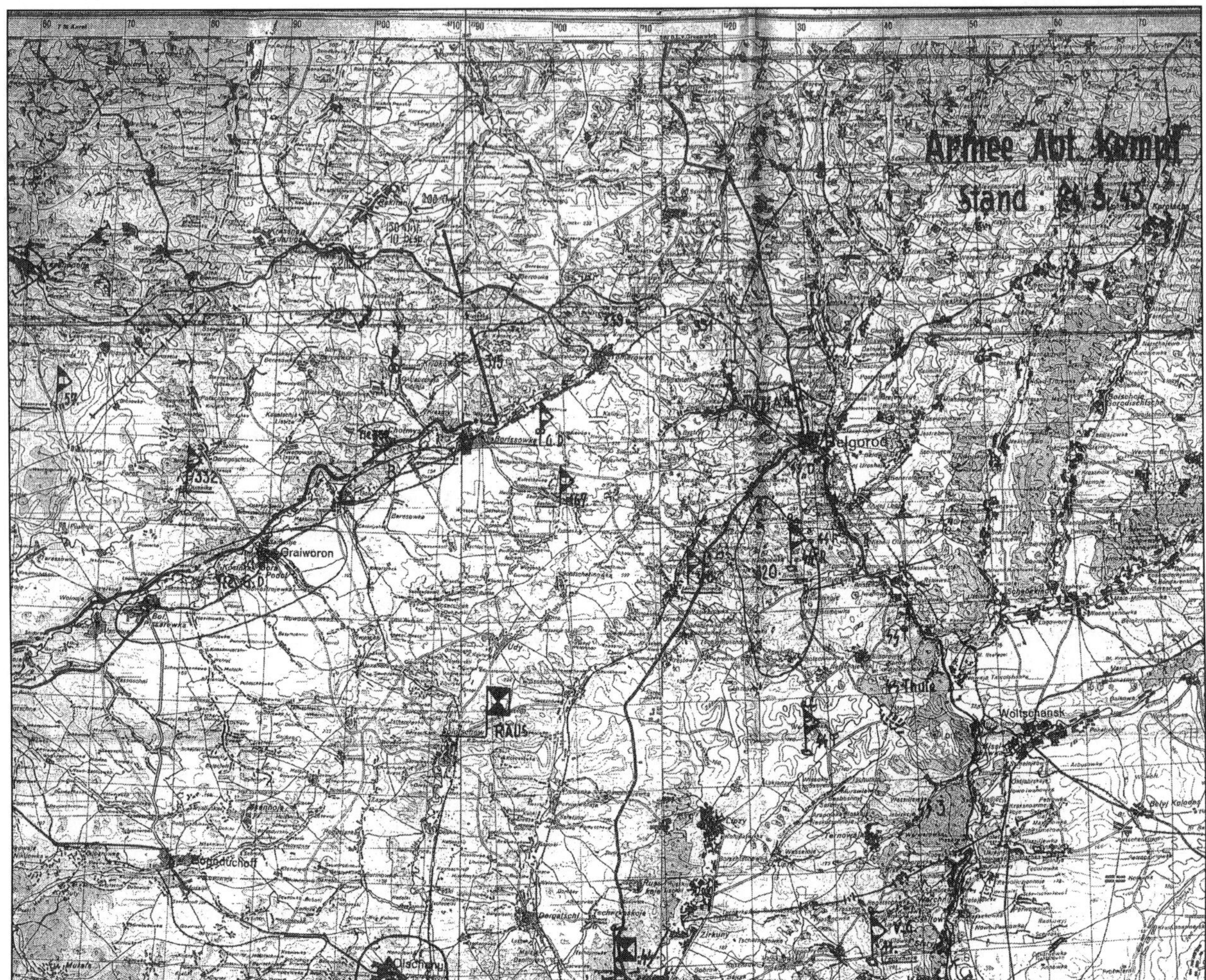

Provisional Army Kempf: Situation as of 24 March 1943

under Corps Raus, along with elements of the SS Panzer Corps, setting the northern boundary in the area to the west of Belgorod. This is where the front line would remain until the 4th of July. The German forces across all the attacking corps (LII [52nd], Raus, SS Panzer, XLVIII Panzer and LVII Panzer) finally settled down on the 25th and the Provisional Army Kempf and the Fourth Panzer Army went over to the defense.

The spring thaw had arrived, the roads had turned into quagmires of mud, and the troops were immobilized across the front. Kursk was still in Soviet hands. In place by late March were all the major formations of the Voronezh Front. The Soviet Fortieth, Twenty-first and Sixty-fourth Armies were in place along the line, while the First Tank Army and Sixty-ninth Army were in the rear. Two of these formations, the Twenty-first and Sixty-fourth Armies, were veteran organizations fresh from their victory at Stalingrad and were rested and refitted. The First Tank Army was a recently created formation. The Sixty-ninth Army, on the other hand, had been badly mauled in the German counterattack, and the Fortieth Army had been engaged in significant combat for a while. General Kirill Moskalenko (Fortieth Army) claimed that in the middle of February his divisions averaged 3,500 to 4,000 men each, while in the Sixty-ninth Army it is claimed that some divisions were as weak as 1,000 to 1,500 men supported by only about 20 guns and 50 mortars.

In the north, Rokossovskii's offensive, deprived of his reinforcing armies, had stalled. The advancing Soviet forces were driven back by German counterattacks starting 7 March, and this major movement of the front halted on the 21st of March. The defining lines of the Kursk bulge had been set.

So ended Germany's last major successful offensive of World War II. South of Belgorod, the Germans had returned to roughly the same line they had occupied before the summer 1942 offensive. North of Belgorod the Soviet Army occupied a very large and obvious bulge around the Kursk area. It was some 150 kilometers deep and 200 kilometers wide. It stretched the length of the front an additional 330 kilometers. It was an obvious point of attack and became the focus for the Battle of Kursk.

The Soviet winter offensive had ended. While the rather ambitious Soviet offensive drive was halted by Manstein's counterattack, overall the Soviet offensives that had started four months earlier on the 19th of November around Stalingrad had dealt the German Army its worst defeat since the Napoleonic Wars and had recovered all that was lost in the summer of 1942. The Soviet offensives had managed to surround and annihilate one German Army and had effectively swept the four German allied armies "off the map," as Manstein stated.

The Soviet winter offensive had cost the Germans and their allies maybe a million men.[5] The Soviet Union had regained virtually all the territory it had lost during the summer. The Soviets had humbled the German Army and had set the stage for the Battle of Kursk. This was done at considerable cost to themselves. The Soviet casualties recorded by Krivosheyev for the first quarter of 1943 (January through March) were 656,403 killed and missing and 1,421,140 wounded.

The two giants had fought themselves to a standstill. The spring thaw and the rains came and turned the southern front into a sea of mud. At this point, both armies sat down to take a break and wait for the summer. On 1 April, German Army strength in the east stood at 2,732,000 men in 147 infantry divisions and 22 panzer divisions and 1,336 tanks. Soviet Army strength for their operating Fronts and armies on 3 April was 5,792,999. According to German intelligence, they were organized into more than 500 divisions and supported by more than 6,000 tanks.[6]

Adolf Hitler had spent most of this time (19 February to 13 March) in his forward headquarters in Vinnitsa, Ukraine. While at Vinnitsa, he met with Colonel General Heinz Guderian, whom he had dismissed from command back in December 1941. On the 20th of February Hitler appointed Guderian to be the Inspector General of Armored Troops. At Guderian's insistence, this position reported directly to Hitler. Guderian, who had not seen Hitler since he was dismissed by him 14 months earlier, noted that he had aged greatly, his left hand trembled, his manner was less assured, and his speech was hesitant. Yet, when Hitler returned to East Prussia on the 13th of March, according to Lieutenant General Walter Warlimont, it was with the air of a victorious warlord, clearly considering himself and his

5 German losses on the Eastern Front were reported as 128,900 for November, 200,690 for December, 152,465 for January, 212,152 for February, and 111,525 for March. These are departures from the field army (killed, missing, and evacuated with wounds or illness). Added to that would be Italian, Romanian, and Hungarian losses. See HERO, *German and Soviet Replacement Systems in World War II*, page 55.

6 David M. Glantz and Jonathan House, *When Titans Clash: How the Red Army Stopped Hitler* (University Press of Kansas, Lawrence, Kansas, 1995), pages 151 and 349–50, note 7. The German strengths are from OKH reports. The Soviet strength was from Central Party Archives that put "operating Fronts and army" strengths at 5,792,000. Oddly enough, Glantz and House take the Soviet tank strength figure from the German OKH intelligence reports.

A report prepared by OKH, Organisationsabteilung (I) dated 18 September 1943 gives the German strength in the east as of 1 April 1943 as 2,719,293 (T78, R411).

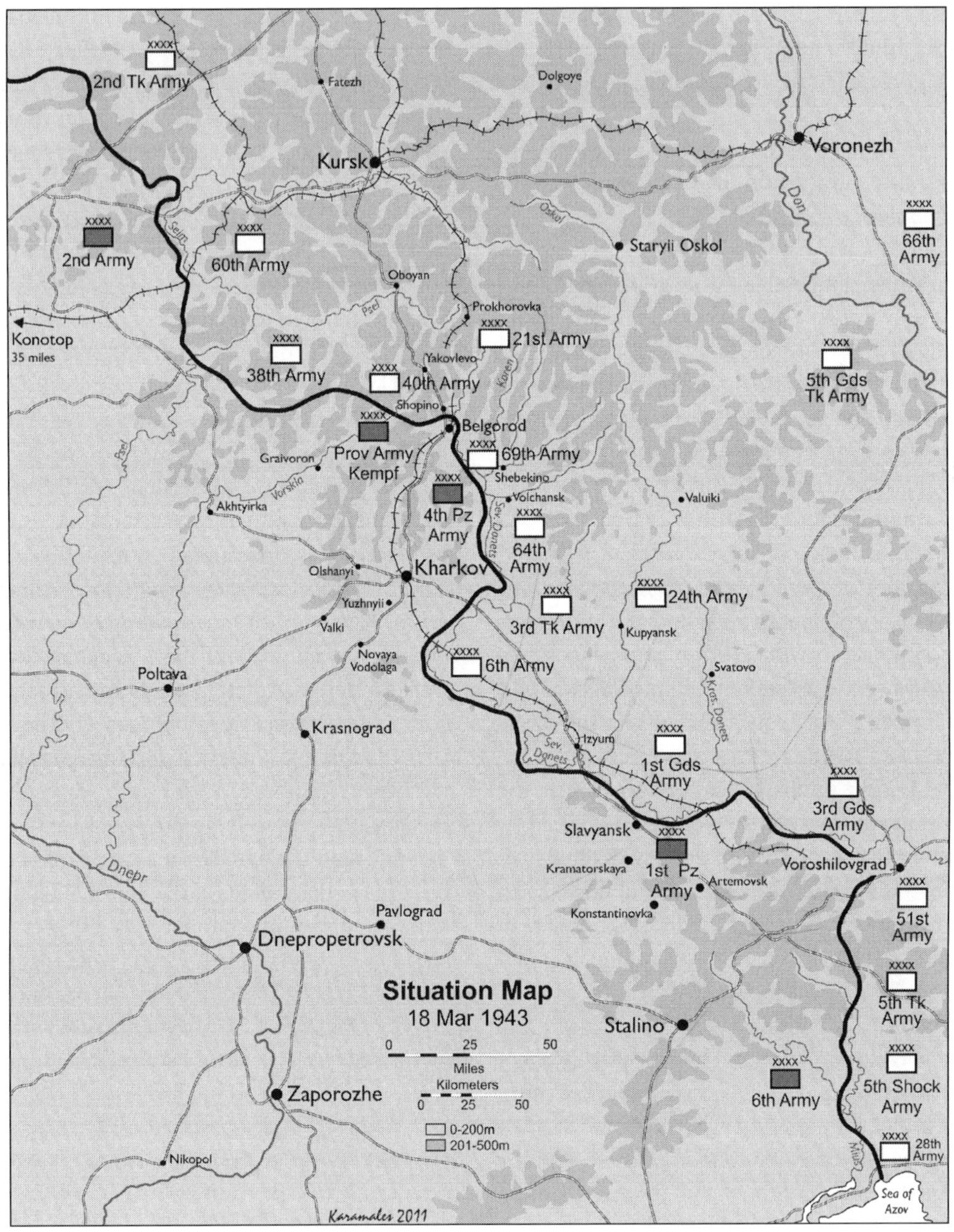

Situation Map
18 Mar 1943
2nd Tk Army
Fatezh
Dolgoye
Kursk
Voronezh
Don
Oskol
Staryii Oskol
66th Army
2nd Army
60th Army
Seim
Oboyan
Prokhorovka
Psel
Konotop
35 miles
21st Army
38th Army
Yakovlevo
40th Army
Koren
5th Gds Tk Army
Shopino
Belgorod
Prov Army Kempf
Graivoron
69th Army
Shebekino
Vorskla
4th Pz Army
Volchansk
Valuiki
Akhtyirka
Sev. Donets
64th Army
Olshanyi
Kharkov
24th Army
Yuzhnyii
3rd Tk Army
Valki
Kupyansk
Novaya Vodolaga
6th Army
Svatovo
Poltava
Krasnograd
Izyum
Krasn. Donets
1st Gds Army
3rd Gds Army
Slavyansk
Kramatorskaya
1st Pz Army
Artemovsk
Voroshilovgrad
Dnepr
Konstantinovka
51st Army
Pavlograd
Dnepropetrovsk
5th Tk Army
Stalino
Miles
Kilometers
0-200m
201-500m
6th Army
5th Shock Army
Zaporozhe
Mius
28th Army
Nikopol
Sea of Azov
Karamales 2011

leadership primarily responsible for closing the front again after the Stalingrad debacle.

This victorious warlord almost did not make it home, for among the cargo of Hitler's airplane was a bomb prepared by two of Kluge's staff officers, Colonel Henning von Tresckow, Kluge's chief of staff, and Major Fabian von Schlabrendorff. They had given a parcel to one of Hitler's staff officers, telling him that it was a gift of a couple of bottles of Cognac for a friend of Schlabrendorff's in Rastenburg. The bombs were timed with a half-hour setting but failed to go off. Schlabrendorff recovered the dormant bombs at Rastenburg and Hitler remained unaware of the attempt on his life.

This was not the only attempt on the Fuehrer's life that month. Earlier, General Hubert Lanz, the head of Provisional Army Lanz, had independently organized his own plot to kidnap and assassinate Hitler. The plot also included Major General Dr. Hans Speidel, his chief of staff, and Colonel Count Hyazinth Strachwitz, one of the most decorated soldiers in the army. They were waiting in Poltava on 9 February 1943 for Hitler to arrive, when at the last moment, as Hitler often did, his plans were changed and he flew to Zaporozhe instead. This ended this attempt, although Major General Hans Speidel later became involved in the 1944 attempt to assassinate Hitler. Even though he was arrested and held for seven months, he would survive the war and later hold a high command in NATO. Count Strachwitz would command the Gross Deutschland Panzer Regiment at Kursk.

THE TIME FROM late March through June 1943 was spent by both armies recuperating, rebuilding and preparing themselves for the third summer of war. The German Army in March 1943 was short some 470,000 men. On 23 January, they had only 495 tanks ready for combat on the entire Eastern Front (as compared to 3,300 in June 1941). Added to the problems faced by the German Army, their forces in North Africa had collapsed in May and they ended up with some 100,000 losses in that theater.

The Germans were able to replace their losses with additional call-ups and rebuild their armies back to their former strength. The German strength on the Eastern Front when they went in on 22 June 1941 was around 3,300,000 men. It had declined to 2,734,448 by 1 July 1942, but was built back up to the 2,900,000 range from October to January. After the winter campaign, it stood at 2,719,293 and was built back up to 3,005,398 by 1 July 1943. This was out of a total armed forces strength of 10,132,898.[7]

The Soviets also rebuilt their forces (see Cycle of War at the end of this chapter). They were also finally seeing a steady flow of lend-lease aid arrive. British convoys had regularly been sailing to Murmansk and Archangel in the north since the fall of 1941, while U.S. aid was beginning to arrive in large quantities through Persia (now Iran) since the spring of 1942. The stage was set for the Battle of Kursk.

7 All data given here is from a report prepared by OKH, Organisationsabteilung (I) dated 18 September 1943 (T78, R411). Contrary to some claims, this was not the strongest the German armed forces were was during the war, for on 1 January 1944, they were reported to have a strength of 10,597,000 (T78, R411, page 6379590). In contrast David M. Glantz and Jonathan M. House, *The Battle of Kursk* (University Press of Kansas, Lawrence, Kansas, 1999), page 16, state that the German armed forces were at 9.5 million on 30 May 1943 and that this was their highest strength of the entire war.

The following chart lists the Soviet casualties by calendar quarter (killed and missing) and total casualties. It also includes total strength.

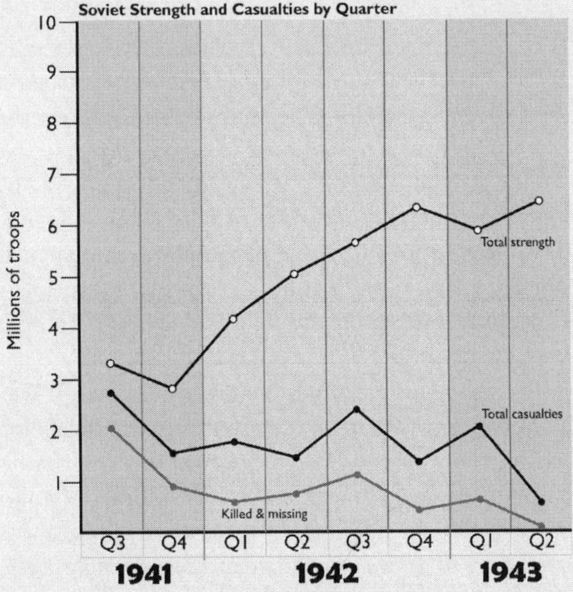

This chart is drawn from figures in Krivosheyev's book.[1] They are a summation of losses for the Fronts, and as such are less than total Soviet losses. Still, they show a clear pattern. The two bloodiest periods of the war are the two German summer offensives in the 3rd quarter of 1941 and 1942. The third and fourth periods with the highest casualties (although not the highest killed and missing) are the two Soviet winter offensives in the first quarter of 1942 and 1943. Then there is the very quiet period of the 2nd quarter of 1943, which was indeed the quietest period of the war, suffering even fewer losses than the Soviet Army suffered in the 3rd quarter of 1945, when Germany surrendered with the fighting ended less than half way through the quarter.

Comparative Losses

Even though there is concern that Krivosheyev's figures underestimate Soviet losses, especially for 1941, a comparison of German[2] versus Soviet losses by quarter is illustrative.

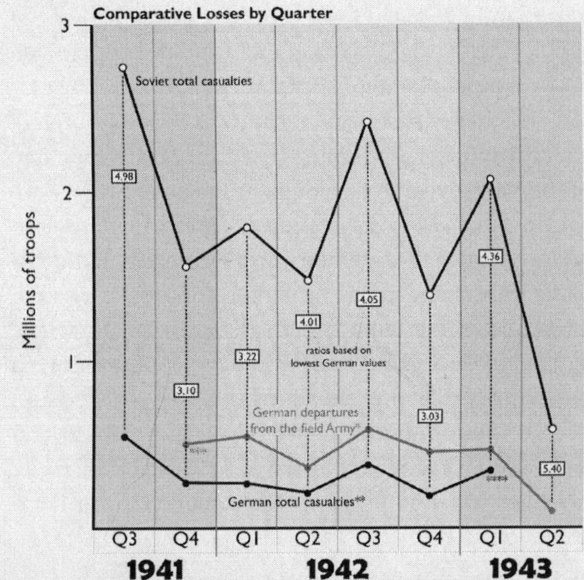

* This includes killed, missing, and evacuated with wounds or illness. It signifies departures from the field army, vice all casualties.
** This is drawn from BA-MA RW 6/v.552 and v.553, *Casualties on the Eastern Front 1941*. It covers from June 22 to the end of 1942. The June casualties (as the Krivosheyev figures do not appear to report these first nine days) are 41,084 and are included in the figures here: the ratio is 5.38 with this data not included. Data provided courte of Niklas Zetterling.
*** Data only provided for December (168,000). This figure was multiplied by three to produce a gross quarterly figure.
**** Data only covers January (260,080) and February (90,815). No attempt was made to estimate March.

1 Krivosheyev, pages 152–153, table 72.

2 German data is from the HERO Report: *German and Soviet Replacement Systems in World War II* (HERO, Dunn Loring, VA, July 1975), page 55. It was drawn from T78, R415, H1/182.

CHAPTER ONE

Preparing for the Showdown

SUMMARY: Mission saw an armored division including a battalion of Tiger Tanks execute a combat exercise with live ammunition south of Kharkov on June 26. Visited infantry division June 27 at front in rain and mud. Saw defenses in West, which are incomplete. Returned to Germany and saw Hitler who said Western defense will be completed in 8 to 10 months and Allies will not attack before that time. Hitler appeared nervous, preoccupied and not in best health. German civilians are depressed; army morale is still good.

FROM A U.S. INTELLIGENCE REPORT ON 23 JULY 1943
FROM THE U.S. MILITARY ATTACHE TO
TURKEY BRIGADIER GENERAL RICHARD G. TINDALL[1]

IN FEBRUARY 1943, while the offensives were still underway to restore the front, Manstein and Army Group South presented a tentative plan to Hitler for a strategic defensive for the summer. The plan was to wait until the Soviets started an offensive and then hit them hard "on the backhand" at the first good opportunity. It envisioned that if the Soviets launched a pincer attack on the Donets area from the north and the south, an operation which may be supplemented by an offensive around Kharkov, then the German front along the Donets and Mius should be given up in accordance with an agreed time table and the enemy should be drawn westward toward the lower Dnepr. Simultaneously, all the reserves that could possibly be released, including most of the armor, were to assemble west of Kharkov. They were to smash any attacking enemy forces around Kharkov and then drive into the flank of those forces advancing in the direction of the lower Dnepr. This would trap the Soviet forces along the coast of the Sea of Azov and allow Manstein to inflict considerable casualties on the Soviets, especially by gathering prisoners of war.

Such a plan requires two major conditions, first, that the army conducting the retreat is sufficiently disciplined to be able to retreat in good order, which the German Army probably was, and second, that the attacking army would get disorganized and weakened as they advanced. This, by nature, tends to happen with any attack. As a force moves away from its starting point, it tends to outrun its supply, exhaust its troops, wear down its equipment and outrun its air support. In the case of the Soviet Army attacks, this was even more so the case, as the lead elements had a tendency to be pushed until they

1 Military Intelligence Division W. D. G. S.; Military Attache Report Germany; Subject: Visit of Turkish Mission to Germany; I.G. No 5840; From M.A. Turkey; Report No. 7844; Date July 23, 1943. This is a U.S. Turkish Military Attache Report of 23 July 1943 prepared by Brigadier General Richard G. Tindall. This report was based on personal conversations with Turkish officers recently in Russia, France and Germany.

exhausted their men, machines and supplies. It was not unheard of for the armored spearhead of Soviet attacks to run out of fuel. As Manstein was showing with his counterattacks in February 1943, the Soviet attacks, when they reach the end of their tether, could easily be slapped back with considerable casualties to the Soviet Army, especially if the Germans conserved and concentrated their armored formations. Still, such a plan required an organized retreat in the face of an aggressively attacking Soviet Army. This is always a risky proposition.

It was also a plan that attempted to address the weakness of the German Army, which was that it really did not have sufficient forces to hold the line along the Eastern Front. With each division holding an average of ten kilometers of front, it was difficult to prevent penetrations and breakthroughs. As such, the plan attempted to make a strength out of their weakness.

This plan did not appeal to Hitler. He was concerned about the economic value of the Donets Basin and the political repercussions of even a temporary evacuation on Turkey and Romania. More fundamental, Hitler had a belief, reinforced by his experience in the Soviet winter offensive of 1941, that one should fight for every inch of ground. He believed that his no retreat orders in 1941 "saved the German Army from a Napoleonic retreat." Also, the risks of such an operation were obvious. It would require a calculated loss of terrain and would start the front in a retrograde maneuver that might never be arrested. Furthermore, it required waiting for the Soviets to initiate the attack, which meant that one could be holding forces in reserve for a considerable time if the Soviets were in no hurry to attack. Germany was expecting an Allied invasion somewhere in the Mediterranean soon and sorely needed to bolster their Italian ally, who had lost an army in the Soviet Union and was about to lose another one in Tunisia. The advantage of striking at a time convenient to the Germans would be that they could then shift their armored forces for operations elsewhere. Waiting until the Soviet Army attacked would take that strategic flexibility away. Germany could be holding reserves in the east waiting for the expected attack, while the allies were invading and Italy was collapsing in the west.

Therefore, Hitler decided to strike first. The bulge around Kursk presented an obvious target, and its reduction, in addition to shortening lines, would also eliminate the jump-off points for Soviet attacks against Orel and Kharkov.

While the "backhand" blow is often described as Manstein's idea (although Manstein credits the anonymous "Army Group South" with the suggestion), according to Major General Theodor Busse, Manstein's chief of staff, it was also advocated by the Chief of the Army General Staff (Col. General Kurt Zeitzler), the Chief of Operations (Lt. General Adolf Heusinger), and the commanding generals of Army Group Center (Kluge) and South (Manstein).

The Germans had been stunned by their defeat at Stalingrad. They had lost around 300,000 troops there. Although this loss did not permanently cripple the German Army, for recruitment during the spring had rebuilt its strength back up to its pre-Stalingrad level, this had become a war of attrition and the losses from all these defeats were telling. The damage done to the German allies was particularly severe, and the reduced presence of the allies could only be compensated for by stretching the German forces all that much thinner. Still, even with that re-building effort, the Germans were really only able to assemble one strategic reserve to strike in one area. The men, formations and equipment lost at Stalingrad were to be sorely missed, as were all the losses from the Soviet winter offensive.

Make no mistake about it, the Germans had been resoundingly defeated, Hitler had been humbled and a German marshal had surrendered for the first time in history. The German Army had been pushed back 400 kilometers from Stalingrad. Now it was time to attack again. This attack was militarily, politically, and psychologically desirable. The German Army immediately began discussing its next summer attack. Even in OKW (the headquarters effectively in charge of every theater but the Eastern Front), the Chief of the Wehrmacht Operations Staff, Col. General Alfred Jodl, on 29

November 1942, prepared an appreciation of the overall situation. He stated that "we must finally establish a firm front in the East so that next spring we can take the offensive at least in one area."[2]

THE ATTACK WAS MILITARILY desirable because of the need to shorten the front, to wound the Soviet Army, to reestablish initiative and to rebuild German confidence.

The Eastern Front covered some 2,000 kilometers, not counting Finland and Karelia. Germany in April 1943 had 177 German and 17 Allied divisions, not counting those in Finland and Karelia, available to cover this front. This resulted in an average frontage of around ten kilometers per division. The perimeter of the Kursk bulge itself was 600 kilometers. If this bulge could be cut off, this would reduce the German lines by 330 kilometers, or the overall German front by one-sixth. This reduced front would be easier to hold and may have allowed Germany to free up to another 30 divisions for operations elsewhere. This argument implies that the Germans were now looking at a more defensive strategy in what had developed into a war of attrition.

The other obvious advantage to a double envelopment of the Kursk bulge is that it would surround and destroy the Soviet forces that were in the forward part of the bulge. It presented another opportunity to wound the Soviet Army.

It was also felt that the German Army needed to reestablish the initiative. The German Army could do the most damage to its opponents in a fluid offensive situation. This meant that it was desirable to create such a fluid situation, which the Germans excelled at and the Soviets did not. In effect, the Germans needed to determine the pace and direction of operations so the fighting could be steered to their advantage.

Finally, while the German Army certainly still had confidence in their fighting prowess, their confidence in their leaders and the course of the war effort certainly had been shaken by the events since November 1942. In addition to the Eastern Front disasters, the German Army had also been rolled back by the British in North Africa and the U.S. had invaded North Africa. There was a large battle building there with the Western Allies that would determine control of the Mediterranean. Furthermore, German cities were now being bombed both day and night by the American and the British air forces. In January, the U.S. Army Air Force flying fortresses (B-17s) staged the first daylight bombing attack on Germany. In March, the British resumed night bombing, now using their four-engine bombers. The war was now being carried to the German homeland.

WAR IS NEVER DEVOID of political and psychological considerations. The Axis allies, Romania, Italy, Hungary and Finland, were concerned. Romania had two armies overrun in the fighting and Italy had lost one. After the disaster at Stalingrad and the subsequent Soviet offensives, these allies obviously needed to be reassured that the German Army was as virile and capable as before. This was best served by unleashing yet another of the successful German summer offensives. The political imperatives for some form of offense were very strong as the axis allies still made a significant contribution to the German war effort. As was stated in Hitler's announcement to his troops before the battle, "The victory at Kursk must have the effect of a beacon seen around the world."

FINALLY, THERE WERE some overriding psychological reasons for the German Army to attack. The German Army had just suffered its first major defeat since the Napoleonic Wars, and in all reality, the greatest defeat in its history. It was beginning to look like they were about to face a similar defeat in Tunisia. There clearly was a strong emotional need to re-establish their superiority over the Russians. It was needed to salve their

2 Gen. Walter Warlimont, *Inside Hitler's Headquarters 1939–45* (Presidio Press, Novato, CA, 1964), page 282.

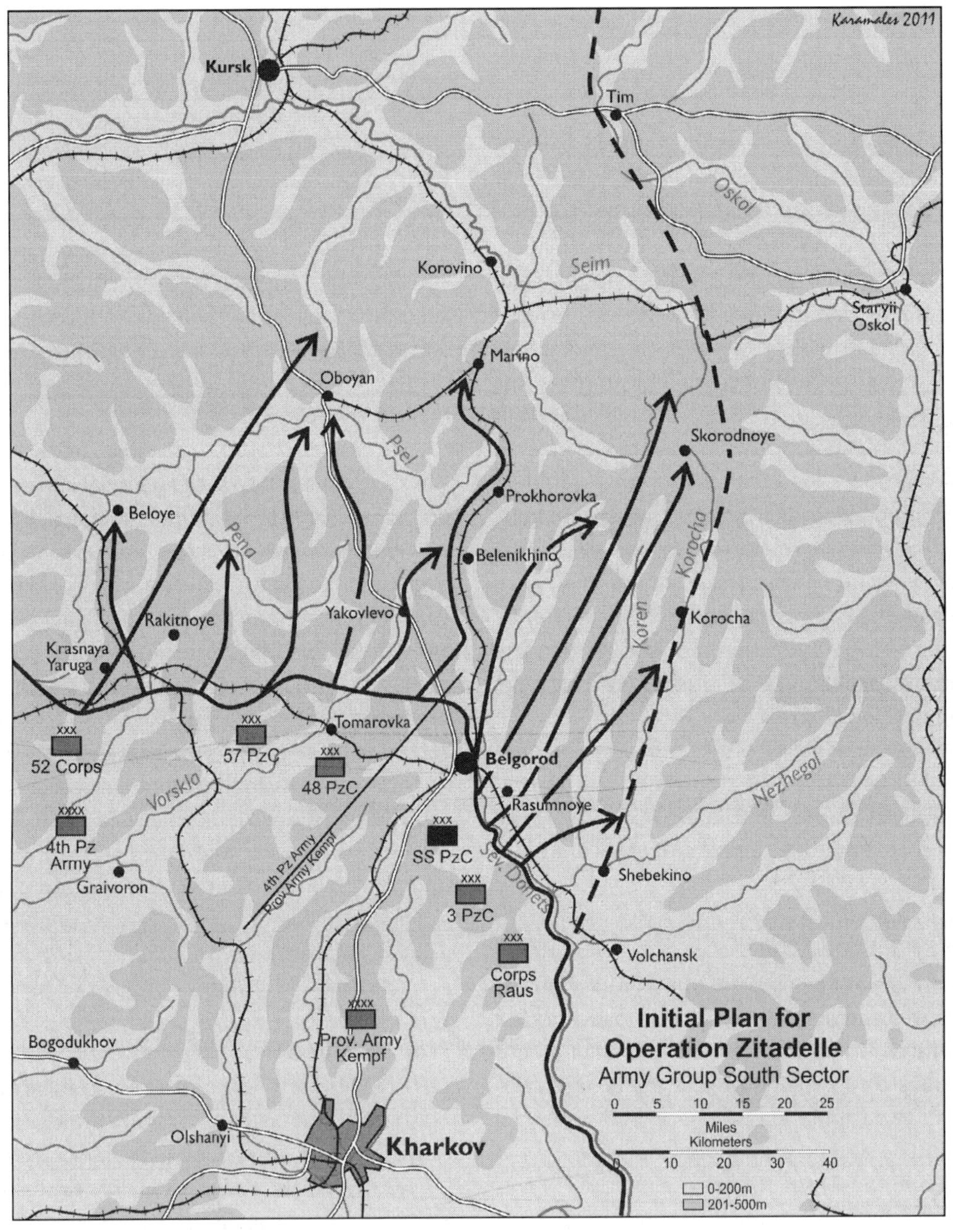
Karamales 2011
Kursk
Tim
Oskol
Seim
Korovino
Staryii Oskol
Marino
Oboyan
Psel
Skorodnoye
Prokhorovka
Beloye
Pena
Belenikhino
Korocha
Koren
Yakovlevo
Korocha
Rakitnoye
Krasnaya Yaruga
Tomarovka
52 Corps
57 PzC
48 PzC
Belgorod
Vorskla
Rasumnoye
Nezhegol
4th Pz Army
4th Pz Army
Prov Army Kempf
SS PzC
Graivoron
Sev. Donets
Shebekino
3 PzC
Volchansk
Corps Raus
Prov. Army Kempf
Bogodukhov
Olshanyi
Kharkov
Initial Plan for Operation Zitadelle
Army Group South Sector
Miles
Kilometers
0-200m
201-500m

own wounded pride, to re-build their confidence, and to shake the Russian confidence. This made it almost imperative that the Germans open up the summer season with yet another attack.

Therefore, there were strong military arguments in favor of an attack, strong external and internal political arguments in favor of an attack, and a psychological argument and need to conduct an attack. While one could also present a strong military argument for remaining on the defensive, the political and psychological arguments were certainly going to be overriding.

The year 1943 was bound to be the last year the German command could expect to operate unencumbered by the threat of a major second front. This made the need to strike in several places and seize the initiative all the more important. The first place chosen was the Kursk bulge. This, of course, was the most obvious target. That this bulge in the line presented such a target was also clear to the Soviet planners. It was some 200 kilometers wide and protruded into the German lines some 150 kilometers. It stretched the length of the front an additional 330 kilometers. Reducing it would shorten the lines along the Eastern Front by more than 15 percent, easing the defensive burden for the overstretched German Army.

The strategic reserves that Germany was going to assemble for this operation were two armies. In 1941, Germany had attacked with 17 armies (four of them allied). In 1942, the German offensive had been reduced to ten armies (four of them allied). Now, the best they could muster for their third summer offensive was four armies (including the dormant Second Army).

In many respects, the attack in the south was merely the continuation of Manstein's spring counteroffensive. Most of the German attacking forces used in the southern part of the Kursk offensive were already in place, as were most of the Soviet defending forces. In effect, the battle was a continuation on 5 July of an attack that had halted on 24 March, with mostly the same players and a whole lot more equipment.

Unlike the 1944 Ardennes offensive, which was clearly Hitler's plan, it does not appear that Hitler produced this battle plan and then pushed it on his generals. The impression that one gathers is that a Kursk-like operation was being discussed by Manstein, Zeitzler, Kluge, and Hitler. Kursk, or the "forehand" blow, as Manstein called it in his book, was not Manstein's preferred course of action. Still, Manstein felt that an attack in May would be effective, although Guderian has him later claiming, somewhat unrealistically, that it needed to occur in April.

If anyone could be assigned responsibility for initiating the idea, it is probably Manstein and the staff of Army Group South. The details of the planning and coordinating the actions of the two army groups would go to the Chief of Staff of OKH, Zeitzler. Once the idea of Manstein's "backhand" was off the table, then most likely the details of the plan were reached by consensus. The decision to choose that option rested with Hitler. The planning for it rested with General Zeitzler and the German OKH staff, leading a number of writers to blame him for the plan. The plan was most likely jointly authored, with the idea originally suggested by Manstein, decided upon by Hitler, and supported by Zeitzler. In the end, as commander in chief of the army, the final decision lay with Hitler.

THE PLAN FOR the Battle of Kursk was announced with Operations Order No. 5, 13 March 1943. It was issued the day Hitler flew back from Smolensk with a bomb that failed to detonate in the cargo hold in his Ju-52. This failed assassination attempt was courtesy of the Chief Operations Officer of Army Group Center, Colonel Henning von Treskow. Operations Order No. 5 was the planning for the next German offensive and was issued while the Germans were still fighting to take Kharkov.

The new German operation, *Operation Citadel* (called *Zitadelle* in German), is clearly spelled out here, with a strong panzer army launching an attack northward from Kharkov in conjunction with the forces from Army Group Center. The initial readiness date given for the south was for a panzer army to be assembled by the middle of April. Still, this is not an attack date. The date for actual operations to begin was before the expected Soviet offensive could get underway at the end of the mud period. Therefore, the earliest date for the operation is the 15th of April, although clearly a date could be set that was later than that.

On 15 April, Operations Order No. 6 announced Hitler's "final decision." *Operation Citadel* was set, with the date to be decided, but no earlier than 3 May. The order warned that the operation would have to be done quickly because the troops were needed for other missions. Second, it warned Army Group Center and South to be on guard against Soviet attacks in other sectors on either side of the Kursk bulge. This problem was particularly acute in the area of the northern attack, as Kluge's forces would be attacking to cut off the Kursk bulge from their own Orel bulge. As such, the same could be done to them as they were trying to do to the Soviet Army. Even in the south, the line of the Donets River projected westward to below Kharkov, creating a potentially dangerous situation.

Army Group South was ready to attack. In the north with Army Group Center, their world still consisted of exhausted units, trying to incorporate new replacements and bring their equipment back up to strength. The organization designated to lead the Northern attack for Army Group Center was the Ninth Army, commanded by Colonel General Walter Model. He protested that Ninth Army's deployment could not be completed by 3 May and insisted that its mission needed to be reduced or the operation had to be put off to at least 15 May.

Meanwhile, Jodl, the Chief of Staff of OKW, had objected to Kursk because it was dangerous to plunder the reserves for operations in the East when there were so many problems in the Mediterranean. Hitler was now having doubts about the details of the plan. A few days after signing the order on the 15th of April, Hitler telephoned Zeitzler, and suggested they substitute the pincer attack, which the enemy would almost certainly be prepared for, with a frontal assault on the center of the Kursk bulge by the combined forces of Army Group Center and South. This proposal alarmed Zeitzler and he flew to Berchtesgaden on 21 April to demonstrate with maps and statistics that such a re-deployment would result in intolerable delays in launching *Citadel*.

Still, it was becoming obvious that the Soviets had guessed that an attack was coming and were preparing for it. Army Group South estimated that from reserves already at hand, the Soviets could throw eight tank corps, five mechanized, and five cavalry corps against the Fourth Panzer Army in the first six days of its attack. On 18 April, German air reconnaissance reported that long truck columns were moving out of Moscow toward Kursk and out of Stalingrad to Valuiki, due east of Kharkov.

THEN CAME A SERIES of short postponements. On 26 April, OKH agreed to postpone the operation two days, to 5 May. On the morning of 30 April, they agreed to four more days of delay due to heavy rains (postponed to 9 May). This was at the request of the Ninth Army commander, General Model. Even after that extension, Model was still indicating that he could not meet the deadline. That afternoon, they ordered that all directives setting a day for *Citadel* be canceled and destroyed. A new date would be set after Hitler had conferred with the commanding generals.

This last decision was the result of the commander of the Ninth Army, Colonel General Walther Model, expressing serious concerns about the operation. He had been studying the aerial reconnaissance of the Soviet defensive systems. He had originally planned to break through the Soviet defenses in two days. Now he was not sure they could do this. Model was looking at the difficulties of trying to force a breakthrough against these strong Soviet positions because of their artillery superiority and, in particular, their strong anti-tank defenses. The result, in Model's opinion, would be an offensive that would be protracted enough that the enemy would have time to move up his reserves. In that case, success would no longer be certain. On 27 April, Model flew to Munich and met with Adolf Hitler on the 28th to relay his concerns. At Hitler's retreat at the Berghof (near Berchtesgaden in Bavaria), he and Model poured over Model's reconnaissance photos in the Great Hall. Twelve months later, Hitler would claim that Model's concerns, with the additional heavy loss of assault troops this implied, gave him cold feet about *Citadel*.

TABLE 1.1
A NOTE FROM THE FILES OF THE INSPECTOR GENERAL OF ARMORED TROOPS

	Tanks	*Tiger*	*Panther*	*Hornet*	*Assault Tank*	*Ferdinand*
Army Group South	616	53		30		
In route by 9 May	30	16				
In route by 1 June	30			15		
In route by 10 June	20	28			40	
	—	—	—	—	—	—
	696	97		45	40	

	Tanks	*Tiger*	*Panther*	*Hornet*	*Assault Tank*	*Ferdinand*
Army Group Center	286	20				
In route by 9 May	29					
In route by 1 June	121			45		
In route by 10 June	63	31	200			86
	—	—	—	—	—	—
	499	51	200	45		86

THE CONFERENCE ON Kursk was called for 4 May. The day before that, Guderian and Hitler met to discuss tank production. A note in the Inspector General of Armored Troops' files appears to show the tank production status for the offensive.[3] See Table 1.1.

Therefore, according to their planning, they had 699 tanks in the south, and 306 in the north. This put the armor strength in the north at 44 percent of that in the south. By delaying the offensive to 9 May, they potentially had 745 tanks in the south (6.6 percent more) and 335 in the north (9.5 percent more). Delaying the offensive to 1 June did little for the south (790 tanks, or 13 percent more than the 3 May strength) but added significantly to the north (501 tanks, or almost 64 percent more in the north). Delaying to 10 June even further reinforced the north, with now a total of 878 in the south (25.6 percent more than on 3 May) and 881 in the north (or around 188 percent more in the north). These figures leave out Sturmgeschuetz IIIs and IVs (assault guns), and the Marders (self-propelled antitank guns), which were a significant portion of German armor strength.

With this delay of the offensive to at least 10 June (after all, these are "in route" dates), the attack in the north almost tripled its armor, and was now equal in tank strength to the southern attack, as opposed to being less than half the strength of the southern attack. Overall, there was now 75 percent more armor for this attack. This was clearly the basis of the discussion in the following day's meeting about delaying the offensive. The reason for a delay would be to build up armor in Army Group Center, with 200 of the newly designed Panther tanks originally slated to go there. The fact that neither the Panthers nor Hornets were really combat capable was another issue, but one can see the basis for the decision to delay the offensive to early June. Faced with a choice of conducting an offensive with the northern attack group not having enough or heavy enough armor to penetrate, or canceling the offensive altogether,

3 T78, R6232, Fuehrervortrag, Zufurung Stand: 3 Mai 1943. Provided courtesy of Frederick L. Clemens, whose research helped clarify my understanding of the deployment of the Panthers.

this briefing provided Hitler with a third option, which was to delay the offensive. Whether this was Guderian's purpose is not known.[4]

Hitler then summoned the senior commanders to Munich for a three-hour conference on 4 May to discuss the battle. Those present at the conference included:

Adolf Hitler, commander of the Army and the Armed Forces
Field Marshal Wilhelm Keitel, the Chief of Staff of OKW,
Col. General Alfred Jodl, Chief of OKW Operations Staff,
Col. General Kurt Zeitzler, the Chief of the Army General Staff,
and his staff (including the first General Staff Officer of the Armed Forces Operational Staff),
Field Marshal von Manstein, commander of Army Group South,
Field Marshal von Kluge, commander of Army Group Center, along with the chief quartermaster of Army Group Center,
Col. General Guderian, the Inspector General of Armored Troops, whose last field command was held under Kluge who had helped get him dismissed,
Col. General Hans Jeschonneck, the Chief of Staff of the Luftwaffe,
General of Infantry Schmundt, Hitler's military adjutant, and
Colonel i.G. Scherff

Guderian claims in his memoirs that Colonel General Walter Model, commander of the Ninth Army, and Albert Speer, the Minister of Armaments, were present during this meeting and that Colonel Wolfgang Thomale showed up for the 4 May meeting (but was not at the 3 May meeting). This has been questioned in some histories, with Ernst von Klink's book stating declaratively that they were not there. Model's objections were probably presented to the meeting in a letter.[5]

Hitler opened the conference with a speech that lasted for three-quarters of an hour. He described the situation on the Eastern Front and then went on to outline the proposed plan and the arguments that Model had presented against them. Model had produced information, based mostly upon air photography, that the Soviet Army was preparing deep and strong defensive positions in exactly those areas where the attack by the two army groups was supposed to go. The Soviets had withdrawn the bulk of their mobile formations from the forward area of the salient, and had strengthened the two bases of the bulge with unusually strong artillery and antitank forces. In particular, Model believed that the German main medium tank, the Mark IV, would not stand up to the new Soviet antitank guns. Model's conclusion was that the enemy was counting on the Germans launch-

4 Below clearly states that in April Guderian supported Hitler's decision to postpone *Citadel* so the panzer force could be strengthened. See Nicolaus von Below, *At Hitler's Side: The Memoirs of Hitler's Luftwaffe Adjutant 1937–1945* (Greenhill Books, London, 2001), page 168.

5 Ernst von Klink, *Das Gesertz Des Handelns, Die Operation "Zitadelle" 1943* (Deutsche Verlags-Anstalt, Stuttgart, 1966), footnote 184, page 140, states that a memo from General of the Infantry Busse, at that time the Chief of Staff for Army Group South, dated 12 April 1958, names the following participants: Field Marshal von Manstein, the Chiefs of the General Staff of the Army and Air Force, Field Marshal von Kluge with the Chief Quartermaster of Army Group Center, Colonel General Guderian, General of Infantry Schmundt, the first general staff officer of the WFSt (Armed Forces Operation Staff) and Colonel i.G. Scherff. Not present were Colonel General Model and contrary to the mention of Colonel General Guderian, Minister Speer and Colonel Thomale.

Below, *At Hitler's Side*, clearly indicates that Model was not there and furthermore states that it was Model who advised Hitler to postpone the offensive for another month to July so as to allow the Ninth Army the maximum number of tanks for the operation. See Below, page 171.

Also see Albert Seaton, *The Russo-German War 1941–1945* (Presidio Press, Novato, CA, 1993, first published 1971), page 356. Most histories, including the usually careful Earl F. Ziemke, *Stalingrad to Berlin: The German Defeat in the East* (Center of Military History, the United States Army, Washington DC, 1987, originally published 1968), page 129, indicate that Model and Speer were there.

ing this attack and therefore the Germans must adopt a fresh tactical approach, in effect, abandon this attack altogether. In Guderian's opinion, the manner in which Hitler expressed this opinion of Model's made it plain that he was impressed by Model's arguments and that he had not decided yet in favor of the attack.

According to Guderian, Hitler polled his generals for their opinion, starting with Manstein. Manstein stated that the attack would have had a good chance of succeeding if it had been launched in April, now its success was doubtful, and he would need a further two full-strength infantry divisions in order to carry it out. Hitler replied that two divisions were not available and Manstein must make do with what he had. Hitler then repeated his question, and according to Guderian, received no clear answer from Manstein.

Manstein, in his memoirs, claims to have urged an immediate attack, claiming that because of the collapse of German and Italian resistance in Tunisia, which was expected any day, this would be followed in a few weeks by a British and American landing in the Mediterranean. This would create more complications, therefore an immediate attack was the best. Manstein states that neither he nor Kluge wanted the attack postponed.

According to Guderian, Hitler then addressed Kluge, who spoke unambiguously in favor of the Kursk operation. He declared that the Ninth Army was not as bad off as Model thought. Jeschonnek added that a delay would not benefit the Air Force. Guderian then claims that he asked to express his views, and stated that the attack was pointless. The German Army had only just completed reorganization and re-equipping of the Eastern Front, and if Germany attacked, they would certainly suffer heavy tank losses which could not be replaced in 1943. Guderian also stated that Germany should be devoting its tank production to the Western Front so as to have mobile reserves available to use against the allied landing that was almost certainly coming in 1944. He also pointed out that the new Panther tank, which Zeitzler was relying on so heavily, was still suffering many teething problems, as is typical of all new equipment, and it did not seem that all these problems could be corrected before the attack. Guderian claims that Speer also supported these arguments from his point of view of arms production. According to Guderian's account, Guderian, Speer, and Model were the only men present at the meeting who clearly opposed the offensive. There is some question whether Speer and Model were actually present at the meeting. Model's immediate superior, Kluge, was in favor of conducting the attack. No decision was reached that day, but Hitler did indicate privately to Model that there would be a postponement.

But, there are sources that contradict Guderian and Manstein. According to the controversial historian David Irving, Field Marshal Wolfram Baron von Richthofen has a description of the conference in his diary. This description was provided to him by General Jeschonnek as Richthofen did not attend. Irving quotes Richthofen's diary as stating:

> [On 27 April] General Model declared he was not strong enough and would probably get bogged down or take too long. The Fuehrer took the view that the attack must be punched through without fail in shortest time possible. [Early in May] General Guderian offered to furnish enough tank units within six weeks to guarantee this. The Fuehrer thus decided on a postponement of six weeks. To get the blessing of all sides on this decision, he called a conference [on 4 May] with Field Marshals von Kluge and von Manstein. At first they agreed on a postponement; but when they heard that the Fuehrer had already made his mind up to that effect, they spoke out for an immediate opening of the attack—apparently in order to avoid the odium of being blamed for the postponement themselves.[6]

As no stenogram exists of this conference, one is left only with the memoirs of two generals and the diary of a person who did not participate. There also are what

6 David Irving, page 514 (or pages 583–584 in his 2001 version of the book that is available on the web). According to emails received from David Irving in 2002 and 2008, this passage is a directly translated quote from the diary, and the diary was stored at the Militargeschichtliches Forschungsamt at Freiburg im Breisgau, Germany. A xerox of the page in question is stored in the Irving Collection at the Institut fur Zeitgeschechte in Munich, Germany. We have not checked these files and cannot confirm the translation.

appear to be the Inspector General of Armored Troops' notes for the meeting for 3 May. These notes clearly show the beneficial effects on tank strength of a six-week delay in the offensive. Guderian's memoirs are quite explicit as to what happened at the conference but appear to be confused as to attendees and dates. Manstein mentions the conference and the issues in a very general sense. The Richthofen entry contradicts the other two memoirs, claiming that Guderian was the source of the six- week delay and that Manstein and Kluge supported the delay. It is impossible to resolve these differences. Guderian probably opposed the offensive altogether, which is what Guderian says. Still, Guderian may have pushed for its postponement. If this is correct, than this was a dangerous bureaucratic political maneuver that did not serve the German Army well.

Hitler's answer to these concerns was that these difficulties could only be overcome by strongly reinforcing both attacking armies with more panzer forces, particularly by the deployment of the newly-developed Panthers, Tigers, and new heavy assault guns. Hitler ended up proposing letting *Citadel* wait until 10 June, when they expected to have the new and heavier tanks available in quantity. Some, if not most of the major commanders objected, maintaining that the delay would benefit the Soviets more than the Germans. As the Germans knew the Soviet tank output was higher than theirs, they were afraid waiting would cancel any gains obtained from the new tanks. Overall it appears that Zeitzler, the Chief of Staff of the German Army, Kluge of Army Group Center, and Manstein of Army Group South, were in favor of the offensive, but wanted it to start soon. The decision to significantly postpone the offensive but continue it regardless appears to have been primarily Hitler's.

Amid all the debates on strategy, the atmosphere was further clouded by the poisoned relations between Kluge and Guderian. In May, after the conference, Kluge sent a letter to Hitler challenging Guderian to a duel and asking Hitler to serve as his second. Needless to say, Hitler refused such an absurd request and asked the two generals to resolve their differences. That did not happen.

Of the eleven principals involved in this conference (including Speer and Model, who probably were not in attendance but intimately involved), only four of them would survive the war (Guderian, Manstein, Speer, and Zeitzler). Two would serve extended jail sentences for their actions during the war (Manstein and Speer). One would be unfairly drummed out of the German Army in disgrace and forbidden to wear his uniform (Zeitzler). Four committed suicide (Hitler, Kluge, Jeschonnek and Model), each for very different reasons. Two were executed for war crimes (Keitel and Jodl), and one was killed in the assassination attempt against Hitler in July 1944 (Schmundt). Five of them left some form of account of the war (Guderian, Keitel, Manstein, Speer, and Zeitzler).

On 6 May, OKH announced that *Citadel* was postponed to 12 June. The next day in a telephone conference with Zeitzler, General of the Panzer Troops Werner Kempf, the commander of Provisional Army Kempf, protested that the delay was undesirable from both a psychological and operational point of view. He believed it would benefit the defender more than the attacker. Zeitzler agreed and said that he was glad to have such an observation from the front to lay before Hitler. Zeitzler obviously did not want to postpone, but the other alternative, which was to cancel the operation, appears to have only been championed by Guderian.

On 10 May, when Hitler was back in Berlin, Guderian was summoned to the chancery to discuss the Panther tank production. There was concern that the production was behind schedule. After the conference, Guderian claims to have seized Hitler's hand and asked if he could speak frankly to him. Guderian urged Hitler to give up the attack on the Eastern Front. Guderian ended his plea with the question "Why do you want to attack in the East at all this year?" Keitel, who was present along with two others, said, "We must attack for political reasons." Guderian replied, "How many people do you think even know where Kursk is? It's a matter of profound indifference to the world whether we hold Kursk or not. I repeat my question: Why do we want to attack in the East at all this year?" Hitler replied, "You're quite right. Whenever

I think of this attack my stomach turns over." Guderian answered, "In that case your reaction to the problem is the correct one. Leave it alone." Guderian claims that Hitler assured him that he had not yet committed himself, and the conversation ended.[7]

On 15 May Hitler presided over another conference of his generals. In that conference, he cited Italy and Hungary as the two critical areas, and emphasized the importance of preventing a second front from opening. The crisis in Italy was his primary concern and he needed to transfer eight armored and four infantry divisions from the East to secure the Italian peninsula. He might also have to occupy the wavering Hungary. Hitler concluded that in the circumstances, he was prepared to consider a strategy of withdrawal in the East, including the evacuation of the Orel bend and the Donets region. In effect, he was looking at shortening the line so as to transfer troops to the west. This was a very different approach than he had taken in the past and was in line with General Jodl's (Chief of OKW Operations Staff) thinking.

Zeitzler had to deal with political problems from the more senior ranking heads of OKW, who were hoping to poach troops from his front so they could shore up their own areas of concern. While OKW was nominally concerned for the entire German war effort and OKH was subordinate to it, their efforts begin to take on the appearance of a bureaucratic east-west war between the two staffs. The fact that both staffs reported directly to Hitler allowed this division of command and the subsequent bureaucratic fighting to fester. Warlimont, in his book on the OKW, complains strongly about Zeitzler's refusal in May and June to provide OKW with any detailed information on the location of units on the Eastern Front or any plans for their movement. As such, it would not be surprising if Zeitzler had a strong desire to conduct an eastern offensive. He had a strong bureaucratic imperative to get an offensive going so that his troops would not be poached for the west.

At this juncture, it must be pointed out that part of the problem with the plans for Kursk was that no one had a real plan for how to resolve the war in favor of Germany. This certainly included Hitler. In 1939 the objective was to defeat Poland, in 1940 the objective was to defeat France and force England to peace, in 1941 the objective was to defeat Russia (and force England to peace), and in 1942, the objective was still to defeat Russia, even if the strategy used was very questionable. In 1943, the objective was no longer to defeat Russia, but to somehow or the other bleed them into exhaustion while they somehow or other dealt with the Western Allies. At this point, Germany was not operating with any clear objective and had no agreed upon plan on how to bring the war to a conclusion politically or militarily. As such, the issue of whether to attack, when, and where, became considerably blurred. It is hard to develop a clear set of operational plans when no one knows what the grand strategic plan is.

DURING THE SPRING thaw, Lt. Stahlberg, Manstein's aide, typed up Manstein's handwritten draft of a memorandum addressed to the "Fuehrer and Supreme Commander of the Wehrmacht." The memo provided a comprehensive appreciation of the situation, with the conclusion that there was no longer any point in hoping for absolute victory in the East. A military stalemate should be sought. A military non-decision should create conditions for the political leadership to end the war by negotiation.

Stahlberg discussed the issue with Manstein after the memo had been sent and confirmed that Manstein felt that a negotiated resolution could be made to the war. Stahlberg pointed out that he did not think that Hitler could negotiate with the allies after all his personal insults of their leaders, his breaking of treaties, "and finally, in the territories we had occupied, acts had been committed on the German side since the beginning of the war which were incompatible with international law." Stahlberg continued:

> Manstein let me talk without contradiction, but when I paused, he said that although he did not dispute my arguments, nevertheless I was wrong.

7 Heinz Guderian, *Panzer Leader* (The Noontide Press, Costa Mesa, CA, 1990), pages 308–309.

> In politics such arguments were insignificant in the last analysis, and above all it was not the job of soldiers to argue about political morality. Germany still held a good many trumps which had not been played. For instance, not one allied soldier had yet landed on the continent of Europe. Of course, he now expected the Americans and British to land in Italy or the Balkans, or on the Atlantic coast in the foreseeable future, and then we Germans could, if necessary, retreat on to the Alps, which could be defended with very limited forces. We still had unsuspected reserves, but reserves were useful only if they were established in good time and if strategic plans were developed in good time.[8]

EVEN ONCE THE DECISION of what to do (attack) and where to attack (Kursk) was decided, the question of when to attack remained. The actual, effective delay of the battle is shorter than what some infer in their writings. Guderian quotes Manstein as stating that the attack should have been made in April. No one else seems to have accepted this date as feasible. Even Manstein claimed that Army Group South would not be ready for offensive operations until mid-April. Furthermore, the Donets did not reach flood stage until late April. As the attack was to be a pincer attack, the northern part of the pincer, led by Model's Ninth Army, had to also be ready. With Model's insecure logistical net, and with the spring thaw in the north coming later, it does not appear that any type of effective two-pincer attack could have been launched in April. A primarily single-pincer thrust from the South may have been possible in the second half of April, but no one seems to have pushed for that.

The first date set for the offensive was 3 May. This was probably the earliest date that it could have been conducted. On 30 April, the reason for the delay of the offensive was heavy rains, so clearly the 3 May date could have not been met. Even then, Model clearly protested that date and requested that the offensive be put off at least to the 15th. As Model was a general not afraid to attack, this is probably a reasonable assessment. Regardless of Manstein's impatience, it simply does not appear that the attack could have gone forth before the 15th. General Busse, Manstein's chief of staff, claims that it could not have gone forward until the 25th. This means that the decision to delay the attack until 12 June amounted to a four-week delay, counting from the 15th. While everyone was discussing a six-week delay on the 3 and 4 May, the start of the offensive was certainly going to have to be delayed until 15 May regardless.

It is the delay past 15 May that must be questioned. At this point, regardless of authorship of the original plan, this delay appears to have been Hitler's decision, and this decision is questionable. To determine whether an earlier attack (say 15 May or 12 June) would have been significantly more successful than the attack conducted on 5 July requires more than looking at the post-war accounts of the German generals involved. It requires a look at the strengths, equipment, and the comparative ratios of the attacking forces and the defending forces on 4 July as compared to 12 June or 15 May. This must be done for both the southern attack and for the northern attack. This comparison must also take into account any weather changes and the effects of further development of Soviet defensive works. This is done in Appendix II of the book *Kursk: The Battle of Prokhorovka* for the southern attack, and it does not appear that the Germans would have gained any advantage in May.[9] As the delay in the offensive was being caused by the delays in preparing the northern attack, then one must also look in depth at the northern attack. This is an effort outside the scope of this book. Perhaps later.

Part of the reason for launching such an attack was to trap the large mobile force of the Soviet Central Front that had been previously on the offensive. At the time of the spring thaw, these forces had collected in the northwest corner of the bulge and a pincer attack on the bulge would have certainly surrounded significant mobile forces. The German OKH intelligence map of

8 Alexander Stahlberg, *Bounden Duty: The Memoirs of a German Officer, 1932–45* (Brassey's [UK], London, 1990), page 294.

9 See Christopher A. Lawrence, *Kursk: The Battle of Prokhorovka* (Aberdeen Books, Sheridan, CO, 2015), pages 1263–1289.

20 March shows the Soviet Second Tank Army with the XVI Tank Corps, XI Tank Corps, and II Guards Cavalry Corps up in the northwest corner. Their April intelligence map still shows the Second Tank Army in the northwest corner, but the tank corps and cavalry corps are now shown as being in reserve positions in the Central Front. The opportunity to surround significant Soviet mobile forces was gone.

This was not an opportunity lost, but more like a possibility that was never realistically there. As these forces were close to the area where the northern pincers were going to attack, for the purposes of trapping this force, the speed of Model's attack was far more important than the speed of Manstein's attack. If Model's attack did not penetrate with sufficient force and speed, then these potentially trapped forces would instead become defensive reinforcements and be well positioned to halt Model's attack or be able to escape. Neither the weather nor Model's forces were in good shape for offensive operations in April. While Manstein may have been successful, without a corresponding success in the north, the Soviet mobile forces were not going to be trapped. By May, when Model was ready, these forces had been re-deployed.

What were left in the Kursk bulge to be trapped were the Fortieth Army, the Thirty-eighth Army, the Sixtieth Army, the Sixty-fifth Army, and the Seventieth Army. Two of these armies, the Fortieth and the Seventieth, were certainly going to be involved in holding the western flank of the German offensive, while the other three were not involved in the action at all. These five armies add up to a sizable collection of 36 infantry divisions and at least 300,000 men. There was little armor.

IN EARLY JUNE, Guderian was still pushing to delay the offensive. Goebbels reports in his diary for 6 June that:

> In the evening we went with Dr. Lay to the KdF House to visit the winners of the Knight's Cross, War Service Cross, and other distinguished soldiers. During the visit, I had a very detailed discussion with Colonel General Guderian. Guderian is pleased that the Fuehrer called off the May offensive. Naturally, Guderian sees the military situation only from the point of view of the panzer forces; however, he is still correct when he states that each month's delay wins us an advantage.
>
> The Fuehrer has Guderian against the expressed fear that it would be considered cowardice because he does not now attack. It is Guderian who has managed to ally these fears. The plan is now not guided by external motives, especially not from motives that stem from the mood of the people. You can make it clear to the people if one is right and sensible.
>
> It is still in doubt this summer, some opportunity to give the enemy a few deafening blows. We have sufficient operating reserves to do this if there is sufficient delay in the arrival of the English-American troops and weapons.[10]

BY THE MIDDLE OF JUNE, according to Colonel Friedrich-Wilhelm von Mellenthin, the chief of staff of the XLVIII Panzer Corps, Field Marshal Manstein and all of his senior commanders saw that it was folly to continue with the operation. Manstein strongly urged that the offensive should be abandoned. General Busse, Manstein's chief of staff, states that Manstein, with Army High Command approval (meaning Zeitzler), had been firmly voicing his opposition to any further postponement of the operations.

Gerd Schmuckle, a junior officer in the artillery regiment of the 7th Panzer Division, reports in his memoirs that he was asked to attend a dinner given by the 7th Panzer Division's commander, Lt. General Baron Hans von Funck in honor of Major General Hans Speidel, who like Schmuckle, was also a Swabian. During the dinner Speidel was critical of Hitler's repeated postponements of *Citadel*.[11]

10 Joseph Goebbels, *Die Tagebucher von Joseph Goebbels* (The Diary of Joseph Goebbels) (K.G. Saur, Munchen, 1993), Part 2, Volume 8, pages 431 & 432. KdF means *Kraft durch Freude*, or "strength through joy." It was a Nazi leisure organization founded by Dr. Robert Ley that was supposed to use recreational activities to foster a national sense of community.

11 Robin Cross, *Citadel: The Battle of Kursk* (Michael O'Mara Books Limited, London, 1993), page 117.

The commander of the 6th Panzer Division, Major General Walter von Huenersdorff, also expressed doubts. On 22 May at a large dinner prepared for his senior officers in Kharkov, he ventured the opinion that there were insufficient forces to breakthrough the Soviet defense in the Kursk salient and that the entire operation violated "the ground rules of leadership." At least one member of the company heard Huenersdorff use the word "idiotic" when referring to Kursk. Note that this opinion is being expressed in late May. One could infer that perhaps *Citadel* was never a good idea, whether done early or later.[12]

Hovering over these proceedings was the worry of what the next Western allied operation might be and when it would occur. The Western allies were clearly getting ready for further operations. After an aerial bombardment that began on 8 May, they invaded the miniscule island of Pantelleria, halfway between Tunis and Sicily, on 11 June.

MEANWHILE HITLER HAD come to rely on the arrival of the Panther tanks to justify the delay in the start of the operation. This desire to bring in new and heavier tanks was certainly in response to Model's concerns about the Soviet antitank defenses and the inability of the Mark IV to cope with them. Hitler was probably the wrong man to make this point to. Like many dilettantes in the military arts, Hitler was fascinated with the technology of war and vastly overrated the value of improved weapons. He truly believed that technology could win the war for him. He had already made absurd statements that grossly overrated the Tiger's contribution to battles.

At this juncture, Germany still had a limited number of Tigers (often called the Tiger I, to distinguish it from the later Tiger II). They had first gone into action in August 1942 in a wasted action near Leningrad. They first saw action in the south at Zimovniki on 7 January[13] and as of the first of April, some 134 were in the German inventory. Production was growing, and by the 1st of July, the Germans had 262 Tigers,[14] of which around 40% (102 Tigers) were committed to the southern thrust of the Kursk offensive with another 45 committed in the north (with only 31 committed to the offensive). It was a good tank, certainly the best heavy tank in the world at that time. It was better armed (although not better armored) than its Soviet counterpart, the KV-1. Eventually there would be seven companies of Tigers in the south and four in the north.

Germany had also been producing a new giant assault gun, the Ferdinand, or Elephant. This odd-ball vehicle was designed by Dr. Ferdinand Porsche,[15] famous for his people's car, or Volkswagen; Auto Union rear-engined formula one cars; and after the war, the sports and racing cars that carried his name. It was one of those arrangements done outside the normal military channels, with Porsche getting approval directly from Hitler for the project. A total of 90 of these 65-ton behemoths, with its high-velocity 88mm gun mounted in a nonrotating turret, and without a machinegun to protect it against infantry, were completed by the end of May. They were dispatched to the Ninth Army and ready for action in early June. None were sent to Army Group South.

Then there was the new German medium tank, the Panther. This beautiful tank design gave the Germans a medium tank that was superior to anything the Soviets possessed. It started production in January 1943, but, as usual, there were teething problems. As late as the 16th of June, Guderian was telling Hitler that the Panther was not ready for action in the east, as was probably also the case on the 18th when he had a conference with Hitler after a visit that same day to Grafenwoehr, where the two Panther battalions were training.[16]

12 Cross, page 117.

13 Zeimke, page 74.

14 Thomas L. Jentz, *Panzertruppen, The Complete Guide to the Creation & Combat Employment of Germany's Tank Force, 1943–45* (Schiffer Military History, Altglen, PA, 1996), page 286.

15 Dr. Ferdinand Porsche was an honorary doctor, receiving his honorary doctorate from the Vienna University of Technology in 1916. His title was "Dr. Ing. h.c.: (Doktor Ingenieur Honoris Causa).

16 Guderian, page 310.

Finally, there were the new assault guns and tank destroyers being built. One was the Hornet or Hornisse (later renamed the Nashorn or Rhinoceros), which was a high-powered 88mm gun on an open-topped lightly armored chassis. In defensive operations, it was an extremely useful weapon. The first 45 were delivered by mid-June and put into the 560th Heavy Panzer Jaeger Battalion as their first operational unit. Still, these otherwise impressive antitank guns were not ready for combat. On 17 June, a visiting officer from the army staff reported that the battalion was not ready for action due to vibration from vehicle movement transmitting to the piece and gun carriage and damaging the sights. A new travel gun lock was required. Furthermore, the steering linkage and brakes were defective and their use could cause the engine to overheat. The battalion reported that all its vehicles were in a complete state of disrepair and must be completely rebuilt at a workshop. Therefore, this unit was shuffled off to the XLII (42nd) Corps in the southern part of Provisional Army Kempf and did not see action in the Battle of Kursk.

Another new assault gun was the Sturmpanzer IV or the Brummbar, which was a 150mm low velocity gun mounted in a heavily-armored Panzer IV chassis. There were also various self-propelled artillery pieces, like the Wespe (Wasp), which was the 105mm field howitzer mounted on the Panzer II chassis; the Grille (Cricket), which was the 150mm heavy infantry gun mounted on a Panzer 38t chassis; and the Hummel (Bumble Bee), which was a 150mm field howitzer mounted on the Panzer III/IV chassis. These were distributed to the armored units, giving them the first truly self-propelled artillery. It was an amazing production effort, originally most of these new weapons were to be ready by 12 May. This included plans to have ready 250 Panthers, 100 Hornets, 40 Brummbars, 100 Hummels, 285 Tigers, 90 Ferdinands, and 90 Grilles. The 200 Panthers and 45 Hornets (Nashorns) headed to Army Group South, 45 Brummbars and 89 Elephants to Army Group Center, with 102 Tigers going to the south and 45 to the center. The other self-propelled artillery went to units in both armies. Kursk would not only be the first combat use of the Panther, but also the Wespe, Brummbar, and Hummel.

Finally, also recently deployed, but not specifically for Kursk, were the Panzer IIIs with flamethrowers, which were part of three German divisions in the south (the Gross Deutschland, 11th Panzer, and 6th Panzer) and the various 5mm and 8mm armor skirts being added to tanks for additional protection against hollow charges and infantry portable antitank weapons.

So, the offensive was delayed from mid-May until 12 June to allow more time to deploy the armor. By 12 June, the Tigers, the Ferdinands, Hornets, and the Brummbars had been deployed (although the Hornets were not working and the Ferdinand battalions had just arrived). The Panthers and a lot of the self-propelled artillery were still not ready. Basically the operation was now being held up waiting for one tank regiment (the Panthers). This was even more mystifying, as the person who had originally complained that his Panzer IVs were not enough to penetrate the Soviet defensive positions quickly (Model of the Ninth Army) was not the one who would be receiving these Panthers. The Panthers, as of the middle of June, were now heading to Army Group South to support Manstein, who had been saying for a month that he was ready to go.

At this stage, it was time to reassess the situation. On 18 June the OKW operations staff submitted an appraisal to Hitler which concluded that *Citadel* should be canceled until the situation was clarified. Their concern was with the west and the possibility of an allied landing in Italy or the Balkans. Army Groups Center and South had noted the continued build-up of Soviet forces and were now expecting the Soviets to launch an offensive. On 19 June, Army Group Center provided the assessment that there would be a Soviet offensive and concluded that the best way to disrupt it would be to launch *Operation Citadel*. In the face of conflicting advice, Hitler went forward and on 21 June, set 3 July as the date for the Kursk offensive. After listening to Model's concerns, and consulting with Kluge and Manstein, on 25 June he authorized a date of 5 July. This date held, some two months later than the first proposed date of 3 May.

On 24 June, in a discussion with Goebbels, Hitler confessed that his grand designs were now lost. The major task now was to hold the Italian mainland. In

HOTH'S REVISED PLANS

Colonel General Hermann Hoth, commander of the Fourth Panzer Army, in early May began to worry about the details of the army's operation. The intelligence he was seeing showed the X Tank Corps assembled in the vicinity of Oboyan and significant concentration of Soviet forces along the Oskol River. He gathered that the Soviet reserves, including several tank corps, would come into the battle from the northeast of his army's area of advance, through Prokhorovka. This caused him to revise his planning for the Fourth Panzer Army's operation. Instead of having both corps advance forward, with LXVIII Panzer Corps going to Oboyan and the SS Panzer Corps going north and across the Psel to the west of Prokhorovka, he slightly revised the path of the SS Panzer Corps within the scope of the original April plans. According to a report written in 1947 by Friedrich Fangohr, Hoth's Chief of Staff, the concern was that around 7th to 9th of July, reinforcing Soviet armor would be arriving in the area of Prokhorovka so as to counter-attack his advancing army in the right flank. He therefore, in response, planned to advance the SS Panzer Corps to the north-northeast, having them cross the Psel and go through Prokhorovka. He had the right boundary of the Fourth Panzer Army moved to encompass Prokhorovka. He requested that Provisional Army Kempf move north to properly cover his flank, with its left wing, the 6th Panzer Division. The Fourth Panzer Army orders for 28 June stat that 6th Panzer Division was to attack from Belgorod via Sabyinino towards Prokhorovka.

He put these ideas forth in a series of meetings with Marshal Manstein starting the 10th of May. Manstein agreed to Hoth's adjustments to the plan. Therefore, when the Fourth Panzer Army orders were issued on 28 June 1943, they included the revised left and right boundaries for the SS Panzer Corps and the intermediate objectives of the Psel River and Prokhorovka for the corps. The XLVIII Panzer Corps objective remained Oboyan, but he had added the caveat that the corps would go around Oboyan to the east. This was the plan in force when the Fourth Panzer Army entered battle in July.[1]

1 For a copy of the Fourth Panzer Army orders for 28 June 1943, see Klink, pages 308–317. Also, there is an extended discussion of this adjustment in Steven H. Newton, *Kursk: The German View* (Da Capo Press, Boston, 2003), pages 77–79 and 357–370.

the east, the army needed to conserve its strength until 1944, to ensure that the front was spared the crisis which had gripped it the previous two winters. The goal of *Citadel* was now merely to provide "a minor correction of the line." Hitler also confessed that success at Kursk would not be sufficient to swing neutral opinion behind a revitalized and victorious Germany.[17] So much for the ". . .beacon seen around the world."

17 Cross, *Citadel*, page 143.

Writer #742 claims that on 27 June, the final attack order was received by the Fourth Panzer Army headquarters. Hitler held a final pre-battle commanders' conference at Rastenburg, East Prussia (known as the Wolf's Lair, now in Ketrzyn, Poland) on 1 July.[18] Attendees included Manstein, Kluge, Hoth, Kempf, Model, most of their corps commanders, and the two air commanders, Colonel General Robert Ritter von Greim and General Otto Dessloch. General Johannes Friessner, the

18 Alexander Stahlberg, an attendee, placed the conference in Munich in his book *Bounden Duty*, pages 303–304, and provided a description of the conference. Writer #742, among others, placed it in Rastenburg.

XXIII (23rd) Corps commander from Model's Ninth Army, left handwritten notes of the conference.[19]

Hitler outlined the situation on all fronts, blaming the Italians as the main cause of German misfortune. He referred to the Hungarians and Romanians as unreliable and stated that Finland was at the end of its strength. For the Eastern Front, he stated that nothing must be given up without a fight. Hitler judged that the situation on the Eastern Front to be such that the Russians could not be allowed to use the winter months to refurbish their troops, else another crisis would ensue. He rejected a recent memo from Army Group Center to evacuate the Orel bulge so as to create an operational reserve. He also again rejected the idea of a "backhand" strike. He decided it would be better to seize the initiative and attack.

Hitler continued, saying it was politically necessary to exhibit a smashing success, first of all to buck up Germany's allies, secondly, to disrupt the Western allies' plans for opening a second front, and lastly, for the folks at home. Hitler justified the long waiting period prior to the beginning of the offensive as critical for the assembly of reserves and for the completion of new weapons, the Tiger, Panther, and Ferdinand tanks. He pointed out that it took time to overcome the difficulties encountered with the new tanks during their trials at the proving ground. Hitler summarized that the attack was a gamble, but he had the feeling that it would succeed. He justified this feeling by reflecting on his previous successful campaigns that had succeeded despite the council of his military advisors: Austria, Czechoslovakia, Poland, and the Soviet Union.

He then ended by declaring that the vengeance weapons for use against England were almost ready, the U-boats had been redesigned, and methods had been developed for defeating the Anglo-American locating devices, so that in a month or two the U-boat war would be resumed. He closed with the remark, "The dice have been cast, the attack has been ordered, all the prerequisites for success are in place."[20]

Breith added in his post-war account that Hitler also discussed the need to hold the Donets Basin and the valuable manganese source at Nikopol and indicated that the delay in the attack was necessary to bolster the defense of Italy.[21]

This was classic Hitler. After a period of considerable doubt, he had now made his decision, and once that course was plotted, he was going to stubbornly stick to it. The refusal to retreat, the over-reliance on technology, the blaming of others for his failures and the use of "vengeance weapons" were themes that would repeat themselves for the rest of the war. Kursk was now Hitler's offensive.

Model used the meeting to present his misgivings one more time to Hitler. Manstein used the opportunity to annoy Goering and the acting commander of the Fourth Air Army, Dessloch, by suggesting that Richthofen, the previous commander, be recalled to the Eastern Front.

They also discussed what to do about the eventuality of a Soviet attack in the north against the Second Panzer Army, for this formation was covering the western and northern part of the Orel bulge and had little armor. A successful Soviet attack there could easily crush the Orel bulge and force the Ninth Army to terminate its attack on Kursk. Hitler suggested that this threat could be parried by using every available German aircraft. At this stage, there were over 700 aircraft in the 1st Air Division, Sixth Air Fleet, in the Orel bulge to support the attack in the north, and over 1,100 aircraft in the VIII Air Corps, Fourth Air Fleet, in the south to support that attack.[22]

Hitler also issued his orders of the day for *Operation Citadel*, one for the commanders and one for the troops. The daily orders for the troops were to be distributed only immediately before the commencement of the attack.

19 Alexander Stalhberg, who was the adjutant to General Manstein and an attendee at the meeting, places the conference at the Nazi party premises of the NSDAP in Koenigsplatz, Munich. He provides a detailed account of the events at the conference. See Stahlberg, *Bounden Duty*, pages 303–304.

20 Klink, pages 197–198.

21 General der Panzertruppen Hermann Breith, *Breakthrough of a Panzer Corps Through Deeply Echeloned Russian Defense During the Battle of Kharkov in July 1943*, pages 1 & 2.

22 Cajus Bekker, *The Luftwaffe War Diaries* (Ballantine Books, New York, 1966), page 432.

As of 1 July 1943, Germany fielded 3.1 million men on the Eastern Front, having effectively rebuilt their army almost back to its 1941 Eastern Front strength. There were an additional 1.3 million men deployed on all the other fronts (including Finland). This amounted to some 29.5 percent of the German Army personnel now facing other threats, real or imagined. The German Army in the East consisted of 168 regular divisions, seven SS divisions, 12 other divisions, 2,269 tanks, 997 assault guns and 500 obsolete tanks (total of 3,766 "tanks"). Committed to the offensive and around the Kursk bulge were 45 divisions (including the Second Army and the XXIV (24th) Panzer Corps) and around 2,700 "tanks" of various types.[23]

In Finland there were seven divisions (including one SS division) and 20 assault guns. The forces facing the west consisted of 69 regular divisions, four SS divisions, 10 other divisions, 873 tanks, 405 assault guns and 100 obsolete tanks (total of 1,378 "tanks"). Some 37 percent of the German armor was now in the west. The Germans had 5,003 "front-line aircraft" in June 1943. In July, only 2,500 of them were on the Eastern Front. The Western allies were now occupying the attention of half the Luftwaffe (the German Air Force). The Axis had 960 front-line German aircraft and around 300 Italian aircraft in the central Mediterranean, and around 800 aircraft on home defense in Germany, along with some 600 night-fighters. The forces in the West were currently unengaged with the Allied armies, but awaiting their next move. After two years of war in the East, the Western allies were finally beginning to draw significant attention from the German Army.

23 Niklas Zetterling and Anders Frankson, *Kursk 1943: A Statistical Analysis* (Frank Cass, London, 2000), page 18, provide a count of 2,451. This includes all tanks and assault guns, whether ready-for-action or not. It does not include artillery observation tanks, self-propelled artillery, self-propelled antitank guns or Pz Is. The count also does not include the 17th Panzer, 23rd Panzer, or Viking SS Division (total of 181 tanks, see page 31).

For most tables in this book unless it states otherwise, our count of "tanks" includes all ready-for-action tanks, all assault guns, and all self-propelled antitank guns (Marders). It does not include artillery observation tanks, munitions-carrying tanks, recovery tanks and self-propelled artillery. In the south alone, there were 113 operational Marders on the 4th and 5th of July.

HERE THERE BE PANTHERS

At the time Germany invaded the Soviet Union in 1941, it had nine major types of tank-like vehicles. They were:

1.) The 5.8 ton Panzer I, armed with two 7.92mm caliber machineguns, had a two-man crew, 13mm frontal armor, first deployed in 1934. There were 843 in the German Army on 1 July 1941 and a handful on 1 July 1943 (mostly used as command tanks at this stage).

2.) The 8.9 ton Panzer II, armed with a 20mm gun and one 7.92mm machinegun, had a three-man crew, 14.5mm frontal armor, first deployed in 1936. There were also flamethrower versions of this tank. There were 1,067 tanks and 85 flamethrower versions in the German Army on 1 July 1941 and 236 on 1 July 1943, plus a few flamethrower versions.

3.) The 19.8 to 21.8 ton Panzer III, armed with either a 37mm or a 50mm gun and two or three 7.92mm machineguns, had a five-man crew, 30mm frontal armor, first deployed in 1937. This was originally the main medium tank in the German Army. There were 1,501 in the German Army on 1 July 1941 and 1,423 on 1 July 1943.

4.) The 20 to 22.3 ton Panzer IV, armed with a short barreled 75mm gun and two 7.92mm machineguns, had a five-man crew, 50mm frontal armor (model F), first deployed in 1938. This was originally supposed to be a support tank but eventually became Germany's main medium tank. There were 531 in the German Army on 1 July 1941 and 1,472 on 1 July 1943.

5.) The 10.5 ton Czech 35t, armed with a 37mm gun and two 7.92mm machineguns, had a crew of four, 25mm frontal armor, first built in 1935 and brought into the German inventory in 1939. There were 189 in the German Army on 1 July 1941 and maybe a handful by 1943.

6.) The 9.4 ton Czech 38t, armed with a 37mm gun and two 7.92mm machineguns, 25mm frontal armor, with a crew of four, 25mm frontal armor, first built in 1939 and entered into the German inventory that same year. There were 763 in the German Army on 1 July 1941 and 204 on 1 July 1943.

7.) The 20.2 ton assault gun mounted on a Panzer III Chassis (the Sturmgeschuetz III), armed with a short-barrel 75mm gun (no machinegun, no rotating turret), with a crew of four, 50mm frontal armor, first deployed in 1940. There were 416 in the German Army on 1 July 1941 and 1,594 on 1 July 1943.

8.) The 6.4 ton antitank gun mounted on Pz I chassis, armed with a 47mm antitank gun (no rotating turret, open top and rear casemate), a crew of three, 13mm frontal armor, first deployed 1940. They were also bringing into service a version of this based upon a captured French tank chassis that was heavier (10.5 tons) and better armored (32mm). The Germans also had captured a considerable number of French tanks, but these were almost never used on the Eastern Front. A total of 202 were converted before the French Campaign, and continued to be used in decreasing numbers through 1943.

9.) A 8.5 ton self-propelled artillery piece on a Pz I chassis, armed with 150mm heavy infantry gun (no rotating turret, open top and rear casemate), with a crew of four, 13mm frontal armor, first deployed 1940. Only 38 were made.

The Germans also had various command tanks in different models (Pz Is, IIIs, Vs, and VIs), most armed with only machineguns (although the recent Pz III and all the Pz V and Pz VI versions were fully armed). There were 331 in the German Army on 1 July 1941 and 412 on 1 July 1943.

(continued)

During the next two years of warfare, the Panzer IIIs and IVs, along with the Sturmgeschuetz IIIs, became the German Army's main tank-like vehicles. These three "tanks" were generally up-gunned and up-armored over the next two years. The other tanks were slowly phased out of service by natural attrition.

At the start of the invasion, the Panzer III was in the process of being upgraded to a 50mm gun, was then given a higher-velocity 50mm gun, and they then created a version using the low velocity short-barreled 75mm gun as a support tank. The frontal armor of the Panzer III was increased from 30mm to 50mm or greater. There was also a flamethrower version created, of which 41 were deployed at Kursk.

The Panzer IV was upgraded to high-velocity long-barreled 75mm gun. Many of the Panzer IVs had 80mm of frontal armor (vice 50mm) by the time of Kursk, although their turret still had only 50mm.

The Sturmgeschuetz (assault gun) III was also upgraded to the high-velocity long-barreled 75mm gun and had its frontal armor upgraded to 80mm. There was also a version of this assault gun created with a 105mm howitzer (the Sturmhaubitze). The Sturmgeschuetz III became very common. The Sturmhaubitze (assault howitzer) were less common with only 68 deployed north and south of Kursk.

Meanwhile the Germans continued developing their armor. They developed a whole range of self-propelled antitank guns mounted on Panzer II and Czech 38t chassis (the Marder IIs and IIIs, respectively), mounting either a German 75mm gun or the captured Russian 76.2mm gun (with a modified muzzle break that increased muzzle velocity).

In early February 1943 Hitler ordered the development and clarified the production schedule of a number of self-propelled artillery pieces by mounting them on existing tank chassis. These were the Hummel (Bumble Bee), a 150mm heavy field howitzer mounted on the Pz III/IV chassis; the Wespe (Wasp), a 105mm light field howitzer mounted on the Panzer II chassis; the Grille, a 150mm heavy infantry gun mounted on the Panzer 38(t) chassis; the Brummbar, a 150mm "assault" howitzer (similar to the heavy infantry gun), mounted on a heavily armored Panzer IV chassis; and the Hornisse (Hornet), a self-propelled 88mm antitank gun mounted on a Panzer III/IV chassis. All but the Grille and Hornet would first be deployed at Kursk. The Grille was deployed before Kursk, while the Hornet was deployed instead with the XLII Corps of Provisional Army Kempf as it was still not combat ready. At this same time, it was ordered that 5mm to 8mm armored "aprons" be produced for installation on the sides of German panzers and assault guns as protection against Soviet antitank rifles.

The Germans also produced a new medium tank intended as a replacement for the Pz IV. This was the vaunted Panther Tank, the Pz V. It weighed 43 tons, had 80mm of frontal armor that was properly sloped, 100mm of front turret armor, and was armed with a 75mm high-velocity gun. It was one of the best tank designs of the war.

They had also produced in the second half of 1942 their first successful heavy tank, the Panzer VI, or Tiger tank. It weighed 57 tons, had 100mm of frontal armor and was armed with an 88mm gun, although one of lower velocity than that used in the Hornet or Elephant. It was first deployed on the Eastern Front in August 1942 and was a significant improvement over what the Germans had before.

Finally, the German designers had been given a free hand by the Fuehrer to develop their own designs. The one of these that actually went into production and was to be ready for the battle was the Ferdinand (or Elephant). It was named after its designer, the famous Ferdinand Porsche of Volkswagen, Auto Union, and later the Porsche sports car fame. This was a 65-ton behemoth, with 200mm of frontal armor, and having the 88mm high-velocity gun mounted in a casemate (non-rotating turret). The early models of this slow tank (top speed 19 mph) lacked any machineguns.

Production of these new tanks was fairly limited. A few tanks had only a limited production, so they only manufactured 90 Elephants, 100 Panzer III Flame tanks, 200 Grilles, and 60 Brummbars (production was later restarted for both Grilles and Brummbars after the initial production run). In other cases, the production lines had just started, so that by 1 July, the Germans had made only 484 Panthers (428 available on 1 July 1943), 347 Tigers (240 available on 1 July 1943), 119 Sturmhaubitze (assault howitzers, 136 claimed to be available on 1 July 1943) and 155 Hornets (131 available 1 July 1943). There were also 971 of the various Marder IIs, IIIs, and similar self-propelled antitank guns available on 1 July 1943.

It was these new tanks (Tiger, Panther, and Ferdinand) that Hitler was hoping would turn the tide of the war. In many respects, Model's complaint that the Mark IV would not do well against the new Soviet antitank guns played into Hitler's obsession with technological answers to these problems. Instead of devising a new plan, or a new strategy, to Hitler the obvious answer was to provide Model with a new tank. As they just happened to be coming off the production line, they could be rushed to the battle, and Model's objection had been answered. If the production run was delayed by the myriad of things that usually delay production runs of new projects, then if one just slips the battle date a little bit the new tanks will be in place. It was a classic case of an over-reliance on technology to solve a strategic problem.

CHAPTER TWO

The Soviets Prepare

> We wanted to meet the German forces' expected offensive with a powerful defense, bleed the enemy, and then, by launching a counteroffensive, defeat him once and for all. It was decided to, simultaneously with a plan for waging a premeditated defense, devise a plan for our offensive activities, without waiting for the enemy's offensive, if the latter should drag out for a prolonged time.
>
> Thus our troops' defense was undoubtedly not a forced measure, but a deeply premeditated one, and the Stavka made the time for launching the offensive dependent on the situation. This meant not hurrying it, but not drawing it out either.
>
> MARSHAL GEORGII K. ZHUKOV
> 1971[1]

THE SOVIETS HAD to face the coming summer of 1943 with some trepidation. Even after their victory at Stalingrad, they had to fear the next German summer offensive. To summarize the previous German offensives:

	Days	Distance Advanced (km)	Kilometers Per Day
Poland 1939	35	350	10.0
Norway 1940	62	550	8.9
France 1940	43	800	18.6
Yugoslavia 1941	12	525	43.8
Greece 1941	24	525	21.9
North Africa 1941	50	520	10.4
Crete 1941	12	250	20.8
Russia 1941 (first part)	28	580	20.7[2]
Russia 1941 (second part)	70	260	3.7
Russia 1942	57	500	8.8

Any rational man, in the face of such a record of performance, could not help but be concerned. Summer was coming, and the Germans were again going to attack. The German summer offensives had always resulted in low casualties for the Germans and high casualties for the opposing forces. Looking at those summer campaigns once more:

1 Georgi K. Zhukov, *Vospominaniya i Razmyshleniya* (Moscow, Izdatelstvo Novosti, 1971), page 440. In the 1992 edition of his memoirs (vol. 3, p. 23), Zhukov has the latter paragraph underlined.

2 Only covers from 22 June through 19 July. The actual first phase of the offensive lasted 97 days but there was little forward advance, although much lateral movement during the rest of that time. This produces an advance rate of 6.0 kilometers per day.

	German Casualties	*Defender Casualties*	*Exchange Ratio*
Poland 1939	44,303	266,000	1 to 6
Norway 1940	2,921[3]	3,737	1 to 1.3
France 1940	156,492	424,840	1 to 2.7
Yugoslavia 1941	558	55,123	1 to 98.8
Greece 1941	10,571[4]	73,840	1 to 7.0
North Africa 1941	1,884	8,440	1 to 4.5
Crete 1941	5,678	3,479	1.6 to 1
Russia 1941 (early days)	54,592	747,870	1 to 13.7[5]
Russia 1941 (first part)	534,000	2,571,205	1 to 4.8[6]
Russia 1941 (second part)	241,078	1,037,169	1 to 4.3
Russia 1942	206,350 ?	568,347	1 to 2.8

THE SOVIET ARMY FACED a decision similar to the Germans for the summer of 1943. This was whether they should attack, or whether they should defend first and attack later. Of course, the Soviet experience with successfully defending against a German attack during summer was not very good. In 1941, they conducted a successful defense of Leningrad and Moscow, but it was late in the year against a very over-extended German Army. There was not a lot of success before that point. Their forces in Ukraine had put up a decent fight in front of Kiev before they were surrounded by Guderian's drive down from Smolensk. They also had success with a counterattack retaking Rostov in late 1941. Beyond that, Soviet defensive efforts in 1941 were desperate, hard fought, and without result until late in the year.

Defensive actions in 1942 were more successful. The Soviet Army effectively held over half the front in 1942 (the areas opposite Leningrad and Moscow) but were pretty much driven back without respite across the entire southern part of the front. Again, only late in the year were the Soviets able to actually force a German offensive to grind to a halt, in this case in the bloody street battles in Stalingrad and in the foothills of the Caucasus.

The Soviet Union had conducted a number of very successful winter offensives against the Germans but they had yet to conduct a successful offense in the summer. The sense was that the German Army dominated the summers and the Soviet Army dominated the winters.

According to the 1944 Soviet General Staff Study, the decision to defend and then counterattack was made in late March. They were to shift the Central and Voronezh Fronts to a "firm and stubborn defense to exhaust and bleed the enemy dry"[7] and then after committing fresh reserves, the main forces of these two Fronts, as well as those of the Western and Bryansk Fronts, would launch a general offensive and defeat the main German grouping.

On 21 April, the commander of the Voronezh Front, General Nikolai F. Vatutin, submitted a report to Stalin on the preparation of forces for the defense and provided an extensive discussion of the preparations for offensive operations across the Ukraine after the defensive phase. Vatutin expected these offensive operations to take two and half months and was hoping to start them in June.[8]

At this stage, Vatutin had most of the forces in place he would have in July, and was rearming and refitting them to bring them up to full readiness. As such, his goal was to have all his units ready for action by 5 May, including having the infantry divisions brought up to 7,000 to 8,000 men and all his armored units brought back up to strength. Furthermore, defensive works were well under way and he was fully expecting a German attack in early May consisting of up to ten German armored divisions and no less than six infantry divisions on the main axis of attack. He specifically noted

3 This includes the 1,317 reported killed and 1,604 reported wounded. It does not include the 2,375 missing, as most of those were lost at sea.

4 Includes 6,000 Italian casualties.

5 From 22 June through early July. Dates for German and Soviet losses do not match.

6 From 22 June to 26 September for the Germans. Soviet dates vary. Figures from the previous line are also part of these figures.

7 Glantz and Orenstein, page 10.

8 Used translation of report provided in Glantz and House, *The Battle of Kursk*, pages 365–373.

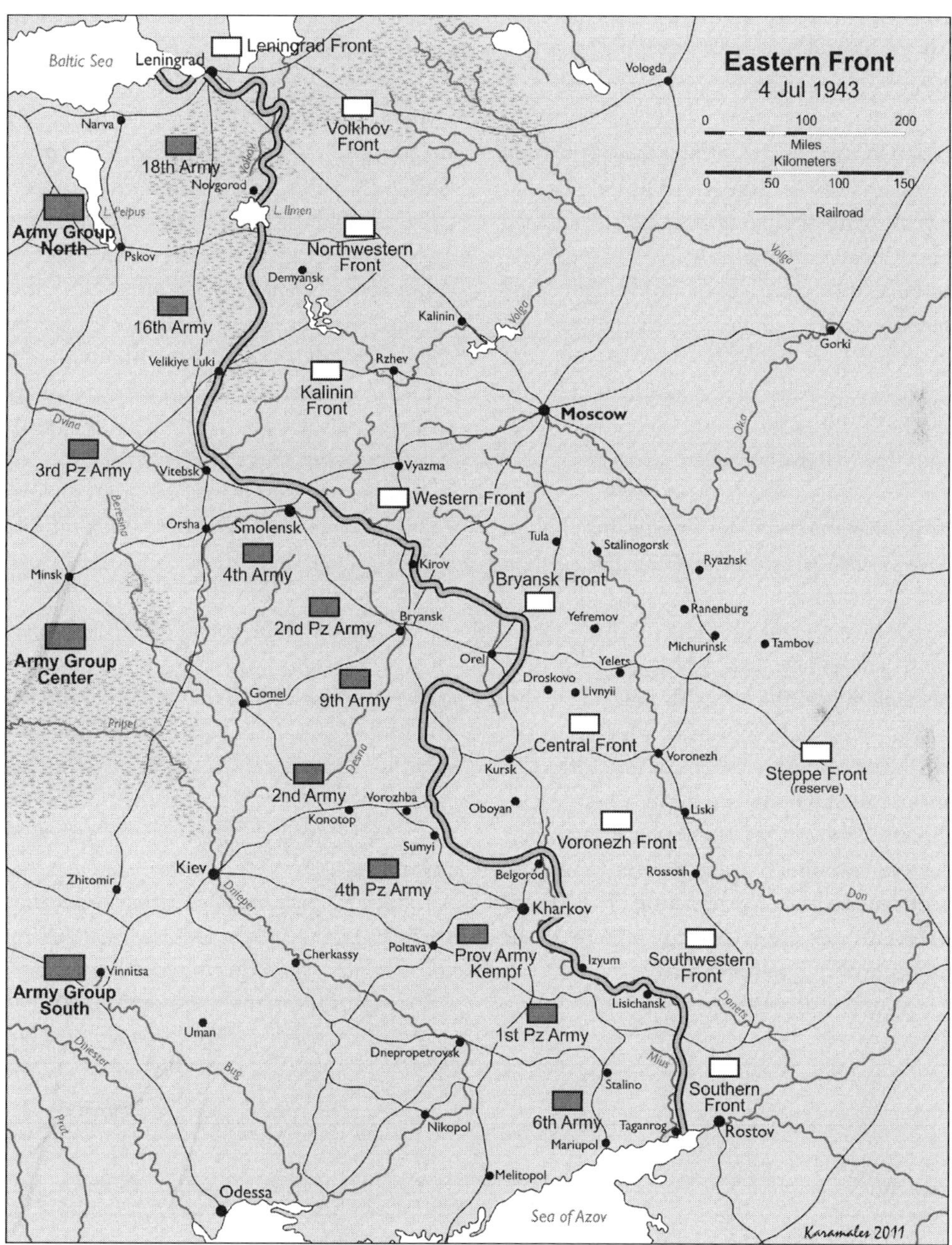

Eastern Front
4 Jul 1943
0 100 200
Miles
Kilometers
0 50 100 150
Railroad
Baltic Sea
Leningrad
Leningrad Front
Volkhov Front
Narva
18th Army
Novgorod
L. Ilmen
L. Peipus
Army Group North
Pskov
Northwestern Front
Demyansk
16th Army
Kalinin
Volga
Gorki
Vologda
Velikiye Luki
Rzhev
Kalinin Front
Moscow
Oka
Dvina
3rd Pz Army
Vitebsk
Vyazma
Western Front
Smolensk
Orsha
Tula
Stalinogorsk
Ryazhsk
Minsk
4th Army
Kirov
Bryansk Front
Ranenburg
2nd Pz Army
Bryansk
Yefremov
Michurinsk
Tambov
Army Group Center
Orel
Yelets
Droskovo
Livnyii
Gomel
9th Army
Pripet
Central Front
Voronezh
Steppe Front
(reserve)
Kursk
2nd Army
Vorozhba
Konotop
Oboyan
Liski
Sumyi
Voronezh Front
Kiev
Belgorod
Rossosh
Zhitomir
4th Pz Army
Don
Dnieper
Kharkov
Poltava
Prov Army Kempf
Izyum
Southwestern Front
Cherkassy
Vinnitsa
Army Group South
Lisichansk
Donets
Uman
1st Pz Army
Dnepropetrovsk
Mius
Southern Front
Stalino
Dniester
Bug
Prut
Nikopol
6th Army
Taganrog
Rostov
Mariupol
Melitopol
Odessa
Sea of Azov
Karamales 2011

in this report that he had no documentary information concerning the German intentions. This would lead one to believe that the Front commanders were not privy to the intelligence coming from the Lucy spy ring, operating from Switzerland. As such, Vatutin was forced to guess the Germans' intentions, and as a result concluded that the Germans would attack along the Staryii Oskol axis with part of their forces pushing towards Oboyan and Kursk. This report also notes that the Germans would be deploying aircraft armed with 37mm guns and the 88mm armed heavy Tiger tank.[9]

The initial part of Vatutin's plan was approved by Stavka (signed by Vasilevskii) on 25 April and the First Tank Army was assigned to the Voronezh Front as of 28 April. He was to be fully prepared for defense no later than 10 May and his Front must be prepared for an offensive not later than 1 June.[10]

By this time, the General Staff, under Vasilevskii, had completed its basic plans for the summer campaign. At this point, Stavka suspected that the Germans might begin their attack within the next few days. On the 8th of May, the Fronts were put on alert in anticipation of a German attack on the 10th, although a warning note had been sent out on the 5th.[11] This alert is in line with the German start date of 9 May, which was the date after the second postponement of four days due to heavy rains. It was the final date they set before they scrapped all plans and ordered the 4 May conference. The Central Front responded that they would have all troops in battle readiness by the morning of 10 May. It appears that the field was not getting full updates of the state of German thinking and planning.

THE EXPECTED GERMAN offensive did not occur in early May, and for reasons not known to the Soviets, continued to be delayed. The long wait began to bother General Vatutin. The always aggressive Vatutin, along with his political officer, Nikita Khrushchev, submitted a report to Stalin on 26 May proposing that a preventive strike be launched against the German forces around Belgorod and Kharkov.[12] This idea was not supported by Zhukov, Vasilevskii, or Antonov, and they reported so to Stalin. According to Vasilevskii, Vatutin more than once brought up the necessity of starting the offensive so as not to miss the summer. Vatutin is quoted as saying "Aleksander Mikhailovich [Vasilevskii]! We'll sleep through it and miss the moment. The enemy isn't attacking, soon it'll be fall and all our plans will be ruined. Let's drop this entrenching and start first. We have enough strength for this."[13]

Vasilevskii noted in his daily conversations with Stalin that he was also ill at ease. Stalin told him that Vatutin had called him and insisted that they launch an offensive no later than the first days of July. Stalin further said that he considered the proposal worthy of the most serious attention and that he ordered Vatutin to report his views to Stavka.[14]

Zhukov states that Stalin was indeed questioning whether to await the enemy offensive or to strike a preventive blow. Zhukov claims that "Stalin was afraid that our defenses might not be able to withstand the enemy onslaught, as in 1941 and 1942." On the other hand, Stalin was not sure that the Soviet troops would be able to break through the German defenses. According to Zhukov, these doubts by Stalin continued until almost mid-May.

It is an interesting comparison. Hitler at this time was having severe doubts about conducting the offense,

9 Used translation of report provided in Glantz and House, *The Battle of Kursk*, pages 365–373.

10 Used translation of report provided in Glantz and House, *The Battle of Kursk*, page 373.

11 Erickson claims this occurred on the 2nd of May, see John Erickson, *The Road to Berlin* (Phoenix Giants, London, 1996, originally published in 1983), page 76. The note of 5 May can be found in Glantz and House, *The Battle of Kursk*, page 373. Glantz and House claim that there were alerts on the 2nd, 8th, and 19th, see *The Battle of Kursk*, page 77.

12 Date provided by Glantz and House, *The Battle of Kursk*, page 77, but there is no source given for this date. This date does not match with the account provided in the 11th edition of Zhukov's memoirs (1992) which states, as in earlier versions, that Vatutin and Khrushchev made their request and this caused Stalin to hesitate as to the course of action. In a passage restored to the 1992 edition, it states "This hesitation continued, as I recall, until the middle of May." See Zhukov, 11th Edition, page 32.

13 Vasilevskii, Volume II, page 24.

14 Stet., 24.

while Stalin was having severe doubts about whether the defense would succeed or the Soviet counterattacks would succeed. If both leaders had paid council to their doubts, then the summer of 1943 could have been very quiet indeed.

According to Zhukov, as a result of repeated discussions and the evidence the staff provided him, Stalin finally "firmly decided" to meet the German attacks and then counterattack. However, after the experiences of 1941 and 1942, one cannot blame Stalin for being concerned. Still, as Chistyakov (Sixth Guards Army commander) reports in his memoirs, he had preliminary instructions from Vatutin to conduct an offensive, so he ended up training his troops for both roles.

In the second half of May, Zhukov was again at Kursk preparing the commands for battle. In his report on 21 May, he indicates that based on an analysis of the disposition of German tank units, the low density of German infantry units, the absence of heavy artillery, and the scattered dispositions of reserves opposite the Central Front, that the Germans would not be able to launch an offensive before the end of May. This clearly reflects German planning, which at this point had set a date of 12 June.

Zhukov states that by the beginning of June, they knew "virtually all the details" of the enemy plan to strike using major armored forces, including the new Tiger tanks and Ferdinand self-propelled guns. This assessment was certainly helped by the good intelligence they were receiving from the Lucy ring. Still, there was a major shortfall in Soviet intelligence. Zhukov claims that Stavka had concluded that the enemy was massing its strongest force against the Central Front around Orel. As he points out, they learned later that the forces facing the Voronezh Front were stronger. In light of the extent of their operations in the south since November 1942, it is somewhat mystifying how they could make this mistake. Almost all of the units they faced in the south they had faced in March, other than a few reinforcing infantry divisions, which they should have certainly anticipated. They should have expected the attack in the south to be as strong as it was. One can only conclude that the Soviet Army may not have properly estimated the strength of the German panzer divisions and especially the strength of the four over-sized panzer grenadier divisions.

By the end of May, the plan had settled into absorbing the German attack and then going over to the offensive in the areas of Voronezh, Central, Southwestern, and Bryansk Fronts. The Supreme High Command Reserves were massed around Livnyii, Staryii Oskol, and Korocha, "ready to form a defense line in the case the enemy succeeded in breaking through in the Kursk salient," according to Zhukov. The Soviet counteroffensive was massive. Whereas the defensive phase would involve parts of two Fronts, the counteroffensive would involve the left wing of the Western Front, the whole of the Bryansk Front, the Central Front, the Voronezh Front, the right wing of the Southwestern Front, and the reinforcing Steppe Front. At the same time, Stavka had also worked out a plan for offensive operations in case the enemy offensive was delayed. So, regardless of German plans, the Soviet Union was going to attack in that area that summer.

What the Soviet Army Knew About

In their staff study prepared in 1944, the Soviets state that in late March and early April, the Germans had assembled 59 divisions in front of the Central, Voronezh, and Southwestern Fronts. Of these, up to 23 to 26 divisions, including 15 to 17 infantry, 6 to 7 panzer, one cavalry, and one panzer grenadier division were opposite the Central Front; up to 16 or 17 divisions, including 12 to 13 infantry and 4 panzer (SS Corps) divisions were opposite the Voronezh Front, and up to 18 divisions, including 9 infantry divisions and up to 9 panzer divisions, were opposite the Southwestern Front.[15]

This is an interesting assessment and it is fundamentally correct. The Germans had seven infantry divisions opposite the southern flanks of the Voronezh Front, and seven divisions from the Second Army to the west of the Voronezh Front. The three SS panzer grenadier

15 Glantz and Orenstein, page 8.

divisions and the Gross Deutschland Division were being moved into reserve in the rear. The 6th, 11th, and 17th Panzer Divisions were in the line and shortly to be moved to the rear. They were opposite the Southwestern Front. To the southeast was the First Panzer Army, with the Viking SS Panzer Grenadier Division, and the 7th, 3rd, and 19th Panzer Divisions.

In light of this estimate, the later post-war Soviet claims that they were somewhat surprised by the size of the German attack in the south is hard to justify. Yet, the Soviet estimates had identified by early April most of the forces the Germans were going to be able to put into the attack. If the Soviets were taken by surprise, it was not due to a lack of information about what forces the Germans had.

The Soviet numerical estimates are interesting, and for reference, we included the actual count, best as we can determine.[16]

	27 March	*4 July*	*Actual Strength*
Personnel	76,000	168,000	338,335
Tanks and Assault Guns	375	1,700	1,709
Guns (all calibers)	500	2,500	3,498
Mortars (all calibers)	500	1,100	3,539

Toward the end of June, it became obvious that the Germans were going to launch their offensive in the next few days. On 30 June, Zhukov was with the Central Front. He received a call from Stalin, instructing him to remain in the Orel sector to coordinate the operations of the Central, Bryansk, and Western Fronts. Stalin had appointed Vasilevskii to be in charge of the Voronezh and Southwestern Fronts.

First, it is clear that they underestimated the strength of the German forces on 27 March and were either underestimating them on 4 July or miscounting them. Part of this underestimation may have been due to them not giving the proper strength to German divisions. Their estimate of German tank strength on 4 July is very accurate. As these estimates are from the Soviet General Staff Study of 1944, they may have had the benefit of hindsight. It does make one suspicious that they may have had access to the German monthly tank status reports. Until we can get access to the Front files and some of the Soviet intelligence files, we cannot confirm what their actual estimates were just before the battle.

The Soviet Army did have a methodology called the correlation of forces. It was expected, as part of the staff planning, that the Soviet commanders would list out what their strength and assets were compared to the opposing force. This useful exercise, although the opposing side came from intelligence data, did force all Soviet commanders to consider the calculus of combat before the battle. In the staff study, they provided the following estimate for the correlation of forces:[17]

	Entire Front	*Main Attack Sector*
Personnel	1 : 2.5	1 : 1.5
Tanks	1.1 : 1	1.6 : 1
Guns	1 : 1.5	1.5 : 1
Mortars	1 : 3.9	1 : 3.8

The first number in the ratio is the German strength; the second number is the Soviets. As can be seen, the Soviets thought they had the Germans heavily outnumbered in personnel, and were outnumbered in tanks and artillery on the main line of attack. This correlation is based upon the forces of the Sixth Guards Army, the Seventh Guards Army's two right flank divisions, the Sixty-ninth Army's two right flank divisions, the First Tank Army, and the V and II Guards Tank Corps. The selection of only two divisions each from the Seventh Guards Army and the Sixty-ninth Army is a little strange as seven divisions from these two armies ended up fighting the various German panzer corps.

An actual ratio, based upon all the forces deployed on the 4th, but using the actual German and Soviet data, produces the following estimates.

16 Soviet estimate from Glantz and Orenstein, page 27. German data from the Kursk Data Base, assembled from German unit records.

17 Glantz and Orenstein, page 29.

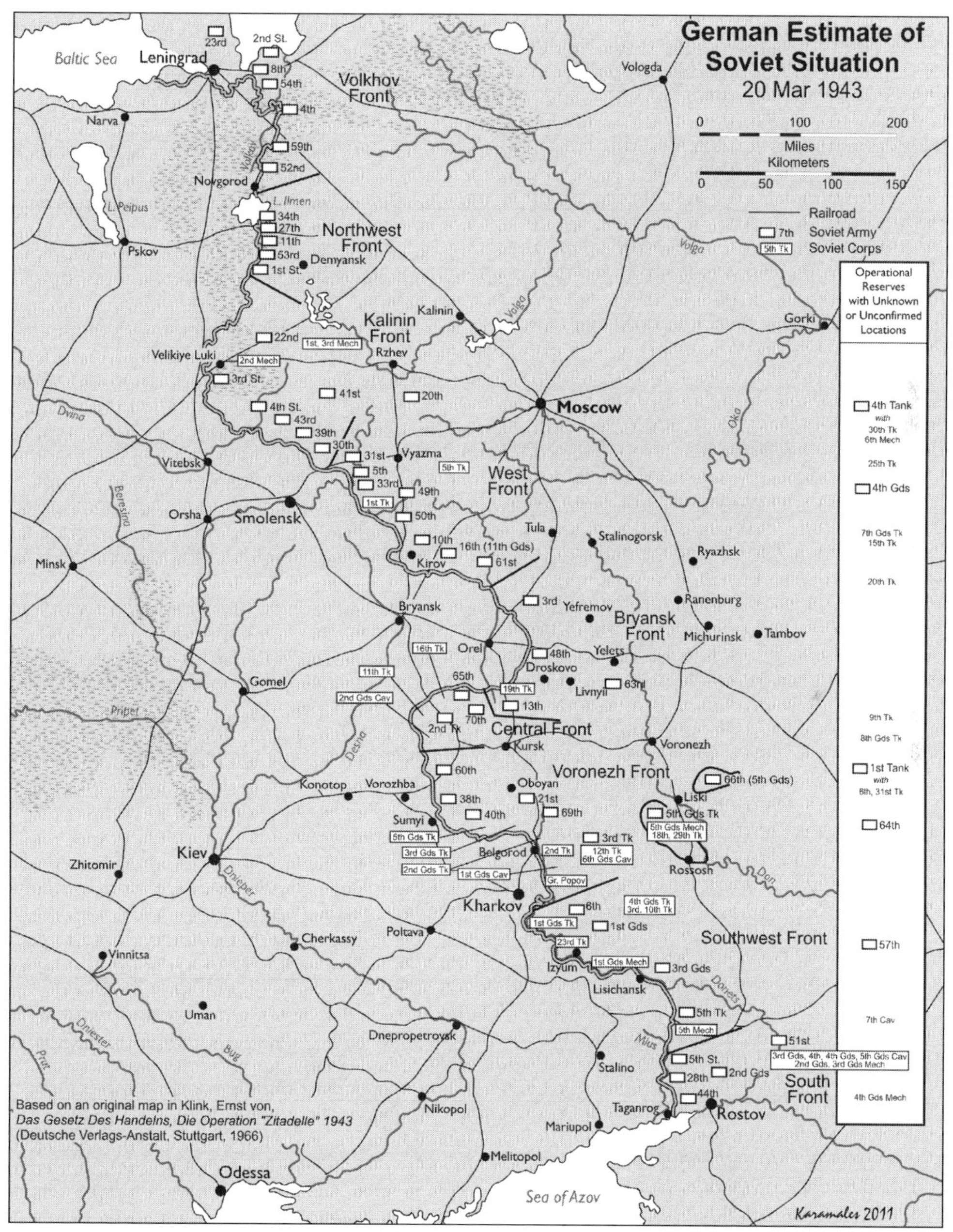
German Estimate of
Soviet Situation
20 Mar 1943
Miles
Kilometers
Railroad
Soviet Army
Soviet Corps
Operational Reserves with Unknown or Unconfirmed Locations
Based on an original map in Klink, Ernst von, Das Gesetz Des Handelns, Die Operation "Zitadelle" 1943 (Deutsche Verlags-Anstalt, Stuttgart, 1966)
Karamales 2011

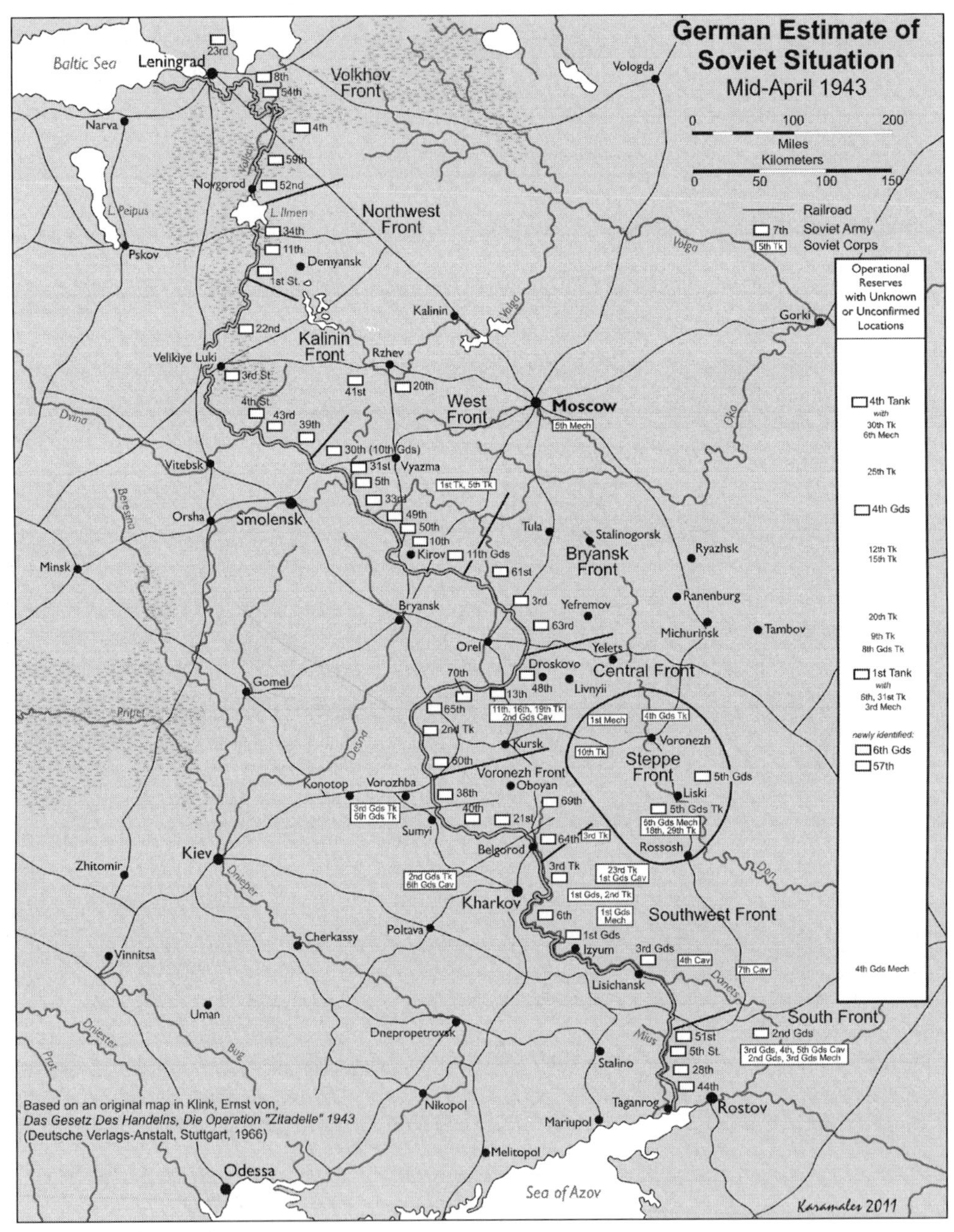

German Estimate of Soviet Situation
Mid-April 1943
Miles
Kilometers
Railroad
Soviet Army
Soviet Corps
Operational Reserves with Unknown or Unconfirmed Locations
Moscow
Leningrad
Kiev
Kharkov
Kursk
Smolensk
Rostov
Odessa
Baltic Sea
Sea of Azov
Volkhov Front
Northwest Front
Kalinin Front
West Front
Bryansk Front
Central Front
Voronezh Front
Steppe Front
Southwest Front
South Front
Based on an original map in Klink, Ernst von, *Das Gesetz Des Handelns, Die Operation "Zitadelle" 1943* (Deutsche Verlags-Anstalt, Stuttgart, 1966)
Karamales 2011

	Total German	*Total Soviet*	*Ratio*
Personnel	338,167	391,111	1 to 1.16
Tanks	1,711	1,537	1.11 to 1
Guns[18]	2,477	4,083	1 to 1.65
Mortars	1,586	5,439	1 to 3.43

As can be seen from the above, this was basically a battle that favored the Soviets in numbers, with the Soviets having the advantage of defensive works, being on defense, and supposedly superior intelligence. About the only significant area where the Germans held a numerical advantage was in field artillery above 105mm, where they had 809 guns compared to 502 guns.

What Did the Germans Know About?

Many of the discussions on Kursk have stressed that the Germans did not realize the extent or degree of the Soviet defenses or that Soviet intelligence deception was particularly good (i.e. Mellenthin, Glantz). However, it does appear that these themes are overstated. The German intelligence maps had clearly identified most of the major Soviet formations they would be facing. Looking at the German OKH enemy location maps of 20 March 1943, in the southern part of the Kursk bulge, they report the Voronezh Front with the Sixtieth (eventually transferred to Central Front), Thirty-eighth, Fortieth, Twenty-first and the Sixty-ninth Armies. The Fortieth Army and Twenty-first Army (Sixth Guards Army) are reported in their correct locations, while the Sixty-ninth Army is where the Seventh Guards Army eventually was (which was correct). They show on the front line around Kharkov the V Guards Tank Corps, the III Guards Tank Corps, the II Guards Tank Corps, and the I Guards Cavalry Corps, as well as "Group Popov," in the line from north of Belgorod to east of Kharkov. Due east of Kharkov they report the Third Tank Army with the XII Tank Corps and the VI Guards Cavalry Corps. Farther east they are showing the Fifth Guards Tank Army with the V Guards Mechanized Corps, XVIII Tanks Corps, and the XIX Tank Corps. East of that they show the Sixty-sixth Army, which they have correctly surmised has been renamed the Fifth Guards Army. Finally, off the map, to the rear, either in the area or moving to the area, they note the First Tank Army, with the VI Tank Corps and the XXXI (31st) Tank Corps, and the Sixty-fourth Army (Seventh Guards Army).

During the Kursk offensive in the south, the Germans faced initially four infantry armies (Fortieth, Sixth Guards, Seventh Guards, and Sixty-ninth) and later the Fifth Guards Army. All of these were identified as of 20 March. If one assumes that a Soviet Army had seven divisions, then this would amount to 28 rifle divisions they could be facing. In the course of the actual operations, they faced a total of 37, of which 29 started with the Voronezh Front. During the operations in July, they faced the First Tank Army and later the Fifth Guards Tank Army. Both of these have been identified. Overall, they faced ten tank and mechanized corps, of which five started with the Voronezh Front at the beginning of the battle and five were sent in as reinforcements. The German intelligence maps on 20 March show four tank corps in the area (and a cavalry corps), four mechanized and tank corps to the rear (and another cavalry corps), and two tank corps far to the rear under the First Tank Army. Of these ten mechanized and tank corps shown, eight actually participated. There were only two mechanized and tank corps they had not identified. One was the III Mechanized Corps, which may have been misidentified as the III Guards Tank Corps north of Belgorod although they also show the III Guards Mechanized Corps way down in the Southern Front near Rostov. The other was the X Tank Corps, which is shown southeast of Kharkov with the Southwestern Front. The only other major formation they have not identified is the XXXV (35th) Guards Rifle Corps with its three divisions. What is clear is that by 20 March, the Germans had identified or had their eye on at least 80% of the major formations that would or could be in position in the Kursk area.

18 Guns include rocket launchers, and exclude 20mm, 37mm, and 40mm AA guns.

The Soviet Build Up

In their preparations for the battle, according to Konev, the forces added to the three Fronts (Central, Voronezh, and Steppe) included 683,000 troops, 11,000 field guns and mortars, 3,800 tanks and self-propelled guns, and 1,900 aircraft. This is added to a force that is stated as having a combined strength on 1 July for the Central, Voronezh, and Steppe Fronts of 1,910,361 troops, 28,304 field guns and mortars, 5,128 tanks and self-propelled guns, and possibly 2,650 planes.[19]

This seems to indicate that the personnel and fighting strengths of these three Fronts were beefed up by at least a third (36 percent) before the main offensive and the artillery was expanded by a similar amount (39 percent). This is a significant amount of replacements to absorb in what appears to be a three month period. Most of the armor (74 percent) was newly arriving as was most of the air force (72 percent).

Just as a comparison, the overall figures for the Soviet Army in summer of 1943, as given by Vasilevskii, are 6.4 million troops, 99,000 field guns and mortars, 2,200 rocket launchers, 9,850 tanks and self-propelled guns, and 8,300 warplanes. Counting the Steppe Front, this would mean that the Soviet Army had committed 30 percent of their soldiers, 29 percent of their artillery, 52 percent of their armor, and 32 percent of their aircraft to the defense of the Kursk bulge.

The Soviets did not build up their formations for the battle by sending new units into the Voronezh Front. Almost all the major formations that fought in the battle were in the area by the end of March. Instead these units were built back up to strength, and supplemented by a large number of separate armor, antitank and artillery brigades, regiments, and battalions.

The Voronezh Front was not brought up to strength by using replacements from the rear, but instead by using their own "internal resources," as the staff study claims. According to the staff study, 27 percent of the Voronezh's replacements came from mobilization of those eligible for military service in the liberated territory, 9 percent were returns to duty from army and

---

19 These figures are from *Voyenno-Istoricheskii Zhurnal* [Military History Journal], 1968, Number 6. "Dokumentyi i Materialyi: Kurskaya Bitva v Tsifrakh."

The Voronezh Front had on 1 July 625,591 people, 9,479 guns, 1,704 tanks and self-propelled guns and 881 aircraft. Of the guns, 1,795 were 45–57mm AT guns, 2,327 were 76mm guns and greater, 4,596 were 82mm and 120mm Mortars, 450 were 20–37mm AA guns, 311 were 76mm to 85mm AA guns, and 272 were BM-8 and BM-13 rocket launchers. The tanks consisted of 105 heavy tanks, 1,114 medium tanks, 443 light tanks, 24 medium self-propelled guns, and 18 light self-propelled guns.

As a double check, our Kursk database shows that the Voronezh Front, not counting the Thirty-eighth Army (which was outside the area we were concerned with) had at the start of the battle 391,111 people, 1,537 tanks and self-propelled guns, 3,836 guns 45mm and above, and 3,843 mortars 82mm and above. See Appendix III of my book *Kursk: The Battle of Prokhorovka* for more details. The higher figures provided by the Soviets for tanks, guns, and mortars are mostly accounted for by the missing Thirty-eighth Army. The personnel strength figures definitely mismatch as our data does not pick up significant supply and transport troops, rear area medical troops, air army personnel, some rear area AA units, etc.

This Soviet record reports for the Central Front 711,575 people, 12,207 guns (11,076 field guns and mortars), 1,785 tanks and self-propelled guns and 1,034 airplanes. For the Steppe Front they record 573,195 people, 9,211 guns (8,510 field guns and mortars) and 1,639 tanks and self-propelled guns. The Southwestern Front records 735 airplanes. The Southwestern Front aircraft are included in the combined figures.

There are additional airplanes in the area that may have been involved. The report footnotes note that these figures do not include about 480 night bombers from long-range aviation and do not include the IX Fighter Corps and 36th and 101st Fighter Division from the Air Defense Command. They also note that other Soviet secondary sources mention a total of 3,130 airplanes not counting long-range aviation, and 2,370 airplanes, not counting long-range aviation and the neighboring Fronts. There is a reported figure of 550 aircraft for the Steppe Front from Dupuy and Martell, *Great Battles on the Eastern Front*, page 76, clearly taken from Soviet sources. These figures are not included in the above aircraft totals.

Vasilevskii, Volume II, page 25; Konev, page 20, and Moskalenko give similar figures, in most cases having rounded them to the nearest hundred or thousand. Due to the centralized nature of Soviet historical writing and the tendency of generals to be assigned ghost writers, the consistency in the numbers between the various accounts is not surprising.

See Konev, "The Great Battle at Kursk and its Historic Significance," *The Battle of Kursk* (Progress Publishers, USSR, 1974), page 20.

Front hospitals, some 33 percent came from taking those fit for duty from rear units and installations, and 31 percent from regular replacements. This system of replacements leaves a little to be desired.

The Soviet Defensive Works

It has been widely discussed in Soviet sources and blindly accepted in western military writing that the Soviet Army defensive positions for the Battle of Kursk were some of the most extensive field fortifications ever prepared. However, it appears from the evidence that this view is overstated. Mines were employed in large numbers, but in insufficient density to prove a significant barrier to the German advance. Other barriers, including antitank ditches, were emplaced, but again, in limited density. Field fortifications were built in sufficient numbers, but only the trench system was truly extensive. Finally, despite three months of preparation, the Soviet forces had completed less than 75% of the fortifications that had been planned. From the evidence, even the completion of the planned works would have been insufficient to halt the German attack. The extent and strength of the actual fortifications were less than what has been implied by previous accounts of the battle.

The Soviets had prepared defensive works with an overall depth of 300 kilometers. Based on the probable times they expected the Germans to begin the offensive, they tried to complete the initial defensive works by 15 April. This was two weeks ahead of the first real date given by the Germans for launching the attack. The Fronts prepared their defensive lines while the local population was extensively enlisted to work on the rear defensive lines.

They also concentrated a large reserve in a defensive line behind the Kursk bulge. This was the Reserve Front (renamed the Steppe Military district on 15 April and later the Steppe Front on 10 July), now under command of General I. S. Konev. At the beginning of July it consisted of the Twenty-seventh Army (Lt. Gen. S. G. Trofimenko), Forty-seventh Army (Maj. Gen A. I. Ryzhov and then Maj. Gen. P. M. Kozlov), Fifty-third Army (Lt. Gen. I. M. Managarov), Fourth Guards Army (formally Twenty-fourth Army) (Lt. Gen. G. I. Kulik), Fifth Guards Army (Lt. Gen. A. S. Zhadov), Fifth Guards Tank Army (Lt. Gen. P. A. Rotmistrov), Fifth Air Army (Lt. Gen. S. K. Goryunov), IV Guards and X Tank Corps, I Guards Mechanized Corps, and III, V, and VII Guards Cavalry Corps.

As part of this defense, the Fronts were instructed to create no fewer than five or six defensive lines along the most important axes. In addition, the eastern bank of the Don (what was referred to as the state defensive line) was also prepared for defense, and later the Steppe Front constructed a defensive line along the eastern banks of the Kshen and Oskol Rivers from Livnyii to Novyii Oskol. The work began in April and continued up until the offensive started on 5 July.

The forward four defensive positions were constructed using the engineers and troops in the area. Civilian labor was used for the positions farther back. The construction and outfitting of the Front rear echelon positions was done by a special set of defense construction directorates. They employed local forces and means. As one would expect, this rear area effort did not amount to much and the defensive positions got progressively weaker the farther one went back. Only the first two defensive lines were of real significance. The details of these works are discussed fully in Chapter Four of my book *Kursk: The Battle of Prokhorovka*.[20]

Just to look at one aspect of their defensive works, as part of these works were a considerable collection of antitank and antipersonnel mines deployed in the first two defensive lines. This means in the first and second

20 See Christopher A. Lawrence, *Kursk: The Battle of Prokhorovka* (Aberdeen Books, Sheridan, CO, 2015), pages 181–215.

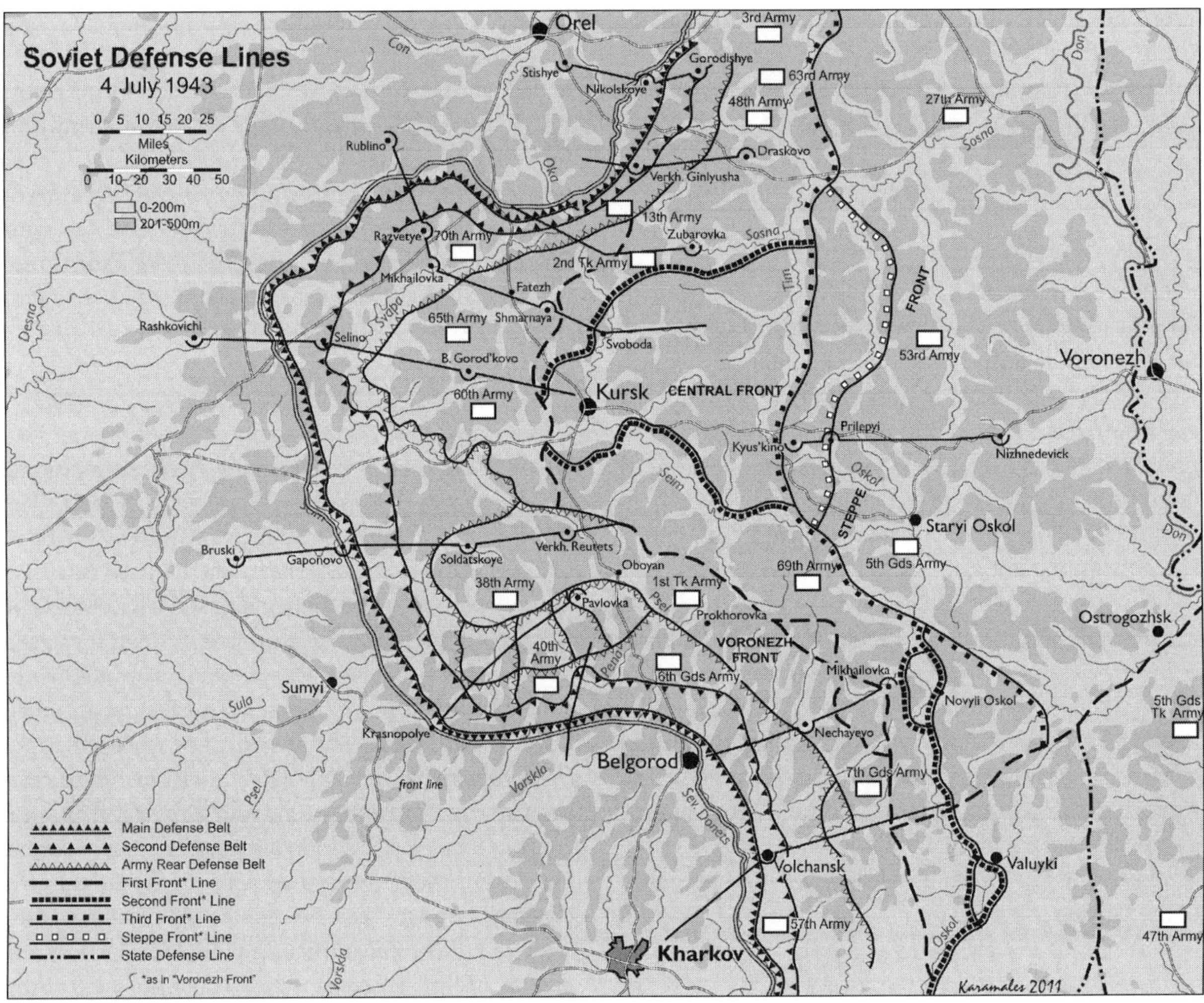

SOVIET DEFENSIVE WORKS FROM SOVIET-ERA SOURCES.

defensive echelons of the Sixth and Seventh Guards Armies. In the case of the Sixth Guards Army, this was 170,210 mines as of 4 July 1943. As of 30 June, it was 88,261 antitank mines and 53,324 antipersonnel mines. The mines were mostly deployed in the first echelon, which had 80% of the mines. They were deployed almost evenly between all four rifle divisions in the first echelon. The situation with the Seventh Guards Army was similar, with 151,954 mines deployed by 5 July (66,814 antitank and 85,140 antipersonnel), of which 92% were in the first echelon. Unlike the Sixth Guards Army, their placement favored the divisions on each end of their line, the 36th Guards Rifle Division which was opposite the German XLII Corps, and the 81st Guards Rifle Division, which was facing the 6th Panzer Division. The Fortieth Army had 59,032 antitank mines, 70,994 antipersonnel mines as well as 6,377 "mine shells" (this is assumed to be artillery shells rigged to explode). The Fortieth Army, to the right of the Sixth Guards Army, was not attacked.

So for the defensive phase of the Battle of Kursk (4-18 July), the Soviet Army laid at least 291,797 antitank mines and 294,378 antipersonnel mines. In the south this produced an impressive 1,666 mines per kilometer and 1,624 antipersonnel mines per kilometers.

Overall, the first defensive line of the Voronezh Front (including the first two echelons of the defending armies) had at least 221,846 antitank and 219,134 antipersonnel mines emplaced before the battle began (excluding the Thirty-eighth Army). The linear density of mines in the area (175.1 kilometers) is some 1,267 antitank mines and 1,251 antipersonnel mines per kilometer. While this appears impressive, what it would really amount to over the entire width of the front is a two-row deep minefield, with a little more than a single mine per meter in each row.

The density of the second echelon tended to be 100 to 200 mines per kilometers, or one per every five to ten linear meters of front. Clearly, the mines in the second echelon were not being laid in belts, but were instead being gathered around defensive points and blocking certain passages.

In contrast, in the third defensive belt was the First Tank Army, which reported having laid some 1,980 antitank mines and 1,520 antipersonnel mines by 4 July. Considering that the frontage of the Army was some 25 kilometers, this was indeed a very thin line of defensive works. The Sixty-Ninth Army, also deployed in the third belt had emplaced as of 4 July 17,671 antitank mines and 16,848 antipersonnel mines.

There were of course, extensive earthworks, trench systems, gun pits and so forth. But again, this was heavily biased into the first echelon, with the army's second echelon being considerably weaker. The front's third echelon was even less prepared and some of the works, including tank ditches, had not been completed.

Comment on Soviet and German Planning

The question facing the Soviets for the summer of 1943 was the same as that facing the Germans: should they attack, or should they defend and then counterattack? In effect, the Soviets were considering a Manstein-like "backhand" approach although not with the dynamic exchange of territory that Manstein was considering. As such, the Soviet plan involved considerably less risk.

The problem in determining who contributed to the German plan is that defeat is an orphaned child. Therefore, the post-war German accounts are filled with explanations of how they did not really support the attack as executed. This leaves to the historian the task of actually trying to figure out who actually did author and support this effort.

Due to the more centralized nature of Soviet history, there is less confusion and contradiction in the accounts. It is clear that the basic plan for the battle was driven by Zhukov and supported and drafted by Vasilevskii. Still, Zhukov did not operate without some problems, as he was not always aware of what national reserves were available. Furthermore, he had to address Stalin's fears about Moscow, and throughout 1942 and 1943 the Soviet Union tended to over-protect Moscow at the expense of the south. Nonetheless, at this stage, Zhukov was left with a freer hand to develop plans compared to his counterparts in Germany.

It is interesting to note, although no one particularly states it, that both sides' battle plans were not based on geographical, economic, or primarily political objectives, they were fundamentally based upon grinding down and destroying each other's army. This was clearly now a war of attrition, with maneuver only used as a means of causing enemy losses.

SOVIET TANKS

The Soviet Union, before the start of World War II, had the most developed tank production program in the world. As such, it started the war with a good number of well-designed tanks, and in 1943 these were still in use. In addition, for the summer of 1943, the Soviet Union was also deploying a number of new tanks. Finally, the Soviet forces were supplemented by U.S. and UK lend-lease tanks which, although sometimes of inferior design, were still useful armor. The tanks used at Kursk include:

Soviet Tanks

T-60 This was a 6.4-ton light tank armed with a 20mm gun and one 7.62mm machinegun, had a two-man crew, with up to 35mm of frontal armor, and a maximum speed of 42 kilometers per hour (kph). It was first deployed in 1941. A development of the T-40, it was first manufactured in two and a half weeks.

T-70 This was a 9.8-ton light tank armed with a 45mm gun and one 7.62mm machinegun, had a two-man crew, with up to 45mm of frontal armor (50mm on turret front), and a maximum speed of 45 kph. It was first deployed in 1942. There were 8,226 of these tanks manufactured. It was developed from the T-60.

T-34 This was a 30.9-ton medium tank armed with a 76.2mm gun and two 7.62mm machineguns, had a four-man crew, with up to 45mm of frontal armor (52mm on turret front side and rear) and a well-designed sloped armor scheme that enhanced its protection and was well armored on the sides and rear as well. It had a maximum speed of 55 kph. It was first deployed in 1940. At the time of its introduction, it was probably the best medium tank in the world.

KV-1 This was a 47.5-ton heavy tank armed with a 76.2mm gun and four 7.62mm machineguns, had a five-man crew, and heavily armored with up to 75mm of frontal armor (90mm on turret front) and a maximum speed of 35 kph. It was well armored on the sides, rear, top and bottom. It was first deployed in late 1939. The tank was named after Marshal Kliment Voroshilov and was one of his few useful contributions to the Soviet Army. At the time of its introduction, it was probably the best heavy tank in the world. There were 3,486 KV-1s and 1,087 KV-1Ss manufactured.

KV-1s This was a faster but more lightly armored version of the KV tank and was present at Kursk. This was a 42.5-ton heavy tank armed with a 76.2mm gun and three 7.62mm machineguns, had a five-man crew, and armored with up to 60mm of frontal hull armor (82mm on turret front) and a maximum speed of 43 kph. It was well armored on the sides, rear, top and bottom. It was first deployed in 1942.

KV-2 This was the KV-1 heavy tank with a large slab-sided turret added to accommodate the ML-20S 152.4mm Howitzer. It weighed 54 tons, was armed with a 152mm gun and four 7.62mm machineguns, had a six-man crew, and heavily armored with up to 75mm of frontal hull armor, although its turret was more vulnerable. It had a maximum speed of 32 kph. It was first deployed in 1940 and a total of 213 were built. The Soviets report 10 KV-2s with the 203rd Tank Regiment. If these were actually a KV-2, vice a KV-1S (which were sometimes called a KV-2), then the KV-2s at Kursk were probably some of the last ones in the Soviet inventory.

Soviet Assault Guns

Su-76 This was a 10.6-ton open-topped, open-backed assault gun mounting the 76.2mm division gun and no machineguns, had a four-man crew, 30mm frontal armor and a maximum speed of 45 kph. Like the German Marders, it was created by using an obsolete chassis, in this case the T-70, and building an armored casemate for the gun. Production of the SU-76 started very late in 1942 although Kursk saw the first large scale deployment of the SU-76M model. The SU-76 would become the second most common Soviet armored vehicle, after the T-34.

Su-122 This was a 30.9-ton assault gun mounting the M-30 122mm howitzer and no machineguns, had a five-man crew, 45mm frontal armor and a maximum speed of 55 kph. It was created using the T-34 chassis and building an armored casemate for the gun. It saw its first action around Leningrad in January 1943.

Su-152 This tank was designed in 25 days in January 1943 by marrying a 152mm Field Gun to a KV-1 tank chassis. Production was started immediately and by May 1943 they had outfitted four regiments, each with 12 Su-152s.

The Su-152 weighed 45.5 tons, was armed with a ML-20S 152.4mm gun and no machineguns, had a five-man crew, 60mm frontal hull armor (75mm on the "turret" front) and a maximum speed of 43 kph. It was well armored on the sides and rear as well. Construction started 1 March 1943 and it was first deployed at Kursk.

Lend Lease Tanks

Stuart The American-built M-3 Stuart was a 10.95-ton light tank armed with a 37mm gun and four 7.62mm machineguns, had a four-man crew, with up to 25mm of frontal armor, and a maximum speed of 56 kph. It was first deployed in 1941. It was one of the better light tanks in the world at the time of its introduction. In 1942 and 1943, the U.S. provided the USSR with 1,676 M3 and M3A1 Stuarts, with 1,232 seeing service in the Soviet Army.

Grant The American-built M-3 Grant (or Lee) was a 27.2-ton medium tank armed with a hull-mounted 75mm gun, a turret-mounted 37mm gun and three 7.62mm machineguns, had a six-man crew, with up to 50mm of frontal armor, and a maximum speed of 40 kph. It was first deployed in 1941 with the British in North Africa. It was a stop gap measure until the U.S. could produce a medium tank with a larger turret mounted gun. Its tall silhouette made it vulnerable, as did the need to expose most of the tank to fire its main gun. Clearly inferior to Soviet and German medium tank designs of the time. There were 1,386 of these tanks sent to the Soviet Union, or about 6% of the production run of 22,743, with 976 serving with the Soviet Army, including a few M-2A1 medium tanks.

Matilda The British-built Mark II Matilda was a 27-ton infantry tank armed with a 40mm (two pounder) gun and one 7.92mm machinegun, had a crew of four and was heavily armored with up to 78mm of armor on its front. It was slow at 24 kph maximum speed. The first 20 Matildas were delivered to the Soviet Union at Arkhangel on 11 October 1941 and by the end of the year, 187 had been delivered. The UK sent 1,084 during the war, of which 918 served. This was a little over one-third of its production run of 2,987.

Churchill The British-Built Mark IV Churchill was a 39.5-ton infantry tank (effectively a heavy tank) armed with a 57mm gun (six-pounder) and two 7.92mm machineguns, had a crew of five, and heavily armored with up to 102mm of armor on its front. It was slow at 25 kph maximum speed. Various armament schemes were tried, with 57mm, 75mm, and 95mm main guns, a version with a 75mm gun in the hull, flamethrower versions, etc. The Mark IV was the version most likely present at Kursk. A total of 344 Churchills were provided to the Soviet Union during the war, of which 253 were Mark IV versions.

Soviet Armored Cars

BA-10 This is a heavy armored car used for reconnaissance, communications, and joint operations with cavalry and motorized infantry, and as a mobile strike vehicle. It was armed with a 45mm gun and two 7.62mm machineguns, had a crew of four, had up to 14mm of frontal armor, weighed 5.14 tons (5.36 tons for the BA-10M) and had a speed of over 80 kph. Versions of this armored car first came into use in 1932 and the BA-10M version came in use in 1937.

BA-20 This is a light armored car used primarily for reconnaissance. It was armed with one 7.62mm machinegun, had a crew of two, had up to 8mm frontal armor, weighed 2.52 tons, and had a speed of around 90 kph.

BA-64 This is a light armored car with four-wheel drive primarily used for reconnaissance. It was armed with one 7.62mm machinegun, had a crew of two, had up to 15mm frontal armor, weight 2.60 tons (2.67 tons for the BA-64B), and had a speed of 80 kph. It first came into use in 1942.

Lend-Lease Armored Personnel Carriers

Bren Gun Carrier This British-designed "universal" carrier weighed 3.5 tons, carried a single 7.7mm machinegun, had 7 to 11mm of armor and a speed of 50 kph. It was first deployed in 1935. There were 2,008 that served with the Soviet Army out of a production run of 89,595.

M-3 Scout Car This is the U.S. M-3A1 White Scout Car. This four-wheel drive vehicle weighed 5.6 tons, was armed with a 12.7mm machinegun and a 7.62mm machinegun, had 12mm of armor, carried 8 men (six dismounts), and had a speed of 105 kph. There were 3,340 sent to the Soviet Union out of a production run of 20,894.

CHAPTER THREE

The Belgorod Offensive

4–8 JULY 1943

Our detractors used to say that the only reason we were able to defeat Paulus's colossal army at Stalingrad was that we had the Russian winter on our side. They had said the same thing about our defeat of the Germans outside Moscow in 1941. Ever since Russia turned back Napoleon's invasion, people claimed that winter was our main ally. However, the Germans couldn't use this excuse to explain their defeat at the Battle of the Kursk Salient in 1943. They fired the first shot; they chose the time, place, and form of the battle. All the cards were in the hands of Hitler and his cutthroats. It was high summer.

NIKITA KHRUSHCHEV
CA. 1970[1]

DEPLOYED ON THE south side of the Kursk bulge, around Belgorod, prepared for the attack, were five German corps assigned to the offense under command of two armies. To the west of Belgorod was the Fourth Panzer Army with three corps. Around Belgorod and to its south was Provisional Army Kempf with two of its three corps in the offensive. A third corps, the XLII Corps of three infantry divisions, was to the south and conducted an insignificant feint on the 5th of July.

Under the Fourth Panzer Army were three corps. Of those, two, the XLVIII Panzer Corps and the SS Panzer Corps, were to lead the attack. The LII Corps was to support the left flank. In the days before the battle the weather was relatively benign, with some scattered showers on the 1st and 2nd, and dry, partly cloudy for the 3rd. The roads were reported as good. On the 3rd of July, the Fourth Panzer Army noted that the front was remarkably calm with minimal air activity. They also noted that their movements were going according to plan. This was also true for the first half of the 4th. The weather for this day included scattered thunderstorm showers, but the roads were still easily passable and the movements went as scheduled. They were now ready to start the attack.

The LII Corps, covering a front of 56.6 kilometers, consisted of two infantry divisions, the 57th Infantry Division on the far left (west) and the 255th Infantry Division on the right. Opposing them was the Soviet Fortieth Army of seven rifle divisions. Then came the powerful XLVIII Panzer Corps with the 332nd Infantry Division on the left, then the 3rd Panzer Division, then the very large Gross Deutschland Panzer Grenadier Division and the 11th Panzer Division on the right. Added to the Gross Deutschland Panzer Grenadier Division was the Lauchert Panzer Regiment with the 200

1 Nikita Khrushchev (translated and edited by Strobe Talbott), *Khrushchev Remembers* (Little, Brown and Company, Boston, 1970), page 208.

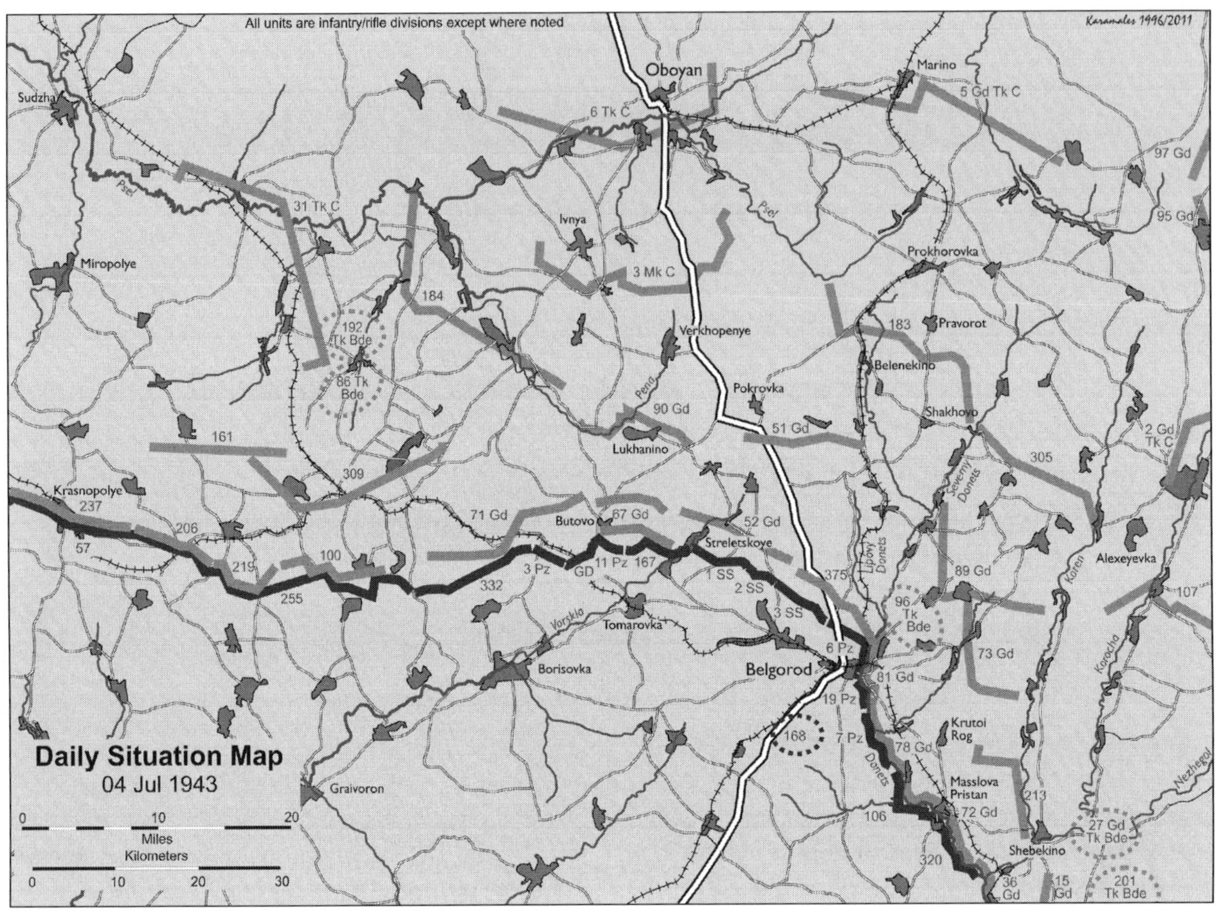

new Panther tanks. To the right of the XLVIII Panzer Corps was the SS Panzer Corps. These two panzer corps were opposite of the Sixth Guards Army with seven rifle divisions.

The SS Panzer Corps was laid out with its three SS panzer grenadier divisions in a line. The Leibstandarte SS Adolf Hitler (LSSAH) Panzer Grenadier Division was on the far left, next to the 167th Infantry Division, which had been placed between the two attacking panzer corps; to the right of it was the Das Reich (DR) SS Panzer Grenadier Division and to the right of that was Totenkopf (T) SS Panzer Grenadier Division. At this point in their life, these divisions were only identified by name, not number, but they would be later numbered in the order they were deployed here from left to right as the 1st, 2nd, and 3rd SS divisions. This was the core of the SS, its three oldest and most senior divisions, ready to attack. These three divisions were deployed along a front of some 19.5 kilometers.

Although the divisions themselves were quite large, there were not a lot of other supporting units for them, with the corps having two artillery battalions (one of them nebelwerfer), two engineer battalions and three construction battalions. The corps also had an extensive collection of bridging columns. The Adolf Hitler SS Division had a nebelwerfer regiment attached and a light field howitzer battalion, in addition to the 315th Infantry Regiment of the 167th Infantry Division. Das Reich had one nebelwerfer battalion attached, as did Totenkopf. Basically the attack force was three SS pan-

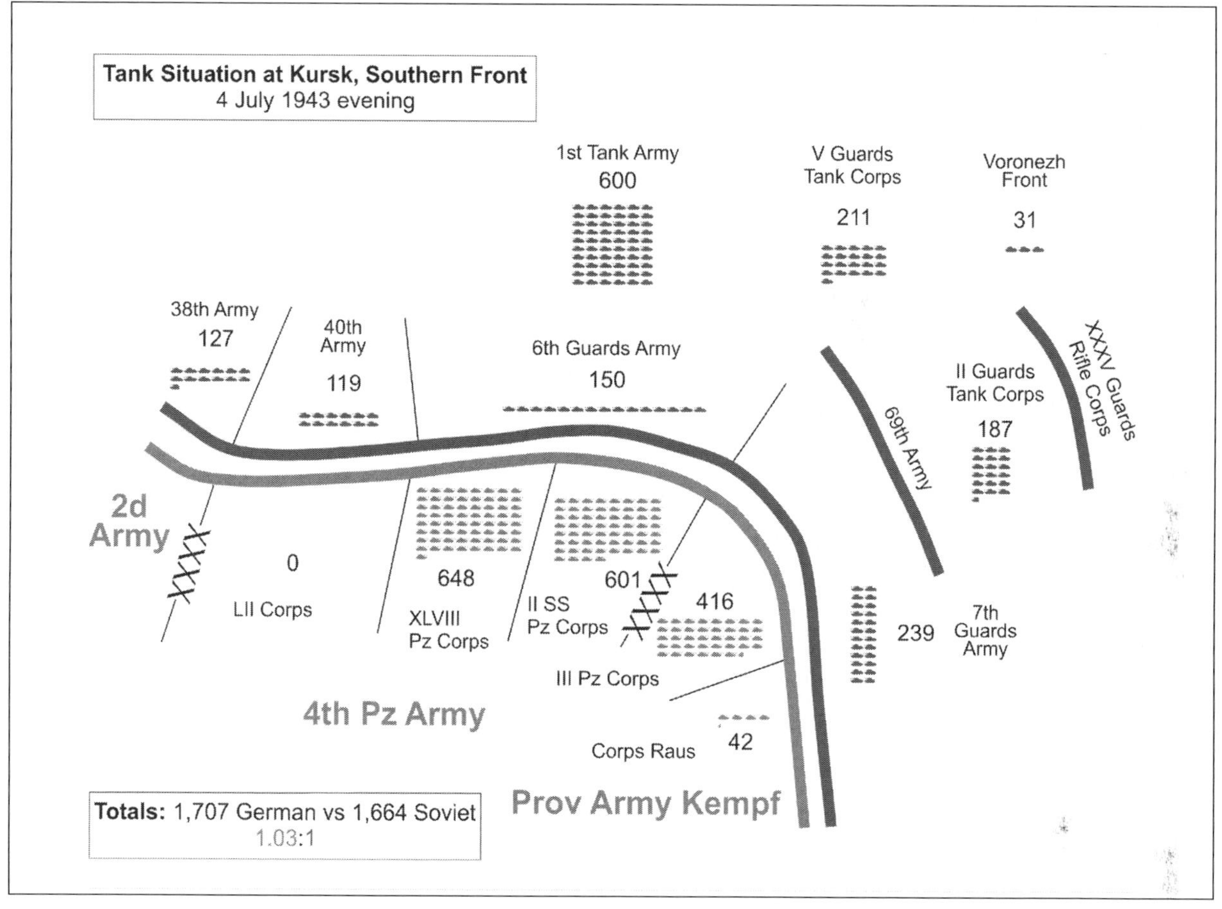

zer grenadier divisions backed up with eight battalions of artillery and nebelwerfers and five engineer and construction battalions. This structure did not significantly change during the battle.

Both of these panzer corps, the XLVIII and SS Panzer Corps, cleared the outpost line during the afternoon of the 4th of July. In the case of the XLVIII Panzer Corps, this turned into a battalion-sized fight at Butovo that went into the evening. The main attack started the next day.

Around Belgorod and to its south was the two participating corps of Provisional Army Kempf. The Donets River ran from north to south, mostly separating parts of the two lines, with the Germans on west bank and the Soviet Army on the east bank. The 6th Panzer Division was located in a foothold on the east bank of the Donets River, around the town of Mikhailovka, along with most of the 168th Infantry Division. The 19th Panzer Division was to its south, partly across the river and with part of the division having to conduct a cross-river attack the next morning. The 7th Panzer Division was going to have to attack across river. They were all part of the III Panzer Corps and supported by the 168th Infantry Division, which was partitioned among them, with a reinforced infantry regiment attached to each panzer division. Also there was the only Tiger battalion in the battle, the 503rd Heavy Panzer Battalion, also partitioned among the three panzer divisions. To the south of the III Panzer Corps were the two divisions of Corps Raus, the 106th and 320th Infantry Divisions. They were on the west bank, covering some 18 kilometers along the river. They were preparing to conduct a cross river attack the next morning. They were to cross the Donets, advance and cross the Koren River, and then advance to and establish defensive positions at the Korocha River, some 18 to 26 kilometers beyond the Donets. They were to protect the flank of the III Panzer Corps so as to provide it room and a base for operation. The III Panzer Corps was to protect the flank of the Fourth Panzer Army and its SS Panzer Corps.

As a result of its clearing operations on the 4th of July, German losses totaled around 657 (129 killed, 516 wounded, and 12 missing). Some 87.5 percent of these losses occurred in the XLVIII Panzer Corps Sector. It was the only sector with significant combat activity. The SS Panzer Corps area had much less, mostly the Totenkopf SS Division, although the Adolf Hitler SS Division probably suffered higher losses than the one wounded it reported for this day. There were virtually no casualties in the other areas as no line of advanced outposts was attacked, except for the 57th Infantry Division. The 332nd Infantry Division also showed some losses, probably due to the artillery exchanges.

It is hard to determine the Soviet casualties for this day. Most of the Soviet reports for the first few days of combat are aggregate reports covering several days, and may include the data from the evening of the 4th. It is hard to determine what percent of those losses are from the 4th as there are not always clear daily casualty reports for this day. As such, our recorded figure of 333 Soviet casualties for this day is most likely low. Still, in the initial move up, with the infantry versus infantry fights that followed, unsupported by significant air or artillery support, the Germans and the Soviets exchanged casualties on roughly an equal basis. This would be one of the few times that this happened on this battlefield. All of the recorded four German tank losses (two Panthers destroyed and two Tigers damaged) on this day were due to mechanical failure.

Still, it is clear that the Soviet outpost line in front of the Sixth Guards Army did serve its purpose in warning the army of an impending German offensive. It also, as the Germans were to discover the following day, successfully masked the details of the Soviet preparations. Finally, they inflicted more than their fair share of casualties, although it did not delay the German offensive effort. It was an effective defensive preparation. The German clearing effort was also effective.

Breaching the First Line: 5 July 1943 (Monday)

The Germans had successfully cleared the outpost line on the 4th and were now prepared to initiate the main assault. This assault was conducted by four German corps, consisting of 14 divisions, including nine armored divisions. Only the two divisions of the LII Corps did not participate in the initial attack.

In the north, from the Orel bulge, the Germans also launched the northern pincer with initially nine divisions, including only one panzer division although joined by three other panzer divisions by the end of the day. The Battle of Kursk had now begun.

The Soviet "Counter-preparation" Artillery bombardment

Much has been made of the effectiveness of the Soviet artillery bombardments that were conducted early in the morning of the 5th. This counter-preparation fire was ordered by either Zhukov or Rokossovskii shortly after 2 AM in the north (Central Front) where Zhukov was located.[2] These bombardments, in both the north (at 0220) and the south (at 0330), supposedly disrupted and delayed the German attack and caused them considerable casualties.

Overall, at least for the south, the effects of this counter-preparation bombardment have clearly been overrated in Soviet literature and must be counted as one of the myths of the Battle of Kursk. It appears to have been fired too early to have caught troops in the open, or con-

2 Zhukov's memoirs indicate that he ordered the fire, while Rokossovskii (Central Front commander) states in his memoirs that he ordered the fire.

centrated, or in their assembly areas. The Germans had not even set a time for the attack in the XLVIII Panzer Corps sector when the bombardment hit. Added to that is that the target selection for the bombardment was somewhat speculative, based upon their estimates of where the Germans may have assembled, with limited knowledge of where they actually were and when. The bombardment would have obviously been much more effective not only if they had waited until the targets were moving, in the open and concentrated, but if they had also waited until they had clear information as to where the targets actually were so they could concentrate on them. At least in the south, it appears that this bombardment wasted considerable ammunition with little effect.

The Fourth Panzer Army Attack

The Fourth Panzer Army unleashed its attack at four points across the front the morning of 5 July. The 3rd Panzer Division attacked from Gertsovka, while the Gross Deutschland Division attacked at two points along the ravine east of Berezovyii. The 11th Panzer Division attacked at Butovo, especially in the areas east of Butovo. The SS Panzer Corps concentrated all its forces to achieve a decisive penetration at Berezov. Defending against these attacks from west to east were the 71st Guards Rifle Division, the 67th Guards Rifle Division and the 52nd Guards Rifle Division.

All German air assets were assigned to the SS Panzer Corps for the morning of the 5th. In the afternoon, they were assigned to the XLVIII Panzer Corps, but their distribution is unknown.

Overall, the Luftwaffe flew 2,387 sorties on the 5th. According the surviving Luftwaffe records, they were flown in support of the SS Panzer Corps. However, according to Major General Hans Seidemann's (commander of VIII Air Corps) post-war account, they were flown in support of both the SS and the XLVIII Panzer Corps. According to the Fourth Panzer Army orders, the SS Panzer Corps was to have all the air support in the morning and the XLVIII Panzer Corps was to have it in the afternoon. From the unit accounts, this appears to be what was done.

There were 371 fighter sorties (Me-109) and 74 reconnaissance sorties. Possibly involved in supporting the ground operations were 536 bomber sorties although some of these may have been striking behind the front lines, 1,071 Stuka sorties which were certainly being used in a close air support role, and 335 ground attack sorties (Fw-190s and Hs-123s). The only surviving detailed air report is from an He-111 squadron and it appears to have been striking the rear part of the first echelon of defense and the second echelon in the SS Panzer Corps area. Germans lost no Ju-87s and only one Fw-190 for the whole day, so German losses from close support were minimal.

The XLVIII Panzer Corps attack was slow-going on the morning of the 5 July. The 3rd Panzer Division and the Gross Deutschland Division had concentrated their attack on the 210th Guards Rifle Regiment of the 71st Guards Rifle Division, while the rest of the Soviet division faced off against the 332nd Infantry Division. The 3rd Panzer Division was still having to untangle from the village of Gertsovka in the morning and was delayed in crossing the ravine west of Berezovyii. They were able to advance in the afternoon to the village of Korovino, which they took by the evening. The 332nd Infantry Division was able to advance to their left and take Voskhod.

The Gross Deutschland Division, with its mix of Tigers, Panthers, other panzers and assault guns got tangled in the ravine east of Berezovyii for an extended fight. They had to bring up engineers, clear mines, and build bridges before they were finally able to work their way across. They then advanced up to the village of Cherkasskoye, which they had mostly cleared by the end of the day. Still, the division had gotten its armor across the ravines and through the Soviet first defensive line. They were now ready to advance to the east and exploit its penetration of the first defensive line.

The 11th Panzer Division had an easier day, taking Butovo from the 67th Guards Rifle Division and then advanced up to Cherkasskoye and points east. The 167th Infantry Division to its right also advanced against the 67th Guards Rifle Division and maintained contact with the SS Panzer Corps on its right.

Results of the XLVIII Panzer Corps Attack

In one day, the XLVIII Panzer Corps had penetrated most of the first Soviet defensive line. Casualties were heavy. The losses for the various units involved were:[3]

	Total	*Killed*	*Wounded*	*Missing*
332nd Infantry Div.	418	39	376	3
3rd Panzer Div.	170	23	145	2
GD PzGr Div.	401	64	332	5
Panther Regiment	4	2	2	
11th Panzer Div.	178	18	159	1
167th Infantry Div.	334	39	285	10
Total	1,505	185	1,299	21

Soviet losses are harder to establish. The 71st Guards Rifle Division reports at 1800 that they had lost 312 men killed and 452 wounded. In the case of the 67th Guards Rifle Division, they report that as of 1700, the 196th Guards Rifle Regiment had lost 58 men killed and 120 wounded. The 199th Guards Rifle Regiment had lost 95 men killed, 123 wounded and 302 missing. An earlier report from the 201st Guards Rifle Regiment placed its losses at only two men killed, five wounded, and one horse killed. These reports were further updated with a claim at 0200 that the 196th Guards Rifle Regiment had lost more than 2/3rds of its personnel and equipment and the 199th Guards Rifle Regiment had lost more than half its personnel and equipment and the 201st Guards Rifle Regiment had lost five killed and ten wounded. The large number of supporting units does not always have good records of their losses. Furthermore, in this type of intense fighting, the more reliable casualty reports are the later counts taken after the units are well to the rear. As such, casualties for any particular day may have to be estimated even though we know the total casualties the unit suffered during the operation. In many cases, the number of missing in action only shows up later in aggregate reports. Overall, it is estimated that on this day, between these two divisions and their attachments they lost some 3,730 people (994 for the 71st Guards Rifle Division and 1,583 for the 67th Guards Rifle Division).

This is around a 2.7-to-1 exchange ratio, in a situation where the defending forces were in prepared positions, in rolling mixed terrain being attacked at around a 2.8-to-1 force ratio.

German armor losses were high. In the case of the 3rd Panzer Division, they started with 79 tanks and 14 Marders, and lost ten this day, including their only assault gun. Of that total, only a Panzer IV long was written off as destroyed. In the case of the Gross Deutschland Division, they started with 158 tanks and 19 Marders, and lost 30 this day, including five of their assault guns. However, only two Panzer IV longs were written off as destroyed.

The Panther regiment started with as many as 198 tanks operational. By the end of the day, they were estimated to be reduced to something like 119 operational. As well as can be determined, two were lost due to friendly fire, one due to hostile fire, six broke down during the march that morning, and up to 19 were lost to mines. The remaining estimated 51 tanks were most likely mechanical failures. The Panther regiment had hardly seen action, but was now down to around 60 percent of its strength. This does not seem to be worth the two-month delay in the start of the offensive for this level of support.

For the 11th Panzer Division, they started with 122 tanks and 9 Marders, and lost 12 tanks, including three assault guns. In general the assault gun losses across these three divisions were similar to the turreted tank losses (9 lost out of 65 assault guns vice 43 lost out of

3 Losses are as reported for the day by each division, except for the Panzer Regiment von Lauchert, which are assumed to be the casualty report for "corps troops" provided by the XLVIII Panzer Corps; and except for the 332nd Infantry Division, which was derived from various periodic casualty reports that cover more than a day. In the case of the 167th Infantry Division, the 315th Infantry Regiment was attached to the SS Panzer Corps, but the casualty figures included below certainly include the regiment. As such, for calculating strengths and losses for each engagement, 1/3rd of the 167th Infantry Division's casualties were counted in the SS Panzer Corps engagements, reducing the total by 111 casualties for the XLVIII Panzer Corps engagements.

294 turreted tanks). In contrast, there were no Marder losses.

This comes out to 52 tanks lost. Considering the limited Soviet armor support, most of these tanks had to be lost due to Soviet antitank guns, artillery and mines. As discussed later, it is estimated that 40 of them were lost due to mines.

Still, at the end of the day, regardless of the losses, the Germans had penetrated the first defensive line in this area, isolated two Soviet regiments from the 67th Guards Rifle Division, and were now in position to move onto and assault the second line.

The SS Panzer Corps

The attack began this day, 5 July, with a concentration of the three SS panzer grenadier divisions and the VIII Air Corps on Berezov. This small town was held by the most eastward regiment of the 52nd Guards Rifle Division, the 155th Guards Rifle Regiment. It was right in the line of the Das Reich sector and the point of concentration for all three SS divisions.

The SS Panzer Corps did start its main attack at 0300 hours (0400 Moscow time), with strong artillery and dive-bomber support. As with the XLVIII Panzer Corps, the artillery preparation was worked out well ahead of time with the initial preparation consisting of 24,464 artillery rounds and 9,270 mortar rounds. The Germans noted that the initial attack ground to a halt in the face of heavy Soviet artillery fire from the east bank of the Vorskla and from the Zhuravlinyii woods, and also because deep minefields were encountered. They noted that only after renewed concentrated artillery barrages onto hill 220.5 and into Berezov, as well as Stuka attacks against the Soviet artillery positions on the height west of the Vorskla and the Zhuravlinyii woods, did the crucial breakthrough effort succeed (see the 1:50,000 scale maps M-37-37-G (map sheet 11) and M-37-38-V (map sheet 14) of the area from Dragunskoye to Shopino).

The Sixth Guards Army reported that by 0900 (Moscow time) the Germans had broken through their forward positions along height 220.5 to Gremuchii. At 1415, the spearhead of the Das Reich SS Division was two kilometers south of height 233.3 (some three kilometers beyond Berezov). A Soviet armored attack (230th Tank Regiment) was defeated, with the Germans claiming seven destroyed tanks. There was tenacious resistance from height 233.3 (which fell at 1600) and from the direction of Byikovka. At 1400 the division's armored group advanced from the Kazatskoye area to Berezov, arriving at about 1630. During the day's fighting around Berezov, height 233.3 and north of it, the Tiger company alone claimed 23 Soviet tanks knocked out (most likely an over-estimate), and it lost two tanks immobilized by mines.[4] The advancing SS Panzer Corps was able to drive through the 52nd Guards Rifle Division, and peel back the 375th Guards Rifle Division by threatening envelopment. This opened a path to the north.

III Panzer Corps

The Donets Triangle

Two branches of the Donets River converge some eight kilometers north of Belgorod to form a single wider river, around a town called Shishino. The river north of Shishino is separated into the two branches, effectively two marshy creeks. The smaller branch is the Lipovyii Donets, which is to the west, and effectively runs to the north (the river flows to the south). The larger branch is the Severnyii Donets, which is to the east, and effectively runs to the north by northeast (the river flows to the south). Although both of these branches are really streams, they are fairly defensible. The area inside the triangle formed by these streams is higher ground, and in some cases noticeably higher ground. These positions provide good oversight of

4 Wolfgang Schneider, *Tigers in Combat, Volume II* (J.J. Fedorowicz Publishing Inc., Winnipeg, Canada, 1998), page 143, is the source for the claim by the Tiger company. The veracity of this claim cannot be confirmed. As there was only one Soviet tank regiment in the area (the 230th) and there were other German armored forces in the area, this claim is probably overstated.

the battlefield to the west of the triangle where the SS Panzer Corps was going to advance. It also provides a good view of the battlefield to the south and east of the triangle where the III Panzer Corps was going to advance. Furthermore the crossings, especially closer to the point where the two tributaries converge, are particularly defensible due to the extended areas of marshy ground around the streams.

These streams define two sides of a triangle, with the base being a connecting line that passes through the area of the towns of Pravorot and Prokhorovka. Therefore, holding these towns would be necessary if one were going to maintain a presence in this triangle.

This was a dominant piece of terrain that very definitely shaped the battle. The Lipovyii Donets formed the right flank of the SS Panzer Corps. The SS Panzer Corps did not make any serious attempts to cross here during the first days of the battle. The boundary line between the two corps was set to run from Bolkhovets (village assigned to the III Panzer Corps) to the road fork north of Blizhnii Ivanovskii (to III Panzer Corps) up the improved road to Shopino (village to SS) to the east edge of the line of villages that run north to Nepkhayevo to the church village Luchki (to the SS) to Olkhovatka (to the SS) to Sarayevka (to the SS) to Subotino (to the SS) to Tim (to the III Panzer Corps). In the most basic terms, everything to the east of Lipovyii Donets, including the entire Donets triangle, was the responsibility of the III Panzer Corps. After Luchki, the SS Panzer Corps right flank line ran northeasterly through Prokhorovka and on to well east of Kursk.

The responsibility for clearing the Donets triangle area belonged to Provisional Army Kempf, and it gave that task to the 6th Panzer Division. This was the division that was to move parallel to the Severnyii Donets and was to cross at Sabyinino, Krivtsovo and points south. This covered four bridges and led to Gostishchevo. As such, if the 6th Panzer Division could get to those crossing points, cross, then push on through Gostishchevo and beyond, then the flank of the SS Panzer Corps would be adequately covered. This implies that the Germans were expecting to cross the Severnyii Donets within a day or two after the attack started and push on into Gostishchevo. This was clearly an optimistic timetable.

In the meantime, covering the right flank of the SS Panzer Corps would temporarily be the responsibility of the Totenkopf SS Division until the 167th Infantry Division was shifted over from its attack up the Vorskla ravine. Then all three SS divisions would be free to attack.

The 6th Panzer Division was to capture Staryii Gorod and Chernaya Polyana, continue the attack over the heights of Dalnyaya Igumenka and seize Sabyinino and Krivtsovo and the Severnyii Donets bridges west of those two places. The division was then to attack in either the direction of Skorodnoye or towards the heights around Verschina. This was clearly heading northeast and leaving the area between the Lipovyii Donets and the Severnyii Donets to be cleaned up by unspecified mop-up forces. The division was to maintain reconnaissance patrols in contact with the SS Panzer Corps. The 168th Infantry Division was to advance due east to form up a defense line to the left of the 106th Infantry Division. Therefore, no significant forces were initially assigned to clean up the area of the Donets triangle!

The real problem with the 6th Panzer Division attack was that the point of attack was painfully obvious. To start with, it was the one place along the Donets River where the Germans already had a bridgehead. As such, the Voronezh Front had piled forces into this area. Directly opposite the bridgehead at Mikhailovka (opposite Belgorod) was the deeply entrenched 81st Guards Rifle Division. The 81st Guards Rifle Division was deployed across only 10.2 kilometers, in two echelons, and had a significant percent of the Seventh Guards Army defensive works allocated to it. This unit's frontage was the narrowest of any of the ten Soviet divisions in the first echelon. Furthermore, it had the 262nd Tank Regiment attached,[5] along with an antitank regiment and four artillery, Katyusha and mortar regiments.

To the right of the 81st Guards Rifle Division was the 375th Rifle Division. Chernaya Polyana was actually in

5 According to David Glantz, this unit was just northeast of Staryii Gorod; Glantz, *Atlas of the Battle of Kursk*, page 13. According to Valerii Zamulin at a meeting in November 2004, this unit was located at the Kreida about two kilometers south of Staryii Gorod. This last location would come under attack from both the 6th and 19th Panzer Divisions.

its zone of defense. The area between the two divisions consisted of marshlands and the Donets River. Furthermore, the division was backstopped to the north by the 89th Guards Rifle Division of the Sixth Guards Army. The 375th Rifle Division had the 96th Guards Tank Brigade attached and this brigade was positioned to the northeast of the 81st Guards Rifle Division and on its side of the Severnyii Donets. As such, the 81st Guards Rifle Division was in a solid defensive position and effectively backstopped by another infantry division and two more armored formations. It was facing parts of the 417th and 429th Infantry Regiments on its side of the river and the forces of the 6th Panzer Division (see the 1:50,000 scale maps M-37-38-V (map sheet 14) and M-37-50-A (map sheet 16) of the area from Shopino to Solomino).

The 6th Panzer Division's objectives for the day included seizing Staryii Gorod and Chernaya Polyana. These two towns were heavily fortified. Staryii Gorod was held by the 81st Guards Rifle Division. On the west bank of the Donets, just north of Belgorod, the 375th Rifle Division held the woods north of Pokrovka and behind it, Chernaya Polyana. The 81st Guards Rifle Division had attached to it four artillery, mortar and Katyusha regiments, an antitank regiment, an antitank rifle battalion and the 262nd Tank Regiment. The 375th Rifle Division, which did not come under pressure on their right from the SS until the afternoon, had four artillery and mortar regiments attached to it. There was plenty of artillery to support these positions north and east of Belgorod.

The division attacked at 0225. The division's panzer regiment lost an estimated 13 tanks this day.[6] At 1030,

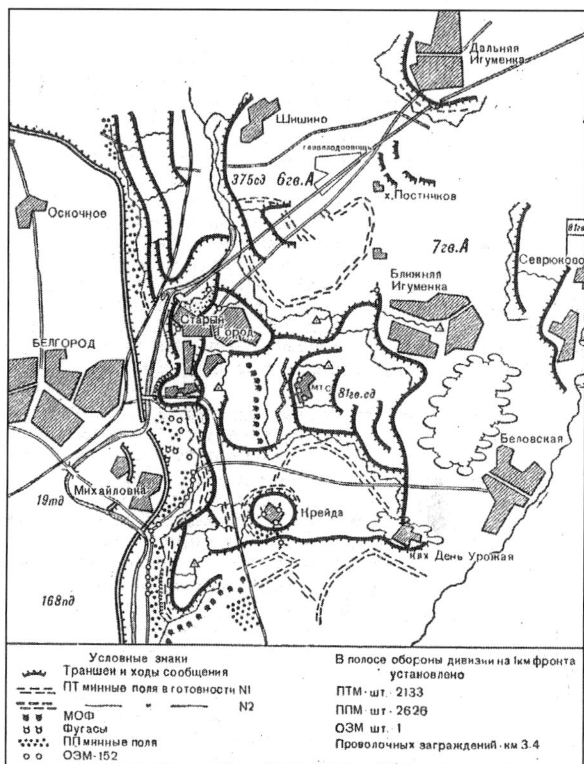

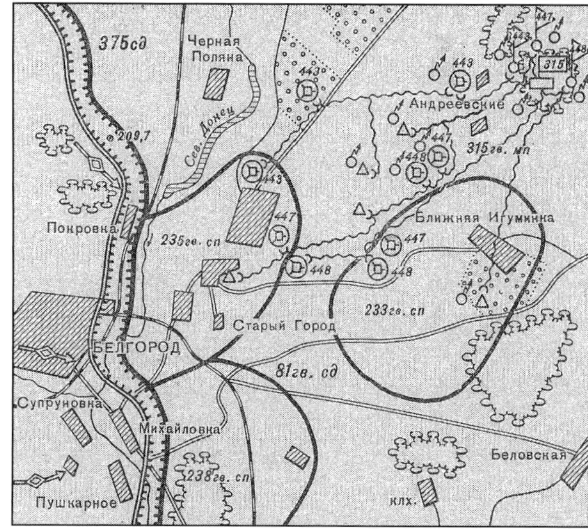

Two Soviet-era maps of the 81st Guards Rifle Division defensive positions.

6 There are no armor strength reports between the 4th of July and 8th of July. On the 7th, the division does report that during the last three days they lost 14 tanks, 2 of them totally destroyed. This report appears low, as the number ready for action on the 8th coupled with the loss report that was provided for the 8th, indicates a decline in tank strength for the 5th through the 7th of at least 33 tanks lost or broken down. While the casualties for the 5th are not known, it is clear that the total losses were heavy during the first three days of the operation.

Elements of the 6th Panzer Division clearly were engaged this day, as they report losing 10 killed, 58 wounded and 4 missing for 5 July. The extent that the panzer regiment was engaged is not known, but based upon this, it is assumed that the division on this day suffered panzer losses. Also, Alfred Rubbel reports the loss of 4 Tigers on this day in his attached Tiger Company.

it headed south to a different bridge in the Mikhailovka bridgehead, but halted before then and waited, probably while the division could see if any real progress could be made by its attacking infantry regiments. At 1700 it received orders to move south and follow the 7th Panzer Division and left Mikhailovka at 2000, and moved through Belgorod and south.[7]

The 6th Panzer Division's failure to advance in the first day of the battle was to create considerable problems for the Germans.

To its south, the 19th Panzer Division was heavily engaged but expanded the bridgehead to the south of Mikhailovka. South of there, the 7th Panzer Division, conducting an opposed river crossing at Solomino, achieved a breakthrough this day, penetrating the 78th Guards Rifle Division. It was able to advance to the Krutoi Log area.

By the end of the day, the bulk of the 7th Panzer Division was massed on the hills north of Krutoi Log. The division had advanced around seven kilometers this day and into the 78th Guards Rifle Division's second echelon. The clearing of the by-passed Razumnoye was to be handled by the 106th Infantry Division. The corps engineers were building a 24-ton bridge at Solomino and the 7th Panzer Division was to build another one with its engineer assets. The defending 78th Guards Rifle Division had fallen back along the line from height 126.3 to Razumnoye to Krutoi Log.

Overall, the III Panzer Corps' attacks this day were moderately successful. The 6th Panzer Division infantry attack stalled and could not get armor support because of the failed bridge. This effectively ended this attack. The 19th Panzer Division had set up a bridgehead on the opposite bank but its forces attacking out of the Mikhailovka bridgehead had only limited success. The division still had not committed its armored group to exploit any breakthroughs. The 7th Panzer Division had made good progress this day, having crossed the river and pushed up between Krutoi Log and Razumnoye. In light of the optimistic expectations of the command, this was not the advance they hoped for. For the purpose of providing flank support to the SS Panzer Corps, little of what was done this day provided that. They really needed to achieve an armor breakthrough and turn towards the north. Still, during the afternoon of 5 July, the corps did regroup under orders from Breith and prepared to take advantage of the one breakthrough it did have by sending the 6th Panzer Division south into the 7th Panzer Division's bridgehead. According to Breith, they were not sure whether to send the 6th Panzer Division north to break through the positions to the east of Belgorod with the 19th Panzer Division or east to further exploit the existing 7th Panzer Division breakthrough. Early on 6 July, he decided to send it east,[8] effectively ending any chance of getting immediate flank support to the SS Panzer Corps.

Corps Raus

As hard as the fighting was in areas where the three German armored corps attacked, the Corps Raus assault was the hardest fought and bloodiest action of the day. There were effectively two lines of defense to cross, one was the Donets River, the other the raised railroad embankment that ran along the east bank of the river. It turned out that crossing the river was the easy part. It was the fight for the railroad embankment that consumed the day. Furthermore, unbeknownst to the 106th Infantry Division, there was another critical defensive structure, a 10-meter-wide tank ditch that the division was not aware of and thus had made no provisions to bridge.

The 106th Infantry Division's attack began at 0225 along the entire length of the Donets, with all three infantry regiments crossing. This developed into an extended and brutal fight. The 106th Infantry Division by the end of the day had lost over 1,000 men. This was more losses than any of the other 14 divisions to its north or west had taken on this day. It was almost 10% of the division strength gone in one day. The unit suffered horrendous casualties and had very little to show

7 Jentz, page 88.

8 Breith, page 6.

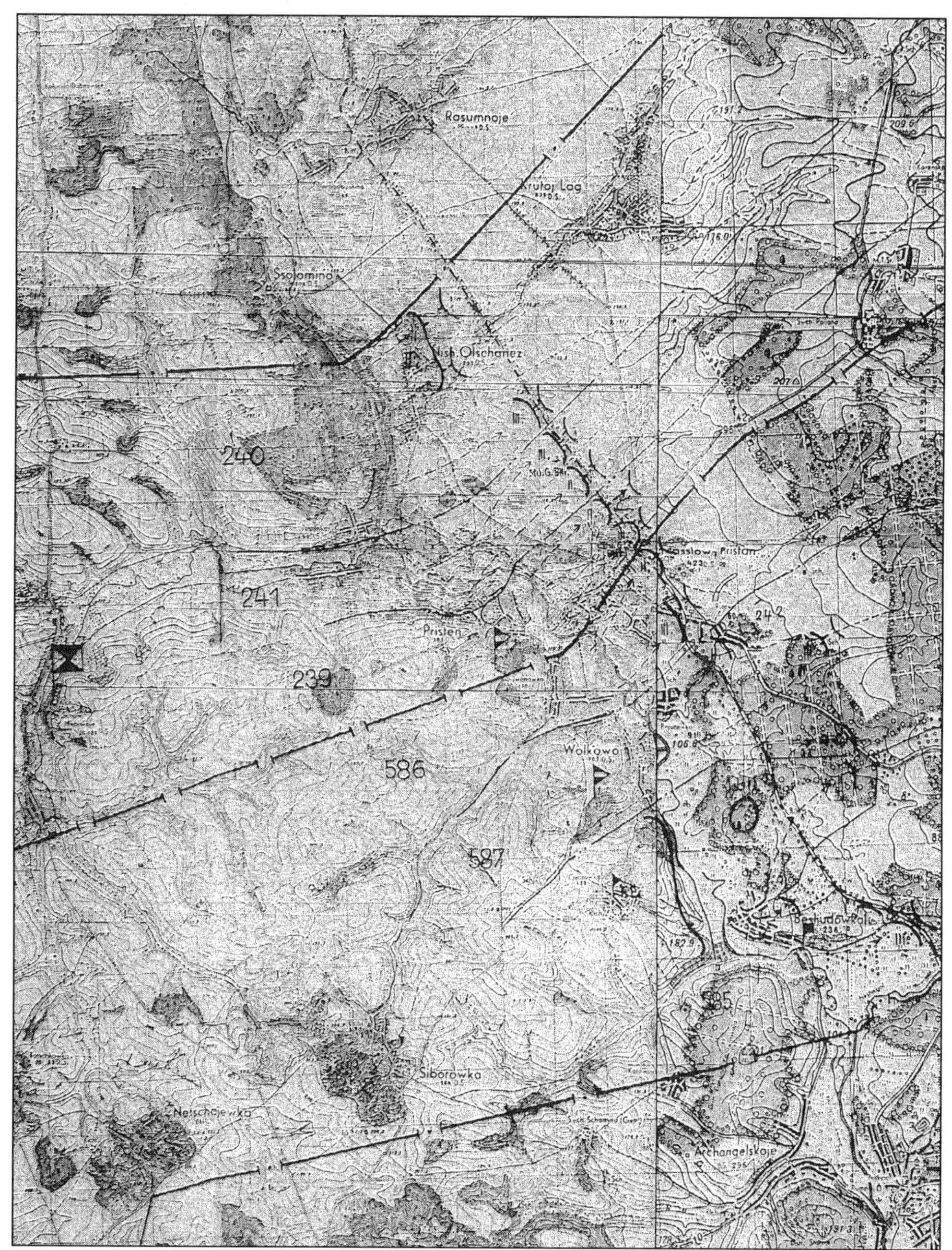

Corps Raus: 5 July 1943, 1630 hours. Note the 320th Infantry Division's advance through the woods.

for it. The division had gotten across the Donets and advanced two kilometers to the railroad embankment. Furthermore, the Soviets were defending this area with mostly the forces they had originally held there. This effort was providing no flank support to the III Panzer Corps. To the south, the 320th Infantry Division was having an even more difficult time.

The 320th Infantry Division also crossed the Donets against little resistance at 0225. The Germans observed that the Soviet pressure and counterattacks were increasing throughout the morning. Still, German force pushed forward and had gotten as far as the east edge of the woods that was three kilometers east of Priyutovka. The Soviets counterattacked this force in the afternoon with tanks. The 27th Guards Tank Brigade was concentrated there. They were reported on the 4th of July to have 48 T-34s and 4 T-70s ready for action. The Soviet infantry, helped by the 27th Guards Tank Brigade, threw the Germans back on Rzhavets and Maslova Pristan.

The Germans, who had not been able to bring up assault guns and towed antitank guns because of the problems with their bridges, were driven back with heavy losses. The 27th Guards Tank Brigade lost six T-34s on this day. The Luftwaffe did dispatch Hs-129s and Stukas to help support the German defense, but the danger had passed by the time the planes reached the battlefield. These German forces were forced to withdraw to the west edge of the woods, putting the entire division again back on the railroad embankment! The Soviet counterattacks had effectively pushed the German forces almost back to the Donets River.

At the end of the day, the 320th Infantry Division had lost at least 1,300 troops, and probably more than 1,600.[9] This was more than 10 percent of the division's strength. It was the most bloodied German division of the day. The division had been seriously hurt by having its 587th Infantry Regiment push beyond the railroad embankment into the woods, only to be thrown back by a Soviet counterattack. In light of the corps' rather optimistic mission, it is hard to criticize the regiment for moving forward through the woods when it had the chance; still, even the Germans noted in the records the increasing build-up of Soviet forces. In the face of such an observed build-up, the decision to advance one unsupported regiment forward looks foolish. It is clear the Corps Raus needed more artillery or better air support to have conducted this crossing. The Soviet counterattack by the 213th Rifle Division and the 27th Guards Tank Brigade had been extremely effective.

Overall, this fight between the 72nd Guards and 213th Rifle Divisions against the 106th and 320th Infantry Divisions was a bloody infantry fight. The Soviets had lost an estimated 1,220 casualties in exchange for an estimated 2,846 German casualties! This was the only time during this battle the Soviets would achieve such a favorable exchange or the Germans would suffer such losses.

Voronezh Front Reserves

The First Tank Army's three corps were moving forward this day into the Sixth Guards Army's second echelon position and would be heavily engaged the following day. At 1640, Vatutin ordered Katukov (First Tank Army) to move forward to cover Oboyan and to prepare a counterattack towards Tomarovka at dawn the next day. The V Guards Tank Corps and the II Guards Tank Corps were ordered at 1635 to move forward. The V Guards Tank Corps was to reach the Luchki, Teterevino and Malinovka area by midnight and was to attack towards Byikovka. The II Guards Tank Corps was to reach the Sazhnoye Machine and Tractor Station and Novyiye Lozyi area by midnight and was to attack towards Gremuchii.[10] These last two corps were later subordinated to the Sixth Guards

9 The reported loss figures for the division for the 5th are 1290 (100 killed, 1100 wounded and 90 missing). This report appears to be a rough estimate and is probably conservative. The division does provide daily casualty reports for the whole period and a total report of casualties covering the 5th through the 20th (3,038, 472 killed, 2,140 wounded and 426 missing), which is higher than the sum of the daily reports. Therefore, it is assumed that the division suffered higher losses than what was initially reported on the 5th, and there are other reports from that day that point towards that being the case.

10 Glantz and Orenstein, pages 87, 154 and 234. Erickson, page 101.

Army. Still held in the rear and out of combat were the Sixty-ninth Army of five divisions and the XXXV Guards Rifle Corps of three divisions.

The Voronezh Front also began sending smaller formations to the battle, with the 180th and 192nd Tank Brigades ordered at 2210 to concentrate in the Oboyan area as part of the First Tank Army's reserve.[11] Late in the evening of the 5th, the Sixth Guards Army was informed that the 14th and 31st Antitank Brigades were going to be transferred to it.[12] This was certainly in response to the Sixth Guards Army's commitment of all four of its antitank artillery units to the battle.

Among the large number of units of the Steppe Front, the X Tank Corps, sitting back at Staryii Oskol, was activated on this day. If the original plan was to include this unit in any defense of the Voronezh Front in case of a major attack, then putting it farther forward would have made more sense. As it was, this corps would spend two days marching some 100 kilometers before it was in position to join combat.

Daily Summary

This day ended with the four German attacking corps having penetrated the first defensive line, although this effort was not completed by nightfall. Still, the Germans had not advanced as far or as effectively as they wished. The XLVIII Panzer Corps, the SS Panzer Corps and the 19th Panzer Division had gotten entangled during the morning in the Soviet defensive works and made little progress. The 6th Panzer Division's attack had just out-and-out failed. Only the 7th Panzer Division had achieved a clean and successful penetration in line with the original plan. In the Corps Raus sector, they had firmly placed themselves on the opposite bank of the river, but at a huge cost. Still, the German attack was underway and now moving forward.

For this day, the Germans lost around 6,334 people (967 killed, 5,099 wounded and 268 missing). Of those, less than half a percent were in the LII Corps area (not including the 332nd Infantry Division), 22 percent were in the XLVIII Panzer Corps area (including the 332nd Infantry Division), 19 percent were in the SS Panzer Corps, 14 percent were in the III Panzer Corps and 45 percent were with Corps Raus. Poor Corps Raus had suffered terribly this day, with the 106th Infantry Division losing 8.2 percent of its strength in one day and the 320th Infantry Division losing 11.6 percent of its strength in one day. There were no other German divisions that suffered comparable losses, for the next highest losses were suffered by the Adolf Hitler SS Division, which lost 602 this day, or 2.9 percent of their strength.[13] In fact, the losses of these two divisions (in terms of either absolute or percentage losses) were the worst of the battle, and no other German unit ever came close to suffering such losses during the next 13 days.

The defending Soviet forces lost a total of around 8,483 casualties (1,634 killed, 3,569 wounded and 3,280 missing). This was a 1.3-to-1 exchange ratio in favor of the Germans in total casualties, and 4.0-to-1 in favor of the Germans in irreplaceable casualties. The three divisions in the Sixth Guards Army that bore the brunt of the attack suffered heavily. The 71st Guards Rifle Division lost 11.1 percent of its strength, the 67th Guards Rifle Division lost 18.5 percent and the 52nd Guards Rifle Division lost 7.7 percent.[14] Overall, the Sixth Guards Army lost 7.4 percent of its strength that day in combat, while the Seventh Guards Army lost only 4.9 percent of its strength that day in combat. For these units, this was only the start of three very difficult days of fighting.

Armor losses during the day strongly favored the Soviets. Their losses were confined to five tank regiments and brigades resulting in an estimated 100 tanks damaged

11 Glantz and Orenstein, page 154.

12 I. M. Chistyakov, *Po Prikazu Rodinyi* [On Orders from the Motherland] (Moscow, 1971), page 96. He states that they were to be transferred from the Fortieth Army, but this is clearly incorrect as the 31st Antitank Brigade was attached to the Sixty-ninth Army on the 5th. The 32nd Antitank Brigade, which was attached to the Fortieth Army, remained with that army.

13 The 19th Panzer Division actually suffered a higher percent of losses with 497 combat losses this day, or 3.6% loss.

14 All these figures for the first three days of battle for these divisions are estimates based upon their cumulative casualty reports and later daily casualty reports.

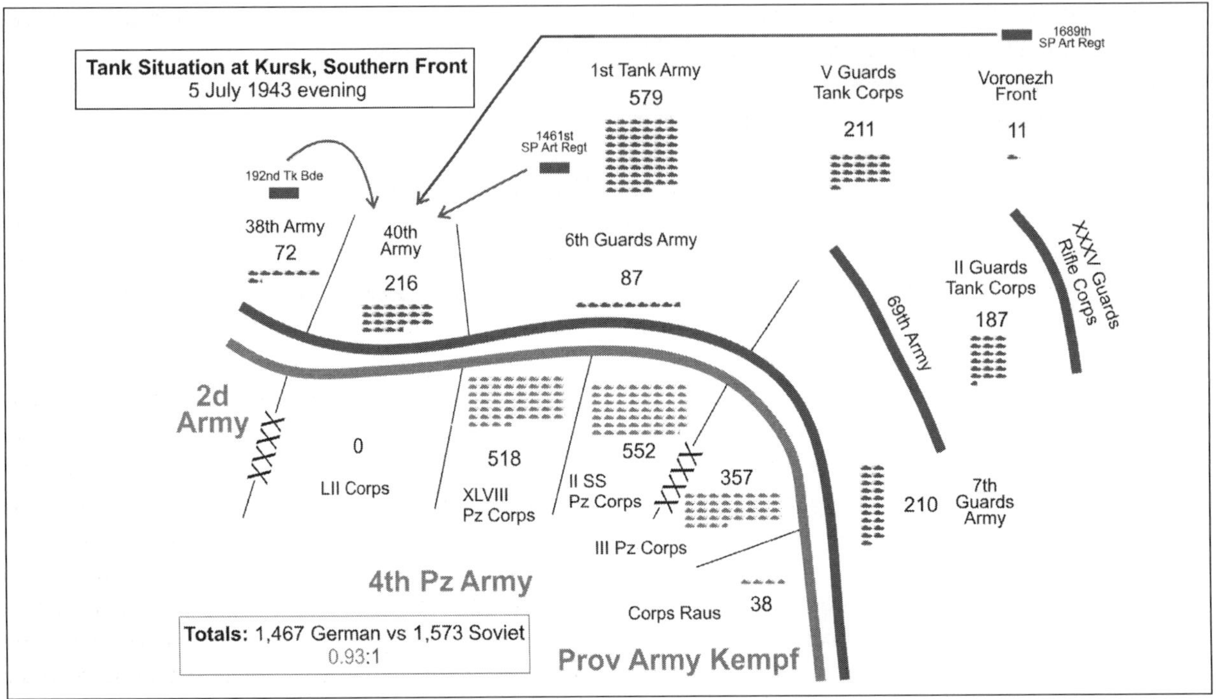

or destroyed. In contrast the Germans lost 250 tanks damaged and destroyed for this day, including mechanical breakdowns (a common problem with the Panthers).

At the end of the day, the opposing armored forces were deployed as shown above.

Exploiting the Breakthrough: 6 July 1943

Having broken the first defensive line, the German Army now advanced up to and attacked the second Soviet defensive line.

The XLVIII Panzer Corps

The 3rd Panzer Division's armored group conducted a surprise advance with some of its tanks from the area east of Krasnyii Pochinok north into Zavidovka at 0920. At this point, they had reached the Pena River. At 1045, they were ordered to secure a crossing over the Pena near Zavidovka as soon as possible and build a bridge there during the night. The division was then supposed to advance on Rakovo. Five minutes later, the division reported an increase in enemy fire from the hills north of the Pena River and also flanking fire from height 210.3, which was behind them.

At this point, the leading tanks of the 3rd Panzer Division had worked their way into Zavidovka only to be hit from all sides by heavy fire from Soviet artillery, antitank guns, and dug-in tanks (T-34s and KV-1s according to the Germans), especially from the north bank of the Pena and from Podimovka, which was out of range of the German artillery and could not be suppressed. There was no place in the town out of enemy sight and the town could be held only by incurring heavy casualties. So, when the tanks ran low on ammunition, they withdrew, claiming to have destroyed one T-34, one American tank and seven antitank guns in the village.

The 3rd Panzer Division had a total of 84 operational

tanks at the start of this day, of which the heaviest were Panzer IVs or Sturmgeschuetz IIIs. During the course of the day, the 3rd Panzer Division lost seven tanks, of which two were written off as totally destroyed.

LT. GENERAL FRANZ Westhoven (3rd Panzer Division commander) forwarded the opinion that crossing the river required proper preparation. Knobelsdorff (corps commander) then ordered the divisions in the corps to create a bridgehead across the Pena with all available forces and to disregard their flanks. Meanwhile, the reconnaissance battalion of the Gross Deutschland Division was supposed to be taking care of height 210.3.

At this point, the 3rd Panzer Division reconnaissance elements were reporting that the Soviet positions on both sides of Rakovo were extremely strong. There were various engineer obstacles, dug-in tanks (again reports of KV-1s and T-34s) and heavy artillery fire that prevented movement across the open space south of the river. The banks of the Pena River and valley near Krasnyii Pochinok were flooded and marshy. The division concluded that the Soviet defense along the Pena River was stronger than the defenses that the division had penetrated the previous day. Westhoven concluded that crossing the Pena River and capturing a bridgehead must be done in one stroke with strong fire support from the corps and army artillery. If not, Westhoven reasoned, the division may be badly cut up by Soviet fire. This was certainly a realistic appraisal of the situation, and halting the attack before it took significant losses was sound generalship. At this point, the 3rd Panzer Division attack had stalled as of noon, 6 July.

At about two o'clock in the afternoon (1400 hours), Hoth (Commander, Fourth Panzer Army) inserted himself into the discussion, and stated that the 3rd Panzer Division should not remain inactive through the rest of the day. Mellenthin (the corps' chief of staff) suggested that the division should regroup and move through Yarki, Lukhanino, Syirtsevo and attack Verkhopenye. The division then reassembled north of the Krasnyii Pochinok and Yarki areas, and at 1715, was reported to be ready to cross the stream at Lukhanino or Alekseyevka by moving behind the Gross Deutschland.

THE 3RD PANZER Division attack here today basically failed. While they were successful in advancing through the 67th Guards Rifle Division positions, they were stopped cold at Zavidovka. Still, it was with foresight that they did not continue a bad plan and seriously hurt themselves trying to achieve the impossible. As it was, the original plan calling for the division to cross at this point must be questioned. It was clearly a solid second defensive position, especially because of the terrain, and this is readily apparent from the topographical maps. It was almost certainly going to be defended, and sending the 3rd Panzer Division to achieve a breakthrough at Gertsovka so that it would only become stalled farther along the route, does not make a lot of sense. The 3rd Panzer Division would have probably been better used to attack farther to the east, supporting the Gross Deutschland and the 11th Panzer Divisions, possibly initially held as a reserve, and its sector assigned the 332nd Infantry Division. Basically, the direction of the division's attack on the 5th turned out to be pointless, and it effectively wasted the entire following day. The breakthrough in the XLVIII Panzer Corps sector was really being conducted by just two armored divisions.

AT THIS POINT, the original plan of the 3rd Panzer Division had been thwarted. The 332nd Infantry Division and the 3rd Panzer Division had driven back the 71st Guards Rifle Division, freeing up the 3rd Panzer Division for further exploitation. But, the plan to have the 3rd Panzer Division cross the river west of Lukhanino was stopped by the deployment of the VI Tank Corps opposite them on the Pena. This would be one of two German panzer divisions that would be halted these first two days by a well developed Soviet defense.

Western part of a First Tank Army map for 5 July 1943, showing the VI Tank Corps positions.

Elements of the Gross Deutschland Division started operations early at 0230 and the 11th Panzer Division was attacking by 0315. They were still fighting to clear out the village of Cherkasskoye. They then had to clear mines along their routes of advance and sort out the traffic problems between them, as both divisions were advancing up the same road.

The 11th Panzer Division started its attack this day at 0315 when one reinforced regiment started out to clear the Butovo road to the north to height 246.0 and to complete the mopping-up of Cherkasskoye. The Soviets, "thoroughly shaken," according to the German accounts, offered little resistance. As of 0545, the 11th Panzer Division had not quite finished mopping up the south part of Cherkasskoye, where several pockets of resistance were still opposing its advance. The division was holding a line running from height 244.5 to the southern outskirts of Cherkasskoye. Several flame-thrower tanks had pushed their way through the town and no more strong resistance was encountered. Southwest of Cherkasskoye, Soviet troops had entered the woods again, making it difficult to clear the mines from the road from Butovo to the northeast. The engineers were working their way south from the northeast, trying to meet the Gross Deutschland engineers clearing from the south, so their tanks could use the road. The Gross Deutschland's tanks were moving up as the mines were being cleared. The road clearing was reported finished at 0715 and Gross Deutschland's tanks began advancing up the road. At around 0740, the two divisions had their dispute over road precedence that required the corps commander to divide their sectors. At 0750 the 11th Panzer Division reported that all the division engineer units had been moved forward and were in the first echelon. However, the roads in the rear needed more repair. The corps engineer officer agreed to clear the rest of the mines from the road and to build a two-lane road between Butovo and Cherkasskoye.

AT 0830, THE 11th Panzer Division and the Gross Deutschland Panzer Grenadier Division began to advance from the line 246.0–232.4. The 167th Infantry Division also joined the operation when its attack jumped off at 0830. At 0840 clearing operations in Cherkasskoye were declared complete by the 11th Panzer Division. After removing minefields and crossing an antitank ditch, the 15th Panzer Regiment encountered Soviet antitank units at the road fork 1.5 kilometers northeast of height 246.0. Pushing past them, by 1330, advance elements of the 11th Panzer Division had reached a mine barrier on the road three kilometers southwest of Dubrova. There they met strong resistance from positions around height 241.1.

At 0930 the advance of the Gross Deutschland Division at 246.0 was making good progress, but Hoernlein (the division commander) expected that the area between 246.0 and Dubrova would be heavily mined, necessitating the commitment of a large group of engineers. At 0935 the division's lead tanks (from the elements of Strachwitz's panzer regiment that had advanced through Yarki) were counterattacked by Soviet tanks two kilometers north of 246.0 (perhaps remnants of the 245th Tank Regiment). Strachwitz asked to have all nearby division forces put under his command for immediate attack, since he had no contact with the Panther regiment. At 1025 there was still no contact with Major Meinrad von Lauchert's Panthers, and the division gave Strachwitz permission to launch his attack. His lead elements came under heavy flanking artillery fire from Alekseyevka. This was certainly from the VI Tank Corps.

The Gross Deutschland Division temporarily had under its command a panzer brigade of two panzer regiments. These were the Gross Deutschland Panzer Regiment, under command of the legendary "Panzer Count," Colonel Hyazinth von Strachwitz and the newly formed Panther Regiment, which consisted of the 51st and 52nd Panzer Battalions and a command group under Major Meinrad von Lauchert. These two regiments were nominally under command of the 10th Panzer Brigade, under Colonel Karl Decker, who only arrived on the battlefield on the 4th without a headquarters or staff. The Panther Regiment had been having repeated breakdowns of their new tanks since they first started moving up to join the Gross Deutschland Division on the 4th. They started the day with maybe as few as 119 tanks operational, and dozens more broke down or were damaged this day. The Panther Regiment was also lagging behind the Gross Deutschland Panzer Regiment during this advance and Decker and Strachwitz were no able to maintain communication. This cumbersome command arrangement was ended by the corps commander, General Otto von Knobelsdorff at 1625, with Strachwitz given command of both regiments and Decker placed in corps reserve.

As the morning developed, the German command debated the best course of action. The SS Panzer Corps was advancing more rapidly than the previous day, so Hoth considered it very important that the Gross Deutschland and the 11th Panzer Division reach the road fork at height 254.5 near Dubrova as quickly as possible, so as not to expose the flank of the SS Panzer Corps. While this desire was transmitted at 1005, at 1025 Mellenthin was still telling the Gross Deutschland Division that is was imperative to take Alekseyevka and then Lukhanino. Finally at 1030, Hoth and Seidemann (VIII Air Corps) arrived at the XLVIII Panzer Corps command post. After an orientation by Knobelsdorff (corps commander) and Mellenthin, Hoth repeated his

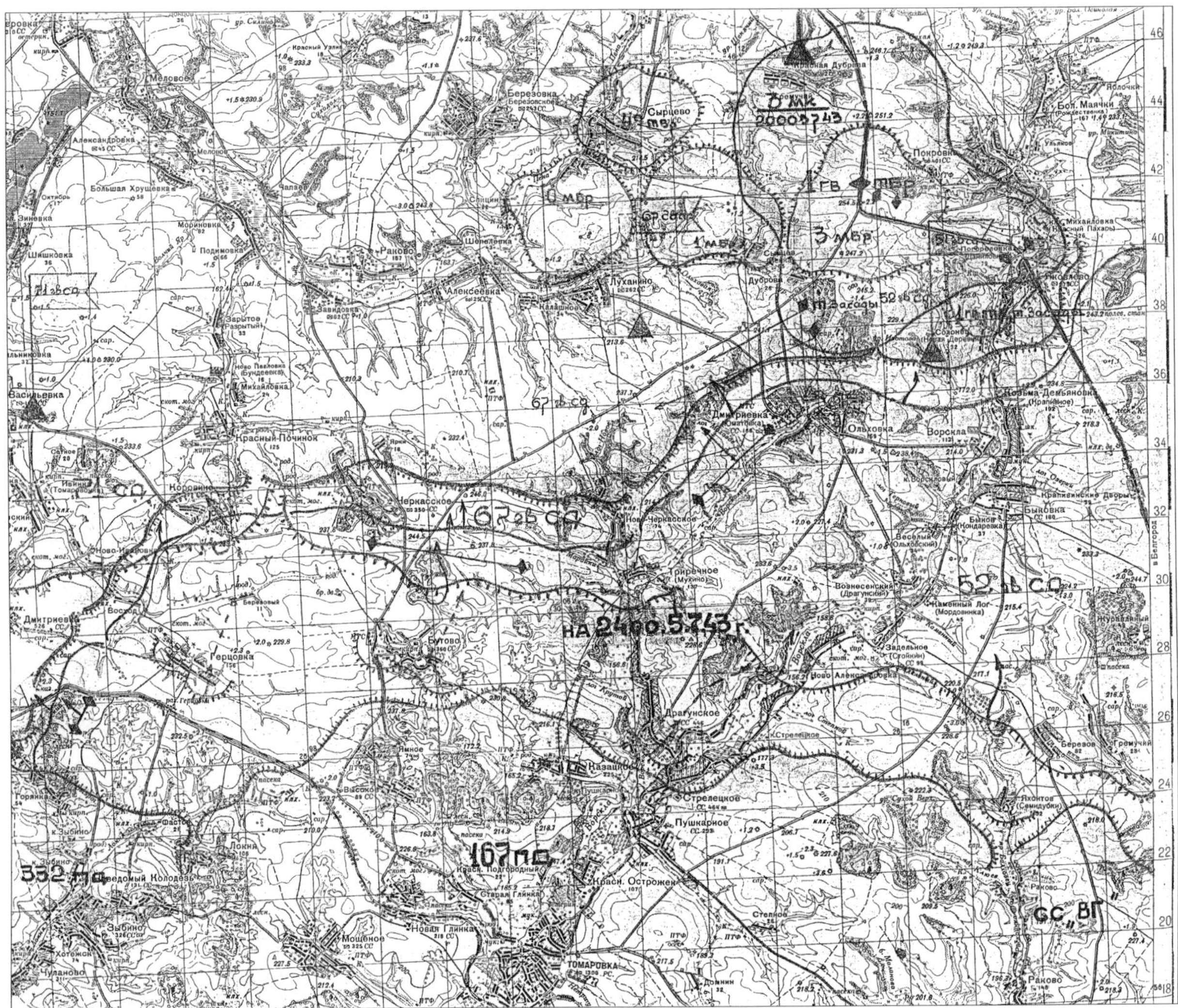

Portion of III Mechanized Corps map showing the corps positions as of 2400 on 5 July 1943.

order to break through the Soviet defense positions, with the main effort being south of Dubrova. He also stated that Lukhanino must be taken by units of the Gross Deutschland Division, but for the time being Alekseyevka should not be attacked.

It took the rest of the morning and part of the afternoon for the two German armored divisions to clear the first defensive line. Between the Russian infantry, antitank guns, mines and tank ditches, it was past noon when the two divisions were able to move into position to attack the second defense line. This defense line was now reinforced by the large III Mechanized Corps from the First Tank Army. At 1430 (Moscow time) the Sixth Guards Army reported that Lukhanino was taken by the Germans.

This effectively was the end of the fight for the first defensive line, leaving the 67th Guards Rifle Division gutted and partially surrounded. The XLVIII Panzer

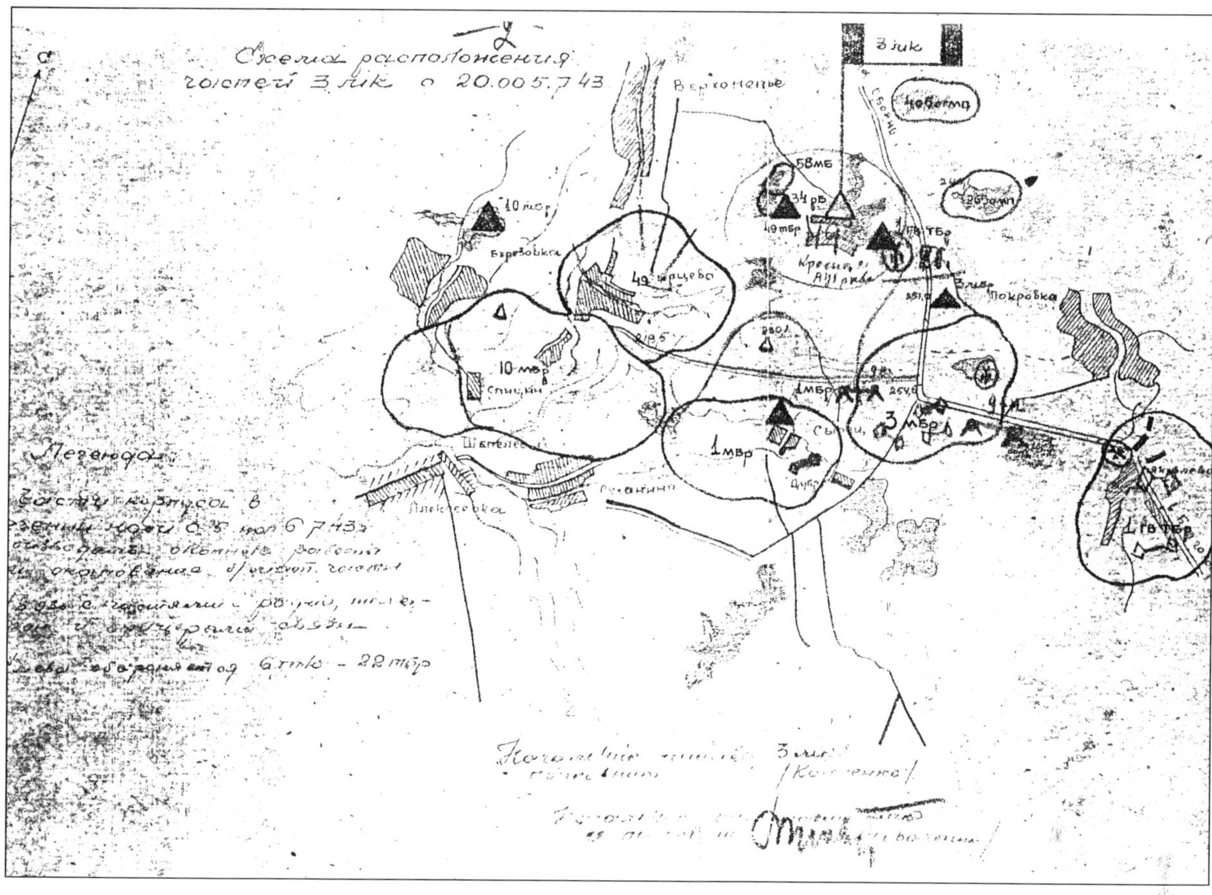

III Mechanized Corps at 2000 5 July 1943.

Corps had penetrated through the first line held by the 71st and 67th Guards Rifle Divisions taking an estimated 2,640 casualties from the afternoon of the 4th to the afternoon of the 6th, versus an estimated 6,021 inflicted on the opposing forces. There were also an estimated 219 tanks lost, including broken down Panthers, versus an estimated 39 tanks lost on the Soviet side. Still, by the afternoon of the 6th the Germans were moving to assault the second defensive line. The Soviet fight along the first line had delayed the German schedule by the better part of a day. Still, that fight had gutted the poor 67th Guards Rifle Division.

The III Mechanized Corps Enters Battle

It is at this point that the III Mechanized Corps enters the fray. Having received their orders to move forward at 1640 (Moscow time) on the 5th, they moved while it was still daylight and after a 20 kilometer march reached their positions by darkness. Because of an absence of transport, the corps' infantry did not reach their new defensive positions until dawn on 6 July.[15] Even the motorized battalions of the mechanized brigades had to walk according to Captain Vasilii Stepa-

15 Glantz and Orenstein, page 235.

novich Surikov,[16] of the 1st Mechanized Brigade. They did not have trucks. They also arrived in positions only in the morning of 6 July!

The first action report from the III Mechanized Corps was a patrol sent out at 2330 on the 5th by the 1st Guards Tank Brigade in the direction of the mound +1.1, three kilometers southeast of Yakovlevo. This force was fired on by the Germans, with the Soviets reporting a loss of one T-34 burned, 10 men killed and 2 wounded. This was certainly the work of the SS Panzer Corps.

The Voronezh Front Armor is Ordered to Counterattack!

At 1640 (Moscow time) on the 5th of July, Vatutin (Voronezh Front commander) personally ordered Katukov (First Tank Army) to move up to cover Oboyan and to prepare to launch a counterattack towards Tomarovka at dawn. The Front's other two tank corps, the V Guards and II Guards, were to concentrate in the east and prepare to attack in the direction of Belgorod.[17] This attack would have launched five armored corps directly into the face of six attacking German armored divisions. It would have been dramatic.

According to unpublished memoirs from the First Tank Army commander, Mikhail Efimovich Katukov:[18]

> Vatutin ordered that the First Tank Army, II and V Guards Tank Corps should counterattack Tomarovka. I was against this decision. Why would we move our dug-in tanks two kilometers forward exposing them to the 88mm guns that can destroy our T-34s? Our 76.2mm guns could not reach the German tanks even at the 1.5 kilometer distance! Luckily for me, I received a phone call from Stalin in the morning of 6 July. I told him that it would make more sense to fight German tanks from prepared positions. "Okay," Stalin said, "You won't counterattack. Vatutin will call you and tell you that."

The Advance on Dubrova

Having effectively dispensed with the organized resistance from the first defensive line by about 1200, the Gross Deutschland Division moved up to the crossing at Lukhanino and also raced across the area from Cherkasskoye to Dubrova to start the assault on the second defensive line. This last maneuver consisted of a twelve kilometer march across the front of the Soviet III Mechanized Corps. The III Mechanized Corps was powerless to stop it, interfere with it or even seriously harass it. As the corps had just moved into those positions during the day, they were in no position to move south across the river and attack the German advance, nor would that have been advisable. Still, the Germans were able to move for some twelve kilometers in front of the Soviet lines due to the shortage of artillery in the III Mechanized Corps. In its organization, the Soviet tank and mechanized corps had 42 (or 54) 120mm mortars. This was their primary artillery piece, with their only guns being the dual-purpose 76mm division guns. None of the tank brigades, regiments or even the entire XXXI Tank Corps had any guns or mortars larger than 82mm. The infantry divisions which they were operating with had 122mm guns, but only 6 of them in the case of the 90th Guards Rifle Division and 11 in the case of the 67th Guards Rifle Division, along with another 24 or 25 120mm mortars. This artillery might have been a useful supplement if they had not already been mixed in with the antitank defensive positions, and as such, many of the guns belonging to the 67th Guards Rifle Division had been lost!

Now the 120mm mortar was a perfectly good artillery piece. It was reliable, and was able to throw a 35 pound shell. Being a mortar though, it had a range of only around 5,700 meters. If the mortars were deployed two or three kilometers behind the lines, then they did not always have the range to hit the road, which was

16 Captain Vasilii Stepanovich Surikov was the Deputy Commander on Political Issues of the Motorized Battalion, 1st Mechanized Brigade, III Mechanized Corps. He was born in 1920. He finished the war in Austria as a Colonel and a rifle regiment commander. After the war, he worked as a teacher. Interview was taken by Major General G. G. Nessonov in 1999.

17 Erickson, page 101. Cross, page 177, records the time as 1630. This is probably a typo, as the structure of his text would lead one to believe that it was drawn directly from Erickson.

18 From notes provided by Col. Fyodor Sverdlov in 1999.

from two to four kilometers from the Pena River. They certainly did not have the range to track and fire on the forces throughout the length of the move along the road. As such the Germans could run right by the Soviet defending forces relatively unmolested. This problem was highlighted in the III Mechanized Corps after action report prepared by Major Petukhov[19] which stated:

> The enemy attacked at 1000 hours on 7/6/43 along the corps' left flank with the intention of reaching the Belgorod-Oboyan road. The corps could do little against the enemy's approaching columns, because it lacked powerful artillery, and the Sixth Guards Army's artillery units were being withdrawn from the battle. . . . The corps neither had, nor was it supported by heavy artillery.

This advance highlights another weakness in the Sixth Guards Army deployment, for they had placed their first echelon well in front of the second echelon (which was along the Pena River and its branches), leaving limited forces between the two echelons. As the high open ground ran between these two echelons, once the Germans had pushed the 196th Guards Rifle Regiment back, they were then able to drive along that higher ground behind the division's other two regiments and deploy to attack the second echelon. In effect, the Soviets had set up a "piecemeal" defense that allowed not only the 67th Guards Rifle Division to be overwhelmed by three Germans divisions, but effectively put only one regiment squarely in the main line of advance.

Part of the problem stems from the Sixth Guards Army decision to deploy the divisions in a single echelon instead of using one regiment to create a second echelon. This change would have made things somewhat stickier for the advance on Dubrova. It would also have made the initial penetration easier as only two regiments, vice three, would have been defending the front. The fundamental problem was the 67th Guards Rifle Division was simply defending too much front against too many enemy to be truly effective. This was a flaw in the initial deployment that must be blamed on the high command (Vatutin and Vasilevskii). There were certainly other forces in the area that could have been brought forward before the battle to reinforce these positions (for example: the three tank corps of the First Tank Army, the second echelon of the Sixth Guards Army, the 184th Rifle Division and others from the Fortieth Army, elements of the Sixty-ninth Army, etc.). Such a change would imply, of course, doing something other than the doctrinal three or more echeloned layered defense lines. Alternatively, the Sixth Guards Army could have simply been deployed on a smaller front.

Around 1500 or a little earlier, the attack on Dubrova started. A mid-afternoon attack by the Gross Deutschland Panzer Regiment on Soviet positions near Dubrova failed. The division remained under flanking fire and heavy pressure from Lukhanino. After crossing the first antitank ditch southeast of Lukhanino, the Panther regiment, followed by the Gross Deutschland Grenadier Regiment and three-quarters of the artillery regiment, advanced toward the second antitank ditch. Encountering heavy resistance and antitank fire, they proceeded to one kilometer north of height 241.1. The Fusilier Regiment, attacking from 213.6 toward Lukhanino and Kalashnoye, reached the eastern edge of Lukhanino and 500 meters south of Kalashnoye by 1710. After reaching height 210.3 (south of Zavidovka), the Gross Deutschland Reconnaissance Battalion began to advance toward Alekseyevka (to the northeast). At 1715, the Gross Deutschland Panzer Regiment was reported advancing west of Dubrova. On its left, the Panther regiment was securing the flank against the Soviet forces deployed along the Pena River to the north. The II Battalion, Gross Deutschland Fusilier Regiment captured height 210.3 finally and eliminated the flanking fire that had been hitting 3rd Panzer Division. After a brief artillery preparation, the I Battalion of the Gross Deutschland Grenadier Regiment forced a crossing over

19 This report, written by Major Petukhov, a General Staff representative with the First Tank Army to the senior General Staff representatives with the staffs of the First Guards Tank Army and the Voronezh Front (from Podolsk archives, archive 3440, schedule 1, file 37), provides a summary of the operations of the III Mechanized Corps from the 6th through the 15th and some rather caustic criticisms of these operations.

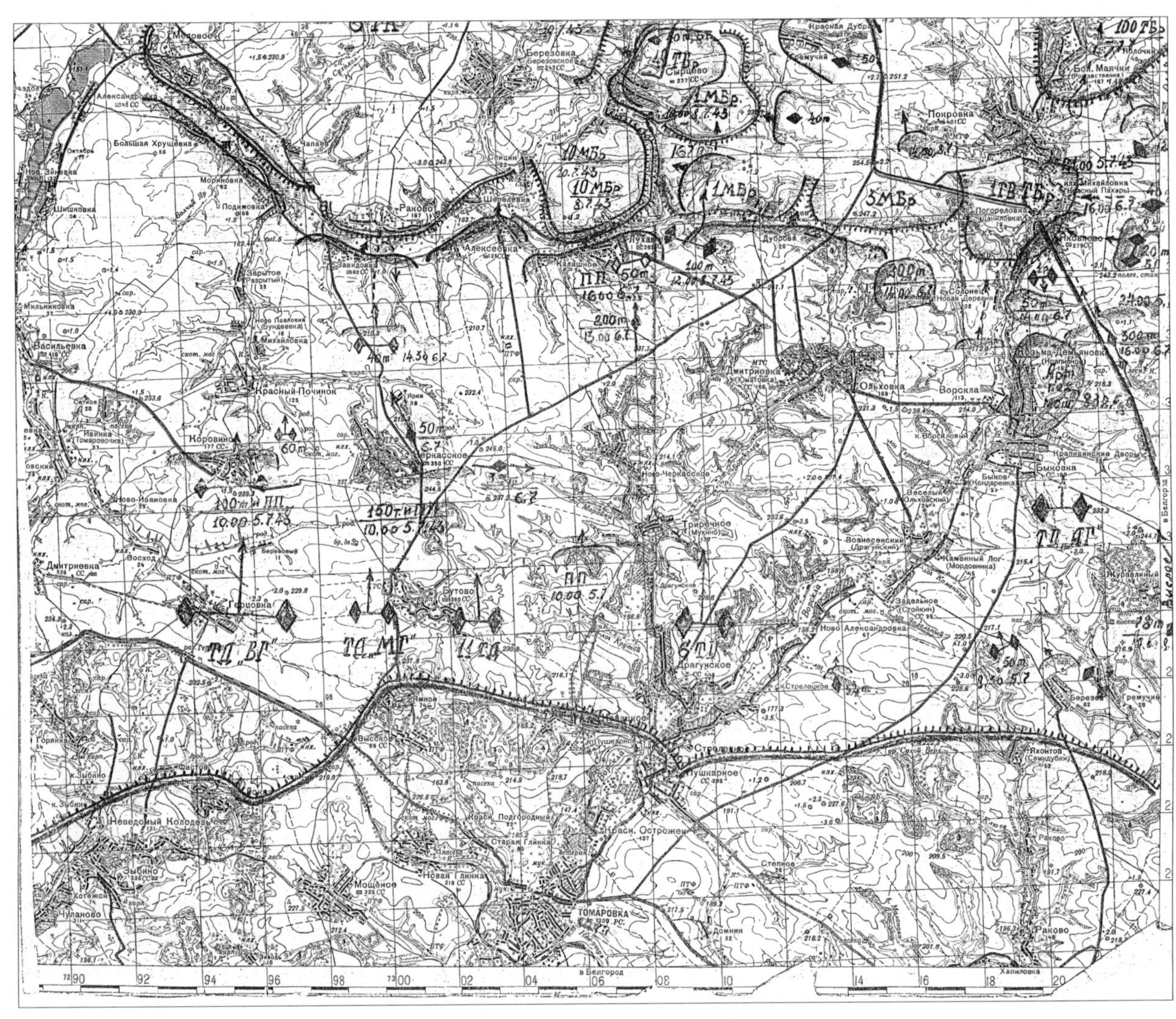

Portion of the First Tank Army map showing the attack on Dubrova.

the ravine near Dubrova, formed a bridgehead, and dug in some 500 meters east of Dubrova for the night.

Meanwhile, at 1500 the 11th Panzer Division was engaged in heavy combat in the trenches and antitank ditches two kilometers southwest of Dubrova, and in the hills around the town. In front of the antitank ditches the engineers, under heavy small arms and antitank fire, were clearing the terrain of mines. At 1640 the lead tanks of the division took hill 241.1. By 1715 the 11th Reconnaissance Battalion had reached the northwest edge of Dmitriyevka, and had taken the antitank artillery positions in the woods northwest of Dmitriyevka (this is a different town than the one farther west that had been on the flank of the 332nd Infantry Division).[20] The main force of the division had broken through the minefields and the first trenches of the Soviet second defense zone and was advancing toward the woods south of Dubrova. The division, after crossing the first antitank ditches, requested air support in front of its forward elements. The Sixth Guards Army reported at 1700 (Moscow time) that Dmitriyevka and Olkhovka had been taken.

AT 1810 THE Gross Deutschland commander (Hoernlein) affirmed earlier reports that the division, having overcome extremely heavily mined barbed wire and antitank ditches in the Olkhovaya and Bolshoi ravines, was attacking Dubrova. The fighting was described as "very intense." At 1820 air reconnaissance reported about 50 or 60 Soviet tanks in front of the leading German tank elements one kilometer southwest of Dubrova (this is certainly the 3rd Mechanized Brigade). At 1910 the division was reported to be involved in heavy fighting with Soviet antitank units south of Syirtsev, and that the division had suffered heavy casualties. At 2100, the division reached the eastern outskirts of Dubrova. It was reported that there were 48 Russian tanks in the forest southeast of the town. The Gross Deutschland Panzer Regiment reported that it would still achieve its breakthrough by midnight, but that the condition of the terrain made encirclement of the Soviets west of Syirtsev impossible (such an encirclement would have included two mechanized brigades from the III Mechanized Corps). It also reported that its tanks were short of ammunition. Knobelsdorff ordered the Gross Deutschland Fusilier Regiment to establish a bridgehead north of the Pena near Lukhanino and for all Gross Deutschland elements to be assembled within that bridgehead. If possible, the panzer elements at Syirtsev were to move there as well. The 3rd Panzer Division was to move through this bridgehead behind the Gross Deutschland.

This last order is a little confusing, as the Gross Deutschland Panzer Regiment was well engaged around Syirtsev and Dubrova and there seemed to be little reason for it to shift back to the west. As the high ground and open terrain ran by Dubrova up to height 254.5, and Soviet forces could indeed be enveloped in the pocket between Lukhanino and Syirtsevo, or at least marginalized and pushed off to the flank. Continuing pressure to exploit a breakthrough at 254.5 seemed to offer more play.

MEANWHILE, THE PANZERS of the 11th Panzer Division were advancing towards Dubrova from the southwest (at 1820). The 110th and 111th Panzer Grenadier Regiments of the 11th Panzer Division were also being brought up to join the armored group. At 1910 the 15th Panzer Regiment was advancing very slowly near height 241.1 because of strong antitank fire. The reconnaissance battalion was attacking Soviet positions on the hill from the south. At 2110 the reconnaissance battalion was ordered to encircle the Izotovo Woods from the south (a path four kilometers southeast of Dubrova) to approach the Soviet positions from the rear. This would effectively envelop the Soviet armor that was reported southeast of Dubrova (probably from the 1st Guards Tank Brigade).

20 In the Belgorod area are several towns of the same name within a short distance of each other. For example, in the SS Panzer Corps attack area there are two Luchkis within six kilometers of each other and also two Prokhorovkas within ten kilometers of each other. In the XLVIII Panzer Corps attack there is a Syirtsev and a Syirtsevo within five kilometers of each other. These are the types of things that truly bedevil historians and sometimes add confusion to the accounts.

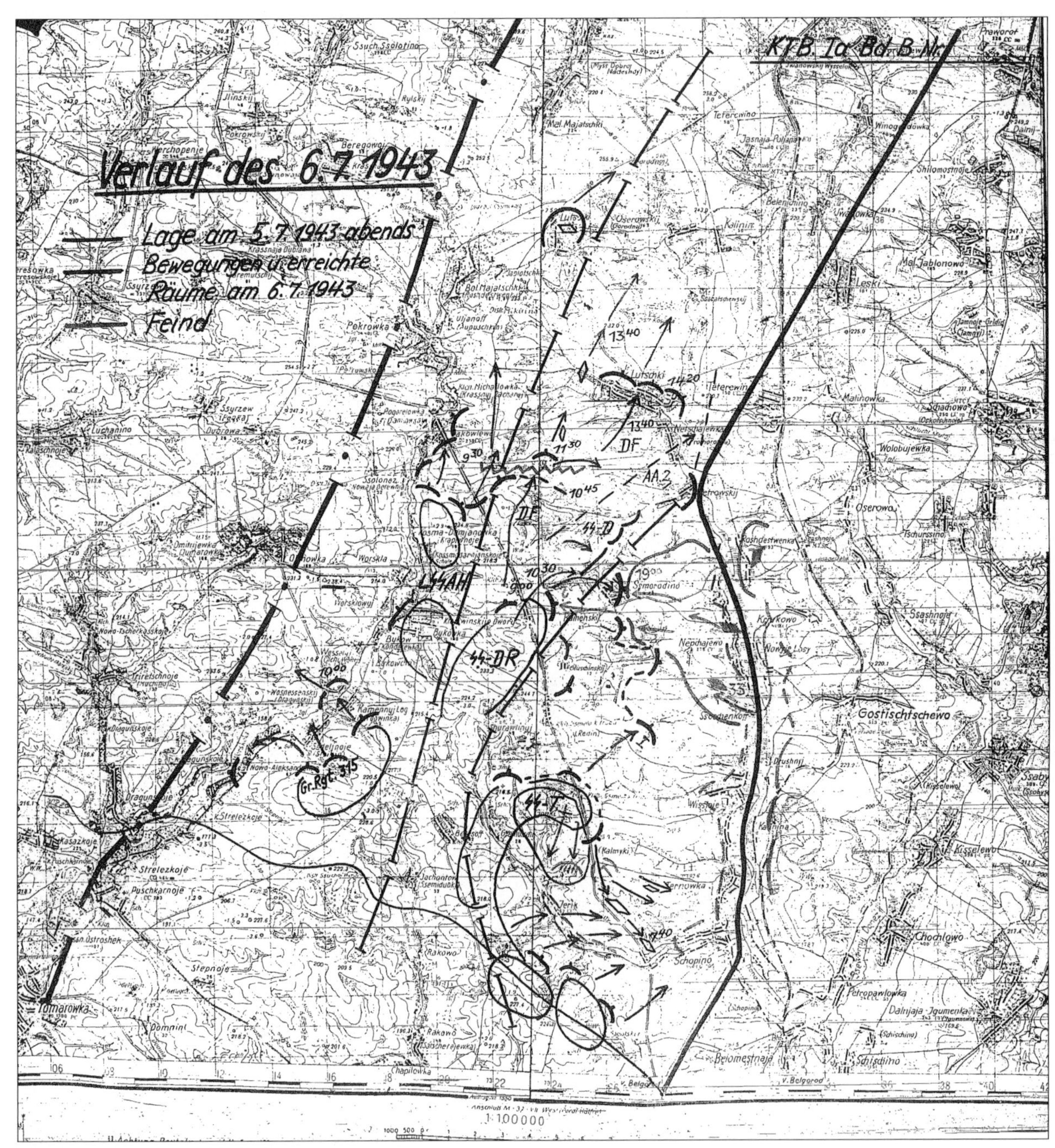

The SS Panzer Corps map showing positions on the 6th of July.

Soviet Losses for the Day

By the end of the day, the 71st Guards Rifle Division effectively had one regiment roughly handled and moved out of position. The 67th Guards Rifle Division was effectively reduced to one very damaged defending regiment, with the rest of its troops streaming back to the rear. The Germans had entirely removed the first line of defense in front of the XLVIII Panzer Corps.

The second line had already come under assault. Opposite the XLVIII Panzer Corps, this defensive line consisted of the VI Tank Corps and the III Mechanized Corps supported by the 90th Guards Rifle Division and the retreating elements of the 71st and 67th Guards Rifle Divisions. The 90th Guards Rifle Division had already been weakened by the attachment of four of its nine infantry battalions forward into the first defensive line, where they eventually disappeared from the records. Overall Soviet losses for the forces fighting the XLVIII Panzer Corps since the attack started late on the fourth is estimated to be 6,459 men.

SS Panzer Corps

The SS Panzer Corps, while not as far forward as they planned, had effectively penetrated the first defensive line on the 5th. Unlike the XLVIII Panzer Corps to its left, the SS Panzer Corps was able to cleanly penetrate into the second defensive line on this day. This was not due to any measurable superior performance on the part of the SS compared to the XLVIII Panzer Corps, but due to less resistance directly in front of them and the failure of the Soviet command to bring any significant armored forces into this second defensive line.

The 52nd Guards Rifle Division, which was the formation that had the misfortune of facing these three very large SS divisions on the 5th, started this day with its forces split. During the night it had tried to withdraw; on its left (facing mostly Totenkopf) the 155th Guards Rifle Regiment fell back and concentrated in the Smorodino area; in the center, the 151st Guards Rifle Regiment withdrew back to the Pokrovka and Bolshie Mayachki area; and on its right, the 153rd Guards Rifle Regiment took up an all around defense along its previous lines, guaranteeing its envelopment along with elements of the neighboring 67th Guards Rifle Division.

By morning the division was reporting one rifle battalion along the line from Trirechnoye to height 233.6 to Voznesenskii and Veselyii. This battalion had been shunted off to the side while the 167th Infantry Division was moving behind them to their west. Four other rifle battalions were compressed in a more defensible area from Solonets to Yakovlevo. As the division had been cut in two by the SS Panzer Corps, in the east there were two rifle battalions on the line of the grove north of Yerik, being pushed farther eastward by Totenkopf. It is not known where the division's other two rifle battalions were located at this time. The division's headquarters had pulled back to Pokrovka from Vorskla village, via the woods west of Yakovlevo. They were now trying to concentrate the division at Pokrovka. The reports for the 5th claimed that the division had lost 700 men killed and wounded, but in light of the overall losses during the battle, the actual number for that day was certainly much higher, possibly more than a thousand.[21]

In the east, the right flank of the 375th Rifle Division had peeled back so that they were defending in the area of Shopino, Ternovka and Yerik. They had been further reinforced in this area with one regiment from the 51st Guards Rifle Division, which was originally in the army's second echelon.

The other two regiments of the 51st Guards Rifle Division were holding in the army's second defensive line with their right flank running from height 226.0 to the southern outskirts of Yakovlevo to the height four kilometers southeast of Yakovlevo. This left the second

21 The corps reported 4,179 casualties for 1 June to 30 July with 739 killed, 2,140 wounded, 1,198 missing and 102 DNBI (Fond: 872, Opis: 1, Delo: 461, page: 222). At 1700 on 9 July the division was reported to have suffered 4,056 casualties since 5 July (Fond: 872, Opis: 1, Delo: 25, page: 16). On 15 July the army reported 6,583 casualties for 4–15 July with 1,689 killed, 2,320 wounded, 6,583 casualties for 4–15 July with 1,689 killed, 2,320 wounded, 2,574 missing (Fond: 335, Opis: 5113, Delo: 238). This seems high and we accept the lower figures which were provided, in part because of the strength figures that were reported (8,919 on 1 July and 3,880 on 12 July). The report of 5 July 700 killed and wounded is assumed not to have picked up those who went missing this day (Fond: 872, Opis: 1, Delo: 25, page: 11).

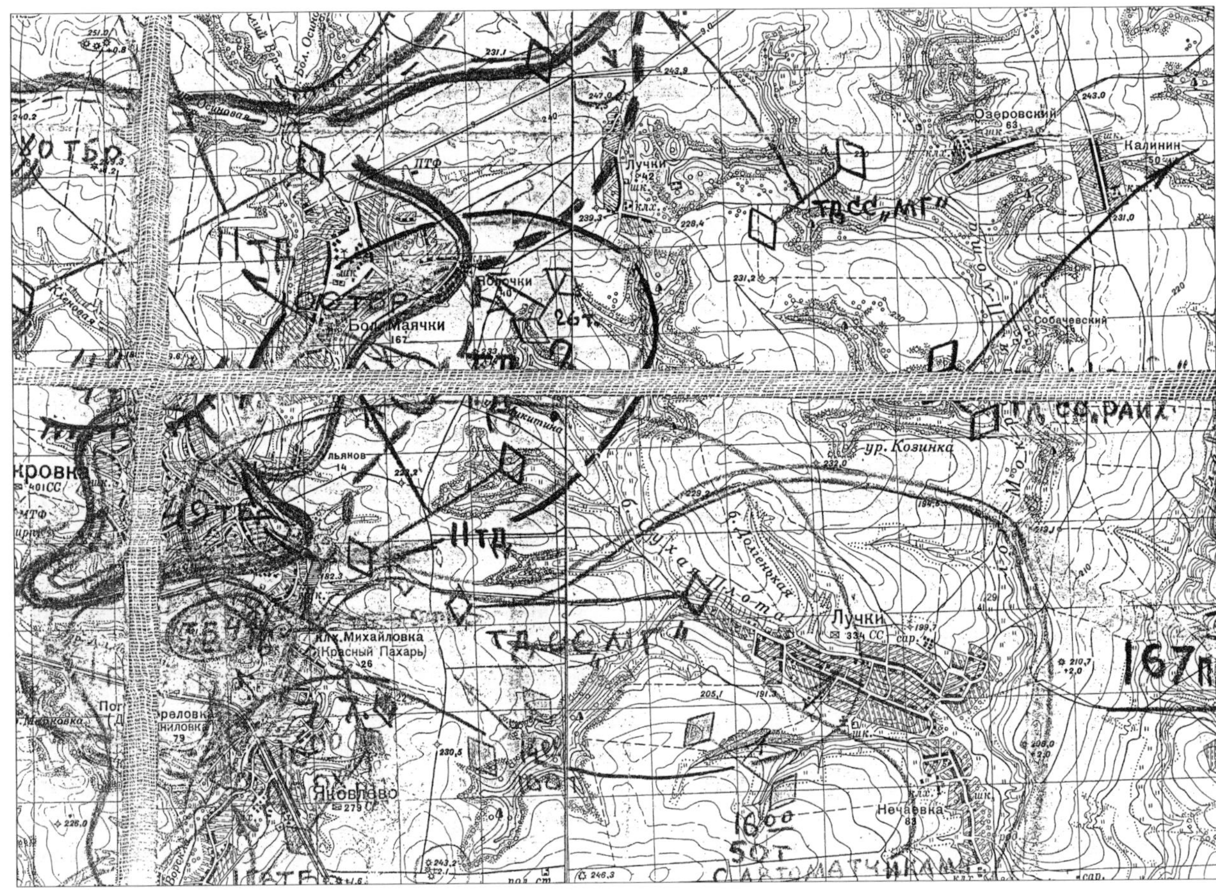

First Tank Army map showing the fight at Pokrovka, 6 July 1943.

defensive line thinly held with little available reserves and a gap in the center of this line. The Sixth Guards Army now had six of its seven divisions engaged, with the oddly placed 89th Guards Rifle Division, along with the 31st Antitank Brigade, as yet unengaged.

There were three armored corps coming up to support this second defense line. In the west arriving in the area of Pokrovka and Yakovlevo was the XXXI Tank Corps from the First Tank Army. It was positioned in the First Tank Army's second echelon but would end up facing the Adolf Hitler SS Division. In the center, arriving in front of the advancing SS Panzer Corps, and taking a position oddly enough well behind the second echelon held by the 51st Guards Rifle Division, was the V Guards Tank Corps. It effectively ended up facing off against the Das Reich SS Division. Finally, to the far east, and coming in on the right flank of the SS Panzer Corps, was the II Guards Tank Corps. It ended up facing mainly the Totenkopf SS Division.

The XXXI Tank Corps was originally supposed to make up the second echelon of the First Tank Army but was quickly thrown into the fighting on the army's left flank to defend against the Adolf Hitler SS Division. It moved forward during the night of 4/5 July to positions running from Ivnya to Vladimirovka to Alisovka, with its main forces concentrated in the Kurasovka area. It then received orders at 1800 (Moscow time) on the 5th to prepare to attack, and then an hour later to take up defensive positions. After a night march, in the morning of the 6th, the corps' 237th Tank Brigade was positioned along height 240.4 to the outskirts of Kruglik, the 100th Tank Brigade from Kruglik to Kulinovka, and the 242nd Tank Brigade from height 232.8 to 248.3. This is some 20 kilometers to the rear of the defense line occupied by the First Tank Army. By 1600 (Moscow time), the 100th Tank Brigade was moved southeast to the area northeast of Yakovlevo to secure the army's left flank and provide a junction with the V Guards Tank Corps. At 1700 (Moscow time), this brigade was ordered by Katukov to move forward to the Bolshiye Mayachki region and the 242nd and 237th Tank Brigades were ordered forward to the Ozerovkskii region by forced march.[22] These latter two brigades never got that far, leaving a gap to the V Guards Tank Corps. By the end of the day, the 100th Tank Brigade occupied a defensive line from Bolshiye Mayachki through Yablochki.[23] This brigade was subordinated to the III Mechanized Corps. As a result of these marches, 15 tanks were reported to have fallen out of column of the XXXI Tank Corps (ready-for-action still included 137 T-34s, 30 T-70s, 2 T-60s and 6 BA-64s, of which the 100th Tank Brigade had 39 T-34s, 11 T-70s, 2 T-60s and 3 BA-64s).

What the Soviet Army was facing on this flank of the First Tank Army was the massing of the Gross Deutschland and 11th Panzer Division armor to their front while the Adolf Hitler SS Division's armor was pushing up from the southeast, effectively pushing against their left flank. This created a dangerous situation for the First Tank Army. This situation was magnified by the failure of the Voronezh Front to position the V Guards Tank Corps directly to the left of the First Tank Army, along the line held by the 51st Guards Rifle Division. This left the SS Panzer Corps with the ability to peel back the flank of the First Tank Army with the Adolf Hitler SS Division while the Das Reich was able to penetrate the 51st Guards Rifle Division and then advance to engage the V Guards Tank Corps.

Still, it would appear that the XXXI Tank Corps was only engaged to a limited extent this day with only the 100th Tank Brigade engaged while the other two brigades were still moving up. It does not appear that the 100th Tank Brigade was engaged before 1600 or 1700 (Moscow time) and we have not noted any casualty reports for the XXXI Tank Corps for this day.

The V Guards Tank Corps Enters Battle

On the 5th of July, Lt. General Andrei Kravchenko's V Guards Tank Corps was still being held in the rear. Its 20th Guards Tank Brigade was located at Sarayevka, with 32 T-34s and 21 T-70s (plus 7 in repair), its 21st Guards Tank Brigade was in Ploskoye, with 44 T-34s (plus 4 in repair) and also 21 T-70s, its 22nd Guards Tank Brigade was in Nagolnoye with 49 T-34s and 21 T-70s, its 48th Guards Tank Regiment was in the woods two kilometers southwest of Vyazovoye with 21 Churchills, its 6th Guards Motorized Rifle Brigade was in Yaryigino and the other units in the corps were located in and around these areas, along with 2 other T-34s, 28 BA-64 armored cars and 20 armored transports (probably British Bren gun carriers). The three tank brigades were reporting four to nine refills of fuel, two to three reloads of ammo, and seven to 12 days of food on hand. This was a unit well-stocked, well-inventoried and ready for battle.

During the afternoon of the 5th, the corps was ordered at 1635 by Vatutin to occupy a defense line from just outside of Yakovlevo to Nechayevka and Teterevino.[24] This put the corps behind the 51st Guards Rifle Division. It appears that they never moved forward to support the Sixth Guards Army's second echelon before the Soviet second defense line was broken. Conducting a night march, as of 0600 on the 6th, they had moved forward 38 kilometers and occupied positions from Teterevino (north) to Ozerovskii to Luchki (north). This provided little direct support for 51st Guards Rifle Division, but did put them directly in the path of the SS Panzer Corps. Of the 125 T-34s that started with the tank brigades and regiment, they reported only 106 arriving in

22 This sentence drawn from Glantz and Orenstein, page 89.

23 This sentence drawn from Glantz and Orenstein, page 89.

24 Glantz and Orenstein, pages 86 and 154.

the concentration area. This means that either 19 broke down en route, or more likely, the number reported ready for action on the 5th was optimistic. The number of T-70s which arrived in the area was three greater on the 6th than the number they reported ready for action on the 5th, while all 21 Churchills had made it without problems. During the march, one T-34 in the 20th Guards Tank Brigade overturned, killing three men and wounding one. As of 0600 that morning, the 6th Guards Motorized Rifle Brigade's "motorized" infantry was still on the march, and measures were being taken to put them on vehicles (the brigade was reported to have around 148 "cars" for its 2,500 men).

The tank corps reported it was involved in difficult defensive fighting since the morning[25] but the first report we have of it in action is an unsuccessful counterattack by the 22nd Guards Tank Brigade from the edge of Kozinka Woods toward height 232.0, and Luchki. Lt. General Kravchenko (V Guards Tank Corps commander) dispatched the 21st Guards Tank Brigade and 48th Guards Tank Regiment (the Churchills) to assist. These forces failed to stem the German attack, which overran the 22nd Guards Tank Brigade at Ozerovskii and Kalinin. By 1630 (Moscow time), two of the corps brigades and the tank regiment were surrounded in the area of Kozinka Woods. The Germans then tried to seize Belenikhino station on the fly and strike at Storozhevoye. The V Guards Tank Corps had only one remaining tank brigade to plug into this gap and no other reserves to halt the envelopment of its main force.[26] As Lt. General Kravchenko reported to Vatutin:

> Using large numbers of tanks, no less than two panzer divisions and motorized infantry, at 1200 on July 6, 1943, the enemy began to move out from the area of Smorodino, Kozmo-Demyanovka, and the woods to the east in two columns to the north and northeast. It is now clear that the enemy directed his main effort against the corps. This was the point of a tank wedge numbering up to 300 tanks and a mechanized division. From the beginning the enemy's air force systematically worked over the corps' positions and concentration points. During July 6, 1943, no less than 1500 air sorties were counted. While the enemy's tank group was advancing, I was given an order by the commander of the XXIII Rifle Corps in your name to move two tank brigades and the Churchill tank regiment out of my area to counterattack the enemy in the area of hills 246.3, 243.2 and the grove to the northeast. Besides this order, issued in your name, a Colonel Nikiforov, empowered by the commander of the Sixth Guards Army, threatened to shoot me if the corps did not counterattack. I fulfilled this order. Despite the fact that a section of the corps defense was weakened, the corps units continued to hold back the main force of the enemy until 2300 on July 6, 1943, as long as they were not completely encircled. By conducting a fighting withdrawal away from the encirclement, the corps occupied a defense along the railroad line from Ivanovskii Vyiselok-Belenikhino-Teterevino (exclusive), with security units one kilometer west of the railroad. Fighting bitterly with strong enemy tank forces, and with no support from neighbors on the right (units of the First Tank Army) and the left (units of the II Guards Tank Corps), on July 6, 1943, the corps lost 110 tanks.[27]

Losing 110 tanks in one day is a stunning failure on the part of the V Guards Tank Corps, even if this figure includes the 21 T-34s that were lost before battle was engaged. It clearly started the morning with at least 193 tanks, and lost at least 46 percent of them in one day. While one could castigate Lt. General Kravchenko for launching an attack without artillery, air, infantry or flank support right into the face of the German combined arms team, it was an attack ordered by his

25 Fond: 3403, Opis: 1, Delo: 18a, pages: 143–156.

26 Valerii N. Zamulin and L. N. Lopukhovskii, "Prokhorovskoye Srazheniye. Mifyi i realnost" [Battle of Prokhorovka. Myths and Facts] from *Voyenno-Istoricheskii Arkhiv, No 9(33) Sentyabr 2002* [Military Historical Archives], page 77.

27 Valerii N. Zamulin and L. N. Lopukhovskii, "Prokhorovskoye Srazheniye. Mifyi i realnost" [Battle of Prokhorovka. Myths and Facts], from *Voyenno-Istoricheskii Arkhiv, No 9(33) Sentyabr 2002* [Military Historical Archives], pages 77–79. Translation courtesy of Gary Dickson.

superior and reinforced with the threat of execution! He faced the combined arms teams of the Das Reich SS Division with its 148 tanks, assault guns and self-propelled antitank guns and maybe parts of the Adolf Hitler SS Division, which had 157 tanks, assault guns and self-propelled antitank guns.

By the end of the day, the Das Reich SS Division was able to capture Luchki, Sobachevskii, Kalinin, height 232.0, Ozerovskii, and the wooded section northwest of Ozerovskii. It lost 30 tanks and assault guns this day.

By the end of the day, the 52nd Guards Rifle Division was reporting that it had two rifle regiments at Syirtsev-Pogorelovka (basically opposite parts of the 167th Infantry Division and the Adolf Hitler SS Division) and two rifle battalions at Yerik and the grove to the north (opposite Totenkopf SS Division). This division was being withdrawn from the fight with the elements of 153rd Guards Rifle Regiment (which had been enveloped) ordered at 1400 to begin its withdrawal well to the rear to the Sukho-Solotino area. The 155th Guards Rifle Regiment was to concentrate in the Sobachevskii area (three kilometers north of Luchki [south]) and the 151st Guards Rifle Regiment in the Malaya Psinka area (on the Psel, seven kilometers north of Prokhorovka). This effectively ended the fighting for this Soviet division. In two days of heavy combat it had been left with the unenviable task of facing three SS panzer grenadier divisions and had lost an "estimated" 1,720 casualties, or about 19 percent of the overall division strength.[28] The army had lost communication with the division around 1700 and did not re-establish it until the following day.

The 51st Guards Rifle Division, which was now in the center of this fight, was stretched from Pokrovka to Mikhailovka to Luchki to Teterevino, or across the entire front of the SS Panzer Corps. In effect, the SS Panzer Corps had indeed pushed a significant penetration through the middle of the 52nd Guards Rifle Division and into the 51st Guards Rifle Division. The Soviet line ran along the length of the Vorskla up to Yakovlevo in the west and was pushed out to Yerik in the east, but this area was on the verge of being surrounded. These two divisions would be two of the more seriously bloodied divisions in the Voronezh Front during this battle.

While Das Reich and Adolf Hitler were concentrating their forces on narrow attack frontages, the Totenkopf SS Division was expanding its frontage to protect the right flank of the corps and to open up the road from Belgorod. While this was not the best use of the corps' offensive resources, since the corps did not have any supporting infantry divisions on this flank, this is the only option that it had. Furthermore, this flank contained a Soviet tank corps and an independent tank brigade.

The II Guards Tank Corps had carried out a night march from the Korocha area. According to a captured prisoner report from the SS Panzer Corps, the 26th Guards Tank Brigade at 1500 (Berlin time?) on the 5th of July was alerted and moved to the area of Petropavlovka, where it arrived at 2400. The Soviets report that by 0400 (Moscow time) on the 6th the corps had positioned itself along the Lipovyii Donets. The 25th Guards Tank Brigade was deployed in the western outskirts of Rozhdestvenka, the 26th Guards Tank Brigade around Nepkhayevo and stretched between Rozhdestvenka and Novyiye Lozyi. Its motorized rifle battalion was on the edge of the woods three kilometers west of Nepkhayevo. The 4th Guards Tank Brigade, along with the 47th Guards Heavy Tank Regiment, was in the area of the woods one kilometer east of Kryukovo, effectively in the second echelon. The 4th Guards Motorized Rifle Brigade was stretched from Novyiye Lozyi to Gostishchevo and was digging in. They held their positions there during the day, trading fire with the Germans starting at 0730 (Moscow time).

This area along the Lipovyii Donets River was also defended by the 375th Rifle Division. Its reported losses the previous day had been relatively light when compared to the neighboring 52nd Guards Rifle Division. In the morning, it was reported to be defending a line running from one kilometer east of Smelo k Trudu Kolkhoz

28 We simply do not know what the losses were for any given day for this division. See footnote 12. The losses given here are derived from a straight line estimate based on interpretation of the unit reports. Using other assumptions, one can make the argument that the division lost around 4,056 casualties on these two days.

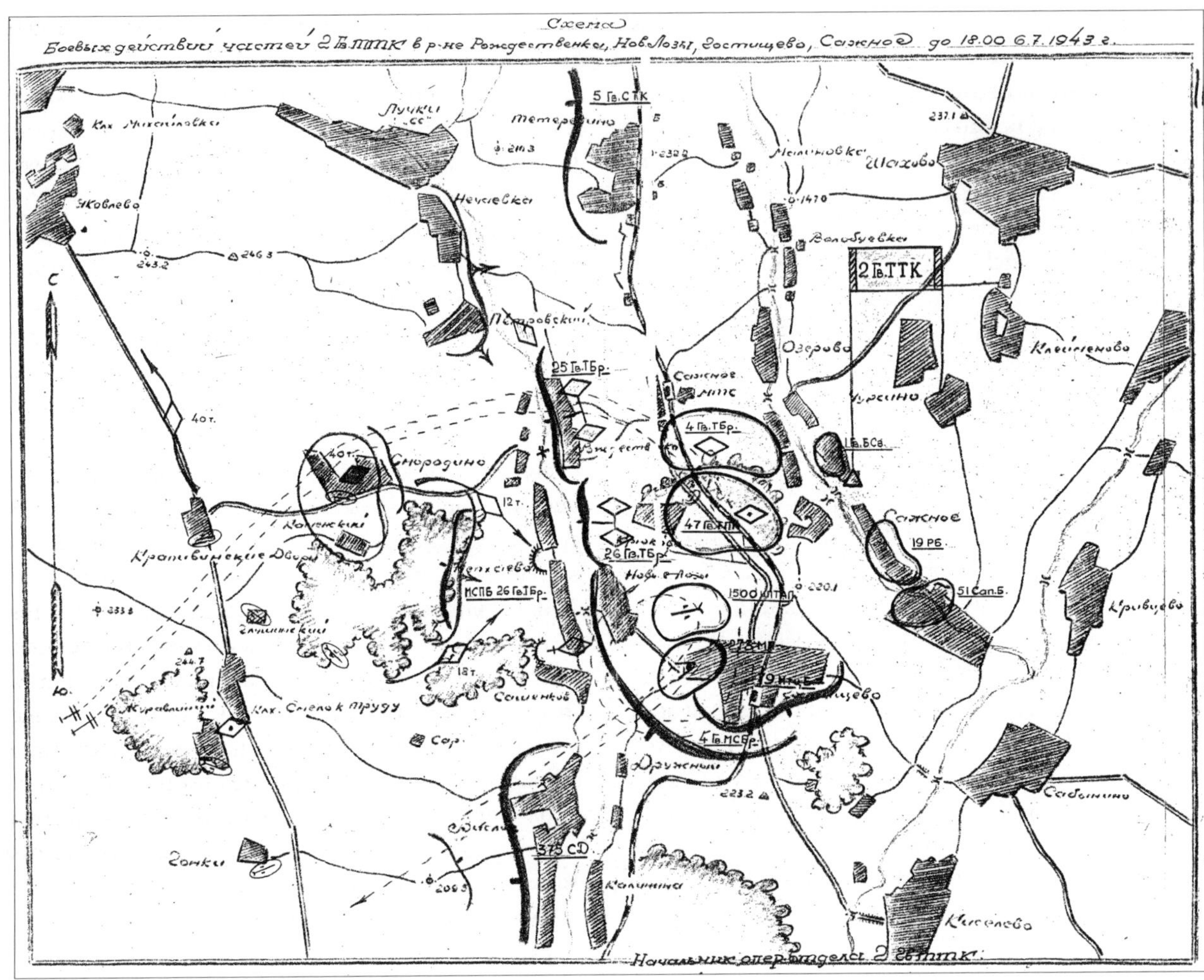

II Guards Tank Corps map for 1800, 6 July 1943.

to Shopino.[29] Also, the 96th Tank Brigade had arrived. It had been sitting in the area of Shishino and Postnikov Sovkhoz since 24 April, and had 42 T-34s, 4 T-70s, 3 T-60s and 1 T-38. It consisted of 1,146 men, broken into two tank battalions, a motorized infantry battalion, an antitank battalion and an antitank company. On the 5th, the 96th Tank Brigade had moved over to defend the crossings at Nepkhayevo, Visloye and Ternovka, now reporting some 46 T-34s and 5 T-70s (they probably repaired some tanks).

Furthermore, as the Germans moved forward, they also began to encounter the defending divisions of the Sixty-ninth Army. The first to be encountered was the 183rd Rifle Division. This division originally was located from Vaselyevka (on the Psel) all the way through Zhimolostnoye to Shipyi, on the Severnyii Donets, a frontage of 38 kilometers. This unit clearly shifted forward along

29 Line went from 1 kilometer east of the Smelo k Trudu Kolkhoz, to south of height 214.5, along the northwest edge of the grove north of Yerik, to height 196.4, to Yerik to Shopino, to height 211.6, to height 190.5, to the grove north of Pokrovka.

the line of the Lipovyii Donets on the 6th, for it records that fighting began at 1050 in the area of Kryukovo and that during the first part of the day, a German infantry regiment and 80 tanks reached the line from Rozhdestvenka to Kryukovo, where it was halted by 1300 hours.

On the basis of an oral order given to them by Chistyakov (the commander of the Sixth Guards Army), the II Guards Tank Corps crossed the Lipovyii Donets in the area of Novyiye Lozyi at 1700 (Moscow time). They then attacked in the direction of Krapivinskiye Dvoryi and the Smelo k Trudu Kolkhoz. According to the corps accounts, "Overcoming the resistance of superior enemy forces, and being subjected to intensive artillery and mortar bombardment, tank fire and enemy air attacks, the corps units by 2000 drove the enemy out of Smorodino, Kamenskii, Glushinskii and the Smelo k Trudu Kolkhoz, where it occupied a circular defense and continued to trade fire with the enemy."

This advance forced the intervention of the armored battle groups of both the Das Reich and Totenkopf SS Divisions, and resulted in a German estimate of 11 Soviet tanks lost. According to the Soviet records, the II Guards Tank Corps lost 28 tanks this day (including 9 Churchills) and 191 men this day. The 96th Tank Brigade reported no losses.

As evening fell, the Soviet forces retreated from the German counterattack to the area of Soshenkov and Nepkhayevo. According to the Soviet records, this withdrawal was ordered by Vatutin (Voronezh Front commander) as a result of its exposed position. The corps was pulled back to the eastern bank of the Lipovyii Donets. By 0600 on the 7th, the 25th Guards Tank Brigade was back on the river, stretched from the outskirts of Petrovskii into Rozhdestvenka, the 26th Guards Tank Brigade continuing this line down into Novyiye Lozyi, and the 4th Guards Motorized Rifle Brigade continued this down into Druzhnyii. The 4th Guards Tank Brigade had been shifted to the corps' right flank to cut the railroad at Teterevino and secure that flank. The corps was down to 86 combat-ready T-34s, 66 T-70s and only seven Churchills.

Meanwhile the Germans had observed a "stronger" Soviet armored force assembling in Ternovka and Visloye. This was the 96th Tank Brigade. The right flank of the SS Panzer Corps was still very much under threat.

What the Soviets had attempted on this day was a coordinated pincher attack with the II Guards Tank Corps attacking from Smorodino to the west and the III Mechanized Corps attacking from Yakovlevo to the east. If successful, such an attack could have pinched off the SS Panzer Corps attack and resealed the front. While the II Guards Tank Corps was well-positioned to conduct this attack, the III Mechanized Corps suffered from coming under attack on the afternoon of the 6th by the advancing German XLVIII Panzer Corps. This severely limited the forces that it could throw into these attacks to the east while still holding against the German advance from the south and southwest. In fact, this effectively doomed this effort, as it divided the strength of the III Mechanized Corps so that it was neither defending in full force against the XLVIII Panzer Corps nor attacking in full force against the SS Panzer Corps. Furthermore, because these attacks were launched early, they did not really hit the SS Panzer Corps in the flank, but effectively went head on with the Adolf Hitler and Totenkopf SS Divisions. Still, the idea that two Soviet armored corps would be able to counterattack and seal off three of the large SS panzer grenadier divisions was probably ambitious to start with.

III Panzer Corps

This was the day that the III Panzer Corps brought its armor to bear, with mixed results. As the day developed, it became clear that the Germans were going to have real problems breaking the 81st Guards Rifle Division positions but had already made a break in the first defense line in the 78th Guards Rifle Division area. The sudden change of plans and the shifts that occurred on this day, while achieving a breakthrough, set the stage for a confrontation between Breith and his commander, General Kempf.

During the night, the 6th Panzer Division was ordered to turn over its sector to the 168th Infantry Division, reassemble behind the lines and prepare to follow the 7th Panzer Division and attack Melikhovo. The division's withdrawal from its former area and the turning over of the sector to the 168th Infantry Division went as planned, with command of the sector released to the 168th Infantry Division at midnight. The Soviets did not attempt to attack or follow the division as it withdrew. The division then assembled in Koloniya Dubovoye and then crossed the Donets bridges at Solomino and Dorogobuzhino to the Krutoi Log area. Alfred Rubbel recalled experiencing great difficulties in traversing the antitank ditch on the other side of the river. There was a long traffic jam of tanks and armored vehicles which again drew the enemy's concentrated artillery fire.

The 6th Panzer Division reentered combat at 1645 on the 6th, with Battle Group Oppeln (formed around the 11th Panzer Regiment)[30] from the 6th Panzer Division and Battle Group Glaesemer[31] from the 7th Panzer Division storming Generalovka despite tenacious Soviet defense supported by strong Soviet artillery and effective close-air support.

The only real success Provisional Army Kempf was having was with the 7th Panzer Division. The division moved out at 0500 from the hills north of Krutoi Log to attack the heights at 216.1, west of Batratskaya Dacha Sovkhoz. The armored group, Battle Group Schulz (commander of the 25th Panzer Regiment),[32] attacked eastward towards Batratskaya Dacha and broke into the second Soviet defense line there and 1.5 kilometers north of height 209.6. This Soviet defense had been reinforced by many tanks. This advance by the 7th Panzer Division enabled the 106th Infantry Division on its right to conduct a successful attack of its own. Battle Group Schulz then seized height 216.1 and established contact with the 106th Infantry Division.

The Seventh Guards Army had committed to fighting the breakthrough, mostly against the 7th Panzer Division, six of its seven armored formations. By the end of the day, 6 July, three of these were already gutted. These Soviet armored formations lost at least 58 tanks and self-propelled guns on the 5th and 6th, while the opposing 7th Panzer Division had lost 67 tanks damaged, destroyed, or broken down.

Kempf's Phone Call

On this day was filed away in the III Panzer Corps files a "Note for the War Diary," with the time of 1745 handwritten on it. It was obviously written by Breith shortly after a phone call from his army commander, General Kempf. It says:

> The commanding general Kempf personally called me with General Speidel on the line to tell me that he feels that the employment of the III Panzer Corps is incorrect. His major complaint is that the corps is going too far east.
>
> . . .
>
> The corps is convinced that the correctness of the decision will yet be proven by success.
>
> The negative judgment of the army commanding general is completely incomprehensible to the corps. When the previously noted phone conversation between the army Chief of General Staff and myself ended (details which are in the memo for the record), General Speidel was not able to raise any points against my position.

The memo was hand dated "6/7" and illegibly initialed.[33] The note also included a complaint about the 19th Panzer Division lacking aggressiveness.

30 Battle Group Oppeln was named after Col. Hermann von Oppeln-Bronikowski (2 January 1899–19 September 1966), the commander of the 11th Panzer Regiment. He had already been awarded the Knight's Cross on 1 January 1943, received Oak Leaves 28 July 1944 and Swords 17 April 1945. He was wounded during Kursk but returned back to command this regiment later. He also won a gold medal in the 1936 Olympics in Team Dressage.

31 Battle Group Glaesemer was named after Col. Wolfgang Glaesemer, the commander of the 6th Panzer Grenadier Regiment of the 7th Panzer Division. He had already been awarded the Knight's Cross on 12 February 1943.

32 Battle Group Schulz was commanded by LtCol. Adelbert Schulz (20 December 1903–28 January 1944), the commander of the 25th Panzer Regiment. He was awarded the Knight's Cross on 29 September 1940 when he was a company commander with the regiment, he was awarded Oak Leaves 31 December 1941 when he was a battalion commander with the regiment. After Kursk, would be awarded Swords on 6 August 1943 and Diamonds on 14 December 1943 (only the ninth one awarded). He was killed in action the following month while commanding the 7th Panzer Division.

33 T314, R197, page 1103.

By the end of the day, the corps had already penetrated deep enough that it could turn north and start clearing the area to the north. Still, the failure of the army to take Staryii Gorod and Blizhnyaya Igumenka meant that they were not in position to provide any form of flank support to the SS Panzer Corps. For them to have value for the overall battle plan, other than as a significant distraction, they needed to get well past these points and start threatening to cross the Severnyii Donets. They were still some 12 to 15 kilometers from that point and were faced with having to turn and advance to the north while the forces in the Seventh Guards Army's second defensive line would accumulate on their flank. If they could turn this into an advance between the two defense lines like the XLVIII Panzer Corps had done on this day, then considerable progress could be made. As it was, with the 81st Guards Rifle Division solidly anchored at Staryii Gorod, the Soviets were still in position to place another east-west defensive line in the path of the German advance. The shifting of the 6th Panzer Division and elements of the 74th Panzer Grenadier Regiment (19th Panzer Division) out of the Mikhailovka bridgehead and putting them back into action through the bridgeheads created by the 19th Panzer Division and the 7th Panzer Division, while it minimized casualties and maximized the maneuverability of the panzer forces, did not do much to help the overall battle plan. While the III Panzer Corps operations on this day were the best for the corps, it may well not have been the best decisions for Army Group South's attack. Perhaps the real problem was that the Germans really did expect less resistance from the Soviet forces than they were getting. As such, their plans were based upon the ability to seize terrain and an advance rate that was unrealistic.

Corps Raus

The 106th and 320th Infantry Divisions were huddled between the railroad embankment and the east bank of the Donets. Corps Raus had made a two kilometer advance, while the armored forces to their immediate left, the 7th Panzer Division, had penetrated seven kilometers into Soviet lines. The corps had lost 2,500 men in the heavy fighting the previous day, but had effectively dislodged the leading two regiments of the 72nd Guards Rifle Division. This division's second echelon was insufficient to halt the corps. The day was spent, after a sharp exchange in the morning, advancing to the second echelon of the army, as it was with most of the other attacking German divisions.

The weight of the III Panzer Corps attack fell on the 78th Guards Rifle Division. For the 5th and 6th of July, it reported losing 3,293 men killed and wounded (missing is not stated), along with 12 120mm Mortars, 60 82mm Mortars, 39 50mm Mortars, 15 76mm guns, 36 45mm guns, 12 122mm guns, 152 Antitank Rifles (out of 197), 4 cars and 123 horses. In contrast, to its north, the 81st Guards Rifle Division reported only 347 men killed and wounded (missing is not stated) and to its rear, the 73rd Guards Rifle Division reported 1,670 killed and wounded (no missing). To the south of it, the 72nd Guards Rifle Division reported 2,738 killed, wounded and missing (439 missing) with only about half the equipment losses, while the 213th Rifle Division reported 1,865 killed, wounded and missing.

The Steppe Front and the Southwestern Front

The evening of the 5th, at 1830 (Moscow time), Vatutin reported the situation to Stalin by telegraph. He informed Stalin that six German panzer divisions were operating in front of the Sixth Guards Army alone, and that the Germans were bringing up fresh reserves (one wonders what the basis was for that statement). Vatutin requested from Stavka four tank and two aviation corps so as to "ensure dynamic operations." Vasilevskii, the Stavka representative, was also there and submitted his report recommending that they release the X Tank Corps and II Tank Corps, sending one to Prokhorovka and the other to Korocha. He also recommended that they move General Pavel Rotmistrov's Fifth Guards Tank Army to the Oskol River south of Staryii Oskol.[34]

34 Glantz and Orenstein, page 91–92.

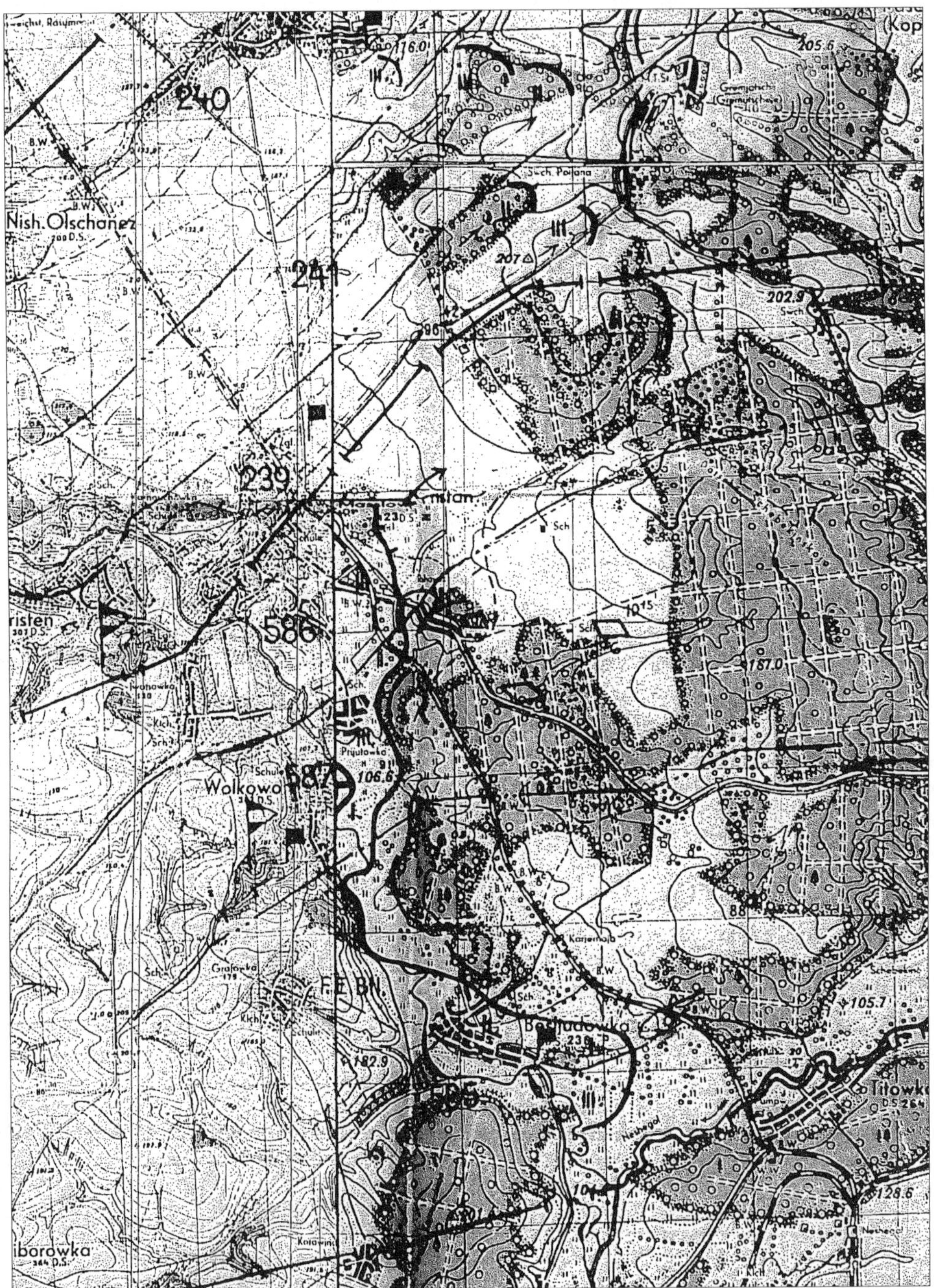

Corps Raus: 6 July, 1500 hours.

The Steppe Front, which controlled the Fifth Guards Tank Army, Fifth Guards Army, Fifty-third Army and other units behind the Voronezh Front, was put on alert this day.

Its nearest forces to the front, the Fifth Guards Army, were alerted on the evening of the 5th. At 1800 on 5 July, at least one division, and probably the entire army, was ordered to cease their training and occupy their defensive positions. The X Tank Corps, which was located at Staryii Oskol, only 115 kilometers from the front, was detached from the Fifth Guards Army on the night of the 6/7th of July and moved south. It was ordered at midnight to move to the Prokhorovka area, began moving at 0400 on the 7th, and by 1900 had concentrated in the Prokhorovka area.[35] This was a move of around 80 kilometers.

The Fifth Guards Tank Army, consisting of the V Guards Mechanized Corps and the XXIX (29th) Tank Corps, was also alerted on the evening of the 5th. The XVIII Tank Corps was now attached to the army. At 2330 on 6 July this army was ordered to move; it moved out at 0130 on the 7th, with its main forces moved to Staryii Oskol by the morning of the 8th.

In the Southwestern Front, the II Tank Corps was also alerted at midnight of the night of 6/7 July and by 0800 on 8 July had concentrated in the Kamyishevka and Pravorot area.[36]

These actions set five more armored corps into motion to reinforce the five armored corps that had become engaged on this day.

Finally, in an action that would have a very limited effect on the battle, but is indicative of how seriously the Soviet command was taking the German attack in the south, at midnight of 5 July, in a phone conversation with Rokossovskii, Stalin promised to transfer the Twenty-seventh Army (Lt. General Trofimenko) from the Steppe Military District to the Central Front. This reinforcing infantry army was effectively due east of the Central Front and consisted of six rifle divisions and a tank brigade. A few hours later, this assignment was withdrawn and the Twenty-seventh Army was prepared for a move south. Instead Rokossovskii would have to hold with his existing forces and furthermore, if there was a breakthrough in the south, he would be responsible for defending the city of Kursk.[37] The Twenty-seventh Army started shifting south on the 6th.[38]

Summary to Date

The Germans had now turned their initial three penetrations, each done with a panzer corps, into a broader advance. The XLVIII Panzer Corps and the SS Panzer Corps were now attacking forward with five armored divisions (3rd Panzer Division was repositioning), supported on the left flank by parts of the LII Corps. The III Panzer Corps had clearly penetrated and was pushing forward aggressively with its three panzer divisions, supported on its right flank by Corps Raus.

The casualties during the day were lower than the previous day, the Germans having lost some 3,973 casualties (556 killed, 3,200 wounded and 217 missing). This compared favorably to the estimated 8,271 Soviet casualties (1,631 killed, 3,436 wounded and 3,204 missing). The Soviet fighting strength was further reduced by the large number of regimental-sized elements either isolated or roughed up and badly pushed out of position. As such, there were disorganized elements and units streaming back to the rear across the battlefield that had little organized combat power.

Still, although the first defensive line was decidedly cracked, the second defensive line was both active and well-manned by Soviet armor. At this point the comparative armor strengths put the Germans in a difficult offensive situation and were going to result in some bitter battles over the next few days. So far, the heavier armor losses had been suffered by the Germans, and this was part of the cost of working their way through the Soviet defensive works and antitank positions. On

35 This sentence from Glantz and Orenstein, pages 92 and 154.

36 Glantz and Orenstein, pages 92 and 154. The unit was alerted at 2345 on the 6th. For more details on its move up to the battle, see Chapters Eleven and Thirteen in my original book *Kursk: The Battle of Prokhorovka*.

37 Erickson, page 100.

38 Erickson, page 103.

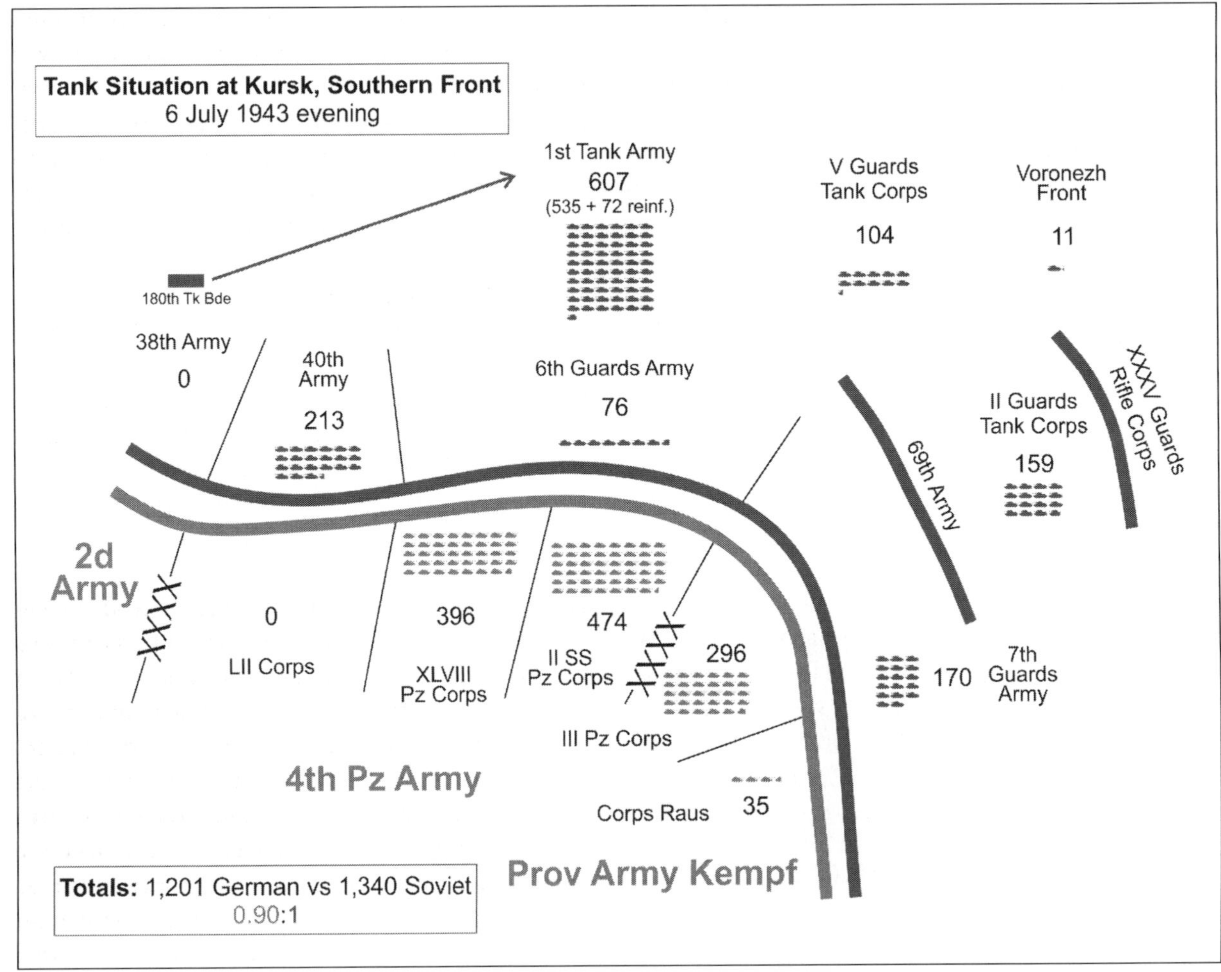

the 6th, the Germans had lost some 276 tanks across the battle front, while the Soviets had lost 243 (including breakdowns in engaged units), with a significant portion coming from the V Guards Tank Corps. This was an almost even exchange rate, unlike the previous day. Along with the losses from the previous day, and the few from the evening advance of the 4th, this resulted in a loss ratio of 1.6 to 1.0 in armor, to the Soviet Army's favor (530 German tanks lost versus 335 Soviet tanks lost).

Still, with the forces the Soviet Army had now brought up, the Germans were now effectively attacking across the front at a 1.5-to-1 force ratio. While the Voronezh Front had almost 400,000 troops not counting the Thirty-eighth Army, they had still only managed to get about 180,000 of them into the line of battle. As such, the Germans still had a relative advantage at the front.

Attacking the Second Defensive Line: 7 July 1943

The German Army had cleared away the outposts on 4 July, had effectively broken the first defensive line on the first day of the battle, 5 July, and spent the second day of the battle moving up to and initiating the attack against the second defensive line. This third day of battle was essentially spent penetrating the second defensive line in the area of the XLVIII Panzer Corps, while the SS Panzer Corps was already through it and the III Panzer Corps effectively turned north and was running beside it.

XLVIII Panzer Corps

On the morning of the 7th, the 3rd Panzer Division was scattered from the 332nd Infantry Division sector across to Lukhanino. The Gross Deutschland Division stretched from Lukhanino to Dubrova and 11th Panzer Division was near Dubrova ready to continue the engagement with the III Mechanized Corps.

In the early morning, elements of the 3rd Panzer Division were covering the western flank of the corps and waiting to be relieved by the 332nd Infantry Division. In response to Knobelsdorff's (the corps commander) decision to move the 3rd Panzer Division behind the Gross Deutschland Division at Lukhanino, four march groups set out at first light towards Lukhanino. By around 0400 the armored group (Kampfgruppe Schmidt-Ott) had reached the area around height 210.7, south of Alekseyevka. At 0720, Westhoven informed Knobelsdorff that he would not be ready to attack before noon. Knobelsdorff ordered that the crossing preparations must be completed by noon.

Other than the late afternoon river crossing, and the action on the division's left flank in support of the 332nd Infantry Division, the 3rd Panzer Division had not been involved in any significant action since noon of the previous day. The division's losses on the 6th were 73 while on the 7th they reported 72 lost in action.

At 0915 the army issued orders that seemed a little optimistic. They stated that the most important mission of the XLVIII Panzer Corps was to make contact with the SS Panzer Corps to prevent a possible Soviet counterattack against this corps from the northwest (this was the threat now being created by the XXXI Tank Corps). It also stated that the 3rd Panzer Division should not advance farther than height 258.5, five kilometers north of Berezovka! This was a point that was only reached days later, and only by coming at it from the northeast! Again, one is left with impression that they considered the Soviet second defensive line penetrated and expected considerable progress on this day, with the 3rd Panzer Division moving through Lukhanino, crossing the Pena from the east, and moving through Berezovka. As we shall see, these routes were well covered by the III Mechanized Corps and the VI Tank Corps.

The Gross Deutschland Panzer Grenadier Division had halted the previous night with its armored group (primarily the panzer regiment, Remer's battalion and some Panthers) thrust into the Soviet line east of Dubrova (height 247.2) and with the Fusilier Regiment with a foothold across the Pena at Lukhanino. During the night the sound of Russian tank engines was heard from the Soviet positions north of the Pena. At 0015, 7 July the division commander (Hoernlein) reported that the Fusilier Regiment had so far failed to establish a bridgehead on the north bank of the Pena, and that only the south part of Lukhanino had been captured. Despite this, Knobelsdorff did not alter the plan to have Gross Deutschland and the 3rd Panzer Division advance through the bridgehead once it was secure.

The issue of Panther losses was raised in the morning message, with the corps stating that the heavy losses of Panthers were not a result of Soviet artillery fire, as up to this time only two Panthers had been penetrated by artillery fire, but was due to mechanical breakdowns. The daily report for the army also noted that 76 of the Panthers were now under control of the quartermaster for the XLVIII Panzer Corps and were being repaired back at work stations. They also reported that more tanks with minor damage were out in the battlefield. On the morning of 7 July, they would report that 43 Panthers were ready for action.

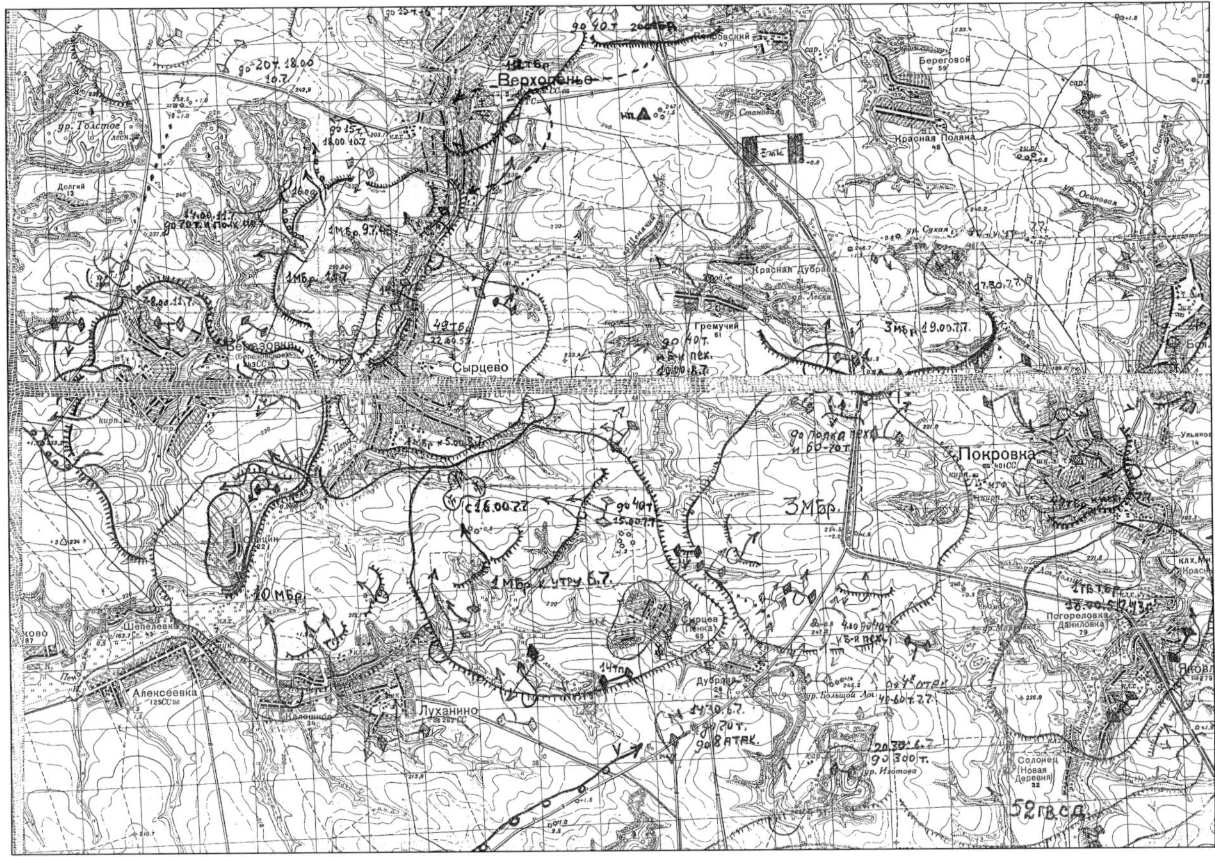

Portion of III Mechanized Corps map showing the situation for 7 July.

Around noon, Hoth reported that the situation changed substantially. What seemed to have changed, in fact, was his understanding of the situation. Strong Soviet armored attacks (from the XXXI Tank Corps) were hitting the left flank of the SS Panzer Corps. Because of this Hoth insisted that the XLVIII Panzer Corps must accelerate their attacks on both sides of Gremuchii and toward Verkhopenye and hit the flanks of the Soviet armor so they could not withdraw. As a result, the 11th Panzer Division was to continue its advance to the hills east of Gremuchii, while the Gross Deutschland Division had to effect a crossing at Lukhanino, from the northeast (!) and then attack the hills southwest of Gremuchii, taking Soviet positions near Gremuchii by double envelopment. This led to the Gross Deutschland attacking in the direction of Syirtsevo.

The assault of Syirtsevo led to heavy losses among the Panther regiment, one of the two panzer regiments now under command of Colonel Strachwitz. The III Mechanized Corps was fighting with its tanks dug-in, camouflaged, well supported by artillery, and protected by minefields. As the two regiments advanced, the Panther regiment came under fire from camouflaged, dug-in T-34s, some firing on the flanks. According to Lt. Rahn, the adjutant for the 52nd Panzer Battalion, the regiment lost as many as 30 Panthers in only a few moments.

The Germans had 200 Panthers at the start of the operation. It appears that only 198 of them were ready for action at the front on the evening of the 4th as at least two of them caught fire and burned on the way to the front. By the evening of the 6th, the German Panther strength was reported as 40. Of those lost, around 40 had been lost due to artillery and mines in the advance to Dubrova and the fighting at Dubrova. The rest, around 120 tanks, were almost certainly mechanical breakdowns. That evening, the corps reported that Panther losses had been extraordinarily high, especially because of mechanical breakdown. They reported that so far, 76 had been lost. There were no Panther strength reports after the morning of the 7th (43 Panthers) until the evening of the 9th (16 Panthers). As Lieutenant Rahn points out, as many as 30 were lost to enemy action on the 7th. This left the regiment with around a dozen tanks.

There is some supporting evidence that heavy losses did occur on the 7th. A list of those killed for the 51st Panzer Battalion shows one killed on the 4th, seven killed on the 5th, two killed on the 6th and 16 killed and one missing on the 7th.[39]

It is this attack, where the Panther regiment was sent into a direct attack through a minefield against dug-in Soviet tanks, that was probably the source of Decker's complaints about how Strachwitz used the Panthers. Decker would later complain to General Guderian about these losses.

39 Kurt Gaetzschmann, *Pz.Abt.51 Heerestruppe—II./Pz.Rgt. 33/9. Pz.Div. 1943–45*. The list shows losses by name, summarized as:

Date	*Number Killed*	*Of those, number that are officers (Lts.)*
27 Feb. 1943	1	
14 Apr. 1943	1	
17 Apr. 1943	4	
4 July 1943	1	
5 July 1943	7	1
6 July 1943	2	1
7 July 1943	16	2
8 July 1843	1	
9 July 1943	3	
10 July 1943	5	
11 July 1943	2	
14 July 1943	1	1

No other people reported killed until 3 August 1943. There is also one man reported missing on the 7th.

THE 11TH PANZER Division jumped off at 0300 on the morning of the 7th. The panzer division was able to envelop and take Dubrova, take heavily defended height 254.5 and push up to the village of Gremuchii. For this day, we record 46 tanks lost (including assault guns and Marders) for the 11th Panzer Division. Of those, only three are recorded as destroyed. There stands today at height 254.5 a plaque honoring the defense by 14th Independent Antitank Artillery Brigade and claiming they knocked out and destroyed 175 fascist tanks.

The 11th Panzer Division, punching directly through a Soviet mechanized corps, seemed to have had a relatively easy day. The Soviet antitank defenses at height 254.5 disappeared without comment from the German records. On the whole this day, poorly documented, was both significant and disastrous for the Soviet defenders, for they had lost the second defensive line, considerable armor, and effectively had one of their mechanized corps divided by the German attack. In fact, the arrival of the 180th and 192nd Tank Brigades from the Thirty-eighth Army was probably critical to shoring up the defenses in front of the 11th Panzer Division for the next day.

From the evening of 7 July, the III Mechanized Corps' units, with the exception of the 10th Mechanized Brigade which retained its original position, "conducted a mobile defense." They stated that superior enemy forces penetrated the corps defense, pushing back the 1st Guards Tank Brigade, 49th Tank Brigade and the 3rd Mechanized Brigade to the north (and leaving the 1st and 10th Mechanized Brigades behind).

Meanwhile, the 167th Infantry Division, operating between the XLVIII Panzer Corps and the SS Panzer Corps, had managed to clear the Vorskla Ravine. The division had counted 1,437 POWs taken in the mop-up of the Vorskla-Vorskolets triangle between 5 and 7 July.

The main body of the 167th Infantry Division (about two-thirds of it) assembled near Dmitriyevka and Olkhovka during the night. The clearing operation was completed "early in the morning." After a confusing flurry of orders, at 1000 the division's new mission was to cover the army's eastern flank between Shopino and Luchki along the Lipovyii Donets, relieving elements of Totenkopf there, and to oppose any Soviet crossings of the river. The division spent the rest of the day preparing for its eastward move to the Donets. No Soviet attacks were reported.

Evening Planning

So ended the day for the XLVIII Panzer Corps. At this point, the German attack had penetrated the second defensive line and was pushing, in the face of significant resistance, towards Oboyan. There is an impression that the German commanders felt during the morning that the Soviet defense in front of them had been defeated. By the afternoon, they had learned otherwise. At 1928, the army stated that there would be no new operation orders for the next day. The XLVIII Panzer Corps should continue to advance to the north in close contact with the SS Panzer Corps. The German orders stated that "The tank battle must be fought out" and that it was possible that in the next few days the Soviets would introduce their reserves!

Still, it is clear the German Army was somewhat confused as to what they were really facing. At 1930, the SS Panzer Corps reported that it had captured a Soviet map showing the deployment of the Soviet formations, including the VI Tank Corps, III Mechanized Corps, one brigade and five tank regiments. At 2000, the army command reported that the Soviet V and VI Tank Corps were advancing south on both sides of the highway from Oboyan to Yakovlevo. They had also identified the II Guards Tank Corps across the Lipovyii Donets. Hoth expressed the opinion that the Soviet tank forces should not be attacked frontally, but should be double enveloped (as usual) by the XLVIII Panzer and SS Panzer Corps.

Even with the captured map, the Germans were still somewhat confused as to who and what they were facing where. This probably is what led to the odd order at 2015, when the corps ordered 11th Panzer Division and Gross Deutschland Division to commence construction of a defense line from the outskirts of Pokrovka to the Sukhaya Woods to Krasnaya Dubrova. It does foreshadow the tactical defensive halts that the Germans would resort to later in the battle.

At 2040 the SS Panzer Corps was ordered to advance immediately so that it could cut off the attacking elements of the Soviet V Guards Tank Corps from its rear echelon and push them towards the west, while the XLVIII Panzer Corps was to break through the Soviet defense near Syirtsevo and by attacking north prevent the withdrawal of Soviet troops to Oboyan. The 3rd Panzer Division, after breaking through the Soviet position on the Pena River east of Berezovka, was to attack north. This ambitious encirclement plan was not immediately executed, for at 2200 the corps was again issuing orders for the next day's attack.

The end of the day summary (at 2400) from the corps concluded that it was now obvious that the Soviets had prepared a deeply echeloned defense system which they were defending stubbornly. South of the Psel River, the Soviets had already committed their reserves, the First Tank Army. It was hoped that tomorrow, 8 July, if the encirclement operation succeeded and the Soviet tank army was destroyed, then the XLVIII Panzer Corps would not meet any more strong Soviet reserve forces in its advance to and across the Psel River. One is left with the impression that the Germans were planning on crossing the Psel the day after tomorrow, if not tomorrow.

Meanwhile the Soviets continued to shift and move forces in front of the German advance, with the Sixth Guards Army now having taken over control of the 309th Rifle Division from the Fortieth Army along with other antitank and artillery units.

SS Panzer Corps

It was now the third day of the offensive and the SS Panzer Corps was still shooting for the objectives that they had planned on reaching the first day of the battle. Needless to say, these original plans were very optimistic.

The Adolf Hitler SS Division started with an attack on Yakovlevo at first light. Its march route at Yablochki (on the way to Luchki) had been blocked during the night so it was also forced to clear it. Both the Adolf Hitler and Das Reich SS Divisions continued their attack to the north and northwest this day at 0600 after a Stuka preparation.

At 0850 the division reported that around 30 tanks had broken through from the northwest against Luchki

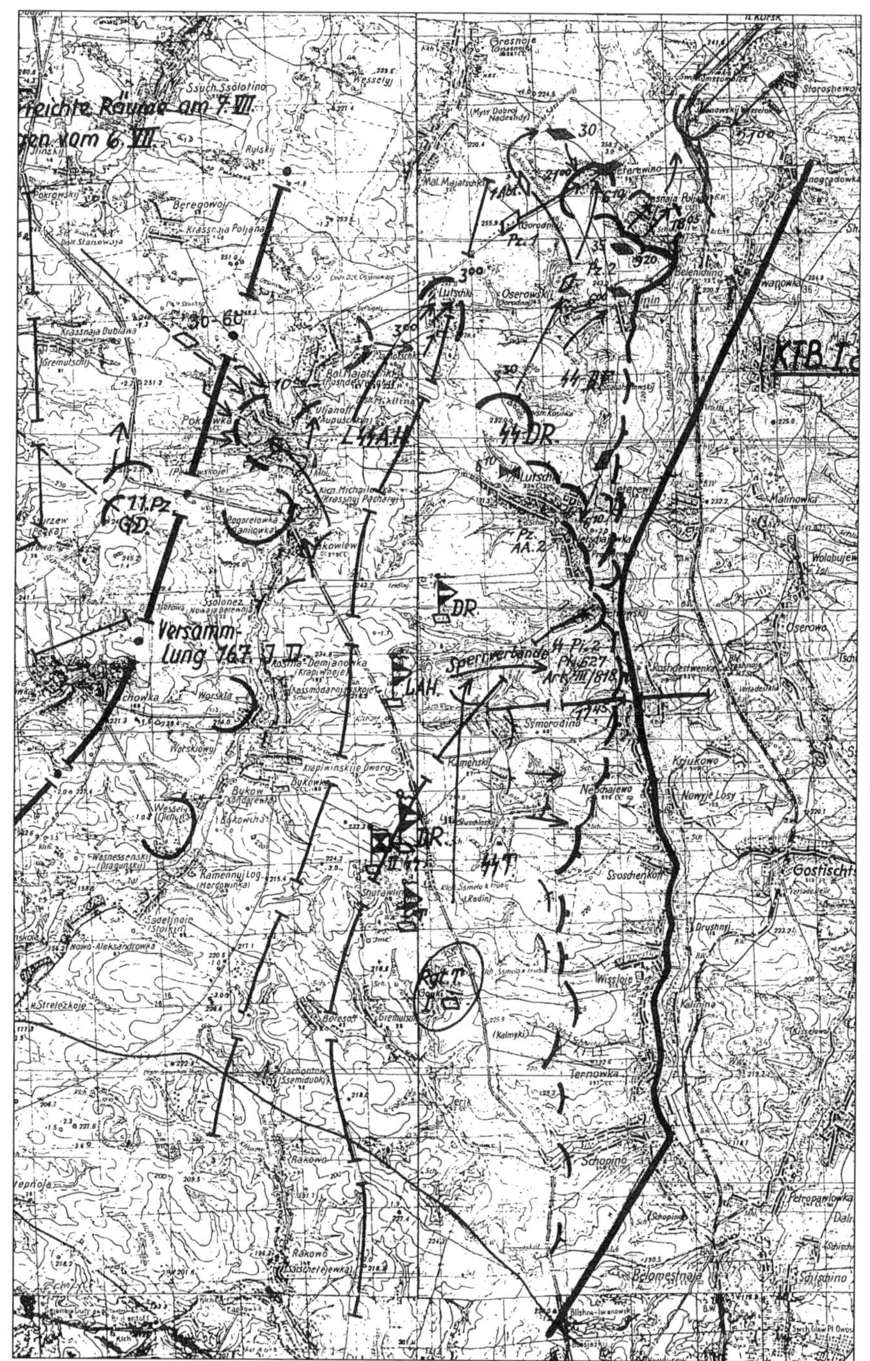

THE SS PANZER CORPS MAP SHOWING POSITIONS ON THE 7TH OF JULY.

(north) but that this attack was repelled. The division spent the rest of the day engaged in heavy defensive fighting against Soviet tank attacks from that direction. This was certainly the XXXI Tank Corps, commanded by Major General Dmitrii Cherniyenko. The division was greatly aided in this defense by the Luftwaffe.

The Das Reich SS Division, having broken through the second defense line the previous day, was now ready to expand and exploit this breakthrough. However, the division was forced to make an early morning counter-attack to win back Petrovskii, as the Soviets had retaken it during the night. It then had the reconnaissance battalion and the Der Fuehrer SS Regiment secure the division's right flank with a line from Nechayevka to height 210.7 to Kalinin.

At 0330, the panzer group moved out to attack Teterevino (north) with the objective of taking and securing that town and the area to its east and north. At 0610, the panzer regiment was locked in a tank fight in Kalinin and Teterevino (north). Soviet tanks were also attacking the reconnaissance battalion at Nechayevka from the north. There were also heavy bombing attacks on Luchki.

Around 1030, the panzer regiment at Teterevino was attacked by about 30 Soviet tanks from the northwest and from Yasnaya Polyana (V Guards Tank Corps). After a difficult fight, around 1200 the Soviets withdrew to the north. During the battle, the panzer group from the Adolf Hitler SS Division shielded to the north and the east. The SS Panzer Corps intelligence officer noted that the Soviet attacks on the 7th showed less planning than the attacks on the 6th and that this resulted in high tank losses for the Soviets.

The V Guards Tank Corps reported that in the morning its defensive line ran from the MTS (Machine and Tractor Station) at Belenikhino to Leski to height 225.0. This was off to the east side of the SS Panzer Corps along the Sazhnovskii Donets. There were now no armored forces to the north of the advancing SS Panzer Corps. After yesterday's losses of 110 tanks, this tank corps was probably down to around 61 T-34s, 35 T-70s and 8 Churchills. As a result of their withdrawal yesterday, the V Guards Tank Corps was now off to the side of the German advance and in more defensible positions. This effectively left the area from Belenikhino to Malyie Mayachki, some eight kilometers, wide open, with little to hold up the Germans.

The Adolf Hitler SS Division's front line at the end of the day ran from the area west of Ivanovskii Vyiselok to Luchki (north) to Yablochki (inclusive) to Pokrovka (inclusive). The Soviet infantry in front of the Adolf Hitler and Das Reich SS Divisions appears to have withdrawn, been pushed aside, or just disappeared during the day. It also appears that parts of the 51st Guards Rifle Division were isolated near Teterevino (south) by the advance of the Adolf Hitler and the Das Reich SS Divisions. The Adolf Hitler SS Division's advance from Luchki through Teterevino to height 258.2 appears to have been against limited resistance, with most of the fighting occurring on the division's left flank against the XXXI Tank Corps. The Das Reich SS Division's push from the south in the morning against Teterevino looks to have cleared the way for the Adolf Hitler SS Division's advance.

To help protect the right flank of the SS Panzer Corps, which would extend by the end of this day to some 30 kilometers across Totenkopf and Das Reich's front, the Totenkopf SS Division moved up to and then went over to the defense on the hills west of the Lipovyii Donets. During the night, strong Soviet tank forces had crossed the Lipovyii Donets into the area of Rozhdestvenka, the hills east of Smorodino and Nepkhayevo. At 0430, Totenkopf kicked off an attack against these forces. By 1030, this flank had been secured. The Soviets had been thrown back to the eastern bank of the Lipovyii Donets and by 1130 the Totenkopf SS Division had advanced in a broad front to take the high ground two kilometers west of the river.

At 0530 on the 8th, Lt. General A. D. Shtevnev (Deputy Commander of the Front for Armored Forces) delivered a Front command order instructing the II Guards Tank Corps to "launch an attack in the direction of Luchki, and, in conjunction with the X Tank Corps, V Guards Tank Corps, and II Tank Corps, surround and destroy the enemy northwest of Luchki and to then develop the attack in the direction of Luchki-Gonki and reach the area of Gonki."

The Soviets still had relatively strong forces to conduct this attack. The V Guards Tank Corps and II Guards Tank Corps had been pulled from the front line and

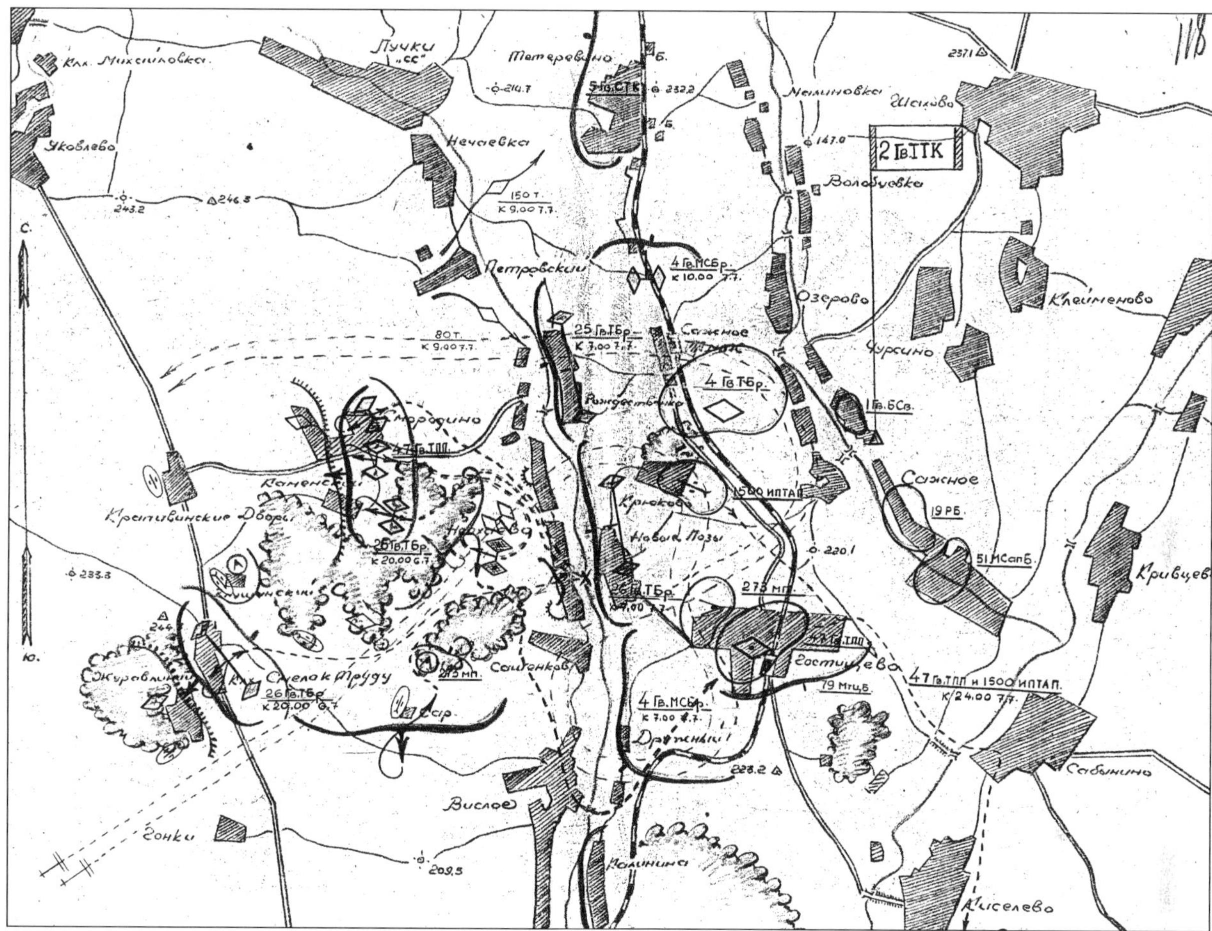

II Guards Tank Corps map for 2400, 7 July 1943.

were in position to launch attacks the following day. The X Tank Corps had just arrived on the battlefield. On this day, they had been subordinated to the Voronezh Front (although they were already on the move), and by 1700 were in the area of Prokhorovka (the soon-to-be-famous one). This was a powerful force, with some 99 T-34s, 64 T-70s, 12 SU-152s and 9 SU-76s. The II Tank Corps was also a new arrival, having come from the Southwestern Front and assigned to the Voronezh Front on the 7th. It assembled in the area of Pravorot and Krasnoye and then moved to the Vinogradovka area on the 8th. It was probably not really positioned for offensive operations that day, but was used as such regardless.[40]

40 It is debatable whether the II Tank Corps would have been able to effectively attack on the 8th. It was still moving up at that time. It did not begin movement to the battlefield until the 7th and concentrated in the Vinogradovka area on the morning of the 8th after a 200 kilometer march. Still, it did attack on the afternoon of the 8th, with little useful effect.

It had at least 168 tanks ready for action.[41] So unlike the rather anemic pincher attack tried on the 6th, using the II Guards Tank Corps and only two brigades from the III Mechanized Corps, this attack would have the full weight of three strong tank corps. The V Guards Tank Corps was considerably weakened from yesterday's fighting, with an estimated force of 61 T-34s, 35 T-70s and 8 Churchills, but the II Guards Tank Corps was in better shape with 82 T-34s and 54 T-70s (not counting the corps reserve of 30 tanks located well to the rear at Bubnovo, 70 kilometers east-northeast of Belgorod, nor the five Churchills from the heavy regiment, which had been separated from the corps).

Still, it is hard to fathom the reasoning behind attacking the SS Panzer Corps when its attacks had yet to be stopped. Furthermore, the objectives of the attack, Luchki and Gonki, were fairly limited. Any envelopments were going to be tactical. This was an attack without a clear purpose. Meanwhile, the SS Panzer Corps was continuing to push forward.

III Panzer Corps

The III Panzer Corps had now deployed, from west to east, the 168th Infantry Division, the 19th Panzer Division, the 6th Panzer Division and the 7th Panzer Division. Two of the three panzer divisions were now attacking to the north and northeast (see the 1:50000 scale maps M-37-38-V (map sheet 14), M-37-38-G (map sheet 15), M-37-50-A (map sheet 16) and M-37-50-B (map sheet 17) in the map section of the area from Shopino to Batratskaya Dacha).

In the original German planning, the actual right flank of the Provisional Army Kempf attack east of the Donets extended all the way to the Koren River. This, of course, required breaking the Seventh Guards Army's second defensive line, which was very much part of the responsibility of Corps Raus. This clearly was not going to happen, so a new German defensive line for the army's eastern flank was being assembled in front of the Soviet Seventh Guards Army's second defensive line. Soviet forces were collecting in the woods between Krutoi Log and Batratskaya Dacha and these needed to be cleared to allow for an organized defensive line. Therefore, the division was ordered for this day to push in concert with Corps Raus to seize the wooded area southwest of height 216.1 and also to attack east of the Razumnaya to Mazikino (five kilometers beyond Melekhovo). At 0615, the 7th Panzer Division continued its attack in the woods northeast of Krutoi Log. No other reports were found for this German division for this day, leaving this day's account incomplete.

The Soviet position to the north of the III Panzer Corps was weak. Much like the XLVIII Panzer Corps had been able to do, the III Panzer Corps was now running on the high ground between the two Soviet echelons. The choice of the routes was initially defined by the course of the Razumnaya and the gullies and forests bounding the south and east side of the area of advance. The terrain led the III Panzer Corps to advance to the northeast and then turn north, some ten to fourteen kilometers beyond the Donets.

Corps Raus

The Seventh Guards Army was putting up a solid line of troops in the area running from Batratskaya Dacha and due south. This turned into a classic infantry fight, with little armor involved on either side. The 73rd Guards Rifle Division, part of the XXV (25th)

41 The II Tank Corps had ready-for-action on the 9th 70 T-34s, 56 T-70s and 11 Churchills. It had 21 tanks in repair (12 T-34s, 7 T-70s and 2 Churchills), with two of the three brigades indicating that they were probably broken down during the march to battle, and that is assumed to be the case for the other brigade. It lost at least 31 tanks on the 8th (for more details see Chapters Eleven and Thirteen in my original book *Kursk: The Battle of Prokhorovka*), in addition to those recorded as broken down. Therefore, this corps started with at least 189 tanks and maybe had as many as 208 (65 per regiment according to Ivanovskii, plus 13 Churchills). If the corps was full strength, one could expect it to have 218 tanks, with 134 T-34s, 63 T-70s and 21 Churchills.

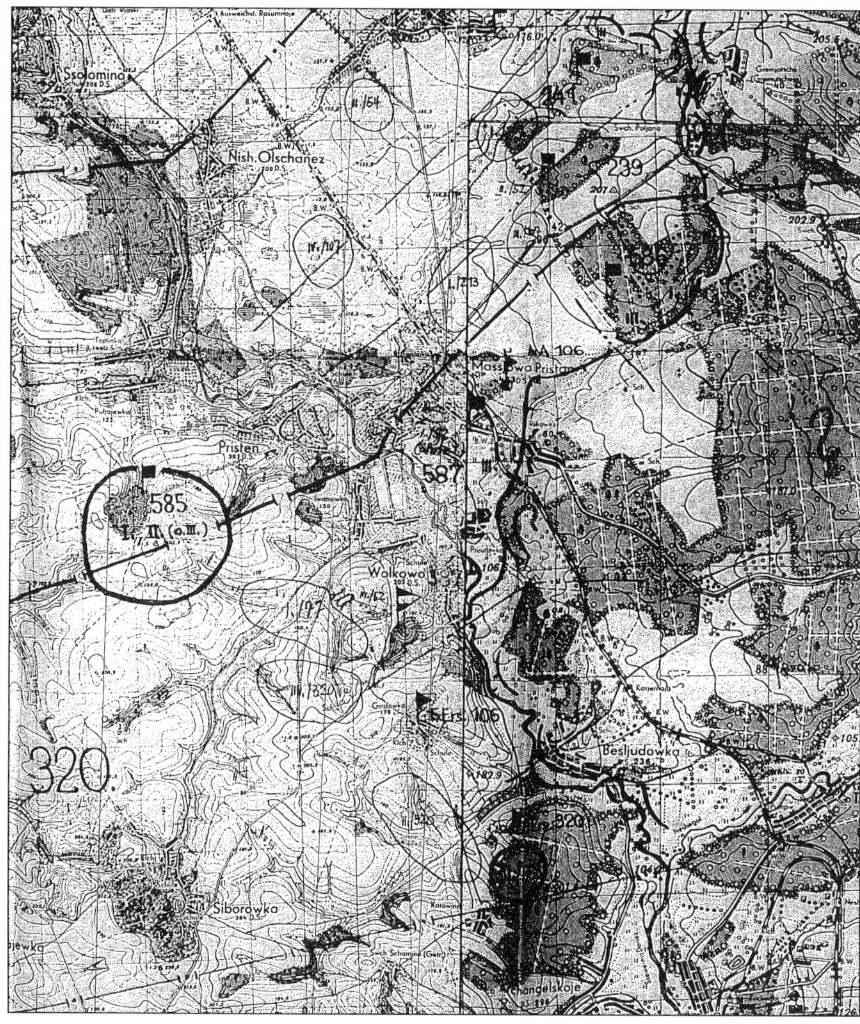

Corps Raus: 7 July, 1800 hours.

Guards Rifle Corps, extended from Solovyev Kolkhoz to Batratskaya Dacha to Gremyachii. It had two regiments of the 78th Guards Rifle Division and the 30th Antitank Brigade under its command along with the lend-lease equipped 201st Tank Brigade (armed with over 30 British Matildas and Valentines) and the 1529th Heavy Self-Propelled Artillery Regiment with 10 Su-152s.

South of Gremycchii was the XXIV (24th) Guards Rifle Corps, now consisting of four divisions (36th Guards, 72nd Guards, 111th and 213th). The 72nd Guards Rifle Division was stretched from Polyana to Bezlyudovka, while by the end of the day the 213th Rifle Division ended up stretched from Korenskaya Dacha to the Nezhegol River. The units from these two divisions were intermingled. The 27th Tank Brigade was stretched from Polyana to Rzhavets to the grove east of Priyutovka, still maintaining a combat strength of 35 T-34s and 5 T-70s. To the south, facing the inactive XLII Corps and deployed in two echelons, were the 36th Guards Rifle Division and the 111th Rifle Division.

Corps Raus was attacking this force with only two infantry divisions, the 106th and 320th. They were supported seven battalions of artillery and by the 905th Assault Gun Battalion and 393rd Assault Gun Battery.

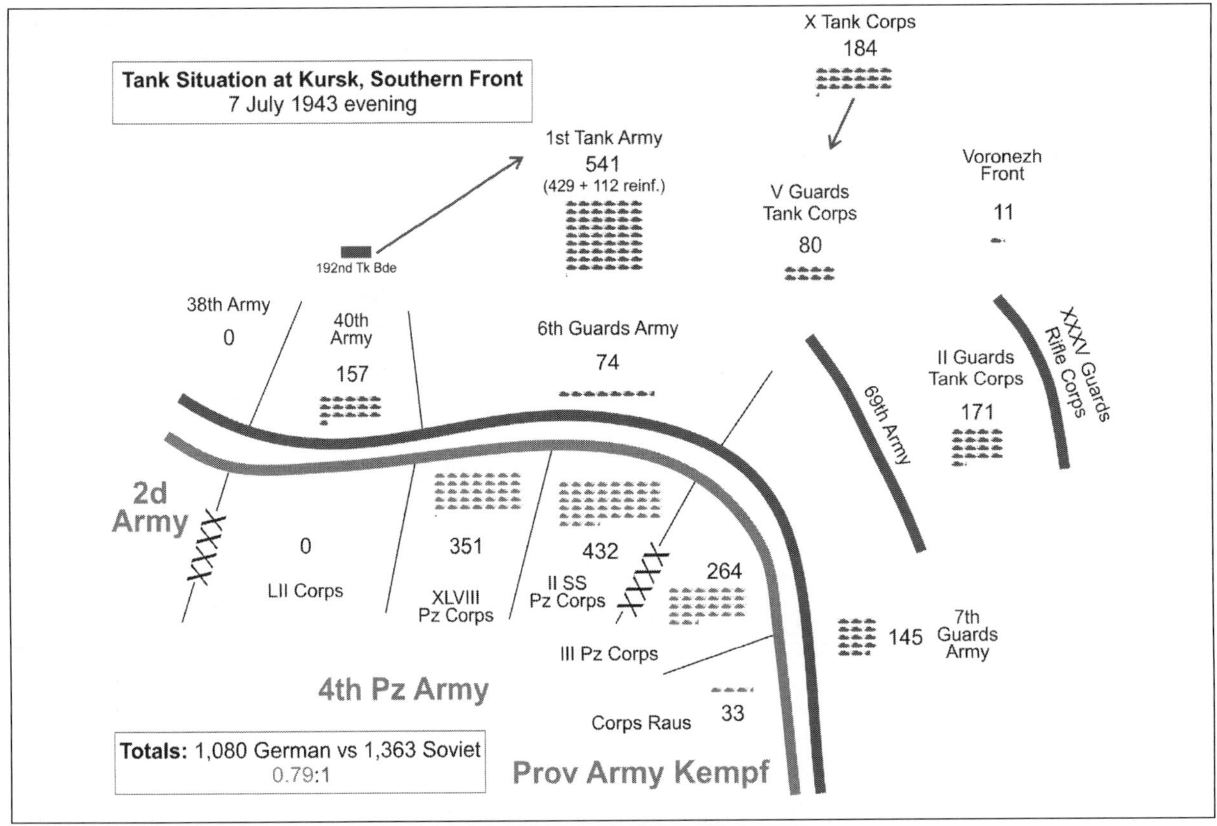

The battalion started with 23 Sturmgeschuetz IIIs and 9 Sturmhaubitzes while the battery had another 10 Sturmgeschuetz IIIs. The 320th Infantry Division had already withdrawn its 585th Infantry Regiment to the west side of the Donets River, to rest and recover.

For the period of 5 to 7 July, the Seventh Guards Army reported losing 12,158 men killed, wounded and missing, 82 tanks, 21 self-propelled guns, 33 120mm Mortars, 81 45mm Mortars, 63 76mm guns, 11 122mm guns and 4 152mm guns. Shumilov finally rolled over to the defense. His plans for the next day were to exhaust the Germans in defensive fighting and, with the arrival of the XXXV Guards Rifle Corps, take the offensive.

At this point, the Corps Raus attack had effectively ground to a halt. The 106th Infantry Division had made limited attacks and a limited advance of around two kilometers against the Seventh Guards Army second defensive line, while the 320th Infantry Division had completely stalled and was reduced to two effective regiments, with its southernmost regiment having been pulled back across the Donets. The III Panzer Corps was supposed to be covering the flank of the SS Panzer Corps, but this was far from occurring. The 7th Panzer Division was now covering the eastern flank of the III Panzer Corps. At a cost of around 4,281 casualties over the three days, the value of what these two divisions were providing to the offensive operation was extremely limited. It would have certainly reduced German casualties if the 106th had followed behind the 7th Panzer Division instead of conducting its own river crossing. It also would have been as effective in covering the flank while the 320th could have covered the rest of the area south of Solomino from the west bank of the Donets. This river crossing, while it may have been useful if the divisions could have reached their planned objectives, was in fact fairly useless and expensive, as it developed.

Both of these divisions had crossed against significant, well-entrenched Soviet forces backed by armor. Furthermore, not only did they not have air support, their enemy did. Under these circumstances the ability of these units to advance and cause the casualties they did is an impressive performance. The 320th had the more difficult circumstances, and in fact seems to have been mishandled, getting the 587th Infantry Regiment rolled out of the woods by an armored attack on the 5th, then being attacked again the following day from those same woods, getting the 585th Infantry Regiment in the south gutted, and never being able to clear all the crossing points and bridges from enemy fire. Still, for a high numbered German division (meaning it was raised later in the war, often with many conscripts and not as many experienced personnel), this formation fought surprisingly well.

Summary to Date

The Germans had now effectively penetrated the main part of the Soviet's two defensive lines. What was left for them to fight in and through were intermediate positions. The two armies were now in an open field battle and almost all of the Voronezh Front reserves had moved into combat, or were to arrive shortly.

The cost of this breakthrough for the Germans was high, with some 14,187 casualties (killed, wounded and missing). They also had at least 697 tanks damaged or destroyed. In contrast, the Soviet defenders had lost 28,930 (killed, wounded and missing) for a loss ratio of 2.04 to 1, and had at least 523 tanks damaged or destroyed.

Although the Germans had penetrated the first two lines, they were two days behind schedule and were now fighting and advancing in an open field battle against the Voronezh Front. The battle had shifted to a new stage.

The Advance Continues: 8 July 1943

At this point, the Fourth Panzer Army had penetrated the first two echelons of Soviet defensive positions. Because of the depth of the Soviet works, the Sixth Guards and First Tank Armies were not fighting without some defensive structures, but fundamentally the advantage they gained in the first three days of fighting from fortified works was gone. The next defensive line was behind the Soviet forces. In the XLVIII Panzer Corps area the next defensive line was actually two lines, with one running from Kurasovka to Korocha and the rearward main defensive line running along the Psel River. While the forward line was some 16 to 22 kilometers behind the Soviet second echelon line, the crossing of the Psel at Oboyan was some 36 kilometers behind height 254.5. In the case of the SS Panzer Corps, the next defensive line was the area in front of Prokhorovka, where the Sixty-ninth Army was originally positioned. Still, these works were not anywhere near the extent or depth of the two lines the Germans had already fought through.

The Voronezh Front was in a losing battle. They had lost their defensive works. The attrition exchange was not favorable, which meant that as the battle continued, the relative strength between the two forces would continue to shift into the Germans' favor. There were two natural defensive lines, one formed by the initial front line position, which had some advantages due to the higher ground it was formed along. Behind that was the strong natural defensive line along the Pena River and extending to height 254.5 and Pokrovka. There was no clear third natural defensive line until the Psel. The positions further back were defensible, but not as defensible as the positions that the Sixth Guards Army, First Tank Army, and their supporting forces had just been rousted out of. In front of the XLVIII Panzer Corps, the width of the front, between the Pena and the Vorskla, also expanded the farther one moved toward Oboyan, except for the brief narrowing at Verkhopenye. In the case of the SS Panzer Corps, the width of the front remained relatively constant until they reached the Psel River and the area in front of Prokhorovka. So, the Soviet defense was not going to benefit from compression of their forces as they were forced farther back.

The one advantage the Soviet forces did have was that they still held very significant defensive positions on the west and east flanks of the German positions. It was here that the battle developed its own peculiar taste,

Portion of III Mechanized Corps map showing the situation for 8 July.

with each panzer corps taking a different approach. In the case of XLVIII Panzer Corps, it ended up crossing over the Pena River to its west and getting tangled up in fighting on that flank, while the SS Panzer Corps choose to place defending forces on its eastern flank and continued pushing forward, leading to a fight in a narrow corridor and to the Battle of Prokhorovka.

In response to the degrading defensive situation, Vatutin and the Sixth Guards Army organized a large attack for this morning, which was supposed to pinch off the German attack by making thrusts from their defensive positions in the east and west against the base of the Fourth Panzer Army. The XXIII Guards Rifle Corps (51st Guards, 52nd Guards, and 375th Rifle Divisions), V Guards and II Guards Tank Corps were to attack in the east along with the newly arriving X and II Tank Corps. This attack was under the overall command of the deputy army commander, Major General P. F. Lagutin. The X and II Tank Corps were to attack from the Vasilyevka and Vinogradovka line in the direction of Yakovlevo and Byikovka. The V Guards Tank Corps was to launch from its positions from Belenikhino to the outskirts of Teterevino against Ozerovskii. The II Guards Tank Corps was to attack from Rozhdestvenka against Luchki. The attack was to be supported by units of the Sixty-ninth Army attacking from the area northeast of Teterevino. From the Fortieth Army would be a two division attack by the 161st Rifle Division and the 71st Guards Rifle Division, which was now attached to that army, in the direction of Gertsovka. The VI Tank Corps was to attack from the Syirtsevo region toward Yakovlevo.[42] The orders for this attack were issued by Vatutin at 2300 on the 7th.[43] The offensive was to begin at 1030 (Moscow time) after a 30-minute artillery preparation. The Front aviation was tasked to support these attacks.[44]

42 I. M. Chistyakov, *Po Prikazu Rodinyi* [On Orders from the Motherland] (Moscow, 1971), page 106, and Glantz and Orenstein, pages 96–97.

43 Erickson, page 104, and Glantz and Orenstein, page 96.

44 Glantz and Orenstein, page 97.

XLVIII Panzer Corps Operations

The XLVIII Panzer Corps was facing a constriction of its front in the area between Verkhopenye and the Vorskla River. After that, the terrain and width of the front expanded. It was evident that Verkhopenye needed to be removed as a defensive point so as to allow the attack to go forward. The Soviets still held significant positions along the Pena, running from Mikhailovka to Verkhopenye. While the river was not very significant, the hills on the Soviet side of the bank were. Added to that, once those positions were penetrated, the area behind the positions consisted of an entangling collection of villages and wooded areas. This position could, and did, serve to constrict the frontage of the German attack, and by its existence, force the Germans to expend effort to clear it. So, not only was the XLVIII Panzer Corps forced to attack forward, but also had to attack to the west. This was a diversion from its main line of attack, and as such weakened its main attack. Again, the terrain, although it might be considered by some to be open and rolling, was in fact shaping the battle in a significant way.

Finally, the Voronezh Front shifted the V Guards Tank Corps to this front after it had been depleted fighting against the SS Panzer Corps. This unit fought the SS on the 8th. On the evening of the 10th of July it was then shifted over to the far left flank of the XLVIII Panzer Corps and re-entered battle on the 12th, on the attack!

Other forces from outside the Voronezh Front also contributed to stopping the XLVIII Panzer Corps. The most significant of these was the X Tank Corps from the Fifth Guards Army. This unit was alerted on the evening of the 5th and actually began moving to the battlefield on the 7th. It arrived at 1700 in the Prokhorovka area and by 2100 had shifted over to cover the Psel to the west of Prokhorovka and to cover Prokhorovka. There it remained, not seeing combat, until the morning of the 9th. It then shifted two tank brigades to the west and reinforced the line at Kruglik and Kalinovka, with its lead elements arriving around 1600 on the 9th. The motorized infantry brigade and one tank brigade remained in the Psel area on the 9th, and then the other tank brigade joined its compatriots to face off against the XLVIII Panzer Corps.

Later additions to the battle against the XLVIII Panzer Corps included the 13th and 66th Guards Rifle Divisions from the Fifth Guards Army, both units arriving in the area on the 11th and attacking the following day. Overall, with the significant exception of the X Tank Corps, the XLVIII Panzer Corps penetration was fought mostly with Voronezh Front assets, with most of them in place and ready for battle on the 12th of July.

Still, the situation as of the morning of the 8th was not promising for the Voronezh Front. Blocking the road to Oboyan were now only five brigade-sized formations, some of them very depleted. The major forces of the Sixth Guards and First Tank Armies had been pushed to the side of the advance. With the XLVIII Panzer Corps having three armored divisions available to freely maneuver, a significant breakthrough to Oboyan was definitely possible. What actually occurred was a bizarre exercise in operational and tactical errors by both sides that resulted in a very confused fight over terrain of questionable value.

The 3rd Panzer Division continued its attack in the morning but not from its crossing at Lukhanino, but from point 0.8, two kilometers northeast of Lukhanino. It had shifted forces there during the night and the attacked at dawn. At the same time, the Gross Deutschland Division continued it attacks on Syirtsevo. It took most of the day for these two divisions to clear these areas south of Verkhopenye. Meanwhile elements of the Gross Deutschland Division took the village of Gremuchii and then advanced on Verkhopenye from the east, taking most of it. The Germans had now secured most of the areas up the Psel River, leaving the VI Tank Corps and parts of the III Mechanized Corps behind the river and on their flank. Meanwhile the 11th Panzer Division held position until just past noon, having built defensive works the night before. Now that the Gross Deutschland Division had pulled "level" with it, it proceeded to advance north, and established flank contact with the SS Panzer Corps.

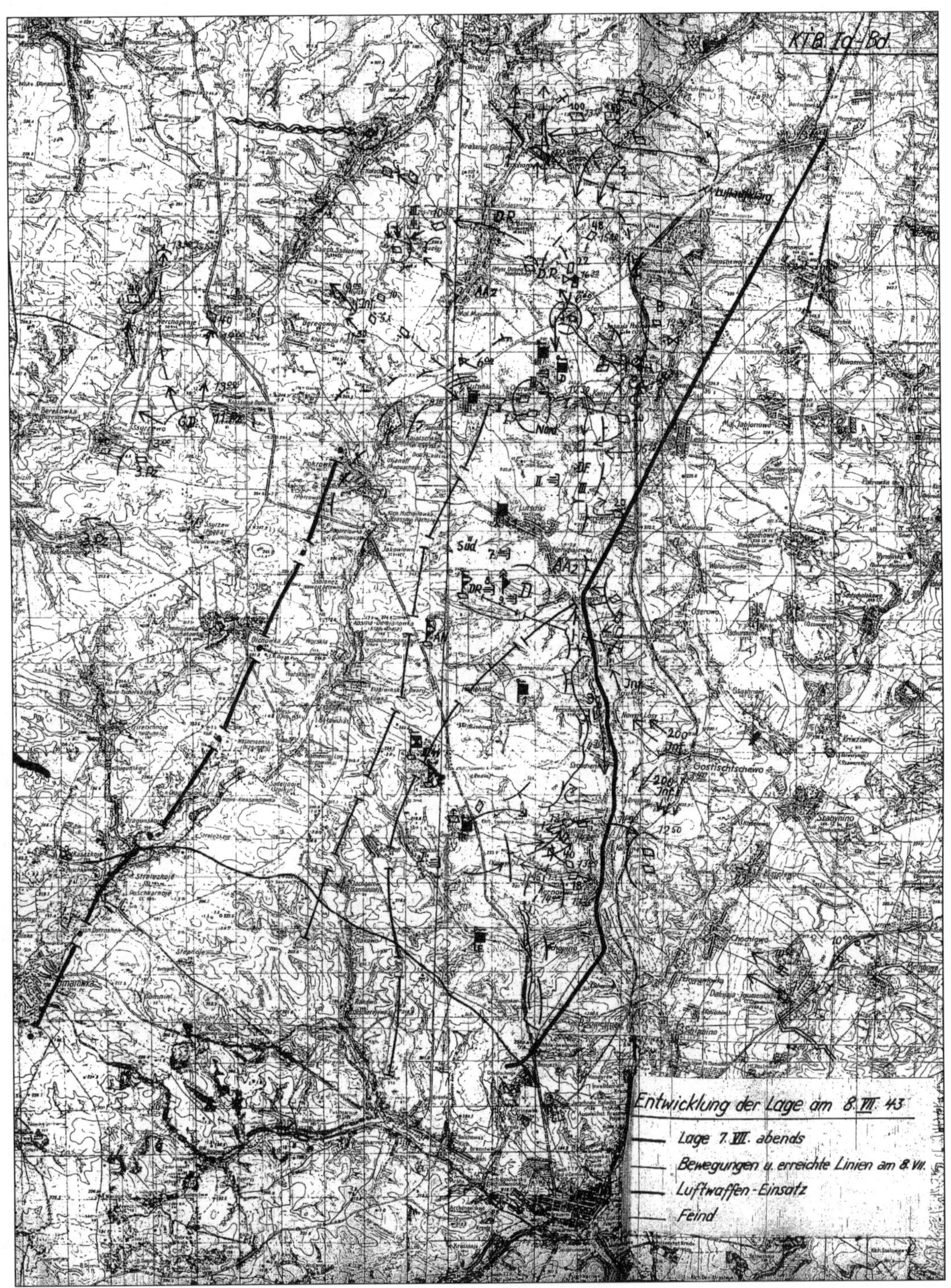

The SS Panzer Corps map showing positions on the 8th of July.

SS Panzer Corps

As a result of the battles over the last two days, the XXXI Tank Corps found itself out of position, withdrawing to the northwest, with the 11th Panzer Division to its south. This created in the mind of General Hoth (the Fourth Panzer Army commander) an opportunity to envelop significant Soviet armored forces. These Soviet tank forces, primarily the XXXI Tank Corps, were accumulating in and around the Vorskla River from Pokrovka and to the north. To encircle them required the SS and XLVIII Panzer Corps to coordinate, and get at least one or more elements around each flank. The SS Panzer Corps was ordered this day was to "push forward so as to cut off the Soviet armor from its rear and push those elements to the west." This was not a particularly useful attempt. First, the rear of the XXXI Tank Corps was to its west. Second, as the XXXI Tank Corps really was only three tank brigades with little other supporting forces, there wasn't much of a rear to get to. Third, it required the help of the 11th Panzer Division to complete the encirclement. The 11th Panzer Division was still quite busy dealing with the elements of the III Mechanized Corps and the various reinforcing tank brigades in front of it. So, while the SS Panzer Corps may have had the freedom to maneuver and try to conduct envelopments, no such luxury existed for the 11th Panzer Division.

What the Germans ended up doing this day was attempting a single-arm envelopment of the smallest tank corps in the battle, while still leaving four tank corps on their right flank. The XLVIII Panzer Corps, which was to help, was in fact getting ready to commit most of its forces to moving west also, meaning away from this operation. As such, this effort turned into a northwest push, which, while helping to clear the flank, did little other than that and distracted the SS Panzer Corps from its primary objective. This attack resulted in the Adolf Hitler and Das Reich SS Divisions heading northwest.

The Voronezh Front's handling of armor could not have been more confused. At the start of the battle, it had five armored corps in the rear. On the 5th, the First Tank Army was moved up (with three corps), arriving into position that evening. The X Tank Corps was also activated on this day. The afternoon of the 5th, the Voronezh Front then moved its other three tank corps (V Guards, II Guards, and the newly attached X Tank Corps), with the V and II Guards arriving in position on the morning of the 6th.

At that point, Vatutin tried to launch an all-out attack with all five tank corps. This was the attack that Katukov (First Tank Army) had intervened directly with Stalin to get canceled. That afternoon, the Voronezh Front then tried to snip off the SS Panzer Corps' advance with a pincher attack with the II Guards Tank Corps and elements of the III Mechanized Corps. This naturally failed, because it was simply not strong enough of an attack. Meanwhile, the V Guards Tank Corps moved up to a position behind the second line of infantry, so that it would not become engaged until after this infantry line was broken. It then attacked without any real air or artillery support, and little infantry. Then after getting major elements enveloped by the SS, it withdrew, leaving the left flank of the First Tank Army hanging, forcing them to commit the weak XXXI Tank Corps to cover that flank.

On the morning of the 8th, the Voronezh Front then tried to launch an attack with four tanks corps (including the newly arriving X Tank Corps and II Tank Corps). This turned into a two corps attack, with later piecemeal attacks by the II Tank Corps.

Katukov was correct in getting the attack on the 6th canceled. If Vatutin's planned attack with five armored corps did not make sense, then his pincher attack with one and a half armored corps made even less sense. The attack on the 8th with four tank corps made more sense, but what actually happened, which was an attack with two tank corps, made no sense at all.

While there were considerable tactical problems in the handling of the First Tank Army's armor, there was at least some sound, fundamental logic behind its placement and actions. However, the positioning and behavior of the rest of the Voronezh Front's armor made little

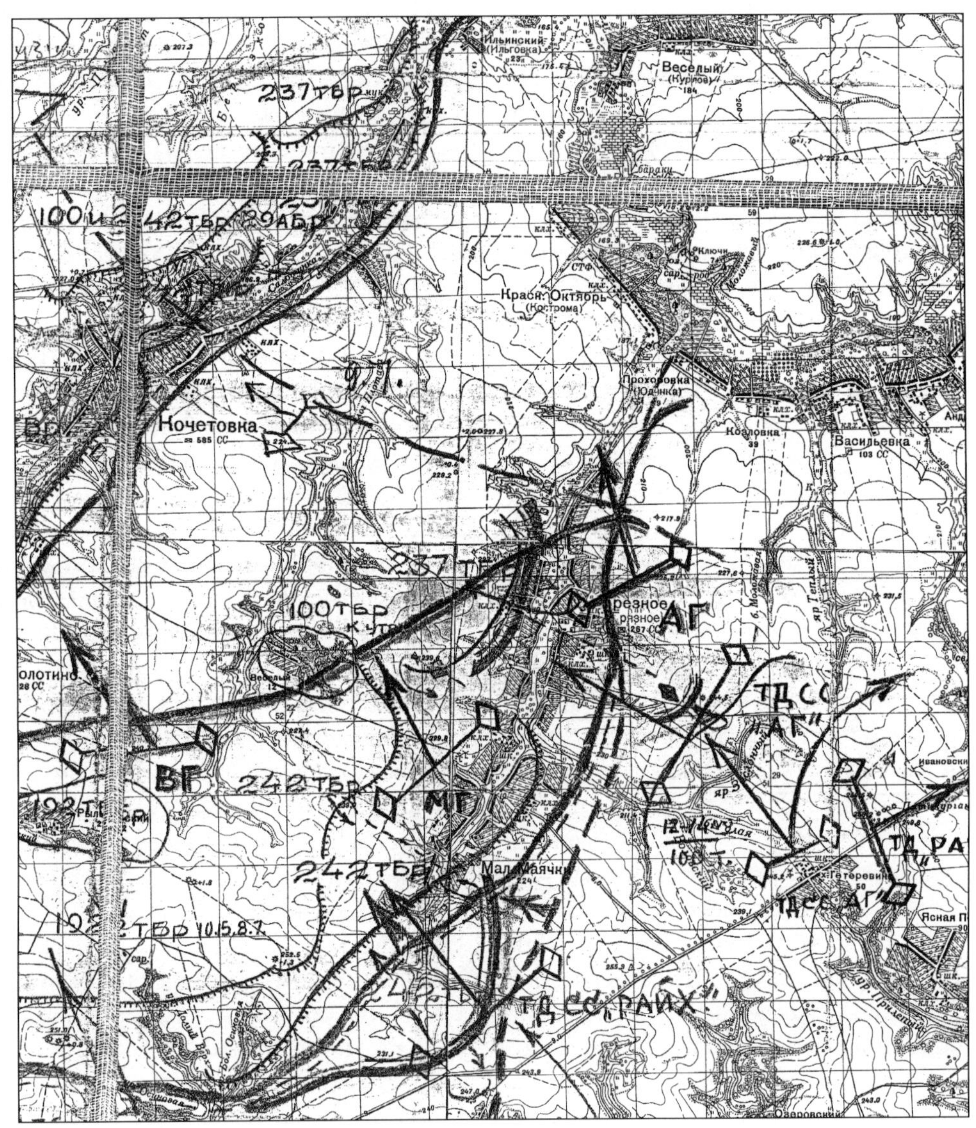

XXXI Tank Corps positions around the 8th of July.

sense. This includes the failure to place the V Guards Tank Corps in the Sixth Guards Army second echelon, the disastrous counterattack with the V Guards Tank Corps on the 6th, the counterattack with the II Guards Tank Corps on the afternoon of the 6th, the withdrawal of the V Guards Tank Corps exposing the First Tank Army flank, the "backfield" shuffle of the X Tank Corps so that it did not really see combat until the 10th, and finally the piecemeal attacks by the II and V Guards Tank Corps on the 8th and the piecemeal attack from the march by the II Tank Corps.

The blame for much of this must go to Vatutin and Chistyakov. The pincher attack on the 6th was ordered by Vatutin and Chistyakov, and the positioning of these tank corps was done by Vatutin. The scale of the disaster would only have been worse if Katukov had not gotten Stalin to override the counterattack orders on the 6th. The attack ordered by Chistyakov on the 8th was also a very poor idea, and as it included elements outside the Sixth Guards Army, was clearly done under the overall direction of Vatutin. Kravchenko, the V Guards Tank Corps commander, appears to have been forced into attacking (and threatened with being shot if he disobeyed), so it is hard to assign him much blame. One does note a lower level of casualties in the neighboring II Guards Tank Corps, commanded by Colonel Alexei S. Burdeinyii, even though both corps launched attacks on the 6th and 8th (see discussion below on the II Guards Tank Corps attack). Burdeinyii seems to have been very careful about husbanding his resources. One does note, though, that Burdeinyii's attack was not launched at 1030 as was the V Guards Tank Corps', but came later, at 1200. This non-synchronized attack was also noted in the 1944 General Staff Study, but no reason was given for it.[45]

Portion of map showing positions of the X Tank Corps and its brigades around Prokhorovka and Psel River for 1700 on 7 July and 2100 on 8 July.

45 See Glantz and Orenstein, page 98.

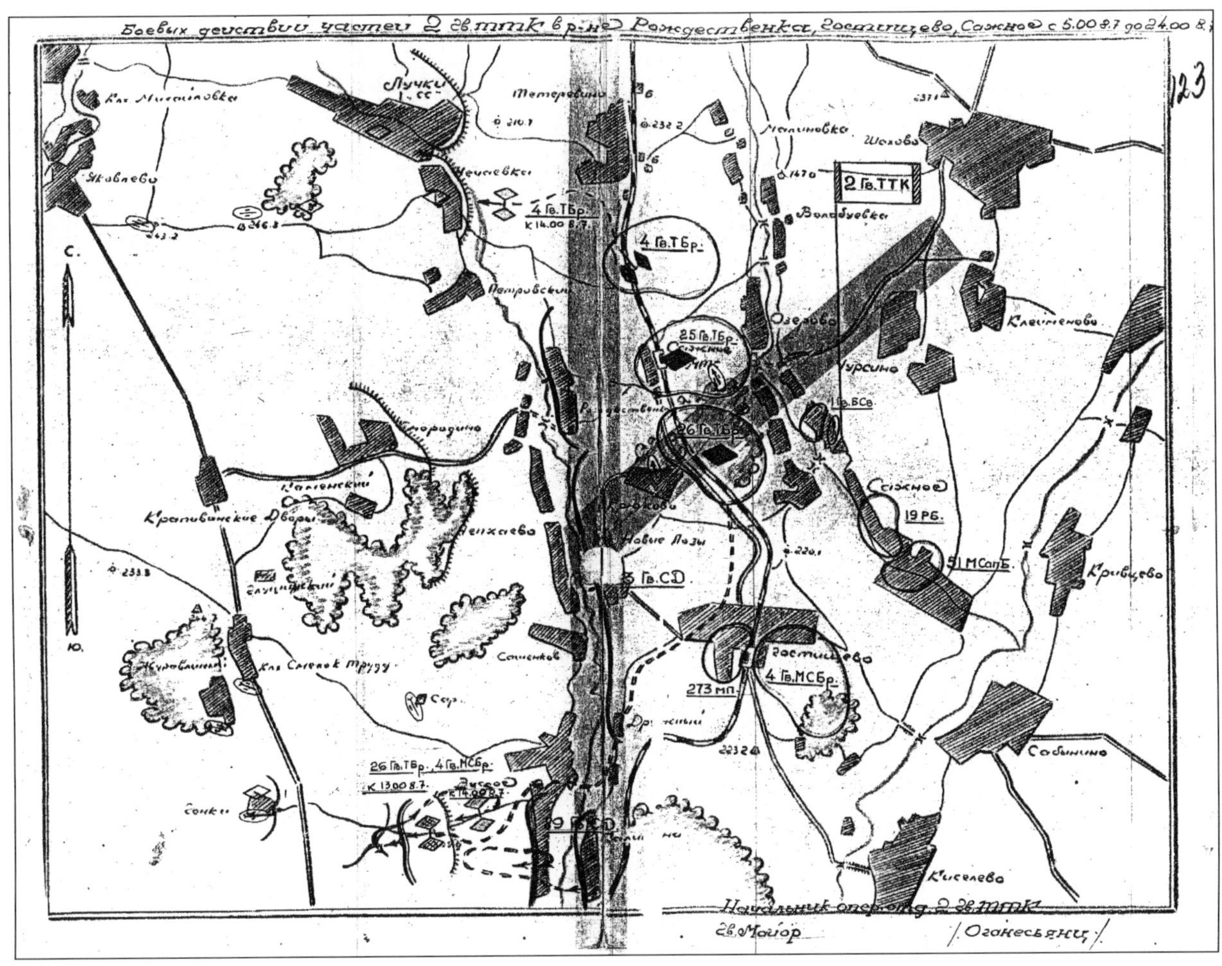

II GUARDS TANK CORPS MAP FROM 0500, 8 JULY 1943, TO 2400, 8 JULY 1943.

Analysis of the Armor Exchange

The interesting aspect of the II Guards Tank Corps operations was that although it had been in action since the 6th, and had launched two major attacks, it was still relatively strong. See Table 3.1 on the following page for a simple comparison of losses from the 5th to the 8th of July across all the Soviet armored formations facing the Fourth Panzer Army.

The opposing German armor had also been attrited at similar rates or lesser rates, especially if one ignores the Panther regiment. See Table 3.2.

We can make a rough comparison here. For the sake of simplicity, XXXI Tank Corps is considered to have faced off against the SS Panzer Corps for this period, while III Mechanized Corps is considered opposite the XLVIII Panzer Corps for this period, less two brigades (1st Guards Tank Brigade and 49th Tank Brigade) fighting the Adolf Hitler SS Division on the 6th and 7th. The two brigades of the III Mechanized Corps that were primarily engaged with the SS Panzer Corps on the 6th and 7th had committed 94 T-34s and 9 T-70s and T-60s with a loss of around 77 T-34s, 5 T-70s, and 1 T-60 over the two days. See Table 3.3.

Here, what is being shown is that in the first four days

TABLE 3.1
SOVIET TANK STRENGTH OPPOSITE THE FOURTH PANZER ARMY, 4 AND 8 JULY 1943

	Total Tanks 4 July	*Total Tanks 8 July*	*Percent of Original Strength*
REMAINING IN FORTIETH ARMY AREA			
59th Tank Rgt	22	22	100
60th Tank Rgt	35	28	80
FIRST TANK ARMY AREA			
VI Tank Corps	164	87	53
1461st SP Artillery Rgt	21	14	67
III Mechanized Corps	231	67	29
86th Tank Bde	62	49	79
180th Tank Bde	72	14	19
192nd Tank Bde	55**	49	89
XXXI Tank Corps	184	120*	65
230th Tank Rgt	39**	9	23
1440th SP Artillery Rgt	21	4	19
EAST OF VORSKLA RIVER			
V Guards Tank Corps	211	43	20
II Guards Tank Corps	187	155	83
II Tank Corps	208	137	66
245th Tank Rgt	39***	6	15
96th Tank Bde	51	46	90
NOT YET SERIOUSLY ENGAGED[46]			
X Tank Corps	184	184	100
203rd Tank Rgt	11	11	100
1689th SP AT Art Rgt	20	17	85
	1817	1062	58

* Exact strength on the 8th is not known. This figure is an estimate derived from the overall loss report and may be too high. Strength on the 9th is recorded in the Kursk Data Base as 54 tanks (30 percent), which is the lowest strength of this unit. It may have been reduced to this level earlier than the evening of the 9th.

** Armed with U.S. Grant and Stuart tanks

*** No records were located on this regiment. Strength, losses and equipment type was keyed to the 230th Tank Regiment, and attrited relative to the infantry divisions the respective regiments were attached to. As such, figures given are an estimate.

46 These numbers are based upon the assumption that the X Tank Corps did not attack on the 8th of July.

Table 3.2
Fourth Panzer Army Tank Strength, 4 and 8 July 1943

	Total Tanks 4 July	*Total Tanks 8 July*	*Percent of Original Strength*
3rd Panzer Division	93	77	83
Gross Deutschland	177	111	63
Panther Regiment	198	13	7
11th Panzer Division	131	66	50
Adolf Hitler SS Division	173	98	57
Das Reich SS Division	166	97	58
Totenkopf SS Division	165	122	74
	1103	584	53

Table 3.3
First Tank Army (less XXXI Tank Corps and 2 Bdes/III Mechanized Corps) versus XLVIII Panzer Corps

	Total Tanks 4 July	*Total Tanks 8 July*	*Percent of Original Strength*
First Tank Army (less XXXI TC & 2 Bdes)	562	273	49
XLVIII Panzer Corps	599	267	45

Table 3.4
Other Voronezh Front armor (including XXXI Tank Corps and 2 Bdes/III Mechanized Corps) versus SS Panzer Corps

	Total Tanks 4/5 July	*Total Tanks 8 July*	*Percent of Original Strength*
Voronezh Front armor	775	390	50
SS Panzer Corps	504	317	63

of combat, both formations had effectively exchanged tanks on an even basis (a 289 decline versus 332, or 0.87 to 1). As around 115 or more Panthers were mechanical breakdowns, the actual exchange on the field of battle was higher (289 versus 217, or 1.33 to 1). A comparison to the SS Panzer Corps is revealing. See Table 3.4.

One can clearly see that in the first four days of the battle, the loss ratio was more favorable for the SS Panzer Corps (385 decline versus 187, or 2.06 to 1) and that it attrited the forces facing it at a rate higher than what it lost.[47]

While these two German corps were fighting side by side, there were some differences in the conditions. The SS Panzer Corps did start with less armor, although the starting tank strengths of the two German corps are similar if one takes out all the Panthers that broke down from the XLVIII Panzer Corps total. The XLVIII Panzer Corps did fight in more difficult terrain. Both corps faced similar infantry, artillery and antitank forces and a similar degree of fortification. The air support appears to have been split evenly between these two formations (although it may have favored the SS). The primary difference in the exchange ratio between the two German corps appears to have been caused by the way the V Guards Tank Corps was handled.

The V Guards Tank Corps in its fights with the Das Reich lost about two or three tanks for every one Das Reich lost. In contrast, from the 6th through the 8th, the II Guards Tank Corps lost 46 tanks (there were also five Churchills lost to the III Panzer Corps) and saw a total decline in tank strength over the three days of 32 tanks (including the five Churchills). The opposing Totenkopf SS Division in those three days lost 30 (six destroyed) tanks with a decline in strength of 28 tanks. This is closer to parity and serves to further contrast the performance of the V Guards Tank Corps as compared to the II Guards Tank Corps. The two brigades of the III Mechanized Corps also lost 83 tanks over the course of two days against the 70 tanks lost by the Adolf Hitler SS Division over the same two days, and the XXXI Tank Corps lost 64 tanks over the 7th and 8th (mostly on the 8th) versus the five tanks lost by the Adolf Hitler SS Division on the 8th.[48]

On the other hand, the forces of the First Tank Army opposite the XLVIII Panzer Corps remained on the defensive. Of course, in making the tank loss comparisons, there is no reason to believe that the primary cause of losses for either side's tanks was attacks by the other side's tanks.

As the armor facing the SS Panzer Corps was constantly attacking, especially when compared to the First Tank Army, which did make use of dug-in tanks, it is surprising that the casualty differences are not greater. When one considers that the Germans were attacking through fortified works and certainly lost a number of tanks to mines and antitank guns, the loss ratios seem to indicate superior use of armor on the part of the Germans.

It has been determined that the German tank losses due to mines was somewhere around 131 for the 5th of July. On the 6th of July, it gets harder to determine the mine losses, and an estimation has placed the losses tentatively at 69 tanks. This is 37.95 percent of the armor loss for those two days and 13.11 percent of total armor losses for 4 to 18 July. After that, it appears that the percentage of tanks lost to mines declined to perhaps five percent or less for the subsequent days. Overall,

47 The loss figures for these calculations are based upon a total decline in number of tanks ready-for-action. *The Dupuy Institute*, in its Kursk Data Base does have a slightly more detailed count of losses, but through the 8th of July, it does not differ significantly from the decline in strength. For example:

	Decline in Strength	*Derived Losses*
XLVIII Panzer Corps	332	361
SS Panzer Corps	187	235

As more tanks were returned to action each day, these figures become further apart. At this stage of the battle, the Soviet decline in strength figures and the Kursk Data Base derived losses are close to the same due to more limited reporting of tank losses in the Soviet records.

48 As the tank losses are determined by a decline in ready-for-action by each tank model from the previous day, then losses could be under-represented on those days that many tanks return from repair. This may have been the case for the 8th of July for both the Gross Deutschland Division and for the Adolf Hitler SS Division.

mines probably caused around 15 to 20 percent of German tank losses during the course of the entire battle.[49]

If one does a loss-exchange ratio analysis, less the German mine losses in the first two days, the following figures are generated:

	Decline in Strength
First Tank Army (less XXXI TC & 2 Bdes)	289
XLVIII Panzer Corps	332
less Panther breakdowns	−115
less mine losses, 5th	−54
less mine losses, 6th	−32
	131

This now shows an exchange ratio of 2.21 to one in favor of the German XLVIII Panzer Corps. A look at the SS Panzer Corps shows a very lopsided result:

	Decline in Strength
Other Voronezh Front Armor	385
SS Panzer Corps	187
less mine losses, 5th	−33
less mine losses, 6th	−14
	140

This shows an exchange ratio of 2.75 to one in favor of the Germans. Still, if one could factor out the other weapons effects, it would appear that the Germans, in their tank operations, were achieving kill ratios of two to one or greater. Furthermore, it does appear that the kill ratios achieved by the SS armor was superior to the neighboring Wehrmacht units, although it also appears that the primary reason for this was the way Soviet armored operations were conducted east of the Vorskla (under Vatutin and Chistyakov's direction) as opposed to those west of the Vorskla (under Katukov's command).

Redirection

The Soviet attacks on the Fourth Panzer Army flanks on this day had burned out with little effect, or as Chistyakov states, "our flank attacks . . . did not yield the desired results and we, having fallen short of Krasnaya Polyana, here halted by a strong enemy force consisting of tanks, aviation and artillery. The Front commander [Vatutin] in order to avoid unnecessary losses, ordered us to consolidate on a new line."[50] At this stage, the Voronezh Front quit trying to conduct major attacks and for the next three days confined themselves to just concentrating on defending. Meanwhile, Chistyakov, the Sixth Guards Army commander, found he needed to pull his headquarters out of Kochetovka, which was now threatened, and pull back to a reserve command post.[51]

49 This has been examined in depth by *The Dupuy Institute* in three reports, *Military Consequences of Landmine Restrictions*, Spring 2000, *The Military Consequences of a Complete Landmine Ban*, Summer 2001, and *A Measure of the Real-world Value of Mixed Mine Systems*, 11 June 2001. See *The Military Consequences of a Complete Landmine Ban*, pages 16–24, for an explanation of how the figures for the 6th were derived. Estimated mine losses come out to:

	5th	*6th*
XLVIII Panzer Corps	40	18
Panzer Regiment von Lauchert	14	14
SS Panzer Corps	33	14
III Panzer Corps & Corps Raus	44	9
19th Panzer Division		14
Total	131	69

50 Col. Gen. I. M. Chistyakov, *Sluzhim Otchizne* [We Serve the Fatherland] (Moscow, 1975), page 153.

51 Col. Gen. I. M. Chistyakov, *Sluzhim Otchizne* [We Serve the Fatherland] (Moscow, 1975), pages 154. On page 156 of this book it states that "Late in the evening of July 8 N. F. Vatutin told me over the telephone that my neighbor to the right, Fortieth Army, is sending me the 14th and 31st Antitank Brigades, and from the Front reserve, the II and V Guards Tank Corps." This statement is contradicted by a statement made in his 1971 book (page 96) that he was informed of the transfer of the two antitank brigades on the evening of the 5th. Even that statement is not correct as the 31st Antitank Brigade was attached to the Sixty-ninth Army, not the Fortieth Army. This is discussed in Chapter Seven of my original book *Kursk: The Battle of Prokhorovka*.

The 8 July date of this report, considering that the V Guards Tank Corps and the two antitank brigades were already well engaged, appears to be an error and probably refers to a report the evening of the 5th.

III Panzer Corps

At this point, in the first three days of fighting across the Donets, the III Panzer Corps had lost 39 percent of its armored strength.[52] These losses were pretty much spread evenly across all three panzer divisions.

This left a weakened offensive force pushing against a Soviet force that was clearly out of position and because of the direction of the German attack, not getting the full benefit of its defensive works. As such, even with the heavy losses, the III Panzer Corps was still able to move forward, but the ability of this corps to maintain the momentum, re-cross the Severnyii Donets in a timely manner, and protect the right flank of the SS Panzer Corps was now questionable.

Corps Raus

While the 320th Infantry Division held onto the southern flank, the 106th Infantry Division got into an extended brawl around Gremyachii. Meanwhile, to the north was the 7th Panzer Division, which had been reduced to protecting the flank. This was soon to be corrected by the insertion of the newly arriving 198th Infantry Division into the sector in front of Batratskaya Dacha. This division was attached to Corps Raus on this day and began moving into the corps area by truck and train. The division would take several days to completely arrive.

The Steppe Front Reserves

Two armies from the Steppe Military District were now on the move to support the Voronezh Front. At 2230 on 6 July, the Fifth Guards Tank Army, now consisting of three armored corps, was instructed to concentrate along the western bank of the Oskol River, south and southwest of Staryii Oskol. By the morning of the 8th, all three of these armored corps had reached their concentration area. There were now three armored corps in position to move into the Voronezh Front's defense as early as the 9th. Instead, it would be three more days before the Voronezh Front saw these forces.

On 8 July, Stavka (Stalin?) ordered the Fifth Guards Tank Army to concentrate in the area of Bobryishevo, Srednyaya Olshanka, and Marino by the end of 9 July, with its forward detachments south of the Psel River in the Oboyan and Veselyii sectors.[53] This would put the Fifth Guards Tank Army in a strong defensive position running behind the First Tank Army anchored on Oboyan. This was in response to the threat developing against Oboyan.

At 0100 on 9 July, the army received an order instructing it, by the end of the day, to reach the area from Bobryishevo (some ten kilometers east of Oboyan) down to Prokhorovka. This order also subordinated the army to the Voronezh Front. It started moving out of its positions at 0200, conducting a 100 kilometer march. By 0600 the army's brigade-sized forward detachment, Trufanov's detachment, was in the woods south of Marino, some 30 kilometers from Oboyan. By 2300, the army concentration was "basically completed," and by the morning of the 10th part of its forces had occupied the defensive line from Oboyan, along the northern bank of the Psel River to Prokhorovka. The army had marched 350 kilometers and was now stretched across the rear of the Soviet positions, backstopping their defense. This army was in a good position to support the Soviet defense by holding in place or by moving forward to reinforce the existing Voronezh Front defensive positions. Still, this force would not see combat until the 12th.

Meanwhile, the Fifth Guards Army was subordinated to the Voronezh Front on the evening of the 8th and was ordered to reach the line of the Psel by the morning of the 11th. This would provide seven more divisions for the Soviet defense. The units began moving out at 0430 on 9 July.

---

52 The 6th Panzer Division started with 113 Panzers and Marders and was down to 80 operational, the 7th Panzer Division started with 118 Panzers and Marders and was down to 65 operational, the 19th Panzer Division started with 93 Panzers and Marders and was down to 52 operational, the 503rd Heavy Panzer Battalion started with 40 Tigers and was down to 21 operational and the 228th Assault Gun Battalion started with 31 Sturmgeschuetz IIIs and was down to 23 operational.

53 Glantz and Orenstein, page 99.

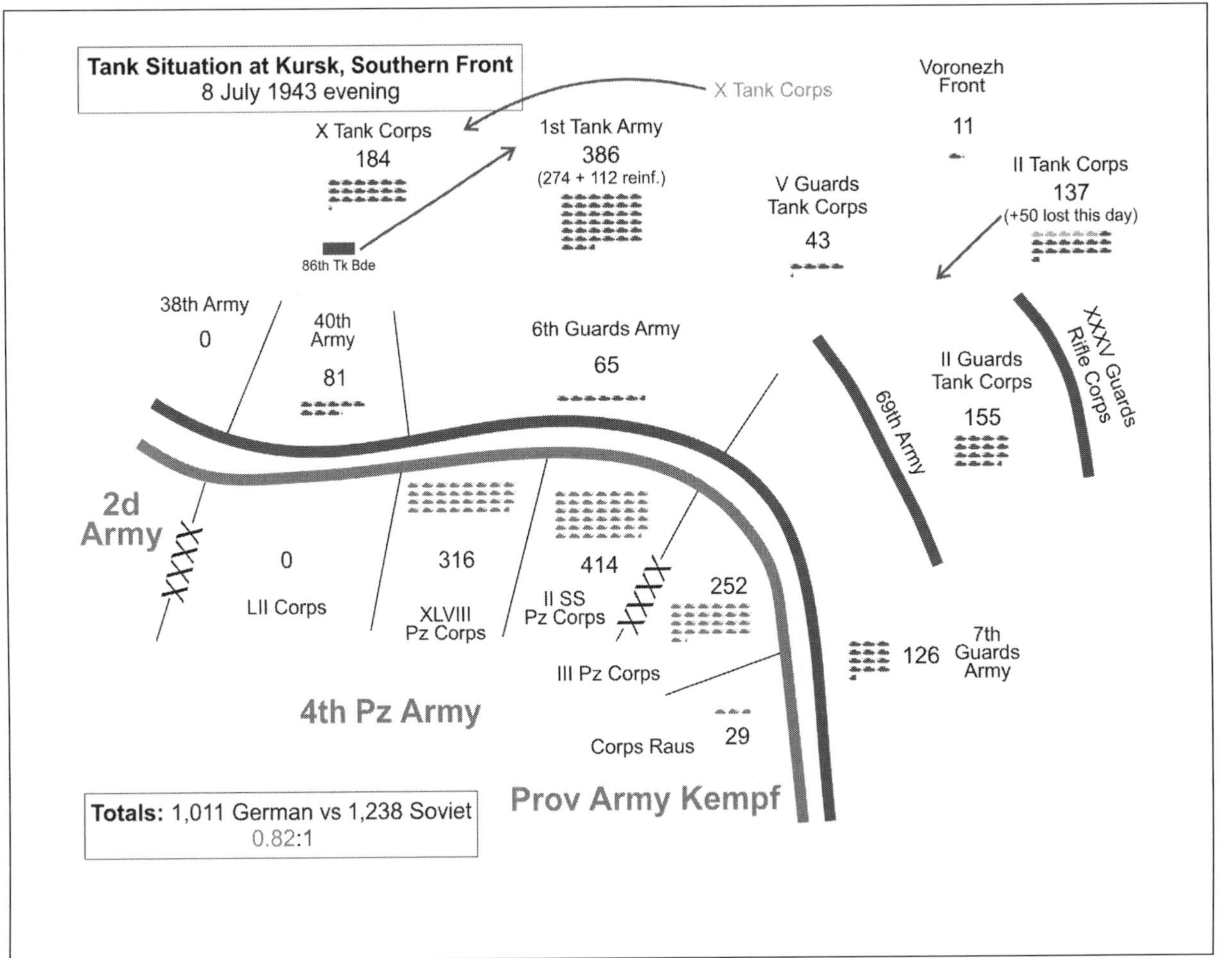

It was also at this time that the X Tank Corps was pulled out of the Psel River bend and Prokhorovka area and moved to the east. At 0035 hours on 9 July, Vatutin called Lt. General Vasilii G. Burkov, the X Tank Corps commander, and ordered him to transfer his Vasilyevka and Komsomolets Sovkhoz sector to the II Tank Corps and subordinate himself to the First Tank Army. Katukov, certainly happy to receive the support, then ordered him to concentrate in the Vladimirovka area.[54] These orders left the Psel River bend to the west of Prokhorovka weakly held on the 9th.

54 Glantz and Orenstein, page 99.

Summary to Date

Finally, this is also probably a good point to stop and take a look at the Soviet armor tactics. At this stage, the Soviets had committed all five of the original Voronezh Front armored corps to action for two to three days. Of those, three were effectively gutted, having lost more than 70 percent of their armor (III Mechanized Corps, V Guards Tank Corps and the XXXI Tank Corps). Two were still in reasonably good shape (VI Tank Corps and II Guards Tank Corps), and there were two new units that had just arrived at the battle (X Tank Corps and II Tank Corps). Two of these gutted armored formations had been tangled up in a fight with one of the opposing SS panzer grenadier divisions for two or three days

(XXXI Tank Corps versus Adolf Hitler and V Guards Tank Corps versus Das Reich). In both cases, they appear to have lost about three times as many tanks as did their German opponents. Based upon these two examples, it appears that in a straight-up armor fight, the Germans did indeed have a three-to-one advantage in casualty effectiveness when facing an equivalent armored formation.

For a number of reasons already discussed, this ratio does not exist for the fight against the III Mechanized Corps. The II Guards Tank Corps' noticeably low losses and continued presence on the SS Panzer Corps' flank speaks well for its commander. Overall, it clearly shows that even after two years of combat, the Soviet armored forces had not developed to the point where they could begin to match the German armor on an even basis. After two years of war this cannot be due to a lack of experience, therefore one is forced to look at the doctrine, the lack of combined arms, the obsession with attacking, the failure to appreciate the value of the defense, the lack of air support, poor commanders, force mix, and a host of other factors as the cause for this continued inferior performance. One must also look at the political system, which failed to develop good commanders or significantly revise the Soviet doctrine even after two years of combat experience.

CHAPTER FOUR

The XLVIII Panzer Corps Heads West

9–11 JULY 1943

During the operation I followed the attack with my division commander in an armored personnel carrier featuring the appropriate radio equipment. . . . During the following days, I got the impression that our division commander Westhoven did not at all conduct this attack with the edge and the willingness to take risks that he usually exhibited. One was almost led to believe that he was more concerned with getting the division back out of this in one piece than actually completing any of the goals that had been set—which he may have considered impossible to accomplish.

CAPTAIN PAUL-GEROGE KLEFFEL[1]

WITH THEIR DEFENSIVE works penetrated and their large counterattack on the 8th having fizzled, the Sixth Guards Army and First Tank Army finally rolled over to the defense for the next three days. It would be a difficult defense, with significant elements out of position on both sides of the German advance and with insufficient forces in front of the advance. As such, the defending Soviet forces spent the next three days trying to restrict and delay the German advance while waiting for reinforcements to arrive and stabilize the situation.

In the case of the Germans, as they advanced, each of their three attacking panzer corps developed their own private battles, with very little connection between them. The area between the XLVIII Panzer Corps and SS Panzer Corps was ground that was split by three creeks running to the northeast. The 11th Panzer Division and SS Panzer Corps connected in this area, but there was no significant action at this juncture. The XLVIII Panzer Corps was biased to the west and heading north and west, while the SS Panzer Corps was biased to the east and heading to the north and northeast. As such, the two corps were heading away from each other.

The space between the SS Panzer Corps and III Panzer Corps was filled with the Soviet forces shoved into the "Donets Triangle." This was an area of high ground created by the fork in the Donets River. The Lipovyii Donets effectively served as the eastern boundary for

1 Lt. General (ret.) Kleffel was interviewed by Maj. Gen. (ret.) Dieter Brand on 21 August 1999 in Hamburg. Lt. Gen. Kleffel had served in the West German Army since 1956, with his last post being the commanding general of III Corps.

TABLE 4.1
DAILY ADVANCE RATE IN KILOMETERS

	3rd PzD	*GD PzGrD*	*11th PzD*	*LSSAH PzGrD*	*DR SS PzGrD*	*T SS PzGrD*
5th	3.8	6.3	3.6	10.7	6.8	6.7
6th	3.5	7.2	12.0	6.8	13.6	4.9
7th	13.2	9.0	7.7	7.6	6.0	4.9
8th	15.0	5.4	6.8	5.6	0	0

the SS Panzer Corps, while the Severnyii Donets created the other side of the triangle that provided the boundary and barrier for the III Panzer Corps. In between these two creeks were a considerable collection of Soviet infantry forces, partially under command of the Sixty-ninth Army. The armor in the triangle still consisted of the persistent II Guards Tank Corps and the 96th Tank Brigade.

Both of the flanking German infantry corps had halted and then held for the rest of the battle. On the western flank the LII Corps held opposite the Fortieth Army while on the southeast flank Corps Raus held opposite to parts of the Seventh Guards Army.

The Fourth Panzer Army Operations

The Fourth Panzer Army attack, having slogged through and penetrated the first two defensive lines in the first three days of battle (5th–7th of July), then made considerable progress in exploiting this victory and driving back the First Tank Army and the Voronezh Front armor reserves (V Guards Tank Corps and II Guards Tank Corps) during the following days. The Voronezh Front had now committed a total of seven tank and mechanized corps to battle (including the reinforcing X and II Tank Corps), had shifted their infantry forces and their supporting armor and artillery units from the Thirty-eighth and Fortieth Armies to be placed in front of the offensive, and had committed almost every one of its divisions and other combat units to the line. The Voronezh Front had now committed everything to the fight. At this point, the Germans were clearly making progress but were now bedeviled by the major forces building up on the flanks of the XLVIII Panzer Corps and the SS Panzer Corps.

The pace of the advance is demonstrated in the recorded daily advance rates in kilometers, shown in Table 4.1 (which, not being in a straight line, exceeds the total depth of the penetration).

At this point, over the next three days the German attack began to slow. A major part of the reason for the slowing of the forward advance of the XLVIII Panzer Corps was the decision made the morning of 9 July to divert the Gross Deutschland Panzer Grenadier Division to take Verkhopenye. The reduced pace of the SS Panzer Corps advance was simply due to increased resistance and the fact that it was effectively only attacking forward with two of its three panzer grenadier divisions.

Still, it was a few basic missteps on the part of the Soviet high command that even allowed this advance to develop. At the start of the battle they had five major armored formations. Deployed from west to east, they were the VI Tank Corps, III Mechanized Corps, XXXI Tank Corps, V Guards Tank Corps, and II Guards Tank Corps. Because of the strength of the Pena River position, the VI Tank Corps ended up on the western flank of the German advance. The II Guards Tanks Corps was always on the eastern flank. This resulted in essentially six German armored divisions fighting against three Soviet tank corps. As the fight developed, the V Guards Tank Corps was also pushed off to the flank, as were two brigades of the III Mechanized Corps. At this point, the Germans still had four armored divisions in position to move forward (from left to right, Gross Deutschland, the 11th, the Adolf Hitler SS, and Das Reich SS). Facing them were three brigades from the battered III Mechanized Corps and the always infantry-shy XXXI Tank Corps. The Voronezh Front had received one additional corps, the X Tank Corps, to place in front of the German advance.

This resulted in some confusion as to where this unit should go. It was first placed in front of the SS Panzer Corps, and then before seeing action, was pulled and placed in front of the XLVIII Panzer Corps. The end result was that there was now a hole in front of the SS Panzer Corps, and other forces were going to be needed to fill that gap.

There were several operational errors here. First, the Voronezh Front simply started with too much armor on the flanks and not enough in the center of the German advance. Second, they did not continue to move forces from the flank to the front of the German advance. Third, they allowed the forces in front of the advance to be pushed to the side (the two brigades of the III Mechanized Corps and the V Guards Tank Corps). This created a situation where they simply did not have enough forces left in front of the German advance to halt it. Fourth, they attempted to halt the advance by several pincher counterattacks before the Germans were sufficiently weakened. This just further weakened the Soviet armored forces.

The X Tank Corps was a welcome addition to the defense, but in fact it was needed in two areas, in front of the SS Panzer Corps and in front of the XLVIII Panzer Corps. What the Voronezh Front needed was at least one more tank corps in front of the German advance, and in light of the fact that it had now let more than three of those corps slide off to the flanks, that corps was going to have to come from elsewhere. This would be from Rotmistrov's Fifth Guards Tank Army and it would be placed in front of the SS Panzer Corps advance.

The XLVIII Panzer Corps

For the XLVIII Panzer Corps, the problems with maintaining the forward advance had actually started on the afternoon of the 6th, when the 3rd Panzer Division arrived at the Pena and discovered the VI Tank Corps in mass on the opposite bank. This Soviet move to occupy the strong line of hills halted the 3rd Panzer Division attack before it started. It was then decided to move the 3rd Panzer Division behind the Gross Deutschland Division and shift it to the Lukhanino crossing that went across the east-west tributary stream that feeds into the Pena. Even this crossing could not be used until it had been cleared from the other side, and the 3rd Panzer Division had moved a significant part of its force across at Dubrova, again behind the Gross Deutschland. Effectively, for the first three days of the attack (5th–7th), the XLVIII Panzer Corps was really only making forward progress with two of its armored divisions. The 3rd Panzer Division was providing only limited support. Even during the following days, the 3rd Panzer Division was almost entirely concerned with dealing with the Soviet forces on the corps' left flank.

Apparently the problem was magnified by a belief by Knobelsdorff (XLVIII Panzer Corps commander) early in the operation that the success of the forward advance was a forgone conclusion. This was stated on the morning of 7 July. Although this may have only referred to the local situation at that time, it appears to have been his bias for the entire operation.

The operations on the following day (8 July) made considerable progress, but again, it was mostly the work of two divisions (Gross Deutschland and 11th Panzer). The 11th Panzer Division had already halted several times to wait for its right flank to be covered by the SS Panzer Corps and for its left flank to be covered by the Gross Deutschland Division. Gross Deutschland's operations were clearly being held up by its limited

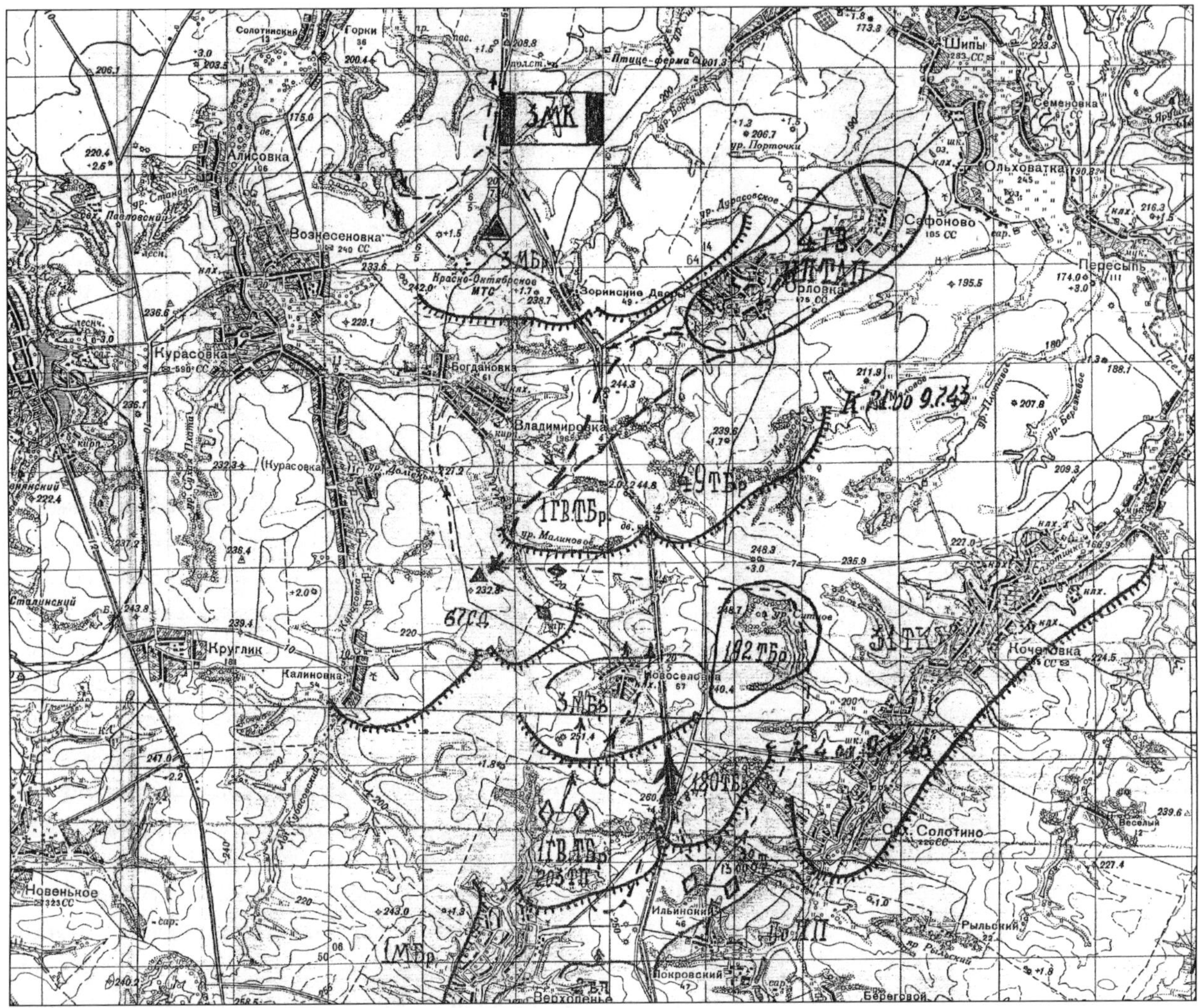

Portion of III Mechanized Corps map showing the situation for 9 July.

attacking frontage and by the enemy resistance. Part of the problem was that the Pena shifted farther to the east as the division moved forward. This meant that effectively the Gross Deutschland Division frontage became narrower as it advanced. Furthermore, Gross Deutschland reported on several occasions receiving fire from the other side of the river. This clearly forced the division to stay to the east and further constricted operations. It would be hard to decide where one should deploy the 3rd Panzer Division in this environment.

Still, as the warfare became more mobile, the Gross Deutschland and 11th Panzer Division were able to make considerable progress and were beginning to move past Verkhopenye. At this point came the critical decision. It became obvious that taking the northern part of Verkhopenye was going to be difficult. The town sat some three kilometers from the only main road heading to Oboyan. While it could be ignored for a brief while, the town had to be taken. As stated in their orders, the Gross Deutschland was in a "hole" around Verkhopenye-Syirtsevo. This put them at a disadvantage as the forces on the west bank of the Pena could both see and fire across this area. The solution that was recommended by Gross Deutschland Division and approved by Knobelsdorff, was to swing north of Verkhopenye and then slice back and around Verkhopenye, unhinging the defense there and allowing them to take the village. This was decided on in the conference around 0930–1000 on the morning of the 9th.

Verkhopenye itself was one of the larger villages in the area. On the east bank of the Pena River it consisted of a row of buildings that ran north-south for about five kilometers and had gardens and outbuildings to their east. At the southern tip of this row was a collection of buildings for the local kolkhoz, and near the middle of the town, on its eastern edge, was a collection of buildings and a church. Just to the east of that were the buildings of the Machine and Tractor Station (MTS). On the other bank of the Pena the town consisted of a row of buildings that ran for six kilometers along the west bank, and for part of that distance, a second row of buildings ran to the west. Like all Russian villages in this area, behind the buildings and houses were gardens, outbuildings, and sometimes walls and fences. There were also two kolkhozes just to the west of the town. It was only a village, but one from which it would be difficult to dislodge a determined defender.

It is not known when this tactical maneuver turned into a decision to move two of the three armored divisions across the Pena, leaving the 11th Panzer Division to conduct the forward push on Oboyan by itself. There were some sound reasons why one needed to clear this flank. Basically, the entire German advance at the point between Kalinovka, Novoselovka, and Kochetovka was across a plain only twelve kilometers wide between the Salotinka River (running through Kochetovka) and the Kurasovka River. This width was further constrained by Verkhopenye and the Pena River line cutting into the flank. Furthermore, the entire advance of the XLVIII Panzer Corps was being supplied by one road. The logistic requirements of three armored divisions are significant and would certainly tax a single road to its limit. Furthermore, the supplying of an entire panzer corps up a single road certainly made them vulnerable to air attacks. The original plan had always been to have control of the road from Zavidovka to Kruglik so as to be able to send the 3rd Panzer Division up that route. Without that road, the XLVIII Panzer Corps was really only left with room for two divisions to operate. Obviously, if one could then unhinge Verkhopenye, this would widen the front and protect the single road the Germans were using. If one could push another five kilometers farther west and clear the intersection at height 258.5, this would help open up the road from Zavidovka to Kruglik. Now they would have a frontage of 17 kilometers to advance over, and have two roads on which to run the supply up. This would clearly be a much better arrangement.

Unfortunately for the German attack, this resulted in two of the three armored divisions becoming involved in clearing the Pena, leaving only one lone armored division to push north. Furthermore, the western push seemed to take on a life of its own as the German attack enveloped considerable Soviet forces. The resulting disruption and casualties were favorable to the Germans, encouraging them to keep doing it. So while the German offensive was supposed to be advancing on Oboyan, in fact over the next few days the XLVIII Panzer Corps got itself into a giant "headhunting" expedition, which while it was wearing down the opposing forces, was not moving forward, but sideways.

There are probably six underlying causes that led to this questionable diversion. First was the failure of the 3rd Panzer Division to cross the Pena on the 6th. This was not because of any shortfall on the part of the division but due to a flaw in the basic attack plan, which had the division attacking against a potentially very strong defensive position with few options to maneuver around it and insufficient force and preparation to penetrate the position.

Second, the Soviet placement of the VI Tank Corps in

that position could not have been more critical or executed in a more timely manner. This placement halted the northern German advance cold and created a continuing problem for them afterwards. While one can criticize many details of the VI Tank Corps placement and its subsequent operations, the basic idea of plopping a tank corps in this defensive position was extremely sound.

Third, there appears to have been an assumption by Knobelsdorff that maintaining forward momentum was not an issue, thereby creating the attitude that these side thrusts could be safely done in force without jeopardizing the overall offensive.

Fourth, there was an over-commitment of forces to this thrust. As the XLVIII Panzer Corps already had a successful drive heading north, diverting the majority of the forces in the drive to the west did not make sense. A partial diversion of the Gross Deutschland Division should have been done for the purpose of clearing Verkhopenye while maintaining forward pressure with the majority of the division. This diversion should not have been for any longer than necessary to get the job done, and then all effort should have again been put forward so as to achieve a breakthrough to Oboyan. The 3rd Panzer Division and the 332nd Infantry Division should have been left to deal with the forces on the west bank of the Pena.

Fifth, the Germans got absorbed in the operation, with the "headhunting" becoming the cause in and of itself. This just further increased the time and effort spent in this diversion and in fact the Gross Deutschland never returned to its northward thrust, becoming fully entangled in the confused fighting in this area.

Finally, it appears the 3rd Panzer Division commander (Westhoven) wasn't trying very hard in this operation as he simply did not believe that it would work from the start. A comparison of combat casualties to date between the various attacking divisions tends to reflect this.

	3RD PZD		GD PZGRD		11TH PZD	
	Total	*Percent*	*Total*	*Percent*	*Total*	*Percent*
4th	155	1.10	36	0.17	121	0.76
5th	170	1.22	401	1.86	178	1.12
6th	73	0.53	175	0.83	93	0.59
7th	72	0.52	224	1.07	136	0.87
8th	77	0.56	375	1.80	108	0.70
Total	547	3.87	1,211	5.62	636	3.97

As one can see, the 3rd Panzer Division's contribution in total casualties was naturally lower, as it was the smallest of the three divisions. By the same token, their percent of losses was also lower, although effectively the same as the 11th Panzer Division. Just in case one thinks that this difference is primarily a result of its maneuvers, one can look at the next three days, when the division was fully engaged, and see that the pattern continues.

	3RD PZD		GD PZGRD		11TH PZD	
	Total	*Percent*	*Total*	*Percent*	*Total*	*Percent*
9th	128	0.94	442	2.16	82	0.53
10th	57	0.42	258	1.29	147	0.96
11th	32	0.24	165	0.83	126	0.83
Total[2]	217	1.54	865	4.02	355	2.22

It would appear that the 3rd Panzer Division's desire to minimize casualties was what was determining its maneuvers, not the other way around.

The XLVIII Panzer Corps Advance Continues, Battles around Verkhopenye-Krasnaya Polyana, 9 July

The operations in front of the XLVIII Panzer Corps on the 9th were basically a continuation of the previous day's operations, with the Soviets replacing their tank losses with additional independent tank regiments and brigades. The battle did go poorly for the Soviets, who in their obsession with holding Verkhopenye and positions behind the Pena, managed to hold the Pena, but allowed

2 Total percent loss is calculated from the division strength before the offensive. Daily percent loss is calculated from the strength the previous day.

the Germans to drive back and split the III Mechanized Corps, bypassing the Soviet positions on the Pena and setting up a scenario where the Soviet forces in the Pena riverbend could be enveloped by attacks from the east and northeast. German armor losses were light this day.

The morning of the 9th was spent with the 3rd Panzer Division attacking to the south of Verkhopenye and the Gross Deutschland attacked the north of Verkhopenye. By 0900 the 3rd Panzer Division was able to report that Syirtsevo was "almost entirely clear," But, across the Pena River there were Soviet forces, with the Germans reporting more than 30 Soviet tanks in firing positions, backed up by heavy artillery and Katyushas. In the western part of Lukhanino, the Soviets had brought into the dense, concealing grain fields a "special unit" equipped with only submachineguns. The 3rd Panzer Division spent the rest of the day clearing the area around Lukhanino and Syirtsevo. As evening fell, there were still Soviet troops in the western part of Lukhanino and in southern Syirtsevo. The fighting continued throughout the night. Still, the 3rd Panzer Division was planning to cross the Pena tomorrow at Syirtsevo and attack towards Berezovka.

While the 3rd Panzer Division seemed to be developing its attack slowly, the Gross Deutschland Division was very active. Its attack to capture the north part of Verkhopenye started slowly in the morning, but by 0700, the division reported that it was engaged in a fierce battle with Soviet tanks and antitank weapons south of the road leading east from Verkhopenye.

With the XLVIII Panzer Corps trapped in a extended fight around Verkhopenye and Syirtsevo, and with the Soviet forces still holding out in north Verkhopenye, the corps sent both the Gross Deutschland's and 11th Panzer Division's panzer regiments to the northwest to seize hill 260.8 at around 1000. They had considerable Luftwaffe support for this attack against dug-in Soviet tanks.

By 1130 the Germans recorded that the Soviet resistance along the front seemed to be weakening. By 1300 the Gross Deutschland Panzer Regiment, advancing now at a good pace, had broken Soviet resistance at Novoselovka and captured the town, destroying many Soviet tanks. The Germans were then able to advance three kilometers north of Novoselovka without much resistance. North Verkhopenye was finally taken in the afternoon, with low German casualties, by slowly and systematically shooting up almost every house with heavy weapons, leaving the town as a heap of rubble.

Knobelsdorff's Decision

At 1450, Knobelsdorff ordered Gross Deutschland to turn off immediately to the southwest toward the road fork at 258.5, with the objective of Dolgii and the hills north of it, in order to block retreating Soviet forces. The decision to turn 90 degrees gave up any chance of achieving a breakthrough to Oboyan. Whether such a breakthrough would have been possible had Knobelsdorff not made that decision is hard to tell. By continuing forward, and leaving the flank to be covered by the 3rd Panzer Division, he would have allowed the VI Tank Corps, two brigades of the III Mechanized Corps, and the 90th Guards Rifle Division to either sit on the corps' flank and counterattack (which to date, had not been very effective for the Soviets), or to shift forces north through Ivnya and back in front of the advancing Germans. Regardless of what was decided, this would have given the Germans at least a free day to continue to push forward with two divisions, and certainly more progress would have been made. Still, there were some other problems with such an advance. First, is was still on a very narrow front and supported by only a single road. This would make it difficult in the long run to sustain an advance unless the area around Verkhopenye was cleared. Furthermore, any successful thrust into the flank of this attack could well have been disastrous. Therefore, Knobelsdorff could not simply ignore the forces on the west bank of the Pena and had to commit at least an armored division to finish clearing the area and securing his western flank.

Still, it was obvious that the real reason he turned two

armored divisions west, was that he saw an opportunity to envelop significant Soviet forces and cause them considerable losses. Needless to say, if the opposing force suffers enough loss, then the offensive's objectives automatically fall. This clearly was an opportunity to do some serious damage to the Soviet Army and could not have really been done using just the 3rd Panzer Division. To do the envelopment required the complete commitment of the mobile formations from the Gross Deutschland and the 3rd Panzer Division. This is what Knobelsdorff did. As an enveloping operation, this was a correct decision. Whether it was time to go "headhunting" and loose focus of the objective is a tougher question.

There was some risk to the operation, for as his armored spearheads pushed west, his northwestern flank would have to be covered by infantry. This problem was noted by Mellenthin in the corps war diary at 1230 on the 10th of July, where he states that he believed it necessary to risk covering the northwest flank with antitank weapons while using the panzer units to destroy the enemy on the west bank of the Pena.

If the objective was to break through the Soviet lines to Kursk and join with the Ninth Army, then this was probably the wrong thing to do. These Soviet forces were out of the way and off to the flank. If a breakthrough could be achieved, then these would have been forces inside the encirclement. As such, they could have been destroyed just as well later. However, if a breakthrough was not achieved, then an opportunity would have been lost to cause additional damage to the enemy

So, was a breakthrough possible? At the close of this day, the following armor was facing the Gross Deutschland Division and the 11th Panzer Division in the north: III Mechanized Corps with a total of 30 T-34s, 21 T-70s and 1 T-60. The three brigades in the north, the 1st Guards Tank Brigade, 49th Tank Brigade, and 3rd Mechanized Brigade are together estimated to have had 14 T-34s, 5 T-70s and 1 T-60 operational, although the repair facilities were probably working hard to put more T-34s back in action.

Added to that were:

59th Tank Rgt: 15 T-34s, 5 T-70s
203rd Tank Rgt: 1 KV-1, 10 KV-2s
230th Tank Rgt: 4 Grants, 5 Stuarts
86th Tank Brigade: 24 T-34s, 7 T-70s, 7 T-60s
180th Tank Brigade: 10 T-34s, 2 T-70s, 2 T-60s
192nd Tank Brigade: 3 Grants, 15 Stuarts

XXXI Tank Corps (moved into second echelon, evening of the 9th): 41 T-34s, 12 T-70s and 1 T-60

and the reinforcing X Tank Corps with 97 T-34s, 9 SU-76s, 12 SU-152s and 64 T-70s.

This is a total of 201 T-34s, 11 KVs, 7 Grants, 12 SU-152s, 9 SU-76s, 20 Stuarts, 95 T-70s, and 11 T-60s.[3] This was still a significant armored force of 240 medium and heavy tanks, self-propelled antitank guns and assault guns, and 126 light tanks. The two German armored divisions could count between them 184 medium and heavy tanks, self-propelled antitank guns and assault guns at the end of the day, and 25 light and flamethrower tanks. It would not have been an easy fight. On the other hand, without the reinforcing X Tank Corps, which made up half of that total, it would have been grim indeed for the Soviet defenders.

By 1800, the Gross Deutschland Panzer Grenadier Division had taken Novoselovka and height 235.9 (west of Kochetovka). Still, as of 1815, the panzer regiment had not yet turned southwest because a reported 200 Soviet tanks were advancing from the north toward height 244.8, north of the road fork. Their lead tanks had attacked the hill at 1745. This force was most likely the newly arriving forces, including the Soviet X Tank Corps. Meanwhile, the reconnaissance battalion was tangled up in combat with a reported 15 Soviet tanks attacking from height 232.8. The units of Gross

3 Just to reiterate a point, these numbers are not gospel, but are a combination of direct reports and reports derived from scattered incomplete reports. This is especially a problem at this juncture with the III Mechanized Corps and the XXXI Tank Corps. The tank figures used here are probably as accurate a figure for unit tank strengths as can be developed from the reports we have seen.

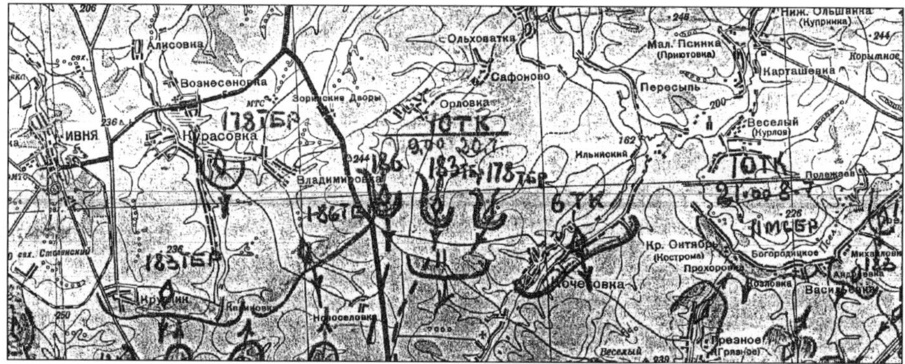

Portion of map showing positions of the X Tank Corps around the Psel River for 2100 on 8 July and its shift to the west, showing location by brigade. Map also shows positions between those two points on 20 July (labeled "9.00 20.7").

Deutschland were now waiting for the 11th Panzer Division to relieve some of its units on the right so it could continue moving its units to the southwest. This relief still had not arrived by the end of the day.

Also by the end of the day, the division had made the turn to the west and southwest with its panzer regiment, the supporting infantry, the reconnaissance battalion and the assault gun battalion. The division's two infantry regiments were left to hold the line facing north and northwest, with the Fusilier Regiment screening the line from the road, to the northern edge of Novoselovka to height 251.4. They were to hold height 244.8 until they could be relieved by the 11th Panzer Division. The Grenadier Regiment was taking up defensive positions on the hills east of Kalinovka with its left on height +1.8 and its front facing the west and southwest.

Meanwhile, the 11th Panzer Division continued pushing forward, taking height 260.8 in conjunction with the Gross Deutschland. The attached 339th Infantry Regiment of the 167th Infantry Division took Krasnaya Polyana and Beregovoi and the 11th Panzer Division took parts of the Sitnoye Woods and Sukho-Solotino. The 11th Panzer Division ended its forward advance at around 1600, having reached their objectives for the day early. The division then shifted laterally to relieve some of the Gross Deutschland units, so that division could push to the west. For various reasons, this relief was slow and delayed the Gross Deutschland's turn to the west and southwest by several hours.

Thrust Around Verkhopenye and the First Attempts to Cross the Pena, 10 July

After the successful, combined operations of the XLVIII Panzer Corps from the 6th through the 9th, the corps direction of effort had clearly split into two separate thrusts. The Gross Deutschland and the 3rd Panzer Divisions turned their attacks to the west to clear the area on the other bank of the Pena, while the 11th Panzer Division continued pushing north towards Oboyan.

The Gross Deutschland move to the southwest was delayed on the 9th because its forces could not be relieved by elements of the 11th Panzer Division. By 1815, 9 July, the Gross Deutschland Panzer Regiment had not yet turned southwest because 200 Soviet tanks were reported advancing from the north towards height 244.8 north of the road fork (X Tank Corps?). At 0330 on the 10th, Gross Deutschland attacked toward height 258.5. The panzer regiment went first, since the rifle regiments were pinned down in their established defense positions by strong Soviet counterattacks supported by tanks. These attacks on the neighboring 11th Panzer Division and the Gross Deutschland's panzer grenadier regiments that were facing north and northwest occurred at 0355, or shortly after the Germans started their attack.

Because of this situation, only the panzer regiment was able to turn southwest. Shortly after starting out, the lead tanks encountered strong Soviet tank forces at 243.0. The Fusilier Regiment, assigned to support the panzers, was unable to follow at first because the ground had been softened by rain (the regiment was truck mounted). It was subsequently held up by strong Soviet forces which appeared in the rear of the panzer regiment, and by intense artillery and rocket fire.

During the early morning fighting, Colonel Strachwitz, commanding the 10th Panzer Brigade (effectively his regiment with a dozen Panthers thrown in), injured his arm from the recoil of his tank gun and had to be evacuated. His command was now taken by Colonel Decker, who had commanded the 10th Panzer Brigade on the 5th and 6th.

As the day developed, the Gross Deutschland Division mopped up the west bank of the Pena at Verkhopenye while the 3rd Panzer Division advanced south of Verkhopenye. At 1300 the Gross Deutschland Panzer Regiment, after heavy fighting around height 243.0, again advanced towards height 258.5. The Germans reported that Soviet tanks kept rolling in from the north and northwest during the early afternoon. This was certainly the X Tank Corps arriving in action.

After heavy fighting en route, at 1845 the Gross Deutschland Panzer Regiment captured height 258.5 after destroying five Russian tanks. The regiment immediately began organizing an all-around defense just north of the hill. Up to that time the division claimed to have destroyed, in that area alone, 49 Soviet tanks, with a further five knocked out by the 3rd Panzer Division. These figures cannot be confirmed from the Soviet records, but may be close to correct although there is some confusion as to the tank losses in the X Tank Corps on this day. Because of the heavy combat, Gross Deutschland reported that it had only six Panthers, three Tigers and about 11 Mk IIIs and Mk IVs (long) still operational! The division's tank status report for 2400 10 July gives a much higher ready-for-action figure (3 Pz II, 8 Pz III long, 13 Pz III Flame, 1 Pz III Command, 2 Pz III Command with 50mm long, 5 Pz III Observation, 2 Pz III Munitions, 5 Pz IV short, 31 Pz IV long, 10 Pz VI, 1 Pz VI Command, 26 StuG III, 17 Marder II).

Command Decisions

The operations this day were more than the XLVIII Panzer Corps bargained for. Even though the flanking operation was conducted by elements of three divisions, most of the real attacks had been the province of the Gross Deutschland and they had been at it since before sunrise. The 3rd Panzer and elements of the 332nd Infantry Division were really only following up after resistance had weakened and the withdrawals had started. This advance had turned out to be more difficult than expected. At 1400, the corps reported that the battles being fought by the Gross Deutschland were considerably harder than at first thought.

At 1700 there was a conference between Knobelsdorff and Hoth. Knobelsdorff pointed out that the corps must be freed as soon as possible for a further thrust across the Psel (to the north). Hoth felt that the 332nd and the rest of the LII Corps could, at best, advance up to height 258.5, as this infantry corps front was getting longer and longer. Furthermore, the 3rd Panzer Division would have to relieve the Gross Deutschland so the Gross Deutschland and the 11th Panzer Divisions could continue operations to the north. The 3rd Panzer Division for the time being would have to remain south of the Psel. Hoth also pointed out that it would not be easy to regroup this thrust to the southwest for the renewed thrust to the north.

At 1930, the corps stated its intention to leave the mopping up of the Pena salient solely to the 3rd Panzer Division and to open up crossings of the Pena for the LII Corps. The 11th Panzer Division and those units of the Gross Deutschland which were relieved would then thrust toward the Psel. There was concern whether the 3rd Panzer Division could handle this mopping up by itself, and regardless, units of the Gross Deutschland would have to remain in the Kalinovka area. Hoth felt that having the 11th Panzer Division advance as far as the hills at Orlovka on the 11th would be sufficient! This town (Orlovka) being some six or seven kilometers in front of the division, with a few Soviet armored corps and infantry divisions in between, was certainly, as we shall see, beyond the immediate reach of this division.

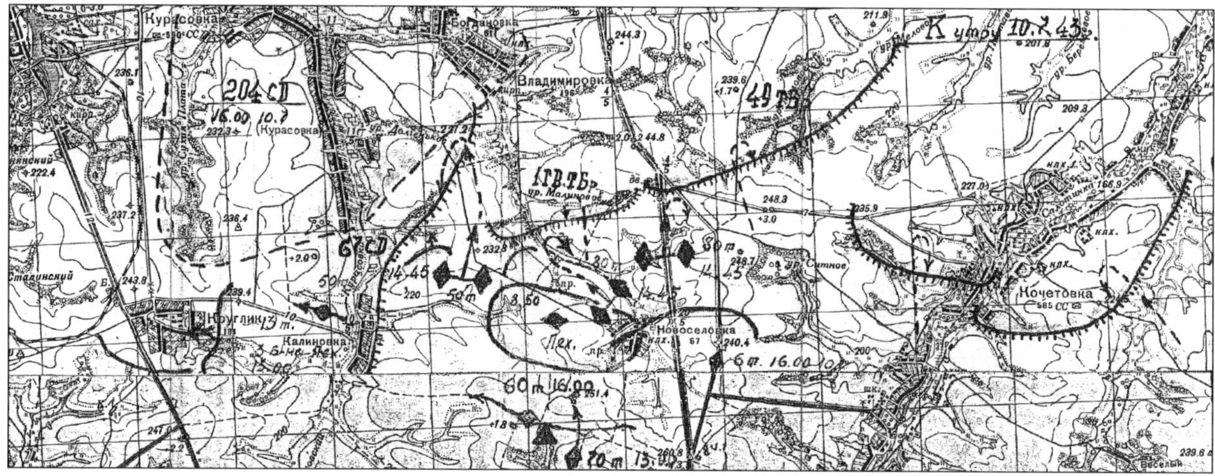

Portion of III Mechanized Corps map showing the situation for 10 July.

The corps mission for the 11th was to open the Pena crossings on both sides of Rakovo and to concentrate all the relieved units of the Gross Deutschland Division to prepare for an attack across the Psel. Furthermore, after the 3rd Panzer Division was relieved by the 332nd Infantry Division, it was to prepare to attack the area of Voznesenovka in order to protect the corps' west flank! This was some 13 kilometers north of height 258.5 and at the same latitude as Orlovka. Apparently, Knobelsdorff and Hoth did indeed consider that they were on the verge of breaking through the Soviet defenses.

Around 2130, reality had set in, with a note in the corps log that it was already obvious that the 3rd Panzer Division would not be able to master the situation in the Pena salient alone the following day. However, they held out the possibility that the situation might change during the night (meaning a large Soviet withdrawal). Therefore the corps was now holding forth two options: either assemble the relieved units of the Gross Deutschland at Novoselovka for a thrust to the north, or to advance farther south on both sides of Berezovka to height 234.8 (north of Rakovo). Hoth decided in favor of the southern advance. So now, this flank operation was clearly going to draw the Gross Deutschland away from its primary thrust north, via Novoselovka, for two full days. Meanwhile, the 11th Panzer Division was supposed to continue attacking northward on its own.

The 11th Panzer Division Advances to Height 244.8—Kochetovka, 10 July

Meanwhile, while the Gross Deutschland Division and 3rd Panzer Division headed west, the 11th Panzer Division was left to continue the panzer corps' northward advance by itself.

The 11th Panzer Division, after being relatively stationary during the afternoon of 9 July, at 1815 received orders to relieve the Gross Deutschland Panzer Regiment. The relief was underway by 1945, but at 2100 it was delayed because the 15th Panzer Regiment was ordered by Mickl (the division commander) to turn toward the east flank toward Sukho-Solotino, where Soviet forces were moving in, apparently driven back by the SS Panzer Corps. Mellenthin (corps chief of staff) stated that he could not understand why an entire panzer regiment had to be committed against this group and that there seemed to have been a misunderstanding in the transmission of orders. (One of the weaknesses of allowing commanders independence is that they occasionally do something they are not intended to.) In this case, while the corps wanted the panzer regiment to support the relief of elements of Gross Deutschland so the corps could go "headhunting" to its left, Mickl had grabbed the panzer regiment and sent it off "headhunting" to its right.

The 11th Panzer Division had limited results for the 10th. The Soviet forces were holding in strength across its front, especially at height 244.8 and were in what the German reports described as an "absolutely dominant position." At 1000 the division, with a little resistance on its right wing, reached the Solotinka River. There were still Russian forces in the north part of Sukho-Solotino. As yet, there was no contact with the SS Panzer Corps.

By 1200, the 11th Panzer Division, relieving the 339th Infantry Regiment, had captured positions at the church in Kochetovka, along with heights 227.0, 235.9, and 248.3 against only slight Soviet resistant. The 339th Infantry Regiment was now free to join its parent division, the 167th Infantry Division. At 1000 the 339th Infantry Regiment was ordered to move immediately to the area east of Bolshiye Mayachki and Kalinin to relieve those elements of the Das Reich SS Division which were committed to the right flank of the SS Panzer Corps.

Meanwhile, the Soviets were reinforcing their troops in front of the left wing of the division on both sides of the highway at the Malinovoye Woods and at 232.8. Around 1330, the 11th Panzer Division launched an attack on height 232.8. It was not until 1600 that they reached the southern slope of that hill. Still, the division was ordered to advance with tanks when the situation permitted, to take heights 244.8 and 248.3 "in order to seize jump off positions for the later advance of the corps towards the Psel River." At 1705, it was concluded that the attack on height 244.8 could not be done this day.

Overall, the division during the day shifted its front line three kilometers to the west. Its forward movement was limited to 1.4 kilometers. Not a whole lot was accomplished on this day and the 11th Panzer Division attack was definitely beginning to stall.

Still, if one looks at the terrain in this area, it was literally the last natural defensive point before one came upon the valley that spreads out in front of Oboyan. Up until this point, the terrain had generally sloped upward in favor of the defender. Once one got past the line of height 244.3 to the Melovoye Woods, the terrain opened up considerably and it sloped downward towards Oboyan. In fact, from the ridge line, one could pretty much see across the entire valley. To have taken this line would have almost certainly opened up the path to Oboyan and forced the Soviet forces to defend along the Psel River. This was a stretch of 13 kilometers of declining terrain beyond height 244.3 down to the villages in front of Oboyan.

The Oboyan position, on the other hand, was quite strong. There were villages a kilometer or two deep along the south bank of the Psel basin, and then two kilometers of swamp and soft ground in front of the Psel. Oboyan itself was a couple of kilometers deep and bounded by villages and orchards. Two kilometers behind it was a line of hills at about 240 meters in height. Therefore, between the swamp lands in front of the Psel and the ridgeline behind it, there was a solid defensive position. Between the Psel and Zapselets branch, this defensible position was also broad. It was also fortified, this being part of the third defensive line. There were further defensible positions behind it (see the 1:50,000 scale map M-37-25-B [map sheet 4] in the map section of the Oboyan area).

Envelopment at Berezovka, 11 July

The Germans were now on three sides of the VI Tank Corps and the Soviet forces holding in and around Berezovka. The Soviet response to the German encircling attempt appears very confused. Getman claims in his memoirs that the VI Tank Corps pulled out of there during the night of 10/11 July, which may very well have been the case. Apparently the 90th Guards Rifle Division and the two brigades of the III Mechanized Corps did not get the word, and during the day, they were slaughtered as a result. Needless to say, having half the defenders withdraw from an encirclement to leave the very weakened other half to be slaughtered and later forced to withdraw in a panic, probably maximized the effect of the German attack. The reasons for this apparent foul-up are not known to this author.

The night before (recorded at 2245), the XLVIII Panzer Corps had arranged with the VIII Air Corps to make strikes between 0545 and 0600 in the area north of Berezovka. The last bomb was to drop at 0600, and the attack by both armored divisions (Gross Deutschland and the 3rd Panzer) was to push south toward height 234.8 at 0600. Artillery was to fire on the woods south and southwest of 258.5 and in the Berezovka area.

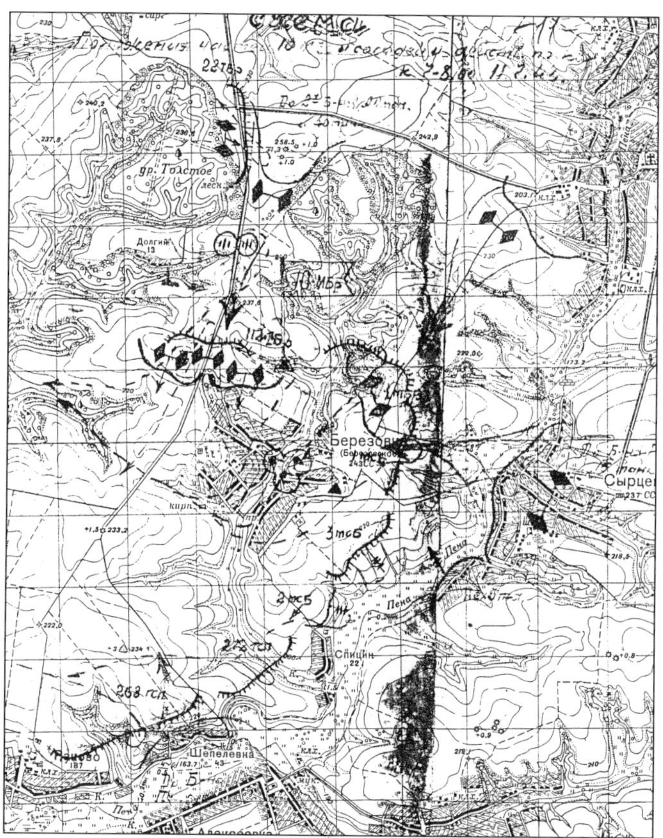

Soviet map dated 11 July 1943 showing the withdrawal around Berozovka and the Pena River.

At 0540, 11 July, Gross Deutschland's advance units occupied height 237.6 at the highway southeast of the Tolstoye Woods. The main force of the division attacked south at 0600 according to plan. The panzer regiment pushed south from 258.5 and inflicted heavy casualties on Soviet troops retreating west from Berezovka. The Soviets counterattacked from the north almost immediately against the corps, and achieved a penetration that touched the right wing of the Gross Deutschland Grenadier Regiment, flanking it from the rear; but the penetration was sealed by a counterattack by elements from the Gross Deutschland and 11th Panzer Division. Strong Soviet pressure continued, however, on the Gross Deutschland front at Kalinovka.

At 0920, a revealing note appeared in the corps diary, to the effect that it had become apparent at this time that the corps had failed to accomplish the expected encirclement, even though significant enemy forces had already been destroyed in the Berezovka area. Most of the Soviet troops seem to have withdrawn to the west and northwest. In effect, the encircling operation had not netted the results hoped for, required too much effort, and could not close the door to the west.

At this stage, the Gross Deutschland Division was in a giant, tangled, and fairly static fight that continued throughout the day. Only at 1610 were the 3rd Panzer Division and the Gross Deutschland Division able to report that they had cleared Berezovka. They used Panthers and shock troops of the Fusilier Regiment to capture the bunkers on the south edge of the town, whose defenders offered "fierce resistance to the last," and from the area on both sides of the highway. Elements of both divisions joined in hard house-to-house fighting in the western part of the village. By the same time, the Gross Deutschland Panzer Regiment had captured height 234.8 and barely cleared the minefield south of it. They also initiated a reconnaissance toward Chapayev.

The 3rd Panzer Division reports stated that the Soviets offered greater resistance in places on this day than on any previous day since the start of the offensive. The 3rd Panzer Division reported that in Berezovka oft times the

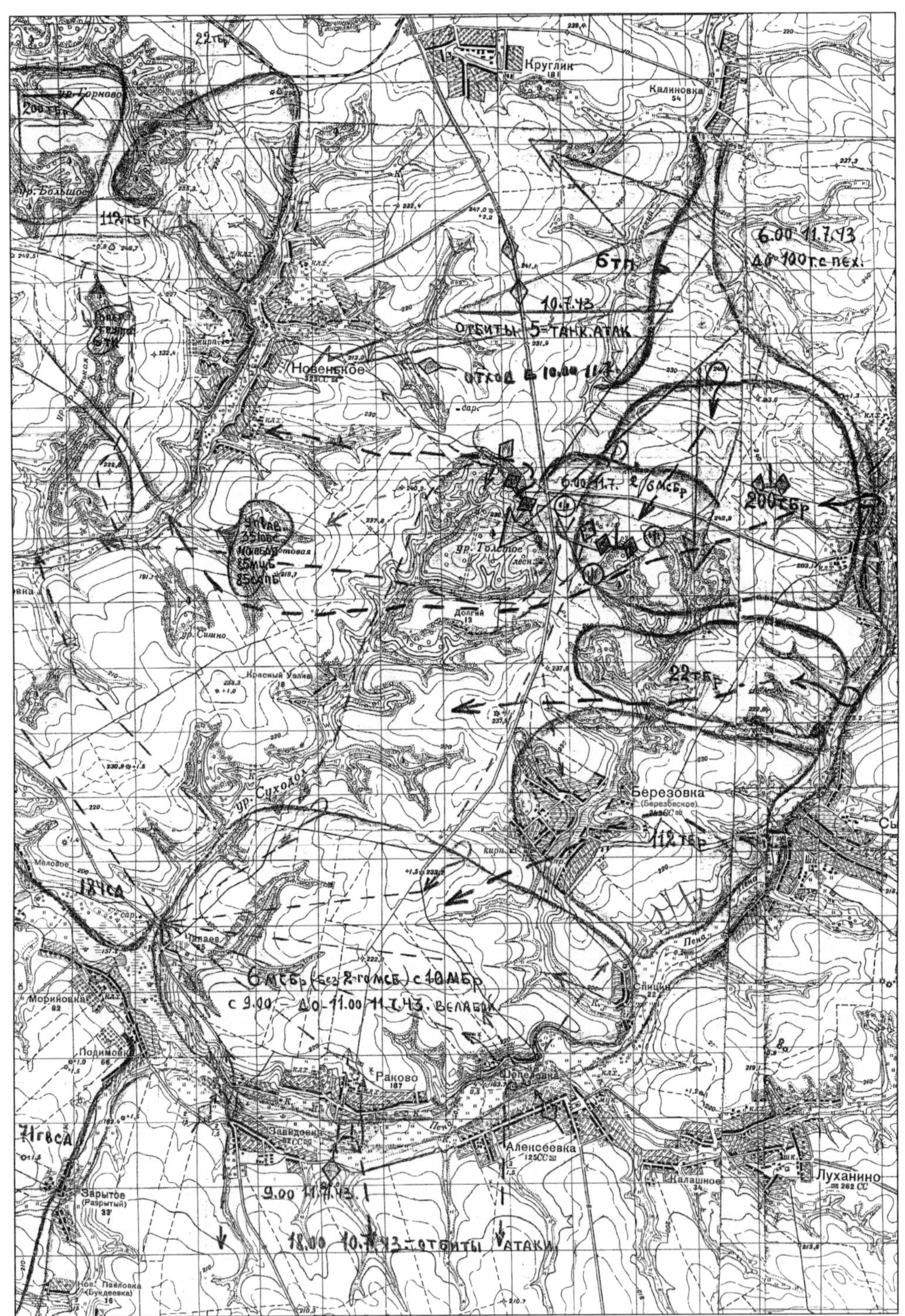

VI Tank Corps map for 11 July 1943.

Soviet defenders would shoot themselves or blow themselves up rather than surrender! The defenders suffered heavy losses from artillery and tank fire. By evening, the 3rd Panzer Division counted 500 Soviet dead and brought in 1,700 prisoners. The Soviets also left behind large quantities of weapons, equipment and ammunition.

As evening fell (1830), the woods on both sides of the road near heights 258.5 and 237.6, especially the Tolstoye Woods, were still occupied by Soviet troops. The Germans were receiving fire from all sides, including antitank and mortars. Many Soviet tanks continued to attack the Gross Deutschland Reconnaissance Battalion at 247.0, south of Kruglik; and the Gross Deutschland Grenadier Regiment was defending against strong Soviet forces at Kalinovka. These attacks continued into the evening.

THE 332ND INFANTRY Division also participated in this operation with its 678th Infantry Regiment. The regiment failed to cross the Pena River on the 10th and ended up holding in Zavidovka for the night. The next day, the division began crossing the Pena to the east at Alekseyevka between 1030 and 1100 with the 332nd Reconnaissance Battalion. This was after the 3rd Panzer Division had already flanked Alekseyevka and Zavidovka from the north with the seizure of height 234.8. The battalion was able to fight through heavily mined areas and establish contact with the 3rd Panzer Division at 234.8 around 1500. It then turned to the west and rolled up the Soviet positions along the river, taking Rakovo, although fighting continued there until 2000 in the evening. The 678th Infantry Regiment was able to cross the Pena at Zavidovka starting at 1615.

For the two days of operations, the Germans had made quite a haul. At a cost of 897 casualties and 50 tanks, they had caused the Soviets an estimated 4,973 casualties, of which at least 2,778 were captured. Furthermore, the Soviets had lost probably at least 74 tanks.[4]

This was a successful tactical envelopment that was now about to get entangled in Soviet defensive stubbornness around Tolstoye Woods.

Attack on Height 244.8, 11 July

The 11th Panzer Division had done an exemplary job over the last six days, repeatedly outmaneuvering and outfighting its opponents. It had continued to advance ahead of its more famous neighboring divisions, the Gross Deutschland and the Leibstandarte SS Adolf Hitler, and had managed to still preserve its combat strength. Its soldiers had demonstrated considerable initiative and its overall performance had been impressive. At this stage, though, it seemed to falter, having had a lackluster day with a slow advance on the 10th and some delays in relieving the Gross Deutschland Division. What transpired on this day did not do anything to add to the commander's credit, as the 11th Panzer Division's attack ground to a rather pathetic halt.

The division was supposed to kick off its drive to the Psel at 0600, but Mickl (the division commander) decided to wait for the weather to clear so he could get Luftwaffe support against the Russian tanks and antitank guns on 244.8. The attack plan called for the 110th Panzer Grenadier Regiment to advance on both sides of the road against 244.8 and then continue on to height 244.3. The first objective for the attack of the 111th Panzer Grenadier Regiment and the 15th Panzer Regiment was height 239.6.

While the division waited, the Soviets launched an attack of their own in battalion strength at 0700 on height 232.8, against the left wing of the division, from the north and from the Kalinovka area. A temporary penetration that also touched the right wing of the Gross Deutschland Grenadier Regiment, flanking it from the rear, was eliminated by counterattacks by elements of the two divisions. By 0800, after strong artillery and rocket barrages, Soviet tanks and infantry recaptured height 207.3, while the II Battalion, 111th Panzer Grenadier Regiment was driven back, suffering heavy losses. According to the corps report, "In an irresponsible manner, the

4 This is data from the Kursk Data Base built from Soviet unit records, as opposed to German estimates.

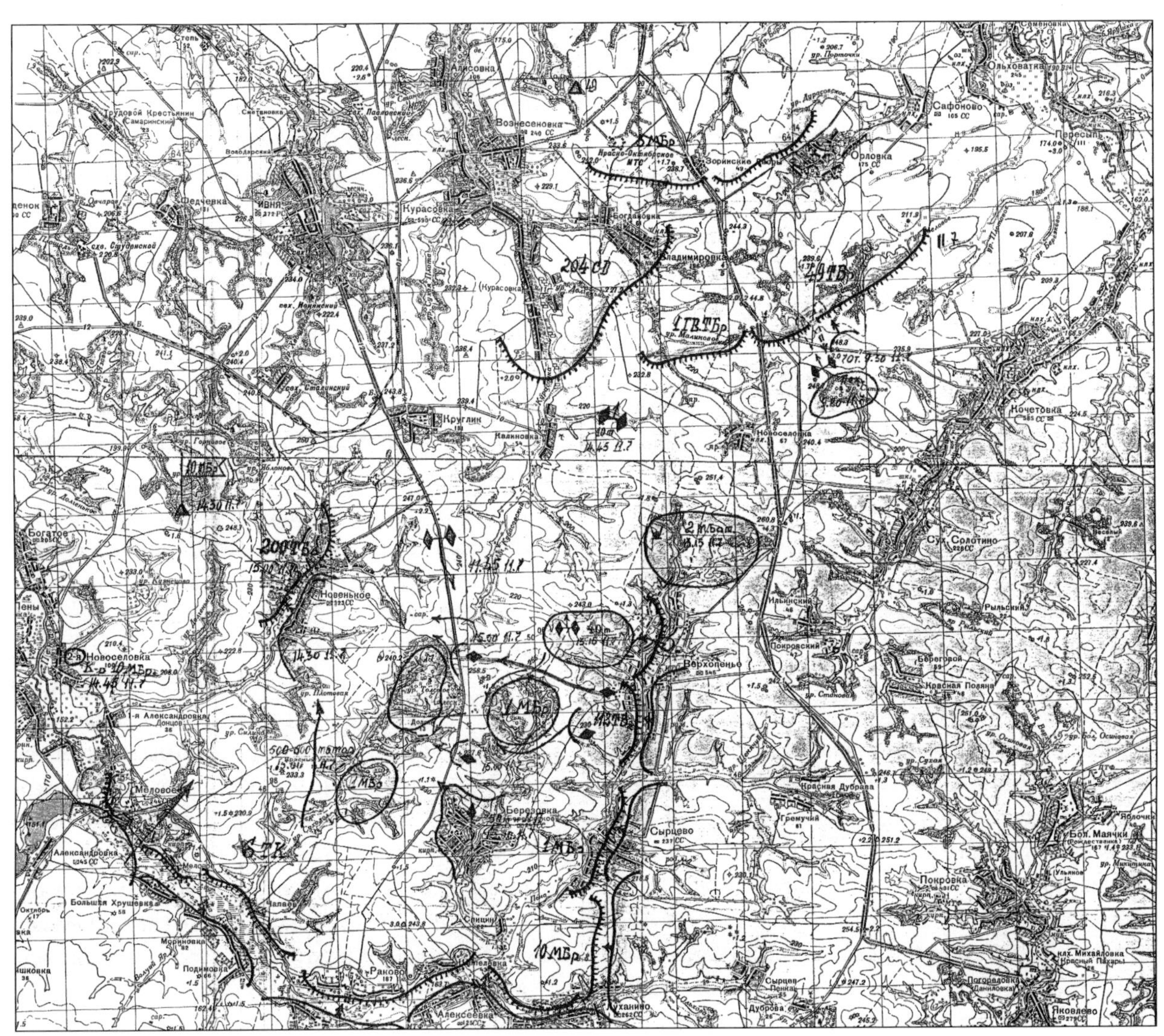

III Mechanized Corps map for 11 July 1943.

assault guns assigned there for tank security withdrew to the rear at the same time to get ammunition, and Soviet infantry and tanks drove the German infantry from the hill. With great difficulty the German forces have occupied a road position just south of the hill." The II Battalion, 111th Panzer Grenadier Regiment took up a new defense along a line extending three kilometers west of 209.3. The battalion-size attack from Kalinovka was driven off by the reconnaissance battalion.

Eventually the Soviet attacks died down and the 11th Panzer Division began to move forward. By 0930, its advance had bogged down in the mud. Tanks were sliding off at inclines of 10 degrees. The division commander halted the attack until 1100 in anticipation of better weather. At 1100 the attack against 244.8 was begun in earnest. Because of heavy cloud cover, promised dive bomber support was unavailable. The start of the attack was "hesitant and uninspired, the artillery preparation completely inadequate" according to the corps reports. Because of the heavy antitank fire, the tanks gained no ground on either side of 244.8 and were firing from a long distance.

Mellenthin (corps chief of staff) arrived at the front to observe the attack and expressed his displeasure to Mickl over the inadequate preparation for the attack. Mellenthin demanded a new attack, with the concentrated effort of the entire artillery and armored force of the division. Believing that the attack could not succeed without sufficient dive bomber support, Mickl proposed that the Gross Deutschland Division join in on 12 July in an attack to capture the hills on the road. Instead, a new attack by the 11th Panzer Division was scheduled for 1700.

At 1630 the reconnaissance battalion destroyed three Soviet scout cars, apparently lost. The Germans claimed the passengers included several senior Soviet officers, including the deputy commanding general of the X Tank Corps! The battalion captured several important maps in his possession. Captured documents and interrogations revealed that the X Tank Corps had three tank brigades and one mechanized brigade approaching in the area west of the highway. Their objective was to strike the flank of the German thrust toward Verkhopenye.

At 1700, parts of the 110th and 111th Panzer Grenadier Regiments, most of the 15th Panzer Regiment and the 911th Assault Gun Battalion jumped off for the planned attack, and advancing rapidly, reached the edge of the woods just north of 235.9 and the center of the woods north of 248.3. This limited attack was to set the division up to take 239.6 and the area to the east.

Overall, this was a day of useless and confusing combat. For some reason, even though they were defending, the Soviets persisted in conducting a series of small disorganized attacks in the morning that frittered away their strength. Still, these attacks met with some success when the 911th Assault Gun Battalion pulled off the field of battle to resupply. This was then followed by a poorly conducted attack on the part of the 11th Panzer Division. Finally, a limited attack was conducted at the end of the day but there was little that could be done to exploit it that day. So ended the German offensive push on Oboyan.

Also soon to be ended were the armor careers of two German armored officers, for Mickl would soon write a poor evaluation of his panzer regiment commander, Colonel Theodor Count Schimmelmann von Lindenburg, and this would be Colonel Lindenburg's last combat armored command. By the same token, the corps commander, General Knobelsdorff, wrote a poor evaluation of Mickl on 30 July and the 11th Panzer Division commander would shortly be transferred to command an infantry division.

THIS ALSO ENDS our discussion of the XLVIII Panzer Corps operations. From the 12th through the 15th they became engaged in an extended operation to the west that I refer to as the Battle of Tolstoye Woods. This battle would entangle the 332nd Infantry Division, the 3rd Panzer Division and the Gross Deutschland Division with the VI Tank Corps, V Guards Tank Corps, X Tank Corps, parts of the III Mechanized Corps and four

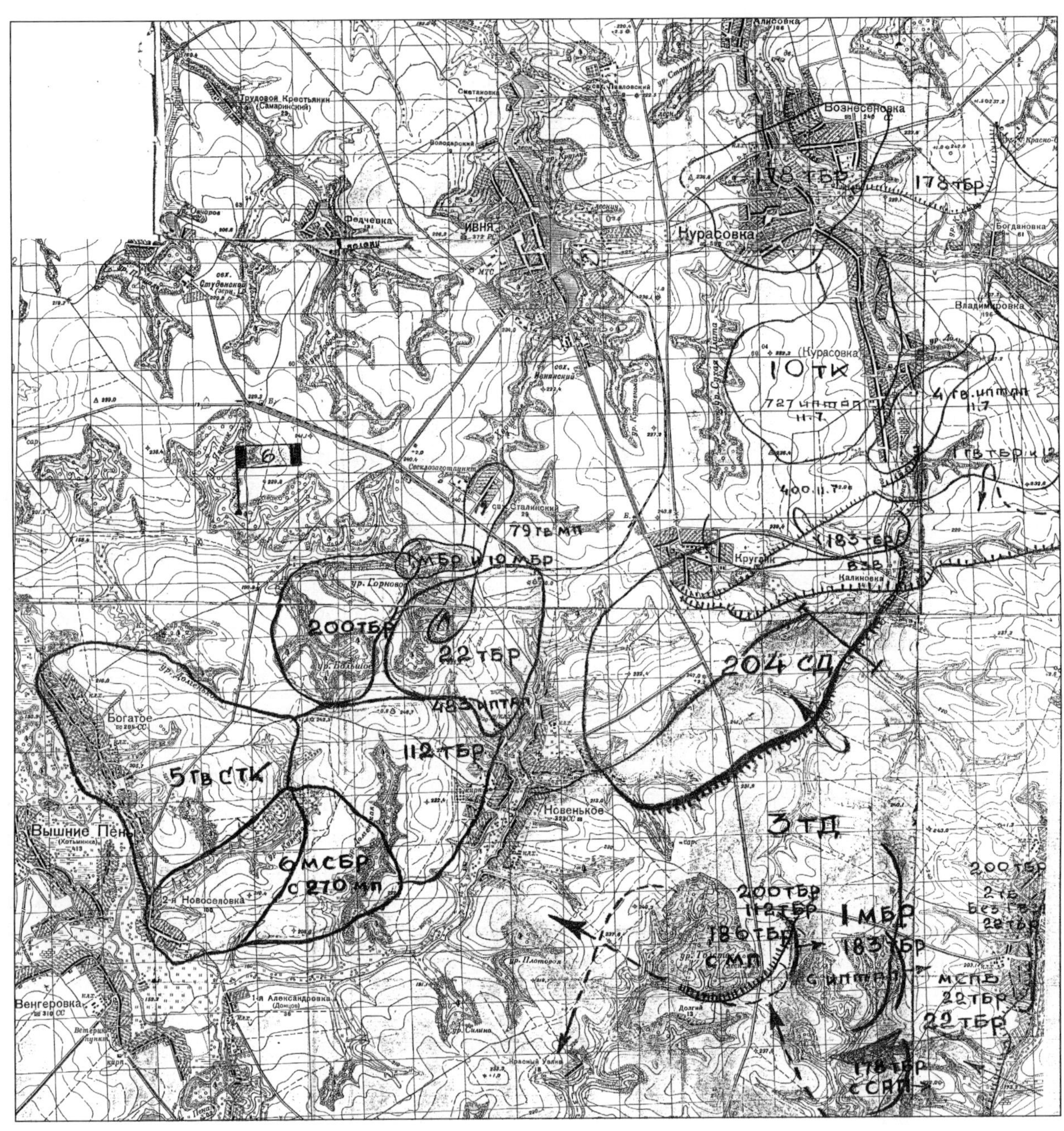

Portion of First Tank Army map showing the Soviet defense from Bogatoye to Kurasovka from 10 through 12 July 1943.

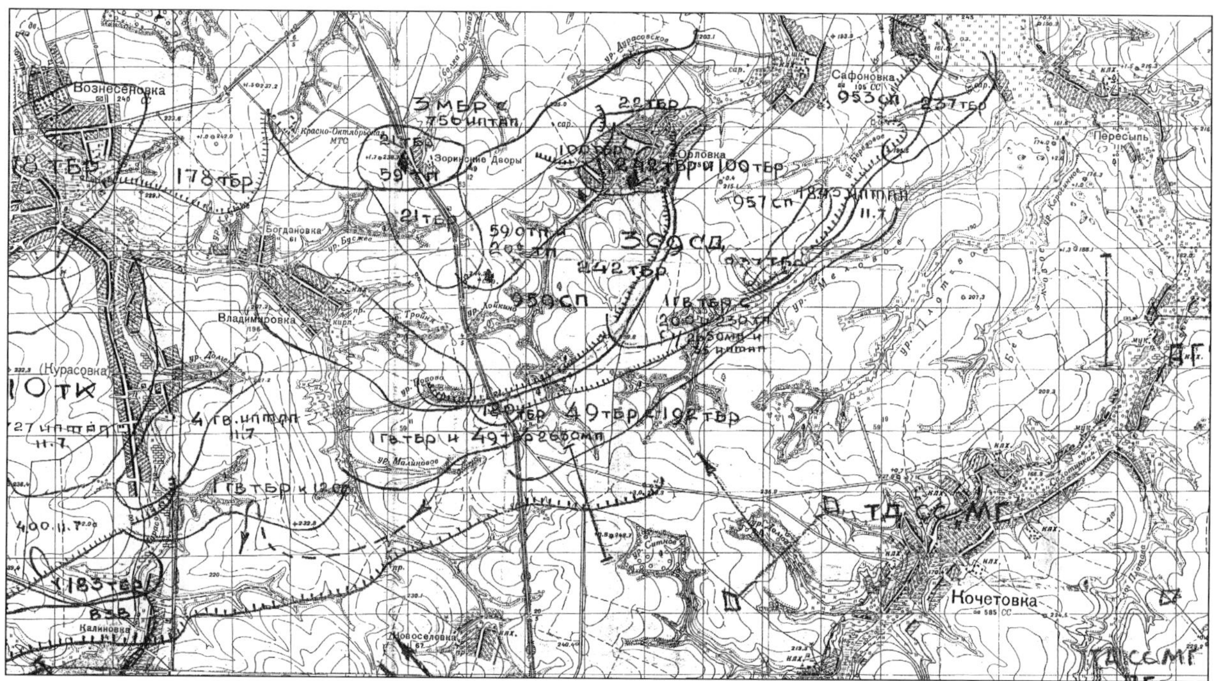

Portion of First Tank Army map showing the Soviet defense from Kurasovka to Peresyip from 10 through 12 July 1943.

rifle divisions in a broad fight over the left flank of the Fourth Panzer Army. Meanwhile the 11th Panzer Division tried to continue pushing forward into three rifle divisions (two from the Fifth Guards Army), backed up by elements of the III Mechanized Corps and the XXXI Tank Corps. These fights are discussed in depth in my book *Kursk: The Battle of Prokhorovka*, Chapters Fifteen and Twenty. We will leave this narrative and focus our attention on the upcoming Battle of Prokhorovka.

We will also cease discussion of the operations of the left flank LII Corps and the right flank Corps Raus. These two infantry corps remained firmly planted on the flanks of the attack for the rest of battle and were involved in very little subsequent combat. Again, their operations are discussed in depth in my original book on Kursk.

Instead our focus for the rest of this book will be on the events leading up to and including the Battle of Prokhorovka, and its aftermath.

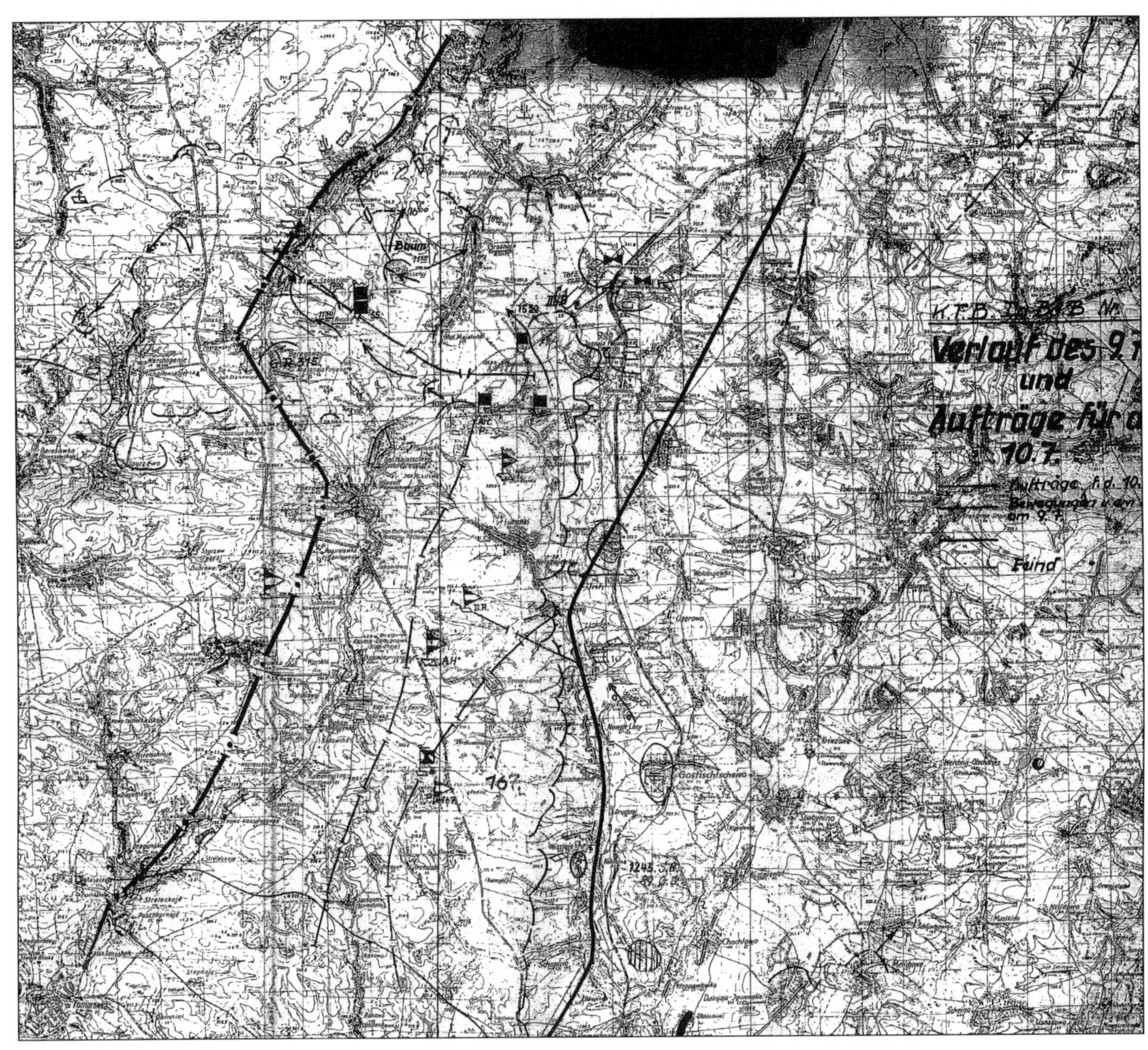

The SS Panzer Corps map showing positions on the 9th of July.

CHAPTER FIVE

The Advance on Prokhorovka

9–11 JULY 1943

> After the reading of the Fuehrer order, the battalion commander spoke to us. No sooner had he finished than a roar of enthusiasm broke loose, culminating somewhere along the line in a chorus. Someone started a tune and immediately everyone joined in. The whole forest echoed with our song and no one seemed to waste a thought on the days full of hardship and sacrifice that lay ahead. Particularly the young, inexperienced soldiers—I was one of them—entered into a veritable state of euphoria and were elated by the expectation of proving our worth in the impending battle. The old foxes, however, who had seen several campaigns, looked upon the whole thing with a noticeable degree of reservation.
>
> PRIVATE (OFFICER CANDIDATE) KURT A. KAUFMANN,
> DAS REICH SS PANZER GRENADIER DIVISION, DESCRIBING THE EVENTS OF 4 JULY 1943[1]

OVER THE NEXT three days the SS Panzer Corps would advance towards Prokhorovka. Still, it spent most of the 9th of July again pushing to the northwest, before it was able to send forces north late in the afternoon. The time lost with these northwestern pushes on the 8th and 9th of July may have already given away the SS Panzer Corps' chance for a breakthrough across the Psel against the very out-of-position Soviet forces.

For this day the SS Panzer Corps decided to halt the Das Reich SS Division so as to secure the east flank, while Totenkopf would move to the left flank of the corps and attack north so as to establish a bridgehead across the Psel at Krasnyii Oktyabr. The corps was then to push northwest to establish communications with the 11th Panzer Division. The Adolf Hitler SS Division was left in a supporting role for Totenkopf's attack.

ADVANCE TO KOCHETOVKA AND THE PSEL

The Leibstandarte SS Adolf Hitler Division ended the previous day with a gap between its right flank north of Luchki (north) and the left flank of the Das Reich SS Division in the area north of Teterevino Kolkhoz. This gap was noted at 1930 and was closed by the 2nd SS Regiment by 0200.

The Soviet X Tank Corps was the major armored formation sitting due north and northeast, directly in

1 Colonel (ret.) Kurt A. Kaufmann was interviewed by Maj. Gen. (ret.) Dieter Brand on 27 July 1999 in Rendsburg. Most of the interview consisted of a copy of a report Colonel Kaufmann wrote 15 years before based on the diary notes he recorded in 1943 as a young soldier during the battle. He retired as a Colonel in the West German Army.

front of this advance. At 2100 on the 8th, its motorized rifle brigade occupied the line of the Psel River and its three tank brigades were deployed in two echelons blocking the road to Prokhorovka. This formation was right where it needed to be when it was needed there. It was then moved! This movement occurred during the night of the 8th and morning of the 9th, as the corps was shifted over to the Kruglik and Kalinovka area to be in front of the XLVIII Panzer Corps. While there was no question this formation was needed over there, as there was a considerable German threat of envelopment of the entire VI Tank Corps and its attached units, this move left a large gap in the Soviet lines in front of the SS Panzer Corps, which was only covered by the very battered 52nd Guards Rifle Division, along with the 11th Motorized Rifle Brigade, the 287th Mortar Regiment, the 178th Tank Brigade and probably the 727th Antitank Regiment (all left behind from the X Tank Corps).[2]

The plan for the morning was to have a regiment-size battle group from both Totenkopf and Adolf Hitler SS Divisions advance again to the northwest to clear the area up to Kochetovka. At 0800 on the 9th, the 1st SS Regiment was ready to advance from both north exits of Bolshiye Mayachki toward Sukho-Solotino. This reinforced regiment (with at least one panzer battalion) jumped off at 1000 in conjunction with the delayed Totenkopf battle group on its right. By 1100 it had reached the line one kilometer north of Ryilskii—Sukho-Solotino (road?) without meeting any resistance worth mentioning. Ryilskii had been occupied without opposition.[3] Patrols sent forward from there revealed that the south part of Sukho-Solotino was also free of Soviet troops. The Soviets had blown up the crossing over the Solotinka River.

The defending 51st Guards Rifle Division was holding Sukho-Solotino, with the 242nd Tank Brigade on its right and the 100th Tank Brigade on its left (both from the XXXI Tank Corps). The XXXI Tank Corps (with the 59th Tank Regiment now attached) was defending along the Solotinka River from Sukho-Solotino to height 188.1 (west of the village of Ilinskii that is on the Psel River). At 1210 (1110 Berlin time), the 51st Guards Rifle Division stated that their two rifle regiments were fighting the Germans who had broken into Sukho-Solotino. Sukho-Solotino was taken and the 51st Guards Rifle Division withdrew. At 0700 the next morning (the 10th), the 51st Guards Rifle Division was reported to be defending along a line running from height 211.9 to southeast of Orlovka to height 188.1 to Ilinskii (on the Psel), well to the rear. Its other rifle regiment was still separate from the rest of the division, defending along the Sazhnovskii Donets, around height 225.0 (south of Leski).

The attacking German regiment from the Adolf Hitler SS Division then halted by 1220 along the line one kilometer north of Ryilskii and Sukho-Solotino.

MEANWHILE, THE TOTENKOPF SS Division was once again mobile, having at 0500 handed over its area to the 167th Infantry Division. This was a later start than they hoped for due to the late relief by the 167th Infantry Division. The Totenkopf SS Division then assembled the reinforced Totenkopf SS Regiment, called Battle Group Baum, around Teterevino and Luchki at around 0810. The new front line of the Totenkopf SS Division started on the right, two kilometers to the northeast of Teterevino. Meanwhile, the always active Soviet defenders sent out an attack with infantry and 30 tanks from the wooded strip just west of Komsomolets Sovkhoz. This may have been from the II Tank Corps and was dealt with by Das Reich SS Division.

At 1000, the late-starting Battle Group Baum began attacking to the northwest towards Kochetovka while

2 The 178th Tank Brigade is reported to be in the old X Tank Corps area along with the 11th Motorized Brigade as of 0600 on 10 July. By 0700 12 July, the Tank Brigade was operating with the other two tank brigades of the X Tank Corps near Novenkoye. It is not known when it moved from its position on the 9th to opposite the XLVIII Panzer Corps. The antitank regiment was reported attached to it at 2100 on the 8th of July and is assumed to have remained attached.

3 Note that the 11th Panzer Division also claimed that it had captured Ryiliskii by 1700 on the 8th. This would, of course, explain why the SS Panzer Corps occupied it without opposition. In general, the connections between the XLVIII Panzer Corps and the SS Panzer Corps appear to have been poorly coordinated.

the Adolf Hitler SS Division attack on Sukho-Solotino kicked off at the same time. Battle Group Baum sent two battalion groups to the north and northeast while the reinforced panzer battalion moved to height 224.5 in the direction of Kochetovka. Forward elements reached Veselyii at 1115 (the Veselyii on the Plotava Woods ravine) and Veselyii was reported captured at 1215. It was not seriously defended as it had been the previous day. At 1150, patrols from Totenkopf had contacted the 11th Panzer Division one kilometer southwest of Sukho-Solotino.

The XXXI Tank Corps reported that at 1300 (1200 Berlin time) it had come under attack by 100 German tanks with infantry and that at 1310, 30 German tanks reached the northern outskirts of Sukho-Solotino. They also reported a simultaneous advance on Sukho-Solotino from Krasnyii Oktyabr (this was probably the Battle Group Baum advance). These advances eventually led to a fight with about 20–30 Soviet tanks near height 224.5, just southeast of Kochetovka. Totenkopf claimed 14 Soviet tanks destroyed and one captured in this engagement. They then turned along the east bank of the Solotinka River and cleared the elongated settlements there.

The Soviets reported that at 1630 100 German tanks with infantry crossed the Solotinka River at several points. The XXXI Tank Corps switched over to "holding actions," having again suffered heavy losses on this day (57 to 70 tanks).[4] In contrast, Totenkopf had 122 tanks ready-for-action as of the evening of 8 July, including 6 Tigers, and lost around 19 (including 3 Tigers and one Sturmgeschuetz III) of them on this day, while the Adolf Hitler SS Division had 98 tanks ready-for-action, including one Tiger, and lost around 10 tanks.

The 29th Antitank Brigade reported that it was engaged in heavy fighting all day along the line height 227.8 to Veselyii to Ryilskii. After the XXXI Tank Corps fell back, the brigade was pulled back at 1900 to a line west of Kochetovka. It reported losses of 10 76mm guns, 15 45mm guns and 15 cars, and then reported at 0400 on the 10th, additional losses of 6 76mm and 1 45mm guns and 5 Studebakers. Equipment remaining was 2 76mm and 5 45mm guns, plus 40 cars.

By 1640, the armored spearheads from Battle Group Baum were in the ravine two kilometers east and north of the Kochetovka. Kochetovka fell to the Germans by the end of the day. By the end of the day also, the XXXI Tank Corps had fallen back to the line running from height 244.3 to height 211.9 to the southern outskirts of Olkhovatka, where it joined up with the 309th Rifle Division. This position had put the corps finally out of contact with the SS Panzer Corps and opposite the XLVIII Panzer Corps. As Senior Lieutenant Yevgenii Mikhailovich Skvortsov,[5] a tank company commander in the 237th Tank Brigade, described the action:

> On the afternoon of the 9th of July, at least 10 Tigers broke into our brigade's position. We destroyed some of them, but we suffered heavy losses ourselves. The German artillery was bombing us constantly for two hours. The aviation damaged only one tank in our company. We had four tanks left, including my tank. In the evening, about 40–50 tanks started to go around our brigade from the west, and about 20 tanks from the east. The attacks from the front continued all the time. Upon the order of Major Protsenko, brigade commander, we retreated to the northwest and took a defensive position near the Oboyan highway, near a village, the name of which I do not remember. We got some gas. Our soldiers finally had good food, for the first time since the 6th of July.

4 The actual reported losses for this day are 56 T-34s (43 burned) and 1 T-70 burned (Fond: First Tank Army, Opis: 3070, Delo: 226). As the totals from the daily reports are less than the total losses later reported for the corps, we estimate the actual losses to be around 70 tanks (with 14 T-70s damaged or destroyed).

5 Colonel Yevgenii Mikhailovich Skvortsov was born in 1923. He lives in Naro-Fominsk, Moscow Region, and was interviewed by Major General G. G. Nessonov in 1999.

THE LAST THREE days of combat had been a most difficult experience for the XXXI Tank Corps. It first entered battle late on the 6th, and spent the next three days in combat with mostly the Adolf Hitler SS Division. During that time it had little support, having been backed up by an antitank brigade, received support from the 192nd Tank Regiment on the 8th, and had supported and fought beside elements (basically a regiment) of the 51st Guards Rifle Division during most of that time. This tank corps lacked its own organic infantry and had minimal artillery support (12 76mm guns and 18 82mm Mortars). The corps went from 152 T-34s, 30 T-70s, 2 T-60s, 6 BA-64s, and 6 armored transports on the 6th, to having only around 41 T-34s, 12 T-70s, 1 T-60, 2 BA-64s, and 3 armored transports by the end of the 9th. This is a loss of at least 130 tanks (at least 134 according to our count), or over 70 percent of the formation's armor strength. In contrast, the Adolf Hitler SS Division lost 47 tanks (five destroyed) from the 7th through the 9th. This comes out to a 2.85-to-one loss ratio in armor (or 2.03 to one if we include the 19 tanks lost by Totenkopf on the 9th). Furthermore, most of the Adolf Hitler SS Division's losses occurred on the 7th, when it was still breaking through the infantry positions. In defense of the XXXI Tank Corps, they were operating at many disadvantages (little artillery, little infantry), and the Germans did have the full range of combined arms available, including air. Still, this was close to a straight fight between two armored forces (184 Soviet tanks versus 120 German tanks), which resulted in a very lop-sided exchange. On the whole, it was a poorly conceived force on the part of the Soviet high command, was poorly deployed without proper support, and while it conducted itself bravely in battle, it did not conduct itself effectively. These losses do not reflect well on its commander, Major General Dmitrii Cherniyenko or the commanders above him. Even Chistyakov (Sixth Guards Army) stated that the Germans on this day had managed to "break the resistance" of the XXXI Tank Corps and 51st Guards Rifle Division and only the timely arrival of the 309th Rifle Division halted the German advance.[6] At this stage, the SS Panzer Corps had now engaged four tank corps, and had gutted two of them (V Guards Tank Corps and XXXI Tank Corps).

AFTER SUKHO-SOLOTINO FELL, the Adolf Hitler SS Division disengaged from combat there and turned itself towards the northeast. The division ended up not involved in any other significant action for this day, due to the need to shift one regiment to fill the gap back to the Das Reich SS Division and the desire to withdraw the panzer regiment from the front line to undergo maintenance. The division then formed a rapid response motorized force and moved it into Luchki (north), holding it there until ordered. In effect, the Adolf Hitler SS Division took a "breather" this day while waiting for elements of Totenkopf to come forward and take over the western part of the SS Panzer Corps' area.

Totenkopf also advanced its other regiment, the reinforced Eicke SS Regiment (Battle Group Becker), relatively unopposed to the Psel River. The regiment arrived in its assembly area at Ozerovskii at 1415 and attacked toward Vasilyevka–Krasnyii Oktyabr at 1550. The Soviet forces in this area were weak. Obviously, Totenkopf had found the seam between the First Tank Army and the armored forces farther to the east. It took Kozlovka at 1845 but its attempt to establish a bridgehead across the Psel failed. By the end of the day the Germans had taken Prokhorovka (a town on the Psel, again, not the soon-to-be-famous one), Kozlovka, and the southwest part of Krasnyii Oktyabr. The only defending forces in the area were the rather battered 52nd Guards Rifle Division and the 11th Motorized Rifle Brigade and possibly the 178th Tank Brigade. These forces were emplaced on the north side of the Psel. They reported coming under attack at 1300 (Moscow time).[7]

---

6 Col. Gen. I. M. Chistyakov, *Sluzhim Otchizne* [We Serve the Fatherland] (Moscow, 1975), page 158.

7 Valeriy Zamulin, *Demolishing the Myth: The Tank Battle at Prokhorovka, Kursk, July 1943: An Operational Narrative* (Helion and Company, Ltd, Solihull, UK 2011), also describes these operations. He has the 11th Motorized Rifle Brigade abandoning Krasnyii Oktyabr under pressure from *Kampf-*

The German advance could now once again be expanded to two attacking divisions. Again, the problems caused by not having enough infantry to cover the flanks resulted in the German attack temporarily losing steam. Totenkopf, with the advance of Battle Group Baum, was able to establish connection with the 11th Panzer Division west of Kochetovka. Meanwhile, its other panzer grenadier regiment had secured the northeast flank of the division and reached the Psel. The gap that the SS Panzer Corps was pushing through was a major hole created by Soviet mistakes. First, they allowed the two tank corps in front of this advance, the XXXI Tank Corps and the V Guards Tank Corps, to be pushed off to the left and right. Then the other two arriving tank corps, the II and X, were also placed on the flank or transferred out of the battle area altogether. There was little to plug into the middle.

Das Reich Now Holds

The Das Reich SS Division spent the day on the defensive opposite the V Guards Tank Corps and II Tank Corps in the north and elements of the II Guards Tank Corps in the south. At 0645, the Germans observed strong tank and infantry forces being assembled in the balkas (gullies) east of Kalinin and across from Der Fuehrer SS Regiment at Ivanovskii Vyiselok and the Komsomolets Sovkhoz. At 0840 Soviet tanks and infantry attacked the positions of the III Battalion, Der Fuehrer SS Regiment along the Ivanovskii Vyiselok to Teterevino (south) road. This attack was repulsed by the combined fire of all weapons, especially the artillery. The Soviet forces retreated.

The II Tank Corps was engaged this day but there is very limited reporting on its activities. At 0700 on 10 July the 99th Tank Brigade was reported to be in the area from the outskirts of Vasilyevka to Andreyevka to Mikhailovka with 15 T-34s and 16 T-70s ready-for-action. The 26th Tank Brigade was positioned along the ravine southeast of Mikhailovka to height 241.6 with 11 T-34s and 14 T-70s ready-for-action. The 169th Tank Brigade was just outside of the southwestern edge of the woods two kilometers west of Storozhevoye, to the northern edge of the woods two kilometers north of Belenikhino with 23 T-34s and 18 T-70s ready-for-action. At the northwestern edge of the woods two kilometers northwest of Storozhevoye was the 15th Guards Heavy Tank Regiment with 11 Churchills ready-for-action. The corps' 58th Motorized Rifle Brigade was still well to the rear, concentrating at Krasnoye.

In their report at 0700 on the 10th, II Tank Corps recorded whether their tanks were knocked out or broken down. This gives us a record of the status of the tank corps except for the losses on the 8th (over 30). At this time the corps had on-hand 57 T-34s (out of 82 recorded) of which 12 were recorded as broken down (14.63% of the recorded strength were broken down); it had 49 T-70s on hand (out of 63 recorded) of which seven were broken down (11.11% of the recorded strength was broken down); and nine Churchills on hand (out of 13 recorded) of which two were broken down (15.38% of the original strength were broken down). While it is not known when these tanks broke down, it is suspected that it occurred on the march to the battlefield. These broken down figures (11 to 15%) are a pretty good indication of the loss of combat power suffered by this tank corps on its march to battle, which was a rather long march of more than 200 kilometers.[8] It had come from the Southwestern Front, where it had been sitting in the region of Urazovo, to the south of Valuiki, and had been resting and recovering for the last two months.[9] The corps was alerted around midnight of the night of

gruppe Becker. He has the Germans taking Kozlovka at 1845 (I assume Moscow time). He has the 52nd Guards Rifle Division defending the Psel.

8 Mikhail Khodarenok provides the same figure we calculated. He has the II Tank Corps receiving the order to move from the Urazovo region to Korocha at 2345 6 July. The corps reached the region of Korocha the evening of 7 July. At 2300 the corps received a new order to move to the region of Pravorot, Vinogradovka. It reached there around 0800 on 8 July. He concludes that "During 23 hours the tank formation moved more than 200 kilometers."

9 E. F. Ivanovskii, *Tankmen Began the Attack [Ataku Nachinali Tankistyi]* (Military Publishing House [Voyennoye Izdatelstvo,] Moscow, 1984).

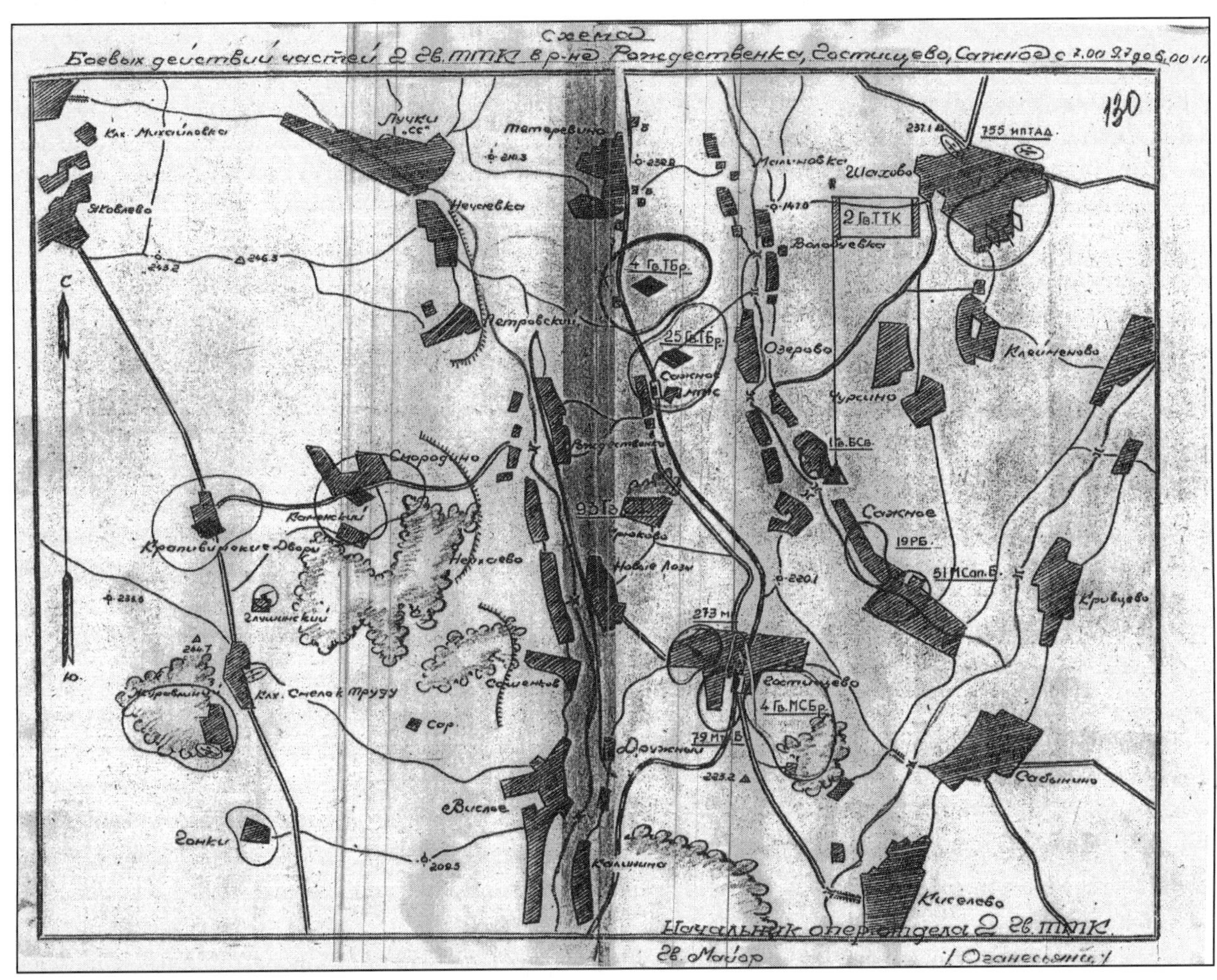

II Guards Tank Corps map from 0700, 9 July 1943, to 0500, 10 July 1943.

the 6th/7th, began moving on the 7th, and supposedly arrived (lead elements arrived?) by the morning of the 8th in the area of Storozhevoye (exclusive), Vinogradovka and Pravorot.[10]

This was an already seriously attrited corps by the morning of 10 July, with II Tank Corps reporting a total of 21 T-34s knocked out, 12 T-34s broken down, 8 T-70s knocked out and 7 broken down, and two Churchills knocked out and two broken down.[11] This indicates that the tank corps probably lost 21 tanks on the march (broken down) over the past couple of days, or that they were not ready to march to begin with. It also indicates that the tank corps lost 31 tanks in combat on the 9th in addition to over 30 tanks lost on the 8th. It appears that the II Tank Corps was primarily engaged with fighting the Das Reich, even though Das Reich lost only a handful of tanks this day (six!).

At 0900, the Soviets launched a tank attack against the positions of the I Battalion, Der Fuehrer SS Regiment east of Kalinin. This attack was also repulsed. At 1125, the division repulsed a Soviet attack by 10–15 tanks with infantry at the railroad booth south of Teterevino (south). The Germans claimed the Soviet infantry suffered heavy losses. The attack may have included the 4th Guards Tank Brigade of the II Guards Tank Corps.

These attacks may also have included the V Guards Tank Corps, but it reported little action this day nor any significant armor losses. Its 20th Tank Brigade transferred its tanks to the 21st Guards Tank Brigade, and the corps' remaining 18 T-34s and 13 T-70s held the line. The 48th Heavy Tank Regiment, which started the battle with 21 Churchills was now reporting four ready-for-action. The 6th Guards Motorized Brigade was reportedly reduced to 902 men (it originally had 2,500), but still had 10 (out of 12) 76mm guns left.

The Deutschland SS Regiment observed large tank concentrations throughout the day in the woods just east of Ivanovskii Vyiselok. Around 1400, 50 Soviet tanks were counted. Over the course of the day, about 100 tanks moved into these woods. Soviet infantry, in about battalion strength, was also reported. The Deutschland SS Regiment also observed a group of 23 tanks in the small woods two kilometers south of the woods east of Ivanovskii Vyiselok. At 1530, the railroad and presumably the concentration areas were bombarded by Stukas and German ground attack aircraft.

It is uncertain who was involved in these actions, but fighting there during the day certainly included the II Tank Corps. It appears that this corps lost 21 T-34s, two Churchills, and eight T-70s in combat this day.

THE II GUARDS Tank Corps regrouped during the night and was now deployed (as of 0700) with the 4th Guards Tank Brigade still south of Teterevino (south). The main body of the corps had disengaged and now was stretched inside the Donets triangle from Gostishchevo to Shakhovo in position to fight the panzer corps on either side of it (SS or III Panzer Corps). The 26th Guards Tank Brigade and the 755th Antitank Battalion were at Shakhovo, while the 25th Guards Tank Brigade was at the Sazhnoye MTS and two kilometers north of there. In the area of Gostishchevo was the 273rd Mortar Regiment, while the 4th Guards Motorized Rifle Brigade was also there and in the woods southeast of Gostishchevo. The 47th Guards Heavy Tank Regiment and the 1500th Antitank Regiment were in the south, already engaged with the III Panzer Corps. The units inside the Donets triangle did little this day and may have suffered virtually no losses, although south of there, the 47th Guards Heavy Tank Regiment was heavily engaged. At the end of the day the corps had 80 T-34s and 50 T-70s, which was 25 fewer tanks than

10 Location on the morning of the 8th comes from Valerii Nikolayevich Zamulin, *Prokhorovka—Neizvestnoye Srazheniye Velikoi Voinyi* [Prokhorovka—the Unknown Battle in the Great War] (Tranzitkniga, Moscow, 2005), page 99. According to other accounts by 0800 on 8 July it had concentrated in the Kamyishevka and Pravorot area. See Glantz and Orenstein, pages 92 and 154.

11 By brigade, this was for the 99th Tank Brigade 12 T-34s knocked out and 4 undergoing repairs, 4 T-70s knocked out and 4 broken down; for the 26th Tank Brigade 6 T-34s knocked out and 3 broken down, and 3 T-70s knocked-out and 3 broken down; and for the 169th Tank Brigade 3 T-34s knocked out and 5 broken down and 1 T-70 knocked out.

it had the previous day. It is hard to tell whether these were combat losses, mechanical breakdowns, or just the record keeping catching up from the previous day. It does appear that the corps' reserve of 20 T-34s and 10 T-70s had now been added into the existing tank brigades.[12] It was still reporting three days of food, 1.5 loads of ammunition, and 1.2 to 1.5 refills of fuel.

The 183rd Rifle Division (Sixty-ninth Army) continued its engagements with the 285th Rifle Regiment, attacking height 258.2 during the night, while other elements of the 183rd Rifle Division attacked Teterevino (south?), but without success. As the division's casualties for the day were low (31 killed and wounded), these attacks appear to have not been pushed forward with much vigor.

Air Support

The Adolf Hitler SS Division reported little Soviet air activity, but a strong friendly air presence. The Das Reich confirmed that Soviet air activity was less than in previous days. At 0734, a flight of about 25 Soviet fighters attacked the command post of the Der Fuehrer SS Regiment south of Kalinin. At 0900 30 fighters attacked the reconnaissance battalion in the area south of Ozerovskii. Totenkopf reports considerable air activity by both sides. At 1700 (Moscow time) two Me-109s strafed the II Guards Tank Corps headquarters at Sazhnoye.

The Soviets reported two fratricidal air attacks, one of 60 Il-2s against the 183rd Rifle Division and a similar size attack of 58 Il-2s against the II Tank Corps.[13]

An Appreciation of the Situation

As was the case with the XLVIII Panzer Corps, it appears that the SS Panzer Corps felt at this stage that it was winning the battle. They reported that the Soviets on their right flank were weakened due to high tank losses from the day before. The Soviet forces in front of them were stronger, but after the heavy blows of the previous day, they were still reeling from the shock. The Soviet tank forces in the Solotinka section (the left flank) were in a delaying fight but not backed up by sufficient infantry forces. It was the impression of at least the SS Panzer Corps' intelligence officer that the Soviets planned to meet the German's thrust from the south and from the north (from the Orel bulge) through flank operations from the east. He concluded that the withdrawal of infantry forces from their positions west of Kursk (around the perimeter of the bulge) was probable, but not yet certain.

One of the prisoners the Germans' interrogated reported that there were German and Romanian prisoners of war at work at the Kursk airport. If this report was true, these may well have been survivors from Stalingrad. It would have been a chilling reminder on this day of the German Army's defeat of the previous winter.

---

12 There is a report of tank strength by brigade for 0700 on 8 July that reports the corps reserve of 30 tanks. On 0700 on 10 July, there is a report of tank strength by brigade that shows no corps reserve. Of significance, the 4th Guards Tank Brigade is only down 2 T-34s and 3 T-70s, while the 25th Guards Tank Brigade has 4 more T-34s but is down 1 T-70, and the 26th Guards Tank Brigade is down 4 T-34s and 3 T-70s. This is after two days of fighting, during which 2 T-34s and 2 T-70s were reported as burned and 6 T-34s and 1 T-70 were reported as knocked out on the 8th and no tanks were reported lost on the 9th, except Churchills (see Fond: II Guards Tank Corps, Opis: 1: Delo: 32, pages: 187–189).

This is also supported by another report of 175 combat-ready tanks on 8 July and 138 combat-ready tanks on 10 July with 20 tanks (11 T-34s, 4 T-70s and 5 Churchills) reported lost on 9 July (Fond: 3400, Opis: 1, Delo: 31, pages: 60–90).

13 Source is Mikhail Khodarenok, "The First Prokhorovka," *Independent Military Review*, 16 May 2003. He quotes Major General Alexei Popov (II Tank Corps) stating in his battle report of 9 July, "I ask to inform Comrade Vatutin that we were bombed by our own airplanes Il-2, totaling 58 airplanes."

Zamulin, *Demolishing the Myth*, pages 288–289, also notes this fratricidal attack against the 183rd Rifle Division and quotes a report from the Chief of Staff of the Sixty-ninth Army that states it came between 0700–0900 against the 285th and 295th Rifle Regiments in the vicinity of Vasilyevka, Komsomolets State Farm and Hill 241.6. According to Zamulin these locations are all in the 285th Rifle Regiment's area. Zamulin was unable to find data on the losses caused by this incident, but I do note that the division suffered only 31 casualties this day.

Advance to Kochetovka and the Psel, 9 July 1943

DURATION One day FRONTAGE 20.4 kilometers TERRAIN Rolling WEATHER Clear to cloudy

	Attacker	*Defender*
Units	T SS PzGrD	52nd Gds RD, XXXI TC & others
Attachments	See below	See below
Strength	19,416	17,690
Armor	109	133 (36 light tanks)
Artillery	145	131
Air Sorties	181	50
Casualties	93 (19 KIA, 69 WIA, 5 MIA)	244 (78 KIA, 124 WIA, 42 MIA)
Armor Losses	18	47
Artillery Losses	1	20
Enemy Captured	N/A	3

Forces Engaged

German Attachments

II/1st Lehr Werfer Regiment
III/55th Werfer Regiment (attached on the 9th)
SS Corps Werfer Battalion (detached on the 9th—not included)

Detached

"T" Assault Gun Battalion (13 StuGs are subtracted from totals above)

Soviet Forces

52nd Guards Rifle Division (all)

230th Tank Regiment (detached on the 9th, not included)
1008th AT Regiment (detached on the 9th, not included)
133rd AT Rifle Bn
I/5th Gds Mortar Rgt
75th Flamethrower Co.
95th Flamethrower Co.
Bn/156th GRR/51st GRD (not included)
28th AT Bde (not included, facing the XLVIII Panzer Corps)

From X Tank Corps

11th Motorized Rifle Brigade[14]
287th Mortar Rgt[15]
178th Tank Brigade[16]
727th AT Regiment[17]

2/3rds XXXI Tank Corps (the 237st and 100th Tank Regiment)

210th ATR Bn
1244th AT Rgt
192nd Tank Bde (detached on the 9th, not included, facing XLVIII Panzer Corps)
59th Tank Regiment (attached on the 9th, not included, facing XLVIII Panzer Corps)
4th Guards AT Regiment (attached on the 9th, not included)

29th AT Bde (independent)

---

14 This unit was reported on 7 July to consist of 13 76mm guns, 12 45mm guns, 6 120mm Mortars, 30 82mm Mortars, 110 LMGs, 45 HMGs and 1,500 Riflemen. Its losses from 5 to 18 July were reported to be 569 killed and 1,556 wounded. Its authorized strength would have been around 3,152.

15 This unit was reported on 7 July to consist of 36 120mm Mortars. Its losses from 5 to 18 July were reported to be 3 killed and 33 wounded. Its authorized strength would have been around 670.

16 This unit was reported on 7 July to consist of 32 T-34s, 21 T-70s, 4 45mm AT guns, 6 82mm Motars, 20 LMGs, 4 HMGs and 428 rifle troops. Its losses from 5 to 18 July were reported to be 34 killed and 134 wounded. Its authorized strength would have been around 1,264 or less.

17 This unit was reported on 7 July to consist of 12 76mm guns and 8 45mm guns. Its losses from 5 to 18 July were reported to be 2 killed and 6 wounded. Its authorized strength would have been less than 500.

The Adolf Hitler SS Division Rests, 9 July 1943

DURATION One day FRONTAGE 18.9 kilometers TERRAIN Rolling
WEATHER Sunny in the morning, dreary and rainy in the afternoon

	Attacker	*Defender*
Units	LSSAH PzGrD	51st GRD & ele. of XXXI Tank Corps
Attachments	See below	See below
Strength	21,037	6,145
Armor	98 (6 light tanks)	40 (8 light tanks)
Artillery	159	24
Air Sorties	182	14 + 17 Night
Casualties	48 (12 KIA, 34 WIA, 2 MIA)	37 (9 KIA, 14 WIA, 14 MIA)
Armor Losses	10	23
Artillery Losses	4	3
Enemy Captured	N/A	0

Forces Engaged

German Attachments
55th Werfer Regiment
861st Light Field Howitzer Battalion

Detachments
III/55th Werfer Regiment

Soviet Forces
2/3rds of 51st Guards Rifle Division (154th & 156th Guards Rifle Regiments; the 158th Guards Rifle Regiment is at Teterevino)
+ 14th Antitank Brigade (attached on the 8th, not included, facing the XLVIII Panzer Corps)
+ 111th Howitzer Rgt (attached on the 9th, not included)
1/3rd XXXI Tank Corps (242nd Tank Brigade)

The 167th Infantry Division Relieves Totenkopf

By about 0500 on the 9th, the Geman infantry division, less one of its three infantry regiments, completed occupation of its new sector along the Lipovyii Donets. It had taken the division a day to move 13 kilometers to the east and adopt a new defensive line. It had left behind its 339th Infantry Regiment, which was attached to 11th Panzer Division and covering that division's right flank. While it was getting into positions during the night, the Soviets attacked with tanks supported by infantry from their bridgehead at Visloye. The attacks hit the 167th Infantry Division positions at heights 229.5 and 209.5 (west of Visloye). The attack was repulsed by artillery fire. The division also reported heavy Soviet air activity during the night, with both bombing and strafing.

At 0820, there were weak Soviet attacks from Nepkhayevo. They were repelled by the reinforced 315th Infantry Regiment. Confusion over the responsibility for sectors prevented the deployment of the 238th

Das Reich Now Holds, 9 July 1943

DURATION One day FRONTAGE 27.0 kilometers TERRAIN Rolling, mixed
WEATHER Sunny, "brutally warm."

	Attacker	*Defender*
Units	II TC, V GTC, 183rd RD & others	DR SS PzGrD
Attachments	See below	See below
Strength	29,776	20,392
Armor	233 (94 light tanks)	97 (1 light tank)
Artillery	193	147
Air Sorties	36	218
Casualties	1,098 (321 KIA, 618 WIA, 159 MIA)	174 (23 KIA, 149 WIA, 2 MIA)
Armor Losses	65	6
Artillery Losses	8	3
Enemy Captured	2	N/A

Forces Engaged

German Attachments
III/1st Lehr Werfer Regiment
SS Flak Platoon (not included)
SS Flak Platoon (not included)
627th Engineer Battalion
III/818th Artillery Regiment

Soviet Forces
II Tank Corps
V Guards Tank Corps
183rd Rifle Division
1/3rd of 51st Guards Rifle Division (the 158th Guards Rifle Regiment)
4th Guards Tank Brigade of the II Guards Tank Corps[18]

18 The corps is reported to have lost 11 T-34s and 4 T-70s on the 9th of July, yet the decline in strength of ready-for-action tanks would indicate a total lost of 14 T-34s and 11 T-70s. This later figure was used, although it may be high and may include tanks not with the 4th Guards Tank Brigade.

Reconnaissance Battalion on the left flank, next to Das Reich SS Division.

At 0500, having relieved the Totenkopf SS Division, the 167th Infantry Division was now attached directly to the control of the Fourth Panzer Army. During the period of the relief, the division temporarily had attached to it the SS Corps Werfer Battalion (less two batteries) and the Totenkopf Assault Gun Battalion.[19]

19 Totenkopf Assault Gun Battalion was attached on the 8th and the SS Corps Werfer Battalion on the 9th.

These were returned to the SS Panzer Corps by the end of the day.

The Soviets had built a temporary bridge at Rozhdestvenka under the cover of tank and artillery fire. The Germans observed infantry groups on the bridge. The Soviets sent out probes in the balka north of the Smorodino–Rozhdestvenka road in the zone of the 627th Engineer Battalion (attached to Das Reich). These patrols were repulsed by the combined defensive fire of all weapons. The German artillery fired harassing missions at the bridge construction site. In the early afternoon, the Soviets were seen moving reinforcements by truck to Rozhdestvenka from the southeast.

These were certainly elements of the 93rd Guards Rifle Division which remained deployed with its 278th and 285th Guards Rifle Regiments in the area from the ravine north of Rozhdestvenka down to Kryukovo, which is where they were the previous day. Their 281st Guards Rifle Regiment was now holding from the mill north of Gostishchevo to the road junction of Novyiye Lozyi and Druzhnyii.

Before noon, the Soviets hit both ravines north and south of the Rozhdestvenka–Smorodino road with infantry. Artillery fire came from the woods west of Kalinin and from the area around Gostishchevo. The bridges at Novyiye Lozyi, Visloye, and Ternovka were opened along with the temporary bridge at Rozhdestvenka. Around 1215, Das Reich expressed concern about its right flank, sending a message back to corps. A couple of minutes later, the corps notified the 167th Infantry Division that it was responsible for the Smorodino to Donets Bridge to Rozhdestvenka road. The resolution of these combats was not reported, but as the 167th Infantry Division held position this day, they were certainly resolved in favor of the Germans. The 93rd Guards Rifle Division reported 13 killed and 96 wounded for the day, while the 89th Guards Rifle Division provided a revised report of 75 killed and 205 wounded. Neither division reported the number of missing, although there were clearly some.[20] The opposing 167th Infantry Division lost 17 killed, 62 wounded and 1 missing on this day, but these figures may have also included losses from the detached 339th Infantry Regiment.

At 1750, artillery observers reported the arrival of friendly panzers in Kiselevo (these would be from the III Panzer Corps) and that friendly forces had appeared behind the Soviet positions on the division's right flank.

20 Based upon the 89th Guards Rifle Division strength reports it is estimated that there were over 1,000 casualties that we did not have reports on for this division alone. These were assumed to be missing.

FINALLY, ON THIS day at 1130,[21] the Sixty-ninth Army, which had only one operational corps (the XLVIII Rifle Corps), was reorganized. The 107th and 305th Rifle Divisions, which had barely been engaged in combat, were to be transferred to the XXXV Guards Rifle Corps. They were replaced in the XLVIII Rifle Corps by the 89th Guards Rifle Division (originally Sixth Guards Army) and 93rd Guards Rifle Division (originally XXXV Guards Rifle Corps). This corps had all its forces on line, from Vasilyevka to Teterevino to Gostishchevo to the outskirts of Khokhlovo. This was a line of over 40 kilometers for three divisions (which were also backed up by two tank corps). Both of these newly attached divisions were still relatively fresh, with the 93rd Guards Rifle Division strength reported to be 8,000 men and 90% of its authorized equipment, while the 89th Guards Rifle Division also had 8,000 men and 95% of its authorized equipment. The 93rd Guards Rifle Division occupied the line from Petrovskii to Novyiye Lozyi (around six kilometers and mostly opposite the 167th Infantry Division), while the 89th Guards Rifle Division was now shifted further south, stretched along the river from Druzhnyii to the outskirts of Petropavlovka (around eight kilometers). It was the 183rd Rifle Division that was stretched beyond reason. It had been deployed with its 285th Rifle Regiment deployed from Vasilyevka to height 258.2 to Teterevino Kolkhoz, which put it right across the route to Prokhorovka. The 295th Rifle Regiment was to its left, from Ivanovskii Vyiselok to Teterevino, and the 227th Rifle Regiment was well to the south, making up a second echelon from Volobuyevka to Sazhnoye to outside of Krivtsovo.[22] This

21 Time from Glantz and Orestein, page 107.

22 Note that this report of the 227th Rifle Regiment's location at 1900 on the 9th (Fond: Sixty-ninth Army, Opis: 10753, Delo: 133, page: 9) is the last location we have reported until the 12th. We do not know exactly what it was doing or even whether it was engaged in combat on the 10th and 11th of July. We have assumed that it was not engaged.

The regiment was reported on the 12th to be in the eastern outskirts of Kalinin in preparation for its attack (Fond: 1433, Opis: 1, Delo: 10). *(continued)*

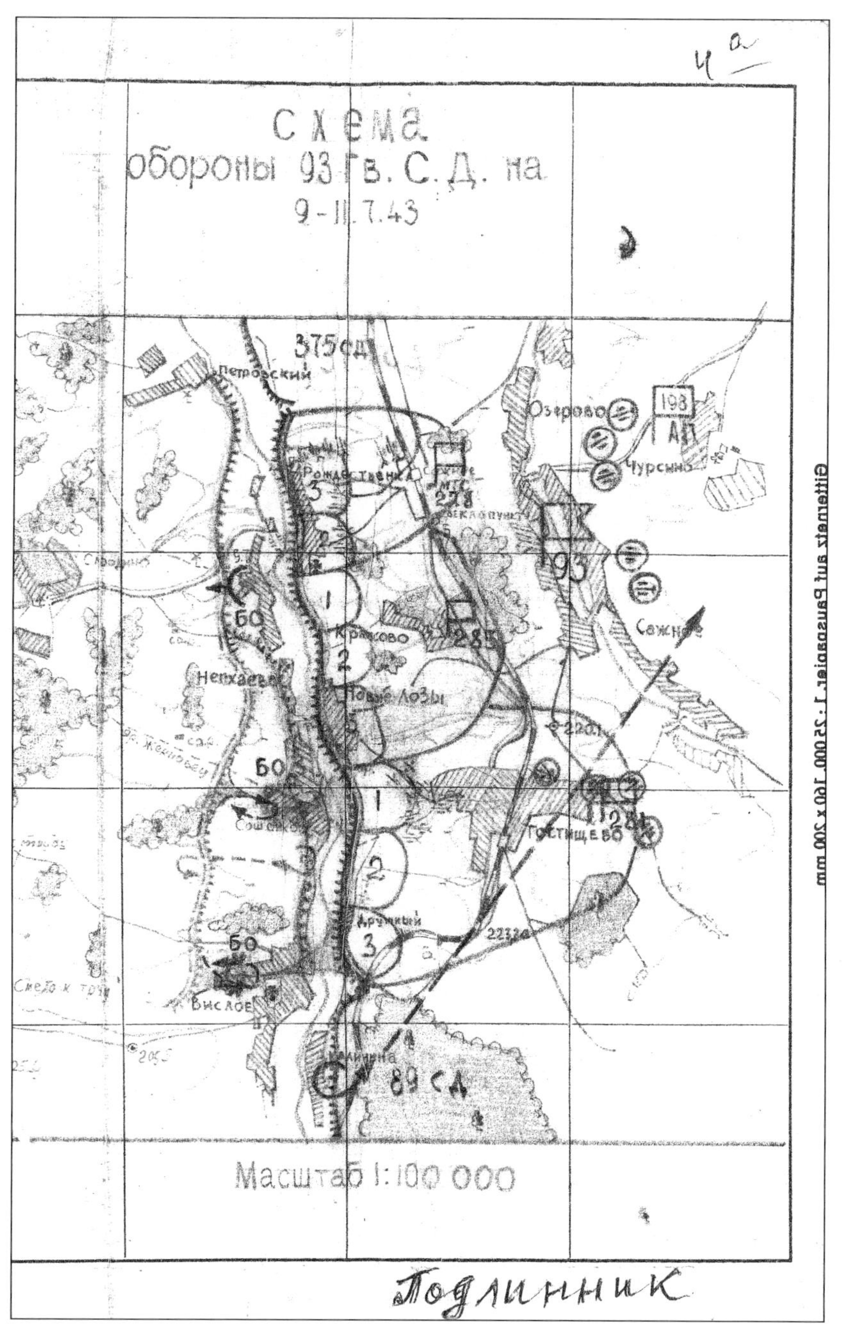

Defense scheme of the 93rd Guards Rifle Division, 9–11 July 1943.

167th Infantry Division Relieves Totenkopf, 9 July 1943

DURATION One day FRONTAGE 19.8 kilometers TERRAIN Rolling, mixed
WEATHER Variably cloudy with evening thunderstorms.

	Attacker	*Defender*
Units	89th & 93rd Gds RD	167th ID
Attachments	See below	See below
Strength	18,637	11,440
Armor	0	13
Artillery	159	130
Air Sorties	17 Night	0
Casualties	559 (88 KIA, 301 WIA, 170 MIA)	82 (18 KIA, 63 WIA, 1 MIA)
Enemy Captured	0	N/A

Forces Engaged

German Attachments
I/1st Lehr Werfer Regiment
"T" Assault Gun Battalion (attached on the 8th)
SS Corps Werfer Battalion (attached on the 9th)

Detached
339th Infantry Regiment (detached on the 8th)

Soviet Forces
93rd Guards Rifle Division
89th Guards Rifle Division
27th Gun Bde (attached on the 9th)

effectively put the 183rd Rifle Division stretched along a 20 kilometer front with the second echelon to its southeast. None of these three divisions were heavily engaged during the day.

The XXXV Guards Rifle Corps, now consisting of the 107th Rifle Division, 305th Rifle Division, and the 375th Rifle Division had been transferred to Sixty-ninth Army control and it had been shifted to the east and was now opposite the III Panzer Corps.[23] This put the Soviet infantry command structure on a more rational basis, with the Fortieth Army controlling the infantry facing the German infantry on the western flank, the Sixth Guards Army in charge of the infantry facing the front of the XLVIII and SS Panzer Corps, the Sixty-ninth Army in charge of the infantry in the Donets triangle, and the II Guards Tank Corps and the Seventh Guards Army in charge of the infantry east of the Donets.

David M. Glantz in his *Atlas of the Battle of Kursk*, page 48, shows the 227th Rifle Regiment in the area of Vinogradovka to Belenikhino on the 10th and 11th. This is the first reference to the 227th Rifle Regiment in this atlas. This would put it opposite the Das Reich SS Division for these two days. It is still shown there on the 12th.

23 Actually we are not certain where the division's 1243rd Rifle Regiment was on this day. It was still in the Shopino area on the 8th (facing Totenkopf) and on the 10th was occupying a line from northeast of Kiselevo to height 211.5 (facing III Panzer Corps).

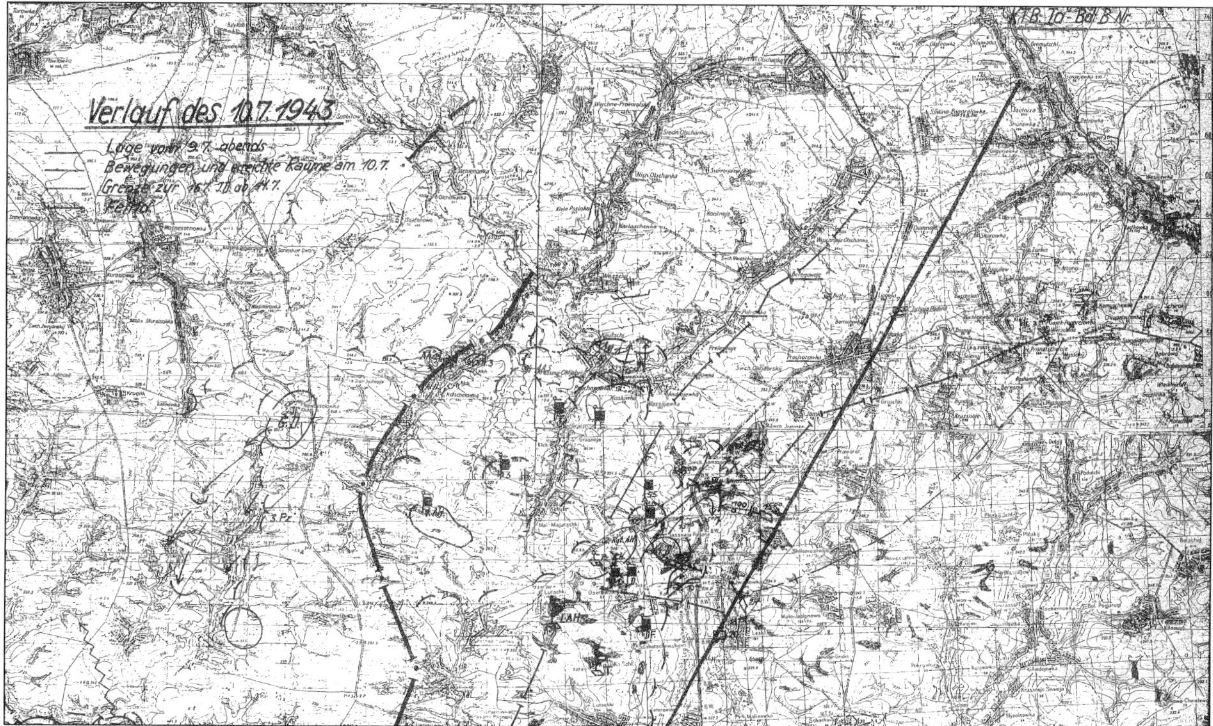

The SS Panzer Corps map showing positions on the 10th of July.

The XXXV Guards Rifle Corps was tasked with defending from Petropavlovka to Staryii Gorod and Myasoyedovo area with the mission of blocking the German advance on Korocha. That the Germans were not intending to push to Korocha was something that the Soviet command had not yet realized. They had probably been deceived by the sweep to the east by the German III Panzer Corps.

The SS Panzer Corps Continues to the Northeast, 10 July

Finally, the SS Panzer Corps was moving towards Prokhorovka again, this time with the Totenkopf SS Division on the left, the Adolf Hitler SS Division in the center, and the Das Reich SS Division on the right. This was still effectively a two-division attack as Das Reich SS Division was tied down defending against the significant Soviet armored forces on its flank. Still, it would contribute a regiment to the attack. Extending the flank back to Belgorod was the 167th Infantry Division.

The giant wedge in the Germans lines, separating the SS Panzer Corps from the III Panzer Corps, had become a major problem. Instead of the III Panzer Corps serving to protect the SS Panzer Corps' right flank, the SS Panzer Corps and the Fourth Panzer Army were forced to commit two divisions to protecting its flank, including one of its SS armored divisions. In light of the terrain and defensive networks to the northeast of Belgorod, the III Panzer Corps maneuvers made perfect sense. Still, what was good for the III Panzer Corps was not good for the SS Panzer Corps. Looking at the III Panzer Corps operations, especially their tank losses, one is hard pressed to accept the idea that they should have indeed attacked head on into strong Soviet positions. This would have certainly bled them dry. As it was, with its penetration, the III Panzer Corps was currently dealing with eight Soviet infantry divisions, a tank brigade, and two tank regiments. They were taking considerable pressure off of the SS Panzer Corps but they were still not covering the flank. One cannot help wondering if the Germans would have been better served to have reduced the III Panzer Corps attack and moved one or two of its divisions into the SS Panzer Corps attack (in particular the 6th Panzer Division).

Because of the gap discovered in the Soviet lines around Greznoye, Totenkopf suddenly found itself on the edge of the Psel from Krasnyii Oktyabr to Kozlovka. At midnight, 9 July, the division formed a bridgehead over the Psel at Kozlovka and sent out patrols to capture hill 226.6. This attack ground to a halt by 0215 before the strong defensive positions on the controlling heights of hill 226.6 and the heavy fire from at least seven Soviet artillery batteries in the area southeast of Veselyii (the village on the Psel River). The division prepared to resume the attack at 1000 with carefully prepared air support. In order to dissipate the Soviet artillery fire, the Adolf Hitler SS Division was to attack at the same time.

In the morning, bad weather conditions, including rain and deep cloud cover, would not allow Luftwaffe support for these attacks. The SS Panzer Corps decided to launch the attacks anyway, and at 1000 Totenkopf attacked across the Psel. Battle Group Becker (the Eicke SS Regiment) was on the right, Battle Group Baum (the Totenkopf SS Regiment) was on the left in the area from Kozlovka to Krasnyii Oktyabr. The artillery preparation consisted of the division's entire artillery regiment and one and one-half rocket (werfer) battalions. At 1100, the Totenkopf SS Division reported in error that it had managed to establish a bridgehead at the little woods immediately southeast of Klyuchi but was encountering heavy resistance in the stream valley north of Koslovka. They reported at 1125 that their advance was proceeding slowly under Soviet artillery and mortar fire and that the river had not been crossed. As of 1300, they had still not crossed the Psel. This effort, even with its artillery preparation, failed. The first weak forces to cross the river were thrown back. The Sixty-ninth Army reported the 99th Tank Brigade (II Tank Corps) entered battle along the Psel, and with the 11th Motorized Rifle Brigade (X Tank Corps), reported kicking the German infantry and tanks out of Prokhorovka (the town on the Psel, not the famous one) and Kozlovka, retaking these towns at 1100 (Moscow time) on the 10th of July.[24]

Finally, at 1515 (Berlin time), the left wing of the Eicke SS Regiment reported forcing a river crossing despite violent resistance, and penetrated into the Soviet first line of defense there at 1542. This attack was supported by artillery fire. At around 1700, after hard fighting, they had pushed through to a point about 800 meters north of the river and were advancing against height 226.6. Meanwhile, Group Baum had crossed the river into the woods at Klyuchi. The Totenkopf SS Division had finally obtained air support and claimed that the Russians were running from the Stukas. With the improvement in the weather conditions in the afternoon, the Soviet dive bombers were driven off and the first objectives reached, with height 226.6 falling to Totenkopf at 1915.

By evening, the Totenkopf SS Division had expanded the bridgehead from east of Klyuchi to over height 226.6 to the bridge one kilometer northwest of Mikhailovka. The reconnaissance battalion had moved to about

24 Zamulin, *Demolishing the Myth*, page 189 also reports a successful counterattack this day:

> "The sharp counterattack of Lieutenant Colonel L. I. Malov's 99th Tank Brigade in cooperation with Colonel P. G. Borodkin's 11th Motorized Rifle Brigade had some success. By 1100, panzers and Panzergrenadiers from the SS Panzergrenadier Division Totenkopf had been driven from the village of Prokhorovka (10 kilometers west of Prokhorovka Station), Kozlovka, and the western outskirts of Vasil'evka. This spoiling attack somewhat delayed the timetable for the enemy's assault upon Prokhorovka Station, but the enemy refused to abandon his plan."

1.5 kilometers south of Veselyii (on the Psel) and was probing toward it. The poor battered 52nd Guards Rifle Division was right in the face of this advance, with its positions at 1700 (Moscow time) reported to be from Klyuchi to height 226.6 to Polezhayev. The Soviets reported that the Germans at 1830 had taken Klyuchi, the southern part of Veselyii (on the Psel) and also Bogoroditskoye.[25] (Bogoroditskoye is often not marked on maps, but it is south of the Psel just west of Vasilyevka).

The 52nd's sister division, the 51st Guards Rifle Division, was disengaging this day and by the end of the day was out of contact with the fighting. Two of its guards rifle regiments (the 154th and 156th) stretched from height 211.9 to height 188.1 to Ilinskii (on the Psel). They had suffered 47 killed and 76 wounded for the day (possibly from engagements with the 11th Panzer Division). The 156th Guards Rifle Regiment reported a strength of 420 men. Over the next few days this division continued to fall back, completely disengaging from combat. Its 158th Guards Rifle Regiment, along with remnants of the 156th Guards Rifle Regiment, were still engaged fighting on the flank of the Das Reich SS Division and had been subordinated to the Sixty-ninth Army.

In light of the reasonably defensible terrain on the opposing bank, the ability of the SS division to force this crossing in the afternoon clearly shows a failure on the part of the Voronezh Front to properly appreciate and defend this terrain. As much as one can criticize the details of the operations of the neighboring First Tank Army, it did manage to hold the southern bank of the Pena in the face of the XLVIII Panzer Corps until itwas flanked at Verkhopenye. The difference, of course, is that it was holding the Pena with a tank corps and a rifle division, while here it had only a very battered rifle division and motorized infantry brigade holding the Psel, and with only part of a tank corps on the flank to counterattack.

There had been good armored forces in the area initially in the form of the X Tank Corps, but most of this unit was shifted to the west the day before the Germans arrived. What was then brought forward to defend the Psel was the Fifth Guards Army, which consisted of seven rifle divisions, but it did not start arriving until the 11th. Effectively at this moment in this area, the Germans were primarily fighting the gutted 52nd Guards Rifle Division and the 11th Motorized Rifle Brigade. The three tank brigades of the X Tank Corps were farther west, although three tank brigades from the II Tank Corps had moved into the area in front of Prokhorovka and one brigade was counterattacking along the Psel. Yet there were seven supporting rifle divisions in the

25 Zamulin, *Demolishing the Myth*, pages 182–183, describes the deployment of the defense along the Psel. No time is given for these dispositions.

"Units of the 52nd Guards Rifle [Division] were dug-in along the northern bank of the bend in the Psel River: its 151st Guards Rifle Regiment was holding the sector stretching from a knoll 500 meters north of Kliuchi to a point 1.5 kilometers southwest of Hill 226.6; its 155th Guards Rifle Regiment lay ready on the sector running between Hill 226.6 and the grove southeast of Kliuchi; its 153rd Guards Rifle Regiment was holding the sector between a path lying 1.5 kilometers east of Hill 226.6 and the village of Polezhaev. The artillery battalions of the 124th Guards Artillery Regiment were positioned behind the trenches of the rifle battalion in two locations: 1 kilometer southwest of Polezhaev and 400 meters southeast of Veselyi. The 11th Motorized Rifle Brigade's 3rd Motorized Battalion was dug in on the crest of Hill 226.6.

Lieutenant Colonel L. I. Malov's 99th Tank Brigade of the 2nd Tank Corps was defending the left (southern) bank of the Psel, in the villages of Vasel'evka and Andreevka. Its defenses were buttressed by two batteries from the 2nd Tank Corps' 1502nd Destroyer Anti-tank Artillery Regiment, as well as the 11th Motorized Rifle Brigade's 1st and 2nd Motorized Rifle Battalions."

Zamulin further states on page 187:

"Thus, on the morning of 10 July . . . In Totenkopf's sector of attack, the 51st Guards Rifle Division of the 6th Guards Army was defending the sector Hill 211.9- Hill 207.8-Il'inskii; 6th Guards Army's 52nd Guards Rifle Division was holding the sector Hill 226.6-Polezhaev (along the northern bank of the Psel River). The positions of the 285th Rifle Regiment of the 183rd Rifle Division and the 11th Motorized Rifle Brigade of the 10th Tank Corps lay in front of Leibstandarte and Das Reich, on the sector Vasil'evka-Molozhavaia gully-Komsomolets State Farm-Ivanovskii Vyselko-Storozhevoe."

The 11th Motorized Rifle Brigade was probably just around Vasilyevka.

Many of the Soviet histories have strange statements, such as, "The enemy understood that he was not going to reach Oboyan and Kursk, and by the evening of 9 July had begun to pull back his troops to another axis. He now directed his spearhead at Prokhorovka, so that, bypassing to the east, he attempted to take Kursk."[1]

This theme shows up in many Soviet histories and some western histories. It appears to have been generated by a wartime misperception that is repeated enough times to became accepted as true. What probably created this perception was that the XLVIII Panzer Corps was attacking forward up to Verkhopenye, when it turned west, while on the 8th and 9th, the SS Panzer Corps pushed due north and northwest so as to destroy and clear the forces south of the Psel. This would have given the impression that pressure was released or halted on the push to Oboyan while the SS Panzer Corps then shifted to the northeast on the 10th.

In fact, the SS Panzer Corps plan of attack always went through Prokhorovka. A simple look at the Fourth Panzer Army or SS Panzer Corps plans or planning maps from 30 June makes this clear. It was Hoth's efforts on the 8th and 9th to push north and northwest so as to destroy Soviet armor that made it look like there was a redirection or change of emphasis.

We still find this focus on Prokhorovka in recent Russian writings. For example, in one recently published book, the author correctly argued that the decision to drive towards Prokhorovka was not made "on the fly." Then there is an extended discussion on how the German plan was now focused on turning the six armored divisions of the Fourth Panzer Army on Prokhorovka. While this is indeed supported by one German account, it is really not a correct depiction.[2] The XLVIII Panzer Corps objective was always Oboyan and this is where they were attempting to advance on the 11th and 12th of July.[3] General Hoth, the Fourth Panzer Army commander, in May and June did modify his army's plan

1 Col. Gen. I. M. Chistyakov, *Sluzhim Otchizne* [We Serve the Fatherland] (Moscow, 1975), page 159.

2 The author makes the argument that the real objective for the Fourth Panzer Army was Prokhorovka. It is clear from the German orders that the LXVIII Panzer Corps objective was Oboyan and the SS Panzer Corps was to advance to its right, which put its advance through the Psel River and of course, Prokhorovka. See Valeriy Zamulin, *Demolishing the Myth*, pages 29–33. His source is Steven H. Newton's book *Kursk: The German View* (Da Capo Press, Boston, 2003), pages 77–79. Newton quotes from writer #742, thought to be Friedrich Fangohr, General Hoth's Chief of Staff.

Zamulin on page 31 quotes Fangohr: "Such a prospect also led General Hoth to modify the mission of the XXXXVIIII Panzer Corps on our left flank. After it initial breakthrough on either side of Cherkasskoe, the corps would not push north to the Psel but keep abreast of the II SS Panzer Corps as it wheeled to the northeast. Such a maneuver would cover *Obergruppenführer* Hausser's flank as he advanced towards the decisive battle with the Soviet reserves and potentially provide additional reinforcements for that engagement. To be sure, we could not as yet determine the manner in which the XXXXVIII Panzer corps might be committed around Prokhorovka, though in no event would we commit General von Knobelsdorff's corps to an attack west of this objective." While he correctly quotes this account, this account does not appear to match the orders and events of the battle as it was actually conducted.

3 The German orders on 1 April 1943 has the "west group" occupy a line of Marino-Oboyan while the immediate objective of "east group," which included the SS Panzer Corps, was the occupation of the intersection at Korocha and the high ground at Skorodnoye and to the northwest of there. This actually puts Prokhorovka on right flank of the advance by the "west group." The two panzer groups were to meet in a pincer movement to reach the line of Skorodnoye-Marino-Oboyan, See page 53–57 of my original book, *Kursk: The Battle of Prokhorovka*.

Hitler's operations order for 15 April had Army Group South breaking through the line Prilepy-Oboyan and linking up with Army Group Center at or east of Kursk. Covering the eastern flank would be force along the line of Nezhega-Korocha-Skordnoye-Tim. The SS Panzer Corps was now part of the group advancing in the center.

to move the SS Panzer Corps to the northeast across the Psel and through Prokhorovka and instructed the LXVIII Panzer Corps to go around Oboyan from the east.[4] The right boundary line for the SS Panzer Corps on their maps on 4 and 9 July reflect this.[5] But, this was clearly part of the plan from the start, not a redirection. Several authors have discussed the redirection to Prokhorovka on the 10th of July by General Hoth. What General Hoth did on the 8th of July was to redirect two reinforced panzer regiments of the SS Panzer Corps to the northwest. They were both recalled back to their divisions at the end of the day. On the 9th it was a push to the northwest by one reinforced regiment from Totenkopf and one from LSSAH.[6]

---

4 There is an extended discussion of this in Newton, pages 357–370. This discussion is based in part upon the post-war paper written by Hoth's chief of staff, General Fangohr. But, as the author notes on page 367, "The barely decipherable handwritten notes from the XLVIII Panzer Corps (sans maps) exercise still survive . . . these notes indicate that Fourth Panzer Army, a full month before the offensive started, envisioned the Grossdeutschland Panzergrenadier Division as the spearhead unit to drive straight north toward the Psel River crossing and directly threaten Oboyan." He also notes the Fourth Panzer Army final attack orders issued on 28 June and 3 July, which states that they were to ". . . move on Kursk and the area to the east, going around Oboyan to the east." This passage appears to have been interpreted by Zamulin to mean through or around Prokhorovka. It appears that XLVIII Panzer Corps objective was to move north of the Psel to the east of Oboyan, perhaps with the crossing point being at Peresyip, on the corps right flank.

Clearly the XLVIII Panzer Corps' objective was to move north and cross the Psel, and this was again discussed in a conference at 1700 on 10 July between Hoth and Knobelsdorff (the corps commander). Hoth's objective for the 11th Panzer Division, on the corps right flank, for the 11th was the town of Orlovka, which is on the high ground around four kilometers from the Psel (see 1:50000 scale map M-37-25-G). The corps' objective for the 12th was the attack across the Psel. See *Kursk: The Battle of Prokhorovka*, pages 699–700. On the morning of 11 July there was a conference between Manstein, Hoth and Kempf at Kempf's headquarters in Dolbino. As part of that discussion, Hoth stated that the desire was to free up the Gross Deutschland Division and move it to crossing the Psel at Peresyip on the 13th. Peresyip is on the Psel just north of Kochetovka. It was in the 11th Panzer Division's sector. This would have moved the Gross Deutschland Division to the corps' right flank, perhaps giving it a northeastern thrust for the 13th. This move never occurred. See *Kursk: The Battle of Prokhorovka*, pages 801 and 804.

I seriously doubt these deployments mean anything more than a tactical move around Oboyan once the LXVIII Panzer Corps, with its three deployed armored divisions, reached Oboyan. The river valley immediately south of Oboyan was clearly going to be difficult to cross while the areas a few kilometers to the east were easier to cross. Still, I doubt the intention was to completely bypass Oboyan and leave it on their flank (see 1:50000 scale map M-37-25-B). Newton's effort is a fairly complex attempt to divine Hoth's planning based upon one post-war interview and a few references in the files. I am not sure it succeeds. Zamulin appears to have relied on this to make Prokhorovka the central objective of the Fourth Panzer Army, which I think is overstating the case.

5 See pages 464 and 724 of my original book, *Kursk: The Battle of Prokhorovka*. Those right boundary lines are unchanged on the map for 9 July, which is included at the start of Chapter Ten. It clearly shows the lines for two divisions moving north-northeast, with the left (west) boundary going through the gully through Solotino and Kochetovka up to the Psel River, and right (east) boundary going just west of Pravorot and just south and east of Prokhorovka.

6 See my original book, *Kursk: The Battle of Prokhorovka*, pages 621 and the maps on pages 624 and 724.

Fifth Guards Army that could have been alerted and brought forward but these were not ordered to move until the 9th, and did not arrive at the front until the 11th. This gap in the movement left the area across the Psel lightly held on the 10th. As such, the Germans were able to force a crossing, giving them play to the north and providing left flank protection through the gap leading to Prokhorovka. Still, this was not a critical error on the part of the Soviets as the Psel bent in a giant semi-circle here and was basically hilly terrain inside this circle. As such, it was relatively easy to defend further back, at the base of the semi-circle. Still, holding this river line would have served to greatly constrict German operations on the 11th and 12th.

WHILE THE TOTENKOPF SS Division waited to cross during the morning, the Leibstandarte SS Adolf Hitler Division initiated its first attack for the day at 1045 (the II Tank Corps claimed that the Komsomolets Sovkhoz came under attack at 0700, Moscow time). This initiated the day-long battles around Komsomolets Sovkhoz and Ivanovskii Vyiselok. This first attack consisted of the 2nd SS Panzer Grenadier Regiment, the assault gun battalion, and the Tiger company (total of 20 Sturmgeschuetz IIIs and four Panzer VIs), supported by the entire artillery regiment and the 55th Werfer Regiment (the III Battalion, which was attached to Totenkopf, returned sometime during the day). This force attacked the line from the railroad at Ivanovskii Vyiselok to the woods southwest of the Komsomolets Sovkhoz. The attack group crossed the railroad embankment at 1130 and at 1145 stormed the southern part of the woods southwest of Komsomolets Sovkhoz.

Meanwhile strong flanking fire from the Prelestnoye to Polezhayev area had stalled the left hand group (1st SS Panzer Grenadier Regiment). The left hand group was now brought in behind the right hand group (2nd SS Panzer Grenadier Regiment) and at 1200 the two attack groups advancing to the same hill, reached the line running from the southwest point of the Sloyevoye Woods to height 241.6. The reinforced reconnaissance battalion, guarding the left flank of the advance, attacked the northwest edge of height 241.6 at 1130. The well dug-in Soviets defended "fanatically" but were nevertheless driven from these positions. Numerous Russians were reported to have deserted. The attack was stalled at around 1300 by a large number of Soviet tanks on the reverse slope of the hill and in the northwest edge of the Sloyevoye Woods. At 1350, the right wing of the second group had crossed the railroad line on both sides of Ivanovskii Vyiselok while the left wing was advancing against hill 241.6. At this point, infantry resistance was not heavy but Soviet tanks were attacking out of the forest south of Stalinskii Sovkhoz. Hill 241.6 was taken at 1420 but was receiving strong flanking fire from the north and the south. The division had also grabbed the southeast point of woods north of Storozhevoye as well. The division's reconnaissance battalion had extended its front to the west and during the night made a solid connection with Totenkopf's right wing.

The defending Soviet forces included the 285th and 295th Rifle Regiments of the 183rd Rifle Division and the 169th and 26th Tank Brigades of the II Tank Corps. The II Tank Corps had the 169th Tank Brigade and the 15th Guards Heavy Tank Regiment (armed with Churchills) in the area around Storozhevoye facing the Adolf Hitler SS Division, while its 99th Tank Brigade was in the area of Vasilyevka, on the Psel, facing Totenkopf. The 26th Tank Brigade occupied the ravine running from Mikhailovka to height 241.1, connecting these two forces, but was involved in the fighting around Komsomlets Sovkhoz. The 183rd Rifle Division reported that it had come under attack from one infantry regiment and 50 tanks in the area of the Komsomolets Sovkhoz, Ivanovskii Vyiselok and Belenikhino. At 0930 (Moscow time) they claim to have thrown back a German attack from height 224.5, but the fighting around the Komsomolets Sovkhoz and Ivanovskii Vyiselok continued throughout the day until at least 2300, when the Soviets fell back, with heavy losses. The 183rd Rifle Division did take noticeable casualties on this day. The II Tank Corps' infantry, the 58th Motorized Rifle Brigade, was still moving up from Krasnoye.

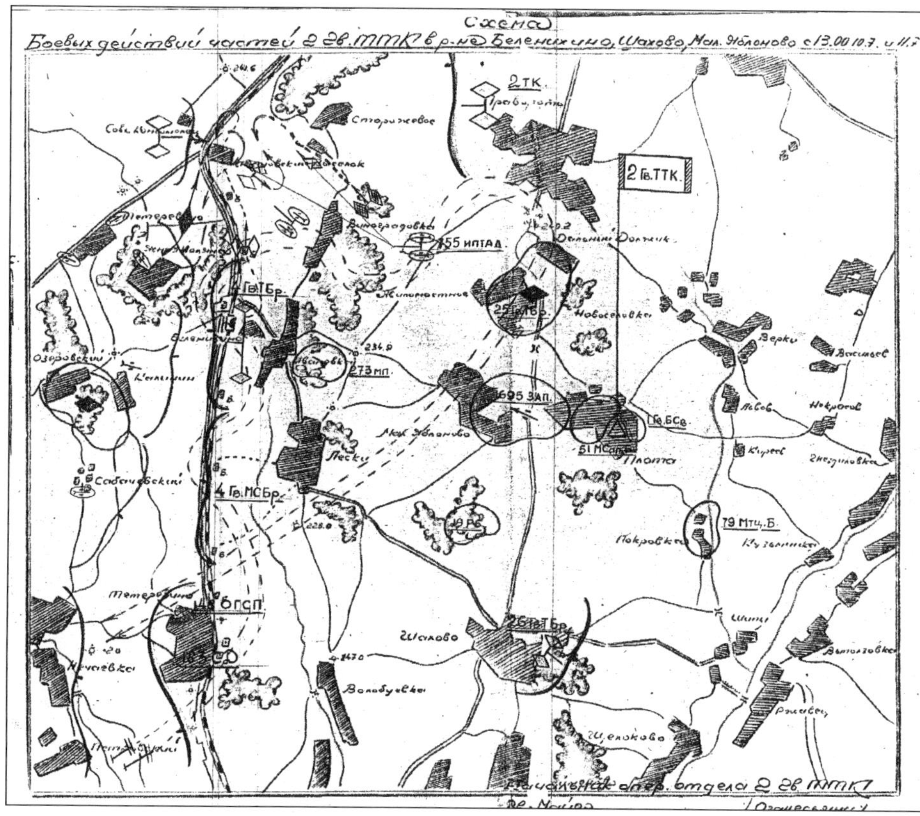

II Guards Tank Corps map for 1300, 10 July 1943 and 11 July 1943.

The Adolf Hitler SS Panzer Regiment was being held in division reserve in an area four kilometers southwest of Teterevino (north). This reserve location was certainly being driven by the Soviet armored groupings reported to the east and southeast of Teterevino.

Meanwhile, the Das Reich SS Division continued to hold the flank of the corps. This division was reporting heavy Soviet movements across the entire division front. The traffic was particularly heavy in areas south and north of Belenikhino. There was heavy artillery and tank fire, especially on the division's north zone. The Soviets probed repeatedly with tanks against the positions of the Der Fuehrer SS Regiment, but later withdrew behind the railroad line. In the Deutschland SS Regiment zone, the Soviets attacked the positions north of Kalinin at 1000 with a company of infantry. This attack was driven off by the combined fire of all weapons. At the same time, the Soviets launched a weak tank attack from Belenikhino against Kalinin. This may have been the same action that the Soviets reported at 1100 (Moscow time), when they stated that German tanks and motorized infantry had broken through the woods and the railroad embankment north of Belenikhino. This forced them to commit the 4th Guards Tank Brigade (II Guards Tank Corps) from the march.

After these attacks petered out, the Das Reich SS Division then began to move forward, starting its advance after the Adolf Hitler SS Division had started its. The

I Battalion, Deutschland SS Regiment pushed into the Lomi Polos ravine,[26] just east of Yasnaya Polyana, with its left wing. At 1345 the III Battalion, Deutschland SS Regiment attacked behind the right attack wing of Group Krass[27] to the railroad bend and reached this at Ivanovskii Vyiselok. The battalion then continued to attack to the southeast, but at 1800 was still holding along the rail line. The foremost elements succeeded in some areas in pushing 1½ kilometers to the east, toward Vinogradovka, but reconnaissance was unable to advance beyond the rail line because of strong antitank and tank defense. The left wing of the Der Fuehrer SS Regiment joined the attack and its forward elements pushed to the rail line just west of Belenikhino.

At 1850, the Soviets reported that German tanks and infantry had attacked Ivanovskii Vyiselok, while at the same time they had attacked along the railroad embankment from Yasnaya Polyana. The 4th Guards Tank Brigade again counterattacked and claimed to have thrown the Germans back to their initial positions. Finally, late in the day, the Soviets threw the 25th Guards Tank Brigade into battle, and by 2200 it had reached the railroad embankment west of Vinogradovka. The Soviets reported continued attacks during the night, with small groups of German riflemen infiltrating the lines of these two tank brigades. Losses were low for the II Guards Tank Corps on this day.

The Soviet defenders on this day held to their positions along the Lipovyii Donets. The entire area of the Donets triangle had now come under command of the Sixty-ninth Army, with the II Guards Tank Corps being subordinated to them on this day. During the morning, the armor of the V and II Guards Tank Corps had disengaged, but by the early afternoon two of the brigades from the II Guards Tank Corps had reengaged.

In the south, facing the 167th Infantry Division were elements of the XXXV Guards Rifle Corps. The line from Rozhdestvenka to Novyiye Lozyi to the outskirts of Druzhnyii was held by the healthy 93rd Guards Rifle Division, and the line from Druzhnyii to outskirts of Khokhlovo was held by the still healthy 89th Guards Rifle Division.

North of them was the II Guards Tank Corps. Its 4th Guards Tank Brigade was around Belenikhino, actively engaged. Its 25th Guards Tank Brigade was in a second echelon position from Dalnii Dolzhik to Zhilomostnoye but was thrown into battle late in the day. Its 26th Guards Tank Brigade was also in the rear, at Shakhovo. Its 4th Motorized Rifle Brigade was west of Leski. Remnants of the 156th Guards Rifle Regiment and the 158th Guards Rifle Regiment of the 51st Guards Rifle Division were stretched between Teterevino (south) to the outskirts of Rozhdestvenka (or at height 225.0 according to a report at 0700 on 10 July).

North of the II Guards Tank Corps were the 183rd Rifle Division and the V Guards Tank Corps. The 183rd Rifle Division was stretched from the Psel to the Severnyii Donets, but had two of its rifle regiments, the 285th and 295th, fighting in the area around the Komsomolets Sovkhoz and Ivanovskii Vyiselok. In the case of the V Guards Tank Corps, only the 6th Guards Motorized Rifle Brigade remained in the line, along with the 454th Mortar Regiment. The rest of the corps (the two remaining tank brigades) pulled back to the rear and shifted over to the area along the Oboyan highway, in front of the XLVIII Panzer Corps. This was a shift of over 25 kilometers and put them in the area of Zorinskiye Dvoryi, Orlovka, and Shipyi. They put an outpost on height 244.3, which was three kilometers south of

26 Listed on maps as "ur. Lomi Polos."

27 This group is not identified but Lt. Colonel Hugo Kraas was the commander of the 2nd SS Panzer Grenadier Regiment, LSSAH Division at this time.

Obersturmbannfuehrer (Lt. Colonel) Hugo Kraas was born 25 January 1911 in Witten in Westphalia. He joined the Nazi party in 1934 and the SA later that year. He joined the German Army in 1935 but moved back to the SS that same year. He was commissioned in 1938 and assigned the LSSAH, where he remained for most of his military career. He took part in Polish, French, and Russian Campaigns. He was awarded the Knight's Cross on 28 March 1943 and took over command of the 2nd SS Panzer Grenadier Regiment before Kursk. He was awarded Oak Leaves in 1944 and ended the war as a Brigadefuehrer (Major General) and in command of the 12th SS Panzer Division (Hitlerjugend). He passed away 20 February 1980.

Zorinskiye Dvoryi, and blocked the road to Oboyan. They then put their equipment into order. At this point, the tank corps was down to 15 T-34s, 8 T-70s and 4 Churchills. This was some 12.80 percent (11.81, 12.70 and 19.05 percent respectively) of its starting strength. They were joined there by "Listratenko's regiment," with 3 T-34s and 5 T-70s. This was probably repaired tanks from the previously withdrawn 20th Tank Brigade.

This was the second shift of the armor across the front, out of the area facing the SS Panzer Corps and into the area opposite the XLVIII Panzer Corps. In both cases, the Soviet tank corps left their infantry brigade behind. As the Soviet tank corps already suffered from a shortage of infantry, this maneuvering just complicated their operational problems and ability to form combined arms' teams.

The II Tank Corps had gotten all three of its armored brigades in action by this time and had suffered significant casualties the previous day and continued to be engaged this day. Its 99th Tank Brigade ended the day along the line from Vasilyevka to Andreyevka to Mikhailovka and was facing Totenkopf. The next morning (at 0700 on the 11th), it was reporting a strength of 993 (usually 1,264 authorized) with 16 T-34s and no reports for T-70s, along with 69 troops killed and wounded. The 26th Tank Brigade was stretched across the area between the Psel and height 241.6 with a strength of 856 men, 3 T-34s and 9 T-70s, having fought with the Adolf Hitler SS Division this day. The 169th Tank Brigade was in the area of Belenikhino and Storozhevoye, with a strength of 878 men, 16 T-34s and 7 T-70s. Also in the area was the 15th Guards Heavy Tank Regiment, which now had four Churchills and a strength of 185 men. They lost 4 tanks and 20 men killed on the 10th. These units were also facing the Adolf Hitler SS Division. All these brigades were down in strength since the report of 0700 10 July, indicating heavy losses and fighting (see discussion above for 9 July). The 58th Motorized Rifle Regiment does not appear to have been in combat this day and was still moving up to battle from Krasnoye. It would enter the line of battle the next morning with 3,100 men.[28] Krasnoye was to the southeast of Prokhorovka and over ten kilometers behind the fighting.

AT THIS POINT, the fighting achieved a certain rational form on both sides, with the Germans steadily and systematically attacking while the Soviets chose to defend without all the heavily armored counterattacks as they had been doing on the 6th, 7th, and 8th. They were still conducting local armored counterattacks, but not in the size and force they had before. As can be seen by the losses on the 10th and 11th, the intensity of the armor battles had declined. A look at the German and Soviet tank losses since the start of the battle against the SS Panzer Corps shows:

Date	*SS Panzer Corps Tank Losses*	*Opposing Soviet Tank Losses*	*Exchange Ratio*
5th	54 tanks	30 tanks	1: 0.56
6th	79 tanks	149 tanks	1: 1.89
7th	55 tanks	86 tanks	1: 1.56
8th	47 tanks	164 tanks	1: 3.49
9th	34 tanks	135 tanks	1: 3.97
10th	3 tanks	55 tanks	1: 18.33
11th	16 tanks	9 tanks	1: 0.56
	288 tanks	628 tanks	1: 2.18

This comparison is a case where one should not place too much reliance in the day-to-day statistics. While the Germans losses, calculated as a decline in ready-for-action, are reasonably accurate during this period for each day and for each division; the Soviet records are not. Overall, the Soviets lost as many or more tanks during this period, as indicated here, but there is some question how many were lost on exactly which day.

For the record, 118 tanks were lost by the Adolf Hitler SS Division while they may have been responsible for

28 And 13 76mm guns, 13 45mm guns, 6 120mm Mortars and 30 82mm Mortars (Fond: 3407, Opis: 1, Delo: 108).

Across the Psel I, 10 July 1943

DURATION One day FRONTAGE 14.0 kilometers TERRAIN Rolling, mixed
WEATHER Heavily overcast, but increasingly clearing. Roads are sodden.

	Attacker	*Defender*
Units	T SS PzGrD	52nd GRD & other elements
Attachments	See below	See below
Strength	19,571	11,402
Armor	105 (limited action)	31 (16 light)
Artillery	149	97
Air Sorties	62	17 + 17 Night
Casualties	374 (77 KIA, 292 WIA, 5 MIA)	452 (108 KIA, 306 WIA, 38 MIA)
Armor Losses	0	0
Artillery Losses	5	3
Enemy Captured	N/A	0

Forces Engaged

German Attachments
II/1st Lehr Werfer Regiment
SS Corps Werfer Battalion (re-attached on the 10th)
III/55th Werfer Regiment (detached on the 10th—not included)
86th Bridge Column B (attached on the 10th)

Soviet Forces
52nd Guards Rifle Division (all)
133rd AT Rifle Bn
I/5th Gds Mortar Rgt
75th Flamethrower Co.
95th Flamethrower Co.
Bn/156th GRR/51st GRD (not included)
28th AT Bde (not included, facing the XLVIII Panzer Corps)

From X Tank Corps
11th Motorized Rifle Brigade
  287th Mortar Rgt
178th Tank Brigade (assumed to have moved today, not included)
  727th AT Regiment (assumed to have moved today, not included)

99th Tank Brigade (II Tank Corps)

Advance on Prokhorovka, 10 July 1943

DURATION One day FRONTAGE 15.1 kilometers TERRAIN Rolling, mixed
WEATHER Until 1400, occasional heavy showers, which hampered movement, clearing after 1500.

	Attacker	*Defender*
Units	LSSAH PzGrD	II Tank Corps (–) & 183rd Rifle Division (–)
Attachments	See below	See below
Strength	21,543	10,322
Armor	94 (6 light)	75 (32 light)
Artillery	173	75
Air Sorties	0	17
Casualties	55 (18 KIA, 34 WIA, 3 MIA)	632 (188 KIA, 373 WIA, 67 MIA)
Armor Losses	2	46
Artillery Losses	4	5
Enemy Captured	N/A	3

Forces Engaged

German Attachments

55th Werfer Regiment (III Bn re-attached on the 10th)
861st Light Field Howitzer Battalion

Soviet Forces

2/3rds of 183rd Rifle Division (285th and 295th Rifle Regiments)
II Tank Corps
  less the 99th Tank Brigade
  less the 58th Motorized Rifle Brigade

255 Soviet tank losses (a 1-to-2.16 exchange ratio). The Das Reich SS Division lost 104 tanks, while they may have been responsible for 274 Soviet tanks (a 1-to-2.63 exchange ratio). The Totenkopf SS Division did not get as much credit, for although it lost only 66 tanks, it is only credited with 99 tanks (a 1-to-1.50 exchange ratio). One must keep in mind that these formations were supported by air, artillery and elements of the 167th Infantry Division and they certainly played a role in causing Soviet tank losses. Furthermore, the assignment of which Soviet units faced which German units is sometimes questionable as the unit boundaries overlapped and sometimes the German units were operating in close coordination with each other.

The reverse comparison can also be made, although it is less clear as there were often two different tank corps facing the same German division and sometimes elements of the same tank corps facing two different German divisions. Still, one can estimate that the XXXI Tank Corps lost 93 tanks while they may have been responsible for 15 German tanks (a 6.20-to-1 exchange ratio). The V Guards Tank Corps lost 166 tanks while they may have been responsible for 62 German tanks (a 2.68-to-1 exchange ratio).[29] The II Tank Corps lost 136 tanks while they may have been responsible for 34 German tanks (a 4.00-to-1 exchange ratio). Note that there is considerable overlap between these three formations and their opponents. Adding them together produces 395 Soviet tanks lost while they may have been responsible for 111 German tanks lost. This is a 3.56-to-1 exchange ratio. Finally, the carefully husbanded II Guards Tank Corps lost 48 tanks while they may have been responsible for taking out 32 German tanks (a 1.50-to-1 exchange ratio).

By comparison, the XLVIII Panzer Corps from the 5th through the 11th took 449 tank losses, including broken down Panthers, and may have been responsible for 471 Soviet tanks. Even if one assumes 120 Panthers broke down, and subtracts them from the calculation, this comes out to a 1-to-1.43 exchange ratio. One could, rather, look at the losses from the 6th to the 11th of July for both German corps. This has the advantage of skipping the 5th, when both German corps were penetrating the defensive lines and not facing much armor. Furthermore, it also eliminates a lot of the Panther breakdown losses and German losses to mines on the 5th. In this case, from 6 to 11 July, the SS Panzer Corps lost 234 tanks and may have been responsible for 598 Soviet tanks. This is a 1-to-2.56 exchange ratio. The XLVIII Panzer Corps lost 317 tanks while they may have been responsible for 438 Soviet tanks. This is a 1-to-1.38 exchange ratio.

This difference in the exchange ratios between the two German corps probably has a whole lot more to do with how their opponents chose to fight than the differences in performance between the two German corps. One does wonder if Katukov's decision to defend with his First Tank Army was the main difference here, as compared to the heavy counterattacking against the SS Panzer Corps that was done under the command of Vatutin and Chistyakov.

Air Support

For this day, the Das Reich SS Division reported that Soviet air activity was moderate. There was occasional bombing of the infantry regiments and low-level bombing attacks against the advance route south of Luchki and on Luchki itself.

The II Guards Tank Corps reported that groups of 2 to 20 German bombers continuously bombed them and their supply columns. They also reported that groups of around six assault aircraft bombed the German positions. The 183rd Rifle Division also reported being bombed.

Intelligence

At this stage, the Germans had clearly identified and named all seven armored corps that they were facing and were well aware that the Fifth Guards Army was moving up. There was only one more surprise in store for the Germans.

29 There were 31 tanks lost by the Das Reich SS Division on the 8th; 16 were assigned to V Guards Tank Corps and 15 were assigned to II Tank Corps.

Das Reich Resumes the Advance, 10 July 1943

DURATION One day FRONTAGE 13.0 kilometers TERRAIN Rolling, mixed

	Attacker	Defender
Units	DR SS PzGrD	II Guards Tank Corps & other elements
Attachments	See below	See below
Strength	19,552	6,814
Armor	98 (1 light)	96 (38 light)
Artillery	145	100
Air Sorties	20	16
Casualties	112 (16 KIA, 94 WIA, 2 MIA)	428 (88 KIA, 182 WIA, 158 MIA)
Armor Losses	1	9
Artillery Losses	5	3
Enemy Captured	N/A	3

Forces Engaged

German Attachments
III/1st Lehr Werfer Regiment
SS Flak Platoon
SS Flak Platoon
627th Engineer Battalion (detached 7/10—not incorporated)
III/818th Artillery Regiment

Soviet Forces
elements of II Guards Tank Corps
 4th Guards Tank Brigade
 25th Guards Tank Brigade
 273rd Mortar Regiment
6th Guards Motorized Brigade (from V Guards Tank Corps)
 454th Mortar Regiment
1/3rd of 51st Guards Rifle Division (the 158th Guards Rifle Regiment)
Probably elements of the 183rd Rifle Division, but they are included in the above engagement. The 227th Rifle Regiment of the 183rd Rifle Division may have also been in this engagement.

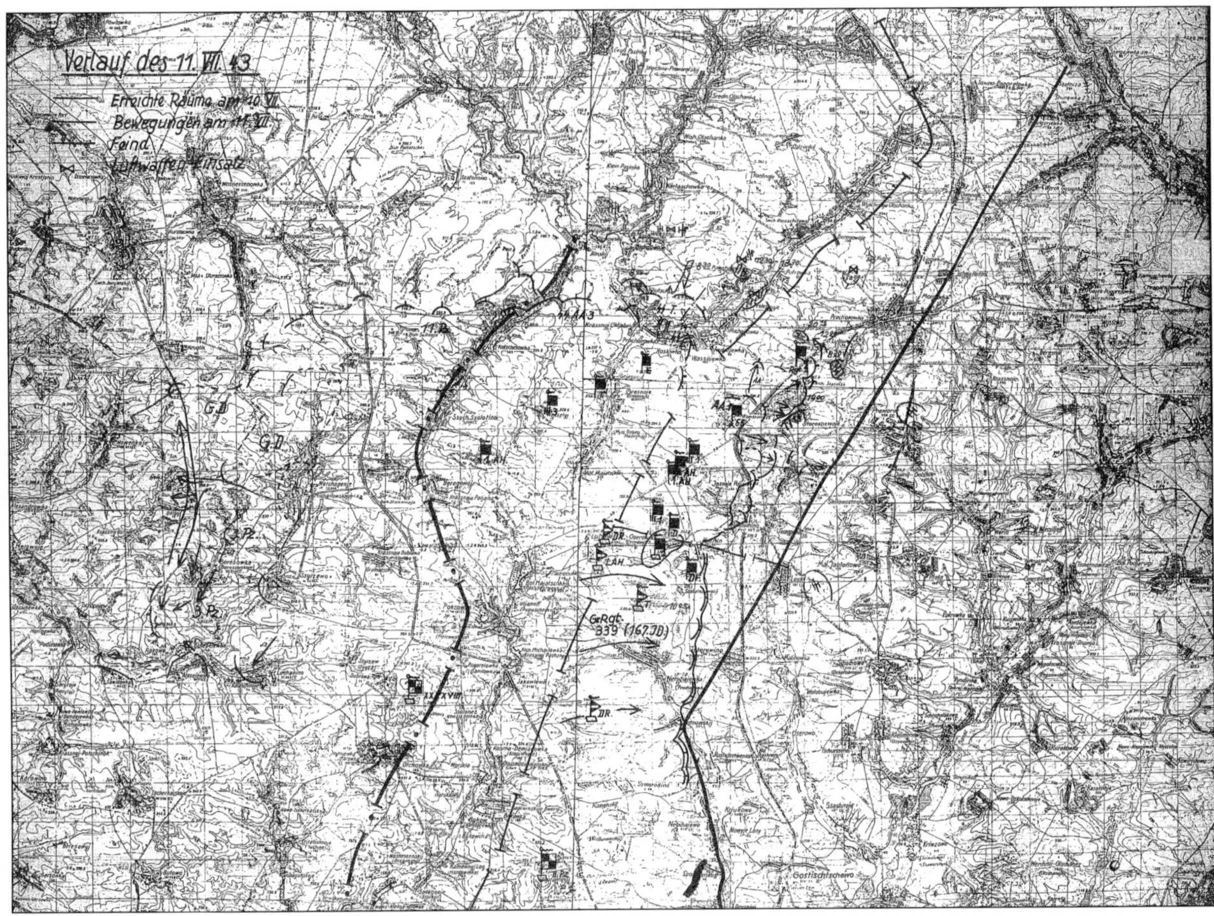

The SS Panzer Corps map showing positions on the 11th of July.

Across the Psel and Onward to Prokhorovka, 11 July

The SS Panzer Corps continued to advance this day into the gathering storm. This was a figurative storm, as the Soviet reinforcements from the Steppe Front were moving forward to battle. It was also an actual storm, as heavy rains fell during the day that severely hampered combat operations. The SS divisions reported that the roads were in poor shape and difficult to move on. This was, of course, the same experience that the 11th Panzer Division was having with its operations. The situation was affecting armor as well as wheeled vehicles. As such, this day was unusually quiet, with the SS Panzer Corps carefully developing its positions.

The Totenkopf SS Division, having actually forced a crossing of the Psel, spent the night establishing defensive positions on the northeast edge of Kozlovka to height 226.6 to the barracks northwest of Klyuchi to the northwest edge of Kochetovka. At 0320 a company strength attack was driven off. Totenkopf was reporting lots of Soviet air activity. At 0415, the Soviets attacked from the northwest in battalion strength, supported by tanks against the barracks 800 meters northwest of Klyuchi. This attack was repulsed by the Totenkopf

SS Regiment, which continued holding the barracks. At 0617, Totenkopf was feeling pressured by the Soviet attacks, complaining that Russian infantry were in the right-hand zone of the bridgehead within hand-grenade throwing range of their positions! There were also Soviet forces in regimental strength advancing from the direction of Veselyii (on the Psel). They reported these attacks repulsed at 0700.

At 0830, another attack, this time in regiment strength, also armor-supported (five tanks according to one German report), occurred in the area. Totenkopf was now complaining of a shortage of artillery ammunition and reported at 1115 having to fetch 1,000 rounds of light field howitzer ammunition from Tomarovka. This attack was also repulsed but apparently it temporarily closed the bridgehead. The Soviet forces involved included the 52nd Guards Rifle Division, which reported fighting in the area of Klyuchi since 0300 (Moscow time), and by noon had driven the Germans out of the town. At 1500, the control of this division was transferred to the XXXIII (33rd) Guards Rifle Corps (Fifth Guards Army), integrating it into their defensive efforts.

Totenkopf intended to bridge the river the night of 10/11 July, as its panzer regiment was still to the south of the Psel, and to launch an attack out of the bridgehead in the early morning, at 0415. This was delayed because the bridging equipment did not arrive. The attack was first postponed to 0700, then 0800, and finally at 1115, the division was estimating that the bridge would not be ready until late afternoon (1800–1900 hours). In order to escape Soviet artillery fire, the bridging column had taken shelter in a balka and didn't arrive at the bridging site until late morning. This delayed the crossing of the armor and Totenkopf's attack to expand the bridgehead. This delay in bridging occurred while Soviet reinforcements continued to arrive throughout the day.

The small towns to the east and southeast of the bridgehead were also heavily occupied by Soviet troops. The Totenkopf Division continued to expand and clean up its positions, with the Eicke SS Regiment penetrating into the sections of Vasilyevka north of the Psel at 1325, and by 1440 had repulsed a Soviet armored counterattack against Vasilyevka. By 1420, the Germans had completed two bridges west of Bogoroditskoye, one of them that could handle the Tigers. At 1445, they ordered the panzer group to cross to the other side of the Psel and into the bridgehead. As of 1545 the VIII Air Corps' air support was assigned predominantly to Totenkopf. After all that effort, Totenkopf then reported at 1615 that poor road conditions made any advance out of the bridgehead impossible until tomorrow at the earliest. The rain had so softened the roads and ground, and especially the already damp river banks, that the tanks got stuck if they tried to cross. This made the bringing of any heavy weapons over the steep north bank out of the question. On top of that, because of the poor weather, they were not going to be able to get Luftwaffe support. This ended Totenkopf's "attack" for the day.

The Soviet defenders were being reinforced by arriving units from Zhadov's Fifth Guards Army. Its XXXIII Guards Rifle Corps was to occupy a line from Semenovka to Veselyii (on the Psel) to height 252.2 to Mordovna. The 97th Guards Rifle Division was on the right from Semenovka to Veselyii, the 95th in the middle from Veselyii up to height 252.2, and the 9th Guards Airborne Division was on the left, from height 252.2 to Mordovka.[30] All these divisions were fresh, but were still moving up into position and joined the fight from the march, although it does not appear that the 97th Guards Rifle Division was engaged in battle this day.

30 Zamulin, *Demolishing the Myth*, page 222, provides the following comment in relation to the defense against the LSSAH Division, which was attacking south of the Psel:

"In addition, the important sector between the river and the rail line was being defended by the 287th Guards Rifle Regiment (and the attached 109th Separate Penal Company) of the 95th Guards Rifle Division, the major portion of which was concentrated on the other side of the river, and the 26th Guards Airborne Rifle Regiment of Colonel A. M. Sazonov's 9th Guards Airborne Division, the bulk of which was located on the other side of the railroad. In essence, no one was responsible for the boundary between the two divisions. This flaw in the defenses, as further events would demonstrate, would lead to grave consequences."

The 95th Guards Rifle Division arrived in battle late this day. It had initiated its night march at 2000 on the 10th, and had arrived at 0400 on the 11th, concentrating in a line running from Veselyii up to Komsomolets Sovkhoz. As of 0400, only the 290th Guards Rifle Regiment had arrived, with one of its battalions detached and located around Prokhorovka. The 284th Guards Rifle Regiment was just behind it and at 0300 reported to be in line from height 236.7 to the northern slope of the ravine one kilometer south of height 236.7 to the grove one kilometer east of the Voroshilov Sovkhoz. The 287th Guards Rifle Regiment and the rest of the division were still moving up. The division's rear units were still in the eastern outskirts of Verkhnyaya Olshanka, some eight kilometers to the northeast. Deployed in front of them were the 52nd Guards Rifle Division and the 11th Motorized Rifle Brigade. The German aircraft were bombing the division, although to date, the only losses they reported were 11 men wounded in the 284th Guards Rifle Regiment when one of their cars had overturned during the marching on the night of 9/10 July. At 2130, the division attacked and moved forward 300 to 400 meters. Their losses for the 11th were reported to be 34 men killed, 79 wounded, and five horses killed.

This attack is recounted by Lt. Ilya Nikolayevich Kozlov, who was a rifle platoon commander:[31]

> I finished the expedited four-month program of the Suvorov Infantry School and became a lieutenant. Since January 1943, I was a rifle platoon commander. In May–June of 1943 our division was part of the Steppe Military Region. We knew that we were preparing for a massive attack because there were a lot of troops in our Military Region (a few field armies and a tank army). Our political commissars were telling us that, trying to pick up our spirit, because we were supposed to participate in this attack too. For two months we had training in all aspects of an attack. We had several company and battalion exercises and a regiment exercise in the middle of June. On the 5th of July 1943, we found out about the massive enemy attack from the north and south towards Kursk. Our political trainers told us about the course of the battle. We also read about it in the division and army papers. The papers mostly described the heroism of soldiers, junior infantry officers, artillerists and tankers. I don't remember when exactly, sometime on the 10th or 11th of July, our division marched to the south from Olshanka. We were supposed to deploy in two trenches, which were prepared there, and not to let the enemy tanks, which were coming from the south, get through. A division was fighting a defensive battle in front of us. All of a sudden, we received an order from the battalion commander to switch not to the defense, but to the offense against the German troops, which had broken through the division located in front of us. We moved forward a little bit, but then were attacked by tanks and infantry. Captain Bugrov, the battalion commander, was a very experienced commander. He participated in the Stalingrad battle. He managed to turn around our battalion under cover of the gun company and mortars. Our artillery was firing at the enemy behind us. My platoon was in the first echelon and we managed to dig in quickly. It was very timely because the German aviation arrived and started bombing us for an hour. After that German tanks and infantry started to show up. I received two additional machineguns. Two battalion 45mm guns were firing behind our platoon, but it seemed to me they could not reach the tanks. Our task was to fire at the German infantry, cutting them from their tanks and making them lay prone so our mortars could shoot at them. We performed this task, although I lost six people who were killed and about 10 to 12 people wounded. It was half of my platoon. About 12 German tanks broke into the area occupied by a company next to us. Our artillery was firing behind us. We never saw these tanks again. They were probably destroyed. By that

31 Major Ilya Nikolayevich Kozlov was interviewed by Col. Fyodor Sverdlov in 1999. After Kursk, he participated in the Kharkhov offensive and the Dnepr operation in the fall. He was awarded the Order of the Red Star during that operation, but nothing for Kursk. After Kursk he was promoted to company commander and in September became a senior lieutenant. He retired as a major, living as a "war invalid" in Korolev, in the Moscow region.

time, our aviation started to strike. It picked up the spirit of my soldiers. Sometimes it was really hard to tolerate the massive mortar and artillery attacks, but none of the soldiers from my platoon ran back. I was giving orders to our mortars and rifles for which enemy units they should fire at. Nevertheless, the battalion commander withdrew us about one to 1.5 kilometers in the afternoon.

The Voronezh Front had left a giant gap in its lines that opened up the Psel for an easy forced crossing. The Fourth Panzer Army and the SS Panzer Corps had essentially missed this opportunity. They had first arrived at the Psel at noon on the 8th with the Das Reich SS Reconnaissance Battalion, but this was not a force that could be sustained there nor could it have crossed the river in the face of the X Tank Corps. On the 9th, Totenkopf did have an opportunity to cross in force, but was delayed in getting started in the morning and did not arrive except with one regiment as of 1845 on the 9th. This force was unable to cross. As the objective of Totenkopf for the day was to cross the Psel, one is left to wonder why only one regiment was sent north while the other regiment and the panzer regiment were sent to the northwest. A dedicated push to the Psel that day certainly could have arrived earlier, as the Battle Group Baum started its attack to the northwest at 1000, while the later arriving Battle Group Becker, which was the force that arrived at the Psel, started moving out only at 1550. There was air support available this day to help make the crossing. This was a real lost opportunity, although the crossing would have probably resulted in an extended engagement with the X Tank Corps. Still, at the minimum this would have kept the X Tank Corps from reinforcing the area in front of Oboyan. This may have created an opportunity for the XLVIII Panzer Corps to break through (assuming they were not continuing to head west, as they did).

The next opportunity to cross was the afternoon of the 10th, which was successfully utilized, but no provisions had been made for bringing the armor across yet. Instead the Germans decided to bring the armor across during the night, but the bridges had not arrived! This delayed the crossing of the armor until late on the 11th and prevented them from attacking in earnest until the 12th.

This failure to bring the bridges forward is hard to explain. It is not as if the Psel River should have been a surprise to the Germans. They had known since the beginning of the operations that they needed to cross it, they observed the river on the 8th, and they planned on crossing in on the 9th with the Totenkopf SS Division. Yet, they did not get the bridges built until after 1400 on the 11th. There was an abundance of bridging units, with the SS Panzer Corps having five, the Fourth Panzer Army controlling two more, and Totenkopf had the 86th Bridge Column B as of the 10th. These could have been brought forward as the division advanced on the Psel. While Totenkopf arrived at the Psel late on the afternoon of the 9th, their bridges were not planned until the night of the 10/11 and were completed later than that. The bridging units should have been with Totenkopf when they first arrived at the Psel. On top of that, not being able or prepared to deal with the soft ground and the embankment on the opposite bank of the river was also poor planning. The blame for this slow river crossing probably lies with the corps commander (Hausser) and the division commander (Priess). The diversion to the northwest to chase the XXXI Tank Corps was probably partially the fault of the army commander (Hoth). By the time the Germans did get their armor across, Zhadov's Fifth Guards Army had arrived.

Leibstandarte SS Adolf Hitler Takes Height 252.2

At 0450 on the 11th, with the Totenkopf on its left and Das Reich on its right, Leibstandarte SS Adolf Hitler Division attacked towards Prokhorovka. Still, its movement out of the assembly area was delayed because of poor road conditions. The 2nd SS Regiment, reinforced with armor, led the attack. It moved along a route that allowed it to be shielded by the Storozhevoye Woods (the large woods 1.5 kilometers southwest of Yamki). At 0625, the German attack was halted by heavy artillery fire from hill 252.4, Prelestnoye and Petrovka. There then was a tank counterattack out of the Storozhevoye Woods.

The Germans discovered antitank ditches to the south of Oktyabrskii Sovkhoz. By 0830, the attack had ground to a halt before strong Soviet positions, including the antitank ditch before hill 252.2. At 0850, they had crossed these antitank ditches, which were part of the Soviet third defensive line that had initially been occupied by the Sixty-ninth Army (specifically the 183rd Rifle Division) before the battle began. The VIII Air Corps then conducted concentrated Stuka attacks in front of the division at 0900.

The division then began to envelop these positions from the right which allowed the attack to go forward again. At 1030 (Berlin time), the regiment began storming the northwest part of height 252.2, just southeast of the sovkhoz. The Germans were receiving heavy artillery fire on their flank from Prelestnoye but claimed to have taken the height at 1200. Around noon, two bomber groups were sent by the VIII Air Corps to the flanking Soviet artillery in Polezhayev and Prelestnoye. The Germans also advanced one battalion on the Storozhevoye Woods.

The Soviets claimed that at 0930 (the same as 0830 Berlin time) the 183rd Rifle Division and the II Tank Corps fought off a German attack of two regiments and 130 tanks, inflicting heavy casualties on the Germans. While the Adolf Hitler SS Division recorded no tank losses on this day, they did lose around 10 Sturmgeschuetzes, a Marder and 337 personnel. During the fighting this day the Tiger company commander, Heinz Kling, was wounded, and Michael Wittmann took over command of the company.[32]

Arriving to defend height 252.2 was the 9th Guards Airborne Division from Zhadov's Fifth Guards Army. The forward elements of the division were less than 15 kilometers from Prokhorovka on the 10th. At 1900 on the 10th, they started marching to their new positions, which included Oktyabrskii Sovkhoz and height 252.2. The regiments were still not in position as of 0600, but at 0800 (Moscow time), the leading III Battalion of the 26th Guards Airborne Regiment entered the fighting along the line of Oktyabrskii Sovkhoz to the railroad booth, supported by the 3rd battery of the 7th Guards Airborne Artillery Regiment. The rest of the regiment joined it as the fighting continued.[33]

As that battle raged, at 1215 the 1st SS Regiment moved through the woods north of Storozhevoye to eliminate the threat to the flank. The reinforced reconnaissance battalion screened the north flank of the division south of Andreyevka, as it had done the day before. The Germans observed that the Soviets were stronger in artillery than in infantry. The SS division was greatly hindered by flanking fire from Petrovka and Beregovoye. They had to give up Oktyabrskii Sovkhoz for that reason.

---

32 This is in accordance with Patrick Agte, *Michael Wittmann and the Tiger Commanders of the Leibstandarte* (Stackpole Press, Mechanicsburg, PA., 2006). According to Wolfgang Schneider, *Tigers in Combat, Volume II*, page 106, it was Waldemar Schuetz who Wittmann replaced. Schneider also does not record any Tiger losses on this day.

33 Zamulin, *Demolishing the Myth*, pages 219–220, provides the following commentary on this fighting:

"It should be noted that a most important factor, which contributed to the SS troops' rapid overcoming of the anti-tank ditch and their tanks' breakthrough to the Oktiabr'skii State Farm was a number of mistakes made by the 9th Guards Airborne Division commander A. M. Sazanov in setting up the anti-tank defense as his forces hastily moved into position in the hours before the SS attack. Firstly, in contradiction to army commander A. S. Zhadov's orders, Sazonov did not throw out an outpost screen or bring up the division's artillery to Prokhorovka as the first order of business, so as to create an operational, strong anti-tank barrier even before the arrival of his division's main forces. . . . Instead of an echeloned artillery position on a tank-vulnerable sector between the Oktiabr'skii State Farm and the rail line, two battalions . . . were placed in reserve in the region of the village of Kusty. Instead, only Senior Lieutenant Svinukhin's 3rd Battalion of the 7th Guards Airborne Artillery Regiment was deployed on this line, in the direct path of the main attack of Wisch's division, and it was given the following assignment: to set up both batteries with their guns facing the railroad (in opposite direction from the anti-tank ditch), and in case of the appearance of an enemy armored train, to destroy it. I will stress that not once during the entire period of the enemy's offensive did the Germans even try to use this archaic form of armor."

Still, the battle raged back and forth over height 252.2 until 1410, when it was finally cleared and held by the Adolf Hitler SS Panzer Regiment and the III Battalion (armored)/2nd SS Panzer Grenadier Regiment. According to some sources, that afternoon or evening there remained on hill 252.2 around 33 panzers. This is in accordance with the post-war accounts of chief of staff Major Rudolf Lehmann. The panzers were then pulled back to behind the tank ditch except for Captain Rudolf von Ribbentrop's 6th Panzer Company. The I/2nd SS Panzer Grenadier Regiment was on the other side of the railroad with the division's assault guns. The II/2nd SS Panzer Grenadier Regiment in the vicinity of the hill and the Oktyabrskii Sovkhoz, digging positions for themselves and antitank guns. On the left flank of the division, the reconnaissance battalion and antitank battalion were digging in around the villages of Pelestnoye, Mikailovka and Andreyevka.[34]

Decisively crippling was the Soviet flanking fire from Yamki and from the hills north of the Psel. The Soviet defending forces were from the 183rd Rifle Division, the II Tank Corps, and one regiment from the 9th Guards Airborne Division. By 1400 (Moscow time) this regiment was reporting losses of 56 killed and 62 wounded and for the day recorded 83 killed and 210 wounded. It also reported that the Germans took the Oktyabrskii Sovkhoz at 1400 (Moscow time). At this point, the 26th Guards Airborne Regiment was suffering from an ammunition shortage. It had one basic load of ammunition before it started its march to the battlefield.

The subsequent fighting in the afternoon for Oktyabrskii Sovkhoz and the Storozhevoye Woods is not well documented. The Germans stated that they finally took Oktyabrskii Sovkhoz at 2015 while they were able to take the southwest part of Storozhovoye Woods at 1700 and reached the southeastern and eastern edge of the woods at 2230 and took Stalinskii Sovkhoz.[35] A German attack against Storozhevoye was driven back by strong artillery fire from the Leski, Vinogradovka and the Pravorot areas.[36]

---

34 According to Zamulin, *Demolishing the Myth*, page 236. Sources are not given, but it appears to be the book *Leibstandarte III* written by Rudolf Lehmann. The estimate of 33 panzers would indicate that the entire II Panzer Battalion was there. Ribbentrop would report that the following day his company started with 7 Panzers.

According to the Kursk Data Base, as of the end of the day on 11 July 1943, the Adolf Hitler SS Division had 2 Panzer Is, 4 Panzer IIs, 1 Panzer III short, 4 Panzer III longs, 7 Panzer III Command tanks, 47 Panzer IV longs and 4 Panzer VIs for a total of 69 tanks in the panzer regiment. They also had 8 Panzer III Observation tanks, 1 Panzer IV Munitions tank, 10 Sturmgeshuetz IIIs, 20 Marders, 5 Hummels, 12 Wespes, and 12 Gilles.

35 Zamulin, *Demolishing the Myth*, pages 220-221, provides the following commentary:

> "The State Farm changed hands several times. Its defense, consisting of the 3rd Rifle Battalion of the 26th Guards Airborne Rifle Regiment together with the 3rd Artillery Battalion of Senior Lieutenant Svinukhin (who was killed later in October 1943 on the Dnepr River) and Major Bugaev's 1st Artillery Battalion of the 95th Guards Rifle Division's 233rd Guards Artillery Regiment, which had been brought up to localize the breakthrough, received the enemy's main assault."

Zamulin also notes an atrocity in a recollection of the battle by Guards Lieutenant A. A. Obisov, the chief of reconnaissance for the 3rd Airborne Artillery Battalion:

> "Much later, already after the liberation of Poltava, I learned that the commander of the 9th Battery, Guards Senior Lieutenant Kronin and the fire direction platoon with several wounded men were taken prisoner at the Oktiabr'skii State Farm. The fascists shot Kronin. The commander of the 9th Battery's fire direction platoon, Lieutenant Dmitrii Lobazov, who was wounded when he was captured, told me about this—we found him [Lobazov] in a hospital after the liberation of Poltava."

36 Rotmistrov provides an account that at 1900 hours (Moscow time) that Marshal Vasilevskii arrived at his command post. They then took a Willy's jeep to survey the jumping off positions of the XVIII and XXIX Tank Corps. On that trip Rotmistrov states that he saw dozens of German tanks in combat formation advancing and firing on the move. Rotmistrov was two kilometers from the Komsomolets Sovkhoz at the time. Rotmistrov, by radio, ordered General Kirichenko (XXIX Tank Corps) to immediately advance two tank brigades and meet the Germans tanks and stop their advance.

This account is from Rotmistrov's memoir, *Stalnaya Gvardiya (Steel Guards)*. It is drawn from Zamulin, *Demolishing the Myth*, pages 228–229. I am not sure how accurate Romistrov's account is. I have not found confirming reports.

MICHAEL WITTMANN

Michael Wittmann became the most famous tank commander in World War II. He was born on 22 April 1914 in the small village of Vogelthal near Oberpfalz in Bavaria. He was the son of a farmer. In 1934, he joined the German Labor Corps and later that year enlisted in the German Army. He left the service in late 1936 as a junior NCO and in April 1937 joined the Leibstandarte SS Adolf Hitler. He was trained in armored cars and joined the unit's scout company. Commanding an SdKfz 232 Armored Car, he participated in the Polish Campaign. In February 1940, he was transferred to the assault gun battery of Leibstandarte. He then participated in the Yugoslavian and Greek Campaigns, where he commanded a platoon of Sturmgeschuetz IIIs. Wittmann then participated in the invasion of the Soviet Union with Leibstandarte and on the 12th of July 1941 received the Iron Cross (second class) for a tank action. He was then wounded but stayed with the unit. On 8 September 1941, he received the Iron Cross (first class) following a fight in the Rostov area where he claimed six kills. He was promoted to the rank of Oberscharfuehrer (Staff Sergeant). He continued fighting in Russia until June 1942, when he was accepted as a cadet for officer training. In December, Wittmann was promoted to Untersturmfuehrer (2nd Lieutenant) and joined the 13th heavy panzer company (the Tiger company) commanded by Haupstrumfuehrer (Captain) Heinz Kling. He was in command of the Panzer III platoon that supported the Tiger tanks. He was transferred east with the division in January 1943. In early spring of 1943, he transferred over to Tigers. *Operation Citadel* was the start of his combat career in Tigers.

During Kursk, he was the 3rd platoon commander in the Tiger company of the Leibstandarte SS Adolf Hitler Division. It was claimed that he destroyed eight T-34s and seven antitank guns on the 5th of July, two T-34s, two SU-122s and three T-60s/70s on the 7th and 8th of July, and eight Soviet tanks, three antitank guns and one gun battery on the 12th. By the end of the operation, it is claimed that he destroyed 30 tanks and 28 guns. These claims cannot be verified among all the losses suffered during those days.[1]

---

1 The claims for 5 July are probably incorrect in at least the tank types. The opposing 230th Tank Regiment was armed with Grants and Stuarts and there were no major formations armed with T-34s in the area on the 5th of July.

The first action report from the III Mechanized Corps was a patrol sent out at 2330 on the 5th by the 1st Guards Tank Brigade in the direction of mound +1.1, three kilometers southeast of Yakovlevo. This force was fired on by the Germans, with the Soviets reporting a loss of one T-34 burned, 10 men killed and 2 wounded.

On 19 July 1943, the 13th company was transferred to the newly formed 101st SS Heavy Panzer Battalion where he served with other SS "Tiger Aces" like Franz Staudegger, Helmut Wendorff and Jurgen Brandt. This battalion was commanded by Heinz Kling. On 13 January 1944, Wittmann was awarded the Knight's Cross with the claim that from July 1943 to the beginning of January 1944 he had destroyed 56 Soviet tanks and another 32 tanks in January. As these were the German propaganda announcements, it is difficult to verify their accuracy, but the SS propaganda company made sure they painted his tank barrel with 88 kill rings and took pictures. His gunner, Balthasar (Bobby) Woll, also received the Knight's Cross. On 20 January, Wittmann was promoted to Obersturmfuehrer (1st Lieutenant). On 30 January 1944, he was awarded Oak Leaves. At this point, Kling's battalion had five Knight's Cross recipients in it (Wittmann, Woll, Staudegger, Wendorff, Kling). In spring of 1944, his unit was transferred to Belgium and he took command of the 2nd company of the battalion. Wittmann married Hildegard Burmester on 1 March 1944. By this time, the German propaganda machine had made him into a major hero. Meanwhile his gunner, Bobby Woll, received command of his own Tiger tank.

On 13 June 1944, Wittmann's company entered action on the Western Front in Normandy against the British in the famous engagement at Villers Bocage. He received the Swords for his Knight's Cross with Oak Leaves for this action. Wittmann was now the most decorated tanker in the German armed forces and was promoted to Haupsturmfuehrer (Captain). He was offered an instructor position, but refused and instead returned to duty. He spent June fighting around Caen, and on 8 August his Tiger was destroyed and the entire crew was killed. The tank was probably killed by rocket fired by a British Typhoon aircraft that hit the Tiger's rear deck and ignited the ammunition. Wittmann and his crew were buried beside their tank at Gaumesnil, near Cintheaux, in an unmarked grave. In March 1983, his grave was discovered and the body identified from dental records.

It was claimed that Wittmann killed 138 or 141 tanks and destroyed 132 antitank guns.[2] Still, he was not the highest scoring "Tiger Ace."

2 There is no way to verify the accuracy of these claims. The claims usually include those accumulated while serving as a gunner and a commander, so duplicate claims are awarded. Many of these claims are repeated from books by Franz Kurowski or Patrick Agte. We have not taken the time to chase every one of these claims down.

THE II TANK Corps, between the fighting of the previous day, this day, and the following day, was being ground out of existence. The extent of the fighting today is not known, for the corps filed a report at 0700 on the 11th and the next report at 1900 on the 12th. One is left to wonder how much was lost on the 11th and how much on the 12th, during the Battle of Prokorovka. Unfortunately, a similar problem exists with the Totenkopf records: we have a tank strength report for the afternoon of the 11th and the next report is for the afternoon of the 13th.

The 99th Tank Brigade started the day with 16 T-34s and an assumed 16 T-70s, and it reported having 10 T-34s and 10 T-70s on the afternoon of the 12th. The 26th Tank Brigade started the day with only 3 T-34s but had 9 T-70s and reported 6 T-34s and 10 T-70s on the 12th. The 169th Tank Brigade started the day with 16 T-34s and 7 T-70s and reported having only 5 T-34s and 6 T-70s some 36 hours later. The 15th Tank Regiment was armed with only four Churchills and did not provide any reports for several days after that. The 58th Motorized Rifle Brigade had arrived, and by morning took up defense from Vasilyevka (on the Psel River) to height 241.6 to the southern edge of the woods north of Storozhevoye. At this point, this brigade consisted of 3,100 men, 13 76mm guns, 13 45mm guns, 6 120mm Mortars and 30 82mm Mortars. Its headquarters was located on the northwestern outskirts of the Oktyabrskii Sovkhoz. Senior Lieutenant Mikhail Fedotovich Sklyarenko, a gun commander with an antitank battery of the 58th Mechanized Brigade, recounts:[37]

On 11 July 1943, severe combat started in the area where our brigade was located. German tanks and infantry were attacking in the direction of Prokhorovka. They came close to the Oktyabrskii State Farm, where our battery was located. Our battery consisted of four 76mm ZIS guns. We received an unexpected command, "Tanks from the front." At the same time, the German artillery started to shell us. There were about 20 tanks in the first line. I could see clearly two in my bead. The range of my gun was 500 to 600 meters. Despite the shells exploding nearby, I quietly aimed and destroyed the tank that was ahead of the other tanks. Then with two shots I destroyed the second tank. The Germans then conducted an artillery attack against our battery. We hid in the trenches prepared in advance, but soon after that returned back to our guns. The tanks started shooting at us. I managed to destroy one more tank from 300 meters. Other guns also destroyed several tanks. The remaining tanks stopped and started shooting. I saw how the battery commander and platoon commander died. They had replaced the artillerists that had been killed. Only two people remained at my gun. I continued shooting, and my colleague was giving me rounds. We destroyed one more tank. All of sudden my gun exploded, probably because of the rounds. I was wounded in the left hip. My teammate put a bandage on my wound, put me in the trench, and continued shooting for another

---

37 Mikhail Fedotovich Sklyarenko was interviewed by Col. Fyodor Sverdlov on 5 November 1998.

Zamulin does include in his book an account from the brigade's chief of the political department dated 12 July 1943. It reports in part:

"After completing a 200-km march, the brigade went into action at 0600 on 11.07.43. Over the twenty-four hours of combat operations, the brigade, according to preliminary data, has the [following] losses in dead, wounded, and missing in action: in the 1st Battalion—300 men; in the 2nd Battalion—150 men; and in the 3rd Battalion—24 dead, 53 wounded and 39 missing in action, for a total of 116 men. In the artillery battalion, 31 men are dead, wounded, or missing in action. Altogether, the brigade has lost 597 men.

Losses in equipment: 76mm guns—3, GAZ trucks—3; personal weapons—200.

The brigade's forces have knocked out or destroyed approximately 40 tanks of which 16 were Tigers, 2 vehicles, a company of infantry, and approximately 50 submachine gunners of the enemy.

In this combat, the artillery battalion's Komsomol organizer, Party member and gun layer Sergeant Borisov particularly distinguished himself, knocking out 7 tanks of the Tiger type from his own gun."

See Zamulin, *Demolishing the Myth*, page 222. The LSSAH Panzer Regiment had only 4 Tiger tanks operational this day. The rest of the losses appear equally inflated, especially as this was just one of several brigades engaged this day with the LSSAH Division.

five minutes. I heard the second gun shooting somewhere nearby. Our tanks started a counterattack on the German flank. It was a severe battle. The sky was black from the smoke. Two nurses carried me to the medical truck [ambulance].

Later I fought in Poland and Germany. I destroyed only two more German tanks. . . . After the war, I worked at the automobile factory all my life. My wounded leg hurts during bad weather.

The II Tank Corps was almost spent. It started with 158 tanks, arrived in the battlefield area with 137 operational tanks, spent the two days in combat and was down to 69 tanks (43.67 percent of original strength) by 0700 on the 11th. Yet it had to spend another 36 hours in the face of the SS Panzer Corps.

The SS Panzer Corps had faced off against four Soviet tanks corps. It effectively ground up the XXXI Tank Corps from the 6th to the 9th, leaving it at 29 percent tank strength (from 184 tanks down to 54). It also fought the V Guards Tank Corps leaving it at 16 percent tank strength before this corps was transferred to face the XLVIII Panzer Corps. It brushed into the X Tank Corps before all but its infantry was transferred to face the XLVIII Panzer Corps, and then it ground up the II Tank Corps. Only the II Guards Tank Corps, sitting on the flank and counterattacking had managed to conserve its strength. It was still at 75 percent of its original strength and had been engaged since the 6th (from 187 tanks down to around 139 or 140 on the 10th and 11th). Just by shear survivability, Burdeinyii's (II Guards Tank Corps) efforts must be complemented. In contrast, the SS Panzer Corps still held 68 percent of its tank strength ready-for-action as of the end of the day on the 11th. Overall, the SS Panzer Corps had seriously engaged four different Soviet tank corps, and had effectively removed two from the battle, and both of the remaining tank corps had been attrited, one heavily. Without more defensive Soviet reinforcements, there is no question that this force would have broken through the Soviet defenses. In fact, two more Soviet tank corps arrived on the field of battle this evening along with one entire guards army.

The Soviets were claiming that the Germans had concentrated 280 tanks in the area of Komsomolets Sovkhoz and advanced on Prokhorovka, with 130 tanks reported at Komsomolets Sovkhoz. This was not a bad estimate of the threat. The Adolf Hitler SS Division as of the evening of the 10th had around 103 tanks and assault guns (and 29 self-propelled artillery pieces) while Das Reich SS Division had around 102 tanks and assault guns.

The SS records note that the Adolf Hitler SS Division attack had to be discontinued because of "Nachhaengens" (giver-uppers, or ones who give up or abandon an enterprise) in both of the neighboring divisions! The validity of this complaint registered about their fellow soldiers is hard to support. Certainly there was little Totenkopf could do until they built their bridge across the Psel.

The SS records for this day also state that a frontal attack on Prokhorovka would have cost enormous casualties due to the strong antitank and artillery defensive fire from the southwest edge of the town, and from the dominating heights of height 252.4. Instead, the command (the SS Panzer Corps?) proposed that they attack Prokhorovka after a thorough Stuka preparation, and after height 252.4 was captured by the Totenkopf SS Division.

This grousing on the part of the Adolf Hitler SS Division about its neighbors is probably not justified. In the narrow confines of the area being attacked and in the face of the organized Soviet opposition, the neighboring divisions would certainly have suffered heavy losses. The decision, whether made formally or not, by the other two divisions not to push aggressively forward may have been the wiser course of action. While it was necessary that the Germans push through and take Prokhorovka, taking Prokhorovka in and of itself was not going to win the battle. It was merely yet another medium-sized village that the Germans needed to pass through to reach their overall objectives, which were still a long way off. Suffering heavy casualties at this one spot on this day made no more sense than suffering heavy casualties to take any other spot on any given day.

Also, the statement that the neighboring units gave up is not fair. The Totenkopf SS Division was having considerable problems moving its armor because of terrain, weather, Soviet resistance, and not having a bridge built in time. It did not get its bridge built across the Psel until after 1400. To push hard so as to make some progress in the late afternoon was not going to be very useful. With elements of the Fifth Guards Army coming into the line, the attack was only going to get more difficult. The inability of the Totenkopf to provide proper left flank support to the Adolf Hitler SS Division's attack was due to many other factors than just simply giving-up.

In the case of the Das Reich SS Division, they were repositioning for the sake of attacking. This required them to pull units out of the line this day. It appears that they had reconstituted their armor reserve, as had the Adolf Hitler SS Division a couple of days earlier, but the Das Reich armor appears to have been tied down in a defensive role.[38] They still had the ever-present II Guards Tank Corps with 136 tanks sitting on their right flank. They could not hastily mass significant forces into the area of attack without making sure they secured the extended line they were protecting. As Adolf Hitler's 2nd SS Regiment had a very difficult fight getting to 252.2, the neighboring forces, having to protect their own flanks, could not be expected to do as well.

On this day, the Adolf Hitler SS Division lost 337 killed and wounded. Totenkopf, on it left, lost 461 killed and wounded while Das Reich, on its right, lost 211 killed wounded and missing. If casualties are a measure of determination, then certainly Totenkopf cannot be blamed and Das Reich was certainly engaged to a considerable degree.

In all reality, the Adolf Hitler SS Division's attack on 252.2 was about the limit of what could be done that day. Its problems this day with the continued flanking fire on Oktyabrskii Sovkhoz and from Yamki really did indicate that this division was not going to go farther forward until its two flanking divisions moved forward. The Adolf Hitler SS Division was certainly not going to clear Prokhorovka or break through the Soviet defenses on this day. A more determined effort would not have taken the city from the Soviets on this day. As the Germans at this time were not fully aware of the size of the armored forces accumulating in and around Prokhorovka, the expressed opinion of the Adolf Hitler SS Division that a little more effort would have yielded the town is clearly in error.

Elements of the Fifth Guards Army were already taking positions around Prokhorovka. While the 26th Guards Airborne Regiment was fighting over height 252.2, the rest of the division moved into position to defend Prokhorovka. The 28th Guards Airborne Regiment, which would cover the Yamki to Grushki area, turned two of its battalions to the west and, supported by the 301st Antitank Regiment, occupied defensive positions at the western outskirts of Prokhorovka. Their other battalion was defending the southern outskirts of the village. The 23rd Guards Airborne Regiment, which was the second echelon unit, had moved forward to place one battalion defending the southern outskirts of Prokhorovka and Mordovka, and two battalions to defend the southwestern slopes of height 252.4. The 95th Guards Rifle Division had also moved elements south of the Psel, and there were additional forces that would be arriving in this area during the evening, including the 42nd Guards Rifle Division and the XVIII and XXIX Tank Corps! This was not a position that was going to fall in one day.

Still, this belief that the Germans were on the verge of punching through the Soviet defense, which was first stated on the 7th in the XLVIII Panzer Corps records, appears to have permeated German thinking during the first week of this operation. They appear to have underestimated the size and tenacity of the forces they were facing and felt, until the 12th of July, that they were about to break through into the open country. The events of the 12th of July were going to disabuse them of that notion.

38 It appears that Das Reich SS Panzer Regiment had enough time to get its armor back in order on the 9th and the 10th. It does not appear to have been heavily engaged during that time and there are a few mentions of its activities in the daily reports. It appears that they only lost 6 tanks on the 9th, 2 on the 10th and 1 tank and a Sturmgeschuetz on the 11th. They do note on the 9th that all tanks that are not required for rapid-response reserves will report for maintenance. Still the division had 97 tanks, Sturmgeschuetz and Marders ready for action on the evening of the 8th (not counting artillery observation tanks), and only 108 of them ready on the evening of the 11th. On the 11th the panzer regiment was being held as ready reserve in the Oserovskii area.

By the end of the day, the Adolf Hitler SS Division had reached the line running from the west part of Storozhevoye and the woods north of there to the course of the road to 500 meters northwest of 252.2 to the north and eastern edges of Oktyabrskii Sovkhoz.[39] This position thrust not only directly towards Prokhorovka, but was also exposed on both its north and south flanks, and could be cut off by counterattacks at its base around Vasilyevka and Yasnaya Polyana. This was a temptation that the Soviets could not resist.

The Das Reich Again Advances

Meanwhile, The Das Reich SS Division started its day by trying to free up forces so as to be able to continue moving forward. The Der Fuehrer SS Regiment was relieved at 0800 and at 1013 the 167th Infantry Division was able to assume responsibility for the zone south of Kalinin. This allowed the two infantry regiments to cover the right flank of the Adolf Hitler SS Division to the southeast and east on the line running from the northeast edge of Kalinin to the east edge of Yasnaya Polyana to the eastern slope of 243.6 (to the road 500 meters northeast of Teterevino) to the railroad booth one kilometer south of Ivanovskii Vyiselok to height 229.3. At 1300, the Soviets attacked to the northwest from the hollow northeast of Vinogradovka. This attack was defeated by a counterattack by the II Battalion, Deutschland SS Regiment. The hills two kilometers northeast of Vinogradovka and the south edge of Storozhevoye were still held by Soviet forces. The Soviets, supported by their armor, continued to offer stubborn resistance throughout the day.

The II Guards Tank Corps remained in position throughout the day and traded fire with the German forces but without taking significant losses. The corps ended the day subordinated to the V Guards Tank Army and was ordered to attack at dawn the following day. At this point, the 25th and 26th Guards Tank Brigades were assembled around Vinogradovka while the 4th Guards Tank Brigade was still holding the line from Belenikhino to Ivanovka. The 4th Motorized Rifle Brigade was also still holding the line from the woods east of Ivanovka to Leski. The corps had also moved the 1695th Antiaircraft Regiment in the area of Vingradovka to Ivanovka. It had been reinforced with the 16th Guards Mortar Regiment (22 Katyushas) that had been placed in the southern part of the woods one kilometer northeast of Ivanovka. Although the entire corps ended the day in the area, it is doubtful if the 26th Guards Tank Brigade saw action this day. It is also unknown what the status and actions were of the previous two antitank regiments that had been attached to the corps (the 1076th and 1510th Antitank Regiments). The tank corps was still reporting 84 combat-ready T-34s and 52 T-70s. Also holding in this area was the 6th Guards Motorized Rifle Brigade (V Guards Tank Corps), which was defending from Belenikhino to the outskirts of Teterevino. The brigade was supposed to turn over its positions there to the 183rd Rifle Division, but for unknown reasons the 183rd was "refusing to take over this sector."

Meanwhile, the Das Reich continued to hold its panzer regiment in ready reserve, this time in the Ozerovskii area. The Tiger company, though, was clearly in action on this day. The company commander was wounded in the arm during the morning and Hauptsturmfuehrer (Captain) Lorenz took over command. At 1200 hours he was killed and his Tiger was destroyed. Obersturmfuehrer Theiss then took command of the company. The Tiger company claimed 10 tanks on this day.[40] The Das Reich SS Division probably only lost two tanks on this day, neither of them reported to be Tigers.[41]

39 Zamulin, *Demolishing the Myth*, page 236, states that there were 33 panzers on Hill 252.2 at the end of the day. This appears to be based upon the book on the book *Liebstandarte III* by Rudolf Lehmann, who was the chief of staff of the LSSAH Division.

40 Wolfgang Schneider, *Tigers in Combat, Volume II*, page 143.

41 This figure appears to contradict the account presented earlier in the paragraph that was drawn from Wolfgang Schneider. For example, in the corps quartermaster log, they report for Das Reich SS Division that as of 7/11, there were three tanks totally destroyed, 1 Pz III, 1 Pz IV and 1 StuG III (T354, R607, p. 507). The German records only show one ready-for-action Pz VI on the 10th and the 11th and 2 on the 12th (for example: T313, R366, pages 8652270 & 2272; T313, R368, pages 8654360; and T354, R605, pages 626, 650 and 674). Still, we suspect the story presented by Schneider is fundamentally correct.

ON ONE OF the days after the 8th of July, possibly this day, Private Kaufmann, in an antiaircraft halftrack, who had experienced his first combat on 5 July, was now about to experience his first wounding.

> We were integrated into the division's armored group and now supported a counterattack by armored personnel carriers and assault guns in ground to ground fighting. Regrettably, I can no longer pin down the time or location. Given that heavy rains had come down in the meantime, the soil was very slippery. So disaster struck when the shear bolt in the right track broke upon longitudinally traversing an incline. We had to stop immediately, because the track would have been reeled off or caught between the rollers and the vehicle's hull. The gun remained ready for fire while our driver set about repairing the damage with the assistance of the ammunition bearers. Fortunately, the Russians did not have visual contact with the location of our breakdown, but they fired their mortars on that sector of terrain on a trial and error basis. For the gunner and myself as loader this was a very uneasy situation.
>
> The shear bolt, about 3¼ inches in length, was designed with a shear point so as to prevent major track damage. It broke easily if experiencing a biased, diagonal load. The drivers knew this, of course, and always carried a "black market" supply. Our driver being thus outfitted as well as due to his skill, was able to exchange the bolt relatively quickly. The objective was to get out of there fast, as the iron content of the air was increasing by the minute.
>
> We had just started moving when another volley of mortar projectiles came down nearby. Two bits from the hail of shrapnel hit me on the right hand, at the thumb and in the palm. The pain was awful and I was bleeding profusely. We stopped behind the next covering terrain feature so as to put on a makeshift bandage on my hand. I then tried to keep a stiff upper lip and continue to do my job as loader. This was only marginally accomplished, however. I had to go back to the battle train with a supply truck that evening and report to the medical detachment. There a medic took professional care of my wounds and said: "Those are only wounds to the flesh, you can stay with the company like this!" I was released with a leather boot on my thumb and a light bandage. Happy about having avoided the field hospital, I took the next ride out to my gun. Soon I no longer felt the small wounds and my combat readiness was retained. I only had difficulty washing for a while, as this had to be done all left-handed.

Air Support

Totenkopf reported moderate levels of air activity for both sides. It reported shooting down one Il-2 at 0615. The Adolf Hitler SS Division reported heavy Soviet air activity for this day, primarily ground attack planes. They reported only moderate support from the Luftwaffe. Furthermore they recorded an incident of fratricide when a German bombing attack on the SPW battalion caused casualties. Das Reich reported that air activity was moderate and the Deutschland SS Regiment shot down a LaGG-3 in the area north of Teterevino and an Il-2 at Ivanovskii.

The 9th Guards Airborne Division, which only had one regiment engaged this day, reported that at 1500, German aircraft in groups of 15–20 planes, bombed the division's defenses. The main attacks were launched against height 252.4, Barchevka, Oktyabrskii Sovkhoz, and height 252.0.[42]

---

42 Zamulin, *Demolishing the Myth*, pages 229–231, has an interview from I. S. Vakhrameev, a soldier in the 1st Rifle Battalion of the 287th Guards Rifle Regiment, who was watching from his battalion's position on Hill 254.2. He reports that the artillery positions in front of him were being attacked at low level by a group of yellowish-brown light bombers that were Italian Caproni. While there were no Italian forces with the German VIII Air Corps there was a Hungarian air division of around 90 aircraft. The Hungarians did purchase dozens of Caproni Ca.135bis bombers, but we have no evidence that they were at Kursk. See page 1392 in *Kursk: The Battle of Prokhorovka*.

That same interview claims that a flight of Il-2s then attacked the advancing German armor with rockets, machineguns and anti-tank bombs, resulting in 20 knocked-out armored vehicles and causing the undamaged German tanks to retreat back to Oktyabrskii Sokhoz.

The 167th Infantry Division Relieves Das Reich, 10 and 11 July

Meanwhile, the two-infantry regiment 167th Infantry Division was expanding its sector so as to relieve the SS Panzer Corps. The night of 9/10 July passed quietly for the division. At 0500, the Soviets began to disengage in the area west of Shopino, Ternovka, and Visloye. The division's patrols were able to maintain contact with the withdrawing Soviet forces. In the 331st Infantry Regiment sector, these patrols were able to advance to the west bank of the Lipovyii Donets. The division then sent patrols across the river to the railroad. These patrols were fired upon in the area of Soshenkov, and the patrols were able to estimate where the new Soviet line was.

The division advanced, with the 331st Infantry Regiment reaching Shopino at 1250. The village was no longer occupied by the Soviets. Meanwhile, part of the 315th Infantry Regiment had penetrated into the west part of Visloye. Soshenkov was now found to be free of Soviets, but they still occupied Nepkhayevo and along the bluff east of the Lipovyii Donets. At about 1400, contact was made with the 168th Infantry Division at Shopino. Reconnaissance over the Donets showed that the Soviets were still along the railroad embankment and edge of the woods east of the Donets. As evening came, the 331st Infantry Regiment patrols had to withdraw to the west bank of the Donets due to increasing Soviet fire. The division reported that the Soviet unit across from it was the 375th Rifle Division, although POWs had been taken from the 93rd Guards Rifle Division as well (the 93rd Guards Rifle Division reported one missing-in-action for this day). This was clearly a case of lagging intelligence, for while the 1243rd Rifle Regiment still may have been in the area on the 9th, the entire 375th Rifle Division was facing the III Panzer Corps on the 10th.

Meanwhile, the 339th Infantry Regiment was handed back over to the division at 1000 and was ordered to move immediately to the area east of Bolshiye Malyachki and Kalinin in order to relieve elements of the Das Reich SS Division in that area.

The next day, the 11th, was fairly quiet. During the morning, German patrols cleared a stretch of Soviet trench east of Visloye, leaving 20 Soviet dead on the field and 14 prisoners in German hands. On the left flank of the division, the Soviets launched a company-strength attack, which was repulsed.

Meanwhile, elements of the 168th Infantry Division were expanding their front and at 1350 reached Khokhlovo and Belomestnaya. This allowed the 167th Infantry Division to move forces from its right flank to its left, allowing it to further relieve the Das Reich SS Division. At 1550, the 331st Infantry Regiment was sent up north to relieve the 627th Engineer Battalion, which had been previously inserted into the line between the 167th Infantry Division and Das Reich. These engineers were needed elsewhere but were not relieved this day.

As Zamulin comments in a footnote to this paragraph (see page 587–588, footnote 66):

"Editor's Note: This eyewitness is referring to the Soviet PTAB (protivotankovaia aviabomba) 2.5, an anti-tank cluster bomblet first used at Kursk. The PTAB 2.5 weighed 2.5 kg, with 1.5 kg of high explosives in a shaped charge warhead. An Il-2 could carry over 200 of these anti-tank bomblets, which could theoretically penetrate 60-70 mm of tank armor—sufficient to penetrate the top armor of even heavy tanks. However, at Kursk the pilots were not familiar with the weapon, and most often dropped them from altitudes too low for the fuses to have time to arm, causing the bombs to fail to detonate. Thus, they were not an effective tank-killer at Kursk. However, this new weapon generated many myths about their effectiveness at Kursk, where they supposedly left hundreds of burned-out German tanks behind after their use. This eyewitness's statement is an example of this. Again, the reader should exercise great caution with respect to Soviet combat reports and eyewitness accounts from this period. I want to thank Boris Kavelerchik for bringing this information to my attention."

Across the Psel II, 11 July 1943

DURATION One day FRONTAGE 14.0 kilometers TERRAIN Rolling, mixed
WEATHER Heavy rainfall. Roads extremely muddy, barely passable for wheeled and tracked vehicles.

	Attacker	*Defender*
Units	T SS PzGrD	52nd GRD & others
Attachments	See below	See below
Strength	19,193	10,948
Armor	116	32 (16 light)
Artillery	145	94
Air Sorties	117	31 + 48 Night
Casualties	462 (77 KIA, 385 WIA, 0 MIA)	500 (123 KIA, 338 WIA, 39 MIA)
Armor Losses	3	6
Artillery Losses	0	3
Air Losses	0	1
Enemy Captured	N/A	0

Forces Engaged

German Attachments
II/1st Lehr Werfer Regiment
SS Corps Werfer Battalion
86th Bridge Column B

Soviet Forces
52nd Guards Rifle Division (all)
133rd AT Rifle Bn
I/5th Gds Mortar Rgt
75th Flamethrower Co.
95th Flamethrower Co.
Bn/156th GRR/51st GRD (not included)
28th AT Bde (not included, facing the XLVIII Panzer Corps and detached on this day)

From X Tank Corps
11th Motorized Rifle Brigade
287th Mortar Rgt

99th Tank Brigade (II Tank Corps)

Arriving on battlefield (loses included but strength not included in engagement strength; figures approx.)
95th Guards Rifle Division (8,845 men & 71 guns)
469th Mortar Regiment (650 men and 36 mortars)
3 batteries from 301st AT Regiment, with 1 battery detached on the 11th (15 guns)

Also in area but not included
97th Guards Rifle Division (8,874 men & 69 guns)
1372nd/29th Antiaircraft Division (401 men and 16 37mm guns)[43]

43 This is the strength on 1 July. The strength for the entire 29th Antiaircraft Division is given as 1,817 men, 112 vehicles, 66 towing vehicles, 48 AA Machineguns, 48 37mm guns and 16 88mm Guns. On 10 July its strength was 1,839 with the same number of guns and one additional vehicle and one additional towing vehicle. On 20 July its strength was 1,838, with one less 85mm gun and 2 less towing vehicles. See Fond: 13701, Opis: 20092, Delo: 9. This was one of the two (out of six) antiaircraft divisions in this battle that did not take any significant losses. The other was the 6th Antiaircraft Division that was part of the Fifth Guards Tank Army.

Height 252.2, 11 July 1943

DURATION One day FRONTAGE 7.4 kilometers TERRAIN Rolling, bare
WEATHER Heavy downpours, which severely hampered combat operations. Roads in very poor shape.

	Attacker	*Defender*
Units	LSSAH PzGrD	183rd RD (–), II TC (–) & 26th Gds AB Rgt
Attachments	See below	See below
Strength	21,487	12,521
Armor	103 (6 light)	37 (14 light)
Artillery	171	86
Air Sorties	220	31 + 12 Fractricide
Casualties	337 (33 KIA, 304 WIA, 0 MIA)	970 (279 KIA, 582 WIA, 109 MIA)
Armor Losses	11	3
Artillery Losses	0	8
Enemy Captured	N/A	4

Forces Engaged

German Attachments
55th Werfer Regiment
861st Light Field Howitzer Battalion

Soviet Forces
2/3rds of 183rd Rifle Division (285th and 295th Rifle Regiments)
II Tank Corps (less the 99th Tank Brigade)

Arriving on battlefield (not included in engagement strength)
26th Guards Airborne Rgt/9th Guards Airborne Division

Das Reich Again Advances, 11 July 1943

DURATION One day FRONTAGE 10.5 kilometers TERRAIN Rolling
WEATHER Light rain, clearing around midday. Roads and tracks somewhat muddy.

	Attacker	*Defender*
Units	DR SS PzGrD	II Guards Tank Corps & others
Attachments	See below	See below
Strength	19,435	13,558
Armor	102	136 (52 light)
Artillery	142	163
Air Sorties	80	30
Casualties	211 (29 KIA, 181 WIA, 1 MIA)	76 (14 KIA, 45 WIA, 17 MIA)
Armor Losses	2	0
Artillery Losses	1	4
Air Losses	0	2
Enemy Captured	N/A	0

Forces Engaged

German Attachments
III/1st Lehr Werfer Regiment
SS Flak Platoon (detached on the 11th—incorporated)
SS Flak Platoon (detached on the 11th—incorporated)
III/818th Artillery Regiment

Soviet Forces
II Guards Tank Corps (less Churchills)
1076th Antitank Regiment
1510th Antitank Regiment
755th AT Battalion
16th Guards Mortar Regiment
6th Guards Motorized Brigade (from V Guards Tank Corps)
454th Mortar Regiment
The 227th Rifle Regiment of the 183rd Rifle Division may have also been in this engagement, but it not incorporated into this record.

The 167th Infantry Division Relieves Das Reich I, 10 July 1943

DURATION One day FRONTAGE 19.8 kilometers TERRAIN Rolling, mixed
WEATHER Variably cloudy with evening thunderstorms.

	Attacker	*Defender*
Units	167th ID	89th & 93rd GRD
Attachments	See below	See below
Strength	14,381	18,077
Armor	0	0
Artillery	119	160
Air Sorties	0	0
Casualties	31 (9 KIA, 22 WIA)	179 (43 KIA, 114 WIA, 22 MIA)[44]
Artillery Losses	0	1
Enemy Captured	N/A	3

Forces Engaged

German Attachments
I/1st Lehr Werfer Regiment
"T" Assault Gun Battalion (detached on the 10th—not included)
SS Corps Werfer Battalion (detached on the 10th—not included)
627th Engineer Battalion (attached on the 10th)
339th Infantry Regiment (re-attached on the 10th)

Soviet Forces
93rd Guards Rifle Division
89th Guards Rifle Division
27th Gun Bde (detached on the 10th)

44 Soviet losses are probably overstated due to averaging of loss reports for the 89th Guards Rifle Division, although it does make a partial loss report of 21 wounded for the day.

The 167th Infantry Division Relieves Das Reich II, 11 July 1943

DURATION One day FRONTAGE 19.8 kilometers TERRAIN Rolling, mixed
WEATHER Rainy, poor road conditions.

	Attacker	*Defender*
Units	167th ID	89th & 93rd GRD
Attachments	See below	See below
Strength	14,350	18,164
Armor	0	0
Artillery	119	132
Air Sorties	0	0
Casualties	8 (1 KIA, 7 WIA)	286 (15 KIA, 165 WIA, 106 MIA)[45]
Artillery Losses	5[46]	0
Enemy Captured	N/A	1

Forces Engaged

German Attachments
I/1st Lehr Werfer Regiment
627th Engineer Battalion

Soviet Forces
93rd Guards Rifle Division
89th Guards Rifle Division
1/3rd 51st Guards Rifle Division (158th Guards Rifle Regiment)

45 Soviet losses are probably overstated due to averaging of loss reports for the 89th Guards Rifle Division.

46 The German artillery losses are a result of bookkeeping adjustment from a 10-day report.

Terrain Photo Section

1 Looking west from road west of Gostichchevo. This is the area where the SS Panzer Corps advanced.

2 Looking west (zoomed) from the road west of Gostishchevo.

3 Looking northwest from road west of Gostichechevo

4 Looking northwest (zoomed) from road west of Gostischevo

5 Looking due east toward Prokhorovka monument (400mm lens), from west of Kochetovka. This gives some idea of the distance between the right flank of the 11th Panzer Division and the tank fields of Prokhorovka.

6 Looking northeast toward Prokhorovka along Yakovlevo-Prokhorovka road (wide view shot), at crest near Prelstnoye-Prokhorovka road intersection.

7 Looking northeast (zoomed shot) at Prokhorovka monument.

8 Looking southeast along the Psel River at Prelestnoye.

9 Looking north (zoomed) at ridge line from Psel River at Prelestnoye.

10 Looking due north at Krivtsovo and the west bank of the Donets River.

11 Looking due north at Krivtsovo (zoomed) and the west bank of the Donets River.

12 Looking south-southwest towards Belgorod from bridge over Donets River at Krivtsovo.

13 Looking west across Donets River from Krivtsovo bridge.

14 Prokhorovka belltower monument southwest of Prokhorovka.

15 Prokhorovka belltower from Rotmistrov's observation post, west of Prokhorovka.

Photo Reconnaisance Section

Start line areas, from west to east

Recommend viewer use a magnifying glass

The area northeast of Belgorod, showing where the Lipovyii and Severnyii Donets meet, 2 June 1943.
The railroad on the left (west) goes to Prokhorovka. The two large villages in the south are Staryii Gorod and Blizhnyaya Igumenka while the three larger villages in the north are Belomestnaya, Petropavlovka, and Dalnyaya Igumenka.

The area north northeast of Belgorod, with the railroad going to Gostishchevo and the pants-shaped woods is clearly visible.
On the Severnyii Donets you can see the towns of Khokhlovo, Kiselevo and Sabyinino. Photo dated 2 June 1943.

Following the railroad out of Gostishchevo to the north, 2 June 1943.

Following the railroad to Prokhorovka to the north, 2 June 1943.

PROKHOROVKA, 2 JUNE 1943.
Compare photo to map M-37-26-V (map sheet 8).

The road leading out of Prokhrovka, 2 June 1943.
The glare in this picture is in the original.

Just west of the Tank Fields, including both towns named Luchki, 2 June 1943.

THE APPROACH ROAD TO PROKHOROVKA, 3 JULY 1943.

PROKHOROVKA, 3 JULY 1943.
Note there are still wooded sections beside the main road.

North of the Psel River Bend, where Totenkopf SS Division and elements of the Fifth Guards Army fought, 14 July 1943.

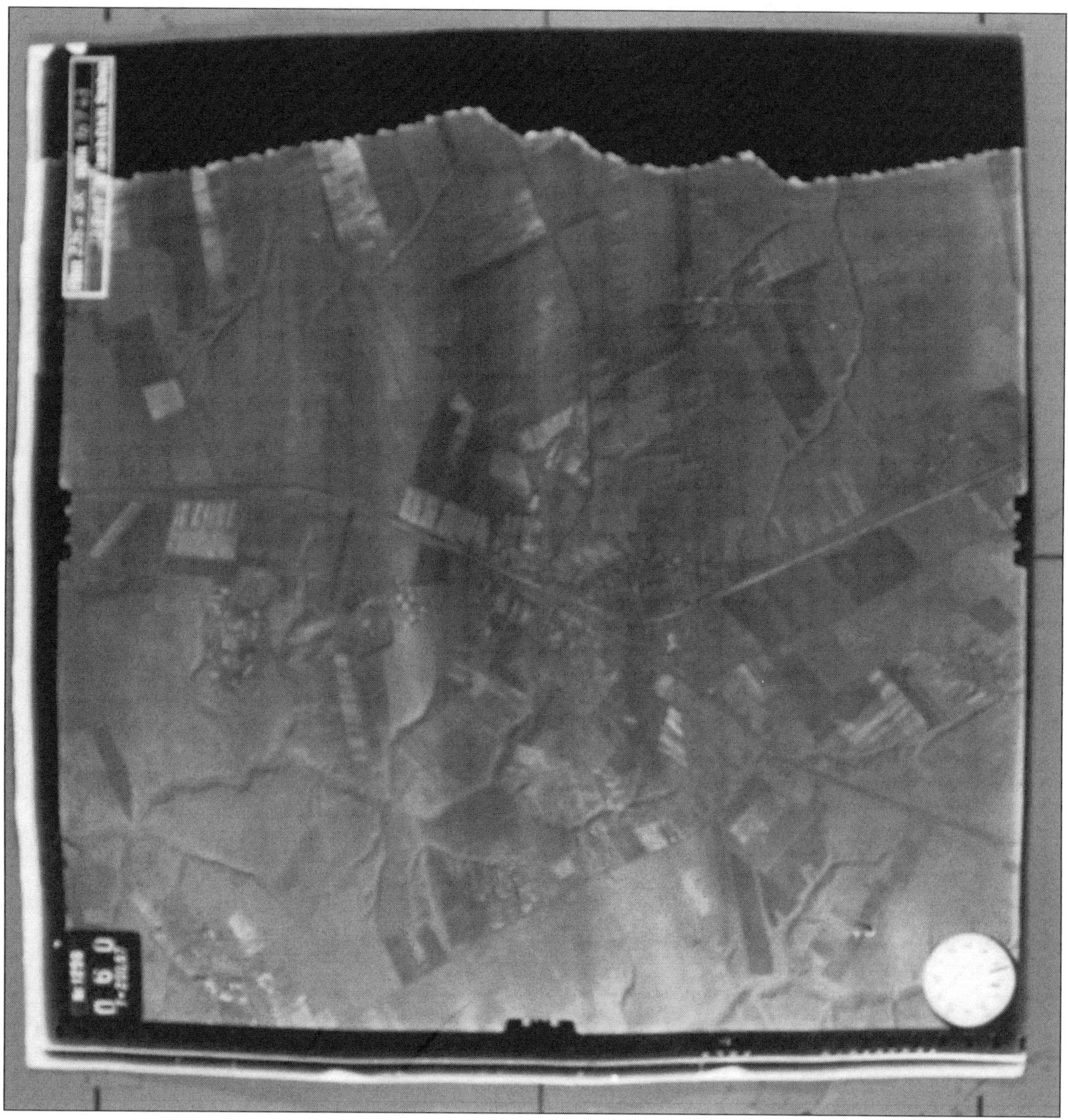

Tank Fields of Prokhorovka, 16 July 1943.

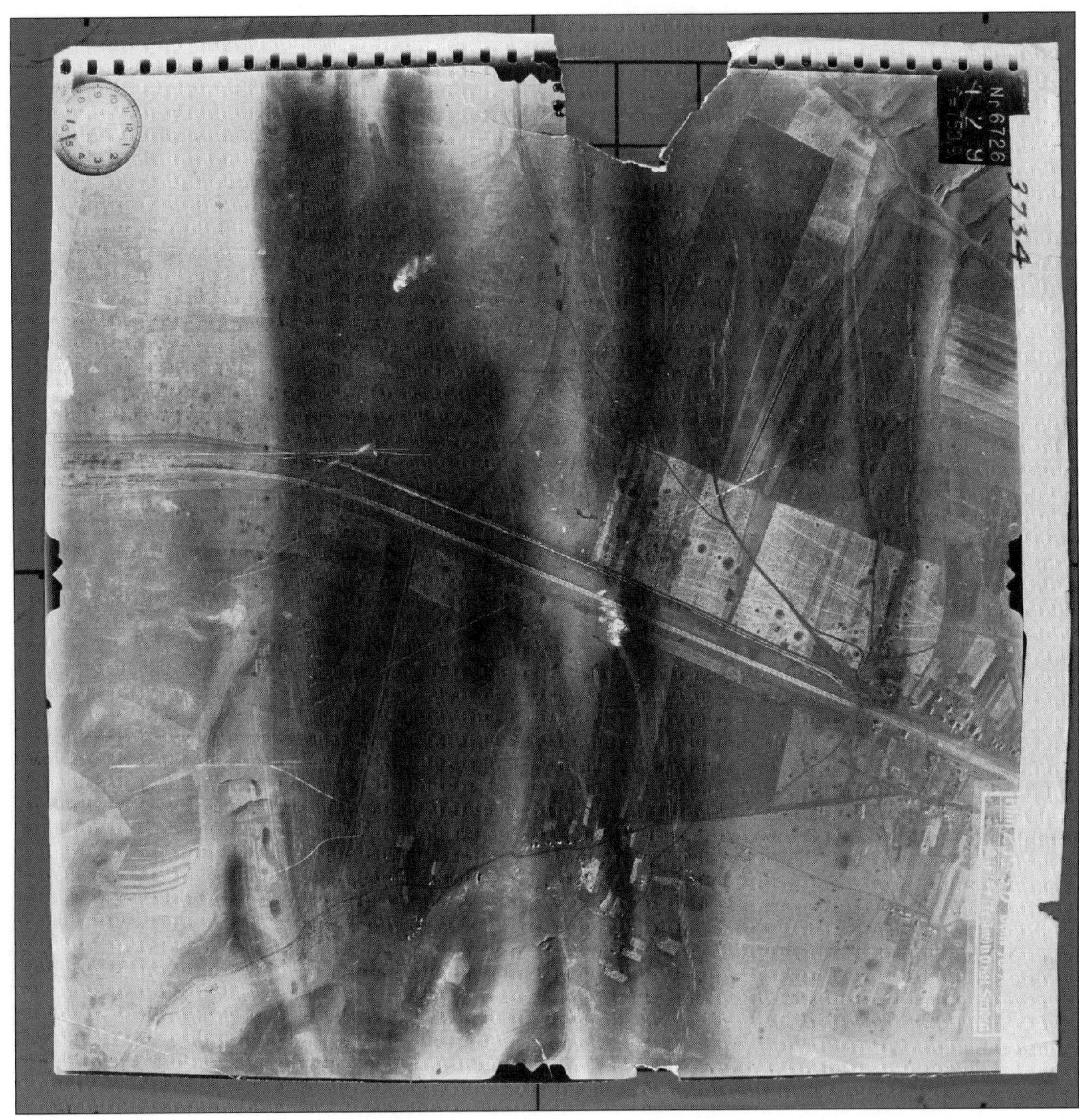

Detailed shot of the area west of Prokhorovka, 16 July 1943. Taken as part of the same reconnaissance mission as the previous photo.

CHAPTER SIX

The Advance on the Severnyii Donets

9–11 JULY 1943

> One event remains firmly implanted in my mind, as it illustrates the steadfastness of Soviet soldiers in their defense. Once again, I had pushed forward with the Tigers . . . I soon noticed that I was right in the middle of an entrenched enemy position. Then I discovered a Russian infantryman in his foxhole about 20 yards to the side of my tank. We both literally stared at the white in the enemy's eye. I signaled for him to get out of his foxhole and also gestured at him with my pistol. Maybe the Russian guy did not understand, in any case, he remained right where he was and kept fixating on me. By then I had enough of this. I grabbed a hand grenade, pulled the lock on it and hurled it towards this Russian. But I had thrown it too soon after engaging. This Russian caught the hand grenade and threw it back without flinching. It went off close to the tank's turret. This conduct displayed by this Russian solider left me so much in awe that I decided in a heartbeat to let this brave man live.
>
> LT. RICHARD ROSEN, 503RD HEAVY TANK BATTALION[1]

The III Panzer Corps

The III Panzer Corps, having now established its eastern boundary, focused its attention on getting to and across the Severnyii Donets. The opposing Sixty-ninth Army started the day concerned about chemical warfare. They had reported in their 0700 operational report that according to a prisoner interrogation, the Germans in the Myasoyedovo area were bringing up

1 Maj.Gen. (ret.) Richard Baron (Freiherr) von Rosen was interviewed by Maj.Gen. (ret.) Dieter Brand on 8 March 2000. Richard von Rosen was born 28 June 1922 and was an officer cadet in the 35th Panzer Regiment in 1940, participated in the Russian Campaign in 1941 with this regiment assigned to the 4th Panzer Division. He was promoted to lieutenant, platoon leader, in the 2nd company of the 502nd Heavy Panzer Battalion (renamed 3rd company of the 503rd) starting in 1942. During 1942 he participated in operations on the "Kalmueck-ensteppe" (semiarid desert in the western Caspian depression between the lower Volga and Kuma depression).

After Kursk he continued service through the war, was wounded five times and was awarded the German Cross in Gold, Iron Cross 1st and 2nd Class, Wound Badge in Gold, and the Armored Assault Badge 3rd Degree.

He studied agriculture after the war and was an advisor with the Blank Office of the federal government starting in 1952. He joined the West German Army in 1956 as a captain and retired as a Major General in 1982.

large quantities of artillery and mortar chemical shells! This concern over chemical warfare was always present, and as such, both sides still carried their gas masks into battle, or kept them nearby in the rear.

The III Panzer Corps Tries to Get to the Severnyii Donets, 9 July

168th Infantry Division

Deployed around the tip of the Donets triangle, this division did little this day, with the exception of the two reinforced regiments still attached to the 19th Panzer Division. During the night, there was only light harassing artillery and mortar fire on the division's southern zone. At 0300, two Soviet companies attacked out of Staryii Gorod against the division's positions along the rail line northwest of Kreida. This attack was beaten back. The Soviets claim that the 81st Guards Rifle Division beat back three attacks from Staryii Gorod between 0400, 1000 and 1400 (Moscow times). This last attack came from Mikhailovka towards Staryii Gorod and was claimed to have been a two-regiment attack supported by 10 flamethrowing tanks. This figure appears to be about twice as many as the Germans had in the area.

The 223rd (238th?) Guards Rifle Regiment was defending Staryii Gorod while the 233rd Guards Rifle Regiment was deployed from Staryii Gorod to Mikhailovka to the fork in the road one kilometer northwest of Kreida.[2] The 235th Guards Rifle Regiment extended from that point to height 130 to the MTS to the Blizhnyaya Igumenka church, where it connected with the 92nd Guards Rifle Division. This last regiment was primarily facing the 19th Panzer Division.

2 This reference to the 223rd Guards Rifle Regiment is cryptic, as this regiment was part of the 78th Guards Rifle Division. The three rifle regiments of the 81st Guards Rifle Division are the 233rd, 235th and 238th. This was probably a typographical error in the original Soviet document (Fond: Sixty-ninth Army, Opis: 10753, Delo: 133). These may have been the unit positions as of 1400.

The 78th Guards Rifle Division reports the 223rd Guards Rifle Regiment at of 1000 on the 9th on the line from Batratskaya Dacha to Gremyachii (Fond: 1225, Opis: 1, Delo: 15, page: 20).

The 19th Panzer Division Continues Attacking

The 19th Panzer Division (without its armored group) moved out from Dalnyaya Igumenka to about 1.5 kilometers east of Shishino. This thrust enveloped the entire 81st Guards Rifle Division and parts of the 92nd Guards Rifle Division. Three Soviet tanks in the northeast part of the Glavplodovoshch Orchard were set afire.

A Soviet breakout from the pocket southeast of Blizhnyaya Igumenka was stopped. The Germans claimed to have destroyed a battalion in the bitter fighting. The Soviets were reported to be still holding a position just northeast of Den Urozhaya Kolkhoz.

At this point, the 19th Panzer Division was missing Battle Group Westhoven (its armored group) and still had one regiment from the 168th Infantry Division attached, along with five Flamethrower tanks from the 6th Panzer Division. As such, it had no significant armored formations and when its armored group of 41 tanks was returned, they were not in the same shape as when they left.

The 375th Rifle Division was positioned to stop the attack from moving farther north or west. It was deployed from Shopino to height 211.6 to height 190.5 to the grove north of Pokrovka to Chernaya Polyana to Glavplodovoshch Sovkhoz to Shishino to Khokhlovo. The 81st Guards Rifle Division, huddled from Staryii Gorod to Blizhnyaya Igumenka, was now effectively isolated and was out of contact with the rear. It was on its third day without food or water and its ordnance was now reported at 0.2 ammo loads. This unit had held as long as it could and was in danger of being enveloped. At the days end, it was finally ordered by Shumilov (Seventh Guards Army) to pull back to the northeast and place itself under command of the Sixty-ninth Army.

The 92nd Guards Rifle Division continued the 81st Guards Rifle Division line with its 276th Guards Rifle Regiment deployed from the western outskirts of Blizhnyaya Igumenka to Andreyevskiye. It would appear that 19th Panzer Division primarily faced the 235th Guards, 276th Guards and 1245th Rifle Regiments.

The Reinforced 6th Panzer Division Crashes Forward

Melikhovo, which had come under attack by elements of the both the 19th Panzer Division and 6th Panzer Division in the late afternoon of the previous day, was finally cleared around 0600 (Berlin time), even though the Soviet records claim that it had been taken at 2000 (Moscow time) the previous day. After a brief wait, Battle Group Oppeln continued its attack onto Shlyakhovoye. The Tigers and the 6th company of the panzer regiment were committed in front in order to pin down the Soviet defenders. Heavy tank fire was received from Shlyakhovoye. The other three companies of the regiment attacked to the west of Shlyakhovoye, and from the northwest edge of Melikhovo, where they advanced along the Dalnyaya Igumenka–Shlyakhovoye road and stormed height 220. The 5th panzer company was then assigned to shield the left flank. Around 0700, Squadron Mueller arrived to reinforce the armored group.

It was early in this fight that Richard Rosen, of the 3rd company of the 503rd Heavy Panzer Battalion (Tiger), was wounded and his participation in the Battle of Kursk ended. He recalled:

> However, the next day [9 July] I received orders from the regiment commander to move my Tigers over into the neighboring attack sector of the 6th Panzer Division, because the Tiger battalion was to be deployed here as a whole.
>
> Shortly after I had started to move, I encountered antitank fire at closest range. Several hits landed on the turret. One must have hit the mantelet for the cylindrical mount. In any case, the gun was torn out of its mounting and the breech hit the turret ceiling. Unfortunately, I had my left arm lying on the breech, so that my elbow was crushed rather badly between breech and turret ceiling. Clearly displaying presence of mind, my driver immediately turned towards the antitank gun at full throttle and ran over it. I no longer took notice of this due to the horrific pain, though.
>
> As my regiment commander, Lieutenant Colonel Schulz signed me out, he called over to me, pointing at his Iron Cross 1st Class: "Rosen, the battle is over." He then recommended me for the Iron Cross 1st Class in respect to the engagements I saw while with his regiment. This was presented to me at a much later date while at home in an army hospital. Indeed, the battle was over for me. A few miles down the road, I met First Lieutenant Scherf, my company commander, who had me brought to the nearest clearing station. Here I received a makeshift bandage on my wounds. I then went along over to the vehicle maintenance company and from there into a private quarter in Kharkov. I was then transferred into a military hospital. My injury was severe enough to have me passed around several military hospitals. I returned as late as May 1944 and went straight to the front in the West.[3]

The battle group had received strong artillery fire throughout its morning advance. The tanks of the 6th and 8th Company had been spotted by the Soviets and remained under observation. The battle group originally sought shelter in the little woods northwest of Shlyakhovoye and in the area around height 230.3, but several tanks were hit and set on fire while sheltering there. This prompted Oppeln to pull his force back to the woods southwest of Melikhovo, leaving behind a tank platoon (the commander was a Lt. Armbruster) and two companies of the II Battalion, 114th Panzer Grenadier Regiment as a shield. The rest of the battle group pulled back for the night. The Sixty-ninth Army reported that the 305th Rifle Division repelled a German attack from Melikhovo towards Mazikino at 0945 (Moscow time) and another at 1530 (Moscow time) towards Shlyakhovoye.

This fighting must have been extremely deadly for the 6th Panzer Division, for it appears to have lost at least 38 of 73 tanks this day (not counting the 5 detached

---

3 Richard Rosen provides a similar, more detailed and slightly different account in his book: Richard Freiherr von Rosen, *Panzer Ace: Memoir of an Iron Cross Panzer Commander from Barbarossa to Normandy* (Greenhill Books, London, 2018), pages 212–214, 220–222. In his book he gives the date of his wounding as 11 July.

flame panzers). The attached Tiger battalion fared no better, with a loss of 19 of 33 tanks (although they may have lost some with the company attached to the 7th Panzer Division). The 228th Assault Gun Battalion was clearly in the middle of the fight also, indicating a loss of 12 Sturmgeschuetz IIIs of 23. The Panzer Group Westhoven, attached from the 19th Panzer Division, would also fare poorly, losing 30 tanks this day.[4] This was a devastating loss of almost 100 tanks in one day!

The rest of the 6th Panzer Division was assembled into an "Attack Group North." The corps had already created an Attack Group South from the 19th Panzer Division less its armored group. This Attack Group North included the Battle Group Westhoven (the 19th Panzer Division's armored group). Attack Group North turned southwest to clear the Soviet elements that had hung in the wake of its advance, and which the 168th Infantry Division had failed to dislodge. This force took height 203.3 and Dalnyaya Igumenka despite heavy resistance from Soviet tanks, and continued to attack south to the line running from the orchard two kilometers west of Postnikov Station to Andreyevskiye. Soviet breakout attempts from the woods two kilometers southeast of Postnikov Station were turned back. Dalnyaya Igumenka had been held by the 47th Guards Heavy Tank Regiment (II Guards Tank Corps) before it fell back to the southeastern outskirts of Khokhlovo with three operational Churchills. The II Guards Tank Corps reported that the Germans took Dalnyaya Igumenka at 1600 (Moscow time).

The attached Panzer Group Westhoven, which had 41 tanks ready-for-action at the end of the previous day was now down to around 18 tanks. They appear to have lost around 30 tanks this day, leaving a gutted regiment to return to its parent division the following day at less than half its tank strength!

This unheralded day of fighting appears to have cost the III Panzer Corps over 100 tanks and assault guns. This was not only the worst day of combat for the corps, but one of the worst for the Germans in the attack in the south. Just to compare:

III Panzer Corps

Day	*Tanks*	*Losses*	*Percent Loss*
4	395	2	0.5
5	393	60	15
6	334	66	20
7	273	54	20
8	241	24	10
9	229	108	47

To put this in perspective, the SS Panzer Corps' worst day had been fewer than 80 tanks lost (on the 6th). The XLVIII Panzer Corps had lost over a 100 tanks a day on both the 5th (estimated at 132 tanks) and 6th (estimated at 130 tanks), but this included probably 80 or more Panthers breaking down over these two days. Furthermore, it was from an initial operating strength of slightly over 600 tanks. No other German panzer corps in this offensive in the south lost more than 80 tanks in a day before this day, or on any day before the end of the offensive! So, this could well be the single worse armor exchange by the Germans in the battle. Except for the XLVIII Panzer Corps on the 5th and 6th of July and the III Panzer Corps on this day, none of the three German panzer corps in this attack appear to have lost more than 80 tanks on any given day.

Even at the famed Battle of Prokhorovka on the 12th of July, the SS Panzer Corps lost fewer tanks. While Rotmistrov and the Fifth Guards Tank Army became renown for this action, the fighting today (9 July) between Andreyevskiye and Melikhovo was truly unheralded, yet not mentioned in major histories of the

4 Most of the loss data is derived from the "Panzerlage am 9.7.43 fruh" and "Panzerlage am 10.7.43 fruh" (T312. R58, page 004374). In the case of the 6th Panzer Division, it shows 70 tanks ready for action early on the 9th and only 22 early on the 10th (but does not report on the 7 Pz IIs). For the 19th Panzer Division it shows 36 tanks early on the 9th and 13 early on the 10th. It also shows losses for 9 July of 21 tanks. There are also other daily strength reports for this division. For the 503rd Heavy Panzer Battalion, it shows 33 Pz VIs early on the 9th and 14 on the 10th with 19 losses. For the 228th Assault Gun Battalion, it shows 23 ready-for-action early on the 9th and 11 the following day, with 12 reported damaged or destroyed on the 9th

battles and the Soviet defenders have not been singled out. So who were these defending Soviet units?

Holding around Melikhovo were the 305th Rifle Division and elements of the 92nd Guards Rifle Division. The 305th Rifle Division reported fighting off a battalion-strength attack from Melikhovo towards Mazikino, supported by 20 tanks at 0940 (Moscow time) and another attack at 1530 (Moscow time) towards Shlyakhovoye. They claimed three German tanks.

The 92nd Guards Rifle Division's 282nd Guards Rifle Regiment, along with the 96th Tank Brigade, was deployed from Andreyevskiye up to the northern outskirts of Melikhovo. The 96th Tank Brigade's 228th Tank Battalion fell back to the northern slopes of height 217.4, having lost eight tanks. The brigade's motorized rifle battalion now moved to the Kiselevo area. The 280th Guards Rifle Regiment, along with the 1004th Rifle Regiment from the 305th Rifle Division, were defending from 500 meters north of Melikhovo to the western outskirts of Mazikino. The 1004th Rifle Regiment was flanked to the north by the 1002nd Rifle Regiment, which anchored its right flank at Sabyinino, while the 1000th Rifle Regiment was to its left. Still, it is uncertain how seriously engaged the 305th Rifle Division was today, as it reported only 50 men killed and wounded.[5]

The 92nd Guards Rifle Division had already been seriously engaged, reporting a strength on the 9th of July of 8,430 men (reported strength on 7 July was 9,489) and on the 10th the corps reported its strength as 5,249. Its casualties were reported through the 9th to be 411 killed, 669 wounded, and 1,104 missing. It was going to have it rough the following day also.

The XXXV Guards Rifle Corps had now joined the Sixty-ninth Army, giving it a second corps. This corps took over the area from Petropavlovka to Staryii Gorod to Myasoyedovo, and took command of the 375th, 81st Guards, 92nd Guards and 94th Guards Rifle Divisions, and the 96th Tank Brigade. These forces were all to the north of the III Panzer Corps. The XLVIII (48th) Rifle Corps now took over command of the 183rd, 89th Guards, and 93rd Guards Rifle Divisions, which were all facing the SS Panzer Corps, and relinquished control of the 107th and 305th Rifle Divisions, which were facing the III Panzer Corps.

The 7th Panzer Division Continues to Hold

During the night, there were local Soviet attacks on both sides of the Solovyev Kolkhoz, which were halted by German counterattacks.[6] The 7th Panzer Division had a quiet day. Elements of the 198th Infantry Division arrived to relieve the south wing of the division. This allowed the 7th Panzer Division to give up defending the area from Batratskaya Dacha Sovkhoz to the point of woods two kilometers south of Myasoyedovo. This relieved the 7th Panzer Division of a five kilometer stretch of front.

There was little change in the Soviet forces opposite them. The 44th Guards Rifle Regiment of the 15th Guards Rifle Division continued holding from height 202.3 to Batratskaya Dacha, while during the night of 9/10 July, its 47th Guards Rifle Regiment was ordered to take over the defensive sector north of there from the 283rd Guards Rifle Regiment of the 94th Guards Rifle Division. It appears the 283rd Guards Rifle Regiment pulled out early, and as a result the Germans were able to penetrate into the woods two kilometers southeast of height 206.9. This resulted in the 47th Guards Rifle Regiment becoming involved in heavy fighting through the night and it was only able to take up its assigned defensive positions by the next morning. The 15th Guards Rifle Division had now committed two rifle regiments forward, stretched from height 206.9 to Batratskaya Dacha, with their third rifle regiment in a second echelon along the Koren River. The 262nd Tank Regiment, down to only six KVs, was also back there. The 94th

5 Fond: Sixty-ninth Army, Opis: 10753, Delo: 133, page: 11. It is distinctly possible that this is not a complete casualty report and the division's losses were much higher on this day.

6 These were probably forces from the 15th Guards Rifle Division. All reports for this day put the 73rd Guards Rifle Division in Batratskaya Dacha and to its south, unlike on the 8th when the 214th Guards Rifle Regiment was fighting in this area.

The 168th Infantry Division Holds, 9 July 1943

DURATION One day FRONTAGE 8.7 kilometers TERRAIN Rolling, mixed
WEATHER Bright, warm, thunderstorms toward evening. Temperature at noon: 31 degree Celsius. Road conditions level four (good).

	Attacker	*Defender*
Units	168th ID (–)	1/3rd 375th RD & 2/3rds 81st Gds RD
Attachments	See below	See below
Strength	8,077	9,342
Armor	6	0
Artillery	48	111
Air Sorties	0	0
Casualties	98 (38 KIA, 52 WIA, 8 MIA)	193 (47 KIA, 62 WIA, 84 MIA)
Artillery Losses	0	4
Enemy Captured	N/A	1

Forces Engaged

German Attachments
2/228th StuG Bn

Detached from the 168th Infantry Division on this day
IV/248th Artillery Rgt
V/248th Artillery Rgt

Still detached from the division
248th Engineer Bn (- 2 cos)
429th Infantry Rgt (- 1 Bn)
442nd Infantry Rgt

Soviet Forces
1/3rd 375th Rifle Division (including the 1241st Rifle Regiment)
263rd Mortar Rgt
1240th AT Rgt
1667th AT Rgt
16th Gds Mortar Rgt

2/3rds 81st Guards Rifle Division (excluding 235th Guards Rifle Regiment)

Guards Rifle Division, along with the 31st Antitank Brigade, was now holding the front from Kalinina to the eastern outskirts of Myasoyedovo to height 206.9 to the western edge of the Solovyev Kolkhoz woods. The 15th Guards Rifle Division was now placed under command of the XXV Guards Rifle Corps, while the 94th Guards Rifle Division was transferred back to the XXXV Guards Rifle Corps, now part of the Sixty-ninth Army.

Air Support

The III Panzer Corps and the 6th Panzer Division reported only light Soviet air activity during the night. The 168th Infantry Division reported bombing attacks on the Belgorod-Kursk highway. The 19th Panzer Division reported weak Soviet air activity this day. The III Panzer Corps reported heavy Soviet air activity in the corps zone during the day.

Commentary

By the end of the 9th, the III Panzer Corps, despite its penetration and efforts, was not going any place important very quickly. Unlike the other two panzer corps, which each had a long single flank to protect, this corps had two long flanks to protect. Furthermore, it

The 19th Panzer Division Continues Attacking, 9 July 1943

DURATION One day FRONTAGE 8.5 kilometers TERRAIN Rolling, mixed

WEATHER Bright, warm, thunderstorms toward evening. Temperature at noon: 31 degree Celsius. Road conditions level four (good).

	Attacker	*Defender*
Units	19th PzD	1/3rd 81st GRD, 1/3rd 92nd GRD & 1/3rd 375th RD
Attachments	See below	See below
Strength	19,347	10,179
Armor	13 (5 light)	0
Artillery	161	107
Air Sorties	0	0
Casualties	472 (85 KIA, 362 WIA, 25 MIA)	935 (178 KIA, 328 WIA, 429 MIA)
Armor losses	6	0
Artillery Losses	0	11
Enemy Captured	N/A	0

Forces Engaged

German Attachments

70th Engineer Bn
2/411th Bridge Column B
842nd Bridge Column J

II/71st Artillery Rgt—detached on the 9th
I/54th Werfer Rgt
II/54th Werfer Rgt
Hq/54th Werfer Rgt

I/61st Flak Rgt
2nd co/503rd Heavy Panzer Bn—detached on the 9th
5 Pz III Flames Tanks (from 6th PzD)—attached on the 9th

429th Infantry Rgt (168th ID), less I Battalion
442nd Infantry Rgt (168th ID)
co/248th Engineer Bn (168th ID)
IV/248th Artillery Rgt (168th ID)—attached on the 9th
V/248th Artillery Rgt (168th ID)—attached on the 9th

Detached on the 9th

Panzer Group Westhoven
Lt Bn/19th Artillery Rgt

Soviet Forces

1/3rd of 81st Guards Rifle Division including the 235th Guards Rifle Regiment

315th Gds Mortar Rgt
290th Mortar Rgt

1/3rd of 92nd Guards Rifle Division including the 276th Guards Rifle Regiment

114th Gds AT Rgt

1/3rd of 375th Rifle Division including the 1245th Rifle Regiment

+ Attachments to the division (only half are counted)
  694th AT Rgt
  88th Flamethrower Company
  192nd Flamethrower Company
  1363/26th Antiaircraft Division
  60th Armored Train Detachment
  137th ATR Bn

Units not included

31st AT Bde—attached to the 81st GRD on the 6th, but included in engagement versus 7th PzD.

The Reinforced 6th Panzer Division Crashes Forward, 9 July 1943

DURATION One day FRONTAGE 5.7 kilometers TERRAIN Rolling, mixed

WEATHER Bright, warm, thunderstorms toward evening. Temperature at noon: 31 degree Celsius. Road conditions level four (good).

	Attacker	*Defender*
Units	6th PzD	92nd Gds RD & 305th RD
Attachments	See below	See below
Strength	22,792	16,241
Armor	158 (17 light & flamethrower tanks)	54 (6 light)
Artillery	143	151
Air Sorties	0	0
Casualties	177 (36 KIA, 139 WIA, 2 MIA)	1,476 (269 KIA, 471 WIA, 7364 MIA)
Armor Losses	97!!!	13
Artillery Losses	0	16
Enemy Captured	N/A	2

Forces Engaged

German Attachments

II/71st Artillery Rgt—attached on the 9th
857th Heavy Artillery Bn
III/54th Werfer Rgt

II/43rd Flak Rgt

228th StuG Bn (- 2nd company)
1st co/503rd Heavy Panzer Bn

Panzer Group Westhoven (from 19th PzD)—attached on the 9th
lt Bn/19th Artillery Rgt (from 19th PzD)—attached on the 9th

Detached

5 Pz III Flame

Soviet Forces

2/3rds of 92nd Guards Rifle Division including the 280th and 282nd Guards Rifle Regiments
114th Guards AT Regiment
305th Rifle Division
1658th AT Regiment
96th Guards Tank Brigade
47th Guards Heavy Tank Regiment (from II Gds Tank Corps, its 8 Churchill's are included)
1500th AT Regiment (from II Gds Tank Corps with 19 45mm AT guns. Strengths not included)

The 7th Panzer Division Continues to Hold, 9 July 1943

DURATION One day FRONTAGE 9.0 kilometers TERRAIN Rolling, mixed

WEATHER Bright, warm, thunderstorms toward evening. Temperature at noon: 31 degree Celsius. Road conditions level four (good).

	Attacker	*Defender*
Units	7th PzD	15th & 94th GRD
Attachments	See below	See below
Strength	19,355	19,658
Armor	52 (4 light)	28 (9 light)
Artillery	127	171
Air Sorties	0	37 + 41 Night
Casualties	367 (58 KIA, 299 WIA, 10 MIA)	270 (49 KIA, 216 WIA, 5 MIA)
Armor Losses	5	0
Artillery Losses	1	0
Enemy Captured	N/A	2

Forces Engaged

German Attachments
9th Bridge Column B
1/505th Bridge Column B
843rd Bridge Column J

99th Flak Rgt Staff
I/38th Flak Rgt
II/38th Flak Rgt
lt Bn/91st Flak Rgt

II/62nd Artillery Rgt

204th Intelligence Troop (not included)
3rd co/503rd Heavy Panzer Bn

198th Infantry Division (losses only)

Soviet Forces
94th Guards Rifle Division
148th Tank Regiment
161st Gun Regiment (detached on the 9th)

15th Guards Rifle Division (at least the 44th and 47th Guards Rifle Regiments)

31st Antitank Brigade

Other Soviet assets (second echelon)

The third regiment of the 15th Guards Rifle Division was on the Koren River in the 2nd echelon. It is included in this engagement. The various attachments to this division (1669th AT Rgt, 2nd Gds ATR Bn, 4th Gds ATR Bn) were not, as was also the case with the nearby 262nd Tank Rgt. In the case of the 1669th AT Rgt, it was detached from the division on this day.

The XXV Guards Rifle Corps also had attached to it the 97th Guards Mortar and 329th Engineer Battalion. These are not included in any engagement in this day.

III Panzer Corps Assets
601st Engineer Rgt Staff
674th Engineer Rgt Staff
925th Bridge Construction Staff
127th Engineer Bn (- co)
531st Bridge Construction Bn
110th Bridge Column B
602nd Bridge Column B
co/538th Road Construction Bn

153rd Flak Rgt Staff

3rd Command of Artillery
612th Artillery Rgt Staff
Pn/13th Light Observations Battery

2nd Fuel Column Troop—attached to corps on the 9th
545th Panzer Recovery Platoon
Hq/503rd Heavy Panzer Bn
2nd co/503rd Heavy Panzer Bn—attached on the 9th

was nowhere near conducting its primary task, which was to protect the flank of the SS Panzer Corps. The fighting here had developed the characteristic of all the fighting around the flanks of the other corps, except it was even more tangled. Again, the Soviet forces tended to hold in place, sticking to the flanks until the Germans finally decided to remove them by envelopment. The resulting withdrawals and captures would then run up the Soviet casualty count. As of 9 July, there were more forces in the III Panzer Corps either holding the flanks or cleaning up and enveloping Soviet forces, than there were making forward progress toward the Severnyii Donets. The III Panzer Corps attack had been pretty much reduced to one combined armored group pushing on Shlyakhovoye. Still, these attacks were actually running parallel to the Severnyii Donets, not bringing the forces nearer to the river. Overall, the German attack, while able to move forward, was clearly not accomplishing its primary goal. The III Panzer Corps losses had become very high, with only 144 tanks and assault guns operational at the end of the 9th, compared to 394 at the start of the attack.

Even so, the corps attack was developing, for they had finally managed to force the 81st Guards Rifle Division to withdraw, and this cleared the area to Belgorod. This also opened up a supply road from Belgorod. The corps now planned to push full force onto Shlyakhovoye, which they presumed was the last enemy defense line.[7]

There is some question about what the 168th Infantry Division was doing at this point. While one of its regiments was clearly supporting the 19th Panzer Division's efforts, the forces in the Mikhailovka bridgehead and elsewhere seemed very quiet. Again, the mission of the III Panzer Corps was to protect the flanks of the Fourth Panzer Army.

III Panzer Corps, 10 July

Having spent the previous day trying to clean up and expand the area facing the Severnyii Donets, the III Panzer Corps now finished cleaning up the area of Blizhnyaya and Dalnyaya Igumenka and prepared to attack northwards to the river. The Soviet withdrawals from this area finally allowed this very tangled northern wing of the III Panzer Corps to clean itself up.

168th Infantry Division

During the morning of the 10th, the 429th Infantry Regiment renewed its attack towards the Blizhnyaya Igumenka and Staryii Gorod, and by noon had reached the main road near the Glavplodovoshch Orchard. The Soviet infantry were either driven from their positions or captured, the 168th Infantry Division reporting that it took 300 prisoners on this day. At 0930, Staryii Gorod was taken with support from the Luftwaffe, some five days behind schedule. Isolated Soviet groups escaped over the Donets towards the north and west by abandoning their weapons. The Germans captured considerable inventory. The holding of this position until they were enveloped was costly for the 81st Guards Rifle Division but they certainly had hindered German operations.

To the left, and on the other side of the Donets, in the 417th Infantry Regiment sector, an early morning attack was launched against the woods 600 meters southwest of the church in Chernaya Polyana. Little progress was made against strong Soviet resistance. Later, about 1115, a reconnaissance attack found the woods to be lightly defended, and a renewed attack resulted in the capture of these woods. Part of the regiment continued the attack through Chernaya Polyana and took the woods two kilometers to the north, while elements were left behind to clear Chernaya Polyana.

Meanwhile, the 442nd Infantry Regiment occupied Blizhnyaya Igumenka in the early morning hours. At noon, the regiment began to assemble in Dalnyaya Igumenka and the area to the north. This regiment was about to be turned back to its parent division, resulting in the 168th Infantry Division having elements of all three of its infantry regiments returned for the first time since the start of this battle.

7 Breith, page 8.

Attack Group South

The III Panzer Corps operations were still split into the Attack Group South, which consisted of mainly the 19th Panzer Division less its armored group and the more powerful Attack Group North.

During the night assault groups from the 73rd Panzer Grenadier Regiment and the 19th Reconnaissance Battalion broke into the Soviet positions three kilometers north of Blizhnyaya Igumenka and found the Soviets withdrawing north. Prisoners and equipment were captured. The 442nd Infantry Regiment occupied all of Blizhnyaya Igumenka area in the morning hours.

At noon, the division began to assemble in Dalnyaya Igumenka and the area to the north. The division spent the rest of the day reorganizing in Dalnyaya Igumenka. It was down to about 88 percent of its starting strength, having lost some 1,728 people. As in almost all combat units, these casualties were concentrated in its forward fighting elements. As such, the 73rd Panzer Grenadier Regiment had already complained of having only two combat-strength companies on the 9th. Now the 74th Panzer Grenadier Regiment was reporting only about 300 men fit for duty (they probably meant 300 infantry fit, as the regiment was most certainly not reduced to 300 men) and the 27th Panzer Regiment reported just 15 operable tanks, including new ones (repaired?) just brought forward. At this point, the offensive strength of the 19th Panzer Division had been severely reduced.

The division did report the appearance of English-made Churchill tanks and claimed two destroyed. This was certainly from the 47th Guards Heavy Tank Regiment, which reported 2 tanks losses for the 9th.[8] The fighting of the III Panzer Corps was now beginning to have a direct impact on the SS Panzer Corps as two of the divisions on its flank, the 89th Guards Rifle Division and the 375th Rifle Division, both in reasonably good condition, were now shifted to stop the III Panzer Corps attack. The 89th Guards Rifle Division was reported to now be defending along the line of the western and southern edge of the woods west of Kiselevo to Kiselevo to the southern outskirts of Sabyinino. The 375th Rifle Division was stretched from the northeastern outskirts of Kiselevo to height 211.5 to the Shlyakhovoye MTS, with its 1243rd Rifle Regiment in the northwest to height 211.5 and its 1245th Rifle Regiment in the southeast. Its 1241st Rifle Regiment was in a second echelon position in the Sabyinino area.

The Sixty-ninth Army Takes Over

The Soviet command had adjusted to the realities of the battlefield, with the Seventh Guards Army now commanding the troops to the east of the German breakthrough, while the Sixty-ninth Army took over command of the troops east of the SS Panzer Corps and north of the III Panzer Corps. In effect, the Sixty-ninth Army was now in charge of the Donets triangle, with the XLVIII Rifle Corps (183rd, 89th Guards, 93rd Guards Rifle Divisions) and the XXXV Guards Rifle Corps (375th, 81st Guards, 92nd Guards, and 94th Guards Rifle Divisions, and the 96th Tank Brigade) under its command. The 107th and 305th were transferred to the Seventh Guards Army. The 81st was now assigned to the XLVIII Rifle Corps. The Sixty-ninth Army also picked up command of the II Tank Corps, II Guards and V Guards Tank Corps.

The II Guards Tank Corps, which had already committed its 47th Guards Heavy Tank Regiment to the fighting south of the Severnyii Donets, had moved its headquarters at 0500 from the Sazhnoye area to the southern outskirts of Kleimenovo, three kilometers south of Shakhovo. At the same time, the corps was subordinated to the Sixty-ninth Army, with orders to hand over part of its defensive area facing the SS Panzer Corps to the 93rd Guards Rifle Division. It was still holding in the Belenikhino and Leski area but was to concentrate and prepare to counterattack to the west against the flank of the SS Panzer Corps and to the south towards Sabyinino. It was also ordered to be ready to counterattack to the southeast and northwest! At 1100, the headquarters had withdrawn to Plota, while

---

8 Operational Report #183 for 0700 on 10 July reports two Churchills burned on the 9th, out of 5 combat-ready. It later reports losses for day as 1 burned and 1 knocked out. It shows 3 ready for action, as it does for the following day's report. See Fond: II Gds Tank Corps, Opis: 1, Delo: 32, pages: 188 & 192.

the 47th Guards Heavy Tank Regiment remained in the area southeast of Khokhlovo with its three Churchills.

During the night of 9/10 July, the 81st Guards Rifle Division broke out of its encirclement. By morning they had concentrated in the northeastern part of the woods 1.5 kilometers northwest of Khokhlovo, with the division's headquarters in Krivtsovo. While this division had been exhausted and had to withdraw when it did, it was reporting on 11 July to still have a personnel strength of 3,500 to 4,000 men. Its equipment, according to their preliminary calculations, was at 40 to 50 percent of authorized strength. Divisional, antitank and regimental artillery had been destroyed. The division had fought for five days with a very limited supply of ammunition, food, and water. It does not appear that they were resupplied during this time.

The 89th Guards Rifle Division was also tangled up in this fight and withdrawal (as were elements of the 92nd Guards Rifle Division, the 375th Rifle Division and the 96th Tank Brigade). Senior Lieutenant Viktor Stepanovich Kozlov[9] had been recently assigned to the 89th Guards Rifle Division:

> It might seem strange, but during the defensive operation of the Kursk battle, I did not have any position. On the 8th of July, 1943, I and six other officers arrived from the hospital to the human resource department with the letter "At the disposal of the Sixth Guards Army commander." All of a sudden the commander himself, Lieutenant General Chistyakov, called us in. He briefly told us about a massive tank attack and that our troops are withdrawing at some positions. He told us about the difficult situation at the left flank, especially at the 89th Guards Rifle Division. He gave us guns and sent us there. He said that our task was not to allow an unauthorized withdrawal of soldiers, especially the escape of separate groups from the field to the east. He told us to relay this order to every commander of a platoon and company. I told Colonel Pigin, the division commander, about it.
>
> In the morning of 9 July, we were already in the front battalions of the division. Dozens of German tanks supported by artillery and aviation were attacking us. In the afternoon I had to command the units, where company commanders were killed. When I saw an unauthorized withdrawal of our soldiers, I would run over there. I warned, then shot twice in the air, but twice I had to shoot the soldiers in the feet. They had dropped their guns and simply ran from the battlefield. Sometimes I would capture them and send them to my commanders.
>
> The situation got worse on the next day. The German tanks, which appeared from the south, got to the rear of the division. None of our soldiers were running away. Everyone tried to stay close to their commanders, because only the commander knew the situation and what to do. Actually there was one incident of escape, but I quickly managed it.

In contrast, the other divisions were in relatively good shape. These units were still reasonably well provisioned, with the 305th, 92nd Guards, and 94th Guards Rifle Divisions all reporting they had five or six days of food and 0.8 to 1 load of ammo. The 305th Rifle Division was reporting 7,821 men, while the 94th Guards Rifle Division was reporting 8,106 men (it reported 9,385 on the 5th of July). The 92nd Guards Rifle Division had been seriously attrited though, and was down to 5,249 men (it reported 9,574 on the 5th of July) and was missing about half of its guns and mortars. This unit reported losing on the 10th of July over 2,000 men![10]

The 92nd Guards Rifle Division at 1800 hours, had its 276th and 280th Guards Rifle Regiments along the line from Kiselevo to height 211.5 to outside the MTS

9 Col. Viktor Stepanovich Kozlov resides in Shcherbinka, Moscow Region. He was interviewed by Col. Valerii Akimov in 1999.

10 There are two different casualty reports for this day, one of 303 killed and 2,077 wounded; and another of 333 killed, 976 wounded and 1,906 missing, for a total of 3,215; with also 141 horses killed and 88 horses missing. These may well have been aggregate reports recording losses for a few days up until the 10th. Still it appears losses were very heavy leading up to and possibly including the 10th.

to Shlyakhovoye. Its 282nd Guards Rifle Regiment was positioned in the second echelon at the garden north of Sabyinino to height 224.4 to the Obyedineniye Kolkhoz garden. The 1004th Rifle Regiment of the 305th Rifle Division had been driven back to a position running from the Dubrov Woods to height 220.1. The division was reported at 1800 to be holding a line from Sabyinino to Shlyakhovoye to Sheino to Ushakovka. The 94th Guards Rifle Division was still holding from Kalinina to height 206.9. The 107th Rifle Division now moved to a second echelon position from Verkhnyii Olshanets to Ploskoye where it entrenched. It suffered eight casualties on this day due to German bombing.

The 81st Guards Rifle Division on the 5th of July halted the attacks by the 6th Panzer Division and parts of the 168th Infantry and 19th Panzer Divisions, and then remained engaged for the rest of the period with the better part of the 168th Infantry and parts of the 19th Panzer Divisions. While it may have lost around 2,296 troops and over half its guns and mortars, the 81st Guards Rifle Division, its attachments and immediate neighbors, had been repeatedly attacked by forces outnumbering them 1.8 to 1, and yet had achieved an exchange rate of 1 to 1.8, and had cost the Germans 88 tanks.[11] It was a most impressive defensive fight by this Soviet division.

Attack Group North

Battle Groups Oppeln (the panzer regiment) and Unrein (formed around the 4th Panzer Grenadier Regiment)[12] defended in place at Melikhovo during most of the day, as they had reached their assigned objectives, while the advance of their neighboring division had bogged down. They endured only occasional Soviet artillery harassing fire. This and some antitank fire was enough, though, to compel the withdrawal of German tanks from height 230.3 to a more sheltered position. Meanwhile, the division brought the road junction west of Melikhovo firmly under German control.

At 1500, Battle Group Unrein advanced from the north edge of Melikhovo into the south part of Shlyakhovoye. Battle Group Oppeln advanced to the crossroads 1.5 kilometers north of Melikhovo, after having to breach a minefield one kilometer west of this crossroads. The Soviets began to withdraw rapidly. At this juncture, as was planned, Battle Group Oppeln stopped supporting this attack on Shlyakhovoye and began to pursue Soviet forces withdrawing to the northeast. Still, despite strong resistance, Battle Group Unrein had Shlyakhovoye under its control by the end of the day and had pushed forward to a line a little north of the town. The expected Luftwaffe support for the attack never materialized and the Germans reported that the weather also hampered their attack.

To the southwest, Battle Group Bieberstein (formed around the 114th Panzer Grenadier Regiment)[13] advanced from the Postnikov Station–Andreyevskiye line to take the Glavplodovoshch Orchard and the area south of Shishino. The 6th Reconnaissance Battalion destroyed the Soviet forces surrounded in the woods two kilometers north of Andreyevskiye and attacked Kalinina from the north and managed to reach positions just to the northwest of the town. Battle Group Quentin moved against the Soviets defending the woods southwest of Kalinina and the "Schipoffue" Kalinina School.[14] Before noon, Soviet infantry attacked the German approach march route from Kalinina. This attack was repelled by part of the I Battalion, 4th Panzer Grenadier Regiment and three Tiger tanks.

11 This is a simple summation of all 12 engagements we recorded the 81st Guards Rifle Division participating in. The 81st Guards Rifle Division made up a little less than half the force across these engagements, so other units also claimed some of the glory in this case.

12 This is Col. Martin Unrein, the 4th Panzer Grenadier Regiment commander.

13 Battle Group Bieberstein was probably named after Konstantin Rogalla von Bieberstein, a major with the 6th Panzer Division who was awarded the Knight's Cross posthumously for Kursk when he was commander of the 114th Panzer Grenadier Regiment. He was killed in action on 14 July and awarded the cross on 24 July 1943.

14 Major Freidrich Quentin was the commander of the 6th Reconnaissance Battalion. He was also a Knight's Cross holder, having been awarded it on 8 February 1943.

The 168th Infantry Division Advances, 10 July 1943

DURATION One day FRONTAGE 8.6 kilometers TERRAIN Rolling, mixed

WEATHER Partly cloudy, occasional light rain in the morning, clearing in the afternoon. Temperature at noon: 19 degrees Celsius. Road conditions good.

	Attacker	*Defender*
Units	168th ID	1/3rd 375th RD & 2/3rds 81st Gds RD
Attachments	See below	See below
Strength	12,421	7,409
Armor	6	0
Artillery	89	48
Air Sorties	14	0
Casualties	118 (19 KIA, 95 WIA, 4 MIA)	259 (59 KIA, 107 WIA, 93 MIA)
Artillery Losses	0	3
Enemy Captured	300[15]	0

Forces Engaged

German Attachments

2/228th StuG Bn

Re-attached to the 168th Infantry Division on this day

442nd Infantry Rgt
IV/248th Artillery Rgt
V/248th Artillery Rgt
co/248th Engineer Bn

Still detached from the division

429th Infantry Rgt (- 1 Bn)

Soviet Forces

1/3rd 375th Rifle Division (including the 1241st Rifle Regiment)

263rd Mortar Rgt—detached on the 10th (not included)
1240th AT Rgt
1667th AT Rgt
16th Gds Mortar Rgt—detached on the 10th (not included)

2/3rds 81st Guards Rifle Division (excluding 235th Guards Rifle Regiment). No attachments (they are in other engagements)

15 The captures probably include some of the Soviet missing reported in the 19th Panzer Division engagement, as most of the 429th Infantry Regiment was still attached to them.

Attack Group South, 10 July 1943

DURATION One day FRONTAGE 12.7 kilometers TERRAIN Rolling, mixed
WEATHER Overcast and rainy, clearing in the afternoon. Temperature at noon: 19 degree Celsius. Road conditions good.

	Attacker	*Defender*
Units	19th PzD	1/3rd 81st GRD, 1/3rd 92nd GRD & 1/3rd 375th RD (all withdrawing)
Attachments	See below	See below
Strength	16,420	9,255
Armor	26 (5 light)	0
Artillery	96	97
Air Sorties	0	9
Casualties	37 (5 KIA, 30 WIA, 2 MIA)	893 (152 KIA, 413 WIA, 328 MIA)[16]
Armor Losses	3	0
Artillery Losses	0	9
Enemy Captured	N/A	0

Forces Engaged

German Attachments
70th Engineer Bn
2/411th Bridge Column B
842nd Bridge Column J

I/54th Werfer Rgt—detached on the 10th (not included)
II/54th Werfer Rgt—detached on the 10th (not included)
Hq/54th Werfer Rgt—detached on the 10th (not included)

I/61st Flak Rgt
5 Pz III Flames Tanks (from 6th PzD)

429th Infantry Rgt (168th ID), less I Battalion
442nd Infantry Rgt (168th ID)—detached on the 10th (not included)
co/248th Engineer Bn (168th ID)—detached on the 10th (not included)
IV/248th Artillery Rgt (168th ID)—detached on the 10th (not included)
V/248th Artillery Rgt (168th ID)—detached on the 10th (not included)

Detached
Panzer Group Westhoven—re-attached on the 10th (included)
lt Bn/19th Artillery Rgt—re-attached on the 10th (included)
ObsBty/19th Artillery Rgt—detached on the 10th (included)

Soviet Forces
1/3rd of 81st Guards Rifle Division including the 235th Guards Rifle Regiment
315th Gds Mortar Rgt
290th Mortar Rgt

1/3rd of 92nd Guards Rifle Division including the 276th Guards Rifle Regiment
114th Gds AT Rgt—detached on the 10th (included)

1/3rd of 375th Rifle Division including the 1245th Rifle Regiment
+ Attachments to the division (only half are counted)
  694th AT Rgt
  88th Flamethrower Company
  192nd Flamethrower Company
  1363/26th Antiaircraft Division
  60th Armored Train Detachment
  137th ATR Bn

Units not included
31st AT Bde—attached to the 81st GRD on the 6th, but included in engagement versus 7th PzD.

16 This figure is probably high for this engagement. Most of these losses come from the estimated 2,141 losses recorded for the whole of the 92nd Guards Rifle Division for this day. It clearly suffered heavily at this time, with the unit reporting a strength on the 9th of 8,430 (Fond: 1260; Opis 1; Delo 13; page: 108) and a 10 July figure of 5,249 (Fond: 906; Opis: 1; Delo: 211, page: 204). There is a report for the 10th stating the unit lost 303 killed and 2,077 wounded and another report for 10 July of 333 killed, 976 wounded and 1,906 missing.

Attack Group North, 10 July 1943

DURATION One day FRONTAGE 6.1 kilometers TERRAIN Rolling, mixed

WEATHER Rainy and overcast before noon, clearing in the afternoon. Temperature at noon: 19 degree Celsius. Road conditions good.

	Attacker	*Defender*
Units	6th PzD	92nd Guards Rifle Division & 305th Rifle Division
Attachments	See below	See below
Strength	18,596	14,314
Armor	50 (5 light)	41 (6 light)
Artillery	114	126
Air Sorties	81	8
Casualties	158 (26 KIA, 131 WIA, 1 MIA)	1,561 (248 KIA, 755 WIA, 558 MIA)
Armor Losses	3	13
Artillery Losses	0	17
Enemy Captured	N/A	1

Forces Engaged

German Attachments

II/71st Artillery Rgt—detached on the 10th (not included)

857th Heavy Artillery Bn—detached on the 10th (not included)

III/54th Werfer Rgt

II/43rd Flak Rgt

228th StuG Bn (- 2nd company)

1st co/503rd Heavy Panzer Bn

Panzer Group Westhoven (from 19th PzD)—detached on the 10th (not included)

lt Bn/19th Artillery Rgt (from 19th PzD)—detached on the 10th (not included)

Detached

5 Pz III Flame

ObsBty/76th Artillery Rgt—detached the 10th (included)

Soviet Forces

2/3rds of 92nd Guards Rifle Division including the 280th and 282nd Guards Rifle Regiments

114th Guards AT Regiment—detached the 10th (not included)

305th Rifle Division

1658th AT Regiment

96th Guards Tank Brigade

47th Guards Heavy Tank Regiment (from II Gds Tank Corps, its 3 Churchill's are included)

1500th AT Regiment (from II Gds Tank Corps with 19 45mm AT guns. Strengths not included)

The 7th Panzer Division Attempts to Push Eastward, 10 July 1943

DURATION One day FRONTAGE 9.0 kilometers TERRAIN Rolling, mixed
WEATHER Partly cloudy, occasional light rain. Temperature at noon: 19 degree Celsius. Road conditions good.

	Attacker	*Defender*
Units	7th PzD	94th Guards Rifle Division
Attachments	See below	See below
Strength	18,406	10,269
Armor	61 (4 light)	0
Artillery	119	82
Air Sorties	0	41 Night
Casualties	19 (3 KIA, 15 WIA, 1 MIA)	236 (40 KIA, 191 WIA, 5 MIA)[17]
Armor Losses	0	0
Artillery Losses	0	1
Enemy Captured	N/A	0

Forces Engaged

German Attachments
9th Bridge Column B
1/505th Bridge Column B
843rd Bridge Column J

99th Flak Rgt Staff
I/38th Flak Rgt
II/38th Flak Rgt
lt Bn/91st Flak Rgt

II/62nd Artillery Rgt—detached on the 10th (not included)
I/54th Werfer Rgt—attached on the 10th (not included)
II/54th Werfer Rgt—attached on the 10th (not included)
Hq/54th Werfer Rgt—attached on the 10th (not included)

204th Intelligence Troop
3rd co/503rd Heavy Panzer Bn

Detached
ObsBty/78th Artillery Rgt

Soviet Forces
94th Guards Rifle Division
148th Tank Regiment

1/3rd of 15th Guards Rifle Division (the 44th and 47th Guards Rifle Regiments are forward)
2nd Gds ATR Bn
4th Gds ATR Bn

31st Antitank Brigade

III Panzer Corps Assets
601st Engineer Rgt Staff
674th Engineer Rgt Staff
925th Bridge Construction Staff
127th Engineer Bn (-co)
531st Bridge Construction Bn
110th Bridge Column B
602nd Bridge Column B
co/538th Road Construction Bn

153rd Flak Rgt Staff

3rd Command of Artillery
612th Artillery Rgt Staff
II/62nd Artillery Rgt—attached on the 10th
II/71st Artillery Rgt—attached on the 10th
857th Heavy Artillery Rgt—attached on the 10th
Pn/13th Light Observations Battery
ObsBty/19th Artillery Rgt (19th PzD)—attached on the 10th
ObsBty/76th Artillery Rgt (6th PzD)—attached on the 10th

2nd Fuel Column Troop
545th Panzer Recovery Platoon
Hq/503rd Heavy Panzer Bn
2nd co/503rd Heavy Panzer Bn

17 The Soviet losses seem very high. The 94th Guards Rifle Division losses were derived from a periodic loss report for 7 through 10 July that was divided evenly over the four days in question. So these were definitely losses, but they were losses that may not have occurred on this day. On the previous days, Soviet losses seem low relative to the 7th Panzer Division.

The Soviet air activity was less than on previous days. The division enjoyed having the Luftwaffe attack targets in front of its positions with Stukas and other close support aircraft.

The 7th Panzer Division Attempts to Push Eastward

Having been relieved by the 198th Infantry Division, this division spent the day reorganizing and preparing to resume offensive operations. While the division was being replaced by the 198th Infantry Division, the Soviets maintained pressure on the division front during the night and going into the next day. After reorganizing, the division began an assault at 1600 to take the north part of the forest north of the forest path. After seizing these woods, the division was to attack the woods and commanding heights two kilometers north of Myasoyedovo with its tank assault groups. Then, together with the 6th Panzer Division, it was to open Myasoyedovo from the north.

The attack into the woods turned into hard fighting, "with many changes of fortune." During the attack, the panzer grenadiers were hit by a surprise attack out of the south by what the Germans estimated to be a regiment. The Germans claimed to have inflicted many casualties on the Soviets and the division ended up holding the north part of the woods. Still, they had not made the advances which had been expected, and the north part of Myasoyedovo remained in Soviet hands.

The 7th Panzer Division was primarily facing the 94th Guards Rifle Division, although elements of the 15th Guards Rifle Division may have been in the area too. The 31st Antitank Brigade was still holding its position in the corridor between the woods, 1.5 kilometers northeast of height 206.9, as it had since the 8th.

Air Support

The 7th Panzer Division reported that Soviet air was very active during the night. Only the 6th Panzer Division reported any German air activity during the day.

The 148th Tank Regiment, still in Shlyakhovoye reported that it was attacked at 1810 (Moscow time) by 51 German bombers, resulting in one killed and one wounded.

Advance to the Severnyii Donets, 11 July

Having now taken a day's rest after the effort to clean up the area in front of the Severnyii Donets, the III Panzer Corps was able to finally advance to this river line, some seven days after they started their attack.

Still, General Breith, the commander of this corps, continued to be contending with some of his division commanders and with his army commander, General Kempf. Another "official note" in the war diary written by his staff officer (1a, the equivalent of a U.S. G-3 staff) reports that at 0830 he gave an order on the phone, in the presence of Breith, for the commander of the 19th Panzer Division to attack Sabyinino when both flanking units advanced because the enemy was emplaced in well built positions at Kiselevo and the heights east of Sabyinino. "He noted [probably meaning General Schmidt *complained about*] the reduced capabilities of his division and mentioned the lack of support by army troops. General Breith said that the enemy is withdrawing northwards from the area of Belomestnaya to the wooded hill north Petropavlovka in order to escape its encirclement by elements of the III Panzer Corps and the 168th Infantry Division, which are already on the Donets in the Shopino-Visloye area. Every attempt will be made to hold the enemy south of Sabyinino in order to contain his strength. There the 19th Panzer Division must attack and penetrate the enemy positions and take Sabyinino and the Donets bridges without reference to the advance of the unit on the right which will attack later due to other conditions. Success is vital for the corps employment in the coming days. This attack must be made with the concentrated strength of the division and supporting artillery. The earlier use of weak recon attacks will not be used."

This last sentence is interesting, as it can be inferred that it is another criticism of General Schmidt's handling of the troops. On the other hand, he did not lose most of his tanks on the 9th, unlike when his panzer regiment was under command of the 6th Panzer Division.

The note continues with "Support of the corps artillery is assured. The 168th Infantry Division assumes coverage of the left flank and rear of the 19th Panzer Division and attacks east of the Donets on Khokhlovo." The note ends with the statement that "The commander of the 19th Panzer Division was briefed on the plan and ordered to begin the attack on Sabyinino." In light of the complaints about the 19th Panzer Division made by Breith to General Kempf on the 6th, there appears to have been continued friction, or at least a difference in attitude, between this division commander and Breith. Breith would give Gustav Schmidt a negative evaluation on the 22nd of July.

At 0835 the diary notes that Breith briefed the chief of staff (1a) of the 168th Infantry Division on the situation and stressed the importance of the division's attack east of the Donets north towards Khokhlovo and a further attack on Sabyinino in order to cover the flank and rear of the 19th Panzer Division.

Then Breith had another debate with his commanding officer, as the diary notes a telephone conversation at 0920 with General Kempf. The diary notes that "The commander of the army said he felt that it was necessary to hold up the corps. The panzer corps commanding general disagrees [Breith]. He believes that the coming day's battles [7th PzD: boot-shaped woods, 6th PzD: Shlyakhovo and Verkhnyii Olshanets, 19th PzD: Sabyinino] will be very difficult. The losses from these battles will permit the breakthrough of the positions and penetration of the rear areas. The situation on the left unit [167th Infantry Division]—SS Panzer Corps is good with the attack on Prokhorovka progressing well. They report that the enemy on the west flank of the corps is becoming extremely weak. Once the identified targets have been reached the corps will be permitted freedom to move north or northeast."[18]

18 T314, R197, page 1362. Note was signed with "1a" and an illegible signature and with some other handwritten notes beneath it.

So, this is the second clear disagreement with General Kempf, first over how the III Panzer Corps was handled on the 6th, and then over wanting to halt the attack on the 11th. It was Breith who was keeping this effort going.

The 168th Infantry Division Reunited

Now reunited with only part of one regiment still detached, the 168th Infantry Division was finally able to advance to the Donets. Elements of the 428th Infantry Regiment jumped off from the Shishino area toward the south edge of Khokhlovo. This attack penetrated into the town center after overcoming Soviet resistance on the south edge of town and a defensive system in the southeastern part of the town. One T-34 was claimed destroyed during the attack and 80 prisoners were captured. Contact was established with the 19th Panzer Division in Khokhlovo. Khokhlovo was defended by elements of the 89th Guards Rifle Division and was reported taken at 1300 (Moscow time). The regiment's advance continued through Kiselevo and into Sabyinino. The southeastern bank of the Severnyii Donets had been cleared.

The 417th Infantry Regiment reached Belomestnaya and heights 190.5 and 211.6. The regiment then took Petropavlovka in the afternoon, crossed the Donets at the tip of the Donets triangle and advanced from the south and west into the southwest part of the "underwear" woods north of the town after beating down stubborn Russian resistance at the edge of the woods.[19] They

19 This account was confirmed by an interview with Lothar Zeidler, a German veteran of the 168th Infantry Division, conducted by the author in 2002 at the National Archives, College Park, Maryland. He recalled that his unit crossed the river and marched up along the rail line to the west of the "underwear" woods unopposed.

Dr. Lothar E. Zeidler was born in February 1924 in Berlin. He was drafted into the German Army in 1943. He served with the 168th Infantry Division on the Eastern Front in 1943–1945, having been twice wounded in combat. He was attached to the division's reconnaissance battalion at the time of Kursk. In 1949 he moved to the United States as an exchange student, after surviving a plane crash that was part of the Berlin airlift. He retired as a professor at Rutgers University in New Jersey.

reported that the Luftwaffe supported the attack on the woods north of Petropavlovka with good results. This was significant progress by this division conducted relatively cheaply. It appears that the Soviets had partially withdrawn from this area.

Kiselevo

At 1830, on 10 July, an armored spearhead consisting of all the 19th Panzer Division's available tanks (around 22 tanks, not counting the Marders) and a panzer grenadier battalion moved out of Dalnyaya Igumenka to take Kiselevo and the bridge at Sabyinino. Both places were reported strongly held by the Soviets. The 92nd Guards Rifle Division was deployed from Kiselevo to height 211.5 to the MTS to west of Shlyakhovoye. Also at Kiselevo was the 96th Tank Brigade. On the 10th, this brigade was still reporting 27 tanks, having lost almost half of its tanks since it first faced the III Panzer Corps on the 8th. To its left was the 305th Rifle Division, deployed from Sabyinino to outside the MTS west of Shlyakhovoye to the Razumnoye railway siding to Mazikino-Ushakovka.

At dawn on the 11th a proper attack on the Soviet positions around Kiselevo was organized with the 19th Panzer Division advancing on it from three sides. At 0930, the division moved out of its assembly area in Dalnyaya Igumenka and advanced to the northwest, with three attack groups, the 73rd Panzer Grenadier Regiment to the south, the 74th Panzer Grenadier Regiment to the east, and the reconnaissance battalion trying to hook around towards the north. The three attack groups received flank fire from the northeast and the heights to the west. The Soviet batteries could not be silenced by either Stuka attacks or German artillery fire.

The 74th Panzer Grenadier Regiment advanced northwest along the ridgeline to the east of Kiselevo where it breached a deep minefield at 1630 and broke into the strongly held Soviet positions east of the town. Mopping up in the area continued into the evening. The Sixty-ninth Army reported that Kiselevo was lost at 1450 (Moscow time).

The 73rd Panzer Grenadier Regiment, supported by the remnants of the 27th Panzer Regiment, attacked to the north, broke into the north part of Khokhlovo, destroyed the Soviets in the south edge of Kiselevo, pushed through that town, and after resupplying the tanks with ammunition, stood ready to attack Sabyinino at the end of the day. The 19th Reconnaissance Battalion, which was on the north edge of Kiselevo, pulled back and joined the advancing 73rd Panzer Grenadier Regiment. The engineers were also kept busy, for during the day, some 800 mines were cleared from both sides of the Khokhlovo-Kiselevo road.

Defending on the western outskirts of Khokhlovo was the 47th Guards Heavy Tank Regiment, now with six operational Churchills and a battery from the 1500th Antitank Regiment. It reported that it fought German armor, with Kiselevo coming under attack at 1130 (Moscow time). At 1200 (Moscow time) it reported that Soviet troops were withdrawing over the Severnyii Donets in the Khokhlovo-Kiselevo area and blowing up the crossing. At 1200 (Moscow time) the tank regiment was ordered to move to Sabyinino to link up with the 96th Tank Brigade. The regiment still had three tanks, a battery from the antitank regiment and an armored car surrounded in the Khokhlovo area. At 1230 (Moscow time), communications with the tanks was interrupted. After this, the regiment commander decided to launch a counterattack on Kiselevo with his two mobile Churchills. This resulted in the regiment taking more losses and they were forced to fall back. The three tanks and the armored car in Khokhlovo were lost but the tank crews and part of the artillery battery broke out of the encirclement. The 47th Guards Heavy Tank Regiment, down to two Churchills, rejoined the II Guards Tank Corps at Leski, becoming its reserve. Kiselevo had fallen in the afternoon, although some mop-up was required.

While the 89th Guards Rifle Division was clearly in Kiselevo the previous day, much of the division was pushed back on this day. It reported that its 267th Guards Rifle Regiment was located from Chursino to the fish hatchery, while its 270th Guards Rifle Regiment was on the line of the western bank of the Severnyii Donets to the fish hatchery to Sheponovo. It had lost communications with its 273rd Guards Rifle Regiment, which had been defending the southern and eastern outskirts of Kiselevo. The 93rd Guards Rifle Division was to the division's right and the 81st Guards Rifle Division was to its left. The 89th Guards Rifle Division complained that the 81st had left its position and opened up the division's left flank! The 375th Rifle Division had been pulled well back, with its 1241st Rifle Regiment in Zhilomostnoye, its 1243rd Rifle Regiment in Maloye Yablonovo, and its 1245th Rifle Regiment to Shakhovo. In effect, these divisions were now making up the second echelon, with the 94th Guards and 305th Rifle Divisions making up the first. The 96th Tank Brigade, which was deployed from Kiselevo to Sabyinino, found itself being cut off from the units it was supposed to be supporting with the German advance to Kazachye and Rzhavets, so it pulled back to Aleksandrovka, having lost another 15 tanks (about half of what it had operational). This was an unusual withdrawal, for the unit could have pulled back into the Donets triangle, but instead found itself to the east of the German III Panzer Corps.

Olkhovatka

Because of the heavy tank losses, the armor in Battle Group Oppeln (6th Panzer Division) was reorganized. A Tiger company under Captain von Kageneck was attached to the battle group, and the II Battalion of the 11th Panzer Regiment was reorganized into two tank companies under 1st Lieutenants Spiekermann and Reutemann.

After a delay caused by the inclement weather, at 0300 the division's attack on Olkhovatka began. It was spearheaded by the Tiger company, which had been reinforced to a strength of 19 tanks; then came two armored companies from the 11th Panzer Regiment. After crossing the Dalnyaya Igumenka–Shlyakhovoye road, the battle group came under heavy tank fire from heights 220 and 230.3. The battle group's advance was also slowed by the presence of a thick minefield. Upon reaching height 230.3, which was held by the 1004th Rifle Regiment of the 305th Rifle Division, one panzer company swung to the east and circled around the wooded strip north of Olkhovatka. The area was secured through the "energetic action" of 1st Lieutenant Spiekermann. The Sixty-ninth Army reported a breakthrough of the 1004th Rifle Regiment at 1800 (Moscow time), with 60 German tanks advancing on Olkhovatka.

The 148th Tank Regiment, which had been defending Shlyakhovoye since the afternoon of the 8th, reported that the Germans had reached the western and eastern outskirts of the town, creating a half-ring around the regiment, and that some of the 305th Rifle Division's units were falling back to Kazachye. The regiment pulled out of Shlyakhovoye on this day, but not before it had lost most its tanks.[20]

The Tiger company and the other panzer company continued pressing straight toward Olkhovatka. The Soviets sought to stop their advance with heavy artillery and gun fire, but this did not substantially slow the advance. In Olkhovatka itself there was no appreciable resistance. After the seizure of Olkhovatka, Battle Group Oppeln continued to press the attack, taking height 224.4 and continuing towards Znamenka. In Znamenka there was only light resistance, and that town too was secured.

By 2000, the tanks from the 6th Panzer Division had reached the antitank ditch east of Verkhnyii Olshanets, took the lightly held village, and arrived at Kazachye at about 2200. It too was easily taken against light opposition. Colonel Oppeln then decided to send a group forward under the battalion commander, Major Baeke to seize a bridgehead during the night.[21]

The 107th Rifle Division had shifted to the north and was now deployed from Novo-Oskochnoye to Shuk-

20 For the 11th, the regiment reports 9 men killed, 9 wounded, 20 missing and 14 T-34s and 3 T-70s burned. Based upon previous reports this would leave the regiment with about 5 T-34s and 5 T-70s. Yet the following day they report 3 T-34s (all tanks are in repair) and 1 T-70 remaining (Fond: 148th IndTRgt, Opis: 661360, Delo: 3, pages: 80–82). The Seventh Guards Army reports for the 9th 19 combat-ready T-34s and 8 T-70s, with 1 T-34 under repair (Fond: 341, Opis: 5312, Delo: 104, pages: 32–82). Therefore, they either lost an additional 10 tanks on or before the 11th. We record them as lost for the 11th.

21 Jentz, page 90.

hovtsevo to Gremyache to the garden east of Inovka (Ionovka?). This would have placed part of the division in the fight today with the 6th Panzer Division as it advanced on Kazachye. Otherwise, it appears to have been unengaged. Also at Novo-Oskochnoye was the 1002nd Rifle Regiment of the 305th Rifle Division. The XXXV Guards Rifle Corps was clearly layering the defense to the northeast of the German armored spearhead.

This attack to the north, while further expanding the penetration, still had not brought the 6th Panzer Division to a position to cross the Severnyii Donets.

The 7th Panzer Division Continues to Expand the Flank

The 7th Panzer Division spent the morning of the 11th reorganizing and resupplying. The division renewed its attack at 1415 with heavy artillery support. The panzer regiment attacked the woods three kilometers north of Myasoyedovo. The attack reached the southeast corner of the woods. At this point, the tanks received heavy flanking fire from dug-in tanks and antitank guns from height 213.7. Heavy artillery barrages forced the Soviet tanks to withdraw from those positions. The tank battle continued into the evening.

At 1445, the two panzer grenadier regiments pushed north and reached height 210.3 and the north point of the boot-shaped woods. The Soviets began large withdrawal movements towards Sheino and the Razumnaya valley. The assault by the two regiments had penetrated halfway into the woods and continued into the evening. The Sixty-ninth Army was reporting that the German attack at 1800 (Moscow time) contained 46 tanks.

By nightfall, the division was stretched from height 210.3 (three kilometers south of Sheino) to the north point of the woods (three kilometers northeast of Myasoyedovo).

Opposing them was the 94th Guards Rifle Division, with the 148th Tank Regiment attached, which was still in its previous position. It was now claiming at 1400 (Moscow time) to have beaten back its eighth attack (for the day?).

It is a little confusing why the 7th Panzer Division was continuing to push to the east and northeast, but this maneuver was certainly holding the Sixty-ninth Army's attention.

Air Support

The 19th Panzer Division reported that during the night and early morning the Soviet air was very active. The 94th Guards Rifle Division reported coming under heavy air and artillery attack.

Commentary

The III Panzer Corps operations at this point were clearly falling far short of their goal. They were not providing flank support except to the extent that they were drawing infantry, artillery, and air to face them, as opposed to the Fourth Panzer Army.

As of the end of the 11th, only the 19th Panzer Division and the 168th Infantry Division were at the Severnyii or Lipovyii Donets and in a position to attack the Donets triangle. The 6th Panzer Division was still pushing north through resistance, trying to get to the river, while the 7th Panzer Division remained on the flank.

This corps, which was the weakest panzer corps at the start, had also suffered the highest losses of the three panzer corps. The XLVIII Panzer Corps, which started with 599 tanks, was down to 283 (47 percent). The SS Panzer Corps, which started with 504 tanks, was down to 341 (68 percent). The III Panzer Corps, which started with only 394 tanks, was now down to 154 (39 percent). Furthermore, the overall strength of its four divisions was down 8.6 percent, and the combat strength in many of its infantry units, where most of the casualties occurred, was perilously low.[22]

22 The 168th Infantry Division was down 10.0%, the 6th Panzer Division was down 3.9%, the 7th Panzer Division was down 8.5% and the 19th Panzer Division was down 12.8% from their starting strengths.

The 168th Infantry Division Reunited, 11 July 1943

DURATION One day FRONTAGE 8.6 kilometers TERRAIN Rolling, mixed

WEATHER Cloudy, warm, thunderstorms in the morning. Temperature at noon: 22 degree Celsius. Roads dried out and passable.

	Attacker	*Defender*
Units	168th ID	elements of the 89th Guards Rifle Division (273rd Gds Rifle Rgt)
Attachments	See below	None
Strength	12,302	2, 429
Armor	6	0 (Germans claim one tank destroyed)
Artillery	89	19
Air Sorties	70 ?	0
Casualties	115 (18 KIA, 94 WIA, 3 MIA)	94 (5 KIA, 54 WIA, 35 MIA)
Enemy Captured	80	0

Forces Engaged

German Attachments

2/228th StuG Bn

Still detached from the division:

429th Infantry Rgt (- 1 Bn)

Kiselevo, 11 July 1943

DURATION One day FRONTAGE 14.8 kilometers TERRAIN Rolling, mixed
WEATHER Cloudy, rainy. Temperature at noon: 22 degrees Celsius. Road conditions good.

	Attacker	*Defender*
Units	19th PzD	elements of the 92nd Guards Rifle Division
Attachments	See below	96th Tank Bde 47th Gds Heavy Tank Rgt (II Gds Tank Corps) Bty/1500 AT Rgt (II Gds Tank Corps)
Strength	16,039	2,883
Armor	28 (5 light)	33 (7 light)
Artillery	96	18
Air Sorties	11	22 Night
Casualties	34 (4 KIA, 29 WIA, 1 MIA)	91 (24 KIA, 54 WIA, 13 MIA)
Armor Losses	13	19
Artillery Losses	0	5
Enemy Captured	N/A	0

Forces Engaged

German Attachments
70th Engineer Bn
2/411th Bridge Column B
842nd Bridge Column J

I/61st Flak Rgt
429th Infantry Rgt (168th ID), (less I Battalion)

Detached
ObsBty/19th Artillery Rgt

Olkhovatka, 11 July 1943

DURATION One day FRONTAGE 9.0 kilometers TERRAIN Rolling, mixed
WEATHER Warm, scattered light showers. Road conditions good.

	Attacker	*Defender*
Units	6th PzD	elements of 92nd GRD & 305th RD
Attachments	See below	See below
Strength	18,692	12,128
Armor	59 (4 light)	27 (8 light)
Artillery	114	105
Air Sorties	6	0
Casualties	107 (17 KIA, 89 WIA, 1 MIA)	663 (110 KIA, 479 WIA, 74 MIA)
Armor Losses	0	27
Artillery Losses	0	10
Enemy Captured	N/A	1

Forces Engaged

German Attachments
III/54th Werfer Rgt

II/43rd Flak Rgt

228th StuG Bn (less 2nd company)
1st co/503rd Heavy Panzer Bn
2nd co/503rd Heavy Panzer Bn—attached on the 11th
Hq/503rd Heavy Panzer Bn—attached on the 11th

Detached
ObsBty/76th Artillery Rgt

Soviet Forces
2/3rds of 92nd Guards Rifle Division
305th Rifle Division
1658th AT Regiment
148th Tank Regiment
107th Rifle Division (losses only)
123rd ATR Bn (losses only)
130th ATR Bn (losses only)

The 7th Panzer Division Continues to Expand the Flank, 11 July 1943

DURATION One day FRONTAGE 5.5 kilometers TERRAIN Rolling, mixed

WEATHER Cloudy, windy and cool. Temperature at noon: 22 degree Celsius. Road conditions good.

	Attacker	*Defender*
Units	7th PzD	94th Guards Rifle Division
Attachments	See below	31st AT Bde
Strength	20,353	9,585
Armor	70 (4 light)	0
Artillery	164	82
Air Sorties	8	22 Night
Casualties	21 (3 KIA, 18 WIA)	354 (116 KIA, 150 WIA, 88 MIA)
Armor Losses	23	0
Artillery Losses	2	21
Enemy Captured	N/A	0

Forces Engaged

German Attachments

9th Bridge Column B
1/505th Bridge Column B
843rd Bridge Column J

99th Flak Rgt Staff
I/38th Flak Rgt
II/38th Flak Rgt
lt Bn/91st Flak Rgt

II/62nd Artillery Rgt—attached on the 11th
I/54th Werfer Rgt
II/54th Werfer Rgt
Hq/54th Werfer Rgt

204th Intelligence Troop
3rd co/503rd Heavy Panzer Bn

Detached

ObsBty/78th Artillery Rgt

III Panzer Corps Assets

601st Engineer Rgt Staff
674th Engineer Rgt Staff
925th Bridge Construction Staff
127th Engineer Bn (-co)
531st Bridge Construction Bn
110th Bridge Column B
602nd Bridge Column B
co/538th Road Construction Bn
153rd Flak Rgt Staff

3rd Command of Artillery
612th Artillery Rgt Staff
II/62nd Artillery Rgt—detached to the troops on the 11th
II/71st Artillery Rgt
857th Heavy Artillery Rgt
Hq/52nd Werfer Rgt—attached to corps on the 11th
I/52nd Werfer Rgt—attached to corps on the 11th
II/52nd Werfer Rgt—attached to corps on the 11th
III/52nd Werfer Rgt—attached to corps on the 11th
Pn/13th Light Observations Battery
ObsBty/19th Artillery Rgt (19th PzD)
ObsBty/76th Artillery Rgt (6th PzD)

2nd Fuel Column Troop
545th Panzer Recovery Platoon
Hq/503rd Heavy Panzer Bn—detached to the troops on the 11th
2nd co/503rd Heavy Panzer Bn—detached to the troops on the 11th

CHAPTER SEVEN

The Situation as of 11 July 1943

By the summer of 1943, before the Battle of Kursk, the Soviet armed forces were superior to the German Fascist forces both quantitatively and qualitatively.

MARSHAL GEORGII K. ZHUKOV
1967[1]

The German Plans for the 12th

The German advance was indeed slowly losing steam. The XLVIII Panzer Corps had spent the last three days pushing two of its armored divisions to the west and the southwest, leaving only the 11th Panzer Division pushing north. On the morning of the 11th the 11th Panzer Division's attack had stalled, although it did have some success in the afternoon.

In the case of the SS Panzer Corps, it still was maintaining two armored divisions moving forward, with only one relegated to the flank, but again its advance was slowing. In the case of Adolf Hitler SS Division, its attack had also stalled. Therefore, of the six attacking armored divisions, only three were attacking north, and two of them had effectively stalled.

In the case of the III Panzer Corps they still had two panzer divisions moving forward, with one relegated to the flank, but the tank strength of these units was perilously low. This attack had been severely weakened and had yet to provide the flank support required for the Fourth Panzer Army. It was not on the verge of breaking through to anyplace that mattered.

The German advance had made its best success in the first three days of the offensive and had slowly declined since then. Just for a comparison, see Table 7.1, based upon distance opposed advance (regardless of direction), which shows that effect.

In the face of these problems, on the morning of 11 July Manstein, Hoth and Kempf met at Kempf's headquarters in Dolbino (15 kilometers southwest of Belgorod) to discuss operations. According to notes on the conference, Kempf pointed out that the 7th Panzer Division would take Sheino this day and with the three panzer divisions they would be able to penetrate (on the 12th?) what they perceived to be the last Soviet defensive position east of Sabyinino. The III Panzer Corps would then be available to advance to the north and link-up with the Fourth Panzer Army. Kempf stated that Breith (III Panzer Corps) was certain the attack would proceed.

Manstein pointed out that the task for Provisional Army Kempf remained to protect the right flank of the Fourth Panzer Army. This meant that the panzer corps must advance into the area southeast of Prokhorovka. Manstein's question at this juncture was whether the III Panzer Corps was able to advance to the north on its own or whether a simultaneous attack to the south from

1 Georgi K. Zhukov, *Marshal Zhukov's Greatest Battles* (Harper and Row, New York, 1969), page 219.

TABLE 7.1
DISTANCE OPPOSED ADVANCE (IN KILOMETERS)

	3rd PzD	*GD PzGrD*	*11th PzD*	*LSSAH PzGrD*	*DR SS PzGrD*	*T SS PzGrD*	*6th PzD*	*19th PzD*	*7th PzD*	*Average*
5th	3.8	6.3	3.6	10.7	6.8	6.7	2.7	3.7	2.3	5.2
6th	3.5	7.2	12.0	6.8	13.6	4.9	6.5	5.9	9.0	7.7
7th	13.2	9.0	7.7	7.6	6.0	4.9	4.9	8.1	11.4	8.1
8th	15.0	5.4	6.8	5.6	0	0	9.0	5.5	0	5.3
9th	2.4	2.7	10.6	5.1	0	0	0	0	0	2.3
10th	5.1	8.1	1.4	0	0	0	2.6	0	0	1.9
11th	10.8	6.8	0	4.1	3.3	6.9	11.1	0	4.2	5.2
Total	53.8	45.5	42.1	39.9	29.7	23.4	36.8	23.2	26.9	35.7

the Fourth Panzer Army would be necessary. Kempf said this would only be known once the high ground east of Sabyinino was occupied, which would be this evening at the earliest.

After Hoth gave a status report which included the stated desire to free up the Gross Deutschland Division and move it to crossing the Psel at Peresyip on the 13th, Manstein pointed out that a drive to the south by the Fourth Panzer Army must be led by more than just one division and must be done immediately. A continuation of the drive to the northeast might still be possible at the moment, and might not be possible later, since the Soviets could deploy new armored forces there. If the attack by the III Panzer Corps did not penetrate, then Manstein decided that it would be switched over to the defensive and be available for use either on the right wing, or north of Oboyan and the area to the west. He also pointed out that the arrival of the XXIV Panzer Corps was anticipated on 17 July and it would presumably be deployed in the west, if the III Panzer Corps were not used there.

Hoth still preferred to keep the SS Panzer Corps moving northeast and recommended using the XXIV Panzer Corps for the drive to the south, but Manstein pointed out that the corps would arrive too late and suggested instead that Hoth could use the 167th Infantry Division to support the III Panzer Corps, at least by mopping-up as far as the Sazhnovskii Donets.[2]

Writer #856 provides a different account of this conference. He states that General Kempf advised the discontinuation of the attack due to dwindling combat strength, the mounting threat to the eastern flank, and the absence of any reserves. Manstein postponed a decision on this until he could visit Breith. As a result of Breith's optimistic estimate of the situation, possibly brought about due to the tactical successes of his units on the previous days, the III Panzer Corps was ordered to continue its attack.[3] Breith also noted in his post-war account that Manstein had come to the corps' command post (seven kilometers east of Belgorod, although it moved on the 11th) on the 11th and had "reluctantly agreed to continue the attack; the German overall situ-

2 T313, R366, provided courtesy of Frederick L. Clemens. George M. Nipe on page 33 of his book provides a very different account of this conference that contradicts this report. No footnotes are provided and no documentation supporting Mr. Nipe's account has been located by this author.

3 Writer #856, pages 47 & 48.

ation had become critical and troops had to be made available to other sectors of the front."[4]

In General Busse's postwar account, in which the Breith and writer #856 accounts are chapters, Busse also adds that Hoth had proposed a continuation of the attack with the limited objective of the destruction of the Soviet forces located south of the Psel River in a coordinated offensive by both armies. Busse states that this was an opinion shared by Manstein and that Manstein's decision to continue the attack after his meeting with Breith was for that purpose.[5] It is hard to evaluate this statement in light of the contradictory conference notes and the fact that the operations and orders for the next day continued to try to push German units across the Psel.

THESE EXCHANGES ARE interesting for several reasons. First, they show that the open right flank of the Fourth Panzer Army had indeed become a major point of discussion. Second, they foreshadow *Operation Roland*, with Manstein's interest in moving more forces to the west side of the advance. Furthermore, the account provides a projected date and location for the use of the reinforcing XXIV Panzer Corps. At this time, the two divisions of the XXIV Panzer Corps were moving up to Kharkov and would be assembled there the following day. Fourth, there is an indication that Manstein was expecting more Soviet armored forces to arrive to cap the SS Panzer Corps' drive to the northeast. Last, it leaves one wondering whether Manstein had indeed given up on breaking through to Kursk and was instead concentrating on conducting operations on the flanks of the main push. It is clear, though, that the decision to continue operations the way they were currently developing was driven by Breith's assessment.

THIS ATTACK WAS slowly losing steam. Much of this was due to the redirection of forces to the flank, which was not going to be immediately corrected. For the following day, the Germans were again trying to focus on moving forward, but these were going to be developing and deliberate attacks, as opposed to any type of sudden breakthrough.

In the case of the XLVIII Panzer Corps, it was going to bring up the Gross Deutschland Division beside the 11th Panzer Division and then have both attack towards Oboyan. Still, it was not expected that the Gross Deutschland Division would be in position until the afternoon of the 12th, so in any case, a major breakthrough was not going to happen there that day.

In the case of the SS Panzer Corps, it had decided to attack height 252.4 first, before the Adolf Hitler SS Division advanced on Prokhorovka. This meant that Totenkopf would first attack six kilometers to the northeast and then turn, re-cross the Psel, and attack three kilometers to the southeast. This was a nine kilometer opposed advance for the 12th. In the course of the last seven days, among the nine armored divisions, in only 12 out of 63 cases did a German armored division make an opposed advance that far in a single day. Most of these cases were after a day of combat where they could exploit the progress from the previous day. In the face of definite opposition, it was probably not possible to complete this advance in a single day. As such, this height could not be expected to fall before the afternoon of the 12th, and probably not until the following day.

4 Breith, page 8.

5 Busse, T-6, pages 22 and 23. Busse also states on pages 23 & 24 that "In the evening of 11 July the Commanding General of Army Group South was informed on the development of the situation in the sector of Army Group Center.... Nevertheless, the decision to go through with the limited-objective attack was adhered to. This was the only way we could hope to hit the enemy forces which had already established contact with our forces and with which, according to all intelligence, we were going to have to contend in the following days. It was hoped that the German units might in this manner gain the freedom of action necessary to withdraw the German lines to the original jump-off position—a move that was certainly going to become necessary later on. For this reason nothing was changed in the order which had just been issued."

This author is troubled by this statement in light of the planned attacks across the Psel on the 12th and 13th by Totenkopf, Gross Deutschland and others.

As the Adolf Hitler SS Division was intending to attack Prokhorovka after a thorough Stuka preparation, and only after height 252.4 had been captured by the Totenkopf SS Division, its advance was definitely halted for the first half of the 12th. In all reality, under any conditions it was not going to break through to Prokhorovka until late on the 12th, and as Prokhorovka was a fairly large village, it would not get clear of the village until the following day. This meant that SS Panzer Corps was going to make, at best, about eight kilometers advance over the next two days. This does not account for the three fresh Soviet armored corps that were being assembled in and around Prokhorovka, which the Germans were not fully aware of.

In the case of the III Panzer Corps, it was finally, if not somewhat belatedly, ordered that evening to concentrate on pushing to the northwest, crossing the Donets and supporting the SS Panzer Corps' envelopment of the Sixty-ninth Army.[6] While this corps was supposed to provide flank support for the Fourth Panzer Army, it had not yet massed the forces necessary to clear the Donets triangle, let alone to actually break through to somewhere that mattered. The high casualties in this corps also limited its potential in future operations.

The Fourth Panzer Army was not likely to break through Soviet positions over the next two days. At best, it was looking at continuing to push them back further, with the consequent attrition on both sides. Still, one gets the impression that many of the Germans thought they were on the verge of breaking through to Oboyan, Prokhorovka, and onward to Kursk. This idea was first expressed on the 7th by the XLVIII Panzer Corps and was probably the underlying reason for the frustration behind the Adolf Hitler SS Division's complaint about not being able to take Prokhorovka on the 11th. Events on the following day would disabuse them of the idea that they were on the verge of a breakthrough.[7]

6 Breith, page 9.

7 Still, some authors accept the Adolf Hitler SS Division's complaint at face value and assume that the Germans could have somehow managed to break through at Prokhorovka on the 11th.

Summary to Date

As night fell on the 11th, the German advance was in trouble. On the far left, the LII Infantry Corps was stretched to the limit. The 57th Infantry Division, a unit with only nine combat battalions,[8] was covering some 40.9 kilometers of front. The other two divisions of the corps were also stretched thin, and the leading 332nd Infantry Division was still unable to get up to height 258.5 so as to cover the left flank of the XLVIII Panzer Corps.

The XLVIII Panzer Corps had managed to divert two of its three divisions off the main line of attack and now needed to get moving forward again. Yet the 3rd Panzer Division was almost certainly going to be relegated to protecting the left flank of the XLVIII Panzer Corps north of height 258.5 in the face of some pretty significant Soviet armored forces. This effectively left the Gross Deutschland and 11th Panzer Division for the forward thrust, and the 11th Panzer Division had just been stopped cold on this day's attacks. The Gross Deutschland was certainly not going to be able to reposition itself until the afternoon of the 12th, and the 11th Panzer Division could no longer continue to successfully attack alone. As the forces they were facing were considerable, in all reality, the XLVIII Panzer Corps attack was stalled, or at best was only going to make forward progress at a reduced rate and with considerable casualties.

On the far right, Corps Raus was solidly emplaced along a line that it could hold without major problems, but it was in a static supporting position with little it could do to add to the offensive. The III Panzer Corps had paid heavily for its advances to date, and was close to exhausted, with only 39 percent of its tanks operational. Furthermore, it was now facing a significant set of terrain features across the Severnyii Donets that was defended by considerable Soviet troops. Its attack had also lost steam, and was again about to stall out due to lack of force.

8 Six infantry battalions, a reconnaissance battalion, an engineer battalion and an attached bicycle security battalion.

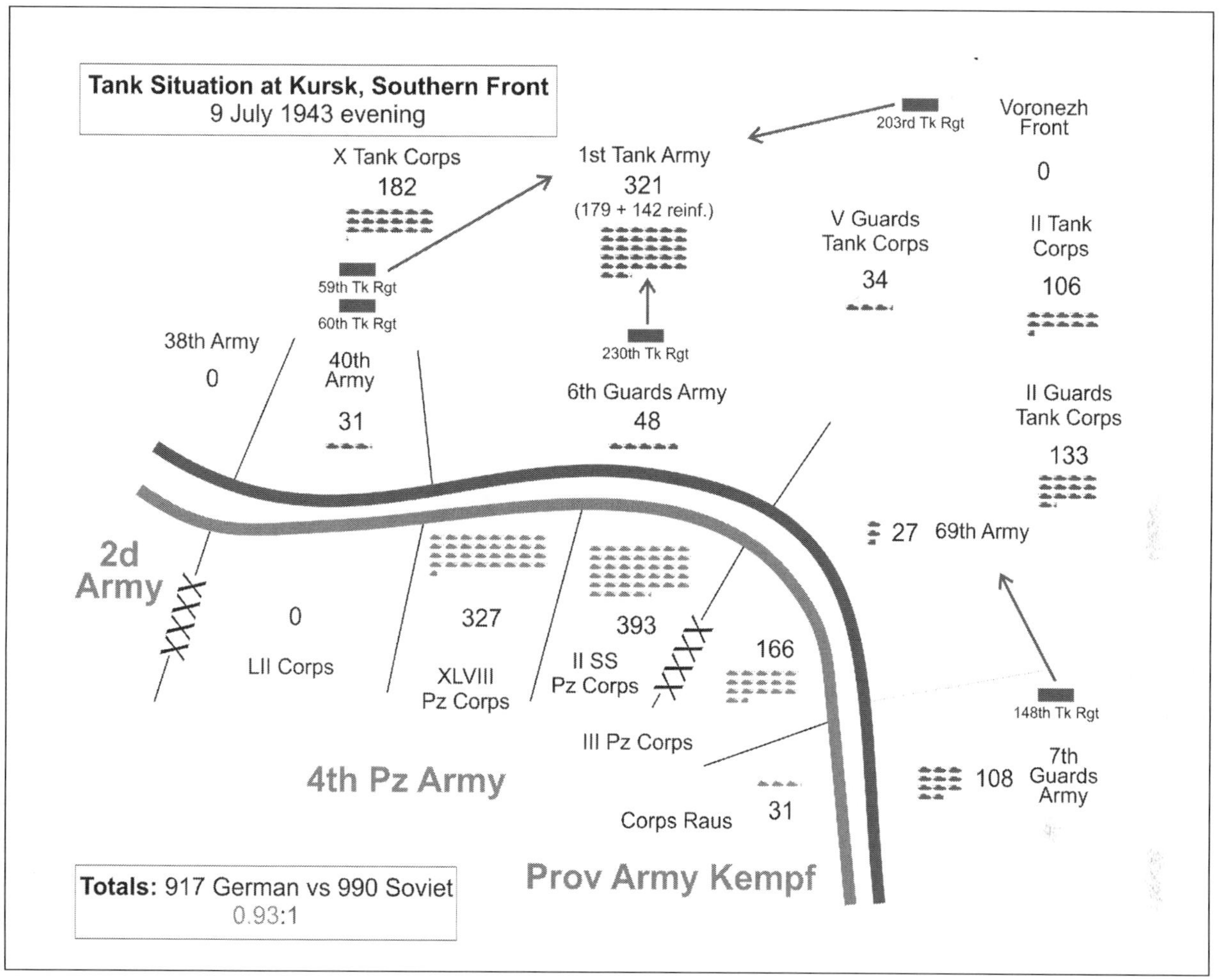

Only in the center was the issue still very much in question, for the SS Panzer Corps appears to have pushed back the Soviet forces enough that if it could push beyond its bridgehead over the Psel and through the town of Prokhorovka, it could still achieve a breakthrough that might also free up the other two corps. Still, there were some problems with the SS Panzer Corps. First, the open terrain it was fighting over was ending. The Germans were looking at having to force themselves across the rough ground around the Psel River and northeast through Prokhorovka, where the attack frontage narrowed down to around six kilometers. Furthermore, their right flank was very extended, with the 167th Infantry Division stretched across some 20 kilometers while the Das Reich SS Division was covering another ten kilometers of flank. In many respects, the panzer group's advance had also been reduced to two divisions pushing forward. Furthermore, the Adolf Hitler SS Division's attack had stalled, and this division was now waiting for the Totenkopf SS Division

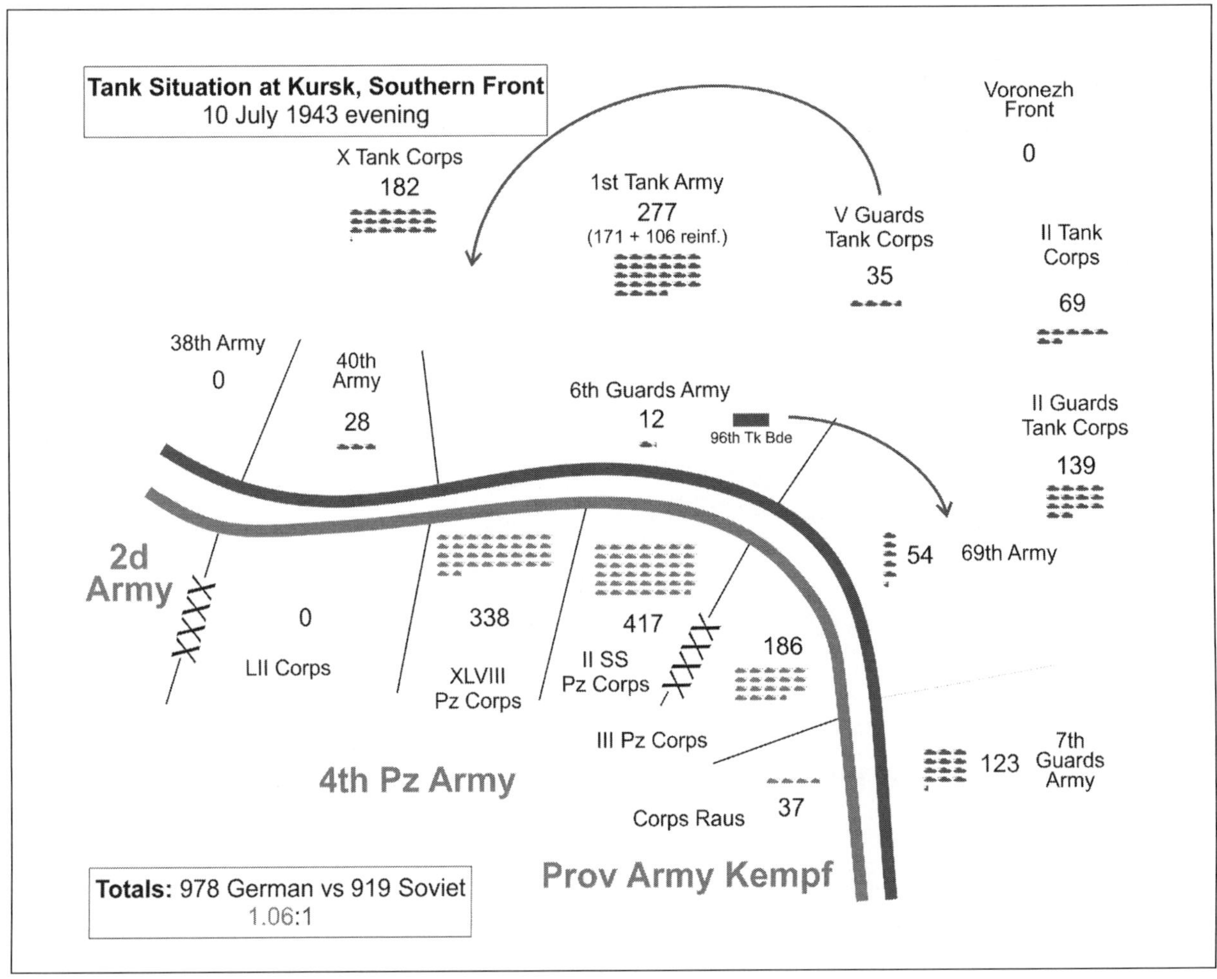

to bring pressure on the flank of the Soviet position at Prokhorovka before it could move forward.

Finally, two more Soviet armies were arriving, fresh and ready to fight, the Fifth Guards Army and the Fifth Guards Tank Army. They were both heading into the Psel River and Prokhorovka area to cap off the SS Panzer Corps push. In all reality, the Battle of Kursk was over, and the German advance had been stopped. The additional forces the Soviets were bringing onto the field were sufficient, such that over the next couple of days, the German advance would slowly grind to an anti-climatic halt. Instead, what happened was the climatic Battle of Prokhorovka, one of the largest tank battles in history.

Just for comparison, when this offensive started, the Germans could count on 1,707 tanks while the opposing Soviet forces in the area had only 1,537 tanks, a 1.1-to-1 ratio. Some seven days later, the Germans were down to 978 tanks, while the Soviets had 804 tanks, a 1.2-to-1 ratio. This included the reinforcing II and X

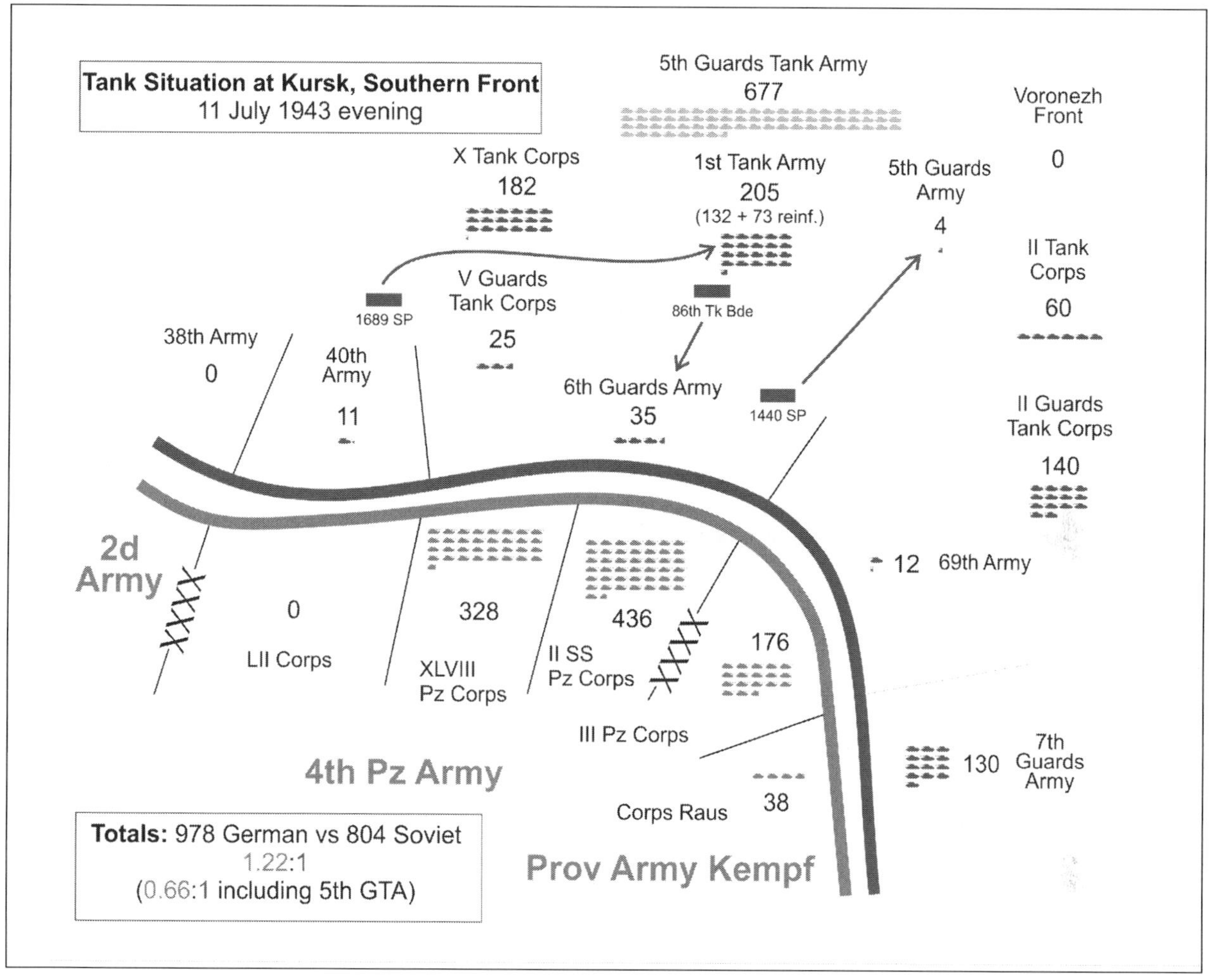

Tanks Corps and the 180th and 192nd Tank Brigades. Their strength on 4 July was 448 tanks. The Germans were down 731 tanks by the 11th, while the Soviets were down 1,181 tanks. This was a 1.62-to-1 attrition rate in favor of the Germans.

The above forces did not include the three corps and 1549th Heavy Self-Propelled Artillery Regiment that was moving into position with the Fifth Guards Tank Army. This meant another 677 tanks were about to arrive on the battlefield.

At this point the Germans had lost a total of 23,903 casualties (3,773 killed, 19,273 wounded, and 857 missing). The forces opposing them had lost 66,233 casualties (14,191 killed, 32,446 wounded, and 19,596 missing). This was a 2.77-to-1 casualty exchange ratio in favor of the Germans.

The Soviet forces were doing better in the armor exchange than they did in the personnel exchange. They lost some 1,519 tanks destroyed, damaged or broken down compared to the German losses of 1,124

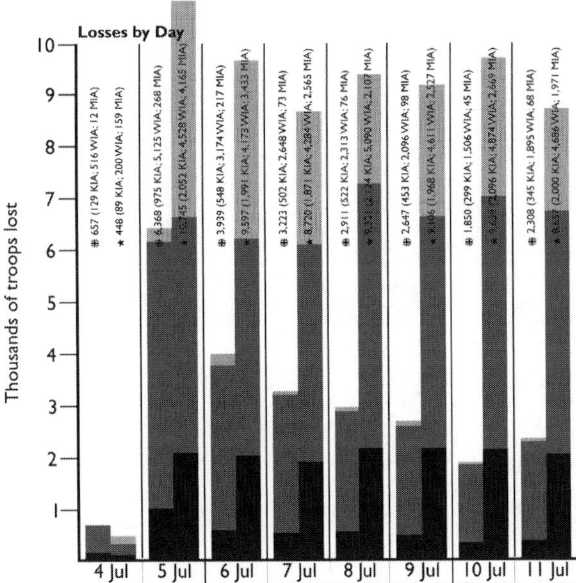

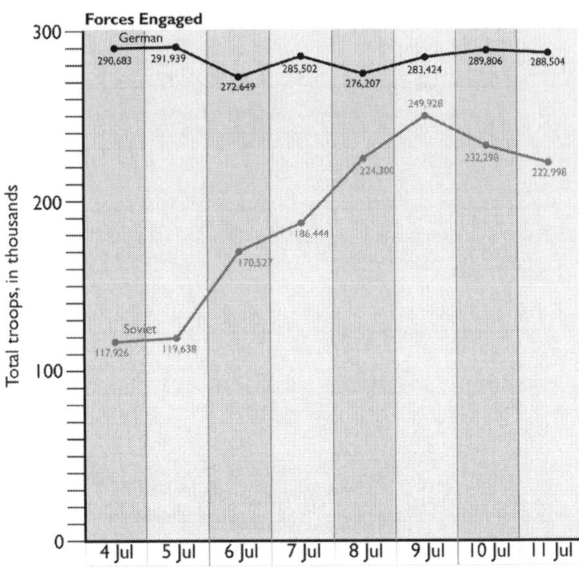

tanks.[9] This was a 1.35-to-1 exchange. Still, the German tank strength was considerable, as they were doing a better job of repairing their tanks and returning them back to battle. As such, the German Army maintained considerable offensive capability, still having 53 percent of its tanks operational since the start of the offensive. But the last four days had not been kind to the Soviet tank force. The forces fielded by the Voronezh Front had lost 889 tanks during those four days while the opposing Germans had lost 426. This fight in more open terrain was a 2.09-to-1 exchange ratio favoring the Germans. Still it would require the reinforcing Fifth Guards Tank Army to turn the balance back to the Soviets. With the reinforcements, the Soviets would be able to outnumber the Germans 1.4 to 1 in tank strength on the field, and this was enough to stop the Germans.

Finally, the Germans had developed an advantage in the first couple of days of the operation, for they were able to deploy all 16 of their starting divisions versus the Voronezh Front, while the Voronezh Front took several days to get all of its forces into the battle. As such, the actual number engaged each day is not representative of the total strength. As the battle developed, the Germans, who initially outnumbered the Soviet forces, found the odds shifting against them. By the time the Soviets were ready to commit their forces from the Steppe Front, the ratio of committed forces was 1.29 to one in favor of the Germans (the attacker). With the committal of the Fifth Guards Army and the Fifth Guards Tank Army, the ratio turned to 0.88 to one, which was the worst ratio that the Germans had faced since the start of the offensive.

9 This count includes some 105 Soviet tanks, mostly damaged from the II Tank Corps and Fifth Guards Tank Army before the 12th. Most of these were march attrition.

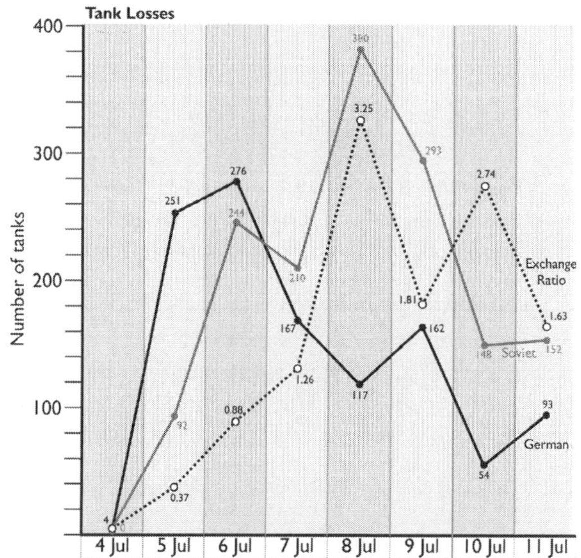

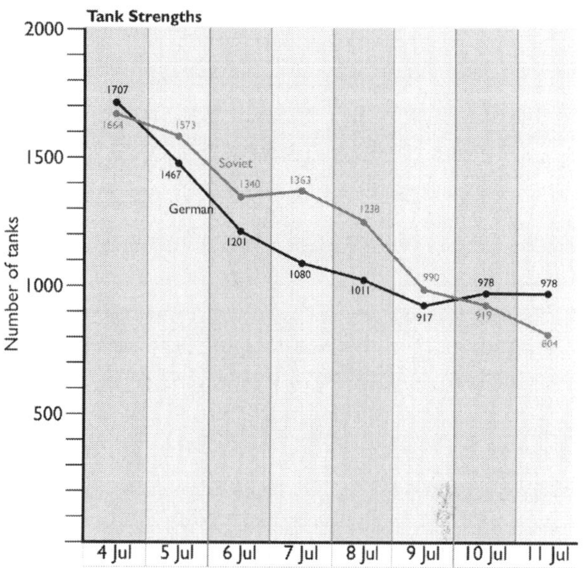

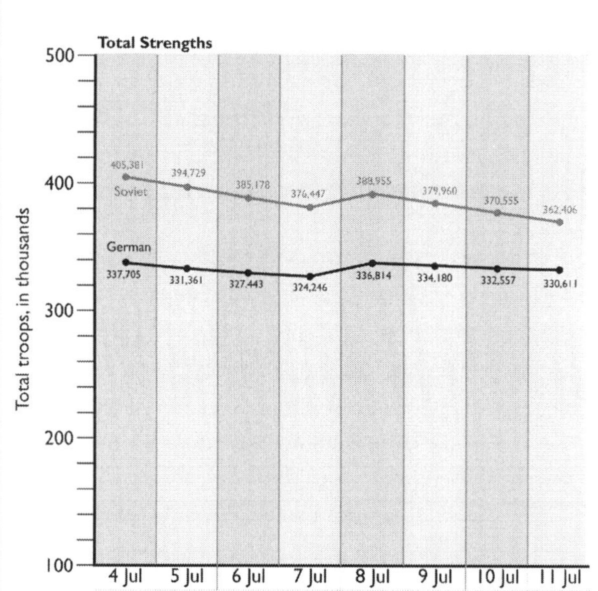

Soviet figures do not include the forces of the Fifth Guards Army, the Fifth Guards Tank Army, or those forces of the Thirty-eighth Army not engaged in the battle. They also only include the X Tank Corps and the II Tanks Corps starting on the 8th. The rest of the Voronezh Front forces engaged in the battle are included, even if some of them did not become actively engaged until several days into the fighting.[1]

1 Figures also do not include the accompanying units with these forces, including the army and corps headquarters, 6th AA Division, 29th AA Division, 12th Mortar Bde, Trufanov's forward detachment (including the 53rd Guards Tank Regiment, the 1st Guards Motorcycle Regiment, and the 689th AT Regiment), 76th Guards Mortar Regiment, 301st AT Regiment, 308th Guards Mortar Regiment, 469th Mortar Regiment, 678th Howitzer Regiment, 1322nd AT Regiment, 1549th Heavy SP Artillery Regiment, 63rd ATR Bn, 256th Motorized Engineer Bn, 377th Motorized Engineer Bn, 431st Engineer Bn, and the 736th, 737th, and 747th AT Bns. It also does not include the 753rd, 754th, 755th and 756th AT Bns that were with RVGK reserve through the 7th.

The total of these figures from 4 July through the 11th are respectively 132,282; 132,929; 133,411; 134,069; 114,446; 114,794; 115,189; and 114,687.

 OTHER GERMAN TANK ACES

A number of soon-to-be-famous German "panzer aces" participated in *Citadel*, including 3 to 5 of the top 10 scoring German tank aces (depending on which list you trust). They include:

ERNST BARKMANN Ernst Barkmann was born 25 August 1919 in Kisdorf in Holstein, the son of a farmer. In 1936 he joined the SS Standarte Germania. Barkmann took part in the Polish Campaign, serving as a machinegunner with the 9th company of Germania SS Standarte and was wounded. In the fall of 1941 he was wounded a second time during the fighting near Dnepropetrovsk and received the Iron Cross (second class). In late 1941 he was transferred to Holland as an instructor, and in early 1942 volunteered for service with the panzer regiment. Barkmann returned to the Eastern Front in the winter of 1942 and was transferred to the 2nd panzer company of the Das Reich SS Division, serving as gunner, and later promoted to command a Panzer III. In early 1943, during the battles for Kharkov, he won the Iron Cross (first class). He served with Das Reich during Kursk.

After Kursk, Barkmann transferred to the 4th company, where he commanded Panther tanks for the rest of the war. In late 1943, Barkmann was promoted to the rank of SS Unterscharfuehrer (Junior Squad Leader or effectively a Corporal or Sergeant). In early 1944, he was transferred with the division to France for rest and refitting, and in June 1944 was committed to Normandy. It was here that he made his reputation in a number of tank engagements with the U.S. forces, including the famous fight at "Barkmann's Corner." For his actions, he was awarded the Knight's Cross on 27 August 1944. He also participated in the Ardennes Offensive and was seriously wounded on Christmas Day 1944. By March 1945, he had returned to action, this time on the Eastern Front. He was wounded again in April 1945 due to friendly fire. Barkmann managed to get to the British zone at the end of the war where he surrendered. He was credited with more than 82 kills.

After the war, Barkmann returned to Kisdorf, where he served as the town's fire chief and mayor. Ernst Barkmann passed away 27 June 2009 at the age of 89.

JURGEN BRANDT Jurgen Brandt was born 2 September 1921 in Rendsburg in Holstein. He was with the 3rd platoon of Leibstandarte's Tiger company, commanded by Michael Wittmann. He is credited with 47 claimed kills. Brandt was killed in action 24 December 1944 in the Ardennes (Battle of the Bulge). He was awarded the German Cross in Gold on 13 January 1945.

PAUL EGGER Paul Egger was born 26 November 1916 in Mautern, Austria. He worked as a clerk until joining the Luftwaffe in 1938. He served as a Stuka pilot during the Polish Campaign and a fighter pilot during the French Campaign and the Battle of Britain. He flew 112 missions, had two claimed kills, and was shot down three times. The last wound relegated him to staff duties.

In May 1941 he joined the Waffen SS and became a tank commander later that year with the Das Reich SS Division. He began earning his reputation in 1941 during the Battle of Kiev, and by the Battle of Kharkov in early 1943 he was credited with 65 claimed kills. He was at Kursk with Das Reich, as photographs showing him near Byikovka on 5 July 1943 attest.

He continued on the Eastern Front until 1944, when he was sent west to fight in Normandy as a platoon commander with the 102nd SS Heavy Panzer Battalion. He returned to the Eastern Front in 1945 and by the end of the war had risen to Sr. Lieutenant (Obersturmfuehrer) and a company commander. He was provisionally awarded a Knight's Cross in the last days of the war, on 28 April 1945. He scored his 113th and final claimed kill on 3 May 1945, escaped from Berlin and surrendered to the U.S. He had been wounded nine times during the war and was the seventh highest scoring tank ace.

He was in captivity for two and one-half years and then made his career as a sports reporter in post-war Germany. He passed away 12 July 2007 in Uberlingen (near Lake Constance), Germany, at the age of 90.

Clemens von Kageneck The oldest of four sons of Major General Karl Graf (Count) von Kageneck (1871–1967), Captain Clemens-Heinrich Graf (Count) von Kageneck was born in Berlin on 17 October 1913. He served with the 3rd Panzer Division for the early part of the war; he took command of the 503rd Heavy Panzer Battalion in May 1943 and commanded it during the Battle of Kursk. He was wounded in July but returned to his unit in October. He was wounded again in December but returned to his unit in January 1944 only to be wounded once again later that month. He was awarded the Knight's Cross on 4 August 1943 and Oak Leaves on 26 June 1944. All of his actions with the 503rd were on the Eastern Front.

Von Kageneck was the older brother of the German Luftwaffe Ace (67 victories, 47 of them on the Eastern Front) and Knight's Cross with Oak Leaves holder Erbo Graf von Kageneck (born 1918) who died of wounds received in aerial combat over North Africa in January 1942 at the age of 23. Another brother, Franz Joseph Graf von Kageneck (1915–1941) was killed in action two weeks earlier in December 1941. The youngest brother, August Graf von Kageneck (1922–2004), survived the war and was a journalist and author.

Clemens-Heinrich Graf von Kageneck was married in 1944 and became a bank manager after the war. His wife passed away in 2003 and he passed away in Bad Homburg on 18 March 2005 at the age of 91. They were survived by seven children and 12 grandchildren.

Heinz Kling Heinrich Kling was born 10 September 1913 in Kassel, Hessen. During Kursk, Captain Kling was the Tiger company commander of the Leibstandarte SS Adolf Hilter. He was later the commander of 101st SS Heavy Panzer Battalion, continuing to command Wittmann, Wendorff, Staudegger and Woll. He was credited with either 67 or more than 51 claimed kills. He was awarded the Knight's Cross on 23 February 1944. He survived the war but drowned in Lake Constance on 30 September 1951 at the age of 38.

Kurt Knispel An ethnic German born 20 September 1921 in Salisfeld (Salisov) in the Sudeten region of Czechoslovakia. After an apprenticeship in an automobile factory in 1940, Knispel joined the army in 1940. In June 1941 he was transferred to a combat unit and participated in Operation Barbarossa as a gunner in a Panzer IV in the 29th Panzer Regiment of the 12th Panzer Division.

In January 1943 he was transferred over to Tiger tanks, already having been credited with 12 kills. He was with the first company of the 503rd Heavy Panzer Battalion during Kursk.

Knispel was the highest scoring "Tiger Ace" of the war, with 168 claimed kills. Of those, 126 were as a gunner, 42 as a tank commander. He was awarded the German Cross in Gold on 20 May 1944. Knispel was never awarded the Knight's Cross due to discipline issues although he was recommended for it four times. He was never promoted above sergeant even though he was a top German tank ace. He died in action late in the war on 28 April 1945 near Znajmo, Czechoslovakia.

Rudolf von Ribbentrop Rudolf von Ribbentrop was a tank company commander at Prokhorovka with the Leibstandarte SS Adolf Hitler Division. He is credited with at least 14 claimed kills from his actions at Kursk. He was awarded the Knight's Cross on 20 July 1943. He was interviewed for this book. *(continued)*

Sr. Lt. Richard Baron von Rosen Richard Rosen was with the 503rd Heavy Panzer Battalion during Kursk. He is credited with about 30 claimed kills. He was interviewed for this book. A brief biography of him is presented in the footnotes of Chapter Six. In 2013, two years before he passed away, he published his memoir of the war.[1]

Alfred Rubbel Alfred Rubbel was transferred to the 503rd Heavy Panzer Battalion just before Kursk. He is credited with over 60 claimed kills during the war. He is the author of several books on Tiger tanks and their units. He was interviewed for this book. A brief biography of him is presented in the footnotes of Chapter Eleven.

Franz Staudegger Franz Staudegger was born 12 February 1923 in Karnten, Austria. During Kursk, he was with the 2nd platoon of the Tiger company of Leibstandarte SS Adolf Hitler Division. On 8 July his tank was not working when his platoon moved out. After his crew repaired it, they were moving up to rejoin their unit when they encountered a Soviet attack. It is claimed that his Tiger tank single-handedly engaged abut 50 T-34s tanks. He used up all his ammunition, destroying 22 tanks and the rest retreated. He was awarded the Knight Cross for this action on 10 July, becoming the first Tiger tank crewman to win this award. He was summoned to Adolf Hitler's headquarters afterwards.[2] As Brigadier General (ret.) Baer recalls his actions:

> On the German side I want to mention SS Sergeant Staudegger. I think his Tiger had been immobilized by enemy fire somewhere southwest of the elevation at 252.2. His crew was either dead or wounded. Staudegger alone killed 20 enemy tanks who were part of one Soviet attack, then destroyed two more in close combat using magnetic charges. I heard this story after it happened and saw his tank later on. Staudegger received the Knight's Cross for his actions.

Staudegger later fought in Normandy and the Ardennes. He was credited with over 35 claimed kills for the war. He passed away 16 March 1991 in Frankfurt, Germany.

---

1 Richard Freiherr von Rosen, *Als Panzeroffizier in Ost und West*, English version published in 2018 as Richard Freiherr von Rosen, *Panzer Aces: Memoir of an Iron Cross Panzer Command from Barbarossa to Normandy.*

2 Probably the most detailed account of this action is in Patrick Agte's book, *Michael Wittmann and the Waffen SS Tiger Commanders of the Leibstandarte in WWII*, pages 103–105 and pages 119–121. The claim of facing 50–60 tanks comes from his Knight's Cross award citation and Nazi-era press (propaganda) releases. The event could not have occurred near 252.2 as it occurred on the 8th of July (or 7 July in some sources). A number of internet sources (but not Agte) mention it occurring at the village of Psyolknee. We have not located a village called Psyolknee on any maps we have. While we do not doubt that some event like this occurred, the details are not supported by anything in either side's unit records.

We have examined the unit records of all Soviet tank corps in the area. The three closest Soviet armor units in the area were the V Guards Tank Corps, the X Tank Corps and the II Tank Corps.

Certainly the V Guards Tank Corps lost a lot of tanks this day with reported losses of 28 T-34s and 9 T-70s: 14 T-34s and 7 T-70s from the 20th Gds Tank Bde and 14 T-34s and 2 T-70s from the 21st Gds Tank Bde. The 22nd Gds Tank Bde reports it has no losses for this day. See Fond: 3403, Opis: 1, Delo: 18a, paqes 143–156. Of course, if the claims for Staudegger are correct, then this would mean that he was responsible for 22 out of 28 T-34s lost by the V Guards Tank Corps on the 8th. As it were, it appears the tank corps was to the east of the Das Reich SS Division and at 1030 has reached the line of Sobachevskii-Kalinin-Belenikhino. In combat report #0112, 2200 July 8, 1943 they place the 20th Guards Tank Brigade two kilometers south of Sobachevskii and the 22nd Guards Tank Brigade in Belenikhino (Fond: 3403, Opis: 1, Delo: 18).

The X Tank Corps is another candidate except it reports that it only lost two tanks between 7 and 11 July (Fond 3410, Opis: 1, Delo: 17, page 10 and Fond: 3410, Opis: 1, Delo: 14, page 5). Unit strength reports for this unit do not contradict these reports. The nearest of its tanks brigades to the northeast of Teterevino on 8 July was the 178th Tank Brigade. The other two tank brigades were to the west of it and moving further west.

The II Tank Corps is the most likely candidate. It attacked in the afternoon and lost at least 31 tanks on the 9th of July. The 26th Tank Brigade did take Teterevino. They do report losses of 6 T-34s knocked out and 3 broken down, and 3 T-70s knocked out and 3 broken down. The first tank battalion of the 99th Tank Brigade did lose its way during the fight and ended up attacking towards Teterevino (see Zamulin, *Demolishing the Myth*, page 146). There it encountered "two Panzer VI" tanks

HELMUT WENDORFF Helmut Max Erst Wendorff was born on 20 October 1920 in Grauwinkel, the son of a farmer. He joined the SS in 1939. During Kursk, he was the 2nd platoon commander in the Tiger company of the Leibstandarte SS Adolf Hitler Division. He was credited during the war with either 84 or 95 claimed kills. He was awarded the Knight's Cross on 12 February 1944. He died in action at Mezieres, France, on 14 August 1944.

KRAFT-HELMUT WALLROTH Kraft-Helmut Wallroth was born 30 July 1916 in Flensburg in Schleswig-Holstein. During Kursk, Captain Wallroth was the Tiger company commander of the Gross Deutschland Division. He had commanded the company since the 13th of January 1943, and continued to command the unit after it was expanded to a battalion in August 1943. He was killed in action on 3 February 1944.

BALTHASAR (BOBBY) WOLL Balthasar Woll was born 1 March 1922 in Wemmetsweiler in Saarland, which was a French administered region of Germany at that time (returned to German control in 1935). An electrician apprentice, he joined the Waffen SS on 15 August 1941 and was assigned to Totenkopf SS Division as a machinegunner. He was wounded in early 1942, was retrained as a tank gunner and assigned as Michael Wittmann's gunner in late 1942. As such, much of his early career was tied to Wittmann. He is credited with over 100 kills. It appears that 81 of these were as Wittmann's gunner (these claims are double counted). He was awarded the Knight's Cross on 16 January 1944, being the only tank gunner to receive that award. He was a tank commander during Normandy, was severely wounded in an air attack, and remained hospitalized until March 1945. He returned to action and survived the war. After the war he returned to work as an electrician and passed away on 18 March 1996 in Bielefeld-Sennestadt, Nordrhein-Westfalen.

NOTE There are not similar public listings or claims for Soviet tank aces.

(Tigers) which brought the battalion under fire. After "suffering tank losses," it retreated. The other battalion of the tank brigade was involved in the attacks to the south with the 169th Tank Brigade. The 99th Tank Brigade does report their losses as of 0700 on 10 July as 12 T-34s knocked out and 4 undergoing report, and 4 T-70s knocked out and 4 broken down. The 169th Tank Brigade report losses of 3 T-34s knocked out and 5 broken down and 1 T-70 knocked out. The 15th Guard Heavy Tank Regiment reports 2 Churchills knocked out and 2 broken down. These reports probably account for the actions of both 8 and 9 July (see Fond: 3407, Opis: 1, Delo: 108, pages 195-216).

The most likely candidate is the first tank battalion of the 99th Tank Brigade. Its composition is not known, but may have been 10 T-34s and 10 T-70s. The 26th Tank Brigade also had 6 T-34s knocked out. One is left with the conclusion from an examination of the Soviet unit records that the claims of 22 T-34s killed by Staudegger on 8 July 1943, along with the 2 T-34s killed by Deutschland SS Infantry Regiment, are probably overstated. The claim that he stopped a panzer regiment is clearly incorrect, as Teterevino was taken and Das Reich reported that they later attacked out of Teterevino with 40 tanks.

CHAPTER EIGHT

The Air War

9–18 JULY 1943

After 20 July [the 1944 assassination attempt on Hitler] everything came out, things I had considered impossible. It was precisely those circles against me who had profited most from National Socialism. I pampered and decorated them. And that was all the thanks I got. I ought to put a bullet in my head. I lacked hard fighters. Model and Dietrich are such. And Rudel [the Stuka pilot]. Now there's a successor for me. Intelligence. What are his views on art and culture?

ADOLF HITLER
1945?[1]

BOTH THE GERMAN and the Soviet air forces primarily supported their ground operations, and as such were fundamentally structured to serve as tactical air forces. Little strategic bombing occurred on the Eastern Front. With the armies of these two nations locked in a life and death struggle, almost all air assets were focused on trying to win the ground war. In effect, strategic bombing was a luxury that neither nation could afford.

Supporting the German Army Group Center and the German forces on the north side of the Kursk bulge was the Sixth Air Fleet under Colonel General Robert Ritter von Greim. Supporting Army Group South was the Fourth Air Fleet under command of General Otto Dessloch. The portion supporting the forces on the south side of the Kursk bulge was the VIII Air Corps under Major General Hans Seidemann.

The Soviet air force had not been able to contend with the Germans for control of the sky since the beginning of the war. Even the German resupply of Stalingrad had been conducted with mostly unescorted transports. During its winter offensive and the German counterattack in March, the Soviet air force was never able to establish air superiority. During most of that period, the German Air Force was able to establish control over any space that it considered important.

Still, the Soviet air force continued to be built up and as such, was becoming a more dangerous and significant threat to German control of the air. First, the Soviet air force had grown larger. In particular, its fighter arm now outnumbered the Germans' on the Eastern Front. Second, they had continued to improve their aircraft and were now fielding planes almost as good as those the Germans manufactured. The Battle of Kursk was the first real attempt in two years to contest the Germans for control of the air.

1 Below, page 223.

The German Air Force during April and May kept their operations somewhat limited, providing support where needed and occasionally striking at and interdicting the Soviet rail lines and rail yards. Mainly they were rebuilding so as to be ready for the offensive scheduled in May. With the offensive delayed, at the start of June the German Air Force took on its first real strategic air campaign on the Eastern Front. This focused on the rail yards around Kursk and on limited strategic bombing of Gorki (the "Soviet Detroit"), Yaroslavl and Saratov.

The Soviet air force spent most of their time between March and July building up for the expected summer offensive. Still, they made a number of efforts to strike at the German rail and airfields. The rail attacks were night harassing attacks, with some occasional successes.

In addition to night harassing attacks on the German rail, the Soviets also launched two sets of airfield raids in an attempt to establish air superiority. This may have been at the instigation of the Voronezh Front command (Vatutin, Khrushchev and Major General Korzhenevich), which suggested around the 21st of April that large air operations be mounted at once to destroy the German aircraft on their airfields so as to weaken the Germans before their offensive.[2]

The first set of airfield attacks was conducted from 6 to 8 May by six air armies (First, Second, Eighth, Fifteenth, Sixteenth, and Seventeenth) against 17 German airfields from Smolensk down to the Sea of Azov. This was a 1,200 kilometer front with a depth of 200 kilometers. On the morning of 6 May this attack was initiated with 434 sorties. The Soviets claimed 500 German losses for a cost of 125 planes.[3] These figures have not been verified, but the claim of German losses is certainly very much higher than what the Germans suffered.[4]

A month later, the Soviets conducted a second operation from 8 to 10 June using the First, Second, and Fifteenth Air Armies and their long-range bombers. The Soviets attacked 28 airfields, focusing mostly on the bomber airfields. This decision to focus on the German bomber fields was probably in response to the German bombing of Gorki on 6 June. The Soviets claimed more than 220 German aircraft destroyed.[5] On the other hand, the German VIII Air Corps and Sixth Air Fleet only record a total of eight losses for these three days, although this probably does not include losses on the ground.[6] It would appear that these two sets of raids mostly damaged the Soviet air force, resulting in high losses for themselves (at least 125 planes) and low losses for the Germans.

Soviet losses from their operations in May and June were probably high. The German High Command War Diary claimed 2,304 Soviet aircraft destroyed in the air or on the ground from 29 April to 30 June. For May, the Germans claimed that 1,257 Soviet aircraft were destroyed, while they lost 143.[7] The accuracy of German claims is discussed later.

THE GERMAN BUILD up in strength over the next three months was considerable, with Seidemann

2 Jukes, pages 50–51.

3 Air Marshal Sergei Rudenko's article on "The Gaining of Air Supremacy and Air Operations in the Battle of Kursk" in *The Battle of Kursk* (Progress Press Publishers), page 188.

4 T312, R1232, the "Einsatzuebersicht Luftw. Kde. Ost am 7.5.43" reports only 1 He-111 lost this day while the NAG 10 reports none (as usual). Have not located German loss reports for the 6th and the 8th or for the Fourth Air Fleet, but there are no indications of heavy losses in any of the unofficial histories of the Luftwaffe. There is no reason to believe that the strike in May was any more successful than subsequent strikes.

5 Air Marshal Sergei Rudenko's article on "The Gaining of Air Supremacy and Air Operations in the Battle of Kursk" in *The Battle of Kursk* (Progress Press Publishers), page 188.

6 T312, R1234. The VIII Air Corps for 8 June reports 1 Ju-87 lost due to flak and 1 Me-109 missing, and "no losses" for the night of 8/9 June; 1 Ju-87 missing for 9 June; and "no losses" for the night of 9/10 June, 10 June, or night of 10/11 June. The Sixth Air Fleet records "no losses" for the 8th of June, the night of 8/9 June, 9th of June. They report 3 He-111s lost for the night of 9/10 June (probably from the raid on Yaroslavl), and no losses of 10 June, and 2 He-111s (probably from the raid on Gorki) for the night of 10/11 June.

7 Jukes, page 56. While these claims have not been verified, the Germans' low losses in May are partly confirmed by the Second Army air liaison officer records. There is not a complete set of reports for May, but the reports that we have usually show low losses for May. This includes reports for the Sixth Air Fleet for May 7th, 14th, 14/15th (a night report), 22nd, 27th, 28th, 28/29th, 29th, 29/30th, 30th, 30/31st, 31st and 31/1st; and for the VIII Air Corps for 28th, 28/29th, 29th, 29/30th, 30th, 30/31st, 31st and 31/1st. The German losses reported for these days are 1 Fw-189,

reporting the entire Fourth Air Fleet having about 1,556 planes at the start of the *Citadel* offensive. Just before the attack, most of the formations were to be transferred to the VIII Air Corps. Remaining in the south was the Romanian Air Corps of around 100 planes and the reconnaissance and harassing squadrons of the I Air Corps and IV Air Corps. All the other formations were attached to the VIII Air Corps before the offensive.

The Fourth Air Fleet was now left with a long-range reconnaissance group of 24 aircraft with its headquarters at Murafa (20 kilometers southwest of Bogodukhov).[8] In the Crimea, the I Air Corps had around 106 aircraft along with a Romanian formation of about 80 aircraft. The IV Air Corps had an estimated 234 aircraft, including 150 from the I Romanian Air Corps. Committed to the Kursk Offensive, under command of the VIII Air Corps, were an estimated 1,112 aircraft.[9] This put over 70% of the aircraft in Army Group South at the disposal of the VIII Air Corps. It was estimated by Seidemann that about 75% of these aircraft were ready for action on any given day.

The Soviet air armies had built up considerable strength. The Second Air Army had a strength of 881 aircraft, while the Seventeenth Air Army had 735. The Fifth Air Army, sitting in reserve, had maybe 430 aircraft. In the north, facing the Sixth Air Fleet, was the Sixteenth Air Army with a strength of 1,034 combat aircraft.[10]

The Soviet air forces, having been in place for three months, were well stocked for the upcoming operations. They had assembled 40,000 tons of fuel for their aircraft, which was enough for 7.5 sorties per plane. This could last for three or four days without resupply. The night bombers had plenty of fuel, with 596 tons of B-70 fuel. This would last for 20 sorties per plane. They had assembled a full range of demolition, fragmentation, and incendiary bombs, rocket rounds, and the new experimental antitank bombs. They had 6,850 tons of bombs, which were more than enough for the upcoming operations.

The Germans chose not to start this battle with the customary strike against the Soviet air fields. Instead, the Germans were only to appear over the battlefield when the offensive started. This was in the hope that somehow Army Group South was going to achieve tactical surprise. This was a vain hope.

In contrast, the Soviets organized for air strikes on the German airfields on both sides of the Kursk bulge for the 5th of July, with the Sixteenth Air Army going after the Sixth Air Fleet in the north, while the Second Air Army, with help from the Seventeenth Air Army, went after the VIII Air Corps in the south. They probably had a good idea of German locations, in part due to signal intelligence received from the British spy John

---

1 Fw-190, 3 He-111s, 2 Hs-126s, 10 Ju-87s, 1 Hungarian Ju-88, 1 Me-109, and 1 Me-110 for a total of 20 planes lost (five from VII Air Corps). Making a straight line estimate from this limited data would produce a monthly loss figure of about 97.

The German claims for Soviet air losses have not been verified. While the claims are very high, they are not out of line with claims that we have been able to verify for July.

8 This is according to Seidemann, page 193. According to Klink, page 336, the Fourth Air Fleet had the 125th Long-range Reconnaissance Group, the 76th Weather Reconnaissance Squadron, a transport squadron, and a "sanitatsflugbereitschaft" (airborne ambulance flight).

9 This is from Seidemann, pages 192–193, and has not been confirmed by other primary documentary sources.

10 The figure of 881 comes from the Second Air Army correlation of forces. The other figures come from *The Battle of Kursk* (Progress Press Publishers), page 189, but as they also use the 881 figure for the Second Air Army, and their strength figures for the Seventeenth Air Army are close to the archival figures we have, these figures appear to be correct. Page 194 gives a combined strength of 1,311 aircraft for the Second and Fifth Air Armies, from which one can derive a strength for the Fifth Air Army of 430 aircraft. This appears to match the archival records we have.

The *Voyenno-Istoricheskii Zhurnal* [Military History Journal], 1968, Number 6. "Dokumentyi i Materialyi: Kurskaya Bitva v Tsifrakh" gives the following figures:

Central Front: 1,034 planes (455 fighters, 241 Assault planes, 260 day bombers, 74 night bombers and 4 reconnaissance aircraft);

Voronezh Front: 881 planes (389 fighters, 276 assault planes, 172 day bombers, 34 night bombers, 10 reconnaissance aircraft);

Southwestern Front: 735 planes (218 fighters, 383 assault planes, 70 day bombers, 64 night bombers).

Their footnotes note that these figures do not include about 480 night bombers from long-range aviation and do not include the IX Fighter Corps and 36th and 101st Fighter Divisions from the Air Defense command. They also note that other Soviet secondary sources mention a total of 3,130 airplanes not counting long-range aviation, and 2,370 airplanes, not counting long-range aviation and the neighboring Fronts. There is a reported figure of 550 aircraft for the Steppe Front from Dupuy and Martell, *Great Battles on the Eastern Front*, page 76, clearly taken from Soviet sources.

VIII AIR CORPS ORDER OF BATTLE SUMMARY

Unit Name	*Number of Planes*
II & III/3rd Fighter Wing	65 Me-109
52nd Fighter Wing (-)*	80 Me-109
1st Ground Attack Wing	85 Fw-190
	16 Hs-123
	33 Hs-129
4th and 8th Sq./2nd Gound Attack Wing	27 Hs-129
Antitank Squadron/51st Fighter Wing	15 Hs-129
2nd Stuka Wing	111 Ju-87
77th Stuka Wing	120 Ju-87
3rd Bombardment Wing	73 Ju-88
27th Bombardment Wing	101 He-111
55th Bombardment Wing (-)	97 He-111
I/100th Bombardment Wing	38 He-111

Unit Name	*Number of Planes*
VI Close-range Reconnaissance Group	34 aircraft
III Long-range Reconnaissance Group	35 Ju-88
Harassing Aircraft Group	60
VIII Air Corps Transport Squadron	13 Ju-52
Royal Hungarian Air Division	90
Total Aircraft	1,093

Seidemann estimated the total strength to be 1,112. He estimated serviceability to be 75%, making around 900 aircraft (Seidemann's estimate) ready for action.

This author is still uncertain whether the 8th Squadron/2nd Ground Attack Wing, III Group/77th Stuka Wing, III Group/3rd Bombardment Wing or some reconnaissance squadrons were at this battle.

* (-) indicates that elements are detached from these units.

Cairncross. Each Soviet air army used a different methodology, with the Sixteenth Air Army endeavoring to conduct their counter-preparation with one massive strike, while in the south, the Second Air Army chose to do this by a series of concentrated blows and echeloned activities during the entire period. This approach may have been influenced by the use of the Seventeenth Air Army, which had farther to fly, making it more difficult to coordinate a massive strike. As it was, the counter-preparation operation did not occur as planned.

The Strike at Dawn

If the real reason for not conducting a strike on the Soviet air force was their desire not to give up tactical surprise, then one wonders how the Germans expected to keep tactical surprise with most of the outpost line in front of the Fourth Panzer Army being forcefully cleared the day before. While the Germans chose to forego the option of launching a surprise air attack, the Soviets did not. Instead, they conducted the "customary" strike at dawn.

In the south, the Soviet counterblow was timed to strike early in the morning against the German airfields around Kharkov. The attacking formations were from

SECOND AIR ARMY FORCES (1–6 JULY 1943)

The Second Air Army was commanded by Lt. General S. A. Krasovskii. The chief of staff was Major General F. I. Kachev. The Deputy Commander of Political Affairs (effectively the Military Council Member) was Major General S. N. Ramazanov. The Chief of the Army Political Division was Colonel A. I. Asaulenko.

	On-hand, 1 July	*Largest Number Flown in a Day*
I Assault Corps	206 Assault	114 Il-2
	82 Fighters	60 Yak-1b
I Bomber Corps	117 Bombers	70 Pe-2
IV Fighter Corps	184 Fighters	38 Yak-1b,
		15 Yak-7b,
		65 La-5
V Fighter Corps	278 Fighters	26 Yak-1b,
		26 Yak-7b,
		100 La-5
291st Assault Division	100 Assault	48 Il-2
	28 Fighters	8 Yak-1,
		4 Yak-7b,
		3 La-5 or
		18 Fighters
208th Night Bomber Division	57 Night Bombers	27 U-2,
		4 R-5
50th Air Reconnaissance Regiment		7 Pe-2
454th Bomber Regiment	21 Reconnaissance	6 Bostons
272nd Independent Army Squadron		

the Second and Seventeenth Air Armies. The Soviets had attempted such strikes in June, but with little success. On the 8th and 10th of June the Sixth Air Fleet had been attacked twice with a very favorable exchange rate for the Germans. A much smaller attempt was also made on the VIII Air Corps on the 8th of June, also with unfavorable results for the Soviets. The Germans with their communications networks, forward observers, radar systems and fighters ready to scramble were clearly prepared to meet such attempts. Why the Soviets thought that it would work now, when it had not worked in the past, is hard to explain.

Between the Second and Seventeenth Air Armies, the Soviets had at least 357 serviceable Il-2s, along with 70 Pe-2s and 38 TB-3s. They had at least 526 fighters available. If they were going to do an airfield strike, it would seem to have made more sense to use the entire force at their disposal for such a strike and to have concentrated on such a strike for most of the morning. Instead they started the day with a limited strike.

 SEVENTEENTH AIR ARMY FORCES (5 JULY 1943)

The Seventeenth Air Army was commanded by Lt. General V. A. Sudets. The chief of staff was Major General N. M. Korsakov. The Deputy Commander of Political Affairs (effectively the Military Council Member) was Major General V. N. Tolmachev. The Chief of the Army Political Division was Colonel V. G. Tochilov.

	Base	*Operational*	*Not Operational*	*Pilots*
I Mixed Corps	Proyezzhaya			
288th Fighter Division	Starobelskaya	2 Yak-1		4
866th Fighter Rgt.	Peski	26 Yak-1	1 Yak-1	34
897th Fighter Rgt.	Peski	20 Yak-1	1 Yak-1	29
659th Fighter Rgt.	Polovinkino	22 Yak-1	2 Yak-1	31
5th Guards Assault Division	Ryibentsovo			
93rd Assault Rgt.	Novo-Pskov	26 Il-2	5 Il-2	35
94th Assault Rgt.	Mokartyatino	30 Il-2	1 Il-2	35
95th Assault Rgt.	Belokurakino	30 Il-2	2 Il-2	37
III Mixed Corps	Novo-Osinovka			
404th Ind. Squadron	Novo-Osinovka	5 U-2	1 U-2	9
207th Fighter Division	Aleksandrovka			
5th Guards Fighter Rgt.	Shchenyachye	21 La-5	1 La-5	33
814th Fighter Rgt.	Uchebnyii Sovkhoz	21 Yak-1/7b	3 Yak-1/7b	41
867th Fighter Rgt.	Bulatselovka	12 Yak-1/7b	3 Yak-1/7b	31
290th Assault Division	Kurilovka	1 Il-2		2
775th Assault Rgt.	Kurilovka	30 Il-2	2 Il-2	38
625th Assault Rgt.	Zatishnoye	33 Il-2	3 Il-2	34
299th Assault Rgt.	Manino	27 Il-2	5 Il-2	31

	Base	Operational	Not Operational	Pilots
IX Mixed Corps	Pokrovskoye			
418th Ind. Squadron	Pokrovskoye	3 U-2		3
295th Fighter Division	Olshana	2 La-5		2
31st Fighter Rgt.	Budennovka	26 La-5	2 La-5	26
116th Fighter Rgt.	Olshanyi	25 La-5	1 La-5	28
164th Fighter Rgt.	Nizhnyaya Duvanka	21 La-5	2 La-5	25
305th Assault Division	Nizhnyaya Duvanka	1 U-2		4
175th Assault Rgt.	Olshanyi	35 Il-2		36
237th Assault Rgt.	Pokrovskoye	30 Il-2	1 Il-2	31
955th Assault Rgt.	Rayevka	27 Il-2		29
306th Assault Division	Nizhnyaya Duvanka	1 U-2		1
672nd Assault Rgt.	Peschanka	34 Il-2		30
951st Assault Rgt.	Lantratovka	29 Il-2	2 Il-2	32
995th Assault Rgt.	Budennovka	28 Il-2	3 Il-2	33
244th Bomber Division	Rogovo	3 U-2		3
449th Bomber Rgt.	Mozhyakovka	24 TB-3		24
860th Bomber Rgt.	Shramovka	17 TB-3	1 TB-3	20
861st Bomber Rgt.	Rogovo	25 TB-3		32
260th Bomber Rgt.	Poddubnoye	10 TB-3	1 TB-3	20
262nd Night Bomber Division	Zapadnoye	2 U-2		3
719th Night Bomber Rgt.	Krinichnyii	8 R-5	1 R-5	22
97th Night Bomber Rgt.	Kovalevka	19 U-2		24
370th Night Bomber Rgt.	Vasiltsevka	19 U-2		31
993rd Night Bomber Rgt.	Ponamarevka	14 U-2		29
39th Reconnaissance Rgt.	Velshanyi	18 Pe-2	1 Pe-2	14
50th Reconnaissance Rgt.	Velshanyi	2 Pe-2	1 Pe-2	4
403rd Ind. Squadron	Ivanovka	7 U-2	3 U-2	11
371st Transport Rgt.	Stepki	14 U-2		22
Totals		750	49	963

The Soviet Second Air Army went forward with groups of six to nine assault aircraft, escorted by the same number of fighters. Attacking the Pomerki and Sokolniki airfields just north of Kharkov were 48 Il-2s with fighter escort from the I Assault Corps while seven fighters from the IV Fighter Corps "blocked" the Pomerki airfield. Attacking the Mikoyanovka airfield was the 291st Assault Division with 18 Il-2s escorted by 18 fighters, while 12 planes from the V Fighter Corps blocked the airfield. They began bombing the German airfields in the area of Mikoyanovka, Sokolniki and Pomerki between 0425 and 0430 (Moscow time). These three locations were widely separated with three German fighter wings located around Mikoyanovka.

The Soviet strike was timed for just when the German operations would be starting. At the bases around Mikoyanovka, the German's 52nd Fighter Wing barely had time to clear the airfield before the Soviet aircraft arrived. Around Kharkov, the Germans were forced to halt bomber operations and instead sent their fighters of the 3rd Fighter Wing scrambling to take off. This included launching fighters through the lines of bombers that were readying to take off. Still, there was enough warning that when the Soviet air arrived, a very strong German fighter force of two fighter wings was waiting for them.

The Second Air Army tried to cover the assault aircraft by blocking the airfields, but it appears the German fighters were airborne when they arrived. The Soviet formations came under continual attack during their approach run and were then attacked again on their return flights. The Soviet fighters were supposed to cover them on the return flight and the IV Fighter Corps flew 50 such covering missions as were half of the V Fighter Corps' 24 missions. In light of the heavy losses inflicted on the Il-2s, this was not a very successful cover. It does not appear that the Seventeenth Air Army flew blocking or covering missions.

Overall, this first Soviet strike consisted of 90 Il-2s and around 131 fighters. Opposing them were two wings of German fighters, potentially around 160 Me-109s. What transpired between Mikoyanovka and Kharkov was one of the largest air fights of the war, creating a spectacle of planes crashing and burning across an 80 kilometer battle area from Mikoyanovka to Kharkov.

This attack was a disaster for the Soviet air forces. Seidemann estimates that 120 enemy aircraft went down in this raid, while the German losses were small. While it appears that Seidemann's estimate is inflated, it was still a disastrous start to a disastrous day for the Soviet air force.

Air Support on the First Day (5 July)

The Germans, with their desire to concentrate all firepower on the decisive point, ended up assigning all the air support in the morning to the SS Panzer Corps, while the XLVIII Panzer Corps received the support during the afternoon. The attacks this day flew forward of the two attacking panzer corps, with the targets including Soviet defensive points; artillery, antiaircraft, and antitank gun positions; tank assembly areas and vehicle columns. They faced strong Soviet antiaircraft fire. This air support included 536 sorties by He-111s and Ju-88s, 1,071 Stuka sorties and 335 ground attack sorties by Fw-190s and Hs-123s. The III Group of the 55th Bombardment Wing flew 82 He-111 sorties this day. Of those, 21 sorties went east of Luchki and 19 went to Byikovka. These strikes, well to the rear, came in at 2600 to 4000 meters (8500 to 13,000 feet). The Luftwaffe ground observers claimed bloody Soviet losses and heavy material losses. Their "confirmed" claims included seven tanks, 30 guns, 70 vehicles, and nine ammunition or supply dumps.

The Second Air Army also started flying air support from the start of the battle, with the majority of it concentrated around the XLVIII Panzer Corps sector. Whereas over 80% of the German sorties this day were ground attack type sorties (1,942 sorties), the Soviets only had a little over 25% of its sorties as ground attack type sorties (334 sorties). There was considerably more weight to the German ground support effort than to the Soviet one.

The Seventeenth Air Army also contributed to the ground war, supporting the Seventh Guards Army. As the German air forces were not active over this area, then this effectively gave the Soviets air superiority over the Corps Raus and III Panzer Corps areas. The I Mixed Corps provided no support (as was also the case with the 244th Bomber Division). The III Mixed Corps sent 45 Il-2s with 62 fighter escorts to attack troops in the western Bezlyudovka and Ivanovka areas. The IX Mixed Corps sent 107 Il-2s with probably an equal number of La-5 escorts to attack German troop concentrations and crossings in the Solomino, Toplinka, Pristen, Pulyaevka, and Ivanovka areas. Most of these attacks were concentrated on Corps Raus, leaving the III Panzer Corps relatively unmolested.

During the day the Germans launched 1,942 ground attack type sorties on the 5th compared to 486 ground attack type sorties by the two Soviet air armies.

This day was a disaster for the Second Air Army. In addition to the heavy losses in their dawn assault on the German airfields, they suffered losses steadily throughout the day with most of their formations. The Second Air Army lost 114 airplanes while the Seventeenth Air Army lost 73. The Germans reported on 19 aircraft lost this day. Of those, 12 were Me-109s. This is a ten-to-one exchange ratio!

This was a staggering lop-sided exchange. The Second Air Army fighters had managed 835 escort and air superiority sorties and were only facing a fighter force that conducted 371 Me-109 sorties this day. The German Fw-190s, a good fighter in its own right, played little role in the air combat with I Ground Assault Group claiming only one kill this day. Yet the Soviets lost 50 fighters, probably to air combat, while the Germans only lost 12 Me-109s and one Fw-190. This is around a four-to-one fighter exchange, and then the Germans fighters were probably able to bag another 56 assault aircraft and bombers, while the antiaircraft fire from both sides accounted for another eight Soviet planes. Most likely, the planes that "failed to return" were from air combat, not antiaircraft fire, which would rarely eliminate an entire flight and leave no reports.

The Seventeenth Air Army losses were less. The I Mixed Corps, which had only participated in a morning airfield strike on the southerly Kramatorskaya airfield, lost nothing. The III Mixed Corps, which had sent out 12 Yak-1s in the morning airfield strike, 45 Il-2s to attack German troops, and 62 escorting Yak-1s, had 14 Il-2s and two Yak-1s fail to return. It also had one other Yak-1 damaged in a dogfight. The IX Mixed Corps, which had sent out 16 Il-2s in the morning airfield strike, 107 to attack German troops, and 124 escorting La-5s, had 45 Il-2s and seven La-5s that failed to return and five Il-2s shot down.

In the face of such heavy fighting, the German VIII Air Corps surprisingly reports no Stuka losses for the day, although the German quartermaster reports do indicate three lost and three damaged. Their losses,

TYPE OF PLANES CLAIMED BY THE GERMANS, 5 JULY 1943[1]

Type	*German Claims*	*Actual Soviet Losses*
Il-2	113	107
LaGG	34	
LaGG-3	9	
La-5	22	7
MiG-1	2	
Yak-1	7	12
Yak-7		3
Fighter		39
Total of Fighter:	74	61
Boston III	1	1
Pe-2	15	18
Total Planes	203	187

1 Records drawn from a listing of O.K.L. Fighter Claims, Film C:2032/II. List was originally assembled by Tony Woods and is available through *The Luftwaffe, 1933–45* website.

as reported by the VIII Air Corps, consisted of 12 Me-109s, four He-111s, a Ju-88, an Fw-190 and an Hs-126. These appear to be permanent losses, and the number of planes damaged and disabled this day was higher. In addition to the noted ace Lt. Walter Krupinski being injured, the German ace Feldwebel (Technical Sergeant) Wilhelm Hauswirth (54 victories) of the 8th squadron was killed. He had claimed his 53rd victory on the 4th and his last on the 5th at 0503. He was then shot down by antiaircraft over the front lines. The III Group of the 52nd Fighter Wing had lost two major aces and four other pilots killed or injured this day.

This day was a disaster for the Soviet air force and very clearly shows the down-side of conducting the "customary" strike at dawn against a ready opponent. The Second Air Army claims that they destroyed 34 German planes at the airfields at Sokolniki and Pomerki, but these claims are not supported by the German records. The rest of the damage claims are very low (burned one hanger, two ammunition dumps blown up, four antiaircraft firing points suppressed, and one fuel tank burned). It appears that their airfield raids accomplished little.

More significant were the continued losses throughout the day. It would appear that there was a gross competency difference between the two air forces and because of this difference in tactical competence, the Germans were able to maintain a very favorable exchange ratio throughout the day.

At the end of the day, the Soviets had lost 187 planes! Of those, 102 were Il-2s. This was 30% of the 337 Il-2s flown that day. The large number of them that simply "failed to return" indicates the nature of the fighting and the losses. It would appear that entire flights of these slow moving aircraft were being eliminated. While the German VIII Air Corps over-estimated Soviet air losses at 220 in air battles and 40 due to flak, it does indicate that most of the Soviet planes were lost to air action, with up to 50 lost in the morning airfield raid (probably most from the Second Air Army).

Overall, 2,387 German sorties were flown by the VIII Air Corps this day. This is more sorties than flown on any single day of the Battle of Britain (13 August to 31 October 1940), although with fewer planes. The two opposing Soviet air armies flew 1,778 sorties, which was more than the British Air Force ever put up during any day of the Battle of Britain and more than the Germans flew on all but one day of that battle. The bloodiest day in the Battle of Britain, "Black Thursday" (15 August) when the Germans lost 75 aircraft and the British 34, was not near as bloody as the 5th of July 1943, when almost twice as many aircraft were lost (206 airplanes). The air fight in the southern part of the Kursk bulge was of the same scale as the far more famous Battle of Britain, while, at the same time, there was a similar size operation occurring in the north!

The Second Day (6 July)

The Soviet air force, after its heavy losses of the previous day, struggled to maintain a presence over the battlefield. Overall, the Second Air Army had managed to put up 823 sorties during the day, which was about 65% of what they did the previous day. The Seventeenth Air Army flew 462 sorties, of which at least 407 attacked targets in the VIII Air Corps area. They actually had more sorties on this day than the previous day.

With the Soviet air force less present, the German VIII Air Corps was now free to concentrate on the second Soviet defensive line. They again provided all their support to the XLVIII and SS Panzer Corps, with the focus being on the SS Panzer Corps. The Soviet second echelon antitank gun and artillery concentrations were attacked continually.

The German fighters and flak were again extremely successful, with the Soviet Second Air Army losing 50 aircraft, including 28 fighters and 22 Il-2s. The Seventeenth Air Army lost 30 aircraft this day, including 21 Il-2s. Of those, it appears that all but two were lost in the Belgorod area (an R-5 and an La-5 on the ground). The Germans lost only seven aircraft this day. Unlike the previous day, this included no fighters, but did include six Ju-87s and one Ju-88.[11] Five of the Ju-87s were lost to antiaircraft fire. With only two planes lost to enemy air, it appears that the Soviet air force was not very aggressive or effective on this day. The loss of 35 fighters without any fighter losses on the part of the Germans is a lop-sided result that is hard to explain. With 78 Soviet losses to seven German losses, it appears that the Germans maintained their ten-to-one kill ratio. The Germans claimed 74 kills for this day.

The Germans conducted 1,686 sorties this day, which was only about 70% of what they had done on the 5th. There were 77 reconnaissance missions (104% compared to the 5th), 323 bombing missions (60% compared to the 5th), 793 Stuka (74%), 240 assault (72%) and 253 fighter missions (68%).

During the day the Germans launched 1,356 ground attack type sorties on the 6th compared to 442 ground attack type sorties by the Soviets.

The Third Day (7 July)

The Soviet air force continued the contest the air space over the battlefield with limited success. The German VIII Air Corps flew 1,829 sorties this day. Their bombers, dive bombers and ground attack units attacked throughout the day ahead of the German armored spearheads in rolling waves of attacks. This was mostly in front of the SS Panzer Corps and elements of the XLVIII Panzer and III Panzer Corps. Their attacks also covered the east flank of the SS Panzer Corps. They struck at Soviet tank assembly areas, battery positions, and vehicle columns. This resulted in significant claims against the Soviet armor.

The Soviet air force continued to resist on this day, resulting in continued high losses for them. The Second Air Army flew 839 sorties this day, while the 17th Air Army continued to bravely provide additional support with an additional 588 sorties. The Germans put up 297 fighter sorties this day while the two opposing air armies provided 999 cover and escort missions. Even in the face of this uneven odds fight, the Germans only lost 10 planes this day, including four Me-109s, while the Second Air Army lost 30 fighters and 13 Il-2s and the Seventeenth Air Army lost 28 Il-2s and six La-5s. This was an eight-to-one exchange, with the loss of 58 Soviet fighters for four Me-109s being hard to explain.

During this day the Germans launched 1,444 ground attack type sorties compared to 400 ground attack type sorties by the Soviets.

An Assessment of the Soviet Air Force

The Soviet air force, over the course of three days, had lost 342 airplanes compared to 36 German planes lost. Among the fighters, it was 16 German Me-109s lost compared to 193 Yak-1s, Yak-7s and La-5s. In defense of Soviet engineering, the Soviet fighters were good planes. They were certainly capable of providing a good fight for an Me-109. The Soviet Il-2s, of which 186 had been lost, were not slower nor more vulnerable than the Ju-87, of which only six had been lost. The difference here was not in weapon quality, but training and doctrine. The Germans were clearly dominating the skies over Russia with their superior skill and tactics.

The Soviet air force had started this battle with well over 1,000 aircraft ready-for-action. With a quarter of them shot down, and certainly many more damaged and therefore not ready-for-action, the Soviet air power was beginning to fade. Their sortie rate per plane went up on this day, so they were able to maintain a similar level of activity with fewer planes, but this higher level of activity was certainly going to result in a further decline in serviceability. After three days of fighting, the Soviet air force had reached the limits of what it could do with its current strategy. On the first day, its loss rate per sortie was over 11 percent! On the 6th and 7th it shifted downwards to six percent, and from there on remained below six percent a day, with the Soviet aircraft taking a more conservative approach compared to the first day of the Battle of Kursk.

It appeared to Seidemann that the "great blood-letting" of 5 July had shocked the Soviet air force into a

11 The Luftwaffe quartermaster reports on the other hand, show four Ju-87s, one Fw-190 and an Me-109 completely destroyed this day.

much more conservative stance. As Seidemann notes in 1947, "At any rate, the Russian aerial formations were rather reluctant. They frequently discontinued their raids when German fighters appeared and exhibited little fighting spirit. Intercepted radio messages indicate that Russian formations were at times instructed not to fight. In this manner German air superiority became evident on the very first day of the offensive. This state of affairs experienced little change during the entire 'Zitadelle' offensive."[12]

It appears that the Soviets, shocked by the high losses on the first day, and having been made clearly aware of German air superiority, chose to be much more selective and cautious for the rest of the battle. This effectively gave the Germans air superiority throughout most of the battle, although the Soviet air was always present, often providing ground support.

Still, according to Seidemann, the Soviet fighter pilots were better trained than before. He noted that a few of the Soviet fighter squadrons were well led and formidable opponents. One gathers that this was not the case with the majority of the Soviet fighter units. He did not consider their aircraft to be better than the German aircraft.

Seidemann referred to the Il-2s as "cumbrous, but heavily-armed" and noted that they frequently fell victim to the Messerschmitts. He also noted that the few U.S. P-39 Airacobras that appeared distinguished themselves by their superior maneuverability and speed over the Il-2s. He also observed that the Soviet bombers were not that common and were limited to bombing the front lines or forward air fields. He stated that their results were not very good.

Seidemann observed that "The Russian pilot proved to be brave, but orthodox and not sufficiently skillful. One gained the impression that Russian flying crews were not sufficiently familiar with the technical aspects of flying and that they were inadequately trained. On the whole, however, the Red Air Force had caught up considerably, particularly as regards numbers. It had turned into a serious adversary."[13]

Lt. General Krupinski commented in 1999 that "The Russian fighters employed strange tactics, which have remained beyond my comprehension. If we encountered bomber formations with fighter support, the enemy fighters kept right on moving in their fixed formation. They always waited for us to attack before engaging in any dogfights. They never attacked on their own initiative. As a fighter pilot, however, one must have the grit to be the first to attack. So we were always calling the shots, which surely helped manifest our notion of superiority."[14]

July 8

The Second Air Army continued the fight, but at a lower loss rate than before. It was no longer concentrating on the XLVIII Panzer Corps area and the forces advancing on Oboyan, but instead was focusing its attention on the eastern flank of the German penetration. Fighters were also providing cover for the area leading to Prokhorovka and for their armored formations in the Donets triangle. It would appear that this was done to try to support and help cover II Guards and X Tank Corps' armored counterattacks on the 8th of July.

The Seventeenth Air Army's support was now waning. It had gone from conducting 176 Il-2 sorties on the 5th to 169 Il-2 sorties on the 6th, to 156 Il-2 sorties on the 7th, to only 76 Il-2 sorties on this day. This was partially due to losses, for the army had lost 118 Il-2s since the start of the operations. They had lost 64 Il-2s in the first day of the operation, but the following day still managed to fly the same number of sorties, probably by using reserve planes and other pilots. On the 7th they still maintained a high number of sorties, as clearly the planes were averaging better than two sorties a day. On this day, the 8th, they appear to have gone back to one sortie per plane, and with the greatly reduced number of planes, this caused the overall number of sorties to drop. After spending three days making more than 150

12 Seidemann, page 202.

13 Seidemann, page 201.

14 Interview with Maj.Gen. (ret.) Dieter Brand on 20 April 1999.

strikes a day to the Provisional Army Kempf sector, the Seventeenth Air Army effort now declined.

The German air continued to be very active with 1,686 sorties. They continued with strong bomber, dive bomber, and ground assault attacks throughout the day. These were conducted in rolling waves along the whole Fourth Panzer Army front. In particular, they continued to concentrate on the SS Panzer Corps' flanks where there were strong Soviet tank concentrations. Soviet tanks were engaged to the northeast of Belgorod in the III Panzer Corps area and forward of the SS Panzer Corps, south of Prokhorovka. The III Group of the 55th Bombardment Wing again split its effort between the two attacking corps of the Fourth Panzer Army. This included sending 22 sorties to Kochetovka and 23 to Verkhopenye. Again, it appears that the He-111s were being used for ground attack strikes on the Soviet second echelon and on the Soviet reserves. The German daytime reconnaissance revealed the assembly of a major Russian tank force around Prokhorovka. This was probably the X Tank Corps.

The Second Air Army losses for the day were 47 planes, including 16 Il-2s and 30 fighters. This was a slightly lower loss rate than the previous days. The German losses declined to five planes but casualties included an Fw-190, two Hs-129s and two Knight's Cross winners in Ju-87s! Lost due to flak east of Verkhopenye was Knight's Cross winner Captain Bernhard Wutka, while lost due to Soviet aircraft was Knight's Cross winner Senior Lt. Karl Fitzner.[15]

During the day the Germans launched 1,380 ground-attack type sorties on the 8th compared to 404 ground-attack type sorties by the Soviets.

July 9

The Germans flew only 28 sorties the night of July 8/9, with the same six bomber sorties against the railroad stations between Kursk and Kastornoye and 20 harassment bombing sorties east of Belgorod in the Koren River area. According to Seidemann, they reported that additional Soviet motorized units were moving up to the front from the direction of Kursk. It is uncertain which Soviet formations were being referred to here.

The Second Air Army and Seventeenth Air Army continued their nighttime activities unabated. The 208th Night Bomber Division sent 60 sorties to bomb the Olkhovka-Byikovka-Yakovlevo area and the roads leading to the front. The 262nd Night Bomber Division attacked the crossing on the Severnyii Donets and German troops in the area of Razumnoye-Krutoi Log-Solomino-Bezlyudovka. The 244th Bomber Division attacked the Rogan and Osnova airfields with 26 sorties and conducted three reconnaissance sorties with 17 TB-3s.

During the day, the I Assault Corps sent out 134 ground attack sorties with their 54 operational Il-2s, striking in the area of Greznoye-Komsomolets Sovkhoz-Krasnaya Polyana-Yakovlevo-Pokrovka-Verkhopenye. The 28 operational Yak-1s carried out 81 escort sorties and sent 25 sorties to patrol and reconnoiter in the area of Tomarovka-Olkhovka-Byikovka. These operations continued to result in high Il-2 losses, with nine of them along with one Yak-1b failing to return from their mission. The 291st Assault Division attacked troops and tanks in the Greznoye-Gremuchii-Verkhopenye area and in Krapivinskiye Dvoryi-Smorodino-Luchki area. Their 38 Il-2s conducted 83 ground attack sorties, supported by 33 escort sorties. This formation continued to be attrited, with six Il-2s lost and two Yak-1s.

15 Rudel claims that during the Kursk battle his training school friend, Flight Lieutenant Wutka, commander of the 8th squadron, was killed. Rudel indicates that the loss may have been as a result of a short circuit when the bomb release was operated, possibly as a result of sabotage. See Rudel, pages 96–97.

The Luftwaffe quartermaster records do record Captain Wutka's death and the loss of his Ju-87 D-3 on 8 July, but they are listed as being from the 9th squadron. The cause of loss is listed as "crashed due to explosion." They also record Sr. Lt. Karl Fitzner's death and the loss of his Ju-87 D-3 from 5/StG 77. The cause of loss is listed as "exploded in the air."

The Second Army air liaison officer records (T312, R1243, page 000095) list them both by name and as Knight's Cross Winners. It does list Wutka as "Captain Wuka," but this is clearly a typo. Bernhard Wutka was awarded the Knight's Cross on 16 November 1942 as a Sr. Lt. with 8./Sturzkampfgeschwader 2. The various listings of Knight's Cross records we have do not list a Captain Wuka. Karl Fitzner was awarded the Knight's Cross on 27 November 1942 as a Lt. with 1./Sturzkampfgeschwader 77.

 THE VIII AIR CORPS SORTIE COUNT

According to the records of the Second Army Luftwaffe liaison officer, the VIII Air Corps flew the following sorties:

		BY TYPE:				
	Total Sorties	*Recon*	*Stuka*	*Bombing (Harassing)*	*Ground Attack*	*Fighter*
June 30	43					
Night	15					
July 1	57					
Night	57			11		
July 2	49					
Night	21			17 (11)		
July 3	78		20			
Night	No report					
July 4	224		132	28		
Night	No report					
July 5	2387	74	1071	536	335	371
Night	No report					
July 6	1686	77	793	323	240	253
Night	64			61 (50)		
July 7	1829	88	746	498	200	297
Night	57			52 (46)		
July 8	1686	77	701	493	186*	229
Night	28			26 (20)		
July 9	1621	97	699	384	183	258**
Night	No report					
July 10	682					
Night	18			14 (8)		
July 11	1039	62	447	197	157	176
Night	61			56 (49)		

* Of it, 53 are tank hunter missions with Hs-129s armed with 30mm cannon.

** Corrected to match the daily total and the summary report for the 5th through the 9th of July.

		BY TYPE:				
	Total Sorties	*Recon*	*Stuka*	*Bombing (Harassing)*	*Ground Attack*	*Fighter*
July 12	654	52	150	13	248	191
Night	No report					
July 13	656	50	239	60	103	204
Night	28			23 (16)		
July 14	1452	83	510	486	135	238
Night	40			36 (23)		
July 15	706	33	191	282	68	132
Night	111			105 (93)		
July 16	499	76	191	30	57	145
Night	85			73 (45)		
July 17	138					
Night	27			25 (18)		
July 18	79	39				40
Night	18			17 (6)		
July 19	92	64				28
Night	18			18 (12)		
July 20	98	84				14
Night	21			21 (15)		
July 21	85	71				14
Night	0					
July 22	74	58				16
Night	6			5		
July 23	46	42				4
Night	30			29 (23)		
July 24	127	68		45		14
Total:	16,792	1,195	5,890	3,964	1,912	2,624
4–18 July:	15,857	808	5,870	3,330***	1,912	2,534
				471 (368) Night Bombing Sorties		

*** Day bombing sorties.

 SECOND AIR ARMY SORTIE COUNT

	Total Sorties	*Recon*	*Ground Attack*	*Bombing*	*Escort*	*Cover & Intercept*	*Other*
Night	10			9			1*
July 4	149	6		143			
Night	48		48				
July 5	1,296	14	202	115	316	531	17 & 19 & 66 & 16**
Night	72			72			
July 6	823	10	237		184	392	
Night	83			83			
July 7	839	10	210		251	368	
Night	96			96			
July 8	957	40	328		114	475	
Night	60			60			
July 9	658	57	217		114	270	
Night	69			68			1*
July 10	463	32	141		81	209	
Night	57	9		48			
July 11	540	8	133		75	324	
Night	109	8		101			
July 12	769	35	220	82	147	285	
Night	156	6		150			
July 13	666	21	222	86	187	150	
Night	200	8		192			
July 14	861	14	191	145	169	241	101***
Night	151	5		146			
July 15	328	24	122		80	102	
Night	219	5		214			
July 16	723	15	143	159	253	145	8***
Night	135	10		125			
July 17	486	34	159	52	154	87	
Night	199	8		190			1*
July 18	435	9	94	93	182	57	
Summation:	11,657	388	2,619	732 1,602 night	2,307	3,779	230

* Special Assignment.

** These are 17 Il-2 missions to attack bridge crossings, 19 fighter missions to block enemy airfields, 66 Il-2 missions to attack German airfields, and 16 unidentified fighter missions.

*** Ground attack by fighters and fighter-bombers.

 SECOND AIR ARMY SORTIES BY PLANE TYPE

		U-2	*R-5*	*Il-2*	*Pe-2*	*Boston*	*La-5*	*Yak-1*	*Yak-7b*	*Yak-9*	*Medium Bomber*	*Fighter*
July 4	Number	6	4		3	3	36	14	38			
	Sorties	6	4		3	3	64	19	60			
July 5	Number	25	4	161	74	6	165	142	40			
	Sorties	44	4	285	123	6	395	372	115			
July 6	Number	27	4	110	7	3	75	88	41		1	
	Sorties	64	6	237	7	3	224	234	118		2	
July 7	Number	26	5	125	7	3	88	78	60		1	
	Sorties	73	8	210	7	3	237	206	176		2	
July 8	Number	28	4	143	10	3	79	89	34		3	
	Sorties	85	6	328	18	3	249	260	99		5	
July 9	Number	26	5	92	10	8	57	78	17		2	
	Sorties	51	5	217	19	8	165	217	32		4	
July 10	Number	24	5	66	2	3	51	51	30	10	3	
	Sorties	53	8	141	2	3	114	110	66	27	8	
July 11	Number	24	5	71	2		67	88	33	40	3	
	Sorties	45	9	133	2		126	158	53	68	3	
July 12	Number	40	4	102	82		19	83	42	80		
	Sorties	101	8	220	82		34	192	68	173		
July 13	Number	47	4	94	79	3	68					171
	Sorties	150	6	222	86	3	154					201
July 14	Number	52	3	82	99	5	56	89	22	29		
	Sorties	192	5	191	145	5	163	287	30	43		
July 15	Number	55	5	66	0	6	37	59	7	21		
	Sorties	146	5	122	0	6	50	115	14	21		
July 16	Number	58	3	86	103	5		34				167
	Sorties	214	5	143	159	5		102				314
July 17	Number	56	4	67	52	7		34			3	89
	Sorties	125	7	159	52	7		89			3	179
July 18	Number	58	6	59	84	5		48				99
	Sorties	190	9	94	93	9		98				141

SEVENTEENTH AIR ARMY SORTIE COUNT (ONLY THOSE THAT WERE IN THE BELGOROD AREA OR ATTACKED THE VIII AIR CORPS)

BY TYPE:

	Total Sorties	*Recon*	*Ground Attack*	*Bombing*	*Armed Recon/ Airfield Attack*	*Escort*	*Patrol/Airfield Cover*	*Intercept*	*Troop Cover*
Night	—								
July 4	—								
Night	—								
July 5	392		152		36	204			
Night	123	24		99					
July 6	407	24	169	36	4	174			
Night	197	19		178					
July 7	588	4	156	34	14	290			90
Night	192	26		166					
July 8	216	8	76			118			14
Night	147			121	26				
July 9	170	8	74			88			
Night	183	19		164					
July 10	61	20	17			24			
Night	149	8		141					
July 11	48	9	19			20			
Night	183	19		164					
July 12	118	3	52		8	55			
Night	164	34		130					
July 13	101	5	35			58		3	
Night	151	32		119					
July 14	141	4	57		10	70			
Night	114	17		97					
July 15	8	4	4						
Night	146	19		127					
July 16	171	4	38		36	87			6
Night	144	45		34	65				
July 17	0								
Night	58				58				
July 18	12				12				
Summation:	4,384	355	849	70 1,540 Night	269	1,188	0	3	110

The IV and V Fighter Corps continued to provide ground cover. The IV Fighter Corps sent up 128 sorties in groups of six to ten planes over Krasnyii Oktyabr, Kochetovka, and Belenikhino and four pairs of fighters reconnoitering the Belgorod-Igumenka road. The V Fighter Corps with 124 sorties sent groups of six to 12 planes over Krasnyii Oktyabr, Novoselovka, and Greznoye. They sent 15 sorties on paired reconnaissance of German tank concentrations in Belenikhino, Kochetovka, and Verkhopenye. It is clear that the Soviets were keeping a good eye and appraisal on the state and focus of the German advance. The two fighter corps lost 17 fighters this day.

The I Bomber Corps continued to stand down, as it had since the 5th. The corps, along with the 454th Bomber Regiment and the 50th Air Reconnaissance Regiment, only conducted reconnaissance flights.

The Seventeenth Air Army only flew 187 sorties this day. The I Mixed Corps sent 64 Il-2s to Razumnoye-Krutoi Log-Maslova Pristan-Solomino, escorted by 37 Yak-2s flying 68 sorties. There was very little enemy air activity in this sector, with only one engagement reported. Still, the corps lost one Il-2, and six others did not return but were assumed to have made forced landings. The III Mixed Corps hit in the same areas, Krutoi Log to Maslova Pristan to Ivanovka, but with only 10 Il-2s. They were escorted by 20 fighters, and eight fighters conducted reconnaissance. Each plane only flew one sortie this day. They lost an La-5 and an Il-2. The IX Mixed Corps remained inactive, while the III Mixed Corps' activity was minimal. Like the IX Mixed Corps the previous day, the III Mixed Corps had also been stood down. While it had not suffered as much as the IX Mixed Corps, it was also a smaller formation, having contributed on the 5th of July 45 Il-2s and 44 Yak-1s to the battle. It lost 14 Il-2s and two Yak-1s on that first day. Over the next three days it only lost nine Il-2s, three La-5s, and three Yak-1s. Its contribution on this day was minimal. This was the last day it would contribute to the Voronezh Front's defense. Its assault aircraft were probably transferred to the I Mixed Corps.

The I Mixed Corps was now carrying the burden of activity. Overall, we are now seeing a decline in the level of activity of the Soviet air, as casualties, damage, serviceability and fatigue reduced their activity. While still fully participating in the night battles, the Seventeenth Air Army was now reduced to providing support with only one of its three mixed corps.

The Germans maintained their presence at the previous levels, including 97 reconnaissance sorties and 258 fighter sorties. There were 384 bomber sorties flown in support of the III Panzer Corps, Totenkopf SS, Adolf Hitler SS, 11th Panzer and Gross Deutschland Divisions. They attacked assembly areas, battery positions and tank concentrations. The III Group of the 55th Bombardment Wing sent 21 sorties west of Verkhopenye to height +1.3, 21 sorties to Kalinovka and 13 to Zorinskiye-Dvoryi. There were 699 Stuka sorties concentrated on supporting the SS Panzer Corps and the 11th Panzer Division, while 183 ground attack plane sorties struck retreating Soviet forces in front of the SS Panzer Corps and XLVIII Panzer Corps "with good effect." The Germans suffered high losses this day, with 11 planes downed, including an Hs-129. This included 7 Me-109s lost this day, the first time since the 5th that the Germans had suffered significant fighter losses. This was in exchange for 22 Soviet fighters downed.

Guenther Rall, at this time the highest scoring ace on the Eastern Front, claimed six planes shot down between July 7 and 9, all of them La-5s. He was himself shot down on the 9th of July but managed to crash land the airplane between German and Soviet lines. He was then recovered by a tank crew of an SS armored unit.[16]

During the day the Germans launched 1,266 ground attack type sorties on the 9th compared to 291 ground attack type sorties by the Soviets. This was the last day of heavy German air presence over the battlefield, although they maintained air superiority for several more days.

16 Letter from Lt. General (ret.) Rall to Maj.Gen. (ret.) Dieter Brand and phone conversation on July 9, 1999. This shoot-down is not recorded in the Luftwaffe quartermaster files.

THE STORY OF LIEUTENANT MOISEI LVOVICH KOROBKOV

The commander of a flight of the 617th Assault Aircraft Regiment of the 219th Assault Aircraft Division of the Second Air Army.

In March 1942 I was called up to the army. I was a sportsman-gymnast, had fine health and therefore was sent to the famous Borisoglebsk School of Airmen (Voronezh region), for the Department of Assault Aircraft. In September 1942 the School was evacuated to the East, just before that we finished studying and became airmen. I took part in air battles during the Stalingrad counteroffensive, received the Orders of the Red Banner and Red Star.

In March 1943 our 219th Assault Aircraft Division was redeployed from the Seventeenth Air Army of the Southwestern Front to the Second Air Army of the Voronezh Front. Just in that time Lieutenant-General of Aviation Krasovskii became the commander of the Second Air Army.

He was my commander during the entire war, until Berlin, and during that time I grew from a pilot-lieutenant to a commander of an assault aircraft regiment, a Lieutenant Colonel. Never was wounded, though took part in combat, without any breaks, from July 1943 until the end of the War.

During the Battle of Kursk I was a commander of a flight (4 assault airplanes), a Senior Lieutenant. It is written in my flight book that from 4 July until 23 August 1943 I conducted 84 battle sorties as part of a pair, flight or squadron. When the weather was good, flights took place two to three times a day. During that time our flight damaged, hit and burned 15 enemy tanks and about 60 trucks with infantry. We took part in air battles, too, brought down 3 enemy airplanes. The hardest battles were during the enemy's offensive from 5 until 20 July 1943. Mainly I attacked tanks and infantry in trucks as the head of a flight or two flights. As a rule, we supported tank armies. In the First Tank Army and from 9–10 July in the Fifth Guards Tank Army we had two our officers with wireless radios. They called the commander of our division, Major General Vitruk, and relayed to him information from the staffs of the tank armies. After that assault airplanes appeared over the battlefield. The division commander defined the quantity of airplanes himself, taking into account our possibilities. Besides those efforts, by order of the staff of the Second Air Army, we reconnoitered and attacked trains with ammunition at the railway stations (2–3 planes, not more). Possibly, such a system of managing was not ideal because we often got contradictory orders.

I remember some successful attacks. 8 or 9 July I and the commander of the squadron, Senior Lieutenant Nikolaev, blew up a railway bridge somewhere to the south from Belgorod. During the same time, leading a group of 7 assault planes, we successfully attacked a tank column of the enemy that tried to break the defense of the First Tank Army near a highway. I remember that attack very well, because we burned a minimum of 4 tanks and because an antiaircraft shell hit my plane. Simultaneously we were attacked by 2 German fighters. But two comrades guarded us and we reached our aerodrome. I was not wounded but for the first time I thought: "Finished, I'll fall down."

I remember, too, the 12th of July. On that day our regiment, headed by the commander of the regiment, Lieutenant Colonel Kryukov, attacked German tanks in front of our tank corps (I don't remember its number) of the Fifth Guards Tank Army. We supported that corps the next day, too. The commander of our division was together with the commander of one of the tank corps and gave all orders.

Such a system was effective and therefore was used in other battles, especially at the main directions of offensives.

I remember a flight when our troops pressed the enemy to the south—it was about 20 July. My partner and I flew a free hunting mission. We found a long column of trucks with infantry. It was without antiaircraft defense—that was not typical. We attacked the column four to five times at a low height while using all of our ammunition. A lot of trucks caught fire, Germans had serious losses. But usually part of our airplanes attacked antiaircraft artillery, while another part—the main target. If enemy fighters appeared, but our fighters were absent, we formed a circle and covered each other. Our planes had two men in them—pilot and gunner. Gunners shot at German fighters. We had losses but brought down German fighters, too. In July my flight brought down 3 German fighters. At the same time, one of my pilots was brought down and perished.

I gained battle experience and bravery (without boasting) quickly enough. After the Battle of Kursk I fought until the end of the war.

After the war I served seven more years in assault aviation. After that I was an instructor in a Military School. In the middle of 1950s the half-wit Khrushchev ordered the reduction of aviation. The School was disbanded, I was retired.

I worked at an aviation factory in Kharkov. I was already married, had two sons. My wife's parents had a little house in Malakhovka (it was a "Jewish district"). In the end of 1980s the parents died, we moved here. I am 75 already. My sons in 1995 moved to Israel (with their families). Both of them are aviation constructors. I can't decide about moving to Israel. I have a lot of friends here, we meet from time to time, remember the past. Live for pension, it is enough for life.

Orders? A lot! I fought two years without any break: Order of Lenin, three of the Red Banner, one of Alexander Nevskii (received in Berlin), three of the Patriotic War; a lot of medals. Here they are, on my uniform. I put it on two years ago, when I took part in a parade of veterans.[1]

---

1 Lieutenant Colonel Moisei Lvovich Korobkov was born in 1924 in Malakhovka, Moscow Region. He is Jewish. Interview taken by Major General G. G. Nessonov in 1998.

Intensity of Combat

From 5 July through the 9th, the Germans had flown between 2,387 and 1,621 daytime sorties each day. The opposing Soviet Second and Seventeenth Air Armies had flown between 1,688 and 828 daytime sorties a day. Starting with the 10th, the rate of activity declined noticeably for the Germans, with them flying only 682 sorties on this day. Between the 10th and the 16th of July, they would fly an average of 817 daytime sorties a day compared to their average of 1,842 for the first five days of the offensive. For the Soviets there was a similar decline, as they flew an average of 714 daytime sorties a day over the next week compared to 1,269 for the first five days of the offensive. The intensity of the air war had clearly declined.

This decline in activity by the Germans was caused by the weather. The results of their transfer of aircraft to Orel would not play a major part in this decline until around the 15th.[17] This decline in activity for the Soviets was caused by the weather, their high losses, and the shifting of most of the Seventeenth Air Army away from supporting the battles around Belgorod. In the case of the Second Air Army, it continued flying sorties at about two-thirds of its previous rate. Both sides were probably affected by the general reduction in readiness and serviceability caused by the heavy action of the previous five days.

Furthermore, the balance of air support was no longer as favorable to the Germans. Instead of flying almost 50 percent more sorties than the Soviets, as they had at the start of the offensive, the Germans were now flying a roughly equal number. Still, this does not mean that the Soviets were contesting or regaining control of the skies. The Soviet loss rate per sortie continued to decline throughout this period and remained lower than it was in the first five days of the offensive. They suffered an average of 6.81 percent losses in the first five days as opposed to 3.57 percent over the next week. In contrast, German losses went up, to a daily loss average of .55 percent in the first five days, as opposed to .88 percent over the next week. In actual count of losses, the Germans lost about the same (52 aircraft from 5 to 9 July compared to 50 from 10 to 16 July). In contrast, the Soviet losses declined noticeably (456 losses from 5 to 9 July compared to 176 losses from 10 to 16 July).

This decline in losses for the Soviets appears to have primarily been caused by their more cautious and selective approach to their missions. Or, perhaps more correctly, high losses of the first five days were a result of an overly aggressive and headstrong approach that was beyond the capabilities of this force. The almost 9-to-1 exchange ratio achieved by the Germans in the first five days of the air battle was certainly attributable to the nature of the operations of the two Soviet air armies. Once they took a more cautious and cost-effective approach, the exchange of casualties declined noticeably to a 3.5-to-one exchange ratio (still very much favoring the Germans). While this was not good, it was much better. Although the overall ratio of daytime sorties was now more favorable to the Soviets, this does not seem to have been a major factor in their reduced loss rates, for the average number of fighter sorties flown by the Germans declined from 282 a day to 181 a day (64 percent) while the average number of Soviet fighter sorties declined from 826 a day to 435 a day (53 percent). So in all reality, over the course of the battle, the force ratios in the air superiority fight actually became more favorable for the Germans. This just further reinforces the point that the high Soviet casualties during the first five days of the operations were as a result of an over-aggressive approach, certainly one beyond the means of the Soviet air force, and that with a more thoughtful approach, casualties could be reduced. Obviously, the Soviet air force was not in position to achieve a favorable exchange ratio, as the differences in experience and training were too great. See Table 8.1.

17 Seidemann, page 204, complains that the combat strength of the VIII Air Corps had waned to about one-third of its original strength. This appears to be grossly incorrect.

TABLE 8.1
INTENSITY OF COMBAT

Date	Total German Daytime Sorties	Soviet Daytime Sorties	Total German Daytime Losses	Soviet Daytime Losses	German Percent Losses per Sortie	Soviet Percent Losses per Sortie
4	224	149	3	4	1.34%	2.68%
5	2,387	1,688	19	187	.80	11.08
6	1,686	1,230	7	77	.42	6.26
7	1,829	1,427	10	86	.55	6.03
8	1,686	1,173	5	60	.30	5.12
9	1,621	828	11	46	.68	5.56
10	682	524	3	25	.44	4.77
11	1,039	588	14	19	1.35	3.23
12	654	887	11	31	1.68	3.49
13	656	767	5	27	.76	3.52
14	1,452	1,002	9	30	.62	2.99
15	706	336	5	11	.71	3.27
16	499	894	3	33	.60	3.69
17	138	486	5	16	3.62	3.29
18	79	447	1	6	1.27	1.34
Total	15,338	12,426	111	658	.72	5.30

THE NIGHT ACTION continued much as before. The Germans maintained an average of 50 sorties a night while the Soviets actually increased their activity from an average of 244 sorties a night in the first five days to 297 sorties a night in the following week. This increase was as a result of more activity by the Second Air Army.

10 JULY

During the night, the 208th Night Bomber Division sent 69 sorties to the Malyie Mayachki, Luchki, Pokrovka, Ryilskii, and Krasnaya Polyana areas and reconnoitered along the Belgorod-Graivoron and Murom-Kharkov areas, and along the roads leading to the front. The Seventeenth Air Army continued its active night bombing campaign with 156 bombing sorties by the 262nd Night Bomber Division against the Donets crossings and along the Razumnoye-Belovskaya-Krutoi Log-Maslova Pristan-Solomino-Bezlyudovka sector. The 244th Bomber Division hit the same area with 24 bomber sorties by TB-3s and also conducted three reconnaissance sorties. There are no reports for the Germans for this night and because of the weather, they may not have flown.

The Second Air Army reported that the weather at night was cloudy, with rain and storms, with visibility of one to two kilometers. During the day the weather was cloudy, with visibility eight to ten kilometers. There was rain in some areas.

This was the first day that the number of sorties by the VIII Air Corps declined considerably, down to 682 for the day. According to the corps, this was because of the poor weather. As the VIII Air Corps was able to raise their sortie count noticeably on the 11th and 14th, any transfers over the last few days had apparently not hamstrung the VIII Air Corps effort. On this day, the

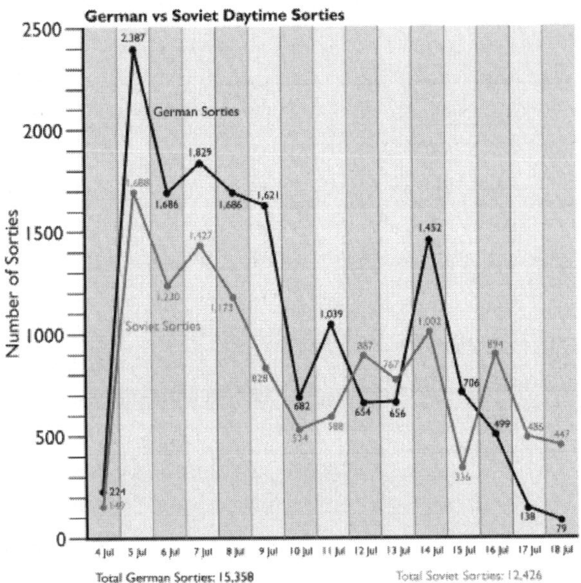
German vs Soviet Daytime Sorties
2500
2000
1500
1000
500
0
Number of Sorties
German Sorties
Soviet Sorties
2,387
1,829
1,686
1,686
1,621
1,452
1,039
682
654
656
706
499
138
79
224
1,688
1,427
1,230
1,173
828
534
588
887
767
1,002
336
894
486
447
149
4 Jul
5 Jul
6 Jul
7 Jul
8 Jul
9 Jul
10 Jul
11 Jul
12 Jul
13 Jul
14 Jul
15 Jul
16 Jul
17 Jul
18 Jul
Total German Sorties: 15,358
Total Soviet Sorties: 12,426

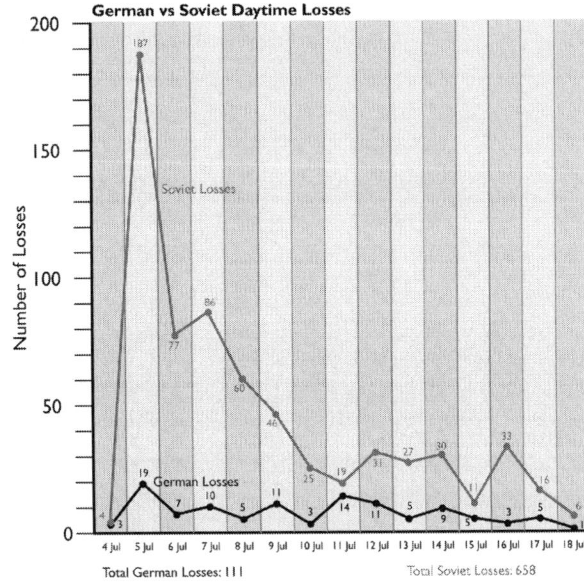
German vs Soviet Daytime Losses
200
150
100
50
0
Number of Losses
Soviet Losses
German Losses
187
77
86
60
46
25
19
31
27
30
11
33
16
6
4
3
19
7
10
5
11
3
14
11
5
9
5
3
5
1
4 Jul
5 Jul
6 Jul
7 Jul
8 Jul
9 Jul
10 Jul
11 Jul
12 Jul
13 Jul
14 Jul
15 Jul
16 Jul
17 Jul
18 Jul
Total German Losses: 111
Total Soviet Losses: 658

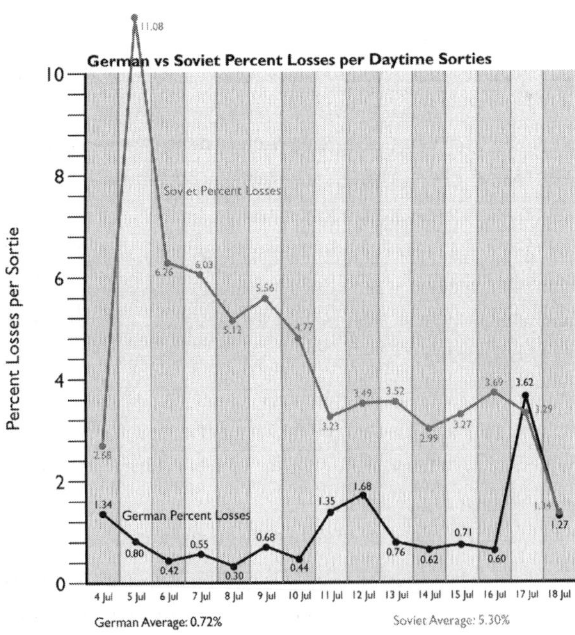
German vs Soviet Percent Losses per Daytime Sorties
10
8
6
4
2
0
Percent Losses per Sortie
Soviet Percent Losses
German Percent Losses
11.08
6.26
6.03
5.12
5.56
4.77
3.23
3.49
3.52
2.99
3.27
3.69
3.62
3.29
2.68
1.34
1.34
0.80
0.42
0.55
0.30
0.68
0.44
1.35
1.68
0.76
0.62
0.71
0.60
1.27
4 Jul
5 Jul
6 Jul
7 Jul
8 Jul
9 Jul
10 Jul
11 Jul
12 Jul
13 Jul
14 Jul
15 Jul
16 Jul
17 Jul
18 Jul
German Average: 0.72%
Soviet Average: 5.30%

XLVIII Panzer Corps received most of the air support, for German air reconnaissance had noted the large Soviet motorized and tank formations moving to the front in this area. Some support was also given to the SS and III Panzer Corps on this day, dissipating the German air strength. The III Group of the 55th Bombardment Wing limited itself to only 34 sorties this day. It struck at Staryii Gorod with 14 and Shlyakhovo with 20.

The Second Air Army continued as before. The I Assault Corps sent 83 Il-2 sorties to strike in the area of Greznoye, Komsomolets Sovkhoz, Veselyii, Krasnaya Polyana, Malyie Mayachki, Kochetovka, Verkhopenye, height 251, Sukho-Solotino, Tavrovo, and Neckuchonoye. They were escorted by 47 Yak-1 sorties. The 291st Assault Division hit the same area, Bolshiye Mayachki, Verkhopenye, Krasnaya Polyana, Gremuchii and Ilinski with 58 Il-2 sorties and escorted with 34 fighter sorties. The Il-2s and fighters of both units maintained an average of more than two sorties per plane per day. The 291st Assault Division lost another five Il-2s while the I Assault Corps lost seven Il-2s and two Yak-1bs.

The two fighter corps continued their defensive patrols, with their IV Fighter Corps in the area of Vladimirovka, Kruglik and Verkhopenye, while the V Fighter Corps patroled in Pokrovka, Kruglik, Verkhopenye, Kochetovka, Orlovka, and Zorinskiye Dvoryi. The IV Fighter Corps flew 107 sorties with five losses. One of those was claimed to be an La-5 that had rammed an Me-109! The V Fighter Corps flew 129 sorties with six losses. This corps, for the first time, showed up in battle with the new Yak-9s! It flew 27 sorties that day with ten Yak-9s. One failed to return from its mission while another was shot down in a dogfight. These were recently arriving reinforcing aircraft that had been sent into battle.

The I Bomber Corps and the 454th Bomber Regiment continued reconnaissance, as probably did the 50th Reconnaissance Regiment. The IV and V Fighter Corps' communications with the Air Force staff broke down this day.

The Seventeenth Air Army effectively ceased to contribute to the fight in the north. The I Mixed Corps again attacked the crossing over the Severnyii Donets in the Yastrebovo-Belovskaya-Bezlyudovo area with 21 Il-2 sorties and 32 fighter sorties. The operations were unusual this day, in that this produced only 17 ground attack, 12 reconnaissance and 24 escort sorties. They used four Il-2s for reconnaissance or escort duty. The planes only flew one sortie this day and had no encounters with German aircraft and no losses. The III Mixed Corps used eight fighter sorties and six fighters to reconnoiter in the Provisional Army Kempf area, without action. That was their only activity for the day. The IX Mixed Corps also flew eight sorties, covering their Velikii Burluk railroad station. They also had no encounters. The 244th Bomber Division conducted two reconnaissance sorties. For all practical purposes, the Seventeenth Air Army had ceased active participation in the daytime battle.

During the day the Germans probably launched around 500 ground-attack type sorties on the 10th compared to 158 ground-attack type sorties by the Soviets.

German "Strength"

On the 10th of July, the Soviets estimated German strength as follows:

Airfield	*Total*	*Fighters*	*Bombers*	*Unknown*
Rogan	50	10	40	
Osnovo	100	15	85	
Tolokonnoye	100	64	36	
Bessonovka	36	36		
Pomerki	30			30
Akhtyirka	6		6	
Kramatorskaya	42	20	22	
Sokolniki	75	61	14	
Total	439	206	203	30

This is intelligence data gathered from reconnaissance flights, and as such should always be viewed with considerable suspicion. It appears that at this stage in the battle, the Germans had 700 or more aircraft operational. These Soviet estimates, however, miss a number of German airfields (Mikoyanovka, Barvenkovo, Varvarovka, Urgim, Dudkovo and Golovino).

11 JULY

This night only saw 18 German sorties, including six bombing missions on the Staryii Oskol railroad station, which left lots of material burning, and eight harassing missions southeast of Belgorod. The Soviets maintained their heavy night attacks, with the 208th Night Bomber Division carrying out 57 sorties in the area of Malyie Mayachki, Luchki, and Ryilskii and the adjacent ravines. The 262nd Night Bomber Division sent 116 sorties into the area of Polyana Sovkhoz, Solomino, Ivanovka and Maslova Pristan. The 244th Bomber Division sent 33 TB-3s to hit Razumnoye-Krutoi Log-Bezlyudovka. Two of these TB-3s also struck at Rogan airfield.

The weather was not good this day. The Second Air Army reported that it was cloudy during the night and day, with intermittent rain and storms.

Although hindered by the poor weather, the Germans picked up the action today with some 1039 sorties. The bombing was again concentrated mostly in support of the Fourth Panzer Army with most of the Stukas directed to their targets (Leitverkehr or control-station traffic). The III Group of the 55th Bombardment Wing supported the III Panzer Corps with 11 sorties at Sabyinino, eight at Sheino, six at Shlyakhovo and 19 at Gostishchevo. The VIII Air Corps only flew 176 fighter sorties this day and took heavy losses, some 14 planes, including three Me-109s. The high losses were reported to be because of the poor weather. Furthermore, the Germans were unable to assess the effects of their attacks due to the poor visibility.

With this poor weather, the level of Soviet activity and losses remained low, with the Second Air Army only putting up 539 sorties this day. The Second Air Army losses were only 18 aircraft this day, including 13 fighters. The army did report 31 engagements this day but that is lower than on previous days.

The I Assault Corps sent another 49 Il-2s to fly 92 sorties against the area of Yakovlevo-Luchki (south) to Teterevino-Kalinin-Ozerovskii-Luchki (north) to Bolshiye Mayachki-Pokrovka-Krasnaya Polyana. They were escorted by 36 Yak-1s conducting 62 sorties at a cost of one Il-2 and two Yak-1s. The 291st Assault Division sent 22 Il-2s on 41 sorties to strike the area of Syirtsevo-Krasnaya Polyana-Ilinskii-Verkhopenye. They were escorted by seven fighters conducting 13 sorties. This light escort did not seem to adversely affect them, as they lost the same as the I Assault Corps.

The two fighter corps continued their patrol over their lines, with the IV Fighter Corps covering the Aleksandrovskoye-Belenikhino-Krasnyii Oktyabr area with 160 sorties while the V Fighter Corps covered the Orlovka-Kalinina-Krasnaya Polyana-Kochetovka area with 170 sorties. The IV Fighter Corps lost 10 planes this day while the V Fighter Corps lost only three.

The I Bomber Corps only flew two reconnaissance missions, while the 454th Bomber Regiment did not fly because of the weather. The Second Air Army headquarters continued to have communication problems by cable, so most of the communications during the day were by radio.

The Seventeenth Air Army continued with only the most tepid support during the day. The I Mixed Corps attacked the Krutoi Log and Polyana Sovkhoz areas with 19 Il-2s escorted by 20 Yak-1s. One of the Il-2s and eight of the Yak-1s also flew reconnaissance sorties in the area of Solovyev Kolkhoz-Batratskaya Dacha and Myasoyedovo. The rest of the Seventeenth Air Army operations were out of the battlefield area.

Seidemann claimed in 1947 that "the Soviet air force began to take an increasing part in the fight. The German advance had considerably shortened the length of the approach run Soviet formations had to make in order to get to the front lines. The German fighters were no longer able to sweep the skies of Soviet aircraft at all times. For this reason, the VIII Air Corps began to move its fighter and ground attack formations forward into the area southwest of Prokhorovka. Two air fields were prepared north of Luchki, but there was no chance to occupy these however."[18]

During the day the Germans launched 801 ground-attack type sorties on the 11th compared to 152 ground-attack type sorties by the Soviets.

---

18 Seidemann, pages 205–206.

 FIRST COMBAT

Lt. Semen Isaakovich Gurvich saw his first combat at Kursk with the 226th Guards Assault Aviation Regiment, 4th Guards Assault Aviation Division:[1]

In March 1943 after I graduated from the Military Aviation School, I was sent to the division of Major General G. Baidukov of the Fifth Air Army. Baidukov was a famous pilot who made a non-stop flight to America with V. Chkalov. My first baptism under fire was in the defensive fighting to the east of Belgorod. Starting from the 5th of July 1943, I flew two to three times a day, as a part of the squadron or sometimes as a part of the regiment, to assault the enemy tanks trying to get to the north towards Kursk. I don't want to brag, I did not have much experience and I was a bit scared. We were fighting enemy fighters every single day. I quickly learned the tactics of mutual aid of our wonderful Il-2s. The Germans called them "black death." My cabin was armored in the back, where German fighters were usually shooting. Soon I learned antiaircraft maneuvers and I felt braver to fly lower and bomb and fire from the lower altitude, which increase the accuracy. I did not like it when some pilots would brag "I have destroyed two German tanks," "I got three tanks." We were bombing the enemy tanks by flying two to four times over them. Sometimes entire squadrons or the regiment was firing. The tanks were on fire, but it was impossible to say who exactly set a tank on fire. When you are bombing in a flight, it was not possible to say who destroyed what.

Approximately on the 10th of July, I was in one of four Il-2s attacking an enemy artillery battalion. I could clearly see that my missiles destroyed one and then another gun, but you don't want to celebrate too quickly during combat. Mortal danger is lying in wait for you every minute. My plane was hit by a shell. Two "Messers" literally attacked me hoping to finish me. My bravery saved me. I flew directly at the front of one plane. The German pilot could not stand it and dodged up. I started a steady fire with bullets and shells. He fell down like a rock. The second plane flew around me at my tail. I heard one shell penetrate into the body. I could smell smoke. I thought to myself "This is the end." I wanted to live. I quickly dropped altitude, flew very low, just above the ground, then above the woods and then turned. The German pilot probably thought that he had destroyed me and turned away. My colleagues went back to the airport but did not say that I was shot down. It was a tradition to wait until the last minute. Even though my plane was damaged, I managed to fly to another airport and landed. They immediately called my commander to let him know where I was. The commander sent a car for me and sent two technicians. They worked for two days almost without any rest and fixed my Il-2. I flew back to my regiment. Starting from the 12th of July, I made at least three flights a day as part of the squadron supporting the offensive of our tanks. There was very heavy fighting. When I looked down, I could observe literally a sea of fire, but our tanks kept moving forward. We supported them well.

I had more air combats. The successful offensive was inspiring me. I gained more experience. We reached Kharkov more than a month later. I made more than 100 combat flights during this time. I made over 200 combat flights over the course of the year. I was awarded the Hero of the Soviet Union in July 1944 for these flights and for the damage caused to the enemy. Before we got to Berlin, I made the same amount of combat flights.

1 Col. Semen Isaakovich Gurvich was interviewed 16 December 1998 by Col. Fyodor Sverdov. In addition to Hero of the Soviet Union, he was awarded four Orders of the Red Banner, two first degree Orders of the Great Patriotic War and two Orders of the Red Star. His family, parents, wife and son, were killed during the war in Rostov-on-the-Don.

12 July

The night leading up to the famous Battle of Prokhorovka was unexceptional. The Germans flew 61 sorties. This included the nightly attack on the rail, now done by seven bomber sorties. They attacked the Staryii Oskol railroad station, which they claimed was left burning and the rails were broken. They also flew 49 harassing bomber sorties against villages and vehicle traffic in the Koren River area.

The Soviets continued their night bombing activity as before, with the 208th Bomber Division bombing the area of Pokrovka-Gremuchii-Bolshiye Mayachki-Yakovlevo-Dubovoye-Pogorelovka-Malyie Mayachki-Ryilskii-Krasnaya Polyana-Luchki (north) and the adjacent ravines, with 109 U-2 sorties while conducting reconnaissance with eight R-5 sorties. The 262nd Night Bomber Division attacked in the area of Belovskaya, Razumnoye, Krutoi Log and Maslova Pristan as well as the river crossings along the Solomino-Bezlyudovka area. This totaled another 140 U-2 bombing sorties and 16 R-5 reconnaissance sorties. They continued to be assisted by the 244th Bomber Division, which hit the Verkhnyii Olshanets-Razumnoye-Kazachye area with 24 TB-3 bombing sorties. As they did the previous night, they also flew three reconnaissance sorties.

The Second Air Army reported that the weather was cloudy at night with intermittent rain, and visibility of six to ten kilometers. It was also cloudy during the day, with visibility of four to ten kilometers, and rain.

During the day, the Germans flew only 654 sorties. They were only able to fly 13 bomber sorties because of the weather. Instead, their air support was provided by only 150 Stuka sorties and 248 ground attack sorties. This was the lowest level of air support that the Germans had provided to the army since the start of the offensive. This, on the day of the highest drama! This effort was capped with only 191 fighter sorties and again the Germans took heavy losses, 11 aircraft, although the records do not record the losses by type.

The Soviet air was still active this day, although most of the strikes occurred well behind the front line. The I Assault Corps launched massed strikes with Il-2s in the Yakovlevo-Luchki (south)-Kalinin-Malyie Mayachki-Veselyii-Sukho-Solotino-Krasnaya Polyana-Pokrovka-Shlyakhovo-Melekhovo-Verkhnyaya Olshanka area. They sent up 72 Il-2s to conduct 142 sorties and 38 Yak-1s to provide 101 escort sorties. This increased effort was at a cost of eight Il-2s and a Yak-1. The 291st Assault Division attacked the area of Pokrovka-Yakovlevo-Bolshiye Mayachki-Luchki-Verkhopenye-Syirtsevo-Dmitrievka-Novo-Cherkasskoye-and the woods south of Dubrava-Lukhanino-Gremuchii. They sent up 30 Il-2s to conduct 78 sorties and 16 Yak-1s to provide 46 escort sorties. This was at a cost of four Il-2s.

The two fighter corps continued patrolling, with the IV Fighter Corps covering the Aleksandrovskoye-Leski-Vasilyevka area with 157 sorties. The IV Fighter Corps now had 40 Yak-9s flying. The V Fighter Corps covered the Voznesenovka-Ivnya-Fedchevka-Kruglik-Prokhorovka-Vasilyevka-Belenikhino-Maloye Yablonovo area with 163 sorties. It also had 40 Yak-9s flying. This put both of the fighter corps over the tank fields of Prokhorovka. Although the Soviet close-air support aircraft were not reported in this area, both the Totenkopf and Das Reich SS Divisions reported Soviet bombing and strafing attacks (see Chapter Nine) and the shooting down of an Il-2 and a Martin (Boston?). Still, the level of air combat activity on this day was low, with the IV Fighter Corps reporting only three engagements and three losses. Of those, one was due to antiaircraft. The V Fighter Corps reported only 11 engagements, with a loss of nine planes, including two Yak-9s.

Finally, after a six-day hiatus, the Second Air Army felt it was safe to sally forth with their Pe-2s again. The I Bomber Corps flew 82 sorties in groups of nine to 26 Pe-2s. These were escorted by the fighters from the IV and V Air Corps. Due to the weather, 14 of the Pe-2s were not able to locate their escorts and so aborted, returning to their airfields with full bomb loads. The weather also affected the 454th Bomber Regiment, which did not send up any sorties this day. The remaining Pe-2s struck the Germans in the area of Bolshiye Mayachki-Pokrovka-Yakovlevo-the woods two to four kilometers east of Yakovlevo. Considering the large number of significant targets on the battlefield, this rear area strike was of limited value to the immediate battlefield. This same tendency appears with the Il-2 strikes. Even though they were ground attack planes, one notices that the areas they were attacking were consistently well to the rear of the front line. As such, it is clear that the Soviet air, unlike the VIII Air Corps, was not conducting close air support. Thus, the use of Soviet air in the Battle of Kursk was more for harassment and attrition. What it did not do, which the German did well, was concentrate on the critical points on the battlefield, in conjunction with the armor and artillery, so as to be able to suppress and take areas with minimal casualties.

The Second Air Army was only supported by the I Mixed Corps during the day. They sent 52 Il-2s on 52 sorties to Verkhnyii Olshanets, Novoye Oskochnoye, Kazachye, Razumnoye, Krutoi Log and the crossings over the Severnyii Donets around the Nizhnyii Olshanets-Solomino area. They also flew 54 Yak-1s to provide 55 escort sorties, eight armed reconnaissance sorties, and three reconnaissance. They lost three Il-2s.

The Second Air Army continued to have communication problems. For the second day in a row it reported that its headquarters and the 208th Night Bomber Division had no cable communications. The day before that (the 10th), the IV and V Fighter Corps had no connections with the staff. The main means of communication between the subordinate units and the headquarters was by radio. They also were using the 272nd Independent Communications Squadron to deliver messages for the army air staff. The Second Air Army would continue to have communications problems on the following days, reporting problems through the 15th and on the 17th, and with minor breaks on the 18th.

Overall, the Soviets lost 30 planes this day, while the Germans claimed only 16 kills. One is left with the impression that the area over the Fifth Guards Tank Army's attack was not seriously contested. Both sides are reported to have flown in that area, with the Fifth Guards Tank Army counting some 1,500 German sorties. The Fifth Guards Army was vocal about its lack of air support (again, see Chapter Nine). It does not appear that the Soviets provided much direct air support for their attack, but that the German air was in operation for the defense. Instead the I Assault Corps and 291st Assault Division concentrated on the rear areas of the two attacking panzer corps.

During the day the Germans launched 411 ground-attack type sorties on the 12th, compared to 354 ground-attack type sorties by the Soviets. This was the lowest level of support provided by the VIII Air Corps since the start of the offensive and considerably lower than the daily average of 1,478 ground-attack type sorties provided in the first five days of the attack. On the other hand, after two days of limited support, the Soviet air forces were making their presence felt again at almost the same level they provided in the first four days of the German offensive. Overall, the influence of air on the fighting this day was low, certainly lower than it had been during the first four days of the offensive. Much of this was due to the weather. It clearly suppressed the German operations and the degree of close air support. It also reduced the Soviet ground attacks. It also appears to have dampened the intensity of the air combat. The plane losses for both sides during this day appear to have been from weather and antiaircraft, with limited losses due to air combat.

The Yak-9

This day is noted for the first extensive appearance of the Yak-9 over the battlefield during the Battle of Kursk. The appearance of this plane, whose cockpit resembled the Fw-190, almost cost Guenther Rall his life. As he tells it:[19]

> On July 12th I went up for a free chase with my adjutant late in the afternoon. The sun stood in the west, a humongous cumulus cloud rose up in the east, which was drenched in glowing red sunlight. We flew at an

19 Letter from Lt. General (ret.) Rall to Maj.Gen. (ret.) Dieter Brand and phone conversation on 9 July 1999. This accident is also not recorded in the Luftwaffe quartermaster files.

altitude of about 4500 meters (15,000 feet) so that I did not notice what went on in terms of intense fighting on the ground that day. I then noticed two dots in front of the glowing red cloud. We attacked immediately, having the sun in our rear. Upon approaching I became unsure whether these were really enemy planes or whether they could be two of the newly commissioned Fw-190 chase planes. I was aware that a squadron with that new type had been sent to the front for *Citadel*, but I had never seen this airplane before. So I pulled up just before the other airplanes in a turn, and that is where I saw the red star on the wing. I immediately commenced the attack, and—coming from the side—I flew directly towards one of the enemy airplanes. Then occurred what is termed a "mid air collision." While my propeller cut off the enemy's wing, his propeller slit my plane open from underneath. The enemy plane immediately fell out of the sky, while I was able to retain lift. The damaged propeller and the hull that was slit open was causing such severe vibrations, though, that I felt the engine would be torn out of the airplane any minute. But I managed to get behind my own lines where I made another crash landing.

13 July

There is no German report for this night. Seidemann claimed that nighttime reconnaissance again showed heavy traffic on the roads to the battle area from Kursk and Staryii Oskol.

The 208th Night Bomber Division flew 156 sorties, bombing the Germans in the area of Olkhovka, Melekhovo, Dalnyaya Igumenka, Verkhnyii Olshanets, Shlyakhovo, Olkhovatka, Byikovo, and Vorskla. The 262nd Night Bomber Division, with 39 U-2s flying 100 sorties, hit the area of Belgorod, Belovskaya, Mikhailovka, Razumnoye, Krutoi Log and Maslova Pristan. Two U-2s and eight R-5s flew 30 reconnaissance missions. The 244th Bomber Division with 13 TB-3s flying 26 sorties attacked Maslova Pristan-Solomino-Bezlyudovka while four TB-3s flying eight sorties performed reconnaissance.

The Second Air Army reported the weather at night as cloudy, but clearing towards the morning, with rain in places. Visibility was four to ten kilometers. It was cloudy during the day, with light rain in places and visibility six to ten kilometers.

The VIII Air Corps sent up 656 sorties today despite inclement weather. There were again only limited (60 sorties) bombing attacks. These included 28 from the III Group of the 55th Bombardment Wing, which sent 22 of them to Veselyii. This unit suffered its first losses for the battle when two He-111s collided with each other in the clouds over the airfield. While two crew members were able to parachute out of one of the stricken planes and save themselves, the two planes and the other eight crew members went down. The VIII Air Corps reported losing two He-111s this day on their own side of the lines. The VIII Air Corps provided Stuka support to the III and XLVIII Panzer Corps with 239 sorties. Seidemann noted the participation in the XLVIII Panzer Corps battles on this day. It was here that the value of the air liaison officers attached to the panzer divisions was again demonstrated. Still, the Luftwaffe was unable to have these officers accompany all divisions, riding in tanks or armored halftracks. Their cumbersome SdKfz 305s (a special purpose 3-ton Opel Blitz truck) were frequently unable to follow the attacking units. Whenever the liaison officer rode with the unit commander in his command tank, however, it was possible to direct German air attack to the most dangerous targets.

The German ground attack planes also flew 103 sorties, attacking strong points and Soviet attack groups in front of the XLVIII Panzer Corps and SS Panzer Corps. Because of the thick clouds and poor visibility, the results could be observed for only a few attacks. Still, they claimed 25 Soviet tanks destroyed this day.

Seidemann reported that at this stage the operational strength of flying formations remained at about two-thirds of reported morning strength. He claimed the Soviet air operated primarily over Prokhorovka and the sector south of Oboyan.

The Soviet I Assault Corps continued to strike behind the front line with 163 sorties striking at Pokrovka-Yakovlevo-Luchki-Bolshiye Mayachki-Malyie Mayachki-Krasnaya Polyana and in the Shlyakhovo-Melekhovo-Dalnyaya Igumenka-Verkhnyii Olshanets area. They were escorts by 112 Yak-1 sorties. The 291st Assault Division sent 59 Il-2 sorties against Greznoye, height 255, Malyie Mayachki, Luchki, Bolshiye Mayachki and northwest of Ozerovskii. They were supported by 42 escort sorties.

The IV Fighter Corps covered the area of Aleksandrovka-Belenikhino-Vasilyevka-Maloye Yablonovo with 61 sorties, and provided 41 sorties for escorts of the Pe-2s in the Prokhorovka-Vasilyevka-Belenikhino-Maloye Yablonovo area. They also conducted six reconnaissance missions. The V Fighter Corps covered the area of Aleksandrovskii-Vasilyevka-Belenikhino-Maloye Yablonovo with 89 sorties and sent out four reconnaissance sorties.

The I Bomber Corps flew 86 sorties, bombing Verkhnyii Olshanets and Shlyakhovo-Melekhovo and conducting some armed reconnaissance missions with single planes. They lost two Pe-2s this day when they crashed into each other over the Ilovskoye airfield. Both planes burned and their crews died. The dangers of flying in difficult weather were demonstrated this day with both the Germans and Soviet bombers suffering similar types of accidents. The 454th Bomber Regiment sent three Bostons on reconnaissance missions but ended the missions early due to the weather. They lost one Boston.

The I Mixed Corps continued attacking in the Seventh Guards Army area, sending 35 Il-2s to strike at Novo-Oskochnoye, Verkhnyii Olshanets and Kazachye. The corps had 37 fighters conduct 58 escort sorties, five reconnaissance sorties and three interception sorties. They had one Il-2 fail to return.

During the day the Germans launched 402 ground attack type sorties on the 13th compared to 343 ground attack type sorties by the Soviets.

14 July

During the night, the VIII Air Corps sent up another 28 sorties, including seven bombers to the railroad station at south Kastornoye and 16 harassing sorties in the Koren and Korocha area.

The Soviets continued to make good use of the night, with the 208th Night Bomber Division sending out 102 bombing sorties and five reconnaissance sorties. The U-2s bombed Kazachye-Shlyakhovo-Olkhovka-Verkhnyii Olshanets-Novo-Oskochnoye-Raevka-Dalnyaya Igumenka-Melekhovo. The 464th Bomber Regiment also flew three of their Bostons that night to reconnoiter and look for the arrival of German reserves. The 262nd Night Bomber Division again bombed the area of Razumnoye-Krutoi Log-Maslova Pristan with 107 U-2 bombing sorties and also conducted 30 reconnaissance sorties. They flew 40 U-2s and 8 R-5s this night. The 244th Bomber Division again attacked in the area of Razumnoye-Krutoi Log and the Donets crossing in the Maslova Pristan-Solomino sector. Twelve TB-3s bombed while two others reconnoitered.

The Second Air Army reported the weather as cloudy at night, with visibility up to three kilometers. During the second half of the night, it was cloudy in the area northeast of Belgorod, with thunderstorms in places. During the day there were brief rains, with visibility up to ten kilometers.

The VIII Air Corps ratcheted up the intensity this day. Seidemann noted that while he received orders on this day discontinuing the offensive, it did not mean an end to the VIII Air Corps actions. They flew some 1,452 sorties this day, the highest level of activity since the 9th. In the late morning, they sent strong bomber units to strike in front of the Gross Deutschland. In the afternoon, they changed the focus of these attacks to the Totenkopf and Das Reich SS Divisions. They flew 486 bomber missions this day. The III Group, 55th Bombardment Wing flew 58 sorties, sending 21 to Avdeyevka and 37 to around Veselyii. Rolling attacks by Stukas were used to try to break the Soviet resistance in front of Gross Deutschland, Das Reich and III Panzer Corps. These 510 Stuka attacks were claimed to have opened the way for the ground troops and resulted in heavy losses in men and material. There were 135 ground-attack sorties used to continually support the attacking spearheads and cover

THE AIR IN THE NORTH

Supporting the Ninth Army attack on the north side of the Kursk bulge was the Sixth Air Fleet, consisting of the 1st Air Division, the 12th Flak Division and the 10th Flak Brigade. Reporting directly to the Sixth Air Fleet was a night fighter group and a long range reconnaissance group. The 1st Air Division, under command of Major General Paul Deichmann, also had three short-range reconnaissance groups reporting to it.

Under the 1st Air Division were a total of ten wings. They had three Bombardment Wings each of three groups (total of nine groups). There were two night bomber squadrons. There were three Fighter Wings with a total of eight groups and one squadron. There were three Ground Attack Wings, with five to seven groups, and four additional tank hunting squadrons. Finally there was a "destroyer" (Me-110) wing of three groups.[1]

Overall, this amounted to around 730 planes.[2] On the first day of the Battle of Kursk, this force was able to fly 2,088 sorties. Its rate of sorties declined in the following days, and it averaged 1,073.5 flights a day. From the 5th through the 15th, inclusive, the force flew a total of 12,823 sorties, which was 89 percent of the number flown in the same time period by the VIII Air Corps. But as the VIII Air Corps was being stripped of air units after the 9th, then perhaps the most useful comparison of relative air support is best measured by comparing the number of sorties from the 5th through the 9th. In that case, the Sixth Air Fleet flew 6,848 sorties while the VIII Air Corps flew 9,209, which is some 74 percent of what the VIII Air Corps flew. Even this does not fully state the difference in air support levels. The VIII Air Corps was literally flying only half the reconnaissance missions that the Sixth Air Fleet was flying, and flew about the same number of fighter missions. If one just compares the number of Stuka missions, bomber missions and "hunting" missions, which are the ground attack missions, then one discovers that the Sixth Air Fleet flew a total of 4,278 ground attack sorties while the VIII Air Corps flew 7,047 from the 5th through the 9th. This puts the Sixth Air Fleet flying only 61 percent of the ground attack type missions that were flown by the VIII Air Corps.

The antiaircraft units attached to the Sixth Air Fleet consisted of the 12th Flak Division with three regiments and the 10th Flak Brigade with five or six flak battalions and two searchlight batteries.

Opposite them was the Soviet Sixteenth Air Army that was attached to the Central Front. Around the rest of the Orel bulge was the Fifteenth Air Army (Bryansk Front) and the First Air Army (Western Front). Without looking into the records and details of their operations, it is difficult to determine how much opposition the Sixth Air Fleet faced. It certainly was fully engaged with the Soviet Sixteenth Air Army (Central Front) during *Operation Citadel*. The degree that the First Air Army (Western Front) and the Fifteenth Air Army (Bryansk Front) were involved was certainly much less. For example, the Sixth Air Fleet's losses from the 5th through the 11th were recorded as 33 airplanes over the seven days, never losing more than seven planes a day (compared to 69 planes lost by the VIII Air Corps in the same period). Starting with the 12th, the Sixth Air Fleet's losses went up precipitously, to 61 airplanes over the next four days (compared to 30 planes lost by the VIII Air Corps in the same period). These losses were certainly due to the initiating offensives by the Western and Bryansk Fronts on the north face of the Orel bulge, and their supporting air operations. The Sixth Air Fleet was not only responsible for supporting the Ninth Army, but also the Second Army and the Second Panzer Army. On the 12th, the Second Panzer Army came under attack by the Soviet Western and Bryansk Fronts as part of the Soviet counterstoke. In contrast, German air losses in the south declined after the 12th of July.

1 The Sixth Air Fleet order of battle was drawn from Klink, page 335, and has not been cross-checked.

2 Hooten, page 195.

the troops. There were 238 fighter sorties this day, but it does not appear that the German Air Force was seriously contested. Even though they lost nine planes this day, three were to flak and one to a bomb explosion. There were only three Me-109s lost this day. It also does not appear that the Germans were seriously contesting the Soviet airspace, for the Soviets were able to fly Pe-2 sorties throughout the day with relative impunity.

The Second Air Army recorded its highest level of activity since the 5th, and the highest daytime activity since the 8th. The I Assault Corps launched another 124 Il-2 sorties in the area of Kazachye-Verkhnyii Olshanets-Novo-Oskochnoye-Shlyakhovo-Melekhovo and in the area of Lukhanino-Berezovka-Butovo-Rakovo-Cherkasskoye-Syirtsevo. These last locales were clearly to the rear and attacks there would have had little direct influence on the fighting, unlike the German Stuka strikes around Tolstoye Woods. These planes were escorted by 40 Yak-1s which flew 199 sorties this day. The 291st Assault Division flew 67 Il-2 sorties to Novo-Oskochnoye-Verkhnyii Olshanets and to the Syirtsevo-Lukhanino-Gremuchii area. They were escorted by 41 fighter sorties.

The IV Fighter Corps patrolled the area of Bogoroditskoye-Pravorot-Shakhovo and escorted the planes from the I Bomber Corps. They launched 209 sorties this day. The V Fighter Corps patrolled the area of Bogoroditskoye-Belenikhino-Shakhovo-Pravorot and the area of Vladimirovka-Verkhopenye-Berezovka-Kruglik with 154 sorties.

The I Bomber Corps, in groups of 9 to 18 Pe-2s, bombed in the Verkhnyii Olshanets-Novo Oskochnoye-Kazatskoye area and the Syirtsevo-Lukhanino-Dubrovo area. A total of 99 Pe-2s flew 145 sorties. This major bombing effort resulted in the loss of four of them, three due to antiaircraft fire.

The I Mixed Corps attacked the Germans in the Kazachye-Novo Oskochnoye-Verkhnyii Olshanets area with 57 Il-2 sorties by 47 Il-2s. The corps' 49 active fighters flew 70 escort missions, 10 armed reconnaissance and four reconnaissance missions. They lost three Il-2s and three Yak-1s.

This increase in activity by both sides did not see a corresponding increase in losses. The Germans lost nine planes this day, of which only five could have been due to aerial combat. The Second Air Army lost 20 planes this day. This included six planes lost to antiaircraft fire. Loss rates remained low for both sides on this day and it appears that the two sides were managing to attack each other's ground forces without too much conflict in the air.

During the day the Germans launched 1,131 ground attack type sorties on the 14th compared to 401 ground attack type sorties by the Soviets.

The Big Transfer (15–17 July)

Sometime around the 14th or just after, the VIII Air Corps was again called on to shift more forces up to the north. At this point, not only had the Ninth Army's attack failed, but the Second Panzer Army was becoming unhinged by the incessant Soviet attacks on the north side of the Orel bulge. Major formations were now shifted north to cover this critical situation. This resulted in the VIII Air Corps being stripped of the 52nd Fighter Wing, 1st Ground Attack Wing, the five Hs-129 squadrons, the 2nd Stuka Wing (starting the 12th?), the 77th Stuka Wing, and possibly several bombardment groups of the 27th and 55th Bombardment Wings.[20] This was at about the limit of what Sixth Air Fleet could accommodate and service, so the remaining

---

20 Seidemann claims that the VIII Air Corps was stripped of another one or two fighter groups, the three groups of the 77th Ground Attack Wing, Rudel's Antitank Group, and several bombardment groups of the 27th and 55th Bombardment Wings, in addition to claiming around the 7th of July that they had transferred the 3rd Fighter Wing, the 2nd Stuka Wing, the 3rd Bombardment Wing and the Hs-129s. According to Hooten, page 196, Col. Helmut Bruck's 77th Stuka Wing was transferred to the 1st Air Division in the north on the 16th of July.

The VIII Air Corps flew no Stuka sorties from the 17th through the 24th, flew no ground attack sorties from the 18th of July through the 3rd of August, no bomber sorties from the 18th through the 23rd, and less than 30 fighter sorties a day from the 19th through the 24th.

formations stayed with the VIII Air Corps. This left primarily the Hungarians to provide air support at Kursk.

This transfer probably involved 500 or more planes, reducing the VIII Air Corps to below 500 planes, or less than half of its initial strength. Air losses from the 4th through the 14th had been at least 97 aircraft.

The VIII Air Corps maintained a healthy 1,452 sorties on the 14th, so it is expected that most of the transfers occurred the following day, when the air corps reported only 706 sorties. At that point, the ability of the VIII Air Corps to maintain air superiority was severely compromised.

15 July

The VIII Air Corps flew 40 sorties this night, having now sent 13 bomber sorties to the Staryii Oskol station and the unloading point at Stretenka (15 kilometers due west of Staryii Oskol). They report train cars and station buildings set on fire. There were also 23 harassing sorties in the Koren and Korocha areas.

The 208th Night Bomber Division attacked the German forces in Komsomolskii, height 255, Yasnaya Polyana, Ozerovskii, Teterevino, the woods west of Belenikhino, Verkhnyii Olshanets, Olkhovatka, Raevka, Kazachye, Rzhavets, Novo-Oskochnoye, Shlyakhovo, and Melekhovo. The 262nd Night Bomber Division hit the area of Razumnoye-Krutoi Log-Maslova Pristan-Solomino. There were 40 U-2s that flew 77 bombing sorties and eight R-5s that flew 15 sorties. The 244th Bomber Division attacked the area of Razumnoye-Maslova Pristan-Krutoi Log-Solomino and reconnoitered. There were 14 TB-3s which flew 20 bombing sorties and two reconnaissance sorties.

The Second Air Army reported that it was cloudy at night with rain and thunderstorms in places, with visibility of one to three kilometers. It was cloudy during the day, with rain and visibility of two to three kilometers.

During the day, the VIII Air Corps flew 706 sorties, which was half of what they had done the previous day. This much lower level of effort included only 132 fighter sorties. There were still a significant number of bomber sorties—282—flown this day. This serious commitment of the entire bomber and dive bomber force, as well as continuing ground attack aircraft support, was focused in the Donets triangle, where the spearheads of the Das Reich SS Division and the III Panzer Corps were converging. In the case of the III Group, 55th Bombardment Wing, they only flew their sorties in the afternoon, with 19 near Marino and Prokhorovka and the other 19 completely outside the Belgorod area. The German air was also used to cover the flank of this movement from strong Soviet tank forces coming from the north (possibly the V Guards Mechanized Corps).

For the first time since the start of the offensive, the German air effort was diverted from the Kursk battles, possibly with the entire bomber force and two close assault groups sent against villages and railroad stations in the Izyum area and striking at the Soviet preparations area. They claim these raids caused heavy losses in Soviet personnel and material. At this point, with possibly over 200 bombers still on-hand, it is estimated that such a raid resulted in at least 100 bombing sorties and at least 40 assault sorties heading south to deal with the latest developing threat from the Soviet Army.[21]

The Second Air Army effort was noticeably reduced because of the weather (as was probably also the case with the German VIII Air Corps). The I Assault Corps was not very active because of the weather. They still managed to send up 46 Il-2s on 97 sorties along with 39 Yak-1s for 65 sorties. This attack struck at Pokrovka-Tomarovka-Shepelevka-Leski-Kalinina-Lukhanino area and the Belenikhino-Leski-Kalinina-Ivanovka-Greznoye area. They lost four Il-2s and two Yak-1s this day. The 291st Assault Division sent up 320 Il-2s on 25 ground attack sorties and 10 Yak-1s on 18 escort sorties. They also suffered the loss of four Il-2s.

The IV Fighter Corps from 0600 to 1600 (Moscow time) covered the area from Aleksandrovka-Pravorot

21 We note that the only unit record we have, the III/55th Bombardment Wing, sent half of their flights to the Kursk battlefield and half to the Izyum area. Obviously the "entire bombing force" did not strike in the Izyum area. There were 282 bombing sorties that day.

and from 1600–2300 (Moscow time) covered the area from Pravorot to Shakhovo. In all, 37 planes flew 58 sorties. They were not heavily engaged, reporting only one engagement and no losses. The V Fighter Corps also covered troops, with 52 planes flying 59 sorties, with also little activity, reporting only six engagements and the loss of only a single Yak-9.

Because of the weather, the I Bomber Corps did not conduct any missions, but the 454th Bomber Regiment sent six Bostons to reconnoiter as far as the line from Tomarovka to Belgorod, also dropping bombs.

The I Mixed Corps conducted almost no operations this day due to the poor weather, including rain and low cloud cover. It sent four Il-2s to attack Kazachye-Novo-Oskochnoye-Verkhnyii Olshanets area and four fighters to conduct meteorological reconnaissance. It reported two engagements, but no losses.

During the day the Germans launched 541 ground attack type sorties on the 15th compared to 126 ground attack type sorties by the Soviets. Still, 150 to maybe more than 300 of these German ground attack type sorties may have been outside the battle area. The weather also clearly played its part in reducing the level of activity of both air forces.

16 July

The 16th of July was also a quiet day in the air, but not nearly as quiet as on the ground. The German night air activity increased considerably, with 111 sorties flown. Twelve bombing sorties struck at Kupyansk railroad station (a little over 100 kilometers east southeast of Kharkov) while 93 harassing sorties struck at Malinovka, Gavrilovka and Andreyevka. All of this was now well out of the Kursk battlefield area and again focused on the developing threats in the south. The 111 sorties flown this night were the highest recorded night activity for the VIII Air Corps since the offensive began.

During the night, the 208th Night Bomber Division again attacked Belenikhino, Yasnaya Polyana, Kalinin, Ozerovskii, Luchki (north), Kazachye, Kurakovka, Novo-Oskochnoye, Verkhnyii Olshanets, Vyipolzovka and Rzhavets. It conducted a rather hefty 214 sorties with 58 U-2s and five sorties with three R-5s. The 262nd Night Bomber Division was also active, with 42 U-2s launching 100 bombing sorties in the area of Novo-Oskochnoye-Verkhnyii Olshanets-Dalnyaya Igumenka and seven R-5s flying 16 reconnaissance missions. The 244th Bomber Division also attacked the area of Verkhnyii Olshanets and Blizhnyaya Igumenka with 12 TB-3s and 27 bombing sorties while two TB-3s flew three reconnaissance sorties.

This day was the last day of any significant air activity in support of the German attack on Kursk. The VIII Air Corps flew 499 sorties during the day, including 191 Stuka sorties. It attacked Soviet tanks and assembly areas in front of the Fourth Panzer Army. The corps only flew 145 fighter sorties this day, complaining that with their depleted numbers, the air corps could no longer completely defend against enemy air attacks, even though the Stuka attacks were restricted to the morning and evening hours. The German fighters escorted the Stukas and conducted free-hunting missions. The VIII Air Corps bomber units were now committed to action in the south with the IV Air Corps. As such, the VIII Air Corps only reported 30 bombing sorties for this day. The III Group, 55th Bombardment Wing recorded 55 sorties this day, including 19 sorties to Krasnyii Oskol. The rest were out of the Belgorod area. These were the last sorties they did in support of this operation. The following day, the entire unit was operating out of Stalino, far to the south.

During the day, Soviet assault aircraft continued to work over the battlefield, with the I Assault Corps flying 104 ground attack sorties with 47 Il-2s and 102 escort sorties with 34 Yak-1s. They attacked Belenikhino, Ozerovkskii, Ivanovka, Leski, Shakhovo, Verkhopenye, Syirtsevo, Berezovka and Rakovo. The 291st Assault Division hit the woods east of Leski, the ravines west of Maloye Yablonovo,[22] Maloye Yablonovo, the Yamnoye-Gridin-Shakhovo road, Shakhovo and the ravines to the west of Shakhovo, the woods and the ravines southeast

22 Almost certainly "log Sukhaya Plota."

of Krasnyii Uzliv, and the woods northeast of Chapayev. This was done with 39 Il-2 sorties and 34 sorties from the escorting fighters.

The I Bomber Corps was again active after a two-day hiatus, with 103 Pe-2s launching 159 bombing sorties at Belenikhino, Kalinin, Ivanovka, Ozerovskii, Byikovka, Streletskoye, Krasnyii Uzliv and Chapayev. This was a bloody series of missions which resulted in the loss of 11 Pe-2s. The IV Fighter Corps provided escort for 12 groups of Pe-2s and also patrolled the Gnezdilovka-Pravorot-Shakhovo-Shchelokovo areas. They lost five Yak-1s, probably on the escort missions. The V Fighter Corps also escorted Pe-2s and patrolled the same area as its compatriot fighter corps, with a loss of seven planes, including three Yak-9s. Five of those planes failed to return from their mission, again leading one to conclude that the majority of fighters lost were on escort missions. The 454th Bomber Regiment reconnoitered in the area of Tomarovka-Belgorod.

The Seventeenth Air Army was beginning to get more active. After having effectively stood down two of its three mixed corps for a week, all three began flying again. The I Mixed Corps bombed around Verkhnyii Olshanets using 33 Il-2s in 38 sorties. They used 40 Yak-1s to provide 42 escort sorties, six sorties to cover ground troops and four reconnaissance sorties. These operations were with light losses, losing only two Il-2s.

The III Mixed Corps sent eight Il-2s to strike at Kramatorskaya airfield. As they had tried before, 10 fighters blocked the airfield beforehand while 22 provided escort. There were also 11 other fighters that conducted reconnaissance unrelated to the Battle of Kursk. They claimed two German planes destroyed and four damaged at the airfield. On the way home, the mission ran into an estimated 60 Ju-88, He-111 and Me-110 bombers (?) escorted by 25 Me-109s and Fw-190s. The German fighters attacked, resulting in a fight. Still, this was not bloody, with only one La-5 failing to return from this mission. The 244th Bomber Division struck at the Rogan airfield this day using 18 TB-3s. The IX Mixed Corps flew 23 fighters as escort for these missions, along with six reconnaissance sorties. They also had an La-5 fail to return.

During the day the Germans launched 278 ground attack type sorties on the 16th compared to 340 ground attack type sorties by the Soviets.

17 July

The Germans continued their heavy night action with another 85 sorties, including 28 bombing sorties at Kastornoye station with a claim of good results, and 45 harassing sorties again in the Koren and Korocha areas.

The Soviets continued to respond with their heavy night bombing campaign. The 208th Night Bomber Division put up 132 sorties. They bombed the Verkhopenye, Spitsyin, Shepelevka, Alekseyevka, Lukhanino. Syirtsevo, Berezovka and Rakovo areas. The 262nd Night Bomber Division expanded its targets to include the VIII Air Corps airfields. They sent only 34 sorties to bomb the Razumnoye-Maslova Pristan-Solomino area and the crossing over the Severnyii Donets along the Solomino-Maslova Pristan sector. They did 39 reconnaissance sorties. Sixteen sorties were sent to strike at Rogan airfields while 20 were sent to bomb the Kramatorskaya airfield. The 244th Bomber Division went after the Sokolniki airfield with 15 TB-3 sorties, the Osnova airfield with 14 TB-3 sorties and sent six sorties on reconnaissance missions. The effectiveness of this new night bombing effort on the airfields was probably minimal. The Second Air Army's 454th Bomber Regiment also sent up three medium bombers for reconnaissance during the night.

The Second Air Army reported that the weather was cloudy at night with visibility of six to ten kilometers. The clouds increased during the day, but visibility remained at six to ten kilometers.

The German VIII Air Corps put up a rather anemic 138 sorties this day. The VIII Air Corps action in support of Provisional Army Kempf and the Fourth Panzer Army consisted of only some close assault and fighter sorties, as most of the remaining German units of the VIII Air Corps were now operating in the area of the IV Air Corps around Izyum. The Hungarian air force had to cover the gap created by all the German transfers, and this is shown by their taking three of five losses this day. The Germans flew no Stuka missions this day.

With the German effort now minimal, and the weather clearer than on previous days, the Soviet air force took over the skies and made their presence felt. The Second Air Army put up 486 sorties during the day. The I Assault Corps struck in the Verkhopenye-Berezovka-Syirtsev-Rakovo-Komsomolets Sovkhoz-Pokrovka area and the Sukho-Solotino-Krasnaya Polyana-Malyie Mayachki area with 115 Il-2 sorties supported by 89 escort sorties. Still, the corps took considerable losses this day, possibly from flak, as they report two Il-2s shot down from antiaircraft fire, and 11 Il-2s force-landed on their side of the lines. The 291st Assault Division attacked the southern outskirts of the woods north of Dolgii, the ravines east of Rakovo, southeast and northeast of Berezovka, south of Zavidovka, Cherkasskoye, Dubrova, and Butovo. This was done with 21 Il-2s which flew 44 sorties escorted by 10 fighters which flew 36 sorties. For some reason, this division decided to drop some 2,000 leaflets this day. This was a small effort compared to the 214,000 leaflets dropped during the night by the 208th Night Bomber Division.

The I Bomber Corps sent 52 Pe-2s to bomb the area of Verkhopenye-Berezovka-Syirtsevo. They were escorted by the IV Fighter Corps, which also patrolled and covered its airfields. They flew 58 sorties with 44 planes. The V Fighter Corps patrolled and covered the Soviet troops in the Vladimirovka-Kruglik-Novenkoye-Melovoye area. They carried out 85 sorties with 35 fighters.

The 454th Bomber Regiment sent up seven Bostons for daytime reconnaissance, looking out to a line from Vorozhba to Sumyi to Akhtyirka to Poltava to Kharkov.

The Seventeenth Air Army, except for its night bombing, had now withdrawn from this battle. The I Mixed Corps did not fly this day, while the III and XI Mixed corps, while very active, were now operating farther south, along the Izyum sector in support of the Soviet offensive initiated in that area on the 17th of July (the Izyum-Barvenkovo Offensive).

It was a quiet day, with the Germans conducting only 138 sorties this day, in contrast with the 486 sorties from the Second Air Army. The Second Air Army only reported 13 engagements this day and lost only six planes downed, of which two were shot down by antiaircraft fire. The Soviets were still not reaping the full benefit of the German surrender of the air. It is clear that with a concerted push, the Soviets could establish air superiority, and this in the face of a German withdrawal on the ground.

The Germans may not have provided any daytime ground attack missions on the 17th compared to 211 ground attack type sorties by the Soviets.

18 July

During the night, the VIII Air Corps sent up only 27 sorties, with seven bombers hitting Kastornoye railroad station and 18 harassing sorties in the Koren and Korocha areas.

The Soviet night activity remained high with 199 sorties. The 208th Night Bomber Division hit the Olkhovka-Novo-Cherkasskoye-Dmitrievka-Trirechnoye-Cherkasskoye-Butovo-Kazatskoye area and the Pokrovka-Yakovlevo area and along the Yakovlevo-Belgorod road. They also conducted reconnaissance and photo reconnaissance missions. They also sent an R-5 on a "special assignment" from which it did not return. Most likely, these various solitary "special assignment" night missions that occurred on the nights of 3/4, 9/10 and 17/18 were to insert agents behind German lines or fly aid to partisans.

The Seventeenth Air Army now withdrew from the night battles around Belgorod and flew no bombing sorties in this area. It did continue its night bombing of the German airfields, with 33 U-2 sorties hitting Kramatorskaya airfield and 25 TB-3 sorties hitting the Sokolniki and Osnova airfields.

The Second Air Army recorded the weather at night as cloudy, with occasional rain and visibility of two to five kilometers.

The Second Air Army was the only air force active during the day. On this day, the Germans only conducted 79 sorties: 40 fighter sorties and 39 reconnaissance sorties. This low level of activity was partially a result of the weather.

The I Assault Corps sent out 53 Il-2 sorties to hit the retreating Germans along the roads in the Yakovlevo, Gostishchevo, Butovo, Streletskoye and Tomarovka areas. They were escorted by 47 Yak-1 sorties, but did not encounter any enemy aircraft and suffered no losses. The 291st Assault Division sent 41 Il-2 sorties to attack Verkhopenye, Gremuchii, Olkhovatka, Lukhanino, Cherkasskoye, Butovo, Greznoye, Sukho-Solotino, and the Malyie Mayachki areas. They were escorted by 16 Yak-1bs flying 51 sorties. They reported only one engagement with no losses from that engagement, but they did lose three Il-2s.

The I Bomber Corps hit the areas of Pokrovka, Yakovlevo, Dubrova, Solonets, Olkhovka, Luchki, Streletskoye and Gostishchevo. They flew 93 Pe-2 sorties with 84 Pe-2s, but nine of those sorties were aborted because of the weather. They were again covered by the IV Fighter Corps, which also covered the fuel at Slonovka Station (southwest of Novyii Oskol). The V Fighter Corps continued covering ground troops. The 454th Bomber Regiment conducted reconnaissance with its Bostons. None of these units encountered any German aircraft.

The Seventeenth Air Army was very active this day, with all three mixed corps flying, but it was all in support of operations in the south except for 12 TB-3 sorties against the Kramatorskaya airfield.

There was little air combat this day, with the Second Air Army reporting only one engagement and losing only seven aircraft, probably all due to antiaircraft or mechanical breakdown. The Germans lost one Me-109, shot down and burned by its own flak from the SS Panzer Corps.

The Germans did not provide any daytime ground attack missions on the 18th compared to 187 ground attack type sorties by the Soviets.

The Rest of the Withdrawal

The German sortie rate for the rest of the withdrawal remained less than 100 during the day, and less than 20 during the night. The daytime missions were mostly reconnaissance and a lesser number of fighter missions. There were no more daytime bombing or ground support missions except for bombing missions on the 24th, although the Stukas of the 77th Stuka Wing did return on the 25th to provide support. The Germans continued sending handfuls of bombers at night to attack the railroad station at Staryii Oskol and on harassing raids in the Koren and Korocha areas. On the 19th, the remaining bombers, Stukas, and ground assault aircraft units were transferred to the IV Air Corps in the Izyum area. The German troops around Belgorod were effectively on their own. The VIII Air Corps was now limited in the day to reconnaissance missions, with some fighter support. They had no bomber, ground attack, or Stuka support. With the Seventeenth Air Army reinforced but diverted to the south, they also played no further role in these battles. The Second Air Army now reduced its effort to a lower level. The Fifth Air Army remained well to the rear. The Soviet air force may have been able to assert control over the air at this point, but it does not appear that either side was interested in serious further conflict. As such, the Soviet Il-2s and Pe-2s were free to bomb where they wished during the withdrawal, but were not as active as they had been in the past.

Summation

This was the last large air offensive the Luftwaffe staged over the battlefield area until the failed *Operation Bodenplatte* (Baseplate) offensive on 1 January 1945 that was launched during the Ardennes Campaign (Battle of the Bulge). Somewhat ignored by air historians, this was a very large air battle. In the 15 days from 4 July to 18 July, the Germans flew 15,857 sorties, or an average of 1,057 a day. The two Soviet air armies flew 16,041 sorties into the Belgorod area or against the VIII Air Corps, or 1,069 sorties a day. That was 11,657 sorties by the Second Air Army and 4,384 sorties by the Seventeenth Air Army.

To again look at the Battle of Britain analogy, during the month of August 1940, the Germans flew only 4,779 sorties and dropped 4,636 tons of bombs. During the month of September 1940, the Germans flew 7,260 sorties and dropped 7,044 tons of bombs, and during the month of October 1940, the Germans flew 9,911 sorties and dropped 9,113 tons of bombs.[23] As the area fought over was smaller than the area of the Battle of Britain, the shorter distances to be traveled by the opposing sides resulted in higher sortie rates.

The tonnage of bombs dropped at Kursk by the VIII Air Corps is not known. The Second Air Army reported that it dropped 1,244 tons of bombs and estimates that the Germans dropped 7,000 tons. In light of the total of 11,641 ground-attack type sorties flown by the Germans and only 4,295 ground-attack type sorties flown by the Soviets from the 4th through the 18th, this estimate of German bomb weight appears to be reasonable. The Germans flew at least 5,870 Stuka sorties, at least 3,330 daytime bomber sorties, and at least 1,912 ground attack sorties. Considering that the maximum bomb load of a Stuka was 1,800 kilograms, of an He-111 was 3,250 kilograms, and for an Hs-123 was 450 kilograms, then one is looking at a maximum weight of 22,248.90 metric tons that could have been dropped. In all reality, these aircraft rarely carried their maximum bomb load. For example, the total weight of bombs dropped by the 644 He-111 H-11R sorties from Rogan for the III/55th Bombardment Wing from 4 to 17 July was 919.7 metric tons, or an average of 1,428.11 kilograms per sortie. Still, it would appear that the Soviet estimate of 7,000 tons of German bombs dropped may have been low and the actual figure could have been around 10,000 to 12,000 tons.

The Soviet air forces flew 3,485 Il-2 ground attack sorties, 732 Pe-2 daytime bombing sorties, 70 TB-3 daytime bombing sorties, and 109 ground attack sorties by fighters and fighter bombers during the offensive. With the maximum bomb load of Il-2s at 600 kilograms, the Pe-2 at 1,200 kilograms, the TB-3 at 4,000 kilograms, and the La-5 FN at 300 kilograms, then the maximum weight of bombs that the Soviets could have dropped during the daytime was 3,282.10 tons, about one-seventh of what the Germans could have done. Most of the sorties were from the Second Air Army, with the Seventeenth Air Army contributing 849 Il-2 sorties and the 70 TB-3 sorties. With 3,142 night attack sorties and a 250 kilogram capacity for a U-2, then we are looking at a maximum figure of around 785.5 tons for the night. These were roughly split evenly between the two Soviet air armies. Of this combined figure of 4,067.60 tons, the Second Air Army made up 2,893.20 tons (compared to 1,244 actually reported as delivered) of this figure and the Seventeenth Air Army made up a maximum of 1,174.40 tons (28.87 percent of the total figure). Assuming the same proportion of delivered bombs to maximum bomb-carrying capacity, then we are looking at around 1,748.96 tons of bombs delivered by both the Second and Seventeenth Air Armies.

The overall losses for this air campaign were 111 German planes and 665 Soviet planes. This lopsided 5.95-to-one exchange ratio is hard to explain, as the Soviets' equipment was as good as the Germans'. It clearly shows the differences in training and experience between the two air forces. In light of the heavy losses the Soviet air force took, no one can question their bravery.

How Effective Were the Two Air Forces in Supporting the Ground Troops?

The Germans flew 11,641 ground-attack type sorties during the day and at least 471 bombing sorties during the night. Of those, there were 368 harassing sorties. As the German harassing aircraft primarily dropped two and four kilogram bomblets, the effectiveness of these harassing missions was probably extremely limited.

The Soviets flew 4,396 ground-attack type sorties during the day and 3,142 bombing (harassing) sorties during the night. Their harassing sorties carried more tonnage of bombs than the Germans, as each U-2 could carry 250 kilograms of bombs.

A simple measurement of effectiveness for this air campaign is the volume of bombs dropped by each side. The Second Air Army states that it dropped 1,244 tons

23 Cajus Bekker, page 255.

of bombs and estimated that the Germans dropped 7,000 tons. Assuming the estimate of German tonnage is reasonable, then this demonstrates a 5.6-to-one difference in weight of bombs dropped by the two sides. The number of daytime ground attack sorties flown was 2.6 times more for the Germans. The weight of bombs delivered per sortie tended to be higher for the Germans due to their more extensive use of two-engined bombers and their higher bomb-load capacities. Just looking at maximum capacity weight each side could have dropped with their sorties, then the Germans could have delivered 6.8 times as many tons of bombs during the day. With the Soviets delivering an estimated 1,750 tons of bombs and the Germans delivering an estimated 10,000 to 12,000 tons, the actual German tonnage figure was probably around six or seven times higher than the Soviet tonnage figure.

One must not forget the German Air Force was more experienced and better trained. The differences in training and capability between the two air forces that were clearly displayed in the air superiority fight certainly also existed in the ground support effort. As such, not only did the Germans provide more sorties and higher bomb weight, but their attacks were certainly better coordinated, better directed and possibly more on target. Also, the Soviet air forces, not having control of the skies and suffering very high losses, were probably under more pressure and haste when conducting their ground attack operations. Overall, the degree of ground attack support received by the German Army was certainly multiples higher than for the Soviet Army. It could be comfortably claimed that the German Air Force provided their ground troops at least ten times the support that the Soviet air force provided to theirs.

Before the battle, the Soviets had stored up in the Second Air Army alone 6,850 tons of bombs. It was clear that they were well prepared for this operation. As it was, because of their inability to maintain control of the air, their high losses, and the limited sorties conducted by their bombers, they only used 18 percent of their available bomb supply. In the case of the I Bomber Corps, which spent most of the offensive grounded, they were the only planes that delivered the 250 kilogram bombs. "The I Bomber Corps light activity and the insufficient activity of the I Assault Corps is explained by the fact that the fighters assigned to escort these units were busy fighting the enemy aircraft."[24] As the report points out, this led to the actual number of bombs dropped on the Germans being much less than were dropped on them.

The Soviet Army clearly was not getting effective support from their air force. On the other hand, the Second Air Army did pepper the battlefield with 90,000 of the 2.5 kilogram antitank bombs (225 tonnes). This was 64 percent of their original supply issue of these bombs.

TABLE 8.2
SUMMATION OF DAYTIME GROUND ATTACK TYPE SORTIES (STUKA, ASSAULT, BOMBING, AND GROUND ATTACK SORTIES)

Date	*German*	*Soviet*	*Ratio*
4	160	0	N/A
5	1,942	486	4.00
6	1,356	442	3.07
7	1,444	400	3.61
8	1,380	404	3.42
9	1,266	291	4.35
10	529*	158	3.35
11	801	152	5.27
12	411	354	1.16
13	402	343	1.17
14	1,131	401	2.82
15	541	126	4.29
16	278	340	.82
17	?	211	N/A
18	0	187	N/A
Total	11,641	4,295	2.71

* Estimated

24 Fond: Second Air Army, Opis: 4196, Delo: 39, page 9.

VIII AIR CORPS LOSSES AND CLAIMS

Date	*German Losses*	*German Claims*	*Date*	*German Losses*	*German Claims*
June 30	0	5	July 12	11	16
Night	0	0	Night		
July 1	0	0	July 13	5	21
Night	0	0	Night	0	0
July 2	1	1	July 14	9	24
Night	0	0	Night	0	0
July 3	0	5	July 15	5	8
Night			Night	0	0
July 4	3	6	July 16	3	24
Night			Night	0	0
July 5	19	260	July 17	5	10
		(220 by air, 40 by AA)	Night	0	0
Night			July 18	1	1
July 6	7	74	Night	0	0
Night	0	0	July 19	0	1
July 7	10	96	Night	0	0
Night			July 20	0	0
July 8	5	43	Night	0	0
Night			July 21	0	0
July 9	11	38	Night	0	0
Night			July 22	2 Hungarian	1
July 10	3	14	Night	0	0
Night	0	0	July 23	0	0
July 11	14	23	Night	0	0
Night	0	0	July 24	1	4

The effectiveness of these bombs as an antitank weapon was limited. No reports have been located of any German tanks lost to them, although certainly some were immobilized or otherwise damaged.

The Second Air Army after-action report singled out the fighters as having worked the hardest of all. They singled out the 737th Fighter Regiment (291st Assault Division) for having carried out five or six sorties per combat-ready plane on some of the most intense days. They also singled out the 8th Fighter Division of the V Fighter Corps for being almost as busy as the 737th Fighter Regiment and from the first day of the operation, took upon itself the full weight of fighting the German bombers.

 SECOND AIR ARMY COMBAT LOSSES, JULY 1943

SHOT DOWN IN AIR COMBAT

	Total	*Pe-2*	*A-20*	*Il-2*	*La-5*	*Yak-1*	*Yak-7*	*Yak-9*
I Assault Corps	44			32		7	5*	
I Bomber Corps	12	12						
IV Fighter Corps	12				3	8	1	
V Fighter Corps	59				31	4	14	10
208th Night Bomber Div.	—							
291st Assault Division	35			27	1	4	3	
454th Bomber Regiment	2		2					
Total	164	12	2	59	35	23	23	10

* The I Assault Corps did not fly any Yak-7s through the 18th of July, so this figure is probably post-Kursk offensive activity.

SHOT DOWN BY ANTIAIRCRAFT FIRE

	Total	*Pe-2*	*A-20*	*Il-2*	*La-5*	*Yak-1*	*Yak-7*	*Yak-9*
I Assault Corps	35			27	2	4	2*	
I Bomber Corps	9	9						
IV Fighter Corps	4				1	2	1	
V Fighter Corps	18				8	3	7	
208th Night Bomber Div.	—							
291st Assault Division	41			36	1	2	2	
454th Bomber Regiment	1		1					
Total	108	9	1	63	12	11	12	

* The I Assault Corps did not fly any Yak-7s through the 18th of July, so this figure is probably post-Kursk offensive activity.

NOT RETURNED FROM MISSION

	Total	*Pe-2*	*A-20*	*Il-2*	*La-5*	*Yak-1*	*Yak-7*	*Yak-9*	*U-2*
I Assault Corps	20			12	1	2	5*		
I Bomber Corps	15	15							
IV Fighter Corps	45				4	28	13		
V Fighter Corps	40				14	7	12	7	
208th Night Bomber Div.	3								3
291st Assault Division	34			28	1		5		
454th Bomber Regiment	1		1						
Total	158	15	1	40	20	37	35	7	3
Total of all causes	430	36	4	162	67	71	70	17	3

* The I Assault Corps did not fly any Yak-7s through the 18th of July, so this figure is probably post-Kursk offensive activity.

SO WHAT DROVE THE SOVIET AIR LOSS CLAIMS?

One surprising feature of the Soviet records is the very large number of claimed kills as compared to the actual German losses. A comparison is displayed below:

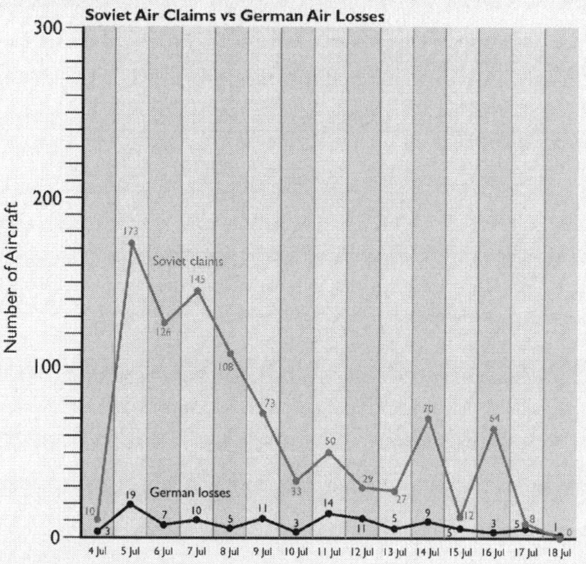

This comes out to a total of 840 claimed kills by the Second Air Army and 88 claimed kills by the Seventeenth Air Army. This does not address the claimed kills by the Soviet ground units. This compares poorly to actual German losses of 111 planes. The Soviets claimed more than eight times what the Germans actually lost.

The reverse tendency is not displayed by the Germans. A comparison of their claims to actual Soviet losses is provided below:

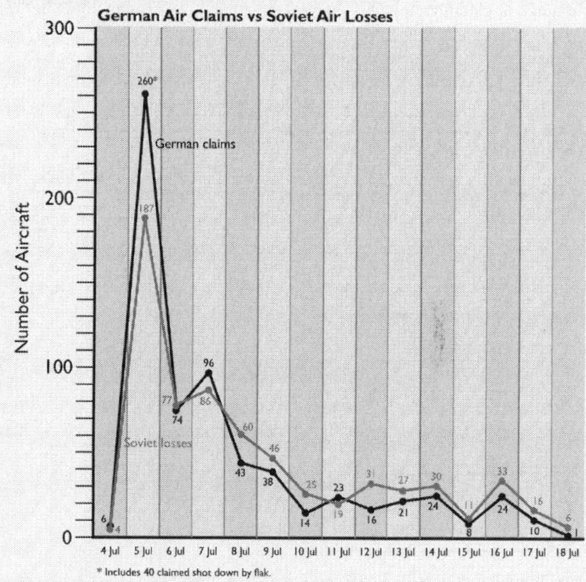

(continued)

This comes out to a total of 658 claimed kills by the VIII Air Corps compared to 658 actual losses by the Second and Seventeenth Air Armies. It would appear that at least for this two-week period, German reporting of air claims was reasonably accurate while the Soviet claims were outrageously high. Also bothersome is that the Soviet claims do not appear to have been related to the German casualties. Instead, if one compares Soviet losses to Soviet claims of German losses, one does find a fit.[1]

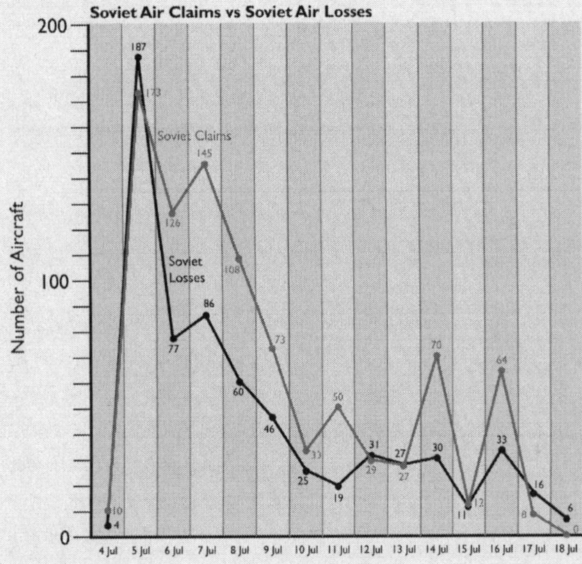

1 This relationship was suggested to me by Dr. Richard Harrison in 1995.

The pattern is fairly clear, the Soviets always claimed more casualties than they lost.[2] With the Soviets losing 658 planes, and claiming 928 German kills, we are looking at the Soviets claiming about 40 percent more kills than they lost. This over-claiming is fairly consistent from day to day, and as shown elsewhere, is not a problem unique to the Soviet air force. The Seventeenth Air Army, possibly as a result of its lower level of activity, did a little bit better in regard to accuracy in its claims.

2 A briefing based upon this data was presented to Col. Fyodor Sverdlov in October 1994, who was a staff officer for the Eleventh Guards Army at Kursk and later a professor at the Frunze Military Academy. After presenting the chart showing Soviet claims to German losses, Sverdlov stated that "the enemy always suffers 30% more losses than you."

 OTHER SOVIET KILL CLAIMS

CLAIMS OF GERMAN PLANES SHOT DOWN BY SECOND AIR ARMY OVER THE VORONEZH FRONT, 5–18 JULY 1943[1] COMPARED TO REPORTED LOSSES BY GERMAN VIII AIR CORPS.

Type	*Number Claimed*	*German Losses*	*Ratio of Claims to Losses*
Ar-66	—	1	—
Do-215	7	—	—
Fiat	5	—	—
Fw-189	3	1	3.00
Fw-190	73	11	6.64
He-111	47	15	3.13
Hs-123	5	—	—
Hs-126	36	2	18.00
Hs-129	—	3	—
Ju-87	223	17	13.12
Ju-88	77	10	7.70
Me-109	341	37	9.22
Me-110	5	—	—
Not Stated	—	14	—
Total	822	111	7.41

GERMAN PLANES CLAIMED BY UNIT, 5–18 JULY 1943[2]

Unit	*Claims*
I Assault Corps	121
I Bomber Corps	16
IV Fighter Corps	175
V Fighter Corps	451
291st Assault Division	48
Total	811

1 Fond: 303, Opis: 4196, Delo: 39, page 9.

2 Fond: 302, Opis: 4196, Delo: 39, page 12.

PERSONAL KILL CLAIMS

While individual Soviet airmen claims of kills cannot be systematically checked, as detailed German logs do not exist, they can be compared to the reported daily losses of the VIII Air Corps. This is illustrative and, not surprisingly, demonstrates that the pattern of over-claiming kills also applies to a pilot's personal totals.

4 July

A list of personal victory claims is provided in the Second Air Army records for the V Fighter Corps for the 4th of July. They also provide the location of the engagement, and all locations are in the Voronezh Front or Fourth Panzer Army area. See Table 8.3.

The VIII Air Corps reports losing 2 Ju-88s and one Me-109 on the 4th of July.

Kozhevnikov is possibly Hero of the Soviet Union Anatolii Leonidovich Kozhevnikov of the 438th Fighter Regiment, who scored 27 victories in his career. Karmin is possibly Aleksandr Leontyevich Karmin of the 27th Fighter Regiment, who scored 19 victories and 14 shared kills in his career. Mikhalev may be Vasilii Pavlovich Mikhalev of the 508th Fighter Regiment who scored 26 victories and 14 shared kills in his career. Stroikov may be Nikolai Vasilyevich Stroikov of the 508th Fighter Regiment who scored 14 victories and 21 shared kills in his career. Orlovskii, Oleinikov, Dernik and Stepanobyim have not been identified.

5 July

The following claims are made for the 8th Guards Fighter Division:

Sr. Lt. Belikov	4 kills
Sr. Lt. Danin	4 kills
Sr. Lt. Sementsov	3 kills
Lt. Nikanorov	3 kills

The following claims are made for the 205th Fighter Division:

Sr. Lt. Gulayev	4 kills
Jr. Lt. Shpak	4 kills
Capt. Nasonov	3 kills

These 25 claimed kills (out of 76 claimed by the V Fighter Corps) exceed the actual 19 losses suffered by the VIII Air Corps on this day.

Hero of the Soviet Union Oleg Stepanovich Belikov of the 19th Fighter Regiment scored 15 kills and 14 fractional kills in his career. Sementsov is probably Hero of the Soviet Union Mikhail Ivanovich Sementsov of the 40th Fighter Regiment who scored 19 kills and 12 shared kills in his career. Nikanorov is probably Hero of the Soviet Union Pyotr Mikhailovich Nikanorov of the 166th Fighter Regiment who scored 17 kills and 5 shared kills in his career. Gulayev is probably two-time Hero of the Soviet Union Nikolai Dmitriyevich Gulayev of the 27th Fighter Regiment who scored 57 kills and 3 shared kills in his career. Danin, Shpak and Nasonov have not been identified.

Ace Claims

A summation of the claimed kills made by Soviet aces that could be compared to the actual German losses is provided in Table 8.4.

It would appear that 55 percent of these claims made by Soviet aces are not correct, or are misidentified as to plane type. As all claims made were of Me-109 or Fw-190s fighters, gull-wing Ju-87s, or twin engine Ju-88s or He-111s, it does not appear that misidentification is the major cause of these incorrect claims. It is not known if this is a representative sample of the accuracy of Soviet ace claims.

Table 8.3

V Fighter Corps Claims for the 4th of July 1943

Pilot	*Claim*	*Location*
Sr. Lt. Kozhevnikov	2 Ju-88	Olkhovka-Aleksandrovka
Sr. Lt. Karmin	1 Ju-87	30 km SW of Belgorod
Jr. Lt. Orlovskii	2 Me-109	Streletskoye
Jr. Lt. Mikhalev & Stroikov	2 Me-109	Shelkovo, Klemenkovo
Jr. Lt. Oleinikov	1 Me-109	Streletskoye, Dmitriyevka
Jr. Lt. Dernik	1 Me-109	Tomarovka
Jr. Lt. Stepanobyim	1 Me-109	own side of lines

Table 8.4

Claimed Kills by Soviet Aces Compared to Actual German Losses

Soviet Ace	*Kill Claims Checked*	*Not a Possible Kill*
Ivan Kozhedub	5	2
Nikolai Gulayev	1	1
Kirill Yevstigneyev	9	8
Arsenii Vorozheikin	2	0
shared kills	1	0
Ivan Syitov	2	2
Fyodor Arkhipenko	2	1
shared kills	4	3
Sergei Glinkin	1	0
Nikolai Dunayev	1	1
Ivan Gnezdilov	2	0
Ilya Andrianov	2	1
Oleg Smirnov	1	0
Aleksandr Vyibornov	1	1
Ivan Ulitin	2	2
Anatolii Shamanskii	2	1*
Anatolii Kozhevnikov	9	3
	—	—
	47	26

(continued)

* Duplicate claim

A SIMILAR TYPE of check of German ace claims is not possible because so many more Soviet planes of different types were shot down each day. Rarely is there a day where a German claim can be disproved, unless one can compare a specific time and location. The claims that were checked are shown below, but little can be determined from this tally.

German Ace	*Claims Checked*	*Not a Possible Kill*
Erich Hartmann	22	3

Overall, in light of Soviet claims from 4 to 18 July reported in excess of German losses by more than eight times, it is not surprising that many individual claims cannot be confirmed. This does bring into question the validity of all Soviet ace totals. On the other hand, the fact that German claims for 4 to 18 July were almost equal to Soviet losses during that time does provide some level of confidence in the accuracy of German claims. Still, one notes that the Luftwaffe claimed 220 planes shot down by air and 40 by antiaircraft on the 5th of July, when the Soviets reported losing 187, so one should not place too much reliance on the accuracy of these claims.

Yet based upon this limited sample, it does appear that the German ace claims are usually valid while the Soviet claims are clearly inflated, and possibly inflated by several times.

CHAPTER NINE

The Tank Fields of Prokhorovka

12 JULY 1943

> To hurry with the counterblow, when the situation has not yet ripened for it, means to prematurely exhaust all one's opportunities for continuing the struggle while it is still going on and has not yet reached its culmination point. This may often place the entire defense under danger of a complete defeat.
>
> BRIGADE COMMANDER GEORGII S. ISSERSON
> 1938[1]

THE RATIONALE BEHIND the Soviet decisions that lead to this dramatic day is somewhat obscure.[2] It appears, from looking at the operations leading up to this point, that the counterattack was deeply ingrained in the Soviet military defensive doctrine. We had already seen six days of continuous local counterattacks across the line from virtually all the armored units and several failed attempts at coordinated pincher attacks. While some of these counterattacks hit weak points in the German lines or their flanks, causing them considerable consternation, most simply went nowhere. These counterattacks often forced the Germans to halt and redeploy, delaying their forward progress, but mostly they just wasted Russian lives and materiel for little practical gain. These constant local counterattacks, conducted without proper reconnaissance or preparation, were sapping the strength of the Soviet armies and making it more difficult to defend. In effect, with their local counterattacking and obsession with attacking, the Soviets made the same mistakes tactically that they had often made strategically during the war.

Still, counterattacking is an essential part of a defense, especially if one can get on the attacking forces' flank, find a weak spot, and hit them before they have a chance to organize a defense. It is a means to damage, entangle, or even throw back the opposing attacking forces, and if properly done with sufficient force, can cripple the attacking force and reverse the fortunes on the battlefield. The German Army made extensive use of counterattacks in defensive situations, and as a matter of habit, often would counterattack a position

1 Isserson, *Osnovyi Oboronitelnoi Operatsii* [*Fundamentals of the Defensive Operation*], published in 1938 by the RKKA General Staff Academy, page 54. Translation provided by Dr. Richard Harrison.

2 Zamulin, *Demolishing the Myth*, on pages 262–263 states that "It is very difficult to establish a chronology of the decisions regarding Voronezh Front's counterattack and the implementation of measures for its preparation. Unfortunately, my research was unable to uncover any sort of schematic map or written plan for the operation." He was the Deputy Director and Director of Research at the Prokhorovka Battlefield Park Museum, 1996–2009.

shortly after it was taken, before the other side had a chance to consolidate. They also counterattacked to restore the line after a penetration. Still, these were different than the often uncoordinated local offensives done by the Soviet Army. It was almost as if the Soviet Army understood that they should counterattack, but did not always understand when or where or how.

There also appears to be almost a psychological, or machismo, aspect to their counterattacks. It's almost as if they were saying, "How dare you attack us, we'll attack you." Courage was not an issue, this was clearly shown in abundance. But rational and practical use of one's assets is in question here. Quite simply, the first goal was to halt the German advance. This is still best done by placing significant forces in front of the advancing forces and attriting and halting the attackers. As the German military theorist Carl von Clausewitz points out, "Defense is the stronger form of combat." Once the enemy has weakened himself attacking, then it is time to unleash coordinated large counterattacks, in this case using combined arms at the German weak points (usually the flanks). These numerous uncoordinated small counterattacks that they had been doing did not fit into any rational defensive scheme.

Still, on the 12th, the decision was made by the Voronezh Front to attack. This time instead of attacking locally with limited efforts, they decided instead to attack across the entire front. The concept of smashing headlong, in a broad general offensive across the entire front of an attacking opponent, must be questioned at its most basic level. Exactly what was the purpose and use of such an attack? First, why would one attack everywhere, when parts of the line are better defended than other parts? Why not attack where you think the enemy is weak, instead of everywhere? Second, why not concentrate your offensive forces at the critical areas you want to attack? Therefore, you will get the best outcome from the attacks and may have enough weight to continue the attack in case the enemy position is penetrated. Third, why attack in the areas where the enemy is attacking? As the self-educated U.S. Civil War General Nathan Bedford Forrest so eloquently stated, "Hit them where they ain't." Work on the enemy's flanks, not across their front, into the face of their attacking forces. Fourth, why attack at all? The Germans were still attacking across the front with their three armored corps. Why not wait until their attacks had truly run out of steam? Attrite them before counterattacking. It appears that the attacks on the 12th were launched too early, too broadly and before the Germans had been exhausted.

On the night of 11 July, Vatutin had reached a decision to launch a counteroffensive with the front forces to encircle and defeat the main German grouping.The basic plan was to launch attacks against the Fourth Panzer Army from the west by the V Guards and X Tank Corps together with the XXII (22nd) Guards Rifle Corps (Sixth Guards Army) in the direction of Yakovlevo and from the northeast with the newly arriving Fifth Guards Tank Army and the XXXIII (33rd) Guards Rifle Corps (Fifth Guards Army) in the direction of Greznoye, Yakovlevo and Byikovka. There would be supporting attacks by the XXIII (23rd) Guards Rifle Corps and the XXXII (32nd) Guards Rifle Corps and by the Seventh Guards Army against Razumnoye.[3]

3 Glantz and Orenstein, page 108. The timing of this decision is as quoted from the Soviet General Staff Study on the Battle of Kursk, done in March-April 1944. The translated passage is quoted as "On the night of 11 July, the *front* commander reached a decision concerning the expediency of launching a counteroffensive. . . ."

Zamulin, *Demolishing the Myth*, on page 263 quotes from the Official History of the Great Patriotic War published in 1962 a passage that states, "On the night of 10 July, the Military Council of the Voronezh Front . . . Pursuant to an agreement with the Stavka, the Voronezh Front command took the decision to launch a powerful counterstroke on the morning of 12 July . . ."

On the other hand, according to Rotmistrov's post-war account, Rotmostrov was summoned to meet with Vatutin near Oboyan during the day on 10 July. They did discuss the counterstroke at Prokhorovka and Rotmistrov received his combat orders and returned to his command post in the afternoon (see Zamulin, pages 268–269). Parts of Rotmistrov's account appear fanciful.

It is possible the decision to attack on the morning of the 12th was made, or at least vetted to *Stavka* on the night 10th. Primary source documents have not been located that can confirm this.

This would be a large simultaneous attack that encompassed six tank corps and well over a dozen rifle divisions. As Vatutin's Stavka representative was Vasilevskii, he clearly had to be aware of such an effort and must have approved of it. The political advisors were Khrushchev and Korniets, who while not in overall command, certainly had some say into whether it should be done or not. Clearly, these four people, along with the Chief of Staff of the Voronezh Front, Lt. General Ivanov, approved or at least acquiesced to this attack. Furthermore, the plan of attack was submitted to Stalin and Stavka on the 11th and quickly approved.[4] It was an attack that was unnecessary, mindless in execution and did nothing but waste lives. It was bad generalship.

Still, in the Fortieth Army, Sixth Guards Army and First Tank Army, the effects of these orders were mitigated by the fact that in many cases they were not seriously executed. Just as some German units appear to have been conserving their strength during the operation, clearly a large number of Soviet units in the western part of the battlefield claimed that they attacked, but did not.[5]

In the Soviet system, especially under Stalin, disobeying an order was not only grounds for dismissal or court-martial, but could result in far worse for the insubordinate and even his family. The Soviet military did not allow or encourage initiative at the local level; orders were expected to be obeyed. As such, when the orders came down to attack, one could not, especially with one's commissar nearby, choose to not execute that order because it really didn't make sense for the situation. Still, the people commanding these units were not fools; they knew their resources and they knew what they were facing. Therefore, many simply took the expediency of claiming that they attacked and then did a reconnaissance in force or a very limited operation. When one looks at the Soviet reports for that day, almost everyone reported that they attacked. Yet when one looks at how far they advanced or what their casualties were, there clearly were many units that were really not attacking. In this case, one cannot rely on just the official accounts or even the unit records to determine what they had done, one must look at the actual casualties and whether the unit moved forward, to determine what occurred. In effect, uncovering the history of this day is an exercise in reading between the lines.

Orders and daily reports in the Soviet Army were usually signed by both the chief of staff and the senior political officer. Therefore, if one was ordered to attack and did not execute this order, then to properly represent the situation to the chain of command required a certain degree of collaboration and acquiescence on the part of the unit commanders, their chiefs of staff, and their political officers. As such, buried within this command-driven army was a situation where one could exercise one's initiative but had to collectively cover-up any direct violations of those orders. Therefore, there was a culture of misinformation buried in the army, and it was a collaborative effort that often had to include the political officers. This culture of misinformation seems to be one of the established contradictions in a Soviet-style army (not that this doesn't happen in other armies). It shows up in spades in their intelligence reports. When one reviews the Soviet intelligence reports, one finds that they clearly show a solid understanding of who and what they are facing, although they often do not have the detailed data of the German reports due to the much lower number of prisoners they are taking. Still, these intelligence reports are clearly a rational attempt to understand and analyze the situation. The Soviet correlations of means and forces, which are mathematical comparisons of what each side had at the start of an operation, are often reasonable estimates of the enemy strength and capability. Their reports on their own losses are usually accurate, as these can be easily verified. Their reports on numbers of enemy seen, planes that flew overhead, etc., all seem to be reason-

4 Erickson, page 106.

5 These operations to the west of the SS Panzer Corps and the subsequent Battle of Tolstoye Woods are not further discussed in this book. They are discussed in considerable depth in my book *Kursk: The Battle of Prokhorovka*.

able estimates. What is always invariably inflated is their estimate of enemy casualties. As Colonel Fyodor Sverdlov, a staff officer in the Eleventh Guards Army during the Battle of Kursk stated, "The enemy always suffers 30 percent more losses than you."[6]

There is no question that the Soviet Army, as a matter of custom, usually reported unusually high losses by their opponent, and these losses usually were in excess of their own. This is not something unique to the Red Army, but it was endemic and occurred regularly in the Soviet Army. As one can see by the same comparison done for the Germans, this tendency did not exist to the same degree in the German Army.[7]

Added to that, if one was ordered to attack, one always reported an attack, even if common sense and individual initiative indicated otherwise. As such, any account of the actions on the 12th of July is simply not going to be correct if one relies primarily on Soviet records or does not compare the accounts of both sides, and furthermore does not compare them to the casualty reports and the actual movement on the battlefield. The inability of Soviet-era historians to make such comparisons, both because of a lack of access to German sources and due to official censorship, has resulted in their accounts of this day being much different than that presented here. The fact that many American and English historians have also presented accounts that parallel those Soviet accounts does not in any way validate them or make them more credible.

The Fifth Guards Tank Army Moves Up

To recap the movements of General Pavel Rotmistrov's Fifth Guards Tank Army: the army, consisting of Major General Boris Skvortsov's V Guards Mechanized Corps and Major General Ivan Kirichenko's XXIX Tank Corps, was initially deployed in the area of Ostrogozhsk, Kamenka and Pukhovo. On 5 July, the army received orders from Lt. General Ivan S. Konev (commander of the Steppe Military District) that the army was to put itself into combat readiness. Major General Boris Bakharov's XVIII Tank Corps, situated in the Rossosh area, was included in the army. At 2230 on 6 July, an order was received from the Steppe Military District instructing the army to concentrate along the western bank of the Oskol River, south and southwest of Staryii Oskol. It was specifically ordered to force march to the concentration area and be ready to operate in the direction of Oboyan and Kursk.

Within two hours of the receipt of the order (at 0130), the army's units left for their new location. A forward detachment under the command of army deputy commander Major General Kuzma Grigoriyevich Trufanov was created consisting of the 1st Independent Red Banner Guards Motorcycle Regiment, 53rd Guards Tank Regiment, 689th Antitank Regiment and a battery from the 678th Howitzer Regiment. These units were pulled from the V Guards Mechanized Corps. The "Trufanov detachment," as it has been called, was the lead for the army and had reached the concentration area by midday. The XXIX Tank Corps followed behind along the same route and had reached the concentration area by the end of 7 July. The V Guards Mechanized Corps, using a different route, had completed its concentration by the morning of 8 July. The XVIII Tank Corps had left the Rossosh area at 1030 on 7 July and reached the concentration area by the morning of 8 July. By day break 8 July, this concentration of the army's main forces was completed, with the arrival of the final rear units taking place at the end of the day.[8]

6 This comment was made on October 1994 while I was presenting the results of my comparison of Germans airplane losses with Soviet estimates of German airplane losses. See Chapter Fourteen in my book *Kursk: The Battle of Prokhorovka*, pages 839–840, for this comparison.

7 In particular, we bring your attention to the tables in the sidebar "Tank Losses Versus Intelligence Reports" in my book *Kursk: The Battle of Prokhorovka*, pages 872-879.

8 "Fifth Guards Tank Army's Combat Activities from July 7–24, 1943" (compiled 30 September 1943 by army commander Lt. General Rotmistrov and military council member Major General Grishin). Fond: 332, Opis: 4948, Delo: 19, pages 1–3.

At 0100 on 9 July, the army received an order instructing it, by the end of the day, to reach the area from Bobryishevo, some ten kilometers east of Oboyan, down to Prokhorovka. This order also subordinated the army to the Voronezh Front. It started moving out of positions at 0200, conducting a 100 kilometer march. By 0600, Trufanov's detachment was in the woods south of Marino, some 30 kilometers from Oboyan. By 2300, the army concentration was "basically completed" and by the morning of the 10th part of its forces had occupied the defensive line along the northern bank of the Psel River from Oboyan to Prokhorovka. The army had marched 350 kilometers and was now stretched across the rear of the Soviet positions.

The most western point of the army was Major General Trufanov's forward detachment, which moved to the Oboyan area and took up defensive positions along the Psel River at Oboyan, running from Trubezh through the southern outskirts of Oboyan to the mouth of the Zapselets River, a front of around eight kilometers. This was a naturally good defensive line with the Psel somewhat wide at this point, and fronted by swamps and soft ground that ran for a kilometer or more before it. The detachment had the mission of preventing the Germans from reaching the northern bank of the Psel River and holding this line and Oboyan until the arrival of units from the Voronezh Front.

To the east of it was the rest of the V Guards Mechanized Corps, concentrated in the Bobryishevo and Nagolnoye area. It was ordered by the morning of 10 July to take up defense positions with two brigades along the northern bank of the Psel River from the Zapselets River to the outskirts of Veselyii. This was a rather extended line of about 30 kilometers. Major General Skvortsov, the corps commander, stationed the 11th Guards Mechanized Brigade with the 104th Antitank Regiment along the Psel from the Zapselets River to Shep (17 kilometers southeast of Oboyan). The 10th Guards Mechanized Brigade, with the 1447th Self-Propelled Artillery Regiment, occupied the line from the outskirts of Shep to the outskirts of Veselyii. The 12th Guards Mechanized Brigade concentrated in the woods northwest of Verkhnyaya Olshanka. The 24th Guards Tank Brigade, with the 285th Mortar Regiment, was in Bolshaya Psinka. The corps headquarters was in Nagolnoye. The defensive line was occupied by 1000.

The XVIII Tank Corps, along with the 1000th Antitank Regiment, had concentrated by 2300 on 9 July from Verkhnyaya Olshanka to Kartashevka to Aleksandrovskii to Prokhorovka to Grigoryevka. They were then ordered to occupy the line from Veselyii to height +1.0 and 226.6 to Mikhailovka to the southern outskirts of Prokhorovka and Tikhaya Padina. The 678th Howitzer Regiment and 76th Guards Mortar Regiment concentrated in the Ploskoye-Kolbasovka area, ready to support the V Guards Mechanized Corps and the XVIII Tank Corps.

The XXIX Tank Corps was ordered to concentrate in an area 10 to 20 kilometers northwest of Prokhorovka while the 53rd Motorized Rifle Brigade, with the 108th Antitank Regiment and the 271st Mortar Regiment, were to occupy a line in the southwest corner of this concentration area. This line was over 20 kilometers in length and some 15 to 20 kilometers behind the line occupied by the V Guards Mechanized Corps and the XVIII Tank Corps.

By the morning of the 10th, the Fifth Guards Tank Army was stretched across the rear of the Voronezh Front along the Psel, backstopping their defense. After three days of marching, this force was certainly tired, and elements were certainly lagging behind along their route of march. There was still broken down armor that was coming up. At this point though, the army was in a good position to backstop the Soviet defense by holding in place or moving forward to reinforce the existing Voronezh Front defensive positions.

During 10 and 11 July, the army's units did not engage in combat. Enemy aircraft at 0830 on 10 July bombed units of the XVIII Tank Corps, during which three men in the 32nd Motorized Rifle Brigade were killed. The 1694th Antiaircraft Regiment, which was covering the corps on this day, did not fire a shot. The following day the 32nd Motorized Rifle Brigade lost

REPORT OF EQUIPMENT AND SUPPLY OF THE FIFTH GUARDS TANK ARMY AT 1700 11 JULY 1943

In Valeriy Zamulin's book, *Demolishing the Myth*, pages 275–276, there is a chart of tank strengths that we did not locate in our original research.[1] It is labeled "Report on the Equipment and Supplies of the 5th Guards Tank Army at 1700 11 July 1943."[2] As it is an informative and interesting chart, it is repeated here:

Equipment	29 Tank Corps	18 Tank Corps	2 Tank Corps	2 Gds Tank Corps	5 Gds Mech Corps	Army-level units	Total
1. Operational							
T-34	120	68	35	84	120	36	463
T-70	81	58	46	52	56	8	301
Mk-IV Churchill	-	18	4	3	-	-	25
Total Tanks	201	144	85	139	176	44	789
Su-76	8	-	-	-	7	-	15
Su-122	12	-	-	-	10	-	22
Total SP Guns	20	-	-	-	17	-	37
Total, Tanks and SP Guns	221	144	85	139	193	44	826
AT Guns: 122mm	-	-	-	-	-	20	20
85mm	-	-	-	12 (a)	-	-	12
76mm	12	12	18	-	43	-	85
45mm	20	12	26	19	23	12	112
2. En Route to Prokhorovka Station							
T-34	8	26	-	-	43	3	80
T-70	4	5	-	-	4	1	14
Mk-IV Churchill	-	2	-	-	-	-	2
Total tanks	12	33	-	-	47	4	96
Su-76	1	-	-	-	2	-	3
Su-122	-	-	-	-	2	-	2
Total SP Guns	1	-	-	-	4	-	5
Total, Tanks and SP Guns	13	33	-	-	51	4	101
AT Guns: 76mm	-	-	-	20	-	-	-
3. In repair shop							
T-34	2	5	7	-	1	5	20
T-70	-	-	2	-	-	1	3
Mk-IV Churchill	-	1	-	-	-	-	1
Total tanks	2	6	9	-	1	6	24
Total Armor							
Total tanks on roster	215	183	94	139	224	54	909
Total SP Guns on roster	21	0	0	0	21	0	42
Total, all armor	236	183	94	139	245	54	951

(a) Other than anti-aircraft guns.

1 Our original archival research effort was conducted from 1993 to 1996 by a team of researchers led by retired Frunze Military Academy professor Fyodor Sverdlov, who this book is dedicated to. He provided supplemental research, including interviews and maps up through 2002.

2 He gives the source as TSAMO RF, Fond: 5 GTA, Opis: 4948, Delo: 67, page: 12.

Table 19 continued

Equipment	29 Tank Corps	18 Tank Corps	2 Tank Corps	2 Gds Tank Corps	5 Gds Mech Corps	Army-level units	Total
4. Supplies (in daily loads)							
Fuel and lubricants:							
For tanks	1.5	1.5	-	1	1.5	-	-
For vehicles	0.5	1	-	1.5	0.3	-	-
Ammunition							
For tanks	1.5	1.5	-	1	1.4	-	-
For AT Guns	1	1	-	1	1	-	-

Source: TsAMO RF, f. 5 gv. TA, op. 4948, d. 67, l.12.

another four men killed by a direct bomb hit. Overall for the day, the corps reported losing 8 T-34s, 3 T-70s, 23 killed and 34 wounded from German air attacks. As Major General Bakharov (XVIII Tank Corps commander) complained, "The corps' concentration area consisted of open terrain, cut up by deep gullies and lacking major roads, lacking woods, and gardens in inhabited areas, which offered the corps' units no cover in the open, which is why the corps' units during 10–11 July were subject to air attacks." The XVIII Tank Corps also sent elements of the 78th Motorcycle Battalion to reconnoiter in the Belenikhino area on the 9th, where they lost four men and two motorcycles. On the 10th, they sent four armored cars to reconnoiter the Kochetovka and Greznoye area.[9]

Still, the Fifth Guards Tank Army was planning to attack. At first it was planning to launch the blow from Belenikhino to the west, but the terrain in this area turned out to be unfavorable for tanks.[10] The planning included a conference at army headquarters on the 10th, attended by Major General Kirichenko of the XXIX Tank Corps and probably a number of other senior commanders. On the 11th, Major General Kirichenko, along with some subordinates, conducted a reconnaissance mission that they returned from by 1300. The XXIX Tank Corps then began to move to its new concentration area at 1530. At this point, the XXIX Tank Corps had 123 T-34s, 81 T-70s, 11 SU-122s and 8 SU-76s. The corps' 25th Tank Brigade also reported a KV-1 and another SU-122. The XXIX Tank Corps moved its headquarters to Mordovka, just east of Prokhorovka.

On 11 July, the II Tank Corps and II Guards Tank Corps were attached to the army. At this stage, Rotmistrov reported the army tank strength at 501 T-34s, 261 T-70s and 31 Churchills, for a total of 793 tanks. He also reported 45 122mm guns (including their two regiments of self-propelled artillery), 124 76mm guns and 330 45mm antitank guns, 1,007 antitank rifles, 495 mortars and 39 Katyushas.

During 11 July, up to 2400, the army's units concentrated in their offensive starting position from Mikhailovka to Prokhorovka to Maloye Yablonovo to Priznachnoye to Skorovka. The army marched another 45 to 60 kilometers. Overall, the army had marched up to 400 kilometers in four days.[11]

The Fifth Guards Army Moves Up

As significant, but having drawn much less attention in the history books, the Fifth Guards Army also moved towards the battle. This army originally consisted of seven infantry divisions and the X Tank Corps and had been in its current position for at least half of May and all of June. At 1800 on 5 July, at least one division, and probably the entire army, was ordered to cease its training and occupy its defensive positions. The X Tank Corps left the Fifth Guards Army on the night of the 6–7th of July and by 1700 on the 7th had concentrated in the Prokhorovka, Yamki and Pravorot area. It was subordinated to the First Tank Army at 2400 on 8 July.

According to Lt. General Alexei Zhadov, by the beginning of July the army's units were sufficiently manned and trained to carry out their tasks. They were well equipped and stocked. By this time, the army had prepared a defense line, consisting of two defensive belts with a forward zone. The forward edge of the first belt passed along the line Zaoskolye to Aleksandrovka to Rusanovka to Skorodnoye to Belyii Kolodez. This was at least 65 kilometers in length. The second belt was laid 10 to 15 kilometers behind the forward edge of the first belt, and passed along the line from Rzhavets

9 "Fifth Guards Tank Army's Combat Activities from July 7–24, 1943" (compiled 30 September 1943 by army commander Lt. General Rotmistrov and military council member Major General Grishin), Fond: 332, Opis: 4948, Delo: 19, pages 3–5, and Fond: XVIII TC, Opis: 1, Delo: 26, pages 6–7.

10 Rotmistrov's report, 30 September 1943, page 6.

11 This recap, including the distances marched, are taken from "Fifth Guards Tank Army's Combat Activities from July 7–24, 1943," compiled 30 September 1943 by army commander Lt. General Rotmistrov and military council member Major General Grishin, pages 1–6.

to Saltyikovo to Bogoslovka to Olshanka. The defensive line was 40 kilometers deep.

Major General A. I. Rodimstsev's XXXII Guards Rifle Corps occupied the army's right flank with the 13th and 66th Guards Rifle Divisions in the first echelon and the 6th Guards Airborne Division in the second echelon. Major General I. I. Popov's XXXIII Guards Rifle Corps occupied the left flank, with the 97th and 95th Guards Rifle Divisions in the first echelon and the 9th Guards Airborne Division in the second echelon. The 42nd Guards Rifle Division was stationed in the second echelon as the army reserve.

On the 8th of July, Lt. General Konev flew to the army's command post and informed them that Stavka had ordered that the Fifth Guards Army be subordinated to the Voronezh Front and that it should reach the line of the Psel by the morning of 11 July. The army was to take up defensive positions and prevent the Germans from advancing to the north and northeast. Konev also informed them that by the end of 9 July, Rotmistrov's Fifth Guards Tank Army would be concentrating to the east of Prokhorovka.[12]

AT 0430, 9 JULY, Zhadov issued orders for the XXXII Guards Rifle Corps to concentrate by the morning of the 11th in the area of Oboyan, Shipyi and Pervomaisk and to securely occupy the line of the Psel River from Oboyan to Olkhovatka. The XXXIII Guards Rifle Corps was to concentrate by the morning of 11 July in the area of Semenovka, Prokhorovka and Verkhnyaya Olshanka. The 42nd Guards Rifle Division was ordered to concentrate by the morning of 11 July in the area of Rzhavchik, the Komsomolskii Sovkhoz, Vikhrovka and Ploskoye.

The units were to move out upon receipt of the order, with the army's artillery to carry out a forced march in order to reach the Psel River by the morning of 10 July, "thus securing the unimpeded movement of the army's main force and preventing the enemy's mechanized units from crossing the river." The army's engineers were to secure the march route across the Donetskaya Seimitsa River. This included repairing six bridges and 60 kilometers of roads along the march route.

There was some German air activity during the march, with the 97th Guards Rifle Division reporting on the 9th that its march columns were being bombed. At this point, the Fifth Guards Army switched to night marches for the night of the 9/10th and 10/11th, with the units moving out at 1900 or 2000 during the night, and trying to get to their destinations by 0400 to 0700 the next morning. On the 10th, the 9th Guards Airborne Division reported single enemy aircraft flying over the division's concentration areas. These were certainly German reconnaissance missions.

The morning of the 10th, a light misty rain fell, and although the cloudy weather and light rain made the movement more difficult, it did serve to provide good cover from the air. The units of the XXXIII Guards Rifle Corps were specifically ordered to put one division along the line of Veselyii up to height 252.2, and another one from height 252.2 to Mordovka. The movement to the Psel River line was carried out in combat formations with strong forward detachments pushed forward.

By 0400 on 11 July, the army claimed to have reached its defensive positions. As the day developed, parts of the army became involved in combat, with the first units coming under artillery fire at 1100.

The XXXII Guards Rifle Corps deployed on the 13th with the 66th Guards Rifle Divisions from the unnamed stream at grid 7606 to the Zapselets River to Zorino to Shipyi, and with the 6th Guards Airborne Division in the second echelon in the Kotovo, Pervomaisk, Pselets, Mashkin area. The XXXII Guards Rifle Corps was shielded by the defending X and XXXI Tank Corps, and the 51st Guards Rifle Division.

The XXXIII Guards Rifle Corps occupied a line from Semenovka to Veselyii to height 252.2 to Mordovka, with the 97th Guards Rifle Division on the right, the 95th in the middle (from Veselyii up to height 252.2), and the 9th Guards Airborne Division on the left. Its deployment to the north of the Psel was shielded by the

12 Gen. A. S. Zhadov, *Chetyire Goda Voinyi* [Four Years of War] (Moscow, 1978), pages 86–87.

defending 52nd Guards Rifle Division. Still, there was "no solid front" in this area, so the 95th Guards Rifle Division and the 9th Guards Airborne Division did not have time to occupy their positions and had to enter the fight from the march.[13] The 26th Guards Airborne Regiment of the 9th Guards Airborne Division became engaged and by 1400 had been penetrated by the German forces that occupied height 252.2. German aircraft, in groups of up to 100 Ju-88s, bombed the units of the XXXIII Guards Rifle Corps.

The 42nd Guards Rifle Division, Zhadov's reserve, concentrated in the area of Glafirovka, up to Svino, Pogorelovka, Dumnoye, Skorovka, 2nd Zhuravka, Setnitsa and Olkhovatka.

As Zhadov summarized the situation:

> I have to admit that we had not anticipated that events at the front would develop so rapidly and that we would not be able to take up defensive positions in time along the line of Oboyan to Prokhorovka. Also, in marching to the front, we did not form strong forward detachments. This led to a situation in which the divisions' main force had to deploy directly under enemy fire.[14]

These Soviet units also did not come forward with a full load of ammunition and it was not possible to bring up more immediately. This was caused by a shortage of wagons and horses in the units. As such, by the end of the day, the Fifth Guards Army would be facing ammunition shortages which would not be rectified until the 14th.[15]

Transport was not the only shortage in these units. The 6th Guards Airborne Division on 10 July had only 6,903 rifles, semi-automatic rifles and submachineguns for its 8,916 men, while the 97th Guards Rifle Division on 10 July had only 7,465 rifles, semi-automatic rifles and submachineguns for its 8,874 men. This may not have been the case for all the units of the army, but still, it is clear that many of the units in this army were still shy of some basic equipment.[16]

Finally, a number of these units added significant amounts of people in the days before the move. For example, the 9th Guards Airborne Division received 583 people on 8 July, the 13th Guards Rifle Division received 736 men between 4 and 8 July, the 66th Guards Rifle Division added in 1,189 men between 1 and 10 July, while the 97th Guards Rifle Division added 1,555 men between 1 and 10 July.[17] This well may have been the source of the small arms shortages in these units, although in general, not every person in a Soviet division was authorized a small arm.

---

13 This claim that they had to enter the fight from the march is from Gen. A. S. Zhadov, *Chetyire Goda Voinyi* [Four Years of War] (Moscow, 1978), page 90.

14 Gen. A. S. Zhadov, *Chetyire Goda Voinyi* [Four Years of War], page 91.

15 Vatutin's After Battle Report to Stalin, page 68, claims that the units only had 0.5 loads of ammunition by the beginning of the offensive. This is certainly a true statement by end of the day of the 12th, but it appears to be true before then. The units did appear to start with one basic load before they moved forward (see below).

In the case of the 42nd Guards Rifle Division, it does note having one basic load on 6 July and only 0.6 loads for shells "at their firing points" with 0.5 loads "in transit" on the 13th. They again report one basic load on the 14th. (Fond: 42, Opis: 3, Delo: ?, pages 310–313, 327, 321). The 97th Guards Rifle Division notes for the 10th of July that the division is particularly short of transport, In moving, the division could not bring with it the necessary munitions supplies and then notes its supply situation, where two of its regiments have only 0.2 to 0.3 loads of mortar, antitank, and artillery rounds. The division started with only 299 carts, 773 horses and 74 cars. (Fond: 1271, Opis: 1, Delo: 3, pages 22–29). The 66th Guards Rifle Division had only 229 wagons, 63 cars, and only 826 horses out of 1,892 authorized. (Fond: 1197, Opis: 1, Delo: 55, pages 2 & 3, 5). The 6th Guards Airborne Division only had 146 two-horse carts, 24 one-horse carts, 794 horses and 65 cars on 10 July. (Fond: 1312, Opis: 1, Delo: 35, pages 80, 83).

16 Fond: 1312, Opis: 1, Delo: 35, pages 80, 83, and Fond: 1271, Opis: 1, Delo: 33, pages 132–133. The 66th Guards Rifle Division reported on 10 July having 5,548 small arms for its 5,522 people but also reported its strength on 1 July as 7,781 men and on 10 July as 8,744 men. (Fond: 1197, Opis: 1, Delo: 55, pages 2& 3, 5).

We only had small arms data for three of the seven divisions in the army, but found the two larger divisions to be shy of equipment. In contrast, it appears that all the units were close to authorized strength for their larger caliber weapons.

17 Fond: 1319, Opis: 1, Delo: 4, pages 44 & 45; Fond: 1075, Opis: 1, Delo: 6, pages 250–54; Fond: 1197, Opis: 1, Delo: 55, pages 2 & 3, 5, and Fond: 1271, Opis: 1: Delo: 33, pages 132 & 133.

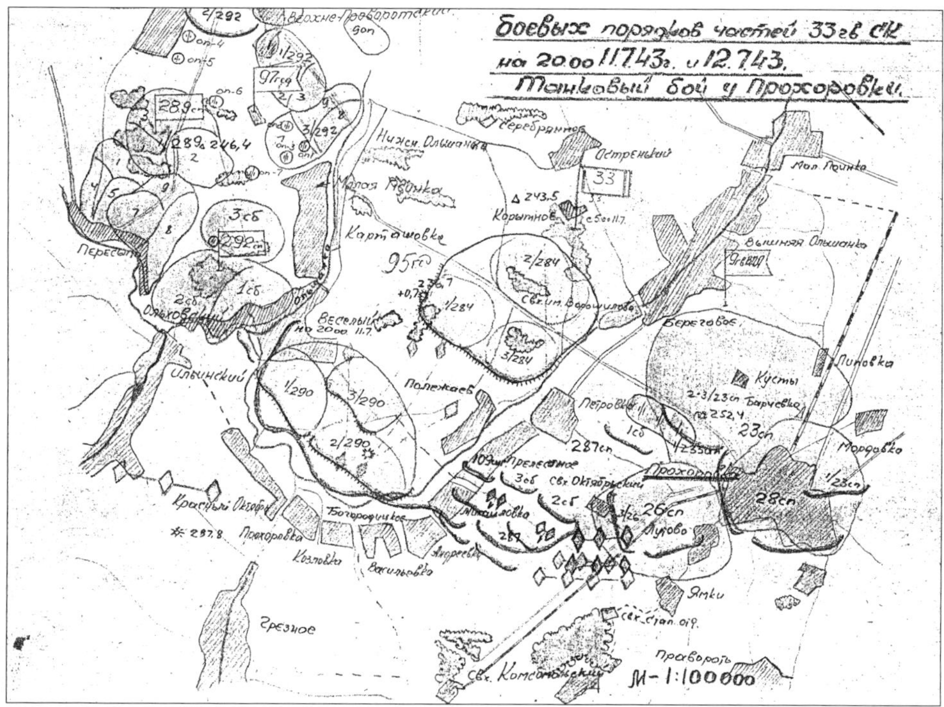

Combat positions assigned to the XXXIII Guards Rifle Corps on 2000 11 July 1943.

At 1315 (Moscow time on 11 July), Zhadov was ordered by Vatutin to launch an attack in conjunction with the Fifth Guards Tank Army with its left flank XXXIII Guards Rifle Corps in the direction of Bolshiye Mayachki and with its right flank XXXII Guards Rifle Corps, in conjunction with the Sixth Guards Army, in the direction of Krasnaya Polyana and Gremuchii.[18]

The XXXIII Guards Rifle Corps was to take advantage of the tank attack. The corps' main blow was to be launched by the 97th, 95th and 42nd Guards Rifle Divisions (attached from the army's reserve). The 9th Guards Airborne Division and the 52nd Guards Rifle Division (now attached from the Sixth Guards Army) were arrayed in defense. The 6th Guards Airborne Division was pulled from the XXXII Guards Rifle Corps and placed in army reserve, around Srednyaya Olshanka, height 243.5, and Ostrenkii, ready to exploit the XXXIII Guards Rifle Corps' success. This position was also a good blocking position to cap off any push from the southwest across the Psel, and as such, this division remained here for the next week.

The XXXII Guards Rifle Corps was left with two divisions, but reinforced by the attachment at the end of the day of the 1440th Self-Propelled Artillery Regiment. It had 14 SU-76s and 8 SU-122s, of which only 2 SU-76s and 7 SU-122s were ready for action.

Still, for the afternoon of the 11th, the Fifth Guards Army reported that the situation was not clear and nothing was known about the enemy. At 1525, the commanders of the two rifle corps and the 42nd Guards

18 The Fifth Guards Army, Fond: 328, Opis: 4852, Delo: 83, page 10, indicates that the orders were changed at 1315 (Moscow time). Gen. A. S. Zhadov, *Chetyire Goda Voinyi* [Four Years of War], page 91, states that the orders occurred in the evening. This was probably a reference to the specific attack order given at 2040.

STRAGGLERS

Any serious march leaves people behind. The nature of the Fifth Guards Army march, some 120 to 140 kilometers, created its fair share of problems. In the case of the 97th Guards Rifle Division, they provided a report of stragglers by regiment for the morning of 10 July, covering two days of marching (from 0700 to 1400 on the 9th and from 2000 on the 9th to 0500 on the 10th). The 289th Guards Rifle Regiment reported "straggling casualties" of 63 men, 25 rifles, 30 submachineguns and 8 light machineguns. The 292nd Guards Rifle Regiment reported 7 men, 3 rifles, and 4 submachineguns. The 294th Guards Rifle Regiment reported 24 men, 18 rifles, 6 submachineguns. In the case of the 13th Guards Rifle Division, they reported for 9 July that 130 men got sunstroke.

The 97th Guards Rifle Division also reported that it was particularly short of transport. In moving, it could not bring with it the necessary munitions. The division's munitions situation at 1200 on 10 July was reported in basic loads in Table 9.1.

The division then claimed that as a result of measures taken (these are not specified), the munitions supply had been raised to 1.5 loads. Still, it appears that some units went into battle not as well supplied as they should have been. By 1400 on the 11th, the 26th Guards Airborne Regiment of the engaged 9th Guards Airborne Division was suffering from ammunition shortages. The 95th Guards Rifle Division reported a similar problem, recording 1.5 ammo loads by 0400 on 11 July, and expending one ammo load in the fighting on the 11th and 12th. As no transport was available, the munitions stocks were not replenished until 2200 on the 12th.

Overall, even before they started the march, the supply situation of the Fifth Guards Army was not lush. A sample of supply by division is provided in Table 9.2 (in basic loads).

It is clear in the days after the offensive started but before the units moved (from the 5th through the 8th), that some additional ammunition and supply was brought up. This is reported by the 9th Guards Airborne Division on the 6th.

IT ALSO APPEARS that the units were given a last minute injection of reinforcements. The 9th Guards Airborne Division reported receiving 583 replacements on the 8th of July. The 13th Guards Rifle Division reported receiving 736 reinforcements between the 4th and 8th of July. The 95th Guards Rifle Division reported receiving 995 cadets from the Guryev and Kuibyishev infantry schools on the 7th of July, and another 100 cadets arrived from the Smolensk machinegun school on the 14th of July.

These reinforcements appear to consist mostly of young new recruits. As recounted by Naum Aronovich Orlov, who was 18 at the time, in June of 1943 he graduated from the Vladimir Infantry School and was sent to the 95th Guards Rifle Division as a platoon commander. As he notes, "I became a guardsman!" They then trained for two weeks and then marched to battle.[1] Captain Semen Dmitriyevich Kravchuk (commander II Battalion, 192nd Guards Rifle Regiment, 66th Guards

1 Letter from Col. Naum Aronovich Orlov, Netania, Israel, to Col. Fyodor Sverdlov, 1999.

Table 9.1
97th Guards Rifle Division Munitions Status in Basic Loads, 1200, 10 July 1943

Weapon	*289th Guards Rifle Regiment*	*292nd Guards Regiment*	*Rifle 294th Guards Rifle Regiment*
Rifle	1.0	1.5	0.7
SMG*	0.8	1.5	0.8
50mm	1.0	0.3	0.3
82mm	1.0	0.3	0.3
120mm	1.2	0.3	0.2
45mm	1.0	0.25	0.2
76mm	1.1	0.25	0.3

* Submachinegun

Table 9.2
Fifth Guards Army Supply Status, early July 1943

Unit	*Date*	*Ammunition*	*Food*	*Fuel*
9th Guards Airborne Division	4th	1.3	3 days	0.30
	8th	1.0	5 days	2.28
13th Guards Rifle Division	8th	1.0		
42nd Guards Rifle Division	6th	1.0		
66th Guards Rifle Division	6th	0.9 to 1.2		
	8th	1.0 to 1.2		
95th Guards Rifle Division	11th	1.5		

Rifle Division) also reports that half the people in his battalion were young soldiers, who arrived only in May.[2]

Overall, it appears that about ten percent of the division strength was added by last minute replacements. Most likely these were sent to the infantry, as this was where the largest shortages tended to be. As such, these replacements were certainly not well-integrated into the unit, and undoubtedly this reduced their combat effectiveness and increased their casualties.

2 Interview with Col. Semen Dmitriyevich Kravchuk was taken by Col. Valerii Akimov in Moscow on 15 November 1998. Col. Kravchuk, on the other hand, was an experienced commander, having been in the withdrawal from Kharkov to the Volga and was in the northern wing of the counteroffensive at Stalingrad. After Kursk, he was in combat up to the Elba River in 1945, where they met the Americans. He retired as a Colonel, residing in Moscow.

Rifle Division received orders to carry out a general reconnaissance with the onset of darkness, so as to improve their positions, take prisoners and determine the Germans' location. It was stated that it was necessary to finish this work by 0300 on 12 July.

At 2040, it was announced that the attack would began on 12 July at 0500 (Moscow time) with a 20-minute artillery preparation. Meanwhile, the army continued to develop its antitank defenses. Strong points were constructed with up to 50 percent of the 76mm division guns in the strong points, in addition to the 45mm guns and the 76mm regimental guns. The entire antitank defense was echeloned in depth, including mobile antitank reserves. The 29th Antitank Brigade was made the army's antitank reserve.

The Other Soviet Forces

Just to make sure their position had plenty of depth, the Soviets also had the Twenty-seventh, Forty-seventh and Fifty-third Armies moving to better positions in case of a breakthrough. The Twenty-seventh Army, consisting of six divisions and a tank brigade, started moving west on the 6th, having originally been designated for operations on the north side of the Kursk salient. It had completed a march to Maloarkhangelsk when it received orders on the 9th to move to the Kursk region and occupy defenses in the Kursk Fortified Region. Also there was the IV Guards Tank Corps, which was originally around Staraya Veduga (well east of Kursk), and had moved north through the Twenty-seventh Army positions and by the end of the 9th was in the Maloarkhangelsk area. The IV Guards Tank Corps then moved south to Kursk and on 11 July, was located in the area between Oboyan and Kursk. Meanwhile the Twenty-seventh Army, following a similar route, would arrive at Kursk on the 14th.[19]

The Forty-seventh Army, with six divisions, which was located behind the Southwestern Front in the area of Olkhovatka, Krivonosovka and Kamenka, began moving the night of 8 July to the northwest and by the 14/15th of July was concentrating in the area of Korocha. The III Guards Mechanized Corps began moving at 1400 on 10 July and also ended up concentrating around Korocha with the Forty-seventh Army.[20]

Between the Fifth Guards Army and the Twenty-seventh Army was the Fifty-third Army of seven divisions, which was occupying the Steppe Front's defensive line along the Kshen River. On the morning of the 9th it was ordered to advance to the Front defensive line along the Seim River with three divisions. By 2300 on the 12th of July it had occupied the line along the Seim River from Nechayevo to Bukino. This was a line of about 40 kilometers in length. It was supported by the I Mechanized Corps, which moved from its position around Nizhnedevitsk (well east of Kursk) at 0900 on 7 July, moved through the Fifty-third Army's positions and then south, where it held on the Seim River.[21] This was a significant force now located within 40 kilometers of the current front line.

Effectively the Soviets had another line of forces forming, consisting of three more armies, each supported by a tank or mechanized corps, with the Twenty-seventh Army north of Oboyan covering Kursk; the Fifty-third Army covering the Seim River behind Prokhorovka; and the Forty-seventh Army covering Korocha. In light of the Fifth Guards Army bringing up its division's strengths by hundreds of men in the days just before battle, and its shortfalls in transports and sometimes small arms, the state of these units would not be expected to be any better.

The Fourth Guards Army had also started unloading in the region of Kastornoye, due east of Kursk, around the 12th, adding a potential reserve behind this newly forming echelon.[22] Furthermore, the Soviets had other forces available, including the VII Guards Cavalry

19 Erickson, page 106, and Glantz and Orenstein, pages 93 and 105.

20 Glantz and Orenstein, page 93.

21 Erickson, page 106, and Glantz and Orenstein, pages 93 and 106.

22 Glantz and Orenstein, page 93.

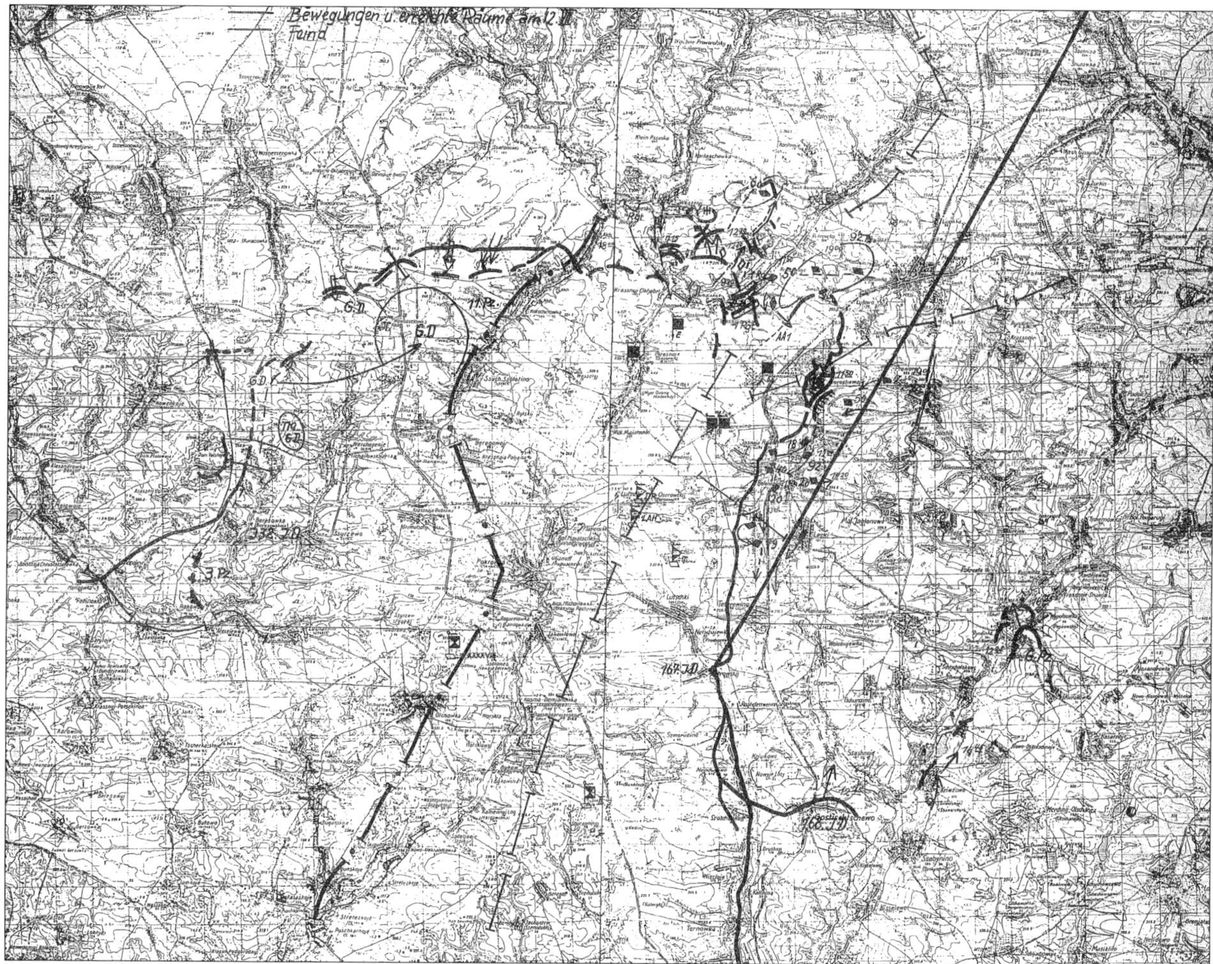

THE SS PANZER CORPS MAP SHOWING POSITIONS ON THE 12TH OF JULY.

Corps, III Guards Cavalry Corps and V Guards Cavalry Corps in the area behind the Southwestern Front, while the Central Front had the just recently engaged III, IX, XVI and XIX Tank Corps on the northern side of the salient that could have been made available for operations in the south.

The SS Panzer Corps' Mission

This engagement has sometimes been described as a meeting engagement, with the Germans about to attack at dawn. In fact, in the area of the "tank fields of Prokhorovka" (the open area southwest of Prokhorovka where hill 252.2 is located), the orders given at 2250 the evening of the 11th told the Adolf Hitler SS Division to hold the current line with its left wing, while its right wing was to push forward to the line east of Yamki. The Totenkopf SS Division was to advance on the left to the Beregovoye-Kartashevka road and roll up the Psel valley from the north and south. The two divisions were then to attack toward Prokhorovka after the elimination of flank threat from the Psel valley. Das Reich SS Division was to hold with its right wing while it took Vinogradovka and Ivanovka with its Deutschland SS

Regiment, following the right flank of the Adolf Hitler's attack. It was then to push forward into the high ground southwest of Pravorot.

The first priority of the day was getting the Totenkopf attack going.

The Nature of the Data

The XLVIII Panzer Corps with its chief of staff, Colonel von Mellenthin, having been an officer of the general staff, had good detailed records throughout its operations, including useful daily summaries of the action. The record-keeping in the SS Panzer Corps, on the other hand, suffered when the fighting got intense. While they kept good status reports, their daily reports of activity seemed to almost disappear when the fighting got the toughest. As a result, on the day of greatest drama, the record keeping for one of the major players almost disappeared.

Some of this can be recreated using interviews. There were also Nazi-era propaganda pieces issued that described the battle. While their descriptions may well be accurate in many cases, the fact that they were issued for propaganda purposes make these extremely suspect sources.[23] In history, any data is not good data, it must be evaluated. Therefore, this description of the Battle of Prokhorovka, with one exception, documents only those things that are clearly recorded and uses only those interviews which we took ourselves. While this leaves out many of the personal battle accounts that have proliferated over the years, our goal is to debunk the myth, not add to it. Therefore, while more detailed and dramatic descriptions of the battle may be found elsewhere, the reader is warned to view them with caution.

The 97th Guards Rifle Division Attack on Kochetovka

Zhadov's Fifth Guards Army moved forward with the 97th Guards Rifle Division on the right while the 95th Guards Rifle Division remained in place on the left. By 1300 on 11 July the 97th Guards Rifle Division was deployed along the Psel from the northern outskirts of Peresyip to the southern outskirts of Veselyii and on to its eastern edge, with the 289th and 294th Guards Rifle Regiments in the first echelon from Peresyip to Veselyii, and the 292nd Guards Rifle Regiment in the second echelon.

At 0830, following an artillery bombardment, the 97th Guards Rifle Division had pushed aside the German forward positions and by 0900 (Moscow time) had advanced to the line from height 183.1 to Ilinskii. At 0930, the 289th Guards Rifle Regiment, on the division's right, had captured height 209.3 and by 1200 had reached the southeastern outskirts of Kochetovka. By this time, the 294th Guards Rifle Regiment had reached Krasnyii Oktyabr. The neighboring 66th Guards Rifle Division had reached the road at height 227.0 to height 235.9 (and pushed down into Kochetovka) while the 95th Guards Rifle Division remained in place.

At 1515 (Berlin time) the Soviets launched another attack from Ilinskii aimed at Kochetovka. This attack by the 97th Guards Rifle Division stalled at Kochetovka, where they were still fighting as of 1900 (Moscow time). Their line extended from the unnamed height southeast of height 209.3 to northeast of height 166.6, and "further to the southeast until the letter 'K' in the sign 'Krasnyii Oktyabr'." By 2000 the 294th Guards Rifle Regiment reached the line "MUK" to the northern slopes of the gully east of "MUK" to the letter "K" in the name Krasnyii Oktyabr. By the end of the day, the 289th Guards Rifle Regiment had stopped on the line 300 meters west of height 209.8 to "MUK," and the 292nd Guards Rifle Regiment was in reserve on height 189.1.[24] It appears

23 For example, see the biography of Joachim Peiper, Commander of Panzer Regiment Leibstandarte by Patrick Agte, see Patrick Agte, *Jochen Peiper, Kommandeur Panzerregiment Leibstandarte* (Kurt-Vohwinckel-Verlag, 82335 Berg am Stamberger See, I. Auglage 1998), pages 132–143.

24 This is how the position is referred to in the notes we received from the Soviet records. While not a particular useful description as we do not know exactly which map they are referring

that most of the weight of this attack fell on the 11th Panzer Division on this day.

The Fight North of the Psel

Totenkopf, whose bridgehead stood across the Psel, was attacked in the morning by elements of the newly arriving Fifth Guards Army, though these Soviet forces had little armor.

The 95th Guards Rifle Division during the night regrouped with the 290th Guards Rifle Regiment stretched from Veselyii to just shy of height 226.6. The 284th Guards Rifle Regiment occupied the southwestern, southern and southeastern slopes of height 226.6 along with the 52nd Guards Rifle Division. The 287th Guards Rifle Regiment was located from Mikhailovka to Prelestnoye to Petrovka. The 11th Motorized Rifle Brigade from the X Tank Corps was still in the area. It deployed two battalions on height 226.6 with the support of the artillery battalion.[25]

Totenkopf reported Soviet attacks on the barracks northwest of Klyuchi at 0330 and 0730. These Soviet infantry attacks were both defeated, the first attack being in battalion strength but without tanks, although the second attack had tank support.[26] At 0630, Totenkopf was complaining about the Soviets conducting a slow infiltration on the flank positions at the barracks west of Klyuchi along with heavy artillery and Katyusha fire. Totenkopf's advance to the northeast was still on hold.

At 0400 (Berlin time) Totenkopf took the panzer battalion that had crossed over the river the previous day, and began advancing against the barracks (at Klyuchi?). They reported taking them at 0715. The 52nd Guards Rifle Division reported a German attack at 0500 (Moscow time) in the morning. The 52nd Guards Rifle Division was now reported to have a strength of only 3,380, although with elements still in the Donets triangle, this was not a complete strength report. This division was low on ammunition but well supplied with food. It was ordered to attack from the area around height 226.6 to Polezhayev and to take Bogoroditskoye, Kozlovka and Vasilyevka and then push on to Greznoye. The 95th Guards Rifle Division was also supposed to attack, but apparently it stumbled in its efforts. As the Fifth Guards Army noted:

---

to or what scale, they are left in this account until such time as we can locate a better description. We were not able to copy the 97th Guards Rifle Division records at that time.

25 The 11th Motorized Rifle Brigade deployment is from Zamulin, *Demolishing the Myth*, page 380. He provides a more detailed description of their deployment on page 383:

> "The Soviet defenses were arranged in two echelons. Units of Lieutenant Colonel G. G. Pantiukhov's 52nd Guards Rifle Division comprised the first echelon. The 151st Guards Rifle Regiment was covering the sector running from a hill lying 500 meters north of Kliuchi to the southwestern slopes of Hill 226.6. . . . The 155th Guards Rifle Regiment was defending Hill 226.6 directly, with its defenses arranged toward the southwest [and south?] in the direction of Kozlovka, Vesil'evka and Andreevka. The 153rd Guards Rifle Regiment's positions extended from the southwest slopes of Hill 226.6 to Polezhaev. The 11th Motorized Rifle Brigade's 3rd Motorized Rifle Battalion had dug-in directly on the crest of Hill 226.6, while its 2nd Rifle Battalion was defending the southeastern outskirts of Vasil'evka and Andreevka, covering bridges over the Psel River."
>
> "The 95th Guards Rifle Division was in the second echelon. Its 290th Guards Rifle Regiment was located on the line: southern outskirts of Veselyi-Kliuchi-woods southeast of Kliuchi. The 284th Guards Rifle Regiment was holding the sector Hill 236.7—Voroshilovski State Farm—Hill 243.5. Prior to the morning of 12 July, its 287th Guards Rifle Regiments had been located northeast of Oktiabr'skii State Farm, fighting together with the 9th Guards Airborne Division's 26th Guards Airborne Regiment for possession of the State Farm and Hill 252.2. Around 0800 12 July, it had been withdrawn into the division commander's reserve in the area of Veselyi."
>
> "At 2215 11 July, Lieutenant General A. S. Zhadov brought up Colonel M. N. Smirnov's 6th Guards Airborne Division to the Sredniaia Ol'Shanka—Hill 243.5—Ostrenkii area. The 6th Guards Airborne Division provided the army a reserve force."

26 I am not sure of the source of this armor, but it probably was the 99th Tank Brigade. The 99th Tank Brigade was in this area on the 11th (as of 0700) but on the 12th was reported to be concentrated in Krasnoye as of 1900. It appears that the tank brigade lost 12 tanks between 0700 on 11 July and 1900 12 July. See Fond: 3407, Opis: 1, Delo: 108, pages 195–216.

In the first two days of fighting, one notes a lack of operational interaction, reconnaissance and coordination among the corps.

Basic shortcomings pointed out by the operational section of the army staff are the absence of artillery interaction with the 95th Guards Rifle Division. The units did not arrive on time at their jump-off positions. Regimental commanders did not understand their orders sufficiently. For example, Lt. Colonel Seletskii and Major Kakmovtsev were called to divisional headquarters at 0800 in order to receive their instructions, when the battle had already begun.[27]

The 95th Guards Rifle Division was moving forward to take over the positions of the 52nd Guards Rifle Division. When the Totenkopf SS Division attacked from Kliuchi and towards Veselyii in the morning (at 0525 Moscow time), they ended up preempting this effort, catching the division on the move and out of position. The entire command staff of the artillery regiment and its battery commanders were away on reconnaissance. The German attack threatened to encircle two battalions of the 290th Guards Rifle Regiment and the attached 108th Penal Company.[28] The regiment commander left his post and then lied to his commander about the positions of his units.[29]

The 11th Motorized Rifle Brigade, left behind by the X Tank Corps, continued to hold on top of hill 226.6 after the Germans took it and fought for two hours before those units withdrew.[30]

At 0830, the 153rd Guards Rifle Regiment of the 52nd Guards Rifle Division advanced in the direction of Polezhayev, but it was repulsed and fell back to the area east of Polezhayev. The 155th Guards Rifle Regiment also pushed forward, but fell back to the north to join up with the 151st Guards Rifle Regiment, fighting in the area between Veselyii and Klyuchi and to the west towards the road intersection. It would appear that the 95th Guards Rifle Division did not support this attack, and overall, little coordinated offensive action was conducted by the units north of the Psel.

Meanwhile, while Totenkopf was about to be hit hard in its right flank by the XVIII Tank Corps, it continued to prepare for its attack to the northeast. The last elements for the SS attack finally crossed into the bridgehead at 0900, and at 0930 the armored group jumped off from hill 226.6 to the northeast. The Fifth Guards Army reported the Germans launched an attack with up to 100 tanks at 1215 (Moscow time) in the direction of height 226.6, which was successful and which then

27 Fifth Guards Army, Fond 328, Opis 4852, Delo 83, page 16.

28 The account of the 290th Guards Rifle Regiment operations is from Zamulin, *Demolishing the Myth*, pages 385–387. Our research for the Kursk Data Base did not indentify the penal company.

29 Zamulin, *Demolishing the Myth*, page 386. This is in accordance with a report filed by the division commander.

30 On 14 July 1943, the brigade's political officer wrote this dispatch:

"At 1200 12 July 1943 the enemy launched a resolute attack on our brigade's defenses. . . . After five hours of uninterrupted, bitter fighting, which included hand-to-hand combat in the trenches; exploiting the lack of steadfastness of our neighbors to the right—the 95th Guards Rifle Division's 156th Guards Rifle Regiment, and on the left—the 52nd Guards Rifle Division's 151st Guards Rifle Regiment, which exposed our flanks by falling back, the enemy succeeded in breaking into the depths of our defense with tanks and motorized infantry and in developing the offensive with attacks on our front, flanks and rear. For the next two hours, the 2nd and 3rd Motorized Rifle Battalions fought in complete encirclement, while the 1st Motorized Rifle Battalion struggled in semi-encirclement. Numerically small and weakened by the breakdown of weapons, the brigade was compelled under the cover of artillery to withdraw from the fight and turn over the defense to units of the 95th Guards Rifle Division and the 42nd Guards Rifle Division. . . ."

". . . Alongside the positive factors in the brigade, there were manifestations of criminal cowardice. The commander of the 1st Motorized Rifle Battalion Captain Timov and his chief of staff Captain Bugarsky ran away from the command post at the very climax of the intense fighting. Battalion commander Comrade Timov lost all control over his men and wound up at the command post of a different unit, while his chief of staff Captain Bugarsky completely ran away to the rear area of his battalion, and for two days of intense combat never showed himself on the battlefield...An investigation into the facts surrounding the criminal cowardliness of the aforementioned commanders is being treated as a case subject to the justice of a military tribunal."

See Zamulin, *Demolishing the Myth*, page 389.

pushed on north to the eastern outskirts of Veselyii and height 236.7. The Fifth Guards Army commander, General Zhadov, was on hill 236.7, the "commanding height" in the area, at the command post of the 95th Guards Artillery Division's artillery commander. The hill ended up being defended by artillery regiment and the antitank artillery battalion.[31] As a result of this attack, the 95th Guards Rifle Division suffered "heavy casualties" and was pushed back to the eastern slopes of height 226.6, where it continued fighting. The 95th Guards Rifle Division only recorded 62 killed and 53 wounded for this day.[32] This is certainly an underestimate for this day and this day's losses may have been 1,000 or more.[33] Any German push to the north or northeast was covered by the 6th Guards Airborne Division, which was hurriedly taking up defensive positions from Srednyaya Olshanka to height 243.5 to Ostrenkii to the heights to the east. All their gun artillery had been moved up to positions for direct fire.

Still, the Soviets tried to maintain pressure on the northern flank of the Totenkopf SS Division with more attacks at 1110 (Berlin time) south of Veselyii and Ilinskii. At least one of these attacks during the day from the north included an estimated 40 tanks. But what temporarily diverted Totenkopf's drive to the northeast was its decision at 1115 (Berlin time) to turn its armor south to cross the Psel at Mikhailovka and move in behind the Soviets south of the Psel. This particular attack did not advance far. But, some of Totenkopf's armor did cross to the south of the Psel this day, most likely at Bogoroditskoye. This would put them in front of the XVIII Tank Corps' attack. They then got into a heavy exchange with the XVIII Tank Corps as a result of its attack along the seam between the Totenkopf and Adolf Hitler SS Divisions. This is discussed further in the XVIII Tank Corps attack. Before the end of the day, the armored group was again able to advance to the northeast.

At 1500 (Berlin time) the Totenkopf armored group was now two kilometers northwest of Polezhayev, having returned to its original objective for the day after having been diverted in the early afternoon towards Mikhailovka (see below). At 1630 (Moscow time), the Soviets reported that the German offensive had been halted, but fighting clearly continued, for at 1835 (Berlin time), the SS Panzer Corps reported that the armored group from Totenkopf were engaged in heavy tank battles about one kilometer northwest of Polezhayev. Meanwhile, the Soviets continued their attacks on the Totenkopf northern flank with an attack at 1725 (Berlin time) with 700 men without tanks southward from Ilinskii.

In the extremely active operations north of the Psel, there is an odd claim in the Soviet records that at 1600 (Moscow time) 36 German tanks from hill 226.6 descended into the depression north of that hill and moved through the ravine west of Polezhayev, and headed towards hill 236.7 (some four kilometers away). Reaching the hill, the tanks spend an hour driving back and forth on it, and then departed into the depression west of hill 236.7.[34] This action is not reported in the

31 Zamulin, *Demolishing the Myth*, page 388, some of which is quoted from Zhadov's memoirs. It is not clearly stated how far the German advance had moved from height 226.6 to height 237.6. The distance between the two heights was a little over four kilometers. Zhadov's account states that fighting occurred on the "southern slopes of the hill." This would put the action within a kilometer of the hill top and in line with the eastern outskirts of Veselyii. This means that the Totenkopf SS Division was able to advance over three kilometers north in the face of the XXXIII Guards Rifle Corps offensive.

32 It reported suffering 96 men killed and 132 wounded for the 11th and 12th, and 34 men killed, 79 wounded and 5 horses killed on the 11th.

33 The division gives a casualty figure for the 11th through the 14th of 948 killed, 1,469 wounded, 729 missing, 56 horses killed and 82 horses wounded. With the reported figures for 11–12 July of 96 killed and 132 wounded, then we are looking at 2,918 casualties for the 13th and 14th. It does not appear that the fighting on the 13th and 14th was significantly more intense than the fighting on the 12th.

34 Zamulin, *Demolishing the Myth*, page 390. The report is from the 52nd Guards Rifle Division. As he notes in his book, "The cited document doesn't give a clear picture of what occurred at this time in the valleys and on the hills in the bend of the river. . . . This gives the readers of the operational summary the impression that the tanks, without encountering any resistance, 'cruised around' the hill for an hour, and then on their own decided to depart into the depression." I gather he does not fully accept this account.

German records and probably overstates the operation. It is hard to understand how they could drive to hill 236.7 without a significant fight. The main attack in the afternoon by Totenkopf's armor was to the northeast between Polezhayev and hill 236.7 and towards height 235.3, which would cut the road between the Kartashevka and Prokhorovka.

Finally, at 1900 (Moscow time) the Fifth Guards Army reported that its troops were encountering difficulties with ammunition supply. In certain units, only half of the basic complement of munitions, fuel and food remained.[35]

The V Guards Mechanized Corps Deploys Against Totenkopf

The Germans were breaking through to the area of Polezhayev farm. The Fifth Guards Army had no more units to the east, with the area being occupied only by headquarters, rear, and army units. This created a threat to the flank of the Fifth Guards Tank Army, forcing Rotmistrov to move the 24th Guards Tank Brigade and the 10th Guards Mechanized Brigade into the area north of the Psel.[36]

With Trufanov's detachment and the 11th and 12th Mechanized Brigades sent south during the day, this was the Fifth Guards Tank Army's last reserve. By 1900 on the 12th, the 10th Guards Mechanized Brigade and the 24th Guards Tank Brigade had concentrated in the Basenkov, Bakhteyevka, Gusek and Pogorelovka area and received orders to attack the Germans at 2000 in the area of the ravine west of Veselyii. At 2030 (Moscow time), the army reported that the Germans (Totenkopf SS Division) had broken through and reached the line of the northern outskirts of Polezhayev to height 236.7. Rotmistrov then threw the 10th Guards Mechanized Brigade into the area of Ostrenkii (Vostrenkoye) with the mission of preventing the Germans from advancing to the east and northeast. The 24th Guards Tank Brigade was thrown into the area of Voroshilov Sovkhoz with orders to attack the Germans in the direction of the grove one kilometer west of the sovkhoz and prevent the Germans from advancing to the east and northeast. Still, these brigades did not report any casualties for this day.[37]

The fight against Totenkopf's advance to the northeast was conducted by elements of the 284th Guards Rifle Regiment and the majority of the 233rd Guards Artillery Regiment, both units part of the 95th Guards Rifle Division. This was a particularly dangerous attack as height 235.3 was almost on the Kartashevka-Prokhorovka road. Taking it would have cut the road and effectively flanked the XVIII Tank Corps. The defensive fight was primarily conducted by Soviet artillery and antitank guns, firing over "open sights" (direct fire).[38] The commander of the artillery regiment was killed at his observation post during the fighting.[39]

By nightfall the Totenkopf armored group had overcome two strong "pakfronts" (lines of antitank guns) and was battling Soviet tank units on the division's

35 A specific example of this is provided in the 95th Guards Rifle Division's journal: "At the time of the division's arrival in the region of defense, it had only a 1 to 1.5 combat loads of ammunition, of which it had already expended up to one day's worth [on the morning of 12 July]. Despite requests for assistance by providing transportation for bringing up more ammunition from the army-level dumps, superior commanders rendered no assistance at all. Available trucks—ten—on 11.07.43 had been sent to the army dumps for ammunition, and the last trucks returned empty at 2200 12.07.43. All this affected the course of the battle.

Moreover, our own aviation twice struck the combat formations of our infantry and artillery, as a result of which two tractors were smashed together with the artillery shells they were towing; (there are) losses in personnel." (See Zamulin, *Demolishing the Myth*, page 389).

36 Zhadov, page 93.

37 Zamulin, *Demolishing the Myth*, page 399, makes the same observation and also notes that Rotmistrov's account of the action here are in error.

38 Zamulin, *Demolishing the Myth*, page 392. Zamulin, page 398, has the losses for the 284th Guards Rifle Regiment this day as 137 men killed in the I Rifle Battalion, 51 in the II Rifle Battalion, and 8 in the III Rifle Battalion.

39 Zamulin, *Demolishing the Myth*, page 394. This was Major A. P. Revin, who in many Soviet-era accounts is reported as killed at a gun, where he had taken the place of a fallen gun layer. This type of narrative embellishment is common in Soviet-era writings.

front and flank. It had captured the hills just west of the village of Polezhayev. At 2245, Totenkopf's armored group reported that it had reached the Beregovoye-Kartashevka road. Its goals were to block it during the night. By the end of the day, Totenkopf reported that it had advanced effectively another three kilometers to put its front line along the western edge of Andreyevka, to height 228.3, to the barracks, to the north edge of Krasnyii Oktyabr, to the northeast edge of Kochetovka.[40] On its far left, Totenkopf had lost contact with the 11th Panzer Division because of the Soviet penetration at Kochetovka.

The Totenkopf SS Division did participate in the legendary "death ride" of the panzers on this day, and its contribution in fighting the XVIII Tank Corps is discussed below.[41] In spite of the XVIII Tank Corps morning attack, the division was able to continue its slow steady advance to the northeast in the afternoon, in an attempt to flank the Prokhorovka position. Still, it was not able to get to height 252.4, and another two Soviet tank brigades had been inserted into its path.

It is hard to determine how many tanks were lost by Totenkopf during the day. A portion of its armored group participated in stopping the XVIII Tank Corps south of the Psel. A portion of its armored group then attacked in the afternoon north of the Psel. The Totenkopf SS Division did provide a report for this day of the number of tanks ready for action but it is probably incorrect, as it shows a decline of only one ready-for-action "Pz III long" from the previous day (from 54 to 53) and an increase of one more "Pz VI" (from 9 to 10). As the unit was heavily engaged this day, this report is clearly not current. On the 11th at 1835 it reported the following ready for action:

Pz III long	54
Pz IV short	4
Pz IV long	26
Pz VI	9
Command tanks	7
StuG III	unchanged (21)
SP AT Guns	unchanged (11)

On the 13th, after two days of attacks they reported the following ready for action as of 1935:

Pz III long	32
Pz IV short	3
Pz IV long	14
Pz VI	0
Command tanks	5
StuG III	20
SP AT Guns	2

This is a decline of 56 tanks over a two day period. On both the 12th and the 13th they were attacking. There is no reason to believe that the majority of those 56 tanks were lost on the 12th. In fact, there is reason to believe that the reverse is true, as their attacks on the 13th appear to have been more extensive. Still, it is hard to believe that they went through the 12th without loss, especially as their armored group was attacking throughout the day and also engaged in an armor fight with the XVIII Tank Corps. Therefore, one can only determine the losses over two days (57 tanks),[42] and estimate that they may have lost 20 to 30 tanks on this day, almost all of them damaged. Among those lost were those that had mechanical breakdowns that were not repaired by the 13th. Obviously, we could not count any tanks knocked out or broken down on the 12th that were repaired before the evening report on the 13th (although the report of the 12th of July does imply that one Panzer VI was placed back in action). When

40 This was a line a couple of kilometers shy of heights 236.7 and 235.3. An examination of the SS Panzer Corps map for 12 July (see page 305) shows them deployed on this line but with arrows going to height 235.3.

41 The phrase "death ride" comes from Alan Clark, page 337, and others.

42 The 10-day status report for the 10th appears to record the tank status for the 11th. It appears to report one more Panzer VI in action, resulting in the difference between 56 or 57 tanks lost. We chose the higher figure.

they were on the offensive, they were facing primarily infantry, antitank guns and artillery. When they were fighting around Andreyevka, they were facing Soviet armor. It is hard to determine which of these tank losses were due to the Soviet defensive efforts rather than to attacks by Soviet armor.

General Popov's Nighttime Counterattack (11/12 July)

The commander of the XXXIII Guards Rifle Corps, Major General I. I. Popov, in order to restore the situation on his left flank, ordered the 95th Guards Rifle and 9th Guards Airborne Divisions to launch a night attack with the 287th Guards Rifle Regiment of the 95th Guards Rifle Division and the 26th Guards Airborne Regiment of the 9th Guards Airborne Division to restore the situation in the Oktyabrskii Sovkhoz and height 252.2 area. These attacks appear to have had little results, and may not have been aggressively pushed. The Adolf Hitler SS Division noted that it was a "notably quiet night." It appears that the primary effort of this attack was to move the 287th Guards Rifle Regiment into the little valley area from Mikhailovka to Petrovka. Here it was out of position and unable to support the rest of the division for the upcoming fight. During the morning, the units of the 42nd Guards Rifle Division and tanks from the XVIII Tank Corps would attack through the 287th Guards Rifle Regiment.

Rotmistrov's Attack

On this day Rotmistrov unleashed the most famous and misunderstood tank attack of the war. He would observe the attack from his forward command post at hill 252.4.

The Fifth Guards Tank Army Attack Plan

As Rotmistrov moved up, he had potentially five armored corps at his disposal. These were the three corps he brought with him as part of the army, and two corps just assigned to his command. Inside the Donets triangle were the II Tanks Corps and II Guards Tank Corps. Just brought up through Prokhorovka and arriving during the middle of the night were the XVIII Tank and XXIX Tank Corps. Lagging behind, and in the second echelon, was the large V Guards Mechanized Corps. These units had marched almost to Oboyan, and had now turned around and marched back to this area to support this attack. The army headquarters was in Skorovka, seven kilometers northeast of Prokhorovka, while Rotmistrov's observation post was at height 252.4, two kilometers northwest of Prokhorovka.

The army's attack was preceded by a 30-minute artillery bombardment. This artillery preparation, while claimed to have lasted 30 minutes, was probably not very significant. The only significant indirect artillery available was the 678th Howitzer Regiment with 20 122mm Howitzers, which was attached to the XXIX Tank Corps except for one battery that was attached to the XVIII Tank Corps.

The Fifth Guards Tank Army did have artillery, but it does not appear that it had deployed them yet. The unit had assembled a long-range artillery group consisting of four howitzer and gun regiments with a total of 56 122mm to 203mm guns.[43] It also had three guards mortar regiments and two battalions with a total of 88 Katyushas.[44] It also had the 285th and 271st Mortar Regiments, each with 36 120mm mortars. On 11 July, the 120mm mortars had 2.2 loads, the 122mm howitzers had 2.1 loads, while the Katyushas had 2.0 loads. With all this artillery, the Fifth Guards Tank Army still only fired 1,800 120mm mortar rounds and only 400 122mm rounds on the 12th. This is effectively 20 volleys from the howitzers of the 678th Howitzer Regiment, or

43 The 522nd Howitzer Regiment had 12 203mm guns, the 1148th Howitzer Regiment had 18 152mm guns, the 142nd Gun Regiment had 18 122mm guns and the 93rd Gun Regiment had 18 122mm guns.

44 Their group of guards mortar regiments consisted of the 16th Guards Mortar Regiment with 24 M-13s, the 80th Guards Mortar Regiment with 24 M-13s, the 76th Guards Mortar Regiment with 24 M-13s and the two independent battalions with a total of 16 M-13s.

overall, between the 120mm mortars and 122mm howitzers, a little over 40 tons of artillery ammunition.[45] In contrast, the SS Panzer Corps on this day consumed an estimated 500 tons of artillery ammunition.[46] It does not appear that the Fifth Guards Tank Army was able to make good use of its assembled artillery on this day and it does not appear that its artillery had a major impact on the defending Germans.

Rotmistrov launched his famous attack with three tank corps. The XVIII and the XXIX Tank Corps attacked across what has become known as the tank fields of Prokhorovka, while the II Guards Tank Corps, with some support from the II Tank Corps, attacked farther south against the flank of the SS Panzer Corps.

The army was ordered to attack in the general direction of Prokhorovka-Aleksandrovskii, and on to Pokrovka and Tomarovka, in conjunction with First Tank Army and Fifth Guards Army. At first it was planned to launch the blow from Belenikhino to the west. However, the terrain in this area turned out to be unfavorable for tanks, so the axis from Prokhorovka to Malyie Mayachki and Pokrovka was chosen.

The Fifth Guards Tank Army at 1000 on 12 July was to attack in the area bounded on the right by the Beregovoye–Andreyevka–outskirts of Krasnaya Polyana–Krasnaya Dubrava and on the left by Pravorot-Belenikhino—height 232.0—the mound +1.1—three kilometers southwest of Yakovlevo. This three-corps attack had a frontage of only nine or ten kilometers, and went head on into the attacking German formations. It was bounded on its right by the Psel River and had no clear terrain boundary on its left. Running down the center of the attack area were the road and railroad that went southwest from Prokhorovka.

The jump-off point for the attack was the line Prelestnoye-Storozhevoye-Maloye Yablonovo, which was to be occupied by 2400 on 11 July. By the end of the 12th the corps was to advance to the line of Krasnaya Dubrava, height 254.5 to Yakovlevo, having in mind advancing further to the southwest. This was a line 20 to 26 kilometers away from the jump-off point. Considering that no one on either side in the past seven days of fighting had achieved such an advance, this again appears to be somewhat optimistic.

Specifically, the XVIII Tank Corps was to break the German's resistance along the line Andreyevka-the grove northwest of the Komsomolets Sovkhoz. This was the open rolling ground between the Psel and the railroad, with an attack frontage of around four kilometers. They were then to advance some 20 kilometers and destroy the Germans in the Krasnaya Dubrava, Bolshiye Mayachki, Krasnaya Polyana area, then turn to the north and support the army's offensive to the south. Its unit boundary on the left was height 252.4 (exclusive) to northwest edge of the grove one kilometer north of the Komsomolets Sovkhoz (exclusive) to the poultry farm on the northern outskirts of Bolshiye Mayachki (exclusive).

The XXIX Tank Corps was to break the German resistance along the line of the grove one kilometer north of the Komsomolets Sovkhoz–Komsomolets Sovkhoz, which basically meant attacking straight down the road. It was then to destroy the German forces in the Luchki-Bolshiye Mayachki-Pokrovka area and by the end of 12 July reach the line Pokrovka to the grove west and south of Pokrovka, and to be ready to advance farther south. Its boundary on the left was Grushki-Storozhevoye-Yasnaya Polyana (exclusive)—height 228.4—the mill on the northern outskirts of Pogorelovka. It also had an attack frontage of about four kilometers. The 678th Howitzer Regiment was to provide support before the attack started.

The II Guards Tank Corps had the task of breaking the German resistance along the line Yasnaya Polyana-Belenikhino. This was an attack area of about two kilometers. It was then to destroy the German forces in the area of Yakovlevo and the woods to the east, and to be ready to further attack south.

45 This is based upon the weight of the entire round as transported (which is heavier than the actual round) so as to match with how we are recording German ammunition weight.

46 Calculated in the Kursk Data Base from the German supply records. It is based upon the weight of the entire round as transported (which is heavier than the actual round). For 12 July the SS Panzer Corps reported firing a total 738 tons of munitions, vice 619 tons for the 11th. See T354, R607, pages 517 and 521.

The II Tank Corps was to remain in its defensive positions while covering the army's concentration for the attack. The corps was given the task of supporting the other corps by fire and to let them attack through its lines and be ready to operate in the direction of Sukhoye Solotino.

The V Guards Mechanized Corps received orders to concentrate by 2400 on 11 July in Sokolovka-Dranyii-Krasnoye-Vyisyipnoi-Sagaidachnoye-Kamyishevka area, constituting the army's second echelon and to be ready to develop the success of the XXIX Tank Corps and the II Guards Tank Corps in the general direction of Prokhorovka-Aleksandrovka-Luchki-Smorodino. Trufanov's detachment was to leave its defensive positions around Oboyan, concentrate around Pravorot, and to become part of the army reserve in order to secure the army's left flank.

In effect, the Soviets were going to make an attack with three armored corps head on into the German SS Panzer Corps. Why Vatutin thought this was going to work better than the attack by one corps and two brigades on the 6th, or the attack by two corps on the 8th, has never been explained. This attack was scheduled to begin at 1000 (Moscow time).

The III Panzer Corps Draws Attention

As a result of its continued pushing in the south, the III Panzer Corps was becoming more worrisome to the Soviet command. At 0500, Vatutin ordered Rotmistrov to throw a strong mobile group into the Ryindinka, Avdeyevka and Bolshiye Podyarugi area to halt the German offensive and dislodge them from their bridgehead at Ryindinka and Rzhavets.[47] At 0800, it was reported at the Fifth Tank Army headquarters that a large German force, supported by about 80 tanks, had broken through to the southwest and had taken Rzhavets and Vyipolzovka, and was moving on Avdeyevka. This was threatening the army's left flank and rear. Therefore, the army decided to send part of its reserve forces, Trufanov's detachment and the 11th and 12th Mechanized Brigades, to the south to deal with this problem. Major General Trufanov was to take command of these forces, one regiment of the 375th Rifle Division, the 92nd Guards Rifle Division, and the 26th Guards Tank Brigade of the II Guards Tank Corps and to destroy the German forces in the Ryindinka-Rzhavets area (the 375th was never redeployed to the south).

This left only the 10th Guards Mechanized Brigade and 24th Guards Tank Brigade to reinforce the attack planned for 1000. As the Voronezh Front became concerned about the III Panzer Corps attacks that morning, the initial time of 1000 that had been set for the attack was moved forward by Vatutin to 0830 (Moscow time)! Why one would move the attack time forward in response to a flank threat is hard to explain.

Now their attack was being even more hastily conducted and most of their reserve, which was their largest formation, was being sent south to deal with another threat. At 0830 (Moscow time), following a short artillery preparation, the army moved into the attack.

The Tank Fields of Prokhorovka

With the XVIII Tank Corps bounded on the right by the Psel River and the XXIX Tank Corps' left flank running from Grushki to Storozhevoye, these two tank corps were primarily attacking the Leibstandarte SS Adolf Hitler Division, whose front line ran from the Psel to Storozhevoye. It was at these flanking points that the division received considerable support during this day from the Totenkopf SS Division at Vasilyevka and from the Das Reich SS Division at Storozhevoye.

At 0500, Adolf Hitler SS Division reported that after a notably quiet night, they were hearing numerous tank noises along their front and heavy enemy air activity. The Soviets then launched an attack at 0515 (Berlin time) with 40 tanks from Yamki to Stalinskoye Otdeleniye Sovkhoz. This would have been the 25th Tank Brigade of the XXIX Tank Corps. They launched another attack from Prokhorovka with 35 tanks on both sides of the Prokhorovka-Teterevino road, which would have been the XXIX Tanks Corps' 32nd Tank

47 Glantz and Orenstein, page 113.

Brigade and 25th Tank Brigade. They also reported a third attack with 40 tanks from Petrovka along the road one kilometer south-southeast of Oktyabrskii Sovkhoz. This would have been the XVIII Tank Corps. The Germans reported that the Soviet attack was well supported by artillery and "proceeded at great speed." They also reported that another Soviet attack in regiment strength at 0600 over the line Prokhorovka–Petrovka was stopped by combined artillery concentrations before it reached the front line. This would have also been from the XVIII Tank Corps.

The 95th Guards Rifle Division's 287th Guards Rifle Regiment was located along the line from Mikhailovka to Prelestnoye to Petrovka. It reported at 1000 (Moscow time), that the units of the 42nd Guards Rifle Division and tanks from the Fifth Guards Tank Army attacked through them. It does not appear that they were otherwise seriously engaged on this day.

The XVIII Tank Corps Attack

The XVIII Tank Corps was arrayed in three echelons. The first echelon consisted of the 170th and 181st Tank Brigades. Each brigade had around 40 tanks, with about half of them T-34s and half T-70s. The second echelon included the 32nd Motorized Rifle Brigade and a mortar battalion with 82mm and 120mm mortars, which was to relieve the two forward attacking brigades by the end of the day. The third echelon consisted of the 110th Tank Brigade, armed as the other two tank brigades were, and the reconnaissance battalion, which had around 15 armored cars and 20 armored transports. This echelon was to cover the corps' rear and the headquarters and to follow the corps' attack all the way to height 251.2, two kilometers north northwest of Pokrovka. The 36th Guards Tank Regiment, with 18 Churchills, was to attack behind the 170th Tank Brigade in the second echelon and was to secure the corps' right flank after they had advanced further.[48] The 36th Guards Tank Regiment lost its regimental commander before the attack began, having been seriously wounded when a bomb fell near his Jeep.[49]

The corps' attack was supported by the 42nd Guards Rifle Division from Zhadov's Fifth Guards Army. This fresh rifle division moved up during the night and reached its jump-off positions by dawn. It was to attack with its right flank passing through Andreyevka and its left flank passing clear of the Oktyabrskii Sovkhoz. It was a narrow attack frontage that reflected that of the XVIII Tank Corps. It appears that the attack was conducted only by its 127th and 136th Guards Rifle Regiments. The attack was supported by the 91st Guards Artillery Regiment in firing positions around Verkhnyaya Olshanka.[50]

Perhaps the strangest attack the Soviets conducted on this day was done by the XVIII Tank Corps. This attack required the two leading Soviet tank brigades to move along the Psel River to the southwest. The 170th Tank Brigade ended up attacking the Oktyabrskii Sovkhoz, which constricted its attack area, effectively attacking uphill towards height 252.2. Meanwhile the 181st Tank Brigade continued to push to the southwest down the Psel into the area between the two SS divisions. These attacks could not only be fired upon from the south and west, but could also be fired upon by Totenkopf's forces on the other side of the Psel. The attack was essentially

48 Zamulin, *Demolishing the Myth*, page 310, states, "Its [XVIII Tank Corps] combat formation was arranged in three echelons: in the first the 181st Tank Brigade (44 tanks) and the 170th Tank Brigade (39 tanks), supported by the 36th Guards Separate Heavy Tank Regiment (19 Churchill tanks); in the second—the 32nd Motorized Rifle Brigade (which had no tanks); in the third—the tank brigade of the corps' forward detachment (38 tanks)."

49 Zamulin, *Demolishing the Myth*, page 340.

50 The 91st Guards Artillery Regiment reported on the 12th that they supported the attack by the 127th and 136th Guards Rifle Regiments with 213 122mm rounds and 740 76mm rounds in support, with 667 122mm rounds and 3,282 76mm rounds remaining (Fond: 42, Opis: 3, Delo: ?, page 4).

The 132nd Guards Rifle Regiment was reported on the north side of the Psel on the 13th. We are not sure where it was on the 12th but it does not appear to have been part of any combat this day. The initial loss reports provide losses for the 127th Guards Rifle Regiment from 10–15 July, for the 136th Guards Rifle Regiment from 12–14 July and for the 132nd Guards Rifle Regiment only for the 13–14th (Fond: 42, Opis: ?, Delo: 21, pages 277, 278 and 280).

through a shallow valley flanked by enemy forces. It was a scenario reminiscent of the famous British charge of the light brigade from the Crimean War, and with similar results.

As the XVIII Tank Corps went forward, it reported that the Germans began to fall back in the direction of height 217.9 and Komsomolets Sovkhoz while the German artillery "rained" intensive fire on the corps units from the Greznoye to Komsomolets Sovkhoz areas. With the Germans occupying the line running from height 252.2 to Komsomolets Sovkhoz to height 217.9, the XVIII Tank Corps attack was heading into a giant semi-circle of higher terrain that the Adolf Hitler SS Division could use to observe and fire upon the attackers. As the corps describes its attack:

> . . . lacking necessary support from our fighter aviation and suffering heavy casualties from enemy artillery fire and bombing—by 1200 enemy aircraft had conducted 1,200 sorties—moved forward slowly.
>
> The terrain in the corps' attack zone is cut by three deep ravines, stretching from the left bank of the Psel River to the Belenikhino-Prokhorovka railroad, which is why the 181st and 170th Tank Brigades, advancing in the first echelon, were forced to attack on the corps' left flank near the enemy strong point at Oktyabrskii Sovkhoz. The 170th Tank Brigade, attacking on the left flank, by 1200 had lost 60% of its equipment.
>
> Despite these losses, overcoming the enemy's fire resistance, the corps units took the Oktyabrskii Sovkhoz and by 1200 were fighting with the 181st Tank Brigade in Andreyevka and up to height 241.6, the 170th Tank Brigade in the ravine southeast of Mikhailovka; the 32nd Motorized Rifle Brigade was fighting for Andreyevka.[51]

By noon (Moscow time), the XVIII Tank Corps' attack had stalled. Its 170th Tank Brigade had been savaged. The brigade had lost up to 60% of its tanks, its brigade commander had burned to death in his tank, and one battalion commander was mortally wounded.[52] Rotmistrov's chief of staff, Major General V.N. Baskakov was stationed at the XVIII Tank Corps headquarters. He heard the exchange between the corps commander Bakharov and the army commander Rotmistrov, where Bakhorov was requesting clarification of his orders and appealing for air support. Rotmistrov replied, "Kirichenko [XXIX Tank Corps commander] has even great losses, but he is hanging on and attacking: you also must attack, your assignment remains the same—attack!"[53]

THE TOTENKOPF SS Division, sitting on the higher ground on the north side of the Psel, could see this attack developing. They noted the gathering enemy forces as early as 0705 (Berlin time). At 0745 (0845 Moscow time) they noted two Soviet regiments and about 40 tanks from the northwest entering Mikhailovka and the hills to the southeast. At 0910, the VIII Air Corps notified the SS that it had dispatched two Stuka groups to strike at the forces moving southwest from Petrovka.

The Totenkopf SS Division reported an attack on Vasilyevka from 0950 to 1100 (Berlin time). This attack penetrated to the center of Vasilyevka in heavy house-to-house fighting. Meanwhile the panzers from the Adolf Hitler SS Division were slugging it out with the enemy tanks advancing southwest from Petrovka. A counterattack by Totenkopf drove the Soviets from Vasilyevka. At 1110 they reported a Soviet attack from Vasilyevka to the southwest. This was probably elements of the Soviet tank force that turned south from the Psel valley and succeeded in breaking though Adolf Hitler's thin flank security and drove through its artillery positions. Most of these Soviet tanks, though, were destroyed by infantry close combat and direct fire from artillery pieces.

---

51 "Account of XVIII Tank Corps' Combat Activities, July 12–24, 1943" (Fond: XVIII TC, Opis: 1, Delo: 48, page 7).

52 Zamulin, *Demolishing the Myth*, page 342.

53 Zamulin, *Demolishing the Myth*, page 345. The source of the quote is not provided, but we gather it is from Baskakov.

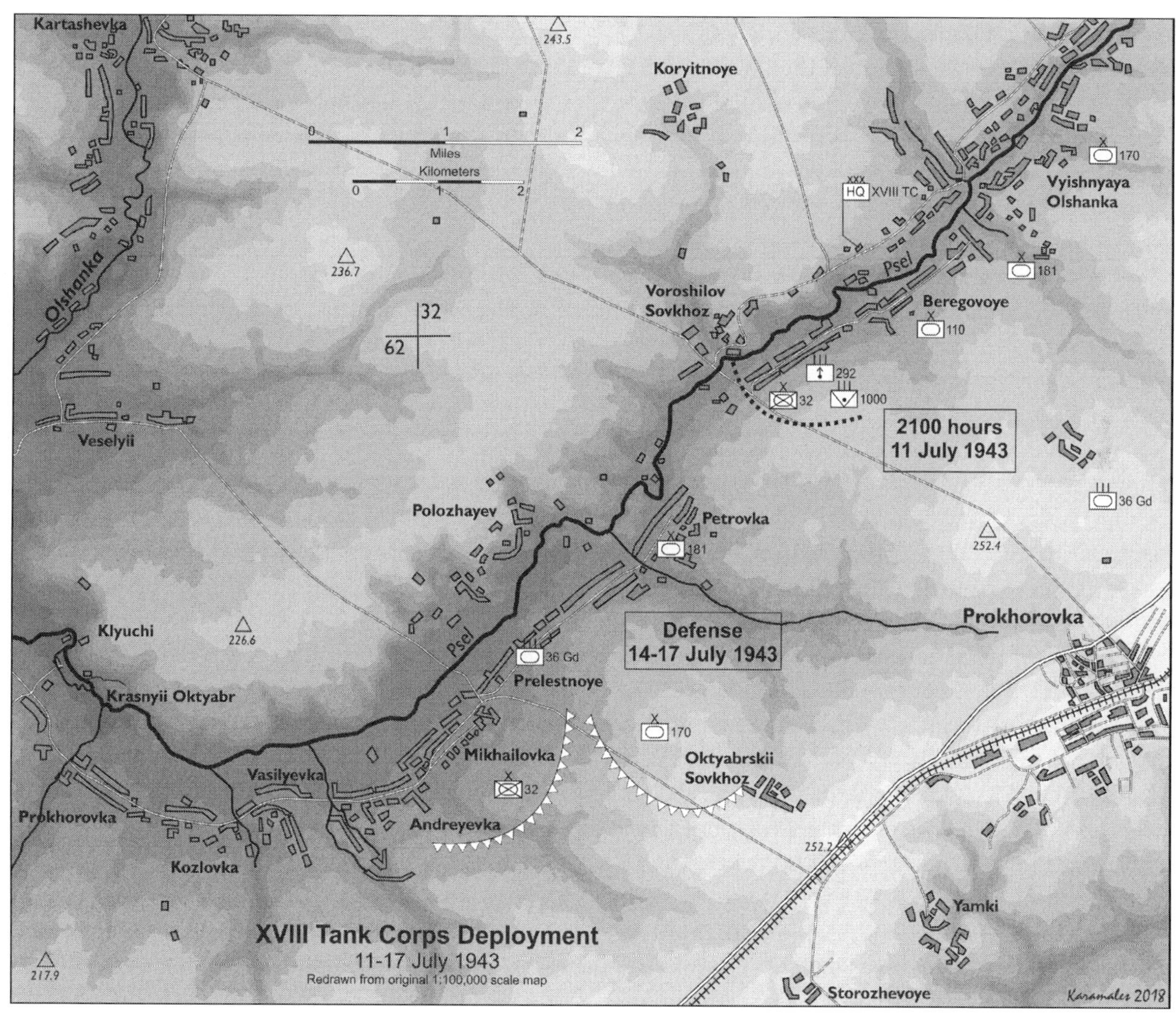
XVIII Tank Corps Deployment
11-17 July 1943
Redrawn from original 1:100,000 scale map
Karamales 2018
Miles
Kilometers
Kartashevka
Olshanka
Koryitnoye
Vyishnyaya Olshanka
XVIII TC
Psel
Voroshilov Sovkhoz
Beregovoye
2100 hours
11 July 1943
Veselyii
Polozhayev
Petrovka
Klyuchi
Prokhorovka
Defense
14-17 July 1943
Prelestnoye
Krasnyii Oktyabr
Mikhailovka
Oktyabrskii Sovkhoz
Vasilyevka
Andreyevka
Kozlovka
Yamki
Storozhevoye

The XVIII Tank Corps original attack had stalled out by late morning. General Bakharov, probably with the encouragement of Rotmistrov, regrouped his forces for another attack. He re-committed the 181st Tank Brigade and the 36th Guards Heavy Tank Regiment to the attack. His third echelon force, the 110th Tank Brigade, was ordered to move forward so as to protect the right flank of his corps (against the Totenkopf SS Division?). In route from Prelestnoye to Mikhialovka, the 110th Tank Brigade was attacked by German aircraft, delaying its arrival.[54] This renewed effort does appear to have helped the XXIX Tank Corps break into the north portion of the Okyabrskii Sovkhoz at 1300 (Moscow time).

Meanwhile, at 1115 Totenkopf, whose armored group was still north of the Psel, told the corps that it would attempt to cross the Psel at Mikhailovka and move in behind the Soviets that were south of the river. Rotmistrov reported that at 1330 (Moscow time), the first echelon brigades were fired on by 13 Tiger tanks from the area of height 226.6, which were moving in the direction of the northwestern outskirts of Mikhailovka. These were certainly Totenkopf's advancing armor which had brought the XVIII Tank Corps under fire on its right flank. He also reported that the 36th Guards Tank Regiment, which was part of the second echelon, encountered heavy fire from "Tigers" and antitank guns in the ravines two kilometers south of Mikhailovka and it suffered heavy casualties. These would have been from the Adolf Hitler SS Division. At 1400 (Moscow time) the Fifth Guards Army claimed that they had captured Mikhailovka (probably done much earlier than 1400) and at the same time repulsed German counterattacks by 50 tanks from the Bogoroditskoye area (south of the Psel, just west of Vasilyevka) and by 13 "Tigers" from the area of height 226.6 (north of the Psel). By 1430 (Moscow time), Rotmistrov reported that after fierce fighting, they had taken the Oktyabrskii Sovkhoz and had reached Andreyevka and Vasilyevka, for an advance of six to seven kilometers. In Andreyevka, the 181st Tank Brigade met a large column of German tanks. As a result of the battle that followed, they claimed the Germans suffered heavy casualties and were thrown back on Kozlovka. These were probably Totenkopf's tanks.[55] At 1330 (Berlin time) German aerial reconnaissance reported that Totenkopf was advancing up the valley. At 1445 (Berlin time), Totenkopf reported that it took the west edge of Andreyevka in an attack. The Fifth Guards Army reported that the corps' further advance was contained by the powerful German artillery and mortar fire from the Greznoye area and by tank fire from the Bogoroditskoye area.

At 1400 (Moscow time), the XVIII Tank Corps reported that the 181st Tank Brigade had occupied the Oktyabrskii Sovkhoz and was fighting along the line from Andreyevka to height 241.6. The 170th Tank Brigade was fighting along the line of the ravine southeast of Mikhailovka, while the 110th Tank Brigade had moved forward and was now 500 meters east of Mikhailovka. Tanks knocked out and burned included 11 Churchills, 6 T-34s and 4 T-70s, although they pointed out that this had not been verified yet. Major General Bakharov requested air support from fighters. The supporting 42nd Guards Rifle Division stated that it took Mikhailovka and attempted to take Andreyevka with its right wing and height 241.6 with its left wing.

The Germans reported for the morning that two Soviet regiments had attacked with about 40 tanks through Prelestnoye, Mikhailovka, and Andreyevka. The attack penetrated east of Vasilyevka and after moving south, turned off opposite the Komsomolets

54 Zamulin, *Demolishing the Myth*, page 347.

55 We are not very clear on this. The Totenkopf SS Panzer Regiment had a heavy company (the Tigers) and two battalions, each of three companies (two medium and one light). The entire panzer group appears to have been north of the Psel River in the morning. During this fight, the Tigers appear to have remained north of the Psel in the area of 226.6. Either the rest of the panzer regiment had move back south of the Psel, or only part of it (one battalion?). That afternoon, the "panzer group" again continued to attack to the northeast, implying that the entire panzer regiment was once again north of the Psel. The division also had an assault gun battalion (the Sturmgeschuetz III) and the self-propelled antitank company (the Marders) which may have also defended Bogoroditskoye in addition to, or instead of, the tanks.

Sovkhoz. The Germans were able to restore the situation here with an attack from the northeast to cut off the Soviet advance.

Meanwhile, Totenkopf at 1455 launched an eastward attack from Vasilyevka that by 1530 had penetrated into the western part of Andreyevka and by 1645 had reached the northeast edge of Andreyevka.

The XXIX Tank Corps Attack

The XXIX Tank Corps attacked along the railroad and highway running from Prokhorovka to Ivanovskii Vyiselok. This rail line was most likely not lined with trees and foliage as it is today. Still this slightly raised track effectively split the battlefield. The XXIX Tank Corps sent armored brigades attacking southwest down both sides of the rail line.

The 32nd Tank Brigade, with around 60 T-34s, was on the right flank of the attack, followed by the 31st Tank Brigade with around 29 T-34s and 38 T-70s. Their left flank was the rail line. On the left flank of the XXIX Tank Corps, and south of the rail line, was the 25th Tank Brigade with about 31 T-34s and 36 T-70s. In the second echelon, behind the attacking tank brigades, was the 53rd Motorized Rifle Brigade. The 108th Antitank Regiment and 76th Guards Mortar Regiment were in the corps reserve.[56]

The 32nd Tank Brigade, with the 1529th Heavy Self-Propelled Regiment and three batteries of the 1446th Self-Propelled Regiment, attacked the Germans head on at Oktyabrskii Sovkhoz and hill 252.2.[57] It appears the 32nd Tank Brigade's second tank battalion hit the outskirts of Oktyabrskii Sovkhoz and hill 252.2 while the first tank battalion crossed the railway embankment to bypass the sovkhoz. With 15 T-34s, the first tank battalion, concealed by a belt of woods, found a gap in the German lines. They dashed past heights 242.5 and 241.6 and were able to enter the southern outskirts of the Komsomolets Sovkhoz from the rear. This was a penetration of the German defenses. Motorized riflemen from the 53rd Motorized Rifle Brigade also followed this route to the Komsomolets Sovkhoz.[58] Some of these units would hold out there until the afternoon.

Meanwhile, the rest of the brigade rolled over the German defensive positions on hill 252.2 and continued on. The 2nd SS Panzer Grenadier Regiment, after taking this position the previous day, occupied the existing Soviet foxholes, trenches and bunkers on the west slope of the hill (the reverse slope) and placed an outpost line facing Prokhorovka. The Soviet armored attack swept over the outpost line and through the German infantry positions on the reverse slope, forcing the German defending infantry, including its halftrack mounted III Battalion, into self defense. The III Battalion was commanded by Sturmbannfuehrer (Major) Joachim Peiper, a Knight's Cross holder.[59] He would become infamous a year and half later when his brigade conducted the

56 Zamulin, *Demolishing the Myth*, pages 309–310, states: "Its [XXIX Tank Corps] attack formation had the 32nd Tank Brigade (63 tanks) and the 25th Tank Brigade (69 tanks) in the first echelon and the 31st Tank Brigade (67 tanks) in the second echelon."

57 The 1529th Heavy Self-Propelled Regiment was armed with 1 KV-1 and 11 Su-152s as documented in the Kursk Data Base. We record it taking no losses. The 1446th Self-Propelled Regiment had ready-for-action 8 Su-76s and 12 Su-122s.

According to Zamulin, *Demolishing the Myth*, pages 284, 286, and 300, the 1529th Heavy Self-Propelled Regiment did not arrive in the area of Prokhorovka until 1800 on the 12th. It had only one combat load of shells as its "rear support" had been held up by the German appearance at Rzhavets. The regiment was previously operating with the Seventh Guards Army.

58 The details of each battalion's operations come from Zamulin, *Demolishing the Myth*, page 314. The T-34 strength figure is from Zamulin. Not sure if any T-70s came with them.

59 Patrick Agte, *Jochen Peiper, Kommandeur Panzerregiment Leibstandarte*, pages 132–143. Translation provided by Maj. Gen. (ret.) Deiter Brand.

Even though I am very bothered by his use of World War II–era propaganda pieces in his writing and his uncritical use of exclusively German sources, his detailed description of the actions on height 252.2 appear to be correct in its general course of events. His account for this day includes quotes from interviews and diaries of a half-dozen veterans. The Adolf Hitler SS Division records provide no details as to what happened on height 252.2 on this day.

Malmedy massacre of U.S. soldiers during the Battle of the Bulge.

Meanwhile, the Soviet armored attack continued on past the hill at high speed, rolled over the 6th Panzer Company, which had been moving forward to reinforce the hill, and then came under direct fire from the German armor from the rest of the II Panzer Battalion. It appears (see below) that the Soviet attack came to a complete halt when it ran into one of its own tank ditches. This attack was halted by German artillery, tank fire, and aircraft.

The Germans reported that a "local modest breakthrough" at 252.2 was resolved by an armored counterattack at 1115 (Berlin time). Control of the height was re-established by a counterattack that included parts of the II Panzer Battalion, and the forces left holding the hill were relieved. According to German reports, on that spot alone 40 Soviet tanks were destroyed in close combat.

The 32nd Tank Brigade was forced to go over to the defensive at 1300 (Moscow time) at Oktyabrskii Sovkhoz with what appear to have been very heavy losses. At 1300, it was also attacked, along with the neighboring 170th Tank Brigade, by Soviet assault aircraft. Another case of "friendly" fire!

The 31st Tank Brigade attacked behind the 32nd Tank Brigade and by 1400 (Moscow time) had reached the area one kilometer northeast of Oktyabrskii Sovkhoz. Upon reaching the northeastern outskirts of the Oktyabrskii Sovkhoz, the brigade was delayed by German artillery and mortar fire and by the "ceaseless" German air attacks.

THE 32ND TANK Brigade suffered the highest losses of any attacking tank brigade of the day, suffering 54 T-34s either burned, knocked out or in need of repair, leaving the brigade with only 6 T-34s. These losses included all 15 T-34s that went to Komsomolets Sovkhoz. Their reported losses at the end of the day were 100 men killed and 130 wounded. These appear to have been caused by more than just stiff resistance. The explanation may lie in an article written in 1989 by Rudolph von Ribbentrop, the former company commander of the 6th Panzer Company. It is quoted here in some length.[60]

> Someone shook me at my shoulder, causing wild dreams and into the sleep of exhaustion after seven days of the heaviest combat in attack, came again and again a shout: "Obersturmfuehrer, Obersturmfuehrer!" Jumping up I banged my head on the hull, because to give a good example as a company commander, I slept in a hole beneath the tank as I always enforce it on my company's soldiers to avoid unnecessary losses . . . by artillery fire at night or by attacks with bombs within the bright shine of American magnesia parachute flares. Into the slowly growing consciousness came the irregular crackling of a two-cycle engine of a DKW motorcycle, an unmistakable sign that one had to be ordered to the battalion, because that motorcycle belongs to the company messenger who was assigned to the battalion. In just that moment came already a voice down into the hole shouting "Oberstrumfuehrer, you have to come to the battalion commander!" During the short drive to the command vehicle of the battalion commander one realized intuitively a somewhat unquiet front line. It might have been as late as half past

60 Rudolf von Ribbentrop, "Erzaehlende Kriegsgeschichte: New geboren—bei Prochorowka" [Tales of War History: Born Again—at Prokhorovka], published in "Der Freiwillge" (The Volunteer), 35th year, issue 7–8, July/August 1989, pages 52 and 56. Provided courtesy of Colonel Dr. Karl-Heinz Frieser of the Militaegeschichtliches Forschungsamt, Potsdam. Correspondence of 30 January 2002 supplemented the article with a German reconnaissance map showing the tank ditch in question. Translation of article was primarily done by Maj.Gen. (ret.) Deiter Brand.

This article ends with a request for donations to the "social organization Paul Hausser." Still, it would appear from the terrain description and other details in the article that this is fundamentally a valid description of the events that he saw, vice a political or propaganda piece. Captain von Ribbentrop (born 1921) is the son of the Nazi Foreign Minister, the infamous Joachim von Ribbentrop, who was tried and convicted at Nuremberg and executed in 1946.

The article has been edited to remove background material and some wordiness.

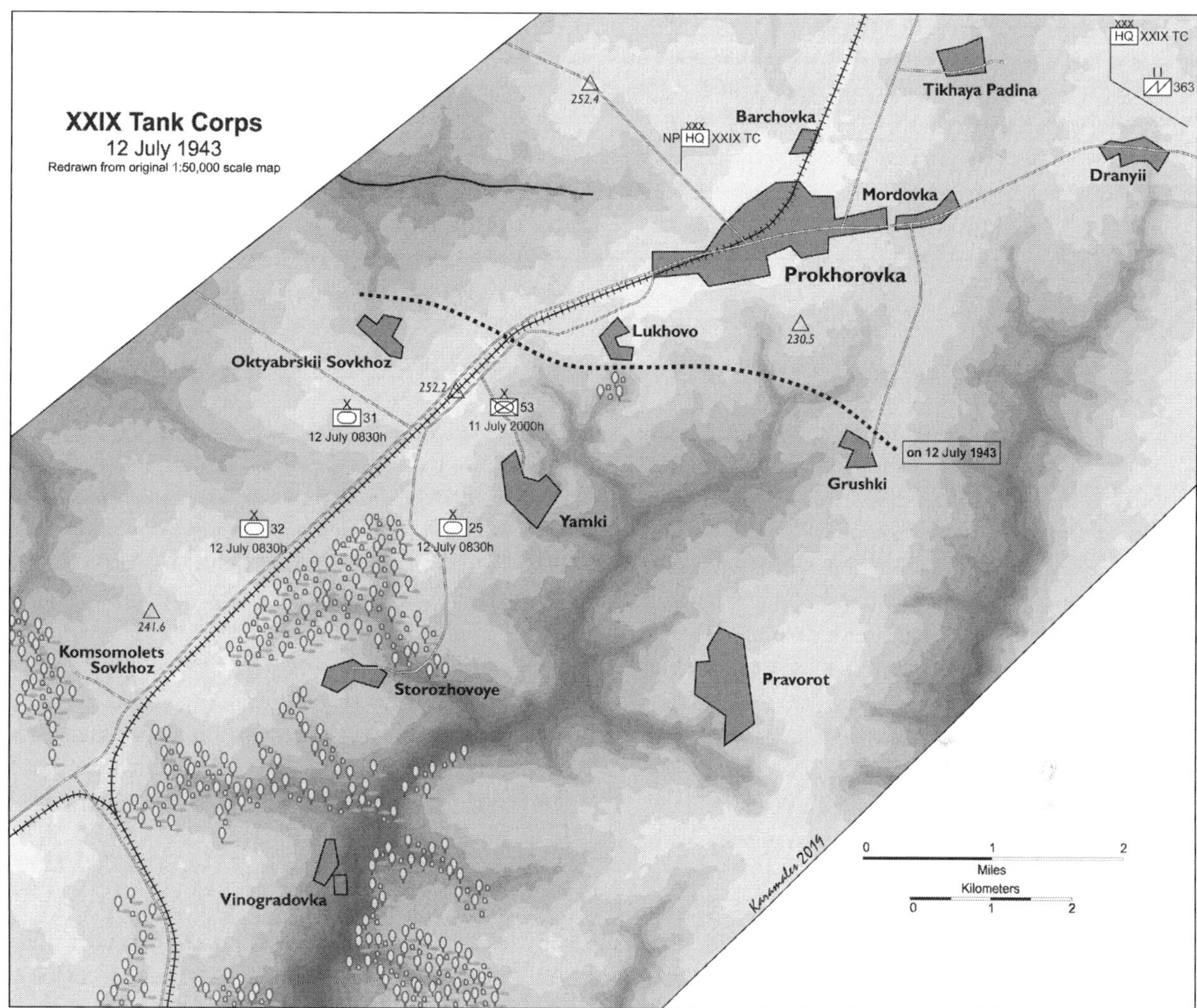

XXIX Tank Corps
12 July 1943
Redrawn from original 1:50,000 scale map
252.4
Barchovka
NP HQ XXIX TC
Tikhaya Padina
HQ XXIX TC
363
Dranyii
Mordovka
Prokhorovka
Lukhovo
230.5
Oktyabrskii Sovkhoz
252.2
31
12 July 0830h
53
11 July 2000h
on 12 July 1943
Grushki
Yamki
32
12 July 0830h
25
12 July 0830h
241.6
Komsomolets Sovkhoz
Storozhovoye
Pravorot
Vinogradovka
0 1 2
Miles
Kilometers
0 1 2

XXIX Tank Corps on 12 July 1943.

five in the morning. The battalion commander stuck his head out of his command vehicle, which was a modified radio vehicle, to explain to me that the infantry had made some observation which made them think that they might have to fight tanks.

Exact reports were not available and therefore I should establish contact with the infantry and be prepared to engage if necessary. There seemed to be some condescension within the sleepy tone of the battalion commander, in the sense that no one could be astonished that in this offensive, which had developed to be a real tank battle, somewhere, some tanks were driving, and it was really unnecessary to hint on that fact. From our perspective as tankers a Russian T-34 looked rather different than it did to an infantry soldier in his foxhole. In view of this rather unconventionally given order, I was disgruntled at first, because the evening before the battalion commander had ordered that our company should stay in reserve—and now this mission, which tankers normally did not like although the combined arms combat together with all the other branches worked excellent. Sitting on the passenger seat of the motorcycle, I drove back to my company, ordered combat readiness, let the motors warm up, got ready with all weaponry and so on, and called a sergeant of my company, Oberscharfuehrer Gebauer, to come with a motorcycle with a sidecar. I wanted to go to the infantry myself, to establish contact, to get the real picture and if necessary, to react immediately. Fortunately, I was not put under control of the infantry, but more so to say "to work together" although this term was not used expressly by the commander. On the other hand the commander's "Sattlebefehl" (order given from the saddle), as we so nicely called it, had the advantage that I had substantial leeway of judgment for self-determined action.

Some remarks with respect to the situation: . . . Out of 22 tanks with which we had started at the morning of the 5th of July only seven were available and combat ready on the evening of the 11th of July. Fortunately, not all of the missing tanks were total losses, as a result, again and again some Mark IV tanks would come back to the company from maintenance.

The day before we had crossed in the fight a Russian tank ditch, alongside of which both the other companies [5th and 7th panzer companies] had taken position in line, while we being the reserve company in this situation, was just behind. This tank ditch, which by nature ran across the front line, had only one single crossing available for the road to Prokhorovka and this bridge had not been destroyed or was repaired. This tank ditch was built in a 'soft' hollow from which according to my remembrance was around 800 meters along a slope with a width of about 300 to 400 meters extending to the direction of Prokhorovka, and on top were somewhere the positions of the infantry. The slope was limited at the right side by the road to Prokhorovka and behind that road an overgrown railway embankment which could be seen more or less as being a tank obstacle.

Along this embankment the front line ran back to where the tank ditch was and then made a turn to the east to contact the Das Reich SS Division. One battalion of our grenadiers had occupied the embankment and at a right angle, another battalion had taken position at the above mentioned hill [hill 252.2]. Our left flank was limbo and had no contact. I drove along the embankment to the front line and reached the command post of the grenadier battalions, which secured our left flank. The command post of the battalion commander was located within a passage through the embankment [most likely at the toll booth, or "BW," as this passage is still there today] and the commander was just going to interrogate a Russian lieutenant taken prisoner. This man—looking like the last of the Teutonic tribe, tall, blond, blue-eyed,—very poised, gave only some replies and finally after having been loosened up by some cigarettes and liquor stated to our surprise "Russian soldiers get bad food but have good morale, German soldiers did get good food, but have bad morale." We all looked a little bit reflective, although we not accept that remark to apply to our own troops.

I did not get any more information with respect to the situation from the infantry commander, he only confirmed the reports that tank noises were being

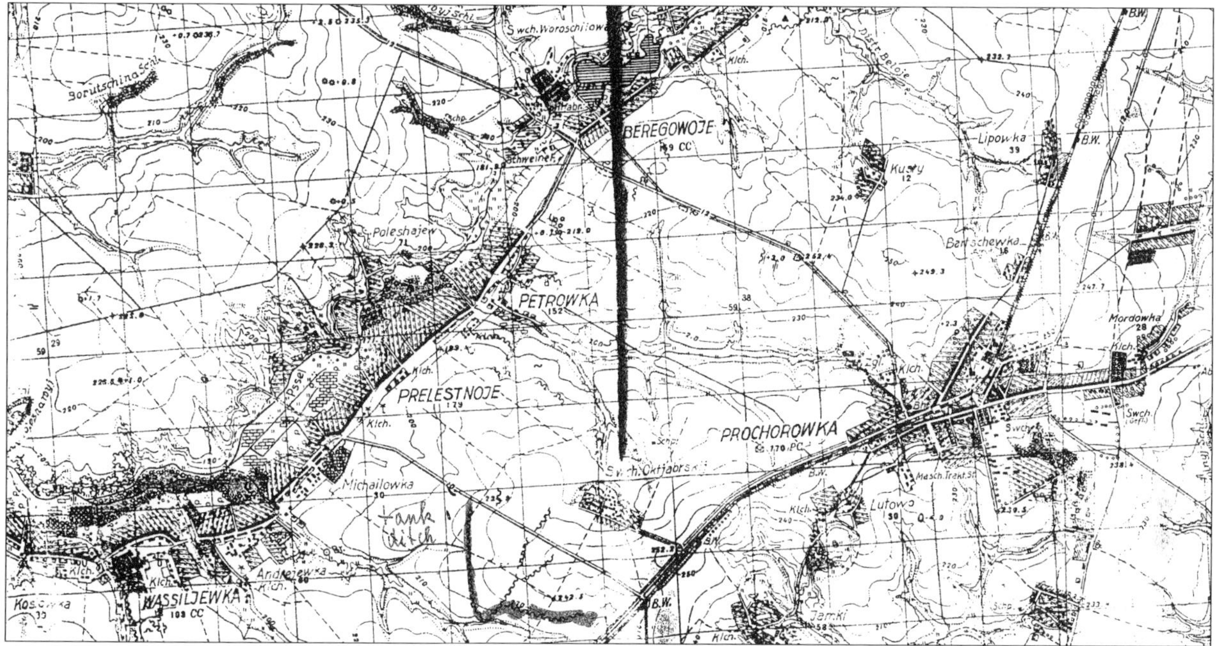

GERMAN COPY OF THE MAP OF PROKHOROVKA WITH THE TANK DITCH MARKED AND LABELED.

heard, but he did not have exact situation reports. We agreed that my company sergeant would stay there with his motorcycle in order to immediately bring me instructions if something concrete would appear.

As I could see our tanks some hundred meters down in the depression at the tank ditch, I decide to go back to the company on foot. At the slope was standing the so called "armored group" consisting of the division's self-propelled artillery battalion, the armored personnel carrier battalion of the famous Jochen Peiper, also widely spread in a way that the slope was riddled with vehicles and weapons of all kinds, but which were not visible to the Russians. In all these units was the deepest silence. . . . As no one could imagine a continuation of the attack on Prokhorovka without our neighbors having closed up, all people slept the sleep of exhaustion because, as mentioned above, seven days of tough fighting with little sleep laid behind us. During the entire war, I personally experienced this lack of sleep as being the worst deprivation compared with hunger, thirst, cold, rain, wetness and so on. . . .

As mentioned above, the company had seven tanks in hand. The highlight of the fighting so far was an attack together with the Peiper battalion on a position of antitank guns which we had overrun and destroyed in full speed like cavalry. I was with my company in undertaking a wide bypass along the horizon to defeat some Russian tanks and antitank guns which had come between our attack formations. The attack was carried out by the so called "armored group." As a company commander unfortunately I had no radio contact with the armored personnel carrier battalion, and just when I commenced the attack together with the Peiper battalion to destroy the antitank gun position, a counter-order was given by my battalion commander, which was not understandable in the given situation. One thing for sure I knew that it was to be absolutely forbidden that the halftracks attack alone the enemy antitank gun position, and therefore I continued the attack in spite of some angry comments by my battalion commander through the radio.

When we gathered having destroyed the entire antitank gun position and having blown up the last Russian antitank gun, I got the most meaningful commendation compared with all I got during the entire war when Peiper, who was revered by all of us, said "At any time we would welcome you (your company) to belong to our band." When I came back later to my own battalion, my battalion commander grumbled some understanding for the fact that it had been impossible to veer off of our running attack and allow exposure of the halftracks to the fire of the antitank guns without tank protection.

When I was still drinking the hot "Muckefuck" (German generic name for malt coffee, a coffee substitute containing no caffeine) with the lower piece of the messkit at my mouth and turned around to look into the direction of the front line I could have imaged suffering hallucinations and depressions. Within a few moments there stood a purple smoke curtain cased by smoke signal cartridges which meant for this day "tank warning!" As this signal could be seen along the entire ridge of the slope before us and also appear more to the right along the embankment, it was immediately clear to me, also without any message or order, that a massive tank attack had been started by the Russians.

Simultaneously dropping the mess kit and ordering "Start the motors and follow me!" I shouted to the company officer Malchow: "We will drive in line some distance up the slope. You with your platoon echeloned on the left side if we are outflanked, I will move with the other three tanks to the center and right. We will take position at the reverse slope and will kill the Russians."

At the same moment I saw the sergeant whom I had left with the infantry commander rushing down the slope in his motorcycle with a huge dust cloud behind him and stretching his fist up into the air which meant "Move immediately!" At this moment, the company started to move and deployed at the slope in a training drill like precision, which caused me with my 22-year-old prime-of-life heart to beat faster. I agreed and in no way doubted that it was an exalting feeling to lead these young but already very combat experienced soldiers into the engagement. When we reached the top of the ridge I realized that in about 200 meters distance following a soft hollow there was another ridge in the terrain at which obviously our infantry had taken position. I ordered by radio to drive with highest speed to the reverse slope in front of us and to open combat there. The hollow stretched to the left and while we were driving down the forward slope we recognized some T-34s which were about 800 meters from us and trying to outflank us. We immediately stopped on the forward slope and opened fire. We succeeded in knocking out some Russian tanks which started burning. Eight hundred meters was an ideal shot for a good gunner! We were waiting for some more tanks to appear down there while I habitually looked around, and in the real sense of the word, it took my breath away because at about 150 to 200 meters in front of us, out of this soft hollow appeared 15, 20, 30, 40 and then a no longer countable number of Russian T-34s, with mounted infantry, which at full speed were storming toward us.

The driver Schuele shouted into the vehicle microphone "Obersturmfuehrer, at right, at right, there they are coming, do you see them?" I saw more than well enough. I said to myself "Now it is out!" which my loader understood as "go out!" and intended to open his hatch and I had to urgently pull him back into the tank. I had already kicked my gunner in his right side, which meant that he had to move the turret to the right because there were the most dangerous targets. At that moment the first round was shot and the first T-34 stood in flames, only some 50 meters in front of us. At the same moment the tank beside me suffered a mortal hit and immediately burned. I saw the Unterscharfuehrer Papke jumping out of the tank, but we never again heard anything about him. Also his right neighbor was mortally hit and immediately started to burn.

Now this wall of tanks was moving on us. Tank aside tank, wave after wave, an unbelievable massing, and above all driving at high speed. Having always been very interested in military history, that this must have been the feeling of the infantry in the big battles of the 18/19th century when a cavalry attack stormed on them and they had no other choice than to fire volley after volley against them and finally hold the rifles together with bayonets fixed against the horses, hoping that they would be skittish and not break into the square.

We could not build a square for defense, we could only fire, at this distance every round was a hit, until a hit would send us burning into the other world. Somewhere in lower consciousness, one realizes that there was only a little chance to survive; on the other hand the situation demanded the next action. Consequently, we killed another three or four T-34s at the shortest distance, i.e., less than 30 meters. Then the loader cried "No more tank ammunition!" In this context one should know that in the Panzer IV, the loader had 18 to 20 rounds at his immediate disposal, half of which or probably a little more were high explosive rounds and the rest were antitank rounds. Now we had shot all the antitank rounds. To stay here was the best way to be recognized by a Russian tank, which had rushed aside of us, and then to be killed. Consequently, first it was necessary to get behind the next ridge and although the Russian tanks had crossed that ridge already, the chance to be recognized there was much lower. So we turned amidst a group of Russian tanks, drove back some 50 meters and turned again at the reverse slope of that ridge we had just crossed before, and had at least a somewhat protected position. In just that moment a T-34 stopped some 30 meters transverse to the right of us, I still see this tank bouncing on its suspension, and it turned its turret in our direction. Again, the thought flashed "The last thing that you will see on this earth will be a fireball and that is the end (and then it is time for leaving off work!)," because I looked directly into the muzzle of his gun. We could not fire at this moment because the gunner was just handing an armor piercing round to the loader, but at the same time, I shouted "Tank! March!" into the microphone. The driver Schueler, being a company commander, I always had one of the best drivers of the battalion, had of course put the tank in gear and the slow Panzer IV start to move. We drove some five meters to the side of the Russian tank which was desperately turning his turret but it did not work quickly enough because of the primitiveness of the T-34. Then after moving 10 meters behind him, we turned again while other Russian tanks with mounted infantry were passing us. We then fired an armor piercing round at a distance of 10 meters at his turret, which immediately blew up the tank and let the turret fly three meters though the air, so that it nearly hit our gun. It escaped through my teeth "This guy will not try to knock us out again!"

I had made a desperate attempt to tear off the swastika flag which was fixed on a box outside and try to pull it inside the tank (the flag should signal our own aircraft that this was a German tank). But, I only succeeded by halves, with the result that it was now fluttering in the wind. This would have to strike the eyes of a Russian gunner sometime soon, and it could be only a question of time when we were lethally hit at the shortest range.

There was only one solution left, that was to remain moving, because a halted tank would have been immediately recognized by the Russians as an enemy tank as they were still driving at full speed. . . . There was no other possibility than to drive within the Russian tank herd and by doing that, it exposed us to a double danger. First, at sometime a T-34 must identify us. That we had survived up to this moment was due to the T-34 not having a tank commander, but instead the gunner had to control the tank. The guy naturally could watch only into the direction where his gun was directed. Otherwise, we would meet our end earlier. Second, there was the danger that we would be engaged by our own tanks, which stood down the slope in a broad line along the tank ditch. After having been wakened up, now urgently began target shooting at the Russian tanks coming down the slope. As this battlefield was covered with dust and smoke and detonations, and additionally, the sun shining directly into their faces, it would have been very difficult to differentiate our tank from a Russian one. Therefore, I repeatedly called by radio my somewhat ridiculous cover name and added "We are driving amidst the Russian tank pack, please don't shoot at us!", but did not get a response. In the meantime, the Russians had driven through the halftrack battalion as well as the artillery battalion and had some vehicles that had been set on fire. But, now the fire of the other two tank companies came to bear.

Also the artillery battalion with self-propelled guns as well as the grenadiers of Peiper's battalion knocked out more and more tanks and kept down the Russian infantry which had jumped off the tanks because of the defenders' fire. The entire battlefield was nothing but one cloud of dust and smoke and from this witch-sabbath approached more new waves of Russian tanks, but at the long slope they were killed by our tanks like hares. This indescribable chaos, dust and smoke, burning tanks and vehicles had probably contributed to our rescue because we were not identified by the Russians. Suddenly I saw a group of Russian infantrymen in front of us and shouted in the larynx microphone to the driver; "Turn a little bit left!" But he had seen them already and from backwards we rolled over these poor guys who within this infernal noise had not realized that a German tank was rolling over them.

I now saw our chance by turning left and oriented into the direction of the road where surely we would meet our own infantry and could maneuver slowly out of the dense Russian herd. In the meantime, the crew was busy passing to the loader the armor piercing rounds from all corners, from the driver, the radio operator as well as the gunner, and whenever the gun was loaded again with an armor piercing round we stopped and killed at the shortest distance one of the T-34s which had bypassed us. It was completely incomprehensible that we had not yet appeared in the sights of a Russian.

This orientation to the left, that was meant to cross over the tank ditch, however, was also made by the Russians. Their attack was launched in an incomprehensible direction. As this tank ditch was marked on all the maps which we had captured, they must have known that this dense massive attack, later I was told that this had been the densest tank mass in a narrow area during the entire war, would last only one kilometer before it must end at their own tank ditch. That this would take away the momentum of the tank attack was foreseeable. Now obviously, the T-34s detected the tank ditch and tried to turn left and cross over the reconstructed bridge. Now the indescribable happened. I succeeded in taking a position behind a killed T-34 in order to participate in the "shooting at moving targets," i.e., the T-34s with the last rounds we had available. As the Russians were now crowded at the bridge and therefore were now flanked and could be killed much easier, the burning T-34s were driving upon one another and ramming one another. That was an inferno of fire, smoke, burning T-34s, dead and injured. Our own chance to survive grew over time, because the slope which I mentioned before was spread with burning T-34s and we had taken a position behind such a wreck. At this moment I got the message from the loader that no more armor piercing rounds were available. We had completely run out of tank ammunition, aside from the high explosive rounds which one could not expect to destroy the well armored T-34.

We participated in fighting the Russian infantry which however, had to be done with highest care, because, as mentioned above, the armored infantry battalion as well as the self-propelled artillery battalion had been overrun and it had to be anticipated for sure that our own soldiers would be as endangered by shooting with high explosive rounds as the Russian infantry would, which now moved purposelessly over the battlefield. So I stopped fire for a while but at the same time the gunner, putting his hands before his face, cried "My eye, my eye!" We had taken a most serious hit directly at the tiny hole in the armor of the turret where the binocular was. The round had not gotten through but had penetrated as much that it pushed the binocular with a terrible hit backward. As a consequence the gunner suffered a serious wound from glass and metal to his head by his eye. Now our tank was no longer combat ready and I decided to take it out of operations, i.e., to cross the bridge over the tank ditch and drive to the rear and first orient ourselves and to try to gather the tanks of the company, if some had survived at all. Now we drove back to the rear area in order to stop at the reverse slope of a small ridge and to take the gunner out of the tank and hand him over to medical service. But, at this moment the company's maintenance sergeant appeared with a repaired Panzer IV so that I only had to change over with my crew and a new gunner in order to go back to combat.

For the crew of the repaired tank which just came from the rear area except for their gunner, this was a bad disappointment that they had to hand over their tank to my crew. But, being the company leader I needed a well cooperating crew with respect to the multiple tasks which had to be done, at the same time like keeping radio contact with the battalion, executing control over my own company, controlling our own tank and executing fire control for our own gunner. We crossed the tank ditch again to drive back to combat. The momentum of the Russian attack had broken down. In the meantime, the battlefield was spread with burning T-34s. I got the message by an orderly officer of the battalion who approached my tank on foot that it was the intention of the battalion commander to start a counterattack and seize back the ridge line. So we drove at high speed up the slope which a while ago we had driven down within the herds of Russians. At high noon the ridge was again in our possession.

The losses to my company were astonishingly low. Destroyed were both the tanks which were set to fire just beside me, two other tanks were heavily damaged, while both the other two companies had no tanks completely destroyed. Also the armored infantry battalion as well as the self-propelled artillery battalion had limited losses.

By prisoner statements, it became known that the Russians had prepared a third wave but did not start this attack after the defeat of the other two waves occurred in relatively short time. Within our lines there stood more than 100 killed Russian tanks.

The commanding general, SS-Obergruppenfuehrer Hausser, convinced himself about the extraordinary success in defense of the Leibstandarte. It was told that he himself marked the killed tanks with a piece of chalk and counted them. . . .

The Russian attack was launched in big masses but at the same time with unintelligible stubbornness. With some intelligent command and control it would have been possible for the Russian tanks to make use of the moment of surprise to inflict heavy losses to the armored group (tank battalion, armored infantry battalion, self-propelled artillery battalion) if not to destroy these elements completely. The fact that the attack of the Russians and their decisive breakthrough would have been heavily influenced by their own tank ditch should have been known to the Russian leaders when planning the attack.

According to Rudolf von Ribbentrop, only his tank company of seven tanks was driving towards height 252.2 while the other two tank companies in his battalion were behind the tank ditch. The legendary "swirling tank battle" of Prokhorovka appears to have been created by this incident, where a single tank company was overrun by one or two brigades of the XXIX Tank Corps.[61] There were no Tigers there![62] Ribbentrop was

---

61 Maj.Gen. (ret.) Dieter Brand interviewed Mr. Rudolf von Ribbentrop in September 2002. Mr. Ribbentrop had nothing to add to his report in the magazine "Der Freiwillige" but confirmed its accuracy. He did discuss the question again with his driver of that day, and he clearly states that there were two companies behind the tank ditch and only their company was driving towards height 252.2. Letter from Maj.Gen. (ret.) Dieter Brand to Christopher A. Lawrence dated 26 September 2002.

There are no reliable detailed descriptions of the division's activities on this day. There are some detailed reports of German heroics at Prokhorovka published at the time. These accounts need to be used with caution, as they are Nazi-era propaganda pieces.

62 From interview with Rudolf von Ribbentrop in September 2002 and documented in an email from Maj.Gen. (ret.) Dieter Brand to Christopher A. Lawrence dated 7 October 2002.

Also see Karl-Heinz Frieser, *Germany and the Second World War: Volume VIII: The Eastern Front 1943–1944: The War in the East and on the Neighbouring Fronts* (Oxford University Press, Oxford, 2017), pages 124–127. He places the company of four Tigers as arriving during the battle and deploying on the division's left wing (see page 126). We have the Tiger strength of the Leibstandarte SS Adolf Hitler Division as 4 on the 11th and 3 on the 12th with one damaged (see the Kursk Data Base).

credited with 14 kills this day and was awarded the Knight's Cross on the 20th.[63]

There is a second source for the tank ditch story, which is Sturmmann Wilhelm Roes of the 7th panzer company. His interview indicates that he was on the other side of tank ditch. He describes the antitank ditch as being 4.5 meters tall on the Russian side and only 1.2 meters on the German side. He describes several Russian tanks driving full speed into the tank ditch (note that Ribbentrop does not describe this). The T-34s were able to continue moving after this, but certainly the shock of such a fall seriously rattled the crew inside. He then states that as they came out of the ditch on the other side, the tank undersides were partially exposed and easy targets.[64]

The XXIX Tank Corps stated that the Germans, employing powerful artillery and mortar fire, plus Tiger tanks firing from ambush and bombers, held the Soviet units offensive along the line Oktyabrskii Sovkhoz to the northern edge of the wood to the hollow one kilometer southeast of Storozhevoye and then started counterattacking. There is no indication in the XXIX Tank Corps or the SS Panzer Corps records of a "meeting engagement" or a "swirling tank battle." Rotmistrov stated that the XXIX Tank Corps attack resulted in a "fierce meeting engagement" with German tanks along the approaches to the road south of the Oktyabrskii Sovkhoz. He stated this attack was halted by German tank and antitank fire as well as aerial bombardment.

According to a recent Russian source, between 1030-1045, the attack was halted at hill 252.2 and the Oktyabrskii Sovkhoz. Rotmistrov then ordered the two corps commanders to conduct a simultaneous strike against the state farm from two sides. But in the given combat environment, it was impossible to coordinate such an attack. Elements of the first battalion of the 32nd Tank Brigade had reached the Komsomolets State Farm early in the fighting. In messages Rotmistrov sent at 1045 he claimed that at 0930 the XXIX and XVIII Tank Corps has reached the line of the Komsomolets Farm.[65] This was overstating their advance.

By 1300, the 32nd and 31st Tank Brigades had gone over to the defensive along this line and Rotmistrov claims that they repulsed four strong German tank counterattacks, "which resulted in heavy enemy losses." Rotmistrov's statement, in light of the unit reports and losses, and the fact the Germans retook the Oktyabrskii Sovkhoz by the end of the day, appears to be incorrect.

This engagement, as noted, appears to have been the genesis of the "swirling tank battle" myth of Prokhorovka. While the Soviets did overrun the mechanized battalion and the self-propelled artillery battalion, they were unable to destroy them. Their fast sweep had caught one under-strength German tank company on the wrong side of the slope. Still, their attack ended up coming to a halt at their own tank ditch and under the guns of two other tank companies. It appears that the attacking force that initially swept over the German positions near hill 252.2 consisted of one or two tank battalions along with supporting forces.[66] It was not the entire tank corps.

ACCORDING TO ONE account of the fight, the lead tank battalion, the 362nd Tank Battalion, early in their advance came under fire from Marders of LSSAH's 1st SS Panzer Jaeger Battalion. As the lead tank battalion, armed with T-34s, crossed the cultivated area of

63 Nipe, page 40, and Franz Kurowski, *Panzer Aces*, page 200.

64 Zamulin, *Demolishing the Myth*, pages 327–328. His footnote does not state the source, only that the story came from the "author's personal archive."

65 Zamulin, *Demolishing the Myth*, page 325.

66 To the west of the rail line was the 32nd Tank Brigade. Its second tank battalion was involved in the attack on hill 252.2 and Oktyabrskii Sovkhoz. They were supported by three batteries from the 1446th Self-Propelled Regiment (two batteries were with the 25th Tank Brigade). It appears that part of its first battalion (with 15 T-34s) crossed over the rail line and moved to Komsomolets Sovkhoz. The 25th Tank Brigade was attacking to the left, east of the rail line. The 31st Tank Brigade joined the attack on hill 252.2 and Oktyabrskii Sovkhoz sometime later.

Stalinskoye creek, they came under artillery fire. The concealed German self-propelled tank destroyers then opened fire while the Soviet tanks were crossing over open terrain. They were then reinforced by the self-propelled guns and the 25th Tank Battalion, which was armed with T-70s. These units continued to advance to the woods with heavy casualties. The 362nd Tank Battalion lost 26 of its 32 T-34s and the two batteries of the self-propelled guns were "completely destroyed." The 362nd Tank Battalion commander was killed, the brigade commander was wounded, as was the commander of one of the motorized rifle battalions. SS Oberscharfueher Kurt Sametreiter would receive the Knight's Cross for this engagement. The 25th Tank Battalion commander took command of all the tanks and the composite tank battalion withdrew behind the infantry's position and to a defensive position a half kilometer southeast of Storozhevoye.[67] The Adolph Hitler SS Division probably had around 20 Marders ready for action and reported two destroyed this day.[68] Around noon the surviving composite tank battalion of mostly T-70s attempted to attack Ivanovskii Vyselok, but with little success.[69]

ON THE OTHER side of the railroad track, the 25th Tank Brigade, with two batteries of the 1446th Self-Propelled Artillery Regiment made more progress. They attacked through Stalinskoye Otdeleniye Sovkhoz and by 1400 (Moscow time) they had taken Storozhevoye and overcome the German fire resistance from Ivanovskii Vyiselok and the groves 1.5 kilometers northeast of Yasnaya Polyana. They also are reported to have taken significant casualties from air and artillery fire (this is Rotmistrov's claim) but no mention is made of the losses to tank fire. Their attack then stalled somewhere around Storozhevoye, tangled up with the Das Reich SS Division.

67 Zamulin, *Demolishing the Myth*, pages 327–328.

68 Captured German Records, U.S. Archives, T313, R389.

69 Zamulin, *Demolishing the Myth*, page 334.

The Das Reich reported in the morning an attack against the small forest east of Ivanovskii Vyiselok with 18 to 20 tanks and against its defenses west of Storozhevoye with infantry and tanks. It reported at 1140 Soviet attacks with tanks and infantry against the II Battalion, Deutschland SS Regiment. After this attack was defeated, at 1255 the battalion attacked Storozhevoye. It reported nine Soviet tanks were destroyed. At 1340, the II Battalion then took the south part of Storozhevoye as well as the little woods south of there. At 1505, the battalion was in the north part of Storozhevoye attacking to the east.

The 53rd Motorized Rifle Brigade, with the 271st Mortar Regiment, meanwhile had advanced into the woods north of Storozhevoye and were able to reach the "glade." Elements of the brigade along with at least 15 T-34s from the first tank battalion of the 32nd Tank Brigade had already penetrated to Komsomolets Sovkhoz in the original attack. Even though two attacking Soviet tank brigades were stalled in front of the German positions around height 252.2, elements of the tank corps had been able to bypass this point and take Komsomolets Sovkhoz. The railroad and the woods north of Storozhevoye probably served to cover the brigade's right flank as it continued forward. After "fierce fighting," by 1400 (Moscow time),[70] they were able to take Komsomolets Sovkhoz. Still, as none of the other armor of the XXIX Tank Corps had been able to come forward with this brigade, they were left in an untenable position and the Das Reich SS Division was attacking Storozhevoye, behind them.

Now, under pressure from German ground forces and air attack, the 53rd Motorized Rifle Brigade was forced to abandon the sovkhoz. The Soviets reported an attack from Yar (ravine) Zaslonnyii which was supported by a claimed 200 German tanks. The 53rd Motorized Rifle

70 1400 according the Fifth Guards Tank Army or 1430 according to Rotmistrov.

The details of the initial penetration to Komsomolets Sovkhoz in the morning by I/32nd Tank Brigade and elements of the 53rd Motorized Rifle Brigade are discussed in Zamulin, *Demolishing the Myth*, pages 314 and 326.

TANK RADIOS

All German tanks were equipped with two-way radios. The Soviets only ensured they had full radio communication in their commander's tanks at the company level and higher. In the case of the Fifth Guards Tank Army, the command tanks were equipped with radios down to platoon level. Even some non-command tanks had radio receivers, allowing them to receive orders from their commander.[1] So, at least a third of the Soviet tanks had radios. The rest of the tanks were commanded by hand signals and in combat simply followed their command tank. This was similar to the situation with their aircraft.

1 Zamulin, *Demolishing the Myth*, page 319–320.

The problem was further magnified for the Soviets in that the commander's tanks had visible radio antennas while the others did not. This allowed Germans to select the command tank among the targets. Even a hit that did not penetrate would often cause the radio to quit working. In the case of the Su-152s, their radios stopped working after five to eight shots from their own guns.[2]

Command of Soviet T-34s was made more difficult as they only had four man crews, with two men in the turret. The German tanks had five man crews, with two men in the turret to operate the main gun in addition to the tank commander. The Soviet tank commander also had to serve as a gunner.

2 Zamulin, *Demolishing the Myth*, page 320.

Brigade fell back to the line of Stalinskoye Otdeleniye Sovkhoz, where it took up defensive positions along with the 25th Tank Brigade, repelling the German's "rabid" tank and motorized infantry attacks. The 15 T-34s from the first tank battalion of the 32nd Tank Brigade were all destroyed. The battalion commander, Major P. S. Ivanov, was killed. His body was found on the 18th beside his burned out tank and he was buried at the sovkhoz.[71]

Supporting the XXIX Tank Corps attack was the 9th Guards Airborne Division. The division started the day deployed from the hollow 1.5 kilometers east of Petrovka to Grushki, covering Prokhorovka. The 28th Guards Airborne Regiment did move forward to join the attack south of the railroad and by 1400 (Moscow time) its I and II Battalions had reached the middle of the woods northwest of Storozhevoye. To the north of the railroad, the 23rd Guards Airborne Regiment advanced, and at 1800 (Moscow time, but this probably was a status report covering the morning's activities) was reported to be in the ravine southeast of Andreyevka, with its III Battalion up to the railroad (in front of height 241.1) and its II Battalion in the second echelon. The 26th Guards Airborne Regiment, which had been pushed off height 252.2 the previous day, was in line behind them but was not committed to the fighting.

They reported overcoming stubborn enemy resistance to capture Oktyabrskii Sovkhoz, height 252.2, Yamki, the Stalinskoye Otdeleniye Sovkhoz, and that they fought to capture the northeast slopes of height 241.6 and Storozhevoye.

According to the Adolf Hitler SS Division's daily report, "thanks to the defense against this massive armored attack, the enemy made little progress, there

71 Zamulin, *Demolishing the Myth*, page 326.

being during the entire day just the small penetration east of Storozhevoye." The situation in that sector was restored at 1330 (Berlin time). There is no record of any counterattacks by the Adolf Hitler SS Division after this.

Rotmistrov summarized the days fighting as "XXIX Tank Corps, attacking along the army's main axis, which coincided with the enemy's main attack axis, took the main force of the blow and made insignificant tactical success and took heavy personal and equipment casualties; however, thanks to its heroism in the unprecedented large tank battle, it inflicted such a blow on the enemy that he was no longer able to attempt such a large offensive along this axis."[72] As shown below, the German tank losses on this day were a fraction of the Soviet losses.

Starting at dawn, two Soviet tank corps had thrown themselves against the Adolf Hitler SS Division with parts of the Totenkopf and Das Reich SS Divisions, and by the early afternoon had fallen back to their defensive positions, effectively gutted. It was an attack that went nowhere at great cost.

The Afternoon Battles

By 1400, Berlin time, it was clear that the Soviet attacks had failed. The XVIII Tank Corps had stalled without taking all of Vasilyevka. They had lost Oktyabrskii Sovkhoz. The German positions stretched in a giant semi-circle around the corps positions from height 226.6 north of the Psel, through Vasilyevka and height 217.9, to height 241.6 and on to height 252.2. They were looking down on the Soviet positions from these heights.

Meanwhile, the XXIX Tank Corps' attack on height 252.2 had been stopped cold, with heavy losses. Their armored attack to the south of the railroad had also been stopped and their supporting infantry had advanced to take Komsomolets Sovkhoz, only to have to retreat to Stalinskoye Otdeleniye Sovkhoz.

It would appear that most of the losses the Soviets took on this day had occurred as part of their morning attack, but still fighting continued until nightfall. At 1401, the Germans reported that the Soviets launched an attack along the line from the east edge of Yamki to the road bend one kilometer west of Prokhorovka. This force was composed of infantry with strong artillery support and supported by tanks. The tanks, the Germans reported, were kept too far behind the attack spearheads, and the entire attack was stopped by combined artillery fire before it contacted the German front line. This may have been the 53rd Motorized Rifle Brigade supported by the gutted 25th Tank Brigade. At this point, the 25th Tank Brigade may well have had no T-34s operational, explaining why the surviving T-70 light tanks would have held back.

The Germans reported an additional concentration of 60 Soviet tanks in the ravine just east of Petrovka and east of Andreyevka, as well as infantry forces one kilometer northwest of Oktyabrskii Sovkhoz, which were shelled by the division's artillery beginning at 1600.

The depleted II Tank Corps was not involved in the morning's fighting, but was deployed in two defensive echelons covering the space between the XXIX Tank Corps and the II Guards Tank Corps. The corps had been reduced to only 55 operational tanks after the previous days of fighting.[73] The II Tank Corps still got partially tangled up in the afternoon's engagements. Two of its tank brigades were well to the rear in Krasnoye and Grushki, and not involved in action this day. However, the 169th Tank Brigade became involved in trying to hold Storozhevoye, defending along a line 0.7 kilometers west of there, but at 1600 (Moscow time) the Soviets reported it was pushed back to a line one kilometer southeast of Storozhevoye.[74] This brigade was

72 Rotmistrov and Grishin, page 9.

73 According to Operational Summary No. 138 at 0700 12 July the 99th Tank Brigade has operational 10 T-34s and 10 T-70s. The 26th Tank Brigade had 6 T-34s and 8 T-70s, the 169th Tank Brigade had 14 T-34s and 4 T-70s and the 15th Guards Tank Regiment had 3 Churchill's. See Zamulin, *Demolishing the Myth*, page 369.

74 Zamulin, *Demolishing the Myth*, pages 376-377 has the brigade holding in Storozhevoye until at least 1800, with pockets of resistant fighting until 2000, or possibly later.

reported to be down to 65 "active bayonets," 5 T-34s and 6 T-70s and to have suffered 79 men killed and wounded this day.

The II Tank Corps' 56th Motorized Rifle Brigade defended along this line from Prokhorovka to Yamki, in the second echelon behind a tank brigade. It was still reporting 1,200 "active bayonets" and 150 men killed and wounded.

BY THE END of the day, the XVIII Tank Corps was halted at Vasilyevka. Its further advance had been halted by German artillery and tank fire from the western outskirts of Vasilyevka. The corps had reached a line 200 meters east of the Bogoroditskoye church, the southern outskirts of Vasilyevka, the two windmills at Prelestnoye, farther along the northern slopes of the ravine southeast of Andreyevka, and to the Oktyabrskii Sovkhoz. Rotmistrov claimed that German fire from assault guns, hull-down tanks and "fierce" aerial bombardment made any further attack impossible. The XVIII Tank Corps pointed out that it had "unexpectedly" encountered a "well-organized and powerful" antitank defense, consisting of hull-down tanks and assault guns along the line of height 217.9 to height 241.6. "Suffering heavy casualties, the corps moved towards its objective with difficulty, but could not carry out its mission."[75] It does not appear that the Soviets ever took height 241.6 during the day. It does appear that the XVIII Tank Corps had ceased further forward movement by 1400 (Berlin time) this day. This was a poor deployment with an entire tank corps now strung out over ten kilometers along the line of villages in the shallow valley along the Psel River from Vasilyevka to Beregovoye.

Toward the end of the day, the XVIII Tank Corps stated that the Germans attempted a frontal tank attack from the Kozlovka-Greznoye area, with a simultaneous attempt to bypass the corps' units from the Kozlovka-Polezhayev direction, using Tiger tanks and self-propelled guns and with an intensive aerial bombardment of the Soviet lines. This was certainly Totenkopf's continued attack north of the Psel River.

---

75 The XVIII Tank Corps reports that "by the end of the day [no specific time provided] had reached the line 200 meters east of Bogoroditskoye Church—the southern outskirts of Vasliyevka—Andreyevka—two windmills at Prelestnoye—further along the northern slopes of the ravine southeast of Andreyevka—the Okyabrskii Sovkohz" (Fond: 18th TC, Opis: 1, Delo: 48, page 7). I believe the Bogoroditskoye Church is the church marked just west of the ravine west of Vasilyevka and is between Kozlovka and Vasilyevka. The XVIII Tank Corps' Combat Report #38, 0300 13 July 1943, reports, "ran into the enemy's well-organized resistance, which featured buried tanks and assault guns along the line height 217.9 to height 241.6." It then reports that "I [Bakharov] have ordered the corps' units to go over to the defense along the following lines." It then gives its positions as: The 32nd Motorized Rifle Brigade, with the 170th Tank Brigade and 36th Guards Heavy Tank Regiment was in the center of Vasilyevka to Mikhailovka to Prelestnoye. The 181st Tank Brigade was in the Petrovka area, and the 110th Tank Brigade was in the area from Petrovka (excluded) to Beregovoye. (Fond 18th TC, Opis: 1, Delo: 26, page 10).

The Fifth Guards Tank Army reports at 1900 that "The corps' further advance was contained by the enemy's powerful artillery and mortar fire from the Greznoye area, and by tank fire from the Bogoroditskiye area." In the 0700 report they record for the XVIII Tank Corps that "by the end of July 12 had taken the eastern outskirts of Vasilyevka, but its further advance was halted by the enemy's artillery and tank fire from the area of the western outskirts of Vasilyevka." (Operational Report #1, 1900, 12 July 1943 and Operational Report #2, 0700, 13 July 1943, Fond: 332, Opis: 4948, Delo: 82, pages 1-2.)

Zamulin, *Demolishing the Myth*, page 354, quotes a very similar report from the Fifth Guards Tank Army, except it claims that "By 1800 the brigades of the [18th Tank] corps had fully seized Vasilyevka and reached Kozlovka." This appears to be optimistic. It then states that "The corps commander ordered the units to dig in on the lines they had attained and to organize all-round defense." It then gives the same positions as was reported by XVIII Tank Corps at 0300 on 13 July 1943. It does not appear that the XVIII Tank Corps "reached" Kozlovka.

The Fifth Guards Tank Army's Combat Activities from July 7–24 compiled September 30, 1943, also reports that: "At 1800 on July 12 the corps' brigades finally took Vasilyevka and reached Kozlovka. The corps, on the [German] line height 217.9 to three kilometers southwest of Kozlovka to height 241.6, encountered heavy enemy fire resistance from assault guns, tanks buried in the ground, and fierce aerial bombardment, which made any further advance impossible." (Fond: 332, Opis: 4948, Delo: 19, Page 8.)

Major General Bakharov (XVIII Tank Corps commander) stated that in order to avoid excessive losses in men and equipment, he ordered the corps' units to take up defensive positions along its new lines. His units consolidated and organized an all-around defense. The 32nd Motorized Rifle Brigade and the 170th Tank Brigade, with the remains of the 36th Guards Tank Regiment, were around the line of villages running along the Psel: Vasilyevka, Mikhailovka, Prelestnoye. The 181st Tank Brigade was in Petrovka (obviously having already withdrawn), and the 110th Tank Brigade was arrayed from the outskirts of Petrovka to Beregovoye, also effectively disengaged.

Up until 1700, according to incomplete data, the XVIII Tank Corps reported 13 German tanks destroyed. At 0700 the following day these claims had been increased to 15 "Tigers" and 300 German troops. There are four different reports of XVIII Tank Corps losses recorded for this day, with the reports made later in the day being worse. One report claimed that up to 20 percent of its motorized infantry and eight senior officers had been put out of action, three of them killed. The highest loss report for the 12th records losses of 43 T-34s, 24 T-70s, and 11 Churchills. It also reports 218 men lost in the tank units and 46 men lost in the motorized rifle brigade. This last figure appears to be low, as they reported at one point that the motorized rifle brigade was down to 260 men.

The corps' actual losses appear to be higher than these reports state. The report at the end of the day records that the 110th Tank Brigade had 15 T-34s and 18 T-70s, while the 170th Tank Brigade had only 5 T-34s and 9 T-70s and the 181st Tank Brigade had 6 T-34s and 8 T-70s, while the 36th Guards Tank Regiment had 8 Churchills. It would appear that the corps lost 81 tanks from all causes on the 12th of July.[76]

While it is dangerous to read between the lines of an official report, it does appear from the XVIII Tank Corps' report of combat activities from the 12th through the 24th of July that Major General Bakharov did not wholeheartedly approve of this attack which destroyed his corps.

The XXIX Tank Corps fared even worse than the XVIII. Because of the nature of its attacks across open ground with the 32nd Tank Brigade, it was completely gutted. It is suspected that most of this damage occurred as a result of their attack in the morning. The supporting 31st Tank Brigade also suffered similarly high casualties.

During the day the 32nd Tank Brigade claimed it was repeatedly attacked from the Oktyabrskii Sovkhoz. It claimed to have destroyed 12 German medium and light tanks along with three Tigers and 400 troops. The 32nd's losses at the end of the day were reported to be 100 men killed and 130 wounded. Overall, 54 T-34s were either burned, knocked out or in need of repair. This was 90 percent of their tank strength, leaving the brigade with only 6 T-34s!

The 31st Tank Brigade claimed that they repulsed four German tank and artillery counterattacks on the Oktyabrskii Sovkhoz. By the end of the day, the brigade was reporting that 20 T-34s and 18 T-70s had been knocked out and burned. This would leave the brigade with only 9 T-34s and 20 T-70s. There certainly were other damaged tanks, as at the end of the day, the brigade reported only three tanks in line, with the location and condition of the remainder being investigated. They claimed to have knocked out or destroyed 12 German medium and light tanks, three Tigers, and killed 400 Germans. Their losses for the 12th were reported to be 14 killed, 27 wounded and 15 missing. During the day, it is claimed that the Germans launched 240 air sorties over the 31st Tank Brigade's units.

The 25th Tank Brigade reported that after suffering heavy personnel and equipment casualties from the German air and artillery fire during their attack in the direction of Stalinskoye Otdeleniye Sovkhoz, they had,

76 Zamulin, *Demolishing the Myth*, page 336, reports the XVIII Tank Corps losses as 43 T-34, 24 T-70s, and 17 Mk-IVs for a total of 84 tanks. Personnel losses are 471 total, with 271 killed and missing.

by the end of the day, concentrated and taken up defensive positions along the hollow one kilometer southeast of Storozhevoye. During the day, the 25th Tank Brigade claimed the Germans flew 400 sorties over it. The brigade claimed at 2400 to have killed 800 Germans, four Tigers, nine Panzer IIIs, while their own losses were reported to be 140 men killed, 180 wounded, 13 T-34s and 10 T-70s irretrievably lost, 11 T-34s and 10 T-70s knocked out or hit by mines and seven T-34s and four T-70s out of action due to mechanical breakdowns. This leaves no T-34s unaccounted for and only 12 T-70s. This was effectively 82 percent of the brigade armor strength gone, along with all of its T-34s.

The 53rd Motorized Rifle Brigade, following its attack, had retreated to a line running from Stalinskoye Otdeleniye Sovkhoz to the hollow east of Yamki. During the day, some 300 wounded men had passed through the brigade medical stations and according to the brigade commander's report, losses were approaching 50 percent.[77]

The XXIX Tank Corps reported at 1900 that the Germans were resisting stubbornly along the line of the road one kilometer southwest of the Oktyabrskii Sovkhoz to the southeast half of the woods to the north of Storozhevoye to the groves southwest of Storozhevoye. They report that the Germans were carrying out raids with large groups of bombers against the corps. The XXIX Tank Corps was also reported to be defending against armored attacks from Komsomolets Sovkhoz.

The XXIX Tank Corps at 0700 on the 13th reported that they had destroyed 26 tanks, of which 11 were Tigers, and 1,800 German troops. This estimate was further revised in the 1900 report for the 13th to be 41 German tanks, including 12 Tigers, and 1,500 troops. Their own losses were reported at 0700 on the 13th as 95 T-34s, 38 T-70s, 8 self-propelled guns, 240 men killed and 610 wounded. This figure does not match the individual brigade figures, which report 105 T-34s and 42 T-70s lost, and so probably does not include those tanks which broke down. Overall, 159 tanks were lost this day from all causes, making this 71 percent of the corps' tank strength. It was the bloodiest single-day tank attack conducted during the battles around Belgorod.[78]

The XXIX Tank Corps also conducted recovery operations, with the evacuation of knocked out tanks being carried out by three turret-less T-34s and an M-3 Grant. During the night, they repaired only three T-34s and one SU-122. Between the two attacking corps, the Soviets had committed six tank brigades to battle this day, with four effectively gutted and another seriously attrited.

At the end of the day, the Adolf Hitler SS Division's front line still ran along the western part of Storozhevoye and the little woods north of there, to the course of the road to 500 meters northeast of 252.2, to the north and east edges of Oktyabrskii Sovkhoz. The Germans held the battlefield.

Officer Cadet Guenther Baer,[79] tank commander in the Leibstandarte SS Adolf Hitler's II Panzer Battalion, recalls that day:

77 This is from combat report #75, 2400, 12 July 1943 (Fond: 29 TC, Opis: 1, Delo: 6, page 93). In operational report #91 , 0400, 14 July 1943 they report losses for 12 July as 517 men killed and missing and 572 wounded (Fond: 29 TC, Opis: 1, Delo; 6, page 104). Zamulin, *Demolishing the Myth*, page 326, reports 1,122 casualties, including 393 dead.

78 Zamulin, *Demolishing the Myth*, page 335, reports the XXIX Tank Corps losses for 12 July as: ". . . 1,991 men, including 1,033 were killed or missing in action. Of the 199 combat vehicles that took part in the fighting, 153 were knocked out." On page 336, he shows their losses as 109 T-34s and 44 T-70s.

79 Brig.Gen. (ret.) Guenther Baer was interviewed by Maj.Gen. (ret.) Dieter Brand on 21 February 1999 in Munster. Gunther Baer was born 19 October 1923. He volunteered for the Waffen SS when he was 18. He went through training with the "Leibstandarte Division" in Berlin-Lichterfelde. At first he served with the guard battalion and stood guard at the Reich chancellery, but starting February 1943 he was with the armored group of the Leibstandarte SS Adolf Hitler Division and saw action during the winter offensive at Kharkov (Manstein's counterattack). At the time of Kursk he was an SS officer cadet with the rank of a sergeant and gunner in a company of the II Battalion of Leibstandarte SS Adolf Hitler Panzer Regiment. Starting 6 July, during the attack, he became a tank commander.

After Kursk, he served in an assault gun battalion and toward the end of the war was an SS second lieutenant and

According to my memory, on July 11th my unit was deployed in conjunction with the 1st SS Panzer Grenadier Regiment east of the railway to Prokhorovka near the Stalinskoye Otdeleniye Sovkhoz. There on that day we saw a special method of engagement used by the enemy. In a large wooded area, enemy infantry had camouflaged themselves in the treetops of what I believed to be large beech trees. They amounted to at least one company, if not a whole battalion. Our infantry suffered heavy casualties when penetrating these woods. We then fought the enemy with machineguns and high explosive shells and made many prisoners.

On the 11th we had been told to prepare for a tough day on the 12th. At my level of tank commander, I don't recall there being talk of a whole enemy tank army scheduled to attack. But the enemy replenishing his reserves from the rear was a known fact.

On the 12th we first warded off an attack of 30 to 40 tanks east of the railway. As usual, the enemy suffered heavily. However, throughout that day, particularly fierce engagements were fought west of the railway where Tigers had been deployed. For this reason we were set to counterattack to the west of the railway towards Mikhailovka as the day went on. We fought throughout the entire day, as the enemy was attacking from Prokhorovka, but also along the flanks, from the Yamki area on the right and the Mikhailovka area on the left.

Time and again we were perplexed at the haphazard manner of their attack. I still recall my platoon leader saying: "If the Soviets would refrain from deploying this huge amount of tanks piecemeal, but instead in the framework of a coordinated attack, we would simply be blown away by their numerical superiority." But they always came in little spurts, 30 to 40 tanks at a time, once from the front, once from the left or from the right. One attack after another was shot to pieces—often in close combat, which saw the infantry destroying many tanks using magnetic charges.

We held our positions on that day and did not retreat.

Heinz Macher,[80] in command of the 130 to 140-man engineer company of the Deutschland SS Regiment recalled:

On July 12, I took part in the attack on Storozhevoye (south of Prokhorovka) with my company. This locality could only be taken after fierce close combat. Enemy tanks were part of the defense inside the village. We fought them with magnetic charges and mines. On that day, the Soviets constantly attacked with their tanks. Throughout the day some armored attack was always in progress. The main burden of our defense was borne by our tanks and assault guns that day, while we fought in conjunction with the II Battalion of the Deutschland SS Regiment in order to capture Storozhevoye. On that day, my company suffered five dead and 10 wounded.

---

company commander. His combat awards include the Iron Cross 1st and 2nd Class, Wound Badge in silver, and Tank Badge in silver and bronze.

After the war, he served with the German Border Police, joining the West German military in 1956 as a captain and commander of a tank company. He rose to become a battalion commander, brigade commander of an armored brigade and finally Deputy Division Commander of the 1st Armored Division. Around 1984, he retired from active duty as a brigadier general.

80 Mr. Heinz Macher was interviewed by Maj.Gen. (ret.) Dieter Brand on 3 March 1999. Heinz Macher, born 31 December 1919, had been in the Waffen SS since 3 April 1939 and took part in the campaigns in Poland, Yugoslavia, Russia and after Kursk, France/Normandy, first as a soldier, and by 1943, as an officer.

At the time of Kursk he was an SS First Lieutenant in the Das Reich SS Division and was commander of the 16th company in the Deutschland SS Regiment. The 16th company was the engineer company for that regiment.

His awards during the war include the Knight's Cross (Kharkov), Oak Leaves (Normandy), German Cross in Gold, Iron Cross 1st and 2nd Class, Close Combat Clasp in Gold, Assault Badge, Golden Wound Badge.

One can see a picture of Obersturmfuehrer Heinz Macher in Bruce Quarrie, *Hitler's Samurai, The Waffen-SS in Action*, page 55.

The II Guards Tank Corps Attack

The II Guards Tank Corps attacked in the Belenikhino and Yasnaya Polyana area against the Das Reich SS Division. At 2400 (Moscow time), the corps' three tank brigades had concentrated in Vinogradovka and Ivanovka. Its motorized rifle brigade and most of the corps' other units were concentrated in the woods east of Ivanovka and Leski. The 47th Guards Heavy Tank Regiment, down to only two Churchills, had returned from its fighting around Khokhlovo and rejoined the corps north of Leski. The order to attack came from Vatutin, transmitted through the commander of the XLVIII Rifle Corps.

Burdeinyii, in order to cover the corps from the southeast and east, placed the 26th Guards Tank Brigade across the road, facing south, from Malaya Yablonovka to Plota. Then around 0900 (Moscow time) he ordered the tank brigade to move down to Shakhovo. This was one-third of his armor. One can infer from this unusual defensive action that he did not have confidence that the forces to the south would hold, or that he would receive word in a timely manner if the Germans did break through.[81]

He then attacked with the other two brigades. Their attacks by-passed Belenikhino from the south and captured the woods west of Belenikhino and the woods east of Kalinin and the unnamed height west of the Sukhaya Plota ravine (this is near Plota). The Das Reich reported in the morning an attack against Yasnaya Polyana with 30 to 40 tanks. At 1200 the division reported a Soviet attack with about 70 tanks and infantry against the I Battalion, Der Fuehrer SS Regiment in the Yasnaya Polyana area. At 1350, this attack was reported as defeated.

At 1205, the Russians attacked the left wing of the II Battalion, Der Fuehrer SS Regiment just north of Kalinin with 40 tanks from Belenikhino and also attacked the battalion's right wing with 10 tanks. They succeeded in breaking through, but this penetration was relieved by a counterattack.

The 167th Infantry Division's 339th Infantry Regiment extended its flank up to Kalinin, and left better records for this day than did the Das Reich SS Division. They first report being attacked at about 0130, with Soviet infantry with "many" tanks attacking the regiments' positions southwest of Kalinin. The attack was repelled with the help of the Das Reich SS Assault Gun Battalion. The Germans claimed eight Soviet tanks destroyed.

The sector was quiet during the morning. At 1015, news of the massive Russian tank attack against the Adolf Hitler SS Division and the Das Reich SS Division reached the 167th Infantry Division's command post. This is one of the few clear references in the German records to a "massive Russian tank attack."[82] At 1155, the division came under attack with armor on the left wing of the 339th Infantry Regiment south of Kalinin. This was hit by division artillery fire, but this did not stop the attack. At 1220, the division requested close air support to attack the estimated 25 attacking Soviet tanks. This German air support and a counterattack from tanks from the Das Reich SS Division caused the Soviet attack to veer south. By 1320, the 339th Infantry Regiment reported that many Soviet tanks were destroyed in front of its left flank, but still the Soviet attack went forward, penetrating the positions of the III Battalion, 339th Infantry Regiment at Petrovskii at 1445. The 238th Reconnaissance Battalion was attached to the penetrated battalion and resolved the penetration by counterattacking the Soviets in the flank. By 1450, the division was reporting that the penetration in the north wing had been forced out and another penetration on the heights of Rozhdestvenka had been mopped

81 This appears to have been done on his own initiative. At 0600, Burdeinyii sent the following dispatch: "To Vatutin, Shtevnev, Rotmistrov. The enemy has seized Rzhavets and Ryidinka with tanks, and is moving on Avdeyevka and Plota. I have decided to position the 26th Guards Tank Brigade east and southeast of Plota." See Zamulin, *Demolishing the Myth*, page 363.

82 German records of this attack are so sparse that, for example, Ziemke's book *Stalingrad to Berlin: The German Defeat in the East*, which was written primarily from German sources, did not even mention the Battle of Prokhorovka or any fighting on the 12th.

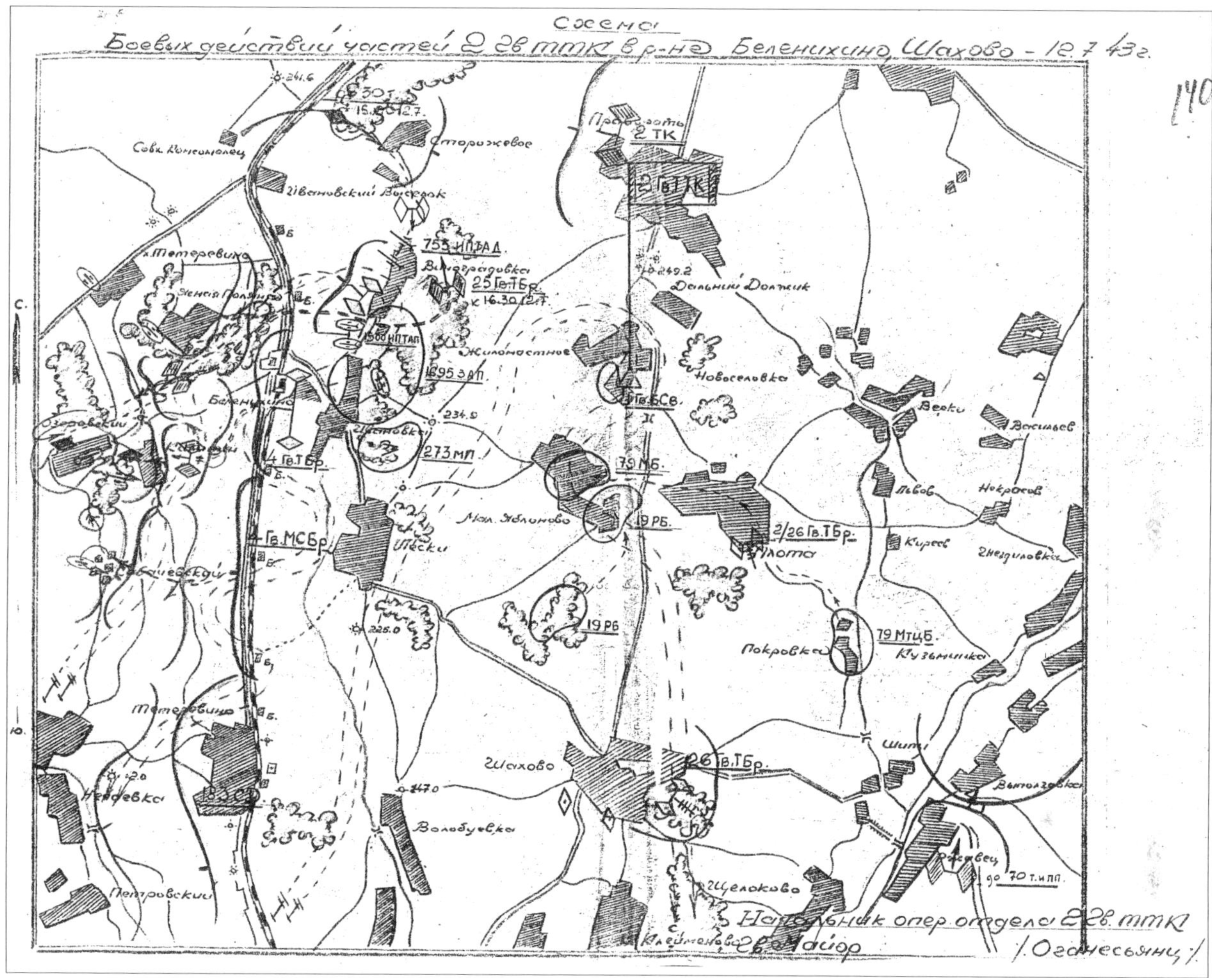

II Guards Tank Corps map for 12 July 1943.

up. Still, continued Soviet pressure compelled the division to request continued support for the 339th Infantry Regiment from the Das Reich SS Assault Gun Battalion.

The II Guards Tank Corps reported at 1430 (Moscow time) that its 25th Guards Tank Brigade had reached the western edge of the woods one kilometer northeast of Kalinin, where it attacked height 243.0. The Germans met the brigade with heavy artillery and mortar fire, and from hull-down tanks. The Germans were well-supported by a large number of aircraft. This halted the brigade's progress. The 4th Guards Tank Brigade, attacking along the corps' left flank, had also crossed the railroad and by 1430 (Moscow time) was fighting for Kalinin, but with no success. It had reached the road south of Kalinin, where it encountered heavy German resistance from the eastern edge of the grove southwest of Kalinin. At 1540 (Berlin time), the panzer regiment, which apparently was back in reserve, reported that two Soviet tank attacks on both sides of Kalinin had been smashed, with 21 Soviet tanks and one Martin (Boston?) bomber destroyed.

Apparently elements of the II Guards Tank Corps were attacked this day by air units of both sides. The 4th Guards Motorized Rifle Brigade was covering the withdrawal of the 4th Guards Tank Brigade from the Kalinin area. The rifle brigade came under a German armor attack and then was hit with a German air attack that is claimed to consist of "28 Ju-87s, 12 Macchi MC.200 Italian fighter-bombers, and 12 Ju-87 G-1 Stuka tank hunters." The Italian aircraft is certainly a misidentification, perhaps for the German FW-190. We also believe there was only one Ju-87 G-1 at Kursk under command of Hans Rudel. Between 1700-1800 (Moscow time) they were then attacked by "Soviet Il-2s and bombers" on the brigade's combat outposts and also the positions of the 4th Guards Tank Brigade. It is stated that these two air attacks cost the 4th Motorized Rifle Brigade 272 casualties. Its I Rifle Battalion lost 141 killed and wounded.[83]

The Sixty-ninth Army's XLVIII Rifle Corps still had command of the 93rd Guards, 183rd, and 375th Rifle Divisions. This corps also joined in the attack on the Das Reich SS Division and the 339th Infantry Regiment. The corps attacked at 1230 from their former defensive positions and by 1400 had captured the fork in the road one kilometer east of Yasnaya Polyana and height 210.7 and were fighting for Kalinin, Nechayevka, Petrovskii, and the woods southeast of Smorodino.

The 183rd Rifle Division had the mission of destroying the Germans in the areas of Kalinin, Ozerovskii, and height 232.0 and as such was operating with the II Guards Tank Corps. Its 296th Rifle Regiment ended up fighting in the area of height 243.0, its 227th Rifle Regiment was on the eastern outskirts of Kalinin, and the 158th Guards Rifle Regiment (51st Guards Rifle Division) was along the 220 contour height on the hill south of Kalinin. At 1900, the division was reported to be on the eastern slopes of height 243.0 to the eastern outskirts of Kalinin to Sobachevskii.

The 375th Rifle Division attacked to the south of the 183rd Rifle Division. It moved up to 1.5 kilometers southeast of Leski and down to Teterevino during the night and attacked at 1200 (Moscow time). This otherwise undocumented attack left the 375th Rifle Division with 406 killed and 603 wounded for the day. At 1900, this division was reported to be just south of Sobachevskii to point +2.0 to Petrovskii.

To the south of it was the 93rd Guards Rifle Division. It moved forward to its jumping off positions with its 285th Guards Rifle Regiment just south of Teterevino, and its other two rifle regiments operating between Petrovskii and Soshenkov. They attacked with minimal casualties (11 killed, 33 wounded) and then consolidated at 1900 (Moscow time) south of Petrovskii to 2.5 kilometers east of Smorodino to the northern part of Nepkhayevo to Gostishchevo. This division was being flanked from the south by the 315th Infantry Regiment from the 167th Infantry Division and by the 417th Infantry Regiment from the 168th Infantry Division.

Then for some reason, after having been held back all day, the II Tank Corps was sent into the attack. It had been holding along the line from Petrovka to Belenikhino during the morning and had covered the army troops' arrivals at their jumping off points. At 1600 (Moscow time), they received orders to attack along the line running from Pravorot to Kalinin. As the II Guards Tanks Corps' attacks along this line had already failed, it made little sense to now send a weaker tank corps into the same attack. Its motorized rifle brigade, which was holding in the second echelon in front of Prokhorovka and Yamki, was sent to Ivanovka, where it became the second echelon force behind the two attacking tank brigades. Its 169th Tank Brigade was still defending the height east of Storozhevoye and was held there to cover the flank. The 99th Tank Brigade from Krasnoye, with 10 T-34s and 10 T-70s, and the 26th Tank Brigade from Grushki, with 6 T-34s, 10 T-70s and 45 "active

83 Zamulin, *Demolishing the Myth*, page 366. The comments concerning aircraft types are mine. The Italian C.200s and C.202s were withdrawn from the Eastern Front on 18 January 1943.

bayonets" were sent to conduct this attack.[84] By 2130, these two brigades had concentrated at Ivanovka with the motorized rifle brigade in the second echelon. The II Tank Corps' reports indicate an estimated 10 tank losses for the day (although this was 15 percent of their tank strength).[85]

The Soviet attacks had been repulsed, but in places the fighting continued into the evening. Local penetrations, including into the left wing of the 167th Infantry Division, were still being resolved as night fell. The division was anticipating further Soviet tank attacks in the Kalinin to Storozhevoye area. It had not received any reports from their assault gun battalion or their flak battalion.

The II Guards Tank Corps by the end of day, in connection with the withdrawal of the 53rd Motorized Rifle Brigade from Komsomolets Sovkhoz and the threat to its right flank that developed as a result of this withdrawal, withdrew to the line of Vinogradovka to Belenikhino, where it consolidated to regroup. It reported at 0700 on the 13th that it had destroyed 21 tanks on this day, of which nine were "Tigers." It revised that report at 1900 to 31 German tanks and 1,000 troops. It reported losing ten T-34s, one Churchill, and eight T-70s by 0700 on the 13th, although their losses for this day were probably more like 39 T-34s, 19 T-70s, and one Churchill.[86] They reported 47 T-34s and 28 T-70s still combat ready, with most of their strength in the unengaged 26th Tank Brigade (30 T-34s, 9 T-70s).

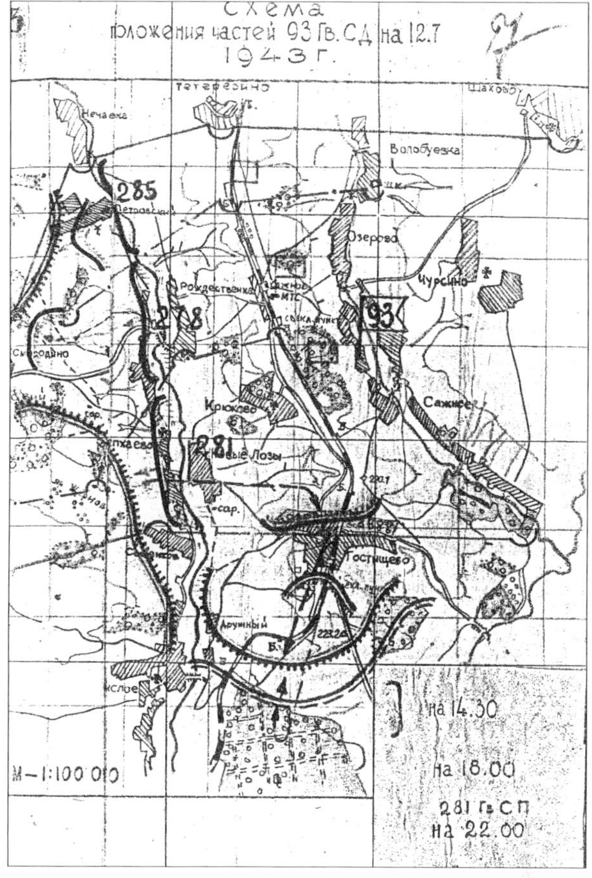

DEFENSE SCHEME OF THE 93RD GUARDS RIFLE DIVISION, 12 JULY 1943.

84 The 99th Tank Brigade was in Krasnoye as of 1900 on the 12th and appears to have already taken its tank losses for the day. It may not have had limited participation in the attack. For the purposes of the statistics in the engagements, we record the 99th Brigade as part of the fight against the Totenkopf SS Division this day vice fighting the Das Riech SS Division.

85 The II Tank Corps lost over 10 tanks this day according to the Kursk Data Base. Zamulin, *Demolishing the Myth*, page 378, reports that the 99th Tank Brigade lost 7 T-34s and 1 T-70.

86 Kursk Data Base.

As Officer Cadet Kendziora,[87] Das Reich SS Division, now commanding a Tiger tank, recalled:

> I did experience the various Soviet attacks on our spearheads on July 12. Combat was often at closest range on that day, because according to my memory, the battle arena was soon dotted with destroyed T-34s. The smoke from these burning tanks very much obstructed our field of vision.
>
> We were particularly impressed by the thrust and relentlessness which marked the Soviet forces' attack—again not as a coordinated effort. Thus, we were able to shoot one attack after another to pieces. Soviet losses were exorbitant, but this did not serve to diminish the Soviet soldiers' fighting spirit. They really fought with the utmost dedication.
>
> I recall one example which I witnessed myself. One T-34 sat ablaze roughly a thousand feet from our positions. The crew had bailed out. I then noticed how an apparently wounded soldier dragged himself back to the burning tank, got in, and then drove the tank against one of ours. I think the latter was an armored personnel carrier. The Soviet tank exploded upon impact. This is a prime example of the doggedness Soviet soldiers showed in combat. They obviously wanted to beat us right there on that battlefield. However, we held the ground against high numerical superiority, on this day and the following days.

Finally, we have the account from Private Kurt Kaufmann, Das Reich SS Division, now a veteran of one week of combat, with the antiaircraft company:

> After a quiet rainy night spent almost without harassment in our tents, the call went out again: "Come on, get ready for attack." With this rather superficial order, which was nevertheless quite the rule on our lowest level of command, our 14th company in the Der Fuehrer SS Regiment entered what was to become the largest armor battle in World War II. At this time the Das Reich SS Division was located 40 kilometers (25 miles) inside the original perimeter of the enemy's system of fortifications. Further advance was to occur in a northeastern direction towards Prokhorovka. South of that city our corps' tanks and Russian T-34s had entered into unrelenting combat throughout several days and nights.
>
> Due to a multitude of reasons, I was only able to keep up entries into my diaries on a fragmentary basis before the beginning of these engagements. . . .
>
> While the attack by the Leibstandarte SS Adolf Hitler Division had been mired down before Prokhorovka on July 11, the assault of our division with the Der Fuehrer SS Regiment in the vanguard allowed us to advance much further—despite massive enemy resistance. We were able to clear a forest as well as the gorge and a salient-like incline to the southeast of that town. Enemy counterattacks with armor support, which saw the first deployment of American-made tanks [U.S. made tanks had been encountered on the 5th and after by the XLVIII Panzer Corps; there are no reports of American tanks in this area, except maybe in the 235th Tank Regiment], forced us to maintain incessant exchanges of fire at closest range. Each enemy assault was annihilated, though, or the Soviet soldiers were taken prisoner. Pursuant to one of those enemy assaults originating in the Storozhevoye area, our attack formation was able to push on and capture this town. This occurred none too soon, as the next armored attack was already charging towards us. We couldn't believe our eyes when we saw about 40 T-34s in a semicircular formation stampeding towards us. It looked like an attack by cavalry. Almost all the enemy tanks were killed by our antitank guns or our own tanks. Some tanks broke into the panzer grenadier positions and were eliminated in close combat using

87 Brig.Gen. (ret.) Kendziora was interviewed by Maj.Gen. (ret.) Dieter Brand on 4 March 1999 in Luneburg. General Kendziora was born 12 February 1925 and had been a soldier since 1 February 1943, at first as gunner in an assault gun and, starting 6 July, as commander of a Tiger tank. He had joined the assault gun battalion in the Das Reich SS Division during the Battle of Kharkov. He became the gunner in the battalion commander's assault gun.

His awards during the war include Iron Cross 2nd Class, Tank Badge in Gold, and Wound Badge.

After the war, he was a battalion commander and brigade commander in the German Army, retiring with the rank of Brigadier General in 1985.

magnetic antitank hollow charges. On our 20mm antiaircraft gun, we had difficulty completing two missions at the same time, namely combating air as well as ground targets. Sorties flown by the enemy increased to such a degree that we had our hands full with that alone. In ground to ground fighting, the antiaircraft gun showed little effect when used against tanks, but was devastating against the accompanying infantry. We were so involved in the engagement that we feared the enemy tanks would roll over us and prepared to abandon the gun. That almost came to pass during one of the ensuing air attacks. Again, a large number of T-34s attacked towards our positions, charging at full speed from a distant forested area. Our own tanks immediately opened fire. In this manner, they could eliminate all enemy tanks that posed an immediate threat to us, but one of them at only 50 yards distance. By then we had already spent two magazines with 40 shots each on this one tank. After a hit by one of our tanks, the Russian crew was able to disembark just before the tank blew up. They came over to our gun, running ducked down with their hands in the air. We were busy ourselves, though, and had no time to take care of prisoners. As a result, they just stood under cover next to our gun. Several enemy tanks had darted past us left and right into the rear of our position. They were all hit by our antitank fire from the flanks or destroyed in close combat. At times all hell broke loose in this battle! The howling of T-34 engines as well as our own Panzer IVs, above that the roaring of airplanes from friend and foe, tank guns barking, bursting of the armor piercing shells, explosion of tanks that were hit, rattle from lighter automatic weapons, dust thrown up and smoke from tanks set ablaze—we were engulfed in a doomsday scenario!

We had dug in our halftrack so deeply that only the gun barrel stuck out of the hole as early as that night. This excellent cover, combined with our camouflage and the discipline in firing we exercised were likely the reasons why we survived the many hours in the midst of battle without a scratch. A T-34 rolling backwards at about 30 yards distance from our position had his running gear shot to pieces by us. Before he could see us several rounds from our own tank hit him. His turret was thus lifted off and fell on its side. The crew didn't stand a chance.

Overall, our division shot 120 enemy tanks on July 12, 1943.

Post-Mortem on the Tank Fields of Prokhorovka

On the 11th (1835 hours), the Adolf Hitler SS Division reported the following tanks ready for action:

Pz II	4
Pz III long	5
Pz IV long	47
Pz VI	4
Command tanks	6
StuG III	10
SP AT Guns	20

There was no report for the 12th. At the end of the day on the 13th, they reported the following ready for action:

Pz II	4
Pz III long	5
Pz IV long	31
Pz VI	3
Command tanks	7
StuG III	20
SP AT Guns	20

As the armor actions were very intense on the 12th and almost non-existent on the 13th, we assume that all tank losses were taken on the 12th. This means that they probably lost around 17 tanks for this day. There were also two Marders reported as killed on this day, even though there was no change to the reported strength from the 11th to the 13th.[88] Of those, we estimate that only 6 were ever written off as totally destroyed.[89] The

88 See T313, R389.

89 This is estimated in part from a report of the number in repair this day of 8 Pz IIIs long, 32 Pz IVs long, 9 Pz VIs and 10 StuG IIIs, as compared to tanks previously lost and previously reported as destroyed.

rest they were able to pull from the battlefield and send back into repair.

In the case of the Das Reich, the figures are more startling:

	11th	*12th*	*13th*
Pz III long	34	42	43
Pz IV long	18	18	20
Pz VI	1	2	1
	11th	*12th*	*13th*
T-34	8	8	11
Command tanks	7	6	8
StuG III	27	27	24
SP AT Guns	12	12	12

This would lead one to conclude that there was only one tank lost by this division on this day. In the case of the Adolf Hitler and Das Reich SS Divisions, there was not significant decline in strength in the following days that would indicate any form of delayed reporting. Therefore, one is left with these reports as the only reasonable estimate of their own losses, especially when one considers the supporting quartermaster and other tanks' status reports. As already discussed, we estimate that the Totenkopf SS Division lost 20 or 30 tanks this day. It is unknown whether they were lost fighting the XVIII Tank Corps, or supporting the fighting against the Fifth Guards Army.

There is no question that the Soviet tank forces suffered heavily. The four tank corps in question were not seriously engaged the following day. On the 13th of July they reported the following number of tanks ready for action:

	T-34s	*T-70s*	*Churchills*
XVIII Tank Corps	15	18	
XXIX Tank Corps	no report		
II Tank Corps	22	20	
II Guards Tank Corps	45	33	2

It is estimated that the losses by corps were:

	Strength 11 July	*Strength 12 July*	*Losses*
XVIII Tank Corps			
T-34s	68	26	45
T-70s	58	35	25
Churchills	18	8	11
XXIX Tank Corps			
T-34s	123	20	105
T-70s	81	39	42
KV-1	1	1	0
SU-122s	12	3	9
SU-76s	8	5	3
	Strength 11 July	*Strength 12 July*	*Losses*
1529th Heavy SP Artillery Regiment			
SU-152s	11	11	0
KV-1	1	1	0
II Tank Corps			
T-34s	28	21	7
T-70s	28	26	3
Churchills	4	4	0
	Strength 11 July	*Strength 12 July*	*Losses*
II Guards Tank Corps			
T-34s	86	47	39
T-70s	52	33	19
Churchills	2	2	1
Totals	581	282	309[90]

This day, neither the Adolf Hitler nor the Das Reich SS Divisions was able to advance. The Adolf Hitler SS Division claimed that it was attacked by at least 115 tanks while the Das Reich SS Division claimed to have been attacked by 110. On this day, the SS Panzer Corps faced around 581 tanks.

The Adolf Hitler SS Division claimed 185 or 192 tanks were destroyed this day; Totenkopf was credited with

90 All data from the Kursk Data Base. The number of tanks ready for action on the 12th subtracted from the figures for the 11th indicates a few less tanks damaged or destroyed. There were either some tanks repaired and returned to action that day or minor errors in the strength or loss reports.

GERMAN INTELLIGENCE MAP, 12 JULY

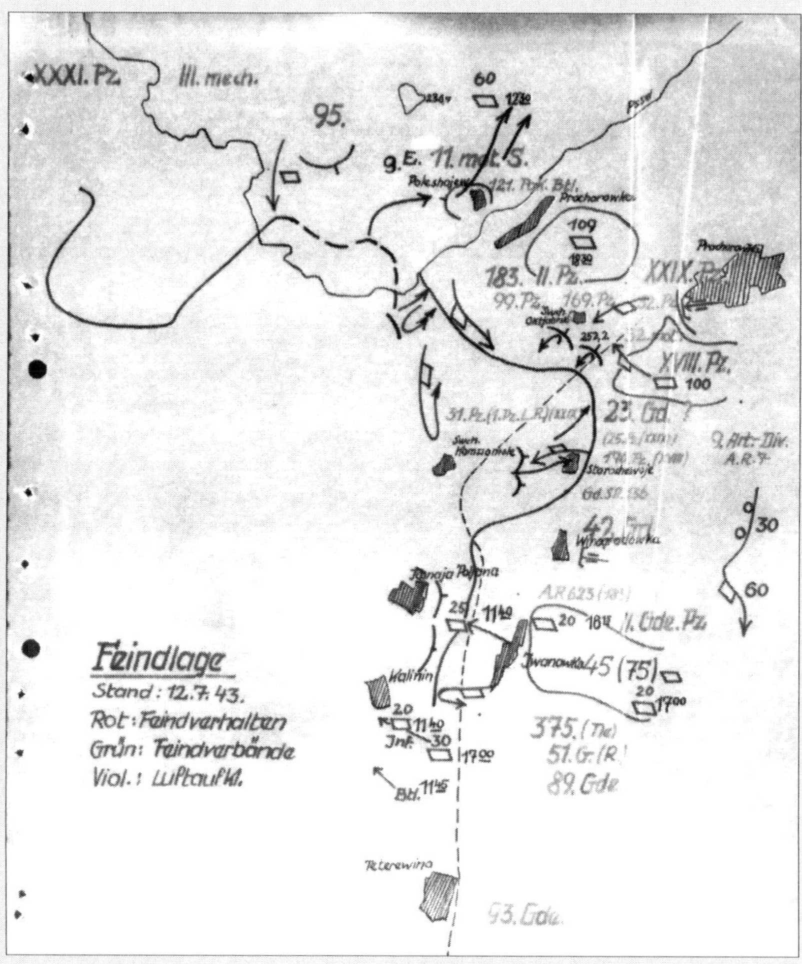

German map of enemy forces, 12 July 1943.

This famous map, which is reproduced in many books, shows the rather confused nature of the fighting and the confusion on the part of the Germans over the units involved.

To start with, while showing the penetration to Vasilyevka, and it being halted by counterattack, the SS Panzer Corps Intelligence Officer also shows a penetration to Komsomolets Sovkhoz by the 31st Tank Brigade (XXIX Tank Corps) from Vasilyevka. This does not appear to have been the case. The location and activities of the 99th and 169th Tank Brigades (II Tank Corps) are also incorrect. The map identifies (and mislocates) only one brigade (170th Tank Brigade) of the XVIII Tank Corps. It does not show the capture of the Komsomolets Sovkhoz by the 53rd Motorized Rifle Brigade, and so on. The German intelligence map does show them losing height 252.2, as does a map from the XXIX Tank Corps, even though German infantry remained on the hill throughout the engagement (or at least on the reverse or south slope of height 252.2).

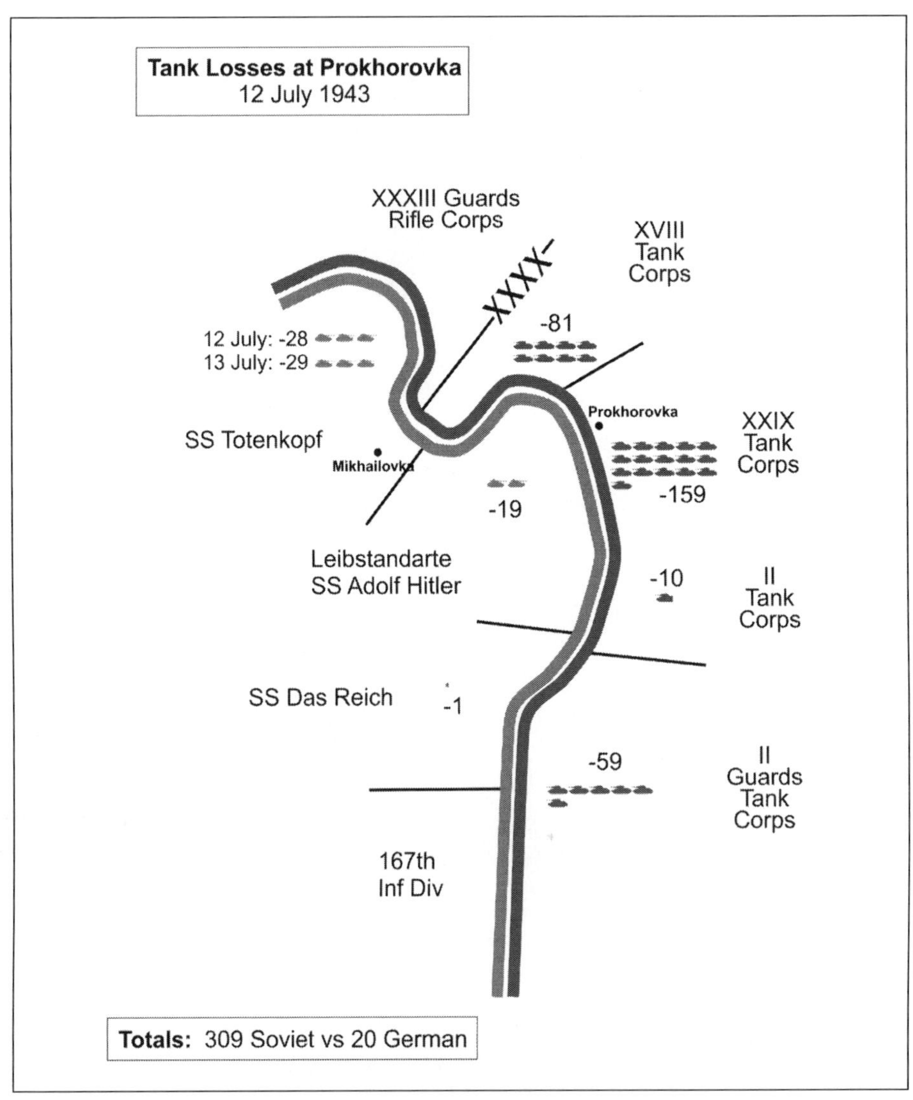

61 tanks, while the SS Panzer Corps initial count for this day was 249 tanks.[91] According to the count from the Soviet records, they lost around 309 tanks in front of the SS Panzer Corps on this day.

The situation with the armor losses is best expressed in the map shown above.

---

91 The claim of 192 tanks by LSSAH came from T354, R605, page 000698, from their daily report for the 13th. The Daily Intelligence Summary by the corps for the 13th, 2100 hours, records 185 tanks by LSSAH, 3 tanks by Das Reich, and 61 tanks by Totenkopf (T354, R605, 000710).

There is a corps report from 2200 on 14 July that provides a night report for 12 July that records 25 tanks for the LSSAH and 75 tanks for Das Reich! This is obviously supposed to be in addition to what was reported for the 13th (T354, R605, page 0000790). So potentially, the LSSAH was claiming 210 tanks for the day, Das Reich was claiming 78 for the day and Totenkopf was claiming 61, for a total of 349.

The Fight North of the Psel, 12 July 1943

DURATION One day FRONTAGE 10.3 kilometers TERRAIN Rolling
WEATHER Overcast with scattered showers. Road and ground conditions poor.

	Attacker	*Defender*
Units	T SS PzGrD	52nd & 95th Guards Rifle Divisions
Attachments	See below	See below
Strength	18,727	20,672
Armor	134	70 (33 light)
Artillery	151	199
Air Sorties	94	24 + 21 Night
Casualties	320 (69 KIA, 235 WIA, 16 MIA)	598 (200 KIA, 359 WIA, 39 MIA)
Armor Losses	28	33
Artillery Losses	1	5
Enemy Captured	N/A	2

Forces Engaged

German Attachments
II/1st Lehr Werfer Regiment
SS Corps Werfer Battalion
86th Bridge Column B (not incorporated)

Soviet Forces
52nd Guards Rifle Division
133rd AT Rifle Bn
75th Flamethrower Co.
95th Flamethrower Co.
Bn/156th RR/51st GRD (not included)

From X Guards Tank Corps
11th Motorized Rifle Brigade
287th Mortar Rgt

99th Tank Brigade (II Tank Corps)

181st Tank Brigade (XVIII Tank Corps)

95th Guards Rifle Division
469th Mortar Regiment
2 batteries from 301st AT Regiment

Also in area but not included:
97th Guards Rifle Division
1372nd/29th Antiaircraft Division
12th Mortar Bde

The Tank Fields of Prokhorovka, 12 July 1943

DURATION One day FRONTAGE 11.0 kilometers TERRAIN Rolling

WEATHER Heavy rainstorms, which severely hampered combat operations.

	Attacker	*Defender*
Units	XVIII & XXIX Tank Corps	LSSAH PzGrD
Attachments	See below	See below
Strength	34,664	21,149
Armor	260 (83 light)	99 (6 light)
Artillery	339	181
Air Sorties	20 Night	131 + 24 Soviet fratricidal sorties
Casualties	2,894 (661 KIA, 1,856 WIA, 377 MIA)	374 (48 KIA, 321 WIA, 5 MIA)
Armor Losses	155	19
Artillery Losses	14	10
Enemy Captured	7[92]	N/A

Forces Engaged

German Attachments

55th Werfer Regiment

861st Light Field Howitzer Battalion

Soviet Forces

XVIII Tank Corps (less 181st Tank Bde)

736th AT Bn

80th Guards Mortar Rgt

XXIX Tank Corps (less 25th Tank Bde & 2 bty/1446th SP Artillery Rgt)

76th Guards Mortar Regiment

1529th Heavy SP Artillery Regiment[93]

678th Howitzer Regiment

2/3rds of 42nd Guards Rifle Division (all casualties)

9th Guards Airborne Division

2 Bty/301st AT Rgt

---

92 Zamulin, *Demolishing the Myth*, page 324, provides the name and report from one of those prisoners, Sturmmann Karl Wuhenpfennig of the 6th/II/2nd SS Panzer Grenadier Regiment.

93 Zamulin, *Demolishing the Myth*, page 286, states that the 1529th Heavy SP Artillery Regiment did not participate in the fighting on 12 July. To quote:

> It had been planned to use the regiment to reinforce the 29th Tank Corps, operating on the axis of the main attack. However, it didn't arrive in the vicinity of Prokhorovka until 1800 12 July, and with only a limited supply of shells (its rear elements had been held up en route due to the enemy's appearance at Rzhavets); thus, the regiment took no part in the fighting on this day.

The II Guards Tank Corps Attack, 12 July 1943

DURATION One day FRONTAGE 8.5 kilometers TERRAIN Rolling
WEATHER Cloudy, dreary and cool. Scattered showers. Roads somewhat muddy.

	Attacker	*Defender*
Units	II GTC, 183rd RD & II TC	DR SS PzGrD
Attachments	See below	See below
Strength	27,124	19,220
Armor	251 (103 light)	108
Artillery	212	144
Air Sorties	24 + 21 Night	57
Casualties	1,559 (495 KIA, 900 WIA, 164 MIA)	243 (41 KIA, 190 WIA, 12 MIA)
Armor Losses	121	1
Artillery Losses	39	1
Air Losses	2	0
Enemy Captured	2	N/A

Forces Engaged

German Attachments
III/1st Lehr Werfer Regiment
III/818th Artillery Regiment

Soviet Forces
II Guards Tank Corps
1076th Antitank Regiment
1510th Antitank Regiment
755th AT Battalion
16th Guards Mortar Regiment
183rd Rifle Division
II Tank Corps (less 99th Tank Bde)
25th Tank Brigade (XXIX Tank Corps)
2 bty/1446th SP Artillery Regiment

Assumed to be withdrawn (not counted)[94]
6th Guards Motorized Brigade (from V Guards Tank Corps)
454th Mortar Regiment

94 On the 11th they were defending from Belenikhino to the outskirts of Teterevino. The brigade was supposed to turn over its positions here to the 183rd Rifle division, but for unknown reasons, the 183rd was "refusing to take over this sector" on the 11th. It is assumed to have been done sometime on the 11th or 12th and they were disengaged. We have no records of any actions by the 6th Guards Motorized Brigade and the 454th Mortar Regiment until 1400 on the 16th, where it is reported to still be defending the line from Dranyii to the southern slopes of point 259.2 to Zelenyii in the Fifth Guards Tank Army sector. This area is four kilometers east of Prokhorovka. It was recombined with the rest of the V Guards Tank Corps on the 18th.

Air Support

The legend of Prokhorovka includes not only a swirling tank battle on the ground, but an equally swirling air battle overhead, amid the majesty of overcast skies and dramatic thunderclouds and lighting. This is the scene displayed in the diorama in the Belgorod Museum and it is correct as far as the weather goes.

The daily report for the SS Panzer Corps notes at 1835 that there had been strong enemy air activity but that because of bad weather, their own air forces could only intervene with weak forces. The Totenkopf SS Division reported heavy air activity by both sides, including bombing and strafing. The Adolf Hitler SS Division reported heavy enemy air activity in the morning. The Das Reich reported at 0710 that 34 Soviet bombers hit the area north of Luchki (north). At 1410, they reported several Soviet bombers bombed and strafed the highway at Luchki (north). They reported shooting down a Martin bomber (Boston?) and an Il-2 during the day.

The XVIII Tank Corps reported up to 1,500 German sorties over their lines. The XXIX Tank Corps and the II Guards Tank Corps reported heavy German aerial bombardment during their attacks. The Fifth Guards Tank Army reported that German aircraft in groups of up to 25–50 planes uninterruptedly bombed the army starting at 0530 (Moscow time). From 0530 until 1700, the army reported 1,500 German sorties. On this day, the Germans flew only 654 sorties. It is not known how many were sent in support of these battles. The only breakdown of missions we have is from a summary of the Red Army Air Force Command, which states that "Enemy aviation with daylight operated in groups of 9 to 30 bombers against the combat formation of our forces, concentrating their effort on the Prokhorovka axis, where up to 400 of the total number of 546 sorties were counted.[95] The Germans reported flying 398 ground-attack type sorties this day, of which 150 were Stuka sorties. As two Stuka groups supported the Germans' morning defense, this could lead to the conclusion that the Stukas only sortied in mass once during this day. The reports from other sectors of the battlefield recorded little German air activity (by either side). Therefore, it would appear that on this day the SS Panzer Corps received the lion's share of the German air support. Still, with the large number of complaints about German air and the high Soviet sortie counts, one cannot rule out the possibility that the German VIII Air Corps report for this day does not record all the sorties flown.

The Fifth Guards Army reported that a group of aircraft bombed the positions of the 95th Guards Rifle Division and the 9th Guards Airborne Division at 0530. The 9th Guards Airborne Division more specifically reported that at 0540, 28 bombers bombed the 23rd Guards Airborne Regiment, which was in the Petrovka area (as were elements of the 95th Guards Rifle Division). The Fifth Guards Army did note, "Our fighter aviation did not securely cover our ground forces."

The 167th Infantry Division

The only division in the SS Panzer Corps that left detailed reports of this day's battle was the 167th Infantry Division, which was holding the far right flank of the SS Panzer Corps. It was stretched across a very difficult to defend 27.2 kilometer front. At this point only two other Germans divisions in this attack were spread across such a front, and they, in sharp contrast, were not facing Soviet armored corps.

The division was deployed with its 339th Infantry Regiment in the north and the 315th Infantry Regiment in the south. During the night of 11/12 July, it was decided that this division should be attached to the SS Panzer Corps and was to move to occupy the heights east of Luchki (south). But communication with the SS Panzer Corps was spotty and there was a great deal of confusion over which units should be deployed where. Lt. General Trierenburg (167th Infantry Divi-

95 Zamulin, *Demolishing the Myth*, page 328. The report was "Operations of Aviation in the Belgorod Defensive Operation." Using intelligence reports to indicate an enemy's action is fraught with problems. In this case, their total sortie count (546 sorties) is close the reported count of German sorties (654) for this day.

sion commander) now decided to pull the 331st Infantry Regiment out of the line during the night and assemble it west of Redin. So instead of being relieved by the 331st Infantry Regiment, the 627th Engineer Battalion was now to be relieved early on the 12th by the 315th Infantry Regiment.

The division's patrols during the night found the Soviets in strength across from the center and left of the division. Two Soviet patrols on the left and a company-strength attack from Nepkhayevo were repelled by fire. The division also reported heavy Soviet air activity during the night.

The actions this day of the division's 339th Infantry Regiment have already been discussed. At the same time as this division was involved with the defensive battles of Prokhorovka, its 315th Infantry Regiment was busy advancing with the 168th Infantry Division on the division's southern flank. After the 168th Infantry Division reported taking Sabyinino and the woods north of Petropavlovka, the 315th Infantry Regiment was ordered to push the division's right wing forward to establish contact with the 168th. It jumped-off at 1300, but was soon met by a Soviet attack that penetrated the 315th's left at 1435.

This attack had penetrated the boundary between the right flank of the 339th Infantry Regiment and the left flank of the 315th Infantry Regiment, moving southeast from Petrovskii. According to Russian deserters, this attack was made by a full regiment (probably from the 93rd Guards Rifle Division). In response, the 331st Infantry Regiment, which was on the march, was ordered to send a battalion back to the Kutovka Woods (the woods in the ravines northwest of Petrovskii), while the 627th Engineer Battalion was sent to block the ravine west of Petrovskii and hinder further Soviet advances to the west. In addition, the 3rd company of the division's engineer battalion and the 3rd company (the flak company) of the division's panzer jaeger battalion were moved to the heights west of Petrovskii.

With the situation on the left flank of the 339th Infantry Regiment finally resolved around 1630, the 2nd squadron (company) of the reconnaissance battalion was now sent south to break through the Soviet positions and re-connect with the left flank of the 315th Infantry Regiment. Meanwhile, the right flank of the 315th Infantry Regiment continued to advance, reporting at 1600 (Berlin time) to have crossed the Donets and was advancing on Kryukovo. At 1400 (Moscow time), the Soviets reported coming under heavy artillery fire at Kryukovo and the grove one kilometer northwest of Kryukovo.

At 1630 the division was ordered by the Fourth Panzer Army to advance, in conjunction with the 168th Infantry Division, with its south wing towards the north in order to roll up the Soviets across from the division center and the north wing. However, the division was still regrouping from the Soviet attacks of this day. By 2100 the squadron from the reconnaissance battalion and the 627th Engineer Battalion cleared up Petrovskii. But, half an hour later the Russians re-entered the town and ejected the reconnaissance squadron, which was forced to withdraw because of an ammunition shortage. The 2nd squadron suffered two killed and ten wounded in this withdrawal. The onset of darkness ended the fighting for the day.

Overall, this was another good performance by this infantry division. Having come under attack on its left flank and center, it was still able to shift the majority of the 331st Infantry Regiment north and continue advancing in the south. Still, its loss of Petrovskii late in the day was going to haunt this division and cost it additional casualties. The division complained of suffering from communications problems throughout the day which hindered coordination and operations. By the end of the day, the Russians were still attacking with strong infantry forces against the front of this division, while the Das Reich was still able to maintain contact with the division at Kalinin.

Meanwhile, the 417th Infantry Regiment of the 168th Infantry Division had already crossed the Lipovyii and Severnyii Donets the previous day and was inside the Donets triangle. Now at the southwest part of the "underwear" woods north of Petropavlovka, it continued its attack through the woods. Strong Soviet resistance was encountered in some places inside the woods but was eliminated by fierce hand-to-hand fighting. When the regiment's I Battalion reached the north edge of the woods, it attacked northeast towards a smaller woods two kilometers southeast of Gostishchevo and succeeded in taking the bunker line at the edge of the woods. Some of the Russians fled from the north edge of the woods into Gostishchevo. The attack was immediately pushed forward and Gostishchevo was taken with minimal Soviet resistance.[96] The Germans claimed 200 captured and uncounted Soviet dead during the attack on the "underwear" woods. This was all completed by 1300 on the 12th of July.[97]

---

96 The daily log for 1600 on 12 July says that Gostishchevo was taken in a "schnellem Nachstossen." "Nachstossen" would indicate a penetrating attack along a narrow front with follow-on elements. On the other hand, if the records contain a typographical error, then the word could be "Nachtstossen," meaning Gostishchevo was taken in a quick night attack (night of the 11th and 12th). We are not sure which is the case. See T314, R194, page 948.

97 At least that is the time a report was filed with the III Panzer Corps. The action may have occurred much earlier than that. See T314, R194 page 948.

This regiment-sized attack, without armor support, had just succeeded in clearing several kilometers of the flank of the SS Panzer Corps, something that Provisional Army Kempf had been trying to do for days. This was clearly not territory that the Sixty-ninth Army wanted to give up, for its 93rd Guards Rifle Division was attacking this day and its southern flank was just one kilometer west of Nepkhayevo. The 89th Guards Rifle Division needed to cover this flank, yet the 93rd Guards Rifle Division reported this day that the 89th was "withdrawing on its own." This probable unauthorized withdrawal clearly created a hole in the Soviet position. An advance by one German regiment, without armor support, should have been relatively easy to halt. Instead, the 417th Infantry Regiment had advanced almost eight kilometers on this day, while the 89th Guards Rifle Division did not take significant casualties. This left the 93rd Guards Rifle Division's flank wide open.

167th Infantry Division, 12 July 1943

DURATION One day FRONTAGE 27.2 kilometers TERRAIN Rolling, mixed

WEATHER 168th ID: Cool, cloudy. Temperature at noon: 17 degrees Celsius. Road conditions good.

	Attacker	*Defender*
Units	375th Rifle & 93rd Gds RD	167th ID & 1/3rd 168th Inf Division (417th Inf Rgt)
Attachments	See below	See below
Strength	18,777	19,107
Armor	0	0
Artillery	126	151
Air Sorties	20 Night	92
Casualties	1,445 (457 KIA, 841 WIA, 147 MIA)	522 (112 KIA, 401 WIA, 9 MIA)
Artillery Losses	6	0
Enemy Captured	3	200

Forces Engaged

German Attachments

I/1st Lehr Werfer Regiment

627th Engineer Battalion (detached on the 12th—but included)

1/3rd of the 168th Infantry Division is counted for this day along with all the casualties in this division.

Soviet Forces

375th Rifle Division

1240th AT Rgt
1667th AT Rgt
137th ATR Bn
88th Flamethrower Company
192nd Flamethrower Company
1363/26th Antiaircraft Division
60th Armored Train Detachment

93rd Guards Rifle Division

1/3rd 51st Guards Rifle Division (158th Guards Rifle Regiment)

89th Guards Rifle Division (losses and enemy captures only)

 TANK LOSSES ON THE MARCH

The XVIII Tank Corps provides the best records of losses to mechanical breakdown from the march. To recount its experience: the XVIII Tank Corps started with an estimated 91 T-34s, 62 T-70s and 21 Churchills. It was ordered to move at 0430 on 7 July, left the Rossosh area at 1030, marched 230 kilometers and by 2200 on 8 July, 15 Churchills, 44 T-34s and 45 T-70s had arrived in the concentration area. This was from an initial strength of 174 tanks, meaning, somwhat alarmingly, 70 tanks were left behind or broke down during the march. As Major General Bakharov noted (XVIII Tank Corps commander), "Such a difficult march could not help but tell on the state of the corps' material and the number of combat and transport vehicles which broke down; the broken country, the bridge with poor carrying capacity, the absence of good fords, all increases the number of accidents and breakdowns."[1]

On 9 July, the XVIII Tank Corps left at dawn, completing a 70 to 75 kilometer march by 1800 hours. At 2320, the corps reported 46 T-34s, 52 T-70s and 17 Churchills. The 110th Tank Brigade had 16 T-34s, 18 T-70s and 6 AA guns. The 170th Tank Brigade had 14 T-34s, 17 T-70s, 29 cars and reported that their remaining tanks were still in transit due to various mechanical problems. The 181st Tank Brigade had 16 T-34s and 17 T-70s, and reported that another 9 T-34s and 7 AA guns were still coming up. The 36th Guards Tank Regiment reported that it actually had 18 Churchills, with only 17 in working order, of which one needed minor repairs. They also reported 3 armored cars, of which one needed repair, and 1 motorcycle, 35 cars and 3 special cars. The 119th Reconnaissance Battalion reported 15 armored cars and 19 armored transports, with one armored transport and one wheeled vehicle having failed to arrive. The 78th Motorcycle Battalion reported 57 motorcycles, 4 armored cars and 7 transport vehicles had arrived, with the remaining transport coming up. The increased tank strength from the previous day was certainly caused by broken down tanks catching up to the unit; still it illustrates the temporary losses caused to any armored unit by simply moving it. They were supposed to be ready for combat the following morning (the 10th).[2]

The following day, at 1620, the 110th Tank Brigade reported that it had 20 T-34s and 14 T-70s, while there were 12 T-34s and 7 T-70s in route, "which had fallen behind due to technical breakdowns." The 170th Tank Brigade reported that 16 T-34s and 4 T-70s had not yet arrived, while the 181st Tank Brigade reported that 13 T-34s, 2 T-70s, 30 trucks and 17 cars were still en route due to technical problems. The 36th Guards Tank Regiment now consisted of 18 tanks, with another 3 tanks coming up. The 29th Reconnaissance Battalion still had 15 BA-64 armored cars, 19 armored transports and 8 trucks, while the 78th Reconnaissance Battalion now had 60 motorcycles, 12 armored cars and 7 transport trucks. It had lost two motorcycles in a reconnaissance mission near Belenikhino the previous day.

As of 1600 on the 11th, the 110th Tank Brigade was now up to 24 T-34s, of which 22 were in working order, and 21 combat-ready T-70s. The 170th Tank Brigade had 22 T-34s and 17 T-70s, while the 181st Tank Brigade had 24 T-34s and 20 T-70s. The 36th Guards Tank Regiment reported 19 Churchills, of which one had broken down, and 2 BA-64 armored cars. The reconnaissance battalion now had 17 BA-64 armored cars, 20 armored transports, and 2 motorcycles. The motorcycle battalion was up to 12 BA-64 armored cars and 65 motorcycles, of which 63 were operational.[3] *(continued)*

1 "Account of XVIII Tank Corps' Combat Activities, July 12–24, 1943" (Fond: XVIII TC, Opis: 1, Delo: 48, Page: 4).

2 Combat Report #34, 2230, 9 July 1943; HQ XVIII Tank Corps (Fond: XVIII TC, Opis: 1, Delo: 26, Page: 6).

3 Next two days from: Combat Report #35, 1620, 10 July 1943; HQ XVIII Tank Corps and Combat Report #36, 1600, 22 July; HQ XVIII Tank Corps (Fond: XVIII TC, Opis: 1, Delo: 26, Pages: 7 & 8).

To summarize material status among the corps' units:

	T-34s	*T-70s*	*Churchills*	*BA-64s*	*Armored Transports*	*Motorcycles*
110th Tank Brigade						
Total available:	32	21				
Ready for action:						
8th						
9th	16	18				
10th	20	14				
11th	22	21				
170th Tank Brigade						
Total available:	30	21				
Ready for action:						
8th						
9th	14	17				
10th						
11th	22	17				
181st Tank Brigade						
Total available:	29	20				
Ready for action:						
8th						
9th	16	17				
10th						
11th	24	20				
36th Guards Tank Regiment						
Total available:			21	3	—	unknown
Ready for action:						
8th			15			
9th			17	2	—	1
10th			18			
11th			18	2	—	1*
29th Ind. Reconnaissance Bn						
Total available:				17	20	
Ready for action:						
8th						
9th				15	19	
10th				15	19	
11th				17	20	

	T-34s	T-70s	Churchills	BA-64s	Armored Transport	Motorcycle
78th Ind. Motorcycle Bn						
Total available:				12	—	unknown
Ready for action:						
8th						
9th				4	—	57
10th				12	—	60
11th				12	—	63
Corps Total						
Total available:	91	62	21	32	20	unknown
Ready for action:						
8th	44	45	15			
9th	46	52	17	21	19	58
10th						
11th	68	58	18	31	20	64

* Assumed

The XXIX Tank Corps demonstrated a similar pattern, reporting on the 10th 120 T-34s on-hand in the three tank brigades, 8 more reported as "delayed," and 75 T-70s on-hand in the three tank brigades with 3 more reported "delayed," while the following day they reported 8 T-34s and 4 T-70s in repair (with now only 74 on-hand in the three tank brigades).

A similar analysis was done by Valeriy Zamulin. He states that the XXIX Tank Corps'

> . . . preparation of the technical services and handling of the march was better organized than the others. After the first 150-kilometer leap, out of the formation's more than 220 combat vehicles, only 12 tanks and one Su-76 self-propelled gun broke down. . . . In the other formations, the percentage of disabled vehicles was significantly higher, especially the V Guards Mechanized Corps. Thus, by 1600 of 10 July, only 62 T-34s and T-70 tanks in total remained in the 11th and 12th Guards Mechanized Brigades and the 24th Guards Brigade.
>
> Altogether on the road from Ostrogozhsk to Prokhorovka Station, in the three corps, two self-propelled artillery regiments, the 53rd Guards Tank Regiment, and the 1st Guards Separate Motorcycle Regiments, from a combined total of 721 armored vehicles, 198 tanks and self-propelled guns lagged behind, or 27.5% of the total number. In addition, by the evening of 11 July, another 24 tanks had caught up, but they were sent immediately for repairs. Thus, altogether in the course of the transfer of the Fifth Guards Tank Army, 227 tanks and self-propelled guns broke down and went out of service, or nearly a third (31.5%) of the army. However, thanks to the intense work of the repair services, at the moment when the army went into battle, about 50% of the disabled vehicles had been returned to service. According to information from army headquarters, at 1700 11 July, a total number of 101 of these vehicles were on their way back to the army.[1]

1 Zamulin, *Demolishing the Myth*, page 167. The formation names are edited from the original to match the format used for this book.

(continued)

Still, the distance marched by the V Guards Mechanized Corps was further than the XXIX Tank Corps. The V Guards Mechanized Corps was the lead unit in the march. The army's forward detachment, the Trufanov Detachment, went all the way to Trubezh, over three kilometers west of Oboyan. The V Guards Mechanized Corps went as far as Bobryishevo, 10 kilometers east of Oboyan. These forces then had to march all the way to back to the Prokhorovka area. The XVIII Tank Corps started its march from Rossosh, over 200 kilometers east-southeast of Belgorod. This gave it a longer march than the XXIX Tank Corps.[2]

Supplies

Furthermore, its does not appear that the XVIII Tank Corps was resupplied on the move. A listing of its supply clearly delineates this problem:

	Tank Ammo	*Tank Fuel*	*Food*
110th Tank Brigade			
9th	2.0 units	1.3 units	10 days
10th	2.0	1.3	7 days
11th	2.0	2.0	6 days
170th Tank Brigade			
9th	1.5	1.0	4 days
10th	1.5	1.0	4 days
11th	1.5	1.0	5 days
181st Tank Brigade			
9th	1.5	.75	3 days
10th	1.5	.50	3 days
11th	1.5	.50	7 days
36th Guards Tank Regiment			
9th	2.5	1.3	14 days
10th	2.5	1.0	2 days of bread *
11th	2.5	1.0	1 day of bread **
32nd Motorized Rifle Brigade			
9th	1.0	0.3	4 days
10th	1.0	1.0	3 days
11th	1.0 ***	1.0	3 days
229th Ind. Reconnaissance Bn			
9th	2.0	2.0	2 days
10th	2.0	2.1	2 days
11th	2.0	3.5	5 days
78th Ind. Motorcycle Bn			
9th	1.5	2.0	7 days
10th	2.0	0.5	2 days
11th	2.0	3.5	2 days

2 See page 914 of *Kursk: The Battle of Prokhorovka.*

	Tank Ammo	Tank Fuel	Food
292nd Mortar Regiment			
9th	1.0	1.0	3 days
10th	1.0	1.0	2 days
11th	1.25	0.5	3 days
1694th AA Regiment			
9th	1.0	1.5	2 days
10th	1.5	1.0	3 days
11th	1.5	.75	2 days
419th Ind. Communication Bn			
9th	1.0	1.5	2 days
10th	1.0	1.5	2 days
11th	1.0	1.0	2 days
115th Ind. Engineer Bn			
9th	2.0	0.2	8 days
10th	2.0	2.0	7 days
11th	2.0	1.0	6 days
1000th AT Regiment			
9th			
10th	1.5	2.0	5 days
11th	1.5	2.0	4 days

* 11 days of other food

** 10 days of other food

*** .75 for 120mm Mortar

From this survey, one is left to conclude that while there was some resupply of fuel and food, it was not significant nor widespread. There appeared to be little resupply of ammunition. What this means is that the 32nd Motorized Rifle Brigade was entering combat with only 80 rounds of 120mm shells per gun. The 181st Tank Brigade only had around 225 kilometers worth of fuel per tank.[3] This figure was based upon "summer dry weather, over unpaved roads of medium quality."[4] In all reality, in a combat environment consumption could be two and half times that rate for an opposed advance.[5] The XVIII Tank Corps was expected to advance more than 20 kilometers on the first day. While the supplies provided were sufficient, if there were any disruptions to the resupply, it could be an issue after a couple of days.

The XXIX Tank Corps appears to have been better supplied, as they reported for the three tank brigades between 1.3 to 3 ammo loads on the 10th and 11th, 1 to 2.5 gasoline refills, 1 to 3.2 diesel refills, and between 5 to 10 days of food. The 271st Mortar Regiment, on the other hand, had only 1.0 ammo load, while the 1446th Self-Propelled Artillery Regiment (SU-122s) had 1.4 ammo loads.

---

3 This figure is for T-70s. T-34s would have been 232.5 kilometers. See *Final Report for the Battle of Kursk; Southern Front: A Validation Data Base* (The Dupuy Institute, McLean, VA., 27 September 1996), pages 46–51.

4 *Brief Tactical-Technical Guide, National Commission for the Defense of the USSR* (Moscow, 1943).

5 See *Final Report for the Battle of Kursk; Southern Front: A Validation Data Base* (The Dupuy Institute, McLean, VA., 27 September 1996), page 46.

CHAPTER TEN

SS Panzer Corps Attack Stalls

13 JULY 1943

> Prayer books are things for women and those who wear panties. We hate the stink of incense; it destroys the German soul as Jews destroy the race. We believe in God, but not in his son, for that would be idolatrous and paganistic. We believe in our Fuehrer and the greatness of our Fatherland. For these and nothing else we will fight. If we must therefore die, then not with "Mary pray for us." We will depart as freely as we have lived. Our last breath: "Adolf Hitler!"
>
> THEODOR EICKE (1892–1943)
> FOUNDER OF THE TOTENKOPF SS
> 1940[1]

NEEDLESS TO SAY, the massive Soviet armored attacks of the previous day surprised the SS with their size and ferocity. Still, the Germans were ready to continue their attack the next day, primarily with a thrust by the Totenkopf SS Division. The SS Panzer Corps advance for this day had been reduced to a single prong thrust by Totenkopf SS Division for the sake of conducting an encirclement to the north of Prokhorovka. The other two SS divisions were to hold position until Totenkopf was successful.

Meanwhile, on the morning of the 12th, Manstein had ordered the XXIV Panzer Corps to move out of the area around Kharkov the night of the 13th and into the area west of Belgorod. Rather than being defeated, Manstein was fully expecting to continue forward and was waiting for the arrival of two more divisions to help.

1 Dr. Chris Mann, *SS-Totenkopf: The History of the 'Death's Head' Division 1940–45* (MBI Publishing Company, St. Paul, MN, 2001), page 42.

TOTENKOPF RETREATS! (THE FIGHT FOR HILL 226.6)

Totenkopf's advance the previous day had forced the commitment of the 24th Guards Tank Brigade and the 10th Guards Mechanized Brigade from the V Guards Mechanized Corps. This was a significant force that included at least 84 T-34s and 16 T-70s. They moved into position the previous evening, but it is not certain to what extent they were seriously engaged.

On this day the Totenkopf SS Division was ordered to continue attacking northeast up the Psel valley with its right wing and to attack with all available armored units along the ridge north of the Psel as far as the Beregovoye to Kartashevka road. They were then to force a crossing of the Psel to the southeast and destroy the enemy southeast and southwest of Petrovka in cooperation with the Adolf Hitler SS Division. The left wing was to hold in its current position, and maintain close contact with the 11th Panzer Division.

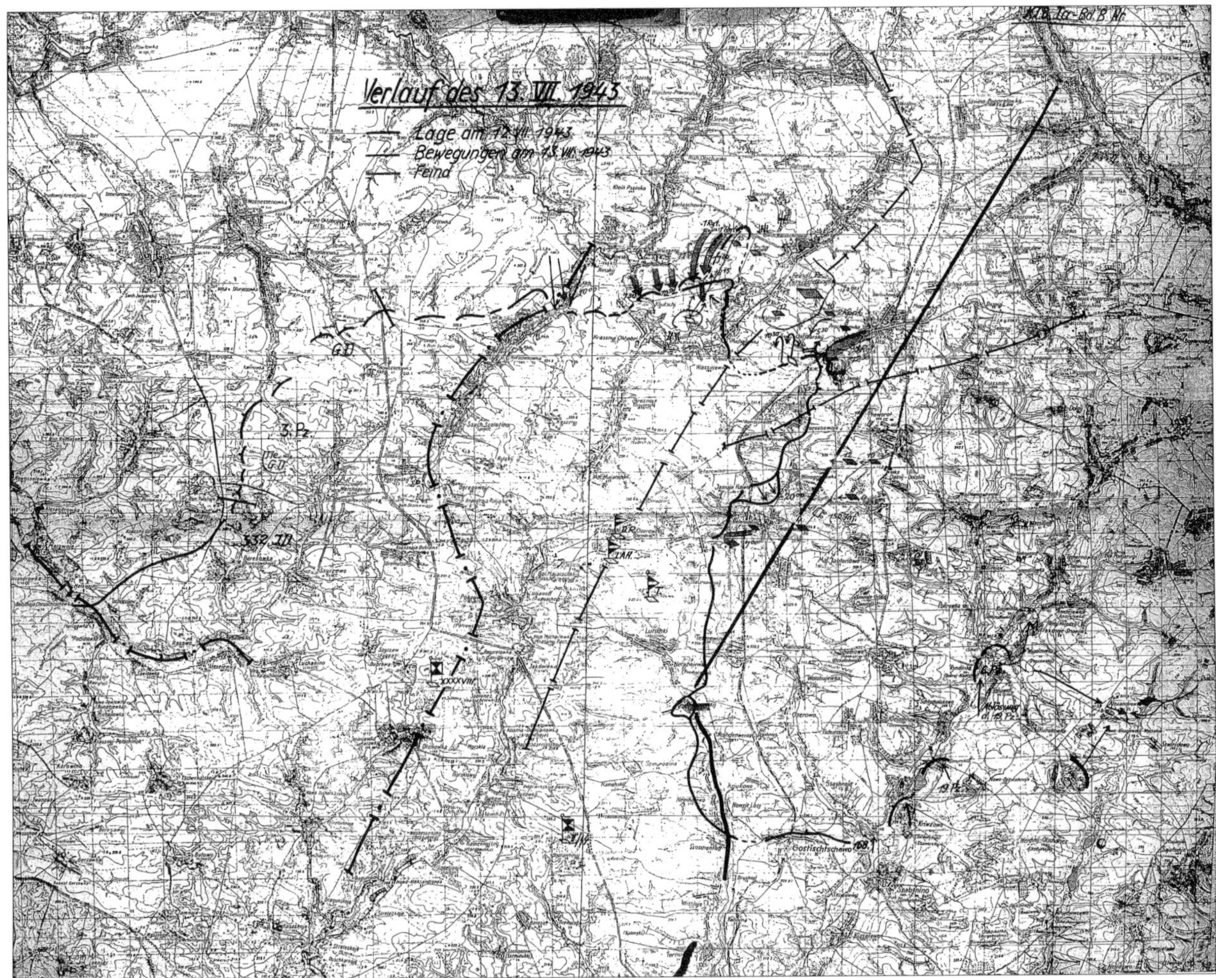

The SS Panzer Corps map showing positions on the 13th of July.

The Soviets, now reinforced with armor north of the Psel, attacked. According to the Germans, the Soviets launched three attacks in the area north of the Psel. One was a strong attack with tank support in the Prelestnoye area. Another was an attack with 15 tanks from height 236.7 to north of Andreyevka. According to the Germans, "the enemy experienced temporary success at the bridgehead." The Soviets also launched a strong attack in the Veselyii area against the west part of the bridgehead with two rifle regiments and 60 tanks.

On the afternoon of 12 July the armored group from Totenkopf had attacked towards the Beregovoye-Kartashevka road. At 2245 the Totenkopf SS Division claimed that its panzer group had reached the Beregovoye-Kartashevka road. Despite strong enemy threats to its flank, and engagements with Soviet tank forces, they had cut the road. But in the early morning hours of 13 July, this unsupported armored group was forced back into the enlarged bridgehead by strong Soviet armored counterattacks from the north. By 1000 on this day, the panzer group had been pushed back from the Beregovoye-Kartashevka road to behind hill 226.6. This was a rather dramatic retreat of six kilometers, although one had the impression that the armored group was indeed thrust forward well in front of the rest of the division!

The 95th Guards Rifle Division was reported to have reached the northern slopes of height 226.6 by 1100 (Moscow time) and taken the first German trench at 1115 (Moscow time).[2] German tanks were reported to have counterattacked at 1130 (Moscow time) towards the eastern slopes, and by 1200 (Moscow time) to have reached the northeastern slopes. At 1100 (Berlin time, 1200 Moscow time) Totenkopf Division reported that it had contained the breakthrough. At 1230, the 95th Guards Rifle Division reported that the Germans had pushed the division's unit out and retaken height 226.6, pushing them back onto the northern slopes of that height. An armor fight clearly developed over height 226.6 but there is little reported on it by Totenkopf. The Germans recorded intercepted Soviet message traffic at 1135 (Berlin time) stating that the Germans had concentrated on height 226.6 and that the Soviets had observed 20 Tiger tanks to the west of the height (Totenkopf only had 12 Tigers and only half of them may have been operational this day). At 1323, the Soviet message traffic again confirmed that they were observing 20 large tanks, although these were now on the eastern and southern slopes of height 226.6 and the Soviet tanks were leading the attack against them. This was certainly the 24th Guards Tank Brigade which was reported to have "driven the enemy out of the Polezhayev—height 226.6 area."

The fight for height 226.6 was clearly resolved in Totenkopf's favor, for by 1500 (Moscow time), the 290th Guards Rifle Regiment was reported still on the southeastern outskirts of Veselyii, while the 287th Guards Rifle Regiment, which the previous day had been in the Psel valley, was on the northwestern slopes of height 226.6 and back to the road junction one kilometer north of height 226.6. The 284th Guards Rifle Regiment, which had been pushed off height 226.6 the previous day, was at that road junction and to the northern spurs of the gully two kilometers northeast of height 226.6. The 24th Guards Tank Brigade was in the hollow 2.5 kilometers north of height 226.6.

Meanwhile, Totenkopf SS Division did push up the Psel, reporting at 1100 (Berlin time) that its attack on Andreyevka was 200 meters from the eastern edge of the village. This attack either stalled or was halted as pressure continued to build on the left wing.

Opposite Totenkopf's left wing was the 97th Guards Rifle Division, which was reported to have attacked at 1000 (Moscow time), but made no progress. Still, these attacks forced them to shift the assault gun battalion over to the left wing of the division in order to reinforce the reconnaissance battalion. There were continued attacks out of Ilinskii supported by strong artillery and Katyushas and the Soviet penetration at Kochetovka was worrying them. This last issue was resolved by an 11th Panzer Division counterattack which kicked off at 1123. At 1700 (Moscow time), the 97th Guards Rifle Division was reported to be along the line of the southern slopes of height 209.3 to the northern outskirts of Krasnyii Oktyabr, putting them a couple of kilometers

---

2 Rotmistrov reported at 1240 to Vatutin: "In Zhadov's sector, Popov's [33rd Guards] rifle corps went on the offensive at 1100 13.07. The delay in the attack occurred because of a lack of artillery shells. I was personally with Comrade Popov in Korytnoe, where I gave the order to the 24th Tank Brigade, the 51st Tank Regiment and the artillery regiment of self-propelled artillery to go on the offensive with the infantry . . . at 1100 with the assignment to destroy the enemy tank grouping in the Polezhaev—Kliuchi—Hill 226.6 area." Quoted from Zamulin, *Demolishing the Myth*, page 462.

As the 95th Guard Rifle Division, which was part of the XXXIII Guards Rifle Corps, was reported to have reached the northern slopes of height 226.6 by 1100 (Fifth Guards Army, Fond 328, Opis: 4852, Delo: 83, page 20), then the attack was probably initiated before 1100. The XXXIII Corps headquarters was at the ravine on the southern outskirts of Koryitnoye. The 95th Guards Rifle Division reported that it took the first German trench at 1115 (Fond: 1267, Opis: 1, Delo: 25). The 97th Guards Rifle Division reported that they attacked at 1000 "but made no progress and remained in its previous positions (Fond: 1271, Opis: 1, Delo: 3). The 95th Guards Rifle Division war diary states that they were engaged with Germans around hill 226.6 between 1010 and 1115 (Zamulin, *Demolishing the Myth*, page 463). Note that in this same report, the 95th Guards Rifle Division reports during a lull later in the day that they brought up ammunition, artillery and 20 tanks (Zamulin, page 464). Clearly the 20 tanks were for some unit other than the rifle division.

from Kochetovka. It appears that it was mostly engaged with Totenkopf this day.

By 1115, the higher commanders (Manstein and Hoth) had given up on the Totenkopf attack's progress and instead decided to start an afternoon attack by Das Reich south of Prokhorovka on Pravorot. The SS Panzer Corps' second attempt to take Prokhorovka had failed.

STILL, THE FIGHTING continued inside the bridgehead for the rest of the day. During the afternoon, the XXXIII Guards Rifle Corps reported that it attacked, but met stubborn German resistance, repelled German counterattacks, and did not make any progress. Totenkopf came back under attack at 1445 (Berlin time) and at 1545 (Berlin time) Totenkopf reported yet another attack out of Veselyii against hill 226.6 in regimental strength. At 1615 they intercepted a Russian radio message that claimed that "the bridgehead will be crushed under all circumstances."

By 1700, the 95th Guards Rifle Division was still fighting along the line from the southern outskirts of Veselyii to the crossroads one kilometer north of height 226.6 to the western outskirts of Polezhayev. The 42nd Guards Rifle Division occupied Polezhayev to Mikhailovka to the ravine southeast of Mikhailovka. The hard-fought 52nd Guards Rifle Division remained unengaged. At 1500, the division became part of the Fifth Guards Army reserve, but remained in its current positions for the day.

This fighting started turning desperate for the Totenkopf when at 1725 it reported that the Soviets had achieved a local breakthrough northwest of hill 226.6 and urgently requested help as they were facing strong infantry forces. At 1730, the bombers that were to support the Das Reich attack were diverted to support Totenkopf. By 1845 Totenkopf had contained the breakthrough and reoccupied its old front but still had not seen the Luftwaffe support.

It appears that the Germans threw in one more attack for the day as the XVIII Tank Corps reported that at 1730 (Moscow time), 10 "Tigers" with automatic riflemen, broke through north of Petrovka and reached the highway leading to Aleksandrovka (the other name for Prokhorovka). The XVIII Tank Corps artillery began firing on them. This penetration, which the Germans did not report, apparently went nowhere.[3]

After regrouping, an armored unit attacked the Germans at 1900 (Moscow time) in the Klyuchi-Krasnyii Oktyabr area. These attacks appear to have also been done by the 24th Guards Tank Brigade. This brigade lost 306 people on this day and 34 of its 56 T-34s. Totenkopf claimed that during one of the Soviet attacks, it is not known which, the 2nd company of the panzer jaeger battalion succeeded in destroying 38 Soviet tanks in 20 minutes.

On the left of the Soviet attacks were supported by elements of the 42nd Guards Rifle Division, which began attacking at 1000 (Moscow time). Its 132nd Guards Rifle Regiment drove the Germans out of Polezhayev. The division's losses for this day were light.

The 10th Guards Mechanized Brigade, on the other hand, recorded surprisingly low losses of five casualties for the 13th and only 131 casualties for the 13th through the 16th. They also reported losing only 11 tanks (10 T-34s and 1 T-70) lost from the 13th through the 16th. This formation may not have been heavily engaged on this day.[4] By the end of the day this brigade had been returned to the commander's reserve. Also, still holding position from Srednyaya Olshanka to height 243.5 to Ostrenkii, was the 6th Guards Airborne Division, which remained effectively unengaged, although it may have provided artillery support.[5]

---

3 Zamulin, *Demolishing the Myth*, page 465, has a similar report, but from the XXXIII Guards Rifle Corps. It states, "According to information from the [42nd Guards Rifle] division headquarters, during one Totenkopf counterattack, six enemy tanks broke through the regiment's positions and penetrate all the way to the Prokhorovka-Kartashevka road, where they were met by the fire of the regiment's reserve elements and compelled to return to their start lines."

4 Although for a variety of reasons, we assigned for the engagement all the armor losses from this brigade to this day.

5 It did report losses of two killed and 15 wounded along with one wrecked 45mm gun for the 12th; eight men wounded and one 45mm gun knocked out for the 13th; and four men killed, 23 wounded and 15 horses killed and two horses wounded for the 14th. These were the only casualties reported for this unit.

It was a dramatic, but poorly documented action that drove the Germans back six kilometers and off height 226.6. The Soviets were then swatted back. The Germans started the day being knocked back by a flank attack that certainly included the 24th Guards Tank Brigade. The Soviets had mostly made use of their infantry forces, and the Germans noted that, compared to previous days, the Soviets threw more infantry [than tanks] recklessly at their lines, while Soviet tanks appeared in decreasing number, reserved for supporting the infantry. Still, with an exchange of possibly 2,007 personnel and 45 tanks for the Soviets compared to 160 personnel and 29 tanks for the Germans, this was a costly but successful fight for the Fifth Guards Army. It didn't hurt that the Germans were attacking into a force twice their size.

Totenkopf made virtually no progress this day and may have suffered significant armor losses. It would appear that this dramatic give-and-take action resulted in the opposing forces being stalemated. At the end of the day, the 10th Guards Mechanized Brigade was moved into the Zhilomostnoye area and placed in the army commander's reserve, probably never being seriously engaged during the course of the day.

Totenkopf's armor losses over the 12th and 13th were 57 tanks, with certainly a fair portion of them lost this day. From the beginning of their attack on 5 July, through the crossing of the Psel on the 10th, the Totenkopf SS Division had lost 64 tanks (and returned to action 15 tanks). In the three days of their offensive across the Psel (11th–13th) they had lost an additional 60 tanks (and returned 21 tanks to action). At the close of the day on the 13th, the Totenkopf armor strength was down to 47 percent of its starting strength, while its personnel strength was down to probably around 88 percent. While the Battle of Prokhorovka was far from being the "death ride" of the panzers, Totenkopf's attack across the Psel certainly was a painful grind that sapped the offensive strength of the division. Credit for this must primarily go to Zhadov's Fifth Guards Army, possibly the 181st Tank Brigade, and the counterattacking 24th Guards Tank Brigade.

Still, it was clear that the Fifth Guards Army had a problem putting up the most effective defense. The Fifth Guards Army again complained in its after-action report that:

> At 2000 the army chief of staff informed the corps and division chiefs of staff that their information continues to be unsatisfactory, in spite of his instructions. During the last two days the army staff has not received a single message describing the course of the fighting, or a single operational or reconnaissance report.
>
> The corps and divisions staffs have forgotten their main responsibility, which is to correctly and on time inform the higher staff. None of these responsibilities for keeping us informed as to the situation of friendly and enemy troops was carried out.
>
> Data as to the battle and the enemy, which might influence the staff's decision should be immediately communicated to the higher staff.[6]

Overseeing the Tank Fields of Prokhorovka

After their dramatic and bloody fight on the tank fields of Prokhorovka, the XVIII and XXIX Tank Corps were ordered during the night to consolidate along their new lines and regroup, so as to be ready in the morning to continue the attack. The XVIII Tank Corps was ordered to provide a covering force from the northern outskirts of Petrovka to height 181.9, to secure the arrival of the 24th Guards Tank Brigade in the Voroshilov Sovkhoz area. The Germans were not active during the night.

Even though these two tank corps received orders on the 13th to attack, they spent the day defending and were not seriously engaged. The XVIII Tank Corps regrouped along the line of Petrovka to Mikhailovka. At 1600 (Moscow time) its 32nd Motorized Rifle Brigade was forward, with its II Battalion, a company of automatic riflemen, and a reconnaissance company

6 Fifth Guards Army, Fond 328, Opis 4852, Delo 83, page 20.

reported deployed from the Psel to the center of Bogoroditskoye (!) to 200 meters east of the Vasilyevka church to the southern salient of Vasilyevka. This position certainly kept the Totenkopf bridgehead under threat of isolation. The rest of the regiment and the 170th Tank Brigade were to the east, from the two windmills at Prelestnoye to the northern slopes of height 252.2 to the western outskirts of Oktyabrskii Sovkhoz. They were supported by the 36th Tank Regiment, with its five Churchills, in the southwestern outskirts of Prelestnoye. The 110th Tank Brigade was east of the area of height 181.9, protecting Prokhorovka from a Totenkopf thrust from the north as was the 181st Tank Brigade, which was in Petrovka. The 78th Motorcycle Battalion and the 2nd company of the reconnaissance battalion took up defense in the area of the Voroshilov Sovkhoz factory.

The XVIII Tank Corps was still operating with the 42nd Guards Rifle Division, which had its 132nd Guards Rifle Regiment north of the Psel, fighting Totenkopf, while its 127th Guards Rifle Regiment was fighting in the streets in Vasilyevka and its 136th Guards Rifle Regiment had consolidated along the road southwest of Oktyabrskii Sovkhoz. The division's losses were light this day.

The XXIX Tank Corps, along with the 1529th Heavy Self-Propelled Artillery Regiment, was on the line from the hollow one kilometer northeast of Oktyabrskii Sovkhoz to Yamki to the hollow 0.5 kilometers southeast of Storozhevoye (the Fifth Guards Tank Army was still claiming that this corps held height 252.2). The 53rd Motorized Rifle Brigade was on the line from 0.5 kilometers southeast of Oktyabrskii Sovkhoz to the southwestern outskirts of Yamki. This brigade organized an antitank defense during the night. Supporting the right side of the brigade was the 31st Tank Brigade, deployed from the hollow 0.5 kilometers northeast of Oktyabrskii Sovkhoz to the road. At 1300, it reported eight T-34s and 20 T-70s in line, and during the night having evacuated eight T-34s from the battlefield. The 32nd Tank Brigade had withdrawn and by 0900 had concentrated one kilometer west of Prokhorovka. It now had 12 T-34s. The 1529th Heavy Self-Propelled Artillery Regiment was in Prokhorovka. The 25th Tank Brigade, with its 50th Motorized Rifle Battalion, 11 T-70s and two antitank guns, were defending one kilometer east of Storozhevoye. The brigade was entrenching, evacuating and repairing knocked-out and damaged equipment. It was ordered at 1600 to attack the Komsomolets Sovkhoz. This attack appears never to have occurred, and at 2100 (Moscow time), the 25th Tank Brigade took up positions in the bushy ravine two kilometers south of Yamki, its left flank stretching to the ravine running in the direction of Pravorot and Vinogradovka, and the brigade facing to the west and southwest. To its left was the 26th Tank Brigade (II Tank Corps), also facing west.

Located with them was the 9th Guards Airborne Division, stretched from Mikhailovka to the railroad booth to Yamki, with the 23rd and 28th Guards Airborne Regiments in the first echelon and the 26th Guards Airborne Regiment in the second. The division was reporting that it was short on ammunition, especially antitank and antitank rifle ammunition. It had no "Molotov Cocktails."

Covering the tank fields from yesterday's fights were the Adolf Hitler SS Division and much of the Das Reich SS Division. The Adolf Hitler SS Division reported a quiet night. At 0530, the Soviets launched a reconnaissance force of two companies along the Prokhorovka to Teterevino road.

The corps ordered the Adolf Hitler SS Division to conduct an armored attack at 1030. The XVIII Tank Corps reported a powerful tank and infantry attack on Polezhayev and Petrovka from the gully south of Andreyevka. The Germans aborted this attack due to the broad tank and antitank defensive line that the Soviets had raised along the north slope (meaning the reverse slope) just south of the Oktyabrskii Sovkhoz. This defensive line completely dominated the crest of the hill. Circumvention of this obstacle was not possible because of the "cloven" (split or divided) nature of the terrain.

This German report effectively matches the XVIII Tank Corps report of deployment along the northern slopes of height 252.2, with parts of the 32nd Motorized

Rifle Brigade and the 170th Tank Brigade deployed from the two windmills at Prelestnoye to the northern slopes of height 252.2 to the western outskirts of Oktyabrskii Sovkhoz. This is what created the antitank defensive line along the reserve slope from Prelestnoye up to almost height 252.2. This left the Germans standing on the south side of that reserve slope about a half to one kilometer south of Oktyabrskii Sovkhoz. At some points the two enemy lines may have been within a half kilometer of each other, with the ridge running west of 252.2 between them. This was only a slight rise, but significant enough. Probably neither side actually occupied height 252.2, which would have been under observation and in direct line of fire from both sides. The rest of the Adolf Hitler SS Division's left flank appears to have followed the reserve slopes back to the west, leaving both sides close to each other, but with the main body of their forces out of sight of each other.

In effect, the Adolf Hitler SS Division's attack was now halted, although not by Soviet attacks and counterattacks, but by a solid defensive line. If this defense line halted the German attack on the 13th, when the Adolf Hitler SS Division was at 93 percent of its tank strength relative to the 12th,[7] then it could have halted the attack on the 12th, when the XVIII and XXIX Tank Corps had 191 T-34s, vice the 46 T-34s they had on the 13th.

The XXIX Tank Corps also reported two German attacks on Stalinskoye Otdeleniye Sovkhoz and Yamki at 1130 and 1500 (Moscow times). Still, the Soviets were not done attacking. At 1230 (Berlin time) they conducted an infantry attack in regimental strength, supported by strong artillery fire and close air support that came out of Prokhorovka and astride the highway. This attack was easily stopped at 1240 by the combined fire from all defensive weapons of the division.

At 1800 (Moscow time) the XVIII Tank Corps conducted an attack with the 3rd tank company of the 51st Tank Regiment, which was occupying defensive positions along the right bank of the Psel. It was ordered to attack Petrovka, which was already occupied by XVIII Tank Corps troops and the 27th Guards Artillery Regiment. As a result, two T-34s were knocked out and another burned by the artillery regiment. This error was caused by a lack of radio communications with the neighboring units.

The Adolf Hitler SS Division now had orders to hold its current line, which was to be fortified along the front and right wing. The division was to prepare to cooperate with Totenkopf SS Division in destroying the Soviet forces to the northeast.

During the day, the division had pushed forward slightly (0.8 kilometers) in the area south of Storozhevoye. It then spent the day at a halt. It is clear that, at least for the time being, the SS Panzer Corps attack in this area had ground to a definite halt.

Officer Cadet Guenther Baer left the battlefield on this day:

> Medical care was indeed good. I was seriously wounded myself on July 13th, receiving two shots in the abdomen. I was brought to the clearing station on a motorcycle's sidecar, where improvised care was administered. I was then brought to the military hospital in Vinniza in a Ju-52 transport plane. I was in surgery that evening.
>
> Problems arose only because the Soviets were specifically targeting our ambulances on the battlefield and often destroyed them. That I had not seen any place before.

The Das Reich "Attack"

The Das Reich SS Division also did not move this day. At 0315, a lone Russian with "a rifle and a knapsack" shot at the guard at the division command post, and then escaped. The Germans claimed that he was part of a partisan band.

Otherwise the night was quiet, although there was some activity in the morning. At 0700 the II Battalion, Der Fuehrer SS Regiment, repulsed an attack by Soviet infantry and seven tanks, and at 0830 a battal-

7 Or 83% if one adds the 99 tanks at the end of the day on the 11th to the 12 that were returned to action on the 12th, compared to the 92 ready for action at the end of the day on the 12th (none were returned to action on the 13th).

ion-sized attack made local penetrations at Yasnaya Polyana, which were resolved by counterattacks. The German observation planes detected rearward Soviet movements to the northeast, covered by tanks, in the Pravorot area. This was interpreted by the Germans as a general withdrawal, which the isolated attacks of the morning were intended to mask. Meanwhile, it was already becoming evident that Totenkopf's attack for this day was going nowhere. So, at 1115, after a briefing by the army, it was decided to stop Totenkopf's attack in the north and instead make an attack in the south. This attack was assigned a jump-off time of 1430 and the VIII Air Corps was requested to provide air support at 1400 hours. Because of the poor weather, Stukas could not be provided but other ground attack aircraft could. The division decided to attack with the panzer group via Belenekhino—Ivanovka and take the high ground southwest of Pravorot. This attack had to be called off because of muddy ground conditions.

After that failure, the division developed a new plan of attack, based upon using the I Battalion, Der Fuehrer SS Regiment to roll up the Soviet positions along the road from the area of the railroad booth south of Ivanovskii Vyiselok to just north of Belenekhino. The III Battalion of the Deutschland SS Regiment was to swivel with the pivot on the left wing at the east slope of the hill west of Vinogradovka and connect with the I Battalion. After taking this ground, which was a necessary prerequisite for a tank advance, and after conducting reconnaissance, a tank attack was to be launched through Vinogradovka to the hills southwest of Pravorot.

By 1550, this attack had not started and at 1730 the air support for this attack was diverted to Totenkopf to help them defend the bridgehead. Only a preliminary attack went forward, capturing the small woods 1.5 kilometers north of Ivanovka at 1930. The Soviet defenders were primarily infantry with few tanks. The trails were still sodden. The attack for this day was then delayed until tomorrow with a jump-off time of 0400.

The Das Reich SS Division's one attack of the day did not accomplish much. It therefore prepared for offensive operations for the following day. Private Kaufmann was part of the Das Reich attacking force on this day:

> Heavy rain came down during the night before July 13, but there was comparatively little enemy action. The unpaved supply routes turned into bogs of mud within a short while. This delayed supply. Our platoon's supply halftrack reached our position with a delivery of provisions, ammunition, and fuel as late as 3 to 4 in the morning. We were already waiting impatiently, because we had already received orders for the continued attack that day. This order was: attack via Ivanovka along a hill range northeastward in the direction of Pravorot. At dawn, the enemy showed substantial renewed activity in our sector. Sporadic attacks had to be fended off until before noon. The first one started between 6 and 7 AM. We counted seven tanks supporting an infantry regiment. They came under fire already at long range from our tanks and were shot to pieces. Their infantry then stopped the attack. We received orders to attack as late as the afternoon. Our section of 20mm antiaircraft guns were now under command of the I Battalion in the Der Fuehrer SS Regiment and had orders to provide support as enemy positions along a railway line were rolled up. It soon became apparent that we were facing nothing but infantry. Nevertheless, progress stagnated compared to previous such engagements. It was difficult to combat the well-fortified and camouflaged pockets of resistance. They were also defended with tenacity and down to the last bullet. It was evening by the time the terrain was in our battalion's hands and a forest north of Ivanovka had been taken. We took a position along the forest perimeter.

The Germans reported that the Soviet response for the day was minor, conducting raids with four tanks south of Belenikhino and with infantry from the east of Vinogradovka. The division records claimed that these were easily repelled.

This does not appear to be entirely correct. The Soviets also organized an attack on Storozhevoye that was the responsibility of the II Tank Corps. At 1000 (Moscow time) its 169th Tank Brigade was on the height east of Storozhevoye, while its 99th and 26th Tank Brigades were in the gully 1.5 kilometers southwest of Storozhevoye (down to the northern outskirts of Vinogradovka) while the 56th Motorized Rifle Brigade was in the hollow 1.5 kilometers "northwest" of Storozhevoye (this would place them northwest of the Storozhevoye Woods; they may have meant southeast of Storozhevoye).[8] They were to attack Storozhevoye and the woods north of there.

The Soviet records we had did not report the details of this attack. Another author had been able to find reports from the 99th Tank Brigade and Sixty-Ninth Army. That author tracks the delay in transmission of the attack order. Rotmistrov issued his combat order to the II Tank Corps at 0335 calling for an attack at 0800 and requesting progress reports every two hours, starting 0600. The order did not reach the II Tank Corps until 0640. The order to attack arrived at the headquarters of the 99th Tank Brigade at 0800. It did not arrive at the headquarters of the 58th Motorized Rifle Brigade until 0830. The corps postponed the attack until 1030.[9] This is not the only case of such a delay.

By 1015 the tank brigades had assembled in the jump-off areas for the attack, but the 58th Motorized Rifle Brigade did not arrive until 1400. Therefore, the tank brigades attacked without their infantry.

Lt. Macher, commanding the engineer company of the Deutschland SS Regiment, recalls it:

> We then prepared for defense in the Storozhevoye area, because a major enemy attack was expected for the 13th. My company was thus deployed on the foremost front line, our sector was approximately 1300 feet wide. We dug foxholes in three rows, 30 to 50 feet apart. Way up front was reserved for the old foxes. But the worst thing on that day was the cloudbursts. Soon our foxholes were flooded. Part of our preparation had of course been coordination with the forward observers of the artillery and our armor, which had occupied positions further behind us.
>
> In my sector, enemy tanks attacked on the 13th. They advanced time and again at high speed and ran right through our position. Many enemy tanks were destroyed by our own armor. We killed three of them in close combat. We suffered casualties because their tanks ran over our foxholes and then swung around, thereby causing the walls to cave in, mauling the soldier inside in the process.
>
> In two instances, we immobilized these tanks in close combat—by blowing up their tracks—but were unable to save our comrades. The enemy tanks were then destroyed by our assault guns.

The account from the 99th Tank Brigade is similar. It states, "Repeated attacks by our tanks and infantry on this axis were not crowned with success. Having a superior position in the arrangement of observation posts and firing positions for artillery and mortars, and having laid minefields, the adversary allowed no possibility to attack Storozhevoye. Our attacking units met particularly heavy fire from the grove lying east of Ivanovskii Vyiselok."[10]

Still, based upon the II Tank Corps reports of tanks ready for action on each day, it appears that the Soviets lost only 6 T-70s on the 13th of July.

The 339th Infantry Regiment of the 167th Infantry Division was still south of the Das Reich. During the night, the 331st Infantry Regiment, which had been held in division reserve, was sent forward to relieve the right wing of the 339th Infantry Regiment. This would also free up the reconnaissance squadron and the 627th Engineer Battalion, which had been sent to the sector. The night was quiet, but German aerial reconnaissance planes reported at 0450 that there was still considerable armor in front of the division, including 15 tanks

8 Fond: 3407, Opis: 1, Delo: 108, pages 195–216.

9 Zamulin, *Demolishing the Myth*, page 469. As he notes "In the operational summary of the 2nd Tank Corps for 13 July, issued at 1600, there is not a single word about it [the attack]."

10 Zamulin, *Demolishing the Myth*, pages 469–470. The Sixty-Ninth Army just noted that "The tank brigades of the 2nd Tank Corps, lacking any infantry cover and without artillery support, halted their advance."

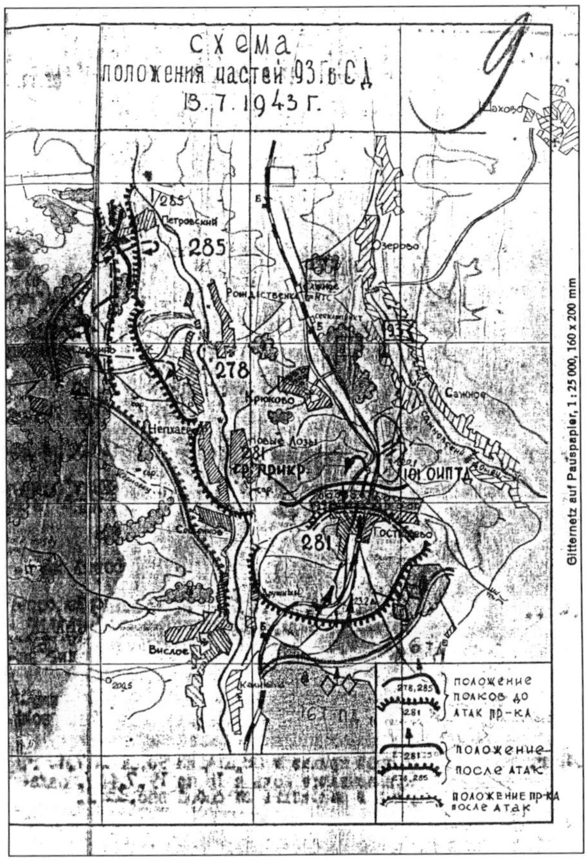

Defense scheme of the 93rd Guards Rifle Division, 13 July 1943.

at the siding near Belenikhino, 20 tanks at Kalinin and 40 tanks at Ivanovka.

To the south of the II Tank Corps was the II Guards Tank Corps. It claimed during the day to have taken Yasnaya Polyana, Kalinin and the height two kilometers south of there, and then was forced to defend against German counterattacks. There is very little else recorded for this day. At 2000 (Moscow time) they claimed to have successfully defended Vinogradovka against a combined tank and infantry attack. At 2100 (Moscow time) Rotmistrov ordered the corps to prevent the Germans from breaking through between Storozhevoye to Ryindinka. At 0200 on the 14th, the corps was holding the line from Vinogradovka to Belenikhino to Shakhovo, with the 25th Guards Tank Brigade pulled from Vinogradovka to concentrate between Maloye Yablonovo and Plota. This unit would not remain there for long, being sent in the morning back to Vinogradovka.

The 167th Infantry Division now had two of its regiments involved in this fight. In the north, the 339th Infantry Regiment during its morning mopping up operations reported capturing numerous prisoners and equipment. The 339th Infantry Regiment and 238th Artillery Regiment were to support the Das Reich's attack on Pravorot at 1400, but this attack did not take place. At 1725 the army told the 167th Infantry Division that it would join in the attack after the SS attack was underway and had become effective. This attack was then postponed until the 14th.

The Sixty-ninth Army still had three divisions in this area facing the SS Panzer Corps. They reported counterattacking at 1430 (Moscow time) and that the 183rd Rifle Division fought for Kalinin and Sobachevskii, but was "halted."[11] The XLVIII Rifle Corps records that following their attack, the three divisions were defending from just off height 243.0 to the eastern outskirts of Kalinin to outside Sobachevskii to height 210.7 to the mound +2.0 to outside Petrovskii to Nepkhayevo. The 183rd Rifle Division was still in the northern part of that line. The 375th Rifle Division was in the center with its 1241st Rifle Regiment on the eastern slopes of the Sukhaya Plota gully to 150 meters west of the barracks, while the 1243rd Rifle Regiment was on height 210.7 to one kilometer north, with two of its battalions now shifted to a line southeast of Shakhovo, due to the threat being created by the III Panzer Corps. The 1245th Rifle Regiment was on the western slopes of height 210.7. The 93rd Guards Rifle Division was south of there and was primarily involved in attacking south this day to retake

11 The Soviet report we have states Klinki, which we assume was a typo of Kalinin ("Sixty-ninth Army Staff Report on Combat Activities, July 5–18, 1943" from Fond: 426; Opis: 10753: Delo: 98, pages 2–4).

Gostishchevo from the 168th Infantry Division. This is similar to the line held at 1900 the previous day, and provides no indication that Kalinin had been taken or any advance had been made. It would appear that the II Guards Tank Corps may have taken Yasnaya Polyana and possibly Kalinin, but did not hold them.

In its center, the 167th Infantry Division also began clearing Petrovskii at 1030. This attack proceeded slowly against the well-entrenched and camouflaged Soviet defenders, so Trirenenburg (the division commander) went to the 331st Infantry Regiment's command post to push it along. By 1330, the German forces in Petrovskii had to be pulled back because the 331st Infantry Regiment was suffering heavy casualties from Soviet fire from the higher east bank of the river.

Overall, it appears that the Das Reich SS Division and 167th Infantry Division conducted limited attacks on this day with limited results. It appears that the Soviets attacks were also limited, and produced no results.

Air Support

Again, the Adolf Hitler SS Division reported lots of Soviet ground attack and fighter plane activity. They complained that support from the Luftwaffe had been weak.

The Das Reich SS Division reported lots of German air reconnaissance over its area. They also reported that Soviet air activity was heavy and there were several bombing and strafing attacks in the area just north of Luchki (north).

The Germans also managed to damage three of their own He-126 reconnaissance aircraft this day with their own AA fire. They halted a further mission late in the day with repeated firing. As the He-126 was a single overhead wing plane with a two-man cockpit, it really did not look like anything else employed by either side during the battle. How this mistake was made is hard to explain.

The XXIX Tank Corps reported that German aircraft carried out reconnaissance flights over them and bombed the 31st Tank Brigade. The 9th Guards Airborne Division reported that groups of 10–12 German planes bombed and strafed the division's units.

The 167th Infantry Division Holds

The 167th Infantry Division was still stretched out along a 27 kilometer front and continued to hold during the limited fighting that occurred on this day. During the night, the 331st Infantry Regiment, which had been held in division reserve, was sent forward to relieve the right wing of the 339th Infantry Regiment. This would also free up the reconnaissance squadron and the 627th Engineer Battalion which had been sent to the sector. The action of these two regiments has already been described above.

At 0720, in the south, the 315th Infantry Regiment reported that the 168th Infantry Division had been forced into a defensive position on the south edge of Gostishchevo. Its 417th Infantry Regiment had been ordered by 1300 on the 12th to leave one reinforced battalion in Gostishchevo and to move the bulk of the regiment to Khokhlovo on the east bank of the Severnyii Donets (seven kilometers to the south of Gostishchevo), where it would take over protection of the left flank of the III Panzer Corps. The Soviets were reported to be moving south in squad and platoon groups, and the division was now concerned about the danger of them infiltrating between the two divisions. At 0830, the Fourth Panzer Army ordered the 238th Reconnaissance Battalion to attach a squadron to the 315th Infantry Regiment to protect the seam between the two divisions. This squadron was sent to the Druzhnyii area. The 315th Infantry Regiment had been mopping up the Soviet remnants on the west bank of the Donets since dawn, but as the afternoon rolled around, the regiment was encountering what it referred to as brave and determined resistance.

The planned attack on Pravorot at 1400, which the 339th Infantry Regiment was to have participated, did not take place. This attack ended up being postponed until the following day.

The Fight for Hill 226.6, 13 July 1943

DURATION One day FRONTAGE 16.6 kilometers TERRAIN Rolling, mixed

	Attacker	*Defender*
Units	T SS PzGrD	95th GRD & others
Attachments	See below	See below
Strength	18,308	37,210
Armor	106	100 (16 light)
Artillery	150	415
Air Sorties	57	44
Casualties	160 (24 KIA, 136 WIA)	2,007 (558 KIA, 1132 WIA, 317 MIA)
Armor Losses	29	45
Artillery Losses	1	6
Enemy Captured	N/A	5

Forces Engaged

German Attachments
II/1st Lehr Werfer Regiment
SS Corps Werfer Battalion
86th Bridge Column B (not incorporated)

Soviet Forces
1/3rd of 42nd Guards Rifle Division (132nd Guards Rifle Regiment)
95th Guards Rifle Division
469th Mortar Regiment
2 batteries from 301st AT Regiment detached on the 13th (not included)
From V Guards Mechanized Corps
24th Guards Tank Brigade
10th Guards Mechanized Brigade
97th Guards Rifle Division
1372nd/29th Antiaircraft Division
12th Mortar Bde less 189th Rgt detached on the 13th
52nd Guards Rifle Division
133rd AT Rifle Bn
75th Flamethrower Co.
95th Flamethrower Co.
Bn/156th RR/51st GRD (not included)
From X Guards Tank Corps
11th Motorized Rifle Brigade
287th Mortar Rgt

Captures include 3 by the out-of-contact 6th Gds Airborne Division
XXIX Tank Corps
1529th Heavy SP Artillery Rgt
76th Gds Mortar Rgt
2/3rds of 42nd Guards Rifle Division (127th and 136th Guards Rifle Regiments)
9th Guards Airborne Division
2 bty/301st AT Rgt (detached on the 13th)

Overseeing the Tank Fields of Prokhorovka, 13 July 1943

DURATION One day FRONTAGE 11.0 kilometers TERRAIN Rolling, bare
WEATHER "Dreary" heavy rains, which made resupplying of combat troops very difficult.

	Attacker	*Defender*
Units	LSSAH PzGrD	XVIII TC, XXIX TC, 42nd GRD & 9th GAD
Attachments	See below	See below
Strength	21,279	32,447
Armor	92 (6 light)	149 (74 light)
Artillery	189	320
Air Sorties	17	44
Casualties	326 (64 KIA, 260 WIA, 2 MIA)	901 (243 KIA, 607 WIA, 51 MIA)
Armor Losses	0	7
Artillery Losses	1	8
Enemy Captured	N/A	4

Forces Engaged

German Attachments
55th Werfer Regiment
861st Light Field Howitzer Battalion
I/1st Lehr Werfer Regiment (attached on the 13th)

Soviet Forces
XVIII Tank Corps
736th AT Bn
80th Gds Mortar Rgt

The Das Reich "Attack," 13 July 1943

DURATION One day FRONTAGE 8.5 kilometers TERRAIN Rolling, mixed
WEATHER Dreary, cloudy and cool. Rain showers in the afternoon.

	Attacker	*Defender*
Units	DR SS PzGrD	II GTC, 183rd RD & II TC
Attachments	See below	See below
Strength	18,959	24,421
Armor	116	90 (48 light)
Artillery	143	173
Air Sorties	0	42
Casualties	61 (17 KIA, 44 WIA)	951 (272 KIA, 575 WIA, 104 MIA)
Armor Losses	4	9
Artillery Losses	1	10
Enemy Captured	N/A	2

Forces Engaged

German Attachments
III/1st Lehr Werfer Regiment
III/818th Artillery Regiment

Soviet Forces
II Guards Tank Corps (less the 26th Guards Tank Brigade)
1076th Antitank Regiment—detached the on 13th (included)
1510th Antitank Regiment
755th AT Battalion
16th Guards Mortar Regiment
183rd Rifle Division
II Tank Corps

The 167th Infantry Division Holds, 13 July 1943

DURATION One day FRONTAGE 27.2 kilometers TERRAIN Rolling, mixed
WEATHER Cloudy, partly rainy. Roads are poor.

	Attacker	*Defender*
Units	167th ID	375th Rifle & 93rd Gds Rifle Divisions
Attachments	See below	See below
Strength	12,769	14,188
Armor	0	0
Artillery	97	88
Air Sorties	0	0
Casualties	104 (26 KIA, 73 WIA, 5 MIA)	109 (18 KIA, 55 WIA, 36 MIA)
Artillery Losses	3	0
Enemy Captured	N/A	1

Forces Engaged

German Attachments

I/1st Lehr Werfer Regiment (detached on the 13th—not included)

Soviet Forces

375th Rifle Division

- 1240th AT Rgt
- 1667th AT Rgt—detached on the 13th (not included)
- 137th ATR Bn
- 88th Flamethrower Company
- 192nd Flamethrower Company
- 1363/26th Antiaircraft Division
- 60th Armored Train Detachment

2/3rds of 93rd Guards Rifle Division (no casualties)

1/3rd 51st Guards Rifle Division (158th Guards Rifle Regiment)

HOPE

Zinaida Nadezhdina[1] was a captain of the medical services, and a doctor-surgeon of the medical sanitary battalion, XXIX Tank Corps. She recounts:

> I was in the woods one kilometer to the north of Prokhorovka where our medical battalion was located on the night of 12 July. Our tank corps was occupying its initial combat lines in front of and to the right of us.
>
> By that time, I was already an experienced doctor. I graduated from the medical school in the fall of 1941 and immediately went to the front. It is not just the service there, one year is counted for three, but it was also good practice. We were attacked by the enemy aviation followed by tanks. I do not remember the details, but after that our corps moved forward. Every hour we were getting more and more wounded. They were delivered in cars, wagons or on stretchers. There were not only tankers there, but also artillerists, infantry and even two pilots. The most severely wounded were tankers, a lot of them had severe burns. We took them to the operating room first. First we did blood transfusions, then performed surgery, and then took them in ambulances to the Front hospitals. We did not have enough of concentrated blood. The number of wounded was increasing. I think the corps' brigades suffered heavy losses during their offensive, and a lot of tanks had caught fire. We did not have a choice, nurses, and later doctors gave the wounded their blood. It was a very simple procedure. A nurse would lie on the bench next to a wounded man. Her blood was transferred right from her vein to his. Each gave up to 200 cubic milliliters of their blood. If it was not enough, another nurse or a doctor would give their blood too.
>
> During the Stalingrad battle I worked for the hospital for the Second Guards Army, which was fighting against the Manstein tank attack after they were surrounded in the city. There were much less wounded then, even though the combat was very severe.
>
> On the 13th of July, the number of wounded increased even more. The army sent us an additional car company for evacuation of the wounded. The same for the 14th of July too. I and other surgeons started operating in the morning of 12 July, and continued working days and nights with one-hour breaks until the evening of the 14th of July. After that, we could take longer breaks.
>
> On the 13th of July, in the afternoon, the nurse put a senior lieutenant on my operating table. He was tall and handsome. He had a bullet in his shoulder and burns on both hands. It was my turn to give my blood. We did a blood transfusion. After the blood transfusion, we were supposed to have some rest, but in this case we could not wait. I operated on him, bandaged him and he was taken away.
>
> Can you imagine that when we were already behind the Dnepr River in November or December of 1943, he found me in my medical battalion. He reminded me that he was Nikolai Mikhailovich Nadezhdin, Senior Lieutenant. Of course, I recognized him immediately. He was appointed deputy chief of staff of one of the brigades of the XXIX Tank Corps. In six months, when our army was in reserve, we got married. Unfortunately, Nikolai has now passed away. He worked for the Tank Academy in Moscow for many years. I worked there too as a doctor. We lived a very happy life, it is not surprising, as Nikolai had my blood!

Nadezhdina is a name based on the Russian word for "hope."

1 Zinaida Ivanovna Nadezhdina was born 1919 in Moscow. She was interviewed in 1999 by Major General G. G. Nessonov.

CHAPTER ELEVEN

Soviet Counterattacks against the III Panzer Corps

12–13 JULY 1943

> First of all, I noticed the large numbers of trucks, all of them of American origin. It looked to me as if every truck had been made in America. . . . It hit me for the first time what massive amount of support the Soviet Union received from the Americans and at the same time I woke up to the fact that in the heart of Russia we were not fighting the Russians alone. However, we did benefit from this support in a way because we captured huge amounts of American field rations. This did us very well. But overall, evidence of this massive support of the Allies for the Soviet Union was real surprise. It did generate some insecurity and caused us to have some second thoughts.
>
> ALFRED RUBBEL, 503RD HEAVY PANZER (TIGER) BATTALION[1]

The III Panzer Corps was still attacking on this day. As such, for the 12th of July, the corps continued forward with considerable progress. It was not halted or stopped by Soviet counter-attacks. The Soviet forces for such attacks had yet to get into position. Their day would come on the 13th.

The Sixty-ninth Army Regroups

As a result of a decision made on the night of 11 July[2] by Lt. General Vasilii Kryuchenkin (Sixty-ninth Army commander) the Sixty-ninth Army pulled back across the Severnyii Donets and regrouped during the night of 11/12 July. The 305th Rifle Division, with the 96th Tank Brigade, pulled back to the previously prepared line running from Vyipolzovka to Aleksandrovka to 1st Novo-Alekseyevskii Vyiselok to Podsumki to Novoslobodka. This was a second echelon position well to the rear. The 94th Guards Rifle Division redeployed with two of its rifle regiments deployed well forward of the 305th Rifle Division from Shukhovtsevo to Mazikino to Sheino to Ushakov, and its third rifle regiment deployed in a rear echelon position from Ploskoye to Novoselovka (on the Koren River). The 107th Rifle Division was now deployed from Razumnaya gully to Shukhovtsevo to Gremyachye to Ploskoye, still making up the second echelon. These units created a solid blocking force to the northeast of the III Panzer Corps, and as such, were no longer on the line of the intended German advance.

Protecting the Severnyii Donets was the 92nd Guards

1 Lt.Col. (ret.) Alfred Rubbel was interviewed by Maj.Gen. (ret.) Dieter Brand on 10 May 1999.

2 Glantz and Orenstein, page 110.

Rifle Division, deployed from Verin to Pokrovka to Ryindinka to Rzhavets to Avdeyevka. This was also positioned to defend against a northeast thrust. The 81st Guards Rifle Division had been withdrawn and was now deployed from Strelnikov to Shchelokovo to Ryindinka. The 89th Guards Rifle Division was holding positions from Kiselevo to Krivtsovo. Sitting on the flank of the SS Panzer Corps was the 93rd Guards Rifle Division from Rozhdestvenka to Druzhnyii. There were no major formations holding the "underwear" woods south of Gostishchevo, although it appears that the 89th Guards Rifle Division was responsible for this. The point of the Donets triangle was being left open!

The 89th Guards Rifle Division had now withdrawn two of its rifle regiments into the Donets triangle and they were deployed from Chursino to Shcholokovo. They had lost contact with their 273rd Guards Rifle Regiment. The division was running out of ammo, food and fuel, but still had almost 8,000 men. This lack of resupply was the same problem that vexed the 81st Guards Rifle Division. This is hard to explain as there are roads running from Prokhorovka to Gostishchevo and then through Kiselevo, Khokhlovo and Shishino and Staryii Gorod. There was also a good road running from Shlyakhovoye to Dalnyaya Igumenka to Staryii Gorod. This road network would have allowed resupply and these roads were not blocked by the Germans during the first days of the offensive. The failure to keep these units supplied was due to some other shortfall in the Soviet Army logistical system, probably transport, availability and priority. The 89th Guards Rifle Division reported receiving reinforcements throughout this period.[3]

The 89th Guards Rifle Division command also had a fright during the previous night as the division staff was withdrawing to Novo-Oskochnoye. At 0200 (Moscow time), the command and staff cars were cut off by a German tank column. They had to break out of this encirclement during the night, but at dawn, were back to work in Plota.

3 They record receiving 35 men on the 5th, 76 horses on the 10th and 164 men in the five days before 15 July.

The Sixty-Ninth Army was also dealing with a problem of unauthorized withdrawals. Early in the morning General Kryuchenkin ordered the head of the army's SMERSH (a name contracted from the Russian words "smert shpionam," which means "Death to Spies") counterintelligence department to organized blocking detachments from his staff. A later report on their efforts state that "In the course of 12 July, 2,842 men were detained. . . . The mass retreat of soldiers and the command staff from the battlefield, which had started at 0500 12 July 1943, . . . was basically stopped at 1600 of the same day and subsequently ceased completely."[4]

The 375th Rifle Division had been pulled back the previous day well to the rear. It was now sent west to counterattack the SS Panzer Corps. This attack was also joined by the 93rd Guards Rifle Division. Vatutin also ordered the Sixty-ninth Army to create a mobile detachment from Fifth Guards Army units which were supposed to be concentrating on the southwest outskirts of Novoslobodka.

With the II Tank Corps and the II Guards Tank Corps transferred to the Fifth Guards Tank Army, the only armor left with the Sixty-ninth Army was the 96th Tank Brigade, which may have been reduced to 7 T-34s and 5 T-70s,[5] and the 148th Tank Regiment, which had maybe one T-70 left operational.[6]

4 Zamulin, *Demolishing the Myth*, page 410. There were seven blocking detachments, each of nine men.

5 They reported losses on the 11th of 13 T-34s and 2 T-60s, which coupled with their other losses since the start of the offensive would reduce them to this level. They reported for the 12th having 14 T-34s and 3 T-70s, but that report probably applies for the end of the day and most likely includes tanks they had repaired (Fond: 3191, Opis: 1, Delo: 3, pages 15–16).

6 Our report indicates that the regiment had 3 T-34s (all tanks were in repair) and 1 T-70 remaining. The Kursk Data Base assumes that the T-70s were also in repair, but it may have been operational (Fond: 148th IndTRgt, Opis: 661360, Delo: 3, pages 80–82).

Trufanov's Detachment and the V Guards Mechanized Corps

With the Fifth Guards Tank Army planning to launch a three tank corps attack at dawn on the 12th, the army's two tank corps nearest to Prokhorovka, the XVIII and XXIX Tank Corps, were sent forward. The forces farthest from the Prokhorovka were made the army's reserve. As such, the V Guards Mechanized Corps was to concentrate by 2400 on 11 July in the Sokolovka-Dranyii-Krasnoye-Vyisyipnoi-Sagaidachnoye-Kamyishevka area, in effect, four kilometers due east of Prokhorovka. They constituted the army's second echelon and were to be ready to develop the success of the XXIX Tank Corps and the newly attached II Guards Tank Corps.

Trufanov's "forward detachment," which was now at the rear of the army's march column, was to leave its defensive positions around Oboyan and become part of the army reserve, concentrating in the Pravorot area in order to secure the army's left flank.

On the morning of 12 July, the Soviet command became concerned about the threat created by the III Panzer Corps. Vatutin responded to this by moving up the jump-off time of the Fifth Guards Tank Army attack from 1000 to 0830. He then stripped the attack of its second echelon, sending Trufanov's detachment to the east and the 11th and 12th Guards Mechanized Brigades to the south. This left only the 10th Guards Mechanized Brigade and 24th Guards Tank Brigade to reinforce the planned attack. These were, for practical purposes, the only uncommitted fresh formations in the Voronezh Front, unless of course, the attack was called off.

Major General Trufanov also took command of the 11th and 12th Guards Mechanized Brigades, one regiment of the 375th Rifle Division, the 92nd Guards Rifle Division and the 26th Guards Tank Brigade of the II Guards Tank Corps and intended to destroy the German forces in the Ryindinka-Rzhavets area (the 375th Rifle Division was never shifted back to the south). Trufanov's detachment was about 16 kilometers by road from the Ryindinka bridgehead. This brigade-sized formation had already moved farther than any other element of the Fifth Guards Tank Army. The detachment still consisted of the 1st Guards Motorcycle Regiment, the 53rd Guards Tank Regiment, the 689th Antitank Regiment, and a battery from the 678th Howitzer Regiment. The 1st Guards Motorcycle Regiment was reported to consist of seven T-34s, 18 armored cars, 217 motorcycles and 20 jeeps (the U.S.-built 1/4-ton truck). The 53rd Guards Tank Regiment had 28 T-34s and 9 T-70s. The 689th Antitank Regiment had 20 45mm guns while the battery from the howitzer regiment would normally have been 4 122mm howitzers.[7]

Instead of moving it to face the threat to the south, Trufanov's detachment was moved east and took up defensive positions around Bolshiye Podyarugi, to the northeast of the German attack. Trufanov's detachment then conducted reconnaissance to the south to locate the Germans. The 53rd Guards Tank Regiment moved to around Novo-Khmelevoi (this village was four kilometers northeast of Aleksandrovka). It then entered combat late in the day when it launched an attack towards Aleksandrovka.[8]

---

7 These are from the army and regimental records we have. Zamulin, in *Prokhorovka: the Unknown Battle in the Great War*, page 318, presents as of 1500 11 July (before the final march from Oboyan back to the battlefield) that the 1st Gds Motorcycle Regiment had 6 T-34s ready for action, 2 in transit and 2 in repair and that the 53rd Guards Tank Regiment had 39 T-34s ready for action, 3 in transit, and 1 T-70 ready for action. This report is mystifying in light of the five Fifth Guards Tank Army reports and two 53rd Guards Tank Regiment reports we have showing the 53rd Guards Tank Regiment with 6 to 9 T-70s from 12 through the 17th of July.

Glantz, in *The Battle of Kursk*, page 416 note 31, claims that the "nucleus" of Trufanov's forward detachment was "twenty-one KV heavy tanks." This is clearly not correct.

8 There is some question as to the extent this formation saw action this day. The Fifth Guards Tank Army reports at 0700 13 July that "53rd Guards Tank Regiment is fighting in the Novo-Khmelevoi area. Losses are being calculated." In the 1900 report for the 13th they report that the "53rd Guards Tank Regiment attacked the enemy in the Aleksandrovka area . . . Losses 9 T-34s, 3 T-70s, 5 men killed, 7 wounded, and 10 missing." (Fond: 332, Opis: 4948, Delo: 82, pages 2 and 3). The 53rd Guards Tank Regiment reports that "During the night of July 12–13 the regiment entered the fighting west of Aleskandrovka." (Fond: 53rd Gds TkRgt, Opis: 20831, Delo: 1, pages 22–29).

Another source claims that the 53rd Guards Tank Regiment entered the fight on the 12th at 2000, attacked the *(continued)*

There is some vagueness in the official accounts of what the 53rd Guards Tank Regiment accomplished this day. This is probably to cover up an embarrassing fight they initiated. Ordered to attack, the tank regiment had to advance through the 92nd Guards Rifle Division's positions. Apparently they were not aware of layout of the infantry defenses. At around 1700-1800 (Moscow time) the tank regiment began to attack in the direction of the village of 1st Novo-Aleksandrovskii Vyiselok. Moving in column towards height 241.5 (north of Aleksandrovka) the tanks opened fire on the move on the combat positions of the 92nd Guards Rifle Division and on the tanks of the 96th Tank Brigade in the Aleksandrovka area. The Soviet troops began fighting each other while Il-2s also attacked the positions of the 92nd Guards Rifle Division. The intervention of more senior officers brought an end to this fight.[9]

Having passed through Aleksandrovka at around 1900, the 53rd Tank Regiment then exchanged fire with German armor. It was noted in one report: "Because of poor reconnaissance, our units ineptly exposed their own flank." The regiment was then ordered to return to its start position. It was then ordered to seize Kazachye by night, so at 2000, while moving through the northern outskirts of Aleksandrovka, it was fired on by German tanks. The regiment commander's tank was knocked out and he was severely wounded. The regiment then took covered defensive positions on the western and southwestern outskirts of Aleksandrovka. They had lost 11 tanks that day.[10]

Meanwhile, the rest of the V Guards Mechanized Corps moved into more critical positions. The 11th and 12th Guards Mechanized Brigades, with the 1447th Self-Propelled Artillery Regiment and supported by 285th Mortar Regiment were to attack the Germans in the Andreyevka-Ryindinka-Rzhavets area. At 0700 on the 13th, it was reported that they had reached and were consolidating along the line of the northern outskirts of Ryindinka, and the Vyipolzovka-Aleksandrovka road. They also joined up with the 26th Guards Tank Brigade of the II Guards Tank Corps. This brigade had been moved to Shakhovo and was defending the route north while the corps' other two tank brigades attacked to the west. By the end of the day, this was the only relatively strong tank brigade left in the corps, with 30 T-34s and 9 T-70s. It does not appear to have been engaged this day.[11]

Germans near Aleksandrovka, and suffered losses of 11 tanks. See Zamulin and Lopukhovskii, *Prokhorovka Battle: Myths and Reality.*

Rotmistrov's report states for the 12th that the 11th Guards Mechanized Brigade had taken Ryindinka from the north and the 12th Guards Mechanized Brigade threw the enemy off height 222.1 and took Vyipolzovo. For the forward detachment, it only states that it "left Oboyan by 1430 and concentrated in Bolshiye Podyarugi," (Fifth Guards Tank Army's Combat Activities from July 7–24, 1943, compiled 30 September 1943 by army Commander Lt. Gen. Rotmistrov and military council member MG Grishin; Fond: 332, Opis: 49498, Delo: 19, page 10). Bolshiye Podyarugi is well to the rear.

For the 13th of July, the Rotmistrov report records the 53rd Guards Tank Regiment attack in the Aleksandrovka area and the loss of 9 T-34s and 3 T-70s. This attack reached the northern outskirts of Aleksandrovka at 2200 and was continued until 2215. We wonder if this refers to events on the 12th, vice the 13th.

Our conclusion is that Trufanov's forward detachment did attack towards Aleksandrovka between 2000 and 2215 on the 12th of July and lost 12 tanks. Their casualties reported at 1900 on the 13th apply to the 12th.

9 Account is from Zamulin, *Demolishing the Myth*, pages 421–423. Primary source is from a report from the Sixty-Ninth Army drawn from the XLVIII Rifle Corps files.

10 Zamulin, *Demolishing the Myth*, pages 422–423. The time of 1900 was provided by the neighboring 10th Antitank Regiment, which reported that 18 tanks were in the Soviet attacking group. The loss claims of 11 tanks are from Zamulin, but do not seem out of line with the other records we have. The Kursk Data Base records 12 tanks lost this day based upon the records we have (Fond 332, Opis: 4948, Delo: 82, pages 2 and 3 and also Rotmistrov's report).

11 Rotmistrov claims, page 10, that "The timely arrival of Gen. Trufanov's units stopped the enemy attack by the end of the day. By 1800 the 11th Guards Mechanized Brigade, reinforced with a detachment from 285th Mortar Regiment, together with the 26th Guards Tank Brigade, had advanced under fire and taken Ryindinka from the north."

"The 12th Guards Mechanized Brigade, reinforced with nine self-propelled guns from the 1447th Self-Propelled Artillery Regiment, threw the enemy off height 222.1 and took Vyipolzovo and reached the road two kilometers southeast of Vyipolzovo.

This account appears to overstate the results for this day. For example, in Zamulin, *Demolishing the Myth*, page 420, he states that the 12th Guards Mechanized Brigade took height

The rest of the corps, the 10th Guards Mechanized Brigade and the 24th Guards Tank Brigade, remained concentrated to the east of Prokhorovka in the Besenkov-Bakhteyevka-Gusek-Pogorelovka area. They were then ordered to attack at 2000 (Moscow time) in the area of the ravine east of Veselyii, where the Fifth Guards Army was fighting with Totenkopf SS Division. These two units concentrated in the Voroshilov Sovkhoz and Ostrenkii area to prepare for the attack but do not appear to have been seriously engaged this day.

The V Guards Mechanized Corps was now scattered to three locales, while the rest of Rotmistrov's Fifth Guards Tank Army spent the day destroying itself in fruitless and foolish armored attacks. Losses reported this day for the V Guards Mechanized Corps, less Trufanov's detachment, were two T-34s, of which one blew up on a mine, two T-70s which blew up on mines, and one antiaircraft gun. It is unknown which brigades these losses were from or whose mines were encountered.

In later Soviet studies of operations, this use of "forward detachments" developed into one of the major events in the legend of Prokhorovka. Trufanov's detachment and its fight against the advancing German III Panzer Corps became in many accounts a major event in the Battle of Prokhorovka. Trufanov's expanded command was significant, but one is often left with the impression that it was his detachment which was the critical element.[12] It was this involvement of the V Guards Mechanized Corps in the south against the III Panzer Corps that has led some historians to define the Battle of Prokhorovka as taking place over two or more days (the 12th and 13th and more) and including two German panzer corps (the SS and the III Panzer Corps). The III Panzer Corps operations were certainly now influencing the Soviet fight against the SS Panzer Corps.

As can be seen, Trufanov's detachment, while providing a nice backstop to the forces defending to the northeast, was in fact not defending on the main axis of attack of the III Panzer Corps. On the other hand, Major General Trufanov, as the commander of four reinforcing armored and mechanized brigades, did play a significant role. Still, the role of Trufanov's detachment has often been grossly overstated and it was certainly not more important then the part played by any other brigade of the V Guards Mechanized Corps. To date, some 18 major Soviet formations, including the 15th, 73rd, 78th, 81st, 89th, 92nd and 94th Guards Rifle Divisions; the 107th, 305th and 375th Rifle Divisions; 96th Tank Brigade; 148th, 167th and 262nd Tank Regiments; 10th, 30th and 31st Antitank Brigades; and the 1438th Self-Propelled Artillery Regiment had all been involved in the fight against the III Panzer Corps. In the end, Trufanov's detachment was only one brigade-size force in a battle that included over two hundred defending brigades and regiments. It was not a brigade at the most critical juncture, nor was it fighting along the major axis of advance, nor did it take exceptionally high losses, nor did it achieve outstanding results.

Gostishchevo

Repeating the account from a previous chapter, the 417th Infantry Regiment of the 168th Infantry Division had already crossed the Lipovyii and Severnyii Donets the previous day and was inside the Donets triangle. Now at the southwest part of the "underwear" woods north of Petropavlovka, it continued its attack through the woods. Strong Soviet resistance was encountered in some places inside the woods but was eliminated by fierce hand-to-hand fighting. When the regiment's I Battalion reached the north edge of the woods, it attacked northeast towards a smaller woods two kilometers southeast of Gostishchevo and succeeded in taking the bunker line at the edge of the woods. Some of the

222.1 by the day's end and "managed to approach the road two kilometers north of Vyipolzovka, where it was met with furious artillery fire and was compelled to dig-in on defense."

12 For example, Erickson claims on page 110 that "Attacking straight off the march, the fresh brigades operating under command of General Trufanov pushed German units back over the northern Donets and out of the village of Rydinka [*sic*]," while Glantz and House, *The Battle of Kursk*, state on page 204 that the attacks "forced German forces out of Rydinka [*sic*]" and that it resulted in a "swirling fight." With a loss of only four tanks during the day in the V Guards Mechanized Corps, three of them to mines, one wonders about the extent of this "swirling fight."

Russians fled from the north edge of the woods into Gostishchevo. The attack was immediately pushed and Gostishchevo was taken with minimal Soviet resistance. The Germans claimed 200 captured and uncounted Soviet dead during the attack on the "underwear" woods.

This regiment-sized attack, without armor support, had just succeeded in clearing several kilometers of the flank of the SS Panzer Corps, something that Provisional Army Kempf had been trying to do for days. This was clearly not territory that the Sixty-ninth Army wanted to give up, for their 93rd Guards Rifle Division was attacking this day and its southern flank was just one kilometer west of Nepkhayevo. The 89th Guards Rifle Division needed to cover this flank, yet the 93rd Guards Rifle Division reported this day that the 89th was "withdrawing on its own." This probable unauthorized withdrawal clearly created a hole in the Soviet position.

It appears that the 89th Guards Rifle Division commander moved his headquarters to the rear on the 11th which put him out of communication with his neighbors and corps command. He then independently made the decision to withdraw the 267th Guards Rifle Regiment from the line along the Donets River from Kalinin [?] to Kiselevo. As was stated by Vatutin in an account from 21 July "Taking advantage of the withdrawal of the 267th Guards Rifle Regiment, the enemy took possession of the forest, which had been defended by this regiment, and then Gostishchevo as well, as the result of which the fulfillment of a combat order, given to another division, could not executed.[13]

An advance by one German regiment, without armor support, should have been relatively easy to halt. Instead, the 417th Infantry Regiment had advanced almost eight kilometers on this day while the 89th Guards Rifle Division did not take significant casualties. This left the 93rd Guards Rifle Division's flank wide open. As the 417th Infantry Regiment was able to take Petropavlovka in the afternoon of the 11th, this withdrawal appears to be unrelated to the Baeke's nighttime dash to seize Rzhavets (see page 382) and started sometime before the middle of the afternoon of the 11th.

The 168th Infantry Division was also receiving support from the 167th Infantry Division. The Sixty-ninth Army reported that a company of German infantry crossed the Lipovyii Donets from Visloye and headed off to attack the height south of Gostishchevo. At the same time, they reported another German company approached Soshenkov from the grove to the west. The 417th Infantry Regiment then moved to take defensive screening positions north of Gostishchevo and along the east bank of the Severnyii Donets along the line of Krivtsovo to Sabyinino to Kiselevo.

MEANWHILE, THE REST of the 168th Infantry Division was moving to protect the east flank of the III Panzer Corps. The 442nd Infantry Regiment had moved to the other side of the corps zone and taken up screening positions along the Razumnaya from Kazachye to Komintern, while the 429th Infantry Regiment prepared to move forward to the fight at Aleksandrovka after assembling in the Verkhnii Olshanets area. The 248th Reconnaissance Battalion cleared the woods to the east, west, and northwest of Znamenka of some hard-fighting Soviet groups, and occupied Novo-Oskochnoye. They claimed taking many Soviet prisoners.

This movement became another point of debate between the III Panzer Corps and General Kempf. The corps decided by 1300 on the 12th that one reinforced battalion of the 417th Infantry Regiment would remain in Gostishchevo while the rest of the regiment would move to Khokhlovo. The other two infantry regiments

13 According to Zamulin, *Demolishing the Myth*, page 406, the 89th Guards Rifle Division commander, Colonel M. P. Seriugun "lost his head" and moved his headquarters to the south, where he encountered German armor. He then quotes a report of the situation from Vatutin, from Order No. 000194 from 21 July 1943.

Vatutin further reports that "Having received information about the appearance of enemy tanks in the region of Verkh. Ol'shanets, Colonel Seriugin abandoned control over the units of his division, and taking command of the training battalion, left with it for the area of Kazach'e, where he intended to set up a new command post. On the move in the direction of Kazach'e, Seriugin bumped into enemy tanks, and was pushed aside to the area of Rzhavets, where he again encountered enemy tanks and was forced to retreat. Cut-off from the units of his division, for fourteen hours he had no direction over them."

and the reconnaissance battalion were assigned to security of the right flank, replacing elements of the 7th Panzer Division there. General Kempf did not agree with the solution to protecting the flanks. He insisted that two-thirds of the division should be on the Donets and only one-third sent to the Razumnaya area. He later modified his disposition to direct one-third of the division to move to the Donets, one-third move to Razumnaya for flank protection, and a regiment group be held in ready reserve in the Verkhnii Olshanets area.[14]

At this point, one infantry regiment of the 168th Infantry Division was now actually screening part of the right flank of the SS Panzer Corps while the other two infantry regiments were shifted to the III Panzer Corps right flank to protect that so its panzer divisions could continue pushing forward.

The 19th Panzer Division Sweeps the Severnyii Donets

At 0745, the two panzer grenadier regiments (the 73rd and 74th) attacked north. The 73rd Panzer Grenadier Regiment advanced against weak Soviet resistance, with the 19th Reconnaissance Battalion screening the right flank. After clearing many minefields it got through Sabyinino and then moved right, northeast up the Severnyii Donets, taking Krivtsovo and Strelnikov before reaching Rzhavets at 1415. There it made contact with units of the 6th Panzer Division.

The 74th Panzer Grenadier Regiment cleared the woods southeast of Sabyinino and then attacked past the east side of the town and took up positions behind the 73rd. Late in the day the 73rd Panzer Grenadier Regiment and one battalion from the 74th took over the Ryindinka bridgehead site and enlarged it. This area had been held by elements of the 92nd Guards Rifle Division and the 81st Guards Rifle Division.

The 81st Guards Rifle Division, which had been in combat since the 5th and had done an exemplary job, had a breakdown in command on this day. The II Battalion of the 235th Guards Rifle Regiment was to defend at the Shcholokovo fish farm along the west bank of the Donets River and prevent the Germans crossing. According to the division commander's report "Having received the order and occupied the defense, the commander of the II Battalion [Captain] Goshtenar took no measures to prevent an enemy crossing. Moreover, at the appearance of an insignificant enemy force, he disgracefully abandoned the battlefield, and retreated without an order from the regiment commander. Goshtenar forgot the glorious traditions of the Stalingrad battles and shamefully fled the battlefield, while his battalion was stopped and returned to its original positions by the division's chief of staff Major Svetnik and the chief of the political department Guards Lieutenant Colonol Bolshakov, who had just arrived. Goshtenar behaved like a coward and betrayed the Motherland. . . . For abandoning his assigned sector without an order and for his disgraceful flight from the battlefield, the commander of the II Battalion of the 235th Guards Red Banner Rifle Regiment will be turned over for a trail by a military tribunal."[15]

Late in the day, the bridgehead came under pressure from the advancing 11th and 12th Guards Mechanized Brigades. According to the Sixty-ninth Army, they had occupied both Ryindinka and Shipyi by the end of day, and these villages were now being defended by two battalions of the 11th Guards Mechanized Brigade and a single battalion from the 12th Guards Mechanized Brigade. The brigade's remaining battalions were concentrated in Avdeyevka. This claim has also been picked

14 See T314, R194 page 948.

15 Zamulin, *Demolishing the Myth*, page 425. It would be interesting to know what the judgment of the military tribunal was.

Zamulin does note that "Elements of practically all the Sixty-Ninth Army's divisions demonstrated instances of fragility: both those that had already been involved in hard fighting for several days in a row and were now badly tattered, and those that had only just moved into the main line of resistance. Units were observed to retreat not only when under pressure from a superior opponent, but also at moments when a few commanders displayed basic faint-heartedness."

up in secondary sources.[16] Still, it does appear that the Germans controlled both of these towns by the end of the day. There is no indication that the Germans were pushed out of Ryindinka.[17]

The Fifth Guards Tank Army Operational Report #2 for 0700 on 13 July states that "The V Guards Mechanized Corps (11th and 12th Guards Mechanized Brigades) reached and consolidated along the line of the northern outskirts of Ryindinka—the Vyipolzovka—Aleksandrovka road . . . during the previous day 4 enemy tanks and 4 guns were destroyed. Losses: 2 T-34s, of which 1 blew up on a mine, 2 T-70s (blew up on mines), 1 antiaircraft gun."[18]

16 The 1944 General Staff Study makes even more extravagant claims, not only claiming to have forced the Germans out of Ryindinka and thrown them back in the Rzhavets region to the eastern bank of the Severnyii Donets, but "utterly smashed" the German 73rd and 74th Panzer Grenadier Regiments. This last event clearly did not occur. They also claimed that one of its brigades reached hill 216.0, which is two kilometers south of Rzhavets and that the 92nd Guards Rifle Division consolidated along the line from Ryindinka to hill 216.0. See Glantz and Orenstein, page 113.

17 Valeriy Zamulin also attempts to address this issue in his book. He states that by 1525 (Moscow time), the 11th Guards Mechanized Brigade had driven the Germans from Shipyi, and at 1900 it took possession of Ryindinka. He does note that the 19th Panzer Division's battle group could not be dislodged from its position on the western bank of the river. He does state that only one document exists that briefly describes the course of the fighting, a dispatch from the 11th Guards Mechanized Brigade chief of political department. He then quotes it, even though it does not claim to have taken Ryindinka or Shipyi. See Zamulin, *Demolishing the Myth*, pages 417–419.

In light of the fact that the German records do not mention loosing Ryindinka and at 0700 the next morning the 11th and 12th Mechanized Brigades are reported to be along the line of the northern outskirts of Ryindinka—the Vyipolzovka—Aleksandrovka road, it does not appear that they took Ryindinka. The Germans reported that a battalion of the 6th Panzer Division was also in the Shipyi bridgehead on the morning of the 13th (see page 393 of this book).

18 Fond: 332, Opis: 4948, Delo: 82, page 2. The claims for kills and losses apply to the entire V Guards Mechanized Corps, including the 10th Guards Mechanized Brigade and 24th Guards Tank Brigade. As the 10th Guards Mechanized Brigade and 24th Guards Tank Brigade do not report any losses for the 12th, then most likely all these claims and losses apply to this action.

The 11th Guards Mechanized Brigade did report 354 personnel losses for the 12th, while the 12th Guards Mechanized Brigade reported 244 killed and wounded from the 12th through the 16th.[19]

The 6th Panzer Division Crosses the Severnyii Donets

During the night the division moved panzer assault groups up to Kazachye at around 2200. A task force from Battle Group Oppeln then bolted forward to seize a crossing over the Severnyii Donets northwest of Rzhavets in a surprise attack during the night.

The attack was lead by Major (Dr.) Franz Baeke, who assembled a task force consisting of the II Battalion, 11th Panzer Regiment and the II Battalion, 114th Panzer Grenadier Regiment. It also included some Tigers. At the head of the column they placed a captured T-34. The column then moved quietly during the night through the Soviet lines and towards the bridgehead when their "trojan horse" T-34 broke down, forcing the column to stop and having to push it out of the way. The column was then able to continue and by coup de main seized the crossing near Rzhavets, although the main bridge had been blown.[20]

As Alfred Rubbel,[21] with the 1st company, 503rd Heavy Panzer Battalion recalls:

19 Fond: 332, Opis: 1943, Delo: 80, pages 14–17.

20 Cross, pages 207–209.

21 Lt.Col. (ret.) Alfred Rubbel was interviewed by Maj.Gen. (ret.) Dieter Brand on 10 May 1999. Alfred Rubbel was born 18 June 1921 and volunteered for the army on 12 May 1939. He served in the Russian Campaign in the 11th Panzer Regiment, 6th Panzer Division (Moscow and Caucasia) as a loader, gunner and tank commander. He was transferred to 503rd Heavy Panzer Battalion before Kursk.

By the end of the war, he was the adjutant in the 503rd Heavy Panzer Battalion (Tiger) in Hungary. Was awarded Iron Cross 1st and 2nd Class and the Tank Badge of the 3rd Degree (for 50 Assaults). During Kursk, these included credit for actions on July 5th (Mikhailovka), 6th (Razumnoye), 7th (Yastrebovo), 11th (Verkhnyii-Olshansk), 12th (Kryukovo) and 12 August (north of Dergachi).

A farmer after the war, he joined the West German Army, rising to a battalion commander and a training group commander at the Armor Training School. Upon retirement, he was employed with industry in tank development.

During the night from the 11th to the 12th of July I participated in the 11th Panzer Regiment's night attack onto Rzhavets led by Major Baeke, which is so well publicized in literature. The attack had been staged to pursue retreating Soviet contingents. The night was dark, visibility was very limited, but there was no fog.

The night attack was led through seven Russian villages. Our fighting force consisted of maybe 20 tanks and easily stretched over an entire kilometer. We were in a convoy along a roadway, so the whole effort was more akin to a move at night than to an attack. I don't recall finding ourselves wedged in between Russian columns as reported in many of those gripping accounts. It was not until the first light of dawn that we came to realize that we were in the middle of a Russian formation, and then the exchange of fire naturally ensued without delay. We decided it in our favor, mostly because the Russians immediately took flight, almost as if in a panic.[22]

According the 11th Panzer Regiment's war diary, the battle group was led by the 7th panzer company, followed by the 7th company of the 114th Panzer Grenadier Regiment, then the 8th panzer company, the rest of the II Battalion of the 114th Panzer Grenadier Regiment, and finally the Tigers. They rolled through Kurakovka at 0030 hours without encountering any Soviet forces. A truck convoy was passed. At 0040 they arrived at Rzhavets, passed through Rzhavets, which still had Soviet guards moving convoys and horse-drawn vehicles, and advanced to the bridge. The column was broken by a vehicle breaking down, and the point of the column, now separated, met a column of T-34s carrying infantry. They tried to pass this column without being recognized while the rest of the battle group caught up and a firefight broke out. The Germans claimed ten T-34s and one T-70 destroyed, of which five T-34s were claimed destroyed in close combat by Major Baeke and Lt. Zobel.[23] The Germans then took Rzhavets and the

---

22 More dramatic, and possibly exaggerated, accounts of Major Baeke's attack can be found in Cross, pages 207–209, and Franz Kurowski, *Panzer Aces*, pages 60–61 (Ballantine, 2002) or page 59 (Fedorowicz, 1992). Kurowski claims that the action has been "reconstructed" from entries in Dr. Baeke's diary but this "reconstructed" account is placed in quotes. This author remains suspicious of the accuracy of this and some other accounts in Kurowski's books.

There is also a Russian account of this night march that has the German column led by several T-34s. It then encounters on the road at Kurakovka a column of Soviet infantry from the training battalion of the 89th Guards Rifle Division moving the opposite way during the night (50 meters visibility). As the two columns pass each other, they get into a fight at point blank range. This account appears to contradict part of the account of Rubbel and other German authors. See Zamulin, *Demolishing the Myth*, pages 404–405. That account is from M.G. Boev, the deputy commander of the training battalion, who was at the head of the Soviet column.

Zamulin, page 407, quotes Vatutin as reporting on 21 July that 89th Guards Rifle Division commander:

> "Colonel Seriugin . . . taking command of the training battalion, left with it for the area of Kazach'e, where he intended to set up a new command post. On the move in the direction of Kazach'e, Seriugin bumped into enemy tanks, and was pushed aside to the area of Rzhavets, where he again encountered enemy tanks and was forced to retreat. . . ."

Zamulin also reports a dispatch sent by the 89th Guards Rifle Division to the commander of the LXVIII Rifle Corps:

> "At the order of the division commander, the division headquarters was being relocated to the area of Novo-Oskochnoe, and at 0200 12.07.43 the vehicle containing headquarters staff, were cut off by a column of up to 300 enemy tanks. The command staff managed to abandon their vehicles before they were destroyed by enemy tanks."
>
> "By dawn, the division command, with the exception of the assistance chief of operations Guards Captain Lebedenko and the division's topographer Senior Lieutenant Levchenko, emerged from encirclement at Plota and returned to normal work. . . ."
>
> "The division's special units, which were relocating together with the headquarters particularly suffered, and are being brought back to order. . . . Losses are being determined."

One must conclude that there was an encounter at 0200 (Moscow time) by the 89th Guards Rifle Division headquarters and its training battalion with a German armor column that lead to it scattering. It may have been with the rear half of Baeke's column as the front had reached Rzhavets at 0040 (Berlin time).

23 These claims are from German 11th Panzer Regiment (6th Panzer Division) war diary. Zamulin, *Demolishing the Myth*, page 407, reports that "the 96thTank Brigade's 331st Tank Battalion engaged two columns of enemy tanks, numbering about 40 vehicles, in the area of Rzhavets. The Battalion's *(continued)*

column continued forward. The infantry of the II Battalion crossed the destroyed bridge and established a bridgehead on the opposite bank of the river. At 0500, the I Battalion arrived at Rzhavets and reinforced this bridgehead.[24]

They then held this bridgehead during the day against Soviet artillery and tank fire. The bridgehead was expanded during the day as the division seized Rzhavets and created another bridgehead at Ryindinka. The units at Ryindinka were relieved by the 19th Panzer Division and establish another bridgehead northwest of Vessilok. Meanwhile, the main part of the division, including those elements that had been operating with the 168th Infantry Division in the south, moved into the Kazachye-Kurakovka area. During the morning, the panzers of Battle Group Oppeln tangled with the Soviet tanks in this area.

During the morning, most of Battle Group Unrein entered the area south of Verkhnii Olshanets, while elements of the battle group were still mopping up in the southeast part of Shlyakhovoye. Battle Group Quentin moved part of its force to assume flank protection east of Shlyakhovoye, and these were supposed to be relieved by elements of the 7th Panzer Division, which never showed up. These reconnaissance forces found Soviet troops in Novo-Alekseyevka, Vyiselok and Aleksandrovka. These places had been reported free of Soviet forces earlier in the morning, and the Soviet forces there were now reportedly being continually reinforced, with at least 25 tanks spotted. This was the 305th Rifle Division which was deployed from Sviridovo to Alekseyevka, the 92nd Guards Rifle Division, which was deployed from Vyipolzovka to Vyiselok, and the 96th Tank Brigade (which only had 12 to 16 tanks). The 107th Rifle Division probably saw combat on this day, but the records only note that its 522nd Rifle Regiment abandoned Verknyii Olshanets and concentrated in the rear at Zayachye. By the end of the day, all three rifle regiments of this division were back in second echelon positions. Meanwhile, elements of Battle Group Quentin also moved back toward Kalinina.

In order to reduce the threat of an attack against the division's flanks, Battle Group Unrein was given part of Battle Group Quentin (the division reconnaissance battalion) and some assault guns, and ordered to attack Novo-Alekseyevka, Vyiselok and Aleksandrovka immediately. Fighting continued in these towns throughout the day. The front line at the end of the day was Kazachye-Kurakovka-Vyipolzovka-directly south of Ryindinka. The important point was that the corps was finally across the Severnyii Donets at three points.

As Alfred Rubbel recalled the advance over the last few days with the 6th Panzer Division:

> I can no longer recall the progress of the attack in terms of a time and location. According to a document which listed the days of deployment, my company and I were used as follows: July 5 at Mikhailovka, July 6 at Razumnoye, July 7 at Yastrebovo, July 11 at Verkhnii Olshanets and July 12 at Kurakovka. The heaviest fighting occurred on July 11 and 12.
>
> I report only my general impressions. The attack was continued towards the northeast. Here, we thought we had overrun the enemy's fortifications in the Generalovka area, thus gaining open space again.
>
> It appeared that the enemy was dodging us according to plan. We saw long columns of Soviet troops, which we fired at with explosive shells but soon aborted such measures because we didn't even have enough ammunition for that.
>
> First of all, I noticed the large numbers of trucks, all of them of American origin. It looked to me as if every truck had been made in America. Also, for the first time in those days we encountered three Churchill tanks, which were swiftly destroyed. Later on we also saw American tanks of the Sherman and

six T-34s and the crew of one gun of an anti-tank battery were pulling out of Kiselevo when they collided with the enemy column. In the subsequent night-time battle, the tanks managed to knock out nine combat vehicles of the 6th Panzer Division and after passing the Bol. Pod'iarugi, the Battalion reached Aleksandrovka at 0400 12 July 1943, where it took up a defense.

If this is again another encounter with Baeke's column, then it would indicate that both the German and Soviet kill claims are overstated.

24 Jentz, page 90.

General Lee types. These however, were not adversaries to be taken seriously for us. For instance, we fought the Sherman tank with the explosive shell with delayed action. The shell penetrated the weak armor and then unfolded its work of destruction when detonating inside the tank. On some days half of all enemy tanks were of American origin.

It hit me for the first time what massive amount of support the Soviet Union received from the Americans and at the same time I woke up to the fact that in the heart of Russia we were not fighting the Russians alone. However, we did benefit from this support in a way because we captured huge amounts of American field rations. This did us very well. But overall, evidence of this massive support of the Allies for the Soviet Union was a real surprise. It did generate some insecurity and caused us to have some second thoughts.

The next few days saw our attack advance swiftly. The Tiger company was usually in the vanguard of the 11th Panzer Regiment. Most of the time the division's armored formation included the armored personnel carrier battalion of the 4th Panzer Grenadier Regiment. We employed the classic approach to an attack in using such an armored formation. We engaged the enemy along a small front line with units grouped deep into our rear and did not worry about any threat to our flanks or rear. In this wedge formation, we were always way ahead of the division's main body.

However, we did not see an intrepid Soviet leadership make use of such a situation either, by attacking us deep in the flank and cutting us off. Instead, the enemy seemed to be falling back from one position to the next. I have never seen a Soviet commander on the lower level attempt to tie us up at the front while attacking our flanks or rear with his main force. Thus, only the exchange of fire at the front line unfolded, where we had the advantage. We would then try to catch the enemy at his flank by maneuvering on the battlefield, which often succeeded.

Therefore, we never did face any particular challenges. All in all the enemy presented himself the same way we knew him from numerous engagements.

The Soviets had no Shermans at Kursk, but did deploy Grants (almost identical to Lees) and Churchills in this area. The Grant's armor was thinner than the Sherman's.

Apparently the Luftwaffe had not been informed that the Germans had seized the bridgehead at Rzhavets, and at 1020 (Berlin time) on the 12th, He-111s bombed the bridgehead, mistaking the Germans for a Soviet armored formation.[25] The bombs hit a conference of staff officers and unit commanders being held by General Huenersdorff next to his command vehicle. Fifteen Germans were killed and 49 wounded. Major Rogalla von Bieberstein, commander of the 114th Panzer Grenadier Regiment, was killed. Among the wounded were Colonel von Oppeln-Bronikowski, the panzer regiment commander, and General Huenersdorff. Huenersdorff would continue to command, only to meet his fate a day later. Oppeln was replaced by lightly wounded Baeke.[26] If this count is correct, the division had lost two regiment commanders on the 12th. The German records, on the other hand, indicate that this event occurred on the 13th (see the account below for the following day).

25 The time of the attack comes from Zamulin, *Demolishing the Myth*, page 419. It is from an VIII Air Corps staff report compiled the evening of 13 July. The report claims that bombing by a squadron of He-111s was due to poor weather conditions, limited visibility and poor navigation. They became lost and combat the Rzhavets area. It was investigated at 1635 the same day and the investigation determined that no one should be accused of criminal negligence since all precautionary measures have been observed.

Most accounts of this incident states that it was because the Luftwaffe had not been informed that the Germans had seized the bridgehead. If this report is correct, then it was a simple navigational error in poor visibility.

26 Cross, page 209, and Kurowski, *Panzer Aces*, pages 62–63. Kurowski claims it was one errant He-111. On the other hand, Franz Kurowski, *Panzer Aces 2*, pages 547–548 claimed that Oppeln's command vehicle was hit by a Soviet antitank gun when he chose to take a shortcut through the Soviet positions after being told to report to the wounded Huenersdorff. This directly contradicts the account he provides in *Panzer Aces*.

168th Infantry Division, 12 July 1943

Gostishchevo The actions of the 417th Infantry Regiment are incorporated in the 167th Infantry Division engagement for this day (see Chapter Nine). The other two infantry regiments saw limited action this day.

Forces Engaged

Attachments
2/228th StuG Bn, with 6 StuGs
lt Bty/I/61st AA Rgt—attached the on 12th

Still detached from the division
248th Engineer Bn (less 3 cos)
429th Infantry Rgt (less 1 Bn)

The 19th Panzer Division Sweeps the Severnyii Donets, 12 July 1943

DURATION One day FRONTAGE 7.8 kilometers TERRAIN Rolling, mixed
WEATHER Cool, cloudy, occasional showers. Temperature at noon: 17 degrees Celsius. Road conditions good.

	Attacker	*Defender*
Units	19th PzD	81st Guards Rifle Division
Attachments	See below	None
Strength	17,884	6,229
Armor	27 (5 light)	0
Artillery	150	31
Air Sorties	0	33 + 5 Night
Casualties	37 (5 KIA, 30 WIA, 2 MIA)	655 (161 KIA, 336 WIA, 158 MIA)
Armor losses	2	6
Artillery losses	2	6
Enemy Captured	N/A	1

Forces Engaged

German Attachments
70th Engineer Bn
2/411th Bridge Column B
842nd Bridge Column J
52nd Werfer Rgt—attached on the 12th (included)
I/61st Flak Rgt (less 1 battery)
 lt Bty/I/61st Flak Rgt—detached on the 12th (included)
429th Infantry Rgt (168th ID), less I Battalion

Detached
ObsBty/19th Artillery Rgt

Arriving Soviet Forces
11th Guards Mechanized Brigade
12th Guards Mechanized Brigade

The 6th Panzer Division Crosses the Severnyii Donets, 12 July 1943

DURATION One day FRONTAGE 12.2 kilometers TERRAIN Rolling, mixed
WEATHER Occasional light rain, cool. Temperature at noon: 17 degrees Celsius. Road conditions good.

	Attacker	*Defender*
Units	6th PzD	92nd Guards, 305th & 107th Rifle Divisions
Attachments	See below	See below
Strength	21,000	23,225
Armor	67 (4 light)	12 (5 light)
Artillery	140	205
Air Sorties	0	35 + 5 Night
Casualties	108 (18 KIA, 88 WIA, 2 MIA)	725 (126 KIA, 521 WIA, 78 MIA)
Armor losses	11	14
Artillery losses	1	14
Enemy Captured	N/A	4

Forces Engaged

German Attachments
II/62nd Artillery Rgt—attached on the 12th
II/54th Werfer Rgt—attached on the 12th
III/54th Werfer Rgt
Hq/54th Werfer Rgt—attached on the 12th

II/43rd Flak Rgt
lt Bn/91st Flak Rgt—attached on the 12th
204th Intelligence Troop—attached on the 12th

228th StuG Bn (less 2nd company)
1st co/503rd Heavy Panzer Bn (included)
2nd co/503rd Heavy Panzer Bn (included)
Hq/503rd Heavy Panzer Bn (included)

Detached
ObsBty/76th Artillery Rgt (included)

Soviet Forces
92nd Guards Rifle Division
96th Tank Bde
305th Rifle Division
1658th AT Rgt—detached on the 12th (included)
148th Tank Rgt—attached on the 12th (not included)
107th Rifle Division
496th Mortar Rgt
123rd ATR Bn
130th ATR Bn
53rd Guards Tank Regiment (losses only)

Myasoyedovo, 12 July 1943

DURATION One day FRONTAGE 5.5 kilometers TERRAIN Rolling, mixed
WEATHER Cool and cloudy. Temperature at noon: 17 degrees Celsius. Road conditions good.

	Attacker	*Defender*
Units	7th PzD	94th Guards Rifle Division
Attachments	See below	148th Tank Regiment (detached—not included)
Strength	17,779	8,326
Armor	49 (4 light)	0
Artillery	135	61
Air Sorties	0	11 + 40 Night
Casualties	19 (3 KIA, 15 WIA, 1MIA)	485 (158 KIA, 263 WIA, 64 MIA)
Artillery losses	1	9
Enemy Captured	N/A	0

Forces Engaged

German Attachments
9th Bridge Column B
1/505th Bridge Column B
843rd Bridge Column J

99th Flak Rgt Staff
I/38th Flak Rgt
II/38th Flak Rgt
lt Bn/91st Flak Rgt—detached on the 12th (not included)

II/62nd Artillery Rgt—detached on the 12th (not included)
I/54th Werfer Rgt
II/54th Werfer Rgt—detached on the 12th (not included)
Hq/54th Werfer Rgt—detached on the 12th (not included)

204th Intelligence Troop—detached on the 12th (not included)
3rd co/503rd Heavy Panzer Bn—detached on the 12th (not included)

Detached
ObsBty/78th Artillery Rgt (included)
Regimental Group—detached on the 12th (included)

Corps Assets
601st Engineer Rgt Staff
674th Engineer Rgt Staff
925th Bridge Construction Staff
127th Engineer Bn (less 1 co)
531st Bridge Construction Bn
110th Bridge Column B
602nd Bridge Column B
co/538th Road Construction Bn

153rd Flak Rgt Staff

3rd Command of Artillery
612th Artillery Rgt Staff
II/62nd Artillery Rgt
II/71st Artillery Rgt
857th Heavy Artillery Rgt
Hq/52nd Werfer Rgt—detached to the troops on the 12th
I/52nd Werfer Rgt—detached to the troops on the 12th
II/52nd Werfer Rgt—detached to the troops on the 12th
III/52nd Werfer Rgt—detached to the troops on the 12th
Pn/13th Light Observations Battery
ObsBty/19th Artillery Rgt (19th PzD)
ObsBty/76th Artillery Rgt (6th PzD)

2nd Fuel Column Troop
545th Panzer Recovery Platoon
Hq/503rd Heavy Panzer Bn—attached on the 12th
1st co/503rd Heavy Panzer Bn—attached on the 12th
2nd co/503rd Heavy Panzer Bn—attached on the 12th
3rd co/503rd Heavy Panzer Bn—attached on the 12th
Regimental Group (from 7th PzD)—attached on the 12th

The day ended with yet another Soviet attack on Rzhavets at 1800, during which the Germans claimed to have shot three more T-34s.[27]

Finally that evening, the 53rd Guards Tank Regiment from Trufanov's forward detachment launched its attack towards Aleksandrovka at 2000. This regiment, supported by three batteries from the 689th Antitank Regiment, at 2200 (Moscow time) had reached the northern outskirts of Aleksandrovka, and then was suddenly attacked from the hollow 1.5 kilometers southwest of Aleksandrovka by 28 German tanks, of which eight were Tigers. This was a Soviet claim; the 6th Panzer Division's 11th Panzer Regiment had around 24 tanks, not including Marders or self-propelled artillery ready for action this day. The 503rd Heavy Panzer Battalion was down to around 17 Tigers ready for action. This action continued until 2215, and then the regiment took up defensive positions along the west and southwest outskirts of Aleksandrovka with 13 tanks, and along the western and southwestern outskirts of Novo-Khmelevoi with six T-34s and seven T-70s. The regiment had lost nine T-34s and three T-70s, but claimed nine German tanks, including two Tigers.[28] The 6th Panzer Division is estimated to have lost 3 tanks on the 12th, while the 503rd Heavy Panzer Battalion lost an estimated 6 Tigers this day. The Soviet antitank regiment was reported to have lost 5 guns this day and a total of 12 45mm antitank guns for the 12th and the 13th. The 53rd Tank Regiment lost 9 T-34s, 3 T-70s, 5 men killed, 7 wounded, and 10 missing on the 12th and possibly including the 13th.

Myasoyedovo

The 7th Panzer Division commenced its attack in the late evening hours of 11 July to seize the north part of Myasoyedovo, and spent the morning of the 12th mopping up in that town and in the boot-shaped woods. At noon, the division supply officer reported much captured Soviet equipment in the boot-shaped woods and requested that the corps' captured equipment recovery unit be dispatched. Breith in his post-war account referred to this action as having been a major victory that resulted in this front quieting down and allowing the division to now be shifted to the north.[29]

Mopping up in the Razumnaya valley between Myasoyedovo and Kalinina was carried out by attached elements of the 168th Infantry Division. The division was relieved about noon by elements of the 198th Infantry Division. The bulk of the division moved through Melikhovo to Kazachye. A regimental group consisting of a panzer grenadier regiment with a tank company and an artillery battalion remained in the Yastrebovo area under corps control.

The 94th Guards Rifle Division was reported to be defending along the line from height 205.6 (1.5 kilometers north-northeast of Mazikino) to Mazikino to Sheino to Ushakovo. It was reported to have repelled infantry and tank attacks during the day.

The 11th of July was probably the last day of combat for the 31st Antitank Brigade. It was reported on the 11th that the brigade had been pulled back for refitting and on the 12th that its "remnants" had gathered in Prokhodnoye (behind the Koren River) and that losses were large and being calculated. The same was the case with the 148th Tank Regiment, which was ordered to move to the Bolshaya Psinka area and then to Kazachye, in order to link up with the 305th Rifle Division. The regiment had 3 T-34s and 1 T-70 remaining, with all tanks in repair. The tanks and four antitank rifle crews reached the Zayachye area under command of the deputy chief of the regimental staff. This ended the 148th Tank Regiment's participation in the Battle of Kursk.

Air Support

The 19th Panzer Division reported that there was some Soviet air activity during the night. Soviet close

27 Jentz, page 91, drawn from 11th Panzer Regiment war diary.

28 The details of this attack are from Rotmistrov's report on 30 September. Although it is in the area of the 13th, we believe that it is providing an account of the actions for the evening of the 12th. See footnote 8 above for a detailed explanation.

29 Breith, page 9.

air support was very active early in the day and again around noon, bombing division artillery positions. The Luftwaffe had only light reconnaissance and fighter activity.

The 6th Panzer Division reported that the Soviet air activity was at its usual level. The 7th Panzer Division reported lively Soviet activity during the night.

The Germans apparently received some air support from the Soviet side with multiple fratricide incidents reported this day. According to one account from the 11th Guards Mechanized Brigade, at 1211 (Moscow time) 25 Il-2s attacked their own troops and again at 1230 with 30 Il-2s. During the night, a U-2 attacked their own troops with incendiary bombs. This regiment was located in the Ryindinka area, across the river from Rzhahavets. At Rzhavets the Germans were also attacked by their own bombers when a squadron of He-111s, in poor weather conditions and with limited visibility, and also because of poor navigation, became lost and bombed the Rzhavets area.[30] This was the infamous attack that hit the command post of the 6th Panzer Division.

III Panzer Corps Attacks the Donets Triangle, 13 July 1943

The problem with the Soviet withdrawal on the 12th was that it set the Germans up for a significant advance that day and allowed them to get multiple footholds across the Severnyii Donets River. The 94th Guards, 305th and 107th Rifle Divisions (XXXV Guards Rifle Corps) were protecting against a northeasterly thrust and most of the Soviet armor in the Donets triangle on the 12th was committed to attacks on the SS Panzer Corps. This left an opening in the Soviet defense that the Germans were able to exploit with their push north. In effect, they were moving laterally across the front of the XXXV Guards Rifle Corps.

The German armor, particularly the 6th Panzer Division, had suddenly found that they could turn north and simply push across the Severnyii Donets, with the XXXV Guards Rifle Corps to the flank and with the only opposition in front of them being three withdrawing and exhausted divisions (81st, 89th and 92nd). The Severnyii Donets crossing was very defensible with raised banks on the northern side and broad stream beds and open areas ahead of them. But, somehow, no one had managed to make sure that there was a secure, established, defensive line on this bank, so the 168th Infantry Division, 19th Panzer Division and 6th Panzer Division had all been able to cross the previous day without much difficulty.

The three reinforcing brigades commanded by Trufanov arrived too late in the day to halt this effort and furthermore, were positioned primarily to the northeast of the German attack, leaving the area to the southwest of Ryindinka lightly held. If Ryindinka could be held, then the Germans could simply roll up the flanks of the units in the Donets triangle.

The Soviet answer was, of course, to counterattack, which they spent the 13th doing. It probably would have been more useful if between the Seventh Guards Army commander and the Sixty-ninth Army commander they had just made sure they had secured against a northern thrust with proper forces, including armor.

While the XLVIII Panzer Corps and the SS Panzer Corps were fighting stiff and sometimes overwhelming defensive battles on the 12th, the III Panzer Corps had actually made considerable progress in its advance and had finally crossed the Severnyii Donets at three points. They came under attack across their entire front on the 13th and as such, made little progress on this day, but this did not remove the threat they posed to the Soviet forces in the Donets triangle.

30 Zamulin, *Demolishing the Myth*, page 419. The Soviet air reports come from a report submitted by the 11th Guards Mechanized Brigade chief of the political department. The report on German fratricide comes from a VIII Air Corps staff report compiled on the evening of 13 July. His source for this German report is given as V. Gorbach and D. Khazanov, *Aviatsiia v bitve nad Orlovsko-Kursk dugoi* [Aviation in the battle over the Orel-Kursk bulge], (Moscow: Moskva 2004), p. 169. We could find no records from the VIII Air Corps during our research for the Kursk Data Base project.

The Sixty-ninth Army's Predicament

The Sixty-ninth Army was now engaged with two different panzer corps and facing threats from three different directions. Its XLVIII Rifle Corps had three divisions facing west against the SS Panzer Corps and two divisions facing south against the III Panzer Corps. Splitting them was the German 417th Infantry Regiment, which had waltzed into Gostishchevo the previous day due to a major mistake by the army (or at least by the 89th Guards Rifle Division). As such its 93rd Guards Rifle Division was flanked and would be forced to turn south to deal with this threat.

The Germans had developed a bridgehead at Ryindinka, from which they were threatening to launch an attack with two armored divisions. Still, the Sixty-ninth Army had received considerable support with the majority of the V Guards Mechanized Corps, under command of Major General Trufanov. These forces were now shifted to their sector and in a position to counterattack the German bridgehead.

On the eastern flank of the III Panzer Corps attack was the XXXV Guards Rifle Corps of four divisions backed up by "Trufanov's detachment." These were in relatively secure positions. Overall, the III Panzer Corps and Corps Raus attack was now drawing off all three divisions of the XXXV Guards Rifle Corps, four of the divisions from the Sixty-ninth Army, one division and tank brigade from the Sixth Guards Army, and four armored or motorized brigades from the V Guards Mechanized Corps.

Gostishchevo

The southern point of the Donets triangle is keyed around the hills and streams to the south of Gostishchevo. To take those, the woods to the north of that and the town of Gostishchevo would make a good start at rolling up this position. The first attempt to penetrate the initial defensive positions around Staryii Gorod occurred on the 5th of July with the 6th Panzer Division's attack and quickly failed. No further significant attempts were made until the 168th Infantry Division began its drive on the 11th. This advance had quickly cleared the path and in a significant surprise advance, took Gostishchevo on the 12th.

Still, for the 417th Infantry Regiment, taking Gostishchevo turned out to be easier than holding it. The first Soviet counterattacks started in the evening hours of the 12th, when two strong Soviet probing attacks came from the north and northwest of Gostishchevo. These were repelled. Yet, the Germans were only holding Gostishchevo with one reinforced battalion while the rest of the regiment was on the Severnyii Donets, in the area of Krivtsovo, Sabyinino and Kiselevo.

The following day the 93rd Guards Rifle Division attacked with a vengeance, taking Gostishchevo and Druzhnyii before it was "halted." This division, which had not yet suffered any significant losses in this battle, lost 130 killed and 718 wounded on this day. The 417th Infantry Regiment was forced back out of the town, and it ended up holding at the north edge of the "underwear" woods. The Soviets then dug in on both sides of height 223.2, the hill between the woods and Gostishchevo. This successful attack was not even noted in the Sixty-ninth Army records for the day, for they had reported receiving no reports from the XLVIII Rifle Corps about the corps or the Germans. The XLVIII Rifle Corps headquarters was in Maloye Yablonovo (near Plota) and the Sixty-ninth Army headquarters was in Korocha, only 35 kilometers away.

The rest of the division area was quiet. The 417th Infantry Regiment continued to defend near Gostishchevo and around Strelnikov, which was some eight kilometers northeast of Gostishchevo. The other two infantry regiments were farther east, defending the flank of the corps in what amounted to an entirely separate operation. They were deployed along the Razumnaya creek with the 442nd Infantry Regiment defending from the south edge of Kazachye down to the Komintern Bridge (7.5 kilometers due south of Kazachye). This was a frontage of around nine kilometers. The 429th Infantry Regiment, after assembling in the woods west of Znamenka, took over the sector from the Komintern Bridge (but not including it) to 500 meters south of the

Svishchev ravine (a point about three kilometers southeast of Melikhovo). This gave this regiment a frontage of around 8.5 kilometers.

The Fight for the Bridgeheads

The 19th Panzer Division was left with the job of securing the bridgeheads that had been grabbed the day before. By early morning, 13 July, the 73rd and 74th Panzer Grenadier Regiments occupied the enlarged bridgeheads, with the 19th Reconnaissance Battalion screening both flanks of the division. The reconnaissance battalion had established contact with the 11th Panzer Regiment (6th Panzer Division) at Rzhavets.

In the area of Sazhnoye, Shakhovo and Shcholokovo were the 81st and 89th Guards Rifle Division. The 81st Guards Rifle Division was deployed from 100 meters west of the edge of Shcholokovo to 200 meters east of Shakhovo. It defended the southwestern outskirts of Shakhovo while the 89th Guards Rifle Division held the river lines west of Shcholokovo and back to Sazhnoye. It was still in good shape, reporting its strength at 7,805 men.[31] The Sixty-ninth Army reported that the Germans attacked in small groups towards Shakhovo and Lomovo and fought with their attacking units.

At 0230 (Berlin time), the Soviets, with six tanks moving south on both sides of the Severnyii Donets, attacked the Ryindinka bridgehead. They entered the town and penetrated to the bridge site, splitting the bridgehead. The 74th Panzer Grenadier Regiment's headquarters was cut off from the III Battalion, which was defending the town. The headquarters had to withdraw to the east bank after a firefight with Soviet infantry and the destruction of one Soviet tank.

At 0400 (Moscow time) the II Guards Tank Corps reported that German tanks and infantry crossed the Severnyii Donets in the Shcholokovo area and attacked the 26th Guards Tank Brigade. This attack was halted at a cost of two T-34s. The brigade would again report coming under attack by German tanks and infantry at 2030 and 2130 (Moscow time) from Shcholokovo.

At 0700 (Moscow time) on the 13th, it was reported that the 11th and 12th Guards Mechanized Brigades had reached and were consolidating along the line of the northern outskirts of Ryindinka, and the Vyipolzovka-Aleksandrovka road. A counterattack was then conducted by Battle Group Richter, which consisted of the 27th Panzer Regiment (now down to 31 tanks), the I Battalion of the 114th Panzer Grenadier Regiment from the 6th Panzer Division, and elements of the reconnaissance battalion. The force cleared the bridge site and by the end of the day had forced the Soviets back to the center of the town (implying that the Soviets had taken the town). The Germans claimed that they had disabled four Soviet tanks during the repeated Soviet counterattacks. The operation was completed by about 1900, and contact was made on the right flank with Battle Group Horst (probably the 73rd Panzer Grenadier Regiment).[32] The Soviet artillery had fired heavy concentrations during their attack. Lt. Colonel Richter (commander 74th Panzer Grenadier Regiment) and Captain Westhoven (his adjutant) were wounded. Major von Mentz assumed command of the 74th Panzer Grenadier Regiment and Battle Group Richter.

This Soviet attack was probably initially successful because the Germans had placed most of their forces facing the more obvious threat. The I and II Battalions of the 74th Panzer Grenadier Regiment were attached to the 73rd Panzer Grenadier Regiment to protect the right wing of the division. These forces were facing strong Soviet positions about 300 meters east of Shakhovo. There was no contact between either side until evening, when a Soviet attack occurred.

The rest of the 19th Reconnaissance Battalion was screening the 6th Panzer Division sector while the motorcycle company (the second company) estab-

31 As they report the same strength figure for the 15th of July, there may be some confusion in the records.

32 Major Johannes Horst was commander II Battalion, 73rd Panzer Grenadier Regiment in April 1943.

lished and held a small bridgehead at Shcholokovo. This bridgehead was ordered eliminated by the 11th Guards Mechanized Brigade and the 26th Guards Tank Brigade, but it appears that this attack never occurred. The 11th Guards Mechanized Brigade ended the day deployed from Ryindinka to Shipyi to Kuzminka, while the 12th Guards Mechanized Brigade was to its left, from Rzhavets to Vyipolzovka. The 11th Guards Mechanized Brigade reported 414 casualties for this day.[33]

Meanwhile, the division's engineer battalion spent the day building a 24-ton bridge at Rzhavets that kept getting shot up by the continuous Soviet artillery barrages, and around 0600, an attack by six of their own He-111s that inflicted serious casualties.

The 6th Panzer Division Pushes Northeast

Those elements of the division that were in the bridgehead south of Ryindinka were relieved during the night and moved to defend Vyipolzovka-southwest Rzhavets. Heavy Soviet artillery and antitank fire was reported there.

The bulk of the division began 13 July in the Kazachye-Vyipolzovka area, preparing to cooperate with the 7th Panzer Division on its right flank, which was aiming to attack and destroy the corps-strength Soviet forces around Aleksandrovka. The division also had a battalion in the Shipyi bridgehead. By 0900 the Germans were prepared to attack height 241.5 from positions in the Kazachye-Kurakovka area.

During the day, strong Soviet infantry and armored forces counterattacked and pushed forward to the German front lines. This was accompanied by what the division described as "overwhelming" Soviet air activity, with bombing and strafing. These attacks were concentrated over Kazachye, which resulted in heavy German losses. The Tiger battalion at Rzhavets reported being attacked by friendly aircraft, which caused heavy losses of men and materiel. This very effective German air attack accounted for five German officers and 15 NCOs and enlisted killed, and seven officers and 49 NCOs and enlisted wounded.[34]

The Rzhavets bridgehead again came under attack, with the Germans claiming another three T-34s, but this time losing four tanks because they were in unsuitable positions. The regiment's diary also reports that they suffered heavy losses where their own bombers dropped bombs on their positions. Colonel von Oppeln-Bronikowski and his adjutant Sr. Lt. Guckel were wounded. Major Baeke took over command of the panzer regiment. At around 1800, he pulled the panzer regiment out and moved it to an assembly area near Kurakovka in preparation for an attack on Aleksandrovka. Huenersdorff was also lightly wounded that day by an enemy air attack and then was mortally wounded the following day when he was hit in the head while in the forward line.[35]

Huenersdorff, who had been wounded on the 13th, continued to command the division. While he was returning to his forward headquarters the next day he was shot in the head by a Soviet sniper or wounded by a fragment. The mortally wounded general was evacuated back to Kharkov where they flew in a brain specialist. There he was also tended to by his wife, Oda, who was in charge of the forward forces' convalescent center of the German Red Cross, but Huenersdorff never regained consciousness and died at 1830 on the 17th. He was 44 years old.[36] The division's panzer regiment was soon named after him. He was temporarily replaced by Colonel Martin Unrein.

33 Fond: 332, Opis: 1943, Delo: 80, pages 14–17.

34 Because of the similarities in casualty figures, this author remains suspicious that this was the same air attack as other authors (Cross, Kurowski) claim occurred on the 12th. The author has not located any reference to the air attack on the 12th in the unit records.

35 See the daily III Panzer Corps war diary entries for the 13th and 14th (T314, R194, pages 000954 and 0000964).

36 Cross, pages 207–208, and Franz Kurowski, *Panzer Aces*, pages 63–64, states Huenersdorff was shot in the head by a Soviet sniper. Franz Kurosowski, *Panzer Aces 2*, page 548, claims it was shrapnel that pierced his steel helmet after his command vehicle had been hit. As this story was written later, it may be a correction of Kurowski's previous account. Jentz, page 92 provides the time of death.

THE 92ND GUARDS Rifle Division took Vyipolzovka at 1400 (Moscow time) on 13 July and continued to attack towards Rzhavets. By 1700 (Moscow time) the division was deployed from Vyipolzovka to outside of Aleksandrovka. The 96th Tank Brigade was with the 92nd Guards Rifle Division and defending the mounds at height 241.5 (just north of Aleksandrovka).

Trufanov's detachment had been holding Bolshiye Podyarugi and Novo-Khmelevoi, while the 53rd Guards Tank Regiment had attacked in the Aleksandrovka area the night before. For this day they were reported to be defending along the line of Avdeyevka to Aleksandrovka to Novo-Khmelovoi where they repelled German tank and infantry attacks. The 689th Antitank Regiment was reported to have lost 5 guns on the 12th and a total of 12 45mm antitank guns for the 12th and the 13th.

While there clearly was an armor engagement near Aleksandrovka, the German attack on Aleksandrovka did not take place because of the Soviet counterattacks and because a 7th Panzer Division attack on height 222.1 failed.

The 94th Guards Rifle Division Attacks

Replaced by the arriving 198th Infantry Division, the 7th Panzer Division was now able to rejoin the attack. The bulk of the division reached the assembly area in the vicinity of Kazachye, Verkhnii Olshanets and Dalnyaya Igumenka during the night of 12/13 July and morning of the 13th, where they reorganized for the next mission. Parts of the division were still moving to this assembly area during the rest of the day.

At 0400, the Soviet 94th Guards Rifle Division launched a surprise attack from the Razumnaya valley near Sheino, deep into the flank of the III Panzer Corps. Only the determined efforts of the 58th Panzer Engineer Battalion and part of the II Battalion, 54th Werfer Regiment, contained the attack. Part of Battle Group Glaesemer (II Battalion, 74th Panzer Grenadier Regiment and I Battalion, 6th Panzer Grenadier Regiment) were pulled out of the march column to launch an immediate counterattack. The Soviets were ejected from the positions they had taken, and after a bitter fight, eliminated. The Germans took 200 prisoners and claimed 400 Soviet dead. According to numerous prisoner-of-war statements, this attack was the end of the 286th Guards Rifle Regiment of the 94th Guards Rifle Division. The rest of Battle Group Glaesemer and the 7th Reconnaissance Battalion moved up to form a screen on the corps' flanks along the line running from Melikhovo to Komintern to Kazachye. The 94th Guards Rifle Division then consolidated and defended. Its casualties during the day were reported to be around 129, from our examination of the Soviet records.[37] This German claim may be overstated. This attack is not mentioned in the Soviet reports we have.[38]

It was reported that by 1100 (Moscow time) a company of the 94th Guards Rifle Division straddled the fork in the road east of Komintern, in order to maintain contact with the 107th Rifle Division, and that a single battalion at 1100 reached the eastern outskirts

37 The division suffered a total of 516 killed, 1,562 wounded and 681 missing from 5 July through 16 July (Fond: 1264, Opis: 1, Delo: 9, page 144). Its reported losses for the 13th were 31 killed and 98 wounded and they were reported by regiment (5 killed and 10 wounded for the 283rd Guards Rifle Regiment, 10 killed and 50 wounded for the 286th Guards Rifle Regiment and 16 killed and 38 wounded for the 288th Guards Rifle Regiment). There are no indications of heavy losses of equipment on this day (Fond: 1264, Opis: 1, Delo: 9, pages 107–147).

Still, we do not think this count is correct. If we subtract from the aggregate casualty report covering 5 through 16 July all the daily casualty reports for this unit and the periodic casualty report covering the 7th through the 10th, we still end up with at least 250 additional casualties that are not accounted for by the daily and other periodic reports. The decline in unit strength figures over time also strongly indicate that the unit suffered at least as many losses from 5 through 16 July as reported in the aggregate report, and maybe more. Therefore, we strongly suspect that the 94th Guards Rifle Division casualty reports for this day do not completely report the situation, especially as they do not report missing.

38 In the Sixty-ninth Army 0700 report for 13 July it states that the division was occupying defensive positions from Mazikino to along the eastern slope of the Razumnoye to the ravine two kilometers northwest of Sheino to the center of Ushakovo. It also states that "The division was not active" (Fond: Sixty-ninth Army, Opis: 10753, Delo: 133, page 22).

of Melikhovo without serious opposition. The division, in order to maintain contact with the Seventh Guards Army, moved a rifle battalion to height 210.3 and the northern edge of the grove west of that height.

During the morning, the order arrived that the 7th Panzer Division was to support the 6th Panzer Division attack with a regimental group. Movement to their jump-off positions was delayed by unfavorable terrain and Soviet action. The jump-off positions were finally reached at 1615. Meanwhile, the 168th Infantry Division was ordered to relieve Battle Group Glaesemer in the afternoon.

The attack of this reinforced regimental group from Rzhavets over Vyipolzovka to the northeast was unsuccessful despite "basic preparation." Flanking fire from the heights west of the Donets halted the attack. Strong Soviet air attacks hit the approach routes and the assembly areas in an effort to disrupt the march and destroy the vehicle concentrations. The division suffered heavy personnel and vehicle casualties.

It is claimed that there was also fighting this morning in and around Avdeyevka, but it is hard to sort out what occurred. It appears that a column from the 12th Guards Mechanized Brigade, consisting of two tank companies from the 55th Guards Tank Regiment, the 1st Motorized Rifle Battalion, a battery of 76mm guns, a company of 120mm mortars and an antitank rifle platoon moved out toward Avdeyevka at 2200 the previous night. This column reached the village of Avdeyevka at dawn and became engaged in a fight. Hard to say what occurred after that, as the Soviet-era accounts appear to be inflated (28 German tanks and assault guns claimed by one company).[39]

In the area was the 107th Rifle Division, deployed from Sviridovo down the Razumnaya gully to Gremyachye to Lomovo to Ploskoye. The 107th Rifle Division was claimed to have repulsed an attack by 15 tanks and a company of automatic riflemen from Shukhovtsevo. The division only reported ten casualties this day although we suspect this is low.[40] The 305th Rifle Division was also in the area. It regrouped during the night and by 0700 on 13 July had consolidated along the line of Aleksandrovka to Sviridovo. As of 1900 it was defending along the line from Aleksandrovka to Sviridovo to Podsumki to Alekseyevka to Ploskoye. Part of this line was back on the Koren River. The Sixty-ninth Army stated that the 305th Rifle Division did not fight during the day.

Air Support

The 168th Infantry Division reported strong Russian bombing and strafing attacks during the night, concentrating on the Kazachye-Rzhavets area and on the front line between Dalnyaya Igumenka and the Komintern bridge.

The 19th Panzer Division reported that in the evening of 12 July and during the night there were heavy Soviet air attacks. There was heavy Soviet close air support all day. There was some German fighter and reconnaissance activity.

The 6th Panzer Division described Soviet air activity as "overwhelming," with bombing and strafing. These attacks were concentrated over Kazachye, which resulted in heavy German losses. The Tiger battalion at Rzhavets reported being attacked by friendly aircraft, which caused heavy losses of men and materiels. The 53rd Guards Tank Regiment (Trufanov's detachment) reported that German aircraft launched a series of strikes.

The 7th Panzer Division reported strong Soviet air attacks on its approach routes and the assembly areas.

39 Zamulin, *Demolishing the Myth*, pages 478–479, provides this account drawn from Soviet-era secondary sources.

40 The division reported a total of 596 casualties between the 9th and 20th while reporting strengths of 8,342 and 188 civilians for the 5th, 8,130 for the 10th and 7,533 and 184 civilians for the 15th (Fond: 1296, Opis: 1, Delo: 52, pages 125, 127, 129, 132 & 135). This is a decline in strength of 813 military personnel and civilians. Or the division had a strength of 7,128 on the 15th with losses of 934 by then (Fond: 906, Opis: 1: Delo: 211, pages 204, 235, 239, 244, 245, 249). We do not know what specific days the casualties occurred but doubt that only 10 casualties occurred on this day (13 July).

Gostishchevo II, 13 July 1943

DURATION One day FRONTAGE 6.0 kilometers TERRAIN Rolling, mixed
WEATHER Cloudy, windy, cool; some rain in the afternoon. Temperature at noon: 19 degrees Celsius. Roads passable.

	Attacker	*Defender*
Units	281st Rgt/93rd Gds Rifle Division	417th Inf Rgt/168th Infantry Division
Attachments	None	None
Strength	3,011	4,649
Armor	0	0
Artillery	23	36
Air Sorties	0	0
Casualties	848 (130 KIA, 718 WIA)	115 (18 KIA, 94 WIA, 3 MIA)
Artillery losses	8	0
Enemy Captured	0	N/A

Note: The Soviet attack probably had more weight to it than the one regiment (1/3rd of a division) shown.

The XXXV Guards Rifle Corps' war diary recorded two German mass air raids in the areas of Vyipolzovka and Aleksandrovka with the participation of up to 250 Ju-86 and Ju-88 bombers. These counts are probably overstated. One of these attacks at 1600 killed the 55th Guards Tank Regiment commander with a bomb fragment.[41]

A Question of Direction

At this point, one must really question the purpose and direction of the III Panzer Corps' operations. It had gotten one infantry regiment of the 168th Infantry Division across the Severnyii Donets, only to leave it insufficiently supported by peeling off its other two infantry regiments to support the III Panzer Corps right flank. As such, the 168th Infantry Division was not able to hold Gostishchevo on the 13th. Furthermore, even though they had established a series of useful bridgeheads around Ryindinka they only occupied them with one panzer division. Instead, the other two panzer divisions seemed to be committed, along with the Tiger battalion, to continuing to push to the northeast. While this push was certainly distracting, and had attracted the attention of parts of the V Guards Mechanized Corps, it was not leading the corps in a direction that protected the flank of the Fourth Panzer Army. The way to do that would have been either to roll up the Donets triangle from the south (meaning through Gostishchevo) or to push from Ryindinka to Shakhovo and then up that road to Prokhorovka (some 18 kilometers north of Shakhovo). Either action, or both together, if successful, would have cleared the Donets triangle and finally freed up the German units tied down on the flank of the SS Panzer Corps.

As it was, by the time the III Panzer Corps was in

41 Zamulin, *Demolishing the Myth*, pages 479–480. The plane count is probably exaggerated as the VIII Air Corps flew at total of 239 Stuka sorties and 60 bombing sorties this day, and there were multiple missions flown in support of all three attacking German panzer corps.

Defense Line along the Razumnaya, 13 July 1943

DURATION One day FRONTAGE 17.5 kilometers TERRAIN Rolling, mixed
WEATHER Cloudy, windy, cool; some rain in the afternoon. Temperature at noon: 19 degrees Celsius. Roads passable.

	Attacker	*Defender*
Units	None	168th Infantry Division (less 417th Inf Rgt)
Attachments		See below
Strength	0	10,784
Armor	0	6
Artillery	0	81
Air Sorties	25 Night	0
Casualties	0	4 (1 KIA, 3 WIA)
Enemy Captured	0	N/A

Forces Engaged

German Attachments
2/228th StuG Bn
lt Bty/I/61st AA Rgt
I/38th Flak Rgt (attached on the 13th)

Still detached from the division
248th Engineer Bn (less 3 cos) (included)
429th Infantry Rgt (less 1 Bn) (included)

position to help the SS Panzer Corps, it was too late. The Adolf Hitler's attack was stalled on the 11th, Totenkopf's attack stalled on the 13th, and only Das Reich was in position to conduct further attacks to the south of Prokhorovka. Still, an advance by the III Panzer Corps on Shakhovo would have helped this attack, but at this stage, even that advance was behind schedule. The real loss of momentum to the SS Panzer Corps attack started on the 6th when Totenkopf had to deploy the majority of its forces to protect the flank and could no longer participate in the attack forward. For the III Panzer Corps to have been really useful to the SS Panzer Corps, it meant that they had to cross the Severnyii Donets by the 6th or 7th, so as to begin forcing the Soviet units opposite Totenkopf to start withdrawing. In this way, the SS Panzer Corps could have maintained all three of their SS divisions pushing forward. Needless to say, the III Panzer Corps was never near that goal.

Although the III Panzer Corps had finally crossed the Donets, the forces it mostly fought were the forces of the Seventh Guards Army. As such, its attack kept this army from being stripped to reinforce the Sixth Guards Army's defense. It drew four of the five divisions of the Sixty-ninth Army and at times one or two divisions from the Sixth Guards Army. It also drew two of the three divisions of the XXXV Guards Rifle Corps to its sector and eventually all three divisions on the 13th. It drew the majority of the V Guards Mechanized Corps from Rotmistrov's reinforcements. So, it did help contribute to the Fourth Panzer Army's attack by drawing attention to itself, but it fundamentally failed in its primary mission, which was to protect the flank of the Fourth Panzer Army. Furthermore, this failed mission was conducted at considerable cost, as these three divisions were the hardest hit of the nine German armored divisions sent into the attack. In the end, the III Panzer Corps could have been more helpful in the overall attack plan and it took unnecessary casualties.

The Fight for the Bridgeheads, 13 July 1943

DURATION One day FRONTAGE 7.8 kilometers TERRAIN Rolling, mixed

WEATHER Gloomy, windy, sometimes rainy in the afternoon. Temperature at noon: 19 degrees Celsius. Roads passable.

	Attacker	*Defender*
Units	19th PzD	81st GRD, 89th GRD, 26th GTB & 11th GMB
Attachments	See below	See below
Strength	16,488	17,402
Armor	37 (5 light)	74 (21 light)
Artillery	129	103
Air Sorties	40	63 + 25 Night
Casualties	34 (4 KIA, 29 WIA, 1 MIA)	1,007 (215 KIA, 505 WIA, 287 MIA)[42]
Armor losses	7	10
Artillery losses	0	6
Enemy Captured	N/A	2

Forces Engaged

German Attachments
70th Engineer Bn
2/411th Bridge Column B
842nd Bridge Column J

52nd Werfer Rgt

I/61st Flak Rgt (less 1 battery)

429th Infantry Rgt (168th ID), less I Battalion (not included)
I/114th Panzer Grenadier Rgt (from 6th PzD)—attached on the 13th (not included)

Detached
ObsBty/19th Artillery Rgt (included)

Soviet Forces
81st Guards Rifle Division
89th Guards Rifle Division
26th Guards Tank Brigade
+ 2 Churchills from 47th Gds Tank Regiment
11th Guards Mechanized Brigade

---

42 Soviet losses were clearly high this day with the 11th Guards Mechanized Brigade reporting 414 casualties (Fond: 332, Opis: 1943, Delo: 80, pages 14–17). The 89th Guards Rifle Division provided only a cumulative casualty report on the 13th which served as the basis for our estimate losses for this day (Fond: 1252, Opis: 1, Delo: 60, page 223). The 81st Guards Rifle Division estimated losses are also based upon cumulative casualty reports this day. The 81st Guards Rifle Division may not have even been seriously engaged this day. German losses were clearly low during this period with the 19th Panzer Division reports on 1,728 casualties from the 5th through the 9th, and 2,118 casualties (266 killed, 1758 wounded, 94 missing) for the 5th through the 20th. This is a difference of 390 and an average of 35 casualties a day from the 10th through the 20th.

The 6th Panzer Division Pushes Northeast, 13 July 1943

DURATION One day FRONTAGE 9.6 kilometers TERRAIN Rolling, mixed
WEATHER Cloudy, windy, cool. Temperature at noon: 19 degrees Celsius. Road conditions good.

	Attacker	*Defender*
Units	6th PzD	92nd Guards Rifle Division, 12th GMB & Trufanov's detachment
Attachments	See below	See below
Strength	21,716	12,577
Armor	60 (4 light)	77 (20 light)
Artillery	139	75
Air Sorties	28	63 + 12 Fratricidal + 25 Night
Casualties	109 (19 KIA, 89 WIA,1 MIA)	213 (58 KIA, 116 WIA, 39 MIA)
Armor losses	12	17
Artillery losses	2	3
Enemy Captured	N/A	0

Forces Engaged

German Attachments
II/62nd Artillery Rgt
II/54th Werfer Rgt
III/54th Werfer Rgt
Hq/54th Werfer Rgt

II/43rd Flak Rgt
lt Bn/91st Flak Rgt
204th Intelligence Troop (not included)

228th StuG Bn (less 2nd company)
503rd Heavy Panzer Bn—attached on the 13th (included)

Detached
ObsBty/76th Artillery Rgt (included)
I/114th Panzer Grenadier Rgt—detached on the 13th (included)

Soviet Forces
92nd Guards Rifle Division
315th Guards Mortar Regiment—attached on the 13th (included)
96th Tank Brigade
12th Guards Mechanized Brigade
Trufanov's detachment

The continued problem of each armored corps commander effectively heading off and conducting his own private war further weakened the effectiveness of the German offensive. As such, there were times, with nine armored divisions in action, when the Germans were really only able to use about four of them to maintain the forward momentum of the offensive, while the rest were involved in either protecting the flank or conducting "headhunting" expeditions on the flank.

As it was, the III Panzer Corps attack was now pushing northeast past Rzhavets up the length of the Severnyii Donets. This was further defining the Donets triangle, and creating a massive defensive feature that could be attacked with considerable loss to the Soviet Army. So, in this sense, the III Panzer Corps operations had become better directed towards causing Soviet casualties than they were towards helping the Fourth Panzer Army achieve a breakthrough.

The 94th Guards Rifle Division Attacks, 13 July 1943

DURATION One day FRONTAGE 4.3 kilometers TERRAIN Rolling, mixed

WEATHER Cool, windy and cool. Temperature at noon: 19 degrees Celsius. Roads passable.

	Attacker	*Defender*
Units	94th Guards & 107th Rifle Divisions	7th PzD
Attachments	See below	See below
Strength	17,085	17,196
Armor	0	51 (4 light)
Artillery	144	143
Air Sorties	62 + 25 Night	39
Casualties	474 (40 KIA, 157 WIA, 277 MIA)	18 (3 KIA, 15 WIA)
Armor losses	0	10
Artillery losses	12	0
Enemy Captured	1 (by the 305th RD)	200

Forces Engaged

German Attachments
9th Bridge Column B
1/505st Bridge Column B
843rd Bridge Column J

99th Flak Rgt Staff
I/38th Flak Rgt—detached on the 13th (not included)
II/38th Flak Rgt

I/54th Werfer Rgt
II/54th Werfer Rgt—detached on the 12th (included)

Detached
ObsBty/78th Artillery Rgt (included)
Regimental Group (included)

Soviet Forces
94th Guards Rifle Division
107th Rifle Division
  496th Mortar Rgt
  123rd ATR Bn
  130th ATR Bn

III Panzer Corps Assets
601st Engineer Rgt Staff
674th Engineer Rgt Staff
925th Bridge Construction Staff
127th Engineer Bn (less 1 co)
531st Bridge Construction Bn
110th Bridge Column B
602nd Bridge Column B
co/538th Road Construction Bn

153rd Flak Rgt Staff

3rd Command of Artillery
612th Artillery Rgt Staff
II/62nd Artillery Rgt
II/71st Artillery Rgt
857th Heavy Artillery Rgt
Pn/13th Light Observations Battery
ObsBty/19th Artillery Rgt (19th PzD)
ObsBty/76th Artillery Rgt (6th PzD)

2nd Fuel Column Troop
545th Panzer Recovery Platoon
Hq/503rd Heavy Panzer Bn—detached to the troops on the 13th
1st co/503rd Heavy Panzer Bn—detached to the troops on the 13th
2nd co/503rd Heavy Panzer Bn—detached to the troops on the 13th
3rd co/503rd Heavy Panzer Bn—detached to the troops on the 13th
Regimental Group (from 7th PzD)

CHAPTER TWELVE

Aftermath of Prokhorovka

13 JULY 1943

> July 12, 1943 along the Belgorod axis will enter the history of the Great Patriotic War as the day of the bloodiest and most bitter collision of tanks, infantry and aviation ever seen by man. This was the most tense day, when two huge forces collided: the crack fascist units and units of the Fifth Guards Tank Army.
>
> MAJOR GENERAL BAKHAROV OR HIS STAFF
> XVIII TANK CORPS, 1943[1]

The Battle of Prokhorovka was not the "death ride" of the panzers. It was not a giant swirling tank battle. It was not a decisive defeat for the German Army. Regardless of the casualties, it was not a decisive defeat for the Soviet Army. There were not 400 German tanks left destroyed on the field of battle and certainly not 100 Tigers. It was not a German victory that would have resulted in the Soviet Army collapsing, given one more decisive push. It was a bloody and unnecessary slaughter for the Soviets that wasted lives and resources on pointless counterattacks. Rolling over to the defense would have done the task at much less human cost.

On the 12th, across the entire front, the Soviets lost some 21,277 men (4,829 killed, 12,900 wounded, and 3,548 missing). The Germans on that day lost 2,702 (487 killed, 2,129 wounded, and 86 missing). This was a 7.88-to-1 exchange ratio in favor of the Germans. This was certainly the best exchange ratio they had for any day of the battle. See Table 12.1 for the total casualties since the start of the offensive.

The cost in killed and missing (complete losses) was even more significant. See Table 12.2.

In armor losses one sees the same pattern. See Table 12.3.

In the air, there was a different pattern, as the Soviets did their heavy attacking in the first three days of the offensive. See Table 12.4.

On the ground, the German attack was halted. The two infantry corps had no further role to play in the battle. The LII Corps' three divisions were simply unable to make any significant progress or support the German armored attack any more than they already had. On the right flank, Corps Raus, although not spread nearly as thin, was in the same situation with its three divisions.

This left the task of further advance to the three armored corps. Of those, the XLVIII Panzer Corps still had some play. The 3rd Panzer Division was pretty much engaged in covering the flank, but still had 63

1 "Account of XVIII Tank Corps' Combat Activities, July 12–24, 1943" (Fond: XVIII TC, Opis: 1, Delo: 48, Page: 10).

Table 12.1
Soviet vs German Casualty Ratio

	Soviet Casualties	*German Casualties*	*Ratio*
5th	10,745	6,368	1.69 to 1
6th	9,597	3,939	2.44 to 1
7th	8,720	3,223	2.71 to 1
8th	9,321	2,911	3.20 to 1
9th	9,106	2,647	3.44 to 1
10th	9,639	1,850	5.21 to 1
11th	8,657	2,308	3.75 to 1
12th	21,277	2,702	7.88 to 1
13th	11,551	1,869	6.18 to 1
Total	98,613	27,817	3.55 to 1

Table 12.2
Killed and Missing

Date	*Soviet Killed & Missing*	*German Killed & Missing*	*Ratio*
5th	6,217	1,243	5.00 to 1
6th	5,424	765	7.09 to 1
7th	4,436	575	7.71 to 1
8th	4,231	598	7.08 to 1
9th	4,495	551	8.16 to 1
10th	4,765	344	13.85 to 1
11th	3,971	413	9.62 to 1
12th	8,377	573	14.62 to 1
13th	4,335	351	12.35 to 1
Total	46,251	5,413	8.54 to 1

Table 12.3
Soviet vs German Tank Losses

	Soviet Tank Losses	*German Tank Losses*	*Ratio*
4th	0	4	—
5th	92	251	0.37 to 1
6th	244	276	0.88 to 1
7th	189	167	1.13 to 1
8th	380	117	3.25 to 1
9th	293	162	1.81 to 1
10th	148	54	2.74 to 1
11th	152	93	1.65 to 1
12th	416	122	3.41 to 1
13th	141	81	1.74 to 1
Total	2,055	1,327	1.55 to 1

Table 12.4
Soviet vs German Air Losses

	Soviet Air Losses	*German Air Losses*	*Ratio*
4th	4	3	1.3 to 1
5th	187	19	9.8 to 1
6th	79	7	11.3 to 1
7th	87	10	8.7 to 1
8th	61	5	12.2 to 1
9th	46	11	4.2 to 1
10th	25	3	8.3 to 1
11th	19	14	1.4 to 1
12th	31	11	2.8 to 1
13th	28	5	5.6 to 1
Total	567	88	6.4 to 1

percent of its tank strength and 97 percent of its personnel strength.[2] As Westhoven had carefully preserved this division, it was still very much combat capable, but its role was certainly going to be reduced to covering the left flank of the advance, once the advance could get going. At this point, it and the Gross Deutschland Division were still tangled up with the Soviet forces on

2 According the Kursk Data Base, on 4 July it had 77 tanks, 14 Marders and 2 Sturmgeschuetz IIIs, on 13 July it had 48 tanks, 10 Marders and 1 Sturmgeschuetz III.

that flank and the plan to get the Gross Deutschland moved back so it could attack north on the 12th had been canceled amid the Soviet counterattacks on that day. As of the 13th, they still had not relocated and any participation in further forward advance would have to occur on the 14th or later.

The 11th Panzer Division, without the support of the Gross Deutschland, was not going to move forward. In fact, they were having a hard time hanging onto Kochetovka and keeping their right flank secure. The XLVIII Panzer Corps attack was clearly stalled and was not going to be able to go forward until forces were repositioned. Even then, in light of the Soviet forces facing it, it was very questionable whether any real forward progress could be made.

In the case of the SS Panzer Corps, the Adolf Hitler SS Division was stopped cold. It had to wait until Totenkopf could free up the Soviet defensive positions by flanking them. Yet the Totenkopf SS Division on the 13th had been rolled back and at a considerable cost in armor. In its three days of attacking, its overall armor strength dropped from 116 tanks on the evening of the 10th to 77 tanks by the evening of the 13th.[3] The Totenkopf attack had clearly failed. The Das Reich was also limited to local attacks, although it was planning something more ambitious for the 14th. In many senses, the SS Panzer Corps situation was similar to the XLVIII Panzer Corps, which is that they could still attack, and with proper preparation make some progress, but there was a very limited chance of a breakthrough or even causing any significant casualties. The best way these two corps could inflict casualties was to continue working on the flanking positions, where the Soviet forces were still somewhat out of position. But this did not do much for any forward progress. Basically, the German attack had failed.

The III Panzer Corps was clearly weakened. Their mobile elements were down to 34 percent of their armor strength and 92 percent of their personnel strength.[4] While they were working on creating a dangerous trap in the Donets triangle, they had not broken the second defensive line of the Seventh Guards Army. Furthermore, they were still some 20 kilometers south of Prokhorovka, and had only just established bridgeheads across the Severnyii Donets. As such, while there were still some offensive opportunities for this force as they now had all three panzer divisions back in action, the overall weakness of the force and its independent and isolated operations resulted in this force being only a limited threat.

Overall, with or without the Battle of Prokhorovka, the German attack had failed, although it had not yet stalled. This battle was not over, for there was still a large tangled fight in the west around Tolstoye Woods and a large salient, which this author has dubbed the Donets triangle, pushed between the SS Panzer Corps and III Panzer Corps on the other flank.

Zhukov Arrives

Zhukov stated that he was called by Stalin on 12 July at the Bryansk command center and ordered to fly to the Prokhorovka area, "where a fierce tank battle was in progress."[5] Zhukov was supposed to study the situation and take over the coordination of the Voronezh and Steppe Fronts.

Marshal Zhukov arrived at the staff of the Voronezh Front's Sixty-ninth Army, where General I. S. Konev, the commander of the Steppe Front, also was. Apparently, Konev's presence there irked Zhukov, who stated in one of the restored passages to his memoirs that they

3 According to the Kursk Data Base, on the 10th there were 84 tanks, including 3 Tigers, 21 Sturmgeschuetz IIIs, and 11 Marders. On the 13th there were 55 tanks, including 1 Tiger, 20 Sturmgeschuetzes, and only 2 Marders. There were also 6 Hummels and 12 Wespes throughout this time.

4 This includes only the four divisions and the attached Tiger and assault gun battalions. It does not include the attached artillery, antiaircraft, engineers, headquarters, and other units, which were considerable. Armor strength declined from 396 to 133. It does not include the 18 self-propelled artillery pieces they had.

5 It is unknown whether this is Zhukov's description of the battle or his paraphrasing of Stalin. See Georgi K. Zhukov, *Marshal Zhukov's Greatest Battles* (Harper & Row, Publishers, New York and Evanston, 1969), pages 240–241.

[Konev and others] knew he had already been entrusted with command of both fronts.[6] The Sixty-ninth Army's headquarters had remained well to the rear, at Korocha, throughout the battle.

That evening, Zukov met there with Marshal Vasilevskii, familiarized himself with the situation, and expressed his "complete agreement" with the steps that Vasilevskii had taken. Vasilevskii had been instructed by Stalin to drive down to the Southwestern Front so that he could organize their counteroffensive in conjunction with the upcoming Voronezh and Steppe Front offensive.[7] Again, Stalin was shuffling the senior military commanders.

Stalin's Phone Call

In the summer of 1964, Colonel Fyodor Sverdlov had to accompany, on a trip to Leningrad, the Deputy Minister of Defense and Main Marshal of Tank Troops, Pavel Alekseyevich Rotmistrov. Colonel Sverdlov was in the neighboring train compartment which, as it turned out, he was sharing with two ladies. So as to give the ladies some privacy, he ended up standing out in the passageway. General Rotmistrov saw the Colonel and invited him into his private two-bed train compartment for tea. Drinking cup after cup of hot tea as the train rolled through the night, Rotmistrov told Colonel Sverdlov about his experiences during the war. As Colonel Sverdlov tells the story:[8]

I asked him which successful battle did he consider the most important. He replied that, of course, it was the meeting engagement at Prokhorovka, during the Battle of Kursk, on July 12, 1943. This was the largest tank battle of the Second World War. "I was then in command of the Fifth Guards Tank Army, along with two attached tank corps, which routed the main fascist tank group, which was aimed at Kursk, and which put a victorious finish on the defensive battle," he said. "The Hitlerites lost 400 tanks and self-propelled guns, including 100 Tigers created specially for this operation. After this battle they were forced to renounce further offensives, as their entire strategic plan for the summer of 1943 was foiled. Thus our tank army effectively carried out its strategic task. To be sure, our losses were no less than the Germans. Of course you don't know that, nor does anyone else."

Here Rotmistrov made a lengthy pause and smiled mysteriously. "But now, 20 years after the war, I can tell you that when Stalin found out about our losses he went into a rage. He called me during the day on July 13 and said, 'I gave you a tank army for a counteroffensive so that you could take Kharkov, and here you've gone and lost half an army. For that I'm going to relieve you of your command and maybe put you on trial, too.' The chief of the General Staff, Marshal Vasilevskii, saved me. The next day he reported to Stalin the true situation. Stalin calmed down a bit and didn't return to the question again, but he never forgave anything. General Vatutin, the Front commander, recommended me for the Order of Suvorov, 1st class, but I did not receive it; but that's not important. After a series of major victories, our Fifth Guards Tank Army successfully attacked in the summer of 1944 in Byelorussia and Lithuania and participated in the liberation of Minsk and Vilnius. The army only included all of two tank corps, because Stalin wouldn't give us the third one, although I asked him several times. But Stalin considered that the pace of our offensive was insufficiently rapid and relieved me of my command. Like I said, he never forgave anything and forgot nothing. I was the commander of Soviet tank

6 Zhukov, 11th edition, page 55. This hinted-at friction between Konev and Zhukov and the fact that the meeting occurred at the Sixty-ninth Army headquarters, vice Front headquarters, was removed from earlier editions of Zhukov's memoirs.

7 Georgii K. Zhukov, *Marshal Zhukov's Greatest Battles*, pages 240–241.

8 This story comes from three sources: a conversation between Christopher A. Lawrence, Richard Harrison and Col. Fyodor Sverdlov in late October 1993; a letter written at my request by him to Richard Harrison on 21 November 1993; and his book, F. D. Sverdlov, *Neizvestnoye o Sovetskikh Polkovodtsakh* [Unknown Facts about Soviet Captains] (Moscow, 1995), page 56. The quoted section is from his letter of 21 November 1993.

troops in Germany and later became an assistant to the Minister of Defense and was awarded the rank of Main Marshal of Tank Troops. Stalin has been dead for ten years, but an unmerited hurt is not forgotten."

Rotmistrov was quiet for a moment, then said, "I've gotten upset again. It's best to get to bed."

The Creation of the Myth

It is not known what Stalin was told by Vasilevskii on the 14th, nor is it known if the Soviet command team realized how poorly they had fared relative to their opponents. Left with only official memoirs, it is hard to tell if the commanders felt at the end of the day that they had indeed achieved a decisive victory, or had the uneasy feeling that they had suffered too many losses, or realized that they had just sent large numbers of their own men to oblivion for little gain. Obviously Stalin had the gut feeling that the operations had been wasteful.

Still, Rotmistrov was not the most senior commander in the Prokhorovka area. The decision to attack was made in conjunction with Vatutin and Vasilevskii, their chiefs of staff, and Khrushchev and the other political commissars. If Rotmistrov's actions were deserving of dismissal and trial, then might not Vatutin, Vasilevskii, and Khrushchev also share in this responsibility? As seen through the purges, trials could result in the severest of punishment and the events and associations in one's past could come back much later as incriminating evidence in someone else's trial. Being part of a failed operation had many potential repercussions.

One cannot help wondering if a few details of the battle were swept under the rug for the sake of protecting Rotmistrov, his commanders, and everyone associated with them.

One must understand and appreciate the practice of the military arts under Stalin. Starting in 1937, Stalin had, as a matter of "policy" managed to arrest and in most cases execute almost 75 percent of the Soviet Army commanders of division or higher. This process slowed greatly after 1937, but in 1941, after the failures on the front, he had arrested and executed the Western Front commander, General of the Army Dmitrii Gregoryevich Pavlov, along with four other generals under his command or on his staff.[9] After 1941, the number of generals arrested and executed declined considerably, and no more major military figures were arrested during the war.[10]

Still, two years after the execution of Pavlov and only six years after the great purge, the fear of arrest was still very much present. As such, those in the Soviet officer corps were very interested in protecting themselves from arrest and it appears that as a result, the Soviet Army developed a habit of lying in its official reporting. It was necessary to do and was very much a part of their system.

Obviously, officers would not lie about things that could be easily checked, like the strength of their units, their losses, their location, etc. All these needed to

---

9 These were Major General V. E. Klimovskikh, Chief of Staff of the Western Front, Lt. General N. A. Klyich, Chief of Artillery of the Western Front, Major General A. T. Grigoryev, Chief of Signal Service of the Western Front and Major General A. A. Korobkov, commander of the Fourth Army.

10 Still, in 1941 some 27 Soviet generals were shot, including those who fought in 1941 and those who were arrested before the war. Source: A. A. Pechenkin, "Generals perished not only in battles," Nezavisimaya Gazeta [Independent Newspaper], 17 June 2005.

A list of generals that were arrested is provided by the website http://handbook.rkka.ru. Its list for 1937 repression includes 3 marshals (all executed or died in captivity), 15 army commanders (all executed or died in captivity), 66 corps commanders (62 executed or died in captivity), 168 division commanders (147 executed or died in captivity), and 338 brigade commanders (289 executed or died in captivity). Most of them were executed in 1937 and 1938. Two of the brigade commanders were returned to duty, deserted to the Germans during the war and were executed after the war by the Soviet Union.

It lists 94 general officers arrested during the war: 1 General of the Army (executed), two Colonel Generals (both executed), 20 Lieutenant Generals (16 executed or died in captivity), and 71 Major Generals (at least 53 executed or died in captivity). It appears, even though this list is not complete, that all of them were arrested in 1941 and most were executed in 1941 or during the first two months of 1942.

be reported so as to determine replacements, supply, combat strength, and so on. This data was needed for combat purposes and being something that could be easily confirmed, the records in these areas needed to be reasonably correct, and they do appear to be.

Where they could distort the record was in describing events and losses caused to the enemy. Both types of distortions regularly occur in Soviet records. This is seen in the many cases where the Soviet units claim they attacked, yet neither the unit nor the opposing German forces record any appreciable casualties, and at the end of the day, the opposing forces are in the same location.

This is also clearly seen in the Soviet claims of German losses, and a number of examples of this have already been provided. This is not to imply that other armies don't over claim enemy kills. It is a common occurrence, and all armies exaggerate the enemy strengths and losses to some extent. It is a common mistake in intelligence reports, and sometimes these exaggerations are by an order of magnitude. As such, no historian should rely on one side's claims of the enemy strength or losses. The unique aspect of the Soviet Army is the extent and consistency with which these exaggerations were done. It would appear that regardless of the situation, they almost always reported higher enemy losses than they suffered. For historians, this problem has been magnified by these claims being repeated as fact in Soviet-era secondary sources.

Therefore, it is understandable, due to the nature of the Soviet system and after Rotmistrov received his phone call from Stalin, that such a misrepresentation of the situation would occur. The only question is who started the legend.

The Battle of Prokhorovka was recorded in Rotmistrov's report of 30 September 1943. As can be seen from comparing the account excerpted below with the more modern-day accounts provided in Appendix VII of my book *Kursk: The Battle of Prokhorovka*, the statements, assumptions and errors in this report are reflected in further Soviet-era accounts. The report is titled "Fifth Guards Tank Army's Combat Activities from July 7–24, 1943," compiled 30 September 1943 by army commander Lt. General Rotmistrov and military council member Major General Grishin.[11] It states in part:

> The enemy, advancing on Oboyan, was hit hard in the area south of Ivnya and, having regrouped his forces, is trying to launch his main blow toward Prokhorovka, with the mission of bypassing Oboyan from the east and continuing on to Kursk. For this reason, the enemy has thrown in the Adolf Hitler Division and the SS divisions Death's Head, Das Reich, among others.
>
> The enemy is preparing a blow aimed at Prokhorovka. According to intelligence data, the enemy has gathered considerable tank, motorized infantry, artillery and mortar forces in this area.
>
> Seven armored divisions were operating in this area: 3rd, 11th, Gross Deutschland, Adolf Hitler, Death's Head, Das Reich, and another of unknown numerical designation.
>
> There are also four infantry divisions: 255th, 167th, 68th and a fourth of unknown numerical designation.
>
> Besides this, the 17th Panzer Division, "SS Viking" and 16th Motorized Infantry Division have arrived from the south.
>
> Overall, the enemy had up to 1,000 tanks. Of these, 150–200 were Tigers. There was also a large amount of artillery, mortars, among which were up to three regiments of nebelwerfers.
>
> Directly against the army the enemy had 700–800 tanks from the Gross Deutschland, Adolf Hitler, Das Reich, 6th, 11th and 19th Panzer Divisions, supported by a large number of bomber aviation. . . .
>
> At 0830, following a short artillery preparation, the corps moved into the attack.
>
> As it was later learned, at the same time the German command also began an attack along this axis, launching his main blow along the railroad toward Prokhorovka, with the mission of taking Prokhorovka at all costs and to secure a springboard for a further attack on Kursk.

11 Fond: 332, Opis: 4948, Delo: 19, pages 5–21.

Thus an unusually large tank battle arose, in which there participated along a narrow section of the front on both sides more than 1,500 tanks, a huge amount of all types of artillery, mortars and aviation. . . .

The enemy also launched his main blow along the railroad toward Prokhorovka, hoping to break the resistance of our units and take Prokhorovka from the march. . . .

The enemy was hit hard by a counterattack from the Prokhorovka area and began to waver and look for a weaker spot in our line. The enemy, having made a breakthrough in the Vyipolzovka-Avdeyevka area, began to throw units in this direction, hoping to develop the offensive along the Severnyii Donets and reach the army's rear. A serious threat developed.

The timely arrival of General Trufanov's units stopped the enemy attack by the end of the day. . . .

The first stage of Fifth Guards Tank Army's offensive action may be considered to have been completed by the evening of July 14.

As a result of the army's offensive actions, the enemy suffered great losses and his offensive was halted; however, the enemy attempted to attack along his neighbor's sectors, where he had some success. As a result, part of the army's forces were thrown into the battle on the enemy's flanks, and until this fighting was completed, the army's center temporarily went over to the defensive, consolidating its achievements. The army's appearance was unexpected for the enemy, which was aided by the army's swift transfer from the Ostrogozhsk-Rossosh area to the battlefield.

The army's swift and well-organized concentration in the area was a surprise for the Germans.

Having taken a powerful blow, the Germans began to waver and search for weak spots. During July 13–14 they felt our weak spots. They began to attack our left flank in the Vyipolzovka-Avdeyevka-Bolshiye Podyarugi direction simultaneously.

They were able to trickle through the Fifth Guards Army's sector in the direction of Veselyii-to the northern outskirts of Polezhayev, but thanks to our timely measures all the enemy's attempts to turn the army's flanks were liquidated. . . .

During the July 12–16 period the army's troops inflicted huge personnel and material casualties on the enemy.

The army destroyed 552 tanks, of which 93 were Tigers; 45 artillery and 29 mortar batteries were suppressed, 769 troop and freight trucks were knocked out; 10 ammo dumps were blown up, and 55 aircraft were shot down. There were 15,620 men and officers destroyed.

The enemy, having suffered huge casualties, could do nothing but withdraw his troops to the Belgorod-Tomarovka defensive positions. . . .

In the course of 13 days the Fifth Guards Tank Army waged fierce actions with the enemy's choice tank and infantry divisions, and inflicted heavy personnel and material losses on him.

During all stages of the operations the army employed various operational-tactical forms of waging battle. The army, in developing an offensive plan, collided with an enemy who also was attacking with a mass of tanks and infantry, supported by a large amount of air power, which on some days carried out up to 1,500 sorties over our units.

On July 12 the greatest tank battle in the history of the Great Patriotic War took place, involving up to 1,500 tanks on both sides.

Having inflicted huge losses on the enemy in personnel and equipment and delayed the enemy's further advance, the army's units had to wage defensive battles in the space of a short time, beat off fierce enemy counterattacks and simultaneously attack along some sectors of the front. . . .

"Vatutin's After Battle Report to Stalin" appears to support these claims:

Rotmistrov's tank army, with II and II Guards Tank Corps, ran into a meeting engagement with the SS Panzer Corps and the 17th Panzer Division, which were moving towards Rotmistrov immediately south of Prokhorovka along a narrow front. As a result, a massive and bitter tank battle took place on a small field.

The enemy suffered a defeat here, but Rotmistrov also suffered casualties and did not advance. . . .

> Simultaneously, both Katukov and Chistyakov launched a series of attacks against the enemy's XLVIII Panzer Corps, causing him significant losses.
>
> The main enemy force, as a result of these battles, was utterly bled white and routed. On July 13 the enemy carried out weak attacks on the Prokhorovka, Oboyan and Ivnya axes, and on the 14th he went over to the defensive here and continued to be active only against Kryuchenkin. However, it was already clear that he had run out of stream against Kryuchenkin as well, and that his strength was at an end. . . .
>
> The enemy, in the fighting from July 4–22, lost the following
>
> killed and wounded—135,000
> planes shot down and knocked out—917
> [missing line in translation]
>
> It should be pointed out that a significant part of the knocked-out enemy tanks were quickly repaired. . . .
>
> The enemy, while withdrawing, left equipment on the field—guns and cars and other military hardware, for the most part, wrecked. He evacuated many knocked-out tanks and cars.[12]

It would appear that the myth of Prokhorovka was created by Rotmistrov, with the understanding, acquiescence, and support of his senior commanders. Rotmistrov would later rise to be a Chief of the Military Academy for Tank Troops from 1958 to 1964, Vasilevskii would rise to head the Ministry of Armed Forces of the USSR and later the Military Ministry of the USSR from 1949 to 1953, Zhukov would be Defense Minister from 1955 to 1957, and Khrushchev would head the Soviet Union from 1953 to 1964. Starting in 1965, the more conservative Brezhnev regime awarded Rotmistrov the Hero of the Soviet Union on 7 May and started the official celebrations of Victory Day on 9 May in the Soviet Union. Over time, the myth of Prokhorovka had become an established part of Soviet military history.

12 "Vatutin's After Battle Report to Stalin," pages 68–70.

Hitler Summons Manstein

On the 13th, Manstein and Kluge (Army Group Center) were summoned to Hitler's headquarters in East Prussia to discuss the offensive. Hitler opened the conference by announcing that the allies had landed in Sicily and that the situation had taken a serious turn. The Italians were not even attempting to fight and Sicily was likely to be lost. Since the next step might be a landing in the Balkans or Lower Italy, Hitler felt that he needed to form new armies there. He decided these forces must be found from the Eastern Front, so *Operation Citadel* would have to be discontinued. This was, of course, what Manstein had been worried about and why he had pressed for an early offensive.[13] In fact, the Allies had landed in southeast Sicily on the 9th and now had eight divisions ashore. They were facing two German armored divisions and ten, mostly poorly prepared, Italian divisions. They had captured the main port in the area, Syracuse, on 10 July and on the 11th, had defeated the counterattacks on the Americans by the two German armored divisions and one of the better Italian divisions. The Allies were now firmly established on the southern third of the island and were advancing.

Meanwhile, Kluge reported that his army was making no further progress and that he now had to divert mobile forces to halt Soviet attacks on the north side of the Orel bulge. Kluge felt that he could not continue *Citadel* or resume it at a later date.[14] In fact, any German progress in the north had effectively stalled on the 9th, and the Germans were stagnated in the fighting around Ponyiri. Furthermore, on the 12th, the Soviets had unleashed a counterattack on the north side of the bulge with the Western and Bryansk Fronts. This was a powerful attack by two Fronts, consisting of two armies, including two tank corps, from the Western Front, and three armies, including two tank corps, from the Bryansk Front. This attack would only get stronger over time as the forces now held in reserve and the forces from the Central Front joined in. At this point, Kluge's

13 Manstein, page 448.
14 Manstein, page 449.

offensive had come to a complete halt, and showed no prospects of it being able to make further progress. He was now in danger of his entire front collapsing. *Operation Citadel* had clearly failed because of the failure of the northern attack, and nothing that occurred in the south was going to change that. While Sicily was one reason Hitler gave for calling off the operation, it was not the reason for the failure of *Operation Citadel.*

On the other hand, Manstein felt that in his sector the battle was reaching its culminating point. He contended that breaking it off at this time would be "throwing victory away." He wanted to continue operations until the Soviet mobile reserves were completely defeated.[15]

Hitler, however, ruled that *Operation Citadel* be canceled due to the threats in the Mediterranean and the problem with Army Group Center, but he did allow Army Group South to continue attacking until it had destroyed the Soviet armor reserves.[16]

So, for the south, *Operation Citadel* continued, now mutated into a "headhunting" expedition. This would result in two major flanking battles, the battle of Tolstoye Woods on the left and the clearing of the Donets triangle on the right. These two battles had already begun when the conference in East Prussia was held on the 13th. In the case of Tolstoye Woods, the XLVIII Panzer Corps had been forced on the afternoon of the 12th to cancel their attack to the north and had started again attacking to the west. On the 13th these forces were now fully committed to the fighting on this flank. In the case of the Donets triangle, on the 13th, the Totenkopf attack around Prokhorovka had already stalled and the attack to clear up the triangle, which was necessary so as to attack Prokhorovka from the south, was about to begin. As such, the decisions made in the meeting on the 13th had no influence on the fighting on the ground through the 15th.

15 From Manstein, page 449. Below, page 174, states that Manstein was unconditionally in favor of continuing the attack, but Kluge doubted he could hold the Soviet attack and wanted the operation called off.

16 Manstein, page 449.

What these decisions would lead to is a change of focus after the 15th, from trying to attack forward to launching yet another attack to the west. This attack would be labeled *Operation Roland* and was scheduled to commence on the 18th.

The XXIV Panzer Corps is Activated

Also, Manstein's reserves were finally activated. At 1700 on the 9th, the Viking SS Panzer Grenadier Division and the 23rd Panzer Division of the XXIV Panzer Corps had been ordered to move up to Kharkov and were transferred on the 10th from command of the First Panzer Army to Army Group South. They were in place around Kharkov by 0300 on the 12th. As of 13 July, the Viking SS Division had 45 tanks, 6 Sturmgeschuetzes and 5 Marders, while the 23rd Panzer Division had 57 tanks and 7 assault guns. The 23rd Panzer Division was otherwise at strength but the already weak Viking SS Division, as of the 13th, still had a shortfall of 2,602 men.[17] At 0920, on 12 July, the units were ordered to move on the night of the 13th into the area of Belgorod.

There were now almost no other reserve forces available in Army Group South. Even though the army had a front of over 650 kilometers to cover, this was the entire effective collection of reserves available for the entire area. Committing the 198th Infantry Division and the XXIV Panzer Corps left the Germans with only the 17th Panzer Division and the 16th Motorized Infantry (now Panzer Grenadier) Division to back the remaining 600 or so kilometers of front. This was clearly too thin.

At 2220 on the 12th, march orders had been drawn up and issued. The units did not move until nighttime on the 13th. By 0530 on the 14th, the two divisions had not left the Kharkov area, with the Viking SS Division assembled in the area of Liptsyi-North Kharkov, and the 23rd Panzer Division assembled in the area of South Kharkov-Merefa.

17 See Chapter Three of my original book *Kursk: The Battle of Prokhorovka* for further details.

The 23rd Panzer Division during the night of the 14th had moved to the area south of Alekseyevka and was still there as of 2100 on the 15th. By 1315 on the 15th, the XXIV Panzer Corps headquarters had moved behind the XLVIII Panzer Corps. The Viking SS Division had moved into the area west of Belgorod.

At 2100 on the 15th the attack was canceled and the two divisions were ordered to march south under command of the First Panzer Army.[18] Manstein specifically complained in his memoirs about this force having been stopped, under orders from Hitler, from being used as part of his offensives.[19]

The Soviet Southwestern Front unleashed on the 17th of July the Izyum-Barvenkovo Offensive. This was not a small offensive, spearheaded by the First Guards and Eighth Guards Armies and supported by the XXIII Tank Corps, I Guards Mechanized Corps, and the Seventeenth Air Army. It was to be assisted from the east by Southern Front's Mius River Offensive, also started on the 17th and consisting initially of the Second Guards Army, the Fifth Shock Army, the Twenty-eighth Army, and supported by the II Guards and IV Guards Mechanized Corps.

The XXIV Panzer Corps' two divisions were redirected to the south. The Viking SS entered combat on the 18th of July, working with the 17th Panzer Division to halt the offensive in the First Panzer Army area. The 23rd Panzer Division was sent even farther south and entered battle on the 19th in the Sixth Army area. The 16th Panzer Grenadier Division, which was also in the area, had already been committed to this fight the day before.

Summary to Date

To briefly summarize the events to date in map form, we present four graphics. First is a Soviet era chart showing all the reinforcements for the Voronezh Front during the Battle of Kursk. The next two charts are the tank status charts for the 12th and 13th. Lastly we present a chart of all the armor losses for both sides, as recorded in the Kursk Data Base, for the 12th and 13th of July 1943.

18 Kriegstagebuch Nr. 2/43, Teil 1, Gen.Kdo. XXIV. Panzerkorps, page 49 (T314, R719, 000065). Some authors put the date earlier than this, for example see Glantz, *The Battle of Kursk*, page 245, where he states "As early as 14 July, Hitler had directed that the XXIV Panzer Corps be moved into reserve behind the First Panzer Army along the Northern Donets near Izyum."

19 Manstein, page 453.

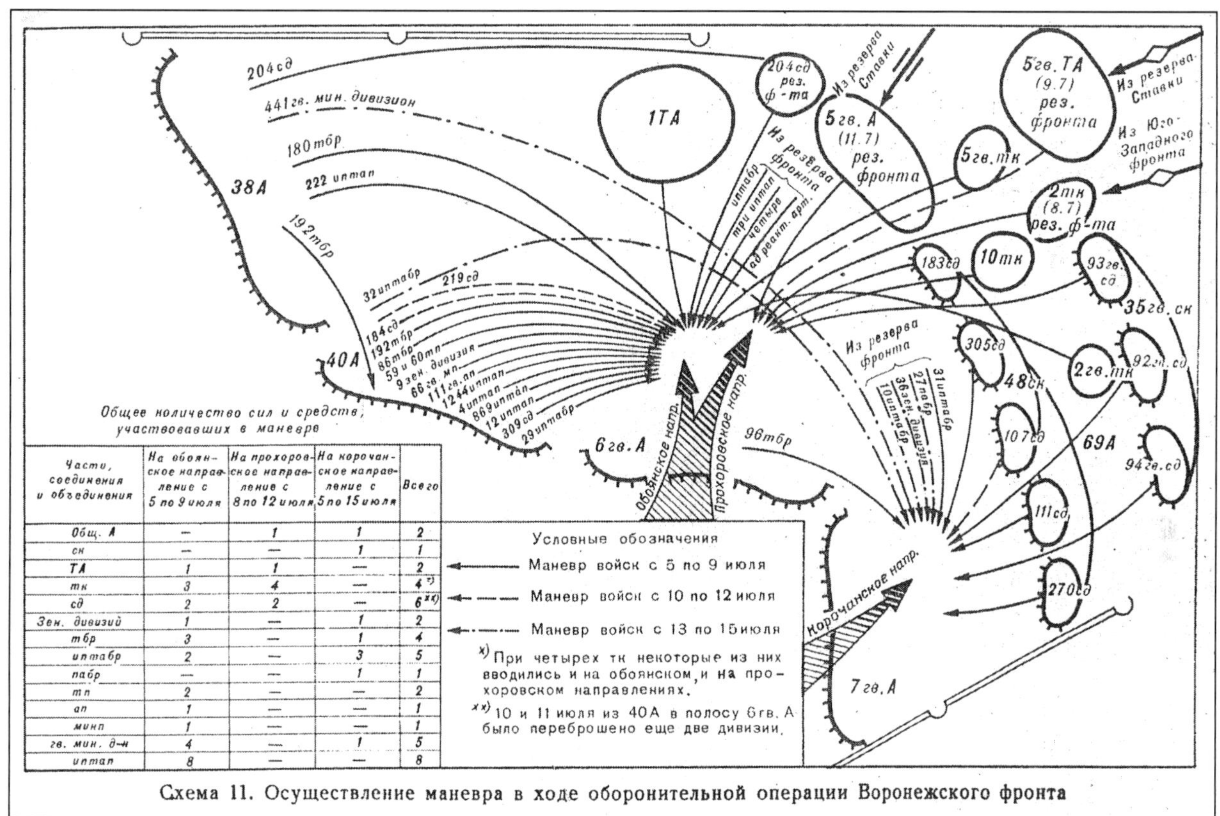

Части, соединения и объединения	На обоянское направление с 5 по 9 июля	На прохоровское направление с 8 по 12 июля	На корочанское направление с 5 по 15 июля	Всего
Общ. А	—	1	1	2
ск	—	—	1	1
ТА	1	1	—	2
тк	3	4	—	4 x)
сд	2	2	—	6 xx)
Зен. дивизий	1	—	1	2
тбр	3	—	1	4
иптабр	2	—	3	5
пабр	—	—	1	1
тп	2	—	—	2
ап	1	—	—	1
минп	1	—	—	1
гв. мин. д-н	4	—	1	5
иптап	8	—	—	8

Схема 11. Осуществление маневра в ходе оборонительной операции Воронежского фронта

Soviet reinforcements during the Battle of Kursk, as drawn from Soviet sources[20]

20 K. S. Kolganov, ed., *Razvitiye Taktiki Sovetskoi Armii v Godi Velikoi Otechestvennoi Voini (1941–1945 gg.)* [Evolution of Tactics of the Soviet Army during the years of the Great Patriotic War] (Voyenizdat, Moscow, 1958), page 873.

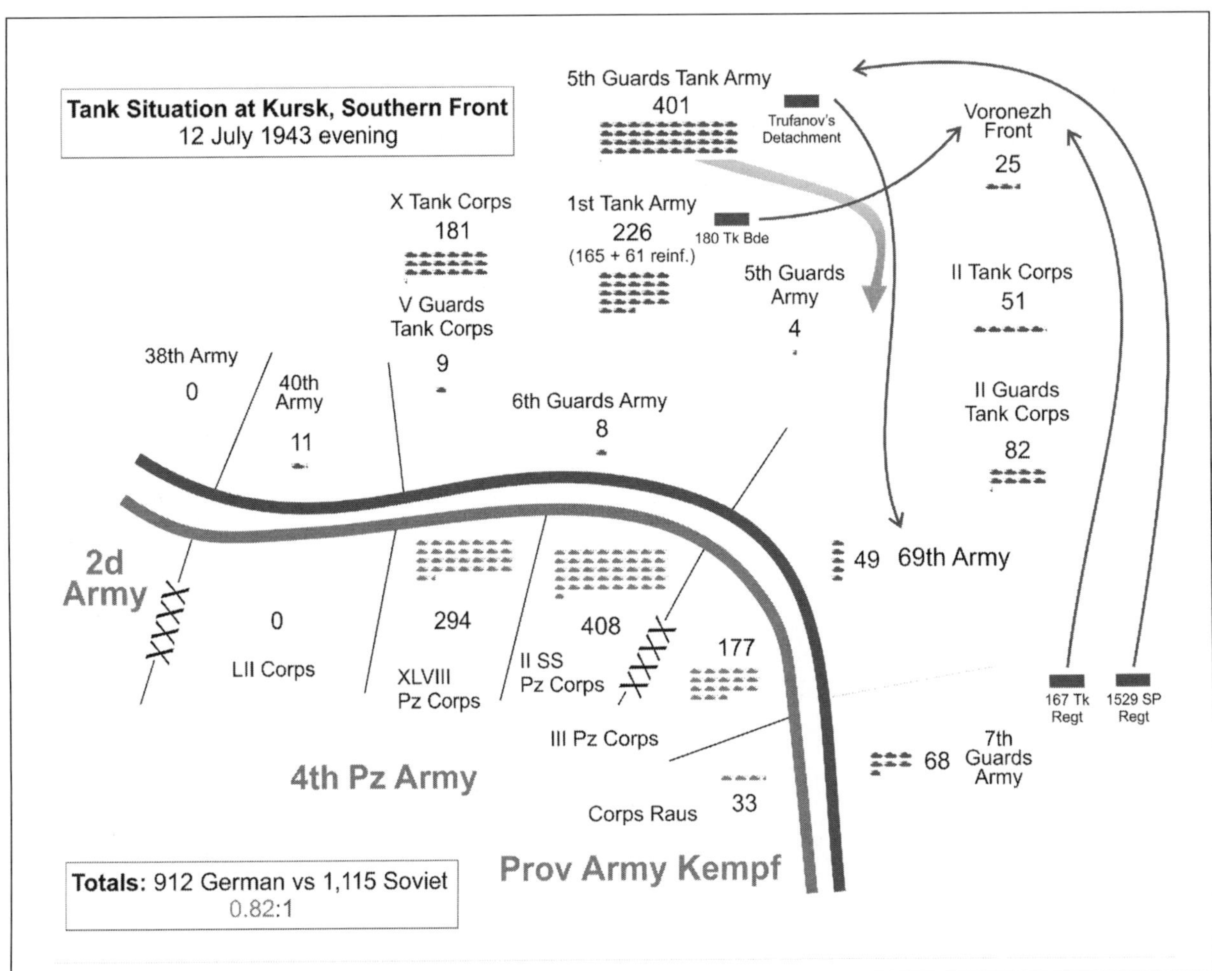

Tank Situation at Kursk, Southern Front
12 July 1943 evening
5th Guards Tank Army
401
Trufanov's Detachment
Voronezh Front
25
X Tank Corps
181
1st Tank Army
226
(165 + 61 reinf.)
180 Tk Bde
5th Guards Army
4
II Tank Corps
51
V Guards Tank Corps
9
38th Army
0
40th Army
11
6th Guards Army
8
II Guards Tank Corps
82
49
69th Army
2d Army
0
LII Corps
294
XLVIII Pz Corps
408
II SS Pz Corps
177
III Pz Corps
167 Tk Regt
1529 SP Regt
68
7th Guards Army
4th Pz Army
33
Corps Raus
Prov Army Kempf
Totals: 912 German vs 1,115 Soviet
0.82:1

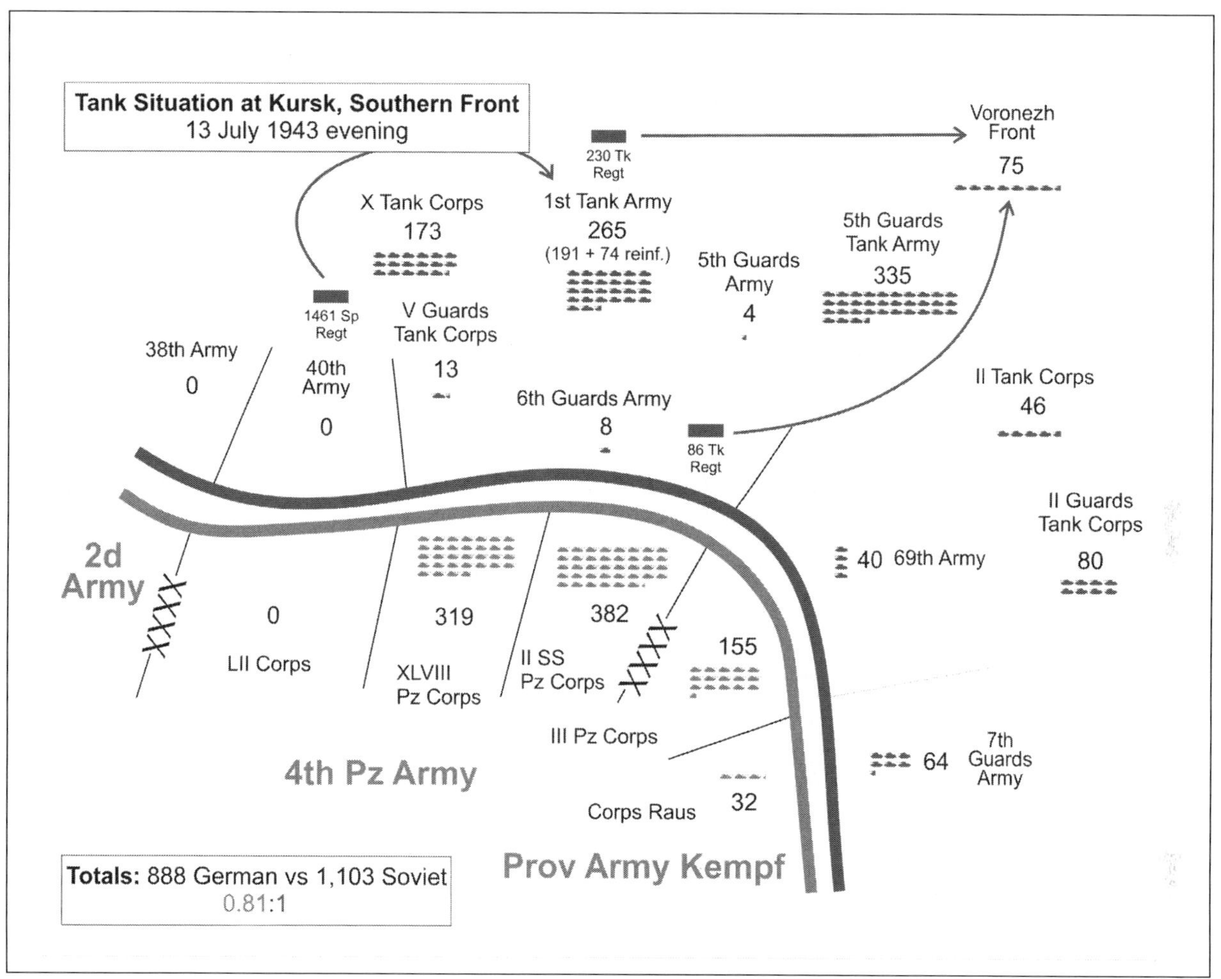

Tank Situation at Kursk, Southern Front
13 July 1943 evening
230 Tk Regt
Voronezh Front
75
X Tank Corps
173
1st Tank Army
265
(191 + 74 reinf.)
5th Guards Tank Army
335
5th Guards Army
4
1461 Sp Regt
V Guards Tank Corps
13
38th Army
0
40th Army
0
6th Guards Army
8
86 Tk Regt
II Tank Corps
46
II Guards Tank Corps
80
40 69th Army
2d Army
0
LII Corps
319
XLVIII Pz Corps
382
II SS Pz Corps
155
III Pz Corps
64 7th Guards Army
4th Pz Army
Corps Raus
32
Prov Army Kempf
Totals: 888 German vs 1,103 Soviet
0.81:1

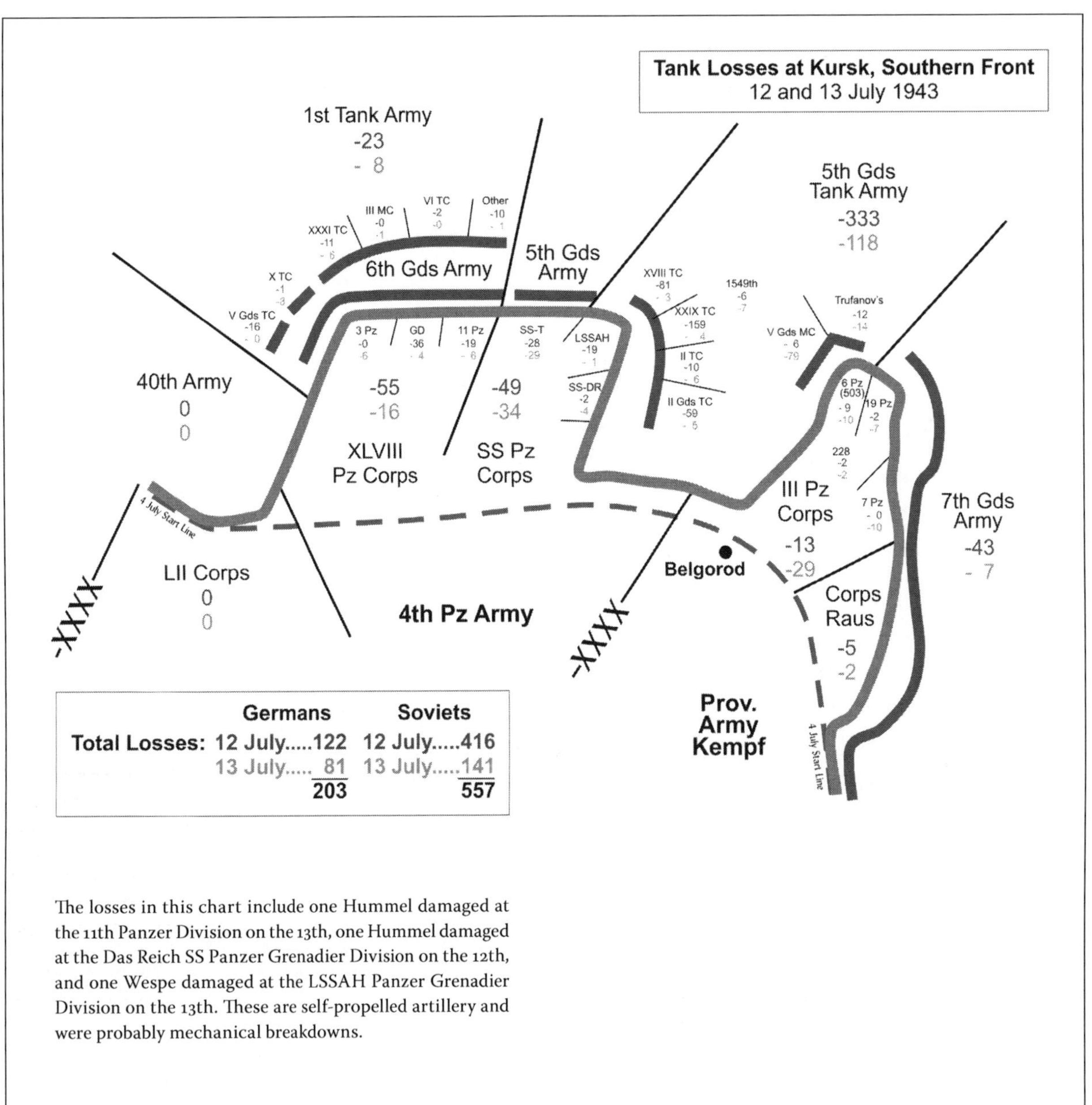

	Germans	Soviets
Total Losses:	12 July.....122	12 July.....416
	13 July..... 81	13 July.....141
	203	557

The losses in this chart include one Hummel damaged at the 11th Panzer Division on the 13th, one Hummel damaged at the Das Reich SS Panzer Grenadier Division on the 12th, and one Wespe damaged at the LSSAH Panzer Grenadier Division on the 13th. These are self-propelled artillery and were probably mechanical breakdowns.

It appears that in many secondary sources in the west, General von Mellenthin has become the "resident expert" on the Soviet fighting man. His oft-quoted passage is over-quoted, and in fact is included later in this book. Still, we also asked German veterans for their comments and impressions of their Soviet foe, and several follow.

Lieutenant von Rodde,[1] Adjutant, 6th Tank Regiment, 3rd Panzer Division:

> When I consider all impressions as a whole, the Soviet soldier fought this battle with all the positive characteristics we knew him to have. He was tenacious, brave, valiant up to self-sacrifice, immeasurably bearable of pain and resourceful in battle. Even when wounded, the Soviet soldier doggedly fought on. The Soviet units in this operation seemed to be even more motivated than previously. This was also noticeable in a reduction in deserters who changed sides. In any case, the Soviet units were better equipped. A certain degree of monotonous leadership style did remain an apparent deficiency among the lower ranks, though.
>
> Although in a way we had a high regard for the Soviet soldier, we felt superior on the battlefield. This was justified as we decided all engagements in our favor, even if this incurred substantial losses at times. We always ruled on the battlefield. If *Operation Citadel* still remained unsuccessful then the reasons for this are found on the operational and strategic level, not with the fighting force.

Captain Frantz,[2] Commander, Gross Deutschland Assault Gun Battalion:

> All in all, as a battle-hardened force we felt we had the edge over the Soviet military. This does not mean that the Russian soldier was lacking in bravery, or rather tenacity. On the contrary, but their soldiers were poorly led. *(continued)*

1 Maj.Gen. (ret.) Franz-Joachim von Rodde was interviewed by Maj.Gen. (ret.) Dieter Brand on 6 May 1999. General von Rodde was born 25 November 1922 and had volunteered as a soldier since October 1940. He was a non-commissioned officer and tank commander in the Russian Campaign, 1941. Underwent officer training and stationed in Kharkov in February 1942. He served as a platoon leader in the summer of 1942 in the Caucasus, Terek, and Sea of Azov areas. He fought in the battles of retreat in winter 1942/43. In July 1943, he was a staff officer for Colonel Schmitt-Ott, commander of the 6th Panzer Regiment. Awards included Iron Cross 1st and 2nd Class, Wound Badge in Gold, Tank Assault Badge 50.

After the war, he was a farmer and then joined the West German Army. He rose to the rank of Major General, holding several command positions, the last one as commander 3rd Armored Division.

2 Mr. Peter Frantz was interviewed by Maj.Gen. (ret.) Dieter Brand on 20 April 1999. Mr. Frantz was born 24 July 1917 in Leipzig. He volunteered for the service in 1936. He became an officer candidate in the 4th Artillery Regiment in Dresden. During the Polish Campaign, he was a staff officer. From 1939 on, he served with the newly created assault-gun units, serving as Platoon leader 16th company (the assault gun company) in the Gross Deutschland Infantry Regiment starting March 1940. He participated in the campaigns in France and the Balkans and from 1941 through 1943, in the Russian Campaign. Throughout this time he remained with the Gross Deutschland Infantry Regiment. He continued with the Gross Deutschland Division when it was created in April 1942, serving first as company commander, and then, beginning 3 January 1943 through 1944, commander of the assault gun battalion in the division.

After that, he was trained as a General Staff officer and ended the war as a Ic (G4) in an armored corps. Awards included Iron Cross 2nd Class (Poland), Iron Cross 1st Class (France), Certificate of recognition from the army's commander in chief (Russia, 1941), German Cross in Gold (Russia, 1941/1942), Knight's Cross (Russia, 1942), Oak Leaves (Russia, 1943 winter offensive in February), and Wound Badge (5 times).

After the war, Frantz was a manager of a pharmaceutical concern. He also served as a reserve officer in the West German Army and as such was the commander of an armored brigade and deputy division commander.

Captain Bergemann,[3] Commander, III Battalion, Gross Deutschland Grenadier Regiment:

We encountered a tenacious adversary in this operation, who fought with bravery. However, we always felt superior to them. This was reflected in the reality of combat. Not a shadow of a doubt should be cast on the often heroic sacrifice the Soviet soldiers made, but we had a better handle on things as regards cooperation of forces and leadership on the lower levels. Added to that, time and again the lone Soviet soldier, occasionally in small groups, changed sides. Each of our Landsers took this as a clear sign that they were on the right side.

Captain Thieme,[4] Commander, I Battalion, 110th Panzer Grenadier Regiment:

I want to stress again that the Soviet soldiers fought with extreme tenacity. Compared to other engagements we made relatively few prisoners. The enemy either fought to the last man or evaded according to plan.

Lt. Schaefer-Kehnert,[5] 119th Artillery Regiment, 11th Panzer Division:

3 Colonel in the General Staff (ret.) Alfred Bergemann was interviewed by Maj.Gen. (ret.) Dieter Brand on 2 October 1999. Col. Bergemann was born Oct. 10, 1915. He had been a soldier since 1 April 1935, serving first in the 16th Cavalry Regiment in Erfurt and then assigned to 3rd Motorcycle Battalion upon establishment of the 3rd Panzer Division. He was involved in the Polish Campaign as a special missions staff officer. Mr. Bergemann then volunteered for the air force and was trained as an observer in a reconnaissance squadron. He was again back with the army starting 1 April 1942 serving in the Gross Deutschland Division, first as a lieutenant with the Ic (executive officer with the G4). Following an injury, he was in the Fuehrer reserve with the division's Ia starting spring of 1943.

He was assigned to the Ia of the Gross Deutschland Division (equivalent to the G3) in July upon assembly for action of that division and was held back as part of the reserve of potential leaders (to replace commanding officers killed or wounded in action). Mr. Bergemann became the commander of the III Battalion of the Gross Deutschland Regiment on the third day of *Citadel*.

He was trained as a General Staff officer following another injury in August 1943 and served as a G4 and a G3 of an army corps. His awards include the German Cross in Gold, Iron Cross 1st and 2nd Class, and Wound Badge.

Col. Bergemann became an officer in the West German Army starting in 1956, having several assignments in HQ AFCENT and ending his career finally as a section chair for NATO matters in Armed Forces Staff, Ministry of Defense, in Bonn. He retired in 1974.

4 Mr. Karl Thieme was interviewed in writing due to his age and illness. Correspondence was conducted by Maj. Gen. (ret.) Dieter Brand in March and April 1999. Mr. Thieme was born 28 May 1914 and had served in the army since 10 January 1936. He had participated in the Polish Campaign, the occupation of Denmark, and the French Campaign as well as the campaign in the Balkans, and had been in action in Russia without pause since June 1941. In July of 1943 he was a captain and commander of the I Battalion of the 110th Panzer Grenadier Regiment, 11th Panzer Division.

During the war he was promoted from Lieutenant and platoon leader to Lieutenant Colonel and regimental commander. His awards included the Iron Cross 1st and 2nd Class, Tank badge, Close combat clasp, German Cross in Gold, Knight's Cross, with Oak Leaves and Swords, Royal Bulgarian Medal of Valor. During World War II, only 19 people in the German Army (vice SS, Air Force or Navy) below the rank of General were issued the Knight's Cross with Oak Leaves and Swords.

After the war, he served as the director of the German Federal Railways' liaison office to the United States military.

5 Prof. Dr. Walther Schaefer-Kehnert was interviewed by Maj. Gen. (ret.) Dieter Brand on Oct. 21 1999. Mr. Schaefer-Kehnert was born 5 February 1918. He was a conscript from 1937 through 1939 and mobilized in 1939. He was trained as a reserve officer and saw action in the campaigns in France, the Balkans and Russia. Served with the 119th Artillery Regiment of the 11th Panzer Division from 1941 to 1944. During the battle, he was a first lieutenant and commander of the 4th battery in the II Battalion of the 119th Artillery Regiment.

Later in the war, he ended up on the Western Front in Normandy, the retreat across France and finally at the Bridge of Remagen. He ended the war as a commander of an artillery battalion of the 11th Panzer Division and a major of reserves. He was wounded four times during the war. Awards include German Cross in Gold, Iron Cross 1st and 2nd Class, and Wound Badge.

After the war, Mr. Schaefer-Kehnert studied agriculture,

The Soviet adversary became ever more tenacious over the years. But we never lost our notion of superiority. However, dealing with them became ever more difficult due to the greater amounts of material the Soviets could dispose of. This culminated in our losing the operational initiative after *Citadel*. After that, the growing superiority in material simply rolled over us.

It was a common sight to have soldiers defect from Soviet units. A few of them were always coming over. However, I never witnessed entire units changing sides.

I recall no incident of soldiers from our division defecting to the Soviets. I don't want to rule it out, I just didn't learn of this ever happening. If it did occur, it was in isolated cases.

In the area of operations of the LII Corps and XLVIII Panzer Corps, the Soviets units opposing them reported capturing from the 4th through the 18th, 227 Germans, among them 4 deserters. The opposing German forces reported capturing 12,436 Soviets, among them 599 deserters. There was clearly a difference in morale and cohesion when one compares the Soviet Army to the German Army in World War II.

Officer Cadet Guenther Baer, tank commander, II Battalion, Leibstandarte SS Adolf Hitler Panzer Regiment:

I cannot refer to any single act [of bravery] by Soviet soldiers, but want to emphasize that the enemy fought with incredible ferocity on the 10th, 11th, and 12th. In fact they fought like fanatics.

Colonel (ret.) Kurt A. Kaufmann of the Der Fuehrer SS Regiment provides an opposing view:

Soviet unit cohesion was by far not as strong as amongst ourselves. I have seen several days where Russians gave themselves up in droves. This was in remarkable contrast to other observations where Soviet soldiers fought heroically down to the last man.

One event remains engrained in my memory. I was on guard duty at the gun one night, I believe in the Luchki area. There I heard Russian folk songs in the distance, which we Germans were also very familiar with. And the chorus drew nearer and nearer! I alerted my comrades and we stood guns at the ready when we noticed the faint image of a group of twenty or thirty soldiers. When called upon they reacted immediately, walked over to us and willingly followed our orders. Apparently, one group had made up their mind to change sides and desert. They seemed to believe that their singing folk songs were a workable substitute for the usual password. And they obviously relied on the assumption that Germans would not fire on Russians approaching with a tune.

This type of conduct was unimaginable for my comrades and I.

At times we collected large numbers of prisoners. I don't remember who led them to the rear, that was always the infantry's business. We with our antiaircraft guns never took care of that.

Richard Rosen of the 3rd company, 503rd Heavy Panzer (Tiger) Battalion:

I want to emphasize once more that we on the lower command levels, i.e. platoon leaders and surely including the company commander, had not expected such fierce fighting and such steadfastness on the part of the enemy. This surprised us all, and the Russians fought so bitterly as to simply gain our respect.

However, this did not serve to diminish the belief in our own superiority over the adversary. We felt superior as always. After all, we had a few command-

---

taught as a professor in Gottingen, and worked for the World Bank in various countries for several years.

Professor Schaefer-Kehnert wrote two letters while at the front on 13, 14, and 15 July 1943 describing the events since July 4th.

ers in our Tiger battalion, who had accomplished in excess of 100 enemy tank kills.

Alfred Rubbel of the 1st company, 503rd Heavy Panzer (Tiger) Battalion:

> The common Russian soldier fought relentlessly and bravely, he would rather be beaten to death in his post than run away. If, however, tendencies within the group triggered such a reaction everyone more or less panicked and took flight. The Russian soldier was by far better accustomed to bearing adversities than were our own men.
>
> When fear took hold everyone appeared paralyzed by it. Hardly anyone had the guts to take the initiative and do something. With us, that was different. It was mostly our battle-hardened sergeants on the lower command level who would take the initiative, maintain order and keep things under control. Generally, however, the Russian soldier fought doggedly and this was more evenly noticeable throughout now compared to the campaigns in 1941 and 1942.
>
> The Russian soldier was a master of making use of the environment, camouflaging his positions and improvising, second to none.
>
> Leadership quality on the lower command level—comparable to our non-commissioned officers—was not good. We experienced for the first time during *Operation Citadel* that tanks were led by tank commanders. Apparently, this was to remove a major deficiency within the Soviet armored corps. Much that would be called the art of war, however, had not been mastered although it was second nature for any of our leaders on the lower command level. This included, for instance, moving forward in a coordinated formation during an attack.
>
> As a military force on the battlefield we always felt we had the edge over the enemy. This was not due to any degree of arrogance, but was well founded in our daily observations in battle. We were simply better in terms of leadership in our units, skill in using our weapons and overall cooperation of forces. To me the decisive factor seemed to be that all leaders from the lowest level of tank commander up through the ranks had been trained to rely on their own judgment in making decisions in respect to the overall objective. That was our strength, not our soldier's bravery, which the Russian soldier had no less to offer.

 OTHER PUBLISHED VIEWS OF THE RUSSIAN FIGHTING MAN

From the 84 Soviet interviews that were done, many of which have been incorporated into this book, and from the opposing 28 German interviews, one can get some feel of the beliefs and motivations of the people who were fighting. A number of books on the Eastern Front have had discussions of the character of the Russian fighting man. One such description is provided by Major General F. W. von Mellenthin, Chief of Staff of the XLVIII Panzer Corps at Kursk, in his book *Panzer Battles*:

> No one belonging to the cultural circle of the West is ever likely to fathom the character and soul of these Asiatics, born and bred on the other side of the European frontiers. . . . There is no way of telling what the Russian will do next; he will tumble from one extreme to the other. With experience it is quite easy to foretell what a soldier from any other country will do, but never with the Russian. His qualities are as unusual and many-sided as those of his vast and rambling country. He is patient and enduring beyond imagination, incredibly brave and courageous—yet at times he can be a contemptible coward. There were occasions when Russian units, which had driven back German attacks with ferocious courage, suddenly fled in panics before a small assault group. Battalions lost their nerve when the first shot was fired, and yet the same battalions fought with fanatical stubbornness on the following day. The Russian is quite unpredictable; today he does not care whether his flanks are threatened or not, tomorrow he trembles at the idea of having his flanks exposed. He disregards accepted tactical principles but sticks to the letter of his field manuals. Perhaps the key to this attitude lies in the fact that the Russian is not a conscious soldier, thinking on independent lines, but is the victim of moods which a Westerner cannot analyze. He is essentially a primitive being, innately courageous, and dominated by certain emotions and instincts. His individuality is easily swallowed up in the mass, while his powers of endurance are derived from long centuries of suffering and privatation. Thanks to the innate strength of these qualities the Russian is superior in many ways to the more conscious soldier of the West, who can only make good his deficiencies by superior mental and moral training.
>
> A feature of the Russian solider is his utter contempt for life or death, so incomprehensible to a Westerner. The Russian is completely unmoved when he steps over the dead bodies of hundreds of his comrades; with the same unconcern he buried his dead compatriots, and with no less indifference he faces his own death. For him life holds no special value; it is something easy to throw away.
>
> With the same indifference the Russian solider endures cold and heat, and the pangs of hunger and thirst. Unheard-of hardships make no impression on his soul. He lacks any true religious or moral balance, and his moods alternate between bestial cruelty and genuine kindness. As part of a mob he is full of hatred and utterly cruel, but when alone he can be friendly and generous. These characteristics apply to the Asiatic Russian, the Mongol, the Turkoman, and the Uzbek, as well as to the Slavs west of the Urals. . . .
>
> To some extent the good military qualities of the Russians are offset by dullness, mental rigidity, and a natural tendency towards indolence.[1]

1 Mellenthin, pages 349–352.

Colonel Albert Seaton, whose background is not known to me, provides another description of the Russian soldier in his book *The Russo-German War 1941–45*, published in 1971.

> The outstanding characteristics of the Great Russian were obstinacy, cunning and stamina and these qualities had been bred into him by the harshness of his climate, the barrenness of his soil, the invasions of the Asiatics, the overlordship of the Tartars and possibly the copious mixture of Finnish blood into his stock. The Great Russian soldier was not lacking in courage, he was tenacious, and irrespective of whether or not he was a true communist, he was usually patriotic with a strong love of his native land. He was gullible and was easily swayed by the propaganda of his commissars, although this was true of most Red Army soldiers, irrespective of race. He had no great love for the life of a soldier, which he endured with patient stoicism, and unless dragooned by his officers and commissars, his military efficiency was poor and he became dirty, indisciplined and unruly or apathetic. All Russians tended to be unpredictable and subject to violent changes in moods and this characteristic was to show itself in the pattern of the fighting in the Second World War. On occasions formations fought to the death with the greatest tenacity. Sometimes they gave themselves up en masse or ran away. Generally they were better in defence than in the attack, but they tended to be slow-witted, slow-moving, ponderous and cautious, and they suffered from the age-old curse of passivity and the lack of originality and initiative. . . .
>
> . . . The other main element in the population was the Ukrainian. His national characteristics resembled those of the Pole, being intelligent, quick-witted, courageous and merry, having panache and elan. He lacked, however, the stolidity of the Great Russian. The White Russian was usually inferior as a soldier to both the Ukrainian and the Great Russian. . . .[2]

In the end, while these statements may reflect one person's observations, they are also tinged with racism.

---

2 Seaton, pages 96–97. I have reversed the order of the discussion on the Great Russian and the Ukrainian and White Russian in my quotation here.

Battlefield Photo Section

All pictures are from named SS photographers and almost certainly of SS units. Most pictures dated the 19th or earlier in July are probably from the Kursk battlefield. They were not captioned, but the photographer is listed (i.e. Groenert, Merz, Buschel).

TANKS

TOP Tiger, Groenert, 19 July 1943. BOTTOM Tiger Tank, Groenert, 16 July 1943.

TANKS
Tiger Tank, Groenert, 16 July 1943.

Tanks in action, Tiger front and center, Groenert, 16 July 1943.

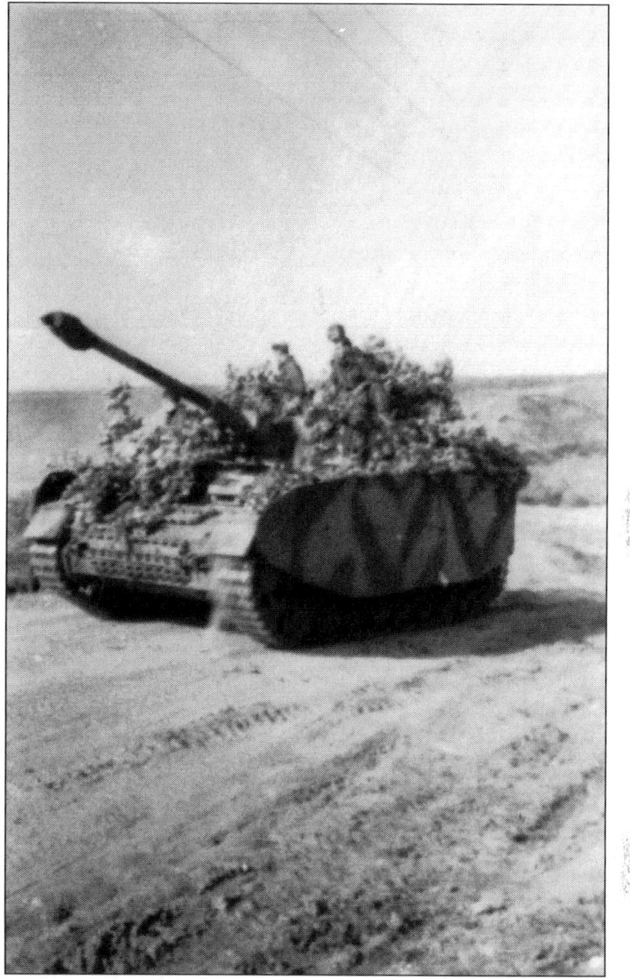

TANKS

A Panzer IV from the front, Merz, 16 July 1943.

A Panzer IV in action, Merz, 16 July 1943.

TANKS

A Panzer IV in action, Merz, 16 July 1943.

Panzer IV, Buschel, 13 July 1943.

TANKS

Panzer III, Groenert, 16 July 1943.

Panzer III, Cantzler, 19 July 1943.

TANKS
German armor from the front, Merz, 16 July 1943.

This looks like the Kursk battlefield, Merz, 15 July 1943.

TANKS

Sturmgeschuetz III crossing an engineered tank ditch crossing, Groenert, 19 July 1943.

Sturmgeschuetz III, Buschel, 15 July 1943.

TANKS

Sturmgeschuetz III, Buschel, 15 July 1943.

Sturmgeschuetz III, Buschel, 15 July 1943.

TANKS
Marder, Groenert, 16 July 1943.

Marder, Buschel, 15 July 1943.

Tanks
Marder, Laux, 13 July 1943.

A pair of Marders, Buschel, 13 July 1943. One notes that most armor pictures in July are taken from the rear.

TANKS

Self-propelled artillery position, King, 13 July 1943.

German self-propelled artillery, Buschel, 15 July 1943.

TANKS

German self-propelled artillery on the move, King, 13 July 1943.

German self-propelled artillery on the move, King, 13 July 1943.

Tanks

German self-propelled artillery deployed, King, 13 July 1943.

This certainly looks like the Kursk battlefield, Buschel, 10 July 1943.

Tanks
German armor, Buschel, 10 July 1943.

Other Vehicles
Armed halftrack, Groenert, 18 August 1943 (this photo is probably from after the Kursk offensive).

Other Vehicles
Armed halftrack, King, 13 July 1943.

German halftrack and infantry, King, 17 July 1943.

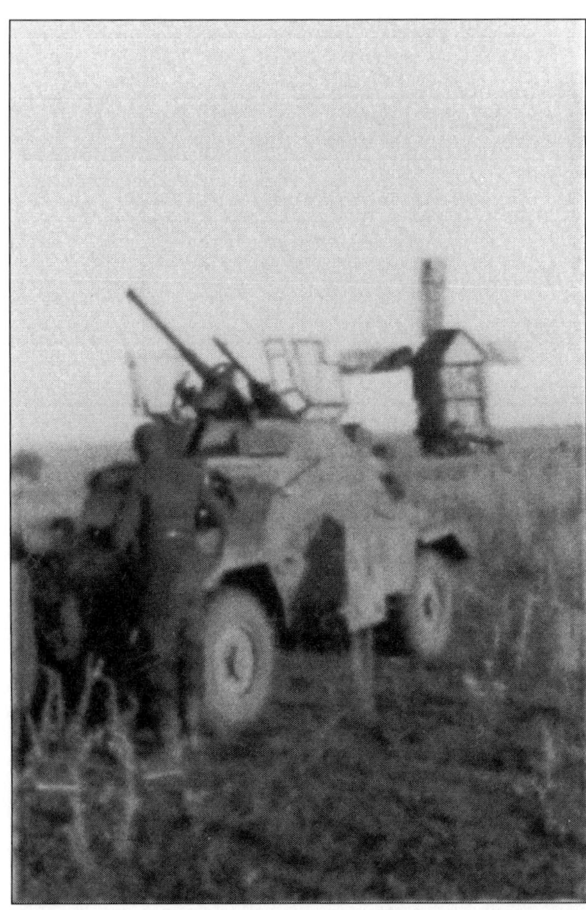

Other Vehicles
German armored car, King, 13 July 1943.

German armored car, Groenert 18 August 1943 (this photo is probably from after the Kursk offensive).

Other Vehicles
Motorcycles, Buschel, 19 July 1943.

Other Weapons
German artillery, Buschel, 10 July 1943.

Other Weapons
German artillery, Buschel, 10 July 1943.

Gun position, Cantzler, 19 July 1943.

Other Weapons

Nebelwerfer and Sturmgeschuetz III, Buschel, 15 July 1943.

Nebelwerfers firing, Buschel, 15 July 1943.

Other Weapons
The trail of the Nebelwerfers, Merz, 16 July 1943.

Battles scenes, village not identified, Merz, 15 July 1943.

Other Weapons
German mortar position, Geyk, 19 May 1943.

Good morning . . . , H. Ahrens, 12 May 1943.

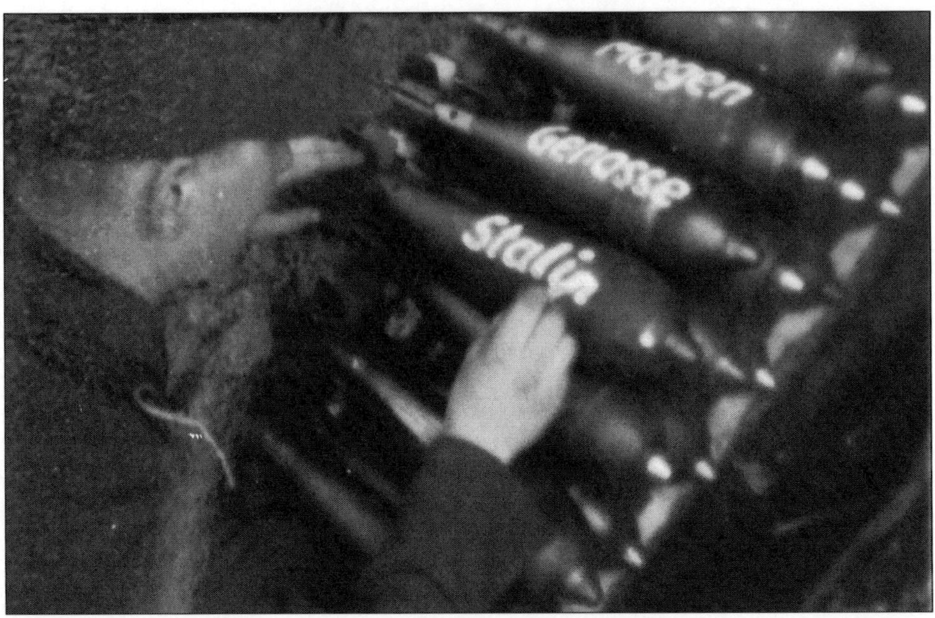

Other Weapons

. . . comrade Stalin, painted on mortar rounds, H. Ahrens, 12 May 1943.

Halftrack and towed antitank gun, Groenert, 16 July 1943.

OTHER WEAPONS
German Panzer III and towed antitank gun, Merz, 16 July 1943.

German 20mm AA guns, Merz, 15 July 1943.

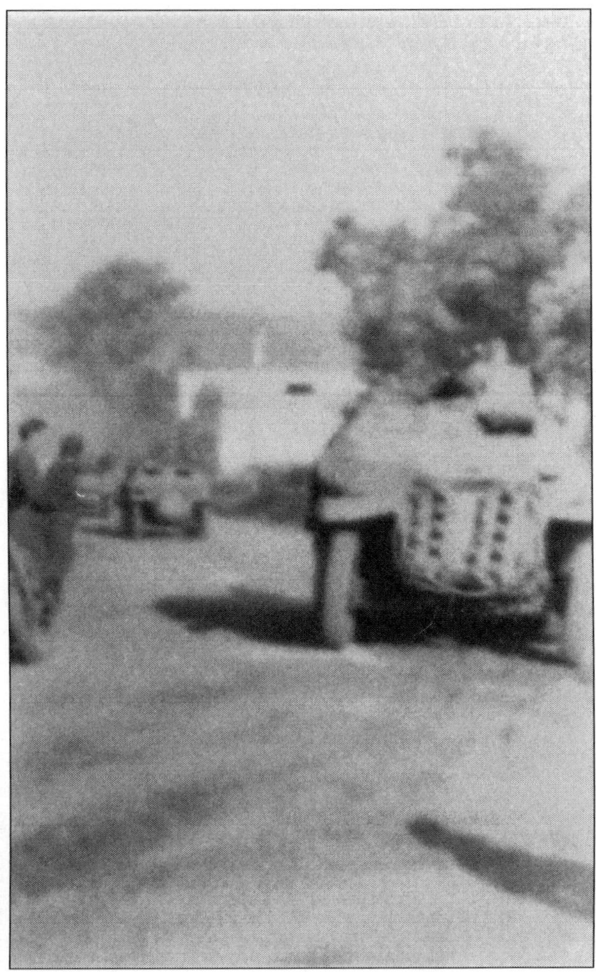

OTHER WEAPONS
German AA machinegun, Buschel, 19 July 1943.

INFANTRY
Halftracks full of infantry moving through village, Merz, 16 July 1943.

INFANTRY
German infantry advancing, Groenert, 19 July 1943.

Infantry at Kursk, Groenert, 19 July 1943.

INFANTRY

Infantry moving through a village, Groenert, 16 July 1943.

German infantry in a tank ditch, Groenert, 19 July 1943.

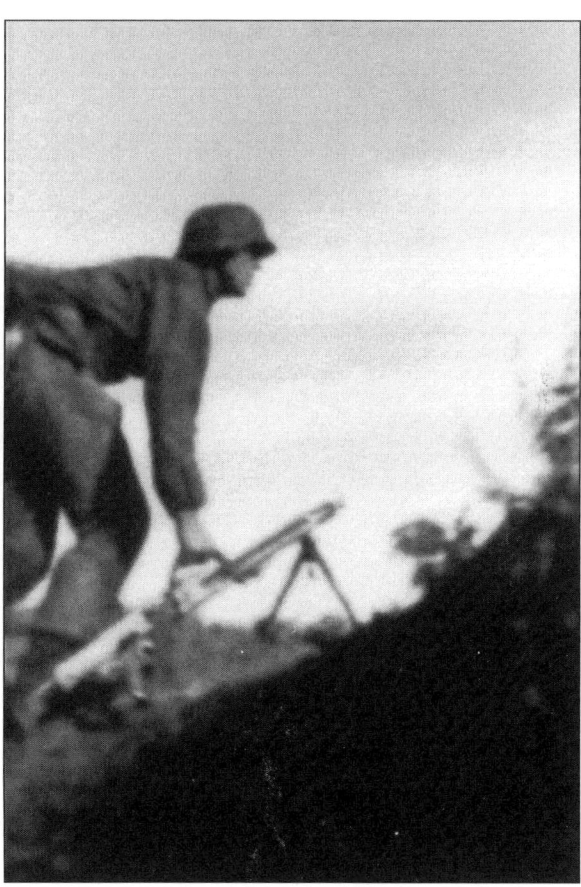

INFANTRY
German infantry in a tank ditch, Buschel, 10 July 1943.

German machinegun, King, 13 July 1943.

INFANTRY
German machinegun, Buschel, 15 July 1943.

PLANES
Stuka in flight, Buschel, 19 July, 1943.

Planes
Fighter on the ground, Laux, 14 July 1943.

Other
Crossroads and traffic control, Buschel, 13 July 1943.

OTHER
Surrendering Russians always make for good propaganda pictures, Merz, 15 July 1943.

SOVIET TANKS
T-34 from the front, Buschel, 15 July 1943.

SOVIET TANKS
T-34 from the rear, Buschel, 15 July 1943.

T-34 from the side, Buschel, 15 July 1943.

Soviet Tanks
German captured T-34 in use, Buschel, 10 July 1943.

Soviet Churchill, Buschel, 10 July 1943.

Commanders Photo Section

SENIOR GERMAN FIELD COMMANDERS

TOP ROW, LEFT TO RIGHT

Field Marshal Erich von Manstein (Army Group South), 4 February 1943.

Manstein, app. 1942.

MIDDLE ROW Manstein in the field, 21 May 1942.

BOTTOM ROW, LEFT TO RIGHT

General Werner Kempf (Provisional Army Kempf), date unknown. PHOTO FROM TURKISH WIKIPEDIA.

Colonel General Hermann Hoth (Fourth Panzer Army), 15 December 1938.

SENIOR SOVIET FIELD COMMANDERS

TOP ROW, LEFT TO RIGHT Nikolai Fedorovich Vatutin (Voronezh Front), 1943.

Nikolai Fedorovich Vatutin, 1943.

BOTTOM ROW, LEFT TO RIGHT Vatutin's chief of staff, Semen Pavlovich Ivanov (1907–1993), 1943.

Vatutin, with Ivanov, his chief of staff, on the right, June 1943.

TOP Vatutin and Khrushchev, on the front, June 1943.

BOTTOM Nikita Sergeyevich Khrushchev, at the front, June 1943.

LEFT Nikita Khrushchev, on the field phone, with the Fifth Guards Tank Army commander, Pavel Rotmistrov, standing in glasses, on the left, 15 July 1943. Zamulin, *Demolishing the Myth*, page 264, provides the following caption for the same photo:

> On 10 July 1943, N.S. Khrushchev reports over the telephone to I.V. Stalin on the arrival of the 5th Guards Tank Army in the area of Prokhorovka Station. Seated next to him is the commander of the Voronezh Front's Armored and Mechanized Forces Lieutenant General A. D. Shtevnev. Standing to Shtevnev's immediate right is 5th Guards Tank Army commander Lieutenant General P. A. Rotmistrov, and standing on Rotmistrov's right is the deputy commander of the Voronezh Front General of the Army I. P. Apanasenko. (RGAKFD).

Note that the decision to attack was probably not made earlier than the night of the 10 July, and the photo was taken during the day. Nor was the Fifth Guards Tank Army at Prokhorovka Station on 10 July. According to Rotmistrov's post-war account, Rotmistrov was summoned to meet with Vatutin near Oboyan during the day on 10 July. They did discuss the counterstroke at Prokhorovka and Rotmistrov received his combat orders and returned to his command post in the afternoon (see Zamulin, pages 268–269).

The photo could have been taken at that time of this meeting. It also may have been taken on a later day.

RIGHT Nikita Khrushchev's grave in Novodevichye Cemetery in Moscow. PHOTO BY TATIANA S. LAWRENCE.

GERMAN AIR COMMANDERS
LEFT TO RIGHT
Major General Hans Seidemann (VIII Air Corps), App. September 1944.

Seidemann, 30 November 1944.

Soviet Air Commanders
LEFT TO RIGHT Stepan Akimovich Kravsovskii (Second Air Army), 1943.

Vladimir Aleksandrovich Sudets (Seventeenth Air Army), 1945.

Sergei Kondratyevich Goryunov (Fifth Air Army), 1945.

THE GERMAN CORPS COMMANDERS

TOP ROW, LEFT TO RIGHT General Hermann Breith (III Panzer Corps) when he was a Major General.

General Paul "Papa" Hausser (SS Panzer Corps) SS-OberstGruppenfuehrer and General of the Waffen SS, probably after 15 July 1943.

LEFT General Werner Kempf (right) in discussion with Hermann Breith (center) and Major General Walter Chales de Beaulieu, 168th Infantry Division (left) on 21 June 1943. PHOTO FROM WIKIPEDIA.

THE SOVIET ARMY COMMANDERS

TOP ROW, LEFT TO RIGHT Ivan Mikhailovich Chistyakov (Sixth Guards Army), 1944.

Mikhail Stepanovich Shumilov (Seventh Guards Army), October 1943.

Vasilii Dmitriyevich Kryuchenkin (Sixty-ninth Army), May 1943.

Pavel Alekseyevich Rotmistrov (Fifth Guards Tank Army), 1943.

BOTTOM ROW, LEFT TO RIGHT Pavel Alekseyevich Rotmistrov, 1943.

Rotmistrov's gave in Novodevishye Cemetery. PHOTO BY TATIANA S. LAWRENCE.

Aleksei Semenovich Zhadov (Fifth Guards Army), 1943.

THE GERMAN DIVISION COMMANDERS
LEFT TO RIGHT Lt. General Wolf Trierenberg (167th Infantry Division), 15 May 1943. PHOTO FROM WIKIPEDIA VIA DEUTSCHES BUNDESARCHIV.

Sr. Colonel (SS Oberfuehrer) Theodor Wisch (Leibstandarte SS Adolf Hitler Panzer Grenadier Division). PHOTO BY HANS HOFFMAN, SEPTEMBER 1941, FROM WIKIPEDIA.

Lt. General (SS Gruppenfuehrer) Walter Krueger (Das Reich SS Panzer Grenadier Division), date 6 September 1943.

TOP ROW, LEFT TO RIGHT Major General (SS Brigadefuehrer) Hermann Otto Priess (Totenkopf SS Panzer Grenadier Division), undated. PHOTO FROM RUSSIAN WIKIPEDIA.

Lt. General Walter von Huenersdorff (6th Panzer Division), date unknown. PHOTO FROM WIKIPEDIA VIA DEUTSCHES BUNDESARCHIV.

Lt. General Baron Hans von Funck (7th Panzer Division). Photo by Hans Hoffman, undated, but labeled as "GeneralLtn. Funk."

BOTTOM ROW, LEFT TO RIGHT Colonel Martin Unrein (6th Panzer Division). Unrein is on the left.

Lt. General Gustav Schmidt (19th Panzer Division), 10 March 1943.

TOP ROW, LEFT TO RIGHT Aleksei Semenovich Burdeinyii (II Guards Tank Corps), September 1943.

Aleksei Fedorovich Popov (II Tank Corps), September 1943.

Vasilii Gerasimovich Burkov (X Tank Corps), April 1943.

BOTTOM ROW, LEFT TO RIGHT Boris Sergeyevich Bakharov (XVIII Tank Corps), 1943.

Ivan Fedorovich Kirichenko (XXIX Tank Corps), August 1943.

Boris Mikhailovich Skvortsov (V Guards Mechanized Corps), June 1943.

SOME GERMAN BRIGADE, REGIMENT AND BATTALION COMMANDERS

TOP ROW, LEFT TO RIGHT Dr. Franz Baeke (Battalion commander, 11th Panzer Regiment, 6th Panzer Division). Major Baeke would eventually be awarded the Knight's Cross with Oak Leaves and Swords. PHOTO FROM WIKIPEDIA.

Otto Baum (Totenkopf SS Panzer Grenadier Regiment), 19 May 1942.

Hellmuth Becker (Eicke SS Panzer Grenadier Brigade).

BOTTOM ROW, LEFT TO RIGHT Standartenfuehrer Heinz Harmel (Deutschland SS Panzer Grenadier Regiment).

Captain Clemens Count von Kageneck (503rd Heavy Panzer Battalion), July 1944.

TOP ROW, LEFT TO RIGHT Sturmbannfuehrer (Major) Joachim Peiper, 1943. PHOTO FROM WIKIPEDIA VIA DEUTSCHES BUNDESARCHIV.

Lt. Colonel Adelbert Schulz (25th Panzer Regiment, 7th Panzer Division), 10 January 1944.

BOTTOM ROW, LEFT TO RIGHT Colonel Schulz, January 1944.

Sylvester Stadler (Der Fuehrer SS Panzer Grenadier Regiment), 27 September 1943.

German Tank Aces and Knight's Cross Winners
TOP ROW, LEFT TO RIGHT Rudolf von Ribbentrop, 23 July 1943.

Staudegger, 23 July 1943.

BOTTOM ROW, LEFT TO RIGHT German tank ace Michael Wittmann, 24 January 1944.

Wittmann, 1944.

Wittmann, November 1944.

GERMAN FLYERS AND ACES
TOP ROW, LEFT TO RIGHT Captain Alfred Druschel I/S.G. 1.

Major Dietrich Hrabak (52nd Fighter Wing), 22 April 1943.

BOTTOM ROW, LEFT TO RIGHT Hrabak, 27 November 1943.

Colonel Hartmann (52nd Fighter Wing), Sept. 1944.

Walter Krupinski (52nd Fighter Wing), undated. PHOTO FROM WIKIPEDIA.

TOP ROW, LEFT TO RIGHT Captain Wilhelm Lemke (3rd Fighter Wing), 27 November 1943.

Captain Kirchner (3rd Fighter Wing), photo by Hans Hoffman, undated.

Guenther Rall (52nd Fighter Wing), 3 November 1942.

BOTTOM ROW, LEFT TO RIGHT Major Hans-Ulrich Rudel, before July 1944.

Rudel, 27 November 1943.

Colonel Hans-Ulrich Rudel, 1945.

SOVIET ACES

TOP ROW, LEFT TO RIGHT Grave of Ivan Nikitovich Kozhedub (1920–1991), the top Soviet ace and thrice Hero of the Soviet Union. PHOTO BY NATALIA GUSEVA.

Bust of Nikolai Dmitriyevich Gulayev (1918–1985), Soviet ace and twice Hero of the Soviet Union. PHOTO FROM GEROI STRANYI WEBSITE AT WWW.WARHEROES.RU.

LEFT Grave of Kirill Alekseyevich Yevstigneyev (1917–1996), Soviet ace and twice Hero of the Soviet Union. PHOTO FROM GEROI STRANYI WEBSITE AT WWW.WARHEROES.RU.

CHAPTER THIRTEEN

Cleaning Up the Donets Triangle

14–15 JULY 1943

> On July 15 at noon, the battalion again attempted to take Pravorot. . . . Armored engagements took place in the course of the next hours, where we could only be mere bystanders. From a tank crew from one of our own tanks that had been destroyed, and who stayed with us briefly, we learned that the Soviets had already lost a total of 450 tanks by the 14th of July. Their reserves seemed immeasurable, because the counterattacks continued with heavy armor support.
>
> PRIVATE (OFFICER CANDIDATE) KURT A. KAUFMANN,
> DAS REICH SS PANZER GRENADIER DIVISION

THE DONETS TRIANGLE was like a wedge shoved into the lines between the Fourth Panzer Army and Provisional Army Kempf. It now extended almost 30 kilometers in front of the III Panzer Corps and for some 30 kilometers in front of the SS Panzer Corps. The main source of supply into the triangle was the road from Prokhorovka heading south. South of Pravorot, the only other roads that lead into the triangle from the west were from Gnezdilovka to Plota and the roads along the Severnyii Donets that passed through Ryindinka and Shipyi to Shakhovo and Plota. These were now cut by the German bridgeheads there. The 81st and 89th Guards Rifle Divisions had already complained of a lack of resupply, although this does not seem to be as a result of the road network. It now appears that this problem was becoming more severe, with the entire Sixty-ninth Army having difficulties not only getting resupplied with food, but also not being provided ammunition or other material. It is not known what arrangements were made to evacuate the wounded. Within this triangle, there were five rifle divisions and two tank corps.

THE SS PANZER CORPS ATTACK

These two days of battle, 14 and 15 July, would see the SS Panzer Corps' last attacks around Prokhorovka, with Totenkopf and Adolf Hitler holding over the next two days while Das Reich tried to develop the attack to the south of Prokhorovka.

Totenkopf

Now with the direction of the SS Panzer Corps' attack shifted to the right, Totenkopf rolled over to holding the northern (left) flank of the SS Panzer Corps. It was now stretched along a front of almost 17 kilometers. Throughout the day, this division came under attack

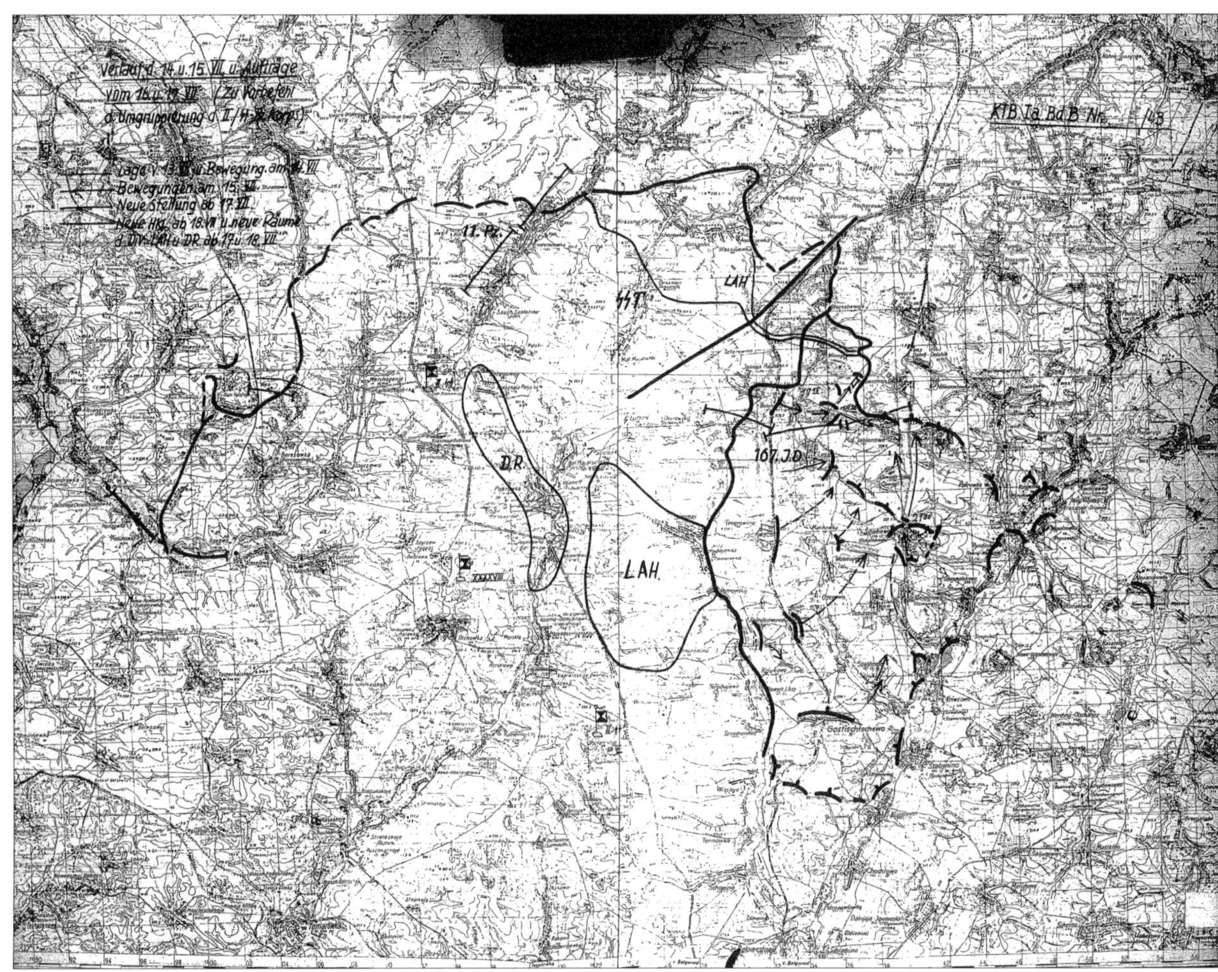

THE SS PANZER CORPS MAP SHOWING POSITIONS ON THE 14TH AND 15TH OF JULY

by Soviet infantry and tanks, predominately in the area of the Totenkopf SS Regiment (covering the north side of the unit).

At 1030 (Moscow time) the Fifth Guards Army attacked along their entire front. The XXXIII Guards Rifle Corps reported encountering heavy German resistance and being subjected to heavy German air attacks. On their right remained the 97th Guards Rifle Division which stated that it failed to make progress due to heavy German resistance. This division recorded casualties for this day as 61 killed and 345 wounded. In the center, the 95th Guards Rifle Division repelled a German counterattack at 1300 (Moscow time) from height 226.6 but was otherwise unable to make any progress. Still it lost 21 killed and 315 wounded on the 14th, but was supplemented with 100 new arrivals from the Smolensk Machinegun School (which was not in Smolensk at this time due to German occupation). On the left, the 42nd Guards Rifle Division repelled a German counterattack at 1330 (Moscow time) from Vasilyevka church, but otherwise made no progress this day. The 52nd Guards Rifle Division was in the second echelon behind the

95th Guards Rifle Division. Also in the area were the 24th Guards Tank Brigade and the 10th Guards Mechanized Brigade.

Totenkopf reported that there was artillery and infantry harassing fire along the whole front. At 0945 (Berlin time) they reported an attack by eight Soviet tanks on the Eicke SS Regiment. At 1045, there was another attack on this regiment in battalion strength. At 1225, there was a Soviet attack in battalion strength without tanks out of the western part of Veselyii against the III Battalion, Totenkopf SS Regiment. At 1325, this attack was defeated using artillery and heavy infantry weapons fire. At 1300 the division received air support, with a flight of He-111s attacking a concentration of Soviet tanks northeast of Veselyii, while Stukas attacked the gully and woods east of Veselyii. There were occasional overflights of Soviet fighters.

At this stage, the Fourth Panzer Army was concerned about a perceived build-up opposite Totenkopf and felt its bridgehead across the Psel was in danger.

THE FOLLOWING DAY both sides were inactive. The Totenkopf SS Division continued to defend its sector, reporting strong artillery and mortar fire during the day. At 1100 (Berlin time), there was an attack by one company from the northeast on the right wing of the Totenkopf SS Regiment, accompanied by three tanks. The attack was repulsed by combined artillery fire. This was probably the 95th Guards Rifle Division, which reported that it tried to take height 226.6.[1]

At 0500 (Moscow time) that morning, the 42nd Guards Rifle Division was pulled out of line and transferred to the Fifth Guards Tank Army. It was sent to Pravorot in response to Das Reich's attacks. The 9th Guards Airborne Division took over its section. The 52nd Guards Rifle Division was shifted over to a second echelon position from Petrovka to height 252.4 to help cover for the removed 42nd Guards Rifle Division. There simply was not much activity in the area now and the Fifth Guards Army still was holding the fresh 6th Guards Airborne Division in reserve, as it had since the 11th.

Air Support

On the 14th, Totenkopf received extensive air support in the afternoon from He-111s and Stukas. It also reported occasional overflights of Soviet fighters and claimed two Il-2s shot down that day. The Soviet 95th Guards Rifle Division noted that the Germans had air support.

The following day, Totenkopf reported heavy Soviet air activity. At 1500, its flak battalion claimed yet another Il-2.

The Adolf Hitler SS Division Holds

Having spent the 12th and 13th waiting for the Totenkopf SS Division to turn the Soviet position north of Prokhorovka, this division continued to hold in place, waiting for the Das Reich SS Division to turn the Soviet position south of Prokhorovka. The division's order on this day was to defend its present positions and prepare to attack with its right wing from Yamki to Prokhorovka as soon as the attack of the Das Reich SS Division through Pravorot to Prokhorovka created the opportunity.

During the night and early morning, the Soviet forces made occasional reconnaissance probes. At 1000 (Berlin time), the Soviets began firing heavy artillery and mortar harassing fire, which continued for the whole day. Late in the afternoon, the Soviets conducted a reconnaissance in force of about two companies from Mikhailovka against the Adolf Hitler SS Reconnaissance Battalion. This Soviet force was pinned down by German artillery fire.

Meanwhile, German patrols revealed new concentrations of tanks in Yamki, further fortifications of Soviet positions on both sides of the highway and south of Oktyabrskii Sovkhoz, as well a major massing of infan-

1 There is also a report by the division that they tried to take the height during the night of 15/16. It is not certain if these are two separate attacks, or there was only one attack made during the night.

Holding Across the Psel I, 14 July 1943

DURATION One day FRONTAGE 16.6 kilometers TERRAIN Rolling, mixed
WEATHER Overcast, scattered showers. Roads in places very difficult to negotiate.

	Attacker	*Defender*
Units	95th GRD & others	T SS PzGrD
Attachments	See below	See below
Strength	33,139	18,148
Armor	66 (16 light)	77
Artillery	305	149
Air Sorties	15	73
Casualties	1942 (497 KIA, 1141 WIA, 304 MIA)	175 (20 KIA, 154 WIA,1 MIA)
Armor Losses	0	8
Artillery Losses	8	2
Enemy Captured	5	N/A

Forces Engaged

German Attachments
II/1st Lehr Werfer Regiment
SS Corps Werfer Battalion
86th Bridge Column B (not incorporated)

Soviet Forces
1/3rd of 42nd Guards Rifle Division (132nd Guards Rifle Regiment)
95th Guards Rifle Division
469th Mortar Regiment

From V Guards Mechanized Corps
24th Guards Tank Brigade
10th Guards Mechanized Brigade

97th Guards Rifle Division
1372nd/29th Antiaircraft Division
12th Mortar Bde—189th Rgt detached on the 13th—rest of Bde detached on the 14th (not incorporated)

52nd Guards Rifle Division
133rd AT Rifle Bn
75th Flamethrower Co.
95th Flamethrower Co.
Bn/156th RR/51st GRD (not included)

From X Guards Tank Corps
11th Motorized Rifle Brigade
287th Mtr Rgt

Captures include 4 by the out-of-contact 6th Gds Airborne Division

try forces in Mikhailovka. A barrage by the entire Adolf Hitler SS Artillery Regiment on Mikhailovka caused a temporary withdrawal of those units.

Still huddled along the Psel River was the XVIII Tank Corps, with 38 T-34s, 46 T-70s and 7 Churchills. The corps maintained its 181st and 110th Tank Brigades back at Petrovka and Beregovoye, and its 29th Reconnaissance and 78th Motorcycle Battalions at Voroshilov Sovkhoz so as to provide a blocking force in case Totenkopf had penetrated to the north of Prokhorovka. The corps was periodically shelled during the day by the German nebelwerfers. The corps' front line ran from the northwestern outskirts of Andreyevka to the southeastern outskirts of Vasilyevka to the southern outskirts of Mikhailovka, then along the northern spurs of the ravine east of Andreyevka to the two windmills at Prelestnoye to farther along the northwestern slopes of height 252.2 to outside of Oktyabrskii Sovkhoz. The

Holding Across the Psel II, 15 July 1943

DURATION One day FRONTAGE 16.6 kilometers TERRAIN Rolling, mixed
WEATHER Heavy rainfall. Road extremely muddy and only in places passable for wheeled vehicles.

	Attacker	*Defender*
Units	95th GRD & others	T SS PzGrD
Attachments	See below	See below
Strength	25,287	17,975
Armor	22	76
Artillery	279	107
Air Sorties	21	0
Casualties	183 (29 KIA, 137 WIA, 17 MIA)	65 (19 KIA, 46 WIA)
Armor Losses	0	1
Artillery Losses	0	0
Air losses	1	0
Enemy Captured	2	N/A

Forces Engaged

German Attachments
II/1st Lehr Werfer Regiment
SS Corps Werfer Battalion
86th Bridge Column B (not incorporated)

Soviet Forces
1/3rd of 42nd Guards Rifle Division (132nd Guards Rifle Regiment)—not included

95th Guards Rifle Division
469th Mortar Regiment

From V Guards Mechanized Corps
24th Guards Tank Brigade

97th Guards Rifle Division
1372nd/29th Antiaircraft Division
66th Guards Mtr Rgt—attached on the 15th (included)

52nd Guards Rifle Division
133rd AT Rifle Bn
75th Flamethrower Co.
95th Flamethrower Co.
Bn/156th RR/51st GRD (not included)

From X Guards Tank Corps
11th Motorized Rifle Brigade
287th Mtr Rgt

II Battalion of the 32nd Motorized Rifle Brigade was no longer thrust to the west threatening Totenkopf's rear and instead was back in Andreyevka and Vasilyevka, having repelled three German attacks during the night of 13/14 July. Toward the end of the day, the 170th Tank Brigade was shifted to reserve at Mordovka at Rotmistrov's orders.

Blocking the path to Prokhorovka was the XXIX Tank Corps and the 9th Guards Airborne Division. The 9th Guards Airborne Division was also concentrating south of the rail line, in the area of the woods around height 245.8 to Storozhevoye to Ivanovskii Vyiselok. It was now being well supported, with one load of ammunition (although there were still no Molotov cocktails) and hot food guaranteed three times a day.

The XXIX Tank Corps spent the night improving its defensive positions. This unit had 33 T-34s, 39 T-70s, 1 KV-1, 3 SU-122s and 5 SU-76s. Its 31st Tank Brigade and the 53rd Motorized Rifle Brigade were deployed from 500 meters northeast of Oktyabrskii Sovkhoz down to Yamki. The 25th Tank Brigade was one kilometer east of Storozhevoye. The 32nd Tank Brigade was moved inside the Donets triangle and was deployed from Maloye Yablonovo to Zhilomostnoye. The corps was also now being backed up by the 1529th Heavy Self-Propelled Artillery Regiment, which had moved into firing position in the Prokhorovka area.

THE ADOLF HITLER SS Division continued to wait the following day for some break in the situation to its front. Its orders were to attack Yamki and secure it after the capture of Pravorot by the Das Reich. No time was set for the start of this attack.

Meanwhile the left wing of the division held position. The armored group, consisting of the Adolf Hitler SS Panzer Regiment, the 1st SS Armored Car Company, and reinforced by heavy weapons and self-propelled artillery, was to jump off at 0230 and advance via Ivanovka to just west of height 234.9, two kilometers east of Ivanovka. The division's armored group was then to be placed under corps command and then attack south together with elements of the Das Reich SS Division.

During the day, the division continued to be harassed by artillery and mortar fire. The heaviest fire was on the eastern edge of the woods south of Stalinskoye Otdeleniye Sovkhoz. There were German casualties. Throughout the day, the Soviets made unsuccessful reconnaissance probes in strengths of up to two companies.

Meanwhile the panzer group, in accordance with corps' orders, reached the area east of Ivanovka after an arduous journey in bad weather, and at 1430 was handed over to corps control, except for one panzer company. This attack by the panzer regiment was then called off by the corps.

Blocking the path to Prokhorovka were still the XVIII Tank Corps, parts of the XXIX Tank Corps, and the 9th Guards Airborne Division. The XVIII Tank Corps had only its 32nd Motorized Rifle Brigade and the 36th Guards Tank Regiment (the Churchills) forward, while the 110th and 181st Tank Brigades remained around Gergovoye and Petrovka. The 170th Tank Brigade remained in reserve in the Mordovka area (just east of Prokhorovka) and was then sent south to height 242.7, three kilometers north of Novoselovka. The XXIX Tank Corps held in place while the 9th Guards Airborne Division now had elements on the north side of the Psel, as its 26th Guards Airborne Regiment was used to relieve the 42nd Guards Rifle Division.

The XVIII Tank Corps claimed that 60 German tanks and a battalion of "automatic riflemen" attacked from the area of the gully south of Kozlovka against units of the 32nd Motorized Rifle Brigade. Thanks to a tank ambush consisting of 10 Churchills and the unit's antitank guns, the attack was defeated with the Germans losing three Tigers. This attack is not reported in the German records and the records do not indicate such losses.[2]

Air Support

The Adolf Hitler SS Division reported heavy German air activity, especially over the Das Reich SS Division and occasional overflights by Soviet fighters. The XXIX Tank Corps reported that it was being bombed by groups of 12–20 German planes from 0800 (Moscow time).

The following day, the Germans reported heavy Soviet air activity. At 1430 (Moscow time) a large group of Ju-88s bombed Prokhorovka. The XVIII Tank Corps complained that the Germans launched a number of powerful air attacks against the corps.

The Das Reich Now Attacks

Having had the Adolf Hitler SS Division attack stall on the 11th, and then Totenkopf's attack stall on the 13th, it was now the Das Reich's turn to try to turn

2 There is a report for the 15th of 4 Panzer IVs and 3 Sturmgeschuetzes lost with the LSSAH even though the daily inventory remained the same.

Overseeing the Tank Fields of Prokhorovka II, 14 July 1943

DURATION One day FRONTAGE 11.7 kilometers TERRAIN Rolling
WEATHER Weather had completely cleared.

	Attacker	*Defender*
Units	LSSAH PzGrD	XVIII TC, XXIX TC, 42nd GRD & 9th GAD
Attachments	See below	See below
Strength	20,952	31,782
Armor	92 (6 light)	169 (78 light)
Artillery	187	303
Air Sorties	24	0
Casualties	151 (21 KIA, 114 WIA, 16 MIA)	661 (144 KIA, 467 WIA, 50 MIA)
Armor Losses	0	1
Artillery Losses	2	5
Enemy Captured	N/A	3

Forces Engaged

German Attachments
55th Werfer Regiment
861st Light Field Howitzer Battalion
I/1st Lehr Werfer Regiment

Soviet Forces
XVIII Tank Corps
736th AT Bn
80th Gds Mtr Rgt
XXIX Tank Corps
1529th Heavy SP Art Rgt
76th Gds Mtr Rgt
2/3rds of 42nd Guards Rifle Division (127th and 136th Guards Rifle Regiments)
301st AT Rgt—attached on the 14th (included)
9th Guards Airborne Division

the positions at Prokhorovka. The division was to take Soviet positions on the east side of the line Ivanovka-Vinogradovka and begin moving up its panzer regiment for an attack on Pravorot. The first attack objective for the panzers was Pravorot, with the division to be ready to move on to Prokhorovka and take it by surprise if possible. If such an attack were successful, it would make the Donets triangle position untenable, because the main road now was cut.

The attack began at 0400 (Berlin time) after a short preparation by the artillery and werfer regiments.[3] The I and III Battalions of Der Fuehrer SS Regiment advanced from the north to Belenikhino and then from the west against the railroad embankment. After overcoming tough Soviet resistance and crossing extensive minefields, the attack penetrated into the north part of Belenikhino at 0700. Meanwhile, Burdeinyii (II Guards Tank Corps commander) had recalled the 25th Guards Tank Brigade from the Yablonovo-Plota area, and by 0700 (Moscow time) it had reached the western part of Vinogradovka.

Following a powerful artillery, mortar, and aircraft barrage, the Germans attacked with tanks at 0800 (Moscow time) the 183rd Rifle Division and II Guards Tank Corps at Belenikhino. After "fierce fighting," the Belenikhino train station was captured at 0830 (Mos-

3 Start time of the attack is also reported as 0355.

Overseeing the Tank Fields of Prokhorovka III, 15 July 1943

DURATION One day FRONTAGE 11.7 kilometers TERRAIN Rolling
WEATHER "Deluges of rain." Roads bottomless and not passable.

	Attacker	*Defender*
Units	LSSAH PzGrD	XVIII TC, XXIX TC & 9th GAD
Attachments	See below	See below
Strength	20,800	26,226
Armor	97 (6 light)	182 (85 light)
Artillery	187	256
Air Sorties	0	21
Casualties	130 (24 KIA, 103 WIA, 3 MIA)	158 (35 KIA, 123 WIA)
Armor Losses	9[4]	1
Artillery Losses	3	0
Enemy Captured	N/A	3

Forces Engaged

German Attachments
55th Werfer Regiment
861st Light Field Howitzer Battalion
I/1st Lehr Werfer Regiment

Soviet Forces
XVIII Tank Corps
736th AT Bn
80th Gds Mtr Rgt

XXIX Tank Corps
1529th Heavy SP Art Rgt
76th Gds Mtr Rgt
9th Guards Airborne Division

4 Three StuG IIIs and 4 Pz IVs reported as lost, even though daily reports indicate that inventory stayed the same or went up.

cow time). Vicious house-to-house fighting followed, during which the Germans claimed to have destroyed 12 Soviet tanks in close combat. The Germans then advanced east along the gully (ur. Polovik) towards Vinogradovka while concentrating tanks and motorized infantry in the woods east of Ivanovskii Vyiselok. At 1145 (Moscow time), the Soviets reported a German breakthrough of about 20 tanks in the Ivanovka area. It was preceded by another artillery and mortar barrage and supported by 100 aircraft (Soviet claim). The Soviet estimate of 100 aircraft may have been correct, for at 1000 hours, the Germans sent three Stuka groups to support Das Reich.

The Germans took Belenikhino at 1130 (Berlin time). The German infantry were well supported by effective artillery fire. The 4th and 25th Guards Tank Brigades could not withstand the German attack and lost 12 T-34s and nine T-70s and fell back along the line from Vinogradovka to Ivanovka. The 4th Guards Motorized Brigade was able to hold its position along the line from Ivanovka to the barracks five kilometers south of Belenikhino.

The II Guards Tank Corps was now holding with its 4th Guards Tank Brigade at Ivanovka, its 25th Guards Tank Brigade from the southern outskirts of Ivanovka to the slopes of the height one kilometer east of Leski, and its 4th Guards Motorized Rifle Brigade holding the slopes of the unnamed heights one kilometer west of Leski to the northwest slopes of height 225.0. The corps' 26th Guards Tank Brigade was still protecting Shakhovo from attack from the south. The corps still had 33 T-34s, 24 T-70s and 2 Churchills, but most of the T-34s were with the 26th Guards Tank Brigade in the south.

By 1245, the panzer regiment had assembled with its forward elements on the east edge of Belenikhino, ready to advance through Ivanovka to height 234.9 as soon as the artillery had eliminated the flanking fire from Leski. The panzer regiment was then to occupy the high ground.

In the attack from the west, the railroad at height 220.3 (south of Belenikhino) was reached. The 167th Infantry Division also joined in this attack on the railroad.

PRIVATE KAUFMANN, WITH the antiaircraft battery Der Fuehrer SS Regiment, recalls (probably supplemented by familiarity with the unit records):

> Our section commander SS Sergeant Trenkel showed up that night and instructed us on the situation. He said that according to the latest reports the enemy was receding in our sector and one could count on continuing the attack by early next morning. That's how it happened. We moved on eastward as early as 4 AM. The intermediate objective was Belenikhino and the elevated terrain beyond, so as to push on towards Pravorot after that. After extremely intense house-to-house fighting in Belenikhino, drawn out over hours from 7 until noon, the village was captured. The Grenadiers had destroyed twelve tanks in close combat this morning. The attack continued from Belenikhino in the early afternoon and Ivanovka was taken after heavy fire on our flanks. Together with an armored company under the I Battalion's command, we reached an elevation situated northeast of Leski after that. From there an attempt was made to push on to Pravorot that night. However, all movement had to be called off due to heavy rainfall softening the soil.

The German attack then stalled. Das Reich reported that its panzer group began moving eastward at 1300, but complained of heavy flanking fire from Leski. Then, for some reason, the corps did not hear from the division from 1330 until 1705, when they stated that the panzers had moved out at 1700. In the meantime, the III Panzer Corps was reporting at 1616 that its tanks were advancing toward hill 234.9 and were wondering where the Das Reich spearhead was.

It does not appear that Das Reich accomplished much between 1330 and 1700. At 1500 (Moscow time), the 183rd Rifle Division reported it was "securely" holding along the line from height 234.9 to Leski. The 183rd Rifle Division and II Guards Tank Corps were backed up by the II Tank Corps, although it does not appear to have been engaged on this day. This corps was holding the heights west of Pravorot to Vinogradovka. It still had 24 T-34s, 24 T-70s and 4 Churchills. Also in the rear, around Novoselovka, was the 10th Guards Mechanized Brigade.

AT 1700 (BERLIN time) the reinforced panzer regiment, after a heavy artillery barrage, was able to resume its advance. At 1800 (Moscow time, 1700 Berlin time) the German aircraft resumed their "massive" strikes against the II Guards Tank Corps units, including attacking the corps headquarters in Zhilomostnoye three times. At 1830 (Moscow time) the Germans launched an attack accompanied by massed bomber and assault aviation strikes. German tanks broke through the 183rd Rifle Division in the direction of Leski and height 234.9 while at the same time attacking Vinogradovka and Ivanovka. In a quick assault, the Germans took Ivanovka at 1715 (Berlin time) and hill 234.9 at 1825 (Berlin time) with their infantry, with the tanks arriving at 1850. The corps then ordered operations to continue during the night so as to take Pravorot. They then pressed northward, becoming engaged in a fight with Soviet tank forces at a point 2.5 kilometers west of Zhilomostnoye (south of hill 242.1) at dusk.

The Das Reich was again ordered to continue its attack during the night, and after taking Pravorot and the high ground just to the north, it was now to attack south with the panzer group from Adolf Hitler, and try to make contact with the III Panzer Corps. This nighttime attack was stopped in its initial phase after it took the high ridge east of the line Ivanovka-Vinogradovka.

THE II GUARDS Tank Corps, suffering heavy losses, at 2100 (Moscow time) fell back to the line running from southwest of Pravorot to Zhilomostnoye to Maloye Yablonovo to Shakhovo. Rotmistrov again committed his reserve, the 10th Guards Mechanized Brigade, from the Tikhaya Padina area (two kilometers northeast of Prokhorovka) to the Zhilomostnoye and Novoselovka area. The 26th Guards Tank Brigade was holding against the III Panzer Corps in Shakhovo, but sometime after 1830 (Moscow time), the brigade's second regiment was shifted from Shakhovo to between height 234.9 and Yablonovo so as to firm up the corps position in the southwest. This significantly weakened the corps defense of Shakhovo, with fatal results.

The Germans took Vinogradovka, Ivanovka, Leski, and Shakhovo during the night from the II Guards Tank Corps. Still, the Germans' attack toward Pravorot was not successful. The II Guards Tank Corps fell back on the line from the height southwest of Pravorot to Zhilomostnoye to Maloye Yablonovo to the height one kilometer north of Shakhovo. Its losses during the night (and the day?) were reported as 17 T-34s and nine T-70s.

The II Tank Corps was now re-engaged to support the II Guards Tank Corps, repelling a German infantry and tank attack from the woods north of Storozhevoye. The corps was concentrated in the area two kilometers east of Storozhevoye. At this point, the Fifth Guards Tank Army and Sixty-ninth Army had almost lost control of the road out of the Donets triangle, leaving the 81st Guards, 89th Guards, 93rd Guards and 375th Rifle Divisions potentially isolated.

THE NEXT MORNING, the Das Reich continued its attack to clear the triangle. This attack had been redirected during the night to drive to the south and advance to the Zhilomostnoye-Pravorot road, instead of continuing the drive against Prokhorovka. This attack started slowly because of weather. The regiments moved up at 0500 (Berlin time) to the security line running from height 234.9 to 232.3 to the east edge of the turtle woods, to the east of Vinogradovka to height 242.1 to the hill 1.5 kilometers north of Vinogradovka to the east edge of Storozhevoye. The bringing up of heavy weapons and the displacement of the artillery was severely hampered by the poor road conditions, especially in the gullies, and was not completed until 1200. Furthermore, the Germans were encountering deep minefields and an antitank ditch in front of Pravorot. At 1230 the Das Reich SS Division reported that the attack was bogged down. The area around Vinogradovka was totally soggy, and there were tremendous difficulties in bringing up supplies and reinforcements. There were strong Soviet antitank and antiaircraft defenses on height 242.7. They concluded that attacking was only possible by night.

While the Das Reich was trying to get ready for its attack, the situation in front of it was rapidly changing, for the III Panzer Corps was now having a very direct influence on the course of the battle. The Sixty-ninth Army had been struggling for several days fighting in what had become a "V", with the SS attacking its western side and the III Panzer Corps driving in from the south and southeast. With the advance during the late evening of the Das Reich SS Division from the west and the 7th Panzer Division from the south, this position had become untenable. The Voronezh Front was forced to conduct a withdrawal so as to save the enveloped forced trapped inside. Unfortunately for the Soviets, it was a withdrawal in poor weather, and as such, the same mud that was slowing down the German attack was also interfering with the Soviet rifle divisions' attempts to pull back their heavy weapons.

At some point during the day, the three rifle divisions of the XLVIII Rifle Corps that were facing the Das Reich SS Division and the 167th Infantry Division began their withdrawal. These divisions were able to withdraw without serious pursuit from the SS Panzer Corps. Of course, the objective of the Das Reich attack, Pravorot, was still being defended by the 183rd Rifle Division, parts of the XXIX Tank Corps, II Tank Corps, and II Guards Tank Corps

The 183rd Rifle Division still held the area southeast of Storozhevoye, but its defensive line now went southeast to Zhilomostnoye and then east toward Novoselovka. It was backed up by the 10th Mechanized Brigade, which claimed that on the 15th it kicked the Germans out of Zhilomostnoye before being involved late in the day in the fighting around Plota. The II Tank Corps, which started the day with all four of its brigades concentrated in the area two kilometers east of Storozhevoye, ended the day with two of its brigades two kilometers southeast of Storozhevoye, while its 26th and 99th Tank Brigades were turned into a mobile tank reserve in the Pravorot area. The corps was still reporting almost the same number of tanks ready for action as on the previous day although it is claimed to have repelled an attack during the day from the Storozhevoye and Vinogradovka area.

The II Guards Tank Corps, after its withdrawal during the night, had halted along a line running from the height southwest of Plota to Zhilomostnoye to Maloye Yablonovo to the height one kilometer north of Shakhovo. It was to be ready to counterattack in the morning to restore the situation. By 0700 (Moscow time) it had deployed in a layered defense facing south, with the 4th and 25th Guards Tank Brigades (which were reduced to a total of 7 T-34s and 5 T-70s) deployed in a second echelon position from height 242.7 to 1.5 kilometers southwest of Pravorot. The 4th Guards Motorized Rifle Brigade was in the northwest and southern outskirts of Maloye Yablonovo to Plota. The 26th Guards Tank Brigade (23 T-34s, 7 T-70s and 2 Churchills) was deployed between Maloye Yablonovo and Plota. It was now primarily engaged with the III Panzer Corps.

At 1200, a battle group of the Das Reich SS Panzer Regiment established contact with the 7th Panzer Division in Yablonovo and blocked the area to the south. By 1430, Leski, on the division's right flank, had been occupied without a fight by the 167th Infantry Division. It appears that most of the Soviet forces in the Donets triangle withdrew ahead of the German advance. Due to the shortening of the front, Das Reich was able to free its engineer battalion and its armored car battalion for other duties.

The Germans claimed that the Soviets were able to reinforce their defenses south and southwest of Pravorot through the commitment of additional antitank, flak and tank forces, but what they were seeing was mostly the concentration of the Fifth Guards Tank Army and Sixty-ninth Army forces that had previously been more dispersed. In the afternoon, the Germans observed "frantic" entrenchment activity along the whole edge of the city. The Germans shelled these activities.

After a short tank battle, the Soviets withdrew from height 242.7 (one and one-half kilometers southwest of Pravorot). During the afternoon, the Germans made preparations for a night attack by the reinforced Deutschland SS Regiment on the hills south of Pravorot, in particular hill 242.7. This attack was to be conducted towards Pravorot and was to fall on the XXIX Tank Corps from the Vinogradovka area and on the II Tank Corps from the Storozhevoye and Vinogradovka areas. The night attack was scheduled for 0200, but never occurred. At 2045, new orders arrived from the army for the corps to hold and reinforce its currently held line. So ended the last SS attack to capture Prokhorovka.

PRIVATE KAUFMANN CONTINUES his account:

> On July 15 at noon, the battalion again attempted to take Pravorot. But soon the attack became mired down in concentrated defensive fire and we had to dig in right there on the spot. As always, this occurred in the following sequence: first cover for every man, every man on his own, then as a joint effort for the halftrack. Armored engagements took place in the course of the next hours, where we could only be mere bystanders. From a tank crew from one of our own tanks that had been destroyed,

Attack towards Pravorot, 14 July 1943

DURATION One day FRONTAGE 8.5 kilometers TERRAIN Rolling
WEATHER Sunny, dry. Roads drying up.

	Attacker	*Defender*
Units	DR SS PzGrD	II GTC, 183rd RD & II TC
Attachments	See below	See below
Strength	18,881	23,715
Armor	120	83 (42 light)
Artillery	142	176
Air Sorties	189	0
Casualties	287 (58 KIA, 229 WIA)	1298 (436 KIA, 766 WIA, 96 MIA)
Armor Losses	4	10
Artillery Losses	0	17
Enemy Captured	N/A	1

Forces Engaged

German Attachments
III/1st Lehr Werfer Regiment
III/818th Artillery Regiment

Soviet Forces
II Guards Tank Corps (less the 26th Guards Tank Brigade and 2 Churchills)
1510th Antitank Regiment—detached the 14th (included)
755th AT Battalion
16th Guards Mortar Regiment
183rd Rifle Division
1852/32nd AT Bde—attached on the 14th (included)
II Tank Corps

and who stayed with us briefly, we learned that the Soviets had already lost a total of 450 tanks by the 14th of July. Their reserves seemed immeasurable, because the counterattacks continued with heavy armor support. The enemy attacked the spearhead and the flanks from our wedged attack formation simultaneously. Time and again, this brought us into severe jeopardy in the course of the following days. Despite heavy losses, the Soviet guards battalions kept trying to run over our positions. On several occasions, their attacks collapsed only a short distance from our positions under concentrated fire out of all barrels. The Soviet infantry suffered horrible losses as a result.

Air Support

The Das Reich SS Division complemented the "untiring attacks" of the Stuka pilots. The Luftwaffe considerably eased the task of the infantry. There was also strong enemy fighter defense over the battlefield. The Soviets reported on the 14th that 50 German aircraft

Attack on Pravorot stalls, 15 July 1943

DURATION One day FRONTAGE 8.3 kilometers TERRAIN Rolling
WEATHER Heavy rain in the morning, clearing in the afternoon. Roads very soft.

	Attacker	*Defender*
Units	DR SS PzGrD	II GTC, 183rd RD & II TC
Attachments	See below	See below
Strength	18,576	26,292
Armor	128	112 (53 light)
Artillery	142	177
Air Sorties	30	21 + 30 Night
Casualties	114 (26 KIA, 88 WIA)	248 (62 KIA, 170 WIA, 16 MIA)
Armor Losses	17	14
Artillery Losses	0	1
Enemy Captured	N/A	0

Forces Engaged

German Attachments
III/1st Lehr Werfer Regiment
III/818th Artillery Regiment

Soviet Forces
II Guards Tank Corps (less the 26th Guards Tank Brigade and 2 Churchills)
301st Antitank Regiment—attached on the 15th (included)
755th AT Battalion
16th Guards Mortar Regiment
183rd Rifle Division
1852/32nd AT Bde
II Tank Corps
10th Mechanized Bde

bombed Pravorot at 0910 and attacked Pravorot again with heavy bombers at 1130. The Germans reported little Soviet air activity for the 15th.

Summation of the Battles of Prokhorovka

On the 15th, the attacks to seize Prokhorovka ended. This village had been the focus of the SS Panzer Corps' attacks since at least 10 July, when Totenkopf had crossed the Psel for the purpose of working around to height 252.4, to its northwest. On the 11th, the Totenkopf SS Division had continued pushing across the Psel, while the Adolf Hitler SS Division advanced directly on Prokhorovka, taking height 252.2 to the southeast of the town. The Das Reich SS Division supported the attack on the right flank.

The following day, the 12th of July, the Soviets unleashed their tank attacks. These halted Adolf Hitler's and Das Reich's forward movement, but not Totenkopf,

TABLE 13.1
THE SS PANZER CORPS LOSSES IN THE ATTACKS AROUND PROKHOROVKA

	TOTENKOPF SS DIVISION		ADOLF HITLER SS DIVISION		DAS REICH SS DIVISION	
	Men	*Tanks*	*Men*	*Tanks*	*Men*	*Tanks*
10th	374	0	55	2	112	1
11th	461	3	337	11	221	2
12th	316	28	374	19	243	1
13th	160	29	326	0	61	4
14th	175	8	151	0	287	4
15th	65	1	130	9	114	17
Total	1,551	69	1,373	41	1,038	29

which continued attacking on the 12th and 13th, finally being ground to a halt by the heavy tank losses they were suffering. The following two days (14th and 15th), having failed to take the town from the front or from the left flank, the Das Reich SS Division then attempted to take the town from the south. This attack also failed even though the defending forces were unhinged by the III Panzer Corps' flanking attacks. The concentrated Soviet forces around Pravorot were extensive and the Germans were hesitant to push into them.

Let's look for a moment at the German losses in these attacks in Table 13.1. The average losses for these divisions for the five days from the 5th through the 9th were 1,184 men and 90 tanks (Totenkopf: 804 men, 64 tanks; Adolf Hitler: 1,612 men, 105 tanks; Das Reich: 1,137 men, 101 tanks).[5] It is clear from the personnel losses that the various attacks on Prokhorovka were carried forward with the same intensity and force that was used to penetrate the first two defensive lines. Still, their armor losses were clearly less. It is also clear that the fighting in the first five days of the offensive was as significant as the fighting around Prokhorovka, and much more so when it comes to armor losses!

5 None of these tank figures include losses in self-propelled artillery or guns (Wespe, Grille, nor Hummel), nor artillery observation tanks. They do include Sturmgeschuetzes and Marders.

For six days, the SS Panzer Corps had tried to take the town from three directions. All attacks failed. The SS Panzer Corps had stalled. In fact, it had been stopped cold by the Soviet defenders. This was not an attack that had failed due to a lack of energy. It was not an attack that had stopped because it had been called off by Adolf Hitler! It was also not an attack that had been defeated by Rotmistrov's counterattack on the 12th. All Rotmistrov's attacks had done was waste Russian lives for little military advantage. **It was an attack that was stopped by a solid Soviet defense with their infantry, antitank guns, artillery and tanks.**

The Germans had continued to attack for three full days after the famous Battle of Prokhorovka, losing more armor in their attacks on the following days than they lost on the day of the famous "death ride" of the panzers. So ended the offensive efforts of the SS Panzer Corps at Kursk.

THE 167TH INFANTRY DIVISION

Meanwhile, the 167th Infantry Division continued to connect the flanks of the two attacking German armies. The night of 13/14 July was relatively quiet except for artillery and rocket barrages on the division's flanks and many probes against its right wing.

At 0830 in the morning the division requested

air support so it could clear up a Soviet penetration at Nepkhayevo (this was probably an existing position, as opposed to a new penetration). The division was informed that German aircraft could not take off because of the weather and that it was sufficient for the division to keep the Soviet penetration from making further progress. It was not necessary to throw the Soviet forces back.

At 0845, the division reported heavy casualties in clearing the west bank of the Donets. The Fourth Panzer Army ordered that pressure should only be applied when weak enemy resistance was encountered. Meanwhile the division was waiting on the SS attack to develop. At 1015 the attack of Das Reich SS Division on Belenikhino was reported to be meeting very strong resistance and getting flanking fire from Leski and Teterevino, so the 167th Infantry Division was requested to provide artillery support, and to do so with the help of aerial observers. At 1030, the 339th Infantry Regiment was ordered to support the SS attack by attacking the woods east of Kalinin with its left wing as soon as Belenikhino was in SS hands. Observers were reporting large groups of Russians heading north and northeast out of Leski.

Belenikhino fell at 1130, but for some reason the report did not reach this division until 1200. At 1215, the 339th Infantry Regiment began pushing its left onto the hills south of Belenikhino and putting out patrols along its whole front. The left wing of the 339th Infantry Regiment was reported to be moving forward at 1350, receiving heavy flanking fire from Teterevino and the railroad embankment. The artillery regiment was requested by Das Reich to fire smoke on the hill north of Leski. By 1700, the 339th's left wing had reached the railroad booth two kilometers south of Belenikhino. The Soviets were occupying prepared positions on the heights west of the railroad. This halted the German advance for the day.

Holding Leski was the 183rd Rifle Division. To the south, positioned around Teterevino was the 375th Rifle Division, which reported no activity on its front this day. Still, something happened, for they recorded either 101 or 1,009 casualties for this day![6] The 93rd Guards Rifle Division held position south of Teterevino down to Gostishchevo, again with little activity for the day.

The 167th Infantry Division was also attacked at Rozhdestvenka during the day, but this was beaten off. German air activity was lively throughout the day. There was little Soviet air activity, just some bombing of the front line.

THE NIGHT OF 14/15 July passed quietly except for some Soviet patrols. The 331st Infantry Regiment extended its left and prepared to attack the heights at Leski the following day. Artillery was moved up to support the attack.

At 0800, the Soviets were reported to be abandoning the west bank of the Donets. At 0803, the Fourth Panzer Army reported (optimistically) that the Soviets were now encircled in the Donets triangle, and ordered the 167th Infantry Division to cooperate with the 168th Infantry Division in rolling up the Soviet positions in the area between the railroad and the Lipovyii Donets towards the north. However, because such an operation would require a complete reorganization of the division's positions, which were concentrated on the left for the attack on the heights at Leski, Trierenburg (167th Infantry Division commander) decided to let the Leski attack proceed. The 331st Infantry Regiment concentrated, while the 315th Infantry Regiment moved

6 The division reported 17 killed, 51 wounded and 33 missing for 14 July, along with reporting that the division remained in its previous position (Fond: 1696, Opis: 1, Delo: 36, pages 250-251). There is a corps report of 385 killed and 624 wounded for this day along with much lower reports for the 183rd Rifle Division and 93rd Guards Rifle Division (Fond: 932, Opis: 1, Delo: 23, page 12). We have no reason to question the reports for the 183rd Rifle Division and the 93rd Guards Rifle Division. Clearly the 375th Rifle Division took very heavy losses at Kursk: 4,898 losses reported for 6th–18th (Fond: 932, Opis: 1, Delo: 23, page 19), and a decline in strength from 8,727 men on the 1st (Fond: 872, Opis: 1, Delo: 468, page 12) to 3,768 men on the 18th (Fond: 426, Opis: 10753, Delo: 110, page 4). It is not known with confidence whether they took over a thousand casualties this day or if it was a previous day.

167th Infantry Division, 14 July 1943

DURATION One day FRONTAGE 27.2 kilometers TERRAIN Rolling, mixed
WEATHER Very cool, poor visibility.

	Attacker	*Defender*
Units	167th ID	375th Rifle & 93rd Gds Rifle Divisions
Attachments	None	See below
Strength	13,109	14,075
Armor	0	0
Artillery	94	88
Air Sorties	0	0
Casualties	104 (26 KIA, 73 WIA, 5 MIA)	1,094 (405 KIA, 664 WIA, 25 MIA)
Artillery Losses	0	4
Enemy Captured	N/A	2

Forces Engaged

Soviet Forces
375th Rifle Division
1240th AT Rgt
137th ATR Bn
88th Flamethrower Company
192nd Flamethrower Company
1363/26th Antiaircraft Division
60th Armored Train Detachment

2/3rds of 93rd Guards Rifle Division (no casualties counted)
1/3rd 51st Guards Rifle Division (158th Guards Rifle Regiment)

to the east to destroy the Soviets. At 0900 the 331st was ordered to push the withdrawing Soviets toward the east, into the 315th, take height 225.0, and tie in with the 339th Infantry Regiment near Leski. The 315th was ordered to push on to the railroad while sending one company south toward Gostishchevo.

At 1200, the 339th Infantry Regiment reported that it was advancing. The left flank of the regiment had reached the lightly defended Leski. At 1330, part of the 315th crossed the Donets and at 1340 had reached Teterevino. At 1415, the 331st was ordered to take the heights south of Plota and west of the Severnyii Donets. By 1450, the division had reached the line running from Shcholokovo to Shakhovo to the heights east of Leski. The division's artillery displaced forward to support the advance, with the light battalions just behind the front line and the heavy battalion in the center of the sector near Volobuyevka.

At 1700 the division still had its right wing across the Sazhnovskii Donets and its left wing at the Leski heights, but it was reporting that communications with the 168th Infantry Division on the right and the SS Panzer Corps on the left were quite bad, and the division had no clear picture of the overall situation in the Provisional Army Kempf sector. At 1800, the 315th Infantry Regiment was ordered to withdraw from the front and assemble in the area of Kleimenovo, Chursino and Sazhnoye, "because the situation indicated that the division would shift its thrust."

167th Infantry Division, 15 July 1943

DURATION One day FRONTAGE 27.2 kilometers TERRAIN Rolling, mixed
WEATHER Variably cloudy, occasional thundershowers. Road conditions improving.

	Attacker	*Defender*
Units	167th ID	375th Rifle & 93rd Gds Rifle Divisions
Attachments	None	See below
Strength	13,005	12,976
Armor	0	0
Artillery	94	84
Air Sorties	0	0
Casualties	104 (26 KIA, 73 WIA, 5 MIA)	1,143 (44 KIA, 147 WIA, 952 MIA)
Artillery Losses	0	10
Enemy Captured	N/A	0

Forces Engaged

Soviet Forces
375th Rifle Division
1240th AT Rgt
137th ATR Bn
88th Flamethrower Company
192nd Flamethrower Company
1363/26th Antiaircraft Division
60th Armored Train Detachment

2/3rds of 93rd Guards Rifle Division (2/3rds of casualties counted)
1/3rd 51st Guards Rifle Division (158th Guards Rifle Regiment)

The division, with considerable independent initiative, had taken over the areas that the Soviets were withdrawing from and re-established a new line. Their front was some 27 kilometers in length. It does not appear that they were heavily engaged during the course of the day.

III Panzer Corps Operations

The III Panzer Corps operations to date had been of little overall value to the conduct of the offensive. Granted, they, along with Corps Raus, had tied up the forces opposite them, including the entire Seventh Guards Army and its two tank brigades and two tank regiments. They also eventually drew in two divisions from the Sixth Guards Army (the 89th Guards and the 375th Rifle Divisions), four divisions from the Sixty-ninth Army, the three divisions of the XXXV Guards Rifle Corps, and the majority of the V Guards Mechanized Corps. Still this corps had not reaped a lot from its efforts, especially in light of the heavy losses suffered by this corps and the supporting Corps Raus. The cleaning up of the Donets triangle was going to be the one big benefit garnished from this corps' operations.

For most of the day of the 14th, however, little was done by the corps to help reduce this triangle. The 168th Infantry Division continued to apply pressure to Gostishchevo while the 19th Panzer Division secured its bridgeheads. The 6th and 7th Panzer Divisions were still off to the east pushing farther east and northeast, well into the second defensive line of the Seventh Guards Army. The III Panzer Corps would not began to push north until late in the day, and with surprising success.

Gostishchevo

In the morning, the 417th Infantry Regiment made a strong probing attack from the north edge of the pants-shaped woods. This attack reached the north edge of the woods east of height 223.2 and recaptured the height itself. The Germans took 22 prisoners and rounded up 38 deserters. During the evening of the 14th, the 417th Infantry Regiment pushed reconnaissance patrols forward to Gostishchevo, which overcame Soviet resistance and reached the line running from the northern wood line, some 1200 meters south of the east entrance of Gostishchevo, to 300 meters north of height 223.2. Gostishchevo and the train station to the south of the town were found to be held by strong Soviet forces.

In addition to elements of the 93rd Guards Rifle Division, the 267th Guards Rifle Regiment (89th Guards Rifle Division) was holding in the southern outskirts of Gostishchevo to the southern slopes of height 223.2 to the eastern outskirts of Shakhovo.[7] They reported that the Germans took Druzhnyii.

Ryindinka Bridgehead

The 19th Panzer Division's orders for this day were to hold the bridgehead, which was clearly a problem the previous day. If Soviet resistance was weak, then the 19th Panzer Division was to enlarge the bridgehead to the woods two kilometers west of Shcholokovo.

Operations had ended the previous day at around 1900, with the Soviet forces driven out of the bridgehead by Battle Group Richter (now commanded by Major von Mentz). During the night, there was light Soviet bombing on positions in the bridgehead and the supply routes. The 19th Panzer Engineer Battalion completed the 24-ton bridge at Rzhavets during the night. Beginning at daybreak and continuing throughout the morning there were continuous, and at times heavy, Soviet air attacks throughout the division sector.

As part of the clearing operation in the Ryindinka bridgehead, Shipyi was attacked early on 14 July. After hard fighting, the stubborn Soviet defense was overcome and the town taken. Soviet counterattacks and an attack in regimental strength out of the woods east of Shakhovo and northeast of Shcholokovo on the left wing were defeated with the help of tanks. According to German accounts, the attacker suffered many casualties and many prisoners were taken. The Soviet forces were reported to be then assembling again in the large ravine northeast of Shakhovo, with at least 10 tanks. The Sixty-ninth Army reported that the Germans advanced with a regiment of infantry and 50 tanks from Shcholokovo and Ryindinka to Shakhovo. The 19th Panzer Division still had 37 tanks operational, including 5 Panzer Is and IIs.

A German reconnaissance patrol that was operating in the wooded gully west of the Shcholokovo bridgehead was surrounded and routed. One sergeant of the 19th Reconnaissance Battalion fell into Soviet hands. South of the city, Soviet patrols trying to cross the river were destroyed or turned back by the train personnel (supply personnel) of the 19th Reconnaissance Battalion.

The 89th Guards Rifle Division had two rifle regiments facing these bridgeheads, with the 270th Guards Rifle Regiment stretched from the grove southeast of Gostishchevo to the eastern part of Sazhnoye to the grove northwest of Krivtsovo. The 273rd Guards Rifle Regiment was on the line northwest of Krivtsovo to the grove one kilometer southeast of Kleimenovo. The division's losses for this day were less than a hundred, even though the 273rd Guards Rifle Regiment claimed that it was fighting to take Krivtsovo and Strelnikov. They reported that by the end of the day, the Germans had managed to take Ryindinka, Shipyi, Shakhovo and Krivtsovo. The 81st Guards Rifle Division covered the area from Shcholokovo to Shakhovo. The 26th Guards Tank Brigade remained south of Shakhovo, trading artillery fire with the Germans.

7 This regiment claimed to have attacked during the night of 13/14 and threw the Germans out of Gostishchevo, but it appears that the 93rd Guards Rifle did that the day before.

The 7th Panzer Division Attacks Again

On this day, 14 July, the 7th Panzer Division, in conjunction with the 6th Panzer Division, was again on the attack. Still this attack was heading to the east and northeast, which did little to directly support Das Reich's or the Fourth Panzer Army's attack. The division was to attack via Vyipolzovka, Krasnoye Znamya and height 222.1 (four kilometers east-northeast of Rzhavets) to take the Soviets from the rear around Aleksandrovka (four kilometers south-southeast of hill 222.1).

During the night, a new battle group was formed to relieve the battle group fighting its way toward height 222.1 via Vyipolzovka and Krasnoye Znamya. The new battle group had the mission of attacking out of Kurakovka toward the northeast over height 218.0 to take height 222.1. The left battle group jumped off at 0530. It took Krasnoye Znamya at 0730 after very hard fighting, but its failure to take Andreyevka by 0715 forced the cancellation of a planned attack by the 6th Panzer Division on Aleksandrovka. In a continued attack from the southeast, a part of the battle group forced its way into Andreyevka and destroyed seven Soviet tanks that were part of strong Soviet tank force (German claims). The battle group attained height 222.1 at 1015, after having to breach numerous minefields.

The right-hand battle group moved forward across two gullies running southeast from Vyipolzovka and Krasnoye Znamya toward height 222.1. The battle group occupied the heights east of height 222.1. The foremost line of penetration during the operation extended along the heights about seven kilometers north of Kazachye (height 222.1 to height 224.3).

In the area were the 92nd Guards Rifle Division, the 11th and 12th Mechanized Brigades of Trufanov's mobile group, and Trufanov's forward detachment. The 92nd Guards Rifle Division ended up falling back to a line running from height 222.1 to point +1.5. This effectively deployed most of the division against the 6th Panzer Division. Across the Donets the 11th Guards Mechanized Brigade was holding from the southern slopes of height 135.09 to the southeastern outskirts of Kuzminka. The 12th Guards Mechanized Brigade was the 7th Panzer Division's primary opponent. It ended the day in Avdeyevka. Trufanov's detachment pulled back from Aleksandrovka, where it faced the 6th Panzer Division, having suffered a loss of 14 T-34s (all irreplaceable losses), probably suffered the previous day.[8] The detachment still had 18 T-34s and 6 T-70s. The 1st Guards Motorcycle Regiment was holding at height 223.5 to the western outskirts of Novo-Khmelevoi, while the 53rd Guards Tank Regiment held the southwestern outskirts of that town.[9] Trufanov's detachment claimed 20 German tanks destroyed, including 10 Tigers. In all reality, the 6th Panzer Division's losses for the 13th and 14th were around 6 tanks, and the entire 503rd Heavy Panzer Battalion is estimated to have lost 11 Tigers during these two days.[10]

The Sixty-ninth Army records that this attack was conducted by a regiment of infantry, supported by 60 tanks (including 10 "Tigers") in the direction of Ryindinka, Vyipolzovka, Krasnoye Znamya, height 222.1, and Novo-Khmelevoi. The 7th Panzer Division only had 41 tanks ready for action this day and probably only 3 operational Tigers attached to it. Vyipolzovka fell at

8 There is some question about this. The loss report is from 1900 on the 14th, but it appears to be a report catching up the status from earlier reports. It is hard to determine what day these losses occurred.

Regardless, it does not appear the units of Trufanov's forward detachment were significantly engaged after the 14th, and most of their losses occurred between 2000 on the 12th and sometime on the 14th.

9 While the Fifth Guards Tank Army consistently reported between 15 to 18 T-34s and 6 T-70s ready for action at 1900 on the 14th, 0700 on the 15th, 0400 on the 16th, and 0400 on the 17th' the tank regiment reported six T-34s and seven T-70s ready-for-action for the 13th and then claimed that it got tangled up in a tank battle north of Aleksandrovka, and lost all tanks but one T-34! It claimed 35 killed and wounded for the 14th. That regiment was reduced to one tank and a composite rifle company (Fond: 53rd Gds TRgt, Opis: 20831, Delo: 1, pages 22–29).

10 The last strength report for the 503rd Heavy Panzer Battalion was 23 tanks on the 10th, which we believe was also their strength on the 11th. They reported at 0725 on the 11th having 17 Tigers with the 6th Panzer Division, 3 with the 7th Panzer Division and 1 with the 19th Panzer Division. The company with the 6th Panzer Division was reported later on the 11th as having grown to 19 tanks. They reported 6 Tigers ready for action for the entire battalion on the 14th.

1200 (Moscow time). The Sixty-ninth Army reports halting the attack by 1630 (Moscow time). Actually, the Germans had halted so they could shift their attack north, which is probably what they should have been doing the whole time. Again the claims of success tied to Trufanov's forces appear to be overstated.

Breith, in his post-war account, does again claim a major victory and that the close teamwork of the 6th and 7th Panzer Divisions had destroyed a large number of Soviet tanks. The question then arose whether they were going to exploit their victory and continue the drive eastward in order to capture Korocha, or turn northwest as planned. The army group decided to conduct the push to the northwest "although the possibilities of an attack on Korocha were fully realized."[11]

New orders from the III Panzer Corps brought about a reorganization. At about 1400 (Berlin time), the 1st company of the 7th Reconnaissance Battalion was sent into the Shcholokovo bridgehead. The rest of the reconnaissance battalion was later ordered forward to strengthen this bridgehead and to reconnoiter the woods south of Shcholokovo. The reconnaissance mission continued into the evening. The bulk of the division started moving to the bridgehead at 1515. The 7th Panzer Division was finally ready to start pushing north. It was to attack west and northwest out of the Shcholokovo bridgehead toward Novoselovka and Zhilomostnoye.

This attack was particularly successful, effectively unhinging the Sixty-ninth Army's position. Shakhovo was occupied by Battle Group Schulz between 2000 and 2130 on the 14th of July. The opposing 81st Guards Rifle Division that was defending the bridgehead gave way, although it is hard to blame it for this. This Soviet division had been engaged in heavy combat since the 5th and had already been enveloped once. It had performed as well as any division on the Soviet side. The 81st Guards Rifle Division suffered 130 casualties on this day. It reported that by 2000 (Moscow time) the Germans had managed to push the division's units out of Shakhovo-Kleimenovo and reach Maloye Yablonovo.

The 26th Guards Tank Brigade was left defending Shakhovo but facing the Ryindinka bridgehead. To shore up the II Guards Tank Corps' position from the southwest, Burdeinyii had sent the brigade's second regiment after 1830 (Moscow time) to the area of height 234.9 to Yablonovo. This left the area around Shakhovo dangerously weak. At 2130 (Moscow time) they reported that the Germans had launched their attack towards Shakhovo. The remaining first regiment of the brigade, consisting of nine T-34s and two Churchills, fought for three hours to hold back the German advance, but was forced to withdraw and take up position along the line from the mound northeast of height 237.1 to Prokrovka (on the Donets). The Fifth Guards Tank Army reported that the force attacking Shakhovo had two infantry battalions and 50 tanks.

This sudden collapse was a major failing on the part of the Soviet defenders, but considering the number of points the Donets triangle was being attacked at, and the general convoluted defense effort required to hold it, it is not surprising that it finally collapsed. This success late in the day sealed the fate of the Donets triangle, and was fundamentally created by the attack of one weakened panzer division. The shifting back of the second regiment of the 26th Guards Tank Brigade to face the SS Panzer Corps certainly weakened the defense of Shakhovo and could not have occurred at a worse time. In the face of attacks from multiple directions, it would have been hard for Burdeinyii to have matched the German forces successfully across the eleven kilometers of front he was trying to cover. The fundamental problem seems to lie with the Sixty-ninth Army. They appear to have put most of their reinforcing forces and armor over to the XXXV Guards Rifle Corps to protect against a northeast push. This appears to have been the wrong emphasis.

The 7th Panzer Division did have some problems with the escaping Russians crossing their main support highway in their rear and temporarily cutting them off.[12]

The Germans then moved the 58th Panzer Engineer Battalion and II Battalion, 7th Panzer Grenadier Regi-

11 Breith, page 10.

12 Breith, page 10.

ment across the Donets during the night to strengthen the bridgehead. Battle Group Steinkeller was supposed to follow them closely, but its relief by elements of the 6th Panzer Division in the hills south of Andreyevka was greatly delayed and did not occur until after 1600.

Aleksandrovka

The 6th Panzer Division was to attack Aleksandrovka at 0715, taking height 241.5 (which was just beyond Aleksandrovka) and then attacking through Novo-Khmelevoi and onto height 233.1. It was to then screen the corps' east flank. This was a drive of some seven kilometers into Soviet lines. It is not clear why this drive needed to be done before setting up a defensive line and turning the III Panzer Corps offensive to the north.

The night passed quietly, but with continuous Soviet air activity. Bombing in the division sector resumed at dawn. The division closed on its assembly area for the attack on Aleksandrovka.

Early in the morning, the 6th Reconnaissance Battalion (Battle Group Quentin) received artillery fire from the direction of Sviridovo, to its right. The Soviets were reported digging in north of the two lakes in the Razumnaya valley and Soviet mine laying was reported about one kilometer west of height 235.

Panzer Group Baeke (Baeke had replaced Oppeln-Bronikowski on the 12th) and Battle Group Unrein attacked at 0700 (Berlin time) after heavy artillery preparation. The defending 305th Rifle Division reported fighting a German attack that started at 0730 (Moscow time) of a regiment and 50 tanks. Again, the Germans only had 28 tanks ready for action plus a handful of attached Tiger tanks. After hard fighting, especially by the panzer grenadier regiment, which faced bitter resistance on the south edge of Aleksandrovka, that town was taken. The supporting 96th Tank Brigade lost four T-34s.

The Soviets then claimed that the Germans regrouped and resumed this attack at 1300 (Moscow time) in the direction of Novo-Khmelevoi and Sviridovo. Panzer Group Baeke then attacked over height 241.5 towards height 231.5 (the distance between these two points was about 1250 meters). The Germans claimed they destroyed 25 Soviet tanks, 41 antitank guns and 12 field guns. The Sixty-ninth Army claims the German advance was halted at 1630 (Moscow time). The 305th Rifle Division by 1800 was defending the mound +1.5 (halfway between 241.5 and 231.5) to Sviridovo to Podsumki. This would put it still in front of height 231.5.

Then the 6th Panzer Division established a defensive line along the heights east of Kazachye to Aleksandrovka to height 241.5 to height 222.1 to Krasnoye Znamya in compliance with the corps' orders. Part of the 7th Panzer Division was relieved in Krasnoye Znamya. The 503rd Heavy Panzer Battalion was also detached from the division and returned to the III Panzer Corps' control.

The other two Soviet divisions in the XXXV Guards Rifle Corps were to the east and southeast of the 6th Panzer Division and mostly out of the line of its offensive. The 107th Rifle Division remained where it was, with the 516th Rifle Regiment deployed from the Lebedki gully to the eastern shore of the southern lake in the Razumnaya gully. This was clearly the engaged regiment, as the other two rifle regiments were away from the front line, with the 504th Rifle Regiment deployed facing the southwest with its right flank starting from the southern lake and then along a southeasterly line to Lomovo, Gremyachii to Ploskoye, while the 522nd Rifle Regiment was in the western outskirts of Zayachye. In effect, two regiments of this division made up a second echelon position going back to the Koren River. They were now joined by the reconstituted 148th Tank Regiment, which came back to the line by moving to Podsumki garden with two T-34s and one T-70. It appears that the 516th Rifle Regiment was bloodied this day as they reported losing up to 228 men on 14 July.[13] As this division was deployed on the 13th up to Sviridovo it is suspected that at least one regiment was engaged with the 6th Panzer Division.

---

13 This is from Operational Report #00304 dated 0400 16 July 1943. This is still a pretty vague casualty report for a day-and-a-half-old report (Fond: Sixty-ninth Army, Opis: 10753, Delo: 133, page 36).

Gostishchevo III, 14 July 1943

DURATION One day FRONTAGE 6.0 kilometers TERRAIN Rolling, mixed
WEATHER Sunny and warm. Road conditions good.

	Attacker	*Defender*
Units	417th Inf Rgt/168th Infantry Division	281st Rgt/93rd Gds Rifle Division & 267th Rgt/89th Gds Rifle Division
Attachments	None	None
Strength	4,534	4,292
Armor	0	0
Artillery	36	33
Air Sorties	0	24 Night
Casualties	117 (19 KIA, 95 WIA, 3 MIA)	359 (78 KIA, 260 WIA, 21 MIA)
Artillery Losses	1	3
Enemy Captured	60 (38 deserters)	0

Defense Line along the Razumnaya, 14 July 1943

DURATION One day FRONTAGE 17.5 kilometers TERRAIN Rolling, mixed
WEATHER Sunny and warm. Road conditions good.

	Attacker	*Defender*
Units	94th Gds Rifle Division	168th Infantry Division (less 417th Inf Rgt)
Attachments	None	See below
Strength	7,462	9,666
Armor	0	6
Artillery	46	72
Air Sorties	24 Night	0
Casualties	76 (14 KIA, 43 WIA, 19 MIA)[14]	0
Armor Losses	0	0
Artillery Losses	1	0
Enemy Captured	0	N/A

Forces Engaged

German Attachments
2/228th StuG Bn
lt Bty/I/61st AA Rgt (not included)
I/38th Flak Rgt—detached on the 14th (not included)

Still detached from the division
248th Engineer Bn (less 3 cos) (included)
429th Infantry Rgt (less 1 Bn) (included)

14 The Sixty-ninth Army reported in the 0400 16 July report that the 94th Guards Rifle Division suffered 836 casualties on 14–15 July and in the 2330 16 July report recorded 760 men lost in the fighting on 15 July (Fond: Sixty-ninth Army, Opis: 10753, Delo: 133, pages 36-40).

Ryindinka Bridgehead, 14 July 1943

DURATION One day FRONTAGE 4.8 kilometers TERRAIN Rolling, mixed
WEATHER Bright, dry. Temperature at noon: 21 degrees Celsius. Roads conditions good.

	Attacker	*Defender*
Units	19th PzD	89th GRD, 26th GTB & 11th GMB
Attachments	See below	See below
Strength	16,458	8,553
Armor	37 (5 light)	64 (21 light)
Artillery	129	56
Air Sorties	29	75 + 48 Night
Casualties	41 (7 KIA, 32 WIA, 2 MIA)	500 (119 KIA, 288 WIA, 93 MIA)[15]
Armor Losses	0	32
Artillery Losses	1	2
Enemy Captured	N/A	3

Forces Engaged

German Attachments
70th Engineer Bn
2/411th Bridge Column B
842nd Bridge Column J

52nd Werfer Rgt
I/61st Flak Rgt (less 1 battery)

429th Infantry Rgt (168th ID), less I Battalion (not included)
I/114th Panzer Grenadier Rgt (from 6th PzD) (not included)

Detached
ObsBty/19th Artillery Rgt (included)

Soviet Forces
2/3rds of 89th Guards Rifle Division
26th Guards Tank Brigade
+ 2 Churchills from 47th Gds Tank Regiment
11th Guards Mechanized Brigade I/54th Werfer Rgt

Detached
ObsBty/78th Artillery Rgt (included)
Regimental Group (included)

15 Soviet losses were clearly high this day, with the 11th Guards Mechanized Brigade reporting 394 casualties (Fond: 332, Opis: 1943, Delo: 80, pages 14-17) and the 89th Guards Rifle Division reporting 35 killed and 60 wounded for 14 July (Fond: 1252, Opis: 1, Delo: 22, page 13). German losses were clearly low during this period with the 19th Panzer Division reporting 1,728 casualties from the 5th through the 9th, and 2,118 casualties (266 killed, 1758 wounded, 94 missing) for the 5th through the 20th. This is a difference of 390 and an average of 35 casualties a day from the 10th through the 20th.

The 7th Panzer Division Attacks Again II, 14 July 1943

DURATION From 1500 until 2130 (6.5 hours) FRONTAGE 2.0 kilometers TERRAIN Rolling, mixed
WEATHER Increasingly cloudy. Roads good.

	Attacker	*Defender*
Units	7th PzD	81st Guards Rifle Division
Attachments	See below	None
Strength	17,694	5,708
Armor	32 (4 light)	0
Artillery	133	23
Air Sorties	0	48 Night
Casualties	11 (1 KIA, 10 WIA)	237 (57 KIA, 73 WIA, 106 MIA)
Armor Losses	0	0
Artillery Losses	0	4
Enemy Captured	N/A	0

Forces Engaged

German Attachments

As above except I/38th Flak Rgt—attached on the 14th at 1600 is now included.

Aleksandrovka, 14 July 1943

DURATION One day FRONTAGE 11.7 kilometers TERRAIN Rolling, mixed
WEATHER Heavy rainfall, clearing in the afternoon. Bright and dry by the end of the day.
TEMPERATURE AT NOON 21 degrees Celsius. Roads in steeper areas impassable, but were good by the end of the day.

	Attacker	*Defender*
Units	6th PzD	92nd Gds RD, 305th RD & others
Attachments	See below	See below
Strength	21,612	19,444
Armor	48 (4 light)	40 (9 light)
Artillery	137	152
Air Sorties	29	87 + 48 Night
Casualties	110 (18 KIA, 90 WIA, 2 MIA)	945 (182 KIA, 596 WIA, 167 MIA)
Armor Losses	8	4
Artillery Losses	0	17
Enemy Captured	N/A	1

Forces Engaged

German Attachments
II/62nd Artillery Rgt
II/54th Werfer Rgt
III/54th Werfer Rgt
Hq/54th Werfer Rgt

II/43rd Flak Rgt
lt Bn/91st Flak Rgt
204th Intelligence Troop

228th StuG Bn (less 2nd company)
503rd Heavy Panzer Bn—detached on the 14th (included)

Detached
ObsBty/76th Artillery Rgt (included)
I/114th Panzer Grenadier Rgt (included)

Soviet Forces
92nd Guards Rifle Division
96th Tank Brigade—detached on the 14th (included)
315th Guards Mtr Rgt
305th Rifle Division
148th Tank Regiment (not included)
Trufanov's forward detachment
1/3rd 107th Rifle Division (but all losses included)
123rd ATR Bn
130th ATR Bn
496th Mtr Rgt

III Panzer Corps Assets
601st Engineer Rgt Staff—detached from corps on the 14th
674th Engineer Rgt Staff
925th Bridge Construction Staff
127th Engineer Bn (less co)—detached from corps on the 14th
531st Bridge Construction Bn—detached from corps on the 14th
110th Bridge Column B—detached from corps on the 14th
602nd Bridge Column B
co/538th Road Construction Bn—detached from corps on the 14th

153rd Flak Rgt Staff

3rd Command of Artillery
612th Artillery Rgt Staff
II/62nd Artillery Rgt
II/71st Artillery Rgt
857th Heavy Artillery Rgt
Pn/13th Light Observations Battery
ObsBty/19th Artillery Rgt (19th PzD)
ObsBty/76th Artillery Rgt (6th PzD)

2nd Fuel Column Troop
545th Panzer Recovery Platoon
503rd Heavy Panzer Bn—attached on the 14th
Regimental Group (from 7th PzD)

The 94th Guards Rifle Division was still holding from 500 meters south of Komintern (the road junction at map coordinate 24-50) down to Mazikino to Sheino to the garden south of the outskirts of Sheino and on to Ushakovo and the northeastern slopes of height 210.3. It reported no losses for this day. Both of these divisions were effectively opposite the 168th Infantry Division.

The Rest of the 168th Infantry Division

The other two infantry regiments continued holding the right flank of the corps. The 429th Infantry Regiment repelled a Soviet reconnaissance patrol on its left wing during the night, but otherwise, there are no other reports of activity.

Air Support

The 19th Panzer Division reported that during the night there was light Soviet bombing on the positions in the bridgehead and supply areas. Beginning at daybreak and continuing throughout the morning there were continuous, and at times heavy, Soviet air attacks throughout the division sector. The 7th Panzer Division reported heavy Soviet air activity during the night and the early morning hours. The 6th Panzer Division reported continuous Soviet air activity during the night, with bombing in the division sector resuming at dawn. The 168th Infantry Division reported heavy Soviet air activity in the Razumnaya sector during the night.

The III Panzer Corps Finally Pushes North

Finally on the 15th, ten days after the start of the offensive, the III Panzer Corps was able to clear the Donets triangle. It had the 417th Infantry Regiment, the 7th Panzer Division, and the 19th Panzer Division pushing north, while the 6th Panzer Division and most of the 168th Infantry Division were relegated to protecting the right flank of the corps.

The Soviet Withdrawal

The 81st Guards, 89th Guards, 93rd Guards and 375th Rifle Divisions were left enveloped by the late evening advance of the previous day. Little was recorded of their activity for this day. The XLVIII Rifle Corps ordered its units to withdraw in the morning. The 89th Guards Rifle Division reported that is was encircled, but by 2200 (Moscow time) had pulled back to a line from Novoselovka to Kuzminka. In the case of the 93rd Guards Rifle Division, it spent the day "fighting in encirclement" and then reported on the 16th to have "left the encirclement" and pulled back to a line from Pravorot to Dalnii Dolzhik.[16]

Table 13.2
From the 89th Guards Rifle Division reports

	15th	*16th*
Men	7,805	4,379
Horses	1,095	895
Machineguns	443	170
AT Rifles	260	154
50mm Mortars	52	5
82mm Mortars	82	6
120mm Mortars	24	18
45mm Guns	26	20
76mm Regimental Guns	12	9
76mm Division Guns	17	17
122mm Guns	2	2
Cars	57	52

This withdrawal was disastrous for the units involved. See Table 13.2 for statistics reported by the 89th Guards Rifle Division.[17]

There were similar losses among the other divisions, although they are not so clearly documented. Overall, it is estimated in the withdrawal from the Donets triangle, the four divisions lost or left behind on the 15th and 16th at least the following: 156 machineguns, 258 antitank rifles, 29 45mm antitank guns, 19 76mm guns, 77 50mm mortars, 95 82mm mortars, 14 120mm mortars and 4 122m guns. Actual losses were probably more than that as we record most of the losses for the 375th

16 Glantz, *The Battle of Kursk*, page 222, does show an encircled group south of Shakhovo on his 15 July map, but does not identify who is in the group.

17 Fond: 1252, Opis: 1, Delo: 60, page 220.

Rifle Division and 81st Guards Rifle Division as combat losses over the course of several days. These losses do not include the 183rd Rifle Division, which was also part of the XLVIII Rifle Corps, but was being driven back, engaged in combat as part of the defense in front of Pravorot. In effect, it ended up covering the withdrawal.

Once back at their new defensive lines, the units began to dig in and put themselves back in order. There was no fighting during the night. By 0200 on the 16th, the 183rd Guards Rifle Division was holding a defensive line in the gully southeast of Storozhevoye to Zhilomostnoye to outside of Novoselovka. It was up to or behind this line that the other four divisions withdrew. The 375th Rifle Division was at Novoselovka. The 89th Guards Rifle Division was deployed down the east bank of the Severnyii Donets from Verin down to just outside of Shipyi. It is reported that it did not fight during the day, although it was still holding a front line position. The 81st Guards Rifle Division was in the rear in the area of Podolkhi (on the Severnyii Donets, northeast of the fighting) with the headquarters on the northwestern edge of Dolgii. It was clearly out of action at this point. The 93rd Guards Rifle Division, which had the farthest to withdraw, ended up sometime on the 16th in a line from Pravorot to Dalnii Dolzhik, and was then pulled back to Krasnoye and out of action.

In effect, the Soviets had abandoned the entire Donets triangle south of Zhilomostnoye and west of the northern branch that feeds into the Severnyii Donets at Shipyi. The front line of the XLVIII Rifle Corps now consisted of the 183rd Rifle Division, 375th Rifle Division and 89th Guards Rifle Division, while the 81st and 93rd Guards Rifle Divisions pulled to the rear and were no longer engaged.

Gostishchevo

With the 93rd Guards Rifle Division withdrawing, the 417th Infantry Regiment's operations became a cautious follow-up. In the morning, weak Soviet resistance was overcome in the woods northwest of Krivtsovo. The Germans claimed 13 POWs and 15 Soviet dead. At 1630, the 417th Infantry Regiment recaptured Gostishchevo. The 417th Infantry Regiment and the 248th Reconnaissance Battalion continued the attack to the north, crossing the Sazhnovskii Donets at Sazhnoye and establishing contact with the 167th Infantry Division.

The 7th Panzer Division Moves North

The attack toward the north from Shakhovo was begun at 0400 (Berlin time) on 15 July, as Battle Group Schulz, with most of the division's tanks, forced the Soviets back toward the line from Zhilomostnoye to Novoselovka. The 26th Guards Tank Brigade came under attack at 0600 (Moscow time), but could not withstand the assault and fell back to a line from height 247.7 to the unnamed height one kilometer northeast of Plota. The Germans took Maloye Yablonovo and Plota at 0645 (Moscow time).[18] The second regiment of the 26th Guards Tank Brigade was kicked off height 247.7 at 0900 (Berlin time).[19] At 0900 (Berlin time) Das Reich reported that elements had made contact with the 7th Panzer Division, but provided no details.

After 1200 (Moscow time), the German armor twice attacked Novoselovka. The 26th Guards Tank Brigade counterattacked, moving forward 300 meters. At 1200 (Berlin time), a battle group of the Das Reich SS Panzer Regiment established contact with the 7th Panzer Division in Yablonovo and this connection left the area to the south isolated. The 7th Reconnaissance Battalion followed the division's attack closely and then broke ahead to clear the road to Pravorot. It claims to have briefly occupied that town! This is a little hard to believe considering the defenses arrayed in front of it. Shakhovo was screened from the west and southwest by Battle Group Glaesemer.

The 81st Guards Rifle Division appears to have simply disappeared during this day. It was reported that by 2000 (Moscow time) on the 14th, the Germans had managed to push the division's units out of Shakhovo-Kleimenovo and reach Maloye Yablonovo. The 81st

18 The 7th Panzer Division reported at 0605 (Berlin time) that it reached the hills between Maloye Yablonovo and Plota and reported at 0800 (Berlin time) that the villages had been cleared.

19 Or at 1000 (Moscow time) . . . one of the few occasions both sides report the same event at the same time.

Guards Rifle Division reports that it was surrounded on the 14th in the area of Kleimenovo and broke out on 15 July in the Podolkhi area. Podolkhi is almost 20 kilometers northeast of Kleimenovo! It was well behind the Soviet lines and there it remained for the next few days. It was covered by the 89th Guards Rifle Division, which by 2200 was deployed from Novoselovka to Kuzminka. This ended the 81st Guards Rifle Division's participation in the battle.

Rotmistrov then ordered the II Guards Tank Corps to counterattack. The 25th Guards Tank Brigade moved to the southern outskirts of Dalnii Dolzhik and attacked towards Maloye Yablonovo. The 26th Guards Tank Brigade moved to the woods 1.5 kilometers southwest of Novoselovka and attacked towards Plota. The 4th Guards Motorized Rifle Brigade moved to the northern slopes of the height north of Plota, to be ready to follow behind the two attacking brigades. The corps' 4th Guards Tank Brigade concentrated in Podolkhi so it could repair its equipment. The Germans reported repelling a counterattack against Yablonovo and Plota by strong Soviet infantry forces, supported by tanks. The II Guards Tank Corps reported losing seven T-34s and three T-70s this day although the decline in tank strength for this day would lead one to conclude at least 16 tanks had been lost.

German patrols of the reconnaissance battalion found strong Soviet forces around Novoselovka and air reconnaissance counted 92 to 150 Soviet tanks in the area north of Pravorot and Novoselovka. This was certainly a mix of Soviet forces, including the 10th Mechanized Brigade, which was being moved into this area, parts of the II Tank Corps and the entire II Guards Tank Corps. Nevertheless, Battle Group Schulz began an attack on strongly defended Novoselovka at 1630, but this attack made no progress. The 7th Panzer Division's front line at the end of the day ran from Plota to height 247.7 to Yablonovo. The forward movement of heavy weapons, artillery and flak was delayed by rainy weather, especially at the Donets River crossing points.

The 19th Panzer Division Breaks Out of the Bridgehead

The III Panzer Corps conducted its breakout of the bridgehead with a night attack. Battle Group Horst (the 73rd and 74th Panzer Grenadier Regiments and a panzer attack group) jumped off at 2000 on 14 July, in support of the 7th Panzer Division attack toward the north and northwest. They reached height #600 (have not been able to identify), northeast of Shakhovo, at 2300. Battalion Group Mentz (the 19th Reconnaissance Battalion and I Battalion, 114th Panzer Grenadier Regiment) seized height 205 (205.1?) north of Shipyi at 2200 on 14 July.

Battle Group Mentz, supported by Battle Group Horst, then advanced against Kuzminka at 0700. The Soviets, including the 11th Guards Mechanized Brigade, defended stubbornly from prepared positions, but height 225 (contour line 225), northwest of Kuzminka, was taken. In late afternoon, the Soviets launched a counterattack from the north.

Battle Group Horst, supported by the 27th Panzer Regiment, undertook mopping-up operations in the large gully northeast of Shakhovo and the hilly area to the north. Soviet resistance was eliminated. The 74th Panzer Grenadier Regiment was returned back to Battle Group Mentz, and Battle Group Horst was given the mission of protecting the flank of this force. This included screening from Pokrovka (the town on the Severnyii Donets) northwest to include Plota.

The 19th Reconnaissance Battalion was able to move into its assigned positions at Shakhovo to the point of woods southeast of Kleimenovo. Two rocket battalions, five artillery battalions and four flak batteries were able to move into positions west of the Donets. During the day, the division bridgehead positions continued to receive Soviet artillery, antitank and mortar harassing fire.

The 6th Panzer Division Holds the Flank

The 6th Panzer Division reported that it halted all offensive activity and began to dig in to preserve present positions, with its panzer regiment pulled back into reserve. They spent the day holding the front line against strong Soviet tank attacks. A Soviet penetration on height 222.1 was eventually cleared up.

Facing the two infantry regiments of the 168th Infantry Division and the 6th Panzer Division was Trufanov's detachment: the 12th Mechanized Brigade and the XXXV Guards Rifle Corps, consisting of the 92nd Guards, 94th Guards, 107th, 305th Rifle Divisions and 96th Tank Brigade. The 305th and 107th Rifle Divisions reported there was no fighting on the 15th, although the 305th may have taken heavy losses leading up to daytime on the 15th.[20] The 107th Rifle Division's 522nd Rifle Regiment, less a battalion, was subordinated to the 305th Rifle Division and was sent to defend Novo-Khmelevoi. This 13 kilometer shift was still behind the lines although closer to them than the regiment's previous position at Zayachye. Otherwise, the Sixty-ninth Army reported that the division was not active today. The 96th Tank Brigade provided fire support with its five T-34s and three T-70s.

The 92nd Guards Rifle Division reported that at 0800 (Moscow time) it repulsed an attack by a company of "automatic riflemen," who tried to reach height 222.1 in small groups. During the afternoon, the Germans again launched an attack in the direction of height 222.1 and Novo-Khmelevoi with one and one-half infantry regiments and 60 tanks. This attack came from Vyipolzovka and the ravine to the northeast. The 94th Guards Rifle Division during the day repulsed two German attacks of up to a regiment in strength, supported by tanks, in the direction of Mazikino. These appear to have been some serious fighting, as the 92nd Guards Rifle Division is reported to have suffered 400 casualties on the 15th while the 94th Guards Rifle Division is reported to have lost 760 men on the 15th.[21]

Defense of Shlyakhovo and Komintern

During the night, at 0230 the Soviets infiltrated what was estimated to be a battalion in the ravine in the Shlyakhovo-Komintern area west of Mazikino. Counterattacks were launched and mop-up progressed throughout the night and into the morning. Fifty-four POWs were taken. The Germans claimed the Soviets took heavy losses. A company-strength reconnaissance probe in the gully 1.5 kilometers southeast of Rayevka was also repulsed. In addition, also at about 0230 two Soviet companies attacked the division's positions between Shlyakhovo and the lake to its north. A prompt counterattack drove them back. The Germans claimed 61 prisoners and 35 bodies counted. Overall (for the day?), the 168th Infantry Division claimed 127 POWs, 23 deserters, and 199 Soviet dead.

Air Support

The 168th Infantry Division and 19th Panzer Division reported that there was heavy Soviet bombing during the night. The 7th Panzer Division also reported many Soviet bombing attacks during the night.

Summary of the Clearing of the Donets Triangle

The Donets triangle had been cleared, primarily by five divisions: the Das Reich SS Division, the 7th and 19th Panzer Divisions, and the 167th and 168th Infantry Divisions. It turned out to be a relatively easy advance because the Soviets had decided to withdraw, so even in the face of poor weather and poor road conditions, the Germans were able to make significant progress on the evening of the 14th and morning of the 15th. This did not translate into being able to make any real progress against the Soviet defensive positions in front of Pravorot and the Germans were again halted in the afternoon.

20 The Sixty-ninth Army in Operational Report #00304, 0400 16 July 1943, states that "During the day the division did not fight. During July 14–15 the division lost 505 men." (Fond: Sixty-ninth Army, Opis: 10753, Delo: 133, page 36). The Kursk Data Base shows significant losses for this unit for this day, as the database reflects losses over a 24-hour period.

21 Fond: Sixty-ninth Army, Opis: 10753, Delo: 133, pages 36, 39 & 40. The 92nd Guards Rifle Division reports 400 lost during the fighting of 14th and 15th at 0400 16 July, and reports 400 lost in the fighting on 15th, at 2330 on 16 July. Not sure if these are reporting the same casualties. Overall losses in this unit were very high.

Gostishchevo IV, 15 July 1943

DURATION One day FRONTAGE 6.0 kilometers TERRAIN Rolling, mixed

WEATHER Heavy rain, clearing in the afternoon. Roads passable only with great difficulty due to rain, impassable in steeper areas.

	Attacker	*Defender*
Units	417th Inf Rgt/168th Infantry Division	281st Rgt/93rd Gds Rifle Division 267th Rgt/89th Gds Rifle Division
Attachments	None	None
Strength	4,417	3,923
Armor	0	0
Artillery	35	30
Air Sorties	0	14 Night
Casualties	38 (6 KIA, 31 WIA, 1 MIA)	634 (42 KIA, 70 WIA, 522 MIA)
Artillery Losses	0	4
Enemy Captured	N/A	0

Defense of Shlyakhovo and Komintern, 15 July 1943

DURATION One day FRONTAGE 17.5 kilometers TERRAIN Rolling, mixed

WEATHER Heavy rain, clearing in the afternoon. Roads passable only with great difficulty due to rain, impassable in steeper areas.

	Attacker	*Defender*
Units	94th Gds & 107th Rifle Divisions	168th Infantry Division (less 417th Inf Rgt)
Attachments	See below	See below
Strength	13,735	9,665
Armor	0	6
Artillery	110	72
Air Sorties	15 Night	0
Casualties	768 (100 KIA, 351 WIA, 317 MIA)	87 (12 KIA, 63 WIA, 3 MIA)
Armor Losses	0	0
Artillery Losses	13	0
Enemy Captured	0	150 (23 deserters)

Forces Engaged

German Attachments

2/228th StuG Bn, with 9 combat-ready StuGs

lt Bty/I/61st AA Rgt (not included)

Still detached from the division

248th Engineer Bn (less 3 cos) (included)

429th Infantry Rgt (less 1 Bn) (included)

Soviet Forces

94th Guards Rifle Division

107th Rifle Division less the 522nd Rifle Regiment (less 1/3rd)

123rd ATR Bn

130th ATR Bn—detached on the 15th (included)

496th Mortar Regiment—detached on the 15th (included)

The 7th Panzer Division Attacks North, 15 July 1943

DURATION One day FRONTAGE 20.4 kilometers TERRAIN Rolling, mixed

WEATHER Rain, clearing in the afternoon. Temperature at noon: 17 degrees Celsius. Roads and trails extremely difficult for wheeled vehicles, passable only with tremendous effort.

	Attacker	*Defender*
Units	7th PzD	81st Guards Rifle Division & 26th Guards Tank Bde
Attachments	See below	+ 2 Churchills from 47th Gds Tank Regiment
Strength	18,337	6,735
Armor	33 (4 light)	32 (7 light)
Artillery	141	23
Air Sorties	30	29 Night
Casualties	25 (3 KIA, 22 WIA)	215 (215 MIA)
Armor Losses	3	12
Artillery Losses	0	3
Enemy Captured	N/A	0

Forces Engaged

German Attachments

9th Bridge Column B
1/505th Bridge Column B
843rd Bridge Column J

99th Flak Rgt Staff
I/38th Flak Rgt
II/38th Flak Rgt

II/62nd Artillery Rgt—attached on the 15th (included)
I/54th Werfer Rgt

Detached

ObsBty/78th Artillery Rgt (included)
Regimental Group (included)

The 19th Panzer Division Breaks Out of the Bridgehead, 15 July 1943

DURATION One day FRONTAGE 17.9 kilometers TERRAIN Rolling, mixed
WEATHER Roads softened by rain, but passable.

	Attacker	*Defender*
Units	19th PzD	89th GRD (2/3rds) & 11th GMB
Attachments	See below	None
Strength	16,421	6,784
Armor	37 (5 light)	0 ?
Artillery	128	51
Air Sorties	30	29 Night
Casualties	34 (4 KIA, 29 WIA, 1 MIA)	622 (145 KIA, 303 WIA, 174 MIA)
Armor Losses	5	0
Artillery Losses	0	1
Enemy Captured	N/A	1

Forces Engaged

German Attachments
70th Engineer Bn
2/411th Bridge Column B
842nd Bridge Column J

52nd Werfer Rgt

I/61st Flak Rgt (less 1 battery)

429th Infantry Rgt (168th ID), less I Battalion (not included)
I/114th Panzer Grenadier Rgt (from 6th PzD) (not included)

Detached
ObsBty/19th Artillery Rgt

The 6th Panzer Division Holds the Flank, 15 July 1943

DURATION One day FRONTAGE 10.0 kilometers TERRAIN Rolling, mixed

WEATHER Morning rainy, clearing in the afternoon. Temperature at noon: 17 degrees Celsius. Roads passable only for tracked and all-wheel-drive vehicles.

	Attacker	*Defender*
Units	92nd Gds Rifle Division & others	6th Panzer Division
Attachments	See below	See below
Strength	18,500	19,850
Armor	45 (14 light)	37 (4 light)
Artillery	108	129
Air Sorties	4 + 29 Night	29
Casualties	708 (158 KIA, 472 WIA, 103 MIA)	103 (16 KIA, 86 WIA, 1 MIA)
Armor Losses	9	15
Artillery Losses	13	0
Enemy Captured	1 + 1 flyer by the 305th RD	N/A

Forces Engaged

German Attachments

II/62nd Artillery Rgt—detached on the 15th (not included)
II/54th Werfer Rgt
III/54th Werfer Rgt
Hq/54th Werfer Rgt

II/43rd Flak Rgt
lt Bn/91st Flak Rgt
204th Intelligence Troop

228th StuG Bn (- 2nd company)

Detached

ObsBty/76th Artillery Rgt
I/114th Panzer Grenadier Rgt

Soviet Forces

92nd Guards Rifle Division
  96th Tank Brigade—detached on the 14th (included)
  315th Guards Mtr Rgt
305th Rifle Division
12th Guards Mechanized Brigade
Trufanov's detachment

III Panzer Corps Assets

674th Engineer Rgt Staff
925th Bridge Construction Staff
602nd Bridge Column B

153rd Flak Rgt Staff

3rd Command of Artillery
612th Artillery Rgt Staff
II/62nd Artillery Rgt
II/71st Artillery Rgt
857th Heavy Artillery Rgt
Pn/13th Light Observations Battery
ObsBty/19th Artillery Rgt (19th PzD)
ObsBty/76th Artillery Rgt (6th PzD)

2nd Fuel Column Troop
545th Panzer Recovery Platoon
503rd Heavy Panzer Bn
Regimental Group (from 7th PzD)

There is no question that the Donets triangle position had reached the limits of its usefulness. With the Das Reich SS Division pushing at the base of the triangle, and the divisions of the III Panzer Corps pushing against the southeast side, it was becoming extremely difficult to defend. Its primary purpose, which was to extend and threaten the flanks of the attacking SS Panzer Corps, had been served. As the German attack on Prokhorovka had ground to a halt, there was no reason to maintain it. Furthermore, the units inside the triangle were not in good shape to maintain it. The Voronezh Front had not done a good job in keeping these units supplied, and as such, many of the Soviet divisions were still operating using the initial issue of ammunition and the rations that they started the battle with.

Given these considerations, the forces in the triangle needed to be relieved. It was simply easier to withdraw from triangle. Under the circumstances, the decision to withdraw made perfect sense. The problem was that the Soviet forces inside the triangle did not have the motor transport to withdraw all their heavy equipment. This situation was certainly not helped by the weather, in particular the rains that left the roads in poor shape. Thus, during the withdrawal, many of the Soviet units were forced to leave behind significant numbers of guns and other heavy equipment. That was the real gain made by the Germans from collapsing the triangle. The total Soviet personnel losses on the 14th through the 16th from the five divisions and two tank corps engaged in the triangle were 7,162.[22] Of these, we record 3,539 as missing, or almost half of the total losses. In contrast, the German losses from the units facing the Soviets over these two days (the Das Reich, 167th, 168th and 19th Panzer Divisions, and the 7th Panzer Division for the 15th) were 931.[23] Where the Soviets really suffered losses was in heavy equipment. As best we can figure, these Soviet units lost some 234 machineguns, 344 antitank rifles, 44 45mm antitank guns, 29 76mm guns, 97 50mm mortars, 127 82mm mortars, 27 120mm mortars, 6 122m guns, 20 T-34s (8 destroyed), 19 T-70s (8 destroyed), and 4 BA-64s (2 destroyed). The III Panzer Corps and Das Reich SS Division claimed at least 2,238 prisoners, including 342 deserters, as well as 361 machineguns, 151 antitank rifles, 55 45mm antitank guns, 33 76mm guns, 6 50mm mortars, 48 82mm mortars, 41 unspecified mortars, 13 120mm mortars, 4 122mm guns, 96 tanks, including 2 T-34s, 8 AA guns, and 5 planes.[24]

It is clear that while the Soviet decision to withdraw was a fundamentally necessary one, its execution was flawed and improvised. They needed to get transports inside the Donets triangle that could have pulled out some of the heavy equipment ahead of the withdrawing units. Considering the rather limited pressure from the south that was put on the triangle

22 This does not include elements of the XXIX Tank Corps or the 10th Guards Mechanized Brigade of the V Guards Mechanized Corps. These losses are derived from multiple records; there was no clear single report on the subject.

23 Only the Das Reich SS Division provides anything like a daily loss report. The other four divisions report losses over a period of days; thus much of this figure is derived from averaging losses over those periods.

24 There is no overall report for the III Panzer Corps during this period but there are reports by division that record, for the 14th at 2245 hours, for the 168th Infantry Division: 190 prisoners including 7 deserters, 2 machineguns, 15 antitank rifles, 2 45mm AT guns, 6 50mm mortars, 5 82mm mortars, 4 120mm mortars; and for the 15th at 2130 hours for the 7th Panzer Division: 119 captured including 32 deserters, 45 machineguns, 23 82mm Mortars, and 1 T-34; for the 19th Panzer Division: 246 captured including 51 deserters, 5 machineguns, 2 76mm guns, 2 82mm mortars, 5 tanks including 1 T-34; for the 168th Infantry Division: 54 captured including 45 deserters; and for the 16th at 2130 hours, for the 7th Panzer Division: 770 captured including 111 deserters; for the 19th Panzer Division: 180 captured, including 29 deserters, 14 machineguns, 7 antitank rifles, 19 45mm AT guns, 14 82mm mortars, and 1 120mm mortar; and for the 168th Infantry Division: 201 captured, including 49 deserters, 38 machineguns, 20 antitank rifles, 5 45mm AT guns, 7 76mm guns, 4 82mm mortars, and 8 120mm mortars (!).

This totals 1,760 prisoners, including 324 deserters, 104 machineguns, 42 antitank rifles, 26 45mm AT guns, 9 76mm guns, 6 50mm mortars, 48 82mm mortars, 13 120mm mortars; 6 tanks including 2 T-34s.

The Provisional Army Kempf reports on 14 July that they had captured some 1,220 prisoners, and killed 60 tanks, 18 guns,

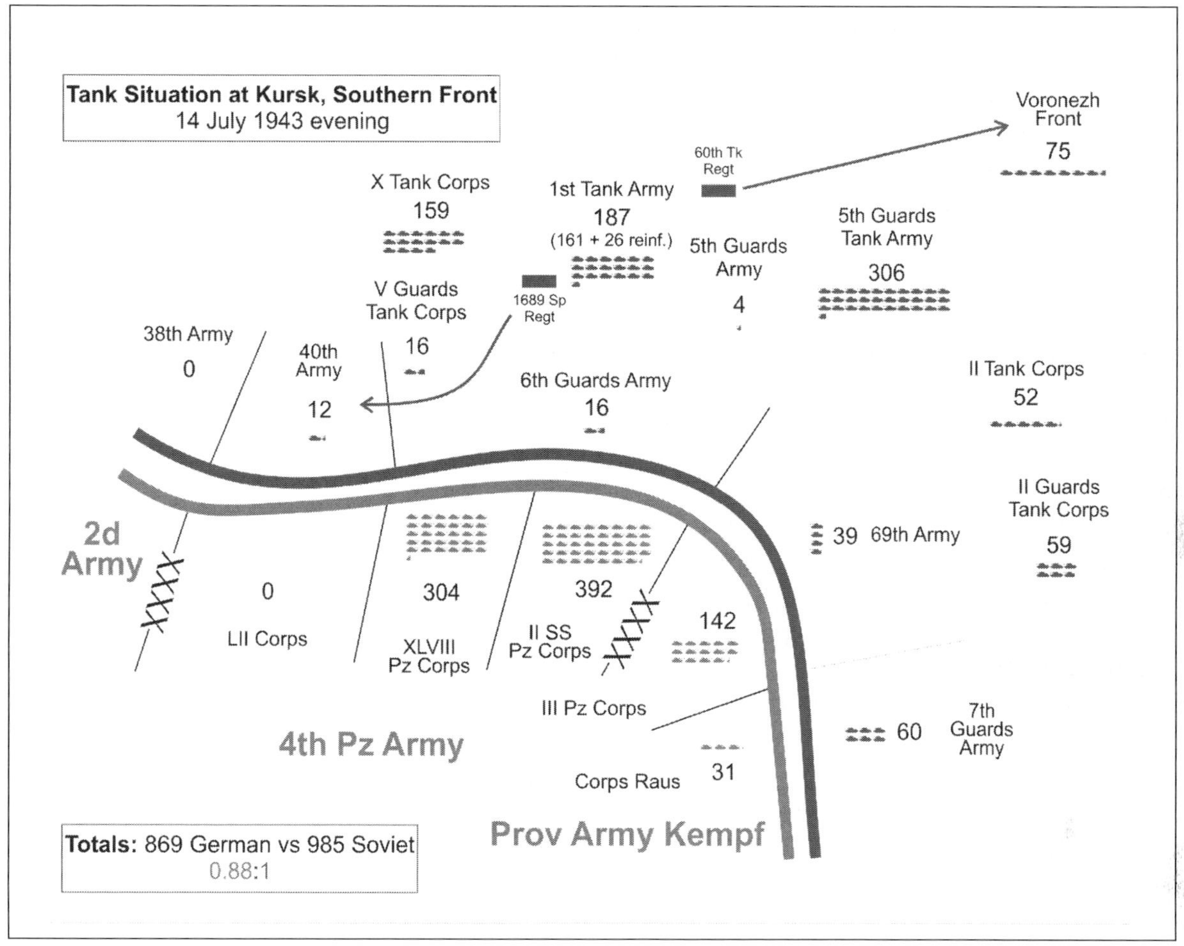

before the evening of the 14th, there was no reason why the withdrawal of some artillery units could not have already started. Considering that most of these units were low on ammunition, an early withdrawal of a third to half of the artillery, while they handed their ammunition to other artillery units, would not have seriously reduced the forces' combat power. It could have saved them some guns. Overall, the withdrawal was poorly planned and poorly conducted.

With the collapse of the Donets triangle, the III Panzer Corps was finally in position to conduct its primary mission, which was to protect the flank of the Fourth Panzer Army. But with the German attack already stalled (and had been canceled), this was now completely irrelevant. Overall, the III Panzer Corps' operations, while dramatic and bloody, served little purpose in the overall plan and did little to help the German Army break through. This was not the fault

58 AT guns, 35 mortars, and 19 antitank rifles. They report for the 15th 1,040 prisoners, 5 guns, 29 AT guns, 16 mortars, 27 machineguns and 10 antitank rifles.

The Das Reich SS Division reports for the 14th 230 captured, 18 deserters, 5 planes, 75 tanks, 8 AT guns, 32 antitank rifles, 90 machineguns, and 6 AA guns. Another report for the 14th records only 25 tanks and 12 AT guns (of which 6 were 76mm). The night report for the 14th and 15th reports 15 tanks, 4 guns, 2 AA guns, 41 AT guns (of it 18 are 76mm), 41 mortars, 77 antitank rifles and 167 machineguns. The division reports for the 15th 248 captured.

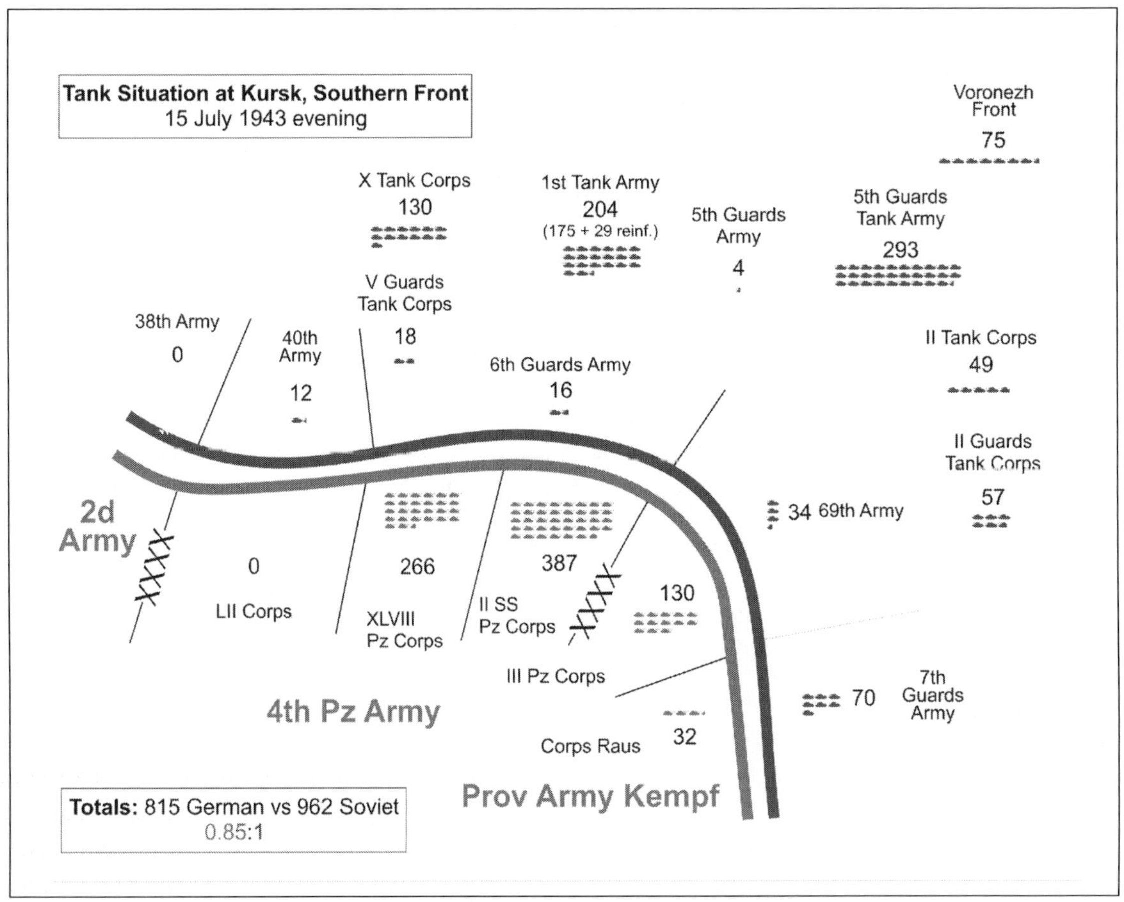

of the local commanders; it was caused by the weaknesses in the initial plans prepared by Manstein, Hoth and Kempf and in their execution by Kempf and Breith.

The disagreement noted in the III Panzer Corps' war diary between Kempf and Breith indicates a lack of a unified vision. Breith's breakthrough and exploitation in the first three days of the offensive was extremely effective. Kempf was also quite correct that the corps really needed to be pointed north if it was going to be useful. In the end, the III Panzer Corps was off fighting its own private little war while the Fourth Panzer Army was busy trying to break through. One must question why the III Panzer Corps exerted so much effort pushing northeast from the 13th through the 15th.

Summary to Date

The front line changed dramatically over these two days, with considerable progress made cleaning up the flanks on the 15th.

Still, the progress did not result in any forward movement or any particular change in the ratio of opposing forces. As shown by the tank strengths, the situation did not really change over the course of two days of fighting.

While the German attack appears to have finally cleaned up the flanks, it did not result in any significant improvement to their situation. The Soviets had deployed and dug-in significant forces along the entire length of the German penetration and had local reserves, even if many of them were previously battered units.

CHAPTER FOURTEEN

The Battlefield Is Quiet

16–17 JULY 1943

> He fell in October 1918, on a day that was so quiet and still on the whole front, that the army report confined itself to the single sentence: All quiet on the Western Front. He had fallen forward and lay on the earth as though sleeping. Turning him over one saw that he could not have suffered long; his face had an expression of calm, as though almost glad the end had come.
>
> ERICH MARIA REMARQUE
> FROM THE 1929 NOVEL *ALL QUIET ON THE WESTERN FRONT*[1]

BY THE 16TH of July, the battlefield had settled. The Soviet attacks on the 12th and 13th gave way to the German flanking operations that cleared out the Tolstoye Woods and the Donets triangle. Now with the lines neatly set, the war stopped for a moment, while both sides considered the next step. Vatutin ordered the Fifth Guards Army and neighboring formations to take up a static defense.[2]

Operation Roland

The morning started with the plans on the German left flank to continue with the relief of the Gross Deutschland, but at 0930, Hoth (Fourth Panzer Army commander) visited the XLVIII Panzer Corps headquarters and ordered the relief operations halted. The attack across the Psel had been canceled and instead Hoth outlined a new plan that would have the army drive west. The idea was to roll up the Soviet First Tank Army, forcing it away from the Psel and destroying it. The Fourth Panzer Army's General Order No. 8 stated that the intent of this operation was to surround and destroy Soviet forces south of the Psel by an attack to the north, followed by a penetration to the west.

The attack was going to be initially conducted by two divisions attached to the XLVIII Panzer Corps while the SS Panzer Corps was to wait until the XLVIII Panzer Corps had penetrated to the west, and was then to cover their advance by moving with most of its forces along the north and northeastern flanks into the high ground south of the Psel. The 11th Panzer Division was to be attached to the SS Panzer Corps while the 7th Panzer Division was to be sent over to the XLVIII Panzer Corps and inserted at the south edge of Kalinovka to be used

1 Books by Erich Maria Remarque (1898–1970) were banned by the Nazis in 1933 and used in the Nazi book burning ceremonies. He left Germany in 1933 and Europe in 1939, but his younger sister, Elfriede Scholz (born 1903), remained in Germany and was arrested in 1943 for stating in private that the war was lost. She was executed on 16 December of that year. The Nazi judge Roland Freisler (1893–1945) stated: "Your brother is beyond our reach, but you will not escape us!"

2 Zhadov, page 95.

in the attack. The 7th Panzer Division, however, was a formation of limited striking power, having on the 17th only around 34 tanks ready for action.

The 7th Panzer Division and the Gross Deutschland Division would attack along the line from height 232.8 to Kalinovka to height 247.0 and seize the high ground east of Gorki and southwest of Voznesenovka (meaning all the high ground both to the southwest and northeast of Voznesenovka). This was a northward attack along a seven kilometer line that started with its right three kilometers northwest of Novoselovka and through Kalinovka, and with its left two kilometers south of Kruglik. The 3rd Panzer Division would initially remain in place to screen the Tolstoye Woods. This division would later join the attack, driving toward the high ground northeast of Novenkoye. The 332nd Infantry Division would again be attached back to the XLVIII Panzer Corps and cover its west flank. The initial objective of the attack was to take the high ground to the south and southeast of Oboyan. Meanwhile, the LII Corps was to try to pin the Soviet forces facing them for the XLVIII Panzer Corps to later destroy. The SS Panzer Corps, after the XLVIII Panzer Corps penetrated to the west, was to advance with the 11th Panzer Division and Das Reich SS Division from height 227.0 to height 248.3 to the Malinovka area railroad station and capture the high ground east and north of Orlovka. The Adolf Hitler SS Division was also to be involved in operations west of Kochetovka.

This resulted in all three panzer corps becoming inactive on the 16th while they prepared, and then for the units to start withdrawing and shifting on the 17th to support this operation. The Das Reich SS Division and all but one regiment of the Adolf Hitler SS Division were to be pulled from the line along with the 7th Panzer Division, and moved to the west. The Das Reich SS Division was to shift behind the 11th Panzer Division while the Totenkopf SS Division was to withdraw from its bridgehead across the Psel the night of 17/18th July. The armored units were to regroup and resupply on the 17th and attack on the 18th.

At 2300 that evening, the XLVIII Panzer Corps received the order to assemble for *Operation Roland*, which had now replaced *Operation Citadel*. As quickly as it came into being, however, this operation disappeared. At 0900 on the 17th, Major General Friedrich Fangohr (the army chief of staff) briefed the XLVIII Panzer Corps on why this attack was being canceled. He noted that it had been recognized that *Operation Citadel* could not be prosecuted further. The exceptionally strong Soviet resistance in front of Model's Army Group Center, combined with the dangerous flank attacks of the Soviets north of Orel, prevented these formations from penetrating towards Kursk. The "rapid link-up" of the two armies at Kursk was deemed impossible.

The cancellation of *Operation Roland*, which the Germans claim would have led to the destruction of "vast enemy forces," was canceled "apparently" due to the Soviet attacks at Mius River and the Izyum areas. The landing of Anglo-American troops on Sicily a few days earlier "probably also influenced the decision." As the briefing notes, the price of trying to hold or increase the narrow gains made must be weighed against the strategic situation.

At this point, all major offensive operations in the south were canceled. The order canceling the attack was received from the army at 1100 and relayed to the divisions at 1200. This cancellation was apparently also relayed to the Soviets, for the XLVIII Panzer Corps intercepted a Russian radio transmission that stated that an intercepted German radio transmission said that the German leadership was withdrawing the units of the Fourth Panzer Army from the Oboyan area. This was a German broadcast that must have been sent in the clear, although the XLVIII Panzer Corps signals officer concluded that the broadcast did not come from his corps.

One wonders how effective *Operation Roland* would have been. It was still initially only a two-division attack that would have certainly run headlong into the significant Soviet forces that were assembled from height 247.0 to 232.8. Neither of these German divisions was in top shape and the Soviet forces had held this area for several days and were still strong.

Exactly how this operation would have resulted in destruction of "vast enemy forces" is not clear. It simply was a sweep of the forward positions of the X Tank Corps and their supporting infantry. This included the 204th Rifle Division, which was backstopped by the 67th Guards Rifle Division and the 219th Rifle Division. They were then to push further into those positions. Again, the Soviets had some depth here with the III Mechanized Corps and 51st Guards Rifle Division still in the rear. There is no question that it would have resulted in more fighting, but it does not seem that this fighting would have been particularly advantageous to the Germans. This attack may have ended up engaging the four major Soviet armored formations in the area, the V Guards, VI and X Tank Corps and the III Mechanized Corps. It may have also engaged some of the four rifle divisions that remained part of the Fortieth Army in addition to five or six rifle divisions in the area that were part of the Sixth Guards Army and the two rifle divisions attached to the V Guards Tank Corps. Unless the operation continued westward, which appears to have been the plan, through the Fortieth Army and into the Thirty-eighth Army, or turned southward into the rear of the Fortieth Army, then no particular advantage or envelopment would have been achieved.

Still, as we saw on the 13th and 14th around Tolstoye Woods, a two-division German attack on this flank was able to go forward. As this was more open terrain, this attack would probably also have gone forward. In light of the weakened state of the German armor, though, it is debatable whether it would have actually been able to crush the V Guards, VI and X Tank Corps. These formations were up to 182 tanks on the 17th, while the two attacking German divisions had 147 tanks.[3] Furthermore, there was nothing that could keep the III Mechanized Corps and XXXI Tank Corps from throwing their tank and mechanized brigades back into combat (another 168 tanks on the 17th). Still, *Operation Roland* had the potential of threatening the Fortieth Army and may have caused serious losses to the Soviets, especially if they choose to respond by counterattacking the right flank of the attack, which in this case would have been where the 11th Panzer and Das Reich SS Divisions were to advance.

The strategic value of this ground was extremely limited. By driving out the Thirty-eighth and Fortieth Armies, the Germans would have pushed their front forward in the south by over 30 kilometers, but would not have actually shortened the overall length of the German line compared to its status on the 4th of July. It may have ground up three more tank corps, of which two were already fairly depleted. It may have forced a number of rifle divisions to displace. It could have resulted in another envelopment that yielded considerable prizes, depending on the speed of the German advance and the quickness in which the Soviets withdrew the Fortieth and Thirty-eighth Armies. It certainly would have taken another three or four days and would have resulted in some losses to the Germans. It also would had made the air war difficult for the Germans, as they had seriously drawn down the VIII Air Corps in the face of a strong Soviet air force.

Instead, what the Germans chose to do was withdraw from the ground they had fought so hard to take. This withdrawal was certainly necessary if one were not going to conduct *Operation Roland,* as the German attack had lengthened their front since the 4th. After Kursk, one armored division was sent to Italy while three armored divisions were sent south to counterattack the Mius River penetration on the 30th of July. The other five armored divisions remained in the Belgorod area. There is no question that conducting *Operation Roland* would have delayed the arrival of these divisions to other areas and further weakened them. While this delay would not have had any impact on the Italian Campaign, the delay by four or five days of the three armored divisions that were sent south to the Mius River would certainly have allowed the Soviets more opportunity to expand their breakthrough and do more damage. Whether the Germans would have done more damage by conducting *Operation Roland* than the Soviets would have done

3 They also had 40 Wespes, Hummels and Grilles, and 5 artillery observation tanks.

by getting another good four or five days out of their Mius River breakthrough is hard to determine without a detailed analysis of that operation. Furthermore, as demonstrated by the actions of 12 July, the exchange ratio from the Germans successfully defending against Soviet offensive actions was better than what they achieved by attacking. Attacking well-developed concentrations of Soviet forces just for the sake of attrition, while the Soviets were breaking through with three armies in another sector of the line, was strategically risky.

It is the decision to cancel *Operation Roland* that Manstein complains about in his book.[4] This was the continued offensive operation to grind down the Soviet reserves that Manstein mentions in his memoirs.[5] With units being ordered withdrawn, and Manstein not allowed to commit his remaining reserves (which instead were committed to trying to restrict the Mius River penetrations which started on the 17th of July), there was no point in continuing operations.

The SS Panzer Corps Withdraws

Over the next two days, the SS Panzer Corps withdrew from combat. Totenkopf was ordered to begin immediately to withdraw all non-essential vehicles and heavy weapons from the bridgehead to the south bank of the Psel. The division was preparing to withdraw the last elements from the Psel bridgehead during the night of 17/18 July.

Totenkopf SS Division Holds

In the case of Totenkopf, on the 16th it reported Soviet artillery and mortar harassing fire across its whole line. The 95th Guards Rifle Division from 0200 (Moscow time) to 0600 conducted a reconnaissance in the area of height 226.6 with a battalion and a reinforced company, but was forced back by German fire.[6] The Soviets were able to take the first line of trenches on the southwestern slope of height 226.6, moving forward 300 to 400 meters, but were then counterattacked on height 226.6 from the southeast. The Germans reported killing 50, taking six prisoners and two antitank guns. At 1120 (Berlin time), the Totenkopf SS Artillery Regiment shelled a Soviet assembly area northeast of Mikhailovka, "shattering" it, according to the German reports.

During the night, the 95th Guards Rifle Division relieved a battalion of the 26th Guards Rifle Regiment, which was holding on the northern slopes of height 226.6. During the first half of the day, the Fifth Guards Army held position and continued to improve their positions. The second half of the day, the army sent reconnaissance detachments forward to observe the German withdrawal. Totenkopf reported only scattered artillery and mortar harassing fire on the 17th. At 1130 (Berlin time), a Soviet attack by two companies from the east against Eicke SS Regiment was driven off by combined fire of all weapons. The 95th Guards Rifle Division's reconnaissance detachment repulsed an armored counterattack and was fighting at around 1600 (Moscow time) on the western slopes of height 226.6.

During the afternoon, Totenkopf began to pull back from some of its positions and to take over parts of the front from the Adolf Hitler SS Division. This led to a reconnaissance in force on the part of the Soviets, with a battalion with 10-15 tanks hitting the northeast bend of the bridgehead. There were still some elements of the Adolf Hitler SS Division there. The division continued to withdraw during the night under the watch of the Fifth Guards Army. They launched another attack by an estimated two companies at 2310 against the left

4 Manstein, page 449.

5 This point seems to have been missed by a number of writers. Glantz and House, *The Battle of Kursk*, briefly discusses *Operation Roland*, pages 219 and 223, and it is mentioned in passing by Zetterling and Frankson, *Kursk 1943*, page 98. In both cases it is referred to as an SS Panzer Corps operation. It is alluded to in Nipe's and Ziemke's writing but not named, but otherwise is not addressed in most other accounts.

6 The Germans report an attack at 0200 (Berlin time) by two Soviet companies against the center of Totenkopf coming from the ravine east of Veselyii.

Holding Across the Psel III, 16–17 July 1943

DURATION Two days FRONTAGE 16.6 kilometers TERRAIN Rolling, mixed
WEATHER 16th: Cloudy but clearing, scattered showers. Roads still soft in places. 17th: Dry, brighter. Roads are dry.

	Attacker	*Defender*
Units	95th GRD & others	T SS PzGrD
Attachments	See below	See below
Strength	25,108	17,910
Armor	22	80
Artillery	279	147
Air Sorties	0	0
Casualties	195 (42 KIA, 153 WIA)	147 (22 KIA, 120 WIA, 5 MIA)
Armor Losses	0	2
Artillery Losses	0	2
Enemy Captured	3	N/A

Forces Engaged

German Attachments
II/1st Lehr Werfer Regiment
SS Corps Werfer Battalion
86th Bridge Column B (not incorporated)
III/55th Werfer Regiment (attached on the 17th—not included)
Leibstandarte SS Adolf Hitler Regiment (attached on the 17th—not included)

Soviet Forces
1/3rd of 42nd Guards Rifle Division (132nd Guards Rifle Regiment)—not included
95th Guards Rifle Division
469th Mortar Regiment—detached on the 17th

From V Guards Mechanized Corps
24th Guards Tank Brigade

97th Guards Rifle Division
1372nd/29th Antiaircraft Division
66th Guards Mtr Rgt—detached on the 17th
201st/12th Mortar Bde—attached on the 17th (not included)

52nd Guards Rifle Division
133rd AT Rifle Bn
75th Flamethrower Co.
95th Flamethrower Co.
Bn/156th RR/51st GRD (not included)

From X Guards Tank Corps
11th Motorized Rifle Brigade
287th Mtr Rgt

Captures include 2 by the out-of-contact 6th Gds Airborne Division on the 17th.

wing of the Totenkopf SS Regiment. At 2355, the withdrawal, having gone according to plan, was completed with the covering SS panzer regiment crossing the Psel at 2210 and the bridge across the Psel was now being dismantled.

Air Support

Totenkopf reported on the 16th that there was strong Soviet air activity, totaling 24 overflights by 284 aircraft. The following day, they also reported heavy Soviet air activity.

The Adolf Hitler SS Division

The Adolf Hitler SS Division also held in place on the 16th, as it pretty much had been since the 11th. It received strong artillery and mortar-harassing fire during the night, along with heavy Soviet patrol activity and aircraft attacks. This included an attack at 0200 (Moscow time) by III Motorized Rifle Battalion of the 32nd Motorized Rifle Brigade, which drove the Germans back to the southern slope of the ravine southeast of Mikhailovka.

Throughout the day, Soviet harassing fire continued at various intensities. The division's patrols explored the area around Mikhailovka and discovered the positions there well fortified and heavily occupied. The opposing 9th Guards Airborne Division, XVIII Tank Corps, and XXIX Tank Corps remained in place, although the XXIX Tank Corps reported repelling a German infantry attack northeast of Storozhevoye and a tank attack from the grove southeast of Vinogradovka.

That evening, as darkness fell, the division began to withdraw to the line on the east edge of height 258.2 to the east edge of Vasilyevka. The 9th Guards Airborne Division noted this withdrawal at 0500 (Moscow time) on the 17th, and its 26th Guards Airborne Regiment advanced, reaching the southern and southwestern slopes of height 252.2 with two of its battalions at 0800 (Moscow time). At 1800 (Moscow time), the division followed-up with small patrols, but according to the Germans, only hesitantly. The SS division had received only weak artillery and mortar harassing fire throughout the day. During the night, the withdrawal was completed except for one regiment which had been left behind.

By the end of the 17th, the Adolf Hitler SS Division had withdrawn back some six kilometers while the 9th Guards Airborne Division's reconnaissance detachment had reached the ravine southeast of Andreyevka to Stalinskoye Otdeleniye Sovkhoz. The remaining regiment was pulled out of the line during the night of 17/18 July.

On the same day, the XVIII Tank Corps had also pulled back, having started its withdrawal between 2100 and 2200 (Moscow time) on the 16th. Its positions were taken over by the 9th Guards Airborne Division. By the end of the 17th it was gathered in the Malaya Poinka, Vyishnyaya Olshanka and height 222.0 area. It left the 36th Guards Heavy Tank Regiment in the southern outskirts of Prelestnoye, where at 1830 (Moscow time) on the 17th, it beat back an attack on Andreyevka by five German tanks (Soviet estimate) from the direction of Prokhorovka. The corps had partially restored some of its strength, now reporting 49 T-34s and 45 T-70s ready for action.

The XXXIII Guards Rifle Corps' Activity

Other than the 95th Guards Rifle Division's limited fighting around height 226.6 on the 16th and 17th, the rest of the Fifth Guards Army's XXXIII Guards Rifle Corps remained in place this day. The 95th Guards and 9th Guards Airborne Divisions remained in line while the 42nd Guards Rifle Division was in a second echelon position between Petrovka and height 252.4 along with the 52nd Guards Rifle Division. The army's reserve, the yet uncommitted 6th Guards Airborne Division, also remained in place. The corps was also backed up by the 24th Guards Tank Brigade, holding in the area of the Voroshilov Sovkhoz. The 95th and 42nd Guards Rifle Divisions sent out reconnaissance probes toward the German lines on the afternoon of the 17th. The 42nd Guards Rifle Division sent out two battalions on the 17th to join the fighting around Vinogradovka.

Overseeing the Tank Fields of Prokhorovka IV, 16 July 1943

DURATION One day FRONTAGE 9.8 kilometers TERRAIN Rolling, bare WEATHER Light clouds

	Attacker	Defender
Units	XVIII TC, XXIX TC & 9th GAD	LSSAH PzGrD
Attachments	See below	See below
Strength	25,805	20,669
Armor	201 (85 light)	105 (6 light)
Artillery	254	184
Air Sorties	0	90
Casualties	177 (41 KIA, 136 WIA)	105 (16 KIA, 86 WIA, 3 MIA)
Armor Losses	1	2
Artillery Losses	1	2
Enemy Captured	4	N/A

Forces Engaged

German Attachments
55th Werfer Regiment
861st Light Field Howitzer Battalion
I/1st Lehr Werfer Regiment

Soviet Forces
XVIII Tank Corps
736th AT Bn
80th Gds Mtr Rgt
XXIX Tank Corps
1529th Heavy SP Art Rgt
76th Gds Mtr Rgt
747th AT Bn—attached on the 16th (included)
9th Guards Airborne Division

Air Support

The division reported heavy Soviet and weak friendly air activity on the 16th and reported little air activity for either side on the following day. The XXIX Tank Corps reported that the Germans on the 16th bombed its positions four times with groups of up to 60 planes.

The SS Panzer Corps reported on the 16th that the Soviets attacked the Adolf Hitler and Das Reich areas with strong air forces, using waves of bombers and ground attack aircraft.

The Das Reich SS Division

Like its neighboring Adolf Hitler SS Division, the Das Reich also held its positions on the 16th and withdrew on the 17th.

During the day, the Soviet air force attacked the division's front line with some of their larger-sized bombs and with strafing attacks. These attacks caused heavy losses of personnel and equipment (total bloody casualties for the day of 224). This was perhaps the single biggest concentrated Soviet air attack of the battle. It included some Il-2s and perhaps over 100 Pe-2s. The Second Air Army reports that the I Bomber Corps with 103 planes carried out 159 sorties in Belenikhino, Kalinin, Ivanovka, Ozerovskii, Byikovka, Streletskoye, Krasnyii Uzliv, and Chapayev areas. These first four locales are in the Das Reich area while the last two are in the 332nd Infantry Division area. They reported dropping eight 250kg bombs, 768 100kg bombs and many of lesser ordnance. They were well escorted, but still these attacks were not without considerable cost, as the Soviets lost 11 of their Pe-2s out of 103 that flew that day.

Meanwhile, the division continued to prepare to withdraw and move to its rear assembly area. Parts of the division started moving out during the early afternoon.

Private Kaufmann, having in the last week seen his first action and received his first wound, was about to celebrate his 18th birthday.

> I particularly recall the 16th of July, because it is my birthday. With the onset of dawn we were continuously attacked by enemy fighters and ground attack airplanes. Given the open terrain our battalion occupied, substantial losses were unavoidable. We fired whatever our barrels could hold up to. We often observed hits, but also noticed how our projectiles bounced off on the armored Ilyushin-2 fuselages. The two ammunition bearers worked tirelessly in reloading the magazines. I had to exchange the heated barrels after every engagement. The three barrels that were part of our equipment never had a chance to cool down anymore. We usually wore asbestos gloves to change the barrels, but in the heat of the moment I had neglected to use those and burned both palms of my hands on the corrugated handles. The resulting pattern on my skin looked pretty neat and reminded me of my birthday in 1943 for a long time to come.

BY EARLY THE next morning the division had been relieved by the 167th Infantry Division. The displacement began at 0300, with the relief of Der Fuehrer SS Regiment completed by 0600.

The Deutschland SS Regiment had some difficulties. Its relieving regiment was in place along the front line at 0615, and the Deutschland SS Regiment began to withdraw at 0700. Somehow, through incongruities in the definition of the boundary between the regiments, the 167th Infantry Division was delayed in relieving its 3rd Company. The company succeeded in disengaging itself, but only with great difficulty and casualties. The Soviet infantry had followed its withdrawal, staying within hand-grenade throwing range.

By 1500, the division, with the exception of a few elements, had arrived in its new assembly area near Pokrovka, some 20 kilometers in the rear. By the night of 16/17 July, the Das Reich SS Panzer Grenadier Division had withdrawn and was finished with the Battle of Kursk. Private Kaufmann recalls:

> It was a surprise to us, when we were pulled rearward from the front on July 17. An infantry division took over our sector. Relief occurred in orderly fashion and without harassment from the enemy. In the framework of an armored unit we marched towards the reserve area south of Luchki. Here our company sergeant major (Spiess) showed up at a late hour and gave out commissary items, some of them labeled: "Only for fighters on the front!" These included cigarettes, chocolate, candy and other luxuries we had long been deprived of. In addition, everyone got a bottle of schnapps, the "Altvater" brand. I have a clear memory of this mild, sweet fruit liquor.
>
> For the first time since inception of *Operation Citadel* our 14th Antiaircraft Company was all together again. Now everyone became aware of our own losses. Fourteen crewmen on the twelve 20mm antiaircraft guns had fallen in battle, a further fourteen had been taken to field hospitals. We didn't know which of them had survived. Five guns mounted on halftracks had been lost. So we had barely half of our original fighting strength left. The mood that evening was thus in stark contrast to the euphoria on the evening of July 4th. It was a strange atmosphere, no one spoke up, everyone looked on soberly, there was no laughter. We were far from any mental crisis but embitterment took its course together with the question why it hit my comrade and not me.

Withdrawing from the Tank Fields of Prokhorovka, 17 July 1943

DURATION One day FRONTAGE 9.8 kilometers TERRAIN Rolling, bare
WEATHER Cloudy, dry. Roads are in good condition.

	Attacker	*Defender*
Units	XVIII TC, XXIX TC & 9th GAD	LSSAH PzGrD
Attachments	See below	See below
Strength	25,628	20,563
Armor	206 (89 light)	117 (6 light)
Artillery	253	182
Air Sorties	0	0
Casualties	5 (2 KIA, 3 WIA)	41 (5 KIA, 34 WIA, 2 MIA)
Armor Losses	1	3
Artillery Losses	2	1
Enemy Captured	6	N/A

Forces Engaged

German Attachments
55th Werfer Regiment
861st Light Field Howitzer Battalion
I/1st Lehr Werfer Regiment

III/55th Werfer Regiment (detached on the 17th—still counted here)
Leibstandarte SS Adolf Hitler Regiment (detached on the 17th—still counted here)

Soviet Forces
XVIII Tank Corps
736th AT Bn
80th Gds Mtr Rgt
XXIX Tank Corps
1529th Heavy SP Art Rgt
76th Gds Mtr Rgt
747th AT Bn
1852/32nd AT Bde—attached on the 17th (not included)
9th Guards Airborne Division

The division remained in the rear on the 17th, seeing no action.

The SS Panzer Corps is Redirected

The purpose of the corps withdrawal was to free up forces for the attack on the 18th. This attack was canceled in the morning. At 1400, the orders were received from the army to transfer the Adolf Hitler and Das Reich SS Divisions to the area west and southwest of Belgorod. The marches to the rear were to be carried out under cover of the darkness, with most of the movement to be executed on the night of 17/18 July and the rest the following night.

The 167th Infantry Division Takes over the Front Line

The night of 15/16 passed quietly. The division now held the line running from Leski to Shakhovo. There was heavy Soviet bombardment in the Leski area while the division continued to mop up the areas east of the railroad during the morning.

At 1320, the SS Panzer Corps reported that part of the corps would be relieved by the 168th Infantry Division

Das Reich Holds, 16 July 1943

DURATION One day FRONTAGE 10.3 kilometers TERRAIN Rolling, mixed

WEATHER Sunny, dry, light cloud cover. Roads still somewhat muddy, but drying up well. Ravines were, however, still quite muddy.

	Attacker	*Defender*
Units	183rd RD & II TC	DR SS PzGrD
Attachments	See below	See below
Strength	13,489	18,445
Armor	49 (21 light)	112
Artillery	101	142
Air Sorties	116 + 43 Night	0
Casualties	30 (9 KIA, 21 WIA)	224 (58 KIA, 166 WIA)
Armor Losses	1	6
Artillery Losses	0	0
Enemy Captured	2	N/A

Forces Engaged

German Attachments
III/1st Lehr Werfer Regiment
III/818th Artillery Regiment

Soviet Forces
183rd Rifle Division
1852/32nd AT Bde—detached on the 16th (included)
II Tank Corps

during the night of 16/17 July in the Yasnaya Polyana and Vinogradovka area. Questions from the 167th Infantry Division as to the details of this operation or requests for orders brought no response from the Fourth Panzer Army headquarters until 1500, when the army called to say that the 167th Infantry Division would be attached back to the SS Panzer Corps as of that moment. An hour later, the division was then assigned instead to the III Panzer Corps, under Provisional Army Kempf. As a result, the division effectively did nothing during the day.

That evening, the Fourth Panzer Army ordered the division during the night to relieve elements of Das Reich SS Division and the 7th and 19th Panzer Divisions. This relief was difficult to carry out because of heavy rainfall inundating the roads, and because it proved impossible to transmit the details of the operations to the units involved.

During the night of 16/17 July, there were many Soviet bombings in the division rear area, especially around Luchki and Yakovlevo. In view of the Soviet situation, attacks were expected at any moment on the division's left wing. The division took over the sector belonging to the 7th Panzer Division during the night and early morning of 17 July, as well as elements of the 19th Panzer Division and Das Reich. The assumption of this new line was completed around 0800. The division also had the 54th Werfer Regiment, the 228th Assault Gun Battalion, and various flak units attached. The division was also supported by units under the 3rd Command of Artillery (under III Panzer Corps) and by an armored reaction force from the 19th Panzer Division.

All during the day, the front line received heavy Soviet artillery, rocket, and mortar fire. During the afternoon, groups of three to four Soviet tanks moved out

Das Reich Withdraws, 17 July 1943

DURATION One day FRONTAGE N/A TERRAIN Rolling, mixed
WEATHER Sunny, dry. Roads dry and in good condition.

	Attacker	*Defender*
Units	183rd RD & II TC	DR SS PzGrD
Attachments	See below	See below
Strength	13,888	18,203
Armor	68 (27 light)	116
Artillery	114	143
Air Sorties	0	0
Casualties	106 (31 KIA, 62 WIA, 13 MIA)	36 (10 KIA, 23 WIA, 3 MIA)
Armor Losses	6	4
Artillery Losses	0	0
Enemy Captured	0	N/A

Forces Engaged

German Attachments
III/1st Lehr Werfer Regiment
III/818th Artillery Regiment

Soviet Forces
183rd Rifle Division
II Tank Corps
1850/32nd AT Bde—attached on the 17th (included)
1854/32nd AT Bde—attached on the 17th (included)

of Pravorot toward the southwest. At 1720, two Soviet battalions supported by 28 tanks (German estimate) attacked the 339th Infantry Regiment sector from the Krutoi ravine. At 1740, the division requested permission to commit the Tiger Company at Plota, which had been allocated to the division, to stop the attack. This permission was not granted until 1825. Meanwhile, the division's artillery regiment fired on the Russian infantry with its light battalions and on the tanks with its heavy battalion, beginning about 1800. The Adolf Hitler SS Division loaned its assault gun battalion to stem the attack. At 1850, the 167th Infantry Division's 238th Antitank Battalion was ordered to bring its guns forward to defend against the tank attack at Vinogradovka. At 1855, the 339th Infantry Regiment, bearing the brunt of the attack, reported five Soviet tanks destroyed, plus two knocked out by mines.

At 1940, General Trierenburg (division commander) arrived at the regiment's command post and directed the Tiger company to the woods at Yasnaya Polyana from where it could support either flank. There were now Russian infantry moving along the railroad embankment at Ivanovskii Vyiselok and another tank attack expected against the highway. The tank attack against Vinogradovka was finally repulsed at 2000. The division was told (by prisoners?) that the Soviets had noticed the relief of the SS and that the attack had been a test of the new unit's armor defenses.

The Fifth Guards Tank Army Attacks Again

Soviet air reconnaissance noted on the 17th the movement of German tanks and trucks south to Belgorod and Tomarovka. At 1000 (Moscow time), Rotmistrov ordered his tank corps to again advance forward with orders to take Vinogradovka, Ivanovka, Belenikhino and to reach the line of the railroad.

The XXIX Tank Corps, along with the II Tank Corps, was to take the Stalinskoye Otdeleniye Sovkhoz, height 246.5 (on the rail line between the two sovkhozes) and the Komsomolets Sovkhoz. It moved forward at 1200 (Moscow time) and by 1800 (Moscow time) the 31st Tank Brigade had its forward units one kilometer south of Oktyabrskii Sovkhoz. Stalinskoye Otdeleniye Sovkhoz fell by 2000 and the brigade ended the day on the railroad west of Stalinskoye Otdeleniye Sovkhoz. The 25th Tank Brigade at 1800 was at the southwestern edge of the woods one kilometer west of Storozhevoye and ended the day in the Ivanovskii Vyiselok area. The 53rd Motorized Rifle Brigade had forward units in the glades of the woods north of Storozhevoye at 1800, and by 2000 had taken height 241.6 (two kilometers northeast of the Komsomolets) and cleaned out the woods north of Storozhevoye. It ended the day on the railroad east of Komsomolets Sovkhoz with forward units in the Komsomolets Sovkhoz area. The corps now had 42 T-34s, 50 T-70s, 1 KV-1, 4 SU-122s and 6 SU-76s.

The II Tank Corps held the line from Yamki to Vinogradovka on the 16th and on the 17th began to advance at 1700 (Moscow time) with the mission of taking Vinogradovka and reaching the line of the railroad. Two battalions of the 127th Guards Rifle Regiment from the 42nd Guards Rifle Division were detached to form a pursuit detachment. These two battalions reinforced this attack and by 1800 (Moscow time) were fighting in the northern outskirts of Vinogradovka. The 99th Tank Brigade led the fight for Vinogradovka, discovering the eastern edge of the town had been mined and was supported by German artillery. It lost six T-34s on mines. At 0200 (Moscow time) on the 18th, the units of this corps were still sitting on the eastern outskirts of Vinogradovka. The corps still had 31 T-34s, 24 T-70s and 5 Churchills.

The II Guards Tank Corps also held in place on the 16th. It was attacked at 1050 (Moscow time) by infantry along the gully north of Plota in the direction of Novoselovka, but this attack was not successful. At 1900 (Moscow time) on the 17th, Rotmistrov ordered the corps forward to take Ivanovka and Belenikhino and reach the line of the railroad. At 2100 its 25th Guards Tank Brigade occupied the southeast outskirts of Pravorot, its 26th Guards Tank Brigade was in Dalnii Dolzhik (just south of Pravorot) and its 4th Guards Motorized Rifle Brigade occupied height 212.0 to the southern outskirts of Zhilomostnoye, ready to attack and take Ivanovka and Belenikhino. The corps' artillery had been centralized for the attack, while the 4th Guards Tank Brigade had handed over its remaining tanks to the 25th Guards Tank Brigade the previous day and remained in the rear. By 0200 on the 18th, the corps' units, advancing under heavy artillery and mortar fire, reached height 234.9, two kilometers east of Ivanovka. The corps had 45 T-34s and 18 T-70s.

The 10th Guards Mechanized Brigade held in Zhilomostnoye on the 16th and was moved to the north of Plota on the 17th. The 24th Guards Tank Brigade was brought down from behind the XXXIII Guards Rifle Corps to Dalnii Dolzhik.

Overall, both sides' casualties during this operation were light, and it is clear this was a very limited attack against a withdrawing force.

Air Support

At 0730 (Moscow time) on 16 July, 25 Ju-88s were reported to have bombed the II Guards Tank Corps. At 1135 (Moscow time) a group of 50 to 60 aircraft bombed the corps' position. From 1300 (Moscow time) groups of 5-15 aircraft constantly bombed the corps' units. Still with all this air activity, the corps only reported 4 killed and 11 men wounded for the day.

On the 17th, the II Guards Tank Corps only reported singular reconnaissance flights from the Germans.

III Panzer Corps

The III Panzer Corps was left conducting some minor clean up operations, but basically the battle was over for

167th Infantry Division Takes over the Front Line I, 16 July 1943

DURATION One day FRONTAGE 29.8 kilometers TERRAIN Rolling, mixed
WEATHER Variably cloudy, changing to thundershowers later in the day. Towards the evening the roads became very soft.

	Attacker	*Defender*
Units	167th ID	375th Rifle & 93rd Gds Rifle Divisions
Attachments	None	See below
Strength	12,900	11,419
Armor	0	0
Artillery	94	75
Air Sorties	0	36 + 43 Night
Casualties	104 (26 KIA, 73 WIA, 5 MIA)	1,353 (1,353 MIA)[7]
Artillery Losses	0	13
Enemy Captured	N/A	0

Forces Engaged

Soviet Forces
375th Rifle Division
1240th AT Rgt
137th ATR Bn
88th Flamethrower Company
192nd Flamethrower Company
1363/26th Antiaircraft Division
60th Armored Train Detachment
93rd Guards Rifle Division

7 The 93rd Guards Rifle Division reported on the 15th to have spent the day "fighting in encirclement" and then reported on the 16th to have "left the encirclement" and pulled back to a line from Pravorot to Dalnii Dolzhik (Fond: 1262, Opis: 1, Delo: 9). At 2330 16 July the Sixty-ninth Army reported that the 93rd Guards Rifle Division was putting itself in order in the area of Krasnoye (Fond: Sixty-ninth Army, Opis: 10753, Delo: 133, page 38).

The division has a reported strength of 9,426 on 5 July and 5,168 on 20 July (Fond: 906, Opis: 1, Delo: 211). This implies at least 4,258 lost in the battle. There are daily casualty reports for the 7th through the 14th and for the 18th. They total 1,551 casualties (269 killed, 1271 wounded, 11 missing). This is considerably fewer than the supposed 4,258 losses. The unreported casualties were assumed to be missing in action and were assigned equally to the 15th and 16th of July, with equipment losses also assigned similarly.

them. As the most depleted of the panzer corps, they were left behind to hold the line while the larger and healthier panzer grenadier divisions withdrew. The 7th Panzer Division was actually withdrawn from the line so it could be re-deployed in the Fourth Panzer Army sector. The other units remained in place, defending.

The 7th Panzer Division

During the night, the division held the line running from Plota to Maloye Yablonovo and repelled several attacks against its right flank. At 0650, the division was reassigned to the Fourth Panzer Army but continued to defend the same positions. Another attack against the right flank of the division was repelled at 0930. The Soviet forces were quiet the rest of the day.

167th Infantry Division Takes over the Front Line II, 17 July 1943

DURATION One day FRONTAGE 16.4 kilometers TERRAIN Rolling, mixed
WEATHER Changeable cloudy to clear. Local showers. Temperature at noon: 20 degrees Celsius. Road conditions "level 4."

	Attacker	*Defender*
Units	375th Rifle Division & others	167th ID
Attachments	See below	See below
Strength	4,890	15,590
Armor	0	9
Artillery	139	139
Air Sorties	0	0
Casualties	0	105 (26 KIA, 74 WIA, 5 MIA)
Armor losses	0	1
Artillery losses	0	0
Enemy Captured	0	N/A

Forces Engaged

German Attachments (all attached 7/17)[8]
228th StuG Bn (-bty)
I/54th Werfer Rgt
II/54th Werfer Rgt
I/38th Flak Bn
Hq/54th Werfer Rgt

Soviet Forces
375th Rifle Division
1240th AT Rgt
137th ATR Bn
88th Flamethrower Company
192nd Flamethrower Company
1363/26th Antiaircraft Division
60th Armored Train Detachment

Also in the area
II Gds Tank Corps (counted against 7th Panzer Division)

8 Werfer regiment assigned to division at 1100, sturmgeschuetz battalion assigned at 1200 (T315, R1482). The III Panzer Corps' quartermaster report for 17 July reports a ration strength of 17,000 men. This clearly includes the attached units (T314, R198).

During the night of the 16/17th, the 167th Infantry Division moved into the 7th Panzer Division's positions. This movement was interrupted by a strong Soviet attack on both sides of Vinogradovka that was supported by an estimated 23 tanks. After the attack was resolved the division continued on to the Olkhovka area, where it went into a temporary assembly area in the rear. It remained there the following day.

The 19th Panzer Division

The 19th Panzer Division also held in place, waiting for its relief by elements of the 167th Infantry Division. During the night, the division repelled Soviet attacks with tanks from Kuzminka and Plota. Artillery fire was directed onto Soviet assembly areas and troop movements. The Soviets reinforced the troops in the gullies in the Severnyii Donets valley. During the night and morning of the 16th, there were also repeated Soviet air attacks on the front and rear. The Luftwaffe was "rarely present."

Another Soviet attack with tanks from the north on division positions near Kuzminka was repelled at 0825. One T-34 was claimed destroyed in close combat. Strong Soviet infantry forces repeated the attack out of the gully north of Plota at about 0900 despite heavy shelling on their assembly area. This attack was also beaten back.

The night was quiet and the following day elements of the division were relieved by the 167th Infantry Division. The 11th Guards Mechanized Brigade was reported, though, to have repelled German infantry and tank attacks from Vyipolzovka to the north from 2300 (Moscow time) on the 16th. The Germans reported repulsing a company-sized Soviet attack from Kuzminka during one of their relief moves (the relief of the I Battalion, 114th Panzer Grenadier Regiment by the 19th Reconnaissance Battalion), but otherwise the relief went as planned and the division was able to assume responsibility for its new frontage at 0300 on the 17th. The division remained in its slightly reduced positions for the rest of the day with no significant activity.

The 6th Panzer Division

This unit continued on the defense over the next two days, as it had done the previous day. Height 222.1 (four kilometers east of Rzhavets) had become the focus of the fight, having first been taken by the Germans on the 14th, was contested on the 15th and would continue changing hands on the 16th and 17th. It is unknown how many times this hill was traded between the two sides over the four days, but it appears that it exchanged hands at least five times. This day started with the hill in German hands.

During the night, the Soviets made probing attacks in company strength against height 222.1. During the morning, heavy artillery fire fell on the division and around midday, the Soviets renewed their attack against height 224.3 (700 meters northwest of 222.1). The attack was stopped by artillery and heavy infantry fire. The Sixty-ninth Army reported that the Germans attacked height 222.1 at 0400 (Moscow time) with a battalion supported by 10 tanks. The attack was repelled by the 92nd Guards Rifle Division by 0830 (Moscow time). At 0920 (Moscow time) the Germans reconnoitered the same height with one company. They were inactive along the rest of the Sixty-ninth Army's front during the day.

At around 1700 (Berlin time), a tank company and II Battalion of the 114th Panzer Grenadier Regiment attacked height 222.1 to support an attack by the I Battalion of the 4th Panzer Grenadier Regiment. The Germans encountered strong Soviet tank forces on the hill and lost two tanks as a result,[9] but appeared to have taken the hill. The Soviets then attacked heights 222.1 and 224.3 around 2000 (Berlin time) on 16 July. These attacks were repelled.

Between 0250 and 1100 on 17 July, the Soviets attacked the 4th Panzer Grenadier Regiment positions on height 241.5 (less than four kilometers southeast of 222.1) with about a company of infantry, but no tanks. The first attack made a small penetration, which was restored by

9 Jentz, page 92.

an immediate counterattack at around 0310 conducted by a tank company, assault guns and the II Battalion of the 4th Panzer Grenadier Regiment. A second attack was beaten off. The panzer regiment then returned to reserve, leaving a platoon to help defend the hill.[10]

A Soviet force composed of tanks and infantry attacked height 222.1 around noon from the area around Poddorozhnaya Woods. This woods and gully came to within 200 meters of the top of the hill. This attack was broken up by counterattacking panzers supported by the division's artillery. Soviet armor again attacked height 222.1 at around 1745, which alerted the panzer regiment, but the German infantry beat off the attack before the German tanks could see action.[11]

The 168th Infantry Division

The 168th Infantry Division was now left to take over and hold a 33 kilometer front against what was still significant opposition. During the night, the division repelled a company-sized unit (60 men) attempting to infiltrate the gully southeast of Kazachye. Six prisoners were taken. An attack of unknown strength against the right wing of the 442nd Infantry Regiment was repelled at 0100. There was nothing else to report for that night, the following day, the following night, or the 17th of July, beyond sporadic artillery and mortar fire and active patrolling on both sides.

The Sixty-ninth Army

The Sixty-ninth Army concluded that they had exhausted the enemy, noting that they were seeing German entrenching activity from Ryindinka to Rzhavets to Vyipolzovka on the night of the 15th/16th. Supported by elements of the Fifth Guards Tank Army, the Sixty-ninth Army held in place and continued fortifying its positions.

10 The movement of the panzer regiment to reserve is from Jentz, page 92.

11 The attack at 1700 is noted in Jentz, page 92.

The XLVIII Rifle Corps was now deployed with the 183rd Rifle Division in the north, in the area it had occupied for most of the battle. Southwest of it was the 375th Rifle Division in the area of Dalnii Dolzhik and Novoselovka. It suffered no reported losses during this time. The neighboring 89th Guards Rifle Division also recorded no activity except for an attack on Kuzminka on the 17th. The 11th Mechanized Brigade also reported fighting in that area. The hard-fighting 81st Guards Rifle Division remained in the rear. The battle was over for them. The 93rd Guards Rifle Division was shifted on the 17th from Krasnoye down to Bolshiye Podyarugi to backstop the 92nd Guards Rifle Division.

The XXXV Guards Rifle Corps had a similarly quiet time. Its 92nd Guards, 94th Guards, 107th and 305th Rifle Divisions remained in place. The 107th Rifle Division's 522nd Rifle Regiment had pulled back farther to the rear to Tonenkoye-Dolgoye. The only significant fighting was around height 222.1 on the morning of the 16th that involved the 92nd Guards Rifle Division and Trufanov's mobile detachment, including the 12th Mechanized Brigade.

The Arrival of the Fifty-third Army

The Steppe Front had provided five armies to backstop the Voronezh Front: the Fifth Guards, Fifth Guards Tank, Twenty-seventh, Forty-seventh and Fifty-third Armies. Sitting to the north of the Fifth Guards Army at the start of the battle was the Fifty-third Army consisting of seven rifle divisions and the IV Guards Tank Corps. This force was closer to Prokhorovka than the Fifth Guards Tank Army initially was. The Fifty-third Guards Army was commanded by Lt. General Ivan Mefodyevich Managarov.

On the morning of the 9th, three divisions of the Fifty-third Army were ordered to move west to a position on the Seim River. It occupied this position by 2300 on the 12th, putting the army within 40 kilometers of the front line. This advance was led by the 252nd Rifle Division. On the 15th, this division was attached to the XXXV Guards Rifle Corps, with a reported strength for the division of 7,477 men and a full compliment of supporting weapons.[12] The 252nd Rifle Division was concentrating on the 17th in the area six to ten kilometers to the northeast of Prokhorovka.

In case anyone harbors the notion that the Voronezh Front was on its last legs and could have been defeated by one final push by Army Group South, the Soviets were prepared to move into place the Fifty-third Army and its seven rifle divisions. Its lead elements had already arrived. This was in addition to the two divisions being held in reserve by the Fifth Guards Army, the relatively strong 42nd Guards Rifle Division, and the fresh 6th Guards Airborne Division. On top of that, the Voronezh Front had a number of seriously attrited organizations resting in the rear, available for recommitment, including the XXXI Tank Corps and the 51st, 52nd, 78th, 81st and 93rd Guards Rifle Divisions. Also with the Fifty-third Army was the I Mechanized Corps, while assembling near Kursk were the Twenty-seventh Army and the IV Guards Tank Corps, and at Korocha were the Forty-seventh Army and the III Guards Mechanized Corps.

Air Support

The 168th Infantry Division reported lively Soviet air activity during the night of the 15/16 with bombing and strafing but little air activity the following night. The 7th Panzer Division also reported frequent Soviet air attacks during the night of 15/16 July. The 19th Panzer Division reported that the night and morning of the 16th, there were repeated Soviet air attacks on the front and rear. The Luftwaffe was "rarely present."

The following day they reported minimal Soviet air activity and no German air presence. The 6th Panzer Division reported for the night of 16/17 July that there was strong Soviet air activity but not as much as previous nights.

12 They report on the 15th 4,242 rifles, 2,110 SMGs, 495 LMGs, 111 HMGs, 2 AAMGs, 43 50mm Mortars, 74 82mm Mortars, 21 120mm Mortars, 48 45mm guns, 31 76mm guns, 12 122mm Howitzers and 209 AT rifles. They report a strength of 7,500 reported on the 17th along with 900 horses and 147 automatic rifles. All the other equipment strengths were the same on the 17th as on the 15th.

The 7th Panzer Division Holds, 16 July 1943

DURATION One day FRONTAGE 9.1 kilometers TERRAIN Rolling, mixed
WEATHER Some clouds, light rain locally. Roads good except in a few locations.

	Attacker	*Defender*
Units	II Gds Tank Corps & 10th Gds Mech Bde	7th PzD
Attachments	See below	See below
Strength	13,817	18,647
Armor	95 (32 light)	42 (4 light)
Artillery	79	141
Air Sorties	10 + 43 Night	82
Casualties	68 (17 KIA, 44 WIA, 7 MIA)	33 (3 KIA, 29 WIA, 1 MIA)
Armor Losses	5	0
Artillery Losses	2	0
Enemy Captured	0	N/A

Forces Engaged

German Attachments
9th Bridge Column B
1/505th Bridge Column B
843rd Bridge Column J

99th Flak Rgt Staff
I/38th Flak Rgt
II/38th Flak Rgt

II/62nd Artillery Rgt
I/54th Werfer Rgt

co/503rd Heavy Panzer Bn—attached on the 16th[14]

Detachments
ObsBty/78th Artillery Rgt (included)
Regimental Group (included)—almost certainly returned to the unit by now

Soviet Forces
II Guards Tank Corps
- 301st Antitank Regiment
- 755th AT Battalion
- 16th Guards Mortar Regiment

10th Gds Mechanized Bde

Also in the area
375th Rifle Division (counted against the 167th ID)
93rd Guards Rifle Division (counted against the 167th ID)

14 The III Panzer Corps' orders for the 15th were that one tiger company ("about 9 Tigers") was to attach itself to the 7th Panzer Division. The company will report to the division at Shakhovo early on the 16th. This means that the Tiger battalion is effectively down to one functioning company with the other two repairing tanks (and presumably withdrawn from battle).

The 7th Panzer Division Withdraws, 17 July 1943

DURATION One day FRONTAGE 9.1 kilometers TERRAIN Rolling, mixed
WEATHER Partly cloudy, light showers in the evening.

	Attacker	*Defender*
Units	II Gds Tank Corps & 10th Gds Mech Bde	7th PzD
Attachments	Same as previous day	See below
Strength	13,749	16,633
Armor	96 (33 light)	33 (4 light)
Artillery	96	114
Air Sorties	0	0
Casualties	16 (2 KIA, 14 WIA)	18 (3 KIA, 15 WIA)
Armor Losses	0	0
Artillery Losses	0	0
Enemy Captured	0	N/A

Forces Engaged

German Attachments
9th Bridge Column B
1/505st Bridge Column B
843rd Bridge Column J

99th Flak Rgt Staff
I/38th Flak Rgt—detached on the 17th (not included)
II/38th Flak Rgt
II/62nd Artillery Rgt
I/54th Werfer Rgt—detached on the 17th (not included)

co/503rd Heavy Panzer Bn—detached on the 17th (not included)

Detachments
ObsBty/78th Artillery Rgt (included)

The 19th Panzer Division Holds, 16–17 July 1943

DURATION Two days FRONTAGE 10.9 kilometers TERRAIN Rolling, mixed
WEATHER 17th: Sunny, bright. Temperature at noon: 23 degrees Celsius. Road conditions good.

	Attacker	*Defender*
Units	89th Gds RD & 11th Gds Mech Bde	19th PzD
Attachments	None	See below
Strength	8,060	16,391
Armor	0	35 (5 tanks)
Artillery	69	128
Air Sorties	43 Night	0
Casualties	281 (15 KIA, 160 WIA, 106 MIA)	78 (9 KIA, 66 WIA, 3 MIA)
Armor losses	0	5
Artillery losses	11	1
Enemy Captured	0	N/A

Forces Engaged

German Attachments
70th Engineer Bn
2/411th Bridge Column B
842nd Bridge Column J

52nd Werfer Rgt
I/61st Flak Rgt (less 1 battery)
429th Infantry Rgt (168th ID), less I Battalion
I/114th Panzer Grenadier Rgt (from 6th PzD)—detached on the 16th (not included)

Detachments
ObsBty/19th Artillery Rgt (included)

The 6th Panzer Division Holds, 16–17 July 1943

DURATION Two days FRONTAGE 14.4 kilometers TERRAIN Rolling, mixed

WEATHER 16th: Clear, warm and dry. Roads had dried. 17th: Bright, warm and dry. Temperature at noon: 23 degrees Celsius. Road conditions good.

	Attacker	*Defender*
Units	92nd Gds & 305th Rifle Division, Trufanov's detachment & 12th Gds Mech Bde	6th PzD
Attachments	315th Guards Mtr Rgt	See below
Strength	16,757	19,752
Armor	21 (6 light)	23 (2 light)
Artillery	92	129
Air Sorties	38 + 137 Night	0
Casualties	191 (47 KIA, 106 WIA, 38 MIA)	207 (32 KIA, 172 WIA, 4 MIA)
Armor Losses	0	1
Artillery Losses	1	3
Enemy Captured	3	N/A

Forces Engaged

German Attachments

II/54th Werfer Rgt—detached on the 17th
III/54th Werfer Rgt
Hq/54th Werfer Rgt—detached on the 17th

II/43rd Flak Rgt
lt Bn/91st Flak Rgt
204th Intelligence Troop

228th StuG Bn (less 2nd company)—detached on the 17th

Detachments

ObsBty/76th Artillery Rgt
I/114th Panzer Grenadier Rgt—re-attached on the 16th

168th Infantry Division Holds, 16–17 July 1943

DURATION Two days FRONTAGE 32.8 kilometers TERRAIN Rolling, mixed

WEATHER 16th: Scattered clouds, local showers. Roads good except for a few locations. 17th: Slightly cloudy, warm. Temperature at noon: 23 degrees Celsius. Roads good.

	Attacker	*Defender*
Units	94th Gds & 107th Rifle Divisions	168th Infantry Division
Attachments	None	See below
Strength	11,938	13,965
Armor	0	8
Artillery	69	107
Air Sorties	33 Night	0
Casualties	129 (14 KIA, 77 WIA, 38 MIA)	232 (37 KIA, 189 WIA, 6 MIA)
Armor Losses	0	0
Artillery Losses	1	0
Enemy Captured	2	N/A

Forces Engaged

German Attachments
2/228th StuG Bn, with 8 StuGs
lt Bty/I/61st AA Rgt

Still detached from the division
248th Engineer Bn (less 3 cos) (included)
429th Infantry Rgt (less 1 Bn) Included)

It is assumed that the 417th Infantry Regiment has relocated with the rest of the division

Soviet Forces
94th Guards Rifle Division
107th Rifle Division less the 522nd Regiment (less 1/3rd)
 123rd ATR Bn
 148th Tank Regiment—attached on the 16th (not included)

III Panzer Corps Assets
674th Engineer Rgt Staff
925th Bridge Construction Staff
602nd Bridge Column B

153rd Flak Rgt Staff

3rd Command of Artillery
612th Artillery Rgt Staff
II/62nd Artillery Rgt
II/71st Artillery Rgt
857th Heavy Artillery Rgt
Pn/13th Light Observations Battery
ObsBty/19th Artillery Rgt (19th PzD)
ObsBty/76th Artillery Rgt (6th PzD)

2nd Fuel Column Troop
545th Panzer Recovery Platoon
503rd Heavy Panzer Bn
 co/503rd Heavy Panzer Bn—detached on the 16th —re-attached the 17th
Regimental Group (from 7th PzD)

167th Infantry Division attached to corps the 16th
7th Panzer Division detached from corps the 17th

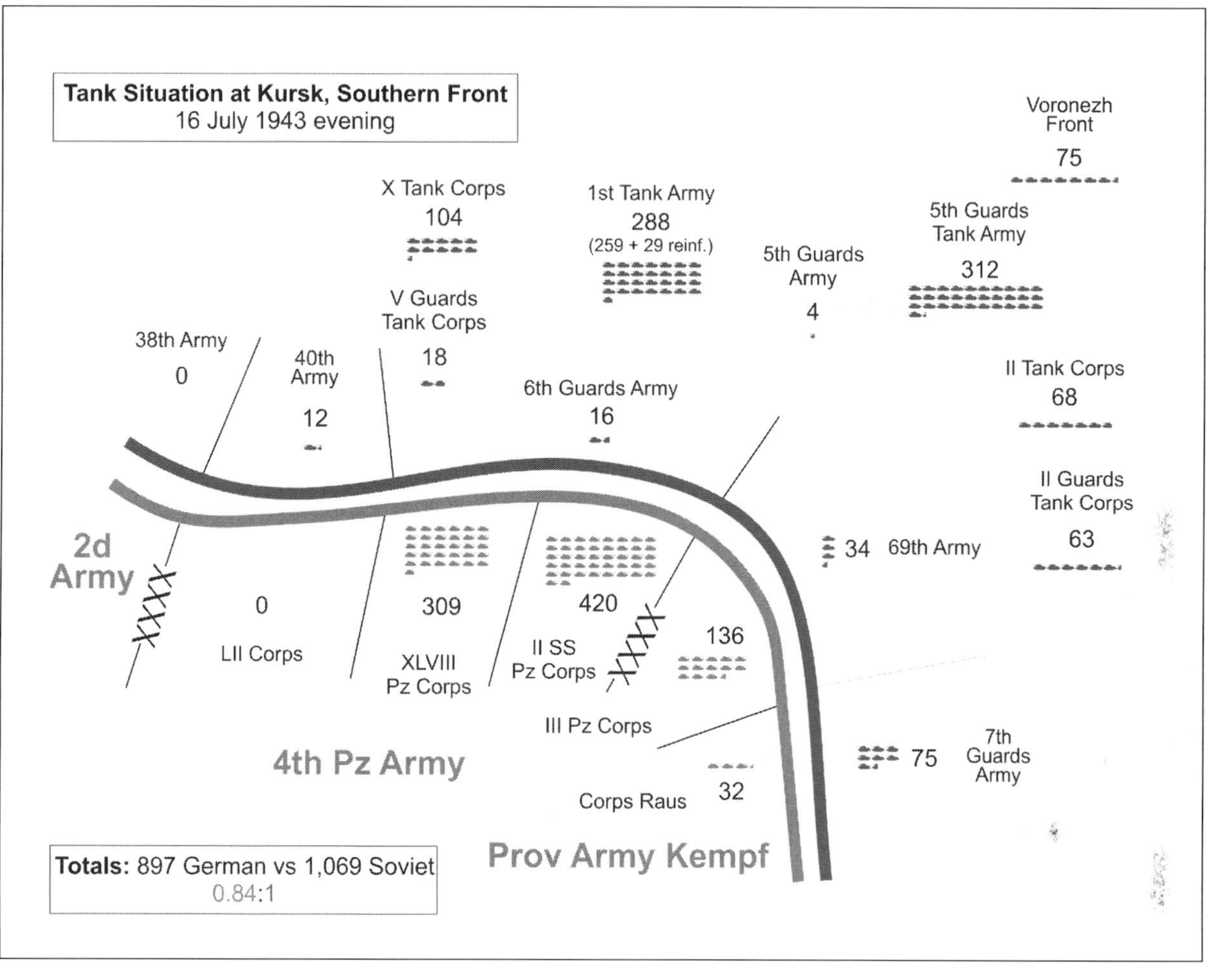

Summary to Date

While the front quieted down, the real turning point over these two days was that the Germans had effectively ceded air superiority to the Soviets. On the 16th, the VIII Air Corps complained that their fighters, with their depleted numbers, could no longer completely defend against Soviet air attacks. This day was also noted for the concentrated Soviet air attacks against Das Reich, which to date, were unheralded in their focus and power. Still, with this newly developed Soviet air superiority, these concentrated attacks were not repeated to the same extent or effect on subsequent days.

The following day, the German Air Force barely appeared over the battlefield, with only 138 sorties that day and five planes lost. The control of the air and the initiative had indeed passed over to the Soviets. The German air had now all been portioned out to the north and the south to deal with all the other threats that the Soviet Army had developed.

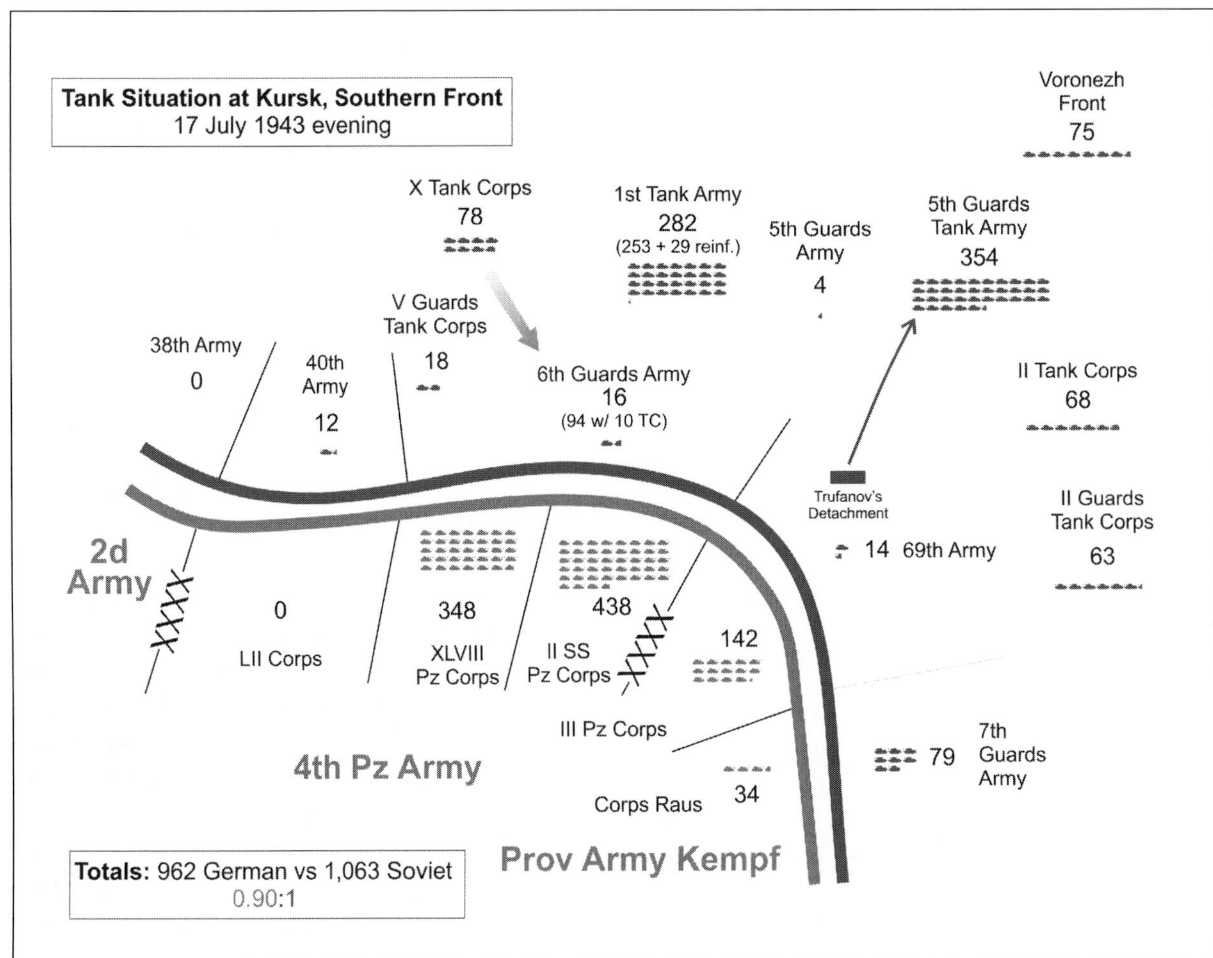
Tank Situation at Kursk, Southern Front
17 July 1943 evening
Voronezh Front
75
X Tank Corps
78
1st Tank Army
282
(253 + 29 reinf.)
5th Guards Army
4
5th Guards Tank Army
354
V Guards Tank Corps
18
38th Army
0
40th Army
12
6th Guards Army
16
(94 w/ 10 TC)
II Tank Corps
68
Trufanov's Detachment
II Guards Tank Corps
63
14 69th Army
2d Army
0
LII Corps
348
XLVIII Pz Corps
438
II SS Pz Corps
142
III Pz Corps
4th Pz Army
Corps Raus
34
79 7th Guards Army
Prov Army Kempf
Totals: 962 German vs 1,063 Soviet
0.90:1

SOLDIERS OF THE FOURTH PANZER ARMY, PROVISIONAL ARMY KEMPF AND THE FOURTH AIR FORCE

In a bold onslaught and by hard fighting, you have broken through strongly fortified positions which the enemy had prepared for their great armored offensive against the center of the army group. With close cooperation of the attached units of the Fourth Air Fleet, you have shattered the greater part of these enemy units.

The enemy on your front, consisting of 10 tank and mechanized corps, lost to your assault 2,000 tanks, comprising two-third of his strength, as well as 1,500 antitank guns and the guns of 80-100 artillery battalions. There are now 32,000 prisoners in your hands and 18,000 dead have been counted, so the enemy's casualties must equal at least 100,000 men. At least 1,000 enemy aircraft were destroyed by you and the attached units of the Fourth Air Fleet. By this, your hard fighting has achieved its objective.

I thank you and your comrades in the air fleet for your bravery, dedication, and boldness.

Meanwhile the enemy is making up for this heavy attack by launching his own attacks at other points along the front. But, he is missing the forces which you have captured.

I know that you will meet the challenge that now confront you just as you always have in the past, in a manner worthy of our fallen heroes.

signed v. Manstein
Field Marshal and
Commander, Army Group South

I am pleased to be able to bring these congratulatory words to the attention of the panzer army.

signed Hoth
Colonel General and
Commander of the Fourth Panzer Army

AUTHOR'S NOTE: This pronouncement was issued around 20 July 1943. It is certainly putting the best face on a failed offensive. The statistics quoted here are surprisingly accurate. Manstein and his staff claim they faced 10 tank and mechanized corps, which is correct. They claim 2,000 tanks. By our count, the Soviets lost 1,379 tanks destroyed or abandoned and 1,092 tanks damaged. They claim 1,500 antitank guns. By our count, the Soviets lost 1,476 45mm AT, 57mm AT and 76mm guns destroyed and 294 45mm AT, 57mm AT and 76mm guns damaged. They claim 32,000 prisoners of war captured. There is no reason to doubt this figure as we count 32,801 Soviet soldiers missing in action. They claim 18,000 dead, our count is 27,046. They claim at least 100,000 casualties, while our count is 126,808 total casualties and is probably low. They claim 1,000 aircraft destroyed, our count is 665. All of our counts cover the period from 4 to 18 July 1943 (see Appendices III and IV in my book *Kursk: The Battle of Prokhorovka*).

Overall, this is an accurate appreciation of the situation, especially as the Soviet offensive in the center of Army Group South was delayed until 3 August 1943. But, it was still a failed offensive and there would be a counter-offensive that they could not stop.

FATIGUE

The underlying restriction on all military operations is the limitations of human beings. They tire, need food, need sleep, become stressed, become ill, and need rest. Most significant of all, they prefer not to die. This makes war something far different than a bloody training exercise.

The soldiers on this battlefield had been in continuous engagements from the 5th through the 15th of July. These eleven days of intense combat took a toll on the physical and psychological condition of the men involved. No amount of training or physical conditioning can remove the basic needs for rest and sleep. In the German Army, they tried to pace the operations. They tried to give their people rest each night, so that there would still be some fight left in them the following days.

The first concerns about fatigue in the German reports show up on the 9th, in a discussion between Hoth (Fourth Panzer Army) and Knobelsdorff (XLVIII Panzer Corps). At this stage, they were already discussing the pacing of the operation to preserve the troops after four days of heavy combat. Hoth ordered that attacks not be made too early in the morning during the days to come so that the troops could get some rest at night. He was concerned about overtiring the troops.

Mentions of fatigue appear more often in the German reports, as continuous battling slowly wore the men out. It was claimed to be the reason for the loss of five tanks in the Gross Deutschland Panzer Regiment on the 14th, and their subsequent withdrawal from battle. Still, the German Army tried to pace operations to allow some rest. By having the battle break each evening with nightfall, many troops were allowed to rest.

The German veterans interviewed claimed to have not had any real problems with fatigue during the battle. This may be due to the 56 years that separated the battle from the interviews, but still, let's look at their observations for a moment:

Lt. Rodde, adjutant 6th Tank Regiment, 3rd Panzer Division:

> Stress during the operation was not considerably higher than what we had seen earlier, but was nevertheless quite a strain. Our tank crews did show signs of the continued exertion after four, five days. The hot summer weather and the humidity after numerous thundershowers did cause an oppressive weather situation. I do not remember any casualties due to physical or psychological exhaustion, though.
>
> But a day of battle made you dog-tired. As a staff officer, I had to manage the war diary. So every night the staff sergeant showed up and requested that I write the daily report. Many times I would write one or two pages and fall asleep on my desk. What I wrote probably didn't make a whole lot of sense. We would usually complete the final draft for the war diary a few days later, but then we would not even remember exactly how things had been. One must take all that into consideration when reading war diaries written by commanders on the lower echelons.

The chapters of this book were mostly drawn from the division, corps and army daily reports. There is no question that these reports are not always complete.

Captain Frantz, commander of the Gross Deutschland Assault Gun Battalion:

I did not notice any signs of excessive stress or battle fatigue among my troops. This was probably due to the fact that *Operation Citadel* was not our toughest assignment. I always insisted that the assault guns would be withdrawn from the foremost positions at night, so that the crewmen could catch a few hours of sleep. There was no sense in keeping the assault guns up front, as we had no night-fighting capability whatsoever.

Captain Bergemann, commander of the III Battalion, Gross Deutschland Grenadier Regiment:

While we were quite challenged during the engagements, but this was by far not the worst compared to what the Gross Deutschland Division had already been through. I never saw any case of battle fatigue or even mental failure of leaders during the operation. What was to come in terms of severe strain immediately afterwards in the battles of retreat at the end of July and August of 1943 simply does not compare to the modest challenges posed by *Citadel*.

I led the battalion until suffering injury at Akhtyirka. The battles of retreat were often a matter of life and death. We never had that notion during *Citadel*.

Officer Cadet Guenther Baer, tank commander, II Battalion, Leibstandarte SS Adolf Hitler Panzer Regiment:

Whenever there was a cessation of fire, it was ordered to sleep. Only one man stayed with the radio. We actually made it quite well through the days of the battle.

Private Kaufmann, antiaircraft battery, Der Fuehrer SS Regiment, Das Reich SS Division:

We had been in action without any major interruption throughout the battle. Interludes at night were always marked by supply arriving and guard duty. The resulting strain made itself felt with everyone after a few days. Apart from sleep deprivation the hot weather depleted our strength. It was not a rare sight to have soldiers fall fast asleep from one minute to the next during brief interruptions of combat. This happened to our halftrack driver who dozed off right in the middle of an engagement while moving from one fire halt to the next. We only noticed after he kept going straight where a better route would have been advisable. We had difficulty waking him up again. I myself fell asleep one night while standing on guard duty and then collapsed. I do not know how long I laid on the ground in deep sleep. Thank God my gun commander woke up and then roused me somewhat roughly. In fact, falling asleep on guard duty was a serious offense, and I could have been punished severely. But my gun commander did not report the incident; he knew all too well how we all felt.

Finally, Alfred Rubbel, with the 503rd Heavy Panzer (Tiger) Battalion, notes:

For us as the fighting force, stress was certainly severe during these days. This was also due to the hot weather and we went to sleep whenever there was a chance. But I did not see any mistakes being committed due to fatigue or psychological stress factors.

CHAPTER FIFTEEN

The German Withdrawal

18–24 JULY 1943

> Thus has been exploded the legend that the German summer offensives are always successful and that the Soviet forces are always compelled to retreat.
>
> JOSEPH STALIN
> 24 JULY 1943[1]

SS Panzer Corps

The SS Panzer Corps had now withdrawn two of its divisions and Totenkopf had now been transferred over to the XLVIII Panzer Corps control as the SS Panzer Corps withdrew from battle. In the case of the withdrawn Adolf Hitler and Das Reich SS Divisions, they started loading their tracked vehicle units on trains that evening for transport to the Donets basin and the two divisions marched to the area southwest of Belgorod and then from there to Kharkov.

The Fifth Guards Army Moves Forward

The Fifth Guards Army had moved forward only very hesitantly the previous day, while continuing to dig in. Toward the end of the 17th, the army had gotten air reconnaissance data indicating the German withdrawal, so Zhadov (Fifth Guards Army commander) had each of his divisions put together a forward detachment, made up of no less than three battalions, reinforced with artillery in order, it appears, to follow and harass the German rearguard.

The XXXIII Guards Rifle Corps was to advance and capture height 226.6 and Klyuchi and to clear the northern bank of the Psel River and height 245.8. Before nightfall, on the 17th, they conducted reconnaissance of the terrain and organized a two-minute artillery barrage to start the attack. The attack was to start at 0500 (Moscow time). The 95th Guards Rifle Division was able to advance forward four kilometers, taking the towns along the Psel River and height 226.6. Meanwhile, the 9th Guards Airborne and the 42nd Guards Rifle Divisions were able to take advantage of Rotmistrov's advance and sent forward reconnaissance detachments to follow the German retreat. By 2000 (Moscow) these reconnaissance detachments were approaching the line from height 217.9 to height 224.5 to height 258.2 to Vinogradovka. This was not without some cost, for the 95th Guards Rifle Division reported losses for the 18th of 20 killed and 141 wounded, while the 42nd Guards Rifle Division reported 56 killed and 67 wounded.

1 From the official order of the day hailing the Kursk victory. This line was personally added by Stalin. See Georgii K. Zhukov, *Marshal Zhukov's Greatest Battles*, page 200.

ZHUKOV'S BRIDGE

Major Valentin Viktorovich Snegirev,[1] the chief of the operational department of the 95th Guards Rifle Division recalls:

> On the 18th of July, 1943, after defeating the massive German tank and infantry counterattacks, our division conducted an artillery preparation and started the offensive from the Veselyii area. Parts of the division forced the Psel River and continued the offensive to the south, towards Greznoye. The division commander and I were at the observation point located on the other side of the Psel River, at the high point. Battalions of the second echelon and artillery were crossing the bridge located behind us, which was built by our engineers. All of sudden a Willys [U.S. built Jeep] drove to our observation point. I looked out and saw Marshal Zhukov stepping out of the car. I saw him the first time in my life, but recognized him immediately because there were many of his photographs everywhere. A short and very thin Lieutenant Colonel with a briefcase (probably Zhukov's aide) was with him. Lyakhov [Colonel A. N. Lyakhov], the division commander, also saw Zhukov. He jumped out of the trench and ran to him and started reporting to him about the offensive being carried out by his division. Zhukov stopped him and asked about the crossing of the Psel River by the troops. Colonel Lyakhov told him about it and showed him the bridge. Zhukov looked at it carefully, and then ordered an engineer battalion sent to the bridge to reinforce it and to put logs on the oozy northern bank of the river, near the bridge. "A lot of tanks will go over this bridge" he said. Then he nodded saying goodbye and left. It was obvious that he came only to the check the crossing over the Psel River. The chief of staff cared even about such details!

1 Col. Valentin Viktorovich Snegirev was born in Moscow in 1918, and was interviewed by Col. Fyodor Sverdlov in 1999.

Totenkopf's Defense

The Totenkopf SS Division had evacuated the Psel bridgehead as of 2400 hours and destroyed the bridge. It spent the day defending against various Soviet attacks. The Soviets initiated a pre-dawn infantry attack in battalion strength against the Totenkopf SS Regiment. This was repulsed. At 1130, an estimated 30 Soviet tanks then broke through along the boundary between the 167th Infantry Division and the Totenkopf SS Regiment. This attack was turned back by a counterattack by the 1st company of the Totenkopf SS Panzer Regiment. The Soviet tanks withdrew to the east. At 1300, the Soviets again attacked the Totenkopf SS Regiment, but this attack was shattered with the help of the III Battalion of the artillery regiment.

Meanwhile the Soviet attacks shifted to the Eicke SS Regiment. At 1400, a Soviet attack of 30 tanks broke through with about 10 tanks. The penetration was sealed off, and with the help of artillery and heavy infantry weapons, the attack was repulsed with what the Germans reported as heavy losses to the Russians.

At 1420, there was a new gathering of Soviet tanks in the area of Ivanovskii Vyiselok. At the same time, an attack of a battalion of infantry with tank support was made against the Eicke SS Regiment. Again, this attack was broken up by artillery and heavy infantry weapons fire. At 1430, a Soviet attack with tank support came at the Eicke SS Regiment from the wooded strip at Komsomolets. At 1530, another attack was made on the Eicke SS Regiment. About 15 Soviet tanks broke through, but four were destroyed by German defensive fire and the Soviet attack stalled and they then withdrew. At the same time, another attack with tank support was repulsed with the destruction of seven Soviet tanks by Totenkopf's tanks. The Germans claimed that of the 70 to 80 tanks that attacked during the day, 35 were knocked out by antitank guns or by counterattack by the panzer regiment. While all these claims are German claims, they are supported by overall Soviet tank losses for the day of at least 32.

Air Support

Totenkopf reported 10 overflights by 66 aircraft. The 167th Infantry Division reported that after 0500 there was heavy Soviet air activity.

Rotmistrov Moves Forward

Rotmistrov continued to push forward with the XXIX Tank Corps while recommitting the XVIII Tank Corps back into action. The XXIX Tank Corps attacked at 0400 (Moscow time) in the direction of the Komsomolets Sovkhoz, taking it after heavy fighting. Still encountering serious resistance from Teterevino to Vinogradovka, the corps advanced to the eastern slopes of height 258.2, where they were halted by heavy artillery and mortar fire. At 1800 (Moscow time) the corps found itself huddled around height 258.2, with the 31st Tank Brigade on the northern slopes, the 53rd Motorized Rifle Brigade on the northeastern slopes, and the 25th Tank Brigade on the eastern slopes. They were halted there for the day, but were able to expand their area of control to Ivanovskii Vyiselok and to the fork in the road two kilometers south of there. The corps lost seven T-34s and 11 T-70s this day, of which three T-34s and four T-70s were destroyed.

The XVIII Tank Corps was committed back into the line, led by the 32nd Motorized Rifle Brigade and initially following behind the XXIX Tank Corps. At 1100 (Moscow time) the corps attacked with artillery support from their jump-off points at Komsomolets Sovkhoz, moving to the right of the XXIX Tank Corps. They came under heavy fire from height 258.2 but advanced their 110th Tank Brigade to the Molozhavaya gully and their other three brigades to the northern slopes of height 258.2. Lacking howitzers, the corps units and their available artillery could not suppress the reinforced firing points of height 258.2, and only by throwing the 32nd Motorized Rifle Brigade into the attack, were they able to claim to occupy the height by the end of the day. On the other hand, it appears that height 258.2 remained in German hands at the end of the day. Their losses were at least 11 T-34s and three T-70s (five T-34s and one T-70 destroyed).

Compared to the 12th, this was considerable progress at considerably less cost; still, it was a bloody rebuff at the hands of the Germans and another lopsided casualty exchange. This was all in the face of the Totenkopf SS Division.

The rest of Rotmistrov's attack fell on the 167th Infantry Division. This was conducted by the II Tank Corps and II Guards Tank Corps. The V Guards Mechanized Corps was concentrated in the Pravorot, Zhilomostnoye, Dalnii Dolzhik, and Krasnoye area in the army's second echelon, ready to join the attack. It did not go forward this day. Trufanov's detachment was concentrated at Priznachnoye and formed Rotmistrov's reserve.

Overall, this attack was aimed in the direction of Komsomolets to Luchki to cutting the Oboyan-Belgorod road with the XVIII and XXIX Tank Corps, and in the direction of Leski to Teterevino (south) to Smorodino for the II Tank, II Guards Tank, and V Guards Mechanized Corps. The forces were then to be ready to advance on Belgorod.

Adolf Hitler and Das Reich Withdraw

Meanwhile, while Totenkopf was holding the line, the Adolf Hitler SS Division withdrew further, to the area west of Belgorod. The march went smoothly although there were several Soviet bombing attacks along the road. This caused no significant disruption. Some units, including the assault gun battalion, remained back in the old deployment area.

Totenkopf's Defense, 18 July 1943

DURATION One day FRONTAGE 16.6 kilometers TERRAIN Rolling, bare
WEATHER Brighter, with occasional showers.

	Attacker	*Defender*
Units	XXXIII Gds RC, XXIX & XVIII TC	T SS PzGrD
Attachments	See below	See below
Strength	46,001	17,260
Armor	219 (95 light)	98
Artillery	423	129
Air Sorties	0	0
Casualties	890 (323 KIA, 564 WIA, 3 MIA)	123 (21 KIA, 99 WIA, 3 MIA)
Armor Losses	38	2
Artillery Losses	2	2
Enemy Captured	7	N/A

Forces Engaged

German Attachments

II/1st Lehr Werfer Regiment (detached on the 18th—not included)
SS Corps Werfer Battalion
86th Bridge Column B (not included)
III/55th Werfer Regiment (detached on the 18th—not included)
Leibstandarte SS Adolf Hitler Regiment (detached on the 18th—not included)

Soviet Forces

97th Guards Rifle Division
1372nd/29th Antiaircraft Division
201st/12th Mortar Bde—attached on the 17th (not included)

95th Guards Rifle Division

42nd Guards Rifle Division

9th Guards Airborne Division

XXIX Tank Corps
1529th Heavy SP Rgt
76th Gds Mtr Rgt
747th AT Bn
1852/32nd AT Bde—attached on the 17th (not included)

XVIII Tank Corps
736th AT Bn
80th Gds Mtr Rgt—detached on the 18th (not included)
361st[r]/80th Gds Mtr Rgt—attached on the 18th (not included)

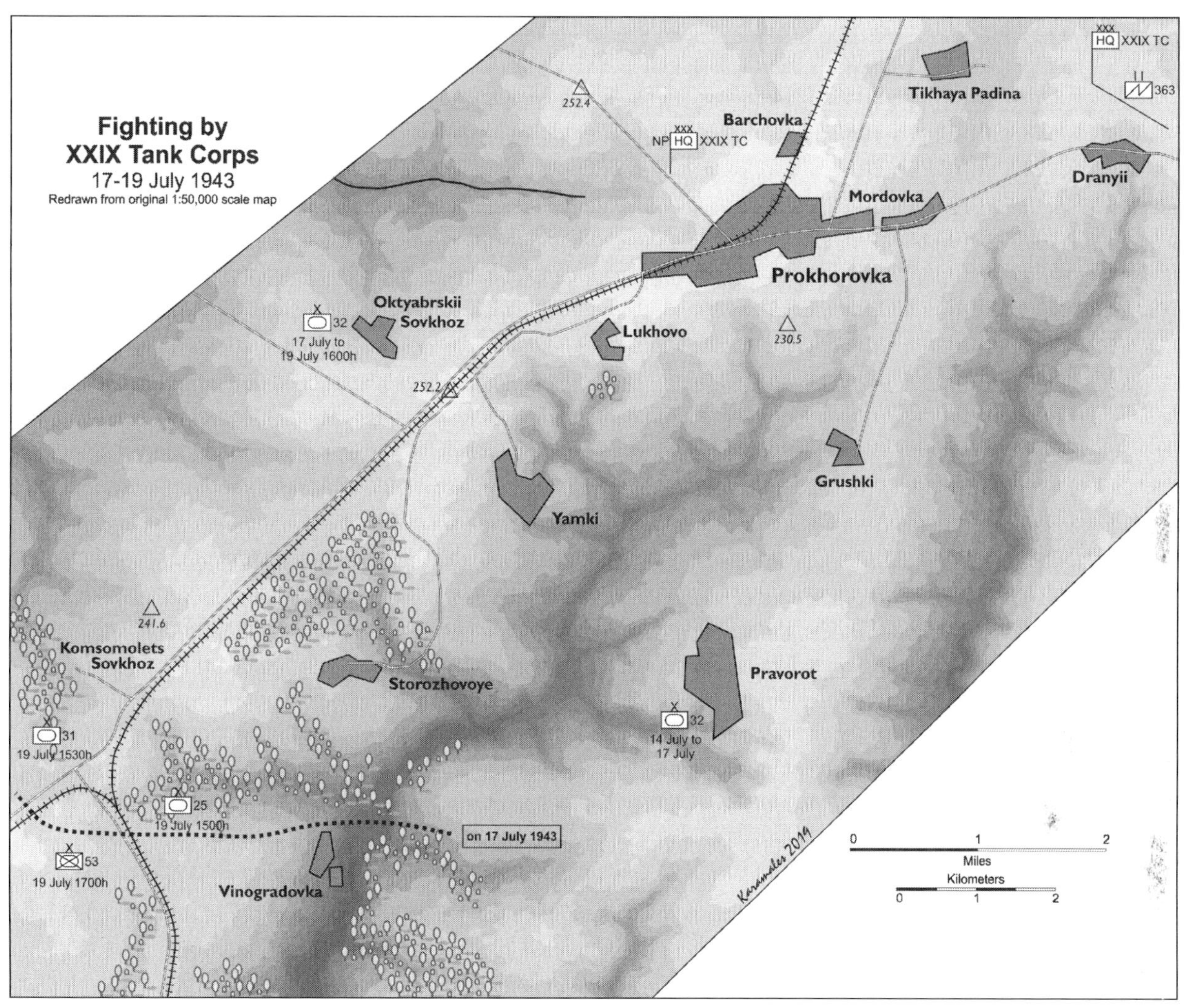

Fighting by
XXIX Tank Corps
17-19 July 1943
Redrawn from original 1:50,000 scale map
XXX
HQ XXIX TC
363
252.4
Tikhaya Padina
Barchovka
XXX
NP HQ XXIX TC
Dranyii
Mordovka
Prokhorovka
Oktyabrskii
Sovkhoz
X
32
17 July to
19 July 1600h
Lukhovo
230.5
252.2
Grushki
Yamki
241.6
Komsomolets
Sovkhoz
Storozhovoye
Pravorot
X
31
19 July 1530h
X
32
14 July to
17 July
X
25
19 July 1500h
on 17 July 1943
X
53
19 July 1700h
Vinogradovka
Karamales 2014
0
1
2
Miles
Kilometers
0
1
2

The Das Reich SS Division also pulled back to the area south of Tomarovka. The withdrawal suffered some delays because of the bridges. Furthermore, the highway around Pokrovka was attacked between 0500 and 0700 by Soviet bombers. The panzer regiment and the assault gun battalion remained back in the division's old deployment area near Pokrovka.

Private Kaufmann recalls an artillery attack on the division:

> On the 18th of July we moved into the area north of Kharkov in the framework of the division in order to assemble for the attack against enemy forces that had broken in there. We encountered great difficulties in digging foxholes in a soil full of rocks and only managed to accomplish this task in haphazard fashion. At about midnight, a plane dropped ten parachute flares from high altitude, which illuminated our sector as if it were daylight. Soon after, a barrage with explosive and phosphorus shells on Katyusha rockets went down. We lay pressing ourselves into the shallow holes and thought our time had come. The barrage lasted only a few minutes—which seemed like an eternity. While our gun crews were the lucky ones again, the Grenadiers did suffer considerable losses. Nothing more happened after that.
>
> There was also no enemy contact on July 19, a dreary, cloudy day.

The Leibstandarte SS Adolf Hitler Division reported 2 killed and wounded for the 18th, and 21 killed, 36 wounded and 23 missing for the period of the 19th through the 24th, with 21 killed, 10 wounded and 23 missing occurring on the 20th. The Das Reich SS Division reported 1 killed and 8 wounded for the 18th, and 8 more wounded for the period of the 19th through 23rd.

The Fight for Height 242.1

While life is unfair, war is even more unfair. The poor bloody infantry always takes the heaviest casualties. Now the panzers, having fought their battle, were withdrawing to the comfort of the rear, leaving the poor infantry the job of holding the front.

The 167th Infantry Division, having halted an armored attack against Vinogradovka at 2000 (Berlin time) was now waiting for the Soviets to launch another attack. The II Tank Corps and II Guards Tank Corps were both concentrating their weight against this one infantry division, with the II Tank Corps concentrating in the north around Vinogradovka and Ivanovka and attacking the 339th Infantry Regiment, while the II Guards Tank Corps attacked height 242.1 and the 331st Infantry Regiment.

At 0100 (Berlin time) the right flank of the 339th Infantry Regiment was attacked by two Soviet rifle regiments with armor support. This attack penetrated to the north edge of Vinogradovka before being thrown back by a counterattack.

The II Tank Corps received orders to attack at 0400 (Moscow time). At 0730 (Berlin time) the 339th Infantry Regiment reported heavy Soviet tank activity in the Pravorot highway sector. Some reports claimed that altogether 100 to 120 Soviet tanks were observed along the division's front! At 1215, a counterattack unit from the 19th Panzer Division arrived in the division's area. At 1300, as its commander was being briefed at the division's command post, a new Soviet attack hit the left wing of the 339th Infantry Regiment with 38 tanks and truck transported infantry. At the same time 30 to 40 Russian tanks were reported at Zhilomostnoye. Calls for close air support went unheeded. These attacks were repulsed by the combined fire of all the division's weapons and partly by tank-supported counterattacks.

During the day the II Tank Corps was able to move forward three to four kilometers and by 2400 (Moscow time) its 56th Motorized Rifle and 169th Tank Brigades were at the railroad booth 0.5 kilometers north of Ivanovka to the northern slopes of the unnamed height east of Ivanovskii Vyiselok. The 99th Tank Brigade had reached the railroad booth two kilometers east of Yasnaya Polyana. The 26th Tank Brigade fought all day for Vinogradovka and by a turning movement from the north was able to reach the railroad booth 0.5 kilo-

The Fight for Height 242.1, 18 July 1943

DURATION One day FRONTAGE 16.4 kilometers TERRAIN Rolling, mixed

WEATHER Cloudy and hotter with occasional thunderstorms. Temperature at noon: 20 degrees Celsius. No change in road conditions.

	Attacker	*Defender*
Units	183rd RD, II TC & II GTC	167th ID
Attachments	See below	See below
Strength	24,539	17,481
Armor	131 (47 light)	18
Artillery	191	147
Air Sorties	23 + 12 Night	0
Casualties	1,069 (311 KIA, 633 WIA, 125 MIA)	190 (37 KIA, 150 WIA, 3 MIA)
Armor Losses	43	1
Artillery Losses	19	0
Enemy Captured	1	N/A

Forces Engaged

German Attachments

228th StuG Bn (–bty) (detached on the 18th—included)
I/54th Werfer Rgt
II/54th Werfer Rgt
I/38th Flak Bn
Hq/54th Werfer Rgt
1st co/503rd Heavy Panzer Bn (attached on the 18th)
127th Engineer Bn (attached on the 18th)
II/38th Flak Rgt (attached on the 18th)

Soviet Forces

183rd Rifle Division

II Tank Corps

1850/32nd AT Bde—attached on the 17th (included)
1854/32nd AT Bde—attached on the 17th (included)

II Guards Tank Corps

301st Antitank Regiment
755th AT Battalion
16th Guards Mortar Regiment
80th Guards Mortar Regiment—attached on the 18th (included)

meters east of the Komsomolets Sovkhoz. The II Tank Corps lost two T-34s and an estimated seven T-70s this day. The 183rd Rifle Division also claimed to have attacked Vinogradovka this day, but with no success.

The II Guards Tank Corps concentrated on taking height 242.1, advancing with its 25th and 26th Guards Tank Brigades while the 4th Guards Motorized Brigade secured the corps' left flank. The expected Soviet tank attack came at 0100 (Berlin time) against height 242.1, on the left flank of the 331st Infantry Regiment. At 0300 (Moscow time) the II Guards Tank Corps' forward detachment reported that it began engaging the Germans in the area of height 242.1. It was able to push them aside and take the hill. At 0330 (Moscow time) the forward detachment was counterattacked and was forced to fall back on the northern slopes of height 242.1. The Germans reported eliminating this penetration of three tanks by counterattack, and then moving their Tiger Company (1st co/503rd Heavy Panzer Battalion) to 242.1.

At 0430 (Moscow time) the 25th and 26th Guards Tank Brigades, covered by artillery and overcoming the German artillery, mortar, and tank fire from the Semidobnoye Woods, started another attack on the height. At 0520 (Berlin time) the Germans reported that 30 Russian tanks carrying mounted infantry attacked the left wing of the 331st Infantry Regiment. At 0500 (Berlin time) the 228th Assault Gun Battalion also moved into the height 242.1—Vinogradovka area to link up with the Tigers and firm up the connection between the 339th and 331st Infantry Regiments. At 0700 (Moscow time) the 25th Guards Tank Brigade had advanced to 100 meters northeast of the Semidobnoye Woods while the 26th Tank Brigade was at the road junction on the eastern outskirts of the woods. At 0600 (Berlin time) the 167th Infantry Division requested close air support, and support from the 7th Panzer Division, but this was too late, as the Soviets overran the division's lines at 242.1. The Tigers shot up many Soviet tanks and the remainder withdrew to the north, but the two Soviet infantry battalions continued to attack, and heavy artillery concentrations fell on the right wing of the 339th Infantry Regiment. By 0930 (Moscow time) the II Guards Tank Corps had again captured height 242.1. The Germans were reporting that there was heavy Soviet air activity with bombing attacks after dawn.

The 228th Assault Gun Battalion was withdrawn from this fight at 1000 (Berlin time) and began moving to the LII Corps area because of a mix-up in orders. This left the situation at the junction of the two regiments very shaky and a renewed Soviet attack penetrated there with tanks. The potentially disastrous situation was resolved by a counterattack by elements of the 238th Reconnaissance Battalion. The assault guns were then ordered to disengage by 1300 and move to Losovo for action with the LII Corps.

At 0930 (Moscow time) the Germans, with a force of 17 tanks (Soviet estimate) and a large number of infantry counterattacked the corps from behind height 234.9, and with six tanks from the Vinogradovka area, supported by powerful artillery and mortar fire. The Soviet tank brigades, having suffered heavy material and personnel losses, fell back on the northeastern slopes of height 242.1.

At 1330 (Moscow time) the Soviet brigades attacked height 242.1 once again and reached its southwestern slopes, where they were once again met with heavy artillery and mortar fire. Following a four-hour battle, the brigades were forced to fall back to the northeastern slopes of height 242.1 with losses, where they consolidated and continued to trade fire with the Germans. Height 242.1 had traded hands at least six times this day!

Thirty Soviet tanks were claimed destroyed by the 1st company of the 503rd Heavy Panzer Battalion and six more by various infantry units of the division. The II Guards Tank Corps lost 29 T-34s and two T-70s this day.

AT 1430, ELEMENTS of the 127th Engineer Battalion were detailed to lay mines in front of the division, and the 538th Road Construction Battalion was ordered to build defensive positions and improve roads in the division area. By evening, repeated Soviet attacks had taken the division's front line and the division began building a new line, registering fires for the next day, and preparing to withdraw to the "Brunhilde" line during the night of 19 July. At the end of the day, the Germans noted that the Vinogradovka and south of Zhilomostnoye attacks were the most heavily reinforced by infantry, leading them to expect more attacks in those areas. The 375th Rifle Division reported that it reached the northern slopes of the ravine south of Zhilomostnoye, but could not advance farther.

III Panzer Corps

While the SS Panzer Corps withdrew from battle, the units of the III Panzer Corps continued to hold the line and start their slow withdrawal back to Belgorod.

The 19th Panzer Division Holds, 18 July 1943

DURATION One day FRONTAGE 6.3 kilometers TERRAIN Rolling, mixed
WEATHER Overcast, occasional rain. Temperature at noon was 20 degrees Celsius. Road conditions good.

	Attacker	*Defender*
Units	89th Gds RD	19th PzD
Attachments	None	See below
Strength	5,396	16,321
Armor	0	30 (5 light)
Artillery	48	127
Air Sorties	0	0
Casualties	0	37 (5 KIA, 30 WIA, 2 MIA)
Armor Losses	0	0
Artillery Losses	1	0
Enemy Captured	0	N/A

Forces Engaged

German Attachments
70th Engineer Bn
2/411th Bridge Column B
842nd Bridge Column J

52nd Werfer Rgt

I/61st Flak Rgt (less 1 battery)
429th Infantry Rgt (168th ID), less I Battalion (not included)

Detachments
ObsBty/19th Artillery Rgt

The 7th Panzer Division Prepares the Next Defensive Line

The 7th Panzer Division, now assembled in the rear, was to shift over to the XLVIII Panzer Corps area and join in *Operation Roland*. As such, it had orders to attack north from a line running from height 232.8 to Kalinovka to height 247.0 to seize the high ground east of Gorki and southwest of Voznesenovka.

At this point, with this division down to only 48 operational tanks and Marders, this was probably optimistic. But it was also irrelevant, as the division's relief of the Gross Deutschland Division west of Novoselovka could hardly begin because of the sodden ground conditions.

With *Operation Roland* canceled, the division was instead ordered to construct defensive positions from Mikhailovka Kolkhoz eastward. Mikhailovka Kolkhoz was just north of Yakovlevo and twelve kilometers southwest of Prokhorovka. This was clearly the start of the defensive line running through Mikhailovka to Luchki that the Germans would fall back to on the 20th. This defensive line in the SS Panzer Corps area covered the withdrawal of Adolf Hitler and Das Reich SS Divisions. The division saw no action this day.

The 19th Panzer Division Prepares to Withdraw

The division's reduced frontage covered from just east of Plota down to Kuzminka. During the day there was little activity other than harassing fire missions by both sides with the I and II Battalions of the 52nd Werfer Regiment claiming to have taken known Soviet targets in front of the unit under very effective fire. Demolition squads from the 19th Panzer Engineer Battalion destroyed all equipment and weapons in the rear area that could not be recovered.

The 6th Panzer Division Prepares to Withdraw

The division was ordered to pull out of the front-line during the day and to organize a rapid-reaction force for the corps' use in case of a Soviet penetration. At 0300 the Soviets attacked Aleksandrovka from the northeast. The attack was repulsed, but not before the Soviets got to within 20 meters of the German positions. During the attack, the Germans claimed that the Soviets lost about 120 killed. The Germans captured six. According to the Germans, taking part in the attack were a number of armed women. They discovered after the attack one such woman, alive, under the bodies of her comrades. This report has not been verified with the Soviet records and this attack is not recorded. Whether it was an attack by women, or just one women was among the men, cannot be determined, but probably the later.

During the day, the division established a rapid-reaction force in an assembly area at Novo-Oskochnoye and Krivtsovo. The commander of this force reported to the 168th Infantry Division. This force could not have been large, for at this point, the division only had a total of 17 tanks operational.[2]

The division got attacked one more time again at height 222.1 at 0200 the night of 18/19 July by an estimated two companies. The attackers made a minor breakthrough, but were thrown back after a brief battle.[3]

The 168th Infantry Division Holds

The 168th Infantry Division remained in place on this day. The night passed quietly except for moderate air activity. The division conducted relief and reorganization of its units during the night. A Soviet patrol of about 15 men tried to infiltrate the position of the 442nd Infantry Regiment but was repulsed.

The day was even quieter with only desultory artillery and mortar fire. Elements of the 651st Engineer Battalion were ordered to clear Soviet minefields and lay new minefields in front of the current division positions. The 576th Road Construction Battalion was ordered to improve and build roads in the division sector.

The Sixty-ninth Army

The Sixty-ninth Army held positions this day, stretched from Zhilomostnoye to the Lebedki gully.[4] Only the 183rd Rifle Division, with its attacks on Vinogradovka, saw any significant action on this day. The 375th Rifle Division advanced to the northern slopes of the ravine south of Zhilomostnoye. The other eight divisions in the army reported no activity for the day,[5] other than some adjustment of the positions of the 92nd and 93rd Guards Rifle Divisions, with the very bloodied 92nd Guards Rifle Division during the night of 17/18 July relieving elements of the bloodied 93rd Guards Rifle Division along the line of Yar (ravine) Podorozhnyii to Yar Zhuravlinyii. This is along the line of the gully just southeast of Avdeyevka and put this division to the left of the 93rd Guards Rifle Division and the 305th Rifle Division to its left. The 93rd Guards Rifle Division had two rifle regiments thrust forward toward Krasnoye Znamya, and deployed from 400 meters southwest of

2 Not counting its 8 Marders.

3 Jentz, *Panzertruppen II*, page 92.

4 This is according to the Sixty-ninth Army. The 107th Rifle Division and 94th Guards Rifle Division were both south of Lebedki gully and may have been detached from the Sixty-ninth Army this day, even though they remained in place.

5 We have the XLVIII Rifle Corps commanding the 183rd, 375th, 81st Guards, 89th Guards and 93rd Guards Rifle Divisions and the XXXV Guards Rifle Corps commanding the 305th, 92nd Guards and 94th Guards Rifle Divisions. Also attached to the XXXV Guards Rifle Corps as of the 15th was the 252nd Rifle Division from the Fifty-third Army. The 107th Rifle Division was detached from the XXXV Guards Rifle Corps on 17 July but did not change location. It had returned to the corps control by the 20th of July. Trufanov's detachment, which was attached to the XXXV Guards Rifle Corps, was returned to control of the Fifth Guards Army on the 17th. Also by the 20th, the 337th Rifle Division from the Forty-seventh Army had been attached to the XXXV Guards Rifle Corps.

The 6th Panzer Division Prepares to Withdraw, 18 July 1943

DURATION One day FRONTAGE 14.4 kilometers TERRAIN Rolling, mixed

WEATHER Cloudy and hot with occasional thunderstorms. Temperature at noon 20 degrees Celsius, Road in steep areas barely passable for vehicles.

	Attacker	*Defender*
Units	92nd Gds, 93rd Gds & 305th Rifle Divisions	6th PzD
Attachments	None	See below
Strength	15,407	18,404
Armor	0	23 (2 light)
Artillery	79	108
Air Sorties	0	0
Casualties	4 (4 WIA)	103 (15 KIA, 86 WIA, 2 MIA)
Armor Losses	0	0
Artillery Losses	18[6]	0
Enemy Captured	1	N/A

Forces Engaged

German Attachments

III/54th Werfer Rgt

II/43rd Flak Rgt
lt Bn/91st Flak Rgt
204th Intelligence Troop

Detachments

ObsBty/76th Artillery Rgt

6 These heavy artillery losses were arrived at by comparing a ready-for-action report from the XXXV Guards Rifle Corps for the 93rd Guards Rifle Division for the 17th (Fond: 906, Opis: 1, Delo: 211) to the division report for the 18th (Fond: 1262, Opis: 1, Delo: 27, page 107). This showed a decline of 18 pieces between these two reports. We suspect this was simply the accounting catching up, as opposed to losses on this day. Also we suspect Soviet personnel losses are under-reported for this day.

The 168th Infantry Division Holds, 18 July 1943

DURATION One day FRONTAGE 32.8 kilometers TERRAIN Rolling, mixed

WEATHER Sunny, warm, thundershowers later in the day. Temperature at noon was 20 degrees Celsius. Roads muddy in places after thundershowers.

	Attacker	*Defender*
Units	94th Gds & 107th Rifle Divisions	168th ID
Attachments	None	See below
Strength	11,806	14,044
Armor	0	0
Artillery	68	107
Air Sorties	12 Night	0
Casualties	43 (7 KIA, 25 WIA, 11 MIA)	117 (19 KIA, 95 WIA, 3 MIA)
Armor Losses	0	0
Artillery Losses	0	4
Enemy Captured	0	N/A

Forces Engaged

German Attachments
2/228th StuG Bn—detached on the 18th (not included)
lt Bty/I/61st AA Rgt (not included)

Still detached from the division
248th Engineer Bn (less 3 cos) (included)
429th Infantry Rgt (less 1 Bn) (included)

Soviet Forces
94th Guards Rifle Division
107th Rifle Division less the 522nd Rifle Regiment (less 1/3rd)
123rd ATR Bn
148th Tank Regiment (not included)

7th Panzer Division Attachments
9th Bridge Column B
1/505st Bridge Column B
843rd Bridge Column J

99th Flak Rgt Staff—detached on the 18th
II/38th Flak Rgt—detached on the 18th

II/62nd Artillery Rgt

Detachments
ObsBty/78th Artillery Rgt
Regimental Group

III Panzer Corps Assets
674th Engineer Rgt Staff
925th Bridge Construction Staff
602nd Bridge Column B

153rd Flak Rgt Staff

3rd Command of Artillery
612th Artillery Rgt Staff
II/62nd Artillery Rgt
II/71st Artillery Rgt
857th Heavy Artillery Rgt
Pn/13th Light Observations Battery
ObsBty/19th Artillery Rgt (19th PzD)
ObsBty/76th Artillery Rgt (6th PzD)

2nd Fuel Column Troop
545th Panzer Recovery Platoon
503rd Heavy Panzer Bn
Regimental Group (from 7th PzD)

167th Infantry Division attached to corps on the 16th
7th Panzer Division detached from corps on the 17th

Gnezdilovka to the southeastern outskirts of Avdeyevka to one kilometer southeast of Krasnoye Znamya to the southwestern slopes of height 222.1 to Yar Zhuravlinyii. The 93rd Guards Rifle Division reported 4 wounded on this day. The 92nd Guards Rifle Division may also have taken some losses this day although none were reported. Even though the 107th Rifle Division was transferred out of the XXXV Guards Rifle Corps on the 17th, it was still deployed in its previous positions defending the Razumnaya gully. The 94th Guards Rifle Division was to its left extending its line down to height 210.3 and to Arkadyevka where it connected with the 15th Guards Rifle Division.

Air Support

The 168th Infantry Division reported that there was moderate Soviet air activity during the night with bombing attacks in the division sector. The 19th Panzer Division reported only light Soviet air activity during the night. At 0530 a large group of Soviet bombers launched a heavy attack against artillery and flak positions in the division's zone. The 272nd Flak Artillery Battalion shot down one Pe-2 in this raid. The 6th Panzer Division reported slight air activity during the night. The 168th Infantry Division reported the Soviet air activity had lessened during the day.

The Rear Area

Not only was the German army pulling back, but they were also evacuating their rear area. The III Panzer Corps' orders for 18 July, issued at 0030, state in part:

> 1.) Evacuation: The entire male population above ten years of age, and all labor-capable female civilians, are to be marched to the rear to one side of the march route. Likewise, all livestock are to be evacuated.
>
> Management of the civilian population is the responsibility of the city commandant in Belgorod.

This of course, was not an exception and completely in line with what many German units were being ordered to do. It is a chilling reminder of the nature of German exploitation of the east. Still, there was some confusion over the execution of this order, as the war diary notes at 1815 on the 18th that "return of the refugees must be stopped immediately. The Army has to build bridges for the civilians." At 2255 the corps operations officer called to repeat the corps' order that ". . . all males fit for military service and of greater than 10 years of age, as well as all able-bodied females fit for labor, are to be rounded up and moved west of the Donets." At 0600 on the 19th, the diary notes that the corps' quartermaster discussed with Provisional Army Kempf the evacuation issues of the civilians and that the ". . . city commandant of Belgorod will provide a reception camp, forwarding the civilians to be handled by the Army Group."

We do not know how many civilians were evacuated from Belgorod or how many were able to return after the war.[7]

The German Withdrawal, Summary for the 18th

The 18th of July was the last day of heavy fighting in the south during the Battle of Kursk until the Soviet counteroffensive started on 3 August. Soviet histories often claim that they drove the Germans back to Belgorod from the 18th to the 24th with their attacks. The Germans claim that they withdrew. There is no question that after the quiet period across the front on the 16th and 17th, there was a final round of combat activity on the 18th and then it declined after that.

On the 16th and 17th, the casualties across the entire front for the Germans were 1,950 killed, wounded and missing, while for the Soviets they were 4,456. On the 18th, the Germans lost 888 while the Soviets lost 4,150. This was clearly a more intensive round of combat this

7 The III Panzer Corps Daily War Diary (T314, R198, pages 000096, 000893 & 000894).

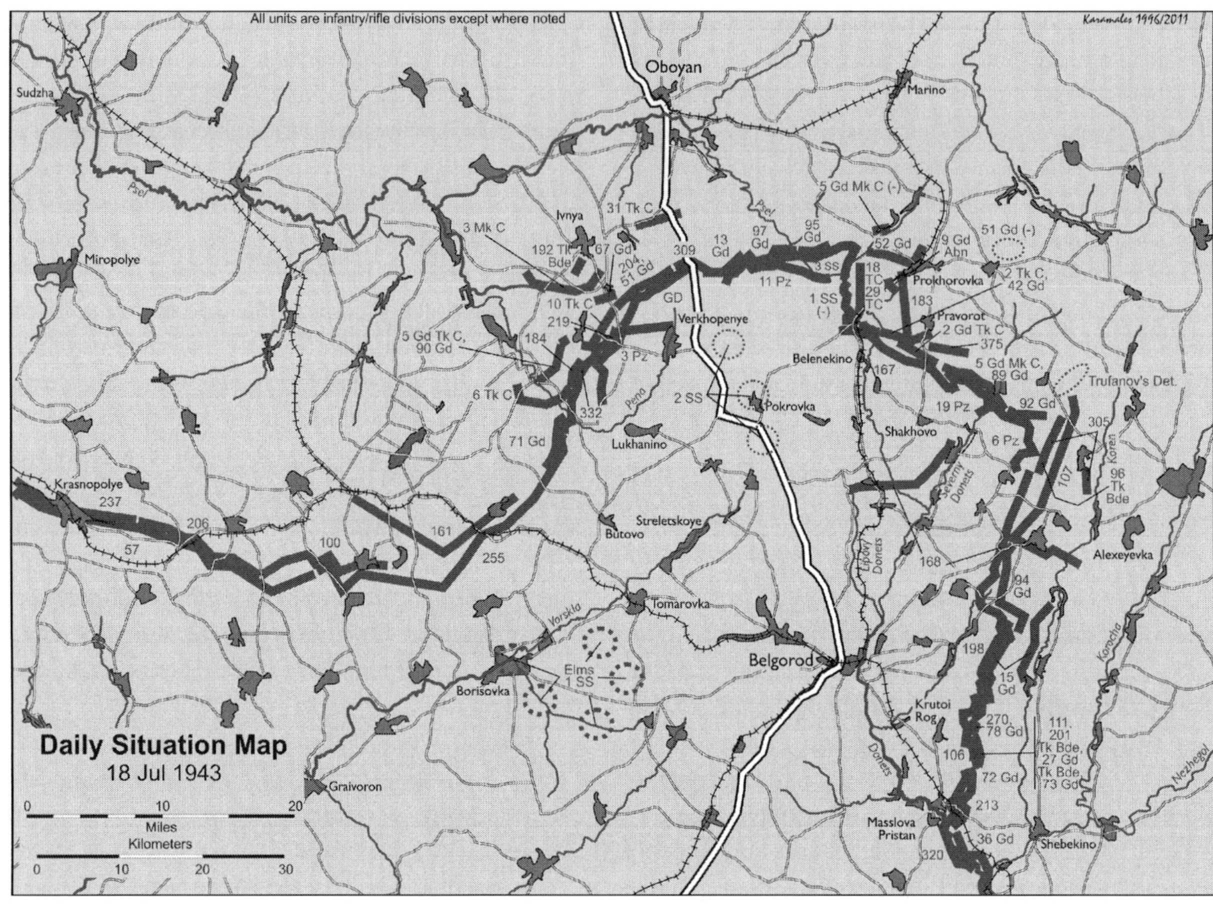

day for the Soviets, but still less than the losses suffered on any day between the 5th through the 15th. It was nowhere near the level of bloodshed of the 12th or the 13th and it does seem that the Soviet attacks were much more restrained. For example, on the 12th, the casualty ratio was 8.5 to 1 in favor of the Germans, while on the 18th, it was 4.7 to 1.

Effectively the German defensive forces had been reduced to 14 divisions in the line, with three of the large panzer grenadier divisions having been withdrawn. These divisions were still in position to re-enter the battle if needed.

The Twenty-seventh and Fifty-third Armies are Brought Forward

In response to the German offensive, the Soviets had formed another line of forces using three more armies, each supported by a tank or mechanized corps. The Twenty-seventh Army, consisting of six divisions and a tank brigade, was north of Oboyan covering Kursk and had gathered there on the 14th. The IV Guards Tank Corps was south of Kursk between Oboyan and Kursk on the 11th of July. These forces would move forward so that by the morning of the 19th they were south of the Psel, to the southwest of Oboyan.[8]

8 Glantz and Orenstein, page 93.

The Fifty-third Army, with seven divisions and the I Mechanized Corps, was behind Prokhorovka on the Seim River between Nechayevo to Bunino. They had been there since the 12th. They then brought it further forward, with the army and the mechanized corps assembling in the area around Skorodnoye by 0800 on the 16th.[9]

On 18 July, Zhukov and Vasilevskii oversaw the attack by the Sixty-ninth Army, Fifth Guards Army and Fifth Guards Tank Army and observed the fighting at Komsomolets Sovkhoz and at Ivanovskii Vyiselok by the XVIII and XXIX Tank Corps. While Zhadov's and Rotmistrov's progress was a disappointing four or five kilometers, the Sixth Guards Army only managed to occupy one height in the Verkhopenye area. Having concluded that Chistyakov's troops were extremely tired, they decided to bring in additional forces from parts of Lt. General I. M. Managarov's Fifty-third Army.[10] As such, the Sixth Guards Army's involvement in the combat on the following days was extremely limited.

The Forty-seventh Army, with six divisions and the III Guards Mechanized Corps had concentrated around Korocha on the 14th and 15th, and remained there for the time being.

The Withdrawal Plans

The German withdrawal was delayed by the limited road net and the weather. At 1630, the army ordered a general withdrawal, and at 1710, that order was rescinded and they instead decided to keep the divisions in line and execute a small rearward jump. At 1800, the 11th Panzer Division and the Totenkopf SS Panzer Grenadier Division were placed under control of the XLVIII Panzer Corps. The Germans planned a series of defensive lines on the 19th and 20th for the units to pull back to during the night. The units were ordered to destroy all bridges and burn all villages in the abandoned area. All vehicles that could not be salvaged were to be destroyed.

For the Fourth Panzer Army (effectively the XLVIII Panzer Corps), the line for the night of the 18/19th was to run from height 258.2 just north of Teterevino to 244.5 to 239.6 to the north edge of Veselyii to Solotino School to along the road to the fork south of 240.4 to 251.4 to 1.8 to 258.5. The line for the 19/20th was to run from north edge of the woods one kilometer southwest of Luchki to Mikhailovka Kolkhoz to height 254.5 to height 230.1 to the hills south of Syirtsevo to the hills north of Spitsin to height 234.8 to the hills southeast of Chapayev. This is roughly where the battle lines had stood on the 6th. After that line was reached, the Totenkopf SS Division was to be disengaged and pulled to the rear.

Meanwhile the roads had become completely soft from the weather and traffic, and the only movement that could be accomplished was by motor vehicles and tracked units, moving cross-country and off the roads. At sundown, it began to rain heavily and on all roads and tracks the thousands of vehicles of the division and army troops, the supply services, the Luftwaffe, and the signals units were bogged in unbroken traffic jams, their forward progress "measured by meters."

The Withdrawal, 19–24 July

What occurred over the six days was a controlled withdrawal on the part of the Germans. As the Kursk Data Base project only covered through the 18th, we did not collect detailed records for both sides on this withdrawal. The records do exist, but we will leave that to someone else to explore fully. What is clear from the material that we did collect is that the German casualties were no higher in the days following the 18th than they were on the 18th. It does appear that the 18th was the most intense day of battle during the withdrawal, and that when the Soviets were able to determine that there was still considerable fight left in the Germans, they did not push their attack more aggressively. This is perfectly rational, even if it does contradict one of the

9 Glantz and Orenstein, page 93.

10 Marshal Zhukov, "In the Kursk Bulge," *Battle of Kursk*, page 49.

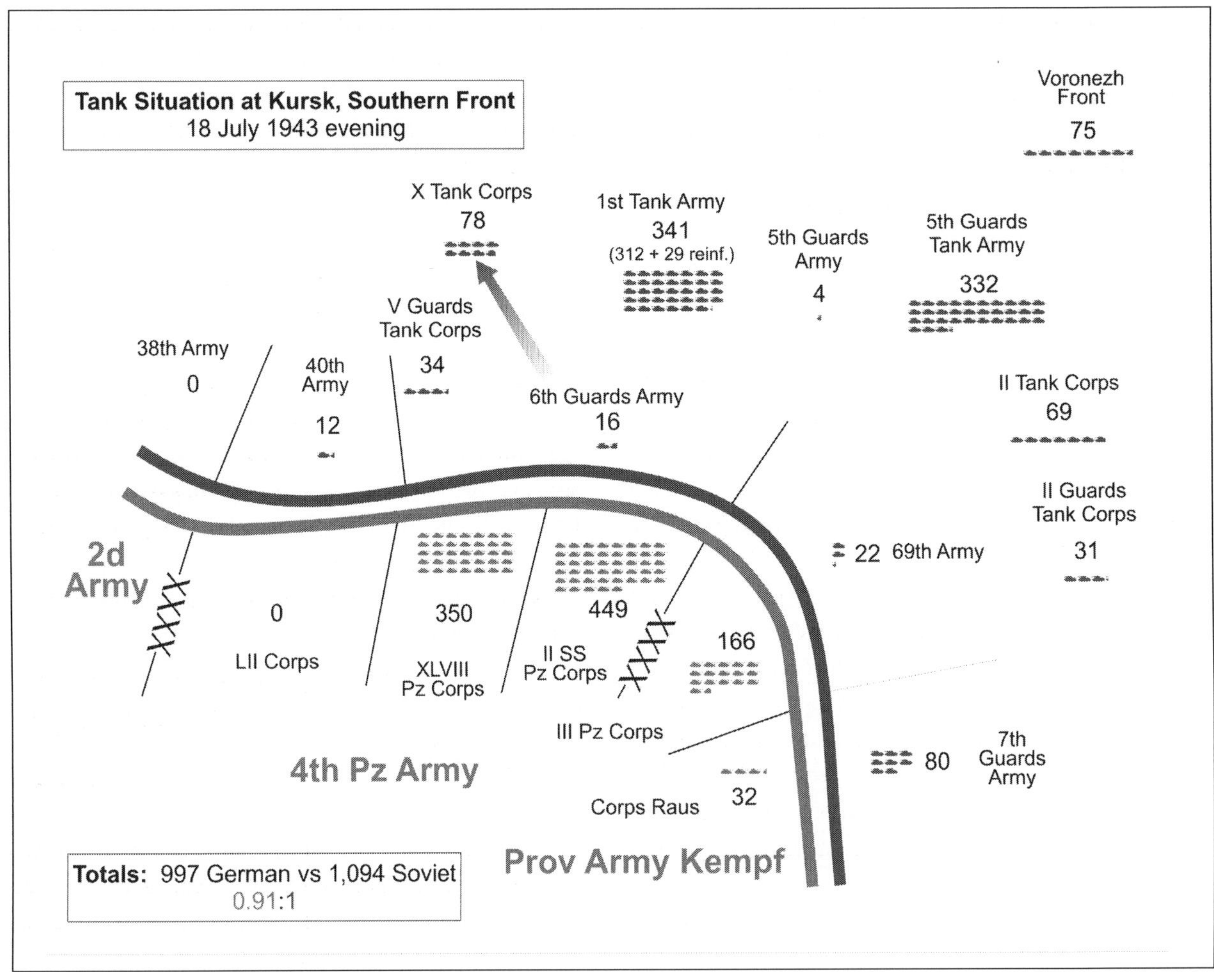

other myths of Prokhorovka. The Germans were able to continue to disengage their armor. The Totenkopf SS Panzer Grenadier Division, and the 7th and 19th Panzer Divisions were pulled back into reserve positions on the night of the 20th. Only the 3rd, 11th and 6th Panzer Divisions remained in line.

The Advance Ends

The advancing Soviet forces had not returned to their starting line. The Germans still held a line from four to fourteen kilometers north of where they started, laid upon a good defensive line of low hills. At this point the Germans had only eleven divisions holding the front. This was three panzer divisions (the 6th, 11th and 19th) and all eight infantry divisions (57th, 255th, 332nd, 167th, 168th, 198th, 106th and 320th). The 11th and 19th Panzer Divisions were in reserve positions with only the 6th Panzer Division in the line. They had been able to disengage and withdraw all four of the panzer grenadier divisions and two panzer divisions. The armored divisions were now under command of the LII Corps. The Soviets had also withdrawn all their major armored formations from the line and were now holding it in the area in the center with the Fifth Guards Army.

The Voronezh Front then consolidated along this new line, as "further advance was made difficult because the enemy is using our old positions and minefields for defensive purposes. As a result, it has become inexpedient to use tanks further along this line." Vatutin ordered the Fifth Guards Tank Army to pull out of the line for refitting, and replenishing fuel, ammunition, and food. Zhadov's Fifth Guards Army took over their positions. The II Tank Corps and II Guards Tank Corps were transferred to Zhadov's Fifth Guards Army and that night the rest of Rotmistrov's Fifth Guards Tank Army withdrew to the rear.

In the restored version of Zhukov's memoirs, he blames the failure to aggressively pursue the Germans not only on the exhaustion of the Sixth Guards Army, Seventh Guards Army and First Tank Army, but also "due to the Fifth Guards Tank Army's insufficient activity." This criticism of Rotmistrov concerning his pursuit and some other issues were deleted from all editions of Zhukov's memoirs before 1992.[11]

The Sixth Guards Army, Seventh Guards Army and First Tank Army played a limited role in this pursuit, for as Zhukov states, they were worn out. On the other hand, Stalin demanded that the Voronezh and Steppe Fronts launch into a counteroffensive around the 23rd or 24th. It took repeated discussion to convince Stalin to wait. The units needed to replenish fuel, ammunition and other stocks. They needed to organize such an attack, conduct reconnaissance and regroup the units, particularly the artillery and armor. They were given eight days to do this.[12]

11 Zhukov, 11th edition, page 58.

12 Marshal Zhukov, "In the Kursk Bulge," *The Battle of Kursk*, page 51.

THIS PHASE OF the Battle of Kursk was clearly over. So was the reign of Europe's first fascist dictator, for also on 24 July, Mussolini was removed as commander of the Italian armed forces by the Italian king and he was arrested the following day.

> Dear mother and father, hi from the front!
>
> Finally, I have my first evening off. For the past two weeks we were fighting to the south of Kursk. Our regiment destroyed about 50 German tanks, but we lost almost all our tanks. The infantry retreated often, so we would stay by ourselves against German tanks. We fought furiously and stopped the Germans. My best friend, Victor Khomenko from Kharkov, died. He was shooting directly at a German tank and set it on fire. The burning tank managed to drive right over him. Our troops are being rearranged now. We are getting additional weapons and soldiers.
>
> Dear mother and father, it is a great victory. We will get together soon in our dear Kharkov. Hugs and kisses.
>
> Semen

The letter above was written 18 July 1943 by Semen Moiseyevich Govzman, a battery commander of an antitank regiment. It was his last letter home, as he died in combat on 25 July 1943.[13]

13 Letter is courtesy of his granddaughter, Maria Ginzburk of Kharkov. Forwarded by Col. Fyodor Sverdlov in a letter dated 19 December 1998.

ZHADOV'S ANALYSIS

From Zhadov's memoirs:[1]

> We immediate participants of the Battle of Prokhorovka are often asked what the reasons are behind the slow pace [of advance] of the Voronezh Front's armies during the counterblow from July 12 to 23.
>
> I will attempt to answer that question on the basis of my experience with Fifth Guards Army's units. The first reason, in my view, is that the enemy, although he suffered heavy losses during the offensive, still disposed of significant forces, especially in tanks and aircraft, for waging an active defense. The German Fascist troops stubbornly resisted our attacking units, often counterattacking with groups of 30 or more tanks.
>
> At the same time, the Fifth Guards Army's units were attacking along a broad front of 50 kilometers and more, and could also not inflict sufficient fire damage on the enemy, because we possessed only our organic forces and equipment, and there were few of these in the army. I, for example, could only maneuver two army antitank regiments, a guards mortar regiment, and an attached mortar brigade, which had only 0.5 of an ammo load. The lack of infantry support tanks with the rifle divisions told particularly in the pace of our advance.
>
> I consider it necessary to point out another reason. The army was committed into battle and we did not understand the situation of this sector, which was extremely difficult and tense. The army staff's information about enemy and friendly troops from the front command was irregular. This, evidently, may be explained by the fact that the enemy was still barreling forward. One can't say that we didn't take an interest in what was taking place in front of us. On July 11 I managed, while looking for this information, to meet General K. P. Trubnikov, the deputy commander of Sixth Guards Army. His information to some degree helped us to pinpoint details of the army's forthcoming actions.
>
> I recall that on July 16 Marshal G. K. Zhukov, Stavka representative and Deputy Supreme Command-in-Chief, arrived at our command post. He was curious as to how the army's commitment into the counterblow on July 12 was organized. He discussed this matter with me and Major General G. V. Poluektov, the army's artillery commander. When we were alone, Zhukov expressed his displeasure with the organization of the army's commitment into the battle and gave me a dressing down because the army, fully-manned, equipped and trained for its mission, had been committed into the battle without tank reinforcements, a sufficient amount of artillery, and extremely short in ammunition supplies. In conclusion, Georgii Konstantinovich [Zhukov] said:
>
> If for any reason the Front staff has not been able to supply the army with everything it needs in a timely manner, then you must insistently request from the Front commander or, in an extreme case, turn to the Stavka. The army commander and the corps and division commanders are first of all responsible for the army's troops and their accomplishment of the mission.
>
> I remembered Marshal G. K. Zhukov's advice the entire war and was guided by it. By the way, the thought of turning to the Stavka for information and help had never entered my head then.

1 Gen. A. S. Zhadov, *Chetyire Goda Voinyi* [*Four Years of War*] (Moscow, 1978), pages 96–98.

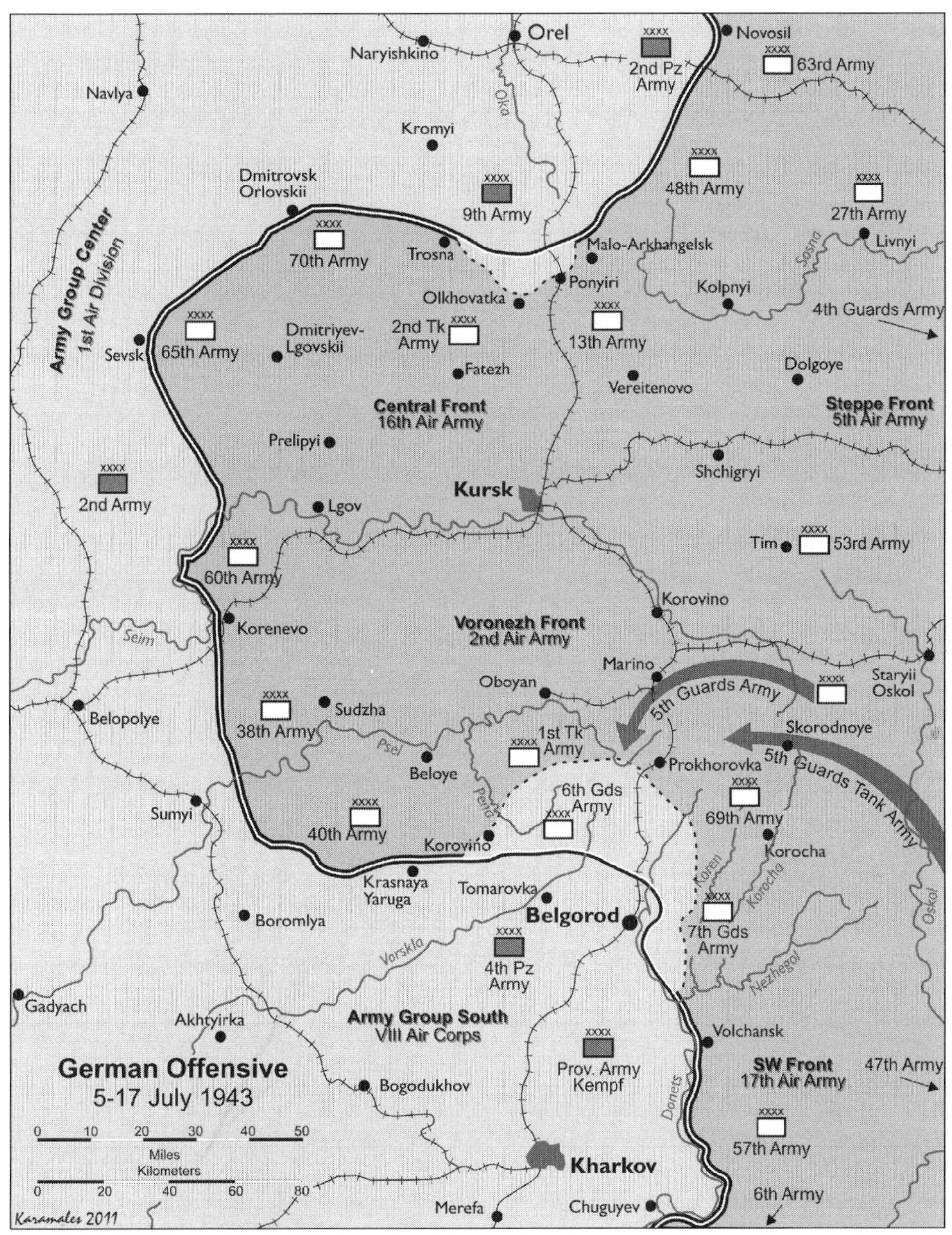
German Offensive
5-17 July 1943
Orel
Naryishkino
Novosil
2nd Pz Army
63rd Army
Navlya
Oka
Kromyi
Dmitrovsk Orlovskii
9th Army
48th Army
27th Army
Livnyi
Army Group Center
1st Air Division
70th Army
Trosna
Malo-Arkhangelsk
Sosna
Ponyiri
Kolpnyi
Olkhovatka
4th Guards Army
Sevsk
65th Army
Dmitriyev-Lgovskii
2nd Tk Army
13th Army
Fatezh
Dolgoye
Vereitenovo
Central Front
16th Air Army
Steppe Front
5th Air Army
Prelipyi
Shchigryi
2nd Army
Kursk
Lgov
Tim
53rd Army
60th Army
Korovino
Korenevo
Seim
Voronezh Front
2nd Air Army
Marino
Staryii Oskol
Oboyan
5th Guards Army
Belopolye
Sudzha
Skorodnoye
38th Army
1st Tk Army
Psel
Prokhorovka
5th Guards Tank Army
Beloye
6th Gds Army
Sumyi
Pena
69th Army
40th Army
Korovino
Korocha
Krasnaya Yaruga
Tomarovka
Koren
Korocha
Belgorod
Boromlya
7th Gds Army
Oskol
Vorskla
4th Pz Army
Nezhegol
Gadyach
Akhtyirka
Army Group South
VIII Air Corps
Volchansk
Prov. Army Kempf
SW Front
17th Air Army
47th Army
Bogodukhov
Donets
57th Army
0 10 20 30 40 50
Miles
Kilometers
0 20 40 60 80
Kharkov
6th Army
Merefa
Chuguyev
Karamales 2011

CHAPTER SIXTEEN

Post-Mortem

I [Zhukov] was making a report to him [Stalin] together with Vasilevskii. Vasilevskii was reporting the true situation, which corresponded neither to our expectations or our intentions. The Germans were doing just the opposite of what we had assumed and what we wanted. This unpleasant report drove Stalin out of his mind. He walked up to Vasilevskii and suddenly asked him pointblank:

"Who are you working for, comrade Vasilevskii?"

He didn't understand. "What do you mean, comrade Stalin?"

"Who are you working for, the English or the Germans?"

Vasilevskii repeated: "I don't understand you, comrade Stalin."

"You don't understand? You make such a report, as if you're working not for us, but for the English . . . ?"

Vasilevskii turned pale, and after this suddenly broke off conversation. We rode together in a car and he could not come to for a long time.

MARSHAL GEORGII K. ZHUKOV
TIME AND PLACE UNKNOWN[1]

THE GERMAN OFFENSIVE phase of the Battle of Kursk was over on the 15th, and by the 20th, five German divisions had been withdrawn for operations elsewhere. The German Army by the 24th had withdrawn back to a few kilometers in front of their start line. Left to hold that line, from left to right, were the 57th, 255th, 332nd, 167th, 168th, 198th, 106th, and 320th Infantry Divisions, backed up by the 6th, 11th and 19th Panzer Divisions. Four large panzer grenadier divisions and two panzer divisions were withdrawn for duty elsewhere.

Of these, the only one that went to Italy was the Leibstandardte SS Adolf Hitler Panzer Grenadier Division, joined later by the II SS Panzer Corps headquarters. The division loaded onto trains at Stalino on the 27th and 28th of July, left the Eastern Front, traveled by train to Innsbruck, Austria, with the lead elements arriving on the 3rd of August, and marched down into northern Italy, arriving in the Po Valley on 8 August.

The relatively undamaged 3rd Panzer Division was placed under command of the II SS Panzer Corps, along with the Das Reich and Totenkopf SS Panzer Grenadier Divisions. On the 30th of July the corps launched a brief counteroffensive in the south to restore the front to the west of the Mius River. That offensive ended on the 2nd of August and the divisions were moved back towards Kharkov. The II SS Panzer Corps headquarters, without any attached divisions, headed to Italy taking command of the Leibstandarte SS Adolf Hitler Division on the 14th of August. The III Panzer Corps took over

1 L.G. Belyayeva, ed., *Marshal Zhukov. Kakim my ego Pomnim. [Marshal Zhukov: How we Remember Him]*. (Izdatelstvo Politicheskoi Literaturi, Moscow, 1988), pages 122–23. Translation provided by Dr. Richard Harrison.

the three divisions that were deployed around Kharkov.

The Gross Deutschland Division and the 7th Panzer Division remained in the east also. The Gross Deutschland was heading north to support Army Group Center, which was in retreat. They were both shortly to be recommitted to try to halt the Soviet Kursk counteroffensive by the Voronezh and Steppe Fronts. In early August, they were joined there by the III Panzer Corps and its three divisions and the now attached Viking SS Panzer Grenadier Division. By 9 August, all divisions involved in the Kursk offensive, except for the Adolf Hitler SS Panzer Grenadier Division, were now reengaged trying to halt the Soviet counteroffensive. They were joined in that effort by the Viking SS Panzer Grenadier Division. These divisions probably should not have tried to leave the area to start with.

The XXIV Panzer Corps, which was Manstein's reserve for this offensive, had already been sent south to Izyum to plug the holes there and had been in combat since the 19th of July.

All this shuffling left the German lines around Belgorod vulnerable to Soviet attack, which indeed did occur in force on 3 August.

Personnel Losses

Army Group South's offensive around Belgorod, from the 4th through the 18th of July, had cost the Germans 34,381 casualties. It had cost the defending Soviets at least 126,808 casualties:

	Total Casualties	*Killed*	*Wounded*	*Missing*
Germans	34,381	5,612	27,627	1,142
Soviets	126,808	27,046	66,961	32,801

This was a 3.69-to-1 casualty exchange ratio in favor of the Germans. Even more extreme were the irreplaceable losses with the Germans having lost 6,754 killed and missing while the Soviet total irreplaceable losses were 59,847. This was an 8.86-to-1 casualty exchange ratio in favor of the Germans.

The losses on each day are enlightening:

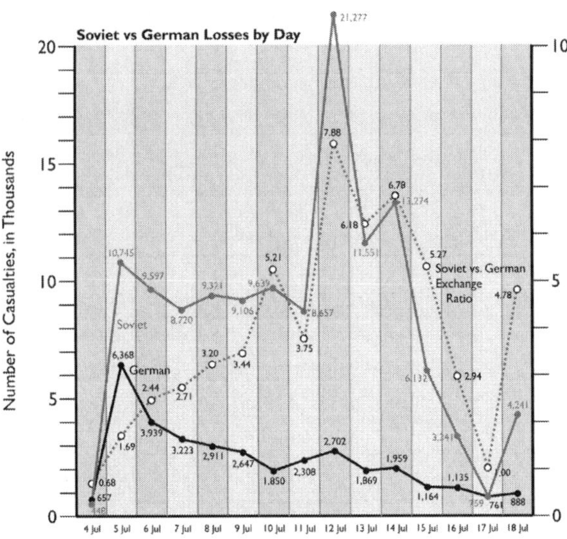

One will note the relatively low ratio of exchange in the first days of the offensive (4 to 6 July), increasing to an exchange rate in excess of three to one for the next few days (7 to 11 July), getting more favorable as the days go on, until the outrageously lopsided exchange ratio on 12 July of 7.88 to 1. In irreplaceable casualties, this is much worse at 14.62 to 1. The ratio then declined over the next six days (13 to 17 July) to less unfavorable for the Soviets, and then when they attacked again, the ratio again became much more unfavorable.

These loss figures were constructed by assembling the data from all divisions and attached units. As such, if they err in any direction, they are too low. The Soviet Voronezh and Steppe Front files are still classified, and as such we were not able to obtain access to them. The Krivosheyev book, however, does provide aggregate figures drawn from these front files. They provide the loss figures in Table 16.1 for the Voronezh and Steppe Fronts for 5–23 July.[2]

This is a total of 143,950 combat losses. As can be seen, there are over 20,000 wounded not accounted for in the Kursk Data Base figures. This certainly cannot

2 Krivosheyev, page 188.

TABLE 16.1.
KRIVOSHEYEV LOSS FIGURES VERSUS KURSK DATA BASE

	Strength	*"Irreplaceable" Losses (killed & missing)*	*"Sanitary" Losses (wounded)*	*Other Losses (DNBI)*
Voronezh Front (5–23 July)	534,700*	27,542	46,350	3,889
Steppe Front (9–23 July)	—	27,452	42,606	4,670
		54,994	88,956	8,559
Kursk Data Base (4 July–18 July)		59,847	66,961	1,116

* Figures include 35 rifle divisions (including the Thirty-eighth Army), five armored corps and six tank brigades. The Steppe Front figures, if they are complete, should account for seven more rifle divisions and five more armored corps.

DNBI stands for disease and non-battle injuries.

be explained by the extra five days of combat covered in the Krivosheyev figures, as the difference in irretrievable losses is fairly close. There are also around 5,000 less irreplaceable casualties in the Krivosheyev figures. Perhaps many of the missing later showed up as wounded. Still, one could conclude that the figures of Soviet losses presented in here underestimate their casualties. Most of this difference is in wounded.[3]

ARMOR LOSSES

Just for comparison, when this offensive started, the Germans could count on 1,707 tanks while the opposing Soviet forces in the area had only 1,537 tanks, a 1.11-to-1 ratio.[4] Still, because of Soviet defensive plans, most of this Soviet armor did not see action until the 6th of July. Some seven days later, just before the Battle of Prokhorovka, the Germans were down to 978 tanks on the 11th, while the Soviets had 1,481 tanks, a 0.66-to-1

3 Various loss reports for Kursk are summarized in Lev Lopukhovskii, *Prokhorovka: Bez Grifa Secretnosti [Prokhorovka: Without the Mark of Secrecy].* (Eksmo, Yauza, Moscow, 2005), page 509. They range for the Voronezh Front from a low of 73,892 killed, missing and wounded from Krivosheyev; a figure of 74,500 according to the commander of the Front; to a figure of 100,932 according to the chief of staff of the Front. We are not sure who and what are being counted in all these figures.

On page 513 are additional loss figures for the Voronezh and Steppe Fronts drawn from archival documents. For the Voronezh Front they show 18,097 killed, 24,851 missing (but a total of 42,977 for these two figures) and 47,272 "sanitary" (effectively wounded) losses from 4 to 16 July; and 2,481 killed, 1,047 missing and 7,155 wounded from 16 to 22 July. These figures total 110,932 and are from Front staff. Total losses for the Front for July are given as 30,003 killed, 31,226 missing and 92,196 wounded. These are from a different set of archival documents. We are not sure if these higher figures include the Steppe Front.

They also provide additional figures for the Steppe Front for 16–22 July of 6,167 killed, 2,490 missing and 25,683 wounded. They provide a total loss figure for July for the Front of 6,258 killed, 2,490 missing and 25,792 wounded. These killed and missing figures for the Steppe Front are much lower than the Krivsosheyev figure of 27,452.

We suspect there is some confusion over who is being counted in these figures. We have *The Dupuy Institute* figure of 126,808 killed, missing and wounded built up from the unit reports; Krivosheyev has a figure of 143,950 killed, missing and wounded from his research; and Lopukhovskii has a figure of 135,272 based upon his research (100,932 Voronezh Front and 34,340 Steppe Front) or as high as 189,038 based upon the total figures for the month of July (154,352 Voronezh Front and 34,686 Steppe Front). This last total seems high.

4 German tank count includes 131 self-propelled artillery (Wespe, Hummel and Grille), 37 Panzer III Observation tanks, and 3 Panzer I and V Recovery tanks. See Appendix III of my original book *Kursk: The Battle of Prokhorovka* for details.

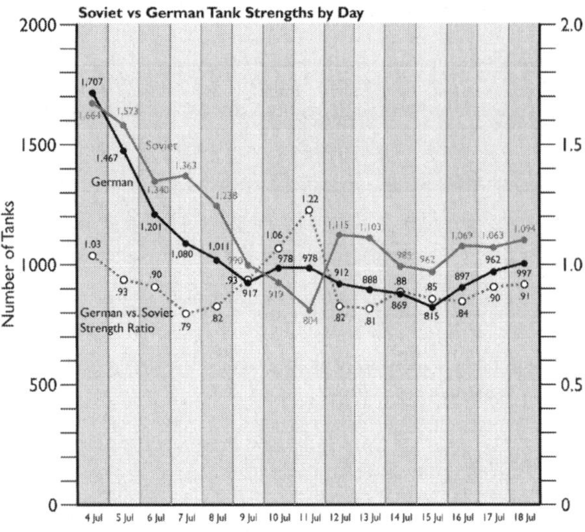

ratio.[5] After the 12th, the ratio shifted back toward the Germans, who had 888 tanks of all types on the 13th to the Soviets 1,103, a 0.81-to-1 ratio.[6] By the end, as both sides repaired their armor, the ratio shifted further back toward the Germans, with their 997 tanks of all types on the 18th, while the Soviets still only had 1,094 tanks, a 0.91-to-1 ratio.[7]

THE SOVIET FORCES did better in the armor exchange than they did in the casualty exchange, having lost some 2,471 tanks destroyed, damaged or broken down compared to the German losses of 1,536 tanks. This was a 1.61-to-1 exchange. Because the Germans regularly submitted daily ready-for-action reports, this is probably a reasonably accurate count of German armor. Soviet reporting tended to be a little more sporadic, so in fact the number of damaged tanks may be slightly higher, as the count of damaged tanks was usually derived by looking at the decline in tank strength by type from one report to the next. Still, these figures are as close as one is going to get with the records that have been located. They certainly are not far from the real story.

The Germans were better able to maintain their tank strength as they did a better job of repairing their tanks and returning them to battle. They also tended to husband their armor resources better and did not suffer the catastrophic daily losses that the opposing Soviet units sometimes took. Over the course of the two-week operation, some German divisions ended up having more tanks damaged than the unit started with initially, but the division never dropped much below half-strength. As such, the German Army was able to maintain considerable offensive capability, still having 48 percent of its original tank strength operational at the end of the offensive (end of the 15th of July).

The Soviets did not do as well in maintaining their armor strength. Being on the defensive, they naturally had more tanks destroyed or abandoned (vice damaged and recovered). Furthermore, their repair facilities did not feed tanks back into the units as quickly or systematically as the Germans did. Added to that, the rather high daily loss rates certainly overloaded the Soviet tank evacuation and repair capabilities. German divisions had a tendency to increase in tank strength from day to day during the quiet moments on the battlefield. The Soviet units usually had to withdraw from battle before there was any significant increase in tank strength from repairs. The Soviet tank corps often had 20 reserve tanks (unmanned) that were fed into the unit to replace losses. The starting strength

5 German tank count includes 125 self-propelled artillery (Wespe, Hummel and Grille), 34 Panzer III Observation tanks, 4 Panzer I and V Recovery tanks, and 3 Panzer IV munitions carriers. See Appendix III of my original book *Kursk: The Battle of Prokhorovka* for details.

6 German tank count includes 122 self-propelled artillery (Wespe, Hummel and Grille), 35 Panzer III Observation tanks, 4 Panzer I and V Recovery tanks, and 3 Panzer IV munitions carriers. See Appendix III of my original book *Kursk: The Battle of Prokhorovka* for details.

7 German tank count includes 123 self-propelled artillery (Wespe, Hummel and Grille), 35 Panzer III Observation tanks, 2 Panzer I and V Recovery tanks, and 3 Panzer IV munitions carriers. See Appendix III of my original book *Kursk: The Battle of Prokhorovka* for details.

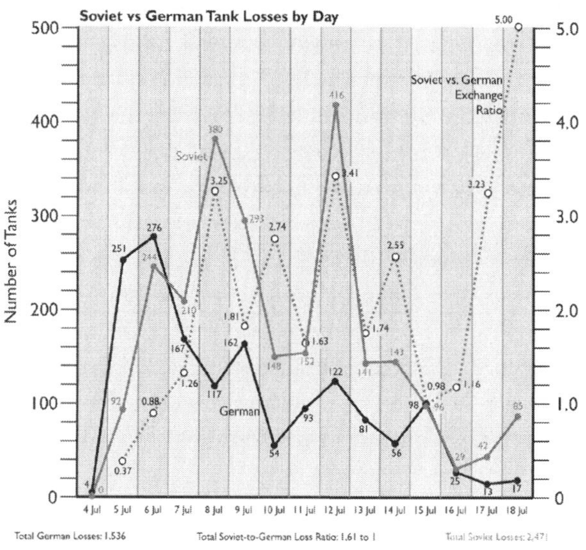

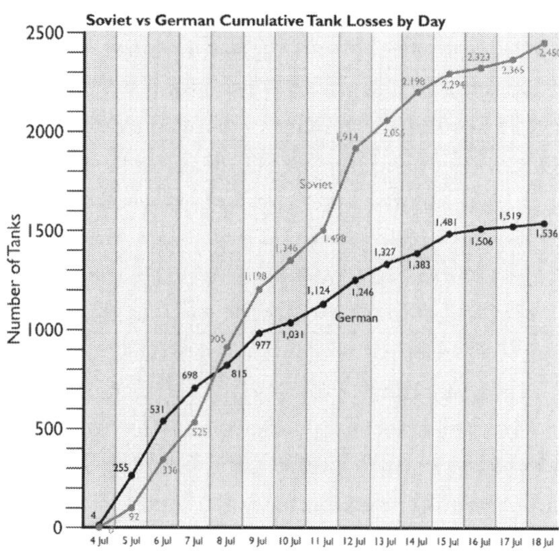

of the Soviet units did not include that reserve and we were not always able to pick up when this reserve was used. The Soviet Army also stripped its independent tank regiments and brigades of armor to transfer over to the corps. These transfers are documented.

Force Ratios

Finally, the Germans had developed an advantage in the first couple of days of the operation, for they were able to deploy all 16 of their starting divisions versus the Voronezh Front, while the Voronezh Front took several days to get all of its forces into battle. On the first day of battle, the Germans had fourteen attacking divisions, yet the opposing Soviet forces consisted of

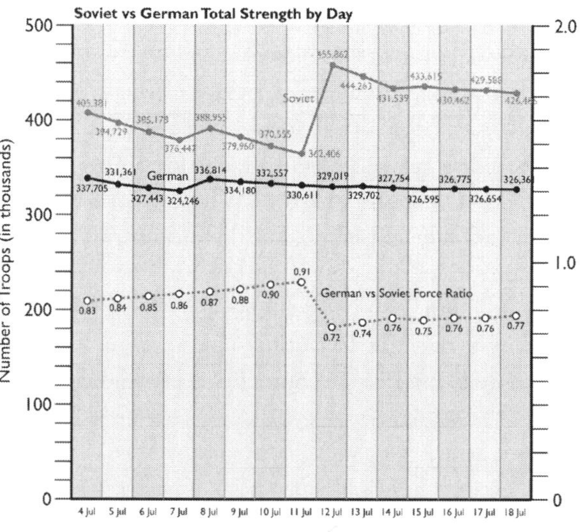

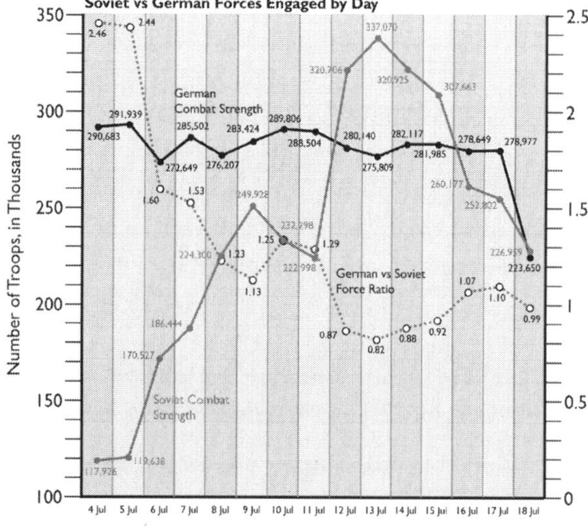

only seven divisions, a force ratio of 2.46 to 1 across the entire line. As such, the actual number engaged each day is not representative of the total strength. As the battle developed, the Germans, who initially outnumbered the Soviet forces, found the odds shifting against them. By the time the Soviets were ready to commit their forces from the Steppe Front, the ratio of committed forces was only 1.29 to 1 on the 11th. With the committal of the Fifth Guards Army and the Fifth Guards Tank Army, the ratio turned to 0.88 to 1 on the 12th, which was the worst ratio that the Germans had faced since the start of the offensive. After that, even with the heavy losses on the 12th and 13th, the ratio remained around one to one. Both sides pulled units from the line, so that when the Soviets attacked on the 18th, they still only had an overall force ratio of around 1.01 to 1. This of course, meant that the Soviet attacks were not going to go anywhere.

Could the Germans Have Broken Through?

Some writers have developed the theme that the Germans were on the verge of winning, and it was only Hitler's decision to call off the attack that prevented a German victory.[8] One thesis is that the Germans were on the verge of penetrating the Soviet defensive positions, and the insertion of the two reserve divisions of the XXIV Panzer Corps would have achieved this breakthrough. Another, more conservative, thesis is that they would have been able to finish grinding up the Soviet First Tank and Fifth Guards Tank Armies and destroyed the Soviet offensive forces. This would have almost certainly required a local penetration and partial envelopment to be successful. Manstein states that, "Speaking for my own army group, I pointed out that the battle was now at its culminating point, and that to break it off at this moment would be tantamount to throwing a victory away. On no account should we let go of the enemy until the mobile reserves he had committed were completely beaten. Nonetheless, Hitler ruled that *Citadel* was to be called off on account of the situation in the Mediterranean and the state of affairs in Central Army Group. The only concession he would make was that Southern Army Group should continue the attack until it had achieved its aim of smashing the enemy's armoured reserves. As a matter of fact not even this could be accomplished, for only a few days later the army group was ordered to hand over several armoured divisions to Central Army Group."[9]

The first thesis, which is that the Germans could have broken through, raises two questions. First, were the Germans on the verge of a breakthrough, and second, would such a breakthrough have been meaningful in the larger context of the operations north and south of Kursk?

The offensive was "canceled" by Adolf Hitler on the 13th. Manstein had activated the XXIV Panzer Corps on the evening of the 9th, they were in Kharkov by the 12th, and on the 15th, they were deployed in the Belgorod area. These reserves consisted of the Viking SS Panzer Grenadier Division (with only 56 tanks) and the 23rd Panzer Division (with 64 tanks). By the evening of the 13th, Manstein's entire attack force (Fourth Panzer Army and two corps of Provisional Army Kempf) had 888 tanks. Therefore, the insertion of these two divisions into the line would have increased tank strength by 120 tanks, or 13.5 percent, and artillery and infantry strength by a lesser amount. While this would have been a notable addition to the line, an overall increase in force strength of only slightly more than 10 percent does not appear to be enough to significantly tip the scale in favor of the Germans.

The question then becomes, where would these two

8 George M. Nipe Jr., *Decision in the Ukraine, Summer 1943, II SS and III Panzerkorps* (J. J. Fedorowicz Publishing, Inc. Winnipeg, Canada, 1996) and *Kursk Reconsidered: Germany's Lost Victory* (article on website www.theblitz.org).

9 Manstein, page 449.

divisions have been inserted? We have found no clear statement in the records as to their intended destination, but it does appear from their deployment for the 15th that they were both going into the Fourth Panzer Army area with one division assigned to each corps. From their deployment positions, they could also have been committed together at one spot in the line. There are arguments in favor of either approach.

Let us look at the status, from left to right, of the six armored divisions in the Fourth Panzer Army. On the evening of the 13th, the 3rd Panzer Division was tangled up still fighting the penetration by the X Tank Corps in the German flank. It was facing the X Tank Corps and others and had only 51 tanks, assault guns, and self-propelled antitank guns operational on the 15th. This force, once the penetration in the flank was cleared up, was going to be reduced to holding the flank, as it did until the 22nd.

The Gross Deutschland Division on the 13th was also tangled up fighting the X Tank Corps penetration. It would not be able to disengage from the line and switch back to the offensive until the 15th. It still had 84 tanks, assault guns and self-propelled antitank guns and 21 Panthers on the 15th. It also had 28 self-propelled artillery pieces. With the 3rd Panzer Division holding its left flank, it could still return to the offensive.

The 11th Panzer Division was halted on the 11th, and had made no further progress on the following three days. It was outnumbered 2.66 to 1 in its sector (see Kochetovka engagement in Chapter Twenty of my book *Kursk: The Battle of Prokhorovka*). It had 80 tanks and self-propelled guns of all types on the 15th.

The Totenkopf SS Division had spent the 12th attacking and on the 13th its attack was thrown back. These two days of actions had cost it at least 57 tanks and it was reduced to 85 tanks, assault guns, and self-propelled antitank guns on the 15th along with 18 self-propelled artillery pieces. This division was stalled and incapable of renewing the attack. It was outnumbered 1.41 to 1 in its sector (see the Holding Across the Psel engagements in Chapter Thirteen).

The Adolf Hitler SS Division had been able to advance on the 11th, but had been slowed considerably, partially because the SS divisions on each of its flanks were unable to keep up, but primary because it was facing significant opposition. It did not advance the following three days, nor did it attempt to. It was outnumbered 1.26 to 1 but had 114 tanks, assault guns and self-propelled antitank guns on the 15th, backed up by 25 self-propelled artillery pieces. The Soviet positions were accessible via well defended, constricted but open ground, and any advance directly on Prokhorovka was going to be costly. As such, this sector of the line was also stalled.

The Das Reich SS Division continued to attack and advance on the 14th and 15th, but with very limited results. As such, it was stalled on the 15th as far as being able to make any progress towards the north. It still had 120 tanks, assault guns and self-propelled antitank guns at the end of day on the 15th, backed up by 25 self-propelled artillery pieces.

What is clear if the attack had continued with the existing six divisions, is that this German attack was not going to go much further. To continue to make forward progress (as opposed to cleaning up the flanks) required the commitment of the two new divisions. Commitment of these new divisions to the sectors held by the 3rd Panzer, Das Reich SS or Adolf Hitler SS Divisions made little sense. Therefore, the reinforcing corps would most likely be placed in the line between Gross Deutschland and the 11th Panzer Division (attacking from Kruglik to height 244.8), or between the 11th Panzer Division and Totenkopf (attacking from Veselyii to Petrovka). Alternatively, they could have sent one division to each location, resulting effectively in a two-division attack in the XLVIII Panzer Corps sector (Gross Deutschland and 23rd) and a weaker two-division attack in the SS Panzer Corps sector (Totenkopf and Viking).

The advantage of splitting the corps was that the Germans would have been able to invigorate two separate attacks. The two-division attack of the XLVIII Panzer Corps would have been able to concentrate 169 tanks (not counting self-propelled artillery) and around

35,000 people against a defender of around 22,000 troops and 130 tanks (see Clearing the Tolstoye Woods engagement in Chapter Twenty of my book *Kursk: The Battle of Prokhorovka*). This area was backstopped with a second echelon and reserves that included the rest of the III Mechanized Corps, the XXXI Tank Corps, 67th Guards Rifle Division and 51st Guards Rifle Division (more than 23,000 personnel and over 120 tanks). Once these forces were added to the fight, the force ratio would have declined to less than 0.8 to 1. Given this, and based upon actions of similar force ratios, one would expect that the Germans would have been able to obtain only a minimal advance although they probably still would have maintained a favorable casualty exchange ratio.

In the SS Panzer Corps area, the Viking and Totenkopf SS Divisions would have been able to concentrate 141 tanks (not counting self-propelled artillery) and fewer than 35,000 people against a defender of 25,000 and 20 tanks (see Holding Across the Psel II engagement). This area was backstopped with a second echelon and reserve forces that consisted of the 6th Guards Airborne Division, most likely the 42nd Guards Rifle Division, 24th Guards Tank Brigade, and most likely the 10th Mechanized Brigade (more than 21,000 personnel and 70 tanks).[10] Once these forces were added to the fight, the force ratio would decline to 0.76 to 1. Again, based on actions with similar force ratios, one would expect that the Germans would have been able to obtain only a minimal advance although they probably still would have maintained a favorable casualty exchange ratio.

If these two German attacks advanced, so to would the 11th Panzer Division, resulting in this developing into a five-division attack. Still, for the first couple of days, the 11th Panzer Division's attacks would have been limited until the positions in front of it started to be turned by the attacks on each flank. Once the positions of Kurasovka, Vladimirovka, heights 244.8 and 244.3, and Veselyii had been taken, then the terrain would have turned in favor of the Germans across the Psel valley. This means that for the next five to ten kilometers, the advantage would have turned to the Germans. The next natural defense line on high ground was the line from the Psel River at Oboyan to the east toward Verkhnyaya Olshanka, where there was another large gully. It is possible that this effort could have pushed the Soviets across the Psel valley to the next natural defensive line on the opposing ridge and possibly caused them to send in additional reserves.

The other option would have been to concentrate both divisions in one sector. This was probably a worse option. First, it would have resulted in only a single attack, allowing the Soviets to concentrate all their reserves at that point. As such, it would have been simpler to respond to. Second, it would have invigorated the attack in only one corps area, leaving the Germans with a three-division attack (as opposed to five divisions) while the other corps was still stagnated. Third, the road and logistical net in the area of Veselyii was extremely limited. As such, committing two new divisions in that area would have complicated supply support for them. Furthermore, the attack frontage would have been restricted to about eight kilometers. On the other had, the frontage in the area between Kruglik and height 244.8 was eleven or so kilometers. Considering the road net, frontage and terrain, attacking in this area seems likely to have been the better option. Therefore, we will examine this option first.

In this case, the three attacking divisions would have consisted of up to 50,000 people and 225 tanks. Facing them would have been around 45,000 troops and 230

10 On 16 July it is reported that the 24th Guards Tank Brigade had 22 T-34s with 306 personnel losses on the 13th and no personnel losses between the 14th and 16th of July. The 10th Guards Mechanized Brigade had 18 T-34s and 15 T-70s with total losses of 131 between the 13th and 16th. The 1447 Self-Propelled Artillery Regiment (which was part of the army) still had 9 Su-76s and 12 Su-122s and had taken no losses. Heavy losses had been taken by other units of the V Guards Mechanized Corps. See Fond: 332, Opis: 1943, Delo: 80, pages 14–17. The authorized strength of a Tank Brigade would be around 1,172 people and for a Mechanized Brigade it would be around 3,800 people.

tanks. This is around a 1.1-to-1 force ratio, and would pose a threat in a day or two, if not responded to, of achieving a penetration.

So what did the Soviets have available for response besides the second echelon forces in the immediate area? In the XLVIII Panzer Corps area, the VI Tank Corps was still refitting and repairing tanks. It could certainly have been shifted and committed (around 6,966 men and 48 tanks on the 15th) and as the attack in front of the SS Panzer Corps would not be invigorated, then some of the forces there, like the 6th Guards Airborne Division, 42nd Guards Rifle Division, 24th Guards Tank Brigade and 10th Guards Mechanized Brigade could be shifted over. All these forces, around 28,000 men and 120 tanks, when committed to action would have reduced the force ratio of a three-division attack to 0.7 to 1. As such, the three-division attack would have almost certainly stalled in front of the Psel River in a couple of days.

In the case of a single three-division push in the SS Panzer Corps area, the forces in the second echelon and not yet committed consisted of 6th Guards Airborne Division, the 42nd Guards Rifle Division, the XXXI Tank Corps and parts of the V Guards Mechanized Corps. These could have been shifted over to support the defense there. Assuming this would take a day or two, it means that around the 16th or 17th, the Germans would have been facing another 26,000 men and 140 tanks in this area and would have been attacking at a force ratio of a little less than one to one although they still would have maintained an edge in armor (205 tanks versus 160). Still, all indications are that this attack also would have stalled, although probably only after some additional losses for the Soviets and more armor losses for the Germans. After all, Totenkopf went through 57 tanks on the 12th and 13th in this area, and some of them were certainly fighting forces they outnumbered in armor strength during that time.

One of the proponents of the arguments that the Germans were almost on the verge of victory suggests that the fresh German panzer corps should have assembled south of the Psel and attacked through the Totenkopf positions.[11] This three division attack, which on the 15th would have consisted of fewer than 50,000 personnel and 205 tanks, would have encountered the better part of the Fifth Guards Army, including all the reserve forces listed in the paragraph above. This is effectively the attack described in the paragraph above, but on an even more constricted frontage. There were also additional forces in this area consisting of the very exhausted 52nd Guards Rifle Division and the fresh 252nd Rifle Division from the Fifty-third Army.

This attack on frontage of eight kilometers would certainly have been able to make some progress, but at considerable cost. Totenkopf had already lost an estimated 1,551 men and 69 tanks in its fighting there from the 10th through the 15th. At this point, with a road running laterally across the back of the Soviet defenses (from Oboyan to Verkhnyaya Olshanka), the Soviets were able to move armor to cap off this attack. Immediately available would have been the XXXI Tank Corps and some of the V Guards Mechanized Corps with some 140 tanks total. This was probably sufficient to hold until further forces were focused in the area. It is clear that the most likely result of such a German attack would have been to stall again, assuming they could have gotten two more divisions across the Psel and into the bridgehead and ready to attack on the morning of the 15th. As the weather at that time was wet, with heavy rainfall and poor surface trafficability, there is every reason to believe that it would have further slowed the German attack, giving the Soviets more than enough time to react.

Finally, as a result of the cleaning up of the Donets triangle (which is assumed would have continued) the Germans had only freed up one division, the 167th

11 George M. Nipe Jr., *Decision in the Ukraine*, page 56–57. Nipe does state that the XXIV Panzer Corps consisted of three divisions, including the 17th Panzer Division. This gives the wrong impression. The 17th Panzer Division was located east of Barvenkovo, over 140 kilometers to the southeast of Kharkov. It was under command of the XXIV Panzer Corps and it could have been incorporated into the German reserves, but as of the 13th, had not been activated for such a purpose and would have taken time to arrive.

Infantry Division, on the 15th. The rest of the German units were still in the line. Conversely, the Soviets were able to free up the battered 89th Guards, 81st Guards, 93rd Guards and 375th Rifle Divisions. Any freed German forces from the triangle could have been committed to the attack, but considering the situation, they would have almost certainly been used for flank protection. As the German attack advanced, it was going to need another division to cover the left flank and one to cover the right flank. As such, these German reinforcements would not have added to the strength of the attack, but they would have allowed the attack to continue forward without having to strip off additional troops to cover the flanks.

Overall, it appears that the Voronezh Front, with existing resources, had the situation under control. The commitment of the two new German divisions would have driven the Soviet forces back further, possibly as much as five to ten kilometers, before additional reinforcements and more favorable terrain would have most likely caused the German attack to again stall. Still, if the Voronezh Front was unable to contain the Germans, the Soviets did have additional forces to call upon. The Fifty-third Army, which consisted of seven rifle divisions, was already along the Seim River between Nechayevo and Bunino. The I Mechanized Corps was also with them. On the 15th of July, parts of the army were on the move and at least the 252nd Rifle Division was within 40 kilometers of the front. These forces would have added at least another 70,000 troops to the battle, noticeably altering the odds. If that were not enough, there were two other infantry armies at hand. On the right was the Twenty-seventh Army with six rifle divisions and a tank brigade, which was at Kursk on the 14th and had the IV Guards Tank Corps in front of it. On the left around Korocha and arriving the night of 14/15 was the Forty-seventh Army with six rifle divisions along with the III Guards Mechanized Corps. These three armies consisted of a total of 19 rifle divisions, three tank and mechanized corps, and one tank brigade. This was certainly more than enough compensation to counteract the Germans receiving two more weak armored divisions.

If still more forces were needed, the Southwestern Front also had three cavalry corps under its command, which would add at least another 50,000 troops and 300 tanks to the fray. Also unloading to the east of Kursk starting on the 12th was the Fourth Guards Army. Finally, there were the armored forces on the northern bulge. These included the III Tank Corps, IX Tank Corps, XVI Tank Corps and the XIX Tank Corps and a number of smaller formations. Some or all of these could have easily been shifted south through Kursk to help defend against the German attack. Also, in the area due east of Orel, the Soviets were about to commit the Third Guards Tank Army to battle. This formation had three tank and mechanized corps and 731 tanks and self-propelled guns.[12] It was released to control of the Bryansk Front on the 14th of July but did not enter combat until the 19th.[13] It could have been shifted south if needed, although it would have been fairly late to arrive and not in the best of shape. While these shifts would have taken considerable pressure off the German Ninth Army, there was little the Ninth Army could do to stop them from occurring. Thus, potentially a total of 19 rifle divisions, three cavalry corps and ten armored corps were available to throw into battle against the two reinforcing German armored divisions. The chances of the Germans being able to get any real and effective penetration were nil. The only other reserve forces the Germans had available were the 17th Panzer Division (78 tanks) and the 16th Panzer Grenadier Division (36 tanks) and scattered assault gun and self-propelled anti-tank gun units.[14] The 17th Panzer Division was located

12 Tank strength is as given by Glantz and House, *Battle of Kursk*, page 58, 230, 421, note 7. Exact date for this strength is not given but it is assumed to be sometime on or before 14 July 1943. Strength is given as 698 serviceable tanks and 32 self-propelled guns (which equal 730) for some point shortly after 14 July, page 236.

13 Glantz and House, *Battle of Kursk*, pages 235–236, page 421, note 7.

14 The 17th Panzer Division reported on the 3rd of July that they had 4 Panzer IIs, 29 Panzer IIIs, 32 Panzer IVs and 2 T-34s. See Zetterling and Frankson, page 31. George Nipe on page 55

east of Barvenkovo, over 140 kilometers southeast of Kharkov, and was effectively the only other major armor reserve for the front. It would have been risky to commit it to action, leaving Army Group South with almost no armor reserve across a 650 kilometer front. The 16th Panzer Grenadier Division was weaker and even further away.

Given that a penetration was pretty much impossible, then the discussion of the effects of such a penetration is academic. Still, one could postulate that the Soviet command could suddenly have been hit with a fit of indecision (which did not seem to be likely at this juncture) and not send any further reinforcements into the bulge. Still with three more armies along with three more tank corps making up the next echelon, it is hard to imagine the Germans obtaining a penetration. But, if one assumes that somehow the Germans may have managed to penetrate through to Oboyan and the line defending in front of Kursk, the situation would still have been difficult for them. The Germans' northern pincer was stalled and the Orel bulge had come under attack on the 12th. The distance from Belgorod to Kursk is about 130 kilometers. This would require manning a left flank with at least four divisions (255th, 332nd and 3rd Panzer were already doing this), and would have taken at least eight divisions on the right flank to protect the flanks of the extended penetration (320th, 106th, 198th, 168th, 6th Panzer, 19th Panzer and 7th Panzer were already doing this). At the point they got to Kursk, the forward offensive force could not have been much more than five divisions (counting the two reinforcing divisions from the XXIV Panzer Corps). To complete the encirclement to the Ninth Army would have required a northern advance of another 80 kilometers, requiring even more flank protection. As such, if the Soviets panicked and withdrew (instead shifting forces to face this threat), then certainly the Seventieth, Sixty-fifth and Sixtieth Armies would have been able to escape. What could be left in the encirclement would be the five divisions of the Thirty-eighth Army and the four remaining divisions of the Fortieth Army. Still, with the Soviet armies advancing on Orel, and the Soviet forces massing opposite Kharkov, the effectiveness and duration of such an encirclement would have been limited. In fact, with the northern pincer of the attack not advancing, then advancing past Kursk with the southern pincer would have been questionable and risky.

Finally, the Germans were losing their air support. Because of the situation in the north, the Germans had shifted more than 500 aircraft to the north around the 15th. The German VIII Air Corps on the 16th consisted of less than 500 planes, compared to its strength of over 1,000 on the 13th. This is less than half of their air strength and is shown in their total sorties flown starting the 15th. The Germans flew 1,452 sorties during the day on the 14th but only 706 sorties on the 15th and were down to 138 daytime sorties by the 17th. This was in the face of an increasingly aggressive Soviet air threat that was putting up almost 500 sorties on the 17th. So, on top of everything else, as the Germans continued their advance, they would either have lost air support, and probably control of the air, or they would have been forced to not reinforce the defense around Orel with air, which would have led to further problems and complications there. In contrast, the Soviets

---

claims 56 tanks around 13 July, drawn from W. Victor Madeja, *The Russo-German War*, Vol. 31 (Allentown: Valor Publishing Company, 1987), page 93. On 10 July, the 17th Panzer Division had 3 Panzer IIs, 46 Panzer III and IVs, 2 command tanks, 7 artillery observation tanks and 20 Marders ready-for-action (see T313, R55, 7292519).

The 16th Panzer Grenadier Division had 29 Panzer III and 7 Panzer IVs on the 17th of July according to Nipe, page 80. On the 30th of June they are showing 3 Panzer IIs, 28 Panzer IIIs, 9 Panzer IVs (T78, R619).

There were also the 203rd and 232nd Assault Gun Battalions with some 58 Sturmgeschuetzes ready-for-action on the 10th, and with the XLII Corps was the 560th Heavy Panzer Jaeger Battalion with 45 88mm Hornets (also called Nashorns) that needed more field work before they could see action. In the Sixth Army area were four assault gun battalions (209th, 210th, 236th and 243rd) that had a total of 80 Sturmgeschuetz IIIs ready for action on 10 July, along with 5 others with the 15th Luftwaffe Field Division.

would still have had the entire strength of the Second Air Army committed, could have thrown in the Fifth Air Army, and included as much of the Sixteenth Air Army as needed. This probably would have resulted in the Soviets effectively having air superiority over the area of the German attack. Starting on the 16th, the Soviet air force began flying more ground attack sorties in the Kursk area than the Germans.

Given all the conditions above, it is easy to dismiss the claims that the Germans were on the verge of a breakthrough.[15]

Still, Manstein wanted to continue the operation so as to cause additional attrition to the Soviet reserves. It would appear that most of the damage had already been done. The Soviet forces were now massed, strength against strength, directly in front of the German forces and in considerable density. This was not only a force that the Germans could no longer get highly favorable exchange ratios from, but one they were going to have a problem penetrating and enveloping. Unless a breakthrough was achieved, there would be no more encirclements and the force exchange ratio was not going to greatly favor the Germans. As such, there was not much to achieve in the way of favorable attrition by continuing operations beyond what they had already done. The best way to cause the Soviets additional casualties was to clean up the areas around Tolstoye Woods and the Donets triangle. After these operations were done, anything else initially required a frontal assault to achieve penetration. As shown from the first days of the operations, the real benefit for the Germans in the casualty exchanged didn't come until the third day of the operation, after they had penetrated the Soviet defensive lines. So again, we are back to having to force a penetration to achieve results. In this case, the overall force-ratio of engaged troops across the front of the entire opposing lines was 0.92-to-1. This is noticeably lower than the ratio of 2.50-to-1 that the Germans started with on the 5th of July. As such, the degree and extent of the penetration would have been considerably less, and the casualty exchange ratio would have certainly stayed well below 2-to-1. As the Germans had such a plan for causing more attrition, which was *Operation Roland*, it would appear that they would have

15 George Nipe's claim that the Germans were on the verge of breaking through requires him to:

1) Mistakenly conclude that the Germans outnumbered the opposing Soviet armor after the Battle of Prokhorovka by 2 to 1 (see page 48 of his book).*

2) Declare that the reinforcing XXIV Panzer Corps consisted of three divisions when it only consisted of two (see page 55 of his book).

3) Ignore the existing local Soviet reserves, which included a number of unengaged divisions from Fifth Guards Army, a number of divisions made available by the withdrawal from the Donets triangle, a number of armored formations that were resting (III Mechanized Corps, XXXI Tank Corps and VI Tank Corps), etc.

4) Ignore the existence of the Twenty-seventh, Forty-seventh and Fifty-third Armies and the three tank and mechanized corps with them.

5) Ignore the ability of the Central Front to shift four tank corps to the south.

6) Ignore the air situation, which clearly now favored the Soviets.

7) Ignore the threats to other places in the German lines.

*It is hard to truly appreciate the logic here unless one goes through his figures in depth. In this case, he totals up strength of all the tanks in the XLVIII Panzer Corps, SS Panzer Corps and III Panzer Corps and compares it to the Fifth Guards Tank Corps (presumably of only three tank and mechanized corps), ignoring the other seven tank and mechanized corps on the battlefield and the numerous tank and self-propelled artillery brigades and regiments.

This error is further magnified by using a figure from Glantz's *From the Don to the Dnepr*, page 361, that appears to be either too low for the 13th of July (". . . 150–200 tanks after the major tank battle at Prokhorovka [12 July] . . .") or a figure from a much later date in July that is misapplied by Nipe to the 13th (see page 55 of Nipe). On the 13th of July, the Fifth Guards Tank Army had around 340 tanks ready for action (including 29 SU-76s, and SU-122s), not counting the attached II Tank Corps (46 tanks), II Guards Tank Corps (80 tanks), 1529th Heavy Self-Propelled Artillery Regiment (1 KV-1, 11 SU-152s) nor the 1549th Heavy Self-Propelled Artillery Regiment (7 Churchills).

also tried something similar if they received the XXIV Panzer Corps. In this case, they probably would have achieved penetration along the line of height 247.0 to 232.8 (effectively Kruglik to Novoselovka). They then would have turned on the Fortieth Army, and possibly the Thirty-eighth Army. With the Fortieth Army having four divisions at risk, while the Thirty-eighth Army had five divisions, then potentially such an operation could bring casualties in excess of 70,000, assuming the Germans could obtain an encirclement with no escape (not very likely). Therefore, we are looking at a force of seven attacking divisions that we assume would be conducting offensive operations for seven days against well-prepared opponents. These seven divisions suffered 10,602 casualties through the seven days covering the 5th through 11th of July.[16] This is a 7-to-1 loss ratio in favor of the Germans. If there were a less than perfect encirclement and let's suppose half the troops at risk were to get out, then we are looking at a 3.5-to-1 loss ratio in favor of the Germans.

While one notes that this is a favorable casualty exchange for the Germans, when the Soviets attacked on the 12th, the Germans achieved better than an 8-to-1 exchange ratio. Therefore, while the continuation of offensive operations for the sake of grinding the Soviets down would have resulted in higher Soviet losses, it would not have been as significant as what would have been caused if the Germans simply presented a solid defense against the attacking Soviets (who did attack on 3 August).

Therefore, we can only conclude that the commitment of Germans reserves and the continued pursuit of the attack would not have resulted in a significant breakthrough or encirclement, and would not have resulted in a casualty exchange-ratio as favorable to the Germans as they would have incurred with a proper defense. Therefore, the further pursuit of this attack did not make sense. What was decided on the 13th, which was to halt the main attack but allow the German forces to clean up the flanks, was probably the best decision at this juncture.

What if the Soviets had not attacked on the 12th and 13th?

The broad Soviet attack across the front on the 12th was clearly a mistake. With the arrival of the Steppe Front forces and other reinforcements, the Germans were no longer threatening to break through at that moment. The Soviets' attacks on the 12th of July had cost them 21,277 troops and 416 tanks, in exchange for 2,702 Germans troops and an estimated 122 tanks. This was almost an 8-to-1 casualty exchange ratio and a 3.4-to-1 tank loss ratio. In the previous three days of fighting (the 9th through the 11th of July), the Soviets had lost 27,402 troops and 522 tanks in exchange for 6,805 German troops and 309 tanks.[17] With the arrival of the Fifth Guards Army and the Fifth Guards Tank Army, the situation and force ratios for the defense had improved. One can therefore safely assume that if the Soviets had defended on the 12th and 13th, the German attack would have stalled and at casualties- and exchange-ratios that were not significantly different than the previous three days. As such, they would have avoided losing more than 10,000 troops and at least 210 tanks, assuming that the German losses would have remained about the same.[18]

16 There were also an estimated 501 disease and non-battle injuries in these units during that time. This estimate does not include the 57th and 255th Infantry Divisions of the LII Corps who were supposed to pin the opposing Fortieth Army but does include the 332nd Infantry Division.

17 We also have the Fifth Guards Army losing 71 tanks during those three days, mostly from their march.

18 If the Germans had an exchange ratio of 1.69 to 1 for the 9th through the 11th (522/309 tanks) then that exchange ratio applied to their 122 losses on the 12th, or their 203 losses on the 12th and 13th would have resulted in 210 or 214 fewer Soviet tank losses than they actually suffered.

The same math applied to Soviet personnel losses on the 12th produces a figure of 10,397 additional men lost.

The Voronezh Front attacks on the 12th and 13th were simply a waste of Russian lives.

Was Hitler Correct to Cancel the Offensive?

Much of the confusion over this question is generated by confusion over what was canceled by Hitler on the 13th. *Operation Citadel* was canceled entirely for the north but in the south operations were allowed to proceed through the 17th, when Hitler then began to take divisions from Manstein. This is clearly stated in Manstein's writings.

What effectively was ended by Hitler was *Operation Roland*. This was a seven to nine division attack that may have yielded more results, but would have been over in less than a week. After that, the fighting would have certainly come to a halt. While canceling this operation by the transfer of troops may have resulted in a lost opportunity to cause more casualties, it certainly did not steal victory from the Germans.

Manstein met with Hitler the day after the suicidal Soviet attacks of the 12th. This was the day of the most unfavorable exchange ratios for the Soviet forces. As such, with an 8-to-1 kill ratio for the day in men, and a 3.4-to-1 kill ratio in armor, it would have been very much to the Germans' advantage to keep the offensive going if it had resulted in the Soviets' persisting in these broad front attacks. Still, it is now clear that they were not going to maintain these attacks and had finally rolled over to a much more passive defense. Faced with a proper and sufficiently strong defense, there was little more that could be gained from a German attack. Yet there were opportunities to do further damage on the two flanks, and Manstein certainly needed to resolve these battles. This he was allowed to do. Regardless of whether the overall offensive was canceled, these two flank battles had to be resolved before he could again move forward. If this is what Manstein requested from Hitler, which appears to be the case, these recommendations are reasonable. If he was looking for any more forward pushes, then his request was not advisable.

Hitler's decision to call off the offensive is certainly understandable. The offensive had clearly failed. In the north, Model had barely gotten off the starting line. In the south, Manstein had made a significant dent, but the attack had stalled. While the German forces may have been able to continue pushing forward, especially if they committed the reserve XXIV Panzer Corps, a breakthrough was not going to be achieved.

One of the reasons that Hitler gave for halting the attack was the invasion of Sicily. He really did need to shore up Sicily and support his Italian allies. He understood that after the disaster in North Africa, the Italians were on the verge of withdrawing from the war. While one can certainly question the value of this ally, it still was the largest ally the Germans had. While they were no longer contributing troops to the war in the east, the Italians still had around 60 divisions in various states to commit to the war effort. Hitler really did have a need to pull forces from the Eastern Front and send them to the west. This was the reason that OKW had originally supported the idea of an early summer offensive in the east to straighten up the lines.

The actual German forces that ended up being sent to Italy from the Eastern Front consisted only of the Adolf Hitler SS Division and the II SS Panzer Corps staff. This has led some Soviet historians to completely dismiss the Sicilian invasion as the reason for Hitler ending the offensive. Still, this was a reason that Hitler gave, and it probably did reflect his thinking at that time, be it right or not.

The real problem was one of timing, for the attack on Kursk had been delayed so much that the Allied landing occurred right in the middle of the Kursk offensive. Therefore, it was no longer possible for Hitler to shore up the Eastern Front and then send forces west. Any forces taken from the Eastern Front would be very much at the expense of that front. As it was, the time it took for those forces to arrive in Italy was sufficiently slow that when they did arrive, it was too late to save Sicily or Mussolini. The Allies landed in Sicily on the 9th of July, although it took them until the 17th of August before they were able to enter Messina, effectively conquering Sicily. On the 24th of July, Mussolini was overthrown, the British crossed the straights of Messina to Italy on the 3rd of September and the Italian government sued for peace on the 8th of September, having been in discussion with the Allies since the 25th of July. The Adolf Hitler SS Division did not arrive in the Po River Valley of Northern Italy until the 8th of August. For Hitler to have gained the benefit from an offensive on the Eastern Front, it really needed to be launched and completed long before the Allies invaded Sicily, for once Mussolini was lost, Italy was lost to Hitler.

Still, it was the OKW's and Hitler's intention to try to pull more forces from the Eastern Front. What stopped this were the overwhelming and extensive Soviet attacks in August that pretty much unhinged the entire southern half of the front. In effect, the additional forces he was hoping to ship west, ended up being reinserted right back into the line in the east to try desperately to hold back the Soviet attacks. As such, the effect was actually the reverse, with the Soviet attacks helping the west. Instead of Hitler conducting Kursk and then shifting to the west to shore up the Italians, Hitler ended up halting Kursk, in part because of the Allied invasions, but he also could never send significant forces to the west because of the deteriorating situation in the east. As such, he lost on both fronts at the same time.

One reason Manstein gave for wanting to continue the attack was the favorable exchange ratios, which he pegged at four times his own losses in killed, wounded, and missing.[19] As we have seen, the overall figure was a little less than that (3.69 to 1). If one subtracts the insanity on the 12th through the 14th of July, the exchange ratio declines to around 2.90 to 1. As such, one would expect that continued operations would not have yielded the same level of results. Furthermore, three major conditions that helped to create these lopsided loss ratios were no longer in effect. First, the concentration and thrust of the initial German attack worked to the Germans' advantage due to poor Soviet deployments: the two-echelon defense approach, and their failure to properly position their armor reserves. Second, the Soviet habit of continuing to attack regardless of the situation, especially the insanity on the 12th, severely depleted their forces. One notes that the Soviet loss ratios are the worst on the days of their heaviest attacks (6th, 8th and 12th). Third, the two weak positions on the flanks, Tolstoye Woods and the Donets triangle, where the Germans could conduct high yield envelopments at low costs to themselves, were already resolved. These untenable and disadvantageous positions were a result of previous operations and were now gone. As such, Soviet defenses now matched German strength with strength, had the right forces in the right places, and had no clear hanging units, exposed flanks, or weak points. As such, the Germans would have found it difficult to maintain the same favorable loss ratios they had earlier.

The reasons Hitler halted Kursk were because the overall attack plan had failed, the forces were needed elsewhere on the front, and he wanted to shift forces to Italy. His decision to halt the attack is perfectly valid. Yet because of continued Soviet attacks, the shift to Italy never occurred. In the end, Army Group South had been stopped by the Voronezh Front and Steppe Front. Hitler's decision just confirmed the obvious.

19 Manstein, page 449.

The Counteroffensives

The Battle of Kursk consisted of four separate major operations. In the north was an attack by the Ninth Army into the Central Front from 5 July to 11 July. In the south was the attack by two armies against the Voronezh Front from 4 July to the 17th. The second phase of the battle consisted of two massive counteroffensives. In the north were three Fronts against two German armies from 12 July to 18 August (*Operation Kutuzov*). In the south was an attack by three Fronts (Steppe, Voronezh and Southwestern) against two German armies from 3 to 23 August (*Operation Rumyantsev*).

This book focuses on the German offensive in the south. According to Krivosheyev, it involved 534,700 Soviet forces and cost them 143,950 casualties. The defensive operation in the north involved 738,000 Soviet forces and cost them 33,897 casualties. The two Soviet counteroffensives were much larger than the German offensives. The one in the north involved 1,287,600 Soviet forces and cost them 429,890 casualties, while the one in the south involved at least 1,144,000 Soviet forces and cost them 255,566 casualties.[20] These counteroffensives have not been adequately described in any book.

20 Figures are from Krivosheyev, pages 187–190. These figures have not been cross-checked, and there are certainly some gaps in them, but they do illustrate the size and the intensity of the subsequent fighting. The figures for the Voronezh and Steppe Fronts in the defensive phase cover the 5th to the 23rd of July. The figures for the offensive in the south do not include the strengths and losses of the Southwestern Front, which joined the attack on the 12th of August.

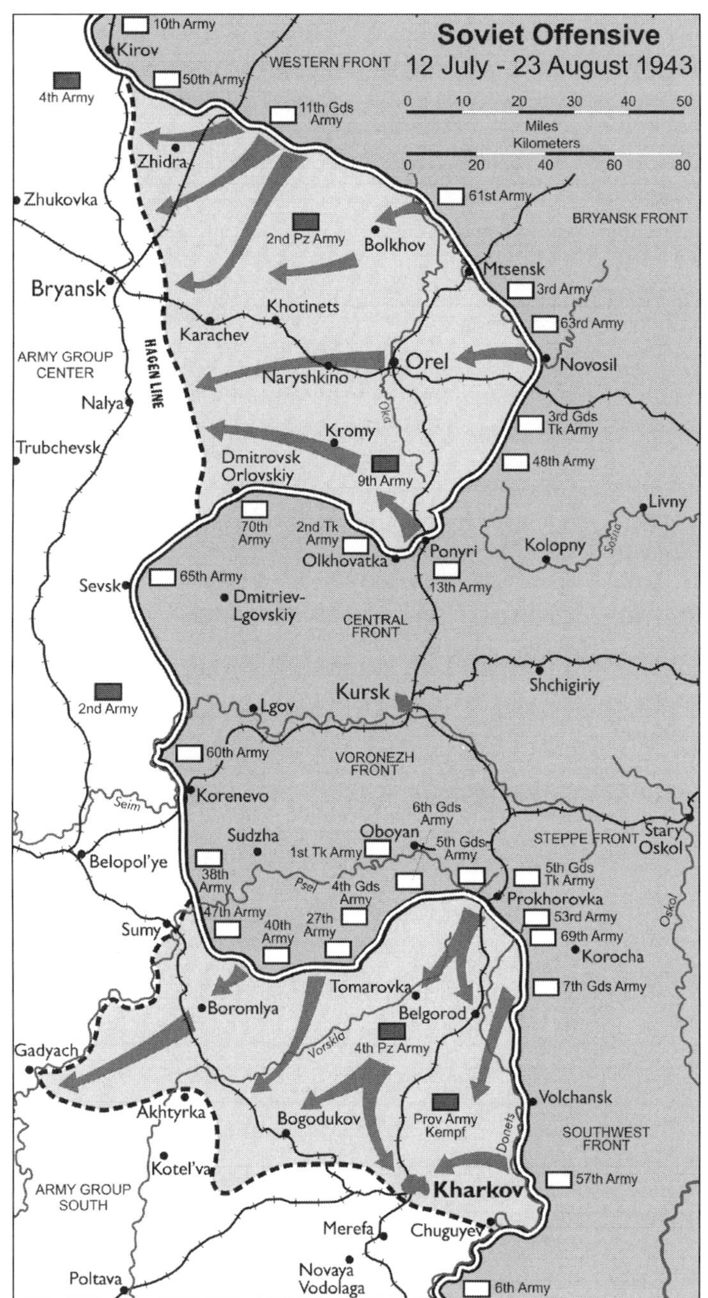
Soviet Offensive
12 July - 23 August 1943
Miles
Kilometers
10th Army
Kirov
50th Army
4th Army
WESTERN FRONT
11th Gds Army
Zhidra
Zhukovka
61st Army
BRYANSK FRONT
2nd Pz Army
Bolkhov
Mtsensk
Bryansk
3rd Army
Khotinets
63rd Army
Karachev
ARMY GROUP CENTER
HAGEN LINE
Orel
Novosil
Naryshkino
Nalya
Oka
3rd Gds Tk Army
Kromy
Trubchevsk
Dmitrovsk Orlovskiy
9th Army
48th Army
Livny
70th Army
2nd Tk Army
Kolopny
Ponyri
Olkhovatka
13th Army
Sevsk
65th Army
Dmitriev-Lgovskiy
CENTRAL FRONT
2nd Army
Kursk
Shchigiriy
Lgov
60th Army
VORONEZH FRONT
Korenevo
Seim
6th Gds Army
Sudzha
Oboyan
5th Gds Army
STEPPE FRONT
Stary Oskol
1st Tk Army
Belopol'ye
38th Army
Psel
4th Gds Army
5th Gds Tk Army
Prokhorovka
47th Army
27th Army
53rd Army
Sumy
40th Army
69th Army
Oskol
Korocha
Tomarovka
7th Gds Army
Boromlya
Belgorod
Gadyach
Vorskla
4th Pz Army
Volchansk
Akhtyrka
Bogodukov
Prov Army Kempf
Donets
SOUTHWEST FRONT
Kotel'va
57th Army
ARMY GROUP SOUTH
Kharkov
Merefa
Chuguyev
Novaya Vodolaga
Poltava
6th Army

Lt. Rodde, adjutant, 6th Tank Regiment, 3rd Panzer Division:

> On our side supply worked as well as we were used to from our combat trains throughout the entire operation. Personnel in the maintenance echelons also made superhuman efforts at times. Their sacrifice is rarely mentioned, but us tankers knew what we had in these men.

Captain Frantz, commander, Gross Deutschland Assault Gun Battalion:

> Supply always functioned rather smoothly. I do not recall any particular action having to be delayed or canceled due to a lack of fuel or ammunition. Our men at the combat train did an excellent job. Medical care was good as well. I did hear that medics working at clearing stations were burdened to the limit in keeping up with the wounded, particularly from the infantry.

Lt. Burchardi,[1] Gross Deutschland Artillery Regiment:

> I do not recall anything going afoul with us. Our supply worked like clockwork and we could rely particularly well on the medical staff.
>
> We would usually transport our fallen soldiers to the rear. It was a matter of honor for our company sergeants to see to an orderly burial for our fallen comrades. It was a rare exception to bury those killed right on the spot.

Private Stark,[2] Gross Deutschland Engineer Battalion:

> Our supply worked very well the whole time. This held true for the medics in particular, which fostered a certain degree of confidence among us.

Lt. Emminghaus,[3] commander, 6th company, II Battalion, Gross Deutschland Fusilier Regiment:

1 Mr. Joachim Burchardi was interviewed by Maj.Gen. (ret.) Dieter Brand on 11 May 1999. Mr. Burchardi was born 10 May 1917 in Dresden and had been a soldier since October 1937. He was originally conscripted but had risen to being an officer since 1 June 1940. He participated in the campaigns into Poland, the Balkans, and Russia in 1941 while with the 4th Artillery Regiment.

During *Citadel*, he was a first lieutenant and O1 (similar to an S3 officer) in the artillery regiment's staff that belonged to the Gross Deutschland Division. During the war, his awards included Iron Cross 1st and 2nd Class, German Cross in Gold and the Assault Badge 50.

Mr. Burchardi spent 5 years after the war as a prisoner of war (POW). He received a university education and served as an officer with the West German Army since 1960. He was promoted up to lieutenant colonel, his last assignment being a teacher in tactics and logistics.

2 Mr. Karl A. Stark was interviewed by Maj. Gen. (ret.) Dieter Brand on 8 May 1999. Mr. Stark was born 20 April 1924. He was conscripted in 1942 and trained as a combat engineer. He had been with the Gross Deutschland Division in Russia since 1943. He was a messenger with the company command squad in a company in the combat engineer battalion. His rank was private. He had been transferred to this unit after basic training in 1943 and had no front line experience. The attacks on 5 July were the first action he saw, they were his "baptism of fire." His awards during the war include a Wound Badge.

He was a bank administrator after the war.

3 Mr. Ottfried Emminghaus was interviewed by Maj. Gen. (ret.) Dieter Brand on 26 May 1999. Mr. Emminghaus was born 1920 in Berlin. He had been a soldier in the 59th Infantry Regiment since 1 October 1939 and served in the French Campaign with the 19th Infantry Division. The 19th Infantry Division was converted into the 20th Panzer Division in late 1940 and Mr. Emminghaus later served as staff officer of the panzer grenadier regiment. During the Russian campaign he was wounded. As an infantryman, he had participated in the French and Russian Campaigns and had substantial battle experience as a result.

He served with the Gross Deutschland Division since its inception in 1942, serving with the Fusilier Regiment since summer 1942. At the time of Kursk, he was First Lieutenant and

Our supply, including the medical service, worked quite well. I don't recall a lack of ammunition in any engagement, ever.

Lt. Neumann,[4] Gross Deutschland Antiaircraft Battalion:

Supply went smoothly and in streamlined fashion.

Captain Bergemann, commander, III Battalion, Gross Deutschland Grenadier Regiment:

Supply functioned smoothly during the entire operation. While we did not have an abundance of provisions, ammunition was never scarce during the operation. Provisions also arrived regularly. The medical service deserves particular regard, as it has a great impact on common soldiers' morale.

Lt. Schoene,[5] commander, 4th company, II Battalion, 15th Panzer Regiment, 11th Panzer Division:

Supply always worked well throughout the whole time. Our supply sergeants regularly showed up with ammunition, fuel and most importantly hot food every evening. That was not always easy as the terrain behind us provided shelter for several scattered Russians. But our supply sergeants were old foxes, all of them. The maintenance echelon, too, which followed in the combat train a few miles behind the fighting units, did an excellent job.

Care for the wounded was good. Often our regiment's doctor was right up front helping to get the wounded out of disabled tanks. I have never seen the Russians firing intentionally on our ambulances.

Lt. Schaefer-Kehnert, commander, 4th battery, II Battalion, 119th Artillery Regiment, 11th Panzer Division:

For us in the artillery, the main adversary was of course the enemy artillery. We had to fear the worst from them. The Soviet air force was also of importance.

During the engagements at *Citadel* it became evident, that the Soviet artillery must have an inexhaustible supply of ammunition at their disposal. We, on the other hand, mainly fired according to

company commander of the 6th company in the II Battalion of the Fusilier Regiment.

His awards during the war included a German Cross in Gold, Iron Cross 1st and 2nd Class, Close Combat Clasp, and Wound Badge.

Mr. Emminghaus was a sales manager and entrepreneur after the war.

4 Brig.Gen. a.D. Neumann was interviewed by Maj.Gen. (ret.) Dieter Brand in Hamburg on 21 August 1999. Horst Neumann was born 22nd of February 1922. He volunteered for the army at age 17 in September 1939. He entered service with the 37th Artillery Regiment in Konigsberg (now Kaliningrad, part of Russia). He joined the army's antiaircraft branch upon inception of same and was assigned to the newly established antiaircraft battalion with the Gross Deutschland Division, serving with that unit until the war's end.

At the time of *Citadel*, he was a lieutenant and antiaircraft combat team commander in the Gross Deutschland Division. His awards during the war included Iron Cross 1st and 2nd Class, Assault Badge, Antiaircraft Combat Badge, Wound Badge (wounded 4 times), and Winter Combat Badge 1941.

A journalist after the war and then entered the West German Army. He underwent General Staff training and his last assignment was General of Combat Support Troops at the rank of Brigadier General. General Neumann retired in 1982.

5 Mr. Eberhard Schoene was interviewed by Maj.Gen. (ret.) Dieter Brand on 1 April 1999. Mr. Schoene was born 17 June 1922 and volunteered for service, starting on 2 January 1941. He was first deployed in Africa, then served as a lieutenant with the 15th Panzer Regiment in Russia starting with summer of 1942. In July 1942 he became a company commander.

He stayed with this regiment together with the 11th Panzer Division until the end of the war. His awards include Iron Cross 1st and 2nd Class, Armored Assault Badge (25)—i.e., 25 armored attacks, Wound Badge in Silver (4 injuries).

Mr. Schoene was a merchant after the war.

observation so as to ensure the effect of what little ammunition we had.

Supply always worked well, i.e. what little there was did in fact reach us at the front. But ammunition was always short. The same holds for supply with provisions and medical care.

Professor Kehnert's observation on Soviet artillery supply is not born out by the Soviet records. The differences in rounds per gun available was such that the Germans had three to five times as many rounds available per artillery piece as the Soviets did. So while the Soviets had 80 percent more guns than the Germans did, the total weight of ammunition dropped on the battlefield was probably around 43 percent of that for the Germans. See the section on "German vs Soviet Artillery Ammunition" in Appendix III of my original book *Kursk: The Battle of Prokhorovka* for details.

Officer Cadet Guenther Baer, tank commander, II Battalion, Leibstandarte SS Adolf Hitler Panzer Regiment:

We never had any problem with supply. Only in the end were we short on the #40 armor piercing shell. But we were supposed to shoot that one only with expressed permission and in emergency situations anyway. We as a tank crew always had several boxes of provisions on our tank.

Private Kurt Kaufmann, Das Reich SS Division:

Supply worked smoothly all along. There was always sufficient ammunition and fuel. The problem was rather getting those supplies to the guns at the front. Our people at the battle train worked tirelessly in accomplishing that mission. A decisive factor was our lack of radio equipment. As a result, we had to find each other at night. This wasted a lot of time, sometimes a gun would stand for hours without ammunition, because the munitions truck drivers or platoon messengers could not find us. Having lone supply vehicles venture through the countryside was by far no harmless task, because scattered Russians were of course everywhere. Our Dutch motorcycle messenger, who often had to run around all by himself was killed on one such mission.

Alfred Rubbel, 503rd Heavy Panzer (Tiger) Battalion:

Logistics of the entire operation always worked well. Whatever we needed was always available. I did not experience a lack of ammunition or fuel at that time.

Our men at the maintenance echelons and repair companies must be highly commended. These people often made a superhuman effort without receiving recognition for it. Our Tigers had the engines, transmissions, gunnery, the drivetrain including tracks, as well as the optics replaced on the front. On occasion, we turned over a Tiger that was pretty much shot to pieces and a few days later it was ready for action again.

German Medical Care

Private Kurt Kaufmann, Das Reich SS Division:

Medical care was also good. The least that can be said is that we felt we were being recovered soon after suffering injury and were receiving professional treatment. While our antiaircraft company had only two medics, medical care was extended by the respective units we were supporting at the time.

THE EFFECT OF WEATHER ON THE BATTLEFIELD

Captain Frantz, commander, Gross Deutschland Assault Gun Battalion:

> The weather was not always favorable. I recall a few awful thundershowers causing the soil to turn into something remotely akin to liquid concrete making any progress with tracked vehicles next to impossible. The valley floors of the various gorges (balkas) usually were swamp areas to begin with. But whenever the sun reappeared the temperature rose quickly—as was typical for summer in southern Russia—and the soil dried out again. Today, however, I no longer recall on which day and in which action we were hampered by these rainfalls.

Private Stark, Gross Deutschland Engineer Battalion:

> The weather did have a strong effect on the troops' state of mind. There was an abundance of heavy downpours. The soil quickly turned into a sticky morass so that every move turned into a major effort. As an engineer one was usually at the mercy of the elements when out on the open field. On occasion, one found cover under a vehicle or in a small hut, more often than not there remained only a shelter half for cover. One would be soaked to the skin in no time and cower down in some hole, wet and filthy. Dealing with this exposure not only to enemy fire but also to the elements without any protection whatsoever was one of those challenges a young soldier seeing his first action had to face.

Lt. Emminghaus, commander, 6th company, II Battalion, Gross Deutschland Fusilier Regiment:

> The weather was a real problem for us during the whole time. When the weather was dry, the black soil of southern Russia almost turned to concrete, the glaring sun soon deprived it of all moisture, the wind carried darkened dust. But as soon as one of the numerous thundershowers came down the soil immediately turned into a stiff black broth, which severely impeded our movement. As infantrymen we were usually exposed to the whims of nature without any protection, the rainfall routinely left us soaking wet. Then we would hope for the sun again, so as to dry the clothes on our body.

Officer Cadet Guenther Baer, Leibstandarte SS Adolf Hitler Division:

> Due to the softened terrain we had several mechanical breakdowns relating to track tension. The radio sets had to be turned off in thunderstorms. We couldn't see anything in the rain, so we had to quit. Only the Soviet infantry kept on fighting without interruption.

Alfred Rubbel, 503rd Heavy Panzer (Tiger) Battalion:

> Combat in these days depended heavily on soil and weather conditions. Time and again there were heavy downpours and thundershowers and after that it quickly turned hot again under the burning sun. As soon as the black soil had dried out it was as hard a surface as tarmac. But after a thundershower it softened up again and turned to black mud within 15 minutes, liable to take one's boots off. After that, only our Tiger tanks could move on. Once the sun came shining through again, the soil in turn dried out in no time.
>
> These repeated downpours also obstructed the exchange of fire because the rain hit our optics making any subsequent observation impossible. Then we had to get out again and clean the optics. This was clearly a design flaw, which we fixed by having a visor against the rain welded onto the optics at our shop.

 GERMAN IMPRESSIONS FROM THE BATTLEFIELD

Lt. Jung,[1] 332nd Antitank Battalion, 332nd Infantry Division:

The most unpleasant part of the entire offensive was the sudden artillery attacks by the Soviets, also often their mortar fire. The Soviet artillery did an excellent job of hitting their targets. Obviously, they had been able to prepare by surveillance and adjustment fire. Possibly, observers remaining behind had very precisely directed the fire. In any case, our attack formations were hit time and again by heavy artillery fire. Therefore, it was impossible to have purely infantry units function in unison with armored formations. They would suffer far too heavily in casualties following such artillery fire.

I witnessed this later on July 14th, when our 678th Infantry Regiment was to attack together with the Gross Deutschland Panzer Regiment. The attack formation was inundated with artillery fire to such a degree that the tanks relieved themselves of the threat by pouncing forward, while the infantry, lacking the protection offered by armor, could not leave their cover.

One event remains ingrained in my memory. I observed how a company commander of an infantry unit in the 3rd Panzer Division had gathered the junior commanders of his unit so as to issue orders. Those five or six men were hunched down within the brush and had laid out their maps. Then, all of the sudden, a mortar attack occurred. One mortar exploded right above this group and tore their bodies literally to pieces. All of them died on the spot.

The other unpleasantry was the Soviets' fighter planes. To be sure, they were not encountered as frequently as was artillery fire, but they always hit us by surprise. They were able to inflict some casualties on our units, particularly when traffic was jammed in a convoy.

As concerns other impressions gathered in this battle, I want to mention our air force. The Stukas were providing excellent fire support for our attack formations. Their fire was usually right on target, and routinely the effect on enemy positions was devastating. After a Stuka attack on an artillery position, only dead could be found in the aftermath. Just as helpful was the assistance provided by our fighter planes against enemy fighters and bombers. When a group of two fighters made their appearance it did not take long for the skies to be swept clean of enemy aircraft. I was witness to at least thirty enemy planes being shot during those days. However, it was evident that we did not have adequate fighter forces to provide permanent air cover for our army units. This is why the enemy fighters and bombers were able to inflict some casualties on our army units.

Lt. Rodde, adjutant, 6th Tank Regiment, 3rd Panzer Division:

Naturally, it was best to combine those units that had similar equipment levels and mobility. This is why we in the armored force very much preferred to have the "real" armored infantry along, namely those who fought directly from their armored personnel carriers and accompanied us in the immediate vicinity. They did, however, also have a tendency of dismounting too late or not at all to fight on foot.

1 Lt.Col. (ret.) Hans-Joachim Jung was interviewed by Maj.Gen. (ret.) Dieter Brand on 21 April 1999. Mr. Jung was born on 27 January 1921 and had entered the army as a volunteer 12 January 1939. He first served with the 8th Antitank Battalion, then with the 102nd Infantry Division and had been with the 332nd Infantry Division since October 1942. In July of 1943 he was a first lieutenant and company commander in the 332nd Infantry Division's antitank battalion. He had some combat experience, having taken part in the Russian Campaign from June 1941 up until being wounded in the spring of 1942.

After Kursk, he served with the Gross Deutschland Panzer Regiment until the war's end. His wartime awards included the Iron Cross 1st and 2nd Class, the "Russian winter battle" badge and the Wound Badge.

Mr. Jung joined the West German Army after the war, retiring in 1977 at the rank of a lieutenant colonel.

Cooperation with the normal infantry was in stark contrast to that, even if their designation was also "panzer grenadier." We often moved this normal infantry piggyback on our tanks until we had to open fire. After dismounting these people ended up sticking to the rear of our tanks like bees to a beehive. It was rather difficult to get them to understand that tanks tended to draw fire and for this reason they should stay clear of our armored vehicles. The inexperienced infantrymen occasionally suffered severe losses due to this practice. . . .

While these [Tigers and Panthers] could fire with a good chance for a hit at ranges far above 1000 meters, we engaged the enemy at ranges between 300 and 1000 meters. This means that the T-34 was far more dangerous for us than for the Tiger or the Panther. The Russian KV I heavy tank we encountered on occasion was a real problem for us.

Sometimes we did receive notification about the assembly of enemy forces in their rear via returning Luftwaffe airplanes. Our Stuka liaison officer would receive these messages on his radio band and hand them to us. Sometimes we could hear the enemy assembling for an attack in the evening. When 40 to 50 tanks are careening through the countryside seeking cover then that does create quite a racket. Drawing the proper conclusions from all this information was something that experience in battle taught us. We did have a few good leaders with the right instincts for this. . . .

I still recall two events particularly well which occurred during the first few days of the operation. We had just obtained the usual hedgehog-position out on an open field one evening, when all of the sudden we were hit by a murderous air attack. A veritable carpet of bombs was raining down on us. This concentration of bombs was also hitherto unseen.

The second thing was a fierce battle against dug-in T-34 tanks when we attempted to penetrate the enemy's second line of defense. According to my recollection it was here in the Syirtsev area where we had the highest casualty rate in the entire operation. . . .

The most dangerous situations were the combination of mine obstacles and massive artillery and mortar fire. Second in line would be fighting the dug-in tanks and the heavy KV I tanks. Furthermore, I should mention the attacks flown by Soviet fighter planes, while counterattacks by Soviet armored formations usually posed no problem for us.

Captain Frantz, commander, Gross Deutschland Assault Gun Battalion

We had relatively few casualties in the assault gun battalion throughout the entire operation. The most dangerous enemy I can recall were the tanks that had dug in up to their turret line. As customary with the Russians, they were extremely well camouflaged. These tanks were relatively successful when exchanging fire, because they could fire a targeted round at short range. Secondly, I should mention the artillery and mortar fire which was usually combined and right on target in hitting our troops. Our infantry, however—lacking armor protection—in turn suffered heavy casualties. Enemy air power did not play any decisive role, and enemy tanks—when attacking—were not very dangerous due to the tactics employed.

Lt. Burchardi, Gross Deutschland Artillery Regiment:

I did not get the impression that the enemy was fighting more tenaciously than we knew him to be. We were surprised by the extensive system of fortifications as well as the superiority in terms of material, particularly that of artillery units. In addition it was obvious that the enemy had been excellently prepared for combat between these systems for defense.

The Soviet artillery fired with remarkable precision. Together with the numerous mortars and in combination with mine obstacles, the Soviet artillery was by far the most dangerous enemy.

The enemy's ground attack airplanes entered into the fight on the ground every now and then and also unloaded their bombs at night. All in all we did not think they were all that significant, though.

Lt. Emminghaus, commander 6th company, II Battalion, Gross Deutschland Fusilier Regiment:

Regarding the enemy, I want to repeat that he staunchly defended his positions. While fighting the enemy positions was our main task, this did not incur the majority of casualties. The worst situations were created when we came upon one of the many minefields, causing our own movement to seize while we were immediately caught under enemy artillery fire. This remains ingrained in my memory. Us infantrymen were particularly afraid of the enemy mortars as well as the Katyusha rocket launchers. These situations caused most of our casualties.

While we did not experience any unexpected situations during the attack, the precision and swift action the enemy exhibited in directing artillery fire on our troop concentrations did indeed surprise us and left us with the impression that we would have to fight our way through deeply stretched defenses. This had not been clear from the beginning. The second thing we did not expect was the enormous use of material by the enemy, particularly in terms of artillery.

A real surprise indeed were the numerous dug-in T-34 tanks. These were for our tanks to deal with, however, not us. Generally, I did witness a few counterattacks by enemy armored formations, but these did not affect us as infantrymen. Our tanks and assault guns clearly ruled on the battlefield. I also remember a few sorties flown by the Red Air Force, which also occurred at night, but did not have any measurable affect on the course of the attack.

Captain Wackernagel,[2] commander, I Battalion, Gross Deutschland Fusilier Regiment:

When I would reflect on what impressed me most in these three days I saw of *Operation Citadel*, I came to these conclusions: first of all, there was this deeply staggered system of defenses, which I had not expected in this fashion. Secondly, the extensive mine fields, which I had not seen in this expanse in any previous engagement. And the third item would be the extremely precise and intense enemy artillery fire, which was proof of an extensive preparation and very skillful leadership of the defense on the part of the enemy.

Officer Cadet Guenther Baer, tank commander, II Battalion, Leibstandarte SS Adolf Hitler Panzer Regiment:

The Soviet soldiers offered fierce resistance whenever encountered. But, this did not impair smooth progress of our armored formations' attack. Later

---

2 Eberhard Wackernagel was interviewed by Maj. Gen. (ret.) Dieter Brand on 10 April 2000. Mr. Eberhard Wackernagel was born 21 September 1917. He was a volunteer and an officer candidate since 1 April 1936. He first served with the 5th Infantry Regiment in Stettin, then with the Gross Deutschland Infantry Regiment. He participated in the French Campaign as First Lieutenant and platoon leader, then company commander. He then fought in the Balkans in 1941 and in Russia 1941–43, during the course of which he was severely wounded several times. He ended the war as a regimental commander on the Western Front. His awards included the German Cross in Gold, Army Leaves of Honor Clasp, Iron Cross 1st and 2nd Class, and Wound Badges.

Upon commencement of *Operation Citadel*, he was a captain and commander of the I Battalion in the Gross Deutschland's Fusilier Regiment. He had belonged to the old Gross Deutschland Regiment since 1939 and participated in all engagements of the regiment since the crossing of the Maas in May 1940. As such, Mr. Wackernagel was one of the seasoned and experienced leaders in the Gross Deutschland Division. He assumed command of the battalion on 21 May 1943 following convalescence after a severe injury.

Mr. Wackernagel studied agriculture after the war, ending his career as director of an agricultural bank.

on, the many minefields and the antitank ditches did. Surmounting these obstacles always took a lot of time and preparation.

We were definitely superior in direct engagement of enemy tanks. Time and again we obliterated the enemy counterattacks without suffering any casualties worth mentioning. Much more dangerous were the defense lines set up with antitank guns. These were extremely well camouflaged and opened fire only at short range.

Minefields and antitank defense lines were the worst for us. Soviet units let us come on to them at closest range—and these defense lines often consisted of 20 antitank guns. I have never before or again seen minefields of the expanse used in this battle. For this reason, combat reconnaissance was very important for us. Often we had very good aerial photographs. Cooperation with the air force reconnaissance worked very well. Most of the time we had at least a vague idea where large minefields and antitank defense lines had been placed.

Then there was the artillery fire. Soviet artillery always fired in a very methodical and precise manner. But even more discomforting for us than the artillery was the fire from enemy mortars. The Soviets had a lot of those. The mortars were so dangerous for us tank crews because of their steep trajectory. A tank being hit by a mortar shell from above usually meant a total loss. My unit lost two tanks with their crews to mortar fire. We always had the advantage against enemy tanks.

The enemy infantry was also not an adversary who could have stopped us. The enemy's air force played no role in our engagements. I don't recall the air force attacking us, but they did attack the supply columns.

My tank company didn't really have any particular casualties. But compared to anything I saw later in the war, our infantry suffered heavily from artillery fire in the night from July 4/5.

What really surprised us was the size of their minefields. Their size and expanse could not be imagined. Other than that nothing surprised us. However, in the course of the attack it became clear just how many tanks the enemy had at his disposal. Their numbers never seemed to be depleted, although we were hitting so many of them. We were not afraid of the enemy, but the amount of his tanks was distressing.

Richard Rosen, 503rd Heavy Panzer (Tiger) Battalion:

I want to emphasize once more that we on the lower command levels, i.e. platoon leaders and surely including the company commander, had not expect such fierce fighting and such steadfastness on the part of the enemy. This surprised us all, and the Russians fought so bitterly as to simply gain our respect.

However, this did not serve to diminish the belief in our own superiority over the adversary. We felt superior as always. After all, we had a few commanders in our Tiger battalion, who had accomplished in excess of 100 enemy tank kills. We did clearly notice the enemy's advantage in terms of material throughout the fighting, though. The most dangerous enemy for us was the SU-152 assault gun and the antitank guns of varying calibers. These caused the greatest number of hits. Some Tigers had been hit so badly that a repair was no longer worthwhile. They were cannibalized for parts at the maintenance company. But the Tiger could take such an awesome amount of hits that it did give us the air of superiority and security in battle. This is why we could roll towards and roll over the antitank lines, i.e. the antitank guns—which the Panzer IV, not to mention the Panzer III, were unable to do because of their weak armor.

I remember only a limited amount of enemy armor, in the first days there was none at all. I did not see any counterattacks by Soviet armored formations in our sector. I also do not remember encountering any American tanks, which were, however, apparently seen by the 6th Panzer Division.

The enemy air force played no significant role in

our attack sector. Actually, I only remember the sole Soviet airplanes which would fly over our positions at night and drop a bomb here and there. Those were the "Ratas" as we called these planes, and we were familiar with them from previous campaigns.

I have not seen any example of failure due to psychological stress. On the contrary, I had unlimited confidence into the leadership capability of my highly experienced commander of the 25th Panzer Regiment, then Lieutenant Colonel Schulz. He proved his worth anew on a daily basis.

I do have a list of the personnel losses in our 3rd company:

July 6	near KRUTOI LOG	2 dead
	near BATRATSKAYA DACHA	4 dead
July 8	near MYASOYEDOVO	1 dead
July 11	???	1 dead
July 12	???	1 dead

This includes some soldiers from our maintenance echelon, who had come to the front to carry out repairs on our tanks and were killed during enemy artillery raids.

We always brought back our dead. They were buried next to the maintenance company at Tavrovo to the west of Solomino.

Alfred Rubbel, 503rd Heavy Panzer (Tiger) Battalion:

Combat was mainly born by the main battle tanks. We ruled on the battlefield. Also, we engaged every fire from enemy armor and always decided such an exchange in our favor. I do recall several counterattacks by Soviet armored formations, but not in large numbers. I did not see the Soviets enter into counterattacks by stampeding ahead in great accumulations of tanks, all of them moving and firing at the same time.

I rarely exchanged fire with enemy main battle tanks at the farthest possible range of 2500 meters, although our excellent 88mm tank gun did give us the capability of opening fire early on. I used the 1000 meter range setting, which gave me a defacto range from 500 to 1600 meters with every round resulting in certain destruction.

Our Tiger tanks could absorb quite a few hits during battle. When our Tiger got hit there was a muzzled explosion. The air immediately reeked of iron oxide, the paint cracked in the interior and often the bolts which held equipment attached to the turret's interior were torn off. This also represented a hazard for the crew. The first reaction was therefore always a roll call to see whether anyone got hurt.

To me the most dangerous place seemed to be the commander's copula. This protruded a whole 40 centimeters past the top edge of the turret. The word had apparently been spread among the Russians to aim directly on the commander's copula with their antitank guns. In any case, we did have a number of battle damages with the copula shot away. Occasionally this would mean the loss of the tank commander, who would have his head torn off in the process.

Our Tiger was most vulnerable on the running gear on its side.

We had fire support from our artillery, an artillery liaison officer was always taken along to the front, occasionally in a Tiger with company headquarters.

However, the artillery was often hard pressed to follow suit with our advance. Quite often, combat situations arose where we would have needed the artillery but it was not available.

Soviet artillery was a stark contrast to that as they had obviously prepared very well for the engagements. As soon as we had to come to a halt on the battlefield, be it due to tank obstacles or other disturbances, we were immediately targeted by enemy artillery fire. This was obviously aimed according to the best observation. A direct hit on the turret of a Tiger usually meant a total loss but did not necessarily entail loss of life among all crew members. But they would most certainly have severe wounds and burns. When caught by artillery fire we always tried to avoid it by moving forward or backwards.

Most unpleasant was the enemy's 173mm artillery [probably means 152mm], featuring an exceptionally high muzzle velocity and penetration capability.

Aside from the artillery I gruesomely remember their mortars. Enemy tank formations, however, were no adversary that could stop us.

The enemy's air force may have flown over our area, but I don't recall any particular effects.

There was no sustained support effort by our Stukas in our sector. While we did observe an attack by three or five planes towards targets in the enemy's rear every now and then, these attacks did not occur close enough to our spearheads for us to make use of them in respect to our own advances.

The Stukas' bombs had a devastating effect on enemy contingents. I passed through several artillery positions which had been hit by Stukas. There were hardly any bomb craters, only large circles of burnt grass. Bodies of the enemy crews had obviously been torn literally to pieces by the pressure waves generated by the exploding bombs and their artillery pieces had been hurled through the air. Such a Stuka sortie, even if it consisted of only a few planes, was much more effective than our own artillery.

Apart from that, cooperation with the air force took place whenever one of their reconnaissance planes returned from a mission over enemy territory, and dropped a message container while flying at low altitude past our line. In this manner we sometimes learned about enemy formations located in assembly areas in the enemy's rear.

I recall a multitude of minefields with wooden box mines. They were practically everywhere. We never had enough engineers along with us so that even us tank crews had to disembark on occasion and make a corridor using the mine-probing rod. The effect of such a wooden box mine on a Tiger tank was only limited. Enough pressure could escape through the gaps between the track-links of our chain-link tracks. Hitting a mine never caused a total loss, but often caused damage on the track and trailing arms. Occasionally this resulted in decreased mobility of the tank necessitating a diversion to the maintenance company.

After hitting a mine my tank went on for another two days with a damaged trailing arm and was even used for combat reconnaissance.

Aside from these minefields there was an incredible variety of other mine obstacles. The Russians were masters in setting up such obstructions. There were entire fields saturated with anti-personnel mines triggered by tripwires. Setting up these obstacles must have been a Herculean effort. There were even dug-in containers full of incinerating oil also triggered by tripwires. These had much the same effect as flame-throwers.

I do not recall too many deserters from the Soviet side during the days of *Operation Citadel*. I also don't recall any large numbers of prisoners taken.

We as tank crews had no time to worry about that anyway and all enemy soldiers approaching us were usually waved to the rear to meet our infantry.

Like all German units we too had a considerable number of Hiwis. As I learned later on, their number was defined in the Authorized organization (Table of Organization and Equipment) to be 40 Hiwis. We only had the most positive relations with these people. They served faithfully, usually in the rear at the combat train, but sometimes also as motorcycle messengers. Some of our Hiwis had relatives living in Kharkov and some of them took their relatives along with them during the retreat following *Operation Citadel*.

Our fallen soldiers were always recovered. We would take them along, wrapped into tent sections, on the rear engine cover. That was a matter of honor for us. The killed were turned over to the company's sergeant major later on, who took care of a dignified and official burial. I never saw us bury our dead right there on the spot. Later on, during the heavy battles of retreat, we were not always able to recover our fallen comrades.

I did not notice any fundamental flaw in our units' preparation during the days of the attack. In hindsight, however, I must note that the very limited level of information we as common soldiers received was a severe deficiency. At the time, I didn't feel that way because we were completely absorbed by the daily business of war. I do want to recall two shortcomings in terms of our units' training, though. It did occur a few times that our Tigers were hit by friendly fire, which originated from the regiment's tanks, but particularly from the assault guns. Given that it was a new tank, many soldiers at the front had no idea of the Tiger's existence. While we did visit a few regiments in June in order to introduce the tank following an order from above, this did not prevent the aforementioned incidents.

The second problem was due to our unarmored infantry's conduct as it accompanied us in immediate vicinity during an attack. We would then take the infantry along piggyback on our tanks as long as possible. When they had to disembark in the course of battle, they would have an incurable urge to attach themselves to the rear of our tanks. One could see why, because the Tiger gave the impression of safety, much like a fortress. On the other hand, this was the most dangerous place, because naturally we attracted the enemy's fire resulting in higher casualty rates with the infantry behind us compared to them fanning out over a wider area. That was a bad habit you couldn't get rid of, and a clear sign of serious flaws in terms of training and experience among the leaders on lower levels in the infantry.

As to my recollection the days of battle during this operation were lacking in any kind of drama of the kind we would experience later on, in liberating the Cherkassyi cauldron, for instance—which was clearly a matter of life and death for 40,000 comrades. Compared to that, the days attacking in the area eastward of Belgorod were almost normal days of combat as the objective was merely territorial gain. This is also apparent in our casualty figures, which were very limited. I believe my battalion only had four or five total losses. Neither do our kill ratios speak for a dramatic attack in our sector. As far as I recall, my company shot maybe 20 enemy tanks or so in these battles, most of them on July 11 and 12. Later on, at Cherkassyi, we destroyed 57 enemy tanks with our 10 remaining Tigers in the time from 2 October through 16 October, 1944. These figures emphasize the varying level of intensity among these battles. However, the situation may have been different for other sectors of the operation, i.e. for the SS divisions or for the Gross Deutschland Division.

DID THE GERMAN SOLDIERS KNOW THEY WERE DEFEATED?

Officer Cadet Guenther Baer, Leibstandarte SS Adolf Hitler Division:

Actually, we thought we were always being successful. But I particularly recall the aforementioned engagement of "parading" enemy tanks at Byikovka and Stalinsk. That same feature was also noticeable in an attack on the Psel sector.

On the evening of the 12th we still thought the attack would continue, particularly given the enormous success we had on that day. Our casualties were not that high and we were still strong enough to fight. Then on the 13th, we heard that the attack may be aborted because there had been a deep penetration in the area of the Das Reich SS Division to our right. That was when we became a bit uneasy. However, the troops remained in the positions that had been reached for several more days. They could make no sense of it when indeed they were eventually called back.

First Lt. Heinz Macher, Das Reich SS Division:

During the days the attack went on, I had gathered the overall impression that we always had an advantage over the Soviet forces. In fact we pretty much decided every engagement in our favor. However, the fighting spirit of the Soviet forces was remarkable. They often fought without ever backing down. As I later learned, some of their troops had already seen action at Stalingrad. Their morale was much different from what we had seen before. Add to that the enemy's advantage in terms of material. The sheer agglomeration of equipment was simply beyond imagination.

Officer Cadet Kendziora, Das Reich SS Division:

When we were ordered to retreat, I believe on the 16th, no one on our level understood this and we were very embittered by it.

Private Kurt Kaufmann, Das Reich SS Division:

The depression that made itself felt towards the end of the battle was by no means caused by a notion that we had been beaten on the battlefield. On the contrary: we felt superior to the enemy at the beginning and we were just that throughout the battle. We decided every engagement in our favor be this attack or defense. We always ruled on the battlefield despite the sometimes incomprehensible and death-defying heroism displayed by the Soviet soldiers who often wanted to run over us in masses and were thus annihilated in such amounts. But one thing had become apparent to every soldier by the end of the battle. The Soviets could apparently avail themselves of inexhaustible reserves. We could destroy as many enemy forces as we pleased, the next morning brought back just as many new ones.

Alfred Rubbel, 503rd Heavy Panzer (Tiger) Battalion:

As the operation was winding down for us in the Kurakovka area when we had been able to make contact with the II SS Panzer Corps, we did not see this as a setback. Up front and in action we sort of took on the next order of business. Throughout *Operation Citadel* we hadn't been of any high morale anyway, as if this were some kind of battle decisive for victory. This was the third year in Russia for us and by now we had seen our ups and downs. We no longer felt any over exuberance or assurance of victory. It was the prevailing opinion in our battalion anyway—and I don't know why—that we would only pursue an offensive of limited scope during the summer of 1943 in order to fall back behind the Dnepr in the fall so as to spend the winter there.

SOVIET LESSONS LEARNED

The Soviet reports in our possession contain a number of observations about the fighting that are worthwhile noting:

Sixth Guards Army (Chisyakov)[1]

Conclusions:

1. The fighting showed that the practice of organizing antitank defense in the form of antitank strong points completely justified itself.

2. While defending, army artillery staffs should draw up a counter-preparation plan, which, when carried out before the enemy attack, is highly effective and even forces the enemy to delay the start of his attack.

3. The artillery, even 45mm guns, fully justified itself in fighting enemy T-6 tanks. The 45mm fire is considered effective only from a distance of 150–300 meters. The other types of guns may fire from a distance of 500–700 meters.

4. Antitank reserves are of enormous importance, but their commitment into battle must be determined upon the clarification of the direction of the enemy's main tank attack.

5. Artillery fire was highly effective during the battle, and prisoner interrogations have shown that nearly 70% of all enemy losses were due to artillery fire, especially from Katyushas.

6. Practice shows that in defense it is necessary to carry out fire over open sights, using all weapons systems, against enemy equipment and personnel. Moving the weapons up to the forward line not only increases the weapons' effectiveness, but is also good training for their crews.

7. During the offensive's first day our aviation was almost completely inactive, particularly fighter aviation. For the most part, the enemy enjoyed success only because he had a great superiority in the air in the direction of the main blow.

First Tank Army, III Mechanized Corps:[2]

3. The enemy attacked at 1000 hours on 7/06/43 along the corps' left flank with the intention of reaching the Belgorod-Oboyan road. The corps could do little against the enemy's approaching columns, because it lacked powerful artillery, and the Sixth Guards Army's artillery units were being withdrawn from the battle. . . .

13. Corps and brigade commanders failed to show the proper initiative in maneuvering equipment. The corps neither had, nor was it supported by heavy artillery.

14. The corp's defensive actions were poorly covered by our fighter aviation.

15. The intelligence branch worked extremely poorly. An accurate account of our losses was not kept.

Fifth Guards Tank Army (Rotmistrov)[3]

Rotmistrov's report of 30 September, which appears to have been the source of the myth of the Battle of Prokhorovka, noted:

New Developments in the Enemy's Tactics and Equipment

1. The presence of a large number of T-5 tanks and heavy T-6s ("Tigers")—15-20% of their overall total—raised the question of means of combating them for the command. In order to solve the problem, the following is demanded: *(continued)*

1 Report on Sixth Guards Army's Artillery Activities in the Defensive Battles from July 4 through 16, 1943; Fond: 335, Opis: 5122, Delo: 109(1), pages 137–138.

2 Report by Maj. Petukhov, a General Staff representative with the First Tank Army, to the senior General Staff representatives with the staffs of the First Guards Tank Army and Voronezh Front, on the III Mechanized Corps activities during the period 7/06–7/15/43; Fond: 3340, Opis: 1, Delo: 37, pages 1–7.

3 Fond: 332, Opis: 4948, Delo: 19, pages 21 & 22.

a) the T-70 has weak firepower and armament completely unfit for waging combat in modern conditions, and should be gotten rid of;

b) the T-34 should be modernized and be fitted with an 85mm gun and have its armor increased;

c) the army should get a new tank with a more powerful gun (100–107mm) and armor up to 200mm thick; the guns' sighting mechanisms should allow for fire at a distance of three kilometers;

d) T-34s should maneuver more on the battlefield, striving to bypass and hit the Germans' T-5 and T-6 tanks from the side.

2. During their July offensive the Germans used their aviation exclusively for launching massed attacks against our troops to a shallow depth along a narrow sector of the front. But these blows were sufficiently massive that they enabled the enemy's ground forces to move forward.

Given a powerful antiaircraft and fighter defense, the effectiveness of these attacks will be significantly weakened.

During the first period of the Fifth Guards Tank Army's operations our fighter aviation was insufficiently active, but in succeeding days this situation was corrected; German bombers began to appear less frequently in the area and losses due to bombing raids dropped sharply.

Engineering troops played a great role in the battle. The Germans, in withdrawing, mined everything possible, ruining roads and destroying bridges.

The sapper's main work is clearing mines, building bridges over crossings, and fixing roads. The pace of the tank formations' advance depends on how quickly the engineering troops cope with these problems.

Among the shortcomings in organizing the interaction of the combat arms is the insufficient linkage of the activities of tanks and artillery. The artillery, as a rule, falls behind and is tardy in occupying new firing positions, particularly antiaircraft artillery.

Interaction with our air force is also not complete, as the result of which there were some incidents of friendly bombing of our troops in the areas of Prokhorovka and Yakovlevo.

The operations' experience showed that the system of troop training preceding the battle, as well as the preparation of staffs at all levels, was correctly organized. Command-staff exercises carried out by the corps and army staffs made it possible to bring them up to speed and train them for battle management in difficult combat conditions.

In the just conducted battles the tank and artillery troops got a lot of experience in fighting with the German T-6 tanks, which are no longer terrifying and invulnerable. The proof of this is the large number of "Tiger" tanks which the army knocked out or destroyed.

From Fifth Guards Army (Zhadov):[4]

At the end of the day the commander of the Voronezh Front noted that the fighting from July 5–14 showed that insufficient attention was being paid to questions of interaction between the combat arms and

4 Fond: 328, Opis: 4852, Delo: 83, pages 23 & 24.

formations. Commanders and their staffs often reduce the varied questions of organizing a battle to giving orders and do not plan the combat activities of the combat arms to the entire depth of the battle and poorly control their units during the battle.

Mutual communications between neighboring units is poorly organized. Under conditions of a rapidly-changing situation this leads to a disruption of control, and the units' disjointed activities. Once an order is given, it must be communicated to those who will carry it out, while leaving them enough time to organize for battle.

Reserve units should not be committed into battle without detailed familiarization with the situation.

There were serious difficulties in supplying artillery ordnance. In this regard, the army commander reported to the Front commander about the low level of supply for guard's artillery regiment from the High Command Artillery Reserve, and that the great distance of the army's artillery depots on July 15 created a threatening situation in the supply of the 122mm artillery (0.1–0.2 ammo loads, or 15-18 rounds per gun), and asked for permission to use shells from the Front depots, in order to increase supplies up to one ammo load (900 rounds).[5]

At 1830 the army commander, in order to put the expenditure of artillery shells in order, notified his corps and division commanders of instances of the thoughtless expenditure of artillery and mortar supplies.

Formation commanders and their artillery commanders removed themselves from planning the battle and fire control when repelling enemy tank attacks. In the majority of cases (95th Guards Rifle Division and 9th Guards Airborne Division), the units open a disorderly fire with all weapons on the attacking enemy tanks, without controlling it or taking distance into account.

As a result of this lack of control, in three days of fighting we managed to knock out or burn only 108 tanks, while losing 95 guns ourselves.[6]

By July 18 it was necessary to create in the units' mobile ammunition supplies in the following ammo loads: 45mm—1; 76mm—0.8; 122mm—0.6; 120mm—1; the expenditure of which was forbidden without the permission of the army commander.

THE SOVIET GENERAL Staff Study also offered a wide range of conclusions that are not repeated here.[7] Written almost a year after the fact back at Moscow, it is a very curious, heavily vetted document. It should be examined with considerable caution.

5 This was obviously to total ammo load for a regiment, as one ammo load for a 122mm Howitzer or Gun was 80 rounds.

6 Certainly the claim of German tanks losses is high.

7 David M. Glantz and Harold S. Orenstein, *Kursk 1943: The Soviet General Staff Study* (self published, 1997). Originally published as *Sbornik Materialov po Izucheniyu Opyita Voinyi, No 11, Mart–Aprel 1944 g.* [*Collection of Materials for the Study of War Experience, No. 11, March–April 1944*] (Military Publishing House of the Peoples' Commissariat of Defense, Moscow, 1944).

VORONEZH FRONT'S LOSS REPORT[1]

24 July 1943

From the period of defensive battles from 4 to 22 July 1943, the Voronezh Front suffered the following losses:

1. From the period of defensive fighting from 4 to 16 July 1943:
   a. Personnel losses: killed—18,097, wounded—47,272, missing—24,851, captured—29. Total —90,249.
   b. Horses: killed—1295, wounded—333. Total —1628.
   c. Material reports from BT and MV units: tanks irretrievably lost—1204, retrieved—655. Total—1859. Assault guns irretrievably lost—29.
   d. Material reports from GMCh unit: vehicles retrieved from battle—16.
   e. Planes: both shot down and recovered—347.
   f. Artillery equipment: guns of all calibers—1605, mortars—1734, light machineguns—4381, medium machineguns—1634, submachine-guns—35,026, rifles—40,520, antitank rifles—3,247.
   g. Automobiles—137.
2. From the period of our counteroffensive from 16 to 22 July 1943:
   a. Personnel losses: Killed—2481, wounded—7155, missing—1047. Total—10,683.
   b. Horses: killed—550, wounded—107. Total—657.
   c. Material reports from BT and MV units: tanks irretrievably lost—367, retrieved—179. Total—516. Assault guns irretrievably lost—28, retrieved—15. Total 43.
   d. Material reports from GMCh unit: vehicles retrieved from battle—4.
   e. Planes: both shot down and recovered—40.
   f. Artillery equipment: guns of all calibers—108, mortars—162, light machineguns—399, medium machineguns—161, submachineguns—872, rifles—1612, antitank rifles—212.
   g. Automobiles—41.

Chief of Staff of the Front:
Lt. General Ivanov

Chief of Operations Department:
Major General Teteshkin

1 *Russkii Arkhiv: Velikaya Otechestvennaya, Vol 15-4(4), Kurskaya Bitva, Dokumentyi i materialyi 27 Marta–23 Avgusta 1943 goda [Russian Archive: Great Patriotic War, Vol. 15-4 (4), Battle of Kursk, Documents and Materiel, 27 March–23 August 1943].* (Terra, Moscow, 1997), pages 272–273, referencing Fond: 203, Opis: 2843, Delo: 301, page 255.

Maps Section

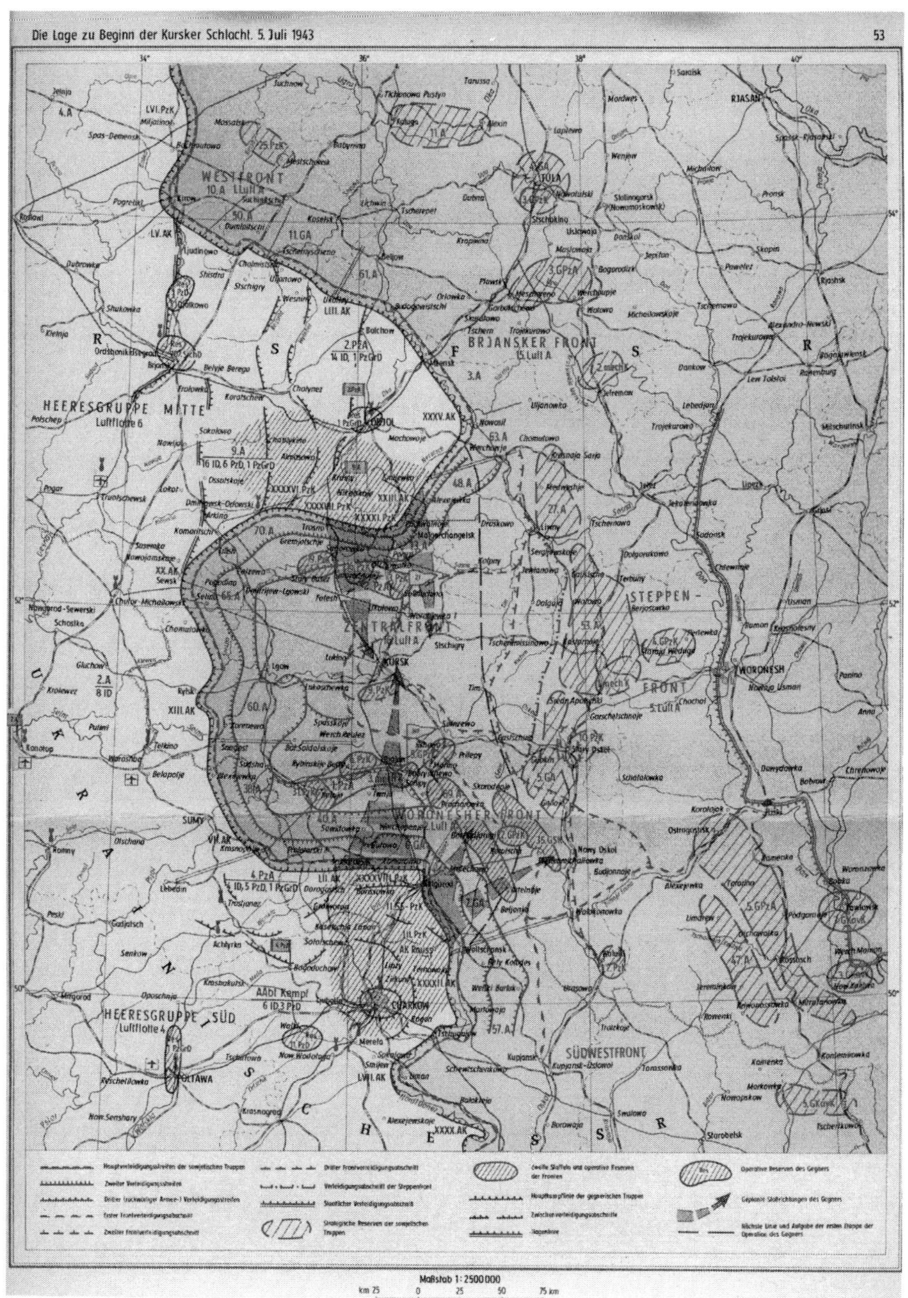

MAP 1: A Soviet map of the Battle of Kursk as translated into German by the East Germans.

It correctly represents the Soviet positions but is riddled with errors on the German positions. For example, the 11th Panzer Division is shown in reserve west of Kharkov as opposed to being in the offensive; the Fourth Panzer Army is shown to consist of five panzer divisions and one panzer grenadier division, vice two panzer divisions and four panzer grenadier divisions; the SS Panzer Corps area of attack is incorrect; the German lines of attack are incorrect; there was no 1st Panzer Grenadier Division in reserve at Poltava, Corps Raus is mis-spelled; and many others.

The map does show the Soviet defensive lines. The key at the bottom shows in order: the Main Defensive Belt of the Soviet Forces, Second Defensive Belt, Third (Rear Army) Defensive Belt, First Front Defensive Line, Second Front Defensive Line, Third Front Defensive Line, Defensive Line of the Steppe Front, and the State Defensive Line. See Chapter Four for a discussion of the significance of these lines.

KARTENBAND, *GESCHICHTE DES GROSSEN VATERLAENDISCHEN KRIEGES DER SOWJETUNION* (MILITAERVERLAG DDR, BERLIN 1975–1985). MAP PROVIDED COURTESY OF ANDERS FRANKSON.

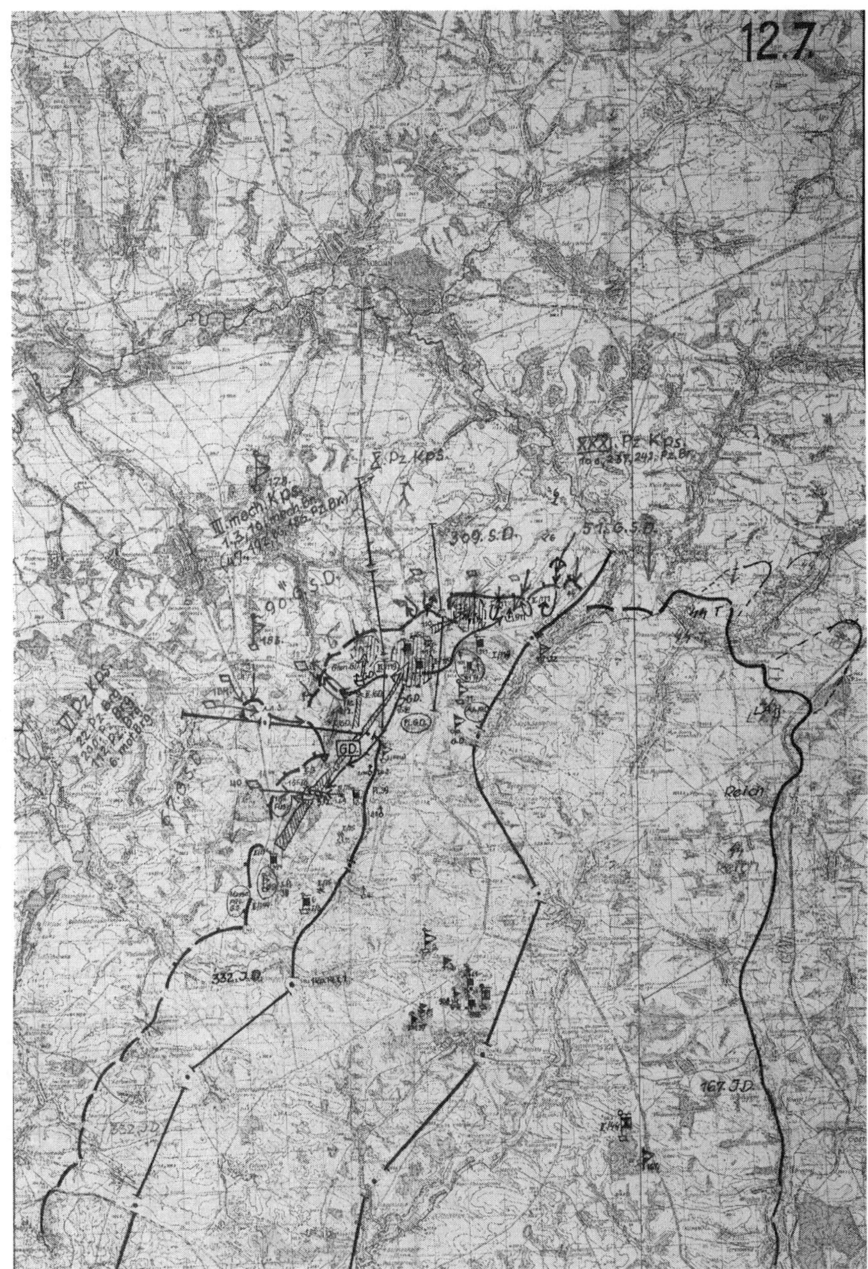

MAP 2: German XLVIII Panzer Corps map for 12 July 1943, 1:100000 scale: covering the area of the XLVIII and SS Panzer Corps offensive, including Oboyan (spelled Obojan on the map) but just shy of Prokhorovka.

There are two kilometers between each grid line and the map covers over 46 kilometers from west to east and over 68 kilometers from south to north. Soviet unit locations and names are based upon German intelligence as of that date, and in some cases are incorrect. COURTESY OF NIKLAS ZETTERLING, BUNDESARCHIV MILITARARCHIV RH 20-8/113 AND RH 24-48/152K.

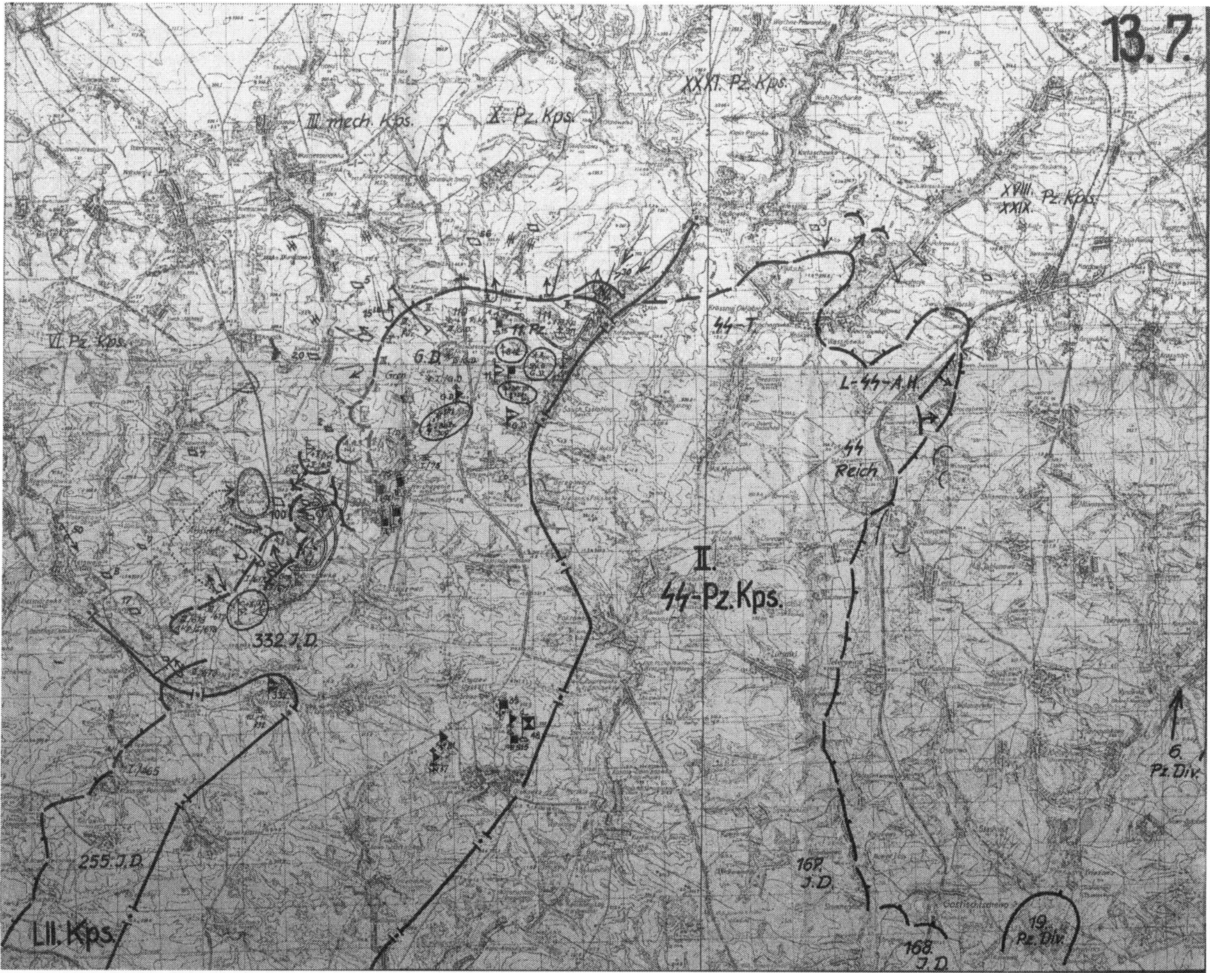

MAP 3: German XLVIII Panzer Corps map for 13 July 1943, 1:100000 scale: covering the area of the XLVIII and SS Panzer Corps offensive and the lead elements of the III Panzer Corps and LII Corps. Map includes Prokhorovka (spelled Prochorowka on the map).

There are two kilometers between each grid line and the map covers 58 kilometers from west to east and over 44 kilometers from south to north. Soviet unit locations and names are based upon German intelligence as of that date, and in some cases are incorrect. COURTESY OF NIKLAS ZETTERLING, BUNDESARCHIV MILITARARCHIV RH 20-8/113 AND RH 24-48/152K.

MAP 4: Soviet General Staff of the Red Army map M-37-25-B from 1942, 1:50000 scale: covering Oboyan (spelled Обоянь) and including the Psel (Псел) River.

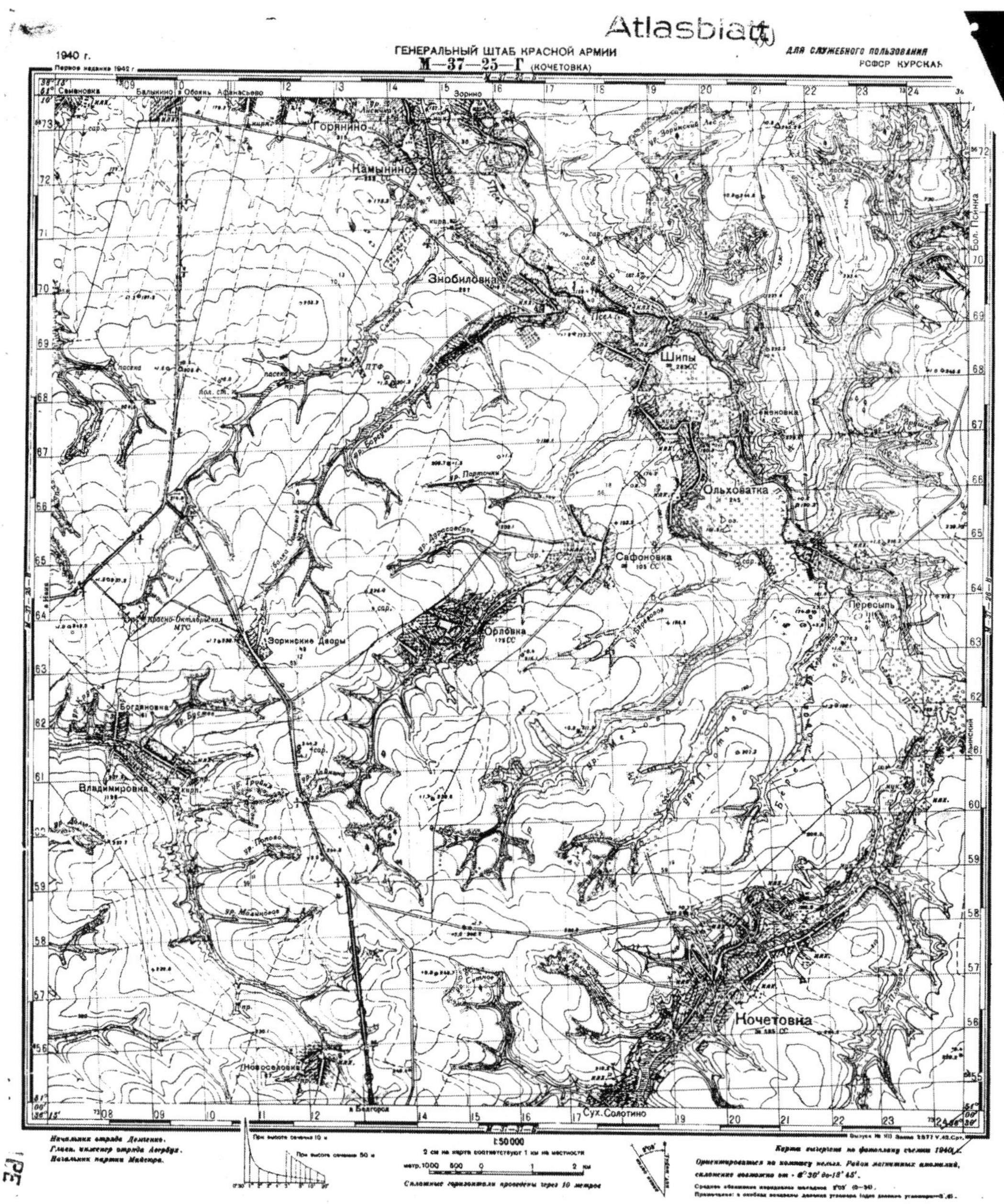

MAP 5: Soviet General Staff of the Red Army map M-37-25-G from 1942, 1:50000 scale: covering Novoselovka (spelled Новоселовка), Kochetovka (Кочетовка) and the Psel (Псел) River.

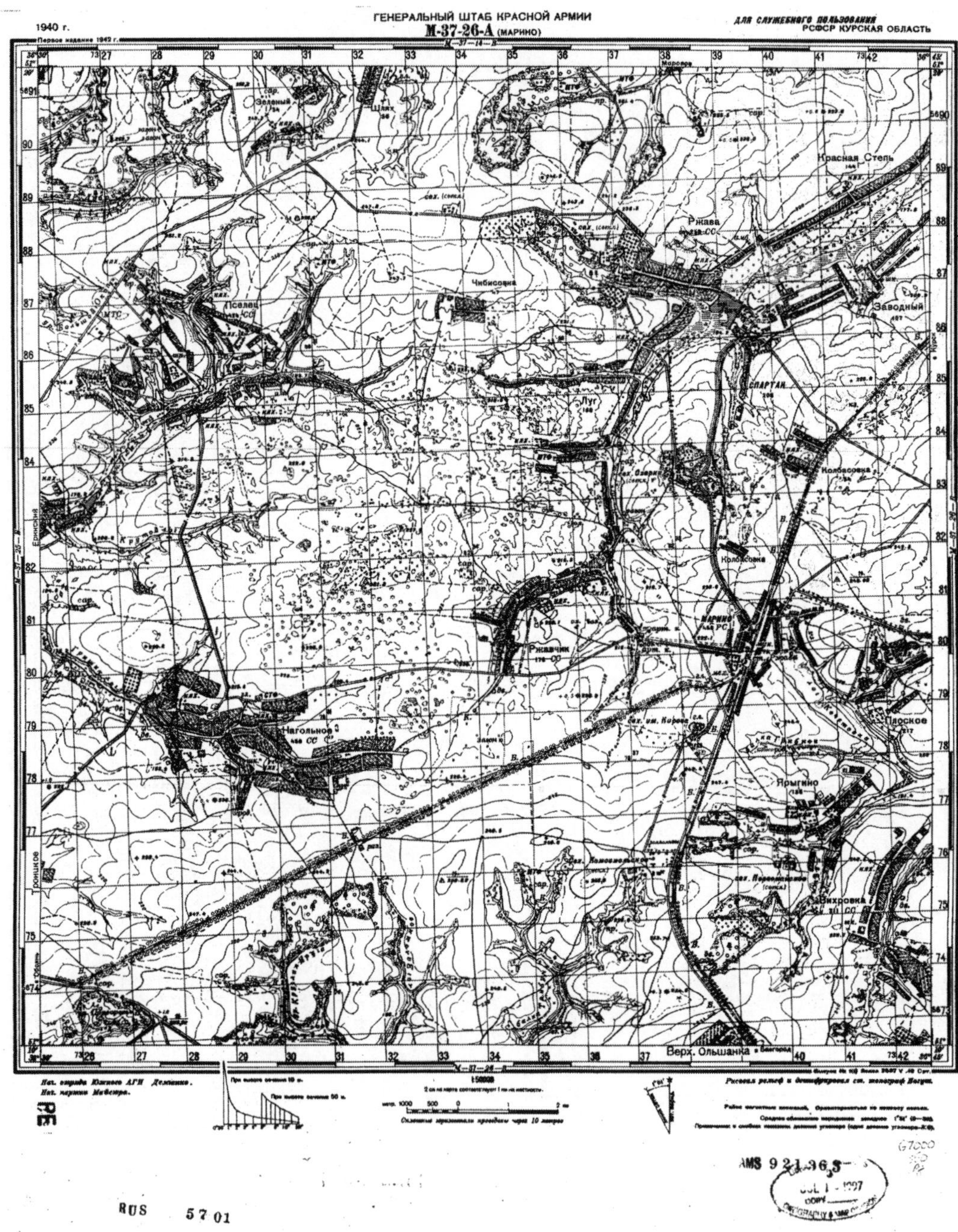

Map 6: Soviet General Staff of the Red Army map M-37-26-A from 1942, 1:50000 scale: covering Marino (Марино) and other areas north of the battlefield.

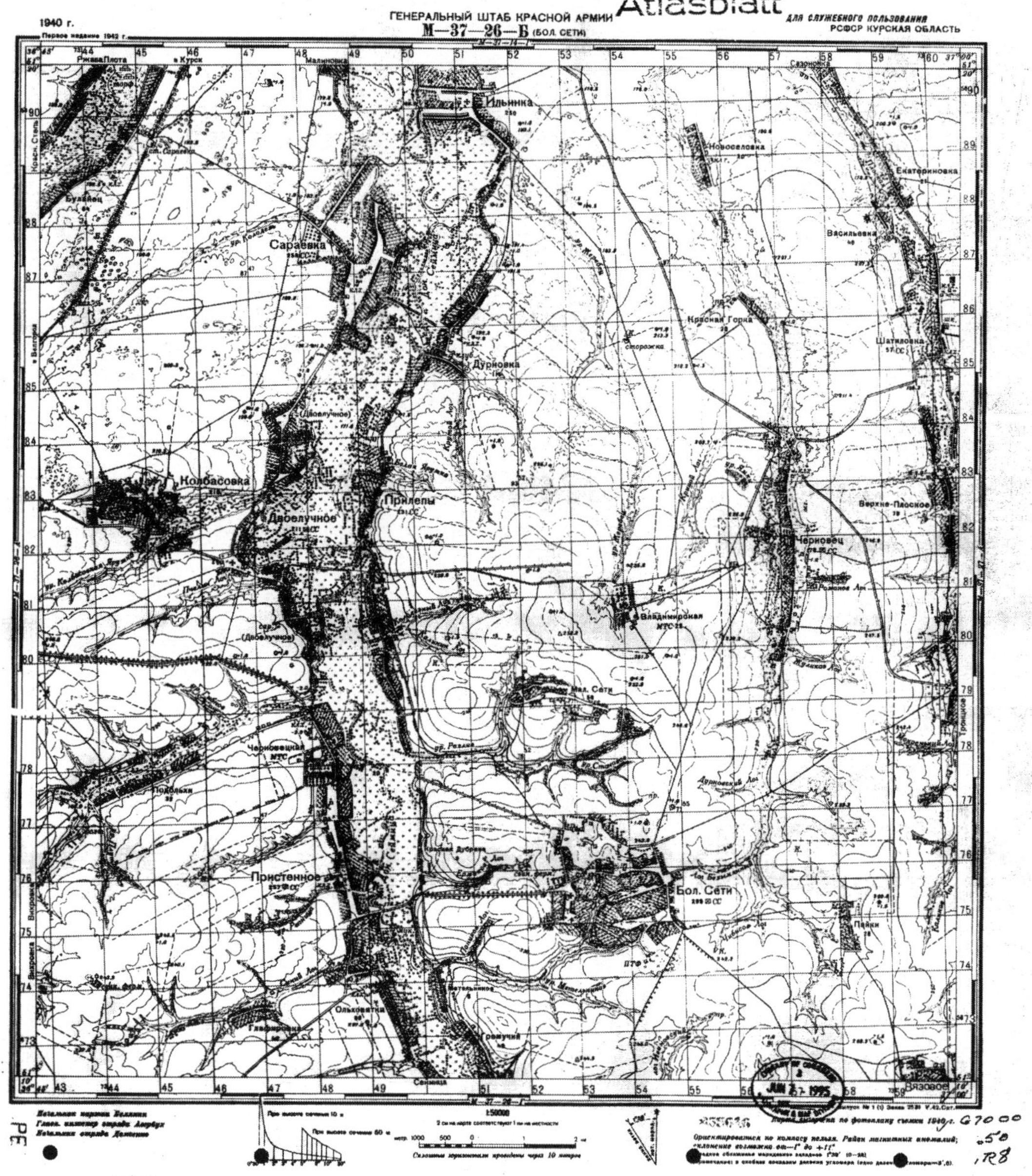

MAP 7: Soviet General Staff of the Red Army map M-37-26-B from 1942, 1:50000 scale: covering the area northeast of the battlefield including the Don Seimitsa (Дон Сеймица) River.

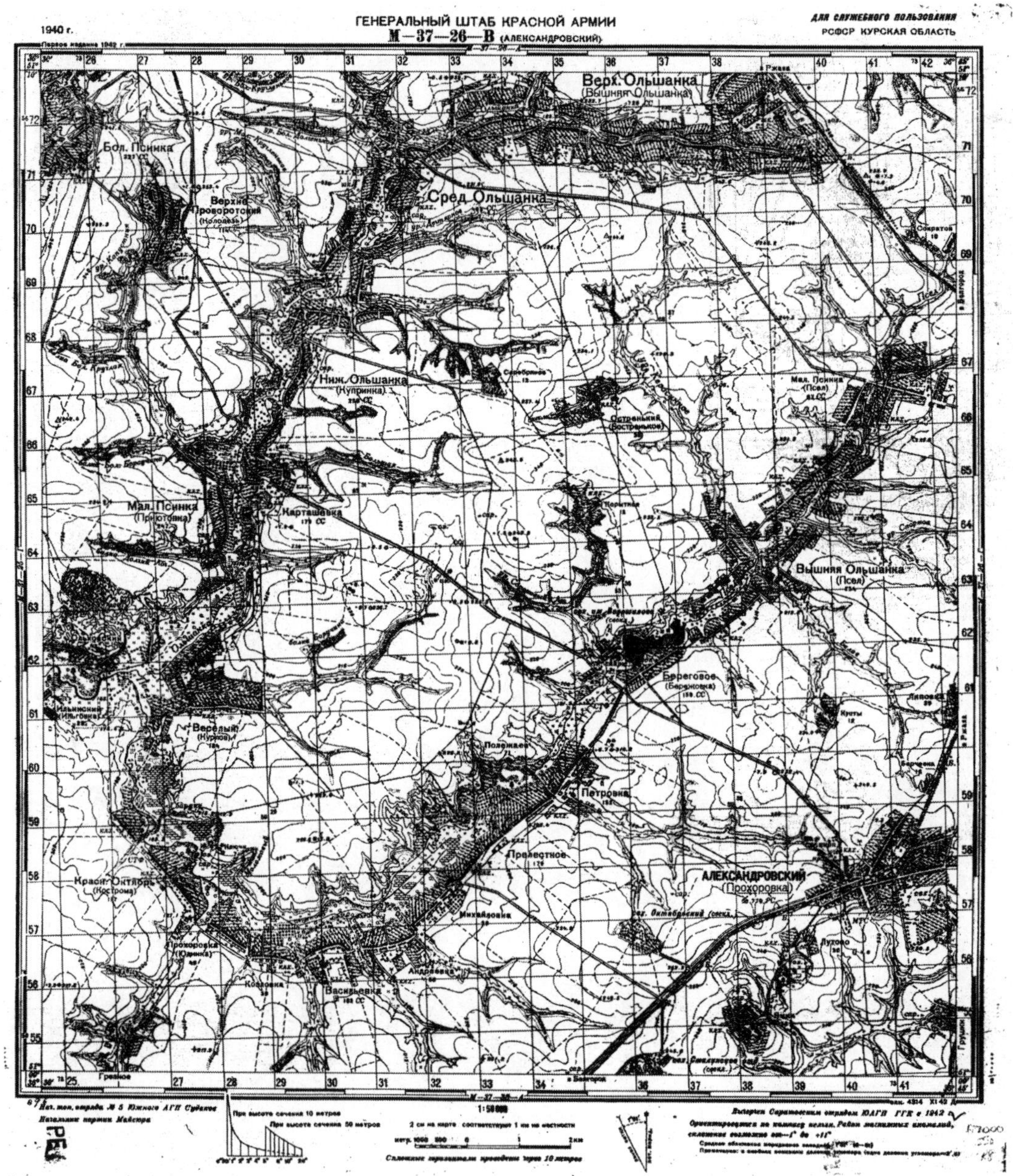

Map 8: Soviet General Staff of the Red Army map M-37-26-V from 1942, 1:50000 scale: covering Veselyii (Веселый), Prokhorovka (Прохоровка), Yamki (Ямки), Stalinskoye Sovkhoz (свх. Сталинское отб) and Oktyabrskii Sovkhoz (свх. Октябрьский).

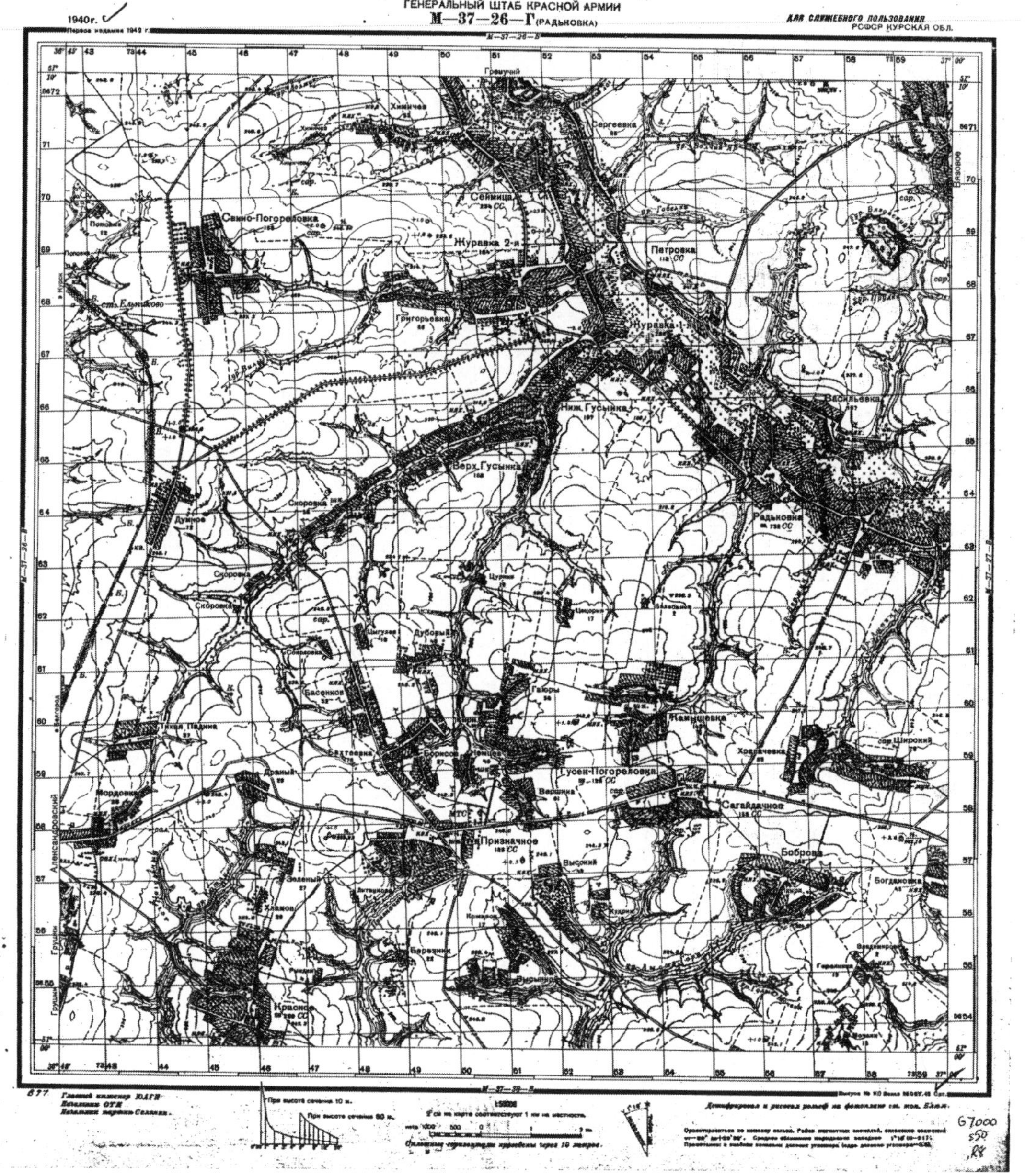

MAP 9: Soviet General Staff of the Red Army map M-37-26-G from 1942, 1:50000 scale: covering the area east of the battlefield including the Don Seimitsa (Дон Сеймица) River.

MAP 10: Soviet General Staff of the Red Army map M-37-37-B from 1942, 1:50000 scale: covering Lukhanino (Луханино), Syirtsev (Сырцев), Pokrovka (Покровка), Yakolevo (Яколево), Syirtsevo (Сырцево) and Verkhopenye (Верхопенье).

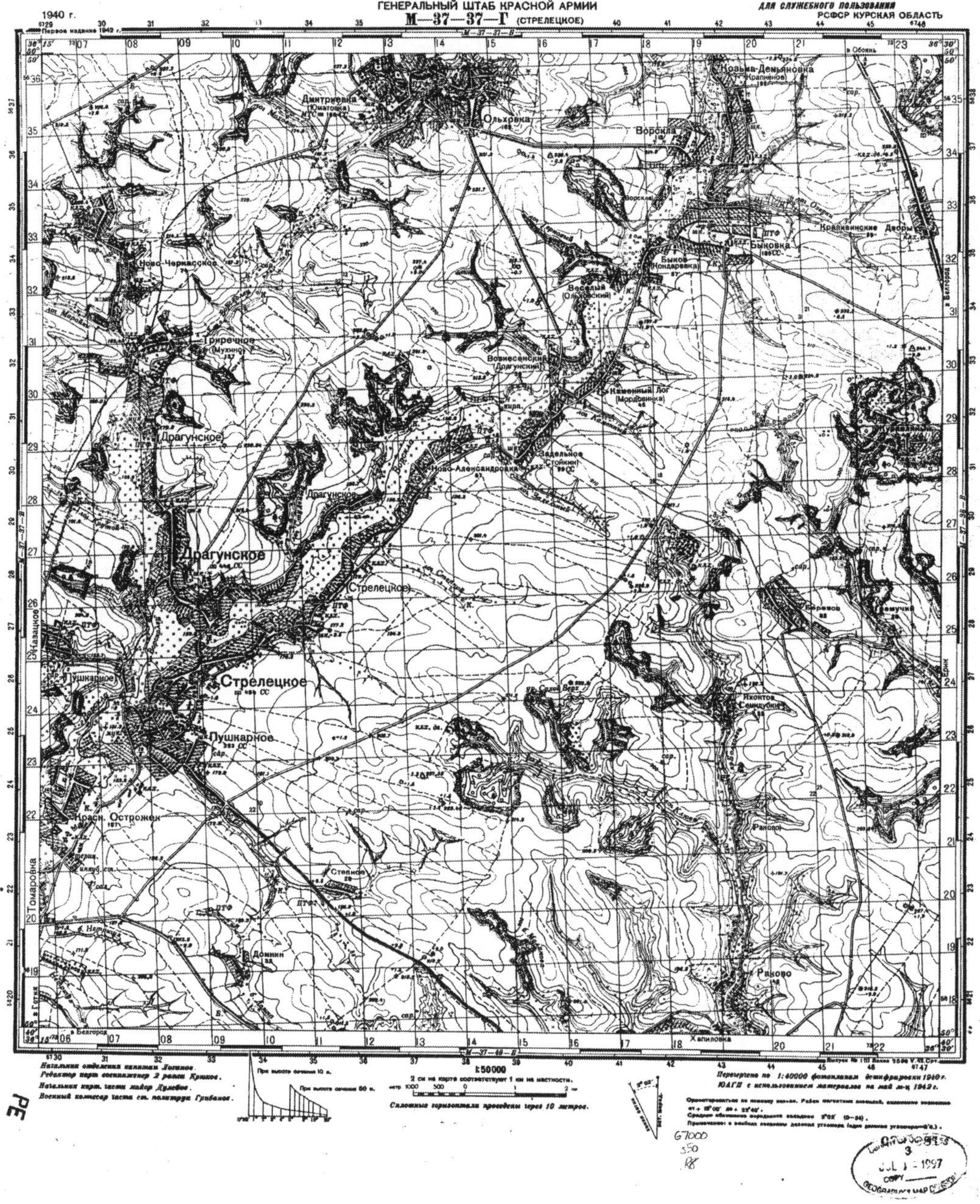

Map 11: Soviet General Staff of the Red Army map M-37-37-G from 1942, 1:50000 scale: covering Dragunskoye (Драгунское), Berezov (Березов), Byikovka (Быковка) and the Vorskla (Ворскла) River.

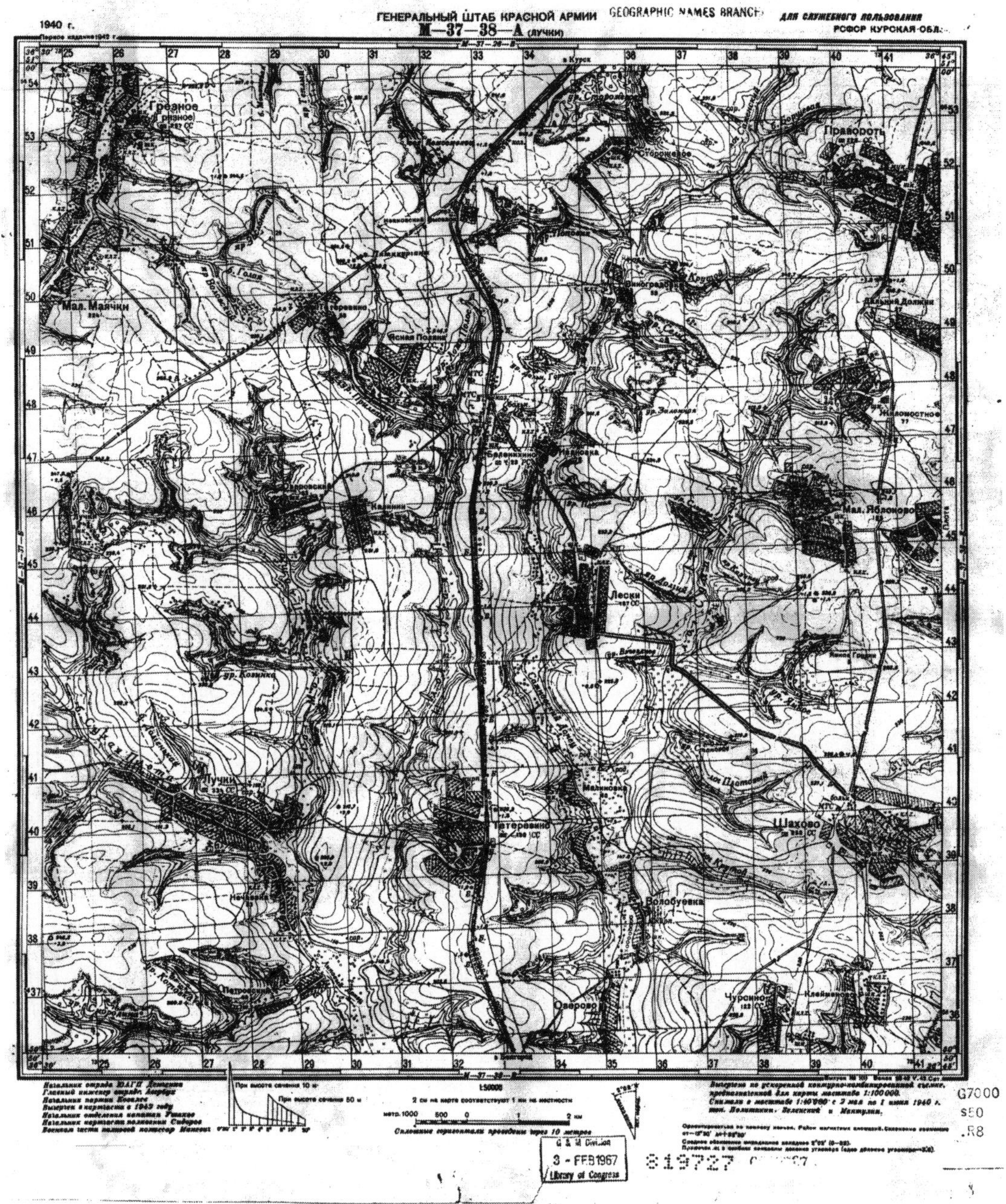

Map 12: Soviet General Staff of the Red Army map M-37-38-A from 1942, 1:50000 scale: covering Luchki (Лучки), Teterevino (Тетеревино), Shakhovo (Шахово), Leski (Лески), Yasnaya Polyana (Ясная Поляна), Storozhevoye Woods (ур. Сторожевое), Greznoye (Грезное), Pravorot (Правопоть) and the Sazhnovskii Donets (Сажновский Донец) River.

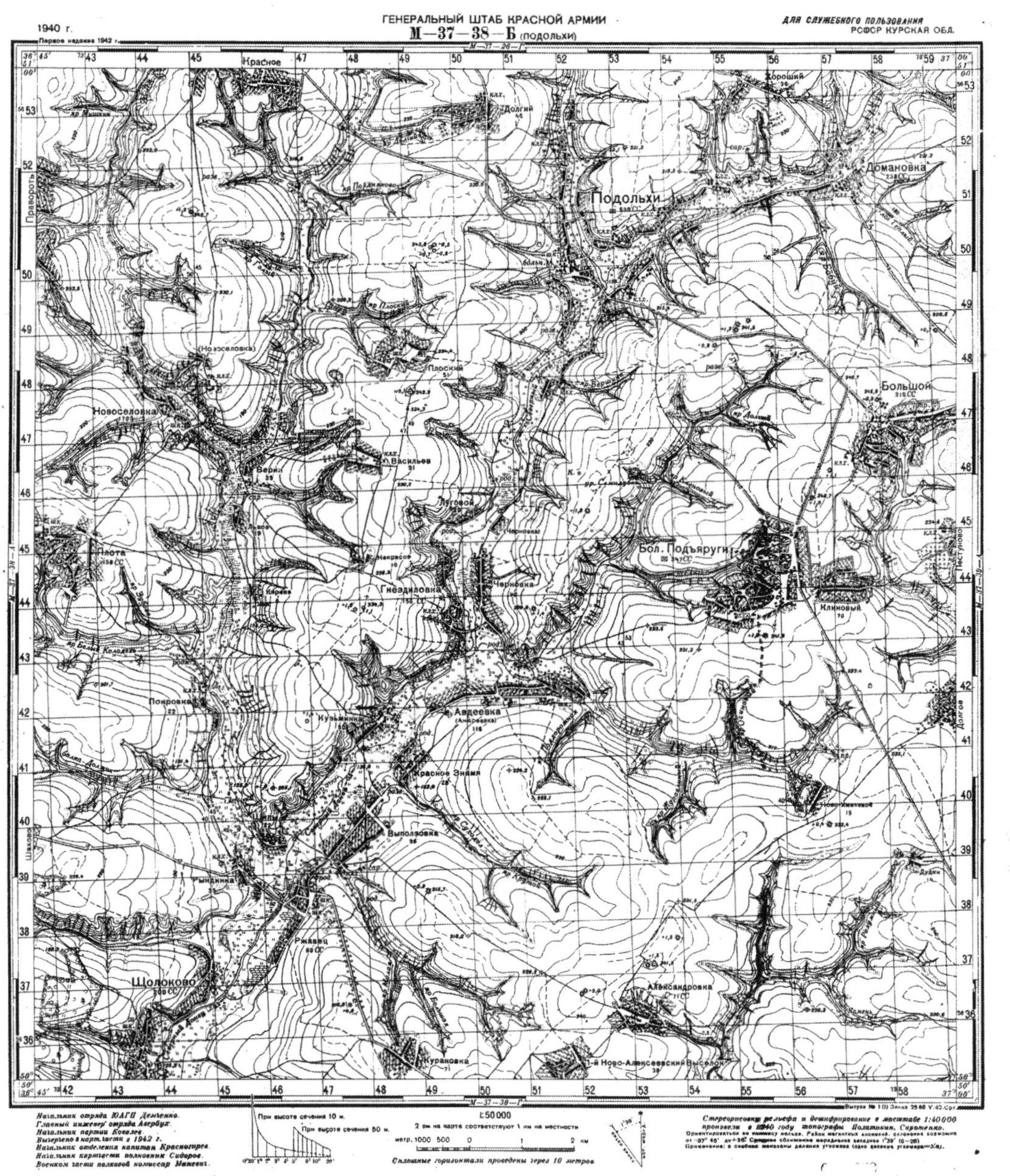

Map 13: Soviet General Staff of the Red Army map M-37-38-B from 1942, 1:50000 scale: covering Shcholokovo (Щолоково), Ryindinka (Рындинка), Avdeyevka (Авдеевка) and the Severnyii Donets (Северный Донец) River.

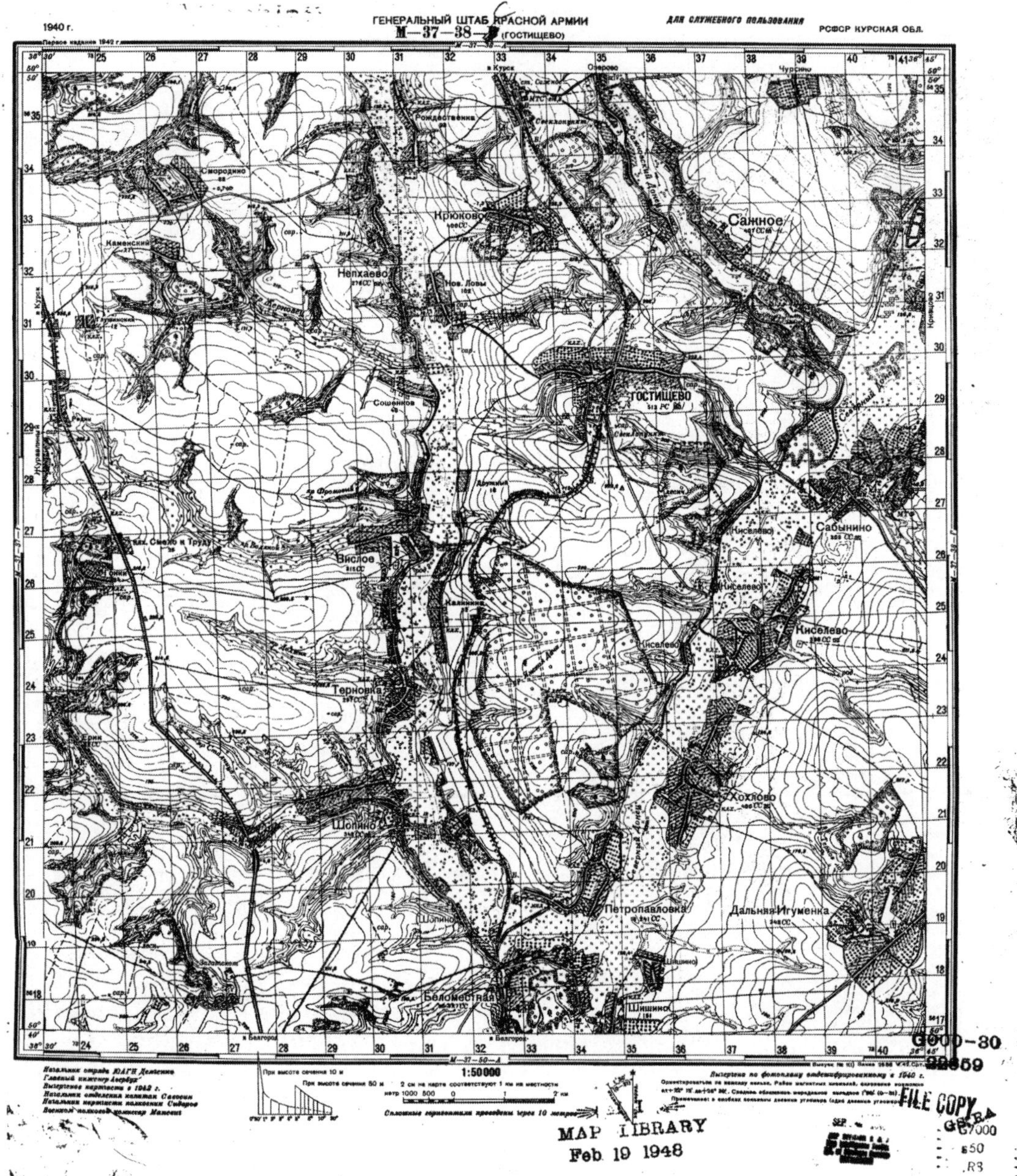

MAP 14: Soviet General Staff of the Red Army map M-37-38-V from 1942, 1:50000 scale: covering the Boldly Towards Labor Kolkhoz (клх. Смело к Труду), Shopino (Шопино), Gostischevo (Гостищево), Sabyinino (Сабынино), Dalnyaya Igumenka (Дальняя Игуменка), and area where the Lipovyii Donets (Липовый Донец) River and the Severnyii Donets (Северный Донец) River meet.

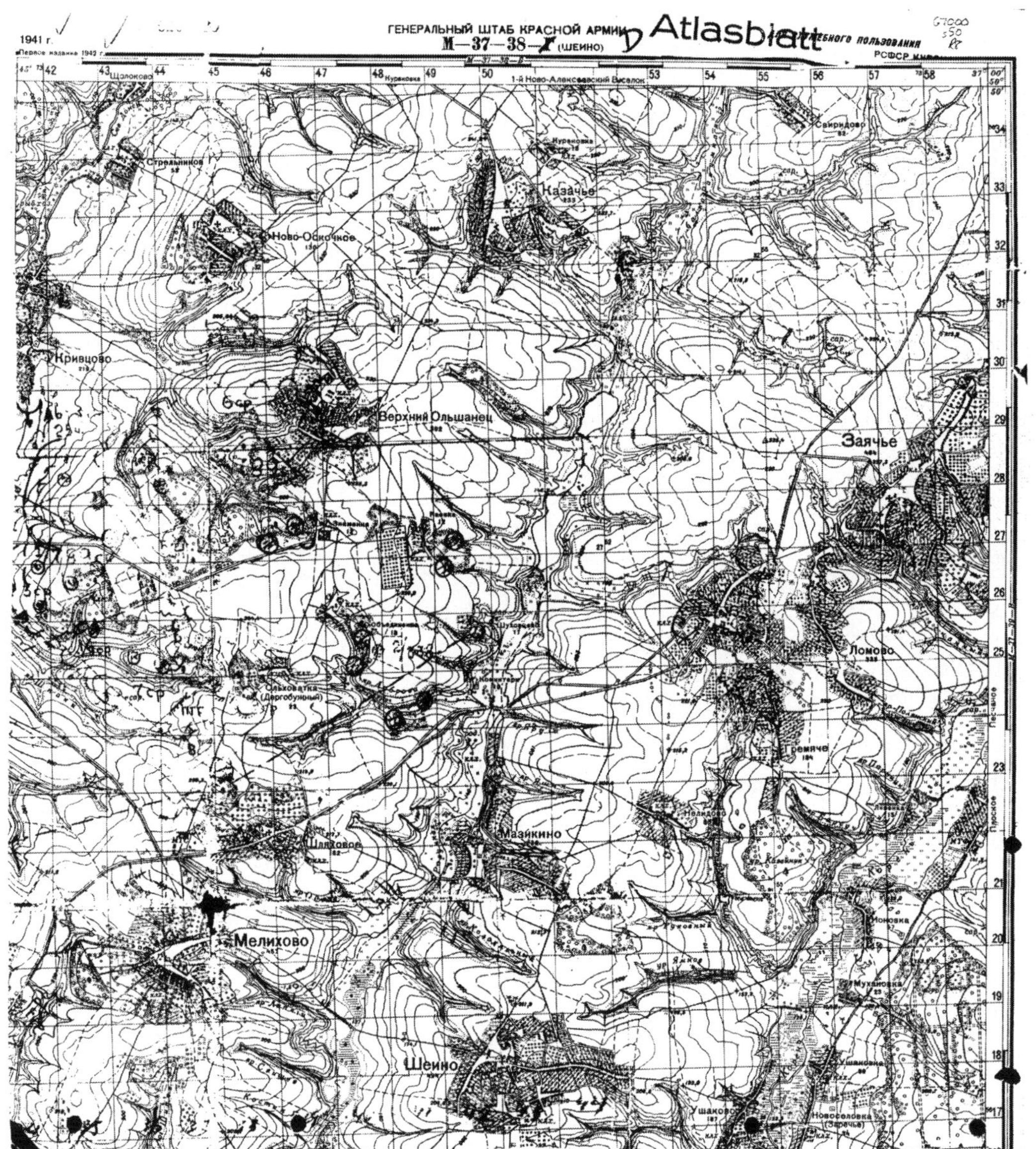

Map 15: Soviet General Staff of the Red Army map M-37-38-G from 1942, 1:50000 scale: covering Melikhovo (Мелихово), Sheino (Шеино), Verkhnii Olshanets (Верхний Ольшанец) and the Razumnaya (Разумная) and Koren (Корень) Rivers.

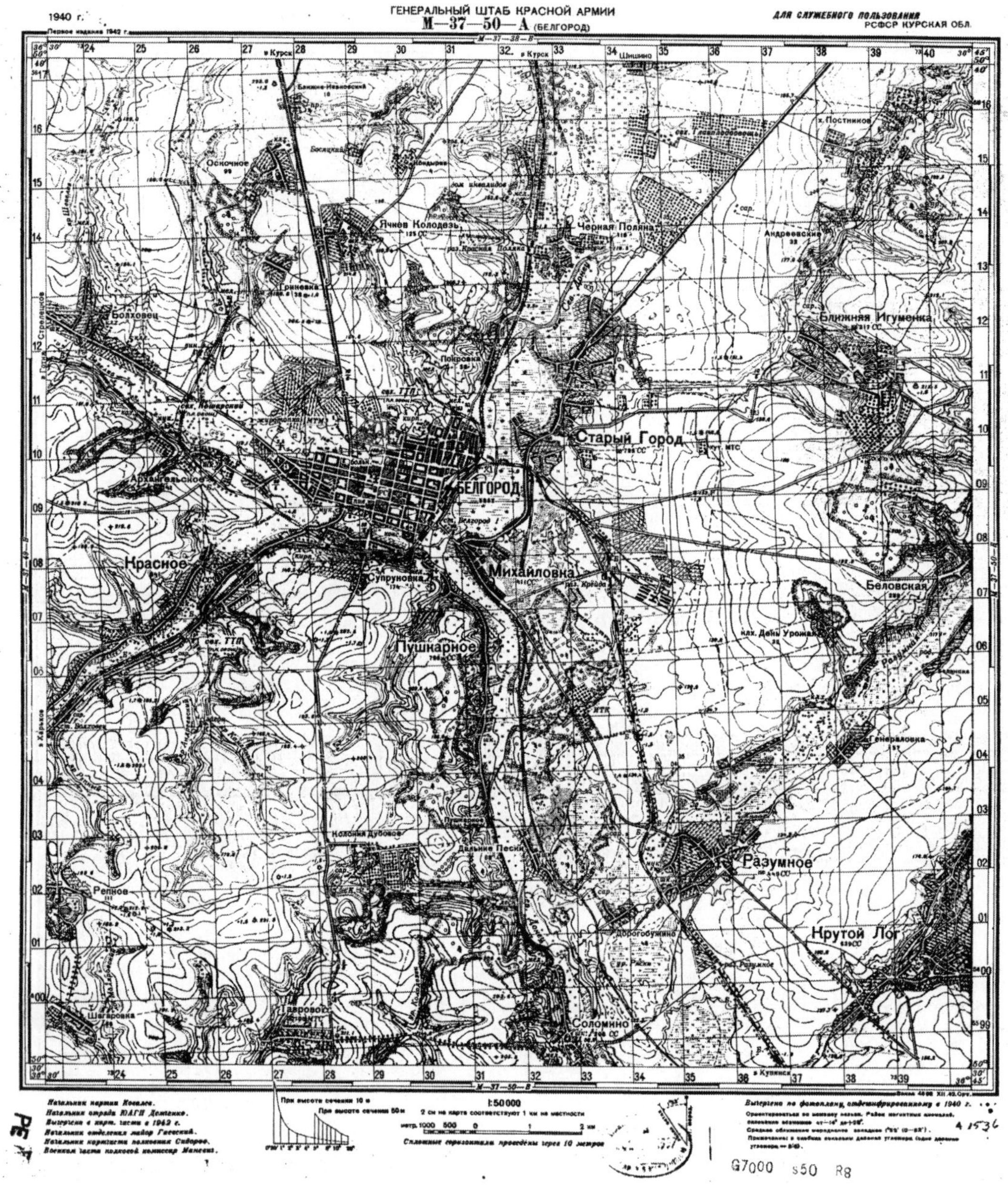

Map 16: Soviet General Staff of the Red Army map M-37-50-A from 1942, 1:50000 scale: covering Belgorod (Белгород), Staryii Gorod (Старый Город), Solomino (Соломино), Razumnoye (Разумное), Krutoi Log (Крутой Лог), Blizhnyaya Igumenka (Ближняя Игуменка), Razumnaya (Разумная) River, and the Severnyii Donets (Северный Донец) River.

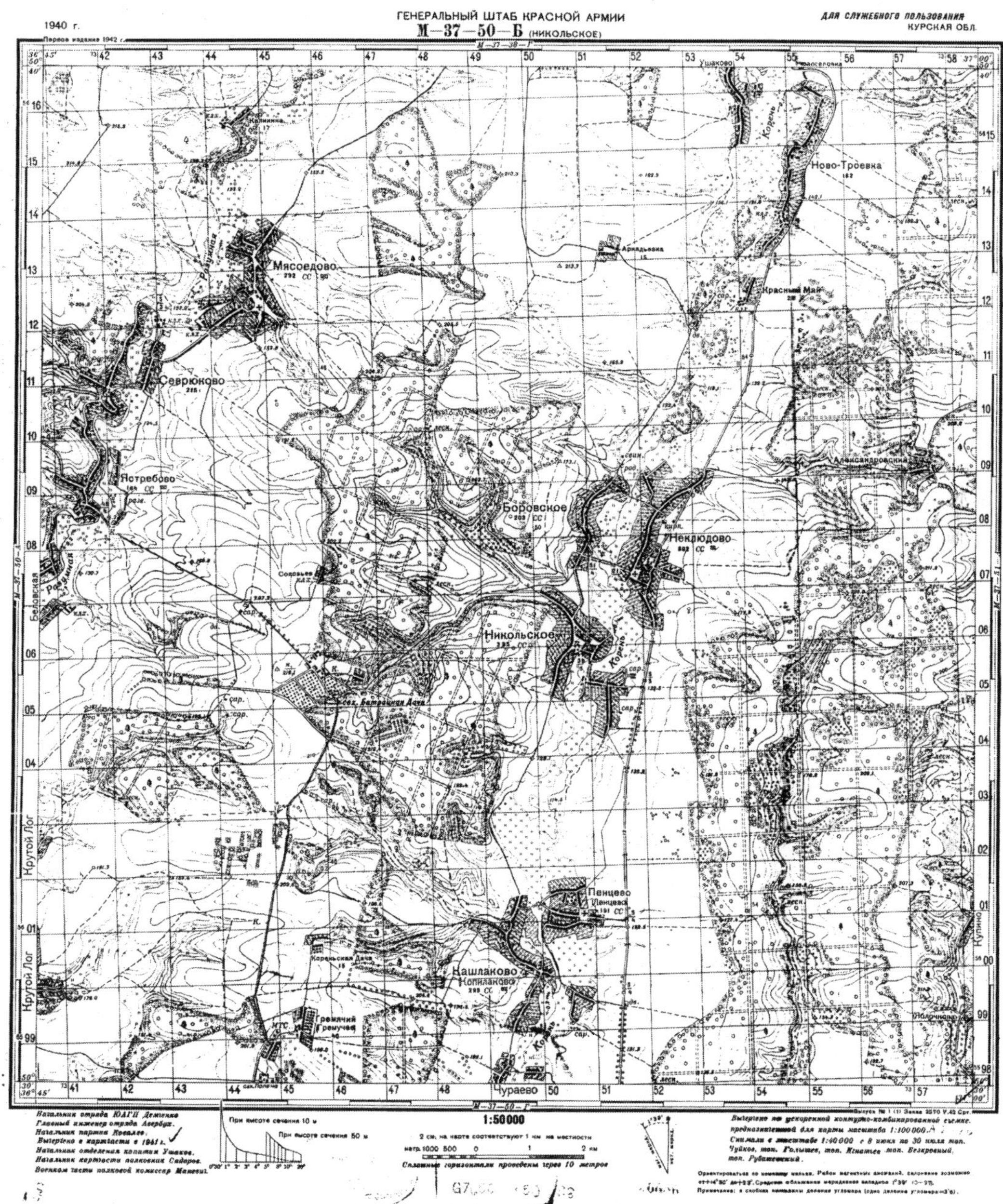

Map 17: Soviet General Staff of the Red Army map M-37-50-B from 1942, 1:50000 scale: covering Gremyachii (Гремячий), Batratskaya Dacha (свх. Батрацкая Дача), Myasoyedovo (Мясоедово) and the Koren (Корень) River.

Appendices

APPENDIX 1

German and Soviet Terminology

Conventions

Unit Numbers The convention followed here is that platoons, companies, regiments and divisions are identified by Arabic numerals, battalions and corps are identified by Roman numerals, while armies are spellled out. However, all battalions numbered above 10 are identified by arabic numerals.

Heights, hills, points Many locales on the battlefield are named for the height in meters identifying them on a map. These places are referred to as "heights," although in some cases, as "hills," especially if the author knew that this height was a clearly defined hill. They are used interchangeably. Some heights are only marked on the maps by a point referencing the additional height above the surrounding terrain (i.e. +1.8 meters). These are referred to as "points."

German Unit Names The units in a German panzer division usually were prefaced by "panzer," for example the 3rd Panzer Reconnaissance Battalion. In all cases, this "panzer" is removed except where the unit is actually an armored unit or refers to their armored infantry (panzer grenadiers), even though they are usually truck-mounted. The same applies for panzer artillery regiments and other units of a German armored division.

Soviet Unit Names The Soviets often referred to units as "independent" or "separate." This was not consistently applied in their own reports and therefore it is not used here. It does not create any problems, as there were no two units in the battle with the same designation except for one being "separate." Also the extended honorific names of the Soviet units are not used in most cases (i.e. 42nd Prilukskaya, Order of Lenin, Red Star, Order of Bogdan Khmelnitskii Guards Rifle Division). For those Soviet units that are referred to as antitank artillery brigades, regiments or battalions, we usually do not include the word artillery.

We do capitalize the first letter of the word "front" when it is used as a formation name (Voronezh Front, Steppe Front) as opposed to when it is used to describe the front or the front line.

German Terminology

I have tried to minimize the use of German military terms in this book, even though many may be well known. The ones regularly used in this book are as follows, and are not italicized.

Abteilung Literally this means a "detachment." It is usually used for a unit larger than a company and up to a battalion in size. It is a term mostly used for artillery units, reconnaissance units and assault gun units (which were part of the artillery arm). It was translated throughout this book as battalion, as for most purposes that is what it is. The Soviet equivalent, the "divizion", is also translated as battalion.

The term is also used to designate provisional or temporary armies, like Army Abteilung Kempf. This is translated as Provisional Army Kempf as opposed to the meaningless (at least in English) Army Detachment Kempf.

Arko This is a German abbreviation for artillery commander. These were regimental-type headquarters set up to command corps and army artillery assets.

Das Reich This means the empire, realm, rule, or nation, as in Third Reich. It was the name given to the "Das Reich" SS Division.

Flak This is a German abbreviation for "Flieger Abwehr Kanone," literally aircraft defense gun or antiaircraft. It is used to refer to antiaircraft units, their fire and the shell bursts from such fire.

Fusilier This is a term from the 17th century that refers to a soldier armed with a fusil, a light flintlock musket. They were originally artillery guards. Although the fusil ceased being used after the Napoleonic Wars, the term has continued to this day as an honorific for certain units. In this book, the term Fusilier is only used to refer to one of the two armored infantry (panzer grenadier) regiments of the Gross Deutschland Division (the other being the Grenadier Regiment).

Grenadier This is a 17th century term that refers to grenade-throwing infantryman. They were usually stronger men who received extra pay. By the Napoleonic Wars, these units had mutated into elite troops. The term continues to this day as an honorific for certain units. During World War II, many German infantry regiments were renamed "grenadier" regiments, but without any other changes being made to the unit. For this book, they are called what they are, which is infantry regiments.

In this book, the term grenadier is only used to refer to one of the two armored infantry (panzer grenadier) regiments of the Gross Deutschland Division (the other being the Fusilier Regiment).

Gross Deutschland This means Greater Germany. It was a regular German Army division (not SS!) recruited from throughout Germany as a whole rather then from traditional regional recruiting areas. This was the reason for this name. The division received preferential treatment in personnel and equipment and was generally considered an elite unit in the German Army. The actual German spelling is Großdeutschland or Grossdeutschland. We chose to "Americanize" the spelling.

Kampfgruppe This literally means "battle group," and is the same as the U.S. combat team or task force. It was a temporary organization created from different units. In practice, a seriously depleted division could also be referred to as a kampfgruppe.

K-Bridge This is a deployable bridge used by the German engineers. There were also B-Bridges, H-Bridges and J-Bridges. They were transported in a platoon-size bridging column that was often named for the type of bridge they carried.

Bridge Set K was the standard box girder pontoon-and-trestle bridging equipment for panzer divisions. Bridge Set B was the standard pontoon-and-trestle bridging equipment for most German divisions. Bridge Set J was designed to carry the new heavy tanks and assault guns.

Landsers A German slang term for a common soldier, similar to "GI."

Lehr This means "training" or "demonstration." It was applied to certain units that were responsible for developing tactical doctrine for their particular arm. They were often used as regular combat units.

Leibstandarte This literally means "life standard" (standard as in a flag or banner) or more correctly "body guard." It was the SS unit originally created as the personal bodyguard for Adolf Hitler.

LSSAH Common abbreviation used for the Leibstandarte SS Adolf Hitler Division.

Nazi This is the German abbreviation for the National Socialist German Workers Party (Nationalsozialistische Deutsche Arbeiterpartei or NSDAP).

This was a very small political party (originally called the German Workers Party) that was formed in 1919 by a toolmaker named Anton Drexler and which Adolf Hitler joined that same year. In 1933, Adolf Hitler, at the head of this party, became Chancellor of Germany. The Nazis were a fascist (dictatorial) and intensely nationalistic political party as well an ideology. Not all Germans were Nazis, although party membership numbered in the millions.

NEBELWERFER This literally means "smoke (or fog) thrower." It was the five- or six-tubed rocket launcher that fired either high explosive or smoke rockets. Neither very accurate nor long-ranged, it could quickly lay down a considerable volume of fire or smoke. It was similar to the Soviet Katyusha.

OKH This is a German abbreviation for the Oberkommando des Heeres (Senior Commander of the Army or German Army High Command). It was the headquarters of the German Army and included the Army General Staff. At the time of the Battle of Kursk, its commander was Adolf Hitler and his chief of staff was General Kurt Zeitzler.

OKW This is a German abbreviation for the Oberkommando der Wehmacht (Senior Commander of the Armed Forces or High Command of the Armed Forces). It was the headquarters and staff for all German armed forces. For most of its existence, its commander was Adolf Hitler, his chief of staff was General Wilhelm Keitel, its chief operations officer was General Alfred Jodl. Most of its officers were from the Army General Staff.

PANZER This means tank or armored. The word was originally used for body armor, but has come to mean a German tank in both English and German. A panzer division is an armored division. A panzer is a tank.

PANZER JAEGER This literally means "tank hunter." For all practical purposes it means antitank and consists of towed 37mm, 50mm and 75mm guns as well as the self-propelled antitank units using 75mm armed Marders.

PANZER GRENADIER This means armored grenadiers or armored infantry. It is a title for the infantry in a panzer division or a panzer grenadier division. It does not usually mean mechanized infantry, as most of the infantry in German armored units were truck transported and fought on foot. Normally only one battalion in a division was actually mounted in halftracks (armored transports).

PANZER GRENADIER DIVISION This means an armored infantry division. Many of these divisions in the German Army were motorized infantry divisions with limited armor assets. The German Army by the middle of 1943 had also created five large panzer grenadier divisions, all of which were committed or held in reserve for the Belgorod Offensive. These large armored divisions included more infantry, more armor and more support troops than either an armored division or a regular panzer grenadier division. They were Gross Deutschland, Leibstandarte SS Adolf Hitler, Das Reich SS, Totenkopf SS and Viking SS Panzer Grenadier Divisions (which was shy on armor compared to the other divisions).

SS This is a German abbreviation for their security section (schutzstaffel). They were a branch of the Nazi party that started as bodyguards for party members and when the party came to power, also provided their concentration camp guards. They were also formed into a military wing to provide a small separate, politically motivated and politically reliable armed force. As such, they had their own training centers, recruitment, rank system, etc. They received preferential treatment in personnel.

STUKA This is a German abbreviation for "sturzkampf," literally diving or falling combat. It came to refer to the most famous of these aircraft, the Junkers Ju-87 dive bomber, their units and also to their dive bombing attacks.

STURMGESCHUETZ This literally means "assault gun." It was a fixed gun mounted on an armored Panzer III chassis. Although part of the artillery branch, it was a "tank-like" vehicle and often used as such.

TOTENKOPF This literally means "Death's Head." It refers to the Totenkopf SS Division. It was originally formed from units assigned to guard concentration camps.

VIKING This means Viking (spelled "Wiking" in German), a Nordic wanderer and warrior from the Middle Ages. It refers to the Viking SS Division, which was made up of mainly Germans, some Dutch and Belgians, but was supposed to rely heavily upon Scandinavian (Danish, Norwegian, Swedish and Finnish) volunteers.

WERFER This means "launcher" and is sometimes used as shorthand for nebelwerfer.

SOVIET TERMINOLOGY

As the Soviet terminology is less well known to many American readers, less of it was used in the text. Still, a few terms and conventions do appear in the book.

BALKA This is a Russian word that translates as gully or ravine.

BOLSHEVIK This means the "majority faction" of the Russian Communist party, even though for most of their history this was not true (the other branch being Mensheviks). This was the faction of the party that was more radical, aggressive and was led by Lenin. It is this faction which seized power and established the USSR.

KOLKHOZ This was a Soviet abbreviation for a collective farm, nominally run by the farmers with some land allotted for personal use.

MECHANIZED As a convention, Soviet armored infantry formations are referred to as mechanized instead of armored infantry, so as to easily distinguish them from the German panzer grenadier (armored infantry) units. As with German panzer grenadiers, they were usually equipped with truck transport as opposed to armored transport. This matches Russian terminology.

MTS This is the Soviet abbreviation for the Machine and Tractor Stations that supplied most of the agricultural machinery used by the kolkhozes.

NKVD This was the People's Commissariat of Internal Affairs. This was the name of the Soviet secret police from 1934 to 1946, replacing the previous name OGPU and later known as the KGB. They served a wide range of functions, including internal and external security and espionage. As they controlled the Ministry of the Interior, they also included border security and NKVD combat units.

RIFLE As a convention, Soviet infantry units are referred to as Rifle instead of infantry, so as to easily distinguish them from the German infantry units. This matches Russian terminology and German usage.

RKKA The Workers' and Peasants' Red Army. This was the abbreviation for the full name of the Soviet Army. It was renamed the Soviet Army after World War II.

SOVIET This means the Soviet Union. It is used in preference to Russia or Russian, since the Soviet Union was a multinational state that had non-Russians in senior positions of leadership (including the head of the state, Joseph Stalin).

SOVKHOZ This was a Soviet abbreviation for a Soviet collective farm. It was usually larger than a kolkhoz and was state-financed and under direct state control and management.

STAVKA This was the staff of the Supreme High Command for the Soviet Armed Forces. It was the supreme Soviet headquarters, headed by Josef Stalin and with Generals Zhukov and others as members. It reported to the State Defense Committee, also headed by Stalin. It was the equivalent of the German OKW.

TANK As a convention, Soviet armored units are referred to as tank instead of armored, so as to easily distinguish them from the German panzer (armored) units. This matches Russian terminology and German usage.

USSR Union of Soviet Socialist Republics, or the Soviet Union. This was the communist state established by the Bolsheviks in 1922 that encompassed most of the areas of the old Russian Empire (it did not include Finland or Poland). It was a larger nation in territory and population than modern Russia.

Transliteration conventions

For German, Americanized spellings were used. Umlauts were not used, and instead the umlaut "a" was replaced with "ae," the umlaut "o" was replaced with "oe," while the umlaut "u" was replaced with "ue."

For Russian, there are several different competing transliteration systems that have fallen in and out of favor over the decades, most individually generated. The Library of Congress system seems to have recently gained popularity. It makes extensive use of the apostrophe to represent soft sounds and uses an "i" for certain variations of Russian letters. This leads to words like "Dal'niaia." The average English language speaking person simply does not know how one is supposed to pronounce an apostrophe. I consider this transliteration system to be an overly scholarly interpretation that loses track of the purpose of a transliteration system, which is to serve people who are not familiar with the language! As the majority of readers have neither the time, inclination nor need to learn the basics of the Russian language, I have used a transliteration scheme that makes use of "y" to represent the soft sound in front of the verbs. This turns "Dal'niaia" into "Dalnyaya" and "Iakovlevo" into the more pronounceable "Yakovlevo." This appears to be a more practical solution for the lay reader.

Specifically, those Russian letters that are transliterated with more than one English letter include the "ж" becomes "zh," the "х" becomes "kh," "ц" becomes "ts," "ч" becomes "ch," "ш" becomes "sh," "щ" becomes

Abbreviations

The following abbreviations are used in this book.

AA	Antiaircraft
Art	Artillery
AT	Antitank
ATR	Antitank Rifle
Bn	Battalion
Bty	Battery (an artillery company)
Bde	Brigade
Co	Company
Col.	Colonel
Col.	Column (a type of bridging platoon)
Con	Construction
D	Division
Eng	Engineer
GD	Gross Deutschland
Gds	Guards
GRD	Guards Rifle Division
Hq	Headquarters
Hvy	Heavy
ID	Infantry Division
KIA	Killed in Action
Lt.	Lieutenant
Lt. Col.	Lieutenant Colonel
MC	Mechanized Corps
MG	Major General
MIA	Missing in Action
Mtn	Mountain
Mtr	Mortar
MTS	Machine and Tractor Station
Pn	Platoon
POW	Prisoner of War
Pz	Panzer
PzD	Panzer Division
PzGr	Panzer Grenadier
PzGrD	Panzer Grenadier Division
RD	Rifle Division
Rgt	Regiment
Sgt	Sergeant
SP	Self-Propelled
T	Tank
TC	Tank Corps
WIA	Wounded in Action

"shch," "ы" becomes "yi," "ю" becomes "yu," "я" becomes "ya." Both "и" and "й" (ikratkoye) are transliterated "i." I did not transliterate "e" to "ye" except when it follows a vowel, otherwise we would have produced spellings like "Vyesyelyii" as opposed to "Veselyii." The hard sound "ъ" is ignored. The soft sound "ь" is represented by a "y" when it precedes a "hard" vowel, otherwise it is ignored. The "ё" (umlaut) is transliterated the same as the "e."

In a few cases, we do not do a direct transliteration as described above where the word or place is commonly known in English. This includes Russia, Moscow and Byelorussia.

Nationalities

There are a number of nationalities referred to in this book. They are briefly defined below.

Caucasian There were a large number of nationalities in the area of the Caucasus Mountains, including Georgians, Armenians, Azerbajainis, Chechens, Ossetians, and others.

Cossacks These are mostly (but not exclusively) a European people who speak Russian. They are descended from horsemen with a tradition of military service and their own independent clan traditions.

Georgians This is a European people in the Caucasus Mountains who speak Georgian, an Indo-European language.

Germans This is a central European people who speak a Germanic dialect and are members of the nation of Germany.

Jewish This is a people scattered across Europe who practice the Jewish religion. They were considered a separate nationality by both the German and Soviet governments.

Kazakhs This is a Central Asian people who speak a Turkish language.

Mongols This is an East Asian people who speak Mongolian. It is also a term applied loosely to the Oriental and Turkish peoples who were commanded by Genghis Khan and his successors in the Middle Ages.

Russians This is an Eastern European people who speak Russian. In some cases, the word is used to refer to the Soviet Army or Soviet soldiers, as the Russians made up the largest national group in the Soviet Union.

Slavs This is a term that covers the people of the central and eastern European language group that includes Polish, Czech, Croatian, Serbian, Russian, Ukrainian, etc.

Tatars This is a loosely applied term that refers to a variety of Mongol or Turkish people, now primarily applied to various Turkish people.

Turkestan This is a central Asian area, populated by a people (Turkmens) who speak a Turkish language.

Ukrainians This is an eastern European people who speak the Slavic language of Ukraine. It is closely related to Russia and mutually intelligible. The original "Rus" state was formed around the Ukrainian city of Kiev. It was the second largest national group in the Soviet Union.

Uzbeks This is a central Asian people who speak a Turkish language.

Comparative Ranks

The German and Soviet ranks systems were very similar and easily comparable, and are also similar to that of the U.S. Army in World War II and now. The confusion to some readers is caused by the U.S. use of the rank of Brigadier General whereas the lowest general officer rank in the German and Soviet Army was Major General. The modern German Army uses a ranking convention for general officers similar to the U.S. See Table I.1.

TABLE APP.1.
COMPARATIVE RANKS

U.S. Army	*German Army*	*SS Rank*	
(Cadet)	Ensign		
2nd Lieutenant	Jr. Lieutenant	Untersturmfuehrer	(Junior Assault Leader)
1st Lieutenant	Sr. Lieutenant	Obersturmfuehrer	(Senior Assault Leader)
Captain	Captain	Hauptsturmfuehrer	(Captain Assault Leader)
Major	Major	Sturmbannfuehrer	(Assault Banner Leader)
Lt. Colonel	Lt. Colonel	Obersturmbannfuehrer	(Senior Assault Banner Leader)
Colonel	Colonel	Standartenfuehrer	(Standard Leader)
(no equivalent)		Oberfuehrer	(Senior Leader)
Brigadier General	Major General	Brigadefuehrer	(Brigade Leader)
Major General	Lt. General	Gruppenfuehrer	(Group Leader)
Lt. General	General of the . . .	Obergruppenfuehrer	(Senior Group Leader)
General	Colonel General	Oberstgruppenfuehrer	(Col. Group Leader)
General of the Army	Field Marshal	Reichsfuehrer SS	(SS Reich Leader)

Note: In this book, the author uses the German ranks, not their translated U.S. comparative rank.

In this book SS officers are usually referred to by their German Army rank equivalent. This expedient was adopted so as not to introduce a lot of German terms to the text, or to use strange sounding English translations of the ranks such as "Assault Banner Leader."

TABLE APP.2.
COMPARATIVE RANKS

U.S. Army	*Soviet Army*
(Cadet)	Ensign
2nd Lieutenant	Jr. Lieutenant
1st Lieutenant	Sr. Lieutenant
Captain	Captain
Major	Major
Lt. Colonel	Lt. Colonel
Colonel	Colonel
Brigadier General	Major General
Major General	Lt. General
Lt. General	Colonel General
General	General of the Army
General of the Army	Marshal of . . .
(no equivalent)	Marshal of the Soviet Union

APPENDIX 2

The Engagements

WITHIN THIS BOOK, after the narrative descriptions of events, are a series of tables that attempt to describe the engagements statistically. These are drawn from the unit records of both sides and are based upon our work with the Kursk Data Base.

The engagements are usually one day in length and are usually one German division versus their Soviet opponents (usually more than a division). There are exceptions. They are longer than a day when nothing really changed from one day to the next and the engagement was otherwise insignificant. They are sometimes shorter than a day when there was a sudden change in the action during the day.

They also sometimes consist of more than a division where the German or Soviet operations were such that it was difficult to determine exactly who was facing and fighting whom. This particularly tends to happen in the XLVIII Panzer Corps' area where the operations of the 3rd Panzer Division and Gross Deutschland Division were tightly integrated and conducted against the same Soviet units. In this particular case, the III Mechanized Corps' large frontage often put it opposite several German divisions at the same time. There is sometimes less than a division in an engagement as elements of the German divisions maneuver on the battlefield.

For these engagements we report the frontage of the unit, usually based upon the German unit's frontage; we provide a basic descriptor of the terrain they fought on based upon definitions that have been traditionally used by *The Dupuy Institute*; and we provide a weather report as summarized from the unit records.

Matching opposing units is also a challenge. Rarely are the two sides so polite as to line up their units so that the left and right divisional boundaries of each side match up geographically. Usually there is some overlap by one side or the other. In those cases where it was close, we just assumed the entire unit was in the engagement. In those cases where it was not, we sometimes had to mathematically divide the unit's strength and losses between engagements.

The attacker and defenders are assigned based upon their role in that particular engagement on that day. In some cases, it is not obvious which definitions should apply, so some judgment had to be applied. The attachments for these units are also included. These attachments sometime make up a significant portion of the combat power of a unit and are included in the strength and loss totals of the side. They are listed by unit. In some cases, there is artillery not attached to these units that is providing direct fire support. We do not always pick these units up as participating in the engagement.

We then provide the total strength of the side. This includes all divisions, Soviet tank and mechanized corps, independent brigades and regiments, units attached to them, and sometimes supporting artillery. It is a simple total of all the people in the unit, regardless of function or mission. The same is the case for the totals for armor and artillery. Artillery includes all towed and halftrack mounted guns of 75mm and greater, regardless of purpose. As such, it includes dual-purpose weapons like the German 88mm antiaircraft guns and the Soviet 76mm division guns.

The total air sorties specifically only address those that are providing direct ground support, as opposed to interdiction, escort, etc. While we have detailed records of the number of sorties flown, exactly where they went on a given day is not very well indicated. As such, considerable derivation was used to assign a specific number of sorties to a specific division-level engagement. This whole process is detailed in Appendix IV. This air sortie data should be taken with considerable caution, as it is usually derived from unit records, as opposed to having been actually reported. Still, we felt a derived number was better than no number at all.

Casualties, armor losses, and artillery losses are from the unit records or derived from them. Casualties are reported as KIA (Killed-in-Action), WIA (Wounded-in-Action) or MIA (missing-in-action). Some of the wounded-in-action may later die. Some of the missing-in-action may indeed be dead, and certainly some of them are wounded. Usually, around 75% of the missing-in-action end up as captured by the other side.

Armor losses are usually determined from the change in strength of the reported ready-for-action vehicles for each day. As such, they represent all losses, whether combat or non-combat, and whether damaged or destroyed. The loss reports by units are much less reliable and usually do not pick up damaged tanks, which make up the majority of tank losses. Almost all German units provide good daily ready-for-action reports. The notable exception is Totenkopf SS Division for 12 and 13 July. The Soviets usually provide daily ready-for-action reports, but sometimes there are periods of three days without any armor reports. This usually occurs during times of heavy fighting. As such the total losses in these cases are usually divided evenly across the days in question. This happens for a time with the III Mechanized Corps and the XXXI Tank Corps.

Artillery losses tend to not be very well documented. Often the German records provide only detailed artillery strength reports every 10 days. As German artillery losses are low, this is not a major issue. Soviet artillery is often poorly reported. In many cases we only know the gun strength at the start of the Battle of Kursk and at the end of the Battle of Kursk. In those cases, we usually tied artillery losses to the personnel losses to be able to derive daily artillery loss figures from the total lost during the battle.

Air losses are only those cases where we feel we have a somewhat reliable report of close air support planes lost as part of these missions. There were considerably more planes lost by each side on each day than what is reported in these engagement sheets.

Numbers of enemy prisoners captured are based upon the records for each side as to who they captured from the other side. We feel these are pretty reliable reports (as opposed to intelligence estimates of enemy casualties). These are worth comparing to the actual number missing. Sometimes they match, sometimes they do not. We do not usually attempt to resolve the difference.

THESE RECORDS ARE our best estimate of the statistics of the fighting in that area on that day. They are not necessarily correct. They are based upon the unit records, but the unit records do not always give an exact count of unit strength on any given day. It is not unusual for a unit to give the losses over a three or five-day period, and leave it for us to determine how many of those occurred on each day. Usually if there is no other evidence, we spread the losses evenly across the days in question. This occurs much more with the Soviet units than with the German units.

In general, German strength, losses, tank strength, tank losses, artillery strength and artillery losses are pretty accurately reported in the records, less the usual vagaries that one should expect for trying to do administrative accounting in the middle of a battle. Still, there are some cases where we do not get daily reports from the Germans. This happens primarily in the III Panzer Corps units and Corps Raus units after the 12th of July. In those cases, we have had to spread the casualties reported for the time period evenly over several days.

The Soviet strength and losses are more difficult to tabulate. In some cases we have estimated the starting strength of Soviet units based upon neighboring units.

It is not unusual in the first couple of days of battle for units to not report any losses until things quiet down a little bit later. It is hard to determine after the fact on which specific days the losses occurred, but estimations were made based upon the data we have. This need for surmising does happen a number of times throughout the battle with a number of Soviet units. The same is the case with tank and artillery losses.

The Soviets have one other peculiarity, in that they often report a higher number of missing in their earlier reporting of casualties than in their later, often post-battle, casualty summations. In these cases, this is probably people returning to the unit after being temporarily separated from it. They also sometimes report lower unit strengths during the battle than they do a few days later. We suspect most of these cases are due to them getting a good count of all their people, as opposed to the unit receiving large numbers of new people.

The details of how the strengths and losses of each and every unit were developed are described for each case in the Kursk Data Base. This large data base, programmed in Access, is available for review at *The Dupuy Institute* but is otherwise proprietary. An earlier version of the data base from 1995 is publicly available, but the data base has been revised and refined considerably since then, especially as part of the writing of this book.

We have provided in this book a detailed description of strength and losses for each engagement for each day. It is not always precisely right, but is as close to correct as we could get with the data we had. It may be possible with more information and research to further refine some of these figures and they should not, regardless, be taken as gospel.

Bibliography

THE FOLLOWING BIBLIOGRAPHY refers only to those books that were actually referenced or reviewed for writing this book. It does not attempt to list all the books on the subject.

SECONDARY SOURCES

Accoce, Pierre, and Pierre Quet, *A Man Called Lucy* (Berkley Medallion Books, New York, 1968).

Aganov, S. Kh., ed., *Inzhenernyie Voiska Sovetskoi Armii 1918–1945* (Voyenizdat, Moscow, 1985).

Agte, Patrick, *Jochen Peiper, Kommandeur Panzerregiment Leibstandarte* (Kurt-Vohwinckel-Verlag, 82335 Berg am Stamberger See, I. Auglage, 1998).

Agte, Patrick, *Michael Wittmann and the Tiger Commanders of the Leibstandarte* (Stackpole Press, Mechanicsburg, PA, 2006).

Amadio, Jill, *Guenther Rall: A Memoir: Luftwaffe Ace & NATO General* (Tangmere Productions, Santa Ana, CA, 2002).

Ananyev, I. M., *Tankovyie Armii v Nastuplenii* [Tanks Armies in the Offensive] (Voyenizdat, 1988).

Axell, Albert, *Stalin's War: Through the Eyes of his Commanders* (Arms and Armour, London, 1997).

Barnett, Correlli, *Hitler's Generals* (Grove Weidenfeld, New York, 1989).

The Battle of Kursk (Progress Press Publishers, USSR, 1974).

Bauer, Eddy, *Illustrated World War II Encyclopedia* (H. S. Stuttman, Inc, Westport, CT, 1978).

Bekker, Cajus, *The Luftwaffe War Diaries* (Ballantine Books, New York, 1966).

Belyayeva, L. G., ed., *Marshal Zhukov: Kakim my ego Pomnim* (Izdatelstvo Politicheskoi Literaturi, Moscow, 1988).

Bingham, James, *Infantry Tank Mk II Matilda, Armour in Profile No. 15* (Great Bookham, UK, 1967).

Boog, Horst, Gerhard Krebs, Detlef Vogel, Derry Cook-Radmore (translator), *Germany and the Second World War: Volume VII: The Strategic Air War in Europe and the War in the West and East Asia, 1943–1944/5* (Oxford University Press, Oxford, 2006).

Bradley, Dermot, Karl-Friedrich Hildebrand, Markus Roverkamp, *Die Generale des Heeres 1921–1945* (Biblio Verlag, Osnabruck, 1993).

Brief Tactical-Technical Guide, National Commission for the Defense of the USSR (Moscow, 1943).

Bullock, Alan, *Hitler and Stalin, Parallel Lives* (Vintage Books, New York, 1993).

Butler, Rupert, *SS-Leibstandarte: The History of the First SS Division 1933–45* (MBI Publishing Company, St. Paul, MN, 2001).

Caidin, Martin, *The Tigers are Burning* (Hawthorn Books, Inc., New York, copyright 1974, pre-publication copy).

Carell, Paul, *The Scorched Earth: The Russian-German War 1943–44* (Schiffer Military/Aviation History, Atglen, PA, 1994).

Carius, Otto, *Tigers in the Mud: The Combat Career of German Panzer Commander Otto Carius* (Stackpole Books, Mechanicsburg, PA, 2003).

Chamberlain, Peter, and Chris Ellis, *British and American Tanks of World War II* (Arco Publishing Company, New York, 1969).

Chamberlain, Peter, and Hilary Doyle, technical editor Thomas L. Jentz, *Encyclopedia of German Tanks of World War Two* (Revised Edition, London, 1993).

Chaney, Otto Preston, *Zhukov* (Revised edition, University of Oklahoma Press, Norman and London, 1996).

Clark, Alan, *Barbarossa: The Russian-German Conflict, 1941–45* (Quill, New York, 1985, originally published 1965).

Clodfelter, Micheal, *Warfare and Armed Conflicts* (McFarland & Company, Inc., Jefferson, NC & London, 1992).

Comnena, Anna, *The Alexiad of Anna Comnena*, translated from Greek by E. R. A. Sewter (Penguin Books, London, 1969).

Conquest, Robert, *The Great Terror, A Reassessment* (Oxford University Press, Oxford, 1990).

Cross, Robin, *Citadel: The Battle of Kursk* (Michael O'Mara Books Limited, London, 1993).

Deutsch, Harold C., and Dennis E. Showalter, eds., *What If? Strategic Alternatives of WWII* (The Emperor's Press, Chicago, 1997).

Drogovoz, I. *Zheleznyii Kulak RKKA: Tankovyie i Mekhanizirovannyiye Korpusa Krasnoi Armii 1932–41 gg.* (Izdatelskii dom, Moscow, 1999).

Dupuy, Trevor N., *Attrition: Forecasting Battle Casualties and Equipment Losses in Modern War* (HERO Books, Fairfax, VA, 1990).

Dupuy, R. Earnest, and Trevor N. Dupuy, *The Harper Encyclopedia of Military History* (Harper Collins Publishers, New York, 1993).

Dupuy, T. N., *A Genius for War, The German Army and General Staff, 1807–1945* (HERO Books, Fairfax, VA, 1984).

Dupuy, T. N., and Paul Martell, *Great Battles of the Eastern Front: The Soviet-German War, 1941–1945* (Bobbs-Merrill Company, Indianapolis, IN, 1982).

Dupuy, Trevor N., ed., *International Military and Defense Encyclopedia* (Brassy's [US], Inc., Washington, New York, 1993).

Dupuy, Trevor N., David L. Bongard, Richard C. Anderson, Jr., *Hitler's Last Gamble, The Battle of the Bulge, December 1944–January 1945* (Harper Collins Publishers, New York, 1994).

Dupuy, Trevor N., Curt Johnson, David L. Bongard, *The Harper Encyclopedia of Military Biographies* (Harper Collins Publishers, New York, 1992).

Dupuy, Trevor N., Curt Johnson, Grace P. Hayes, *Dictionary of Military Terms, A Guide to the Language of Warfare and Military Institutions* (H. W. Wilson Company, New York, 1986).

Dyer, D. P., *Infantry Tank Mark III "Valentine," Bellona Military Prints No. 34 & 38* (Great Bookham, UK, 1972 & 1974).

Ellis, John, *World War II: The Encyclopedia of Facts and Figures* (The Military Book Club, USA, 1995).

Erickson, John, *The Road to Berlin* (Phoenix Giants, London, 1996, 1983).

Ferguson, Niall, *The Pity of War, Explaining World War I* (Basic Books, New York, 1999).

Forty, George, *Tank Aces from Blitzkrieg to the Gulf War* (Sutton Publishing, Stroud, UK, 1997).

Frieser, Karl-Heinz, *Germany and the Second World War: Volume VIII: The Eastern Front 1943–1944: The War in the East and on the Neighbouring Fronts* (Oxford University Press, Oxford, 2017).

Funk & Wagnalls Standard Reference Encyclopedia (Standard Reference Works Publishing Company, Inc., New York, 1962).

Galland, Adolf, *The First and the Last, The Rise and Fall of the German Fighter Forces 1938–1945* (Bantam Books, New York, 1982).

Garlinski, Josef, *Swiss Corridor* (J. M. Dent & Sons, Ltd., London, 1981).

Glantz, David M., *From the Don to the Dnepr, Soviet Offensive Operations December 1942–August 1943* (Frank Cass, London, 1991).

Glantz, David M., *Stumbling Colossus: The Red Army on the Eve of World War* (University of Kansas Press, Lawrence, KS, 1998).

Glantz, David M., and Jonathan M. House, *The Battle of Kursk* (University of Kansas Press, Lawrence, KS, 1999).

Glantz, David M., and Jonathan House, *When Titans Clash, How the Red Army Stopped Hitler* (University Press of Kansas, Lawrence, KS, 1995).

Glantz, David M., and Harold S. Orenstein, *Kursk 1943: The Soviet General Staff Study* (self published, 1997). Originally published as *Sbornik Materialov po Izucheniyu Opyita Voinyi, No 11, Mart–Aprel 1944 g.* (Collection of Materials for the Study of War Experience, No. 11, March–April 1944) (Military Publishing House of the Peoples' Commissariat of Defense, Moscow, 1944). Full title: *Upravleniye po Ispolzovaniyu Opyita Voinyi Generalnogo Shtaba Krasnoi Armii, Sbornik Materialov po Izucheniyu Opyita Voinyi, No 11, Mart–Aprel 1944 g (Directorate for the Use of War Experience of the Red Army General Staff, Collection of Materials for the Study of War Experience, No 11, March–April 1944).*

Goode's School Atlas (Rand McNally & Company, New York, 1943).

Gorlitz, Walter, *History of the German General Staff, 1657–1945* (Praeger, New York, 1957).

Gorlitz, Walter, *Strategie der Defensive: Model* (Limes Verlag, Wiesbaden & Munchen, 1982).

Gorlov, Sergei Alekseyevich, *Sovershenno Sekretno: Alyans Moskva-Berlin, 1920–1933 gg.* (OLMA-PRESS, Moscow, 2001).

Great Patriotic War: 1941–1945 Encyclopedia (Sovetskaya Entsiklopediya, Moscow, 1985).

Halder, Franz, *The Halder War Diary* (Presidio Press, Novato, CA, 1988). Edited by Charles Burdick and Hans-Adolf Jacobsen.

Handbook on U.S.S.R. Military Forces (War Department Technical Manual TM 30-430, War Department, November 1945).

Harrison, Richard W., *The Russian Way of War, Operational Art, 1904–1940* (University Press of Kansas, Lawrence, KS, 2001).

Harrison, Richard W., *Architect of Soviet Victory in World War II: The Life and Theories of G. S. Isserson* (McFarland & Company, Jefferson, NC, 2010).

Hart, Sir Basil Liddell, editor-in-chief, *History of the Second World War* (Marshall Cavendish USA Ltd., New York, 1973; 1966).

Hart, S., and R. Hart, *German Tanks of World War II* (Brown Books, Dallas, 1998).

Hinsley, F. H., et al., *British Intelligence in the Second World War* (three volumes, HMSO, London, 1979–1988).

Hooten, E. R., *Eagle in Flames, The Fall of the Luftwaffe* (Arms & Armour Press, London, 1997).

Irving, David, *Hitler's War* (Viking Press, New York, 1977).

Istoriya Velikoi Otechestvennoi Voinyi Sovetskogo Soyuza, 1941–45 (*The History of the Great Patriotic War of the Soviet Union, 1941–45*) (Voennoye Izdatelstvo, Moscow, 1960–65), Volume 3.

Istoria Vtoroi Mirovoi Voinyi, 1939–1945 (The History of the Second World War, 1939–1945) (Moscow, 1973–80, Volume 7).

Jentz, Thomas L., *Germany's Panther Tank* (Schiffer Military/Aviation History, Atglen, PA, 1995).

Jentz, Thomas L., *Panzertruppen: The Complete Guide to the Creation & Combat Employment of Germany's Tank Force, 1933–42* (Schiffer Military History, Altglen, PA, 1996).

Jentz, Thomas L., *Panzertruppen II: The Complete Guide to the Creation & Combat Employment of Germany's Tank Force, 1943–45* (Schiffer Military History, Altglen, PA, 1996).

Jukes, Geoffrey, *Kursk: The Clash of Armor* (Ballentine Books, New York, 1969).

Jung, Hans-Joachim, *The History of PanzerRegiment Gross-Deutschland* (J.J. Fedorowicz, Winnipeg, Canada, 2000).

Just, Gunther, *Stuka Pilot Hans-Ulrich Rudel* (Schiffer Military History, Atglen, PA, 1986).

Kennedy, Paul, *The Rise and Fall of the Great Powers, Economic Change and Military Conflict from 1500 to 2000* (Random House, New York, 1987).

Khodarenok, Mikhail, *Pervaya Prokhorovka* (The First Prokhorovka), *Nezavisimoye Voyennoye Obozreniye [Independent Military Review]*, 16 May 2003.

Kinder, Hermann, and Werner Hilgemann, translated by Menze, Ernest A., *The Anchor Atlas of World History* (Anchor Books, New York, 1974).

Klink, Ernst von, *Das Gesetz Des Handelns, Die Operation "Zitadelle" 1943* (Deutsche Verlags-Anstalt, Stuttgart, 1966).

Kohn, George C., *Dictionary of Wars* (Facts on File Publications, New York, 1986).

Kolomiyets, Maksim, *Panteryi na Kurskoi Duge* (Panther's at the Kursk Bulge) (Izdatelstvo Strategiya KM, Moscow, 2002).

Kolomiyets, M., and I. Moshchanskii, *Tanki Lend-Liza* (The Tanks of Lend-Lease) (Eksprint, Moscow, 2000).

Kolomiyets, M., and M. Svirin, *Kurskaya Duga* (Kursk Bulge) (Eksprint, Moscow, 1998).

Kolganov, K. S., ed., *Razvitiye Taktiki Sovetskoi Armii v Godi Velikoi Otechestvennoi Voini (1941–1945 gg.)* (Voyenizdat, Moscow, 1958).

Koltunov, G. A., and B. G. Solovyev, *Kurskaya Bitva* (The Battle of Kursk) (Voyennoye Izdatelstvo, Moscow, 1970).

Koltunov, G. A., and B. G. Solovyev, *Ognennaya Duga* (Voyenizdat, Moscow, 1973).

Koltunov, G. A., and B. G. Solovyev, *Kurskaya Bitva* (The Battle of Kursk) (Voyennoye Izdatelstvo, Moscow, 1983).

Kratkii Taktiko-Tekhnicheskii Spravochnik (A Short Tactical-Technical Handbook) (Moscow, 1943).

Kries, John F., *Air Warfare and Air Base Air Defense* (Office of Air Force History, United States Air Force, Washington, DC, 1988).

Krivosheyev, G. F., ed., *Grif Sekretnosti Snyat: Poteri Vooruzhennyikh sil SSSR v Voinakh, Boyevyikh Deistviyakh i Voyennyikh Konfliktakh. Statisticheskoye Issledovaniye* (The Mark of Secrecy has been Removed: Losses of the USSR Armed Forces in Wars, Combat Actions and Military Conflicts. A Statistical Study) (Voyennoye Izdatelstvo, Moscow, 1993).

Krivosheyev, G. F., ed., *Belikaya Otechestvennaya bez Grifa Sekretnosti: Kniga Potep* (The Great Patriotic War without the Mark of Secrecy: Book of Losses) (Veche, Moscow, 2010).

KTO byil Kto v Velikoi Otechestvennoi Voine 1941–1945 (Who Was Who in the Great Patriotic War 1941–1945) (Izdatelstvo "Respublika", Moscow, 1995).

Kurowski, Franz, *Infantry Aces* (Ballentine Books, New York, 2002).

Kurowski, Franz, *Panzer Aces* (Ballentine Books, New York, 2002) and (J. J. Fedorowicz Publishing, Winnipeg, Canada, 1992).

Kurowski, Franz, *Panzer Aces 2* (J. J. Fedorowicz Publishing, Inc., Winnipeg, Canada, 2000).

Langer, William L., *An Encyclopedia of World History*, (Houghton Mifflin Company, Boston, 1952).

Larionov, V., N. Yeronin, B. Solovyov, V. Timokhovich, *World War II: Decisive Battles of the Soviet Army* (Progress Publishers, Moscow, 1984).

Lawrence, Christopher A., *Kursk: The Battle of Prokhorovka* (Aberdeen Books, Sheridan, CO, 2015).

Lincoln, W. Bruce, *Red Victory, A History of the Russian Civil War* (Simon & Schuster, New York, 1989).

Longford, Elizabeth, *Wellington: The Years of the Sword* (World Books, Suffolk, 1971).

Lopukhovskii, Lev, *Prokhorovka: Bez Grifa Secretnosti* (Eksmo, Yauza, Moscow, 2005).

Losik, O. A., *Stroitelstvo i Boyevoye Primeneniye Sovetskikh Tankovyikh Voisk v Godyi Velikoi Oteschestvonnoi Voinyi* (Formation and Combat Use of Soviet Tank Troops During the Years of the Great Patriotic War) (Moscow, 1979).

Lucas, James, *Hitler's Enforcers, Leaders of the German War Machine 1933–1945* (Arms and Armour Press, London, 1996).

Lucas, James, *War on the Eastern Front, The German Soldier in Russia, 1941–1945* (Military Book Club, USA, 1991).

Madej, W. Victor, ed., *The Russo-German War: June 1941–June 1943* (Game Publishing Company, Allentown, PA, 1983).

Madej, W. Victor, ed., *The Russo-German War: July 1943–May 1945* (Valor Publishing Company, Allentown, Pennsylvania, 1986).

Madeja, W. Victor, *Russo-German War: Summer-Autumn 1943* (Valor Publishing Company, Allentown, PA, 1987).

Mann, Chris, *SS-Totenkopf: The History of the 'Death's Head' Division 1940–45* (MBI Publishing Company, St. Paul, MN, 2001).

Mattson, Gregory L., *SS-Das Reich: The History of the Second SS Division 1941–45* (MBI Publishing Company, St. Paul, MN, 2002).

Mawdsley, Evan, *The Russian Civil War* (Allen & Unwin, Boston, 1987).

McEvedy, Colin, and Richard Jones, *Atlas of World Population History* (Penguin Books, Ltd, Middlesex, England, 1978).

McGuirl, Thomas (text research), Remy Spezzano (photo research), et al., *God, Honor, Fatherland: A Photo History of Panzergrenadier Division Grossdeutschland on the Eastern Front 1942–1944* (RZM Imports, Inc., Southbury, CT, 1997).

Mikoyan, A. I., *Tak Byilo* (Moscow, Vagrius Publishers, 1990).

Medicus, Thomas, *In den Augen meines Grossvaters (In the Eyes of my Grandfather)* (Munich, Deutsche Verlags-Anstalt, 2004).

Muller, Richard, *The German Air War in Russia* (The Nautical & Aviation Publishing Company of America, Baltimore, MD, 1992).

Murzayev, N., *Pekhota Ognennoi Dugi: Strelkovyie Soyedineniya i Chasti v Kurskoi Bitve* (Tsentralno-Chernozemnoye Knizhnoye Izdalelstvo, Voronezh, 1987).

The Military Balance, 1997/98 (The International Institute for Strategic Studies, Oxford University Press, London, 1997).

Nechayev, Gen.Lt. E. A., ed., *Meditsinskoye Obespecheniye Sovetskoi Armii v Operatsiyakh Velikoi Otechestvennoi Voinyi, 1941–1945 gg.* (The Soviet Army's Medical Service in Operations of the Great Patriotic War, 1941–1945) (Volume I, Voyennoye Izdatelstvo, Moscow, 1991).

Naimark, Norman M., *The Russians in Germany: A History of the Soviet Zone of Occupation* (The Belknap Press of Harvard University Press, Cambridge, MA, 1997).

Newton, Steven H., *Kursk: The German View* (Da Capo Press, Boston, 2003).

Nipe, George M. Jr., *Decision in the Ukraine, Summer 1943, II SS and III Panzerkorps* (J. J. Fedorowicz Publishing, Inc. Winnipeg, Canada, 1996).

Pavlov, Ivan Vladimirovich, and Mikhail Vladimirovich Pavlov, *Sovetskiye Tanki i Samokhodno-Artilleriiskiye Ustanovki (1939–1945 gg.)* (Arsenal-Press, Moscow, 1996).

Paul, Wolfgang, *Brennpunkte: Die Geschichte der 6. Panzerdivision (1. leichte) 1937–1945* (Krefeld, Hontges, 1977)

Perechen Obyedinenii i Soyedinenii Sovetskikh Vooruzhennyikh sil, vkhodivshikh v sostav deistvuyushchei armii v period Velikoi Otechestvennoi voinyi 1941–1945 (Institut Voyennoi Istorii, Moscow, 1992)

Quarrie, Bruce, *Hitler's Samurai, The Waffen-SS in Action* (Arco Publishing, Inc., New York, 1983).

Ready, J. Lee, *World War Two: Nation by Nation* (Arms and Armour Press, London, 1995).

Restayn, J., and N. Moller, *Operation "Citadel": A Text and Photo Album, Volume 2: The North.* (J. J. Fedorowicz Publishing, Inc., Winnipeg, Canada, 2006).

Reynolds, Michael, *The Devil's Adjutant: Jochen Peiper, Panzer Leader* (Sarpedon, New York, 1995).

Rosen, Richard Freiherr von, *Panzer Ace: The Memoirs of an Iron Cross Panzer Commander from Barbarossa to Normandy* (Greenhill Books. London, 2018).

Ryabkov, Andrei, *Boyevoi Put divizii i brigad strelkovyikh i vozdushno-desantnyikh voisk Krasnoi Armii v Velikoi Otechestvennoi Voine* (Spravochnik, Sankt-Peterburg, 2008)

Salisbury, Harrison E., *The 900 Days: The Siege of Leningrad* (De Capo Press, New York, 1985).

Samokhodnyie Ustanovki Krasnoi Armii (The Red Army's Self-Propelled Guns) (Moscow, 1945).

Schneider, Wolfgang, *Tigers in Combat, Vol. I* (J.J. Fedorowicz Publishing, Inc., Winnipeg, Canada, 1994).

Schneider, Wolfgang, *Tigers in Combat, Vol. II* (J.J. Fedorowicz Publishing Inc., Winnipeg, Canada, 1998).

Schrank, David, *Thunder At Prokhorovka: A Combat History of Operation Citadel, Kursk, July 1943* (Helion & Company, Solihull, England, 2013).

Seaton, Albert, *The Russo-German War 1941–1945* (Presidio Press, Novato, CA, 1993, 1971).

Seidl, Hans D. *Stalin's Eagles, An Illustrated Study of the Soviet Aces of World War II and Korea* (Schiffer Military History, Atglen, PA, 1998).

Shirer, William L., *The Rise and Fall of the Third Reich, A History of Nazi Germany* (Simon and Schuster, New York, 1960).

Slaughterhouse: The Encyclopedia of the Eastern Front (The Military Book Club, Garden City, NJ, 2002).

Sokolov, B. V., *Tainyi Vtoroi Mirovoi* (Mysteries of the Second World War) (Veche, Moscow, 2000).

Spaeter, Helmuth, *The History of the PanzerKorps Gross-Deutschland, Volume 2* (J. J. Fedorowicz Publishing, Winnipeg, Canada, 1995).

Spielberger, Walter J., *Panther & Its Variants* (Schiffer Military/Aviation History, Atglen, PA, 1993).

Strokov, ed., *Istoriya Voyennogo Iskusstva* (Voyenizdat, Moscow, 1966).

Sverdlov, F. D., *Neizvestnoye o Sovetskikh Polkovodtsakh* (Unknown Facts about Soviet Captains) (Moscow, 1995).

Sverdlov, Fyodor, *Tankmen* (Novosti Press Agency Publishing House, Moscow, 1984).

Tank KV: Kratkoye Rukovodstvo Sluzhbyi (The KV Tank: A User's Manual) (Voyennoye Izdatelstvo, Moscow, 1942).

Ismagilov, R., et al., *Tanki Mira* (Tanks of the World) (Rusich, Smolensk, 2001).

Tarrant, V. E., *The Red Orchestra, The Soviet Spy Network Inside Nazi Europe* (Cassel, London, 1998).

Tarrant, V. E., *Stalingrad, Anatomy of an Agony* (Leo Cooper, London, 1992).

Taubman, William, *Khrushchev: The Man and His Era* (W.W. Norton & Co., New York, 2003).

Thomas, Franz; Gunter Wegmann *Die Ritterkreuztrager der Infanterie* (Biblio Verlag, Osnabruck, 1998).

Thomsett, Michael C., *The German Opposition to Hitler, The Resistance, the Underground, and Assassination Plots, 1938–1945* (McFarland & Company, Inc., Jefferson, NC, 1997).

Time Almanac 1999, Borgna Brunner, ed. (Information Please, New York, 1998).

Toliver, Col. Raymond F., and Trevor J. Constable, *The Blond Knight of Germany* (Ballantine Books, New York, 1970).

Toliver, Col. Raymond F., and Trevor J. Constable, *Horrido! Fighter Aces of the Luftwaffe* (Bantam, New York, 1979).

Torchinov, V.A., A.M. Leontiuk, compilers, *Vokrug Stalin: Istoriko-Biograficheskii Spravochnik* (Filologicheskii Fakultet Sankt-Peterburgskogo Gosudarstvennogo Universiteta, St. Petersburg, 2000).

Tsirlin, A. D., et al., *Inzhenernyie Voiska v Boyakh za Sovetskuyu Rodinu* (Voyenizdat, Moscow, 1970).

Urlanis, B., Ts., *Istoriya Voyennyikh Poter* (History of War Losses) (Poligon, Saint Petersburg, 1994).

Voyennoye Iskusstvo vo Vtoroi Mirovoi Voine i v Poslevoyennyii Period (Strategiya i Operativnoye Iskusstvo) (Military Art in the Second World War and the Postwar Period (Strategy and Operational Art)) (Moscow, 1988).

Voyennoye Iskusstvo vo Vtoroi Mirovoi Voine (Strategiia i Operatiynoye Iskusstvo) (Military Art in the Second World War (Strategy and Operational Art)) (Moscow, 1973).

Voyenno-Istoricheskii Zhurnal (Military History Journal), 1968, Number 6. "Dokumentyi i Materialyi: Kurskaya Bitva v Tsifrakh."

Volkogonov, Dmitri, *Stalin, Triumph and Tragedy* (Prima Publishing, Rocklin, CA, 1992).

The War in the East. The Russo-German Conflict, 1941–45 (Simulations Publications, Incorporated, New York, 1977).

Warlimont, Gen. Walter, *Inside Hitler's Headquarters 1939–45* (Pesidio, Novato, CA, 1964).

Weal, Elke C., John A. Weal, and Richard F. Barker, *Combat Aircraft of World War Two* (Macmillan Publishing Co., Inc., New York, 1977).

Werth, Alexander, *Russia at War, 1941–1945* (Carroll & Graf Publishers, Inc., New York, 1964, 1984).

Whiting, Charles, *Jochen Peiper: Battle Commander SS Leibstandarte Adolf Hitler* (Leo Cooper, Barnsley, South Yorkshire, 1999).

Zalesskii, K. A., *Stalin's Empire: A Biographical Encyclopedia Dictionary (Imperiya Stalina. Biograficheskii entsiklopedicheskii Slovar)* (Veche, Moscow, 2000).

Zamyatin, MG N. M., Cols P. S. Boldyirev, F. D. Vorobyev, LtCols N. F. Artemyev, I. V. Parotkin, *Bitva pod Kurskom* (The Battle of Kursk) (Voyennoye Izdatelstvo Narodnovo Komissariata Oboronyi, Moscow, 1945).

Zamulin, Valeriy, *Demolishing the Myth: The Tank Battle at Prokhorovka, Kursk, July 1943: An Operational Narrative* (Helion and Company Ltd, Solihull, UK, 2011).

Zamulin, Valerii Nikolayevich, *Prokhorovka: Neizvestnoye Srazheniye Velikoi Voinyi* (Prokhorovka: the Unknown Battle in the Great War) (Tranzitkniga, Moscow, 2005).

Zetterling, Niklas and Anders Frankson, *Kursk 1943: A Statistical Analysis* (Frank Cass, London, 2000).

Zetterling, Niklas, *Normandy 1944, German Military Orgazniztion, Combat Power and Organizational Effectiveness* (J. J. Fedorowicz Publishing, Inc., Winnipeg, Canada, 2000).

Zetterling, Niklas, and Anders Frankson, *The Korsun Pocket: The Encirclement and Breakout of a German Army in the East, 1944* (Casemate, Philadelphia & Newbury, 2008).

Ziemke, Earl F., *Stalingrad to Berlin: The German Defeat in the East* (Center of Military History, the United States Army, Washington, DC, 1987, 1968).

Zolotarev, V. A., G. A. Sevostyanov, eds. *Velikaya Otechestvennaya Voina, 1941–1945*, Vol 2. (Nauka, Moscow, 1998–99).

PUBLISHED ACCOUNTS FROM PARTICIPANTS

Below, Nicolaus von, *At Hitler's Side: The Memoirs of Hitler's Luftwaffe Adjutant 1937–1945* (Greenhill Books, London, 2001).

Chistyakov, Gen-Col. I. M., et al., *Po Prikazu Rodinyi* (On Orders from the Motherland) (Moscow, 1971).

Chistyakov, Col. Gen. I. M., *Sluzhim Otchizne* (We Serve the Fatherland) (Voyenizdat, Moscow 1975). Second Edition issued in 1985.

Getman, Gen. A. L., *Tanki Idut Na Berlin* (The Tanks are Heading to Berlin) (2nd edition, Moscow, 1982).

Goebbels, Joseph, *Die Tagebucher von Joseph Goebbels* (The Diary of Joseph Goebbels) (K.G. Saur, Munchen, 1993).

Guderian, Heinz, *Panzer Leader* (abridged) (Ballantine Books, New York, 1967)

Guderian, Heinz, *Panzer Leader* (The Noontide Press, Costa Mesa, CA, 1990).

Heiber, Helmut, and David M. Glantz, eds., *Hitler and His Generals: Military Conferences 1942–1945* (Enigma Books, New York, 2003).

Ivanovskii, E. F., *Tankmen Began the Attack [Ataku Nachinali Tankistyi]* (Military Publishing House (Voyennoye Izdatelstvo, Moscow, 1984).

Katukov, Marshal M. E., *Na Ostriye Glavnogo Udara* (To the Spearhead of the Main Blow) (Moscow, Voyenizdat, 1974, and 2nd edition, Moscow, 1976).

Khrushchev, Nikita (translated and edited by Strobe Talbott), *Khrushchev Remembers* (Little, Brown and Company, Boston, 1970).

Khrushchev, Nikita, *Khrushchev Remembers, The Glasnost Tapes* (Little, Brown and Company, Boston, 1990).

Konev, Marshal I. S., *Zapiski Komanduyushchego Frontom, 1943–1944* (A Front Commander's Notes, 1943–1944) (Moscow, 1972).

Krasovskii, Aviation Marshal S. A., *Zhizn v Aviatsii* (A Life in Aviation) (Moscow, 1960).

Krivoshein, S. M., *Ratnaya Byil* (A War Story) (Moscow, 1962).

Manstein, Erich von, *Lost Victories* (Henry Regnery Company, Chicago, 1958).

Mellenthin, MG F. W. von, *Panzer Battles* (Ballentine Books, New York, 1984).

Moskalenko, Marshal K. S., *Na Yugo-Zapadnom Napravlenii, 1943–1945* (On the Southwestern Axis, 1943–1945) (Moscow, 1972).

Ribbentrop, Rudolf von, "Erzaehlende Kriegsgeschichte: New geboren—bei Prochorowka" (Tales of War History: Born Again—at Prokhorovka), published in "Der Freiwillige" (The Volunteer), 35th year, issue 7–8, July/August 1989.

Rotmistrov, P. A., *Tankovoye Srazheniye pod Prokhorovkoi* (The Tank Battle at Prokhorovka) (Moscow, Voyennoye Izdatelstvo, 1960).

Rotmistrov, P. A., *Stalnaya Gvardiya* (Steel Guards) (Moscow, Voyennoye Izdatelstvo, 1984).

Rudel, Hans Ulrich, *Stuka Pilot* (Bantam Books, New York, 1979, originally published 1958).

Stahlberg, Alexander, *Bounden Duty: The Memoirs of a German Officer 1932–45* (Brassey's [UK], London, 1990).

Vasilevskii, Marshal A. M., *Delo Vsei Zhizni* (The Cause of a Lifetime) (Sixth edition, Moscow, 1989).

Zhadov, Gen. A. S., *Chetyire Goda Voinyi* (Four Years of War) (Moscow 1978).

Zhukov, Marshal G. K., *Vospominaniya i Razmyishleniya* (Memoirs and Reminiscences) (Moscow, Izdatelstvo Novosti, 1971).

Zhukov, Marshal G. K., *Vospominaniya i Razmyishleniya* (Memoirs and Reminiscences) (eleventh edition, Moscow 1992).

Zhukov, G., *Reminiscences and Reflections* (Progress Publishers, Moscow, 1985).

Zhukov, Georgi K., *Marshal Zhukov's Greatest Battles* (Harper and Row, New York, 1969).

REPRINTS FROM ARCHIVAL SOURCES

Russkii Arkhiv: Velikaya Otechestvennaya, Vol 15-4(3), Preludiya Kurskoi Bitvyi, Documentyi i materialyi 6 Dekabrya 1942 g.–25 Aprelya 1943 g. (Terra, Moscow, 1997).

Russkii Arkhiv: Velikaya Otechestvennaya, Vol 15-4(4), Kurskaya Bitva, Dokumentyi i materialyi 27 Marta–23 Avgusta 1943 goda (Terra, Moscow, 1997).

Russkii Arkhiv: Velikaya Otechestvennaya, Vol 16-5(3), Stavka Verkhovnogo Glavnokomandovaniya, Dokumentyi i materialyi 1943 god (Terra, Moscow, 1999).

Russkii Arkhiv: Velikaya Otechestvennaya, Vol 23-12(3), Generalnyii Shtab v Godyi Velikoi Otechestvennoi Voinyi, Dokumentyi i Materialyi 1943 god (Terra, Moscow, 1999).

Limited Publication Sources
(*The Dupuy Institute* and HERO reports are available through the website www.dupuyinstitute.org)

Anderson, Richard C., Jr., "Artillery Effectiveness versus Armor," *The International TNDM Newsletter*, Volume I, Number 6, pages 26–29.

Bergstrom, Christer, Copies of research for *Black Cross, Red Star* series of books on the air war in the east, provided May 2002.

Bauman, Walter J., *Quantification of the Battle of Kursk* (U.S. Army Concepts Analysis Agency, provided in a letter to Chris Lawrence from Walter J. Bauman dated 19 August 1998).

Chrisman, Jeff, Copies of research on panzer commanders.

The Dupuy Institute, *Final Report for Capture Rate Study, Phases I and II* (The Dupuy Institute, McLean, VA, 6 March 2000).

The Dupuy Institute, *Final Report for The Battle of Kursk; Southern Front: A Validation Data Base* (The Dupuy Institute, McLean, VA, 1996).

The Dupuy Institute, *The Kursk Data Base* (The Dupuy Institute, McLean, VA, 1996, revised 2002). Christopher A. Lawrence, Program Manager.

The Dupuy Institute, *A Measure of the Real-world Value of Mixed Mine Systems* (The Dupuy Institute, McLean, VA, 20 June 2001).

The Dupuy Institute, *The Military Consequences of a Complete Landmine Ban* (Vietnam Veterans of America Foundation, Washington, DC, Summer 2001).

The Dupuy Institute, *Military Consequences of Landmine Restrictions* (Vietnam Veterans of America Foundation, Washington, DC, Spring 2000).

The Dupuy Institute, *Photoguide for Belgorod Trip, 18–20 September* (The Dupuy Institute, McLean, VA, 1995).

The Dupuy Institute, *Soviet Barriers and Fortifications on the Southern Front, Battle of Kursk, 4–18 July 1943, A Supplemental Appendix to the Kursk Data Base* (The Dupuy Institute, McLean, VA, 1996).

Gaetzschmann, Kurt, *Pz.Abt.51 Heerestruppe–II./Pz.Rgt. 33 9. Pz.Div. 1943–45* (Self-published, 1984).

Glantz, David M., *Atlas and Survey: Prelude to Kursk, The Soviet Central Front Offensive, February–March 1943* (Self-published, 1998).

Glantz, David M., *Atlas of the Battle of Kursk* (Self-published, 1997).

Glantz, David M., *Atlas of the War on the Eastern Front (1941–1945)* (Self-published, 1996).

Glantz, David M., Letter to Christopher A. Lawrence dated 14 August 1995 regarding Soviet Army order of battle and establishment (TOE) strength during the Kursk Operation.

Historical Evaluation and Research Organization (HERO), *A Study of Breakthrough Operations* (HERO, Dunn Loring, VA, October 1976).

Historical Evaluation and Research Organization (HERO), *German and Soviet Replacement Systems in World War II* (HERO, Dunn Loring, VA, July 1975).

Isserson, G. S., *Osnovyi Oboronitelnoi Operatsii* (*Fundamentals of the Defensive Operation*), published in 1938 by the RKKA General Staff Academy.

Jung, LtCol. Jakob, *Consumption of Ammunition by Land Forces Since 1939* (unpublished Bundeswehr study, Bergisch Gladback, FRG, 1986).

Kelley, Greg, with Jason Long, *Romanian Armour in World War II* (Web published, 5/99), (http://orbat.com/site/sturm vogel/romafv.html).

Sverdlov, Fyodor D., Unpublished research notes on Soviet captures of German Prisoner of War, faxed to *The Dupuy Institute* between 26 June 1998 and 14 August 1998.

Sverdlov, Fyodor D., Battle summary prepared for *The Dupuy Institute* (not published, 1998).

Sverdlov, Fyodor D., Interviews with Soviet soldiers and airmen at Kursk, prepared for *The Dupuy Institute* by him and associates, 1998–2000.

Sverdlov, Fyodor D., Soviet commander biographies prepared for *The Dupuy Institute* in 2000.

Whiting, Theodore E., Carrel I. Tod, and Anne P. Craft, *The United States Army in World War II, Statistics, Lend-Lease* (Office of the Chief of Military History, Washington, DC, 15 December 1952).

Foreign Military Studies

The U.S. Army historical section in Europe produced a series of reports written by various senior German officers after the war, usually from 1946 to 48. These reports are very useful, but often fairly general. They tend to reflect the views of one individual and are sometimes written with only a minimal amount of research and primary source documentation. They are usually secondary sources and should be used with caution. The major ones used for this study are:

Breith, General der Panzertruppen Hermann, *Breakthrough of a Panzer Corps Through Deeply Echeloned Russian Defense During the Battle of Kharkov in July 1943* (D-258).

Busse, General der Infantrie Theodor, *The "Zitadelle" Offensive ("Operation Citadel"), Eastern Front, 1943* (T-26).

Guderian, Generalobert a.D Heinz, *Representation of Armored Interests, 1938–1945* (P-041a, Historical Division, Headquarters, United States Army, Europe, 1952).

Moebius, Rolf, *German Heavy Armor* (D-226).

Poppe, Generalleutnant Friedrich, *Teilnahme der 255. Infanterie Division an der Kursk Offesnive Juli–August 1943 mit anschliessendem ausbrechen aus einem Kessel auf Achtyrka (Unternehmen Zitadelle)* (D-336).

Seidemann, Hans, *The 'Zitadelle" Offensive, Eastern Front, 1943: Luftwaffe Participation* (manuscript T-26, written in Newstadt, 1 November 1947 by Writer No. 737, General Seidemann).

Von Strachwitz, Hyazinth *Ein Beitrag zur Geschichte des deutschen Widerstandes gegen das nationalsozialistische Regime* (A Contribution to the History of German Resistance to the National Socialist Regime) (MS #B-340, Allendorf, February 1947).

Wienskowski, Hellmuth von, *Materialsammlung fur die Darstellung des deutschen Angriffs auf Kursk (operation Zitadelle) im Juli 1943* (Chapter 12, T-9, 11 January 1953).

Wienskowski, Hellmuth von, *Materialsammlung fur die Darstellung der russischen Offensiven gegen die deutschen Heeresgruppen A, sud und Mitte vom Juli bis September 1943* (Chapter 12, T-9, 31 October 1953).

Zeitzler, Generaloberst A. D. Kurt, *Das ringen um die grossen entscheidungen im zweiten weltkriege* (D-406).

Commitment of German Armor 1943–45, MS #C-033, October 1948, author unknown, but an addendum was added by LtG. Oldwig von Natzmer, who was chief of staff of Gross Deutschland Division during Kursk.

German Order of Battle Charts (D-427).

German Tank-Strengths and Loss Statistics (P-069).

Writer No. 742, *"Zitadelle" [Operation Citadel], Fourth Panzer Army Attack, July, 1943* (T-26, Part B, Chapter II).

Writer No. 750 *The Battle Fought by the Second Panzer Army and the Ninth Army in the Orel Bend Between 5 July and 18 August, 1943* (T-26, Part B, Chapter III).

Writer No. 762, *The "Zitadelle" Offensive, Eastern Front, 1943, Luftwaffe Participation in the Area of the German OREL Armies* (T-26).

Writer No. 856, *The "Zitadelle" Offensive, Eastern Front, 1943, Sector of Provisional Army Kempf* (Part B, Chapter I, T-26).

Articles and Websites

Fesenko, Col. Yu. (Doctor of technical sciences), Maj. S. Zhuravie, "The Battle of Kursk and 'Desert Storm,'" *Voyennyii Vestnik* [Military Herald], 1993, #5.

Frieser, Karl-Heinz, "Schlagen aus der Nachhand—Schlagen aus der Vorhand. Die Schlachten von Char'kov und Kursk 1943," from Foerster, Roland G., *Gezeitenwechsel im Zweiten Weltkrieg?* (Verlag E.S. Mittler & Sohn, Hamburg, 1996).

Frolov, Aleksander, "Citadel—93, The Americans are Programming the Battle of Kursk," *Sovetskaya Rossiya*, 13 July 1993.

Galitsan, Col. A., and Col. L. Pavlov, "Nekotoryie Osobennosti Operativnogo Iskusstva i Taktiki," *Voyenno-Istoricheskii Zhurnal* #7, 1973.

John, Mark (Reuters), "General who foiled coup attempt on Hitler dies," *The Seattle Times*, 6 October 1997.

"General Remer, Ein Leben fur Deutschland," *National Journal*.

Holm, Michael, *The Luftwaffe 1933–45* (website).

Khrushchev, Nikita S., *Special Report to the 20th Congress of the Communist Party of the Soviet Union, Closed session, February 24–25, 1956* (The New Leader, 1962).

Koltunov, G. A., "Kursk: The Clash of Armor," article in *The History of the Second World War*, 1966. (Marshall Covendish, USA Ltd., 1974).

Kozlov, Col. L., "Sovershenstvovaniye Protivotankovoi Oboronyi Strelkovyikh Soyedinenii," *Voyenno-Istoricheskii Zhurnal* #3, 1971.

"Kurskaya Bitva v Tsifrakh," *Voyenno-Istoricheskii Zhurnal* #6, 1968.

Lee, Martin A., "The Strange Saga of Hitler's Bodyguard," *The Consortium*, 1997.

Lexicon der Wehrmacht (http://www.lexikon-der-wehrmarcht.de).

Long, Jason, *Panzerkeil* (http://www.sturmvogel.orbat.com/Panzerkeil.html).

Miller, Michael D., Axis Biographical Research http://www.geocities.com/~orion47/).

Nipe, George M. Jr., *Kursk Reconsidered: Germany's Lost Victory.* (Article at www.theblitz.org).

Parada, George, "Hans-Ulrich Rudel," *Achtung Panzer* website, 1999.

Pechenkin, A. A., "Generals perished not only in battles," *Nezavisimaya Gazeta* (Independent Newspaper), 17 June 2005.

Remer, Otto Ernst, "My Role in Berlin on July 20, 1944," *The Journal of Historical Review*, Volume 8, No. 1: pages 41-53.

Ritterkreuztraeger 1939–1945 (http://www.ritterkreuztraeger-1939-45.de).

RKKA in World War II (http://www.armchairgeneral.com/rkkaww2).

The Russian Battlefield (http://www.battlefield.ru).

Sazonov, Col. I., "Razvitiye Takticheskoi Oboronyi v Velikoi Otechestvennoi Voine," *Voyenno-Istoricheskii Zhurnal* #9, 1968.

Sokolov, B. V., "The Cost of War: Human Losses for the USSR and Germany, 1939–1945," *The Journal of Slavic Military Studies*, Vol. 9, No. 1 (March 1996), pp. 152–193 (Frank Cass, London, 1996).

Stevenson, Richard W. "John Cairncross, Fifth Briton in Soviet Spy Ring, Dies at 82." *New York Times*, 10 October 1995.

Weber, Mark, "War Hero Fled to Spain to Avoid 'Thought Crime' Imprisonment: [Otto Ernst] Remer Dies in Exile," *The Journal of Historical Review*, Volume 17, Number 1, January/February 1998.

Wendel, Marcus, Axis History Factbook (www.axishistory.com).

Zamulin, V. N., and L. N. Lopukhovskii, "Prokhorovskoye Srazheniye. Mifyi i realnost" (Battle of Prokhorovka. Myths and Reality), *Voyenno-Istoricheskii Arkhiv* [Military Historical Archives], *No 9(33) Sentyabr 2002*, (Tsera, Moscow, 2002 & 2003); *No 10(34) Oktyabr 2002; No 11(35) Noyabr 2002; No 12(36) Dekabr 2002; No 1(37) Yanvar 2003; No 2(38) Fevral 2003; and No 3(39) Mart 2003.*

German Archival Material

The author conducted extensive research of the files for:

- Commanding General of the Army (OKH)
- OKH Quartermaster Reports
- Inspector General of Infantry
- Commanding General of Armaments and Replacements
- Army Group South
- Fourth Panzer Army
- Provisional Army Kempf
- All five participating corps
- All 17 participating divisions
- Second Army (for Luftwaffe data)
- Luftwaffe records (T321, R154)
- Selected Federal German Archives Records

Also reviewed:

- Army Group Don
- Army Group B
- First Panzer Army
- Sixth Army
- Ninth Army
- XVII Corps
- XXIV Panzer Corps
- LVII Panzer Corps
- Tigerfibel, Tiger I (RG 242, D656/27)

Soviet Archival Material

The author conducted extensive research of the files for:

- National Commission for the Defense of the USSR
- Second Air Army
- Fifth Air Army
- Seventeenth Air Army
- All seven participating armies
- Thirty-eighth Army
- All 11 participating rifle corps
- All 10 participating tank and mechanized corps
- All 37 participating airborne, rifle and guards rifle divisions
- 252nd Rifle Division
- All six participating separate tank brigades
- All 59th, 60th, 148th, 167th & 245th Tank Regiments
- 1st Guards Motorcycle Regiment
- 5th, 6th, 9th, 26th & 29th Antiaircraft Artillery Divisions
- 14th, 27th, 28th, 29th, 30th, 31st & 32nd Antitank Brigades
- 27th, 33rd & 36th Gun Artillery Brigade
- 12th Mortar Brigade
- 29 different artillery, mortar and guards mortar regiments

U.S. Archival Material (from National Archives and Library of Congress)

Headquarters, Third United States Army, Office of the Assistant Chief of Staff, G-2, Interrogation Report No. 30, 15 August 1945. Interview conducted by Edmund L. King, Major, Infantry, Chief of Interrogation Section.

Office of Strategic Services, Research and Analysis Branch, Current Inteligence Series no. 13, "The Kursk-Orel Campaign July 5–August 10," 13 August 1943.

War Department, Officer of Assistant Chief of Staff, G-2, "Magic" Summary, Nos. 454, 455, 458, 460, 465, 468, 469, 474, 475, 483, 488, 490, 501, 502, 572 and 624 from 23 June to 10 December 1943.

1:50,000 Soviet 1942 maps that were captured from the Germans

1:50,000 German 1942 maps that were copied from Russian maps

U.S. Turkish Military Attache Report of 23 July 1943 prepared by Brigadier General Richard G. Tindall.

The Interviews

The Battle of Kursk was in 1943. The men in battle, many as young as 17, would now (in 2000) be at least 74 years old. Many of the surviving veterans are older than that. This book was the last chance for many of these veterans to tell their stories. For this book we interviewed 28 German veterans and 84 Soviet veterans. The interviews were originally intended to supplement the accounts, but the depth, interest and details of many of these stories resulted in them becoming a significant part of this book. In most cases the veterans were interviewed in person by a volunteer, usually retired military, who was working for the author. The interviews were not recorded, as this was felt to greatly hinder conversation. Instead, the interviewer took notes and prepared a transcript of the interview later. As such, what is being "quoted" from the veterans in this book are not direct quotes, but are summation, sometimes very detailed, of what the interviewee said. As such, all the interviews are placed in italics. They are not placed in quotation marks, and the words used are not necessary a direct quote from the interviewee. Where it is, we placed the interview in quotes.

The German Interviews

For this book, 28 German veterans of the battle were interviewed. The sole interviewer was Dieter Brand, Major General (Ret.) Bundeswehr. General Brand personally knew four of the people due to their service together in the Bundeswehr (the post-war West German Army). Twenty-six of the interviews were conducted in person, with one conducted by letter and phone and one by letter. All the German interviews were translated by Wulf-Deitrich Brand.

The depth and detail of the German interviews was quite good. This is certainly due to the interviewer. A significant number of these veterans had been interviewed before, many had studied the battle since and some had even written books (Jung and Rall). As such, it is possible that some of the German interviews were influenced by post-war accounts.

The Soviet Interviews

For this book, we collected over 80 Soviet interviews. The interviews were conducted by Col. Fyodor Sverdlov, Col. Anatolii Vainer, Major General G. G. Nessonov, or Col. Valerii Akimov. The first two gentlemen were World War II veterans and Col. Akimov is also a combat veteran (Afghanistan). Most of the Soviet interviews were translated by Tatiana S. Lawrence. These were supplemented by two interviews conducted by the author, both in conjunction with his trips to Belgorod.

The Soviet interviews were not conducted with the same depth and detail as the German interviews. As such, they were not used to the same extent as the German interviews.

Sources for the Chapters

Most of this book was developed from the archived records of the Soviet and German Armies. Chapters Three through Fifteen, except where footnoted, were written entirely from the unit records and interviews, with precedence given to the unit records. For this project, we reviewed the division, corps and army records for all units on both sides involved in the action. We have not listed individual records or footnoted them, due to space considerations. The records used are on file at *The Dupuy Institute* and listed in detail in the *Final Report for The Battle of Kursk: Southern Front: A Validation Data Base* (The Dupuy Institute, McLean, VA, 1996).

The accounts of the fighting on the 12th and 13th of July (Chapters Nine, Ten, and Eleven) were supplemented by other secondary sources. These are noted in all cases where this occurs.

Chapter Eight on the Air War for the German side was drawn from a mix of existing Lufwaffe records and a wide variety of secondary sources. For the Soviet side it was drawn from the unit records and some supporting secondary sources.

Biographical Information

CHRISTOPHER A. LAWRENCE is a professional historian and military analyst. He is the Executive Director and President of *The Dupuy Institute,* a non-profit organization dedicated to scholarly research and objective analysis of historical data related to armed conflict and the resolution of armed conflict. *The Dupuy Institute* provides independent, historically-based analysis of lessons learned from modern military campaigns.

Mr. Lawrence was the program manager for the Ardennes Campaign Simulation Data Base, the Kursk Data Base, the Modern Insurgency Spread Sheets and for a number of other smaller combat data bases. He participated in studies on casualty estimates (including estimates for Bosnia and Iraq) and studies of air campaign modeling, enemy prisoner of war capture rates, medium weight armor, urban warfare, situational awareness, counterinsurgencies and other subjects for the U.S. Army, Department of Defense, the Joint Staff and the U.S. Air Force. He has also directed a number of studies related to the military impact of banning antipersonnel mines for the Joint Staff, the Los Alamos National Laboratories, and the Vietnam Veterans of America Foundation.

His published works include papers and monographs for the Congressional Office of Technology Assessment and Vietnam Veterans of America Foundation, in addition to over 40 articles written for limited distribution newsletters and over 60 analytical reports prepared for the Department of Defense. He is the author of *America's Modern Wars: Understanding Iraq, Afghanistan and Vietnam* (Casemate Publishers, Philadelphia & Oxford, 2015), *Kursk: The Battle of Prokhorovka* (Aberdeen Books, Sheridan, CO, 2015), and *War by Numbers: Understanding Conventional Combat* (Potomac Books, Lincoln, NE, 2017).

Mr. Lawrence lives in Virginia near Washington, D.C., with his wife and son.